American Family Law in Transition

American Family Law in Transition

Walter O. Weyrauch
University of Florida
College of Law

and

Sanford N. Katz
Boston College Law School

The Bureau of National Affairs, Inc., Washington, D.C.

Library of Congress Cataloging in Publication Data

Weyrauch, Walter O. (Walter Otto)
    American family law in transition.

    Includes bibliographies and index.
    1. Domestic relations—United States—Cases.
I. Katz, Sanford N.   II. Bureau of National
Affairs (Washington, D.C.)   III. Title.
KF504.W49   1983   346.7301'5   82-17908
                      347.30615

International Standard Book Number: 0-87179-390-3
Printed in the United States of America

To
Our Families
and
Our Students

Preface

This book is novel in several respects. It attempts to develop a theory of family law from legal practice. The facts in a case, as they present themselves to the practicing lawyer, tend to be diffuse and complex. For example, in a particular case whether there was a marriage or not may be often obscure. Although a judge has the power to come up with a clear result, perhaps by attaching a fictitious intent to the parties, it may sometimes be difficult for the lawyer to say whether a particular set of facts constitutes engagement, marriage, business partnership, nonmarital cohabitation, cotenancy, employment, or something else. Traditional legal theory provides little guidance because it tends to lead to neat classifications in pairs of conceptual opposites, such as marriage or no-marriage, to the exclusion of other viable choices. Beginning with an open-ended checklist of multiple choices, the lawyer selects those that are strategically most advantageous to the client. What may appear later in court as facts is really only a reflection of reality as seen and presented by the lawyer for judicial decision. Inclusion of these intellectual steps into the analysis of law must lead to a broadening of legal theory.

The emphasis of this book is on practice, creating a perspective for those confronted with family law problems, including aspects of planning, counseling, and trial strategy. The cases, rather than merely illustrating narrow holdings of law, become data of human behavior. They should be read as an assemblage of factors which often arose almost accidentally. Their haphazard nature leaves room for strategic alternatives that, as we may speculate, have been on the lawyer's mind at an earlier phase, or that may be pursued in the future. The Comments should be read in conjunction with the cases, for it is in these sections that the signposts for new theory are developed. Perhaps the most appropriate parallel to the method we employ would be literary criticism where a story, poem, or essay is followed by a critique, which in turn feeds back into the literature under consideration.

Some may feel that an approach of this nature leaves the reader and student with no incentives to develop their own theories. Nothing could be further from our intent. Full disclosure of reasoning that is never meant to be final must elevate the quality of discussion to a higher level of awareness. To hold back a critical evaluation on the assumption that readers or students might develop their own reasoning abilities may impede, rather than lead to, enlightenment.

We are concerned with a theory of practice. The intellectual tasks of the practicing lawyers are necessarily more complex and sophisticated than those faced by trial and appellate judges. By a process of reduction, aided by lawyers, judicial jobs have been simplified. Since practice is in flux, this book attempts to develop a theory of family law in transition. Yet if the emphasis of our book is on the increasing autonomy, both of the family and of the individual, it should be recognized that this did not come about through the legislatures, or realistically through the courts, but through the creative imagination of practitioners acting on behalf of clients. Broad social changes facilitated their tasks. We have avoided being encyclopedic because this would have frozen our efforts. Any encyclopedic undertaking reflects and implicitly accentuates the past. This is, of course, a useful and necessary exercise, but it would have impeded a theory of process. It also assumes a closed intellectual system.

The choice of our publisher was meant equally to sustain our effort and bring it to the awareness not only of legal scholars and students but also of those who are "in the trenches" of legal controversy and litigation—the legal practitioners. In a true sense they have helped to create the theories discussed in this book and, in finding them confirmed, may feel encouraged to argue them explicitly in court and to use them in practice.

Walter O. Weyrauch
Sanford N. Katz

October 1982

Acknowledgments

This book is the product of years of collaboration. During this time we have benefited from general discussions and constructive criticisms of the manuscript by our colleagues Mary Ann Glendon, Ruth-Arlene Howe, Stanley Ingber, and Winston P. Nagan. We are grateful for the thoughts they shared with us.

We wish to acknowledge the editorial guidance of Jill White, William A. Schroeder, and Melba McGrath. Mary G. Harreld, Jonny J. Frank, Phillip L. Weiner, Kenneth H. Ernstoff, and Daniel F. Polsenberg, while students at Boston College Law School, provided technical assistance. Gyorgy Lang was most helpful in responding to our reference calls and we thank him. Dean Richard G. Huber of Boston College Law School and Deans Joseph R. Julin and Frank T. Read of the University of Florida College of Law have supported our efforts, and we appreciate their kindnesses over the years. We wish to acknowledge our gratitude to Debra F. Simmons and her staff at the Boston College Law School Word Processing Center for the great amount of help they provided. For maintaining her good humor in assisting us in duplicating materials, we wish to thank Betty Capstick. For her patience, skill, and help beyond the call of duty in preparing the manuscript for publication, we are grateful to Mary Nardone.

We appreciate the skill and cheerfulness of our editor, Louise Rosenblatt, who guided our book through the production process. For reviewing the manuscript, we acknowledge with thanks Richard E. Crouch, consulting editor of BNA's *Family Law Reporter*.

Contents

Chapter 2   Informal Marriage   115

1

Marriage as Contract or Partnership (Co-Ownership) for Profit

The structure of the American family has dramatically changed within the past few decades. In a still continuing process, the nature and functions of marriage as a legal and social institution are being transformed.

Antenuptial Agreements. While formal engagement, as traditionally understood, has declined, it has been revived in other forms. One example is cohabitation as a form of "trial marriage," which, as discussed in Chapter 2, often becomes a substitute for marriage. Another example is the increased importance and recognition of antenuptial agreements. In the past such agreements were a rare practice confined to the elderly and rich who wished to preserve their assets, but they are now entered into by young couples attempting to articulate their mutual expectations. Reversing earlier patterns, the courts tend to accept their validity even if they contemplate and regulate the possibility of future divorce or dissolution of a marriage not yet in existence. Premarital contracts herald changed attitudes on marriage. Indeed, while in the past the nature of marriage was incidentally determined and judicially tested in actions for annulment of marriage, the emphasis now shifts to a wider judicial acceptance of antenuptial agreements. Thus the nature and terms of marriage are increasingly left by the courts to the parties themselves rather than imposed on the parties by a formal pronouncement of policy through the State.

Marriage today is often perceived as neither a sacrament nor a status necessarily assumed for life. The relationship contemplated by parties in modern forms of antenuptial agreements is not dissimilar from that of other long-term contracts, such as partnership, cotenancy, and sometimes employment. Since the parties to a possible future marriage deal with each other on an assumed level of equality and equal bargaining power, their agreement, if it leads to marriage at all,

1

tends to reflect financial and personal expectations like sexual preferences, whether to remain childless, when and how many children to have, and choice of career and domicile. Some of these stipulations, even if drafted upon instructions of the parties to a lawyer, are not meant to be legally enforceable. Yet they have functions comparable to the requirement of legal consideration or form in the law of contracts, namely to safeguard deliberation and to determine the intent of the parties.

Thus marriage itself, not merely the antenuptial agreement, is subject to substantial freedom of contract, with religion and the State assuming a more passive role than in the past. However, contrary to most commercial contracts, marriage is not based on a printed form, although in the duties imposed by law it still has some of the elements of a contract of adhesion. In other words, marriage is less of a "take-it-or-leave-it" proposition than it used to be.

The Nature of Marriage. Although the evolution of the marriage relationship is still ongoing, some patterns can be discerned. A family based on marriage is still perceived as the most desirable and productive unit of society, although no longer necessarily the most stable. While procreation may still be a purpose of marriage, other forms of productiveness are being increasingly recognized, for instance, the educational and financial advancement of both spouses, not just the husband, by joint effort. With such ends in view, the parties to marriage are paying closer attention to the economics of the relationship than in the past. Indeed, marriage is acquiring some of the characteristics of a pooling of resources for speculative investment, or of a co-ownership in present and future property similar to a business partnership for profit (although this language is rarely used).

This egalitarian model of marriage seems, in accordance with the aspirations of women's liberation, to be more viable than older conceptions in which one party, the husband, was seen as the dominant force or master. One aspect of this evolution is that it takes advantage of already existing case law, for example, past cases dealing with family-operated small businesses. Even in noncommunity property jurisdictions, the wife who minded the store or kept the books could be given equal rights in accumulated assets under theories of an implied partnership. The trend is toward giving a similarly favorable treatment to the wife as homemaker and mother, whether the courts refer to implied contract or partnership or special equities.

Of course, a change of perspectives on marriage does not occur with equal force in all segments of the population. For the most part, it reflects changed attitudes within the middle classes, especially among some of its young members of marriageable age. Corresponding trends in family law may therefore be seen as an accommodation to value changes among those who traditionally have had a decisive impact on the shaping of American law and policies. Insofar as more and more middle-class wives and mothers are working, it could perhaps be said that the young middle-class family has taken on some characteristics of working-class families. Furthermore, new trends are mainly found in pioneering appellate opinions in a strictly legal context. These sources are likely to neglect the psychological and emotional aspects of marriage. They are based on individual litigation and not on a poll of national opinion. On the other hand, the mere fact that certain issues, which nobody would have thought of 20 years ago, are now litigated is in itself evidence that changes in the conception of marriage have taken place.

Incidents of Marriage. A number of consequences, recognized in various degrees, follow from the new egalitarian nature of marriage. The wife no longer necessarily changes her name upon marriage. She has an increased personal and economic interest, because of her own career aspirations, in preserving her identity apart from the husband's. Young people may marry to facilitate each other's education and establishment in a professional career. For example, the young wife, instead of the parents as in the past, may help finance the education of her husband. She may defer her studies and accept minor employment. The husband, after he graduates, is expected to pay in turn for the wife's education. If the marriage is dissolved, as often happens and as some contractual understandings even contemplate, payment of "rehabilitative alimony" may be contingent upon the wife's diligent studies. Support obligations are viewed as mutual. In case of injury to the husband, loss of consortium is available to the wife too. Husband and wife are expected to collaborate in all marital tasks, including child care and housework.

Other consequences are still in a speculative stage. A shift of marriage toward "co-ownership for profit" may lead to a reexamination of cases dealing with outside interference. Injunctive relief, perhaps even damages under some name other than "alienation of affection," may become possible again, similar to remedies available if business is interfered with. The increased recognition of proprietary rights resulting from marriage may reopen the discussion of how to deal with "trespassers." The drive for recognition of homosexual and plural marriages, so far unsuccessful, will continue in the courts. State and federal legislatures will probably take a conservative stand in these matters, perhaps for purely fiscal reasons, and confer statutory benefits, for instance, in matters relating to welfare, taxation, and immigration, only upon those who are "really married."

The influx of contractual aspects into marriage, if they take the form of implied partnership, may lead to increased liability of women. As a "partner," a wife may become liable for necessaries and debts of the husband. Her liability, as in partnership, will be joint or several, and it may sometimes be difficult for her to establish that a business of the husband is not also hers. Neither spouse may be able to claim the traditional immunities since they are incompatible with partnership notions. Lawsuits between spouses, such as requests for accounting, may become common even without dissolution of marriage. And there will be little reason to retain a right to refuse to testify in legal matters relating to the other spouse.

General Considerations. The changes in marriage, even when seemingly minor, indicate shifts in basic values. Romantic conceptions of marriage, based on love, appear somewhat muted. Honesty and respect for the partner's continued integrity as a person and individual are being emphasized. The economic aspects of marriage encourage, perhaps even dictate, the need for separate bookkeeping. There is a trend toward retaining a degree of what is considered a desirable emotional detachment. The technical aspects of sexual relations are of increasing interest, while the differences between the sexes decrease. Marriage is valued for simplifying the gratification of physical needs at lower risk and cost. The trend favors birth control, artificial insemination regardless of source, abortion, and sexual tolerance.

The State cannot possibly cope with ever increasing complexities of modern life and the multitude of required tasks. As its policing power is relaxed, many tasks, in part by default, may have to be delegated to the family. It may be that the resultant increased autonomy of the family will also increase self-sufficiency and self-reliance. On the other hand, marriage is no longer absolutely necessary. It has become one of several legally recognized life styles.

Party Autonomy in Marriage

Functional Relation Between Antenuptial Agreement, Engagement, Cohabitation Contract, Informal Marriage, and Business Partnership

Stanard v. Bolin

Supreme Court of Washington

88 Wash.2d 614, 565 P.2d 94 (1977)

HAMILTON, Associate Justice.

This appeal presents the question of whether the common-law action for breach of promise to marry should be abolished. The trial court concluded that the action was contrary to public policy and dismissed the plaintiff's (appellant's) complaint with prejudice under CR 12(b)(6) for failure to state a claim upon which relief can be granted. We accepted review and conclude that the action is not contrary to public policy.

* * *

In October, 1974, plaintiff and defendant (respondent) were introduced to each other by mutual friends, and their courtship developed soon thereafter. During the course of their courtship, defendant assured plaintiff that he was worth in excess of $2 million, was planning to retire in 2 years, and that the two of them would then travel. Defendant also promised plaintiff that she would never have to work again and that he would see to the support of her two teen-age boys. He also promised to see that the plaintiff's mother would never be in need.

On September 22, 1975, plaintiff accepted defendant's proposal of marriage. Thereafter, defendant took her to a jewelry store and purchased an engagement ring and matching wedding rings. The parties found a suitable home for their residence and signed the purchase agreement as husband and wife. At the insistence of defendant, plaintiff placed her home on the market for sale and sold most of her furniture at a public auction. The parties set December 13, 1975, as their wedding date, reserved a church, and engaged a minister to perform the service. Dresses for plaintiff, her mother, and the matron of honor were ordered, and a reception was arranged at a local establishment. The parties began informally announcing their plans to a wide circle of friends. After the wedding date was set, plaintiff's employer hired another person and requested plaintiff to assist in teaching the new employee the duties of her job.

On November 13, 1975, defendant informed plaintiff that he would not marry her. This came as a great shock to plaintiff and caused her to become ill and lose sleep and weight. Plaintiff sought medical advice and was treated by her physician. Plaintiff also had to take her home off the market and repurchase furniture at a cost in excess of that which she received for her older furniture. In addition, plaintiff was forced to cancel all wedding plans and reservations, and to explain to her matron of honor, her mother, and her children, that she was not marrying. Plaintiff was also obliged to return wedding gifts and to face her friends and neighbors, each of whom felt entitled to an explanation.

In her first claim for relief, plaintiff sought damages to compensate her for her pain, impairment to health, humiliation, and embarrassment. Plaintiff's second claim sought damages to compensate her for her loss of expected financial security.

The breach-of-marriage-promise action has its origins in the common law. Professor Clark, a well-known authority on family law, has posited that 17th Century English conceptions of marriage as largely a property transaction caused the English common-law courts to intervene in a subject matter which, up until the 17th Century, had been almost exclusively under the jurisdiction of the ecclesiastical courts. See H. Clark, THE LAW OF DOMESTIC RELATIONS IN THE UNITED STATES 2 (1968) (hereafter cited as Clark). In any event, the action was carried forward into the common law of Washington (see RCW 4.04.010) and was recognized by this court as early as 1905. See *Heasley v. Nichols*, 38 Wash. 485, 80 P. 769 (1905). Because the action has its origins in the common law and has not been acted upon by the legislature, it is proper for us to reexamine it and determine its continued viability in light of present-day society. [Citations omitted.]

The breach-of-promise-to-marry action is one not easy to classify. Although the action is treated as arising from the breach of a contract (the contract being the mutual promises to marry), the damages allowable more closely resemble a tort action. Thus, the plaintiff may recover for loss to reputation, mental anguish, and injury to health, in addition to recovering for expenditures made in preparation for the marriage and loss of the pecuniary and social advantages which the promised marriage offered. In addition, some states allow aggravated damages for seduction under promise to marry and for attacks by the defendant on the plaintiff's character. Furthermore, some states allow punitive damages when the defendant's acts were malicious or fraudulent. For a comprehensive discussion of the damages allowable under a breach-of-promise-to-marry action and a collection of cases, see Annot., *Measure and elements of damages for breach of contract to marry,* 73 A.L.R.2d 553 (1960), and C. McCormick, HANDBOOK ON THE LAW OF DAMAGES 397–406 (1935).

The action in its present form is subject to almost uniform criticism by the commentators, although our research has not disclosed any cases in which a court has abolished the action.[1] In essence, these criticism are: (1) the action is used as an instrument of oppression and blackmail; (2) engaged persons should be allowed to correct their mistakes without fear of publicity and legal compulsion; (3) the action is subject to great abuse at the hands of gullible and sympathetic juries; (4) it is wrong to allow under the guise of contract an action that is essentially tortious and penal in nature; and, (5) the measure of damages is unjust because damages are allowed for loss of social and economic position, whereas most persons marry for reasons of mutual love and affection. [Citations omitted.] Although some of these criticisms are not without merit, we do not believe they justify an outright abolishment of the action.

When two persons agree to marry, they should realize that certain actions will be taken during the engagement period in reliance on the mutual promises to marry. Rings will be purchased, wedding dresses and other formal attire will be ordered or reserved, and honeymoon plans with their attendant expenses will be made. Wedding plans such as the rental of a church, the engagement of a minister, the printing of wedding invitations, and so on, will commence. It is also likely that the parties will make plans for their future residence, such as purchasing a house, buying furniture, and the like. Further at the time the parties decide to marry, they should realize that their plans and visions of future happiness will be communicated to friends and relatives and that wedding gifts soon will be arriving. When the plans to marry are abruptly ended, it is certainly foreseeable that the party who was unaware that the future marriage would not take place will have expended some sums of money and will suffer some forms of mental anguish, loss to reputation, and injury to health. We do not feel these injuries should go unanswered merely because the breach-of-promise-to-marry action may be subject to abuses; rather, an attempt should be made to eradicate the abuses from the action.

One major abuse of the action is allowing the plaintiff to bring in evidence of the defendant's wealth and social position. This evidence is admissible under the theory that the plaintiff should be compensated for what she or he has lost by not marrying the defendant. [Citations omitted.]

Although damages for loss of expected financial and social position more closely resemble the contract theory of recovery than the other elements of damages for breach of promise to marry, we do not believe these damages are justified in light of modern society's concept of marriage. Although it may have been that marriages were contracted for material reasons in 17th Century England, marriages today generally are not considered property transactions, but are, in the words of Professor Clark, "the result of that complex experience called being in love." Clark, *supra* at 2. A person generally does not choose a marriage partner on the basis of financial and social gain; hence, the plaintiff should not be compensated for losing an expectation which he or she did not have in the first place. Further, the breach-of-promise-to-marry action is based on injuries to the plaintiff, and evidence of the defendant's wealth tends to misdirect the jury's attention when assessing the plaintiff's damages towards an examination of the defendant's wealth rather than the plaintiff's injuries.

---

[1]The action has been abolished or modified by statute in some states. See Ala. Code tit. 7, §114; Cal. Civ. Code Ann. §43.5 (West); Colo. Rev. Stat. §13-20-202; Conn. Gen. Stat. Ann. §52-572b (West Supp. 1977); Fla. Stat. Ann. §771.01 (West); Ind. Code Ann. §34-4-4-1 (Burns Supp. 1976); Me. Rev. Stat. Ann. tit. 14, §854 (West); Md. Cts. & Jud. Proc. Code Ann. §5-301 (1974); Mass. Gen. Laws Ann. ch. 207, §47A (West); Mich. Stat. Ann. §25.191; Nev. Rev. Stat. §41.380; N.H. Rev. Stat. Ann. §508:11; N.J. Stat. Ann. §2A:23-1 (West); N.Y. Civ. Rights Law §80-a *et seq.* (McKinney); Pa. Stat. Ann. tit. 48, §171 (Purdon); W. Va. Code §56-3-2a (Supp. 1976); Wis. Stat. Ann. §248.01 (West Supp. 1976); Wyo. Stat. §1-728.

Professor McCormick has concluded that evidence of the defendant's wealth has a more potent effect upon the size of the verdict than any instruction on damages. See C. McCormick, HANDBOOK ON THE LAW OF DAMAGES 399, n.36 (1935). If this is so, then it presents a very strong reason for disallowing any evidence of the defendant's wealth and social position. We conclude that damages for loss of expected financial and social position should no longer be recoverable under the breach-of-promise-to-marry actions. This means that evidence of the defendant's wealth and social position becomes immaterial in assessing the plaintiff's damages.

Other damages subject to criticism are those damages given for mental anguish, loss to reputation, and injury to health. It is argued that these injuries are "so vague and so little capable of measurement in dollars that they give free rein to the jury's passions, prejudices and sympathies." See Clark, *supra* at 12. This argument has little merit, for it places no faith in the jury's ability to evaluate objectively the evidence regarding plaintiff's injuries and render a just verdict. If a jury's verdict is tainted by passion or prejudice, or is otherwise excessive, the trial court and the appellate court have the power to reduce the award or order a new trial. [Citations omitted.] Lack of ability to quantify damages in exact dollar amounts does not justify abolishing the breach-of-promise-to-marry action. In her complaint plaintiff alleged that she had suffered pain, impairment to health, humiliation, and embarrassment as a result of the defendant's breach of his promise to marry. If this is true, and we must assume it is for purposes of review, then she is entitled to compensation for these injuries.

* * *

We also do not believe the action should be abolished so that engaged persons are free from compulsion to choose whether to end an engagement. Although the policy of the state should not be to encourage a person to marry when he or she has begun to have second thoughts about a prospective mate, it is also the policy of the state to afford an avenue of redress for injuries suffered due to the actions of another. Allowing recovery for injuries, which are foreseeable at the time of entering into the relationship, should not be denied on the presumption the defendant would rather enter into the marriage than pay damages for the injuries caused. Furthermore, it is hard to conceive of a plaintiff suing a defendant in order to coerce the defendant into a marriage which would be unstable at best. It is possible that there may be such a plaintiff, but that is no reason for abolishing the action for all plaintiffs, for that would cause most plaintiffs to go uncompensated for their injuries at the expense of a few unworthy plaintiffs.

In conclusion, we have decided that the breach-of-promise-to-marry action should be retained as a quasi-contract, quasi-tort action for the recovery of the foreseeable special and general damages which are caused by a defendant's breach of promise to marry. However, the action is modifed to the extent that a plaintiff cannot recover for loss of expected financial and social position, because marriage is no longer considered to be a property transaction.

The judgment of the trial court is reversed on plaintiff's first claim for relief, and remanded for further proceedings consistent with this opinion. The judgment is affirmed on plaintiff's second claim for relief, which sought damages for loss of prospective economical and social advantage.

UTTER, Associate Justice (dissenting).

The majority, in a well-written opinion, has set forth the historical background of the action for breach of promise to marry. It states the policy reasons for abolishing the action, but chooses to retain its major underpinnings. The sole change is to modify the doctrine to the extent that a plaintiff can no longer recover for loss of expected financial and social position, but may still recover foreseeable special and general damages caused by breach of a defendant's promise to marry.

I believe the change advocated does not go far enough. Motive of the defendant may still, apparently, be considered in assessing damages. *Warner v. Benham*, 126 Wash. 393, 218 P. 260 (1923). Where the breach of promise to marry is wanton or deliberate, the effect is to allow exemplary damages, contrary to the public policy of our state. *Wyman v. Wallace*, 15 Wash. App. 395, 549 P.2d 71 (1976). In *Wyman*, at page 398, 549 P.2d at page 73, the Court of Appeals abolished the action for alienation of affections of a spouse by an unrelated third person on the ground, among others, that "the element of punishment is so inextricably interwoven into any award of damages for alienation of the affections of a spouse that the true nature of the award is punitive." This is no less true in this case than it was in *Wyman*. In addition, in 1973 our state adopted a new dissolution of marriage act. RCW 26.09. The establishment of the fact that a marriage is "irretrievably broken" is now a sufficient ground for dissolution, with no finding of fault necessary. The trial judge observed in his memorandum decision on motion to dismiss:

> "The current public policy expressed in the 1973 Dissolution Act is to disregard fault in the judicial determination of property rights at the dissolution of a marriage. Fault is not to be considered in determining which party shall have the decree. There are no damages as such in a dissolution. Is it not obvious, however, that one of the parties to a dissolution suffers at least as much humiliation, embarrassment, mental suffering and loss of financial expectation and security as does a party to the breakup of an engagement?
>
> "It is significant that there was no divorce by judicial decree at common law when the breach of promise action came into being. *Tupper v. Tupper*, 63 Wash.2d 585 [388 P.2d 225]. Should not the public policy declared in the divorce statutes be applicable to engagements? I believe it is."

The majority lists the almost uniform criticisms of the action by commentators: "(1) the action is used as an instrument of oppression and blackmail; (2) engaged persons should be allowed to correct their mistakes without fear of publicity and legal compulsion; (3) the action is subject to great abuse at the hands of gullible and sympathetic juries; (4) it is wrong to allow under the guise of contract an action that is essentially tortious and penal in nature * * *."

I believe these criticisms are sufficient grounds, given the recently enunciated policy of the state in the dissolution of marriage act, to justify our abolition of this now obsolete, judicially created, cause of action.

Chaachou v. Chaachou*

Supreme Court of Florida

135 So.2d 206 (Fla. 1961)

Per curiam.

On this appeal we are confronted with the culmination of one of the most protracted and bitterly contested divorce proceedings in the annals of Florida jurisprudence.

---

*[*Fredericka Phillips Chaachou, Appellant v. Khudourie Chaachou; Paris Corp., a Fla. Corp.; Columbia Corp., a Fla. Corp.; and The K. Chaachou Foundation, a non-profit Fla. corporation, Appellees.*]

We quote in full the findings of facts, the conclusions of law and the final decree of the chancellor which is under attack herein:

"By her Complaint filed July 11, 1952 alleging a common law marriage with the defendant, Khudourie Chaachou, plaintiff, Fredericka Phillips Chaachou, seeks divorce on the ground of extreme cruelty, an award of alimony, suit money, counsel fees, and a decree for special equities in certain properties mentioned in the Complaint, which consists of four Miami Beach hotels and a residence at 5041 Collins Avenue, Miami Beach.

"The defendant, Khudourie Chaachou, and all corporate defendants on August 6, 1952, filed their joint Answer to the Complaint denying generally all its allegations including the alleged marriage, and admitted only that the defendant, Khoudourie Chaachou, was born in Bagdad, Iraq, had become a naturalized American citizen, that he was engaged in the wholesale rug business in New York City, and that he was involved in the automobile accident which plaintiff alleged initiated her coming to Miami Beach and becoming both the defendant's wife and his business partner.

"On July 16, 1952, the cause was referred to a Special Master by Division A of this Court, before which this cause was then pending 'for the purpose of taking testimony of the respective parties of this cause upon the issue of temporary alimony, temporary suit money and temporary counsel fees to be awarded to the plaintiff, and for the purpose of filing his recommendations to the Court both on the facts and the law with all convenient speed.' To aid the Master in reaching a conclusion on the purposes for which this cause was then referred to him, the parties produced forty-seven witnesses whose testimony appears on more than 2,000 legal size pages, and submitted to him eight written depositions and over 150 exhibits, more than 100 of which were received in evidence.

* * *

"In *Chaachou v. Chaachou* (Fla. Sup. Ct., Rehearing denied June 21, 1954) 73 So.2d 830, the Supreme Court of Florida found the Master to be in error (as was Division A of this Court confirming his report) when he recommended against the existence of a common law marriage between the parties. The Supreme Court held (73 So.2d 830, at p. 837):

" 'The summary of the evidence heretofore given as to the actual marriage, the corroborating evidence with reference thereto, cohabitation and repute, shows beyond question, prima facie, a common law marriage, which shifted the burden to the respondent. He has not met the burden placed upon him by law.'

* * *

"At the final hearing beginning on August 29, 1960, this Chancellor saw and heard the testimony of twenty witnesses, whose testimony covers 861 legal size pages; and in addition received and read nineteen exhibits, one of which (Plaintiff's Exhibit 3–8) consisted of twenty-one letters, all except two being written by the defendant, Khudourie Chaachou, to plaintiff's counsel. At the conclusion of the final hearing the parties filed extensive briefs advocating their positions. Midway during the final hearing of this cause Mr. John Carruthers II, who filed defendants' counterclaim of adultery, and who had represented the defendants in the last appellate proceeding in this cause, asked leave to be relieved of his representation, which was granted.

"During the course of this litigation, including interlocutory and final hearing, this Chancellor has seen and heard a total of forty-nine witnesses, whose testimony covers 3,161 legal size pages, and has received in evidence and read fifty exhibits, including five depositions. In order to properly evaluate the equities of this cause, the record made before the Master on the original reference, which record was initially before the Supreme Court of Florida in *Chaachou v. Chaachou* (Rehearing denied June 24, 1954) 73 So.2d 830, has been reviewed. This record consists of an excess of 2,000 pages of testimony, 100 filed exhibits, and eight depositions.

"From this massive record it appears, and is so found, that the equities of this cause are with the plaintiff, and she is entitled to the relief prayed for in her Complaint.

"Plaintiff bases her claim for divorce on the ground of the defendant Chaachou's extreme cruelty, and there is ample evidence to sustain this ground. The plaintiff and the defendant Chaachou are both naturalized citizens, becoming such in 1950 and 1942 respectively. The plaintiff was born in Turkey of Armenian parents, and the defendant Chaachou was born in Bagdad, Iraq, of Jewish parents. The early history of their business acquaintanceship is recorded in *Chaachou v. Chaachou*, 73 So.2d 830, 832. It is apparent that plaintiff came to Miami Beach from Atlanta at defendant Chaachou's request in the Fall of 1942, and assumed the management of the Savoy Plaza Hotel which he had recently purchased for $165,000.00. Defendant Chaachou owned the Imperial Persian and Chinese Rug Company of New York City, which his counsel represented to the Court in this cause on September 12, 1952, was 'probably the largest rug importing business in the United States.' On Plaintiff's advice, after she began operating the Savoy Plaza Hotel, defendant Chaachou bought the Coral Reef, the Somerset, and the Astor hotels, also located in Miami Beach. Shortly after their purchase, these hotels were released by the military forces, which had been occupying them during the war, and the plaintiff took over their active management and operation also. According to the appraisal report of Adrian McCune, M.A.I., Plaintiff's Exhibit 3-1, these hotels are located near the southerly end of Miami Beach. They are not in the class with those more recently constructed further north along the ocean. But when they were acquired and for almost ten years thereafter, these hotels, because of plaintiff's good management and the scarcity of hotel accommodations at Miami Beach, enjoyed an extraordinary patronage and produced a large amount of revenue.

"That the plaintiff worked hard and effectively in the operation and management of these hotels for almost ten years after they were acquired is beyond dispute. Defendant Chaachou testified:

" 'A. Well, Fredericka was really my right hand. She was behind the desk; she was watching every hotel; she was a hostess, entertainer. She was on every occasion—really, she took my place. She had a free hand. Whatever she do or whatever she spend or whatever else she do—I think I was approximately more than busy man with four hotels on my hand and my importation and exportation in New York. I was hundred per cent practically depending on her, whatever she said goes, * * * she was really equipped for that business at that time.'

"When asked at the Master's hearing in what capacity plaintiff worked at the Savoy Plaza Hotel, which was the first one he bought, defendant Chaachou testified:

" 'Capacity of everything—as a hostess, housekeeper, manager, taking care of everything—entertainer.'

"When questioned on his deposition, which was received in evidence before the Master, if he had used the plaintiff as intermediary in the transfer of funds, he testified:

" 'A. I used the plaintiff as everything—in business and socially, as a hostess and so forth.'

"The plaintiff had been an interior decorator in Atlanta before she came to Miami Beach. Her description of what she did when she took over the management of the Savoy Plaza Hotel appears in her testimony, which is undisputed. She testified:

" 'I did everything that the hotel can be operated. I used to decorate; I used to be on the desk; I used to rent rooms; I looked at them, and many other things I did. I ripped the hotel, put a new bar downstairs, opened a door from the beach, all of this operation, and redecorate the hotel.

" 'When I came that hotel used to take $25 a month a room. I put everybody out. I redecorated the hotel. When I was operating, the hotel was getting $25, $18 a day.'

"Plaintiff testified that she made substantial savings on her interior decoration of the hotels, testifying:

" '* * * I saved $10,000 or $15,000 or $20,000 a year from my decorating.

" 'Q. During what year? A. All the time I had to decorate.

" 'Q. Because you did the decorating? A. I saved a lot of money. Material that sells $25 a yard, I but $2.35.'

"While she was at their summer residence in Tannersville, New York in November, 1951, defendant Chaachou telephoned her to fly to Miami Beach and redecorate three of the four hotels in order to get them ready for the coming season. She did this, replacing the tile, repairing the furniture, hiring the carpenters, and doing whatever was necessary to get them ready.

"On cross-examination she testified:

" 'Q. As a matter of fact during the last several years since Avak came to Miami Beach, you have been less and less active in the operation of the Savoy Plaza Hotel and other business owned by Mr. Chaachou, isn't that true? A. Sir, I was very active all the time.

" 'Q. Even in the past few years? A. I worked so hard until this last month ago, sir, if you don't believe me, ask thousands of people.
* * *

" 'A. I used to go to the bank. I used to rent rooms during the season. I used to be as hostess. I used to redecorate. Every hotel needs redecorating, and put everything. And this year I was every day in the kitchen. I was in the dining room. Sometimes they need help in the dining room. Even 3:00 o'clock in the morning, A.M., I used to work sometimes with the help. I worked very hard.

" 'Q. What hotel did you rent rooms in? A. Every hotel I have rent rooms, sir. I have rent rooms this year at Somerset. I have rent rooms in Savoy Plaza this year.
* * *

" '* * * I was the key of everything in these hotels.'
* * *

" '* * * When everybody comes, they want room, they want Mr. Chaachou. I'm eating, or whatever, I go.'
* * *

" 'I work all them. If switchboard short, I go to the switchboard. Everything has to be done, I do it.'
* * *

" 'Sir, whatever my husband ask, I do, any time. It doesn't matter if midnight or nothing. It is our hotels, and for our profit. * * * If he orders me anything, I'm in it. I never say no. I'm right ready to go whether midnight, morning, or any time.'

"She summarized in her testimony her work in connection with these hotels when she said:

" '* * * I used to work in my business 14, 15, 16 hours, doesn't matter when. He is in the office. Everything I used to control, no time, no hours. Every morning I used to get up, go to my business. Every night, sometimes until 1:00 o'clock. We used to go home together, and I come back until 1:00, 2:00 o'clock I have to be in the hotel.

" 'Q. You were the one? A. Sure, it is mine. I work with my heart and soul, sir * * *.'

"The comprehensive appraisal reports of McCune Company and Bishop & Company show that the Savoy Plaza, Somerset, Astor, and the Coral Reef hotels have a total of 343 rentable rooms. The Savoy Plaza is valued at $160,000.00, the Somerset at $230,000.00, the Astor at $160,000.00 and the Coral Reef at $525,000.00, and these values are equal to or in excess of the purchase price which the defendant, Khudourie Chaachou, paid for them. That they were good revenue producers during the ten year period from 1942 to 1952 is plainly evident. The defendant, Khudourie Chaachou, testified that the profit from them was $250,000.00 a season. The plaintiff persuaded the defendant, Chaachou, to buy the Coral Reef Hotel for $250,000.00 while the Army was still in possession, and even against his lawyer's advice to buy up the outstanding lease for $225,000.00 which lease had an unexpired term of six years. When the Army released this hotel in 1945, the plaintiff redecorated the same in time for occupancy for the 1945 Christmas Season. The plaintiff testified:

" '* * * I worked very hard to put that hotel in order. Christmas, 1945, I opened that hotel. We were very, very successful, that hotel. The cheapest rent that hotel took was $25 a day without American Plan.

" 'The cigar stand—just the cigar stand, $12,000 we got from the cigar stand. It was a most successful year. I remember that the rooms I rented $55 a day for four people, one room, without food.

" 'Six months we were very successful, but I was very tired because we were running other hotels. I suggested, "Let us re-lease this hotel again." and so we put the agency to lease the hotel again, and we re-leased this hotel for five years, $112,000 a year.'

"When the lease mentioned in the plaintiff's testimony had expired, the defendant, Khudourie Chaachou, sold the hotel on June 6, 1951, for $1,225,000.00 and took back a mortgage to himself for $1,100,000.00 to evidence the balance of the purchase price. The mortgagor paid approximately $256,000.00 on this mortgage before he defaulted, so that it is apparent that this hotel produced the defendant, Chaachou, at least $816,000.00 in revenue by the time the parties separated or soon thereafter. This revenue was the direct result, in large measure, of the plaintiff's advice and her labor. The plaintiff's testimony seems fully justified in this record when she said: 'Since I came into his life we have made lots of money'.

"That the defendant, Chaachou, led the plaintiff to believe, and that she did believe during this period, that she was his partner in these hotel operations, can hardly be doubted. A large part of this ten year period when she acted as such, the defendant, Chaachou, was engaged in the operation of his extensive rug business in New York, and left the actual running and management of the hotels to the plaintiff.

"The defendant, Chaachou, deliberately kept the plaintiff in ignorance of all financial matters, and she followed his wishes in this regard. He kept exclusive possession and control of all financial records. He handled them to suit himself and instructed her not to ask questions about them. All checks purporting to represent her share of her partnership income, which he gave her from time to time, she endorsed and delivered back to him on his pretext that he was 'investing' the same for her. At one time he told the plaintiff that he had $55,000.00 of her money invested, and on another occasion said it was $75,000.00 but neglected to tell her and she did not know of what the investment consisted. Whenever it was necessary for her to sign documents or papers she obeyed his instructions without question and signed at the place he indicated for her signature. This was true of all of her income tax returns which he caused his accountant to prepare for her signature. When a copy of her 1946 income tax return was produced upon her counsel's demand at trial, which defendant, Chaachou, had kept in his possession and which had been prepared by his accountant, it reflected partnership returns from the four hotels of $26,000.00 which she testified she never received. This return reflected a deduction of $1,200.00 for 'Entertaining prospects and guests at taxpayer's home in capacity as manager and partner re: Coral Reef, Somerset, Astor and Savoy Plaza Hotels, Miami Beach, Fla. including special parties for Professional Women's Club of Miami, Fla.'

"Time after time in the record of this cause the plaintiff testified that she trusted the defendant, Chaachou, and it is evident that she did not only in her finances but in her personal relationship with him. She testified:

"'* * * I have trusted in him, and he took everything, of the books and everything else, and I took care of everything that goes into hotel, sir.'

"She also testified:

"'A. Armenian girls, when they are married to a man—they obey the husband no matter what he says.
"'Q. Is that the reason you signed this way? A. Yes sir; whatever he told me, I do exactly like he wants me to do.'
* * *
"'Q. Did you ever read your income tax returns before you signed them? A. No, sir.
"'Q. Why didn't you? A. Because my husband used to tell me, "You don't have to read. Don't ask any questions to the accountant. Just do what I am saying." So I just think, well, he knows, and I just signed whatever he wants me to do.
"'Q. Don't you think it was rather foolish for a person just to sign, and not know what he was signing? A. No, sir; because I trusted him.
"'Q. Why did you trust him? A. Well, he is my husband.
"'Q. Is that reason enough for you? A. Well, that is enough reason. I have been obedient, because he has a violent temper. When I did not do something, he gets very upset. Sometimes he hits me.'

"She testified that the only checking account that she had was one in which defendant, Chaachou, put enough money for her to issue a check for the payment of her income tax, and that he had control of all the money. That when they got married, he gave her $100.00 a week allowance, which he later reduced to $75.00 a week, and finally to $50.00 just before they separated.

"She described her last meeting with the defendant, Chaachou, in the business office of the Savoy Plaza Hotel, on June 18, 1952, as follows:

" '* * * I was very tired, and I went to his office to talk to him after the season, I presented the bill that Dr. Minoyian sent, to write a check, and he says, "I am not paying any more of your bills," and he threw the bill at me. Then I said "When are we going to vacation, because I am exhausted, and tired, and I want to go to the summer home to rest. You look tired too. We will go." He said. "You are not going this year to the summer home." I asked him why, and he says, "Because I am selling the house."

" 'That time I said, "Well, then I need some money. I want to get my allowance, so I can go and shop for a few things," and he says, "I am not giving you any more allowance either. I am sick and tired of you. I want you to get out of my life, and stay out."

" 'I said, "What do you mean, I should get out of your life?" He says, "I told you I want you to get out of this building too. If not, I will throw you with the law," and I said, "What are you saying? Why are you talking like that? Are you sick, or you are not feeling good"? He says, "No. I mean it, what I am saying. You have to get out of my life."

" 'I says, "Well, if I have to get out, all right. Let us come to an understanding of my share. I have worked with you all these years, and I don't know what I have, what I don't have, and if you don't want, we will go to court." He says, "Go to court. Go to court, and if the court decides a million dollars, I am going to give it to you. I told you, you have no share. You spent everything. You have no more allowance coming."

" 'I said, "Khudourie, please honey, I don't want you to act like this. I don't want no lawyers. You know I never had lawyer, or anything like that together." "No," he says, "You got to go to court to finish this." I said, "Do you know any lawyer I can go to?" He laughed. He says, "Any lawyer I know?"

" 'I said, "Didn't you promise me that you are going to love me, honor me, keep me forever?" He says, "Man can promise and take it back." I said, "What do you mean? This is no Bagdad or Russia. If you want to take your promise, we have to go to court to let the judge decide, and you give me my share. We will leave each other, divorce each other." "Oh," he says, "Divorce—don't you know that legally you are not married to me. I have affidavits to that." I said, "Put the false affidavits one side. You get them to sign affidavits. I know the kind people. Please, Khudourie, don't let Satan destroy you. We have done everything together. The Lord gave all this money to be used for His glory. I don't want you to mistreat me." He says, "Get out of my life. You have to go, and take your—" I said, "Where am I going?" "Take the jewelery I bought you, sell it, buy a home. Get out of my life."

" 'Then I was so shocked—I was so shocked that I can't tell you.
* * *'

"Following this episode the defendant, Chaachou, wrote the plaintiff two letters which were introduced in evidence in this cause, the first dated July 1, 1952, and the second July 7, 1952. In the former letter defendant, Chaachou, advised the plaintiff:

" 'Since you have neglected and not performed your duties for the past seven or eight days, and inasmuch as we were unable to

contact you several times each day during the above mentioned period, we hereby notify you that your services are no longer required.
    * * *

    " 'Due to the termination of your services, the rent of your apartment will be $15.00 per day and is payable weekly in advance. Otherwise your apartment will have to be vacated by July 5th or before.
    * * *'

"In the latter letter he told her that:

    " 'Inasmuch as your Rent started from Saturday July 5th and has not been paid in advance to date, we hereby give you three days notice to vacate your apartment or pay your rent of $15.00 daily or $105.00 per week, in advance, according to the Florida State Law.'

    "Throughout this entire record on the four occasions that plaintiff has been extensively examined by counsel for both sides, she has steadfastly maintained that she was defendant Chaachou's partner in his hotel business. That she worked with defendant, Chaachou, under that belief and that he encouraged her in her thinking is evidenced from the record. Indeed corroboration of her testimony was furnished by the defendant's admission that 'she had a partnership' and by two documents which he offered in evidence purporting to constitute her a partner in the net profits derived from the operation of the Savoy Plaza and the Astor hotels, which were dated prior to the marriage of the parties and which the plaintiff testified she read for the first time from the witness stand. The plaintiff testified that the defendant, Chaachou, advised her that she was a partner, not only in 20% of the net profits of the Savoy Plaza Hotel but of its ownership as well, and that as he acquired each of the remaining three hotels, he repeated a similar statement to her, with reference to them. The defendant denied this and attempted to reduce her to the status of an employee to avoid his obligation to her, not only financially but as her husband. Whatever partnership existed between the parties became merged in their larger partnership of marriage and its terms are now too indistinct to be specifically enforced as such. To allow him, however, to enjoy the fruits of his wife's labor from which he benefitted so substantially, as shown by this record, without any compensation to her for her contribution to the wealth he derived from these hotels, would constitute a gross inequity and result in his unjust enrichment, which should not be permitted under the rule announced by the Florida Supreme Court in the cases of *Windham v. Windham*, 144 Fla. 563, 198 So. 202; *Strauss v. Strauss*, 148 Fla. 23, 3 So.2d 727; *Engebretsen v. Engebretsen*, 151 Fla. 372, 11 So.2d 322; *Giachetti v. Giachetti*, 157 Fla. 259, 25 So.2d 658.
    * * *

    "Considering the fact that the value of all the hotels is equal to or in excess of defendant, Chaachou's original purchase price, and the large revenue which he derived from them through his wife's assistance and efforts, it is equitable that she should be, and she is hereby, awarded a special equity of three-twentieths (3/20ths) value of each of said four hotels, including its furniture, furnishings and fixtures, as shown by the appraisal report of Adrian McCune, M.A.I., filed in this cause, and that she be, and she is hereby, granted an equitable lien on each of said hotels, its furniture, furnishings and fixtures, as security for this value award.
    "With reference to the residence at 5041 Collins Avenue, Miami Beach, the plaintiff testified it was a present to her on the occasion of her marriage to the defendant, Chaachou. In this she is corroborated by two witnesses who assert that they heard the plaintiff say in the defendant, Chaachou's presence, on the occasion of the wedding reception, that the

defendant had given her the home. (John Kulhanjian, 27–28; Mary Kulhanjian, 2859.) The plaintiff selected the residence and spent five months, with defendant's consent, in furnishing and redecorating it so that she and the defendant could get married and move into this residence when he returned from New York in December of 1944. After their marriage the plaintiff and the defendant, Khudourie Chaachou, lived in this home for almost six years until he ordered her to leave her home and take up residence at the Savoy Plaza Hotel for no apparent reason, except that at about this time he testified 'he was more inclined to get rid of her anyway.'

"Counsel takes the position that this being an oral contract was within the statute of frauds, but the cases do not so hold. *Exchange National Bank of Tampa, etc. v. Bryan*, (1936) 122 Fla. 479, 165 So. 685; *McDowell v. Ritter* (1943) 153 Fla. 50, 13 So.2d 612. In the last mentioned case the Supreme Court, speaking through Mr. Justice Terrell, said:

> " 'The law is settled that the statute of frauds applies only to executory contracts and has no application to agreements fully performed on both sides.'

"That rule seems to be applicable to the instant case, and, therefore, the residence at 5041 Collins Avenue, Miami Beach, Florida, will be awarded to the plaintiff.

"On the question of divorce little need be said. Mrs. Chaachou testified that for no apparent reason her husband put her out of the house just before Christmas in 1949, and insisted that because of her pressing duties at the Savoy Plaza Hotel she should take up her residence there. In obedience to his command, she did move into the Savoy Plaza Hotel, but left her personal things at her home, and went back to her home each morning to have breakfast with him and returned each evening, until she found that defendant, Chaachou, was keeping company with one of his secretaries.

"If denying the fact of marriage, putting her out of the house, vigorously contesting the marriage, withholding from her support, when she was destitute, charging her with adultery after she had proven her marriage, and maligning her character by sending numerous letters to her attorneys (introduced collectively as Plaintiff's Exhibit 3–8) does not constitute extreme cruelty, it is difficult to think what would.

"On the question of adultery the defendant, Chaachou, undertook to prove same by (1) various acts of the plaintiff and one Avak Hagopian, and (2) testimony of John Durgin.

"Incidentally, it appears from the record that Mrs. Chaachou was born on March 3, 1906, and is therefore 54 years of age. She was 46 at the time the Complaint was filed. Avak is 34 years of age and was 26 at the time the Complaint was filed. Mrs. Chaachou has a son older than Avak.

> " 'The rule has commonly been abbreviated into the statement that proof of inclination and opportunity is sufficient to prove adultery; but this statement is correct only when it is understood that inclination means more than ordinary human tendencies, and must extend to proof of conduct reasonably suggesting specific libidinous tendency of each of the parties toward the other, and opportunity must be understood as meaning more than mere chance and must include the elements which would prove guilt beyond a reasonable doubt. However, according to some authority, whatever the disposition of the parties, the mere fact that the parties may have been in each other's company, under such circumstances that the act might have occurred, will not justify the conclusion that it actually did occur. There must be some circumstances, in addition to the disposi-

tion and opportunity, tending to rebut the presumption of innocence, although proof of circumstances which lead a reasonable man
to believe that the offense has been committed, in addition to an
adulterous inclination and an opportunity to commit the crime, will
justify a conviction,' Adultery, 2 C.J.S. *Adultery* §24, p. 492.

"Of Avak, Mrs. Chaachou said:

" 'Q. What place, if any does Avak Hagopian have in your life?
A. Avak Hagopian is like my own son. I have done more to (sic) him
that I have to (sic) my own son. The reason is that he is a man of God,
lives according to the Lord's Will and he was helpless when he was
here. He didn't know language (sic). It was a different country,
strange. I have to interpret for him. I have to write letters for him.
And they were writing letters from all over, and without me he
couldn't do all this work, and I drove him wherever he wanted, because of motherly love I have towards him, like I to my own son.
" 'Q. What association, if any, has Avak had with your family?
A. He is just like one of our family.
" 'Q. Is he presently related to you in any way? A. Yes. He is
married to my sister's daughter.
" 'Q. Did you ever sit on Avak's lap in the same chair with him?
A. Never, never.
" 'Q. Were you ever in Avak's room either you or Avak or both of
you were in your sleeping garments? A. Never. Mr. Niles, I haven't
lost my self-respect yet. I am a Christian. I love my God.'

"The plaintiff introduced in evidence at the final hearing of this
cause a letter (Exhibit 3-11) over the signature of K. Chaachou, dated
November 17, 1959, addressed to Mr. and Mrs. A. Balian of Auburn,
New York, the body of which reads:

" 'Reverend Avak and his foster mother, Fredericka, will be in
Rochester Friday, November 25th, Saturday, the 26th, and Sunday,
the 27th of November.
" 'If you wish them to visit the Syracuse Church at your city,
kindly communicate with them at that time—so that they can make
a definite date in preparation.'

"The defendant attempted through various witnesses to show that
the plaintiff had the *opportunity* to commit adultery with Avak. Avak
stayed at the defendant's hotels at the defendant's suggestion. The defendant had full knowledge of his being there, his whereabouts at all
times and the opportunities that were afforded him to commit adultery
with the plaintiff. There is not one word in the testimony that either the
plaintiff or Avak had the *inclination* to commit adultery with each other.
He not only stayed at the hotels operated by the defendant in Miami
Beach, but he went to the defendant's place at Tannersville in the
Catskill Mountains of New York at the defendant's suggestion. He did
not appear at the trial as a witness. The proof falls far short of that required to establish that the plaintiff committed adultery with Avak.
Mrs. Chaachou testified positively that she had never had sexual intercourse with any man other than Khudourie Chaachou since she married
him in December, 1944.
"Some years after this case was commenced, the defendant asked
leave to file an amended answer charging the plaintiff with adultery. His
motion to amend had two affidavits attached to it. One of them by one
Donald Young.
"Donald Young was called as a witness in the case. The sum and
substance of his testimony was that he saw the plaintiff and Avak up in
Tannersville, sitting on a bench in broad daylight and Avak had his arm

around her. Both were fully clothed. This is far short of proving adultery. Now it may be conceded that the affidavit that this man made and which was attached to the defendant's answer charging adultery went further, but he repudiated everything else, except that they were sitting on the bench in broad daylight, and the man was leaning over her with his arm around her.

"Richard Bluver was a witness who testified that he had stayed at the Savoy Plaza (one of Chaachou's hotels) and that he met the plaintiff there in the drug store and they had a conversation which lasted about an hour. This was in 1949 or 1950, and that she told him that she was married to the 'healer'. Suppose she did, it was false, if she said it, because she wasn't married to the 'healer'. This witness also said that he read Chaachou's advertisement in a newspaper in which he offered $100,000 reward for information connected with the alleged plot against him in this case.

"Joseph W. Price said that he was a Minister of the Gospel, and that he was in Jacksonville to some kind of a meeting and came back in an automobile with Mrs. Chaachou and Avak. They spent the night in Winterhaven. There was another couple in the car, and when they pulled up to the motel, Mrs. Chaachou suggested that they would need three rooms, and he said, 'No, we will need four rooms and then she said "one for you and Mrs. Price, one for Mr. Richer and one for Avak and I'', and when I looked surprised she said "why Reverend Price it wouldn't be wrong for me to share a room with this child that God has given me," and I said "well if you think so, it is up to you", and she said "well, maybe I had better not", to which I replied "well, it would look better if you didn't" '. 'She rented the rooms and brought him his key and he didn't know what the procedure was.' At any rate, even if this transpired, if doesn't appear that she actually occupied the room with Avak. Chaachou gave this witness $500.00 at one time and presently holds a mortgage on his house for $2,200.00. Also this witness admitted that, following this motel incident, he twice invited Avak to preach in his church, and that he believed him to be a 'sincere and honest man.'

"Mack Davis, Jr., * * * was a bell hop at the Savoy Plaza Hotel. He also worked at Chaachou's residence. He testified that Mrs. Chaachou and her sister and the sister's daughter, Doris, and Avak occupied several rooms on the third floor of the hotel and that on some occasions he would go up to the suite and Mrs. Chaachou and Avak would be sitting on the same chair in one of the rooms. The door was not locked; he knocked and she told him to come in, which he did, and no comment was made about the situation. He also said she had on a negligee. This happened several times. He never told Chaachou about it and that is all there is to it. Mrs. Chaachou categorically denied this.

"Now except for the testimony of John Durgin which we will take up later, this is the sum total of the defendant's testimony about the plaintiff's adultery. * * * It is wholly insufficient to make out the charge of adultery.

"Honi soit qui mal y pense.

"The only other bit of evidence regarding the plaintiff's alleged adultery was from the witness John Durgin who testified that on an occasion he visited the plaintiff at her residence on Collins Avenue and went to bed with her.

"As to that Mrs. Chaachou said:

" 'Q. Now, you heard the testimony of Mr. John Durgin? A. Yes, sir.

" 'Q. Tell the court whether or not the incident about which he testified to in which he said you went to bed together ever took place.

A. Mr. Niles, such a ridiculous, horrible lie I have never heard in my life.

" 'Q. Answer the question yes or no. A. Of course not, Mr. Niles.

" 'Q. Did you ever pick him up and take him to your house? A. Never in my life.

" 'Q. Were you ever alone with him under the same roof? A. I never had any association with that man until I saw last year he came to the house with the sheriff.

" 'Q. I ask you, Mrs. Chaachou, did you ever have any conversation—A. No.

" 'Q. Please let me finish my question Ma'am. Did you ever have any conversations with Mr. Durgin about Mr. Chaachou? A. No.'

"This Chancellor saw and heard Mr. Durgin. Apart and aside from the inherent improbability of his testimony, his manner on the witness stand was not at all convincing. He may have been influenced by Chaachou's newspaper advertisements offering $100,000.00 to any one who would furnish testimony in his behalf. This Chancellor believes him to be a liar and a perjurer and so brands him.

"On the question of alimony, this Chancellor, under date of October 24, 1956, made an order awarding the plaintiff $750.00 per month as temporary alimony. This was affirmed by The Supreme Court in certiorari proceedings (92 So.2d 414). It would seem that sum is sufficient for permanent alimony and it will be so ordered.

"The defendant has indicated his intention of pulling up stakes and leaving the State of Florida. If he carried out his threat the plaintiff may find that the award of alimony is ineffective. He will, therefore, be required to put up a surety bond, payable to the plaintiff in the sum of $180,000.00, conditioned upon the prompt and faithful payment by him of the alimony herein decreed to be paid to her during the remainder of his natural life. The injunctive order of this Court will be continued in effect until the bond is approved.

"Many times during the pendency of this litigation, defendant has failed to pay temporary alimony and it has been necessary for this Chancellor on numerous occasions to issue rules to show cause why he should not be held in contempt for his failure to make these payments. He has never actually been sent to jail for that reason, although he was sentenced to serve a period of confinement in the county jail for failure to permit the appraisers appointed by this Chancellor to inspect his property. He purged himself before the order took effect.

* * *

"Concerning the corporate defendants, they are merely the alter ego of the defendant, Khudourie Chaachou. Owning all of their capital stock, with himself as President, they constitute but an agency or a convenient manner in which the defendant, Khudourie Chaachou, has chosen to hold the naked legal title to the Somerset, Astor and Savoy Plaza Hotels. They have no interest in this controversy apart from that of the defendant, Khudourie Chaachou, and except for the mechanics of working out the Final Decree they are unimportant to the outcome of this cause. In equity all of the hotels are the property of the defendant, Khudourie Chaachou.

"Wherefore, the premises considered, it is

"Considered, Ordered, Adjudged and Decreed as follows:

"1. That the equities of this cause are with the plaintiff, and she is entitled to the relief for which she prays in accordance with this opinion.

"2. That the plaintiff, Fredericka Phillips Chaachou, and the defendant, Khudourie Chaachou, be, and they are hereby, divorced each from the other *a vinculo matrimonii*.

"3. That the temporary alimony heretofore ordered for the plaintiff in the amount of $750.00 each and every month be made permanent, and that the defendant, Khudourie Chaachou, pay her on the first of each and every month the sum of $750.00, and that he send the same to her at her residence.

"4. That the defendant, Khudourie Chaachou, post with the clerk of this Court a good and sufficient bond in the sum of One Hundred Eighty Thousand (180,000.00) Dollars, to be approved by this Court, conditioned to pay the plaintiff the permanent alimony herein awarded as and when the same becomes due. That when said bond is posted and approved, the injunctive order of this Court dated the 10th day of April, 1959, and duly recorded in Chancery Order Book 1387 at Page 96, shall stand cancelled and vacated without further order of this Court.

"5. That the plaintiff be, and she is hereby, awarded a special equity equal to three-twentieths (3/20ths) of the value, as shown by the appraisal report of Adrian McCune, M.A.I., in each of the following described hotel properties:

"(a) The Savoy Plaza Hotel, located at 425 Ocean Drive, Miami Beach, Florida, the legal description of which is: Lot 6, Block 116, Ocean Beach No. 4, according to the plat thereof as recorded in Plat Book 3 at Page 151 of the Public Records of Dade County, Florida.

"(b) The Astor Hotel, located at 956 Washington Avenue, Miami Beach, Florida, the legal description of which is: Lots 1 and 2, less the west 135 feet, Block 35, Ocean Beach Number 3, as recorded in Plat Book 2 at Page 81 of the Public Records of Dade County, Florida.

"(c) The Coral Reef Hotel, located at 3601 Collins Avenue, Miami Beach, Florida, the legal description of which is: Lots 1, 2, 7, and 8, Block 25, Ocean Front Amended, according to the plat thereof as recorded in Plat Book 5 at Pages 7 and 8 of the Public Records of Dade County, Florida.

"(d) The Somerset Hotel, located at 335 Ocean Drive, Miami Beach, Florida, the legal description of which is: Lot 4, Block 115, Ocean Beach No. 4, according to the plat thereof as recorded in Plat Book 3 at Page 151 of the Public Records of Dade County, Florida.

"6. That three-twentieths (3/20ths) of the value of said hotel properties, according to the appraisal report of Adrian McCune, M.A.I., equals the sum of One Hundred sixty-one thousand, Two Hundred fifty ($161,250.00) Dollars, and there is hereby created and established upon said described hotel properties a first lien in plaintiff's favor in the said amount. That in the event the defendant, Khudourie Chaachou, shall not deposit with the Clerk of this Court within thirty (30) days from the date of this decree, for the use and benefit of the plaintiff, said sum of One Hundred sixty-one thousand, Two Hundred Fifty ($161,250.00) Dollars, then the Special Master appointed in this cause shall thereafter sell said hotel properties for cash to satisfy said lien of the plaintiff at public auction at the South front door of the Dade County Court House, at Miami, Florida, after first giving thirty (30) days public notice of the time, place and manner of said sale in some newspaper of general circulation in Dade County, Florida, four (4) insertions of such notice in such newspaper at least seven (7) days apart shall be taken and deemed sufficient public notice, and said hotel properties shall be sold on the first Monday succeeding the last advertisement of said hotel properties between the hours of eleven A.M., and two P.M., on that day; that upon the said sale of said hotel properties by said Special Master, the lien of the plaintiff shall thereupon be reduced to the proceeds of said sale."

* * *

* * * Appellees raise twelve points for review.

Of these twelve points there are but two which merit our consideration here. First, it is contended that the chancellor's decree is erroneous in that it is based on the uncorroborated testimony of Mrs. Chaachou as to the grounds for divorce. It is also contended that the chancellor erroneously considered as grounds for divorce, matters which arose after the filing of the complaint. Concerning the grounds for divorce, the chancellor included in his final order the following statement:

> "If denying the fact of marriage, putting her out of the house, vigorously contesting the marriage, withholding from her support, when she was destitute, charging her with adultery after she had proven her marriage, and maligning her character by sending numerous letters to her attorneys (introduced collectively as Plaintiff's Exhibit 3-8) does not constitute extreme cruelty, it is difficult to think what would."

It does appear that the only testimony as to the grounds for divorce was given by Mrs. Chaachou. There was, however, documentary evidence, in the form of the letters referred to by the chancellor introduced as to acts of cruelty which occurred following the institution of the action for divorce. The question then is whether this documentary evidence relating to matters occurring following the filing of the complaint may be used to corroborate the testimony of the appellant. It is the opinion of this court that these matters were properly received in evidence and that when considered in conjunction with the testimony of Mrs. Chaachou provide an adequate evidentiary basis for the chancellor's granting of the divorce on the ground of extreme cruelty. When thus considered, the evidence discloses a course of cruel conduct toward appellant which began before and continued after the filing of the suit and thus serves to corroborate the appellant's testimony concerning the appellee's vilification, harrassment and mistreatment of her during the existence of the marriage.

In the annotation on the subject of corroboration in divorce suits contained in 65 A.L.R. 169, upon which this court relied in the case of *Martin v. Martin*, Fla., 66 So.2d 268, it is pointed out that circumstances which develop during the trial of a divorce action may furnish the necessary corroboration. For example, in *McAllister v. McAllister*, 28 Wash. 613, 69 P. 119, it was held that the defendant husband's apparent insouciance exhibited at the trial toward his pregnant, penniless wife was corroborative of her testimony concerning his cruel treatment of her.

Regarding the letters from appellee which were received into evidence and considered by the chancellor, it has frequently been held that such communications between the parties may be considered as corroboration in a divorce proceeding. 65 A.L.R. 169 at page 179. See also *Hunt v. Hunt*, 61 Fla. 630, 54 So. 390, wherein this court considered such a communication in connection with a charge of desertion.

The chancellor did not err, moreover, in taking into account as evidence of cruelty the appellee's answer charging appellant with adultery, a charge which, as the chancellor found, was wholly lacking in substance. In *Grossman v. Grossman*, Fla., 90 So.2d 115, 117, it was held that a prior unfounded action for divorce brought by a husband could be considered as an act of cruelty on his part. The court quoted from Nelson, DIVORCE AND ANNULMENT (2d ed.) Section 6.23, page 278-279, wherein it is stated: "The malicious institution of unfounded and unwarranted litigation by one spouse against the other may amount to cruelty or personal indignities." In *Wright v. Thomas*, 306 Ky. 763, 209 S.W.2d 315, it was held that in a divorce proceeding instituted by a wife, the husband's counterclaim for divorce containing an unfounded charge of lewd and lascivious conduct on the part of the wife amounted to cruel and inhuman treatment. See also *Wetherington v. Wetherington*, 57 Fla. 551, 49 So. 549, holding that a husband's false charges of adultery may constitute extreme cruelty.

For the foregoing reasons, it is our opinion that the chancellor's findings regarding extreme cruelty are amply supported and corroborated by competent evidence of record, and that he did not err in granting the divorce in favor of the appellant.

* * *

The remaining points raised by the appellees have been considered and are found to be without merit. For the foregoing reasons the order of the chancellor, except as herein modified, should be and the same is hereby affirmed.

It is so ordered.

Comments

Stanard v. Bolin and *Chaachou v. Chaachou* should be read together, although they are seemingly unrelated. *Stanard* involves damages for noncohabitation, while *Chaachou* can be viewed as "damages" for cohabitation. The factual situations in the two cases are in contradiction to each other, the first case dealing with a mere promise to marry, while the second supposedly involves an already consummated marriage, albeit in the form of common law marriage. Obviously the level of execution of the contract is considerably higher in *Chaachou* than in *Stanard*, but this is a matter of degree. Since the conduct of the parties is more determinative of legal consequences than any of their express statements, we are dealing basically with implied contract. *Chaachou* could have been argued under a theory of engagement to marry, but this would have been done by the defendant. His point would have been that the plaintiff must fail because of the statutory abolition of actions based on breach of promise to marry in Florida. There was also an appearance of marriage in *Stanard*. The parties purchased real estate and signed as husband and wife. Whether a theory of engagement or marriage is applied in either case traditionally depends on the intent of the parties and the circumstances.

The reality of litigation is, however, more complex. What appears to be the intent of the parties may be an application of public policy by way of legal fiction. Since the judge, in finding the supposed intent, has to rely on the circumstances as pleaded by the lawyers, the representation of reality and the application of legal theories may be remote or even opposite to what actually took place and what the parties wanted.

The pleadings of the facts in *Chaachou*, for example, determined to some extent the choices of facts and theories available to the court. Other possible facts and theories are incidentally mentioned in the opinion, for example, that the case could have been based on a theory of a business partnership or a personal service contract. Even a landlord-tenant relationship is mentioned. It is conceivable that the plaintiff "wife" would have fared better under a theory of partnership than under a theory of marriage. It is also conceivable that the case could have been settled, even after a divorce action had been filed, under a theory of business partnership, which also would have avoided liability for income tax that had to be paid on alimony. Of course, the defense could also have proceeded, and in fact did alternatively proceed, under theories other than marriage, for instance, that the plaintiff, according to the intention of the parties, was merely in an employment relationship and could be fired for cause.

Another aspect of *Chaachou*, essentially overlooked, is that it can be viewed as an early precedent for a cohabitation contract, comparable to *Marvin v. Marvin* (pp. 172–185), decided 15 years later by the California Supreme Court. The court mentioned in *Chaachou* that "[w]hatever partnership existed between the parties became merged in their larger partnership of marriage." This theory of merger appears to be unsound, since husband and wife can have business contracts with each other. More important is the continuing inference, even after the abolition of common law marriage in Florida, that the plaintiff would have recovered under contract in any event, even if common law marriage had not been available in the state, simply because no merger would have taken place in that case.

Both *Stanard* and *Chaachou* can be viewed in the light of policies that led to anti-heart-balm legislation in many states, namely, that actions of this kind can be used for blackmail purposes. The same can be argued of cohabitation contracts as in *Marvin v. Marvin* (see pp. 172–185). Yet it should not be overlooked that these policies are possibly dated. Whether or not claims of women are viewed as being in the nature of extortion depends on the climate of the times. Perhaps more acute is the question raised in *Stanard* in the dissenting opinion: how actions for breach of promise can be reconciled with the availability of no-fault divorce. Fault obviously is involved in the adjudication even if punitive damages are not assessed. Thus in the State of Washington an engaged man may be in a worse position than if he had married; in the case of a short marriage his wife may have received very little, if anything. A similar problem has been raised in the State of California in the case of cohabitation contracts, as expressed in the dissenting opinion of Mr. Justice Clark in *Marvin*. That fault is involved in *Stanard* can hardly be doubted. It is no accident that the pleadings of the plaintiff fiancee were couched in a form and style identical to a request for a divorce based on extreme cruelty when she stated through her lawyer that she was in great shock, became ill and lost sleep and weight, and had to consult a physician. Here, too, the styles of action for breach of promise and divorce based on fault are very similar.

The attorneys in *Stanard* and *Chaachou* may not have been sufficiently aware that they could have used the amorphous mass of information they had in several different ways. For example, in *Chaachou*—which took almost 10 years of litigation—greater efforts should have been made at an early phase to persuade the parties to settle by dissolving not marriage, but partnership, perhaps by conveying straight title in one or two of the hotels to the plaintiff.

References

Shultz, *Contractual Ordering of Marriage: A New Model for State Policy*, 70 CALIF. L. REV. 204 (1982).

Weitzman, *Legal Regulation of Marriage: Tradition and Change—A Proposal for Individual Contracts and Contracts in Lieu of Marriage*, 62 CALIF. L. REV. 1169 (1974).

Weitzman, L., THE MARRIAGE CONTRACT—SPOUSES, LOVERS, AND THE LAW (1981).

Weyrauch, *Metamorphoses of Marriage*, 13 FAM. L.Q. 415 (1980).

Antenuptial Agreement as Safeguard to Deliberation

*Ante-Nuptial Agreement From Transcript in the Case of Ball**

160 Fla. 601, 36 So.2d 172 (1948)

THIS AGREEMENT, Made and entered into in duplicate this 15th day of June, A.D. 1933, by and between RUTH L. PRICE, now living in the City of Washington, D. C., and EDWARD BALL, of Duval County, State of Florida,

WITNESSETH:

That Whereas, a marriage is contemplated by and between the parties hereto; and, whereas, said parties propose to enter into and solemnize such marriage at an early date; and, whereas, the parties hereto know that marriage is a most serious and solemn relationship, and is not to be entered into lightly;

And, Whereas, many marriages are wrecked by constant bickering and dissension over various matters, oftentimes trifling and insignificant, we herewith make and declare, for our future guidance, a set of rules, by which we will and shall be governed during our married life, to wit:

First: It is agreed by and between the parties hereto to be faithful and loyal, each to the other, in thought, speech and action, at all times and under all circumstances.

Second: It is agreed by and between the parties hereto that each will maintain and exhibit toward the other a courteous and considerate attitude in all relationships and under all circumstances.

Third: It is agreed by and between the parties hereto that if for any reason either of the parties hereto should find a person that the other party is acquainted with to be objectionable, then, and in that event, the other party hereto shall not cultivate or retain an acquaintance or friendship with such person, nor shall either party show that person any favorable attention;

(a) Neither of the parties hereto shall cultivate or retain a friendship with any person who, after a short period of time, shall not prove to be mutually agreeable and satisfactory to both parties.

---

*[Found in J. Carson, A PRACTICAL TREATISE ON THE LAW OF THE FAMILY, MARRIAGE AND DIVORCE IN FLORIDA 100–104 (1950).]

(b) Neither of the parties hereto shall at any time develop or cultivate a close friendship with a person of the opposite sex.

Fourth: It is agreed by and between the parties hereto that no kins person of either of the parties hereto shall be entertained or remain as a guest in the home of the parties hereto for a period longer than one week, unless both parties hereto are mutually agreeable to the prolongation of such visit or entertainment.

(a) No other guest shall be entertained for any period of time, except upon the mutual invitation willingly and freely extended by both parties hereto.

Fifth: It is agreed by and between the parties hereto that when both of the parties hereto enjoy good health, we shall set aside three nights a week to entertain our friends and acquaintances, or to call on our friends and acquaintances, or to seek such other recreation as may be desirable. On the other four nights of each week we shall remain quietly at home, seeking such recreation and genuine happiness as is only to be found outside of the frivolities and ostentations of our present day social life.

Sixth: It is agreed by and between the parties hereto that the property owned by the respective parties to this Agreement at the time of their marriage shall continue and remain their several separate, individual and respective properties, and each party hereto shall be at liberty to make such sale, transfer or other disposition of such party's separate and individual property as that party may desire, without objection or interference from the other party.

(a) That the earnings, increase and/or profits from such respective, individual and separate properties of the parties hereto shall become and remain a part of such separate, individual property.

(b) That the income and earnings (except that from the separate, individual properties heretofore mentioned) of the parties hereto after their marriage shall become and remain community property and that each party hereto shall at all times have an equal right and ownership in this property, except as in hereinafter in Section Seven (7) provided.

(c) Other than incidental and current household expenses, neither of the parties hereto shall disburse, invest, loan, or make any other disposition of the community property until the same shall have been fully discussed and mutually agreed to by and between the parties hereto.

Seventh: It is agreed by and between the parties hereto that in the event either party hereto violates this Agreement to the extent that such party hereto shall become involved in an affair with a person of the opposite sex, that such offending party, shall thereby immediately forfeit to the other party hereto all interest and rights of every kind and nature in the community property and shall thereupon forthwith convey and deliver the same to the other party, and that involvement in such an affair shall automatically terminate this Agreement, other than the provisions of this Section, which shall remain in full force and effect;

(a) Conclusive proof of the involvement in such an affair shall be cause for an immediate separation of the parties hereto, and, in the event there is such an offending party, such offending party shall have no claim against the other party hereto of any kind or nature whatsoever.

Eighth: It is agreed by and between the parties hereto that each of them shall take a proper pride in their personal appearance and that each of the parties hereto shall at all times be neat and orderly, both in their personal attire and personal habits.

Ninth: It is agreed by and between the parties hereto that each will welcome from the other a suggestion or constructive criticism looking towards the improvement of the happy and cordial relations of the parties hereto.

(a) Such suggestions or constructive criticisms are to be made only when there is no third person present, and such suggestions and criticisms shall not be made with a frequency to constitute fault-finding or nagging, as these two latter qualities are at all times to be most studiously avoided.

Tenth: It is agreed by and between the parties hereto that each shall make a confidant of the other and that neither party hereto shall have any other confidant, and that on all occasions and under all circumstances each party hereto shall reveal in the frankest and fullest detail any and all matters affecting either of the parties hereto.

Eleventh: It is agreed by and between the parties hereto that neither of the parties hereto shall ever speak of the other party hereto to a third person except in such a way as will reflect credit on the party so spoken of.

(a) Neither of the parties hereto shall under any circumstances discuss with a third person anything relating to the purely personal relations of the parties hereto.

Twelfth: It is agreed by and between the parties hereto that in the event the parties hereto have any child or children, that when one of the parties hereto shall have reprimanded, admonished or punished such child or children that even though the other party hereto may not have felt that such reprimand, admonishment or punishment was justified, no objection shall be raised to such reprimand, admonishment or punishment in the presence of the child or children; as the parties hereto realize that discipline is necessary and must be mutually enforced for the welfare and successful training and raising of a child or children.

Thirteenth: It is mutually agreed by and between the parties hereto that in the event the parties hereto have a child or children, that such child or children shall have the benefit of a public school education up to and including the high school and that thereafter the parties hereto shall mutually decide whether it is desirable for such child or children to have any additional educational facilities.

Fourteenth: It is agreed by and between the parties hereto that additional rules or regulations, properly executed and attested, may be added from time to time, if the parties hereto shall mutually decide that such additional rules or regulations are desirable.

Fifteenth: It is agreed by and between the parties hereto that neither party will indulge in or take up any form of recreation or sport unless both parties hereto shall simultaneously take up such form of recreation or sport, except such as may be engaged in within the home of the parties hereto.

Sixteenth: It is agreed by and between the parties hereto that a vacation or pleasure trip will be taken only when it is possible and convenient for both parties to take such vacation or pleasure trip.

Seventeenth: It is agreed by and between the parties hereto that when either of the parties are preparing to leave their place of abode or home, that such party, prior to leaving, will advise the other party where he or she proposes to go and the length of time expected to be away from the place of abode or home, so that the other party will not be caused any uneasiness or worry by the absence of such party.

Eighteenth: It is agreed by and between the parties hereto that the violation of any one of the hereinbefore mentioned rules (except Rule No. Seven, for violation of which rule penalty is hereinbefore specifically provided and set forth in said Rule No. Seven) shall cause the party violating such rule or rules to forfeit to the other party an amount which shall equal one percent (1%) of such party's portion of the monthly community earnings or income for each such violation of each rule or rules so violated in any one month, and it is further agreed by and between the parties hereto that the habitual and continued violation of any of the rules herein set forth (except Rule No. Seven, for violation of which rule penalty is hereinbefore specifically provided and set forth in said Rule No. Seven) shall be cause for a separation of the parties hereto and that in such an event the parties hereto shall equally divide and apportion between themselves any and all community property and thereafter each shall go their separate and individual way, without claims of any kind or nature whatsoever against each other.

Nineteenth: The parties hereto hereby convenant and agree, each with the other, to fully and faithfully keep, perform and abide by all rules, matters and things hereinbefore agreed to and set forth; and do hereby further convenant and agree to devote themselves to the purpose of promoting a successful marriage, with harmony, contentment and happiness as the sole objective.

IN WITNESS WHEREOF, the parties hereto have hereunto set their hands and seals the day and year first hereinbefore written.

Signed: RUTH L. PRICE (SEAL)
Signed: EDWARD BALL (SEAL)

Antenuptial Regulation of Dissolution of Marriage

Ball v. Ball

Supreme Court of Florida

160 Fla. 601, 36 So.2d 172 (1948)

CHAPMAN, J.

The record in this case discloses that Edward Ball and Ruth Latham were married in Washington, D. C., on June 17, 1933, and shortly thereafter established a home on the St. Johns River on the outskirts of the City of Jacksonville, where they lived together as husband and wife until the month of January, 1943. During the month of May, 1943, Mrs. Ball left the home and instituted a suit for divorce in the Circuit Court of Duval County, Florida, on the ground of mental cruelty and in her bill of complaint prayed for a divorce and other relief.

On December 6, 1943, the defendant and cross-plaintiff, Edward Ball, filed an answer to the bill of complaint and a counterclaim in which he prayed for affirmative relief. On May 30, 1944, the court below, on motion of counsel for Mrs. Ball, entered an order dismissing her bill of complaint with prejudice to her right to again maintain a suit for divorce upon the facts alleged in the bill of complaint. In the same order the defendant, Edward Ball, was permitted to prosecute his counterclaim seeking or praying for an annulment of the marriage contract and antenuptial contract of the parties entered into shortly prior to their marriage.* * *

On February 1, 1946, by leave of the Court, the cross-plaintiff filed an amended counterclaim and, in part, alleged that the cross-defendant and the cross-plaintiff in early 1933 became engaged to marry and frequently exchanged ideas as to the responsibilities and obligations of marriage and the rearing and education of children which might be born to them as a result of their contemplated marriage, and their views on this point were set out in Sections Twelve and Thirteen of their antenuptial agreement signed by them on June 15, 1933, and are *viz.*:

> "Twelfth: It is agreed by and between the parties hereto that in the event the parties hereto have any child or children, that when one of the parties hereto shall have reprimanded, admonished or punished such child or children that even though the other party hereto may not have felt that such reprimand, admonishment or punishment was justified, no

objection shall be raised to such reprimand, admonishment or punishment in the presence of the child or children; as the parties hereto realize that discipline is necessary and must be mutually enforced for the welfare and successful training and raising of a child or children.

"Thirteenth: It is mutually agreed by and between the parties hereto that in the event the parties hereto have a child or children that such child or children shall have the benefit of a public school education up to and including the high school and that thereafter the parties hereto shall mutually decide whether it is desirable for such a child or children to have any additional educational facilities."

No child was born to the marriage.

The amended counterclaim alleges that the antenuptial contract and the marriage between the parties are invalid and should be annulled because of fraud practiced on the cross-plaintiff by the cross-defendant. Some weeks prior to June 19, 1928, the cross-defendant consulted Dr. George B. Norberg, of Kansas City, Missouri, and was advised to undergo a surgical operation, which was performed at the Trinity Lutheran Hospital on June 19, 1928, by Dr. Norberg. The cross-defendant's right ovary and the right Fallopian tube were removed. The left ovary was not removed but cysts found thereon were punctured. The left Fallopian tube was either removed or some effort or steps taken by the surgeon to make the same patent. The cross-defendant was sterile on June 17, 1933, and for some time prior thereto, and cross-defendant knew it or had good reason to believe that she was sterile.

The amended counterclaim further alleged that it was the duty of the cross-defendant, before the marriage ceremony was performed, to make known to the cross-plaintiff the fact that in the year 1928 she had a surgical operation involving her genital organs. It was her lawful duty to give to the cross-plaintiff all the information in connection with such matters, things and conditions as were known to her and also all of the knowledge and information that she could have obtained by the exercise of ordinary diligence. The defendant failed and neglected to give the plaintiff any information whatever regarding the surgical operation and the cross-plaintiff did not know that the cross-defendant had ever had an operation involving her genital organs or that her genital organs had been diseased. He did not know prior to marriage or prior to the filing of her suit on the 24th of May, 1943, of the diseased condition of her genital organs and he learned for the first time of the surgical operation and the diseased genital organs after she had instituted suit against him for divorce.

The amended counterclaim also alleges that the cross-plaintiff performed his full duties as the husband of the cross-defendant, administered to her needs and wants in sickness and in health and transferred to her stocks and bonds and caused the title to described interests in real estate to be placed in her name. A bank account in the joint names of the parties was opened and the husband deposited therein income and earnings as provided for by the terms and provisions of the antenuptial contract and that the cross-defendant now holds this property, because of her fraud and deception, in trust for the cross-plaintiff as his trustee.

The counterclaim prays for a decree declaring the antenuptial contract and the marriage contract void ab initio and that all property transferred by the cross-plaintiff to the cross-defendant in contemplation of marriage be transferred or conveyed to him.

The cross-defendant, Ruth Latham Ball, in answering the amended counterclaim, admitted her marriage to Edward Ball; that she had been previously married at the age of 24 and lived with her former husband about seven years and she had no children; she married the cross-plaintiff in good faith at the age of 33 and he was 45, and prior to the marriage ceremony she signed the antenuptial agreement referred to; and she lived with the cross-plaintiff as his wife for approximately ten years, and no children were born to the marriage.

The cross-defendant in her answer admitted that prior to June 19, 1928, she consulted Dr. Norberg, a surgeon at Kansas City, Missouri, and, after an examination, he learned that she had a cystic ovary and a diseased appendix and advised her to undergo a surgical operation. For a short period of time prior to the operation until several hours afterward she was unconscious from the effect of an anaesthetic and of her own knowledge does not know and has never known whether her right ovary was cystic and greatly enlarged or whether her right Fallopian tube adhered around the cyst and stretched from its normal length of $2\frac{1}{2}$ or 3 inches to about 8 inches, or whether her left ovary was cystic and degenerated or whether her left Fallopian tube was diseased and the fimbriated end closed as alleged; she was advised by Dr. Norberg, shortly after the operation, that he had removed her appendix and one ovary. She had no further knowledge or information about the operation than as conveyed to her supra by Dr. Norberg, excepting the information appearing in a pleading to the contrary filed December 6, 1943.

Since the filing of the original counterclaim on December 6, 1943, by investigation and inquiry, she learned and believes that in said operation her appendix, right ovary and right Fallopian tube were removed and her left ovary was treated but not removed, and also that her left Fallopian tube was treated but not removed. She denied that on June 17, 1933, at the time of her marriage to the cross-plaintiff she was sterile. She denied that on said date, or any time prior thereto, she knew or had good reason to believe that she was sterile, but, on the contrary, she alleged that she was not sterile.

Answering further she admitted the operation was performed by Dr. Norberg at the Trinity Lutheran Hospital and a record of the operation was kept by the hospital, but she failed or omitted to inspect the hospital record as kept during her operation. She inquired of Dr. Norberg, after the operation and prior to her discharge on June 3, 1928, whether she could have a child and that he told her he saw no reason why she could not have a child and that he thought the best thing she could do would be to go home and have a baby. She alleged that all that was known to her of said operation at the time of the marriage was the removal of her appendix and one ovary.

The answer of the cross-defendant admits that she did not inform cross-plaintiff that one of her ovaries had been removed in the surgical operation but prior to her marriage she did inform him that she had previously had a major operation and after marriage he knew or should have known that a major operation involved her genital organs. That the cross-plaintiff did not know that she was sterile because in fact she was not and is not sterile. After informing the cross-plaintiff of the major operation prior to marriage, his lack of information as to the diseased condition of the genital organs was due solely to his failure to make inquiry after being advised and informed of the major operation by the cross-defendant.

Cross-defendant's further reply to said amended counterclaim says

"that notwithstanding the averments thereof, which the cross-defendant has hereinbefore and here again denies, said marriage is nevertheless valid by virtue of its ratification by the cross-plaintiff in this: That in the early years of their married life together she repeatedly discussed with the cross-plaintiff her failure to become pregnant and manifested to him her distress that she had not done so; that the cross-plaintiff never at any such discussion, or at any other time, voiced or otherwise disclosed any concern or interest in, or questioned her concerning, her failure to become pregnant; that he never at any time complained to her or expressed any disappointment concerning her failure to become pregnant; that in the early part of the year 1938, of her own volition, she consulted a competent physician as to why she had not become pregnant; that said physician, after a physical examination and an investigation from which he learned that in said surgical operation her right ovary and right Fallopian tube had been removed, and that her left ovary had been treated by puncturing cysts contained therein, and that her left Fallopian tube had been treated by cutting off the thickened sacculated end and bringing the mucosa and serosa together, advised her that a slight operation would probably fix her so she could have children; that she promptly told the cross-plaintiff what the physician had said; that the cross-plaintiff then advised her to wait and never thereafter referred to said conversation or the subject thereof; that notwithstanding said next hereinabove alleged facts and circumstances the cross-plaintiff continued to live and cohabit sexually with her as his wife until on or about January 1, 1943, and thereby the cross-plaintiff ratified said marriage."

The Chancellor appointed Herbert Lamson as Special Master, with instructions to take the testimony of the parties and report the same, with his findings of law and fact. Many hearings were had before the Special Master and several hundred pages of testimony taken. The Special Master reported to the Chancellor that the equities of the cause were with the cross-plaintiff and a decree granting the relief prayed for should be entered. Exceptions were made to the report of the Special Master and, after argument before the Chancellor, the exceptions were sustained and the cross-plaintiff's amended counterclaim by an appropriate order was dismissed, and he appealed.

* * *

We have on many occasions ruled that to constitute fraud a misrepresentation must be of a specific material fact that it is untrue and known to be so and stated for the purpose of inducing another to act, upon which statement the other relies in acting to his injury. [Citations omitted.] There is involved in the matter of false representation as a basis for the rescission of contract the element of resulting injury to the person seeking relief which is not supplied by the bare allegation of such injury. There must appear such facts as show a connection between the representation as made and the value as affected by it. This material element of the alleged fraud must not be left to conjecture and averment. *Stokes v. Victory Land Co.,* 99 Fla. 795, 128 So. 408.

On the question of the ratification of fraud by a litigant, Pomeroy's *Equity Jurisdiction,* 5th Ed., says, if the plaintiff is a party to the fraud to such an extent that he is *in pari delicto* with the defendant, he cannot obtain relief as equity generally does not relieve a person from the consequences of his own fraud. If he is not *in pari delicto,* and is comparatively the more innocent of the two, he may obtain relief by doing full equity to those parties, if any, who have sustained an injury by his partial wrong. (Par. 916, pp. 595, 596.)

"Ratification.—While the party entitled to relief may either avoid the transaction or confirm it, he cannot do both; if he adopts a part, he adopts all; he must reject it entirely if he desires to obtain relief. Any material act done by him, with knowledge of the facts constituting the fraud, or under such circumstances that knowledge must be imputed, which assumes that the transaction is valid, will be a ratification. (As said by the American Law Institute, 'The power of avoidance for fraud or misrepresentation is lost if the injured party after acquiring knowledge of the fraud or misrepresentation manifests to the other party to the transaction an intention to affirm it, or exercises dominion over things restoration of which is a condition of his power of avoidance.* * *' ('The victim of the fraud cannot both affirm and disaffirm, he cannot claim under and against the fraudulent transaction'.)

"917.—Promptness—Delay Through Ignorance of the Fraud.—The most important practical consequence of the two principles above mentioned is the requisite of promptness. The injured party must assert his remedial rights with diligence and without delay, upon becoming aware of the fraud. After he has obtained knowledge of the fraud, or has been informed of facts and circumstances from which such knowledge would be imputed to him, a delay in instituting judicial proceedings for relief, although for a less period than that prescribed by the statute of limitations, may be, and generally will be, regarded as an acquiescence, and this may be, and generally will be, a bar to any equitable remedy.

"To this rule there is one limitation: it applies only when the fraud is known or ought to have been known. No lapse of time, no delay in bringing a suit, however long, will defeat the remedy, provided the injured party was, during all this interval, ignorant of the fraud. The duty to commence proceedings can arise only upon his discovery of the fraud; and the possible effect of his laches will begin to operate only from that time."

* * *

A pertinent question presented on this record is, Did the appellee know or have good reason to believe that she was sterile on June 17, 1933? It is not disputed that the appellee advised the appellant that she had, during June, 1928, submitted to a major operation. The parties apparently were content to let the matter rest, as they married and lived together for a period of approximately ten years. The appellant had the opportunity prior to marriage to explore the extent of the major operation by ascertaining whether or not the operation involved her genital organs, the hospital where the operation was performed, the names of the attending nurses, and the name and address of the operating surgeon, and the information was then available as was shown to have been some ten or twelve years later. It is suggested that the law made it the duty of the appellee to voluntarily disclose to her intended husband the several details of the major operation and if it involved her reproduction organs, which operation it is contended rendered the appellee sterile. Her answer in effect was that she told him of the major operation but did not express a view or make a statement about her possible sterility.

Our study of the evidence leads to the conclusion that the appellee at the time of the marriage did not know nor did she have good reasons to believe that she was sterile. The appellant simply failed, which is clearly established when considering all the evidence, to carry the burden of proof as required by law by proving as alleged that the appellee was sterile or had good reasons to believe that she was sterile. We do not overlook the hospital records, the explanation thereof by the appellee, Dr. Mumford's testimony, the opinions of expert witnesses, and the many disputes and conflicts in the testimony. It is the writer's view that knowledge and information of her sterility became positively known to her, if at all, for the first time in January, 1944, as a result of the Rubin's test as given by Dr. Te Linde.

The comments of the Chancellor below on this point are significant and are *viz.*:

"* * * Mrs. Ball's action in having the (Rubin's) test performed is of great significance to the issues in this case, in a way overlooked by counsel, that is, her motive. Regardless of the result of the test, she could have had but one thing in mind when she had it performed; To prove that she possessed the organs necessary to conception. Here is a woman charged with knowledge of her absolute sterility for more than fifteen years and fraudulent concealment thereof for more than ten years. What did she do when that charge was made in defendant's counterclaim? Her lawyer leaves to examine a hospital record on which the charge is based and she sets out on her own to seek irrefutable evidence that the charge is untrue. To me, it is unimportant that the result of the test disappointed her. What is important is that in January, 1944, she still did not know that she was physically incapable of bearing children. Certainly then, she had no such knowledge in June, 1933. An obvious objection can be made: She very guilefully stated that she had had the test made in order to induce the conclusion here reached. The answer to that proposition lies in (1) her obvious reluctance to testify that the test was made and (2) the fact that neither she nor her counsel up to this time have sought to give her action the significance here attributed to it."

* * *

Affirmed.

Rosenberg v. Lipnick

Supreme Judicial Court of Massachusetts

377 Mass. 666, 389 N.E.2d 385 (1979)

HENNESSEY, Chief Justice.

Charlotte Rosenberg brought this action in the Probate Court against the executors of the estate of Perry Rosenberg, her husband (decedent), seeking invalidation of an antenuptial agreement executed by her and the decedent and a declaration that she is entitled to her statutory share of his estate and a widow's allowance. On the plaintiff's motion, the action was referred to a master. The master made findings of fact and concluded that the agreement is valid and that the plaintiff is not entitled to a statutory share of the estate or to a widow's allowance. The Probate Court judge confirmed the master's report and entered judgment for the defendants. The plaintiff duly appealed.

The plaintiff argues, and the argument finds support in the record, that both the master and the judge viewed this court's decision in *Wellington v. Rugg*, 243 Mass. 30, 136 N.E. 831 (1922), as controlling. In that case the court held that a husband's simple failure voluntarily to disclose the value of his property prior to executing an antenuptial agreement was not sufficient to invalidate the agreement. Rather, the party seeking invalidation must show fraud.

The plaintiff filed an application for direct appellate review, asking this court to overrule *Wellington*, and hold that (1) an antenuptial agreement which fails to make a full and fair provision for the wife is not enforceable if the husband failed to disclose his assets prior to execution of the agreement, and (2) the representatives of the husband have the burden of proving full and fair disclosure. We granted the plaintiff's application because of the importance of the issues involved.

Although we agree that the *Wellington* principles should be abandoned,[1] we do not think it wise to act retroactively. The *Wellington* decision has remained undisturbed law in this Commonwealth for over a half-century, and numerous agreements have undoubtedly been fashioned in reliance on its rule. Accordingly, we have reviewed this case for error under the law as it existed in 1959. We have discerned none and thus affirm the judgment for the defendants. However, we take this opportunity to delineate new rules that shall apply to antenuptial agreements executed after the publication date of this opinion.

---

[1] Of course, any rules that we might fashion instead would necessarily be framed in terms of the respective contractual positions of the parties, rather than in terms of "husband" and "wife." See art. 1 of the Declaration of Rights of the Massachusetts Constitution, as amended by art. 106.

The plaintiff, who was fifty-eight years old, met the decedent, who was sixty-nine years old, in February of 1958. Both were gainfully employed. The plaintiff was a widow, the decedent was a widower, and each had children by previous marriages. After a courtship of approximately eighteen months, the decedent proposed marriage and told the plaintiff that he would like her to sign an antenuptial agreement. The agreement provided that the plaintiff would accept $5,000 from the decedent's estate in lieu of dower or any other rights that she might have were she to survive him.

The plaintiff took the agreement to her brother, a practicing attorney, who asked her whether she had any knowledge of her prospective husband's resources. When she stated that she did not, he told her that he thought the agreement was unfair and called for some explanation. She expressed her desire to sign it, notwithstanding her brother's observations. As he did not want to advise her against the proposed marriage, her brother recommended that she ask the decedent to sign an agreement surrendering any claim against her estate in the event that he survived her. She responded that the decedent had already told her he wanted nothing from her, whereupon her brother drafted a second agreement by which the decedent had no claim to her estate. Both agreements were executed on October 29, 1959. The plaintiff and the decedent were married on November 7, 1959.

At the time of their marriage, the decedent owned a dwelling and a block of stores in Chelsea, Massachusetts. He occupied one of the stores from which he operated his business as an electrician. The block of stores was sold in 1974 for $20,000. The dwelling was sold in 1960; however, no evidence was introduced as to its sale price.

Samuel Shapiro, one of the defendant executors and the decedent's accountant, testified that in 1960, the decedent received dividends from listed companies. Shapiro could not state the amount of such dividends. Neither could he remember whether the decedent received any interest on savings or what the decedent's income taxes were at that time.

The decedent died on July 4, 1976. His estate has an approximate total value of $119,000: $55,000 in stocks and bonds; $51,800 in mortgages, notes and cash; $12,000 in life insurance; and $200 in miscellaneous assets.

During their marriage, the decedent supported the plaintiff, although the plaintiff purchased some of her clothes with her own money. She continued to be employed at the time of the hearing and had assets totalling approximately $45,000, although her living expenses exceeded her income.

1. The plaintiff contends that the $5,000 to which she is entitled under the antenuptial agreement is grossly disproportionate to the amount to which she would have been entitled but for the antenuptial agreement. The plaintiff further contends that the agreement should have been declared void in the absence of compelling evidence that the agreement was fair when made or that the plaintiff had agreed to take the reduced share with full knowledge of the decedent's assets. The rule in *Wellington v. Rugg, supra,* is clearly contrary. That case holds that nothing short of proof of fraud will invalidate an antenuptial agreement, irrespective of the unfairness of the agreement's provisions. The following language is controlling:

> "[T]he allegation that the intestate 'concealed' the amount of his property in the absence of anything to show that he made false representations respecting it or prevented the plaintiff from obtaining whatever facts she desired concerning its character or value is immaterial. The failure on his part to inform her of what he owned falls far short of fraudulent concealment. So far as appears had she so wished, she could have made inquiry of him, and also could have made such investigation as she saw fit before making the contract. Notwithstanding the confidential relations between the parties, the simple failure voluntarily to disclose the amount of his property does not constitute actionable fraud."

Id. at 35–36, 136 N.E. at 834. Cf. *Anderson v. Anderson,* 354 Mass. 565, 238 N.E.2d 868 (1968) (finding fraud in antenuptial agreement purporting to limit the rights of the wife in the event of divorce).

Given our view that *Wellington* governs the rights of the parties now before us, we need not decide whether the agreement's provisions were manifestly unfair to the plaintiff.[2] The master found that the plaintiff failed to establish that the decedent either misrepresented or fraudulently concealed the extent of his assets prior to execution of the agreement. In light of the master's finding, which the judge confirmed and which is supported by the record, the plaintiff cannot prevail under the *Wellington* rule. Accordingly, we affirm the judgment for the defendants.

2. Massachusetts stands alone in requiring the party seeking invalidation of an antenuptial agreement to show fraud. See 2 A. Lindey, SEPARATION AGREEMENTS AND ANTE-NUPTIAL CONTRACTS §90 (rev. ed. 1977); Annot., 27 A.L.R.2d 883–906 (1953 & Supp. 1978). The great majority of cases in other jurisdictions hold that the parties to an antenuptial agreement generally do not deal at arm's length. Rather, they occupy a relationship of mutual trust and confidence and as such must exercise the highest degree of good faith, candor, and sincerity in all matters bearing on the proposed agreement. 2 A. Lindey, *supra* at §90–42–43. The burden is not on either party to inquire, but on each to inform, for it is only by requiring full disclosure of the amount, character, and value of the parties' respective assets that courts can ensure intelligent waiver of the statutory rights involved. [Case citations omitted.] See generally Annot., 27 A.L.R.2d 883, §§3, 4 (1953 & Supp. 1978).

Although the *Wellington* court specifically acknowledged that a confidential relationship exists between parties to an antenuptial agreement, *Wellington v. Rugg, supra,* 243 Mass. at 36, 136 N.E. 831, its holding treats them as though they stood at arm's length. The decision cites G. S. Bower on ACTIONABLE NON-DISCLOSURE §135 (1915), *Potts v. Chapin,* 133 Mass. 276 (1882), and *Windram Mfg. Co. v. Boston Blacking Co.,* 239 Mass. 123, 131 N.E. 454 (1921), all of which speak to rights between parties functioning in a commercial context. *Wellington, supra,* 343 Mass. at 35, 136 N.E. 831. Quoting from *Windram,* the *Wellington* court, 343 Mass. at 36, 136 N.E. at 834 stated: "Mere silence on the part of the defendant is all that is charged. But failure to disclose known facts does not amount to fraud, and is not the basis of an action for deceit, unless the parties stand in such relation to one another that one is under legal or equitable obligation to communicate the facts to the other." Although the court chose to view the confidential relationship between the parties in *Wellington* as not giving rise to an obligation to disclose, that case has been cited in subsequent opinions which impose a duty to disclose on parties occupying an obviously less delicate relationship. See, e.g., *Goodwin v. Agassiz,* 283 Mass. 358, 186 N.E. 659 (1933) (holding that the existence of a fiduciary relationship between corporate director and stockholder may give rise to a duty of disclosure).

While we have, in fairness, followed the *Wellington* case in the instant matter, we think that to the extent that *Wellington* negates any duty of disclosure, we should abandon that precedent in favor of the more enlightened rules of other jurisdictions. Thus, in future cases involving agreements drawn after the publication date of this opinion, we shall feel free to hold that the parties by definition occupy a confidential relationship and that the burden of disclosure rests upon both of them.

In judging the validity of such an antenuptial agreement, other relevant factors which we may consider are whether (1) it contains a fair and reasonable provision as measured at the time of its execution for the party contest-

---

[2] The master made no finding of fact with respect to this issue.

ing the agreement; (2) the contesting party was fully informed of the other party's worth prior to the agreement's execution, or had, or should have had, independent knowledge of the other party's worth; and (3) a waiver by the contesting party is set forth.[3] It is clear that the reasonableness of any monetary provision in an antenuptial contract cannot ultimately be judged in isolation. Rather, reference may appropriately be made to such factors as the parties' respective worth, the parties' respective ages, the parties' respective intelligence, literacy, and business acumen, and prior family ties or commitments.[4]

We add that, even if we were to apply these factors and the "fair disclosure" rule to the instant case, it could be argued that the plaintiff here is not entitled to relief. This result might well be urged from all the circumstances, including the fact that she was advised by counsel that she should request disclosure but decided not to for fear it might result in no marriage. Neither was there the slightest evidence of coercion by the decedent against the plaintiff.

The right to make antenuptial agreements settling property rights in advance of marriage is a valuable personal right which courts should not regulate destructively. Neither should the exercise of that right be looked upon with disfavor. Thus, we recognize that antenuptial agreements must be so construed as to give full effect to the parties' intentions, but we are concerned that such agreements be executed fairly and understandingly and be free from fraud, imposition, deception, or over-reaching.

Judgment affirmed.

-----

[3] See, *e.g., Del Vecchio v. Del Vecchio*, 143 So.2d 17 (Fla. 1962); *Hartz v. Hartz*, 248 Md. 47, 234 A.2d 865 (1967); *Kaufmann Estate*, 404 Pa. 131, 171 A.2d 48 (1961); *McClellan Estate*, 365 Pa. 401, 75 A.2d 595 (1950). See generally 2 A. Lindey, Separation Agreements and Ante-Nuptial Contracts §90–36–37 (rev. ed. 1977). Cf. *Friedlander v. Friedlander*, 80 Wash.2d 293, 494 P.2d 208 (1972) (antenuptial agreement made in contemplation of divorce).

As to the burden of proof in cases contesting the validity of antenuptial agreements, see, *e.g., Del Vecchio v. Del Vecchio*, 143 So.2d 17 (Fla. 1962); *Guhl v. Guhl*, 376 Ill. 100, 33 N.E.2d 444 (1941); *In re Estate of Parish*, 236 Iowa 822, 20 N.W.2d 32 (1945); *Burns v. Spiker*, 109 Kan. 22, 202 P. 370 (1921); *Denison v. Dawes*, 121 Me. 402, 117 A. 314 (1922); *McClellan Estate*, 365 Pa. 401, 75 A.2d 595 (1950); *Friedlander v. Friedlander*, 80 Wash. 293, 494 P.2d 208 (1972); *Bibelhausen v. Bibelhausen*, 159 Wis. 365, 150 N.W. 516 (1915). See also 2 A. Lindey, Separation Agreements and Ante-Nuptial Contracts §90–83–85 (rev. ed. 1977); Comment, *Husband and Wife—Antenuptial Contracts*, 41 Mich. L. Rev. 1133, 1137 (1943), and cases cited.

[4] See, *e.g., Estate of Nelson*, 224 Cal. App.2d 138, 36 Cal. Rptr. 352 (1964); *Del Vecchio v. Del Vecchio*, 143 So.2d 17 (Fla. 1962); *Megginson v. Megginson*, 367 Ill. 168, 10 N.E.2d 815 (1937); *Parker v. Gray*, 317 Ill. 468, 148 N.E. 323 (1925); *Achilles v. Achilles*, 151 Ill. 136, 37 N.E. 693 (1894); *Hartz v. Hartz*, 248 Md. 47 (1967); *Rocker v. Rocker*, 42 Ohio Op.2d 184 (1967); *Bauer v. Bauer*, 1 Or. App. 504 (1970); *Kaufmann Estate*, 404 Pa. 131 (1961); see generally, 2 A. Lindey, Separation Agreements and Ante-Nuptial Contracts §90–37–38 (rev. ed. 1977).

Posner v. Posner

Supreme Court of Florida

233 So.2d 381 (Fla. 1970)

Roberts, J.

This cause is before the court on rehearing granted on petition for certiorari to review the decision of the Third District Court of Appeal in *Posner v. Posner*, Fla. App. 1968, 206, So.2d 416. Both parties had appealed to the appellate court for reversal of the decree of the Chancellor entered in a divorce suit—the wife having appealed from those portions of the decree awarding a divorce to the husband and the sum of $600 per month as alimony to the wife pursuant to the terms of an antenuptial agreement between the parties, and the husband having attacked, by cross-appeal, the award of $600 per month support money for each of the two minor children of the parties.

The three appellate judges who considered the appeals agreed upon the affirmance of the decree of divorce to the husband and the award for child support of $1,200 per month. However, each took a different position respecting the antenuptial agreement concerning alimony. Their respective views were (1) that the parties may validly agree upon alimony in an antenuptial agreement but that the trial court is not bound by their agreement; (2) that such an agreement is void as against public policy; and (3) that an antenuptial agreement respecting alimony is entitled to the same consideration and should be just as binding as an antenuptial agreement settling the property rights of the wife in her husband's estate upon his death. They have certified to this court, as one of great public interest, the question of the validity and binding effect of an antenuptial agreement respecting alimony in the event of the divorce or separation of the parties. We have concluded that jurisdiction should be accepted, as authorized by Section 4(2), Article V, Florida Constitution, F.S.A.

At the outset we must recognize that there is a vast difference between a contract made in the market place and one relating to the institution of marriage.

It has long been the rule in a majority of the courts of this country and in this State that contracts intended to facilitate or promote the procurement of a divorce will be declared illegal as contrary to public policy. See *Gallemore v. Gallemore*, 1927, 94 Fla. 516, 114 So. 371; *Allen v. Allen*, 1933, 111 Fla. 733, 150 So. 237. The reason for the rule lies in the nature of the marriage contract and the interest of the State therein.

At common law, the so-called "matrimonial causes", including divorce, were cognizable only in the Ecclesiastical Courts. Because of the Church's view of the sanctity of the nuptial tie, a marriage valid in its inception would not be dissolved by an absolute divorce *a vinculo matrimonii*, even for adultery—although such divorces could be granted by an Act of Parliament. Therefore, the divorce was only from bed and board, with an appropriate allowance for sustenance of the wife out of the husband's estate. See *Ponder v. Graham*, 1851, 4 Fla. 23; CHITTY's BLACKSTONE, Vol. I, Ch. XV, 432, 441. We have, of course, changed by statute the common-law rule respecting the indissolubility of a marriage valid in its inception; but the concept of marriage as a social institution that is the foundation of the family and of society remains unchanged. See 38 AM. JUR., *Marriage*, Sec. 8, p. 185. Since marriage is of vital interest to society and the state, it has frequently been said that in every divorce suit the state is a third party whose interests take precedence over the private interests of the spouses. [Citations omitted.]

The state's interest in the preservation of the marriage is the basis for the rule that a divorce cannot be awarded by consent of the parties, see *Underwood v. Underwood, supra*, 12 Fla. 434, as well as the doctrine of corroboration applicable in divorce suits, see *Pickston v. Dougherty*, Fla. App. 1959, 109 So.2d 577. In the *Underwood* case this court said that it "would be aiming a deadly blow at public morals to decree a dissolution of the marriage contract merely because the parties requested it"; and in the *Pickston* case it was noted that the "prime object of the corroboration doctrine is to prevent collusion and to forestall any attempt which might otherwise be made to destroy the marital relationship falsely."

And it is this same public policy that is the basis for the rule that an antenuptial agreement by which a prospective wife waives or limits her right to alimony or to the property of her husband in the event of a divorce or separation, regardless of who is at fault, has been in some states held to be invalid. [Citations omitted.] The reason that such an agreement is said to "facilitate or promote the procurement of a divorce" was stated in *Crouch v. Crouch, supra,* as follows:

> "Such contract could induce a mercenary husband to inflict on his wife any wrong he might desire with the knowledge his pecuniary liability would be limited. In other words, a husband could through abuse and ill treatment of his wife force her to bring an action for divorce and thereby buy a divorce for a small fee less than he would otherwise have to pay."

Antenuptial or so-called "marriage settlement" contracts by which the parties agree upon and fix the property rights which either spouse will have in the estate of the other upon his or her death have, however, long been recognized as being conducive to marital tranquility and thus in harmony with public policy. See *Del Vecchio v. Del Vecchio,* Fla. 1962, 143 So.2d 17, in which we prescribed the rules by which the validity of such antenuptial or postnuptial property settlement agreements should be tested. Such an agreement has been upheld after the death of the spouse even though it contained also a provision settling their property rights in the event of divorce or separation—the court concluding that it could not be said this provision "facilitated or tended to induce a separation or divorce." See *In re Muxlow's Estate,* 1962, 367 Mich. 133, 116 N.W.2d 43.

In this view of an antenuptial agreement that settles the right of the parties in the event of divorce as well as upon death, it is not inconceivable that a dissatisfied wife—secure in the knowledge that the provisions for alimony contained in the antenuptial agreement could not be enforced against her, but that she would be bound by the provisions limiting or waiving her property rights in the estate of her husband—might provoke her husband into divorcing her in order to collect a large alimony check every month, or a lump-sum award (since, in this State, a wife is entitled to alimony, if needed, even though the divorce is awarded to the husband) rather than take her chances on being remembered generously in her husband's will. In this situation, a valid antenuptial agreement limiting property rights upon death would have the same meretricious effect, insofar as the public policy in question is concerned, as would an antenuptial divorce provision in the circumstances hypothesized in *Crouch v. Crouch, supra,* 385 S.W.2d 288.

There can be no doubt that the institution of marriage is the foundation of the familial and social structure of our Nation and, as such, continues to be of vital interest to the State; but we cannot blind ourselves to the fact that the concept of the "sanctity" of a marriage—as being practically indissoluble, once entered into—held by our ancestors only a few generations ago, has been greatly eroded in the last several decades. This court can take judicial notice of the fact that the ratio of marriages to divorces has reached a disturbing rate in many states; and that a new concept of divorce—in which there is no "guilty" party—is being advocated by many groups and has been adopted by the State of California in a recent revision of its divorce laws providing for dissolution of a marriage upon pleading and proof of "irreconcilable differences" between the parties, without assessing the fault for the failure of the marriage against either party.

With divorce such a commonplace fact of life, it is fair to assume that many prospective marriage partners whose property and familial situation is such as to generate a valid antenuptial agreement settling their property rights upon the death of either, might want to consider and discuss also—and agree upon, if possible—the disposition of their property and the alimony rights of the wife in the event their marriage, despite their best efforts, should fail. In *Allen v. Allen, supra,* 150 So. at page 238, this court said that the agreements relating to divorce that are held to be illegal as contrary to public policy are those "withdrawing opposition to the divorce or not to contest it or to conceal the true cause thereof by alleging another" and that they "have no reference to bona fide agreements relating to alimony or the adjustment of property rights between husband and wife, though in contemplation of divorce, if they are not directly conducive to the procurement of it."

We know of no community or society in which the public policy that condemned a husband and wife to a lifetime of misery as an alternative to the opprobrium of divorce still exists. And a tendency to recognize this change in public policy and to give effect to the antenuptial agreements of the parties relating to divorce is clearly discernible. Thus, in *Hudson v. Hudson,* Okl. 1960, 350 P.2d 596, the court simply applied to an antenuptial contract respecting alimony the rule applicable to antenuptial contracts settling property rights upon the death of a spouse and thus tacitly, if not expressly, discarded the contrary-to-public-policy rule.

* * *

The trend of recent cases involving postnuptial agreements is well summarized by the court in *Schulz v. Fox,* 1959, 136 Mont. 152, 345 P.2d 1045, 1050, as follows:

> "The conclusion to be drawn from these cases is that any agreement the purpose of which is to facilitate the granting of a divorce without proper grounds existing, is void, but that where proper grounds do exist, an agreement with respect to a property settlement, when not brought about by duress or coercion, cannot be said to perpetrate a fraud upon the court and will not be held void. * * * All of the well reasoned cases we have read look to the collusive intent, that is, as to whether the divorce was on proper grounds and as to whether the Court's interest in the continuity of the marriage status or support of spouse and children has been protected."

We have given careful consideration to the question of whether the change in public policy towards divorce requires a change in the rule respecting antenuptial agreements settling alimony and property rights of the parties upon divorce and have concluded that such agreements should no longer be held to be void *ab initio* as "contrary to public policy." If such an agreement is valid when tested by the stringent rules prescribed in *Del Vecchio v. Del Vecchio, supra,* 143 So.2d 17, for ante- and post-nuptial agreements setting the property rights of the spouses in the estate of the other upon death, and if, in addition, it is made to appear that the divorce was prosecuted in good faith, on proper grounds, so that, under the rules applicable to postnuptial alimony and property settlement agreements referred to above, it could not be said to facilitate or promote the procurement of a divorce, then it should be held valid as to conditions existing at the time the agreement was made.

The question of the future binding effect of such antenuptial agreements when presented to the Chancellor for approval and incorporation in the final decree, and the question of the modification thereof upon a showing of a change in circumstances after the entry of the decree of divorce, should be decided under applicable statutory law and judicial decisions relating to postnuptial contracts settling the alimony and/or property rights of the parties.

Section 61.14, Florida Statutes, F.S.A. (Ch. 16780, 1935) among other things, provides:

> "(1) When a husband and wife have entered or hereafter enter into an agreement for payments for, or instead of, support, maintenance or alimony, whether in connection with an action for divorce or separate maintenance or with any voluntary property settlement or when a husband is required by court order to make any payments to his wife, and the circumstances of the parties or the financial ability of the husband has changed since the execution of such agreement or the rendition of the order, either party may apply to the circuit court of the circuit in which the parties, or either of them, resided at the date of the execution of the

agreement or reside at the date of the application or in which the agreement was executed or in which the order was rendered, for a judgment decreasing or increasing the amount of support, maintenance or alimony, and the court has jurisdiction to make orders as equity requires with due regard to the changed circumstances and the financial ability of the husband, decreasing or increasing or confirming the amount of separate support, maintenance or alimony provided for in the agreement or order.''

We must assume that the parties to this litigation knew of the existence of §61.14, Florida Statutes, F.S.A., when they made their agreement in 1960 and that their capacity to make the agreement was and is limited by same.

In summary, we hold that the antenuptial agreement, if entered into under the conditions outlined in *Del Vecchio v. Del Vecchio, supra*, 143 So.2d 17, was a valid and binding agreement between the parties at the time and under the conditions it was made, but subject to be increased or decreased under changed conditions as provided in §61.14, Florida Statutes, F.S.A.

Accordingly, the decision under review is quashed with instructions to the District Court of Appeal, Third District, to vacate that portion of the final decree of the trial court relating to alimony and support money and remand same for further proceedings in the trial court not inconsistent with this opinion.

It is so ordered.

* * *

SPECTOR, District Court Judge (concurring specially):

* * *

A review of the cases which have considered the court's statutory power to modify agreed or awarded alimony makes it clear that such power should be exercised only in the face of the strongest and most compelling reasons. See for example *Ohmes v. Ohmes*, 200 So.2d 849 (Fla. App. 1967), and cases cited therein. Mere ability on the part of the husband to pay more than the amount awarded or agreed upon is not a proper basis for relief under the subject statute. The husband's ability is to be considered only after the wife has convincingly demonstrated an increased need on her part because of her changed circumstances. Only upon the making of such a showing can the court inquire into his ability to pay more.

The question of alimony in the case *sub judice* is one which was agreed upon by the parties prior to marriage in an agreement which we here hold to be valid in view of the *Del Vecchio* case, *supra*. In arriving at that conclusion, the court is unconcerned with whether the husband was initially able to pay more alimony than the amount agreed to in the antenuptial agreement since the very purpose of such an agreement is to provide a mutually satisfactory substitute for such determination of ability. If events have since transpired which have changed the wife's circumstances so as to warrant invoking the relief provided by Section 61.14, Florida Statutes, F.S.A., the trial court is empowered to grant such relief. We are not unmindful that the nation is experiencing an inflationary trend or condition, and this circumstance too may well be the basis of a finding by the chancellor that circumstances have so changed as to require equitable adjustment under the subject statute.

* * *

Volid v. Volid

Appellate Court of Illinois

6 Ill. App.3d 386, 286 N.E.2d 42 (1972)

BURMAN, J.

This is an appeal from an order of the Circuit Court directing plaintiff, Peter Volid, (1) to pay temporary alimony in the amount of $1,250 per month to his wife, Rita W. Volid, (2) permitting Rita Volid to remain in the marital home pending proceedings for divorce and separate maintenance, and (3) requiring Peter Volid to pay the expenses of the home exclusive of utilities. The trial judge specifically found that there was no just reason for delaying enforcement or appeal of the order, and the plaintiff appeals.

The parties were married on December 31, 1965. At the time of the marriage, Peter Volid was a wealthy 60-year-old man who had been married three times previously and who had children and grandchildren. Rita Volid was a 40-year-old school teacher who had never been married before. Three days before the marriage, on December 28, 1965, with the advice of their respective counsels they entered into and executed an antenuptial agreement.

* * *

Paragraph 4 provides in relevant part:

"The parties hereto agree that in the event that a Decree of Divorce or Separate Maintenance shall be entered in a proceeding between them, First Party (Peter Volid) may have an obligation under such Decree to pay reasonable alimony or support to Second Party (Rita Volid). In the event a Decree so provides, it is agreed that the First Party shall pay to Second Party as and for an equitable lump sum settlement in lieu of all rights to alimony or support, and in lieu of all property rights, if any, and in settlement of her rights, if any, of dower, homestead, inheritance, and all and every other such right which may have arisen as a result of their marriage * * * the sum of FIFTY THOUSAND DOLLARS ($50,000.00) * * * if such decree shall be entered within three (3) years from the date hereof; if such Decree shall be entered on a date more than three (3) years from the date hereof, then First Party shall pay to Second Party as and for a lump sum settlement in lieu of the rights referred to above, the sum of SEVENTY-FIVE THOUSAND DOLLARS ($75,000.00) payable at the rate of SIX HUNDRED DOLLARS ($600.00) per month for One Hundred Twenty-Five (125) successive months, commencing one (1) month after the entry of such Decree * * *. The parties further agree that the purposes of this paragraph 4 are to promote marital harmony and to discourage either party from obtaining monetary benefits by a breach of the marital relationship and the institution of a legal proceedings for separation or divorce."

Paragraph 8 states:

"Each of the parties hereto has made a full and complete disclosure to the other of the assets owned by such party at the present time, and the waiver, release and relinquishment of the rights of each party, as hereinabove set forth, has been made with full knowledge of the extent of the wealth of the other party. A schedule of all of the properties, real, personal and mixed, now owned by First Party and the estimated values thereof and a statement of his income have been examined by the Second Party and her Attorney."

The agreement was subscribed to by both parties. The signature of Peter Volid was witnessed by his attorney, Harry Adelman, and the signature of

Rita Wilkes (now Rita Volid) was witnessed by her attorney, Henry Kenoe. According to a notarized certificate attached to the agreement, Rita Volid on the day the agreement was executed stated under oath that (1) she was aware of Peter Volid's wealth and income and the share of it to which she would be entitled upon marriage if the agreement were not executed, (2) that she was satisfied with the provisions in the agreement made for her, and (3) that the agreement was executed as a free and voluntary act by her for the purposes stated therein.

On August 7, 1969, more than three years after the marriage, Peter Volid filed a complaint for divorce in the Circuit Court of Cook County based upon the alleged mental cruelty of his wife. Rita Volid in answering the complaint denied the allegations of mental cruelty toward her husband. She counterclaimed for separate maintenance and sought temporary support. After hearing evidence, the court granted her request for temporary alimony and possession of the marital home.

* * *

The purposes of the agreement were "to promote marital harmony and to discourage either party from obtaining monetary benefits * * * by the institution of a legal proceedings for separation or divorce." An award of temporary alimony in addition to the payment of $75,000 would provide Rita Volid more than the amount agreed upon in lieu of alimony.

The defendant urges strenuously that the provisions of Paragraph 4 have no effect on the award of temporary alimony because the provisions in antenuptial agreements attempting to limit temporary support have never been enforceable in Illinois and would be in violation of public policy. In support of this contention she cites and relies upon a series of cases, amongst which are *VanKoten v. VanKoten,* 323 Ill. 323, 154 N.E. 146; *Berge v. Berge,* 366 Ill. 228, 8 N.E.2d 623, and *Threw v. Threw,* 410 Ill. 107, 101 N.E.2d 515, where provisions of separation agreements which were executed after marriage and which in effect relieved a husband of any obligation to support his wife during the marriage were held to violate public policy. These cases are distinguishable in two main respects. First, the agreements involved in the three cases were executed after the marriage, whereas here the contract was entered prior to the wedding as an inducement to the marriage and before the rights and obligations of husband and wife were undertaken. Second, the agreement here did not attempt to avoid the duty of support, but made a generous provision for the defendant in the event the marriage was terminated. In fact, in view of the age of the parties at the time of the marriage and in view of Rita Volid's knowledge of her prospective husband's prior marriages, it must be noted that the antenuptial agreement may have provided more ultimate support than would a court grant in the exercise of its discretion if the parties were not bound by the agreement. See: *Tan v. Tan,* 3 Ill. App.3d 671, 279 N.E.2d 486.

* * *

In cases from other jurisdictions which we have reviewed at length, antenuptial agreements which totally eliminated the right to support or which made inadequate provision for support have been held to violate public policy. [Citations omitted.]

The reasons given in these cases for holding as void provisions eliminating the obligation of support upon divorce are (1) that the state's interest in the preservation of the marriage relationship could be defeated by agreements which provide for, facilitate, or tend to induce a separation or divorce of the parties after marriage and (2) that the state has an interest in seeing that a divorced woman has adequate support so that she will not become a charge of the state. The assumptions on which these reasons are based should be examined. It is often declared that the state has a vital interest in the maintenance of the family, but this interest does not require that persons, once married, must live together forever without regard to the breakdown of their relationship. The necessity of granting divorces is recognized, and the grounds upon which one can be granted are expanding. Where no minor children are involved, as here, and where the husband and wife can function in society separately and independently, the interest of the state in the continuance of the marriage is small.

The most frequent argument made for holding agreements limiting alimony invalid is that such agreements encourage or incite divorce or separation. There is little empirical evidence to show that this assertion is well founded. It is true that a person may be reluctant to obtain a divorce if he knows that a great financial sacrifice may be entailed, but it does not follow from this that a person who finds his marriage otherwise satisfactory will terminate the marital relationship simply because it will not involve a financial sacrifice. It may be equally cogently argued that a contract which defines the expectations and responsibilities of the parties promotes rather than reduces marital stability. [Citations omitted.]

Many cases state categorically that a husband has a duty to support his wife. This is unquestionably true when the wife is in need of such support. However, when a marriage breaks down and the husband and wife are divorced, the wealth and income of the wife are always considered in determining whether an alimony award should be made and if so in what amount. [Citations omitted.]

When the rules regarding the husband's duty of support were first enunciated, the roles of a husband and wife were more rigid and defined. The husband worked and brought income into the family while the wife maintained and managed the household. The woman generally did not seek outside employment partly, because "her place was in the home", and partly because few opportunities for meaningful employment were available. Married women nowadays are increasingly developing career skills and successfully entering the employment market. Where a woman is trained, healthy, and employable, and where a woman's efforts have not contributed to her husband's wealth or earning potential, the necessity for an alimony award upon breakup of the marriage is not great.

The reasons given to justify the invalidation of all antenuptial agreements which limit the obligation of support upon divorce do not warrant the condemnation of all such agreements in the name of public policy. The law gives certain rights to both spouses upon marriage, but these rights may be waived or terminated upon divorce. Upon marriage, a spouse receives inchoate rights to dower and inheritance, but these rights may be waived or limited by contract. * * *

* * *

Once it appears (1) that some marital rights may be waived before the wedding and (2) that the right to support can be terminated upon divorce, it would be anomalous to hold that the parties cannot plan and agree on a course of action in the event that the marriage is unsuccessful and ends in divorce. Particularly is this true where the parties are older and where there is little danger that either party would be without support. The incidence of divorce in this country is increasing, and consequently more persons with families and established wealth are in a position to consider the possibility of a marriage later in life. Public policy is not violated by permitting these persons prior to marriage to anticipate the possibility of divorce and to establish their rights by contract in such an event as long as the contract is entered with full knowledge and without fraud, duress or coercion. See: *Posner v. Posner*, 233 So.2d 381 (Fla. 1970); *Hudson v. Hudson*, 350 P.2d 596 (Okl. 1960).

Peter Volid agreed to pay and Rita Volid agreed to receive the sum of $600 per month for 125 successive months in lieu of all rights to alimony or support. It is not our province to make contracts, but to construe them. Courts cannot make for the parties better agreements than they themselves have been satisfied to make. *Green County, Kentucky v. Quinlan*, 211 U.S.

582, 29 S. Ct. 162, 53 L.Ed. 335. The court in the exercise of its discretion awarded temporary alimony in the amount of $1,250 per month. The order should have contained a provision that any temporary sums for her support which are paid will ultimately be deducted from the lump sum settlement agreed to by the parties. Upon the entry of a decree payments of $600 per month are to be made until the balance is paid.

* * *

Reversed and remanded with directions.

Comments

Antenuptial agreements, which are of increasing importance, are related not only to engagement, marriage, and divorce, but also to cohabitation contracts. During the past 20 years they have undergone considerable change in form and content. *Posner* is a leading case, widely cited throughout the country in support of the theory that parties should also be able to regulate incidents of marriage breakup. According to the older viewpoint alluded to in the case, such regulation was against public policy. Perhaps the conception of marriage as a personal relation entered for life made any contemplation of divorce seem an impairment to the marital intent. There was also the traditional notion of the State as a third party to the marriage contract which intervened in party autonomy. These considerations had fictitious elements because they were never meant to correspond fully to reality. Marriage was treated "as if" it were intended, necessarily and without reservation, for life; participation of the State was meant further to protect this assumption.

The defendant in *Ball v. Ball*, Ed Ball, who died in 1981 at the age of 93, was a multimillionaire and an extremely powerful figure in Florida politics for over half a century. He was an iron-willed trustee of nearly $2 billion in assets of the estate of Alfred I. du Pont. These facts are vital, although not referred to in the antenuptial agreement reproduced on pp. 24–27 and the following divorce and annulment action on pp. 27–32. The agreement is startlingly modern in many ways, for instance, in the details of attempting to regulate the life style of the marital parties. Today, young people without means often enter into these kinds of agreements in an effort to be honest with each other. It should be noted, however, that the Price-Ball agreement does not provide for a disclosure of assets. That this is highly recommendable as an effort to demonstrate fairness is brought out in *Rosenberg* (pp. 32–35).

Today parties go even beyond what was attempted in *Ball* by trying to regulate sexual preferences and other intimate details of personal life. Whether these agreements are legally enforceable appears to be secondary; their main function, at least today, is to safeguard deliberation. Nevertheless, they may have legal significance insofar as they regulate what exactly is meant to be "the essence" of this particular marriage. Thus, again as in *Ball*, they may be used later as evidence in possible annulment actions. In fact it is arguable that the increased importance of antenuptial agreements may bring about a revived importance of annulment. This may counter arguments that in a time when dissolution of marriage is possible without fault of the parties, there is no real need for annulment as a legal institution.

It should be noted that all the gynecological detail in *Ball* came about because it was pleaded by the attorney for the defendant husband. We may mention in passing that Mr. Roberts, the defendant's attorney in *Ball*, wrote the opinion in *Posner* 22 years later as Justice of the Florida Supreme Court.

References

Montgomery, *Meet Victor Posner, Music Virtuoso Who Plays the Market— The Tycoon Finds His Place in the Shade, in Florida; Voice Behind the Counter*, Wall St. J., June 23, 1981, at 1, col. 4.
Nordheimer, *Ed Ball at 91: Embattled, Implacable*, N.Y. Times, Mar. 11, 1979, §3, at 1, col. 1
Nordheimer, *Edward Ball, Head of Alfred du Pont Trust, Dies at 93*, N.Y. Times, June 25, 1981, §D, at 23, cols. 3–6.

Bibliography

Bartke, *Marital Sharing—Why Not Do It by Contract?*, 67 GEO. L.J. 1131 (1979).
Branca & Steinberg, *Antenuptial Agreements Under California Law*, 11 U.S.F.L. REV. 317 (1977).
Clark, *Antenuptial Contracts*, 50 U. COLO. L. REV. 141 (1979).
Clark, H., THE LAW OF DOMESTIC RELATIONS IN THE UNITED STATES chs. 1, 16 (1968).
Glendon & Lev, *Changes in the Bonding of the Employment Relationship: An Essay on the New Property*, 20 B.C.L. REV. 457 (1979).
Haskell, *Premarital Estate Contract and Social Policy*, 57 N.C.L. REV. 415 (1979).
Levin & Spak, *Judicial Enforcement of Cohabitation Agreements: A Signal to Purge Marriage From the Statute of Frauds*, 12 CREIGHTON L. REV. 499 (1979).
Note, *Antenuptial Contracts to Circumvent Equitable Distribution in New Jersey Under the Revised Divorce Act*, 12 RUTGERS L.J. 283 (1980).
Note, *Breach of Promise to Marry: Relic Revised to Exclude Expectation of Damages*, 53 WASH. L. REV. 751 (1978).
Note, *Marriage Contracts for Support and Services: Constitutionality Begins at Home*, 49 N.Y.U.L. REV. 1161, 1184–1190 (1979).
Note, *Rosenberg v. Lipnick: Status of Antenuptial Agreements in Massachusetts*, 15 NEW ENG. L. REV. 351 (1979–1980).
Sheresky & Mannes, *A Radical Guide to Wedlock*, SAT. REV., July 29, 1972, at 33, *reprinted in* Krause, H., FAMILY LAW—CASES AND MATERIALS 100–08 (1976).

Shultz, *Contractual Ordering of Marriage: A New Model for State Policy,* 70
CALIF. L. REV. 204 (1982).

Swisher, *Divorce Planning in Antenuptial Agreements: Toward a New Objectivity,* 13 U. RICH. L. REV. 175 (1979).

Weitzman, *Legal Regulation of Marriage: Tradition and Change,* 62 CALIF. L.
REV. 1169 (1974).

Weitzman, L., THE MARRIAGE CONTRACT—SPOUSES, LOVERS, AND THE LAW
(1981).

Younger, *Marital Regimes: A Story of Compromise and Demoralization, Together with Criticism and Suggestions for Reform,* 67 CORNELL L. REV.
45 (1981).

Marriage as Status or Contract

From Status to Contract

Maynard v. Hill

United States Supreme Court

125 U.S. 190 (1888)

Appeal from the Supreme Court of the Territory of Washington.

This is a suit in equity to charge the defendants, as trustees of certain lands in King county, Washington Territory, and compel a conveyance thereof to the plaintiffs. The lands are described as lots 9, 10, 13, and 14, of section 4, and lots 6, 7, 8, and 9, of section 5, in township 24 north, range 4 east, Willamette meridian. The case comes here on appeal from a judgment of the supreme court of the territory, sustaining the defendant's demurrer, and dismissing the complaint. The material facts, as disclosed by the complaint, are briefly these: In 1828, David S. Maynard and Lydia A. Maynard intermarried in the state of Vermont, and lived there together as husband and wife until 1850, when they removed to Ohio. The plaintiffs, Henry C. Maynard and Frances J. Patterson, are their children, and the only issue of the marriage. David S. Maynard died intestate in the year 1873, and Lydia A. Maynard in the year 1879. In 1850 the husband left his family in Ohio and started overland for California, under a promise to his wife that he would either return or send for her and the children within two years, and that in the mean time he would send her the means of support. He left her without such means, and never afterwards contributed anything for her support or that of the children. On the 16th of September following he took up his residence in the territory of Oregon, in the part which is now Washington Territory, and continued ever afterwards to reside there. On the 3d of April, 1852 he settled upon and claimed, as a married man, a tract of land of 640 acres, described in the bill, under the act of congress of September 27, 1850, "creating the office of surveyor general of public lands in Oregon, and to provide for the survey, and to make donations to settlers of the said public lands," and resided thereon until his death. On the 22d day of December, 1852, an act was passed by the legislative assembly of the territory, purporting to dissolve the bonds of matrimony between him and his wife. The act is in these words:

"An act to provide for the dissolution of the bonds of matrimony heretofore existing between D. S. Maynard and Lydia A. Maynard his wife.

"Section 1. Be it enacted by the legislative assembly of the territory of Oregon, that the bonds of matrimony heretofore existing between D. S. Maynard and Lydia A. Maynard be, and the same are hereby, dissolved.

"Passed the house of representatives, December 22, 1852.

"B. F. HARDING, Speaker of the House of Representatives.

"Passed the council, December 22, 1852.

"M. P. DEADY, President Council."

The complaint alleges that no cause existed at any time for this divorce; that no notice was given to the wife of any application by the husband for a divorce, or of the introduction or pendency of the bill for that act in the legislative assembly; that she had no knowledge of the passage of the act until July, 1853; that at the time she was not within the limits or an inhabitant of Oregon; that she never became a resident of either the territory or state of Oregon; and that she never in any manner acquiesced in or consented to the act; and the plaintiffs insisted that the legislative assembly had no authority to pass the act; that the same is absolutely void; and that the parties were never lawfully divorced. On or about the 15th of January, 1853, the husband, thus divorced, intermarried with one Catherine T. Brashears, and thereafter they lived together as husband and wife until his death. On the 7th of November, 1853, he filed with the surveyor general of Oregon the certificate required under the donation act of September 27, 1850, as amended by the act of the 14th of February, 1853, accompanied with an affidavit of his residence in Oregon from the 16th of September, 1850, and on the land claimed from April 3, 1852, and that he was married to Lydia A. Maynard until the 24th of December 1852, having been married to her in Vermont in August 1828. The notification was also accompanied with corroborative affidavits of two other parties that he had, within their knowledge, resided upon and cultivated the land from the 3d of April, 1852.

* * *

Mr. Justice FIELD * * *

As seen by the statement of the case, two questions are presented for our consideration: *First,* was the act of the legislative assembly of the territory of Oregon of the 22d of December, 1852, declaring the bonds of matrimony between David S. Maynard and his wife dissolved, valid and effectual to divorce the parties? and, *second,* if valid and effectual for that purpose, did such divorce defeat any rights of the wife to a portion of the donation claim?

The act of congress creating the territory of Oregon * * * declared that the legislative power of the territory should "extend to all rightful subjects of legislation not inconsistent with the constitution and laws of the United States." * * *

* * *

Marriage, as creating the most important relation in life, as having more to do with the morals and civilization of a people than any other institution, has always been subject to the control of the legislature. That body prescribes the age at which parties may contract to marry, the procedure or form essential to constitute marriage, the duties and obligations it creates, its effects upon the property rights of both, present and prospective, and the acts which may constitute grounds for its dissolution.

* * *

When this country was settled, the power to grant a divorce from the bonds of matrimony was exercised by the parliament of England. The ecclesiastical courts of that country were limited to the granting of divorces from bed and board. Naturally, the legislative assemblies of the colonies followed the example of parliament and treated the subject as one within their province. And, until a recent period, legislative divorces have been granted, with few exceptions, in all the states. Says Bishop, in his *Treatise on Marriage and Divorce:* "The fact that at the time of the settlement of this country legislative divorces were common, competent, and valid in England, whence our jurisprudence was derived, makes them conclusively so here, except where an invalidity is directly or indirectly created by a written constitution binding the legislative power." Section 664. Says Cooley, in his *Treatise on Constitutional Limitations:* "The granting of divorces from the bonds of matrimony was not confided to the courts in England, and, from the earliest days, the colonial and state legislatures in this country have assumed to possess the same power over the subject which was possessed by the parliament, and from time to time they have passed special laws declaring a dissolution of the bonds of matrimony in special cases." Page 110. Says Kent, in his *Commentaries:* "During the period of our colonial government, for more than a hundred years preceding the revolution, no divorce took place in the colony of New York, and for many years after New York became an independent state there was not any lawful mode of dissolving a marriage in the lifetime of the parties but by a special act of the legislature." Volume 2, p. 97. The same fact is stated in numerous decisions of the highest courts of the states. Thus, in *Cronise v. Cronise,* 54 Pa. St. 260, the supreme court of Pennsylvania said: "Special divorce laws are legislative acts. This power has been exercised from the earliest period by the legislature of the province, and by that of the state, under the constitutions of 1776 and 1790. The continual exercise of the power, after the adoption of the constitution of 1790, cannot be accounted for except on the ground that all men, learned and unlearned, believed it to be a legitimate exercise of legislative power.* * *"

The facts alleged in the bill of complaint, that no cause existed for the divorce, and that it was obtained without the knowledge of the wife, cannot affect the validity of the act. Knowledge or ignorance of parties of intended legislation does not affect its validity, if within the competency of the legislature. The facts mentioned as to the neglect of the husband to send to his wife, whom he left in Ohio, any means for her support or that of her children, in disregard of his promise, shows conduct meriting the strongest reprobation, and, if the facts stated had been brought to the attention of congress, that body might and probably would have annulled the act. Be that as it may, the loose morals and shameless conduct of the husband can have no bearing upon the question of the existence or absence of power in the assembly to pass the act. The organic act extends the legislative power of the territory to all rightful subjects of legislation "not inconsistent with the constitution and laws of the United States." The only inconsistency suggested is that it impairs the obligation of the contract of marriage. Assuming that the prohibition of the federal constitution against the impairment of contracts by state legislation applies equally, as would seem to be the opinion of the supreme court of the territory, to legislation by territorial legislatures, we are clear that marriage is not a contract within the meaning of the prohibition. As was said by Chief Justice MARSHALL in the *Dartmouth College Case,* not by way of judgment, but in answer to objections urged to positions taken: "The provision of the constitution never has been understood to embrace other contracts than those which respect property or some object of value, and confer rights which may be asserted in a court of justice. It never has been understood to restrict the general right of the legislature to legislate on the subject of divorces."* * * It is also to be observed that, while marriage is often termed by text writers and in decisions of courts as a civil contract, generally to indicate that it must be founded upon the agreement of the parties, and does not require any religious ceremony for its solemnization, it is something more than a mere contract. The consent of the parties is of course essential to its existence, but when the contract to marry is executed by the marriage, a relation between the parties is created which they cannot change. Other contracts may be modified, restricted, or enlarged, or entirely released upon the consent of the parties. Not so with marriage. The relation once formed, the law steps in and holds the parties to various obligations and liabilities. It is an institution, in the maintenance of which in its purity the public is deeply interested, for it is the foundation of the family and of society, without which there would be neither civilization nor progress. This view is well expressed by the supreme court of Maine in *Adams v. Palmer,* 51 Me. 481, 483. Said that court, speaking by Chief Justice APPLETON:

> "When the contracting parties have entered into the married state, they have not so much entered into a contract as into a new relation, the rights, duties, and obligations of which rest upon their agreement, but upon the general law of the state, statutory or common, which defines and prescribes those rights, duties, and obligations. They are of law, not of contract. It was a contract that the relation should be established, but, being established, the power of the parties as to its extent or duration is at an end. Their rights under it are determined by the will of the sovereign, as evidenced by law. They can neither be modified nor changed by any agreement of parties. It is a relation for life, and the parties cannot terminate it at any shorter period by virtue of any contract they may make. The reciprocal rights arising from this relation, so long as it continues, are such as the law determines from time to time, and none other."

And again:

> "it is not then a contract within the meaning of the clause of the constitution which prohibits the impairing the obligation of contracts. It is rather a social relation like that of parent and child, the obligations of which arise not from the consent of concurring minds, but are the creation of the law itself, a relation the most important, as affecting the happiness of individuals, the first step from barbarism to incipient civilization, the purest tie of social life, and the true basis of human progress."
> * * *

* * *

In *Noel v. Ewing,* 9 Ind. 37, the question was before the supreme court of Indiana as to the competency of the legislature of the state to change the relative rights of husband and wife after marriage, which led to a consideration of the nature of marriage; and the court said:

> "Some confusion has arisen from confounding the contract to marry with the marriage relation itself. And still more is engendered by regarding the husband and wife as strictly parties to a subsisting contract. At common law, marriage as a *status* had few elements of contract about it. For instance, no other contract merged the legal existence of the parties into one. Other distinctive elements will readily suggest themselves, which rob it of most of its characteristics as a contract, and leave it simply as a *status* or institution. As such, it is not so much the result of private agreement as of public ordination. In every enlightened government it is pre-eminently the basis of civil institutions, and thus an object of the deepest public concern. In this light, marriage is more than a contract. It is not a mere matter of pecuniary consideration. It is a great public institution, giving character to our whole civil polity."

In accordance with these views was the judgment of Mr. Justice STORY. In a note to the chapter on marriage in his work on the Conflict of Laws, after stating that he had treated marriage as a contract in the common sense of the word, because this was the light in which it was ordinarily viewed by jurists, domestic as well as foreign, he adds: "But it appears to me to be something more than a mere contract. It is rather to be deemed an institution of society founded upon consent and contract of the parties, and in this view it has some peculiarities in its nature, character, operation, and extent of obligation different from what belong to ordinary contracts." Section 108n.

* * *

* * * When, therefore, the act was passed divorcing the husband and wife, he had no vested interest in the land, and she could have no interest greater than his. Nothing had then been acquired by his residence and cultivation, which gave him anything more than a mere possessory right to remain on the land so as to enable him to comply with the conditions, upon which the title was to pass to him. After the divorce she had no such relation to him as to confer upon her any interest in the title subsequently acquired by him. A divorce ends all rights not previously vested. Interests which might vest in time, upon a continuance of the marriage relation, were gone. A wife divorced has no right of dower in his property; a husband divorced has no right by the courtesy in her lands, unless the statute authorizing the divorce specially confers such right.

It follows that the wife was not entitled to the east half of the donation claim. To entitle her to that half she must have continued his wife during his residence and cultivation of the land. The judgment of the supreme court of the territory must therefore be affirmed; and it is so ordered.

Ponder v. Graham

Supreme Court of Florida

4 Fla. 23 (1851)

Appeal from judgment of the Circuit Court of the county of Leon, rendered at the Spring term, 1850, the Honorable THOMAS BALTZELL, Judge, presiding.

Mary Graham filed her petition in the Circuit Court of the County of Leon, representing that her husband, Archibald Graham, died on or about the 2d January, 1848, after having in his life time made and executed his last will and testament—that said will and testament bears date 16th November, 1847, and that one John R. Cannon, and the defendant, William G. Ponder, were therein named and appointed executors—that defendant alone qualified and took out letters testamentary—that the provision made in the said will is not satisfactory to petitioner, and that she, in due form, and in proper manner, signified her dissent thereto, within the time limited by law. The petitioner further states, that her deceased husband died seized and possessed of a large estate, real, personal, and mixed—out of which, petitioner prays that dower may be allotted to her, under the law in such case made and provided.

The defendant for answer, or plea to said petition, alleged that the said Mary Graham ought not to have her dower, as in her petition she claimed and prayed, because the said Mary never was *accoupled* to the said Archibald Graham, deceased, in lawful matrimony. To this plea, there was a replication, affirming that petitioner was *accoupled* in lawful matrimony with the said Archibald Graham, and issue thereon. The jury found for the petitioner; and thereupon it was adjudged and ordered, that said petitioner is entitled to an assignment of dower, and a writ of dower issued as prayed for, commanding the sheriff to summon five discreet free holders as commissioners, to allot and set off, by metes and bounds, to Mary Graham, widow of Archibald Graham, one-third part, according to quantity and quality of the real estate of which the said Archibald died seized, whereof the said Mary had not relinquished her right of dower, and at the same time to allot and set off to the said widow her portion, or one-half of the personal estate of the deceased.

* * *

The facts of the case are succinctly these: The respondent, then Mary Buccles, about the year 1820, in South Carolina, intermarried with one Solomon Canady. Some time afterwards, they removed to, and resided in, Georgia, but soon, in consequence of domestic dissentions, separated.—Mary went to reside with Graham, a bachelor, and continued to live with him, under circumstances from which an adulterous cohabitation might be inferred.

In 1832, and while the said cohabitation continued, a bill was passed by the Legislative Council of the then Territory of Florida, entitled "An act for the relief of Mary Canady."

By this act, the Legislative Council, for the cause expressed in the preamble, assumed to judge and declare that the said Mary Graham was thereby divorced from her said husband, Solomon, and that the bonds of matrimony subsisting between them, were thereby to be entirely and absolutely dissolved, as if the same had never been solemnized. (See pamphlet acts of 1833, page 123.) There does not appear to have been any petition, affidavit, or proofs—a reference to a committee to ascertain the facts, or any notice to the absent husband. In 1834, the cohabitation between Mary and the testator still subsisting, the ceremony of marriage is celebrated between them, and from this time up to the period of the testator's death, which occurred in 1848, he lived with her, and acknowledged her as his wife, and in his will he provides for her by that name, and in that relation.

* * *

SEMMES, *Justice,* delivered the opinion of the court.

* * *

The main question raised in this case, as to the power of a Legislative body, *as such*, to grant divorces, is not altogether a new one. It has been investigated by some of the American Courts, and grave constitutional questions have been necessarily involved in the discussion; and yet the question still remains an open one—opinions clashing—nothing settled. It is to be regretted that amid this conflict of opinion, upon a question of such deep interest, we are unable to avail ourselves of the investigation of any one of the great jurists of our country, to relieve the subject from embarrassment and difficulty, and that while almost every other legal question of importance has had light and authority imparted to it, this, one of the most important of all, has been allowed to slumber on in doubt and uncertainty.

The Legislatures of some of the States of the Union exercise exclusive jurisdiction over this subject; one or more of them by reason, as is contended for by their courts, of the absence of any constitutional inhibition—while others claim this authority by reason, it is said, of an inherent power, analogous to that of the Parliament of Great Britain. Some exercise the power as a constitutional right, while others claim it as an original right, and without the sanction of constitutional authority.

No one doubts the right of the people by their constitution, to invest this power in the Legislature, or any where else; but the question is, when the constitution is silent on the subject, in what department of government does this authority rest? I believe that much, if not the whole difficulty, has arisen from overlooking some of the great principles which enter into the constitutional government of the States, and from not preserving the obvious distinction between legislative and judicial functions—by confounding the *right* which a legislative body has to pass *general laws* on the subject of divorce, with the *power* of dissolving the marriage *contract*.

* * *

The act of the counsel undertakes to determine questions of fact and law exclusively within the province of the courts. If, as is contended with much reason, there were no existing causes of divorce, as set forth in the preamble to this act, then the dissolution of the marriage contract was a mere assumption of power, exercised in the most arbitrary manner.

An act declaring that to be a crime which, by the laws of the land, was no crime, and punishing an innocent party, by depriving him of important legal rights without a hearing, without notice, and who had not, in any mode, made himself amenable to our laws, such proceeding could not be justified, on any principle of natural right, or common justice. But assuming the fact to be so—that the grounds on which the legislature acted were recognized by our law as causes for divorce—then the legislature, assuming the high prerogatives and character of judicial tribunal, proceeds to determine the facts and administer the law—upon *ex parte* showing, pronounces judgment against an absent defendant, and declares a forfeiture of his marital rights, for causes happening in a foreign jurisdiction, and to whose laws he was alone amenable. Is there no distinction between making a law and expounding and administering a law? Between declaring that certain acts may work a forfeiture, and passing judgment of forfeiture? Between enacting a law affecting the remedy, and pronouncing a judgment dissolving a contract? Had any court dissolved this marriage contract, with the facts before it disclosed in this record, it would have been but a poor compliment to its own sense of justice, or the high and solemn trust with which the law had clothed it.

* * *

It is said, and the doctrine is broadly intimated in several of the authorities, that a legislature in this country can grant divorces, in analogy to the Parliament of England. I can see no parallel in the two cases. Political writers in England claim for their Parliament omnipotent power. It is said that in that country "there is no written constitution, no fundamental law, nothing visible, nothing tangible, nothing real, nothing certain, by which a statute of Parliament can be tested." See 3 DALLAS's REPORTS, 308; and yet, with all this acknowledged and untrammelled power, it does not assert or exercise the right of dissolving the marriage contract; to the extent and in the summary mode adopted by the Legislatures of some of the States.

Parliament never decrees a divorce, *a mensa et thoro*—that power belongs exclusively to the courts. Parliament never even decrees a divorce *a vinculo*, but for adultery, and that upon a judgment *a mensa et thoro*, first pronounced by the Ecclesiastical Courts, and unless sufficient cause is shown, a verdict for damages in a Court of Common Law is requisite, before Parliament will take jurisdiction. The whole proceedings, from the libel filed in the Ecclesiastical Court, up to the final decree by Parliament, are, in every essential requisite, *judicial*. The formal petition to the House of Lords, with an office copy of the judgment and proceeding in the court, notice to the defendant, the examination of witnesses, the hearing of counsel, and the judgment pronounced, all clothe it with a judicial character, of which it is impossible to divest it—done, it is true, by Parliament, but by virtue of its omnipotent power.

* * *

* * * There is another point presented by the record in this case, which I think it my duty briefly to consider—it is, whether this act of the legislature is not unconstitutional, on the ground that it impairs the obligation of a contract.

It is insisted that marriage is but a *civil relation*, and not embraced within the definition of a *contract*, as used in the constitution. In England, as well as in this country, all legal writers consider it *as purely a civil contract*. It is true it is a civil relation, but *non constat*, it is not a contract in the strict legal definition of the term. Every contract creates a legal relation between the parties. Blackstone says that "the law of England considers marriage in *no other* light than as a civil contract, and viewing it in this civil light, the law *treats* it as it does all other contracts." 1 BLACKSTONE'S COMMENTARIES, 448. Rutherford says the contract of marriage creates important legal rights in the person and property of the other. 1 INSTITUTES, 314. See, also, Bacon, 476, 488. The contract creates mutual rights, duties and obligations, deeply interesting to society, it is true, but none the less important and valuable to the contracting parties. It is municipal, as it affects the public—it is a contract, as it affects the rights of the person and the rights of property—it has all the attributes of a pure contract, whether we consider the capacity of the parties to contract, the subject matter or the consideration; and the rights growing out of it can be asserted and enforced in a court of justice. A man has as good a right to the property acquired by marriage, as that acquired under any other contract. Mr. Justice Story says, "As to the case of the contract of marriage, which the argument supposes not be within the prohibitory clause, (of the constitution,) because it is a manner of civil institution, I profess *not to feel the weight of the reason assigned for the exception. In a legal sense, all con*tracts, recognized as valid in any country, may be properly said to be matters of civil institution, since they obtain their obligation and construction *jure loci contractus.*" 4 CONDENSED SUPREME COURT REPORTS, 520. I know of no reason why the word contract, as used in the constitution, should be restricted to those of a pecuniary nature, and not embrace that of marriage, involving, as it does, considerations of the most interesting character and vital importance to society; to government, and the contracting parties. It is comprehended by the words of the constitution, and there is no rule of construction that would exclude it, in the absence of any thing to show that it is not within its spirit. 9th Gill and Johnson. And what was the *obligations* of the contract, but the rights and duties which grow out of it? A legislative act which discharges the duties and destroys the rights acquired under any contract, must, of necessity, impair its obligation. A law affecting the remedy, does not impair the obligation, but an act of the legislature dissolving the contract, *destroys* the obligation.

In every respect in which I have been able to see this case, I can find no reason to sustain the act of the legislature. It appears by the record, that the parties were domiciled in the State of Georgia, where, it is alleged; the desertion and ill treatment occurred. The wife, living with the testator, Graham, removed to Florida—while the husband returned to Carolina, his former residence. The bill was introduced into the legislature one day, and passed the next. It is very clear that this divorce would not be recognized by the courts of Georgia or Carolina, were any rights asserted under it in those States. There was an utter want of jurisdiction over the person, as well as the subject matter, and an act thus passed in defiance of the maxim, *audi alteram partem*, has no merit to recommend it to this court. The husband, in this case, in the language of Chief Justice Story, "had as good a right to his wife as his property acquired under the marriage contract—he had a legal right to her society and fortune, and to divest him of these rights, without his default, and against his will, was as flagrant a violation of the principles of justice, as the confiscation of his estate." 4 CONDENSED SUPREME COURTS. [sic]

I am, therefore, of opinion that the act of the Legislative Council of February 11th, 1832, was in conflict with the organic law of Florida and the Constitution of the United States, and is, therefore, void.

Per Curiam—Let the judgment of the court below be reversed.

Ryan v. Ryan

Supreme Court of Florida

277 So.2d 266 (Fla. 1973)

DEKLE, J.

We have for consideration three certified questions of law submitted by the Circuit Court of the Eleventh Judicial Circuit concerning the constitutionality of Florida's new dissolution of marriage law, * * *

The three questions certified to us are as follows:

"1. Whether Florida Statutes Chapter 61 which abolished former grounds for divorce and provided as sole ground for divorce that:
   (1) the marriage is irretrievably broken, and/or
   (2) insanity or mental incompetence
is constitutional in that it does not *impair* the *obligation* of the *marriage contract* nor *adversely affect property rights* of the parties?
"2. Whether Florida Statute Chapter 61 which provides for the granting of a dissolution of marriage upon the court's finding that the marriage is irretrievably broken is unconstitutional in that it is *vague, uncertain and indefinite?*
"3. Whether Florida Statute Chapter 61 is unconstitutional because it *applies retroactively* to marriages entered into prior to July 1, 1971?" (emphasis added)

These questions seek our constitutional interpretation of the new "no-fault" divorce law. The first question has two parts: Does the new dissolution law "impair the obligation of the marriage contract" in violation of Fla. Const. art. I, §10, F.S.A.; does it "adversely affect property rights of the parties." We shall examine and decide these related issues together.

PROPERTY RIGHTS

Fla. Const. §10 of the Declaration of Rights (Art. I) states that: "No * * * law impairing the obligation of contracts shall be passed." The respective parties argue at length with regard to whether or not marriage is a contract thus protected, citing various cases on the point.

This Court said as early as *Ponder v. Graham*, 4 Fla. 23, in 1851, that marriage is a contract. We have consistently since that time referred to "marriage contracts" for over 120 years of Florida Jurisprudence. As recently as *Belcher v. Belcher*, 271 So.2d 7 (Fla. 1972), we referred to the obligation of the husband to support his wife during continuation of the marriage contract, thus still holding our view of marriage to be a "contract" rather than a mere "relationship" as suggested in *Gleason v. Gleason*, 26 N.Y.2d 28, 308 N.Y.S.2d 347, 256 N.E.2d 513 (N.Y. Ct. App. 1970), and in an 1888 U.S. Supreme Court case cited by appellee, *Maynard v. Hill*, 125 U.S. 190, 8 S. Ct. 723, 31 L.Ed. 654. In that U.S. Supreme Court holding, however, and in others it is pointed out that the contracts which were designed to be protected under the constitutional provision are those contracts providing certain, definite and fixed private rights of property which are vested in the contract.

The query arises then whether dower or curtesy is a "property right" of a spouse thus protected. The inchoate right of dower is statutory and not a matter of contract, even though such right does indeed grow out of the marriage by virtue of the parties having "contracted" for that marriage. See also 52 AM. JUR.2d, *Marriage*, §5.

Dower is not a vested right. We have said that because of its defeasible nature dower is not to be given consideration in divorce or dissolution of marriage proceedings. *Bowler v. Bowler,* 159 Fla. 447, 31 So.2d 751 (1947).
* * *
Next we inquire: Is *potential alimony* such a "property right" under the contract of marriage as to be "impaired" contrary to Fla. Const. §10 Decl. of Rights? Under the foregoing analysis of dower we must hold likewise that this contingent interest does not fall within the constitutional prohibition. The same result is true as to equitable interests claimed in the property of a spouse by virtue of contributions of services or other considerations within the marriage, other than interests which have already vested. (Actual transfers and independent interests not inherent in the marriage stand independently.) Such a potential equitable interest as alimony is not yet vested but arises upon subsequent judicial determination (or settlement). True, an ultimate award of such an interest upon a termination of the marriage contract (or a legal separation) stems from the marriage. Without it, such an interest would not have arisen. But these potential interests are not those property rights contemplated by the constitutional prohibition.

VAGUE and INDEFINITE CHALLENGE

The next question of law concerns that part of F.S., Section 61.052, F.S.A., reading:

"(1) No judgment of dissolution of marriage shall be granted unless one of the following facts appears, which shall be pleaded generally:
"(a) The marriage is irretrievably broken. * * *"

The quoted language read in context with the remainder of the statute expresses the purpose and intent of the Legislature with sufficient clarity to render it invulnerable to attack that it is unconstitutionally vague and indefinite.

The word "irretrievably" is defined: "impossible to recoup, repair or overcome." WEBSTER'S THIRD INTERNATIONAL DICTIONARY (1966), page 1196.

When compared with the fourth statutory ground for divorce, "extreme cruelty," in the former statute (§61.041(4), F.S. 1969, F.S.A.), the new language for dissolution of marriage, "irretrievably broken," appears to us to be no more susceptible to the charge of vagueness than were the words, "extreme cruelty." "Extreme cruelty" in the former divorce law was held in case after case to envision a great variety of faults and wrongdoings that were deemed sufficient for the granting of divorce, but the phrase was never invalidated for vagueness or overbreadth. For example, in *Diem v. Diem,* 141 Fla. 260, 193 So. 65, 66, this Court held the phrase, "extreme cruelty," as a ground for divorce to be "relative." The Court added:

"What constitutes it may be determined by the degree of one's culture, his emotions, nervous reaction or moral sense."

* * *
It is the duty of a court to recognize a reasonable construction of a statute which supports its constitutionality. The Legislature does not have to give a detailed and carefully outlined plan of each and every step to be followed in each and every circumstance which could arise. * * * Under the principles enunciated above, the statute meets the challenge of constitutional vagueness.

PLEADINGS

It is sufficient in the petition simply to allege as an ultimate fact that the marriage is "irretrievably broken"; however, the chancellor must determine from the particular facts of each case whether a marriage is "irretrievably broken," subject, of course, to appellate review. Just as "extreme cruelty" was held in divorce cases to cover a wide range of factual predicates for divorce, so the phrase "irretrievably broken" embraces numerous factual bases for dissolution of marriages. However, by the express language of the new statute now, dissolution of marriage is no longer granted because of the fault or wrongdoing or misconduct of one or both parties, as was the case under the grounds for divorce under former Section 61.041, F.S. 1969, F.S.A. The new statutory test for determining if a marriage is irretrievably broken is simply whether for whatever reason or cause (no matter whose "fault") the marriage relationship is for all intents and purposes ended, no longer viable, a hollow sham beyond hope of reconciliation or repair.

PROOF

It is suggested that a circuit judge would hesitate to adjudicate that a marriage is *not* "irretrievably broken" under the present statute when the petitioner simply says that is the fact; that the judge becomes nothing more than a ministerial officer receiving the "irretrievably broken" message and having so received it, being thus compelled to drop this legislative guillotine upon the marriage, thus excising the troublesome mate from the petitioner because the petitioner has subjectively and unilaterally determined that his marriage is irretrievably broken.

We do not view the matter of dissolution as being such a simple, unilateral matter of one mate simply saying "I want out." All of the surrounding facts and circumstances are to be inquired into to arrive at the conclusion as to whether or not indeed the marriage has reached the terminal stage based upon facts which must be shown. Even in uncontested dissolutions, the court would properly make inquiry to determine this fact, for the statute itself in §61.052 provides in subsection (2) the basic predicate: "Based on the evidence at the hearing. * * * [and even] (a) * * * if the respondent does not * * * deny that the marriage is irretrievably broken, the court shall enter a judgment of dissolution of the marriage, *if the court finds that the marriage is irretrievably broken.*" (emphasis added)

It is argued that the provision in the statute for continuing the proceedings for a period not exceeding 90 days to allow the parties to effect a reconciliation, is inconsistent with the objective of determining if in fact there is no further chance for the marriage to succeed. Actually, this further test of the marriage supports the requirement that the court must make a determination, beyond a petitioner's bare assertion, that in truth and in fact the marriage is "irretrievably broken."

And so it is that in every instance the court should make that determination by proper inquiry. It is never a simple matter of "Is your marriage 'irretrievably broken'?" "Yes, your honor, I believe it is." And that ends it, like the oriental ritual of the husband severing his marriage by tossing three stones in the sand one by one and in sequence saying, "I divorce thee; I divorce thee; I divorce thee." There must be appropriate *evidence* (albeit uncorroborated as the statute allows) that in truth and in *fact* the marriage is irretrievably broken.

In *Posner I,* 233 So.2d 381 (Fla. 1970), quoting from *Underwood v. Underwood,* 12 Fla. 434, we stated the law still to be as follows: (233 So.2d p. 383)

"* * * it 'would be aiming a deadly blow at public morals to decree a dissolution of the marriage contract merely because the parties requested it * * *.' "

FORMER DEFENSES ELIMINATED

The new Act includes a provision, §61.044, entitled "Certain Existing Defenses Abolished" and provides:

"The defenses to divorce and legal separation, of condonation, collusion, recrimination, and laches are abolished."

The heretofore well-known defenses of condonation and recrimination found their genesis in the equitable "clean hands" doctrine but even prior to this new legislation enactment, we had to some degree modified strict recrimination as a defense in the case of *Stewart v. Stewart*, 158 Fla. 326, 29 So.2d 247 (1947). There the Court found both pairs of hands so unclean that it was hardpressed to apply the doctrine against both parties and therefore proceeded to call it "a qualifying doctrine" and frankly stated that if the doctrine were applied strictly it would in such circumstances result in "great inequity" in that neither party to the suit had been free from fault. That opinion in *Stewart* did however reiterate that the application of the doctrine of clean hands still existed as a matter of judicial discretion and public policy.

FRAUD

Now we find, however, that by virtue of the new legislative action that the clean hands principle has been eliminated in marriage dissolution except for fraud and deceit which are always available in our courts. A contrived, false or fraudulent creation of the ground upon which dissolution is sought, for the very purpose of terminating the marriage through what amounts to misuse and, in effect, a fraud upon the courts could no more be tolerated in this than in any other litigation. The courts will not knowingly become a party to contrivance or fraud, even in the simplified basis for divorce which has now been created by the new statute. This is inherent in the judicial process. It is not limited to a future discovery of the fraud but may become apparent in the proceedings for dissolution, in which event the court should deal directly with it in such proceedings. In this there may be a direct fraud perpetrated upon the other spouse by misrepresentations, concealments or untruths, manifesting itself either in the course of the proceeding or at a later time. The courts will not indulge or reward falsehood and when such a purposeful inducement or fraud upon the other spouse or the court is made to appear by the evidence, then there would be a failure of proof that the marriage was irretrievably broken. The proof having failed in such instance, there would accordingly not be sufficient evidence upon which to grant the relief sought. This is not based upon a continuation of "fault" as a basis for relief which was required under the former divorce law but as a matter of fraud and deceit. This recognition of such a fundamental concept of equity is necessary in order to preserve the integrity of the judiciary, lest it become a party to a fraud or allow a misuse of the judicial machinery. Not even under statutory imposition can an independent judiciary which is the ultimate protector of right and justice, be subjugated and undermined.

We recognize that the new "no fault" concept was a principle basis of the new legislation for a desired simplification of the procedure aimed at reducing the trauma of the dissolution experience. That is a legislative judgment. The foregoing remaining intolerance of fraud or deceit is a judicial prerogative, to protect against fraud by a party and misuse of the courts and which we view as legally consistent with the new law.

NOT RETROACTIVE

The third question is directed to the constitutionality of the Act as allegedly applying *retroactively* to marriages prior to the Act, that is, prior to July 1, 1971, and thus void under Fla. Const. art. I, §10, and the federal constitution. We have heretofore held that the authority to regulate marriages and correspondingly to provide for their dissolutions is vested in the Legislature. It is inherent in the state's police power to do so in the regulation of society and its relationships, including the very essential and important family relationship within marriage. The marriage contract perhaps more than any other has a vital and essential effect on the very life and society of the State and therefore is a very proper subject of the State's police power; the subject of marriage (and correspondingly the dissolution thereof) has a very definite bearing upon the public interest with which the Legislature is concerned and charged with its regulation.

The Legislature as representative of the people should regulate marriage and the family relationship, and those matters affecting the members of the family in that affinity, in such manner and from time to time as the wisdom of the people may be reflected in the actions of their elected representatives. You might say: "For better, for worse." It must be remembered that the State has always been considered a "third party" or "third interest" in divorce and the family tie.

Petitioner challenges the authority of the Legislature to extend the law to "grant" dissolutions upon a new, simplified test of whether the tie is "irretrievably broken." It is urged as unconstitutional to apply the new law to existing contracts of marriage entered into under the prior law which, it is claimed, was a part of that marriage contract—now being "broken" by legislative action without due process of judicial considerations of notice and hearing. The only trouble with this contention is that the "remedy" (the procedure provided in the new law for dissolution) is the ongoing prerogative of the Legislature which also legislates the marriage in its creation. "* * * the Lord gave, and the Lord hath taken away."

There is, as we have said, no impairment of contract here. Neither is there denial of due process in the manner in which the machinery is set up for judicial determination regarding termination of the marriage. The law provides that consideration be given to support provisions and to any interest of the wife in property of the husband by way of special equity or otherwise. Due process basically is met upon a provision for notice and opportunity to be heard. Of course these are included in the new law, as such requirements were also included in the law in existence when past marriages were entered into. Accordingly, it cannot be maintained with validity that the new provision regarding the same subject matter is void because it affects "retroactively" those earlier marriage "contracts" and the applicable procedures and remedies, which are subject to proper change from time to time.

LEGISLATIVE PREROGATIVE

An additional argument is that the new dissolution of marriage law constitutes an encroachment upon the judiciary. In all candor we must recognize that the matter of divorce is a legislative prerogative. We do not have ecclesiastical courts. In the language of the poet, it might be said as to the role of the courts upon such legislative action: "Theirs not to make reply; Theirs not to reason why. * * *" The change in philosophy, a different approach to the dissolution of marriage (a legislative prerogative) may add to today's moral erosion of contemporary standards in reflecting an unprecedented disregard, even scorn, for law and basic morality. It may also be that the family relationship and provisions for support are no longer protected by the laws of this state by requiring proof of misconduct before such rights can be taken away, but these matters of individual rights, social mores and of state policy are to be settled in the caldron of the people's representative government, the Legislature, by such representatives as the people choose to elect, upon whatever they may have represented to the people that their standards are. If the electorate finds it has been misled in such standards, or wishes to change them, the polls will open again.

* * *

Better we weep over questioned legislation, or judicial decisions for that matter, and strive within the proper channels for desired change, than destroy the system, for whatever well intended purpose. Such is the reasoning behind the oft-mentioned reference to our legal system as one "of laws, not of men." Sometimes it is not easy, but it is imperative to the survival of the democratic process.

* * *

Appellant urges *Ponder, supra,* as a basis for voiding the legislative provision for "no fault divorce." The dissolution of marriage provided in the new law is not, however, "a legislative divorce" which was granted in the early day of *Ponder, supra,* by the Legislative Council of Florida without reference to the courts. *Ponder* is not then precedent for a prohibition of the Legislature to regulate and provide grounds and procedures for dissolution of marriage.

Ponder involved an 1832 act of the Legislative Council of the Territory of Florida entitled "An Act For the Relief of Mary Canady" wherein that body proceeded *ipso facto* to dissolve or annul outright the bonds of matrimony of the said Mary and one Solomon Canady. That, of course, is quite different from a *judicial* consideration of the dissolution of marriage for which the present Legislature has provided in the proceeding in the courts. In *Ponder,* Mary, being then married to Mr. Canady, came to Florida where she proceeded to cohabit with one Mr. Graham and thereafter that early Legislative Council of the Territory saw fit to "dissolve" her previous marriage. This was of course an invasion of the judiciary and recognized as such by the holding in *Ponder* that such individual act was unconstitutional. It does not, however, stand as precedent here. The decision in *Ponder* in rejecting such "legislative divorce" actually reflects a healthy respect for the judiciary's role and also a repugnance for legislation which has solely such a private limited purpose.

* * *

ROBERTS, Justice (dissenting).

Section 61.011, Florida Statutes, F.S.A., entitled, "Dissolution in Chancery," provides that proceedings under this act relating to dissolution of marriage are to be in chancery (equity).

One of the most elementary and fundamental concepts of equity jurisprudence and a universal rule which affects the entire system of equity jurisprudence is the maxim that "He who comes into equity must come with clean hands." This principle is founded upon conscience and good faith.

* * *

Under the majority view a wrongdoing husband can come home every Saturday night for five years, drunk and penniless because of skirt-chasing, gambling, or some other misdeeds; then, he may beat, bruise and abuse his wife because he is unhappy with himself, and then he will be permitted to go down and get a divorce on printed forms purchased at a department store and tell the trial judge that the marriage is "irretrievably broken." Or, the offending wife, after jumping from bed to bed with her new found paramours, chronically drunk, and when at home nagging, brawling and quarreling, all against the wishes of a faithful husband who remains at home nurturing the children is permitted to divorce her husband who does not desire a divorce, but rather, has one forced upon him, not because of anything he has done, but because the offending wife tells the trial court that her marriage is "irretrievably broken."

In my opinion, the offending spouse should not have standing to obtain a divorce if the innocent one invokes the doctrine that,

"He who comes into equity must come with clean hands."

It is the duty of this Court to seek a construction of a statute which would support its constitutionality.

By merely retaining the "clean hands" doctrine, I could agree that the "no-fault" divorce statute is constitutional, but absent this,

I must respectfully dissent.

Comments

Maynard, Ponder, and *Ryan* relate to the nature of marriage as seen in the light of Sir Henry Sumner Maine's famous statement, "that the movement of the progressive societies has been a movement *from Status to Contract.*" In legal practice this statement has never had the same significance it has had for scholarship, but relational and contractual aspects of marriage have lived side by side relatively undisturbed. These cases illustrate that legal practice can live with and accommodate apparent contradictions with ease. *Maynard* stands today for the proposition that marriage is something more than a mere contract, that it is a status or a relationship and, as such, subject to regulation by the government. The case is cited in the context of constitutional attacks on legislation having an impact on marriage. *Ryan* is an illustration citing *Maynard* in upholding the Florida no-fault divorce statute.

Ponder, on the other hand, an early Florida case decided in 1851, 37 years earlier than *Maynard,* continues to be relied on for the seemingly opposite proposition that marriage is contract rather than a mere relationship, and that legislation regulating marriage could conceivably impair the obligation of contract if it affects vested rights. *Ponder* is primarily cited in support of the theory that marriage is contract, notwithstanding the contrary characterization by the United States Supreme Court in *Maynard.*

This illustrates how the significance of landmark cases is often entirely removed from the facts and the holdings. They introduce key words and phrases that are subsequently cited regardless of whether or not such reference is historically defensible or logically consistent. In actual practice, consequently, *Maynard* can be cited whenever an argument in support of the police power of the state to regulate marriage is made, while *Ponder* can be cited in support of the contractual autonomy of marital parties to regulate their own affairs. In an extreme case this may be done within the same case, and *Ryan* demonstrates this capacity to draw from contradictory sources for support.

The facts in *Maynard* and *Ponder* have almost nothing to do with modern reality. They arose out of frontier conditions. David S. Maynard was a powerful figure of American history. Initially trained as a doctor, he founded a medical school in Ohio and later, after his move across the country, became one of the founders of the State of Washington and the city of Seattle. The same legislature of the Territory of

Oregon, having jurisdiction over what later was to become the State
of Washington, granted Maynard his divorce from his first wife, created King County upon his suggestion, declared him to be notary for
King County, and established the county seat on his land claim. Obviously he was a man who could demand and receive almost anything
from the legislature. That Archibald Graham was a man of substantial means is mentioned in *Ponder.* That he too was politically influen-
tial can be inferred from the circumstances and the tone of the special
legislation that was enacted by the territorial legislature of Florida in
his interest and presumably upon his instigation. Tallahassee, the
seat of the legislature and his place of domicile, had been founded as a
city and capital of the new territorial government less than 10 years
when the Legislative Council passed the act for the relief of Mary
Canady. Graham appears to have been one of the first prominent settlers in the area. By neglecting these facts and emphasizing certain
fundamental considerations relating to marriage, to the power of the
courts and legislatures, and to the United States Constitution, the
courts facilitated a process that has led to the conceptually ambivalent, but eminently practical, solution that the current legal situation
reflects.

   Ponder established Florida as a leading jurisdiction for a theory of
marriage as contract, modified by later Florida cases to a theory of
marriage as partnership. The materials in this book attest to the increased national importance of this view, and numerous Florida cases
have confirmed the pattern, for example, *Chaachou v. Chaachou* (pp.
8–22), *Ryan v. Ryan* (pp. 53–59), *Steinhauer v. Steinhauer* (pp. 70–75),
Brown v. Brown (pp. 92–98), and especially *Gates v. Foley* (pp.
292–294). *Ryan v. Ryan,* on the other hand, is important for another
reason. It demonstrates an early split within no-fault divorce jurisdictions, namely, into those that genuinely try to avoid fault and those
that have judicially encouraged its reinstitution. Florida has taken an
early lead in the latter direction. Not only is the majority opinion
"weeping" over the questioned legislation, it also establishes that the
judge is not merely a ministerial officer who must uncritically accept a
request for dissolution. He should have the power and indeed the duty
to inquire about the reasons why the marriage is "irretrievably broken." The answer to this question, as we shall see, reestablishes the
possibility of fault, both in the courts and, more importantly, in the
negotiations in lawyers' offices prior to the filing of the petition for
dissolution of marriage.

References

Hunter, *An Essay on Contract and Status: Race, Marriage, and the Meretricious Spouse,* 64 Va. L. Rev. 1039 (1978).
Mueller, *Inquiry Into the State of a Divorceless Society: Domestic Relations,
   Law and Morals in England From 1660 to 1857,* 18 U. Pitt. L. Rev. 545
   (1957).

Note, *Marriage as Contract: Towards a Functional Redefinition of the Marital Status,* 9 COLUM. J.L. & SOC. PROBS. 607 (1973).

Prosch, T., DAVID S. MAYNARD AND CATHERINE T. MAYNARD: BIOGRAPHIES OF TWO OF THE OREGON IMMIGRANTS OF 1850 (1906).

Rehbinder, *Status, Contract, and the Welfare State,* 23 STAN. L. REV. 941 (1971).

Master-Servant Relationship Versus Partnership in Marriage

Eggleston v. Eggleston
Supreme Court of North Carolina
228 N.C. 668, 47 S.E.2d 243 (1948)

SEAWELL, J.

The plaintiff brought this suit against her husband for alimony without divorce under G.S. §50-16, joining with this cause of action (b) a cause of action to have herself declared a business partner with her husband and to have her rights under the partnership adjudicated and an account taken * * *.

* * *

* * * The case then proceeded to trial, the issues being answered as to both causes of action unfavorably to the plaintiff, who, having taken exceptions hereinafter noted, along with numerous others, preserved them for review by moving to set aside the verdict of the jury for errors committed during the trial, and this motion having been declined, objected and excepted to the judgment, and appealed.

* * *

The Question of Business Partnership:

The plaintiff sought to show the existence and nature of the alleged partnership between herself and her husband by evidence of dealings inter partes for a long period of years and her contributions to the joint undertaking; and by introducing the joint partnership income tax returns for the year 1945 made by herself and husband to the Federal and State taxing authorities, respectively, with other evidence pertinent to this transaction.

More particular reference to these returns will be made further on. For clarity we may say here that in both of the returns it is declared that a partnership existed between the plaintiff and the defendant for the calendar year 1945, manifesting partnership on equal shares as to the net income. After this suit was brought the defendant filed "amended" or "corrected" returns, in point of fact *individual* returns, eliminating the partnership feature.

The evidence by which plaintiff sought to show the alleged partnership may be summarized as tending to show the following facts and conditions:

When they first moved into the filling station on the Draper road and started business she helped display the stock; while defendant went out into the "territory" plaintiff was in charge of the filling station, worked there with no assistance except casual help from little boys to whom plaintiff paid small sums; plaintiff had access to the funds, taking in the money and keeping it in the cash drawer; she put her "inheritance money," about $125, in the business at this early stage; she sometimes bought, but buying was mostly done by defendant. As more filling stations were added, plaintiff went and put up signs in the windows, displayed stock and helped them get set up in the business. She worked regularly during this period, living in the service station for 15 years, and except for a short period of time and vacations in the summer, was there continually, often being compelled to let her housework go. She had often gone without food all day except what she could pick up at the filling station. She sold things out of stock, serviced cars, putting in gas and oil; carried water from the pump in tubs, as there was, for a long time, no running water; washed cars, often making $5 a day in this way. Plaintiff handled the paid and unpaid bills, made out statements and sent them out. Later plaintiff took a bookkeeping course and learned to type, and thereafter kept books for the business. After plaintiff and defendant moved into the new home in 1940 until 1946, while plaintiff did not go to the filling station every day because of her illness, the help came to her to inquire about the business and for direction in matters with which she was familiar, and she continued in charge during Mr. Eggleston's absence. Between 1940 and 1946, when they separated, she went down and did book work. During 1945 plaintiff and her brother, Pickett Parker, did the book work together. Plaintiff took part in the conduct of the tire business, sold tires, entertained presidents of tire companies in her home; sold and delivered tires in the service station and in the territory, took orders and saw that they were delivered; delivered tires in the territory; met people on the highways with tires, delivering and taking orders.

All this proffered evidence was rejected upon objection made seriatim by defendant, and in the same manner plaintiff excepted.

The plaintiff then testified that during the year 1945, she was not certain of the date, defendant came into the kitchen where she was cooking supper, put his arm around her, started kissing her and told her she was his business partner.

> "I asked him what he meant and I said I had been his business partner for twenty years. He said I had always been worried about losing a great deal of the business at his death, and he had fixed it so I would not even have to pay inheritance tax on my part of the partnership. He talked to me about it and ten days or two weeks later he signed—he said of course I would have to pay income since I was a partner in the business and he brought some papers in for me to sign. I signed three different sheets, I think, income papers and different papers, and a blank check."

After identification, plaintiff then introduced in evidence copies of the joint partnership income tax returns made by herself and husband for the calendar year 1945 to the Federal and State taxing authorities, respectively. These returns manifest a taxable net income for that year of $20,801.29 and indicated that Mattie P. Eggleston, the plaintiff, and Frank Eggleston, the defendant, were partners upon equal shares in the business, entitling each to one-half of said net income. The partnership appears as "Eggleston Brothers Filling Station." Accompanying these returns there was a partnership return of estimated tax for the year 1946.

Thereupon plaintiff sought to testify that she signed the documents above mentioned in good faith and upon objection by the defendant the evidence was excluded.

At the same time she offered to testify that she believed the defendant when he told her she was his partner and this also was excluded.

On review the rights of the plaintiff and the validity of the trial which purports to deal with them, must be made to depend on the whole evidence, both competent evidence excluded and the evidence which ran the gamut. So, before examining the instructions given the jury on the 4th issue relating to the partnership, it is necessary to turn to the evidence of the plaintiff as above noted—principally her own testimony—of the dealings between herself and husband with relation to the business in which she claims partnership.

This evidence was excluded apparently upon the theory that her complaint setting up the creation of the partnership restricts her to the transactions involved in the filing of the income tax returns, and especially to its organization on January 1, 1945. We are of the opinion that such a restriction does not necessarily follow from the allegations in her complaint, as a whole, liberally construed. However, this may be, the evidence as to her contributions to the business and the circumstances under which the services were rendered are of such a nature as to support her further contentions as to the creation of the partnership, strengthening the plausibility and credibility of that claim both as a moral and legal consideration for the formation of the partnership, however and whenever it occurred. Its exclusion was error. But we do not mean by this to limit its effect to the function of supporting evidence for a partnership subsequently created. In our view of the case the whole evidence directed to the existence of the partnership must be taken together, and so taken was competent to be submitted to the jury for their consideration and evaluation.

Under the common law as a consequence of the fictional merger of husband and wife into one person, and other disabilities of the wife incident to coverture, there could be no contract and, therefore, no business partnership between husband and wife. [Citations omitted.] That incapacity has been removed in many states by the enactment of "Married Women's Acts"—statutes directly or impliedly giving them the power or the right to contract. The broad general powers of contract given under most of these statutes has in many instances been extended by judicial interpretation to authorize the formation of partnership with the husband. In this State, the "Martin Act," Chapter 109, Laws 1911, G.S. §52-2, has been held to vest the wife with the power to contract with the husband so as to create a business partnership. * * *

"A contract, express or implied, is essential to the formation of a partnership." 40 Am. Jur., *Partnership*, p. 135, sec. 20, see notes 14, 15. but we see no reason why a course of dealings between the parties of sufficient significance and duration may not, along with other proof of the fact, be admitted as evidence tending to establish the fact of partnership provided it has sufficient substance and definiteness to evince the essentials of the legal concept, including of course, the necessary intent. * * *

Not only may a partnership be formed orally, but "[it] may be created by the agreement or conduct of the parties, either express or implied." *Sterman v. Ziem*, 17 Cal. App.2d 414, 62 P.2d 160, 162. As stated in *Niroad v. Farnall*, 11 Cal. App. 767, 106 P. 252, "A voluntary association of partners may be shown without proving an express agreement to form a partnership; and a finding of its existence may be based upon a rational consideration of the acts and declarations of the parties, warranting the inference that the parties understood that they were partners, and acted as such." Of significance on this issue is the statement of the plaintiff, "We divided the profits," and that when they came to a temporary separation the defendant agreed to keep her interest intact. * * *

Where the fact at issue is the existence of partnership the admissions against interest of the person denying the partnership are significant in establishing it. The use and the function of the partnership tax returns as evidence was not per se to create the partnership but, together with other evidence directed to the fact, to establish its existence. They must be considered within the light of the circumstances, their purpose and the deliberation required in their composition. While a mere casual remark made on the streets might not be sufficient as evidence of the existence of a partnership, the tax returns in evidence are of greater significance on account of the solemnity of the oath under which they are made and the deliberate and comprehensive statement of the relation of the parties they contain. While we doubt the propriety of admitting the evidence of the amended or corrected returns, because of their self-serving nature, the hasty effort of the defendant to regain his lost status did not cancel out the evidence afforded by the original returns or such legitimate inferences as the jury under proper instructions might have drawn from them as evidence of the existence of the contract or such inferences as they might legitimately draw from the entire transaction as to the credibility of the defendant. The facts presented in the evidence of the plaintiff make out a case sufficient to "hold water taxwise" as creating a partnership. See "Husband and Wife, or 'Family' Partnerships," INDIANA LAW JOURNAL, Vol. 20, p. 65, containing copious citations of authority applicable to the case at bar.

It is proper to say here that the services rendered by the wife to her husband are presumed to be gratuitous. [Citations omitted.] The presumption is not conclusive; [Citation omitted] and may be overcome by evidence tending to show that the services were not gratuitous. *Stewart v. Wyrick,* 228 N.C. 429, 45 S.E.2d 764. That was a matter for the jury.

The court excluded evidence of the plaintiff that she had acted in good faith in signing the papers, including the partnership returns of income tax, and believed what the defendant had stated to her concerning the partnership to be true. This was error. It had a substantive bearing on the existence of the partnership; and the plaintiff had the right to say that she acted in good faith and not as a participant in a fraudulent attempt to deprive the Government or the State of its taxes.

* * *

* * * First, it is not necessary to a partnership that property or capital involved in it should belong in common to the parties to the contract. On the contrary, a familiar type of partnership, as indicated by the evidence in this case, occurs where the services of the one party is balanced against the capital furnished by the other; and the statement that the property must be held in common before plaintiff can recover is error; second, the partnership sought to be established did not necessarily involve a gift of property by the husband, and it was error to make her rights depend upon the laws respecting gifts inter vivos; third, while in partnership, as in any other kind of contract, there must be an intent, it was error to instruct the jury that before they could find for the plaintiff they must be satisfied by the greater weight of the evidence that the defendant, by the making and filing of the partnership income tax returns in evidence, intended to make his wife a partner. The instruction to that effect has a further infirmity that the plaintiff has not contended and could not contend that the partnership was created by these documents, but only introduced them as evidence of its existence.

A further instruction to the jury to the effect that they were not concerned with the question whether the defendant made and filed the partnership income tax returns for the purpose of defrauding the Government, as that was a matter between defendant and the Government, was calculated to impress the jury that such a thing, if true, need not reflect upon his credibility, and to relieve him from the most damaging situation he had to confront on this issue.

The Case for Alimony:

The trial of the cause of action for enforcing partnership rights with that for alimony led to considerable embarrassment in the admission and rejection of evidence, and placing the admitted evidence in the proper cubicle for consideration. Thus, it is apparent that much of the evidence rejected by the court as not competent on the partnership issue was competent in the proceeding for alimony, and, therefore, was erroneously excluded in its relation to that subject. However, we need only refer briefly to certain salient features of the evidence and pertinent instructions to the jury to make our conclusion understood.

The evidence of the plaintiff tends to show that within a year after the marriage her husband beat her violently with his fists, leaving her bruised and bleeding about the face and mouth, and that he was convicted of the assault; that he was of a violent disposition, quick tempered, addicted to drink, and insanely jealous. She testified that on numerous occasions during the subsequent years she was the victim of brutal and unprovoked assaults, specifying that on one occasion he beat her severely with a shoe, until her body was covered with bruises; again that he threatened her life, locked her in the bathroom and kept her there for hours; that on another occasion, when she questioned the size of the dose of medicine he had been requested to give her, he grew furious and took her by the hair, choked her, and forced her to take it, and another dose of like size that had not been prescribed; that he questioned her fidelity because he saw a sailor going to the house in his absence—the sailor proved to be her brother, just returning from the service—and furiously upbraided her. She further testified that she had frequently been compelled to leave home because of his cruel treatment, and in many instances he persuaded her to return, promising to reform. That he threatened her life, and because of this mistreatment, and others she detailed, and because of fear for her life she was compelled to seek final refuge in the home of her parents. The incidents, she testified, ran through the whole twenty years of their married life.

The defendant denied all the charges except one. He admitted slapping her during the first year of their marriage, but testified that she had first assaulted him with a fire poker. His testimony represented his wife as morose, moody, capricious, and wanting to engage in fanciful enterprises beyond their means, and attributed her dissatisfaction to that state of mind. He testified that he had always contributed adequately to her support, or attempted to do so.

* * *

Because of the errors noted the plaintiff is entitled to a trial *de novo*, and it is so ordered.

McGehee v. McGehee

Supreme Court of Mississippi

227 Miss. 170, 85 So.2d 799 (1956)

ARRINGTON, J.

Mrs. Tina Van Zandt McGehee, complainant in the court below and appellant here, filed bill of complaint against Leo R. McGehee, her husband, defendant below and appellee here, for appointment of a receiver and for dissolution of partnership business. The defendant answered the bill and denied the existence of a partnership and other material allegations of the bill. From a decree dismissing the bill, the complainant appeals.

The evidence shows that the appellant and the appellee were married in March 1937; that in December 1937 they entered into business for themselves; that they borrowed $300 from the bank, with both of them signing the note and appellant's sister endorsed it. With the $300 they bought a truck and rented an office and went into the moving business. The appellant ran the office and the appellee drove the truck. Both of them devoted practically all of their time to the business; neither drew a salary for their work, but funds for living expenses were taken from the business and all profits were put back into the business; that as a result thereof, from this beginning, the business has grown to the extent that it is now worth in excess of $200,000. The various businesses are Leo Van Lines, Mississippi Moving and Storage Company, and Mississippi Storage Company, all located in Jackson, Mississippi, with branch offices at Gulfport and Greenville, Mississippi and Shreveport, Louisiana.

The evidence further shows that all bank accounts have been joint, and that all notes for money borrowed for operating expenses of the business were signed by both parties. There was no oral or written agreement evidencing the partnership at the beginning of their operations, however, according to testimony of their counsel, who had represented them since 1946, the appellant and appellee came to see him with reference to the appellee transferring one-half interest of certain real estate which was used in the business to the appellant. After this conference, the attorney wrote to the Collector of Internal Revenue requesting an opinion as to whether a gift tax would be due if the transfer were made. This letter is as follows:

"June 24, 1952

"Collector of Internal Revenue
"Jackson, Mississippi
"Attention: Mr. W. C. Eastland
"Dear Sir:

"Pursuant to our telephone conversation, I am taking this opportunity of writing and explaining the situation concerning two of my clients. It is the express purpose of this letter to give you these facts and to request from your department a ruling, based on the facts set out in this letter.

"The clients, which we will call Mr. A and Mrs. A, were married on March 24, 1937. Three months prior to that time they jointly purchased an automobile for approximately $300.00, he paying one-half and she paying one-half. At that time they were both employed. In December of 1937, they decided to go into business for themselves, and they borrowed $300.00 from the Jackson-State National Bank of Jackson, Mississippi. Both Mr. and Mrs. A signed the note and Mrs. A's sister endorsed the note. With this $300.00 they bought a truck. They then rented a van and rented office space in Jackson and started in business. There was no written lease covering the space rented for the office; however, the rent was only $6.00 per month. Mrs. A was in complete charge of the office and Mr. A drove the truck. In the latter part of 1938, a certificate of public convenience and necessity was issued to Mr. A; however, Mrs. A was still in complete charge of running the office, Mr. A being in charge of the outside operation.

"In 1944, commercial property in the city was purchased by Mr. and Mrs. A, with the title being taken in Mr. A. The down payment on this property was $1,500.00, which was paid out of the funds which they had earned in their business, and the balance of the purchase price was paid in regular monthly installments out of the income from the business.

"Since that time, additional real property has been purchased and additional certificates have been obtained, all being taken in the name of Mr. A. All of the real property has been paid for out of the funds earned in the business, as well as all payments on certificates and expenses involved in obtaining certificates.

"Prior to 1945, the income tax returns were prepared and filed by Mr. A himself and he is not sure whether or not separate returns were filed for himself and his wife. In 1945, a C.P.A. was employed to file his return, and the C.P.A. promptly divided the business operations into two separate businesses and filed one return in Mrs. A's name and the other return in Mr. A's name. This procedure was followed until the joint property law was made available to people in Mississippi, and since that time a joint return has been filed.

"Mrs. A is generally recognized as the office manager for the business. She has at all times been in complete charge of the office and Mr. A has been in charge of the outside operation. Mrs. A spends the full working day every day in or about the office, and, as previously stated, she is recognized by the general public as being in complete charge of the office, having under her supervision and control some 25 or 30 employees at the present time.

"In building up this business all bank accounts have always been joint, Mr. and Mrs. A, and all loans have been signed by both Mr. and Mrs. A. No salary has been drawn by either Mr. or Mrs. A from the business, such funds as are needed for their expenses being drawn by either of them.

"*It seems to us that Mr. and Mrs. A have been partners in this business from the very beginning. Certainly, there could be no facts in any other partnership* that are not present here except that formal partnership papers have not been drawn by them. Mrs. A takes the position that all of the real property and other assets of the business were put in her husband's name simply for convenience, and that she is the true equitable owner of one-half of all the assets. Mr. A agrees with this and is entirely agreeable to putting the record title to one-half of these assets in Mrs. A's name. Upon advice of the writer, this has not actually been done, since there is some question concerning a gift in the event such an instrument is executed. It is submitted that the execution of such an instrument would constitute solely placing the record title in Mrs. A's name, whereas she has at all times owned the equitable title. (Emphasis ours.)

"We would appreciate it if your department would give us a ruling as to the ownership of this property as it now stands, under the facts as above outlined. The parties are desirous of putting the record title exactly where the equitable title now stands and has always stood, and it is our opinion that no gift tax would be due and no gift tax return should be filed."

The Collector of Internal Revenue advised the attorney that no gift tax would be due, and deeds were executed accordingly and delivered to the appellant. Although the evidence in this case is voluminous, we are of the opinion, after a careful examination of the record, that this letter by their attorney, who had represented them since 1946 and was thoroughly familiar with the business, gives a fair and accurate history of the business.

Later, according to the record, the appellant and appellee did not agree as to the operation of the business and dissension and confusion prevailed, and in June 1954 the appellant and appellee went to their attorney's office to discuss their problem. According to the testimony of counsel, the appellant wanted the appellee to "put in her name a one-half interest in all of their assets and upon his failure to do so by 12 noon, then she would immediately have a bolt and lock put on the business and close it up and file suit for divorce on Monday morning." The appellee was not agreeable to this and the matter was discussed between them and their attorney for several hours without reaching an agreement; that later, the attorney's partner was called in to relieve him, and the discussion was continued with the appellee. A tentative agreement was reached between the appellant and appellee, and this agreement was later drafted and executed by the parties on June 8, 1954, as follows:

"Partnership Agreement
"This Agreement in Writing, this day entered into by and between Leo R. McGehee and Tina Van Zandt McGehee, husband and wife,
"Witnesseth:

"Whereas, the parties have engaged in the operation of the moving and storage and furniture businesses hereinafter mentioned, for a long period of years; and

"Whereas, certain of said businesses have been conducted in the name of Leo R. McGehee, individually, and certain in the name of Tina Van Zandt McGehee, individually; and

"Whereas, certain of the properties used in the operation of said businesses are not now owned by the parties hereto on an equal basis; and

"Whereas, it is the desire and intention of the parties to recognize the equal ownership of all said properties, and the equal responsibility and authority for the management of said businesses; and

"Whereas, it is the desire and intention of the parties to enter into this agreement, whereby said equal ownership, responsibility and authority shall be maintained by the parties on a permanent basis;

"Now, Therefore, it is mutually understood and agreed between the parties hereto as follows, to-wit:

"The parties hereto shall be equal partners in the ownership and operation of the local and long distance household goods moving business conducted under the trade name of Leo Van Lines and Mississippi Moving and Storage Company, and in the local moving and storage business conducted under the name of Mississippi Storage Company, and in the retail furniture business conducted under the name of Mississippi Moving and Storage Company, all of which businesses are now being conducted by the parties in the City of Jackson, Mississippi and elsewhere with general offices located at 410 South Gallatin Street, Jackson, Mississippi.

"The assets of the partnership, to be equally owned by the parties, shall include the following:

"All operating rights, franchises, permits, and certificates of public convenience and necessity heretofore issued to Leo R. McGehee, d/b/a Leo Van Lines and/or Mississippi Moving and Storage Company by the Mississippi Public Service Commission, the Interstate Commerce Commission, and the regulatory agencies of the other states in which operations have been conducted.

"All office equipment, motor vehicles, supplies, and miscellaneous equipment of all kinds used in the operation of said businesses.

"All accounts receivable of said businesses and all cash on hand and in banks.

"All inventories of furniture and other merchandise on hand at the company offices in Jackson, Mississippi and elsewhere.

"All real estate owned by the undersigned, including the buildings and lands located at 410 South Gallatin Street, 140 North Gallatin Street, and 1058 Arbor Vista Boulevard, in the City of Jackson, Mississippi.

"It is agreed that appropriate applications will be filed with the Mississippi Public Service Commission, the Interstate Commerce Commission, and other necessary and appropriate regulatory agencies for the transfer of said franchises, certificates and permits, and that this agreement is subject to the approval of said transfer by said agencies.

"Appropriate deeds of conveyance shall be executed to effect the equal ownership of said real properties.

"The parties shall, from time to time by mutual consent, divide the duties and responsibilities of management of the affairs of said partnership.

"The parties shall have an equal interest in the assets of said partnership, and shall share equally in the profits and losses of the businesses now conducted or hereafter to be conducted by said partnership. It is recognized and agreed that this division of ownership and this division of responsibility and authority embodied in this agreement is entered into by the parties for the purpose of insuring the stability of the operation of said businesses and the personal and business affairs of the parties. In order to accomplish this purpose it is understood and agreed that this agreement shall of necessity be permanent, and that it shall not be altered or terminated as long as the undersigned shall remain husband and wife, and that if the parties shall at any time be legally separated or divorced that this agreement shall thereupon be terminated, and the assets of the partnership divided equally between the parties, and that such division shall constitute a final and complete division of the property and property rights of the undersigned, and shall be in lieu of all other claims between the parties for separate maintenance, alimony or otherwise.

"In the event of dissolution of said partnership during the lifetime of the parties, and one party desires to continue the operation of said businesses, such partner shall have the right to purchase the interest of the retiring partner in the assets of the partnership, and to defer the payment of the purchase price therefor over a period of five years from the date of such dissolution.

"Witness Our Signatures, in duplicate, on this the 8 day of June, 1954.

"/s/ Leo R. McGehee
"/s/ Tina Van Zandt McGehee"

(Duly acknowledged by both parties, and filed and recorded in the office of the Chancery Clerk of Hinds County, Mississippi on September 2, 1954.)

A few weeks after this agreement had been executed, the parties were unable to work in the business as they formerly had because of disagreement, and as a result, the appellant left the business and filed the bill now before the Court.

The chancellor held the partnership agreement invalid on three grounds: (1) That there was no consideration; (2) duress of the appellant in threatening to close the business and apply for a receivership and to file suit for divorce; and (3) that certain provisions of the agreement were never carried out. We deal with these questions in the order stated.

Forbearance to sue is a sufficient consideration for a promise, and the forbearance of appellant to sue appellee for her claimed half interest in the businesses was a sufficient consideration to support the partnership contract. We need not consider whether appellant would have prevailed in the suit with which she threatened the appellee. Appellant had reasonable grounds to believe she had a valid claim to one-half the property involved, and if it be conceded that the claim had elements of doubt as to its validity, it is nevertheless sufficient consideration for the contract. [Citations omitted.]

We are of the opinion that appellee failed to prove duress. The substance of the proof on the question of duress was that appellant threatened to file suit against appellee to enforce her alleged rights to one-half of the property.

* * *

Appellee is in no position to complain that the partnership was not carried out by the parties. The franchises standing in the name of the appellee could not be transferred to appellant by her act alone, and appellee did nothing to comply with the terms of the contract in that regard. The fact that appellant did not convey one-half of the home property to appellee does not invalidate the contract, especially since appellee failed to do that required of him in reference to the franchises which were far more valuable than the home.

Appellee contends that the consideration for the contract was founded on the work and labor of appellant in the businesses, and that Section 454, Code of 1942, providing that husband and wife shall not contract with each other so as to entitle one to claim or receive any compensation from the other for work and labor, renders the contract invalid. We are of the opinion that Section 454 has no application to this case. This court has held that a married woman may lawfully enter into a partnership with her husband. *Jones v. Jones,* 99 Miss. 600, 55 So. 361.

If we should hold that the partnership contract was void either because of failure of consideration or duress, it would necessarily follow that appellee perpetrated a fraud on the United States when he caused his attorneys to urge on the Collector of Internal Revenue Department by the 1952 letter that a partnership then existed in order to save gift taxes. In such a situation, there is a presumption against fraud, bad motives and dishonesty. The partnership agreement expressly recognized prior equal ownership of the property involved, as well as equal responsibility and authority in the operation of the business, and is in full accord with the previous operation of the businesses and not inconsistent therewith.

We hold that the partnership agreement was valid. The case is reversed and remanded for further proceedings not inconsistent herewith.

The attorneys referred to in the foregoing opinion are not the attorneys now representing the parties in this suit.

Reversed and remanded.

Steinhauer v. Steinhauer

District Court of Appeal of Florida

252 So.2d 825 (4th D.C.A. Fla. 1971)

MAGER, J.

This is an appeal by Jerome Steinhauer, appellant-defendant, from a final judgment of divorce entered in favor of Lossie S. Steinhauer, appellee-plaintiff. The final judgment of divorce awarded plantiff custody of their only child and awarded plaintiff lump sum alimony, property rights and child support. This appeal is concerned with that portion of the trial court's order awarding the entire marital home to the plaintiff "on account of her special equity therein and as for lump sum alimony"; and that portion of the order wherein the trial court specifically reserved jurisdiction for the award of alimony in the future if the circumstances justify such an award.

There is little if any factual dispute in this case; there is, however, an obvious conflict between the respective parties' interpretation of such facts as they relate to the final judgment. Plaintiff and defendant were married for approximately twenty-five years before divorce proceedings were instituted. The plaintiff-wife is 57 years old and the defendant-husband is 49 years old. For the last twenty years of their marriage both parties worked together in a drapery business known as Steinhauer Interiors. The wife entered into the interior design business shortly after the marriage of both parties in 1945. The husband worked with the wife in the interior design business for over twenty years. The parties maintained two checking accounts. One account was designated as "Jerome Steinhauer and Lossie Steinhauer" and the other account was designated as "Steinhauer Interiors." The record reflects that both parties had access to both accounts and that both parties wrote checks against both accounts. The evidence is not clear as to when the "Jerome Steinhauer and Lossie Steinhauer" account was opened; it appears however that the "Steinhauer Interiors" account was opened some time in 1964 or 1965. The record reflects that while both parties worked side by side in the interior design business, each party apparently had separate jobs and customers in their interior design business. The husband's earnings from his customers went into the joint account and the wife's earnings from her customers went into the "Steinhauer Interiors" account. The record reflects that the wife actually ran the business and that the husband worked with her performing such tasks as the measuring and the installing of fabrics, picking up of furniture, delivering of furniture, upholstering of furniture, picking up and delivering of fabrics.

We are given some indication from the husband's uncontroverted testimony as to the purpose of having these separate accounts and as to some of the functions the husband performed in connection with his wife's jobs or customers:

"Q (By Mr. Maloney) All right, sir. The purpose, again, you say was to keep your earnings pretty much in this account Jerome and Lossie Steinhauer, and Lossie Steinhauer's earnings in her account, Steinhauer Interiors; is that correct?
"A What was the purpose of it?
"Q Yes.
"A So that there wouldn't be confusion between her jobs and my jobs.
"Q All right. Well, did you feel that she had any separate funds of her own at all, or did you feel that you had equal right to any proceeds that were put into the Steinhauer Interiors account?
"A Well, I had as much right in the Steinhauer Interiors account as she had because I had done work for her on her jobs. I done all different kinds of work for her on her jobs.
"Q So you feel that the money was—
"A As much mine as it was hers.
"Q Okay.
"A Just like the money in my account was as much mine as it was hers. But she did help me on my jobs, too.
* * *
"Q Tell the Court, please, about your participation in your wife's jobs. What did you do?
"A Well, from its inception, if it was a drapery job I sometimes went and picked up fabrics for her, depending on who was making the draperies. I sometimes took the materials to the place to make the draperies. I hung all of them. I hung traverse rods. I picked up furniture, delivered furniture, done the upholstery work, just about everything that I could do to expedite her jobs.
"Q Now, when you did this work did you ever submit a bill to your wife?
"A No, sir.
"Q Were you ever paid for the work you did on your wife's jobs?
"A No, sir. I assumed it was a partnership and that when I worked for her she would work for me, and it would be evenly divided.
"Q Now, will you explain to the Court, please, how one account rather than another account was used for the purpose of paying regular bills?
"A It depended on which one had the most money, as to what bills would be paid.
"Q Does this explain why some bills were paid by you and some were paid by your wife?
"A That's correct.
"Q Out of different accounts?
"A Out of different accounts."

With particular regard to how the business was characterized the uncontroverted testimony of the husband indicated:

"Q (By Mr. Maloney) Now, sir, Steinhauer Interiors, is that a partnership?

"A Well, when a husband and wife are in business from 1947 on up to a few months ago, they both work in the business, there was never any record of anything made as a partnership or a corporation. We just worked with each other, for each other.

"Would you call that a partnership? I would say so.

"Q The answer is yes?

"A Yes.

"Q Okay. Now, what was the division, or was there any division as to the profits of the partnership?

"A There was no division.

"Q How about for income tax purposes?

"A We both filed together, jointly."

With respect to the filing of a joint return the partnership return filed for the year 1968 indicated that the husband worked in the business only 20 per cent of the time. The uncontroverted testimony of the husband in explaining why the tax return showed his participation only 20 per cent of the time was:

"Q (By the Court) According to the partnership return, your wife devotes 100 percent of her time to Steinhauer Interiors and you devote 20 percent of your time?

"A I beg your pardon, sir? Who said that?

"Q That is what the tax return says. I want to know what you do with the other 80 percent of your time.

"A There's a misunderstanding then, sir. There's no truth in that at all.

"Now the tax return may say that that is supposedly 20 percent, but the reason for my putting on the tax return that amount toward her was because of her retirement for social security purposes, so that she would get her social security first, which she does because of her age. But we both devoted full time to the business. There's no such thing as 80/20. It was 50/50, or 100 and 100."

Again, under questioning from the court with respect to the husband's role in the business and the characterization of such business as a partnership, the following uncontroverted testimony of the husband reflects:

"Q (By the Court) Well, you had your jobs and she had her jobs?

"A That's correct.

"Q Under the name Steinhauer Interiors?

"A Yes sir. It got so that we couldn't work together on the same job, planning it. There were differences of opinion, so we had to separate our customers where she had her customers and I had mine. And then I would go on her installations and pick-ups and deliveries to help her.

"So I was devoting a lot of my time to her jobs, and then whatever time I could devote to my job, I would do.

"Q And you lumped these together under the partnership return; is that correct?

"A Yes, sir. It was a partnership. There was no difference of anything at all. This has not come up until I've left the house, that there was any difference at all. There's a witness outside, Mrs. Dilullo. She's a customer. She's an old customer. We've done about three houses for her and I've worked on every one of them, on every one of the jobs, put labor in it. My wife—it's her customer. And my wife planned the job and I done all the installation on the job."

The foregoing testimony demonstrates that both marital partners participated together during their twenty-five year marriage in a joint effort to develop a source of income to sustain the parties and their children during their lifetime together. The trial court, however, found that the wife possessed a special equity in the marital dwelling. This finding appears to have been based upon contributions made by the wife towards the purchase of their current (Tyler Street) home in early 1966. The record reflects that the husband and wife owned together by the entireties a home located at 1810 N.W. 94th Street (1810), and the wife owned, in her separate name, a home located at 1800 N.W. 94th Street (1800). The 1800 dwelling was rented out by the wife and the proceeds were used to pay the mortgage payments on the 1810 dwelling. Although the wife owned the 1800 dwelling, the record indicates that the husband helped in the actual construction of the 1800 dwelling. In 1966 both dwellings were sold. The wife realized a net gain of $8,184.95 from the 1800 dwelling and these proceeds were deposited in the "Steinhauer Interiors" account. The net proceeds of the sale of the 1810 dwelling were $10,178.39, and this was deposited in the "Jerome and Lossie Steinhauer" account. In February 1966 the parties purchased the Tyler Street home for $25,000.00. Approximately $2,500 was the down payment with $4,184.00 paid at the time of closing. Of this total cash payment of $6,684.00, some $4,600.00 came from the "Steinhauer Interiors" account and presumably the remaining $2,000.00 was drawn against the "Jerome and Lossie Steinhauer" account. All checks, however, *were signed by the husband.* In addition, the husband made a $9,000.00 payment from the "Jerome and Lossie Steinhauer" account in order to reduce the mortgage on the Tyler Street home. At the time of trial the mortgage balance was approximately $6,968.00, leaving an approximate equity of just over $18,000.00. The mortgage payments were made out of the "Steinhauer Interiors" account with the bulk of the checks being signed by the husband during 1966, 1967 and 1968; the wife apparently began signing the checks sometime in 1968 and during 1969. It was during this latter period that the marital difficulties seemingly intensified. The record is not clear as to when the parties actually separated, although there is an indication that the husband ceased doing any more work in the interior design business in January of 1969.

Upon divorce the wife ordinarily becomes the owner of an undivided one-half interest as a tenant in common with the husband in land formerly owned by the spouses as an estate by the entirety. [Citations omitted.] However, upon proper pleadings and sufficient and proper proof, the husband's interest in the estate by the entireties can be awarded to the wife as lump sum alimony or to the extent that she establishes a special equity therein. [Citations omitted.]

In determining whether or not the award in question should be considered as lump sum alimony and deemed to have been properly made, the divorced wife's ability to be employed and earn a living, the needs of the wife and the children and the husband's capacity to meet such needs are all relevant material factors in determining the wife's need for alimony. [Citations omitted.]

In the case sub judice, the court specifically found that the wife's income and assets presently *exceeded* those of the husband. It would appear therefore that the award of the entire one-half of the husband's interest in the marital domicile to the wife as "lump sum alimony" would not be consistent with the wife's financial situation.

With respect to whether the wife's contributions were of such a nature as to create a special equity in the marital dwelling, it is our opinion that the circumstances do not support such a determination. We are cognizant of the fact that the wife ran the business and perhaps through her ability and ingenuity the business thrived; we are not unmindful of the contributions made from the sale of her separately owned property towards the jointly owned dwelling. But we are equally not unmindful of the fact that the husband worked side by side with his wife over twenty years in building up the business; both parties seemingly considered their business relationship as a "partnership"; there was a continuous use of the funds of both accounts by the husband with the approval of the wife.

From the foregoing we are not convinced that the wife has established the burden of proof necessary to acquire a legal or equitable interest in the husband's property. *Zuidhof v. Zuidhof,* Fla. App. 1971, 242 So.2d 739. As Justice Adkins observed, "The unity concept of marriage has given way to the partner concept whereby a married woman stands as an equal to her husband in the eyes of the law." *Gates v. Foley,* Fla. 1971, 247 So.2d 40. In *Gates,* the Supreme Court of Florida determined that based upon recent changes in the legal and societal status of women in our society the wife would now be permitted to recover for the loss of her husband's companionship, affection, and sexual relationship (consortium).

As observed earlier, by operation of law each party is entitled to one-half interest in property held by the entireties, *i.e.,* the marital dwelling, joint bank account, etc. This division is consistent with the partnership concept and gives true meaning to the equality of the status of women. As our Constitution states, "There shall be no distinction between married women and married men in the holding, control, disposition, or encumbering of their property, real or personal." Art. X, Sec. 5, Const. of Fla., F.S.A. In direct contrast to the foregoing is the general proposition that a transfer of property from a husband to a wife (as joint tenants) is presumed to be a *gift*; whereas, a transfer from a wife to a husband (as joint tenants) of her separate property is *not* presumed to be a gift, the burden being on the husband to establish that fact. *Olsen v. Olsen,* Fla. App. 1967, 195 So.2d 864. This presumption is seemingly premised upon the inequality of the marital partners and the subservient status of the wife. We cannot accept the concept that a wife is anything less than an equal partner with the husband in the marital relationship. Our own Constitution and statutes place the woman on a status equal (not inferior) to the man. [Citations omitted.]

We do nothing but give lip service to the concept of unity and equality of the marital partners when at the outset we balance the scale in favor of one of the partners. *Property or assets held by the entireties should be presumed to have been acquired by the joint efforts of both parties.* The partners are deemed equal and are entitled to equality in treatment; but the facts of each marital situation are not the same and therefore we should seek to formulate a general rule that has as its cornerstone the equality of the parties and a presumption of an equal partnership; any unequal distribution ought to be made dependent upon a preponderance of the special fact circumstances of each case with the burden resting upon the person asserting a disproportionate distribution.

A jointly held domicile therefore ought to be divided equally between each partner with the wife's and husband's financial contributions to the acquisition of such property to be considered as gifts to each other. To establish a special equity, the wife's contributions must be shown to have been "above and beyond the performance of ordinary marital duties." See *Eakin v. Eakin,* Fla. 1958, 99 So.2d 854. A financial contribution by the wife should be interpreted as being within the realm of "ordinary marital duties" or a prima facie presumption of a gift. Such presumption must be considered to be a reciprocal presumption—each partner should be presumed to have made a gift to the other based upon the marital relationship.

The dissolution of the marital relationship is rarely without difficulty; it invariably has its share of physical, mental, parental and financial implications. We do little to minimize and mitigate these difficulties when we, without regard to the reciprocal relationship, "reward" one marital partner a greater interest in jointly held assets because that marital partner may have been a better bookkeeper and can better account for every dollar expended on behalf of the other partner. [Citation omitted.]

We are most reluctant to disturb a chancellor's determination on questions of alimony or special equity. We are, however, of the opinion that the evidence below does not support the award of the husband's interest in the marital domicile on the basis of a special equity or lump sum alimony. The rationale for the decision which we reach herein is well stated in the Gates case:

"The law is not static. It must keep pace with changes in our society, for the doctrine of stare decisis is not an iron mold which can never be changed. Holmes, in his *The Common Law* (1881), p. 5, recognizes this in the following language:

'The customs, beliefs, or needs of a primitive time establish a rule or a formula. In the course of centuries the customs, belief, or necessity disappear, but the rule remains. The reason which gave rise to the rule has been forgotten, and ingenious minds set themselves to inquire how it is to be accounted for. Some ground of policy is thought of, which seems to explain it and to reconcile it with the present state of things; and then the rule adapts itself to the new reasons which have been found for it, and centers on a new career. The old form receives a new content, and in time even the form modifies itself to fit the meaning which it has received.'

"It may be argued that any change in this rule should come from the Legislature. No recitation of authority is needed to indicate that this Court has not been backward in overturning unsound precedent in the area of tort law. Legislative action could, of course, be taken, but we abdicate our own function, in a field peculiarly nonstatutory, when we refuse to reconsider an old and unsatisfactory court-made rule."

* * * We therefore reject a rule that would create a presumption of gift for one partner but not for the other in property held by the entireties. The partners are equal—the presumptions are equivalent. This conclusion should not be interpreted as precluding the establishment of a special equity where facts, circumstances and the application of equitable principles so require. In determining whether a special equity exists we hold that each party is entitled to the same presumptions with respect to their contributions to each other; and in particular regard to the facts of this case we find that the wife's contributions were not shown to have been "above and beyond the performance of ordinary marital duties."

It should be pointed out that the wife has retained and still continues to run the drapery business, the husband apparently having made no claim to it.[2] For that reason as well as the husband's current financial capabilities the trial court properly reserved jurisdiction for the award of alimony in the future should the circumstances justify such an award.

* * *

Accordingly, the judgment of the trial court is affirmed in part and reversed in part, and the cause is remanded for further proceedings not inconsistent with this opinion. Nothing contained herein shall preclude the trial court from reviewing and revising the awards heretofore made to the wife inasmuch as such awards may have been gauged or influenced by the award of the entire marital dwelling to the wife.

---

[2] The record indicates that the husband is currently employed as a salesman for another business earning an average gross income of $160.00 per week. Part of this earning is based upon commissions.

Owens v. Owens

Supreme Court of Delaware

38 Del. Ch. 220, 149 A.2d 320 (1959)

WOLCOTT, J.

This is an appeal from a judgment of the Chancellor denying at the suit of a wife the eviction of her husband from premises owned by the wife formerly occupied as the marital domicile of the parties, and ordering the entry of a money judgment upon the husband's counterclaim.

The facts are briefly summarized. In the spring of 1953 the plaintiff, at that time a widow, was the owner of certain real estate in Dewey Beach, Sussex County. At that time she decided to erect on a vacant portion of her real estate a three-unit apartment house. She, at that time, made the acquaintance of the defendant, a general contractor, and entered into a contract with him for such construction. In August of 1953, she borrowed sufficient money secured by a mortgage on her property to pay the cost of construction, and upon completion of the construction in May, 1954 paid the defendant in full.

Meanwhile, the acquaintance between the plaintiff and defendant ripened about the middle of November, 1953 into an engagement to be married. Their marriage finally took place in August, 1954 and they established their marital domicile in one of the apartments owned by the plaintiff.

Commencing in the spring of 1954, prior to the marriage of the parties, the defendant began to improve the plaintiff's property, including an additional piece of real estate purchased by her. Thus, the defendant improved the grade of the premises, and erected a garage building with two apartment units on the second floor. Part of the improvements to the premises were paid for by the proceeds of a loan secured by a mortgage on the plaintiff's real estate. The balance was paid by the defendant. The Chancellor found as a fact that the defendant put into the improvements approximately one-third of his estate, or the sum of approximately $23,000.

The plaintiff and defendant lived together as man and wife in apparent harmony until the fall of 1956, at which time incidents took place as a result of which, on October 15, 1956, the plaintiff left the marital domicile. The defendant remained living in the former marital domicile.

The plaintiff sought to prove that she left her husband because of his physical violence to her and because of her fear of future physical violence. The defendant categorically denied any physical violence. He, in fact, claimed that his wife had left him without lawful cause. The Chancellor found as a fact that the plaintiff had no lawful cause to leave her husband.

After final hearing, the Chancellor held that since the plaintiff had left her husband without cause, she could not evict him from the apartment which had been their marital domicile, but could operate her other rental properties for her own profit, and directed the imposition of a lien on the plaintiff's property in favor of the defendant in the amount of $19,616.32, which amount he held represented the extent of his own assets used to improve the plaintiff's property not intended as a gift from him to her.

From this judgment the plaintiff appeals.

First, the plaintiff argues that the Chancellor's finding, that she left her husband without lawful cause, is erroneous. * * * Second, the plaintiff argues that the Chancellor's finding that the defendant did not intend to make a gift to her of the amounts of his own assets used to improve her property is erroneous and should be reversed for the reason that, under such circumstances, a husband presumptively intends a gift to his wife, and that this presumption may be rebutted only by clear and convincing proof, which, it is argued, is lacking in the case at bar.

Thirdly, the plaintiff argues that the Chancellor committed error in holding that a wife, leaving her husband in possession of the former marital domicile owned by her, may not thereafter dispossess him unless her leaving was with lawful cause.

The first two matters argued by the plaintiff are fundamentally questions of fact to be resolved by the trier of fact. Ordinarily, on appeal a finding of fact if supported by the evidence will not be overturned by this court. *S & S Builders, Inc. v. Di Mondi,* 11 Terry 223, 126 A.2d 826.

With respect to the Chancellor's finding that the plaintiff left the defendant without lawful cause, the argument is made that since the evidence in support of the defendant's position consisted of his testimony alone, and since the plaintiff's witnesses—who, incidentally, were connected by relationship or marriage—testified to the contrary, this Court should make its own finding of fact to the effect that the leaving was lawful. We disagree. It seems clear to us from the record that the issue of fact of necessity had to be resolved by considerations of credibility. The Chancellor heard the testimony from the stand and, it is obvious, accepted the defendant's version of the circumstances as the more credible. He apparently believed the defendant and did not believe the plaintiff. We accept his finding.

With respect to the Chancellor's finding that the defendant had sufficiently rebutted the presumption of gift arising from the improvement of his wife's property, we think the same observation is applicable. The Chancellor heard the witnesses and, under the circumstances, we think his finding must be accepted.

With respect to the third question, a different situation presents itself. It is fundamentally a question of law. The question for our decision is the right of a wife, who owns in her sole right the property in which the marital domicile had been established, and who, without lawful cause, leaves her husband, to sue to repossess her property and to evict her husband from the former marital domicile.

Initially, we observe that under the law of this state a wife may not sue her husband in the Superior Court for any purpose, *Plotkin v. Plotkin,* 2 W.W. Harr. 455, 125 A. 455, although it is well established that a wife, because of her inability to sue her husband at law, may bring suit in equity against him for the enforcement of certain rights, *e.g.* the specific performance of a separation agreement, *Peters v. Peters,* 20 Del. Ch. 28, 169 A. 298, and for separate maintenance, *DuPont v. DuPont,* 32 Del. Ch. 413, 85 A.2d 724. The Chancellor's holding denies to a deserting wife the aid of the processes of equity to recover her sole property in his possession if that property had formerly been the marital domicile.

There is no reported decision in Delaware specifically governing the case at bar. It is a case of first instance. The courts of our sister states which have had this problem before them have divided upon it.* * *

It is sufficient to state that one of the two lines of decision takes the view that a wife whose sole and separate property is secured to her by statute is entitled to be protected in her property even against the retention of possession by her husband, whom she has deserted, of the former marital domicile owned by her. These courts take the view that if by statute the common law inability of a wife to control her separate property has been removed, the courts are bound to protect her statutory rights irrespective of the effect upon the marital relationship.

Those courts which follow the opposing line of authority do so on the ground that a court should not lend its process in aid of a deserting wife since to do so would be a disruption of the marriage relationship which has always been sought to be preserved by the courts.

* * *We think our choice must be governed by two statutes enacted by our General Assembly. The first of these is 13 Del. C. §311, the so-called Married Woman's Property Act. This act provides that the property of a

married woman, together with "all the income, rents and profits thereof, shall be deemed to be her sole and separate property." The act further authorizes a married woman to sell or otherwise dispose of her separate property as though she were unmarried, but preserves the husband's common law right of curtesy in her real estate. This latter provision would, of course, be a possible deterrent to a sale of the property by the wife, but has no bearing at all on her right to possession and to the rents and profits.

It is difficult to see how the act could have conferred much broader powers on a wife in the management of her separate property. It excepts no property of the wife from the embrace of its provisions, but for the proviso continuing the husband's right of curtesy. Therefore, to follow the line of authorities holding that a wife may not evict her deserted husband from her property formerly used as the marital domicile would be to write into our act a judicially created exception to its terms. If we write the exception into the act, the anomalous situation would result that a deserting wife may evict her husband from only that part of her separate property which had not been used as the joint residence of the parties, despite the clear language of the act which in terms applies to all her property. This, it seems, would be to penalize a generous wife who has relieved her husband of his legal duty to provide a home.

Furthermore, the wisdom of engrafting such an exception on the Married Woman's Separate Property Law is doubtful. Since the reason given for the exception is the desire of courts to preserve the marital status, it should follow that the enforcement of the exception would restore the status and effect a reconciliation. It would hardly seem, however, even if the economic coercion of an inability to obtain possession of her own property led to the errant wife's return to cohabitation, that her return would in fact be a reconciliation based upon love and affection and thus a real preservation of the marital relationship. The preservation would be forced at best.

Furthermore, it is now apparently the policy of the State of Delaware not to compel the continuance of a marital relationship between unwilling parties, even though the conduct of neither the husband nor wife has been such as heretofore would have justified the entry of a divorce decree. In 1957 the General Assembly amended 13 Del. C. §1522 by the addition of a further ground for divorce consisting of living separate and apart for three consecutive years without any reasonable expectation of reconciliation. The referred-to addition to the grounds for divorce, obviously, makes divorce upon such ground available to either husband or wife at their sole option and without the fact of the other party to the marriage having given cause for the separation.

Under these circumstances, therefore, and because of our reluctance to write into an otherwise clear statute an exception to its provisions by judicial fiat, we hold in accordance with the line of authorities of other states—which is certainly the numerical majority of such states and is stated by the commentator in 21 A.L.R. 745 to be also the weight of authority—that a wife who leaves her husband without him having given her lawful cause to do so may evict him from possession of all real estate owned by her as her sole property.

One further point remains to be considered and that is, since this plaintiff is a deserting wife at whose door the fault of this controversy may be laid, whether or not the Chancellor, in his discretion, may deny her relief. We think not. * * * We have held that she has a legal right to possession of her property and, such being the case, the Chancellor has no discretion to deny her enforcement of that legal right.

By reason of the foregoing, we affirm that portion of the judgment of the court below imposing a lien upon the plaintiff's property and we reverse that portion of the judgment which continues the defendant in possession of the wife's premises. A mandate will be issued providing for the above, and with the direction to award such appropriate relief as may be required to put the plaintiff back into possession of her separate property.

Comments

Eggleston, McGehee, Steinhauer, and *Owens* illustrate that ordinary business law practice can require a full mastery of family law. The idea that a business lawyer can avoid divorce litigation is mistaken. Of course, these cases seem to deal primarily with relatively small businesses, but they involve bread-and-butter legal practice in small and medium-sized American towns. And big business and family law matters are also sometimes closely interwoven, as evidenced by the Ford and Rockefeller empires or by the business affairs of the Onassis and Niarchos families. Marriage breakup in such situations inevitably involves liquidation of business relations. The liquidation of partnership and distribution of assets, in many instances, is not only a functional parallel to dissolution of marriage, but indistinguishable from it.

Chaachou v. Chaachou (pp. 8–22) is an example of a complete merger of business law and family law. It demonstrates that a lawyer must acquire the capability of thinking simultaneously on both levels in making his legal analysis. There is some indication that damage may have been done when the lawyers in *Eggleston, McGehee,* and *Steinhauer* considered the tax aspects—the possibility of tax savings—in isolation when they should also have considered the impact of partnership concepts on the marriage. At least in *Eggleston* and *McGehee,* the legal contract of partnership seemed to have hastened the breakup of marriage. Perhaps such breakup was socially desirable under the facts of the cases, including the more favorable financial position of the wives as business partners. Yet the lawyers who handled the tax matters may have felt themselves to be primarily representing the husband, while inadvertently giving the wives the possibility of an out under favorable financial conditions.

McGehee and *Owens* foreshadow the possibility of increased litigation between husband and wife during an existing marriage. Both cases were outside of divorce litigation, although they were likely preludes to marital dissolution. The appointment of a receiver in an action for dissolution of partnership, and the successful eviction of the husband from property owned by the wife during existing marriage, show the range of possibilities. Actions for accounting are also likely to increase. More often than not, as here, the wife may appear as plaintiff.

Steinhauer demonstrates, however, that the wife may have the dominant economic role in contemporary marriage. In such instances, it is the husband who would benefit from the conceptions of partnership. *Owens*, on the other hand, is based on extraordinary facts. The husband began as an independent contractor, doing construction work on income-producing property for his future wife. Marriage may have been a device which, in effect, lowered the cost of construction for the wife. For the husband it was a speculative business investment that did not pay off, although his rights were somewhat protected by the imposition of a lien on his wife's property. A partnership agreement could also have been made in this case, but it was apparently not thought of and made part of the pleadings.

Any of these cases poses the underlying question as to the nature of the relationship between husband and wife within the business context. That relationship could be master-servant, principal-agent, employer-employee, employer-independent contractor, or partnership. It could also have mixed elements of these relationships. In *Steinhauer* the husband could have been a partner for tax purposes and perhaps also for purposes of external liability, but merely an employee in the internal relationship to his wife. Whether the classification in the construction of the agreement is a matter of fact or of law may vary from jurisdiction to jurisdiction; it also depends on the nature of the proceedings. In divorce litigation the chancellor in equity would decide largely on both the facts and the law and, consequently, his findings might be difficult to reverse on appeal unless they are clearly unreasonable.

These cases show the survival of concepts of law that originated in bygone times. The presumption of gift in marriage was mentioned in *Steinhauer* and *Owens*. The latter also talked about the husband's legal duty to provide a home for his wife. Oddly, the court used this legal point in a reverse fashion: Since the wife had no legal duty to provide a home for her husband, she could evict him from property she owns. It seems clear that the traditional duties of support would have to be revised drastically under a partnership concept of marriage. The duties to support might become mutual or be supplanted by mutual rights in marital property.

Although the cases spanned almost 30 years, in all of them the lower courts took a more traditional view of the relations between husband and wife than the appellate courts. In *Eggleston*, *McGehee*, and *Owens*, this resulted in lower court decisions favoring the husband, which had to be reversed on appeal. Since less than 1 percent of family law cases are appealed, actual court practice may in fact be considerably more conservative than these relatively progressive appellate cases indicate. In other words, the law moves faster in the appellate courts than on the trial court level in family law matters. The legal practitioner must continue to be familiar with conceptions that may have been changed in the appellate courts and by the legislature.

Reference

Note, *The Implied Partnership: Equitable Alternative to Contemporary Methods of Postmarital Property Distribution*, 26 U. FLA. L. REV. 221 (1974).

Bibliography

Clark, *The New Marriage*, 12 WILLAMETTE L.J. 441 (1976).

Clark, H., THE LAW OF DOMESTIC RELATIONS IN THE UNITED STATES ch. 7 (1968).

Donahue, *Comparative Reflections on the "New Matrimonial Jurisprudence" of the Roman Catholic Church*, 75 MICH. L. REV. 994 (1977).

Eekelaar, J. & Katz, S., MARRIAGE AND COHABITATION IN CONTEMPORARY SOCIETIES (1980).

Gelfand, *Authority and Autonomy: The State, The Individual, and the Family*, 33 U. MIAMI L. REV. 125 (1978).

Glendon, *American Family in the 200th Year of the Republic*, 10 FAM. L.Q. 335 (1977).

Glendon, *Marriage and the State: The Withering Away of Marriage*, 62 VA. L. REV. 663 (1976).

Glendon, *Modern Marriage and Its Underlying Assumptions*, 13 FAM. L.Q. 441 (1979).

Glendon, M., THE NEW FAMILY AND THE NEW PROPERTY (1981).

Kulzer, *Law and the Housewife: Property, Divorce and Death*, 28 U. FLA. L. REV. 1 (1975).

Kurtz, *The State Equal Rights Amendments and Their Impact on Domestic Relations*, 11 FAM. L.Q. 101 (1977).

Mackin, *Conjugal Love and the Magisterium*, 36 JURIST 263 (1976).

Note, *The Implied Partnership: Equitable Alternative to Contemporary Methods of Postmarital Property Distribution*, 26 U. FLA. L. REV. 221 (1974).

Poulter, *Definition of Marriage in English Law*, 42 MOD. L. REV. 409 (1979).

Shultz, *Contractual Ordering of Marriage: A New Model for State Policy*, 70 CALIF. L. REV. 204 (1982).

Weitzman, L., *Legal Regulation of Marriage: Tradition and Change—A Proposal for Individual Contracts and Contracts in Lieu of Marriage*, 62 CALIF. L. REV. 1169 (1974).

Younger, *Marital Regimes: A Story of Compromise and Demoralization, Together with Criticism and Suggestions for Reform*, 67 CORNELL L. REV. 45 (1981).

Marriage as Speculative Investment

Marriage for Educational Advancement

Colvert v. Colvert

Supreme Court of Oklahoma

568 P.2d. 623 (Okla. 1977)

LAVENDER, Vice Chief Justice:

James R. Colvert, Jr. (husband) petitioned for a divorce from his wife, Cynthia M. Colvert (wife), in March 1975. On her cross-petition, the wife was granted a divorce by reason of the fault of the husband based on incompatibility. Trial was held December 31, 1975, and judgment granted January 5, 1976. Wife was awarded custody of a three year old son and child support of $200 per month. A division was made of the personal property. This did not involve large values or sums.[1] There were two automobiles. The husband received the 1974 Maverick. The wife received the 1972 Dodge Dart. Wife was decreed an alimony judgment, as property division of $35,000 payable in monthly installments. The monthly amounts were on an increasing scale. Commencing July 1, 1976, and continuing for one year, the monthly amount was $100. The increase was to $250 for the next two years, then $500 per month for another two years. Thereafter, the installment was $1,000 per month until paid in full

Husband's motion for new trial and petition-in-error make the principal issues of this review the amount of alimony and child support.

The parties were married June 1, 1968. At that time, he was a graduate student and she was an undergraduate student at the University of Oklahoma. The husband entered the University of Oklahoma medical school in 1972. At time of the divorce, he was less than six months from graduation and an M.D. degree. The wife graduated from the University of Oklahoma and became a registered pharmacist in early 1972. At time of the divorce, she

---

[1]The trial court awarded parties certain personal property. Values are shown as indicated by evidence of record.

HUSBAND:	VALUE:
Clothing and personal effects	
1974 Ford Maverick automobile	$1,000 to $1,200
Savings account	500.00
Checking account	199.00
Two year old, $10,000 face value life insurance policy with no cash value	–0–
Twenty shares of Occidental Petroleum Co. stock which Appellant received from his father as a gift	280.00

WIFE:	VALUE:
Clothing and personal effects	
1972 Dodge Dart	$1,000.00
Two savings accounts from her earned income, totaling	2,792.00
Checking account	60.00
1974 Federal tax refund	933.67
1974 Oklahoma tax refund	108.66
Household furnishings	

was employed as a pharmacist with a yearly income of approximately $16,000. Marriage problems and separation came in early 1974 with attempts at reconciliation for about a year. At trial, he claimed no income. He showed a debt of $10,000 from student loans he received commencing in the spring of 1974. His father had paid most of his medical tuition and books. Since about 1971, and particularly after she became a registered pharmacist and he entered medical school, the wife was the principal breadwinner who supported the family. An exhibit at trial showed their contribution to the family income from marriage, 1968, through divorce, 1975.[2]

Husband argues error for the decree gave the wife a property right in his yet to be received certificate to practice medicine. He places great stress on comments of the trial court at the close of the trial as to the trial court's intentions concerning judgment and the court's reasons.[3] If there is such a property right, then the husband would assert a like property right in his wife's certificate to practice pharmacy. He argues the alimony and child support awards to be based on speculation and excessive so as to be abusive of the trial court's discretion. We do not agree.

The judgment sought to be reviewed is contained in the January 5, 1976, decree of divorce. * * * That decree contained a judgment for alimony "as property division and in settlement of all of her property right against the plaintiff, in the total sum of $35,000." The decree gave no property rights in the yet to be received certificate to practice medicine. The decree gave the wife alimony designated as property settlement, rather than support, as al-

---

[2]As reflected in husband's Exhibit No. 1 in the record filed in the appeal:

	HUSBAND	WIFE	TOTAL
1968	$ 2,650.54	$ -0-	$ 2,650.54
1969	3,465.64	782.64	4,248.28
1970	3,372.20	888.01	4,250.21
1971	2,280.00	5,130.54	7,410.54
1972	1,140.00	9,806.40	10,944.30
1973	918.06	11,578.66	12,491.17
1974	133.50	15,729.21	15,862.71
1975	-0-	16,800.00 (plus bonus)	

Total 1968 through 1973:

$13,834.44	$28,186.25	$43,020.69

Total 1968 through 1974:

$13,967.94	$43,915.46	$57,883.40

[3]Comments of the court read in part:

"* * * This is an unusual case in that, as we sit here today, the Plaintiff doesn't have a great deal of money.

"However, the Court takes into consideration that the defendant has made most substantial contributions to his education to this point and he stands about six months away from the doors opening to great affluence beyond any question and any doubt.

"I want the record to clearly show that I feel that where there has been a marriage of this length and where there has been the wife as the primary breadwinner, and I find that to be a fact in this case and she has most substantially contributed to the obtaining of an education, particularly in a field which everyone knows is extremely lucrative as far as money is concerned, that the Court should consider the certificate to practice medicine as property acquired during the marriage, having most substantial value.

"It would, indeed, be a tremendous injustice if the Court treated it otherwise and gave alimony in the way of support because that would mean that the wife would have to remain a celibate or else not ever recover anything in the way of her investment.

* * *

"When a man brings a child into this world that becomes his first and primary obligation. In the nature of a judgment for property division, I award the defendant judgment against the plaintiff for the sum of $35,000.00. The first payment will be due July 1, 1976, and for one year the payments will be $100.00 a month starting on July 1, 1977, through June 30, 1979. The court sets the payments at $250.00 a month from July 1, 1979 through June 30, 1981. The Court sets the payments at $500.00 a month and at $1,000.00 a month thereafter until they shall have been satisfied in full."

lowed by 12 O.S. 1971, §§1278 and 1289. The trial court's remarks reflect consideration of the husband's future earning capacity in fixing that amount of alimony.

Although the statute, 12 O.S. 1971, §1278, provides the wife shall be allowed alimony out of the husband's real and personal property, where a divorce is granted by reason of his fault, alimony may be allowed in a proper case where the husband has no estate. *Mathews v. Mathews*, 186 Okl. 245, 96 P.2d 1054, 139 A.L.R. 202 (1939). That opinion, p. 1056, quotes at length from *Nixon v. Nixon*, 106 Kan. 510, 188 P. 227 (1920) that discusses a like Kansas statute from which §1278 was adopted. *Nixon, supra,* though basing the doctrine of alimony upon the common-law obligation of the husband to support his wife, refused to limit alimony under the statute to the husband's present property. Alimony, under such a statute, may be based upon the husband's earning capacity, present or future, and in an amount beyond the value of his estate or property at the time the marriage is dissolved. In *Smyth v. Smyth*, 198 Okl. 478, 179 P.2d 920, 923 (1947) this court, in allowing alimony from property not finally distributed in an estate, quoted from 17 Am. Jur., *Divorce & Separation*, §598 as follows:

> " 'Next to the fortune of which he is already possessed, consideration (as to alimony) should be given to the husband's earning capacity, future prospects, and probable acquisition of wealth from any source whatever. * * *.' " (Explanation added.)

In the present case, prior to marital problems, the family unit made an investment, not in personal or real property, but in husband's professional education as a doctor. That effort was enhanced and made possible by the wife becoming the principal support for the family through her own education, profession, and work. As indicated in *Mathews, supra,* in its quote of *Nixon, supra,* at p. 1056, to limit §1278 to the amount of alimony allowed by present property of the husband would be "an oversight in the letter of the law, against its spirit and intention."

We note the increased scale of the installment payments. The husband testified of plans to graduate from medical school about July 1976, of a first year of post-graduate training, then a required two years active duty with the Army, resume his post-graduate training at a salary of about ten to twelve thousand dollars per year, and after that, the opening of his own practice of internal medicine. On his internship, or the first year of training, he would receive approximately $850 per month. His military duty would be at the base pay of a Captain of some $1,260 per month base pay with other allowances, including a $100 per month professional incentive pay, a subsistence allowance, and a B.O.Q. allowance of $160 per month.

Syllabus by this court in *Reed v. Reed*, Okl., 456 P.2d 529 (1969) states:

> "There is no rule available by which to measure or determine the amount of alimony to be awarded a party as each case depends on its own facts and circumstances; and the awarding or denial of alimony rests within the sound discretion of the trial court, and in the absence of abuse of such discretion the judgment of the trial court awarding or denying alimony will not be set aside on appeal."

Alimony decreed to the wife as a sum of money, payable either in gross or in installments and with the divorce granted by reason of the fault of the husband, as allowed under §1278, is not limited to the value or amount of the husband's property. His earning capacity, present and future, is an element that may be considered in fixing the amount. Section 1289 allows the trial court at the time of the decree to designate all or a portion of each payment as support or as pertaining to a division of property.

Here, the trial court did consider the husband's earning capacity, both present and future. He designated the alimony award as pertaining to a division of property. He gave a monthly child support award of $200 per month. Under the circumstances of this case, we find the alimony and child support awards to be reasonable. *Reed, supra.* There was no abuse of the sound discretion of the trial court. * * *

Husband would seek a property right in the wife's certificate to practice pharmacy. He argues, without citing authorities, the license should be considered jointly acquired property and her future income should be considered. Husband points to no evidence as to why he has a property interest in that certificate. His income contribution to the family from 1968 through 1971 comes from his statutory obligation of support, rather than an investment in her certificate to practice pharmacy. Earning capacity, present and future, is an element of consideration in fixing amount of alimony under §1278 and when divorce is granted by reason of the fault of the husband. This is the circumstance of the present case. We do not agree with this position of the husband.

Husband's reply brief would stress and compare contributions and gifts during the marriage by the parents of the two parties. We dismiss that consideration as not controlling and without merit.

* * *

Affirmed.

Morgan v. Morgan [I]

Supreme Court, Trial Term, New York County

81 Misc.2d 616, 366 N.Y.S.2d 977 (1975)

BENTLEY KASSAL, J.

* * *

The parties were married on January 27, 1967 when the husband was in his third year pre-law course at the University of North Carolina and his wife, a sophomore, studying biology, at the Florida State University. Recognizing that both could not simultaneously continue their education and be self-supporting, they agreed it would be preferable for him to finish his undergraduate and law school education while she worked. She commenced working full-time, earning a monthly salary of $328.00 until the day before she gave birth to a son, on August 9, 1967. She resumed working a few months later, in January 1968, on a part-time basis, took care of her own and other children, on an exchange basis, and did typing at home for students, as well as her husband's theses. This continued until she and her husband separated in October 1972.

In the interim, Mrs. Morgan has become very proficient at shorthand and typing and also worked as a data analyst. I am satisfied that she is very skilled and, as an executive secretary or technician, could probably command an annual salary of at least $10,000 in normal economy and, very possibly, even in the present employment market.

In February 1973, she returned to the campus to pursue a full time educational career by undertaking a pre-medical course at Hunter College and her grades have been exceptional—a 3.83 general average (out of a 4.0 maximum) and an A score in the organic chemistry course, ranking 5th in a class of 70.

For his part, the husband has progressed well in his profession, having graduated from Columbia Law School after being selected for its Law Journal. His career started, as planned, with a one year stint as a law clerk to a

Federal Circuit Judge and he immediately thereafter became an assistant at a prominent Wall Street law firm. His starting salary, in August 1972 was $18,000 per annum with $500 increases on November 1, 1972, March 1, 1973, April 1, 1973, a $3,500 increase on November 1, 1973, a $1,500 increase on May 1, 1974 with the most recent increase of $3,000 on November 1, 1974, to a present salary level of $27,500. In all, he has done well and his future appears very promising.

* * *

At a time when some call for treating the marriage contract as any other contract, it is particularly appropriate to speak of the wife's duty to mitigate the damages to the husband upon breach. I agree that "when she can, she should also be required to mitigate the husband's burden either by her own financial means or earning potential or both." *Doyle v. Doyle,* 5 Misc.2d 4, 158 N.Y.S.2d 909. But it is a corollary to the rule of mitigation that the injured party may also recover for the expenses reasonably incurred in an effort to avoid or reduce the damages. *Norske Ameriekalinje v. Sun Printing & Pub. Ass'n,* 226 N.Y. 1, 8, 122 N.E. 463, 465. In this case, any possible short-term economic benefit which would result from the wife's returning to a position similar to the one she held over two years ago, is far outweighed by the potential benefit, economic, emotional, and otherwise, of her pursuing her education.

In coming to the conclusion I do, I am seeking to effect a balancing of many factors—the parties' financial status, their obligations, age, station in life and opportunities for development and self-fulfillment. As noted in *Phillips v. Phillips,* 1 A.D.2d 393, 395, 150 N.Y.S.2d 646, 649, affd. 2 N.Y.2d 742, 157 N.Y.S.2d 378, 138 N.E.2d 738, times have changed, owing not alone to the co-equal status which a married woman shares with her husband, but also to the increase in the number of married women working in gainful occupations. [Citation omitted.]

Further, I would like to cite a study by the Special Committee on Divorce of the National Conference of Commissioners on Uniform State Laws, entitled "Uniform Marriage and Divorce Legislation: a Preliminary Analysis," which, in setting forth some of the factors to be considered in determining whether alimony is indicated and the quantum thereof, lists the following, among others:

> "(b) The time necessary to acquire sufficient education or training to enable the party seeking maintenance to find *suitable* employment." (Emphasis added.)

Two of *Webster's Dictionary's* synonyms for "suitable" are "appropriate" and "fitting." True, plantiff could spend her life working at what she has been doing for the past seven years, after she, of necessity, agreed to help provide her husband with education for his "suitable employment" but that would not in my judgment be appropriate for the wife, a person with the capabilities of becoming a doctor.

The provisions of Section 236 of the Domestic Relations Law direct, *inter alia,* that the Court consider the "ability of the wife to be self supporting," as well as "the circumstances of the case and of the respective parties." "Self-supporting," in my judgment, does not imply that the wife shall be compelled to take any position that will be available when her obvious potential in life, in terms of "self-support," will be greatly inhibited.

Cognizance must also be taken of other language in the very same section, namely, "* * * the court *may* direct the husband to *provide suitably* for the support of the wife *as, in the court's discretion, justice requires,* * * *" (emphasis added). This has been interpreted to vest broad discretion in the court, "unfettered by" literal readings of the law. [Citations omitted.] Obviously two households cannot be maintained as cheaply as one and we therefore encounter the threshold issue of whether the wife—a very capable woman, probably able to earn at least $10,000 annually as a secretary or

office worker—shall be compelled to contribute this sum, or a fair share
thereof, to her own support, at this time, or shall she have an opportunity to
achieve a professional education based upon her potential, which will be comparable to the one her husband received as a result of her assistance by working during their marriage.

In my opinion, the answer to this issue is that under these circumstances,
the wife is also entitled to equal treatment and a "break" and should not be
automatically relegated to a life of being a well-paid, skilled technician laboring with a life-long frustration as to what her future might have been as a
doctor, but for her marriage and motherhood.

I am impressed by the fact that the plaintiff does not assume the posture
that she wants to be an alimony drone or seek permanent alimony. Rather she
had indicated that she only wants support for herself until she finishes medical school in 5½ years (1½ years more in college and 4 years in medical school)
and will try to work when possible.

In this regard, she merely seeks for herself the same opportunity which
she helped give to the defendant.

Accordingly, I am directing that the defendant shall pay a total sum of
$200 weekly for alimony and child support, so long as she does not remarry
and continues to be a full-time student, undertaking a pre-medical or medical
course. (I am taking into consideration plaintiff's agreement to work during
her vacation periods when not prohibited by school work.) Completion of her
medical school training and the awarding of an M.D. degree shall be deemed a
sufficient change of circumstances and I am granting leave to the defendant
to apply at such time for an appropriate modification to delete the alimony
feature of this award.

Morgan v. Morgan [II]

Supreme Court of New York, Appellate Division

50 A.D.2d. 804, 383 N.Y.S.2d 343 (1976)

MEMORANDUM DECISION.

Judgment, Supreme Court, New York County, entered June 23, 1975,
unanimously modified, on the law and the facts and in the exercise of discretion to reduce alimony to the sum of $75 weekly, and otherwise affirmed,
without costs and without disbursements.* * *

The alimony of $100 per week awarded below was predicated upon plain-
tiff's ambition to obtain entrance to medical school and receive an M.D. degree. It is not disputed that the plaintiff has present earning ability, which
the court below believed might be at least $10,000 per year. A wife's ability to
be self-supporting is relevant when determining the amount of support a husband is to provide * * *.

Absent a compelling showing that the wife cannot contribute to her own
support, courts have "imputed" or deducted a wife's potential earnings from
the amount which would otherwise be found payable as alimony by her ex-
husband. * * * While this Court recognizes plaintiff's goal in medicine, this
pursuit was never in the contemplation of the parties during marriage and
appears to be of recent origin. The law requires that the alimony award
should be predicated upon the present circumstances of the parties. Although the wife's ambition is most commendable, the court below was in

error in including in the alimony award monies for the achievement of that goal.

* * *

Comments

Student marriages pose special legal problems which are often overlooked in legal practice. These often short-term marriages among young people are treated, especially in view of the possibility of no-fault divorce in most jurisdictions, as if they involve no serious property and alimony considerations. Since the parties have lived on a minimum subsistence level, they are not yet accustomed to any particular "station in life" for purposes of support. Unless children were born from the relationship, the only issue may appear to be who gets the car. Actually, the problem is much more serious. These marriages involve a pooling of resources for purposes of financial gain, a goal to be achieved through education. Since parents decreasingly pay for the higher education of their children beyond the age of maturity, now 18 years, and in some jurisdictions have no legal obligation to do so (see *White v. White,* pp. 564–569), young persons are left to their own devices. Usually it is the young woman who forgoes her own educational or career opportunities in order to earn a living for herself and her husband. A variety of reasons, for example, the birth of a child, may make it difficult or impossible to reenter education after the husband is established. Not infrequently the marriage breaks up immediately upon the husband's graduation or, as in *Colvert,* even prior to graduation. The growing case law from various jurisdictions deals primarily with instances in which a man's prospects for professional status and high income have made women more inclined to invest their time and efforts.

Colvert, involving a woman pharmacist who financed the medical education of her husband, speaks of an investment in professional education that was made by "the family unit." The archaic notion of husband and wife as "one" was resurrected for purposes of protecting the wife's equity. In granting the wife $35,000, payable in monthly installments, the court used ambiguous language, simultaneously characterizing the payments as alimony and as property division. Fundamentally, this kind of language is not recommended because of the unclear tax consequences. Should the payments be treated as income of the wife, as in the case of alimony, and thus become deductible for the husband—tax consequences that are avoided in the case of a property division? As expressed in footnote 3 (p. 83), the lower court wanted to sidestep some of the negative consequences of a pure alimony award, for instance, termination in case of the former wife's remarriage. The husband's present and future earning capacity was treated as an already vested right of sorts. This appears to be in line with modern conceptions of property which embrace entitlements and perhaps even capacities and rights that, in the past, would have been considered incipient or inchoate.

Sometimes courts apply terms like "franchise" to the practice of medicine, which implies possession of property, regardless of whether the practice, as a business, has any actual value.* Here, too, older legal notions continue to be effective, as, for instance, when the husband in *Colvert* was denied any rights in the capacity of his wife to practice pharmacy. Whatever he contributed was characterized as "support," and therefore not subject to any recovery in whatever form. If the "pooling of resources" aspect of marriage were fully realized, the different treatment of the pharmaceutical education of the wife and the medical education of the husband would be less significant. The main question would be who has contributed what to the relationship.

Morgan was a rare instance of a lower court proving to be more progressive than an appellate court. The widely publicized trial court opinion talks in terms of equal opportunity for the wife, who had financed her husband's law study with her earnings from clerical work and who now had a chance for a medical education. The husband, upon divorce, was ordered to help finance her education as long as she continued as a full-time premedical or medical student. The appellate court reversed the decision—seemingly under legal theories of alimony, but in reality because of a fundamental difference in values.† Since the wife had the capacity to earn $10,000 per year, this amount accordingly was to be imputed to whatever the husband had to pay. That she had acquired the capacity by deferring her own studies in order to help her husband is "irrelevant" under this viewpoint.

Neither opinion is persuasive in itself, unless one injects fundamental feelings about the nature of marriage. The trial court opinion may represent the law of the future; the appellate opinion is rooted in the past. Another impressive aspect of the lower court opinion is that it recognized the contractual aspect of marriage that may impose a duty to mitigate the damages upon breach. Thus the earnings or earning potential of the wife might have to be considered upon divorce. This concept of mitigation of damages, a judicial invention of the nineteenth century to ease the financial burdens of entrepreneurs, has found an unexpected revival in modern conceptions of alimony, especially if it is viewed as fundamentally rehabilitative in nature. From this perspective, the lower court and appellate court in *Morgan* disagree on the meaning and function of "rehabilitation" of a spouse after divorce.

The main solution for young student wives is an antenuptial agreement, in which the wife agrees to finance her husband's education upon his promise to pay for hers thereafter. A woman's bargaining power may be sufficiently great to facilitate such an agreement prior to marriage. Note, however, that in *Morgan* the woman was ap-

---

*See *Daniels v. Daniels,* 20 Ohio Op.2d 458, 185 N.E.2d 773 (1961).

†The wife went on to medical school and received her medical degree in 1980. She invited the trial judge to her graduation ceremony. The judge, in an interview, stated that what impressed him the most about Mrs. Morgan at the time of trial was the fact that she received an "A" in biochemistry. (Dullea, *Controversial Alimony Case Ends Happily With a Degree,* N.Y. Times, June 6, 1980, §B, at 4, cols. 5 & 6.)

parently pregnant prior to marriage, a factor that probably affected her bargaining power severely. Nevertheless, the husband appears to have been sufficiently ambitious to have agreed, at that stage, to anything that would finance his law studies. These are unpleasant realities of life that tend to be overlooked by young persons in love. Love can, for instance, be invoked by the person who is in an inherently advantageous position, in order to extract services and other benefits from the weaker party that ordinarily could only be obtained at greater cost. If a question were asked by the weaker person, why such services should be rendered, the answer could be, "But don't you love me?". A lawyer might be able to prevent exploitation if his counsel is sought early enough.

Homemaker as Partner

Lacey v. Lacey

Supreme Court of Wisconsin

45 Wisc.2d 378, 173 N.W.2d 142 (1970)

ROBERT W. HANSEN, J.
In objecting to the division of property in this divorce case, the husband cites the 1914 case in which this court suggested: "* * * a clear third of the whole is a liberal allowance to the wife, * * *."[1]
This statement has been repeated so often in subsequent decisions that one well respected law text concludes that Wisconsin, alone among all states, has adopted one-third of the marital estate to the wife as the standard to start from, to be increased or decreased only by special circumstances.
However, the varying percentages for distribution reached or upheld in these same subsequent decisions vary so often and so greatly that another well respected law text lists Wisconsin with what appears to be a majority of other states in having no formula or standard, with the facts and circumstances of the individual case to determine the proper ratio or percentage for apportionment of assets in divorce actions.[3]
When leading test authorities disagree as to whether the formula to be used derives from the facts in a given case or, whether special circumstances merely justify deviation from a general standard, the time has come to clarify the situation. That endeavor best begins with setting forth in full the statement, now fifty-five years old, in which the dower-type allowance to the wife was termed "liberal." The statement then made reads:

> "The nearest approach thereto is this: Except in some extraordinary circumstances, the maximum for the wife is one-half. That may be reduced to one-third or even less. * * * The general level to start from is one-third. Since the early suggestive guide in respect to the matter, it has been pretty well established that a clear third of the whole is a liberal

---

[1] Citing *Gauger v. Gauger* (1914), 157 Wis. 630, 147 N.W. 1075.

[3] 27B C.J.S. *Divorce* §295(1) at p. 285: "The division of property or adjustment of property rights upon a divorce generally depends on the facts and circumstances of the particular case (citing eighteen states, including Wisconsin) and rests largely in the discretion of the court (citing twenty-three states, including Wisconsin) * * *."

allowance to the wife, subject to be increased or decreased according to special circumstances. * * *"[4]

Read as an entirety, it is clear that one-third to the wife was not laid down as either a maximum or a minimum. Phrases such as "extraordinary circumstances" and "subject to be increased or decreased" are not to be disregarded in analyzing what was said. The reference to one-half or more to the wife in some situations as well as the reference to one-third or less to the wife in other situations are both parts of the same "suggestive guide." We do not read the quote as establishing an exact formula or mandatory measuring stick for property division in divorce cases. We find in the full quotation a clear recognition that the formula to be followed in a particular case depends upon and derives from the material facts and factors present in such case. To extact the reference to either "one-half" or "one-third" as possible ratios is at least to shift emphasis and perhaps to distort meaning. The inbuilt flexibility of the 1914 suggestion is lost if a phrase or sentence therefrom is substituted for the full statement.

* * *

The division of the property of the divorced parties rests upon the concept of marriage as a shared enterprise or joint undertaking. It is literally a partnership, although a partnership in which contributions and equities of the partners may and do differ from individual case to individual case. In a brief marriage, particularly as to property which the husband brought to the marriage, one-third to the wife may be too liberal an allowance. In a long marriage, particularly as to property acquired by the parties during the marriage, a fifty-fifty division may well represent the mutuality of the enterprise. In determining the proportion of contribution by husband and by wife in the acquisition of property, more than economic factors are involved. We do not deal with two people with no more in common that two strangers or business associates. The contribution of a full-time homemaker-housewife to the marriage may well be greater or at least as great as those of the wife required by circumstances or electing by preference to seek and secure outside employment. The formula for division derives from the facts of the individual case. If it is argued that this approach gives great leeway and also places a heavy responsibility on trial courts in divorce cases, there is no gainsaying that fact. However, both flexibility and responsibility are called for by the endless variety of human situations that come to court in family cases. No two are exactly alike.

* * *

The application of the general concept and consideration of the specific factors involved in determining the fairness of the property division ordered in the case before us is no easy matter. In fact, it cannot be done because of gaps in both the trial court decision and its finding of facts. It is true that the sequence of events set forth in the record does give a general picture of the property holdings involved, and the manner of their acquisition, but it gives no more than that.* * *

* * *

Additionally, neither the findings nor the written decision of the court indicate any of the factors considered and found material by the trial court in making the apportionment of the assets between the parties. If on review the equitableness of a division of property is to depend upon the material facts and factors present in the case, it follows that a firm foundation for such division must be laid by including in findings or decision the factors found relevant and considered by the judge in reaching his decision as to property division. Even if we were to revert to the starting point concept of one-third or one-half as a beginning, the special circumstances relied upon for ending up

----

[4] *Gauger v. Gauger, supra,* at p. 633, 147 N.W. at p. 1077.

far from the starting point would have to be detailed to explain the variance. If the findings of fact or the written decision do not indicate the basis on which the property was divided, and the reasons for so doing, review of the fairness of the result reached become not just difficult, it becomes impossible.

* * *

Judgment reversed and remanded for further proceedings consistent with this opinion.

Brown v. Brown

District Court of Appeal of Florida

300 So.2d 719 (1st D.C.A. Fla. 1974)

RAWLS, Chief Judge.

The primary question posed by appellant-wife in this appeal from a final judgment dissolving the marriage of the parties is that of money and custody of the children.

* * *

In the year 1952, these parties entered into the holy estate of matrimony. When the coverture was consummated neither party possessed any estate of material value. At the outset of the marriage enterprise, the wife, a registered nurse, continued working and the husband, a graduate of the University of Florida (with a major in accounting), was employed. Not too long after this martial venture was launched, the husband received a promotion resulting in the parties moving to Lancaster, Pennsylvania, where the wife continued her nursing career until six weeks prior to their first child being born. At this point in time, the wife exchanged her career as a nurse for that of a mother and housewife.[1] During the next eighteen or so years, the husband successfully pursued his career as an accountant, reaching the top echelon of his profession upon earning the coveted title of "Certified Public Accountant." While the husband accumulated material wealth, the wife dutifully kept house and assumed the primary responsibility for raising and caring for the four male children born of this marriage.[2] When the marital partnership was dissolved after 21 years of coverture, the husband's financial statement reflected a net worth of $232,843.00, together with an annual earning capacity in the range of $36,000.00 to $40,000.00. The wife's material assets at the time of, and pursuant to, the judgment of dissolution when translated into money amounted to the following: 1) rehabilitative alimony—$6,000.00; one-half equity in residence—$3,000.00; one-half equity in beach cottage—$12,500.00; one-half interest in Hall note—$2,000.00; one-half interest in Jad note—$4,200.00;[3] aggregating the sum of $27,700.00.

We first consider the question of money and material goods. There are indications from the record of the proceedings below that members of the

---

[1] Other than working for a short period as a nurse in 1957, the wife has foregone her profession and practiced the time honored and revered profession of being a mother and housewife. The wife again worked outside of the home from October, 1964, through June, 1965, and the following two "tax seasons" to assist her husband in opening up a new accounting practice. Other than the above related "outside home" work activities, the wife has devoted her time and skills to being a housewife.

[2] In 1973 the sons were 10, 13, 16 and 18 years of age.

[3] Appellee husband cross-assigns as error this item.

Bench and Bar consider that this Court has virtually eliminated alimony.[4] In addition, we have before us a factual situation which is still prevalent even in this modern day of women's liberation, *i.e.*, a wife who has foregone pursuing a professional career and the accumulation of a personal estate in order to be a full time mother and homemaker while the husband remains in the market place providing for the material needs of his family and accumulating a sizable personal estate. For these reasons, the time has come for us to pause and pursue an in-depth consideration of the law of alimony in Florida.

In order to fully explore the subject of alimony, the husband's testimony as to his mental attitude towards the future of the marital venture is material. We observe that the materiality is not by reason of "fault" or "no fault," but is being considered in analyzing the financial status of each party of this marital partnership at the time of its inception and its dissolution. In answer to the question: When was it that you decided to leave? The husband answered, "1964. I made a vow to myself at that time and that vow was that if I ever made enough money that I could support her and those children and have enough groceries for myself, I was going to leave." This statement indicates the husband's motivation to accumulate wealth in his own name in order to prepare for the divorce he had long desired.[5]

For at least forty years prior to the recent enactments repealing "divorce" and instituting "dissolution of marriage" (commonly referred to as "no fault"), the courts awarded a divorced wife periodic alimony almost as a matter of constitutional right. In *Phelan v. Phelan*, 12 Fla. 449 (1868), the Supreme Court defined alimony as: "Permanent alimony is not a sum of money or a specific proportion of the husband's estate given absolutely to the wife. It is a continuous allotment of sums payable at regular periods for her support from year to year." The Court in further discussing alimony stated:

> "The actual income of the husband appears from the cases to be as a general rule the precise fact to be regarded. 2 Hag. Con., 199, 201; 3 Hag. Ec., 472; 5 Eng. Ec., 186; 2 Phillim., 40.
>
> "But this is not a fixed and absolute rule, and there are circumstances which vary it. Before an allotment of permanent alimony is made, the ability of the husband should be made to appear as well as the other considerations which are to be estimated in connection with his faculties, in determining the amount."

This definition of "permanent alimony" was reaffirmed by the Supreme Court in *Welsh v. Welsh*, 160 Fla. 380, 35 So.2d 6 (1948), where it is interesting to note that although she owned substantial property in her own name and was working, the Court awarded her $150.00 per month periodic alimony. The Court observed in *Welsh* that Chapter 23,894, Acts of 1947, had been amended to permit the award of lump sum alimony but refused to apply same retroactively. So, at this point in our judicial construction of alimony, a wife was entitled to periodic alimony based upon her needs and her husband's ability to pay.

The next development in the law of alimony was the appearance of the doctrine of "special equity." As early as 1919 in *Carlton v. Carlton*, 78 Fla. 252, 83 So. 87 (1919), the Supreme Court in a per curiam opinion after noticing that the wife, mother of six children, had contributed generously in funds and by *her personal* exertion and industry through a long period of time to the acquisition and development of his home and other property and the establishment of his fortune, held that the wife possessed a special equity in the property which she aided in acquiring and possessing.

---

[4] The husband's lawyer declared to the trial judge, "Let's assume the district court of appeals virtually eliminated alimony."

[5] The husband admitted that he had for more than one year prior to his testimony been engaged in an adulterous affair with another lady.

In *Heath v. Heath,* 103 Fla. 1071, 138 So. 796 (1932), the Supreme Court utilized the doctrine of special equity to relieve a wife from the harshness of the statutory prohibition of awarding alimony to an adulterous wife. Bottoming the decision in Heath, the Court stated:

> "The provisions of section 4987, Comp. Gen. Laws, section 3195, Rev. Gen. St., to the effect that no alimony shall be granted to an adulterous wife, do not preclude the ascertainment and allowance by the court of an amount to the wife for her special equity in property and business of the husband toward which she is shown to have contributed materially in funds and industry through a period of years while the marriage remained undissolved."

* * *

As previously recited, lump sum alimony was statutorily authorized in 1947. In 1963 the legislature added the phrase "or both in its discretion" at the end of the last sentence of former Florida Statute 65.08.

In *Gordon v. Gordon,* 204 So.2d 734 (Fla. App.3rd 1967), the Third District Court of Appeal, in reviewing the dissolution of a marriage of 27 years, observed that the chancellor made provisions for the custody and support of three minor children. The Court next commented upon the relative material assets of the parties which reflected that the wife was possessed of $90,000.00 in assets while the husband had a net worth of approximately $60,000.00. In approving a lump sum alimony award to the wife of $5,000.00, the appellate court held that the chancellor abused his discretion in failing to reserve jurisdiction to modify the alimony awarded to the wife (upon a showing under F.S. §65.16) by providing for periodic payments in the future, if necessary. * * *

* * *

In 1955 in *Kahn v. Kahn,* 78 So.2d 367 (Fla. 1955), Justice Roberts, speaking for our Supreme Court, announced:

> "Times have now changed. The broad, practically unlimited opportunities for women in the business world of today are a matter of common knowledge. Thus, in an era where the opportunities for self-support by the wife are so abundant, the fact that the marriage has been brought to an end because of the fault of the husband does not necessarily entitle the wife to be forever supported by a former husband who has little, if any, more economic advantages that she has."

This pronouncement marks the entry in the jurisprudence of this state of the concept of rehabilitative alimony. Rehabilitative means the restoration of property that has been lost. The concept of rehabilitative alimony appeared in the statutory scheme of this state in 1971 when the legislature made a major change in F.S. §61.08. The salient provisions are:

> "61.08 * * * (1) * * * the court may grant alimony to either party, which alimony may be rehabilitative or permanent in nature. In any award of alimony, the court may order periodic payment or payments in lump sum or both.
>
> * * *
>
> "(2) *In determining a proper award of alimony, the court may consider any factor necessary to do equity and justice between the parties.*" [Emphasis supplied.]

In 1966, our sister court, the Third District Court of Appeal, in *Sommers v. Sommers,* 183 So.2d 744 (Fla. App. 3rd 1966),[6] clearly stated the rule that

---

[6] Also see *Chestnut v. Chestnut,* 160 Fla. 83, 33 So.2d 730 (1948), wherein Justice Terrell, speaking for the Supreme Court, stated: "It [alimony] is awarded on the theory that marriage is a partnership to which the wife has contributed and when she withdraws from it she is entitled to reimbursement that she may not become a public charge."

prevailed as to awarding alimony prior to the dissolution of marriage act in 1971 (Chapter 71–241, Laws of 1971) as:

> "The accepted principles are that a divorced wife is entitled to alimony which will permit her to live in a manner commensurate with that provided by her husband during coverture, if he has the ability to pay."

An in-depth review of this Court's decisions after the 1971 statutory changes is now in order to determine the current status of alimony in our state.

In *Beard v. Beard*, 262 So.2d 269 (Fla. App. 1st 1972), the trial court found (as is probably true in more than 90 percent of marriage failures) that although neither party was without fault, "the preponderance of the equities lies with appellant husband and he is entitled to a divorce from appellee wife on the ground of habitual intemperance and indulgence in alcoholic beverages." Next, what did the trial court do in Beard as to the material assets accumulated during their 21-year partnership as husband and wife? The trial court awarded the wife the exclusive use of the marital home; the exclusive use of an automobile in her possession; one-half of a $15,900.00 joint savings account owned by the parties; a $1,400.00 savings account in the wife's name; and permanent periodic alimony of $100.00 per week. It is the last item which this Court reversed. After observing that the husband had a net income of $9,500.00 along with the custody and responsibility of supporting a minor child of the parties, we noted that payment of the periodic alimony would leave the husband the sum of $4,300.00 from which he would be required to purchase or rent a place of abode for himself and his minor daughter as well as pay all of their normal living expenses. At the same time, the wife had demonstrated her ability to support herself by having been employed in a supervisory position (with seven employees under her supervision) until sixty days prior to her instituting suit. The opinion carefully points out that:

> "In view of the temporary impairment of her health at the time judgment was rendered, some months may have been required before she was able to completely overcome her drinking problem and regain her health sufficiently to enable her to return to work. * * * The elimination of alimony from the final judgment is predicated upon the conclusion that appellee has now had ample time to regain her health and again become employable but is without prejudice to her right to petition the court for a modification of the final judgment, as amended, upon a proper showing of a change of circumstances and a need for reasonable support not attributable to her own fault."

It is upon these facts that this Court stated:

> "They [husband and wife] now occupy a position of equal partners in the family relationship resulting from marriage, and more often than not contribute a full measure to the economic well-being of the family unit. Whether the marriage continues to exist or is severed through the device of judicial decree, the woman continues to be as fully equipped as the man to earn a living and provide for her essential needs. The fortuitous circumstance created by recitation of the marriage vows neither diminishes her capacity for self-support nor does it give her a vested right in her husband's earnings for the remainder of her life."

Reversing an alimony award requiring a husband to support an alcoholic wife for the remainder of her life by contributing more than he would have remaining from the fruits of his labor to support himself and his minor daughter, does not appear to us as a decision that virtually eliminates alimony.

Thigpen v. Thigpen, 277 So.2d 583 (Fla. App. 1st 1973), is next. There, the parties had lived together for approximately 24 years. The wife had demonstrated her ability as an able office manager for some 15 years prior to the dissolvement of the marriage. The substantial material assets of the marital venture were *equally* divided between the parties. The husband was employed as a salesman at the time of the dissolution with an average take-home pay of approximately $750.00 per month. Appellee wife had declined two jobs during this same period of time due to an allergy she was suffering caused by use of cosmetics which affected her feet and prevented her from wearing dress shoes but not sandals or slides. In setting aside permanent alimony, payable monthly in the sum of $450.00, this Court held, inter alia:

> "We have carefully considered the pertinent evidence contained in the record but fail to find any reasonable basis on which the alimony [periodic] award made to appellee can be sustained. The very heart of an alimony award is and always has been the need of the demanding spouse for support and the ability of the other spouse to respond. *The new concept of the marriage relation implicit in the so-called 'no fault' divorce law enacted by the legislature in 1971 places both parties to the marriage on a basis of complete equality as partners sharing equal rights and obligations in the marriage relationship and sharing equal burdens in the event of dissolution.*" [Emphasis supplied.]

After this extensive (some readers might well add exhausting) review of the question of alimony, it is our considered judgment that a new day has been created by the 1971 legislative enactment and decisions construing same in the following respects: 1) Periodic alimony is no longer payable as nourishment or sustenance of wife or payable at regular periods for her support from year to year in the nature of an obligation to a stranger. (*Welsh v. Welsh, supra*). Periodic alimony is primarily payable from one spouse to another, based upon the need of the receiving spouse and upon the ability to pay by the contributing spouse, giving special attention to facts as to the advisability of rehabilitative alimony. Lump sum alimony is no longer frowned upon in adjusting the material wealth of the parties at the time of dissolution of the marriage. The overriding tenor of this Court's decisions in both *Beard, supra,* and *Thigpen, supra,*[7] is "a new day is born. Husband and wife are now truly partners in the marital venture sharing equal rights and obligations."

The ultimate question is now reached. How shall the material wealth of a marriage which is being dissolved be divided when one partner, the wife, has contributed her time to the marital home and children of the parties while the husband has pursued the accumulation of material goods. The evolution of the law of alimony that we have reviewed in length shows that today the contributions of each party to the accumulation of material assets must be considered in dissolving the marital partnership. Either spouse may contribute either by working in the market place or by working as a homemaker. The fact that in one marital venture a spouse is gainfully employed in the market place and pays a housekeeper to rear the children and keep house is not distinguishable from the spouse who devotes his or her full time to the profession of homemaker. The primary factual circumstance is each spouse's contribution to the marital partnership. In the case *sub judice,* the wife has been short changed. The wife has not been adequately compensated for the contribution that she made as a full time mother and homemaker to the equal partnership marriage. We hold that the trial court abused its discretion in awarding the wife a pittance of the material assets accumulated in the husband's name during 21 years. In so holding, we emphasize even though the cited authorities on the subject speak of "equal partners" and complete equality as partners, we are not engrafting upon the jurisprudence of this state the law of

---

[7] It is noted the counsel for appellee in the instant cause was counsel for appellees in *Beard* and *Thigpen.*

community property. On the question of alimony the judgment is reversed with instructions to the trial court to enter an award of lump sum alimony sufficient to compensate the wife for her contribution to the marriage.

We next turn our attention to the question of child custody. The trial court placed the custody of the four children with their mother with the right of the three oldest boys to live with their father if they so chose without further order of the court. Allowing minor children to pick and choose at their will the parent with whom they will reside only invites them to "play one parent against the other." Such conditions are not in the best interest of the child. The portion of the final judgment concerning the custody of the children is remanded with instructions that those children who are still minors shall be placed in the exclusive custody of the wife with visitation rights to the husband.

* * *

The case is remanded to the lower court for proceedings in accordance with this opinion.

* * *

BOYER, Judge (dissenting).

I respectfully dissent from the carefully and thoroughly prepared opinion of Chief Judge Rawls.

The law is well settled that courts should practice self discipline and refrain from entering into the legislative field: Further, the Supreme Court of Florida has clearly announced pre-emption unto itself of judicial innovations in the law. (*Hoffman v. Jones,* Sup. Ct. Fla. 1973, 280 So.2d 431)

Alimony came about during the era that women in general and wives in particular were placed on a pedestal by male chauvinists. Women apparently found being worshipped on a pedestal to be distasteful and commenced a virtual worldwide drive to be removed from their place of superiority to a position of equality. Why one enjoying a position of superiority would intentionally seek a lower position of equality eludes the writer, but it is a fact of social history. "Success" has been marked by a loss of many heretofore existing superior rights, among them being dower and alimony as a matter of right. The legislature, in its infinite wisdom, responding to the movement for women's liberation, adopted that which is commonly referred to as "no-fault divorce." Drastic changes in the law of domestic relations was thereby wrought. That act clearly and unambiguously provides for "rehabilitative alimony."

* * *

The majority opinion recites that we have before us a factual situation wherein the wife has foregone pursuing a professional career and the accumulation of a personal estate in order to be a fulltime mother and homemaker while the husband has remained in the market place providing for the material needs of the family and accumulating a sizable personal estate; arriving at the conclusion that "in the case *sub judice,* the wife has been shortchanged." Such recitations are, in my opinion, assumptions. The evidence does not necessarily lead to that conclusion. Just because a woman has borne children during a marriage does not mean that she is Whistler's mother. There is a vast difference between the physical act of bearing a child and the fact of being a mother as that term is generally eulogized and used in the traditional American concept. I do not here mean to malign the appellant in the case *sub judice.* She might well be the ideal mother from every standpoint. She might have also been the wife that every man dreams of. However there is nothing in the evidence of this cause to justify us so finding, or finding to the contrary. She may have contributed to the marriage "as a fulltime mother and homemaker" but on the other hand she may not have. The trial judge was in a much better position to make that determination than are we. For aught that we know the appellee may have had good cause to "await the day" that the children would be grown and the marriage relationship terminated.

* * *

In reviewing the final judgment appealed we should not overlook the unquestioned findings of the trial judge that the wife is a registered nurse and a real estate saleslady. It certainly appears to me that the $500 per month rehabilitative alimony plus the $500 per month child support was adequate.

In my view the majority opinion constitutes a substantial departure from this Court's holdings in *Beard v. Beard* and *Thigpen v. Thigpen*, both cited therein.

I must further dissent to the provision in the majority opinion instructing that the minor children be placed in the exclusive custody of the mother. Again, in my opinion, the record is not sufficient to justify that holding. If the case is to be reversed then the instruction to the trial judge should be to take such evidence as may be necessary to determine the proper custodian for the children, taking into account their best interests. [Citations omitted.]

The findings and holdings of the trial court are fully sustained by the record. For us to hold otherwise is to substitute our judgment for his. He observed the parties and the witnesses. He also had an opportunity to observe the children.

I would affirm.

Comments

The position of married women is perhaps nowhere more behind the times than in the legal treatment of the homemaker. Since the husband traditionally is entitled to consortium, namely services, society, and sexual relations, a homemaker is still often viewed as merely doing what the law requires of her. *Brown v. Brown,* in many other respects a progressive opinion, used somewhat patronizing language in stating that "the wife dutifully kept house," while the husband was engaged in his career and in accumulating wealth. Any special compensation—for example, by separate contract benefiting the wife—may even be viewed as lacking consideration because of a preexisting legal duty. The same basic attitude results in the view that a woman as mere homemaker is not established as a partner in the legal sense. As in the small business cases, the wife, to be legally recognized as a partner, must engage in something more than keeping house—in other words, be active beyond the call of duty. It is the attorney's task to find these additional facts by taking an extensive and detailed history of both the marriage and the business.

Meanwhile, the courts have shown an increasing tendency to give greater recognition to the homemaker. In the exercise of judicial discretion, judges, aided by lawyers, have developed patterns of thought that may eventually evolve into rules. They refer to two methods of placing a value on the homemaker's economic contribution: "replacement value" and "opportunity lost." Replacement value indicates how much it would have cost to hire one or more persons, with all the necessary skills to raise children and run a household. United States Department of Labor statistics are used to determine these costs. Opportunity lost refers to the occupation the spouse would have pursued "but for" the marriage. To measure this value, it is necessary to determine the most rewarding occupation available to the spouse, given her education and special skills, at the time of and during the marriage.

In effect, of course, it would be impracticable, if not impossible, to grant actual damages in these cases because the amounts involved would be prohibitively high. Courts therefore use the formulas of replacement value and opportunities lost to support a partnership position of the wife, or, by way of equitable distribution, to give her a substantial share of the marital assets.

Even though the judges in both *Lacey* and *Brown* used partnership language, they did not award the wife an equal share in accumulated assets. As the judge in *Lacey* pronounced, one third is the general level from which to start, although one half, and in rare instances more than that, is not entirely foreclosed. In *Brown*, although recognizing that the lower court had not treated the wife as an "equal partner," the judge hastened to add that such recognition is not to be understood in the sense of community property.

Even in these advanced opinions one is left with the discretion of the chancellor, who ordinarily may be inclined to give the wife less than half of the accumulated assets if she was merely a homemaker. The only way for women to avoid the risk of unfavorable judicial discretion is by antenuptial agreement. Of course, by extreme additional effort in marriage, a woman may bring about a situation that can be characterized as a business partnership; or she may suggest a move to the West Coast, where women's rights are better protected by community property law. The dissenting opinion of Judge Boyer in *Brown*, more than anything else, illustrates the depth of male frustration with the clearly noticeable trend toward full recognition of wives, in any form, as marital partners.

The recent legislative and judicial trend toward "equitable distribution" may, instead of granting relief from unfettered judicial discretion, increase the powers of the judge and expand the jurisdiction of the court. Equitable distribution increasingly subjects all property of the spouses to judicial distribution upon divorce, regardless of whether it was accumulated during the marriage through common effort or originated from other sources, like inheritance. The adjective "equitable" injects potential consideration of conduct and thus of fault, and also invokes continued and even increased emphasis on judicial discretion. Whether or not equitable distribution favors homemakers may depend on personal preference of individual chancellors or the skills of attorneys who represent the participants. While these considerations are not adverse to the economic interests of the practicing bar, they may neglect, as Professor Mary Ann Glendon has pointed out (see References below) the interests of the parties in the majority of divorces involving marriages of relatively short duration with minor children. *Brown*, which, together with *Canakaris v. Canakaris*,* paved the way for judicial equitable distribution in Florida, is somewhere in between. It did involve a marriage of 21 years' duration,

---

*382 So.2d 1197 (Fla. 1980).

but also minor children. Perhaps this made *Brown* suitable for laying the foundation for a principle of sweeping universality.

References

Comment, *The Development of Sharing Principles in Common Law Marital Property States*, 28 UCLA L. Rev. 1269 (1981).

Glendon, *Property Rights Upon Dissolution of Marriages and Informal Unions*, in The Cambridge Lectures—1981 (Butterworth, Toronto, forthcoming).

Knight & Elser, *Critical Factors Which Influence Equitable Distribution Awards*, 55 Fla. B.J. 581 (1981).

Weitzman, L., The Marriage Contract—Spouses, Lovers, and the Law 80–97 (1981).

Importance of Bookkeeping and Accounting

In re Marriage of Mix

Supreme Court of California

14 Cal.3d 604, 122 Cal. Rptr. 79, 536 P.2d 479 (1975)

Sullivan, Justice.

In this action for dissolution of marriage, appellant Richard Mix (Richard) appeals from an interlocutory judgment of dissolution declaring that appellant and respondent Esther Mix (Esther) are entitled to have their marriage dissolved, awarding custody of the minor child of the parties to Esther, and dividing their community property. Richard attacks the finding that, except for the property specifically found to be community, all property both real and personal standing in Esther's name or being in her possession at the time of the separation was her separate property.

Richard and Esther were married on September 4, 1958, and separated on December 14, 1968. There is one child of the marriage, a boy born February 24, 1960. At the time of marriage Esther was an attorney admitted to practice in California and Richard a musician and part-time teacher. Thereafter, they continued to pursue their respective careers. At the start, Esther was an associate in a law firm earning approximately $400 a month; by the time of her separation, she had become a 40 percent partner in the firm and earned about $25,000 annually. Richard's career as a musician, including regular employment with the Sacramento Symphony Orchestra, proved to be a good deal less remunerative; his annual income was generally between $1,000 and $3,000.

At the time of her marriage Esther owned considerable property. This included interests in income producing real property, a residence, a life insurance policy and bank accounts of indeterminate amounts. At that time Richard closed his savings account and the parties changed his checking account at the Bank of America into their joint account. In this new checking account, the parties deposited all their earnings as well as Esther's income from her separate property. This practice continued until 1963 when Esther opened an account in her name alone at the California Bank. In this account she deposited more of her income both from her law practice and her various investments.

The trial court found, so far as is here pertinent, that specific items of property were community property and, on the basis that it would effectuate a substantially equal division, awarded them as follows: (1) to Esther, the equity in the home of the parties, an Oldsmobile automobile, the interest in Esther's law partnership, an undivided one-sixth interest in 10 acres of real property, the household furniture and furnishings, and a tennis club membership; (2) to Richard, two sailboats, a Volkswagen automobile and the sum of $6,137. As previously stated, the court found that all other property, both real and personal, standing in Esther's name or being in her possession was her separate property. This is the finding upon which the present controversy centers.

We therefore find it convenient at this point to list the items of separate property which are the subject of the controversy:

1. *Proceeds of sale of Balboa Circle home.* Upon their marriage Richard and Esther moved into the latter's home on Balboa Circle in Sacramento, where they resided until 1966. The property was encumbered by a mortgage securing a loan which at the time of the marriage had an unpaid balance of about $15,000. During the marriage Esther paid the loan installments and the taxes on the property by checks drawn on the commingled bank accounts. Checks were drawn on the same accounts to pay for capital improvements. After she commenced the present action, Esther sold the home and deposited the net proceeds of $22,312.48 in an account in the Capital Federal Savings and Loan Association. Richard claims a community interest in the proceeds on the basis that the loan installments and the capital improvements were paid from the commingled accounts.

2. *Equitable Life Insurance Policy.* Esther had a life insurance policy issued to her in 1957 as a condition to obtaining a loan on the Balboa Circle home. The premiums were included in the loan payments and were accordingly paid during marriage by checks drawn by Esther on the commingled bank accounts. Richard maintains that 90 percent of the cash value of the policy constitutes community property.

3. *Cash on Hand.* Richard claims the balance of $3,392.15 in Esther's separate account on the day of trial after payment of the community obligations following separation, was community property. He also claims a community interest in the $1,000 balance owing on a loan Esther made to one Harvey Shank.

4. *Real property.* Prior to her marriage Esther and her law associate, later her law partner, each acquired an undivided one-half interest in a lot improved with a single family residence on 18th Street in Sacramento. In 1965 the house was destroyed by fire. Esther and her law partner used the $12,000 collected from insurance on the property together with $29,000 in borrowed money to build a fourplex on the lot. Richard claims a community property interest in the building, but not in the land, on the asserted basis that the building was constructed during marriage and that Richard was an obligor on the note.

In October 1958, a month after her marriage, Esther and her law partner each acquired an undivided one-half interest in unimproved real property on 20th Street in Sacramento. In purchasing her interest, Esther used separate funds on deposit in an account in her name in the Wells Fargo Bank which was one of the accounts she had before her marriage. Subsequently she and her partner borrowed $54,600 to construct an office building on this property, Richard being a trustor on the deed of trust and obligor on the note. Esther invested an additional $9,000 in the project, $4,000 from the commingled bank accounts and $5,000 from her separate property. Richard claims a community interest on the alleged grounds that the property was acquired during marriage, that he was involved in its financing and that the $4,000 contribution had come from commingled funds.

About three months later, in January 1959, Esther, her law partner, and two other persons each acquired an undivided one-fourth interest in an unimproved parcel of land on Newman Court in Sacramento. Esther testified that she paid $6,466.44 for her interest, withdrawing that amount from her account at the Wells Fargo Bank. The joint venturers borrowed $124,000 and built an apartment house on the property. Their loan was secured by a mortgage on the property. Subsequently Esther contributed an additional $4,121.91 to the joint venture, withdrawing the funds from the joint checking account maintained by her and Richard. The latter claims that Esther's interest in the joint venture is community property on the basis that she acquired it during marriage and also contributed the above funds from the commingled bank account.

In 1963 the same joint venturers purchased an additional parcel of land on Newman Court, borrowed $324,000 and built an apartment house on the property. The loan was secured by a mortgage on the property. Esther later contributed $5,100.92 to the joint venture for the acquisition of the property, again using funds from the joint account. Richard makes the same claim as to the community property character of this property.

After making a general finding that all of the foregoing property which stood in Esther's name was her separate property, the trial court went on to state:

> "All of such property which was acquired during the marriage of the parties in the name of petitioner [Esther] was taken in petitioner's name with the knowledge of respondent [Richard] and with the understanding of the parties that it was to be held as petitioner's separate property. Said property was purchased with petitioner's separate funds which were identified and traced by petitioner. Any improvement made during marriage to petitioner's separate property, and any separate property purchased with funds from any bank account in which both separate and community funds were comingled [sic], were made either by respondent or with his knowledge and consent with the intent that such improvements or property would belong to petitioner, and there was at all times a sufficient balance of separate property deposited to such accounts to cover all such amounts withdrawn. All borrowed funds used to improve petitioner's separate property were the proceeds of loans obtained upon the hypothecation of such separate property, and in making such loans the lender did not rely on the credit of the community. Such funds are the separate property of petitioner."

It thus appears that the trial court rested its finding as to Esther's separate property on two independent bases: (1) that Esther had adequately traced the source of the funds withdrawn from the commingled bank accounts for use in connection with the aforementioned properties to her separate funds; (2) that there was an agreement between Richard and Esther that all property purchased by the latter in her own name during marriage was to be her separate property.

The following legal principles apply: "All property of the wife, owned by her before marriage, and that acquired afterwards by gift, bequest, devise, or descent, with the rents, issues, and profits thereof, is her separate property." (Civ. Code, §5107.) Property purchased with the wife's separate property funds is her separate property. [Citations omitted.] The wife's earnings during the marriage are community property and are subject to her management and control. (§5124.)

Real or personal property, or any interest therein or encumbrance thereon, acquired by a married woman by an instrument in writing is presumed to be her separate property. (§5110.) However, "[p]roperty acquired by purchase during a marriage is presumed to be community property, and the burden is on the spouse asserting its separate character to overcome the presumption. [Citations.]" (*See v. See* (1966) 64 Cal.2d 778, 783, 51 Cal. Rptr. 888, 891, 415 P.2d 776, 779.) This presumption applies to property purchased during the marriage with funds from a disputed source, such as an account or fund in which one of the spouses has commingled his or her separate funds with community funds. [Citations omitted.]

"The mere commingling of separate with community funds in a bank account does not destroy the character of the former if the amount thereof can be ascertained." (*Hicks v. Hicks* (1962) 211 Cal. App.2d 144, 154, 27 Cal. Rptr. 307, 314; [other citations omitted]. As the court in *Patterson* stated: "If the property, or the source of funds with which it is acquired, can be traced, its separate property character remains unchanged. [Citations.] But if separate and community property or funds are commingled in such a manner that it is impossible to trace the source of the property or funds, the whole will be treated as community property * * *." (*Patterson v. Patterson, supra,* 242 Cal. App.2d at p. 341, 51 Cal. Rptr. at p. 345.)

During the marriage of Richard and Esther the law bestowed on Richard the management and control of the community personal property other than Esther's earnings and on Esther the management and control of her community property earnings and separate property rents, issues and profits, with other exceptions not here applicable. (§§5124, 5125, and see fn. 5, *ante;* see also §§5113.5, 5128.) Thus under the law and the undisputed facts Esther had the management and control of the commingled bank accounts at the California Bank. Because the presumption in section 5110 that any interest in property acquired by a married woman in writing is her separate property will have no further effect after the wife acquires joint management of all community property on January 1, 1975 (see fn. 6, *ante*), it should likewise not apply when the wife had management and control of the bank account in question. Otherwise, the wife managing a commingled account could by this device insulate herself from the rules applicable to commingling. We conclude therefore that the controlling presumption in this case is the one that property acquired during marriage is community property. [Citation omitted.]

The presumption that all property acquired by either spouse during the marriage is community property may be overcome. Whether or not the presumption is overcome is a question of fact for the trial court. [Citations omitted.]

Generally speaking such post-marital property can be established to be separate property by two independent methods of tracing. The first method involves direct tracing. As the court explained in *Hicks*:

"[S]eparate funds do not lose their character as such when commingled with community funds in a bank account so long as the amount thereof can be ascertained. Whether separate funds so deposited continue to be on deposit when a withdrawal is made from such a bank account for the purpose of purchasing specific property, and whether the intention of the drawer is to withdraw such funds therefrom, are questions of fact for determination by the trial court."

(*Hicks v. Hicks, supra,* 211 Cal. App.2d 144, 157, 27 Cal. Rptr. 307, 315; 7 Witkin, Summary of Cal. Law (8th ed.) §33, pp. 5126–5127.) The second method involves a consideration of family expenses. It is based upon the presumption that family expenses are paid from community funds. [Citations omitted.] If at the time of the acquisition of the property in dispute, it can be shown that all community income in the commingled account has been exhausted by family expenses, then all funds remaining in the account at the time the property was purchased were necessarily separate funds. [Citation omitted.]

The effect of the presumption and the two methods of overcoming it are succinctly summarized in *See:* "If funds used for acquisitions during marriage cannot otherwise be traced to their source and the husband who has commingled property is unable to establish that there was a deficit in the community accounts when the assets were purchased, the presumption controls that property acquired by purchase during marriage is community property." (*Id.* at p. 784, 51 Cal. Rptr. at p. 892, 415 P.2d at p. 780.) Throughout the marriage Esther commingled her community property earnings from her law practice with the rents, issues and proceeds from her separate property in several bank accounts. She concedes that she made no attempt to trace the source of the property by resorting to the "family expense method." We are satisfied from our review of the evidence that Esther failed to keep adequate records to show that family expenses had exhausted community funds at the time of the acquisition of any of the property here in dispute.

Esther contends, however, that she introduced sufficient evidence to trace the source of the funds used to acquire each item of disputed property to her separate property in accordance with the "direct tracing test" described in *Hicks v. Hicks, supra,* 211 Cal. App.2d 144, 27 Cal. Rptr. 307 (see p. 84, *ante*), and that therefore the trial court's finding to that effect is supported by substantial evidence.* * *

Esther introduced into evidence a schedule compiled by herself and her accountant from her records which itemized chronologically each source of separate funds, each expenditure for separate property purposes, and the balance of separate property funds remaining after each such expenditure. She received $99,632.02 attributable to her separate property; expended $42,213.79 for separate property purposes, leaving an excess of separate property receipts over separate property expenditures in the amount of $57,418.23 throughout the course of the marriage. Each year from 1958 to 1968, excepting the year 1961, there was an excess of separate property receipts over separate property expenditures, leaving a balance of separate funds. The 1961 deficit did not, however, exhaust the balance of separate funds carried forward from prior years. The schedule demonstrated that Esther's expenditures for separate property purposes closely paralleled in time and amount separate property receipts and thus established her intention to use only her separate property funds for separate property expenditures.

Richard contends that the schedule contains a fatal flaw in that the entries of receipts and expenditures are not tied to any bank account or bank accounts. Therefore, he argues, the schedule shows merely the availability of separate funds on the given dates but fails utterly to demonstrate the actual expenditures of those funds for the enumerated separate purposes. Esther concedes that she was unable to support the schedule by correlating each itemized deposit and withdrawal on the schedule with an entry in a particular bank account due to the unavailability of various bank records as well as to the lack of such records of her own. Richard urges that this state of the evidence demonstrates that Esther has failed to meet her burden, that she has therefore not overcome the community property presumption, and that her claims to specific property as being her separate property must fall.

We agree that the schedule by itself is wholly inadequate to meet the test prescribed by *Hicks v Hicks, supra,* 211 Cal. App.2d 144, 27 Cal. Rptr. 307, and to support the trial court's finding that Esther "identified and traced" the separate property. However, the schedule was not the only evidence introduced by Esther to effect the tracing. She personally testified that the schedule was a true and accurate record, that it accurately reflected the receipts and expenditures as accomplished through various bank accounts, although she could not in all instances correlate the items of the schedule with a particular bank account, and that it accurately corroborated her intention throughout her marriage to make these expenditures for separate property purposes, notwithstanding her use of the balance of her separate property receipts for family expenses.

The trial court evidently believed Esther. "The testimony of a witness, even the party himself, may be sufficient." (6 Witkin, CAL. PROCEDURE (2d ed.) §248, p. 4240.) Viewing this evidence in the light most favorable to Esther, giving her the benefit of every reasonable inference, and resolving all conflicts in her favor, as we must under the rules of appellate review * * * we conclude that there is substantial evidence to support the trial court's finding that Esther traced and identified the source and funds of her separate property. * * *

Since we conclude that the judgment can be upheld on the basis of an adequate tracing of Esther's separate property, it is unnecessary for us to consider whether it can also be upheld on the independent basis of an agreement between Richard and Esther as to the separate character of the properties in controversy.

The judgment is affirmed.

Comments

No-fault divorce and community property do not necessarily mean that all litigation is simple. In some jurisdictions, such as California, the emphasis may shift away from a determination of fault toward determining exactly what is half of the accumulated community property. The litigation of the issue of how to split the assets may be extremely bitter and protracted. *Mix,* in which the roles were reversed and the wife was the dominant party, illustrates the possible extent of involvement. The wife had considerable means to begin with, and contributed her income as a lawyer to the marriage, while the husband, a musician, had a negligible annual income. The wife acquired substantial real estate on her own initiative; expenses were paid out of commingled accounts. The husband tried to avail himself of a presumption that all the property was community property and as such should be split evenly. The wife, because of her inadequate bookkeeping, was practically unable to prove the contrary. Only the benevolence of the trial judge who, as a fact finder, ruled in her favor saved her from severe financial loss.

How precarious the wife's position was becomes apparent if, hypothetically, the sex roles are reversed with otherwise identical facts. Assume the more usual situation: the husband is the man of means and a successful lawyer while the wife has minimal income as a musician. Very likely the presumption of community property would not have been overcome. The ruling would have been against the husband who had failed to keep adequate books. As seen from this perspective it becomes clear that probably the wife is winning in *Mix* only because the courts were falling back into the older legal pattern of inequality by being overprotective of "the weaker sex."

The case has significance beyond community property jurisdictions. The same problems would arise if marriage is treated as partnership. Presumptions would operate in favor of equal division of partnership assets. Perhaps *Mix* could be used to support a presumption that property acquired during the marriage is partnership property, unless it can be traced to separate property. As marriage develops in the direction of partnership, California precedent becomes increasingly persuasive across the nation. It would be therefore recommendable in divorce litigation, regardless of what state is involved, to research the more complex questions also under California law. Since California appears to lead in development of family law, as for example in no-fault divorce and cohabitation contracts, it becomes an experimental field. Sometimes California precedent may be sufficiently persuasive elsewhere to bring about change.*

The least that can be said about *Mix* is that it argues for the importance of bookkeeping in modern marriage. Even with bookkeeping, however, certain questions are raised. For example, where in the ledger should a spouse's interest in a law partnership appear? And, if a spouse's interest in his or her professional partnership (whether the partnership concerns law, medicine, dentistry, accounting, architecture, and so on) is treated as a marital asset (as in *Mix*) for purposes of equitable distribution at dissolution, how is the fair value of the partnership to be determined? Needless to say, all the tools of discovery as well as valuation experts (often accountants) in the speciality of the partnership must be used. Such items as a partnership buy-out agreement, profit sharing and pension plans (both vested and nonvested), work in progress, accounts receivable, and good will need to be examined. It should be noted that lawyers may be reluctant to have their law partnership's finances scrutinized by another lawyer. Thus, an attempt to pursue a valuation of a law partnership could prompt an early negotiated settlement regarding the nonlawyer spouse's share in the marital property.

References

Bruch, *The Definition and Division of Marital Property in California: Toward Parity and Simplicity,* 33 HASTINGS L.J. 769 (1982).

Diamond, *No-Fault: New Emphasis in Divorce Cases—Focus Shifts From Placing Blame to Splitting Up Assets,* Los Angeles Times, Feb. 14, 1977, Part I, at 1, col. 1

Raggio, *Professional Goodwill and Professional Licenses as Property Subject to Distribution Upon Dissolution of Marriage,* 16 FAM. L.Q. 147 (1982).

Weitzman, *The Economics of Divorce: Social and Economic Consequences of Property, Alimony and Child Support Awards,* 28 UCLA L. REV. 1181, 1214–1215 (1981).

---

*For an illustration, see the reliance by the Supreme Court of Florida in *Posner v. Posner* (pp. 35–39) on the law of California.

Personal Liability of Wife Toward Creditors

Kennedy v. Nelson

Court of Appeals of Alabama

37 Ala. App. 484, 70 So.2d 822 (1954)

CARR, Presiding Judge.

The plaintiff below brought suit against Guy Nelson and his wife, Mrs. Annie Ray Grisham Nelson, for work and labor done. The cause was tried without a jury, and the trial resulted in a judgment in favor of the plaintiff against Mr. Nelson, but in favor of the defendant, Mrs. Nelson. The plaintiff brings this appeal from the judgment in Mrs. Nelson's favor.

In material reviewable aspects the facts are not in dispute.

Mrs. Nelson was the sole owner of an eighty-two acre tract of land. She and her husband had lived on this farm for many years. Up until the year 1951 Mr. Nelson had looked after the farming and rental interests for his wife. Some disagreements arose over the management, and in 1951 Mrs. Nelson rented the place to her husband. The latter was to pay $100 a year for the pasture lands and one-third of the crops on the cultivated portion.

During the year 1952 the appellant contracted with Mr. Nelson to do some grading on the pasture lands. Mrs. Nelson did not in any manner participate in the plan, nor did she become a party to the agreement. In fact, the appellant did not know that Mrs. Nelson owned the farm until some time after the work was completed.

It appears that Mrs. Nelson knew the grading was in progress because the work was done not a great distance from her residence. The bill for the labor was mailed to Mr. Nelson, and he alone was pressed for payment.

Mr. Nelson did not consider the work satisfactorily done, and according to his claim he refused payment on this account. When it appeared that prompt payment would not be made, the appellant endeavored to get Mrs. Nelson to sign a note for the amount claimed. This she refused to do.

From this brief delineation of the evidence it is clear that if the appellant is entitled to recover against Mrs. Nelson this right must arise from the doctrine of principal and agent or from ratification of the contract.

We held in *Turner v. Rhodes,* 22 Ala. App. 426, 116 So. 412, that the relationship of husband and wife does not *per se* raise a presumption that the former acted as the agent of the latter.

Appellant's position is not strengthened by the mere fact that the property of the wife was benefited by the improvements. *Fries v. Acme White Lead & Color Works,* 201 Ala. 613, 79 So. 45.

In other words, a party may choose the person with whom he deals. It may result that one has benefited by the contract of another to which he is not a party, but the law will not imply a promise to pay for this gain which inures incidentally by the performance of the agreement.

A very comprehensive statement of the law is found in the early case of *Wadsworth v. Hodge,* 88 Ala. 500, 7 So. 194, 196:

> "The contract must be either originally that of the wife, through herself or her authorized agent, or else the husband or other agent must assume to contract for her and in her own behalf, and such contract be subsequently ratified by her, with full notice or knowledge of its nature. In the absence of a contract of this character, no lien will attach to her property; and, where the credit is given solely to the husband, he alone

is bound, although it may appear that the wife knew that the building
or improvements were in process of erection on her land, and said
nothing, or that she and other members of the family afterwards occupied the building as a dwelling."

The question of instant concern has been reviewed by our appellate
courts in various aspects a number of times. We will discuss and cite some
cases which bear analogous factual foundations to the case at bar.

In *Hawkins Lumber Co. v. Brown,* 100 Ala. 217, 14 So. 110, the suit was
to recover for the price of lumber used in improving the dwelling on the
property of the wife. The purchase of the material was made by the husband
and credit was given to him solely. There was no evidence that in the transaction he undertook to act as the agent of his wife.

In response to a review the Supreme Court held that under these circumstances the statute did not create a lien upon the property of the owner
for the price of the lumber.

In the case of *Hanchey v. Powell,* 171 Ala. 597, 55 So. 97, the vendor
knew that lumber he sold was to be used for repairs on property owned by
the wife. The court observed that the lumberman did not sell the material to
the wife or to her husband as her agent, but it was sold to the latter individually, and under this state of facts the wife was not "originally or
primarily liable for the debt * * *."

* * *

In the case of *Womack v. Myrick Lumber Co.,* 200 Ala. 591, 76 So. 949,
950, the materialman furnished lumber to improve two dwellings on lots belonging to the wife of the purchaser. The account was stated on the vendor's
books in the name of the husband, agent.

The court held that this was not conclusive of the matter, but it was
essential to show that either the husband acted with authority as the agent
of his wife or that "being fully advised of the facts, she, the owner, ratified
the acts of R. J. Womack (husband) in the premises."

The court observed in *Fries v. Acme White Lead & Color Works, supra*
[201 Ala. 613, 79 So. 48]:

"If there was no such contract in this case, no liability was assumed
by appellant, and none attached, for which she may be subjected in this
suit; for if by express contract credit was given solely to the husband he
alone is bound, although it may appear that the wife knew that the
building or improvements were in process of erection on her land, and
said nothing, or that she and other members of the family afterwards
occupied the building as a dwelling."

We are unable to find any evidence in this record which would authorize
us to hold that Mrs. Nelson ratified the agreement between her husband and
the appellant, and became liable for the debt on this account.

In this aspect the only proof which has any tendency to establish this
doctrine is the fact that Mrs. Nelson knew the grading was in progress and
that she took no steps to disclaim any liability for payment for the work.

According to the authorities, this alone is not sufficient.

* * *

Appellant urges that the long relationship between Mr. and Mrs. Nelson in the management of the latter's farm gave rise and application to the
doctrine of implied agency.

We are, of course, faced with the testimony that this long standing relationship terminated in 1951.

This question seems to be answered adversely to the position of appellant in 41 C.J.S., *Husband and Wife,* §293(b), pages 777–778:

"Where the husband, in dealing with the wife's separate property,
acts as her agent, persons dealing with him are bound to take notice of

his authority as in the case of other agents, and are bound to inquire as to the extent of his authority; and persons having notice of the husband's agency will not be protected as to transactions with him hostile to her interest and beyond the apparent scope of his agency. * * *

"Where one deals with the husband as principal, no fact of undisclosed agency appearing, the wife cannot be charged with liability; and it is not sufficient to charge the wife that the purchases were for the benefit of her separate estate."

* * *

As we have indicated, the case was tried without a jury. There is no indication that appellant's rights were infringed by the procedure.

It is well settled that in matters of this character the sound discretion of the trial judge is invoked. We are clear to the conclusion that we would be out of harmony with the authorities to declare that in the instant case this discretion was abused. [Citations omitted.]

We have responded to the questions which are properly presented for our review.

It is ordered that the judgment below from which this appeal is taken be affirmed.

Affirmed.

Northampton Brewery Corporation v. Lande

Superior Court of Pennsylvania

138 Pa. Super. 235, 10 A.2d 583 (1939)

BALDRIGE, Judge.

This is an appeal from the order of Bluett, J., of the Municipal Court granting the prayer of the petitioner to charge the interest of the defendant, an alleged partner in a partnership with a debt owing the plaintiff.

Broadly stated, the question before us is whether a husband and wife may be partners in carrying on a business; more particularly, whether the court below was correct in holding the relationship existing between the appellant and her husband, in conducting a restaurant and grill at 732 Vine Street, Philadelphia, was that of partners rather than of tenants by entireties.

* * *

At common law, married women, lacking contract capacity generally, could not become partners. Modern legislation has removed almost entirely the legal incapacities of married women. In most jurisdictions they may become members of partnerships and even partners with their husbands. CRANE ON PARTNERSHIP, page 32. There can be no doubt that under the existing law in this state a husband and wife may be partners in a business. Any previously existing incapacity of a married woman to contract in this respect has been removed by statute. This court, in *Loeb v. Mellinger*, 12 Pa. Super, 592, 597, held that a married woman can engage in a trade or business on her own account since the Act of June 8, 1893, P.L. 344, 48 P.S. §32. In *Italo-French Produce Co. v. Thomas*, 31 Pa. Super. 503, we stated that a married woman had the right, if she chose, to become a partner of her husband in a mercantile business, and be subject to the same rights and exposed to the same liabilities as any other member of the same partnership.

* * *

A partnership is defined under our Uniform Partnership Act of March 26, 1915, P.L. 18, §6, 59 P.S. §11, as "an association of two or more persons to carry on as co-owners a *business* for profit." (Italics supplied.) In ascertaining whether a partnership exists, it is necessary to consider all of the attending facts and circumstances, and, if the evidence is sufficient, it is for the jury's consideration.

A plain distinction exists between a partnership of a husband and wife and a tenancy of entireties, which is recognized by section 7 of our Uniform Partnership Act of 1915, supra, 59 P.S. §12, as follows: "In determining whether a partnership exists, these rules shall apply * * * (2) Joint tenancy, tenancy in common, *tenancy by the entireties*, joint property, common property, or part ownership does not of itself establish a partnership, whether such co-owners do or do not share any profits made by the use of the property." (Italics supplied.)

* * * [T]he difference between a tenancy by entireties and a partnership conducted by husband and wife as partners is that the partnership involves, in addition to co-ownership of property, the element of carrying on a business of commercial enterprise for profit.

* * *

The court below, without hearing any testimony under the petition, concluded that it had already adjudicated in the previous proceedings between the same parties that the relationship between Beatrice Lande and her husband in conducting the tap room and grill was that of partners. Accordingly, it made an order directing that a receiver be appointed to determine the value of the appellant's interest in the partnership. The appellant, in addition to contending that the parties were tenants by entireties only, alleges that the court below could not determine what the relationship was of her and her husband in conducting the grill without taking testimony. The learned judge below in his opinion stated that the question had already been adjudicated in this court in previous attachment proceedings when a considerable amount of testimony was taken and it was found that under the law a partnership did exist. A motion for a new trial prevailed in the attachment proceedings and the case was tried again before Judge Crane, who likewise, determined the existence of a partnership and found for the plaintiff against the garnishee. After the death of Judge Crane, a motion for a new trial was argued before Judge Glass, who, in a lengthy opinion, called attention to the fact that the record showed that

> "David Lande * * * testified that the restaurant business conducted under the name of The Keg and Dave's Grill were both registered in the name of David Lande and Beatrice Lande * * * that both he and his wife signed the petition for registration under the Fictitious Name Act and that neither registration had been cancelled; * * * that the liquor licenses at both addresses are in the name of Beatrice Lande and David Lande; that those licenses have been renewed every year since 1936, and that both signed the petition for a liquor license and for the renewals * * * that bank accounts were opened in both names * * * that the leases to both places of business are in the names of both of them; that the money that went into each of the businesses aforesaid was borrowed from the banks by both himself and his wife, Beatrice Lande; that the income tax returns for 1936 and 1937 were joint returns of Beatrice and David Lande * * * that he draws and signs the checks and that Beatrice Lande, his wife, can if she wants to; that neither he nor his wife draw a salary."

There can be no dispute as to these facts and as to the manner in which both David Lande and Beatrice Lande conducted the grill and restaurant on

Vine Street. The real dispute is to the legal conclusion to be drawn from these facts, namely, for the purpose of this case, were they partners or tenants by entireties? We think the trial court was entirely correct in treating the facts as already adjudicated. * * *

* * *

The order is affirmed, at appellant's costs.

Farm Bureau Agricultural Credit Corp. v. Dicke

Court of Appeals of Ohio

29 Ohio App.2d 1, 277 N.E.2d 562 (1972)

GUERNSEY, Judge.

This is an appeal by the defendants Donald W. Dicke and his wife, Virginia, from a judgment in a declaratory judgment action determining the rights of the plaintiff credit corporation and said defendants to funds in the possession of the Sheriff of Auglaize County. It appears that on October 18, 1963 * * * the plaintiff took a cognovit judgment against Donald W. Dicke on a note of which he was the sole maker, issued execution thereon and that on October 19, 1963, the Sheriff attended a public sale of farm chattels which had been in possession of Donald W. Dicke and his wife, Virginia, where he attempted to levy, or succeeded in levying, execution against a part of the proceeds of sale in the hands of the auction clerk. These are the funds to which right of ownership is now disputed. The trial court held, in essence, that the chattels which were sold were the partnership property of Dicke and his wife, that the note upon which judgment had been taken was a partnership obligation, and that the funds derived from the sale of the partnership property were subject to the levy of execution on the judgment against Dicke.

* * *

Appellants' sixth assignment of error is that the trial court committed error in its decision in applying a theory of implied partnership. This we shall discuss together with the seventh assignment that the order of the court is against the manifest weight of the evidence and contrary to law. There was sufficient evidence of probative value with respect to the contributions of capital and labor, the manner of use of a joint bank account, and the frequent representations or acknowledgements, when borrowing money, of joint or common ownership of the chattels involved, that the farm business relationship between the appellants was that of a partnership and that the farm chattels sold at public sale were partnership property. On this state of the evidence we may not conclude otherwise as a matter of law and the fifth assignment of error must be found without merit.

However, the issue then resolves itself as being whether the plaintiff, having taken judgment individually against Donald W. Dicke, may levy execution on said judgment against partnership property owned by both Donald W. Dicke and his wife, Virginia, the funds produced by the sale of partnership chattels retaining the same character and being partnership funds. [Citations omitted.]

We might conclude, notwithstanding that the plaintiff claims, and the trial court found, that the money which was loaned, evidenced by the obligation sued upon, was loaned for partnership use, that since the claim was merged in a judgment individually against Donald W. Dicke, it thereby became his sole obligation which could not be asserted against partnership property. We do not, however, have to rely on such conclusion, arrived at in such manner, for we may arrive at the same conclusion in a different manner.

R.C. §1775.08 prescribes among other things, that:

"(C) Unless authorized by the other partners * * *, one or more but less than all the partners have no authority to:
"* * *.
"(4) Confess a judgment;
"* * *."

This means, of course, that one partner, unless authorized, may not confess a judgment against the partnership, but does not preclude him from confessing a judgment against himself alone. It is likewise obvious that the mere existence of the partnership relation does not, in and of itself, extend the authority of the other partners to one partner to confess judgment. In other words, the authority is not implied by the partnership relationship but must be expressly granted or appear from other circumstances.

Here there is no evidence in the record of any authority expressly or otherwise granted by Virginia Dicke to her husband to confess judgment against their farming partnership and the plaintiff having taken a cognovit judgment against the husband, under such circumstances, may have recourse only against the individual property of the husband and not against partnership property. His interest in partnership property was subject, of course, to a charging order obtained in the manner prescribed in R.C. §1775.27, but not subject to a levy of execution in the manner here attempted.

We conclude that the trial court committed error as a matter of law prejudicial to the appellants in holding and declaring that the funds herein involved were subject to the levy of execution on plaintiff's judgment, that said levy was valid, and that the funds be paid to the plaintiff.

Judgment reversed.

Comments

We have already seen that the conception of marriage as partnership can be a mixed blessing for women, as when, for example, they have higher income and assets than their husbands. Apart from this, wives become increasingly liable for marital debts under conceptions of partnership. They gain a vested interest in the partnership in exchange for the possibility of being liable to outsiders. *Northampton* involved a restaurant, jointly operated by husband and wife. The wife defended herself against the brewery's claims by stating that she was a tenant by the entireties rather than a partner and as such was not liable. The court disagreed and charged her interest in the partnership. This was a small business case; but if marriage is viewed as a pooling of resources for mutual profit, there is no reason why this holding could not be extended. In *Farm Bureau* a married woman who operated a farm jointly with her husband escaped liability on a promissory note signed by him, but only because of a mere procedural technicality.

Once the possibility is seen that a wife may be liable, conscious efforts may be made in marriage, parallel to those in business organizations, to avoid liability. It might be possible to operate the economic aspects of a marriage as a closed corporation. In *Kennedy*, the wife, as sole owner of an Alabama farm, changed her management contract with her husband into a lease. In a principal-agent or employment relationship, she would have been liable for the debts incurred by her husband; as a landlord she was not. Ancient conceptions of feudal law of property, shielding the landlord from liability for activities of the tenant, came to her aid.

As suggested above, marriage should be seen in the context of alternatives available in business, where it is always important to minimize liability. But litigation often becomes arrested in one legal theory, because attorneys have traditionally not been trained to think on multiple levels of analysis. The courts are then limited to whatever theory happens to be submitted to them in the pleadings.

Once a legal theory is chosen, further consequences flow from it. For example, in *Kennedy*, if the wife is classified as a landlord in a lease with her husband, her knowledge of what she saw becomes irrelevant. If the problem is seen as agency, then knowledge can become significant as ratification. The argument of a lease seems to have been facilitated in *Kennedy* by an express agreement between husband and wife. More problematical are the *Northampton* and *Farm Bureau* holdings, because they found partnership by implication. As always, the implied contract can be used as a judicial tool to apply public policy in a covert fashion that, in some instances, may approach legal fiction. The wife may be treated as if she were a partner for purposes of attaching personal liability to her or, on the positive side, to give her a better share in her husband's property as a matter of law.

Reference

Weyrauch, *Metamorphoses of Marriage,* 13 Fam. L.Q. 415 (1980).

Bibliography

Bruch, *The Definition and Division of Marital Property in California: Toward Parity and Simplicity,* 33 Hastings L.J. 769 (1982).

Erickson, *Spousal Support Toward the Realization of Educational Goals,* 1978 Wis. L. Rev. 947 (1978).

Fethke & Hauserman, *Homemaking: The Invisible Occupation,* 71 (2) J. Home Econ. 20 (1979).

Freed & Foster, *Divorce in the Fifty States: An Overview,* 15 Fam. L.Q. 229 (1981).

Glendon, M., THE NEW FAMILY AND THE NEW PROPERTY (1981).

Hauserman & Fethke, *Valuation of a Homemaker's Services*, 22 TRIAL LAW. GUIDE 249 (1978).

Hennessey, *Explosion in Family Law Litigation: Challenges and Opportunities for the Bar*, 14 FAM. L.Q. 187 (1980).

Krauskopf, *Recompense for Financing Spouse's Education: Legal Protection for the Marital Investor in Human Capital*, 28 KAN. L. REV. 379 (1980).

Martin, *Social Security Benefits for Spouses*, 63 CORNELL L. REV. 789 (1978).

Note, *Conceived in Inequality—The Consortium Doctrine: Constitutional Challenges Must Be Made*, 12 NEW ENG. L. REV. 135 (1976).

Note, *Divorce After Professional School*, 44 MO. L. REV. 329 (1979).

Note, *Education Acquired After Marriage*, 12 J. MAR. J. PRAC. & PROC. 709 (1979).

Note, *Equitable Distribution vs. Fixed Rules: Marital Property Reform and the Uniform Marital Property Act*, 23 B.C. L. REV. 761 (1982).

Note, *Restoration of Property: Illusory Barrier to Interspousal Gifts*, 67 KY. L.J. 173 (1979).

Veitch, *Essence of Marriage*, 5 ANGLO-AM. L. REV. 41 (1976).

Weitzman, *The Economics of Divorce: Social and Economic Consequences of Property, Alimony and Child Support Awards*, 28 UCLA L. REV. 1181 (1981).

2

Informal Marriage

The legal reaction to informal cohabitation can be viewed as a key to an understanding of ceremonial marriage in its various forms. Throughout the Middle Ages, informal sexual unions prevailed. Form requirements were introduced by church and state as a means of asserting political power and controlling the population. At the Council of Trent in 1563, the Catholic Church, reacting to the threat of the Protestant Reformation, established ceremonial requirements for the validity of marriage: assistance of a priest and the presence of two or three witnesses after the publishing of the banns.

Much later, England, through Lord Hardwicke's Act of 1753, imposed comparable requirements for marriage; but informal cohabitation continued to exist, especially among the lower classes and in the colonies. The legal system reacted with indifference or tolerance so long as its value preferences were not infringed upon.

In American law, extralegal marital patterns were absorbed gradually into the legal system, and today informal marriage has become more prevalent in all segments of the population than it has been for generations. Its contemporary legal status is due to the creative imagination of practicing lawyers who pressed claims in behalf of women clients. Eventually their arguments were successful in the courts, and there are now enough data for legal theory.

The Dispensability of Marriage. A striking feature of marriage in the formal, legal sense is that, except as a symbol, it is decreasingly necessary. Each point discussed in Chapter 1 attests to this. The shift toward antenuptial agreements and marriage as partnership emphasizes individual autonomy and contract. In a resurrection of equitable maxims such as "equity considers as done what ought to be done" and proprietary theories of equitable conversion, parties to informal cohabitation may be considered to be in a quasi-marital state, at least for purposes of entitlements and property allocation. Consequently, whether the stage of a mutual "conveyance" or "closing" of marriage under statutory requirements is ever reached is in-

115

creasingly irrelevant for the relation of the parties between themselves and also for governmental purposes of welfare and taxation.

On the other hand, what is done in fact also becomes the legal equivalent of what ought to be done in equity. To use the traditional frame of reference and language of a chancellor, if one behaves like a married person, regardless of whether he is married, he is taken by his word and treated as if he were married. And if an individual who ought to be married behaves like an unmarried person, he too is often treated as though married. This means that the legal effects of marriage, although sometimes for limited purposes, may be imposed on the parties if circumstances, as seen by the court, warrant it. In other words, the legal consequences of formal marriage and informal cohabitation are becoming more and more assimilated to each other. To some extent this means also an assimilation of form and substance because lacking formality of marriage no longer necessarily results in absence or loss of substantive rights. This evolution is facilitated because the courts seemingly make only ad hoc adjustments to remedy the hardships in specific cases pending before them, while gradually they affect the conceptions of marriage.

Common Law Marriage. From its inception in early American case law, it was never clear whether common law marriage was a matter of procedure or of substantive law of the family. Like the procedural presumption of marriage, it required cohabitation and repute of being married. Strictly considered, it was not really informal, since it had its own special form requirements. The substantive requirements of common law marriage, namely, cohabitation and repute, merged into the evidentiary requirements for any marriage, whether or not ceremonial and licensed. When the substantive aspects of common law marriage appeared to decline through legislative abolition in an increasing number of states, the "procedural marriage" by presumption survived and became important as a judicial remedy in hardship cases.

Common law marriage was often used in an ad hoc fashion many years after the fact of cohabitation. If an alleged husband and father had died, perhaps in war or in an industrial accident, and his purported wife and children claimed benefits as heirs or survivors, courts tended to be lenient and treat the claim as if there was a marriage. This was accomplished using the concept of common law marriage, if it was available under state law; otherwise the courts used the presumption of marriage.

Procedural Marriage and Other Escape Doctrines. Most Americans rely in their daily transactions on a presumption of marriage that often amounts to an irrebuttable legal fiction based on public policy. Marriage certificates are practically never required to be shown or recorded, not even in real estate transactions. In general, word of being married is accepted without question. If death intervenes, past cohabitation and repute of having been married will do in any American jurisdiction. Marriage certificates are often misplaced, and descendants would face an impossible task if they had to trace the marital history of their ancestors through documents. Whether there was a formal marriage or informal cohabitation thus fades into insignificance.

Sometimes, of course, the evidence is clear that no formal marriage exists. The parties may not dispute this; they may never have intended a marriage and they may never have complied with any of the statutory requirements. Or the marriage may have been illegal because one of the parties was already married or they were closely related. Even in these instances the courts, if "equity" warrants it, grant relief by applying a host of legal theories. They may rule that a party who is in bad faith is estopped to deny that he is married or, in some jurisdictions, they may talk of putative or de facto marriages.

An express agreement, enforced by the courts, may take the place of formal statutory marriage. Sometimes referred to as contract cohabitation, these agreements are more likely to be honored if they use the language of property. Since common law judges are traditionally property oriented, sexual cohabitation becomes less objectionable if it is presented in terms borrowed from the law of property rather than the law of personal service contracts. Personal services in the sphere of intimate relationships are still often stigmatized as prostitution. It is relatively easy to express the incidents of marriage, whether formal or not, in terms of landlord-tenant relationships, co-ownership, or perhaps even co-tenancy at will. Marriage as partnership is really only an application of these theories. It treats marriage, following the spirit of the Uniform Partnership Act, as a co-ownership for profit.

If an express agreement is missing, the courts may imply one. They may find a partnership for purposes of distribution of property, or they may apply theories of unjust enrichment or quasi-contract. They may imply a resulting trust, or impose a constructive trust. What started out as barely concealed legal fiction, namely, treating the parties for limited purposes as if they were married, has in the language of modern courts increasingly come to approximate the reality of marriage. Considerations of fault and moral blame, while still operative, are deemphasized.

Impact on Family Law. The legal consequences of this situation are manifold. They affect not only formal marriage but also the laws of the family and of inheritance. There is scarcely a situation today where it can be positively stated that a permanent sexual union is for all purposes void under the law. Even homosexual unions, at least in the case of sex-change operations, might now be recognized. Also, under conceptions of privacy, standing to attack the validity of a relationship may be denied to all but the parties themselves. Death of a party, consequently, must heal any defect. Now that illegitimate children can inherit from their natural fathers, formal and informal marriage, except for ease or difficulty of proof, have essentially the same consequences. The underlying reasoning seems to be that if both formal and informal marriage are partnership, any marital cohabitation inevitably has proprietary consequences that must be recognized by the legal system like any other accumulation of wealth.

This state of affairs has created an infinite number of problems that are now being litigated in the courts. While common law marriage as a legal institution is relatively clear, its conceptual equivalents are hazy. How, for instance, does one enter a "procedural marriage" or, perhaps more importantly, how does one get out of it? Rebutting a presumption, if available, may become an alternative for divorce or dissolution. How can one avoid the consequences of an implied contract or partnership that in fact may never have been intended, but that now creates entitlements akin to those resulting from marriage? Obviously, in regard to their functions the evidentiary presumption of marriage is confused with the substantive implied contract of cohabitation.

What can be done to clarify the confusion that exists between engagement, common law marriage, and informal cohabitation? How can the abuses be avoided, abuses that resulted in the past from actions for breach of promise to marry and that today result from implied contract cohabitation? The most obvious remedy appears to be an express cohabitation contract that regulates and limits mutual property rights. Of course, claims of prostitution or lack of cohabitation are still possible. Parties may avoid the consequences of marriage in any form by clearly establishing a reward for a meretricious relationship; or, more simply, they may establish intimate relations without living together. The confusion of public records because of informal cohabitation is unavoidable and perhaps of little consequence. In the last analysis, social dynamics appear to be stronger than the capacity of the government to regulate.

Implications of social class continue to be present. Many of the current judicial theories on informal marriage appear to be tailored to the needs of the middle classes, as, for example, when these theories inject notions of property into marriage and the family. Moreover, it is the middle classes who find their way to a lawyer, who, upon request, may draft a contract expressly regulating their informal cohabitation. And in dealing with such parties, courts are more likely to apply theories of trust, unjust enrichment, or estoppel. However, if claims originate from the lower classes, in the absence of clearly established formal marriage or express contract, judges may impose a presumption of marriage, if one of the parties is deceased, or imply a contract, if they are both still alive. Thus the substantive functions of rules of evidence become increasingly clear. Furthermore, express contract and implied contract, although they share the same conceptual underpinning, are not necessarily part of the same social frame of reference. With express contract, party autonomy is more or less real, or at least a possibility; while with implied contract of cohabitation, party autonomy may have elements of a legal fiction judicially imposed upon the parties.

References

Baade, *The Form of Marriage in Spanish North America,* 61 CORNELL L. REV. 1 (1975).

Daube, *Historical Aspects of Informal Marriage,* 25 REVUE INTERNATIONALE DES DROITS DE L'ANTIQUITÉ 95 (3e Serie 1978).

Note, *Marriage as Contract: Towards a Functional Redefinition of the Marital Status,* 9 COLUM. J.L. & SOC. PROBS. 607 (1973).

Schwab, Eheschliessungsrecht und nichteheliche Lebensgemeinschaft— Eine rechtsgeschichtliche Skizze—, 1981 Zeitschrift für das gesamte Familienrecht 1151 (exhaustive treatment of sources from the Middle Ages and Antiquity).

Stein, *Common Law Marriage: Its History and Certain Contemporary Problems*, 9 J. FAM. L. 271 (1969).

Common Law Marriage

Substantive Versus Procedural Marriage (Marriage by Presumption)

Campbell v. Christian

Supreme Court of South Carolina

235 S.C. 102, 110 S.E.2d 1 (1959)

LEGGE, Justice.

James Woodrow Campbell, a resident of Anderson County, died on February 25, 1956. His will dated September 9, 1947 was offered for probate in the Probate Court for that county and was there contested by the appellant, Betty I. Campbell, upon the ground that it had been revoked by her marriage with Campbell on July 17, 1954. The Judge of that Court admitted it to probate and held that the said marriage was invalid because the respondent Beulah Poole Campbell was then decedent's common-law wife. * * *

* * *

Campbell was born on January 12, 1875, and was eighty-one years old at the time of his death in February, 1956. In February, 1894, when he was nineteen, his first child, Myrtis, was born to Emma Hickman, whom he never married. It should be said, in passing, that he supported Myrtis thereafter until her marriage in 1918, and that by his will, after provision for nine cash legacies aggregating $2,525, he left his residuary estate to her and his daughter Cornelia in equal shares and appointed both of them as executrices.

At some time prior to February, 1921, Campbell married Mattie Grey. They had no children.

While married to Mattie, Campbell had illicit relation with Beulah Poole, an illiterate, ignorant girl; and on November 18, 1921, she bore him a child. He was then forty-five, she fourteen.

On January 11, 1923, Mattie having died, Campbell married her niece, Gertrude. One child, Cornelia, was born to them on November 16, 1923. During this marriage, Campbell's relations with Beulah continued, with the result that she had two more children by him, one on January 28, 1925, the other on January 18, 1928. On December 10, 1927, he divorced Gertrude in a Florida proceeding, the validity of which is not in issue.

About a year after the divorce, Beulah came into his home and took the name of Campbell, and they lived together for more than twenty-four years, during which five children were born to them, one in 1931, one in 1932, one in 1935, one in 1938, and one in 1943. In the spring of 1954 he deserted her and moved to another house in the city of Anderson.

Shortly thereafter the appellant, who had been living in Georgia, came to Anderson. In response to a newspaper advertisement she entered Campbell's employ as cook and housekeeper, and on June 10, 1954, they executed a written contract to that effect, which, after reciting her agreement, in consideration of $15 per week and board and lodging, "to cook for J. Woodrow Campbell, keep his house clean, and attend to the washing and other household duties," proclaimed that "she will occupy a separate room and she will be known as an employee of J. Woodrow Campbell," and that "the relationship of employee and employer will be and is the only relationship which will exist between the parties thereto." On July 17, 1954, they drove across the Georgia line and the Ordinary of Hart County performed a ceremony purporting to unite them in holy wedlock. He was then seventy-nine, she forty-two.

There is in the record before us considerable evidence that from the time that Campbell took Beulah into his home, a year or so after his divorce from Gertrude, he and she lived together as husband and wife, and that they were so recognized in the community. An elderly neighbor, who had known Campbell throughout the latter's life, testified that "they lived openly as husband and wife"; that "he carried the children around with him and they went by the name of Campbell and went to school under the name of Campbell"; and that the general public considered them as man and wife. One of Campbell's sons testified, without objection, that when strangers came to the house Campbell, after introducing himself, would introduce Beulah as his wife. His daughter Myrtis testified that during the many years that Campbell and Beulah lived together she visited in their home and understood that they were married; and that the people of the community knew them as man and wife.

In evidence are the birth certificates of five of the children, from which we note the following:

1. That of the child born November 18, 1921, names Beulah Poole as its mother, does not name its father, and states that the child's parents were not married.

2. That of the child born January 28, 1925, names James Woodrow Campbell as its father and Beulah Poole as its mother, and states that the child's parents were not married.

3. That of the child born January 18, 1928, names the parents as Woodrow Campbell and Beulah Campbell, and states that they are married.

4. That of the child born June 8, 1935, names the parents as Woodrow Campbell and Beulah Campbell, and states that they are married.

5. That of the child born July 3, 1943, names the parents as James Woodrow Campbell and Beulah Poole, and states that they are married.

Appellant, contending that Beulah's own testimony shows the relationship between her and Campbell to have been that of concubinage, not common-law marriage, points to the following portions of it:

> "Q. You hadn't had any signed contract or anything at that time that you were his wife, did you? A. No.
> "Q. And he never did tell you that you were his wife, did he? A. I had sense enough to know that I didn't marry him.

"Q. Both of you were not married then, were you? A. No, we weren't married.

    * * *

"Q. Did you ever try to get him to take you to the preacher? A. No, we talked about it but we never did get to it.

"Q. Did you try to get him to? A. No, I did not. I wasn't going to beg him. If he didn't want to marry me, I wasn't going to beg him.

    * * *

"Q. You don't think you had any right to take out a warrant against him for marrying Betty? A. No, I didn't think that I did.

"Q. That was because you didn't consider you and he were married? A. That is right.

    * * *

"Q. Did you and he ever go to church together? A. No sir, he went to church sometimes and carried the children.

"Q. He didn't take you? A. I didn't go.

"Q. Did you want to go? A. Yes, sir, I would like to have gone some, but I didn't get to.

"Q. And that is because you were uncertain about your relationship to him, weren't you. A. Yes, sir."

Throughout the record of this case Beulah appears as a woman illiterate, uneducated, and of childlike simplicity. It is not improbable that when she made the statements above quoted she was thinking of a ceremonial, rather than actual, marriage. Nor is it improbable that she, like many others whose intellectual and social horizons are thus limited, had the notion that a marriage is not legal unless solemnized by a religious, or at least an official, ceremony. The trial judge did not discuss her testimony, and therefore we cannot say with certainty how he construed her statements as to nonmarriage; if he viewed them as referring to ceremonial marriage we could not condemn such inference as unreasonable. But whether he so viewed them or not, we do not think that they are conclusive of the issue. Against them stands evidence that after Campbell's divorce the relationship between him and Beulah, which theretofore had been illicit, underwent a fundamental change; that whereas before it they had lived separately, after it they resided together, openly and continuously, over a period of at least twenty-four years, during which they were known and recognized in the community as husband and wife; and that the children born to them during this cohabitation were declared to the public authorities charged with the duty of registering their births, as having been born in wedlock. In short, they are contradicted by the conduct and general repute of both parties over a period of many years.

"Assertions of both parties that their relation was one of open concubinage, or admission of nonmarriage by one party, fortified by strong circumstances, may suffice to overcome the presumption of their marriage from cohabitation and reputation. Such an admission by the parties does not suffice to overcome the presumption, however, where it is shown that the admission may well have been made with reference to a ceremonial marriage, and not uttered with the idea of negativing broadly the existence of the marital status." [Citations omitted.]

Illicit relationship, though accompanied by cohabitation, is not transformed into the legal state of marriage by mere lapse of time. But mutual recognition of the marriage relation, at a time when the parties are able to enter into the marital contract, has long been accepted as ground for upholding the marriage. Where the evidence is in conflict, determination of the issue is for the trier of the facts. [Citations omitted.]

In the case at bar there was ample evidence, to which we have already referred, to support the conclusion that after the barrier to their marriage had been removed by Campbell's divorce from Gertrude, he and Beulah entered into a new mutual agreement whereby their previously illicit relationship was terminated and a valid common-law marriage established. That Campbell some twenty-five years thereafter declared, in his application for a license to marry Betty, that he was not married, is of no legal consequence; for once his marriage to Beulah became complete, as the trial judge held it to be, no act or disavowal of it on his part could invalidate it. [Citation omitted.]

* * *

* * * [I]t is rarely possible to fix precisely the time at which a common-law marriage may be said to have come into being. [Citation omitted.] But it is clear from the evidence that it was entered into within a year or so after Campbell's divorce, which had been obtained on December 10, 1927. It would seem, then, that their illegitimate children living on May 2, 1951 became legitimate upon the approval that day of the Act of the General Assembly (47 Stat. at Large 265) now Section 20-5.1 of the 1952 Code.

Affirmed.

Thomson v. Thomson

Kansas City Court of Appeals, Missouri

236 Mo. App. 1223, 163 S.W.2d 792 (1942)

SPERRY, Commissioner.

Martha S. Thomson, filed a claim in probate court seeking the statutory allowance of $400 for a widow, and an allowance for a year's maintenance and support, from the estate of Peter Thomson, deceased, whose widow she claims to be. Her claim was allowed for $400 absolute allowance and for $1,400 maintenance. Earl P. Thomson, a son of deceased and administrator of said estate, and Grace Richardson, a daughter of deceased, defendants, appealed to the circuit court. The cases were consolidated in circuit court, and a trial of the cause resulted in a judgment sustaining the allowances made by probate court. From that judgment both defendants prosecute their appeals to this court.

The sole question presented here is whether or not the evidence supports the judgment of the court to the effect that Martha S. Thomson, claimant, is the legal widow of Peter Thomson, deceased. * * *

Peter Thomson and Anna George were married in 1894, and the two defendants herein are the children of that marriage. Anna George Thomson died in 1914, but her mother made her home with Thomson thereafter until her death in 1919. Earl came home from the army in 1918 and was introduced to claimant, under the name of Martha Evans, by his father. Grace also met claimant at about that time, at the Thomson home, and claimant was introduced to her also as Martha Evans. The Thomson family, then living at the home, consisted of Peter, Earl, Grace, the grandmother, and a housekeeper. Claimant did not live there but only came there occasionally. Grace was married and, shortly thereafter, on October 11, 1919, she left home. For a period of about ten years thereafter she did not return home but saw her father occasionally.

Claimant's sister testified in her behalf and stated that, from the date of her marriage in 1911, until 1930, she resided at Chicago, and only returned to Kansas City occasionally for visits to her sister and her father and mother; that their parents lived at 2510 Indiana, in Kansas City, where claimant and witness grew up; that she visited here in April, 1921, and was in the Thomson home; that claimant was living there at that time and was employed as house-keeper; that claimant was then the legal wife of one Fred C. Edelen, who was living but was a mental case; that she requested claimant to move to and live in their father's home because their mother was ill; that deceased said: "Well, this will be her home some day," and that witness answered; "It isn't now because she has a living husband"; that claimant's name at that time was Edelen. The witness further testified that she returned to Chicago; that Fred C. Edelen committed suicide in May, 1921; that witness returned to Kansas City, on a visit, at about Christmas time, 1921; that she visited in the Thomson home and, while there at dinner with deceased and claimant, deceased said to her: "Well, kid, I finally got her to marry me"; that deceased talked with her several times about being married to claimant; that she told him that her wedding anniversary was August 7th, and deceased said: "Well, kid, I got you beat. My first anniversary was 8th of August, and I had another one, that is where I have got it over you, I was married in October, too." She stated that deceased and claimant accompanied witness and her husband on recreational trips out to parties and banquets almost weekly over a period of years and deceased always introduced claimant, and referred to her, as his wife and that she was so accepted and known among their friends and acquaintances; and that deceased and claimant were generally reputed to be husband and wife in the community in which they lived. She also testified that deceased and claimant made a number of trips to Canada to visit deceased's relatives and that she received mail from them while they were on such trips. She identified an envelope and letter which was addressed to claimant, and also a postal card addressed to her from Canada, as being in the handwriting of and signed by deceased. Said letter and card were placed in evidence and the letter closed as follows: "Your loving husband, Peter." The envelope was addressed to "Mrs. Peter Thomson, 1239 Ewing Ave., K. C. Mo." The postal card was signed "Your loving husband, Peter."

* * *

John B. Gage, mayor of Kansas City, testified to the effect that, as an attorney, deceased consulted him about preparation of a will for him; that he prepared a typewritten draft of such a will for deceased and at his request, which draft was offered in evidence and was identified as being the one prepared by witness. It bore date of 1938, but was never executed and was delivered by Mr. Gage, together with other papers belonging to deceased, to the administrator after death of Thomson. In the draft of the alleged will, which was in evidence, deceased's home at 1239 Ewing Avenue, Kansas City, was bequeathed to "my beloved wife, Martha S. Thomson," and provison for payment of certain trust funds was therein made "to my wife, Martha S. Thomson." It was further provided therein that such bequests were to be in lieu of "all dower and marital rights she may have in my estate."

J. Francis O'Sullivan, a lawyer, testified that he lived for many years in the general vicinity of the Thomson home and that he had been employed by deceased to represent him as an attorney on different cases; that deceased introduced claimant to him as "Mrs. Thomson" and that the Thomsons were generally reputed to be husand and wife, in the neighborhood where they resided.

R. L. Dominick, vice-president of the Gate City National Bank, testified that deceased transacted business with the above mentioned bank, through the witness, for about 25 years; that claimant was introduced to him by deceased as "his wife"; that she had accompanied deceased to the bank and that she and deceased had executed deeds of trust, on real estate owned by deceased, as husband and wife; and he identified one such instrument which was executed by deceased and claimant, to the bank, in 1937, and which was signed by deceased and claimant, in witness' presence, as husband and wife, and was so acknowledged before a notary public who fully corroborated the testimony of Mr. Dominick. Mr. Dominick also identified one other such deed of trust, signed and acknowledged by deceased and claimant as husband and wife, which instrument was so executed in the presence of witness.

Mr. Hensley, vice-president of the Produce Exchange Bank, testified that he was formerly employed by the Gate City National Bank and, as notary public, took the acknowledgment of deceased and claimant, as husband and wife, to deeds of trust executed by them. He corroborated much of the testimony of Mr. Dominick.

Certain deed record books were identified and introduced in evidence. They disclosed that deceased and claimant had executed a number of deeds of trust on real estate, and had therein acknowledged themselves, under oath, to be husband and wife. One deed of trust, dated September 10, 1919, was signed by deceased and he acknowledged himself, under oath, to be single and unmarried. In a deed of trust dated November 24, 1923, deceased and claimant signed and acknowledged same as husband and wife, as they did in various others shown to have been executed in 1924, 1927, and 1937. All such instruments which were in evidence, and which bore date prior to 1921, were signed and acknowledged by deceased as a single person.

Dr. Fricke testified that he was the family physician of the Thomsons from 1937 until the death of deceased; that deceased introduced claimant to him in his office as his wife; that he treated claimant in the Thomson home; that he knew her as Mrs. Thomson; and that deceased and claimant were generally reputed to be husband and wife in the neighborhood where they resided.

Claimant was not permitted to testify in her own behalf, on objection as to any matter which occurred prior to issuance of the letters of administration.

On behalf of defendants Earl Thomson testified that his father "Asked me if I cared if he got married, I told him: 'No,' I says 'You didn't say anything when I told you I was going to get married. You told me I was twenty-one years old' * * * In 1921, just before I got married, * * * I was married October 19, 1921." He testified that his father never told him that he was married; that, in 1921, when Earl introduced his sister's brother-in-law to claimant, she said: "I beg your pardon, but it is Mrs. Thomson," that his father was in the house at the time but did not hear the conversation.

Grace Richardson testified that her father never told her he was married to claimant and that the people in the neighborhood did not believe they were married. She also gave testimony to the effect that while she and her father were visiting in the home of her father's sister in Canada the latter urged her to go home to her father's house; that the sister told deceased that, since he was married, claimant should invite witness to their home, and that deceased became angry, shook his cane at his sister and told her he would invite whom he pleased to live in his home.

Other witnesses testified to the effect that neighbors of the Thomsons questioned the fact of their marriage and denied that deceased had, to their knowledge or in their presence, introduced claimant as his wife, or had held her out as such. There was evidence which tended to prove that the marriage records of Jackson, Cass, and Lafayette counties contain no reference to a license having been issued for the marriage of claimant and deceased. No marriage license was offered in evidence and no witness testified regarding issuance of any; nor was there any evidence regarding the performance of any marriage ceremony.

It is claimant's contention that the evidence herein is sufficient to prove that deceased and claimant were married; and that the countervailing evidence was insufficient to overcome, or to seriously challenge such fact, so that the proof of marriage becomes conclusive.

Defendants contend that, at most, the evidence tended to establish a common law marriage and that common law marriages were outlawed by statute enacted in 1921, which statute became effective prior to the death of claimant's husband, Edelen, in May, 1921. * * * Therefore, if claimant's case rests on a common law marriage she may not prevail because until after March 31, 1921, she had a legal husband living and, hence, could not have entered into a valid common law marriage with deceased prior to that date.

Claimant did not attempt to prove by direct or by record evidence that a statutory marriage was entered into between herself and deceased. She contends that her evidence was sufficient to give rise to the presumption that she and deceased were married; that there was insufficient contradictory evidence to overcome said presumption; that said presumption became final; and that, since they were married, it is presumed that said marriage was legal according to the requirements of the laws of Missouri. Her position is that the same quantum and quality of evidence which proves a marriage, under the rule pertaining to presumption, proves a legal marriage, whatever may be the requirements of the law regulating marriages.

There is strong evidence tending to prove the fact that Thomson and claimant conducted themselves as husband and wife, that they so cohabited, and that the local repute was that they were married.

* * *

"Independent of any direct or documentary evidence, a marriage may be circumstantially established by the fact that a man and woman have for a considerable period of time openly cohabited as husband and wife and recognized and treated each other as such, so that they are generally reputed to be married among those who have come in contact with them. Such circumstances justify a finding that at the commencement of the cohabitation the parties actually entered into a marriage; * * *" 38 C.J. page 1337.

* * *

"If a marriage in fact is established by evidence or admission, it is presumed to be regular and valid, and the burden of adducing evidence to the contrary rests on the party who attacks it, even though it involves the proving of a negative." 38 C.J. 1325, 1326.

"* * * where man and woman are living together as husband and wife, marriage should always be presumed. * * * A marriage which is once shown is presumed to have been in compliance with legal requirements as to its celebration." 35 AM. JUR. pages 303, 305.

There is strong circumstanial evidence tending to prove the marriage of claimant and deceased; and there is no substantial evidence, circumstantial or otherwise, tending to contradict the positive evidence of marriage. The fact that the records of Cass, Lafayette and Jackson counties failed to disclose the issuance of a license is wholly insufficient to overcome the proof of marriage here established by circumstantial evidence. [Citation omitted.]

* * * Our statutes on marriage provide the procedure to be followed in order that a legal marriage may be entered into; but they do not provide that legal marriages can only be proved by offering evidence tending to establish the fact that such statutory steps were taken. Marriage statutes, such as ours, are intended to prescribe the manner by which legal marriages may be contracted; but they do not prescribe a rule of evidence by which marriages may be proved. [Citation omitted.]

* * *

It would be most unwise to hold that a marriage cannot be proved except by the introduction of evidence tending to prove issuance of a license and performance of a ceremony. To so hold would be to render it utterly impossible for many couples who were so married to prove the legality of their relationship and the legitimacy of their children. All history teaches us that there is no permanency in the preservation of written records; and the present day bombing and total destruction of entire cities and towns, accompanied by the almost total extinction of the population of such places and the forced migration and dispersal of the survivors, constitute a cogent argument in support of the wisdom of the ancient rules of evidence which permit proof of marriage by evidence other than that of issuance of a license and proof of performance of a ceremony. Upon such proof, in that manner, of the fact of marriage, it follows that the presumption of legality must follow as a rule of necessity.

* * *

The judgment is affirmed.

Religious and Ethnic Factors

Parkinson v. J. & S. Tool Company

Supreme Court of New Jersey

64 N.J. 159, 313 A.2d 609 (1974)

PASHMAN, J.

This is an appeal by Ruth Parkinson from a judgment of the Appellate Division which affirmed a denial of dependency benefits by the Judge of Compensation. Appellant, though not legally married, was living as husband and wife with decedent Richard Parkinson, who, it is conceded, died from an accident arising out of and in the course of his employment. [Citation omitted.]

The sole issue is whether claimant is a "dependent" within the terms of N.J.S.A. 34:15–13(f) according to guidelines we enunciated in *Dawson v. Hatfield Wire & Cable Co.*, 59 N.J. 190, 280 A.2d 173 (1971).

Ruth and Richard Parkinson, lifelong Roman Catholics, were legally married before a Roman Catholic priest in 1927. Two children were born of this marriage which terminated in 1939 when Ruth obtained a divorce decree in the New Jersey courts. Richard thereupon left the state but returned in 1950 to resume life with Ruth and their children. Prior to doing so, and as a step toward remarriage, the couple visited the pastor of their local church, informed him of the divorce and requested that he remarry them. Consent to remarriage was withheld. The priest explained that they were "already married in the eyes of God." The couple accepted the priest's explanation, assumed they were married and resumed cohabitation. No civil ceremony followed.

Appellant testified that she understood the nature of her divorced status under the law, that she was no longer legally married. In the eyes of the Catholic Church, however, a religious ceremony lasts until death; only ecclesiastical authority can dissolve or annul the marriage. Monsignor Smith, an ecclesiastical attorney and expert on canon law, testified that the advice offered by the pastor, since deceased, would be the church's teaching as regards marriage. People reconciled after a divorce and returning to the same authority which married them initially is such an uncommon occurrence that most priests, even those more steeped in canon and civil law, are unqualified to grapple with its legal disposition. Since there is no canon covering these facts, even when proper advice is afforded, no new marriage occurs. On cross-examination, the Monsignor offered what would be his advice to such a couple: a "renewal of consent," *i.e.*, an expression of matrimonial consent by recalling their original marriage vows, coupled with obtaining a new marriage license. In the eyes of the church, it is not a new marriage, but merely a repetition of what already has occurred. It would suffice however for the civil authorities.

The Judge of Compensation found, however, that while the couple had remained married in the eyes of God, and recognized as a marital entity by the public, the civil authority, by virtue of the divorce, did not accept the remarriage. Accordingly, under strict statutory law, Ruth Parkinson did not qualify as a dependent for workmen's compensation benefits. The Appellate Division agreed and rejected appellant's contention that she qualifies as a *de facto* wife under *Dawson, supra.* For reasons hereinafter stated, we reverse, and remand to the Division of Workmen's Compensation for an award of death benefits.

The relevant Workmen's Compensation statute, N.J.S.A. 34:15-13(f) provides in part:

> "The term 'dependents' shall apply to and include any or all of the following who are dependent upon the deceased at the time of accident or the occurrence of occupational disease, or at the time of death, namely: * * * wife * * *."

Appellant concedes that she is not a lawful *de jure* widow, but respectfully urges that we accept her claim as a *de facto* widow, and therefore should be entitled to benefits under the reasoning we have set forth in *Dawson.* In that case, Mamie Dawson, legally married to decedent Charles Dawson in 1949, brought a dependency claim following his fatal work-connected injury. At the Compensation hearing, employer challenged Mamie's rights to dependency benefits, attacked her marriage as meretricious, and offered that decedent had previously been married in 1942, had fathered two children and had never secured a divorce. Dependency benefits were denied. The lower courts reasoned that a knowingly meretricious relationship is generally sufficient to defeat recovery. Justice Mountain, for the majority, fashioned an equitable result and reversed. He pointed out that the claimant entered her relationship in complete good faith, with no suspicion, let alone knowledge, of decedent's prior marriage. The couple had lived together in an open and unchallenged relationship as man and wife until decedent's death. The evidence was uncontradicted that Mamie Dawson had been dependent on decedent. It was only after the latter's death that employer challenged this relationship, and then only to be relieved of its dollar liability. We there concluded that the terms "wife" and "widow" as used in the statute include *de facto* widows where good faith coalesces with "* * * a *de facto* relationship of man and wife continuing unbroken over an extended period of years having had its genesis in a ceremonial marriage * * *." 59 N.J. 196, 280 A.2d 176.

The Appellate Division refused to apply the *Dawson* rationale because Ruth and Richard Parkinson lacked the "ceremonial" requisite. Justice Mountain stated in *Dawson*:

> "* * * We deem it significant that petitioner and decedent entered upon a ceremonial marriage, carrying with it, as all ceremonial marriages do in varying degree, elements of solemnity, publicity and prior deliberation not characteristic of a common law union."

Id. at 196, 280 A.2d at 176.

Employer maintains that without the ceremonial marriage, *Dawson* is inapplicable, for otherwise the Court would be creating a paradox. It would allow claimant to use the legal system when it suits her—to secure a divorce and obtain compensation benefits—but to ignore it for purposes of the ceremonial marriage requirement. To employer, this would flout the fairness and equality of our system of laws.

We disagree. This position misreads both the underlying rationale of the marriage ceremony and the equitable policies we postulated in *Dawson*.

Solemnity, publicity, and deliberation distinguish a legitimate marriage ceremony from an illegitimate common law union. Inherent in the common law marriage are a non-recognition of the legal process, and a lack of commitment which often gives rise to an impermanent and ephemeral arrangement, such that economic support, let alone dependency, may be withheld randomly. The union, which in the eyes of the public remains an uncertainty, may dissolve at any time. Such a couple may not both use an identical surname, file joint tax returns, or be deemed an entity for census-taking, welfare or social security eligibility. Oftentimes while they both may reside at one address, only one name may appear, and the other party may have legal residence elsewhere. Children of such union, moreover, might be deprived of parental guidance since they may never be certain who are their real parents. The Legislature and this Court have both declared that common law marriages are prohibited. N.J.S.A. 37:1-10;[2] [other citations omitted].

A different drama unfolds in the situation before us. Prior to resuming cohabitation in 1950, Ruth and Richard Parkinson, after some deliberation, visited a priest, expecting to arrange for a second church wedding. They had initiated the nuptial process with such a visit once before in 1927. As lifelong Roman Catholics, they were sensitively aware of this requirement. With but a limited sixth-grade parochial school education, however, Ruth was somewhat unsophisticated in understanding the interrelationship between the dual civil and religious mantles cloaking the priest. She had sufficient knowledge that the first ceremony performed by the priest was legally sanctioned. She had little reason to believe differently this time when informed that her marriage was still recognized "in the eyes of God." Words to this effect were expressed in the earlier marriage. Having been uttered by one legally considered an authoritative voice, Ruth and Richard accepted without question its plain and purported meaning. To all parties concerned, it was tantamount in both tenor and spirit to a veritable ceremony. Hence a re-affirmance of the earlier marriage was effectuated.

It has been contended that Ruth was opportune in utilizing the legal system. When she secured the divorce, she showed no hesitation in going to the courts; when she sought to remarry, she ignored the civil authorities. Such reasoning might be relevant if Ruth's legal status were at issue. But it is the "good faith wife" that concerns the Court. And nowhere has it been implied that petitioner lacked the reasonable and sincere belief in fulfilling this role, nor been suggested that she disregarded the duties and responsibilities of the marital institution.

Dawson speaks of good faith where the spouse thinks she is a wife, fulfills the role of a wife, is treated by the decedent as a wife, and is the dependent widow whom the Legislature seeks to aid. Her needs have been the same, and have arisen in the same way, as if the divorce had never occurred, and as if the priest had married them *de novo*. It is understandable that given Ruth Parkinson's limited sixth-grade education, she acted no differently than any one else in her position. When she wanted a divorce, she went to see a lawyer; when she wanted to get married, she went to see a priest. What could be more logical to a simple person with an inveterate

---

[2]This statute says in part:
"All common law marriages entered into after December 1, 1939 are invalid * * * and failure in any case to comply with both prerequisites (license and marriage performed by one authorized to solemnize marriages) which shall always be construed as mandatory and not merely directory, shall render the purported marriage absolutely void."

Roman Catholic background? We do not question that for Ruth and Richard to be legally man and wife she would have had to comply with our marriage statute. That is not subject to argument. But she does not claim to have been a legal wife, rather a *de facto* one. Ruth Parkinson fulfills the good faith condition of the *de facto* spouse we have set forth in *Dawson*.

* * *

Ruth and Richard Parkinson withheld nothing from each other. No concealed impediments nor factors known to either party challenged otherwise legitimate aspects of the marriage. It was the priest, a third party, whose misguided decision proved inaccurate. Yet this marriage is devoid of any putative characteristics. Therefore, both Ruth and Richard had the *bona fides*, if not the strict legal requirement; in *Dawson*, only the widow-claimant acted *bona fide*. Lack of strict legal requirements was not the fault of Ruth Parkinson. To deny her benefits for the unintentional mistake of another is seriously to penalize her for a wrong she did not wilfully commit. This is the very antithesis of the beneficent purposes for which our compensation statute speaks. We pointed out in *Dawson*:

> "Workmen's Compensation legislation seeks to place upon industry the burden of bearing the loss inevitably resulting from accidents arising out of the business employment relationship * * * [when] such loss is occasioned by the work-connected death of an employee upon whom a wife—*or one living in such a relationship*—has been economically dependent. * * * The test of the relationship of husband and wife should not be quite the same in the context of this type of law, designed to supply a social need and to remedy a social evil, as in the area of familial law where questions of property, inheritance, legitimacy of offspring and the like rightly demand a more rigid adherence to conventional doctrine." (Emphasis added).

59 N.J. at 196–197, 280 A.2d at 176.

* * *

Our equitable and humanitarian approach is predicted on a sensitive but frank awareness of the failings of the human being. By such a recognition we are insuring to the greatest extent possible the fulfillment of the high purposes of our socially important and ever broadening compensation act.

Reversed.

CLIFFORD, J. (dissenting).

* * *

The majority agrees that for petitioner and decedent to have "legally" been man and wife, they would have had to comply with the marriage statute. The language of that statute is "broad and sweeping" and its terms are "unusually peremptory," *Decunzo V. Edgye*, 19 N.J. 443, 450, 117 A.2d 508 (1955). However, the Court puts aside the legal requirements for the relationship of "wife" as one of those dependent upon the deceased workman at the time of the accident, N.J.S.A. 34:15–13(f), and again bestows its judicial blessing upon a *de facto* relationship on the authority of *Dawson v. Hatfield Wire & Cable Co.*, 59 N.J. 190, 280 A.2d 173 (1971).

I find no authority prior to *Dawson* for carving out a *de facto* marriage relationship for the singular purpose of creating a status entitling one to dependency benefits. Chief Justice Weintraub pointed out in his concurring opinion in *Dawson* that when the compensation statute speaks of a "wife," he assumed "for present purposes that a *de jure* wife was intended," 59 N.J. at 198, 280 A.2d at 177, but he was of the view that the employer lacked the necessary standing to challenge the validity of the ceremonial marriage in that case. Justice Francis, concurring and dissenting in part, likewise saw the doctrine of a *de facto* wife being accorded the status of a lawful wife for purposes of workmen's compensation as "contrary to the intention of the

Legislature and the express language of the Workmen's Compensation Act,'' 59 N.J. at 200, 280 A.2d at 178. He said:

> "Thus there comes into existence a *quasi*-marital status which was hitherto unknown to, and in fact contrary to, the law of our State, and which is to be employed in the administration of death benefits under the Workmen's Compensation Act. As I see the legislative intention under that act and under the public policy revealed by our marriage laws, a woman is either a legal wife or she is not a wife. Unless the parties are competent to marry and actually comply with the statutory ceremonial prerequisites, they do not become husband and wife regardless of the good faith attending their assumption of the relationship. To illustrate, no matter how fervently and sincerely a man and a woman agree to become husband and wife and to live together as such, in New Jersey they never acquire that status legally regardless of the length of time they live together. The Legislature has condemned common law marriage as 'absolutely void.' ''

N.J.S.A. 37:1-10.

I agree with this perception of the legislative intention under the Workmen's Compensation Act.* It thus leads me to conclude that petitioner has failed to establish that she was the lawful wife of decedent. I therefore reach the same result as did the Judge of Compensation and the Appellate Division and would deny dependency benefits under N.J.S.A. 34:15-13.

---

*I should add that I also find Justice Francis's analysis and reasoning in *Dawson* compelling and would have been drawn to the same conclusion as he and on the same basis—that is, the strong presumption of validity of the second ceremonial marriage fortified by a presumption that the first marriage was terminated by divorce.

Prefatory Remarks to Walker v. Matthews

The style and tone of this 1941 opinion of the Supreme Court of Mississippi belong to a bygone era. Today the seemingly benevolent account of the decedent's life is justly felt to be unbearably patronizing and demeaning to blacks. The first sentence of the opinion characterizes the decedent as a "negro" and thereby implies that the following facts have something to do with his race. This impression is reinforced by reference to the other participants by first name if they are black and by prefix "Mr." or "Mrs." if they are white. The judicial sense of humor appears to be misplaced and strained.

A comparison of *Walker* with *Campbell v. Christian* (pp. 119-122), a 1959 opinion of the Supreme Court of South Carolina demonstrates that, whatever the behavior pattern involved, it may be influenced by factors other than race, for example, economic matters. *Campbell* does not mention race; but had the parties been black, according to then prevailing judicial custom in the South, it probably would have been stated. Many other cases in this chapter, although their language is more circumspect than the style in *Walker*, indicate the potential weight given to ethnic factors; see, for example, *Sousa v. Freitas* (pp. 150-153; Portuguese immigrant) and *Omer v. Omer* (pp.

215–218; Israeli immigrants). *Tyranski v. Piggins* (pp. 218–220) involves the separate families of a teamster and in this respect resembles the facts in *Walker*.

In spite of its objectionable language, *Walker* is a case of continued importance. Perhaps no other case demonstrates as clearly the relationship between common law marriage and marriage by presumption. In the last analysis, the outcome of the case seems to be unaffected by the race of the participants. Perhaps because all of them were black, their relationships were judicially examined with some level of neutrality, albeit in a style that today is offensive.

Reference

Bell, *Racism in American Courts: Cause for Black Disruption or Despair?*, 61 CALIF. L. REV. 165 (1973).

Walker v. Matthews

Supreme Court of Mississippi

191 Miss. 489, 3 So.2d 820 (1941)

ROBERDS, Justice.

On the night of August 19, 1940, George Matthews, a negro, some seventy years of age, died, intestate, at his home five miles northwest of Meridian in Lauderdale County, Mississippi, where he lived alone. He had some ten thousand dollars in cash, other personal property of small value, and his home, consisting of eighty acres of land.

Immediately there was a scramble for his property. Mack Walker and Harriett Davis, claiming to be second cousins and heirs at law of Matthews, filed a petition in the chancery court of Lauderdale County under sections 359 and 360 of the Code of 1930 to have determined who were his legal heirs. They made parties to this petition a number of persons claiming to be collateral heirs of decedent and also one Mattie Tate Matthews and one Fannie, or Tiney, Collins Matthews, claiming to be widows of decedent, and one Will Matthews, son of Fannie Matthews, claiming to be the lawful son and heir of George Matthews.

The chancellor on the hearing limited the evidence and trial to the questions (1) whether either Mattie or Fannie was the lawful widow of decedent, and, if either, which one, and (2) if Fannie were such widow, whether her son, Will, or Pippen-Cat, as he was usually called, was the legitimate child of George Matthews and entitled to inherit his estate along with his mother Fannie; for if there is a widow or a child entitled to inherit, the collateral heirs are excluded.

After an extended trial, lasting some four days, the chancellor found that Fannie was the common law wife of George Matthews and Will was his legitimate son and that they, Fannie and Will, were his only heirs at law. From that finding and decree this appeal is taken.

The questions, therefore, for decision on this appeal are (1) whether Mattie or Fannie or either is the lawful widow of George Matthews, and, if either, which, and (2) if either is his widow, whether such widow is entitled to inherit his property, and (3) whether Will is his legitimate son and entitled to share in such inheritance.

We will try to weave into the warp of the life of this Lothario the woof of his nuptial and concubinage experiences in an effort to picture the fabric of his earthly existence. He appears to have about lived to the limit of his physical and mental powers. He was a fireman on a railroad, and, like the sailor with a sweetheart in every port, it was his desire to have one at each depot along his route. As he neared the end of life's run we find him returning to the old home, and, as his engine was pulling into the terminal and its fires were burning low, sitting on his front porch, murmuring over and trying to read his Bible. That night the fires went out.

In 1898 he was a young man, living on this same farm with his mother, his father being dead. Already he was the father of an illegitimate child, and, wonder of wonders, the mother of this child, who testified on the hearing, did not claim to be his common law wife. He had already served a term in the Mississippi penitentiary.

His mother died in 1899. He went away for awhile, and when he returned he brought back a girl named Lillie Mason. Just where he met her is not shown. She was born and reared and had lived at Marion Junction, Dallas County, Alabama. He brought her either from Mobile or New Orleans, the witnesses were not sure which place he said. He said he had married her and he introduced her as his wife. He lived with her as his wife at the old home place. He held her out in the community as his wife. It is not shown whether there was a license or a marriage ceremony at any place. He would go away for short times and leave Lillie with Mr. and Mrs. Pearce, neighbors, living about 150 yards from his home. Mr. Pearce operated a store. He testified in the case. At the time of the trial he was mayor of Shuqualak, Mississippi. George told Mr. and Mrs. Pearce to take care of Lillie while he was gone and to let her have from the store what she needed and he would pay for it. This was done. Lillie worked and cooked for Mr. and Mrs. Pearce during the times George was gone and apparently some of the time when George was at home. This situation continued until 1902, when George got a job as a railroad fireman with the Southern Railway Company. His first run was from Selma, Alabama, to Rome, Georgia. Later he fired on a switch engine on the yards at Selma. Selma was a division point on the railroad. It was necessary that George live in Selma to do his railroad work. George carried Lillie to Selma in 1902 and placed her in a house "just across the railroad from the depot." Here they lived together as man and wife, holding themselves out as such, until she died in 1911. George paid all the expenses of her last illness, engaged a nurse for her and buried her at the family cemetery, "Shady Rest," at Masillon, about two miles west of Marion Junction. George and Lillie had no children. The testimony is abundant to prove all the common law elements of a common law marriage between them beginning in 1899 and continuing until the death of Lillie in 1911.

We now take up the thread of Fannie Collins. She was reared in Choctaw County, Alabama. Lauderdale County joins Clarke County, Mississippi, on the north; Choctaw County, Alabama, lies immediately to the east of Lauderdale and Clarke Counties; on the east of Choctaw County is Maringo County and on the east of Maringo is Dallas County. Therefore, Choctaw County is between Selma and Meridian. George appears to have met Fannie at Christmas 1902 and Fannie's pleadings say she and George began to live together about January, 1903. There is proof to the effect that George and Fannie then lived together for awhile at Marion Junction, which is twelve miles west of Selma. This was a junction point on the railroad; the trains operated over a "Y" to change their courses to Akron, Meridian and Mobile. Some of the train crews had a meal there; the trains remained there from ten to thirty minutes. It is claimed for Fannie that she and George lived at Marion Junction as man and wife until their son Will was born, October 16, 1903, and there is proof to that effect, although it is far from satisfactory. Fannie then claims, and there is proof to sustain the claim, that she and

George went through a ceremonial licensed marriage on April 1, 1904, at the house of her grandmother, Martha Pressley, four miles west of Enterprise, Clarke County. Will was left at Martha's and Fannie and George went back to Marion Junction and continued to live there as man and wife, according to Fannie's proof, until around the first of 1905, when Fannie left George and went back to her mother's in Choctaw County. At any rate, on March 11, 1905, about eleven months after she claims to have married George, we find Fannie going through a statutory, licensed, ceremonial marriage at Butler, county site of Choctaw County, Alabama, with one George Jones, sometimes called Seale or Brewster. In this license she is designated Tiney Collins. Tiney and Jones lived together as man and wife in the neighborhood where they were married until the fall of 1911, when Fannie left Jones and went to Quitman, Clarke County, Mississippi. Some of the witnesses say she went with a man named Brown. She appears to have worked at Quitman for a short time at a hotel, when she went to Louisiana, in which state she seems to have since resided and in which she lived at the time of the trial. Tiney and Jones had at least two, and maybe, three, children. It is claimed Will, or Pippen Cat, was their child. Later, after going to Louisiana, Fannie went by the name of Munday and at the time of the trial was known as Marsh. In 1912 Jones was killed near Butler, Alabama.

We go back now and take up another thread. During the last illness of Lillie in 1911 George had procured a nurse for her whose name was Mattie Tate. She lived at Selma and was around 16 years old, about George's favorite age. Shortly after the death of Lillie and in 1912 George brought Mattie to Meridian, and there at Black's Hotel, operated by a negro, he went through a marriage ceremony with Mattie. The record is not specific whether it is claimed a license had been issued, but none is shown to have been issued, although witnesses detail the wedding ceremony. About this time George was transferred from Selma to Mobile, where he fired on a switch engine until he retired on a railroad pension around 1938. He carried Mattie to Mobile and there they lived as man and wife, the exact time not being shown, perhaps from three to five years. Anyway, during that time, whatever its duration, they lived in the same house, held themselves out as man and wife and were known to the public as man and wife.

Sometime later, apparently during the period from 1914 to 1917, the time not being definitely shown, Mattie left George and returned to her old home at Selma, where she had continued to live to the time of the trial. On April 12, 1937, she married one Josh Minter in Dallas County, Alabama, under a statutory license, the application for which, made by Minter, said it was his second and Mattie's first marriage, and gave her name as Mattie Tate. She has two living children by Minter and at the time of the trial they were living together as man and wife at Selma. George and Mattie had no children.

Mattie's departure did not seem to greatly disturb George. We find him next at Hot Springs, Arkansas, at the boarding house of one Susie Cole. He proceeded to marry the landlady's daughter, Jessie. This was a licensed, statutory marriage; it took place in Garland County, Arkansas, May 17, 1921. George, in some of his later conversations, intimated he did not marry Jessie; she married him. He said "she pulled down the shades and called the officers." Anyway, they were married and George until the day of his death recognized Jessie thereafter as his lawful wife. All of his railroad passes were issued to him and Jessie as his wife, even up to the last year of his life, although Jessie died September 13, 1927. In his application for railroad retirement pension October 29, 1937, he referred to Jessie as his wife.

Jessie did not like Mobile. She would go there about twice a year and remain with George a week or two. George did not appear to encourage these visits, because, as he said, each time she came it cost him $100. In fact, George gave evidence of his feelings towards his marriages, by saying to witnesses that his first marriage to Lillie cost him $2.50; his second to Mattie $5; and his third to Jessie $500. At this ratio George could not have married many more times. George and Jessie had no children.

So far as the record shows, this ends his matrimonial adventures, although after he came back to the old home on his retirement he did approach a lady friend of long ago with the suggestion he had plenty with which to take care of her if she cared to come and live with him. She did not accept.

We shall now undertake to unravel this tangled skein, apply the rules of law and presumptions and determine the rights of the parties.

And the first knot is that of Lillie and Fannie, and we find and hold that Lillie was the wife of George Matthews before and during the time of his relations with Fannie, and, being the husband of Lillie, he could not and never did become the legal husband of Fannie. We reach this conclusion through these processes:

1. George brought Lillie from another state. They said they were married. He introduced her as his wife and he lived with her as such. There is no other proof as to whether there was, or was not, a statutory or common law marriage in the other state. In the absence of all proof to the contrary we must presume they had legally become man and wife in the other state. * * * A contrary rule would be dangerous to society. A man goes away to another state for a time; he returns with a woman and they announce they have married; they live together as man and wife; they hold themselves out in the community as man and wife; this situation continues for thirteen years and until the death of the woman. What shall the law presume, in the absence of proof to the contrary? That they are living in a lawful or a criminal state? As was said in *Travers v. Reinhardt*, 205 U.S. 423, 27 S.Ct. 563, 567, 51 L.Ed. 865, "The law has wisely provided that marriage may be proved by general reputation, cohabitation, and acknowledgment; when these exist, it will be inferred that a religious ceremony has taken place; and this proof will not be invalidated because evidence cannot be obtained of the time, place, and manner of the celebration of the marriage. * * *"

2. The testimony is abundant to show all the elements of fact of a common law marriage between George and Lillie from 1899 to her death in 1911. The Chancellor stated his findings in these words:

> "It is also in evidence that in 1899 George, who had been away from his home west of Meridian for some months, came back home with a woman named Lillie, and that he told people that she was his wife, and lived with her as such. There is no proof they were ever ceremonially married, or that they were ever married in any way anywhere, but he told people around there that she was his wife. This woman stayed around there sometime; George would go away and be gone two or three months and come back, then he would stay with her awhile and leave again. That kept up until 1902 when George went to Selma and got a job as fireman on the locomotive of the Southern Railway, when he took Lillie and installed her in a house right across from the depot in Selma, and that he continued to live with her there until she died in 1911."

We construe the evidence as establishing such facts much more strongly than did the Chancellor. It is true that common law marriages were not recognized in Mississippi from 1892 to 1906, *(Olivari v. Clark*, 175 Miss. 883, 168 So. 465), but they were recognized in Alabama during the time George and Lillie lived together in that state. *White v. Hill*, 176 Ala. 480, 58 So. 444. The lower court attached much importance to the idea that the relation being unlawful in Mississippi it is presumed to have continued in that status in Alabama. The proof disproves the presumption. The only reason the relation was unlawful in Mississippi was because the law did not recognize common law marriages, not because the elements thereof were not shown as facts.

But the same facts were shown to exist after they went to Alabama and until the death of Lillie and common law marriages were there recognized. * * * Under the proof in this record George and Lillie became common law man and wife in Alabama and under the law of comity it will be recognized here. DIVORCE AND SEPARATION IN MISSISSIPPI by Amis, p. 24, §10, citing *Carroll v. Renich*, 7 Smedes & M. 798, 26 Cyc. 829 to 831.

This status existed before and when George met Fannie; therefore, Fannie could not have become his wife. This makes it unnecessary for us to decide whether the facts disclosed by this record are sufficient to constitute George and Fannie common law husband and wife had there been no legal impediment to such status. It is also unnecessary for us to say what effect her statutory licensed marriage to George Jones in March, 1905, had upon her right to inherit the property of George Matthews.

It also follows from the foregoing that Will, or Pippen Cat, is not the legitimate son of George Matthews, if, in fact, he is his son at all. The great weight of the evidence shows he is in fact the son of George Jones and not of George Matthews, but it is not necessary for us to say whether we would reverse the finding of the chancellor on that question. It, therefore, follows that Will is not an heir at law of George Matthews.

We come now to the rights of Mattie. George went through a ceremony of marriage with her in Meridian, Mississippi, in 1912. It is not clear whether it is claimed there was a license. No license is shown to have issued and the witnesses do not undertake to say whether the preacher had a license at the time of the ceremony. Apparently he did not have such license. However, the ceremony was public evidence of their intention to assume the status of man and wife. There was no impediment and common law marriages were then recognized in this state. They moved to Alabama and lived together as man and wife for some time, the exact time not being shown, but the evidence is sufficient to establish a common law marriage. However, Mattie is not entitled to inherit from George for these reasons:

1. After their separation both George and Mattie went through statutory marriages, under regular licenses, and each thereafter recognized these marriages as valid and lawful, George with Jessie Cole until his death and Mattie with Josh Minter to the time of the trial, and, presumably, at this time, Mattie and Josh having at the time of the trial two living children. In Mississippi, and most of the states, the fact of a subsequent marriage is of itself sufficient to raise a presumption that a former marriage has been terminated by a decree of divorce, in the absence of proof to the contrary. The presumption may be rebutted by proof but there is no proof here to rebut it. The proof could have been made, since George and Mattie, after their separation, have lived only in Mobile and Dallas Counties, Alabama, and George in Lauderdale County, Mississippi, for about a year and a half before his death.
* * *

2. Another question which arises is whether Mattie is now estopped to claim she is the lawful wife of George and lay claim to his property as such. She went through a statutory, licensed marriage with Josh Minter. The application for the license gave her name as Mattie Tate and stated this was her first marriage. She is now living with him as man and wife at Selma and they have two children. * * * In *Joy v. Miles et al.*, 190 Miss. 255, 199 So. 771, we said:

"When the proof discloses, as it does in this case, that a wife seeking to set aside an invalid divorce decree obtained by her husband had become married to another man subsequent to the rendition of such decree, it cannot be said that she comes into a court of equity with clean hands asking for affirmative relief. Moreover, even if it be true—and the chancellor found to the contrary—that she did not know of the decree at the time of her second marriage, such want of knowledge would afford less excuse for having entered into the bigamous relationship with her second husband than if she had known of the divorce proceedings, since she did know that her former husband was still alive, and that she herself had not obtained a divorce. Nor does the fact that she did not remarry until after her former husband had married another woman, following the rendition of the divorce decree in his favor, prevent his second wife from pleading such fact in defense of a suit to set aside the decree of divorce for the sole purpose of enabling the complainant in such a suit to obtain the life insurance left by the divorced husband at the time of his death, and which was payable to his widow."

The majority rule is that desertion or abandonment is generally held to be a bar to any right to share in the estate of the deceased spouse. Annotation 71 A. L.R. p. 285.

We hold that under the facts of the case at bar and the applicable rules of law Mattie Tate (Minter) is estopped to assert heirship to the estate of George Matthews, deceased.

Reversed and remanded.

Comments

Campbell and *Walker* are based on similar factual backgrounds set in the rural Deep South. The facts are not as unusual as one might think. In searching titles and determining whether real estate is marketable, complex facts concerning multiple possible wives have to be analyzed. Had an effort been made, for example, to sell the 80 acres of farmland in *Walker*, the same kind of considerations would have been necessary. The lawyer has to delve into the past lives of people regardless of his personal moral beliefs or perhaps prejudices. Even the regional aspects of these cases are less significant than appears. The same problems arise in matters relating to inheritance or to land title in metropolitan centers. The tone of the cases is therefore not only misplaced but also misleading.

Especially if the persons in issue are no longer alive, legal presumptions become important for untangling chaotic facts from the past. The possibility of common law marriage is closely interwoven, as *Walker* illustrates, with the possibility of applying presumptions of marriage. Common law marriage continues to be a factor even in jurisdictions that have legislatively abolished it. The persons involved may have lived temporarily in other jurisdictions that still recognize common law marriage. In view of the presumption of marriage they may even be presumed to have entered a valid marriage somehow and somewhere. Since ordinarily common law marriages were not abolished retroactively, the possibility of a common law marriage in the past, when it was still legal in a specific state, may be sufficient to cloud the title of real estate today.

Since the legal requirements for common law marriage and for the presumption of marriage are identical, namely, cohabitation and repute of being married, one may wonder how effective the abolition of common law marriage is. The presumption of marriage is available in all American jurisdictions, regardless of whether or not they still recognize common law marriage. *Thomson* arose in a jurisdiction, Missouri, that has not recognized common law marriage since 1921. Nevertheless, as a result of their long-standing cohabitation, the claimant widow and the decedent were presumed to be married. Even the claimant's failure to prove her marriage by documentary evidence did not harm her presumed marital status. The outcome would have been the same had Missouri still recognized common law marriage.

The same result would also have been reached in *Walker* if none of the jurisdictions mentioned in the case had recognized common law marriage. The presumption of marriage and common law marriage are therefore interchangeable in many situations. This has to be kept in mind in jurisdictions, such as Massachusetts, that do not recognize common law marriage. There too cohabitation and repute of being married may result in legal marriage. That this result is reached by way of presumption makes little difference. In fact, there are strategic advantages in arguing presumption rather than substantive law of marriage. Presumptions are based on popular feelings and predispositions reduced to rules of evidence. They carry considerable persuasive weight with the courts. The presumption of marriage, for example, is said to be one of the strongest in law. Essentially it is based on the presumption that people do not engage in immoral or illegal behavior. To what extent this presumption corresponds to reality is another question. The sexual mores have substantially changed, as illustrated by *Marvin v. Marvin* (pp. 172–185), while the rules of evidence originate from another era with different customs that nevertheless are still effective in court.

Parkinson illustrates that religious factors can continue to have an impact on the contemporary secular law of marriage. Here the marriage of Roman Catholics continued to be recognized, at least for workmen's compensation purposes, although the parties had been divorced. The advice of the Catholic priest that they were still married "in the eyes of God," and consequently did not need to remarry, may appear to be shockingly irresponsible. Yet lawyers often render legal advice strictly on the basis of secular law and thereby invite misunderstanding in the parties, just as the priest in this case rendered advice strictly on the basis of church law, with serious consequences. Legal practice requires an awareness of the beliefs—whether based on religion or on popular conceptions of the law—of clients.

Parties may not only believe that they are married, they may also erroneously believe themselves to be divorced. It has, for example, occurred with some frequency that lawyers have issued a receipt reading "$50 for divorce"—meant to be a retainer for future legal action, but understood by the client to be a fee for divorce already obtained. In these instances, further prosecution of the case is then dropped because the party never reappears. In fact relying on the receipt, the party may have remarried. In other words, the possibility of error is ever present, but it can be controlled to some extent if the lawyer is aware of widespread common misunderstandings. Sometimes it is possible to cure past confusion and error with presumptions—for example, that the parties are married or that a divorce was somehow and somewhere obtained for a prior marriage. Since it is often impossible to overcome these presumptions, we really deal with legal fictions that are used to straighten out past facts. Sometimes a lenient statutory interpretation may help, as in *Parkinson*, especially in workmen's compensation cases. But had the issue been inheritance of real property, the same court might have applied a more stringent test and ruled that no marriage existed.

References

Weyrauch, *Informal and Formal Marriage—An Appraisal of Trends in Family Organization*, 28 U. CHI. L. REV. 88 (1960).
Weyrauch, *Informal Marriage and Common Law Marriage*, in SEXUAL BEHAVIOR AND THE LAW 297 (R. Slovenko ed. 1965).

Fung Dai Kim Ah Leong v. Lau Ah Leong
Circuit Court of Appeals
27 F.2d 582 (9th Cir. 1928)

DIETRICH, Circuit Judge. This is an appeal from a decree of the Supreme Court of Hawaii, affirming a dismissal by the circuit court of the appellant's bill of complaint, by which she sought to establish an interest in property held by the appellee. In the opinion below (29 Hawaii 770), may be found a comprehensive statement of the facts; for our purpose, details are unnecessary.

Both parties are of Chinese blood and nativity. In 1884 plaintiff, a girl 17 years old, came to Hawaii, where defendant was then residing, and after some negotiations a marriage was agreed upon and a wedding ceremony was held, all in accordance with Chinese customs, but without a license, as required by the laws of Hawaii. They immediately assumed, and thereafter for 35 years maintained, the relations of husband and wife. In the course of time the plaintiff bore to defendant 13 children, and, besides performing the domestic duties of a housewife, assisted him in carrying on his mercantile business. Success attended their joint efforts, with the result that at the time of the trial there was an accumulation of several hundred thousand dollars' worth of property. Following a decision of the Supreme Court of Hawaii in 1920 (*Parke v. Parke*, 25 Hawaii, 397), expressly overruling an earlier decision of that court and holding that a license was prerequisite to a valid marriage, defendant ceased to recognize plaintiff as his wife, and denied her any interest in the property accumulated during the long period they had lived together. That what was done would, in the absence of the territorial statute requiring a license, have constituted a valid common-law marriage, there can be no doubt, and that in believing they were living together in lawful wedlock they acted reasonably finds confirmation in the fact that not only was defendant advised by competent legal counsel that the marriage was valid, but such was the effect of a decision of the highest court of the territory. *Godfrey v. Rowland*, 16 Hawaii, 377.

Conceding that "there is great inherent justice in the complainant's claim," the Supreme Court was nevertheless of the opinion that the legal obstacles to its recognition are insurmountable. Under the civil law it was thought little difficulty would be encountered, but under the common law, which prevails in Hawaii, no basis for relief was found. There are but few reported decisions involving questions of the property rights of a putative wife, where for one reason or another the supposed marriage turns out to be void, but in the majority of those which have come to our attention relief of some character has been granted. [Citations omitted.]

In these cases the principles invoked are not always the same, and, it may be conceded, in finding a basis for relief, some of them have put a strain upon statutory provisions the relevancy of which is not entirely obvious. But in all of them there is evinced a purpose to prevent a result so inherently wrong as to shock our common conception of fundamental justice.

Directly to the contrary is *Schmitt v. Schneider,* 109 Ga. 628, 35 S.E. 145. This was the only decision the court below found to be in point upon that side of the question, but the following may be cited as having some bearing in defendant's favor, though in the main they have to do with questions of the availability of certain specific remedies at law. *Bell v. Bennett,* 73 Ga. 784; [other citations omitted]. *De France v. Johnson* (C.C. Minn.) 26 F. 891. In the last case, strangely enough, the principle of estoppel was recognized as having efficacy to protect the innocent mortgagee, but not the putative wife, by whom the mortgage was given, though she was equally innocent.

The conclusion of the court below is made to rest upon a statutory provision prescribing as a rule of decision the common law of England, and the assumption that, however harsh and unjust the result, the plaintiff is without remedy under that law. This statute, first enacted in 1892 (section 5, c. 47, Session Laws of 1892), and, with slight amendment, now section 1, Rev. Laws of Hawaii 1925, provides that "the common law of England, as ascertained by English and American decisions, is declared to be the common law of the territory of Hawaii in all cases, except as otherwise expressly provided by the Constitution or laws of the United States, or by the laws of the territory, or fixed by Hawaiian judicial precedent, or established by Hawaiian usage," etc.

* * *

The precise case we have here could never have arisen under the common law of England, for under that law the parties would be husband and wife. Besides, plaintiff is seeking relief in a court of equity, * * * If, then, there is "great inherent justice in plaintiff's claim," for what reason shall a court of equity, invested with this broad power, hold itself incompetent to grant her a measure of relief? The parties were qualified to contract marriage; they agreed upon it, and actually established and for 35 years maintained the marital status. The plaintiff fully performed her agreement of marriage up to the point where, because of the law as then interpreted and the acts of defendant, it became impossible for her to go further. The contract of marriage turns out to be invalid only because of a failure to comply with a formality which at the time was not thought to be requisite. Had the parties entered into an understanding by which orally the plaintiff agreed to purchase and pay for, and defendant agreed to sell, a town lot, such an agreement might be invalid under the statute of frauds, for want of the requisite writing. But if, pursuant to the agreement, plaintiff went into possession, improved the lot, and made the stipulated payments, a court of equity would afford her relief.

True, for reasons of public policy, as well as because of defendant's voluntary present disqualification, a court cannot compel performance to the extent of establishing the personal status originally contemplated; but because plaintiff is remediless in that respect, shall the court also deny her a measure of the pecuniary relief she here seeks? In decrees for separate support and maintenance, we have examples of relief respecting the economic side of the marital relation, without destroying the personal status established thereby. The common-law conception of marital unity by which the identity of the wife was merged into that of the husband has undergone a great change, in some jurisdictions recognized by statutory law, and almost universally by common understanding and assent. If we assume that, as defendant contends, under the common law, in case of a void marriage, the putative wife was without remedy, we should not feel it incumbent to extend such a rule, the reasons for which no longer exist, to a specific case like this, which could never have arisen under the common law.

In common usage, equity protects relationships and vindicates rights not recognized in a court of law, and we are of the opinion that there is here substantial ground for the exercise of its jurisdiction. It may be that plaintiff cannot refer her right to any contractual or trust relation, within the strict legal definition of these terms; but that consideration is not conclusive, for otherwise there would be no place for the growing law of quasi contracts. Technically speaking, there was no partnership, no agreement of trust to cover the plaintiff's money contribution to the business enterprise, and no contract, express or implied, for compensation for her labor and service. But there was the underlying understanding, and the expectation, that she would receive a pecuniary benefit. She looked forward to support and maintenance in the years of her declining capacity to care for herself, which now have come upon her, and in certain contingencies to alimony, or dower. Owing to a mutual mistake of both parties respecting the fact of the existence of a valid marital status, the agreement cannot be fully executed, and plaintiff's expectations cannot be fully realized. We are inclined to think that this is such a mistake as warrants the interposition of a court of equity to grant appropriate relief. POM. EQ. JURIS. (4th Ed.) vol. 11, p. 1704 *et seq.*, particularly pages 1731–1734, 1782; *Moore v. Shook,* 276 Ill. 47, 114 N.E. 592.

Quasi contractual obligations have been defined as "legal obligations arising without reference to the assent of the obligor, from the receipt of a benefit the retention of which is unjust, and requiring the obligor to make restitution." Woodward's LAW OF QUASI CONTRACTS, p. 4; Maine's ANCIENT LAW (4th Ed.) p. 344. The action upon such an obligation "lies for money paid by mistake, or upon a consideration which happens to fail, or for money got through imposition (express or implied). * * * In one word, the gist of this kind of action is that the defendant, upon the circumstances of the case, is obliged by the ties of natural justice and equity to refund the money." Woodward, *supra,* p. 4; and see, also, pages 295, 296; also *Moses v. McFarlen,* 2 Burr. 1005.

In commenting on *Cooper v. Cooper,* 147 Mass. 370, 17 N.E. 892, 9 Am. St. Rep. 721, cited *supra,* at pages 324 and 325 of KEENER ON QUASI CONTRACTS, the learned author says:

> "Had the plaintiff in this case surrendered to the defendant money or other chattels to which the defendant asserted a right because of his marital rights as husband, it does not seem possible that a court would hold that, because of the loss of the right to sue in tort by the death of the intestate, no claim could be asserted against his estate for the value so received by him. And yet in point of principle it is submitted that it is impossible to distinguish between the receipt of money or other property by the defendant and the receipt of services. The plaintiff whether she conferred a benefit on the intestate by rendering services, or by delivering to him money or other personal property, in either case parted with a right in rem under a mistaken supposition, induced by the fraud of the defendant, that the defendant was entitled thereto."

And

> "whatever power, therefore, courts of equity possess to prevent and remove the consequences of fraud, they also possess in dealing with the effects of mistake."

POM. EQ. JURIS. (4th Ed.) vol. 11, pp. 1782, 1783.

As we have seen, by express statute the courts of Hawaii are clothed with wide equity jurisdiction, and more recently the court from which comes *Cooper v. Cooper,* has said: "If our statutes had given jurisdiction of libels for nullity of marriage to courts having full equity powers, there might be some reason for holding that such courts could, as a condition of granting the relief prayed for, require that property brought by the defendant to the plaintiff should be restored to the former, or that an equitable division of any accumulated property should be made" [citations omitted].

We conclude that plaintiff is entitled to a measure of relief. Upon the question of what standard should be applied in determining the amount and character thereof, the decided cases, as already indicated, are not in harmony, and perhaps no specific general rule can be formulated. Each case must be adjudged in the light of its own peculiar facts and the local laws. Here, we think, it will be proper for the court in further proceedings to take into consideration the relative contributions of property, and of personal service in point of value, made by the two parties in the accumulation of the property standing in the defendant's name, the amount and value of such property at the time their de facto marital relations ceased, the amount of property accumulated by plaintiff during the same period and standing in her name, the local statutes affecting the marital relation and divorce, and alimony and dower, or other pecuniary interests of the wife, whether absolute or contingent, present or in expectancy.* * *

By suggesting certain considerations, it is not to be inferred that upon further proceedings they should be deemed exclusive. The fact that during the period of cohabitation between the parties hereto the defendant entered into what now turns out to be a legal marriage with another woman may have some bearing upon the question, and other material circumstances may develop at the hearing affecting the equities.

Reversed, with directions for further proceedings not inconsistent herewith.

Comments

As in *Parkinson* (pp. 126–130), *Ah Leong* shows the impact of religious and ethnic factors on adjudication. In both instances the wife thought herself to be married according to strongly held religious beliefs. No explanation is given in *Ah Leong* about the details of a customary Chinese wedding ceremony, but we may assume that religion is also involved. Either court was willing to treat the woman as having been in good faith, as a so-called "putative spouse," unaware of the legal requirements of marriage. Additional factors in *Ah Leong* were 35 years of cohabitation as husband and wife with 13 children, assistance in the successful business of the assumed "husband," and a change in judicial attitude toward informal marriage in Hawaii. Yet the true importance of the case lies in the fact that it was decided 50 years earlier than *Marvin v. Marvin* (pp. 172–185); its reasoning closely paralleled, and to some extent went beyond, this well-publicized recent California holding. *Ah Leong* is not referred to in *Marvin,* although it was also decided in California by the Ninth Circuit Court of Appeals, sitting on appeal from the territorial Supreme Court of Hawaii. Uninhibited by local Hawaiian precedent, the federal court took an independent look at what it perceived to be the common law of quasi-marital cohabitation.

The Ninth Circuit Court of Appeals in 1928 suggested remedies for claims of women after prolonged cohabitation—for example, express or implied contract for compensation of labor and services; partnership; quasi-contract; unjust enrichment; and equitable relief for lost reasonable expectations relating to support, dower, alimony, or other pecuniary interests, whether absolute or contingent, present or inchoate. As in *Marvin,* the court concluded with a broad invocation of equitable powers, stressing that each case must be judged in the light of its own peculiar facts and that the remedies suggested in the opinion should not be deemed to be exclusive. Perhaps most startling and innovative is the comparison in *Ah Leong* between marriage and real estate transactions. After implying that a de facto wife merits the same protection by estoppel theories as an innocent mortgagee, the court compared a marriage void for lack of form to an oral understanding to purchase land that might nevertheless be enforced in equity after part performance. Clearly, to paraphrase the language of the court in *Ah Leong,* the plaintiff, after 35 years of cohabitation and 13 children, should not be worse off than a grantee who "went into possession, improved the lot, and made the stipulated payments."

Workmen's Compensation

Burgess Construction Co. v. Lindley

Supreme Court of Alaska

504 P.2d 1023 (Alaska 1972)

BOOCHEVER, Justice.

This is an appeal by Burgess Construction Company and Employers Commercial Union Companies, the employer and insurance carrier for the deceased workman, from the judgment of the superior court affirming the decision of the Alaska Workmen's Compensation Board that appellee was a surviving wife entitled to compensation benefits for the death of her husband in a job-related accident.

Appellee, Jeanne L. Lindley, was legally married to deceased in 1951 and had four children. In 1967, appellee obtained a divorce from Ronald Lindley and was awarded $75 per month in alimony. Appellee never remarried between her divorce and the death of Ronald Lindley. Ronald Lindley, subsequent to his divorce from appellee, remarried twice, and was divorced from each of these subsequent wives. In 1968, Jeanne and Ronald resumed living together but never went through another formal marriage ceremony. Appellee testified at the hearing that the only reason they did not marry again was because of financial inability to go outside of Ketchikan for a ceremony and the embarrassment that a ceremony in Ketchikan would cause their children and friends who were under the impression that they had in fact remarried.

The couple lived together until the death of Ronald Lindley on December 10, 1970.

Appellants do not contest the fact of the accident or its job connection. They further concede the payment of benefits to the minor children. Their sole argument on appeal is that under AS 25.05.011[1] appellee was not legally married to deceased at the time of his death; and that therefore, appellee was not entitled to benefits under the workmen's compensation statutes as a "surviving wife."

* * *

No definition of the term "surviving wife" is provided by the workmen's compensation statute but the terms "married" and "widow" are defined by the Act. AS 23.30.265(15) provides

" 'married' includes a person who is divorced but is required by the decree of divorce to contribute to the support of his former wife; * * * AS 23.30.265(21) provides

" 'widow' includes only the decedent's wife living with or dependent for support upon him at the time of his death, or living apart for justifiable cause or by reason of his desertion at such a time; * * *"

It is clear under the statutory definition of "married" that the decedent, though divorced, was "married" for the purpose of the Workmen's Compensation Act, for the divorce decree required him to contribute to appellee's support. It follows that under the Act appellee would be regarded as his "surviving wife." She qualifies as a "widow" for she was living with decedent at the time of his death and was dependent upon him for support.[3]

Under the marital and domestic relations laws of the State of Alaska "[n]o person may be joined in marriage in this state until a license has been obtained for that purpose as provided in this chapter. No marriage performed in this state is valid without solemnization as provided in this chapter."[4] We have held that common law marriages are thus not valid in Alaska.[5] The subject case involves similar contentions to those ruled upon by the United States Court of Appeals for the Ninth Circuit in *Albina Engine & Machine Works v. O'Leary*[6] wherein the court stated:

"Neither the Oregon Workmen's Compensation Act nor the Longshoremen's and Harbor Workers' Act relate to or affect the marriage relationship as such. And the laws of the state regarding marriage are only tangentially relevant as they may bear upon the existence of the status of "wife" or "widow" for the purpose of identifying recipients of benefits under these remedial statutes.

"The application of state domestic relations law, developed in other contexts, to the solution of problems under workmen's compensation statutes, produces results which at best have only a fortuitous relation to

----

[1] AS 25.05.011 provides:
"*Civil Contract.* (a) Marriage is a civil contract requiring both a license and solemnization which may be entered into by
"(1) a male who is 19 years of age or older with a female who is 18 years of age or older, who are otherwise capable, or
"(2) those who qualify for a license under §171 of this chapter.
"(b) No person may be joined in marriage in this state until a license has been obtained for that purpose as provided in this chapter. No marriage performed in this state is valid without solemnization as provided in this chapter."

[3] The appellee, the appellants and the State of Alaska urged us to consider the equal protection argument which would result from the denial of benefits to a common law wife in such circumstances but we decline to consider this question at this time.

[4] AS 25.05.011(b).

[5] *Edwards v. Franke*, 364 P.2d 60, 63 (Alaska 1961).

[6] 328 F.2d 877, 879 (1964).

the remedial purposes of the compensation acts, and often are in direct conflict with them. When the state law does provide a definition of marital status deliberately shaped to compensation act purposes alone, there is no reason why that definition should not be applied under the federal statute in preference to one drawn from the state's general domestic relations law."

The *Albina* case is discussed in *Holland America Insurance Company v. Rogers,* 313 F.Supp. 314, 320 (N.D. Cal. 1970) as follows:

"The *Albina* case reiterates the accepted approach to dealing with problems of marital relations: that marriage is not a monolithic institution, but consists instead of separate and severable incidents. Thus where the policy of a state may preclude its courts from "recognizing," say, a marriage of one man to two women, it may be permissible for both women to recover property from his estate on his death as his "wives," for recognizing a marriage for the purposes of the one incident would not violate the state's public policy as might recognition of it for other purposes. Similarly, in the instant case, this Court need not "recognize" the marriage of Angela Spies to Julian Spies in order to find that she is nonetheless entitled to at least some of the incidents of marriage, including the right to collect death benefits under a federal workmen's compensation law upon his death."

While, for some purposes, appellee would not have been recognized by the Alaska courts as married to the decedent, appellee qualifies for benefits as a "surviving wife" under terms of the Alaska Workmen's Compensation Act discussed above. The grant of benefits by the Workmen's Compensation Board under the facts of this case is within the liberal humanitarian purposes of the Act while a different reading of the statute would clearly frustrate this purpose.

The decision of the superior court is affirmed.

[Concurring opinion omitted.]

West v. Barton-Malow Company

Supreme Court of Michigan

394 Mich. 334, 230 N.W.2d 545 (1975)

PER CURIAM.

The Appeal Board and the Court of Appeals erred in summarily relying upon *McDonald v. Kelly Coal Co.,* 335 Mich. 325, 55 N.W.2d 851 (1952) to deny plaintiff dependent's death benefits. *McDonald* is readily distinguishable from the instant case. A review of the particular facts in this case reveals that plaintiff was a dependent of the deceased within the meaning of Part II, §6 of the Workmen's Act.

On January 9, 1967, Clarence West died as a result of injuries sustained in the course of his employment with Barton-Malow Construction Company. Plaintiff, Alzalee West, made claim for dependent's death benefits under the Workmen's Compensation Act.

For the 13 years preceding the death of Clarence West he and plaintiff resided together in the City of Detroit. During this time plaintiff held herself out as the wife of West and depended on him for her sole support. From the record there is no reason to doubt that West likewise considered plaintiff to be his wife. He depended on her to manage his household affairs and shared the wages he earned with her. A legal dispute arose in this case, however, because plaintiff and West were not formally wed, plaintiff remaining legally married to another man as a result of a short-lived marriage that took place in Texas in 1943.

Without elaborating on their specific rationales, both the Appeal Board and the Court of Appeals summarily concluded that *McDonald* barred Alzalee West's claim for relief.

McDonald v. Kelly Coal Co., supra, does not control the resolution of this action. In *McDonald* the claimants were a mother and her children who had been living with Milton McDonald for less than a year at the time of his death. In construing Part II, §6, the Court offered the following:

> "We are of the opinion that in order to create a family relationship there must exist a condition devoid of moral turpitude. In the case at bar, the responsibility for the support of the two children rests upon their mother and father. Deceased had no such obligation. The tie that bound the children to deceased was the illicit relationship between their mother and deceased. Public policy does not sanction the payment of compensation arising out of meretricious cohabitation. We hold that plaintiffs were not members of deceased's family within the meaning of the Compensation Act."

335 Mich. 325, 330, 55 N.W.2d 851, 853.

The Court in *McDonald* was confronted with a relationship of short duration based on "meretricious cohabitation." In contrast, the facts of the present case reveal a long and continuing relationship with deceased and plaintiff treating each other, and holding themselves out to the public, as husband and wife. Plaintiff did secure an attorney in 1965 to commence divorce proceedings but no formal action had resulted by the date of the claim due to financial difficulties. A final judgment of divorce was obtained on June 2, 1967. If we read meretricious as the dictionary defines it—the relationship of a prostitute or a woman given to indiscriminate lewdness—we find no support whatsoever in the record for describing the relationship that existed between deceased and plaintiff as one based on meretricious cohabitation.

A proper resolution of this case demands that plaintiff's status be examined in terms of the words of, and the legislative purpose underlying, Part II, §6. In relevant part that section provides:

> "In all other cases questions of dependency, in whole or in part, shall be determined in accordance with the fact, as the fact may be at the time of the injury. Where a deceased employee leaves a person wholly dependent upon him or her for support, said person shall be entitled to the whole death benefit. * * * *No person shall be considered a dependent unless he or she is a member of the family of the deceased employee,* or unless such person bears to said deceased employee the relation of husband or widow, or lineal descendant, or ancestor, or brother or sister." (Emphasis supplied.)

From a reading of the words of the statute it is evident that the Legislature did not intend to establish a strict definition of an eligible dependent. Instead, the Legislature employed words with expansive meanings and intended, we believe, to allow the administrative agency and the courts to interpret the statute in light of the individual factual situations that would arise.

An example of this type of construction that reflects the expansive nature of the words of Part II, §6 is found in the case of *Holmberg v. Cleveland-Cliffs Iron Co.,* 219 Mich. 204, 189 N.W. 26 (1922). In *Holmberg* this Court affirmed an award of dependent death benefits ruling that Mrs. Holmberg was a "dependent member" of her cousin's "family" because her cousin had provided monetary support to Mrs. Holmberg after her husband had abandoned her. The Court wrote:

> "Was plaintiff a dependent member of Mr. Franzen's family at the time of his death? This court has had occasion, in insurance cases, to define the meaning of the term 'member of the family,' and has adopted the liberal view thereof. *Carmichael v. Benefit Ass'n*, 51 Mich. 494, 16 N.W. 871.
> "In *Hosmer v. Welch*, 107 Mich. 470, 65 N.W. 280, it was stated:
> " 'The term "family" is elastic, and will be liberally construed. It is not confined to a husband and wife and their children.' "

* * *

Turning to the facts of the case before us today, we are of the opinion that plaintiff is also an eligible dependent. Factually, plaintiff was totally dependent upon Clarence West for her support. Legally, we find that plaintiff fits within the scope of the statutory definition of an eligible dependent. She was, it is true, not legally married to deceased; however, the record indicates without contention that she did bear to Clarence West the relationship of a wife for the 13 years preceding his untimely death. During those years plaintiff was responsible for maintaining their household while deceased undertook the responsibility for furnishing them both with monetary support. In name and in outward appearance plaintiff and deceased were Mr. and Mrs. West.[3] From our reading of the record there is no evidence that would indicate that the propriety of their relationship was ever questioned by anyone except the compensation carrier herein.

In finding plaintiff to be an eligible dependent, it is not our intention to reduce by any degree the importance of the formalities surrounding marriage. Our concern rather is to effectuate the purpose of Part II, §6 of the Workmen's Compensation Act.

The Court of Appeals is reversed and this case remanded to the Workmen's Compensation Appeal Board for the entry of an order in conformity with today's opinion.

* * *

FITZGERALD, Justice (dissenting).

In this case the majority finds that a woman legally married to one man is entitled to workmen's compensation benefits attributable to the death of another man as a member of that man's "family" under M.C.L.A. §412.6; M.S.A. §17.156. We are of the opinion that the public policy of this state will not sustain such strained interpretation.

Marriage to another while a former marriage is legally valid is prohibited by M.C.L.A. §551.5; M.S.A. §25.5. Such marriages, even if solemnized, are declared to be void by M.C.L.A. §552.1; M.S.A. §25.81. Plaintiff's deceased cohabiter had no legal obligation to support plaintiff. That plaintiff be "family" under the Workmen's Compensation Act is, in this state, a legal impossibility. [Citations omitted.]

We cannot presage the impact of this decision upon the laws of this state, or other consequences which may flow from the Court's decision today. Suffice it to say, the decision represents a departure from legislatively established public policy which we cannot endorse.

---

[3] Plaintiff's actions also negate any inference that she intended to look to her first husband for support or to possibly claim any benefits that would flow to her as his legal wife. She commenced divorce proceedings against him while West was alive, but due to economic difficulties did not complete them before West died. Thereafter she did complete the divorce and consequently terminated any arguable claim that she might have had to her first husband's resources and future benefits.

Bibliography

Bell, *Racism in American Courts: Cause for Black Disruption or Despair?*, 61 CALIF. L. REV. 165 (1973).

Clark, H., THE LAW OF DOMESTIC RELATIONS IN THE UNITED STATES ch. 2 (1968).

Hood, *Common-Law Marriage in Oklahoma: A Survey,* 49 OKLA. B.J.Q. 1505 (1978).

Kogel, O., COMMON LAW MARRIAGE AND ITS DEVELOPMENT IN THE UNITED STATES (1922).

Note, *Common Law Marriage and Unmarried Cohabitators: An Old Solution to a New Problem,* 39 U. PITT. L. REV. 579 (1978).

Stein, *Common Law Marriage: Its History and Certain Contemporary Problems,* 9 J. FAM. L. 271 (1969).

Weyrauch, *Informal and Formal Marriage—An Appraisal of Trends in Family Organization,* 28 U. CHI. L. REV. 88 (1960).

Weyrauch, *Informal Marriage and Common Law Marriage, in* SEXUAL BEHAVIOR AND THE LAW 297 (R. Slovenko ed. 1965).

Other Informal Marriages for Limited Purposes

Putative Marriage

Hupp v. Hupp

Court of Civil Appeals of Texas

235 S.W.2d 753 (Tex. Civ. App. 1950)

McDONALD, Chief Justice.

According to the findings of the jury and the evidence in harmony with them, T. R. Hupp, now deceased, was at all times material to this suit married to Zula Hupp. At some time prior to the year 1936 T. R. Hupp became acquainted with the appellee, who will be referred to as Ann Hupp. It is Ann Hupp's claim that she and Hupp were married in 1936, she believing that T. R. Hupp and Zula Hupp had been divorced. T. R. Hupp and Ann moved to Texas, and lived together until his death in 1948. Through their joint efforts and contributions they accumulated property of the value of some twenty thousand dollars. In this suit, brought against Hupp's administrator, his heirs, and Zula Hupp, Ann Hupp seeks to recover judgment for one-half the value of said property, either on the theory that she was entitled thereto as the putative wife of T. R. Hupp, or on the theory that she and Hupp accumulated the property in a partnership or joint venture. Ann recovered judgment, and the defendants have appealed relying on seventeen points of error.

* * *

The jury found that there was not a ceremonial marriage between Ann and T. R. Hupp. Defendants argue that there cannot be a putative marriage where there has not been a ceremonial marriage. In other words, they say that a common law marriage, which would have been a valid marriage if one of the parties had not been married to another, cannot serve as the basis for asserting a putative marriage. The San Antonio Court of Civil Appeals declared in *Papoutsis v. Trevino,* Tex. Civ. App., 167 S.W.2d 777, writ dismissed, that "one asserting under a putative marriage cannot claim good faith in the absence of a ceremonial marriage attended by the formalities prescribed by law." See also, *In re Greathouse's Estate,* Tex. Civ. App., 184 S.W.2d 317. *Smith v. Smith,* 1 Tex. 621, 46 Am. Dec. 121, was relied on as authority for the pronouncement. We do not join in the view announced by the San Antonio Court. The Supreme Court, in *Smith v. Smith,* had before it a marriage relationship which began in 1830 and was governed by the laws of Mexico. The court referred to the fact that a common law marriage was not recognized in that jurisdiction, and said, among other things, that a claim of good faith could not be made under such circumstances in the absence of a ceremonial marriage. In the case then under review there had been in fact a ceremonial marriage. The facts of the three Court of Civil Appeals cases also cited in *Papoutsis v. Trevino* did not present the question now under discussion.

A putative marriage based on a common law marriage relationship was sustained in *Lawson v. Lawson,* 30 Tex. Civ. App. 43, 69 S.W. 246, writ refused, and the Supreme Court cited *Lawson v. Lawson,* without a hint of criticism, in *Barkley v. Dumke,* 99 Tex. 150, 87 S.W. 1147. The opinion in the latter case refers to the fact that *Smith v. Smith* was decided under the rules of the Spanish law, and not under the laws prevailing after Texas adopted the provisions of the common law in 1840. * * *

While a different rule might well prevail under the Spanish law, which does not recognize what we know as common law marriages, every reason that exists for allowing relief to a party who has entered into a putative marriage relationship applies with equal force to the situation where the putative marriage was entered into as a common law marriage as where it was entered into pursuant to a marriage ceremony.

Defendants argue that the evidence was insufficient to warrant finding that there was a partnership or a joint venture, that it was insufficient to show what property was subject to plaintiff's claims, if any she had, or the value of the accumulations resulting from the joint efforts and contributions of Ann and T. R. Hupp, or that certain items of property or money represented such accumulations, and complaint is made of the form of the issues submitted to the jury which inquired about some of such matters. Since we have no way of knowing what the proof may be on another trial, it would probably not be helpful to counsel or the trial court to discuss such questions against the background of the record now before us. We may, however, say this much: If there was a putative marriage, and if the proof does not show the amount of contributions or efforts of either party, the rules seems to be that each of the putative spouses is entitled to half of the joint accumulations. *Lawson v. Lawson, supra.* Attention of the parties is also called to the rule that partners are presumed equal where partnership is shown, and nothing more. *Johnston v. Ballard,* 83 Tex. 486, 18 S.W. 686; *Bivins v. Proctor,* 125 Tex. 137, 80 S.W.2d 307. It would be elemental that the person claiming to be a putative spouse or a partner would have the burden of identifying any particular piece of property as being a part of the accumulations of the parties during the putative marriage or partnership.

* * *

In answer to another contention made by defendants, we refer to the rule which permits proof of a marriage to be made by general repute as to the status of the parties in the neighborhood where they reside and are known. 28 Tex. Jur. 737. But it was not proper to endeavor to prove a divorce between T. R. Hupp and his first wife by the testimony of a witness that he had seen a copy of a divorce decree. If there was such a decree, a certified copy of it would ordinarily be the best evidence of it.

* * *

Reversed and remanded.

Comments

Good faith is only one of many factors that may have an influence on determining a woman's claims after years of cohabitation. The women in *Burgess* and *West* were hardly in good faith about being married. In *Burgess* there had been a marriage of 16 years, resulting in four children, that ended in divorce. Although the claimant had never remarried, her former husband remarried and obtained divorces twice within a span of one year. After these two intervening marriages, the former spouses resumed living together without formal remarriage. In *West* the claiming woman, during the 13 years of cohabitation, continued to be legally married to a man with whom she had lived for only a short time. In both instances factors of social class and poverty seem to have been responsible, at least in part, for the fact that the women continued to live for many years in relationships that had only the appearance of marriage.

The economic factors in the two cases give clues to why they were decided in favor of the women. They might have become public charges had they not won. In spite of the absence of good faith, the courts felt compelled to point out that the women were not really bad. Although not conforming to the laws of marriage and divorce, the woman in *Burgess* had in fact lived up to the expectation of marriage to the same partner for life. The woman in *West* did not conform, in the view of the Supreme Court of Michigan, to the dictionary definition of "meretricious," namely being "a woman given to indiscriminate lewdness." Such tolerance cannot necessarily be expected from the courts. It is more likely to be found in workmen's compensation cases than in any other areas of law. Yet the court in *Burgess* pointed out a truth of more general application that will be found frequently in this book, namely, that marriage can be valid for some purposes but not recognized for some others. Even a bigamous marriage can have some of the legal consequences of a regular marriage. According to the dissent in *West*, this is, of course, a legal impossibility.

Hupp adds one more dimension to the question of who can be acting in good faith. The defense had claimed that the plaintiff could not be a "putative wife" because she had never attempted a licensed marriage. If this were the law, the realm of protected relationships would be drastically reduced. Courts are prone to leave avenues open for equitable relief, if they feel so inclined. Here we have the competing claims of wife no. 1 and wife no. 2 after the husband had died.

While some legals rights of wife no. 1 from a continuing marriage appear to have been undisputed, wife no. 2 had helped in accumulating the property in years of apparent marital cohabitation. Whether she believed in good faith that the prior marriage had terminated in divorce is left open. The court indicated that she might be entitled to half of the property in any event, under a theory of either putative marriage or partnership.

Here, as is often the case, rules of evidence may not have been sufficiently explored by the lawyers. Unless there were clear facts to the contrary, plaintiff wife no. 2 could have claimed a presumption that the prior marriage had been terminated by divorce. It would have been incumbent upon wife no. 1 to overcome this presumption by showing that no divorce had been obtained—an especially difficult, if not impossible, task in view of the fact that the presumption might even have covered the possibility of a divorce in a jurisdiction other than Texas, including neighboring Mexico. The presumption that a prior marriage had been terminated by divorce would even apply in favor of a subsequent common law marriage, as might have been the case here. The contemporary lawyer should be concerned with being liable under theories of malpractice for overlooking the possible application of a presumption in favor of his client. The presumption, incidentally, would exclude rights of wife no. 1 in the estate altogether.

Reference

Baade, *The Form of Marriage in Spanish North America*, 61 CORNELL L. REV. 1 (1975).

Sousa v. Freitas

California Court of Appeal, 1st District, Division 2

10 Cal. App.3d 660, 89 Cal. Rptr. 485 (1970)

DAVID, J.

Plaintiff Maria Jacinto de Sousa, now some 82 years old, illiterate resident of Santo Espirito, on the island of Santa Maria, Azores, Republic of Portugal, was found by the trial court to be the lawful wife of Manuel Sousa Freitas at the time of his death. Hence, she was awarded a decree imposing a constructive trust as to her marital interest on the properties of his estate, as against Catherine E. Freitas, found to be only his putative wife, and the Bank of America National Trust & Savings Association, as executor. The appellants contest such determinations.

Three years after his marriage at Santo Espirito in 1908 and establishing their residence there, followed by the birth of a son, Manuel Joaquin de Sousa emigrated to California, and for a short period remitted small sums to his family. In 1915, Sousa secured a decree from the Superior Court of Alameda County changing his name to Manuel S. Freitas. Though it would seem that a wife or a child is a person vitally concerned, the Code of Civil

Procedure sections 1275–1279, inclusive, makes no provision for personal service of such an application upon them unless as a "near relative" when the father of a petitioner is not living (Code Civ. Proc., §1276). Maria, his wife, did not know of this change of name until long after 1916.

In 1916, Manuel S. Freitas secured a divorce from Maria S. Freitas, meaning Maria Jacinto Sousa. Service was made by publication, the affidavit stating the defendant lived in "Santa Maria, in the Republic of Portugal," though Manuel well knew Santa Maria was only the island on which his wife lived in Santo Espirito at the home they occupied together; and that there, his wife was not and never had been known as Maria Sousa Freitas. There is evidence that he was not there known as Freitas, contrary to his declaration for change of name. Her testimony was that he was always known as Sousa there.[1]

Testifying in the trial court for appellants, Manuel's brother bore the name of Sousa; and appellants' exhibits in the form of letters from the son of Manuel and Maria to his father show the complete home address as Azenka, Santo Espirito, Santa Maria, Portugal.

By reason of the name change and incomplete address the trial court is supported in the finding that Maria "had no notice or knowledge of said divorce action, was not served as a party to said action, and was not a party to the judgment for divorce rendered in 1919. No other action was taken by either plaintiff or her said husband to terminate their marriage, and at all times until the date of death of said decedent, plaintiff believed that she was the legal wife of decedent; said plaintiff, not having been served with process in the aforementioned divorce action, had no opportunity to impose any valid and meritorious defense to any cause of action for divorce which the decedent could or might have brought during his lifetime." The basis for Manuel's action was her alleged refusal to come to him in America; her claim is, that he did not send for her, nor provide the funds. This was a sufficient meritorious defense. [Citation omitted.]

The trial court concluded that the plaintiff was not a party to nor bound by the change of name proceeding by her husband, and that the purported decree of divorce did not terminate her marriage because Manuel S. Freitas perpetrated extrinsic fraud on plaintiff by designating his defendant wife in the divorce proceedings as Maria S. Freitas. We have noted also the important variance in the address; but whether inadvertent or deliberate, the evidence would indicate that Maria might have received the summons had

---

[1] In Spain, Portugal and in Latin-American countries, there is a custom whereby a child bears or may be known by the names of both father and mother, and the name of the mother, appearing last may be used as the family name; or is sometimes expressed only as an initial following the father's family name. Manuel Sousa was the son of Jose Joaquim de Sousa and Bernardina Jacinta de Freitas; and his cousin and wife Maria Jacinta de Sousa is the daughter of Manuel Joaquim de Sousa and Bernardina Jacinta de Chaves. Upon marriage, her surname (sire's name) remained Sousa; and although Freitas under the old custom might describe himself "Manuel Sousa de Freitas," the name Freitas still would not identify her in this island kingdom of cousins. On Santa Maria, there is testimony neither Manuel nor Maria was ever known by the name "Freitas." His brother testifying on the trial gave his surname as "Souza."

There were so many Maria Joaquin Sousas on Santa Maria—cousins bearing the same name—that Maria Sousa for better identity carried also her grandmother's name of Figueiredo. The son of Maria and Manuel Sousa, left with his mother when Manuel emigrated, also was called Jose Sousa Figueiredo.

It therefore seems inevitable that the identity of "Maria S. Freitas," without any designation of place of residence, whether town, locality or parish, on the island of Santa Maria, would be unknown. Thus whether by inadvertence or design, she was deprived of the notice that Code of Civil Procedure section 413 requires that "a copy of the summons and complaint to be forthwith deposited in the post office, directed to the person to be served, at his place of residence. * * *"

"Residence" in this connection means the address at which letters would be most likely to reach the defendant. [Citations omitted.]

it been addressed in her proper name or in one which she recognized as her own or by which she was known in the community. [Citation omitted.]

The trial court necessarily concluded that the marriage ceremony between Manuel S. Freitas and Catherine E. Afflech was invalid.[2]

But from December 29, 1919 until Manuel's death on August 4, 1962, Catherine E. Freitas lived with him in good faith, believing she was lawfully married to him. All of the property held by him at his death was the product of their joint efforts. Maria was not named in Manuel's will, which devised and bequeathed all of his estate to Catherine.

Therefore, we review the determinations of the trial court, relative to the trust imposed upon the estate, securing the rights therein declared in favor of plaintiff Maria Sousa.

These were (1) all of the property was community property of Manuel S. Freitas and Maria Jacinto Sousa, at the time of his death; (2) that as widow, Maria is the owner of an undivided one-half interest as a community interest in all of said real and personal property and income and proceeds thereof; (3) that as putative spouse Catherine is entitled to the other one-half of all such real and personal property with the proceeds and income thereof.

We are impelled to modify such findings and conclusions.

As against the other spouse or his heirs it is well settled that a woman who lives with a man as a wife in the belief a valid marriage exists is entitled to share in the property accumulated by them during its existence. The proportionate contribution of each is immaterial in this state, for the property is divided as community property would be upon dissolution of a valid marriage. [Citation omitted.]

The putative wife's share is not community property. But what is the situation when the legally recognized spouse steps forward to assert her community property interest in and to the same property, as against the putative spouse? There is scant authority. In *Union Bank & Trust Co. v. Gordon* (1953) 116 Cal. App.2d 681 [254 P.2d 644], the "legal" spouse was estopped to assert her claim, since she herself had remarried in reliance upon the invalid divorce. In *Estate of Ricci* (1962) 201 Cal. App.2d 146 [19 Cal. Rptr. 739], where decedent apparently made no disposition of his community interest by will, the award of one-half to each of the legal and the putative spouses was affirmed. (There, the putative wife appealed, claiming the entire estate was the result of her joint efforts with decedent.) This was an equity decision, in the teeth of Probate Code section 201 under which the legal wife would have inherited his portion. The trial court followed this precedent.

But here, the decedent already had by will vested his half of the community property in the defendant putative spouse, a valid disposition under Probate Code sections 201 and 201.5.

By definition, the one-half of the community property so devised was his; and did not include the other half to which the competing claims apply. Stated another way, in accordance with the views expressed by Professor William E. Burby in FAMILY LAW FOR CALIFORNIA LAWYERS, pages 359–360 (quoted in *Estate of Ricci, supra,* 201 Cal. App.2d 146, at pp. 148–149): " 'It seems obvious that one-half of the property in question belongs to the putative spouse. The other half belongs to the legal community (husband and legally recognized spouse) and should be distributed as any other community property under the same circumstances.' " Under this analysis by the recognized expert in community property law, Catherine is entitled to one-half of the property in her own right; plus the half of the community

---

[2]We note that this marriage was on the day the divorce decree was signed, but on the day before it became effective by entry of judgment, no *nunc pro tunc* entry ever having been made; as well as the absence of valid service of summons and complaint on Maria Jacinto Sousa by publication.

property decedent was entitled to devise, or another one-quarter of the whole; and the plaintiff is entitled to one-quarter of the whole estate only. (*Blache v. Blache* (1945) 69 Cal. App.2d 616, 624 [160 P.2d 136].) In effect, the innocent putative spouse was in partnership or a joint enterprise with her spouse, contributing her services—and in this case, her earnings—to the common enterprise. Thus, their accumulated property was held in effect in tenancy-in-common in equal shares. Upon death of the husband, only his half interest is considered as community property, to which the rights of the lawful spouse attach.[3] We do not undertake to state that this analysis would be equitable in all cases, but we are satisfied that it is under the facts here.[4]

The findings and conclusions are modified to state; (1) one-half of the property was community property of Manuel S. Freitas and Maria Jacinto Sousa, at the time of his death; and Maria Jacinto Freitas is the owner of an undivided one-fourth interest as a community interest in all of said real and personal property and income and proceeds thereof; (2) that as a putative spouse, Catherine is entitled to one-half of all such real and personal property and income and proceeds thereof; and as legatee and devisee of the deceased to an additional one-fourth thereof, being his disposition of his half interest in the community property, under Probate Code, sections 201 and 201.5.

* * *

As so modified the judgment is affirmed. * * *

---

[3]Various analogies have been drawn to characterize the nature of the property acquired during the putative marriage to protect the innocent de facto spouse. Consult: W.Q. de Funiak, PRINCIPLES OF COMMUNITY PROPERTY (1943) pages 124–132, section 56; FAMILY LAW FOR CALIFORNIA LAWYERS (1956) *supra*, chapter 13, William E. Burby, "Significant Aspects of Community Property Law," sections 5, 6, pages 359–361.

[4]Some cases, based upon the Spanish law of community property have adopted the view that the lawful wife rightfully takes one-half and the putative wife one-half, leaving the husband nothing, upon the ground that by his conduct he has forfeited his community property rights in the community acquired during the putative marriage, as in Louisiana: *Waterhouse v. Star Land Co.* (1916) 139 La. 177 [71 So. 358, 359–360]; *Fulton Bag & Cotton Mills v. Fernandez* (La. App. 1935) 159 So. 339, 343.

The court in *Estate of Ricci, supra*, 201 Cal. App.2d 146, seems to have followed this rule, while in *Blache v. Blache, supra*, 69 Cal. App.2d 616, 624, it was not followed.

Pursuant to Civil Code section 4452, operative January 1, 1970, property acquired during the putative marriage is termed "quasi-marital property" and is divided equally between the parties under Civil Code section 4800; but no resolution is made of the conflicting claims of the lawful and putative spouse.

Quasi-Contractual Marriage

Sanguinetti v. Sanguinetti

Supreme Court of California

9 Cal.2d 95, 69 P.2d 845 (1937)

SEAWELL, Justice

Plaintiff Angelina Sanguinetti and defendant Joe Sanguinetti were married on February 2, 1927, and separated on September 24, 1934. On October 8, 1934, plaintiff filed her complaint herein, setting forth two causes of action, the first for divorce on the grounds of extreme cruelty, and the second for annulment based on the fact that at the time of her marriage to Sanguinetti she had a former husband living. Sanguinetti filed an answer and also a cross-complaint wherein he prayed for a divorce from plaintiff on the ground of her extreme cruelty and for an annulment. The court granted the defendant an annulment on his cross-complaint. It appears from the findings that plaintiff had married Antonio Depaoli on June 30, 1914, and on July 23, 1923, had procured an interlocutory decree of divorce from him. But at the time of her marriage to defendant herein, more than three years later, a final decree of divorce had not been entered and was not thereafter entered until January 12, 1934. The court herein found that both parties believed the second marriage legal, and that defendant did not know it was illegal until the filing of the complaint herein.

* * *

The court further held that plaintiff was entitled to recover from defendant the sum of $1,250 as the reasonable value of her services to defendant during the time they lived together, and that plaintiff was entitled to an equitable lien to secure payment of this sum on the defendant's San Francisco real property. Defendant appeals from this provision of the judgment.

* * *

* * *

* * * By her complaint plaintiff prayed for monthly alimony and that the San Francisco real property be assigned to her. She did not ask judgment for the value of her services, but the complaint contained a prayer for general relief. Upon an annulment plaintiff would not be entitled to alimony. [Citations omitted.] Since the appeal is on the judgment roll alone, it may be presumed in support of the judgment that plaintiff's right to recover for her services was made an issue in the trial by consent of the parties and evidence introduced on said issue. [Citations omitted.] In an action for divorce or for annulment in the event the marriage sought to be dissolved by divorce has not been validly contracted, it is sound practice to dispose of the property rights of the parties in the same action, thus avoiding multiplicity of suits. [Citations omitted.]

Where a "putative" marriage has existed, that is, where one or both parties to an invalid marriage have in good faith believed such marriage to be valid, upon an annulment or declaration of invalidity the courts will recognize the right of the de facto wife in property acquired by the parties through their joint efforts, and which would have been community property had the marriage been valid, and will make an equitable division of such property. * * *

* * * Here no joint property was found to exist. The recovery allowed plaintiff is for the reasonable value of her services rendered to her supposed husband. A legal wife upon divorce has no right to recover for services rendered in the maintenance of the joint domicile, but may obtain alimony for her future support in proper cases. The putative wife, as noted above, has no right to an allowance of alimony.

Where an invalid marriage has been procured by fraud of the de facto husband, who is aware of the invalidity of the marriage, the right of the wife who has acted in good faith to recover the reasonable value of her services over and above the value of the support and maintenance furnished her by her supposed husband, has been sustained in a number of jurisdictions, including this state. [Citations omitted.]

The basis of recovery for services * * * is quasi-contractual. The supposed husband has been unjustly enriched by the amount by which the reasonable value of the services rendered to him by his de facto wife exceed the amount devoted by him to her support and maintenance. These services would not have been rendered but for a belief in the validity of the marriage and the continuance of the incidents of status incident to a valid marriage.

It is just and equitable that the de facto husband should make compensation for what has been rendered to him under a mistaken belief in the validity of the marriage which was induced by his own fraud. The law raises the promise to pay in such cases. Cases in other jurisdictions which deny recovery to the de facto wife do so on the ground that as the wife never contemplated she should be paid, a contract will not be implied. *Cooper v. Cooper,* 147 Mass. 370, 17 N.E. 892, 9 Am. St. Rep. 721; *Cropsey v. Sweeney,* 27 Barb. (N.Y.) 310.

In the instant case, however, the invalidity of the marriage was due to no fraud or fault of the defendant. He was free to marry. Both parties believed their marriage in 1927 valid. A final decree of divorce was entered in plaintiff's action against her first husband on January 12, 1934, at which time plaintiff and defendant were living together as husband and wife. After entry of the final decree in plaintiff's action against her first husband, plaintiff and defendant were free to legalize their relationship of seven years' standing by contracting a valid marriage. The termination of said relationship cannot, therefore, fairly be said to arise from the invalidity of their marriage, but was due, rather, to circumstances existing at the time of their separation.

In the instant case both plaintiff and defendant alleged grounds for divorce, in addition to the invalidity of their marriage in 1927. During the seven-year period they lived together plaintiff rendered services for defendant, which, in view of the court's finding, we must assume exceeded by $1,250 the value of the maintenance and support supplied her by defendant. * * * To the extent that the value of plaintiff's services exceeded the value of the maintenance provided her, she has not received consideration therefor. She rendered these services in good faith under the belief that she was the wife of defendant, and in expectation of the continuing benefits of that status. If these continuing benefits were cut off, not because of the original invalidity of the marriage, but because the de facto husband committed acts of cruelty which if the marriage had been valid would constitute cause for divorce, we are of the view that the putative wife was entitled to be paid in so far as her services exceeded in value the support provided by her supposed husband.

* * *

It cannot be held that the court was without right to decree a lien for the amount of $1,250 awarded plaintiff on the San Francisco real property of defendant. Under section 140, Civil Code, the award of alimony in divorce actions may be decreed a lien on separate property of the husband. * * * There are no statutory provisions concerning the property rights of a putative wife. The judgment in the instant case is not for the division of joint property accumulated during the putative marriage, but for a sum found due plaintiff from defendant. Whether in a particular case a lien should be granted the putative wife is a matter to be determined by the trial court. Since the evidence is not before us, it cannot be held that the court below abused its discretion.

* * * The portion of the judgment appealed from by defendant is affirmed.

Lazzarevich v. Lazzarevich

California District Court of Appeal, 2d District, Division 3

88 Cal. App.2d 708, 200 P.2d 49 (1948)

VALLEE, J.

Two appeals are pending in this non-jury case from a judgment rendered in favor of plaintiff in the sum of $2,350. Plaintiff appeals upon the judgment-roll. Defendant appeals upon a Settled Statement pursuant to rule 7(b), Rules on Appeal.

Plaintiff commenced the action on August 14, 1946. The first cause of action sought recovery of the reasonable value of work and services performed by plaintiff for defendant from July, 1935, to April, 1946, in maintaining a home for defendant and their son, "cooking for him, washing defendant's clothes, and performing the entire household services for defendant," during all of which period she "believed that she was the legal wife of defendant." The second cause of action sought recovery of contributions made by plaintiff to the household expenses from January 17, 1943 to June 13, 1945, consisting of earnings received by plaintiff while employed in a defense plant and during the period she believed she was defendant's lawful wife. Defendant answered, denying generally all allegations of the complaint and alleging, as an affirmative defense, that the causes of action were barred by the statute of limitations. (Code Civ. Proc. §§337, 339.) He also alleged, as additional affirmative defenses, that the services rendered by plaintiff in his behalf were voluntarily rendered without any agreement or understanding that she would be compensated therefor; and that plaintiff had been fully compensated for all services rendered by her in his behalf.

The Settled Statement reveals the following facts: The parties were married in Los Angeles on March 18, 1921. One child, a daughter, was born, the issue of this marriage. Subsequently defendant (as plaintiff) filed an action for divorce in Los Angeles County. An interlocutory decree was granted the husband and entered on March 18, 1932. On September 6, 1933, without the husband's knowledge or request, his attorney had a final decree of divorce entered. Subsequent to the entry of the interlocutory decree and several months prior to the entering of the final decree, and thereafter, defendant continually sought a reconciliation with his wife. They became reconciled in July of 1935. Both parties testified that before the reconciliation occurred defendant informed plaintiff that no final decree had been entered. Defendant testified that he so believed and so informed plaintiff. The parties then took a trip to Reno, Nevada, the Pacific Northwest, and on their return stopped at Merced, California. While there, defendant made inquiry of the county clerk concerning the remarriage of the parties. He was informed that since no final decree had been entered in the divorce action no remarriage was necessary. This information defendant imparted to plaintiff. Thereafter, on April 23, 1936, a son was born to the parties. As an aftermath of domestic difficulties which arose between them, plaintiff, on August 1, 1945, consulted her attorneys about a divorce. On August 10, 1945, she was informed by them that the court records disclosed the entry of a final decree of divorce on September 6, 1933. Plaintiff testified that she would not have lived with defendant if she had not believed that she was his wife. The parties remained separated from August 1, 1945, until October 1, 1945, when the plaintiff, upon the promise of defendant that he would remarry her if she would return to him, again became reconciled. They again separated on April 1, 1946. From July, 1935 on, defendant owned a half interest, as a partner, in Economy Plumbing Company. During the periods from July, 1935, to August, 1945, and from October, 1945, to April, 1946,

plaintiff performed the usual household duties of a wife, excepting that during the period from January 17, 1943, until June 13, 1945, she worked in a defense plant. During this latter period she did not render to defendant the same amount of household services as she had when she was not employed, but during this period she contributed all of her salary, $172.50 a month, to the household expenses. It was agreed between the parties that plaintiff would contribute her salary to the living expenses and the money saved by defendant thereby would be put into War Bonds for their mutual benefit.
* * *

* * * The court concluded that: (1) plaintiff was entitled to recover the reasonable value of the services rendered for defendant during the period she lived with him under the mistaken belief that she was still married to him and for contributions made to him within that period, except that recovery for services rendered and for contributions made prior to August 14, 1944, was barred by the statute of limitations (Code Civ. Proc. §339, subd. (1); (2) plaintiff was entitled to a judgment in the amount of $625, being at the rate of $50 per month for a period of seven and one-half months between August 14, 1944, and April 1, 1946, and at the rate of $25 per month for a period of ten months within said period; (3) plaintiff was entitled to judgment in the sum of $1,725 for contributions made by her to defendant for a period of ten months between August 14, 1944, and April 1, 1946.

Upon his appeal defendant contends that the plaintiff is not entitled to a judgment for the value of her services or for contributions because she has received one-half of all the property acquired by the parties after their reconciliation and that he, therefore, has not been unjustly enriched. This contention is not tenable.
* * *

In view of the findings, which are not challenged here, that material misrepresentations as to the marital status of the parties were made by the defendant, we think the present case falls squarely within the principles set forth in section 40 of the Restatement of the Law of Restitution. This section reads in part: "A person who has rendered services to another * * * is entitled to restitution therefor if the services were rendered * * * (a) because of the fraud or material misrepresentation of the other * * *" In comment b the following appears:

> "The rule stated in this Clause [(a)] is applicable both where the services are obtained by a consciously false statement and where they are the result of an innocent but material misstatement. The fact that the one rendering the services does not expect to be compensated therefor or otherwise to receive benefit is immaterial. * * * Where domestic services are rendered to a supposed spouse because of an innocent misrepresentation of marital status, the one rendering the services has the burden of proving that the services are of greater value than the benefits received."

(See also, Illustration 4.)
* * *

The present action is one in quantum meruit seeking the recovery of the value of services rendered and contributions advanced by plaintiff during the putative marriage. The action is not one seeking an equitable division of whatever property, if any, may have been acquired by the parties during that period. The issue concerning an equitable division of the property was not presented by the pleadings or the evidence. While it is true, as defendant points out, that the Settled Statement shows there was some evidence that two parcels of real property acquired during this period now stand in the names of the parties jointly, there is nothing in the record before us to indicate the value of the property or the source or amount of the funds used to acquire the property. No attempt was made by defendant to go behind the joint tenancy and establish that it was the intention of the parties to hold the property as community property irrespective of the terms of the joint tenancy deed, [citations omitted.] or that plaintiff received her interest in the joint tenancy property in compensation for services rendered, or that plaintiff did not acquire that interest by gift, or by devise, or from her own funds. In the absence of evidence that the property was acquired with community funds with the intention that it should remain community property, the joint tenancy stands as such,—the interest of each party being separate property. *Siberell v. Siberell, supra; Tomaier v. Tomaier*, 23 Cal.2d 754, 146 P.2d 905. The record before us is devoid of evidence indicating the amount of defendant's earnings during the period of the de facto marriage or the amount in his bank account. The meager evidence appearing in the Settled Statement, contrary to defendant's contention, reveals that there was little, if any, community property existing at the time the action was filed, defendant testifying that at the time of the trial he had less than $1,000. There is no evidence which would have warranted the trial court in finding that the services rendered by plaintiff prior to August 10, 1945, were voluntarily rendered without any agreement or understanding that she would be compensated therefor, or that she had been fully compensated therefor, or that she has received one-half of all the property acquired by the parties after their reconciliation in July, 1935. The trial court did not err in rendering judgment in favor of plaintiff for services rendered and for contributions advanced by her prior to August 10, 1945.

A different result must obtain as to services performed by plaintiff after August 10, 1945. As we have noted, the parties separated on August 1, 1945. On August 10, 1945, plaintiff discovered that the final decree of divorce had been entered on September 6, 1933. On October 1, 1945, she went to live with defendant and continued to do so until April 1, 1946. The essence of the right of a putative wife to recover for services rendered the putative husband is her belief in the validity of a marriage between them. After August 10, 1945, plaintiff was no longer an innocent, deluded, putative wife. She no longer believed that she was defendant's wife. She knew that she was not. The relationship between the parties was meretricious after October 1, 1945. Plaintiff was fully aware of the nature of the relationship. The fact that she returned to defendant upon his promise to remarry her is of no import. The "[e]quitable considerations arising from the reasonable expectation of the continuation of benefits attending the status of marriage entered into in good faith" which had existed prior to August 10, 1945, did not exist thereafter. *Vallera v. Vallera*, 21 Cal.2d 681, 685, 134 P.2d 761, 763. In the absence of an express agreement that plaintiff would be compensated for services performed after the date she has no right to compensation therefor. * * *

The only point made by plaintiff on her appeal is that the court erred in concluding that she was barred by the statute of limitations from recovery for services rendered and advances made by her to defendant prior to "a date two years prior to the date of the commencement of her action." She argues that she should have judgment "for reasonable value of all of the services rendered by her for respondent during the full period of 126 months, based upon the value of such services as found by the trial court, and for all of the advances made by appellant to respondent at the rate of $172.50 per month for a period of twenty-nine months"; that the statute of limitations did not begin to run until the cause of action accrued (Code Civ. Proc. §312), and that the action did not accrue until August 10, 1945, on which date she discovered that she was not legally married to defendant. The point is good.
* * *

The statute of limitations begins to run on a cause of action based on an implied or quasi-contract when the cause of action accrues, and depends largely on the facts of each particular case. * * * In commenting on *Cooper* *v. Cooper*, 147 Mass. 370, 17 N.E. 892, 9 Am. St. Rep. 721, cited *supra*, at pages 324 and 325 of KEENER ON QUASI CONTRACTS, the learned author says:

> "Had the plaintiff in this case surrendered to the defendant money or other chattels to which the defendant asserted a right because of his marital rights as husband, it does not seem possible that a court would hold that, because of the loss of the right to sue in tort by the death of the intestate, no claim could be asserted against his estate for the value so received by him. And yet in point of principle it is submitted that it is impossible to distinguish between the receipt of money or other property by the defendant and the receipt of services. The plaintiff whether she conferred a benefit on the intestate by rendering services, or by delivering to him money or other personal property, in either case parted with a right in rem under a mistaken supposition, induced by the fraud of the defendant, that the defendant was entitled thereto."

And

> "whatever power, therefore, courts of equity possess to prevent and remove the consequences of fraud, they also possess in dealing with the effects of mistake." POM. EQ. JURIS. (4th Ed.) vol. 11, pp. 1782, 1783.

Fung Dai Kim Ah Leong v. Lau Ah Leong, 9 Cir., 27 F.2d 582, 585.
* * *

Since the contributions made and advanced by the plaintiff and the services for which she seeks recovery prior to August 10, 1945, were rendered by her under the mistaken belief that the marriage had not been dissolved, it is obvious that her cause of action for services rendered and contributions advanced could not accrue until she discovered that the marriage had been dissolved. In a situation such as this, the law not ony implies a promise to pay, but must, of necessity, imply a promise to pay at the termination of the services, occurring at the time of discovery of the fact that the marriage had been dissolved, which, in the instant case, occurred on August 10, 1945. While factually dissimilar, we believe this case falls within the principle announced in those cases holding that where there is an express or implied promise to pay on the termination of the services, the cause of action does not arise until the termination of the services and the statute of limitations does not bar any part of the period of continuous services. [Citations omitted.]

The court found that plaintiff during a period of 126 months, from July 31, 1935, until April 1, 1946, performed work and services for defendant. The court also found that the reasonable value of the services performed during the period of 126 months was $50 a month for ninety-seven months and $25 a month for twenty-nine months. Plaintiff performed the services for which she is entitled to recover for 120 months prior to August 10, 1945, the date she discovered that the final decree of divorce had been entered September 6, 1933. As we hold that plaintiff is not entitled to recover for six months after August 10, 1945, for which the court found that the reasonable value of the services was $50 a month, the number of months that she performed services of the reasonable value of $50 a month is ninety-one months. Under the findings, plaintiff is entitled to recover the sum of $10,277.50 from defendant, as follows: For services rendered, $5,275.00, being ninety-one months at $50.00 a month and twenty-nine months at $25.00 a month; for contributions, $5,002.50, being twenty-nine months at $172.50.

The judgment is modified by striking therefrom the figures "$2350.00," and inserting in lieu thereof the figures "$10,277.50." As so modified, the judgment is affirmed, plaintiff to recover costs of appeal.

Comments

Sousa, Sanguinetti, and *Lazzarevich* were cited as precedents in *Marvin v. Marvin* (pp. 172–185) and thus are stepping-stones toward contract cohabitation and theories of equitable relief. In these three cases, the women believed themselves to be married in good faith while in fact they were not. In *Marvin* there was cohabitation with some of the appearances of marriage, but no corresponding marital intent of the parties. Thus the cases come from opposite sides. *Sousa* shows the clearest case of good faith: an American woman having married an immigrant from the Portuguese Azores, relying on a California divorce he had secured from his wife who had stayed behind. Although the court did not expressly state that fraud was committed, the facts are reasonably clear in this regard. The question was whether the property left after his death should be split equally between the two "wives" or whether the American wife, although her marriage of 43 years proved to be void, was entitled to a larger share.

The court, applying partnership language to the void marriage, came to the conclusion that the good faith American wife was in any event entitled to half of the accumulated property as a partner, which means that only the remaining half was part of the estate and as such was to be split. Although the court talks in terms of a continuing Portuguese marriage, the opinion in effect gave greater rights, namely three fourths of the estate, to the American woman. As in many California cases dealing with conceptions of community property, *Sousa* is of potential interest to the rest of the nation. The same mathematics could be applied if marriage itself is viewed as partnership. A wife as "partner" could equally claim her own interest in the partnership, plus half of the remaining interest of the husband's estate. In other words, California cases can conceivably be used as precedents in non-community-property states, if the facts justify an argument based on partnership in jointly operated small businesses, for example.

While in *Sousa* the putative wife was treated as an entrepreneur who was fully compensated by the profits from the joint venture, the women in *Sanguinetti* and *Lazzarevich* appeared to be in the role of domestic servants who, in the absence of a valid marital contract, could only be compensated under theories of unjust enrichment. In both instances it is probable that negligence of the attorneys brought about, or at least contributed to, the mistaken belief that a valid marriage existed. The duty is clearly upon the attorney, in any jurisdiction, to clarify with the parties what steps are necessary to secure a divorce and at what point they are free to remarry. *Lazzarevich* is a blatant case of insufficient communication between attorney and client, which today would be subject to a malpractice claim. Had California been a common law marriage jurisdiction the continued cohabitation of the parties, who did not realize that their divorce had become final, would have constituted a valid, new marriage.

There is a further disturbing point about these cases, which is common to many cases dealing with marriage and divorce. The facts of these cases may have taken on an artificial clarity, due in the last analysis to the language the lawyers used in their pleadings. Had the lawyers in interviews with their clients searched for complexity rather than clarity of facts, they might have left room for presumptions. On the other hand, in all three cases relatively fixed legal consequences may have been dictated by the access to divorce records. Official documentary evidence may have precluded any possibility of doubt.

Reference

Weyrauch, *Informal and Formal Marriage—An Appraisal of Trends in Family Organization*, 28 U. Chi. L. Rev. 88 (1960).

Marriage by Estoppel

Edgar v. Richardson

Supreme Court Commission of Ohio

33 Ohio St. 581 (1878)

Error to the District Court of Wood county.

The original action was brought in the Court of Common Pleas of Wood county, in 1866, by the plaintiff, William Edgar, to recover of the defendant, Fidelia Richardson, forty acres of land in her possession. The plaintiff averred, in his petition, that he was the owner of the land and entitled to its possession. The defendant answered, averring that her name is Fidelia Edgar, and denied the averments of the petition. At the trial a jury was waived, and the case was tried to the court which found the issues for the defendant, and rendered judgment in her favor.* * *

The case, as disclosed by the bill of exceptions, is substantially, as follows: Both parties claim title under John Edgar who died childless and intestate. His title to the land was such that, under the statute, it descended to the wife, relict of the intestate. In 1841, he was married to Sarah Ann Dubbs, who survived him and conveyed the land to the plantiff; this constitutes the plaintiff's title to the land.

To defeat this title, the defendant relies on the following facts: After the marriage of Edgar and Sarah Ann, they lived together about fourteen years, when Edgar took up his residence on the land in question, in Wood county; but his wife refused to live with him, and after about a year, applied in Lucas county for a divorce. Edgar opposed the divorce, and she was defeated. She then went away and remained for about three years, when she returned to her father's house, in the neighborhood of her husband, in Wood county, and said to her relatives and acquaintances that during her absence she had obtained a divorce, but then, and ever afterward, refused to tell where she was during that time. Edgar continued to reside on his farm, and Sarah Ann, soon after her return, made Toledo her place of residence, where she stated and caused it to be believed that she had obtained a divorce from John Edgar. After waiting a few years, Edgar desired to marry if he could be made certain that a divorce between him and Sarah Ann had been obtained. Accordingly, Edgar sent the father of Sarah Ann to Toledo to ascertain from her the truth about her having obtained a divorce. She assured her father that she went away and did not let Edgar know where she was, so that she could obtain a divorce from him, and did obtain a divorce, and showed him some papers to confirm it; and, on being told that Edgar desired to marry again, she said that she wished he would marry again. Soon after this occurred, Edgar communicated what he had done and the information obtained to Fidelia Richardson; thereupon, on the 28th day of May, 1862, he and Fidelia were married, and lived together as husband and wife until his death in 1866. About the same time that Edgar married Fidelia, Sarah Ann married one McKessick, with whom she has ever since lived as her husband. The plaintiff excepted to the admission of the evidence proving the statements of Sarah Ann about her having obtained a divorce from John Edgar.

To rebut the evidence introduced by the defendant, of the admissions of Sarah Ann that she had procured a divorce from Edgar, the plaintiff gave in evidence the deposition of Sarah Ann McKessick that she married John Edgar in 1841, and never was divorced from him.

　　* * *

DAY, J. The errors assigned present two questions: 1. Did the court err in permitting the defendant to prove admissions of the grantor to the plaintiff, that she and her husband, John Edgar, were divorced; 2. If not, is the judgment unsustained by the law and the evidence.

1. The plaintiff sought to establish his title to the land in dispute through a deed to him from Sarah Ann Edgar; he was, therefore, in privity of estate with her; and, for that reason, her admissions before the conveyance, which would have been admissible against her had she been plaintiff in the action, were admissible against him. 1 Greenl. Ev., §189.

He could recover only upon the strength of her title, which depended solely upon her being the wife relict of John Edgar, deceased. To establish that fact, the plaintiff proved that Sarah Ann married Edgar in 1841, and that he died in 1866 without issue. The plaintiff rested on the presumption that she continued to be the wife of Edgar until his death. To rebut this presumption, the defendant was permitted to prove, by said Sarah Ann's admissions during the time she claimed to be Edgar's wife, that she had procured a divorce.

This evidence was objected to, on the ground that a divorce is a matter of record and cannot be proved by secondary evidence. This objection loses much of its force from the fact that the person who made the admissions, and whose interests were affected thereby, refused to disclose where the record could be obtained, thus putting it out of the power of the defendant to prove the alleged divorce by the record if it existed; therefore, the admissions of Sarah Ann, were, by reason of this concealment, the best evidence attainable by the defendant.

But admissions of a party relating to the contents of written instruments, in general, are not regarded as secondary evidence, and though they relate to a record, if the place where it can be obtained be concealed by the party, they should form no exception to the rule.

　　* * *

There was, then, no error in admitting the evidence of the admissions of Sarah Ann, the grantor of the plaintiff, made during her alleged coverture, tending to show that she was not the wife relict of John Edgar, deceased.

2. The remaining question arises upon the overruling of the motion for a new trial. The ground of the motion was, that the judgment was against the law and the evidence.

The plaintiff made a *prima facie* case, entitling him to recover. If, therefore, the judgment in favor of the defendant can be sustained at all, it must be upon the ground that the evidence was such as to warrant the court in holding either that Sarah Ann was in law estopped from denying her declarations, that she was divorced from her husband, John Edgar, or that she had in fact obtained such divorce.

The court made no special finding of facts from the evidence; therefore, in looking to the evidence, we must, as a reviewing court, assume, in support of the judgment, the facts to be what the evidence would finally warrant the court to find as the facts of the case.

It is clear that Sarah Ann undertook, and intended to induce the belief, in whatever neighborhood she resided, that, during her absence of three years in parts unknown, she had obtained a divorce. It is also quite clear, that, after waiting in doubt about the matter for five years, John Edgar, desiring to marry again, if he might lawfully do so, sent her father to learn from her what he might rely upon as the truth about her having obtained a divorce; that she sent back to him assurances of having obtained a divorce; and that she intended to induce him to believe it, knowing that he might, in reliance on such belief, materially change his condition. The evidence further leaves the strong impression that both Edgar and Fidelia Richardson believed, and upon the faith of Sarah Ann's declarations consummated their marriage.

It is true that Sarah Ann had no direct communication with Fidelia; but she undoubtedly intended that her assurances of a divorce sent to Edgar should be communicated, as they in fact were, to the woman he desired to marry. The very object of such assurances was to induce his marriage; and, from the nature of the transaction, it must have been equally her intention that another should be influenced thereby.

Though Sarah Ann did not directly bring about the marriage of Edgar and Fidelia, the court was warranted in finding, from the evidence, that she induced them to believe that, as against any marital right of her's, they might lawfully marry.

Having acted upon her assurances, and in accordance with her expressed wishes, a strong case was made, which, but for reasons not affecting the substantial justice of the case, called for the application, as against her, of the principles of the law which would estop her from denying the truth of her declarations.

But, conceding that the declarations of Sarah Ann do not strictly rise to the degree of an estoppel, or cannot be regarded as conclusive, still the question remains, whether the court was clearly unwarranted in finding, from the evidence, that Sarah Ann had been divorced. This question is left to be determined solely upon her own acts and declarations during the alleged coverture, and her testimony in the case. But the point for our determination, as a reviewing court, arising upon this state of the case is, not whether such divorce had in fact been obtained, but whether a finding by the court below that it had, would be clearly unwarranted by the evidence.

In support of a finding that the divorce had been obtained, there are the declarations of Sarah Ann, strenuously persisted in during a series of years, that it had been obtained. These declarations are corroborated by undisputed facts. She tried to get a divorce with the knowledge of Edgar; after she was defeated by him, she went to parts unknown, avowedly for the purpose of getting a divorce; she was absent during a period sufficiently long to get it; she exhibited to her father papers to show that she had; she induced her husband to marry again; she married again herself. If not divorced, she knowingly was instrumental in bringing herself and her husband into a state of bigamy, and two other persons into that of adultery. Surely, since she concealed the place where the divorce was obtained, a stronger case to establish a divorce, as against her, could not be made. But now, to establish her heirship to the property of the decedent, she has, in a distant state, given her deposition that she never obtained a divorce. In the light of the evidence in the case, her testimony in a matter affecting her own interest cannot be regarded as conclusive.

Her declarations may not rise to the degree of an estoppel against her to deny the truth of her declarations. Nor was the court below estopped from regarding her declarations, supported by the corresponding acts of her life for many years, as more convincing than her testimony now given to win the estate left by the husband she deserted, and, if her declarations be not true, had fraudulently led into the belief that, as against any marital claim of her's, he might safely die intestate. We cannot say that manifestly the court would not be warranted in finding in accordance with her declarations, corroborated by the acts of her life. Clearly such a finding would be supported by evidence—evidence, too, the truth of which Sarah Ann cannot deny without impeaching her own credibility, and can deny only for the purpose of obtaining what, in justice, should be denied to her.

Since, then, the court of common pleas would not be clearly unwarranted in finding, from the evidence, a state of fact that would in law sustain its judgment in favor of the defendant, the judgment of the district court affirming that of the common pleas must be affirmed.

Judgment affirmed.

Mason v. Mason

District Court of Appeal of Florida

174 So.2d 620 (3d D.C.A. Fla. 1965)

PER CURIAM.

We adopt that portion of the opinion of the chancellor which is quoted below as the opinion of this court.

"THIS CAUSE came on to be heard on the Complaint of Plaintiff, LUCY DAVIS MASON, for Declaratory Relief, the Answer, Counter-Claim and Cross-Claim of Defendant, SALLY MASON, the Answer to Counterclaim by Plaintiff, and the Answer of MARTIN W. GARY, Administrator Ad Litem of the Estate of WEARY M. MASON, deceased to Defendant's Cross-Claim, and the amendment to Answer of Defendant, SALLY MASON, and the Court having heard the testimony of the Parties and considered the evidence, the Court finds as follows:

"1. That LUCY DAVIS MASON was married to the late WEARY M. MASON, on the 9th day of April, 1922, at Reddick, Florida; that a divorce suit was filed by WEARY M. MASON in the Circuit Court for Marion County, Florida, (Chancery No. 10936) against Plaintiff, but no Final Decree of Divorce was ever entered therein; that the marriage of Plaintiff to the said WEARY M. MASON was never dissolved by a Decree of Divorce prior to the death of the said WEARY M. MASON on or about February 3, 1962.

"2. That Defendant SALLY MASON entered into a marriage with WEARY M. MASON during his lifetime on or about March 10, 1942, at Dade City, Florida in the innocent belief that the said MASON was a single man; that thereafter, said Defendant lived with the said MASON as his wife until his death on or about February 3, 1962.

"3. That Plaintiff knew of the marriage of the late WEARY M. MASON to Defendant SALLY MASON, and that they were living together as husband and wife in Miami, Florida; that, notwithstanding said knowledge, Plaintiff asserted no rights or claims under her marriage to the late WEARY M. MASON during his lifetime.

"4. That during the purported marriage of Defendant and the said MASON, the Defendant and the said MASON acquired the following properties in the names of the said MASON and Defendant as husband and wife, which were still so held at the time of the death of said MASON * * *.

* * *

"5. That the funds for the purchase and payment of said properties were contributed by the late WEARY M. MASON and Defendant, the Defendant having contributed substantial amounts from her own funds therefor, as well as having paid substantial sums from her own funds for improvements to the properties during the lifetime of the said MASON and since his death.

* * *

"[T]he late WEARY M. MASON led the Defendant, SALLY MASON, to enter into a marriage contract with him on March 10, 1942, to live with him and care for him, and to the taking of title to the above-described properties in their names as husband and wife, believing that they were in fact and in law husband and wife, and the said WEARY M. MASON was at the time of said marriage, at the time of the purchase of the properties above-described and at all times during his lifetime estopped to deny the validity of his marriage to the Defendant, and estopped to deny the right of said Defendant to take title to said properties by survivorship, which such estoppel is binding upon the Plaintiff as the heir-at-law of the said WEARY M. MASON.

"[B]y reason of the aforesaid estoppel, the titles to the above-described properties are declared vested in Defendant SALLY MASON * * *."

See *Alexander v. Colston*, Fla. 1953, 66 So.2d 673.

Affirmed.

Warner v. Warner

Supreme Court of Idaho

76 Idaho 399, 283 P.2d 931 (1955)

TAYLOR, Chief Justice.

The parties were married in November, 1947, and divorced in February, 1948; married again in November, 1948, and again divorced June 5, 1950. During the course of this second marriage they adopted a boy, who at the time of the trial herein was five years of age. By the decree of June 5, 1950, custody was awarded to the mother (appellant) and the father (respondent) was ordered to pay $20 per month for child support.

Shortly after this divorce, plaintiff moved to California and later married one Crim, who obtained a divorce from her in June, 1951. In the early spring of 1951, while plaintiff was married to Crim, defendant went to California and "I primarily looked her up to see Spence [the child], but, as all things happen, we became affiliated." He spent two or three weeks with the plaintiff on that occasion. She told him she would divorce Crim and return to Idaho. In August, 1951, she came back to Idaho and entered the employ of the defendant in a club which he had opened in American Falls. This club was closed in October. Whereupon, plaintiff took up residence with the defendant at the South Fork Lodge in Swan Valley. During the winter of '51–'52 they lived as man and wife in North Hollywood, California, defendant during that time being employed by Lockheed. In April, 1952, they separated and defendant returned to Idaho. In December, 1952, plaintiff married one McCarley in Ely, Nevada.

In March, 1953, defendant again went to Los Angeles to see the plaintiff. Concerning this visit he testified:

> "I spent several weeks with her again as a family. When she wasn't at my place, I was at her place. * * * I asked her to come back to Idaho and try it again, that I thought we still had enough between us to warrant one more attempt."

She agreed and in April, 1953, they returned to the South Fork Lodge in Swan Valley, where they thereafter continuously lived together as husband and wife until this action was commenced in August, 1954. During this time they held themselves out to the public as husband and wife and introduced each other, and publicly referred to each other, as such. Plaintiff testified that before they returned from California she asked defendant to help her to get a divorce from McCarley; that defendant promised her if she would come back to him he would marry her; he would be kind to her and the boy and not beat her anymore; that he would share with her the property he then owned and any property thereafter acquired; that relying upon these promises she returned and lived with him as his wife; that he was good to her about a month after their return, but thereafter pursued his previous course of cruelty, slapping her and striking her with his fist; that on several occasions she asked him to enter into a ceremonial marriage and that "if I ever mentioned it he got mad, and usually slapped me around." As to the occasion which caused the final separation, she testified:

> "Well, he—the last time he hit me he hit me in the head, and I couldn't hardly eat, or open my mouth, and he laughed and thought it was real funny, but it wasn't, and I decided that I am getting too old to take those beatings any longer, I can't take them.
> "It knocked me down the last time he hit me. He hit me right here on the side of the head (Indicating). I had pains for about two months. I was even afraid he had injured me some way."

She did not leave immediately on this occasion, testifying:

> "I thought I would wait and when he wasn't there and leave, I didn't want to get—He threatened to have—to beat me to where I wouldn't look presentable if I ever left, and I didn't—want to take that chance."

About a month later, while he was on a hunting trip, she left the home and commenced these proceedings. The court required the defendant to pay an attorney's fee of $150 and $75 for support of plaintiff pending the action.

About three weeks before the trial, having 'phoned plaintiff's father that he had come to see the child, the defendant went to the home of her parents in Twin Falls, Idaho, where plaintiff was then living. The plaintiff took the child out to meet him in the street rather than risk a disturbance in the house. Concerning this occasion she testified that he jerked her into his car, leaving the boy in the street, and drove down to his hotel and demanded that she go to his room to sign a paper. Upon her refusal, he said:

> " 'All right, then, you take your choice, either I'll take you out in the country and beat the hell out of you, or you go in and do it.' "

Fearing him, she went to the room. As to what there occurred, she said:

> " 'He wanted me to sign—write a letter and sign it calling this all off, and telling a bunch of—telling that it was a bunch of lies and everything, and I told him he could kill me first, so he just about did. He beat me up,

and then left me in the hotel room with no money. I started down the street with my clothes half off, and some friend took me home. I was hysterical. * * * and beat me, and ripped my clothes off of me, and when I finally got home they had to take me to the doctor, and I lost my voice for three days."

Although this last beating occurred after the action was commenced and no supplemental complaint was filed, no objection to the testimony was made.

We also note as a part of this statement of facts that the defendant does not deny the beatings testified to by plaintiff.

The defendant testified that he did not know of the marriage to McCarley until after the parties had returned from California; that he had offered to help her to get a divorce in Idaho, but would not pay her expenses to California for that purpose. He denied any promise to share property with the plaintiff, and denied that he promised to marry her, and testified he did not consider her his wife. In conflict with this, he also testified:

"Q. Yes. and you—while you were there [California], and ever since, you have lived with her as husband and wife, haven't you? A. Yes, I believe it's been assumed by the public that we were man and wife.

"Q. Yes. And as a matter of fact, you held yourself out as man and wife since then, haven't you? A. I was proud to, yes.

"Q. Well, I am asking you if you haven't held yourself out as man and wife? A. Yes, I was proud to, yes.

"Q. * * * So that when you testified a moment ago that her folks upon several times—'my wife has been taken from me several times by her folks,' you considered Carmen as your wife, didn't you? A. Over a period of the last eight years, yes.

"Q. Yes, over a period of the last eight years you have considered her as your wife, that is correct, isn't it? A. When she wasn't, I have waited for her, I suppose."

* * *

The evidence is quite conclusive that these parties entered into the relationship of marriage by mutual consent and by mutual assumption of marital rights, duties, and obligations, insofar as they were capable. The trial court made no contrary finding on this issue, but found that "plaintiff remains married" to McCarley and "that the parties are *in pari delicto* in this case." In its conclusions of law the court held:

"III. That plaintiff and defendant did not marry or become husband and wife under the common law on or about March 27, 1953, or at any time since because of plaintiff's incapacity to consent to such a marriage by reason of the plaintiff being, then and now, already married to one Olvis B. McCarley and that such a marriage would be illegal and void from the beginning."

It is apparent that the trial court based its judgment in this case entirely upon want of capacity in the plantiff, not upon a lack of consent or mutual assumption of marital rights. The evidence as to the McCarley marriage consists of certified copy of the marriage certificate, and plaintiff's admission on the witness stand. Plaintiff testified that she believed that marriage had been dissolved "according to what I hear"; that she did not know where McCarley was; and that she did not think he knew where she was; and that she had not been served with process in any divorce proceedings by him. For aught that appears in this record that marriage could have been dissolved by action of McCarley either before these parties resumed marital relations in March, 1953, or during the time they lived together as husband and wife. If McCarley obtained a divorce before March, 1953, then there was no impediment to the marriage then agreed upon between these parties. If the impediment was removed during the period of their subsequent marital relationship, and they thereafter continued that relationship, then a common law marriage would result. *Huff v. Huff*, 20 Idaho 450, 118 P. 1080; [other citations omitted].

The evidence is wholly insufficient to show that the impediment to plaintiff's marriage was not removed by death or divorce. The record being silent on that question, the presumption of the validity of her marriage to defendant is not overcome.

* * *

" 'The presumption of marriage, from a cohabitation, apparently matrimonial, is one of the strongest presumptions known to the law. This is especially true in a case involving legitimacy. The law presumes morality, and not immorality; marriage, and not concubinage; legitimacy, and not bastardy. Where there is enough to create a foundation for the presumption of marriage, it can be repelled only by the most cogent and satisfactory evidence.' *Hynes v. McDermott*, 91 N.Y. 451, at page 459, 43 Am.Rep. 677 * * *."

Smith v. Smith, 32 Idaho 478, at page 482, 185 P. 67, at page 69.

* * *

The case of *Thomey v. Thomey*, 67 Idaho 393, 181 P.2d 777, is in some respects parallel to this. There the parties entered into a common law marriage relationship, knowing that the plaintiff had a husband living. The defendant assured her that it "did not matter, that she could get a divorce later, and that whatever property was accumulated would belong jointly" to them. The parties lived together in such relationship for four years, at which time the wife procured a divorce from her first husband, after which they continued their relationship for nine years, without any marriage ceremony. The court held a common law marriage resulted. In that case the trial court concluded the defendant was estopped to deny the existence and validity of his marriage to the plaintiff, and its judgment was upheld by this court.

Here we think the defendant by his conduct is estopped to deny the validity of his marriage to plaintiff. It is evident that he wanted her to live with him as his wife. While the evidence is conflicting as to what, if any, promises he made to induce her to return, it is quite evident that he did persuade her to come back, and that his present denial of the marital relationship, and of any promise to share property, is actuated by his desire to deprive her of her property rights. It is also reasonable to conclude that she would not have returned without some inducement offered by him. [Citations omitted.] This conclusion of estoppel is further strengthened by defendant's conduct in living with the plaintiff as her husband after her divorce from Crim from about August, 1951, until April, 1952. Had it been in his interest to do so, he might have claimed a common law marriage arising out of this relationship as an impediment invalidating plaintiff's subsequent marriage to McCarley.

The fact that the relationship of the parties may have been meretricious in the beginning, or that they may have been in pari delicto, does not defeat her rights in the property accumulated during such relationship. A court of equity will protect the property rights of the parties in such cases, either according to their agreement in respect to property, or according to principles of equity and justice. [Citations omitted.]

We conclude that the parties are husband and wife and that the plaintiff is entitled to a decree of divorce on the ground of extreme cruelty.

* * *

The judgment is reversed and the cause remanded with directions to enter judgment in conformity herewith.

Comments

Marriage by estoppel belongs to the realm of legal fictions. The parties are treated *as if* they were married. The statement implies that in reality they are not. Sometimes, as in *Mason*, the party estopped toward one person to assert that no marriage exists may be legally married to another person. The application of estoppel to marriage may therefore lead to situations in which a husband appears to be married to two wives. In *Mason* the husband continued to be legally married to wife no. 1 while, according to the court's reasoning, he was estopped toward wife no. 2, who consequently could claim all rights as a widow. Wife no. 1 was also estopped because she did not step forward to assert her rights from the marriage. In effect this means that wife no. 1 had an affirmative duty toward wife no. 2 to inform her that there never was a final divorce.

Mason invites speculation about the nature of estoppel. Assume, for example, that the husband had still been alive. Both he and wife no. 1 could have asked for a divorce, assuming other requirements were met, because they continued to be legally married to each other. On the other hand, neither he nor wife no. 2 could have asked for a divorce because they were in fact not married. It is questionable whether the husband would be estopped from raising the lack of marital status in the divorce action itself, although in regard to the economic consequences of marriage the estoppel theory would likely work in favor of wife no. 2. Both wife no. 1 and wife no. 2 would probably be entitled to support under theories of marriage and estoppel. Wife no. 2 could ask for an annulment of marriage because of bigamy. Some jurisdictions would deny the husband the right to an annulment action because of his bad faith, while others would stress the public interest in a clarification of status regardless of good faith.

On the whole, estoppel seems to affect financial matters far more than actual marital status. From that standpoint, talk about marriage by estoppel is a misnomer. Yet in actual litigation the lines are blurred, as for example in *Edgar* and *Warner*. In these cases marriage by estoppel and marriage by presumption are commingled, although conceptually this does not seem to make sense. Marriage by presumption results in real marriage, while estoppel is a mere fiction of marriage which in fact does not exist. On the other hand, a presumption, if practically irrebuttable, becomes a legal fiction too. For instance, in *Edgar*, wife no. 1 was caught in her own lie and treated as if she had obtained a divorce. By somewhat circular reasoning, the court treated her earlier statements that she had obtained a divorce as if they were true. They raised a presumption of divorce which she failed to overcome. If she had submitted a divorce decree, she would have failed because she would not then have been married. Had she admitted to having lied, she would have been estopped to assert her marriage toward the bona fide wife no. 2. The overriding concern seems to be an understanding that the more recent wife has better rights, especially if the cohabitation is of some length. The rights of an original wife are somewhat improved, if she is in good faith and was not remiss in asserting herself.

Essentially, these cases demonstrate that legal fictions can bring about just results under the appearance of marriage, regardless of the absence of legal marriage. Note also the overlap between estoppel and implied contract of cohabitation. The misrepresentation leading to estoppel can sometimes be viewed as a promise, and the reliance on the misrepresentation can be characterized as an acceptance. There is an element of artificiality in these legal distinctions, and they can be used interchangeably, provided the functional relationship is seen. *Warner* mentions promises that were made by the husband; it also applies a presumption of marriage and states that the defendant is estopped to deny the validity of his marriage. It even mentions that there might be a real common law marriage that invalidates an intervening marriage. The mere promise implies that there might have been a contract, but not necessarily a marriage. The presumption is a real marriage until overcome by contrary evidence. The estoppel implies that there was no marriage, but that the defendant is treated as if there were one. The common law marriage is a real marriage. The court therefore applied four conceptually independent theories, two of them implying that there was a marriage and two that there was not. The outcome of these contradictory theories was identical. The wife was entitled to a property settlement on a theory of marriage or quasi-marriage.

Reference

Weyrauch, *Informal and Formal Marriage—An Appraisal of Trends in Family Organization,* 28 U. Chi. L. Rev. 88 (1960).

Bibliography

Baade, *The Form of Marriage in Spanish North America,* 61 Cornell L. Rev. 1 (1975).

Bailey, *Legal Recognition of De Facto Relationships,* 52 Austl. L.J. 174 (1978).

Bates, *Presumption of Marriage Arising from Cohabitation,* 13 U.W. Ont. L. Rev. 341 (1976).

Blumberg, *Cohabitation Without Marriage: A Different Perspective,* 28 UCLA L. Rev. 1125 (1981).

Bruch, *Nonmarital Cohabitation in the Common Law Countries: A Study in Judicial-Legislative Interaction,* 29 Am. J. Comp. L. 217 (1981).

Bruch, *Property Rights of De Facto Spouses Including Thoughts on the Value of Homemakers' Services,* 10 Fam. L.Q. 101 (1976).

Casad, *Unmarried Couples and Unjust Enrichment: From Status to Contract and Back Again?,* 77 Mich. L. Rev. 47 (1978).

Fineman, *Law and Changing Patterns of Behavior: Sanctions on Non-Marital Cohabitation*, 1981 Wis. L. Rev. 275 (1981).

Folberg & Buren, *Domestic Partnership: A Proposal for Dividing the Property of Unmarried Families*, 12 Willamette L.J. 453 (1976).

Glendon, *Marriage and the State: The Withering Away of Marriage*, 62 Va. L. Rev. 663 (1976).

Glendon, M., The New Family and the New Property (1981).

Glendon, M., State, Law and Family: Family Law in Transition in the United States and Western Europe (1977).

Note, *Cohabitation: New Views on a New Lifestyle*, 6 Fla. St. U.L. Rev. 1393 (1978).

Note, *Policy Considerations in the Enforcement of Nonmarital Cohabitation Property Rights*, 8 N.M.L. Rev. 81 (1978).

Note, *Property Rights of Unmarried Cohabitants—A Proposal*, 14 Cal. W.L. Rev. 485 (1979).

Note, *Rights of the Putative Spouse*, 1978 S. Ill. U.L.J. 423 (1978).

Samek, *Synthetic Approach and Unjustifiable Enrichment*, 27 U. Toronto L.J. 335–63 (1977).

Skolnik, A., *The Social Contexts of Cohabitation*, 29 Am. J. Comp. L. 339 (1981).

Weyrauch, *Informal and Formal Marriage—An Appraisal of Trends in Family Organization*, 28 U. Chi. L. Rev. 88 (1960).

Weyrauch, *Informal Marriage and Common Law Marriage*, in Sexual Behavior and the Law 297 (R. Slovenko ed. 1965).

Cohabitation Contract

Cohabitation Contract as Substitute for Marriage, Trial Marriage, or Holdover Marriage

Peck v. Peck

Supreme Judicial Court of Massachusetts

155 Mass. 479, 30 N.E. 74 (1892)

Lathrop, J. This is a libel for divorce on the ground of desertion, filed February 2, 1891. The justice of the superior court who heard the case found that no valid marriage was proved and ordered the libel to be dismissed. The case comes before us on a report of the evidence, from which it appears that on October 5, 1877, the parties, having for three years before had their domicile in the state of California, executed the following contract at Portland, Or., which was witnessed by two persons:

> "We, the undersigned, hereby enter into a copartnership on the basis of the true marriage relation. Recognizing love as the only law which should govern the sexual relationship, we agree to continue this copartnership so long as mutual affection shall exist, and to dissolve it when the union becomes disagreeable or undersirable to either party. We also agree that

all property that shall be acquired by mutual effort shall be equally divided on the dissolution of said copartnership. Should any children result from this union, we pledge ourselves to be mutually held and bound to provide them support whether the union continues or is dissolved."

It is further found that the parties thereafterwards lived together under said contract, and held themselves out to be husband and wife, in the state of Oregon, for about three months; in California for about one year; in Iowa, for about three and a half years; in New York, for about three months, and at Boston, in this commonwealth, from 1886 to the time of the alleged desertion, on or about January 15, 1888, and that both said parties have resided in this state from said alleged desertion to the day of the filing of the libel; that the libelee was a spiritualist public speaker, who, on account of peculiar religious and business motives, and by consent of the libelant, retained the name of Mrs. H. S. Lake, the name of her former husband, who died before the year 1877, and there never was any ceremony, act, or solemnization of marriage between them, save as herein stated. The report also sets out the laws relating to marriage of the states of California, Oregon, Iowa, and New York, but does not refer us to any decisions of the courts of those states construing the laws set forth.

There is nothing in the law of California, where the parties had their domicile, or in the law of Oregon, where the contract was signed, which recognizes an agreement to live together, "so long as mutual affection shall exist," as a marriage contract. We have, therefore, no occasion to consider whether, by the law of either of those states, there can be a marriage by a mere contract, without a ceremony. There being no marriage, their subsequent cohabitation points only to the illegal contract under which it began. There is no room for any presumptions. We find nothing in the laws of the states where they lived together which recognizes such a cohabitation as a marriage. [Citations omitted.] Decree affirmed.

Marvin v. Marvin [I]

Supreme Court of California

18 Cal.3d 660, 134 Cal. Rptr. 815, 557 P.2d 106 (1976)

TOBRINER, J.

During the past 15 years, there has been a substantial increase in the number of couples living together without marrying.[1] Such nonmarital relationships lead to legal controversy when one partner dies or the couple separates. Courts of Appeal, faced with the task of determining property rights in such cases, have arrived at conflicting positions: two cases (*In re Marriage of Cary* (1973) 34 Cal. App.3d 345, 109 Cal. Rptr. 862; *Estate of Atherley* (1975) 44 Cal. App.3d 758, 119 Cal. Rptr. 41) have held that the Family Law Act (Civ. Code, §4000 *et seq.*) requires division of the property

---

[1]"The 1970 census figures indicate that today perhaps eight times as many couples are living together without being married as cohabitated ten years ago." (Comment, *In re Cary: A Judicial Recognition of Illicit Cohabitation* (1974) 25 HASTINGS L.J. 1228.)

according to community property principles, and one decision (*Beckman v. Mayhew* (1975) 49 Cal. App.3d 529, 122 Cal. Rptr. 604) has rejected that holding. * * *

We conclude: (1) The provisions of the Family Law Act do not govern the distribution of property acquired during nonmarital relationship; such a relationship remains subject solely to judicial decision. (2) The courts should enforce express contracts between nonmarital partners except to the extent that the contract is explicitly founded on the consideration of meretricious sexual services. (3) In the absence of an express contract, the courts should inquire into the conduct of the parties to determine whether that conduct demonstrates an implied contract, agreement of partnership or joint venture, or some other tacit understanding between the parties. The courts may also employ the doctrine of quantum meruit, or equitable remedies such as constructive or resulting trusts, when warranted by the facts of the case.

In the instant case plaintiff and defendant lived together for seven years without marrying; all property acquired during this period was taken in defendant's name. When plaintiff sued to enforce a contract under which she was entitled to half the property and to support payments, the trial court granted judgment on the pleadings for defendant, thus leaving him with all the property accumulated by the couple during their relationship. Since the trial court denied plaintiff a trial on the merits of her claim, its decision conflicts with the principles stated above, and must be reversed.

1. *The factual setting of this appeal.*

Since the trial court rendered judgment for defendant on the pleadings, we must accept the allegations of plaintiff's complaint as true, determining whether such allegations state, or can be amended to state, a cause of action. * * *

Plaintiff avers that in October of 1964 she and defendant "entered into an oral agreement" that while "the parties lived together they would combine their efforts and earnings and would share equally any and all property accumulated as a result of their efforts whether individual or combined." Furthermore, they agreed to "hold themselves out to the general public as husband and wife" and that "plaintiff would further render her services as a companion, homemaker, housekeeper and cook to * * * defendant."

Shortly thereafter plaintiff agreed to "give up her lucrative career as an entertainer [and] singer" in order to "devote her full time to defendant * * * as a companion, homemaker, housekeeper and cook"; in return defendant agreed to "provide for all of plaintiff's financial support and needs for the rest of her life."

Plaintiff alleges that she lived with defendant from October of 1964 through May of 1970 and fulfilled her obligations under the agreement. During this period the parties as a result of their efforts and earnings acquired in defendant's name substantial real and personal property, including motion picture rights worth over $1 million. In May of 1970, however, defendant compelled plaintiff to leave his household. He continued to support plaintiff until November of 1971, but thereafter refused to provide further support.

On the basis of these allegations plaintiff asserts two causes of action. The first, for declaratory relief, asks the court to determine her contract and property rights; the second seeks to impose a constructive trust upon one half of the property acquired during the course of the relationship.

Defendant demurred unsuccessfully, and then answered the complaint. Following extensive discovery and pretrial proceedings, the case came to trial.[2] Defendant renewed his attack on the complaint by a motion to dismiss. Since the parties had stipulated that defendant's marriage to Betty Marvin did not terminate until the filing of a final decree of divorce in January 1967, the trial court treated defendant's motion as one for judgment on the pleadings augmented by the stipulation.

After hearing argument the court granted defendant's motion and entered judgment for defendant. Plaintiff moved to set aside the judgment and asked leave to amend her complaint to allege that she and defendant reaffirmed their agreement after defendant's divorce was final. The trial court denied plaintiff's motion, and she appealed from the judgment.

2. *Plaintiff's complaint states a cause of action for breach of an express contract.*

In *Trutalli v. Meraviglia* (1932) 215 Cal. 698, 12 P.2d 430 we established the principle that nonmarital partners may lawfully contract concerning the ownership of property acquired during the relationship. We reaffirmed this principle in *Vallera v. Vallera* (1943) 21 Cal.2d 681, 685, 134 P.2d 761, 763, stating that "If a man and woman [who are not married] live together as husband and wife under an agreement to pool their earnings and share equally in their joint accumulations, equity will protect the interests of each in such property."

In the case before us plaintiff, basing her cause of action in contract upon these precedents, maintains that the trial court erred in denying her a trial on the merits of her contention. Although that court did not specify the ground for its conclusion that plaintiff's contractual allegations stated no cause of action,[3] defendant offers some four theories to sustain the ruling; we proceed to examine them.

Defendant first and principally relies on the contention that the alleged contract is so closely related to the supposed "immoral" character of the relationship between plaintiff and himself that the enforcement of the contract would violate public policy.[4] He points to cases asserting that a con-

---

[2]When the case was called for trial, plaintiff asked leave to file an amended complaint. The proposed complaint added two causes of action for breach of contract against Santa Ana Records, a corporation not a party to the action, asserting that Santa Ana was an alter ego of defendant. The court denied leave to amend, and plaintiff claims that the ruling was an abuse of discretion. We disagree; plaintiff's argument was properly rejected by the Court of Appeal in the portion of its opinion quoted below.

No error was committed in denial of plaintiff's motion, made on the opening day set for trial, seeking leave to file a proposed amended complaint which would have added two counts and a new defendant to the action. As stated by plaintiff's counsel at the hearing. "[T]here is no question about it that we seek to amend the Complaint not on the eve of trial but on the day of trial."

* * *

[3]The colloquy between the court and counsel at argument on the motion for judgment on the pleadings suggests that the trial court held the 1964 agreement violated public policy because it derogated the community property rights of Betty Marvin, defendant's lawful wife. Plaintiff, however, offered to amend her complaint to allege that she and defendant reaffirmed their contract after defendant and Betty were divorced. The trial court denied leave to amend, a ruling which suggests that the court's judgment must rest upon some other ground than the assertion that the contract would injure Betty's property rights.

[4]Defendant also contends that the contract was illegal because it contemplated a violation of former Penal Code section 269a, which prohibited living "in a state of cohabitation and adultery." (§269a was repealed by Stats. 1975, ch. 71, eff. Jan. 1, 1976.) Defendant's standing to raise the issue is questionable because he alone was married and thus guilty of violating section 269a. Plaintiff, being unmarried could neither be convicted of adulterous cohabitation nor of aiding and abetting defendant's violation. (See *In re Cooper* (1912) 162 Cal. 81, 85-86, 121 P. 318.)

The numerous cases discussing the contractual rights of unmarried couples have drawn no distinction between illegal relationships and lawful nonmarital relationships. (Cf. *Weak v. Weak* (1962) 202 Cal. App.2d 632, 639, 21 Cal. Rptr. 9 (bigamous marriage).) Moreover, even if we were

tract between nonmarital partners is unenforceable if it is "involved in" an illicit relationship [citations omitted.]. A review of the numerous California decisions concerning contracts between nonmarital partners, however, reveals that the courts have not employed such broad and uncertain standards to strike down contracts. The decisions instead disclose a narrower and more precise standard: a contract between nonmarital partners is unenforceable only *to the extent* that it *explicitly* rests upon the immoral and illicit consideration of meretricious sexual services.

* * *

Although the past decisions hover over the issue in the somewhat wispy form of the figures of a Chagall painting, we can abstract from those decisions a clear and simple rule. The fact that a man and woman live together without marriage, and engage in a sexual relationship, does not in itself invalidate agreements between them relating to their earnings, property, or expenses. Neither is such an agreement invalid merely because the parties may have contemplated the creation or continuation of a nonmarital relationship when they entered into it. Agreements between nonmarital partners fail only to the extent that they rest upon a consideration of meretricious sexual services. Thus the rule asserted by defendant, that a contract fails if it is "involved in" or made "in contemplation" of a nonmarital relationship, cannot be reconciled with the decisions.

The three cases cited by defendant which have *declined* to enforce contracts between nonmarital partners involved consideration that was expressly founded upon an illicit sexual services. In *Hill v. Estate of Westbrook, supra*, 95, Cal. App.2d 599, 213 P.2d 727, the woman promised to keep house for the man, to live with him as man and wife, and to bear his children; the man promised to provide for her in his will, but died without doing so. Reversing a judgment for the woman based on the reasonable value of her services, the Court of Appeal stated that

> "the action is predicated upon a claim which seeks, among other things, the reasonable value of living with decedent in meretricious relationship and bearing him two children * * *. The law does not award compensation for living with a man as a concubine and bearing him children. * * * As the judgment is, at least in part, for the value of the claimed services for which recovery cannot be had, it must be reversed."

(95 Cal. App.2d at p. 603, 213 P.2d at p. 730.) Upon retrial, the trial court found that it could not sever the contract and place an independent value upon the legitimate services performed by claimant. We therefore affirmed a judgment for the estate. (*Hill v. Estate of Westbrook* (1952) 39 Cal.2d 458, 247 P.2d 19.)

In the only other cited decision refusing to enforce a contract, *Updeck v. Samuel* (1964), 123 Cal. 2d 264, 266 P.2d 822, the contract "was based on the consideration that the parties live together as husband and wife" (123 Cal. App.2d at p. 267, 266 P.2d at p. 824.) Viewing the contract as calling for adultery, the court held it illegal.[8]

---

to draw such a distinction—a largely academic endeavor in view of the repeal of section 269a—defendant probably would not benefit; his relationship with plaintiff continued long after his divorce became final, and plaintiff sought to amend her complaint to assert that the parties reaffirmed their contract after the divorce.

[8]Although not cited by defendant, the only California precedent which supports his position is *Heaps v. Toy* (1942) 54 Cal. App.2d 178, 128 P.2d 813. In that case the woman promised to leave her job, to refrain from marriage, to be a companion to the man, and to make a permanent home for him; he agreed to support the woman and her child for life. The Court of Appeal held the agreement invalid as a contract in restraint of marriage (Civ. Code, §1678) and, alternatively, as "contrary to good morals" (Civ. Code, §1607). The opinion does not state that sex-

The decisions in the *Hill* and *Updeck* cases thus demonstrate that a contract between nonmarital partners, even if expressly made in contemplation of a common living arrangement, is invalid only if sexual acts form an inseparable part of the consideration for the agreement. In sum, a court will not enforce a contract for the pooling of property and earnings if it is explicitly and inseparably based upon services as a paramour. The Court of Appeal opinion in *Hill,* however, indicates that even if sexual services are part of the contractual consideration, any *severable* portion of the contract supported by independent consideration will still be enforced.

The principle that a contract between nonmarital partners will be enforced unless expressly and inseparably based upon an illicit consideration of sexual services not only represents the distillation of the decisional law, but also offers a far more precise and workable standard than that advocated by defendant. Our recent decision in *In re Marriage of Dawley* (1976) 17 Cal.3d 342, 551 P.2d 323, offers a close analogy. Rejecting the contention that an antenuptial agreement is invalid if the parties contemplated a marriage of short duration, we pointed out in *Dawley* that a standard based upon the subjective contemplation of the parties is uncertain and unworkable; such a test, we stated, "might invalidate virtually all antenuptial agreements on the ground that the parties contemplated dissolution * * * but it provides no principled basis for determining which antenuptial agreements offend public policy and which do not." (17 Cal.3d 342, 352, 551 P.2d 323, 329.)

Similarly, in the present case a standard which inquires whether an agreement is "involved" in or "contemplates" a nonmarital relationship is vague and unworkable. Virtually all agreements between nonmarital partners can be said to be "involved" in some sense in the fact of their mutual sexual relationship, or to "contemplate" the existence of that relationship. Thus defendant's proposed standards, if taken literally, might invalidate all agreements between nonmarital partners, a result no one favors. Moreover, those standards offer no basis to distinguish between valid and invalid agreements. By looking not to such uncertain tests, but only to the consideration underlying the agreement, we provide the parties and the courts with a practical guide to determine when an agreement between nonmarital partners should be enforced.

Defendant secondly relies upon the ground suggested by the trial court: that the 1964 contract violated public policy because it impaired the community property rights of Betty Marvin, defendant's lawful wife. Defendant points out that his earnings while living apart from his wife before rendition of the interlocutory decree were community property under 1964 statutory law (former Civ. Code, §§169, 169.2) and that defendant's agreement with plaintiff purported to transfer to her a half interest in that community property. But whether or not defendant's contract with plaintiff exceeded his authority as manager of the community property (see former Civ. Code, §172), defendant's argument fails for the reason that an improper transfer of community property is not void *ab initio,* but merely voidable at the instance of the aggrieved spouse. [Citations omitted.]

In the present case Betty Marvin, the aggrieved spouse, had the opportunity to assert her community property rights in the divorce action. [Citation omitted.] The interlocutory and final decrees in that action fix and limit

---

ual relations formed any part of the consideration for the contract, nor explain how—unless the contract called for sexual relations—the woman's employment as a companion and housekeeper could be contrary to good morals.

The alternative holding in *Heaps v. Toy, supra,* finding the contract in that case contrary to good morals, is inconsistent with the numerous California decisions upholding contracts between nonmarital partners when such contracts are not founded upon an illicit considerations, and is therefore disapproved.

her interest. Enforcement of the contract between plaintiff and defendant against property awarded to defendant by the divorce decree will not impair any right of Betty's, and thus is not on that account violative of public policy.

Defendant's third contention is noteworthy for the lack of authority advanced in its support. He contends that enforcement of the oral agreement between plaintiff and himself is barred by Civil Code section 5134, which provides that "All contracts for marriage settlements must be in writing * * *." A marriage settlement, however, is an agreement in contemplation of marriage in which each party agrees to release or modify the property rights which would otherwise arise from the marriage. [Citation omitted.] The contract at issue here does not conceivably fall within that definition, and thus is beyond the compass of section 5134.[9]

Defendant finally argues that enforcement of the contract is barred by Civil Code section 43.5, subdivision (d), which provides that "No cause of action arises for * * * [b]reach of a promise of marriage." This rather strained contention proceeds from the premise that a promise of marriage impliedly includes a promise to support and to pool property acquired after marriage [citation omitted] to the conclusion that pooling and support agreements not part of or accompanied by promise of marriage are barred by the section. We conclude that section 43.5 is not reasonably susceptible to the interpretation advanced by defendant, a conclusion demonstrated by the fact that since section 43.5 was enacted in 1939, numerous cases have enforced pooling agreements between nonmarital partners, and in none did court or counsel refer to section 43.5.

In summary, we base our opinion on the principle that adults who voluntarily live together and engage in sexual relations are nonetheless as competent as any other persons to contract respecting their earnings and property rights. Of course, they cannot lawfully contract to pay for the performance of sexual services, for such a contract is, in essence, an agreement for prostitution and unlawful for that reason. But they may agree to pool their earnings and to hold all property acquired during the relationship in accord with the law governing community property; conversely they may agree that each partner's earnings and the property acquired from those earnings remains the separate property of the earning partner.[10] So long as the agreement does not rest upon illicit meretricious consideration, the parties may order their economic affairs as they choose, and no policy precludes the courts from enforcing such agreements.

In the present instance, plaintiff alleges that the parties agreed to pool their earnings, that they contracted to share equally in all property acquired and that defendant agreed to support plaintiff. The terms of the contract as alleged do not rest upon any unlawful consideration. We therefore conclude that the complaint furnishes a suitable basis upon which the trial court can render declaratory relief. (See 3 Witkin, CAL. PROCEDURE (2d ed.) pp. 2335–2336.) The trial court consequently erred in granting defendant's motion for judgment on the pleadings.

---

[9]Our review of the many cases enforcing agreements between nonmarital partners reveals that the majority of such agreements were oral. In two cases (*Ferguson v. Schuenemann, supra,* 167 Cal. App.2d 413, 334 P.2d 668; *Cline v. Festersen, supra.* 128 Cal. App.2d 380, 275 P.2d 149), the court expressly rejected defenses grounded upon the statute of frauds.

[10]A great variety of other arrangements are possible. The parties might keep their earnings and property separate, but agree to compensate one party for services which benefit the other. They may choose to pool only part of their earnings and property, to form a partnership or joint venture, or to hold property acquired as joint tenants or tenants in common, or agree to any other such arrangement. (See generally Weitzman, *Legal Regulation of Marriage: Tradition and Change* (1974) 82 CAL. L. REV. 1169.)

3. Plantiff's complaint can be amended to state a cause of action founded
upon theories of implied contract or equitable relief.

As we have noted, both causes of action in plaintiff's complaint allege
an express contract; neither assert any basis for relief independent from the
contract. In *In re Marriage of Cary, supra,* 34, Cal. App.3d 345. 109 Cal.
Rptr. 862, however, the Court of Appeal held that, in view of the policy of
the Family Law Act, property accumulated by nonmarital partners in an actual family relationship should be divided equally. Upon examining the
Cary opinion, the parties to the present case realized that plaintiff's alleged
relationship with defendant might arguably support a cause of action independent of any express contract between the parties. The parties have
therefore briefed and discussed the issue of the property rights of a nonmarital partner in the absence of an express contract. Although our conclusion that plaintiff's complaint states a cause of action based on an express
contract alone compels us to reverse the judgment for defendant, resolution
of the *Cary* issue will serve both to guide the parties upon retrial and to resolve a conflict presently manifest in published Court of Appeal decisions.

Both plaintiff and defendant stand in broad agreement that the law
should be fashioned to carry out the reasonable expectations of the parties.
Plaintiff, however, presents the following contentions: that the decisions
prior to *Cary* rest upon implicit and erroneous notions of punishing a party
for his or her guilt in entering into a nonmarital relationship, that such decisions result in an inequitable distribution of property accumulated during
the relationship, and that *Cary* correctly held that the enactment of the
Family Law Act in 1970 overturned those prior decisions. Defendant in response maintains that the prior decisions merely applied common law principles of contract and property to persons who have deliberately elected to
remain outside the bounds of the community property system.[11] *Cary,*
defendant contends, erred in holding that the Family Law Act vitiated the
force of the prior precedents.

As we shall see from examination of the pre-*Cary* decisions, the truth
lies somewhere between the positions of plaintiff and defendant. The classic
opinion on this subject is *Vallera v. Vallera, supra,* 21 Cal.2d 681, 134 P.2d
761. Speaking for a four-member majority, Justice Traynor posed the question: "whether a woman living with a man as his wife but with no genuine
belief that she is legally married to him acquires by reason of cohabitation
alone the rights of a co-tenant in his earnings and accumulations during the
period of their relationship." * * * *Vallera* explains that "Equitable considerations arising from the reasonable expectation of the continuation of
benefits attending the status of marriage entered into in good faith are not
present in such a case." (P. 685, 134 P.2d p. 763.) In the absence of express
contract, *Vallera* concluded, the woman is entitled to share in property
jointly accumulated only "in the proportion that her funds contributed

---

[11]We note that a deliberate decision to avoid the strictures of the community property
system is not the only reason that couples live together without marriage. Some couples may
wish to avoid the permanent commitment that marriage implies, yet be willing to share
equally any property acquired during the relationship; others may fear the loss of pension,
welfare, or tax benefits resulting from marriage (see *Beckman v. Mayhew, supra,* 49 Cal.
App.3d 529, 122 Cal. Rptr. 604). Others may engage in the relationship as a possible prelude
to marriage. In lower socio-economic groups the difficulty and expense of dissolving a former
marriage often leads couples to choose a nonmarital relationship; many unmarried couples
may also incorrectly believe that the doctrine of common law marriage prevails in California,
and thus that they are in fact married. Consequently we conclude that the mere fact that a
couple have not participated in a valid marriage ceremony cannot serve as a basis for a court's
inference that the couple intend to keep their earnings and property separate and independent: the parties' intention can only be ascertained by a more searching inquiry into the
nature of their relationship.

toward its acquisition." (P. 685, 134 P.2d p. 763). Justice Curtis dissenting, argued that the evidence showed an implied contract under which each partner owned an equal interest in property acquired during the relationship.

The majority opinion in *Vallera* did not expressly bar recovery based upon an implied contract, nor preclude resort to equitable remedies. But *Vallera's* broad assertion that equitable considerations "are not present" in the case of a nonmarital relationship (21 Cal.2d at p. 685, 134 P.2d 761) led the Courts of Appeal to interpret the language to preclude recovery based on such theories. [Citations omitted.]

Consequently, when the issue of the rights of a nonmarital partner reached the court in *Keene v. Keene* (1962) 57 Cal.2d 657, 21 Cal. Rptr. 593, 371 P.2d 329, the claimant forwent reliance upon theories of contract implied in law or fact. Asserting that she had worked on her partner's ranch and that her labor had enhanced its value she confined her cause of action to the claim that the court should impress a resulting trust on the property derived from the sale of the ranch. The court limited its opinion accordingly, rejecting her argument on the ground that the rendition of service gives rise to a resulting trust only when the services aid in acquisition of the property, not in its subsequent improvement. (57 Cal.2d at p. 668, 21 Cal. Rptr. 593, 371 P.2d 329.) Justice Peters, dissenting, attacked the majority's distinction between the rendition of services and the contribution of funds or property; he maintained that both property and services furnished valuable consideration, and potentially afforded the ground for a resulting trust.

The failure of the courts to recognize an action by a nonmarital partner based upon implied contract, or to grant an equitable remedy, contrasts with the judicial treatment of the putative spouse. Prior to the enactment of the Family Law Act, no statute granted rights to a putative spouse. The courts accordingly fashioned a variety of remedies by judicial decision. Some cases permitted the putative spouse to recover half the property on a theory that the conduct of the parties implied an agreement of partnership or joint venture. (See *Estate of Vargas* (1974) 36 Cal. App.3d 714, 717–718, 111 Cal. Rptr. 779; *Sousa v. Freitas* (1970) 10 Cal. App.3d 660, 666, 89 Cal. Rptr. 485.) Others permitted the spouse to recover the reasonable value of rendered services, less the value of support received. (See *Sanguinetti v. Sanguinetti* (1937) 9 Cal.2d 95, 100, 102, 69 P.2d 845.) Finally, decisions affirmed the power of a court to employ equitable principles to achieve a fair division of property acquired during putative marriage. [Citations omitted.]

Thus in summary, the cases prior to *Cary* exhibited a schizophrenic inconsistency. By enforcing an express contract between nonmarital partners unless it rested upon an unlawful consideration, the courts applied a common law principle as to contracts. Yet the courts disregarded the common law principle that holds that implied contracts can arise from the conduct of the parties.[16] Refusing to enforce such contracts, the courts spoke of leaving the parties "in the position in which they had placed themselves" (*Oakley v. Oakley, supra*, 82 Cal. App.2d 188, 192, 185 P.2d 848, 850), just as if they were guilty parties "*in pari delicto.*"

---

[16]"Contracts may be express or implied.

These terms, however, do not denote different kinds of contracts, but have reference to the evidence by which the agreement between the parties is shown. If the agreement is shown by the direct words of the parties, spoken or written, the contract is said to be an express one. But if such agreement can only be shown by the acts and conduct of the parties, interpreted in the light of the subject-matter and of the surrounding circumstances, then the contract is an implied one."

(*Skelly v. Bristol Sav. Bank* (1893) 63 Conn. 83, 26 A. 474, 475, quoted in 1 Corbin, CONTRACTS (1963) p. 41.) Thus, as Justice Schauer observed in *Desny v. Wilder* (1956) 46 Cal.2d 715, 299 P.2d 257, in a sense all contracts made in fact, as distinguished from quasi-contractual obligations, are express contracts, differing only in the manner in which the assent of the parties is expressed and proved. (See 46 Cal.2d at pp. 735–736, 299 P.2d 257.)

Justice Curtis noted this inconsistency in his dissenting opinion in *Vallera*, pointing out that "if an express agreement will be enforced, there is no legal or just reason why an implied agreement to share the property cannot be enforced." (21 Cal.2d 681, 686, 134 P.2d 761, 764; see Bruch, *Property Rights of De Facto Spouses Including Thoughts on the Value of Homemakers' Services* (1976) [10] FAMILY L.Q. [101].) And in *Keene v. Keene, supra,* 57 Cal.2d 657, 21 Cal. Rptr. 593, 371 P.2d 329, Justice Peters observed that if the man and woman "were not illegally living together * * * it would be a plain business relationship and a contract would be implied." (Diss. opn. at p. 672, 21 Cal. Rptr. at p. 602, 371 P.2d at p. 338.)

Still another inconsistency in the prior cases arises from their treatment of property accumulated through joint effort. To the extent that a partner had contributed *funds* or *property*, the cases held that the partner obtains a proportionate share in the acquisition, despite the lack of legal standing of the relationship. [Citations omitted.] Yet courts have refused to recognize just such an interest based upon the contribution of services. As Justice Curtis points out, "Unless it can be argued that a woman's services as cook, housekeeper, and homemaker are valueless, it would seem logical that if, when she contributes money to the purchase of property, her interest will be protected, then when she contributes her services in the home, her interest in property accumulated should be protected." (*Vallera v. Vallera, supra,* 21 Cal.2d 681, 686–687, 134 P.2d 761, 764 (diss. opn.); see Bruch, *op. cit. supra,* [10] FAMILY L.Q. [101]; [other citations omitted].

Thus as of 1973, the time of the filing of *In re Marriage of Cary, supra,* 34 Cal. App.3d 345, 109 Cal. Rptr. 862, the cases apparently held that a nonmarital partner who rendered services in the absence of express contract could assert no right to property acquired during the relationship. The facts of *Cary* demonstrated the unfairness of that rule.

Janet and Paul Cary had lived together, unmarried, for more than eight years. They held themselves out to friends and family as husband and wife, reared four children, purchased a home and other property, obtained credit, filed joint income tax returns, and otherwise conducted themselves as though they were married. Paul worked outside the home, and Janet generally cared for the house and children.

In 1971 Paul petitioned for "nullity of the marriage."[17] Following a hearing on that petition, the trial court awarded Janet half the property acquired during the relationship, although all such property was traceable to Paul's earnings. The Court of Appeal affirmed the award.

Reviewing the prior decisions which had denied relief to the homemaking partner, the Court of Appeal reasoned that those decisions rested upon a policy of punishing persons guilty of cohabitation without marriage. The Family Law Act, the court observed, aimed to eliminate fault or guilt as a basis for dividing marital property. But once fault or guilt is excluded, the court reasoned, nothing distinguishes the property rights of a nonmarital "spouse" from those of a putative spouse. Since the latter is entitled to half the "quasi marital property" (Civ. Code, §4452), the Court of Appeal concluded that, giving effect to the policy of the Family Law Act, a nonmarital cohabitator should also be entitled to half the property accumulated during

---

[17]The Court of Appeal opinion in *In re Marriage of Cary, supra,* does not explain why Paul Cary filed his action as a petition for nullity. Briefs filed with this court, however, suggest that Paul may have been seeking to assert rights as a putative spouse. In the present case, on the other hand, neither party claims the status of an actual or putative spouse. Under such circumstances an action to adjudge "the marriage" in the instant case a nullity would be pointless and could not serve as a device to adjudicate contract and property rights arising from the parties' nonmarital relationship. Accordingly, plaintiff here correctly chose to assert her rights by means of an ordinary civil action.

an "actual family relationship." (34 Cal. App.3d at p. 353, 109 Cal. Rptr. 862.)[18]

Cary met with a mixed reception in other appellate districts. In *Estate of Atherley, supra,* 44 Cal. App.3d 758, 119 Cal. Rptr. 41, the Fourth District agreed with *Cary* that under the Family Law Act a nonmarital partner in an actual family relationship enjoys the same right to an equal division of property as a putative spouse. In *Beckman v. Mayhew, supra,* 49 Cal. App.3d 529, 122 Cal. Rptr. 604, however, the Third District rejected *Cary* on the ground that the Family Law Act was not intended to change California law dealing with nonmarital relationships.

If *Cary* is interpreted as holding that the Family Law Act requires an equal division of property accumulated in nonmarital "actual family relationships," then we agree with *Beckman v. Mayhew* that *Cary* distends the act. No language in the Family Law Act addresses the property rights of nonmarital partners, and nothing in the legislative history of the act suggests that the Legislature considered that subject. The delineation of the rights of nonmarital partners before 1970 had been fixed entirely by judicial decision; we see no reason to believe that the Legislature, by enacting the Family Law Act, intended to change that state of affairs.

But although we reject the reasoning of *Cary* and *Atherley,* we share the perception of the *Cary* and *Atherley* courts that the application of former precedent in the factual setting of those cases would work an unfair distribution of the property accumulated by the couple. Justice Friedman in *Beckman v. Mayhew, supra,* 49 Cal. App.3d 529, 535, 122 Cal. Rptr. 604,

---

[18]The court in *Cary* also based its decision upon an analysis of Civil Code section 4452, which specifies the property rights of a putative spouse. Section 4452 states that if the "court finds that either party or both parties believed in good faith that the marriage was valid, the court should declare such party or parties to have the status of a putative spouse, and shall divide, in accordance with Section 4800, that property acquired during the union * * *." Since section 4800 requires an equal division of community property, *Cary* interpreted section 4452 to require an equal division of the property of a putative marriage, so long as one spouse believed in good faith that the marriage was valid. Thus under section 4452, Cary concluded, the "guilty spouse" (the spouse who knows the marriage is invalid) has the same right to half the property as does the "innocent" spouse.

Cary then reasoned that if the "guilty" spouse to a putative marriage is entitled to one-half the marital property, the "guilty" partner in a nonmarital relationship should also receive one-half of the property. Otherwise, the court stated,

"We should be obliged to presume a legislative intent that a person, who by deceit leads another to believe a valid marriage exists between them, shall be legally guaranteed half of the property they acquire even though most, or all, may have resulted from the earnings of the blameless partner. At the same time we must infer an inconsistent legislative intent that two persons who, candidly with each other, enter upon an unmarried family relationship, shall be denied any judicial aid whatever in the assertion of otherwise valid property rights."

(34 Cal. App.3d at p. 352, 109 Cal. Rptr. at p. 866.)

This reasoning in *Cary* has been criticized by commentators. (See Note, *op cit., supra,* 25 HASTINGS L.J. 1226, 1234–1235; Comment, *In re Marriage of Carey* [sic]: *The End of the Putative-Meretricious Spouse Distinction in California* (1975) 12 SAN DIEGO L. REV. 436, 444–446.) The Commentators note that Civil Code section 4455 provides that an "innocent" party to a putative marriage can recover spousal support, from which they infer that the Legislature intended to give only the "innocent" spouse a right to one-half of the quasi-marital property under section 4452.

We need not now resolve this dispute concerning the interpretation of section 4452. Even if *Cary* is correct in holding that a "guilty" putative spouse has a right to one-half of the marital property, it does not necessarily follow that a nonmarital partner has an identical right. In a putative marriage the parties will arrange their economic affairs with the expectation that upon dissolution the property will be divided equally. If a "guilty" putative spouse receives one-half of the property under section 4452, no expectation of the "innocent" spouse has been frustrated. In a nonmarital relationship, on the other hand, the parties may expressly or tacitly determine to order their economic relationship in some other manner, and to impose community property principles regardless of such understanding may frustrate the parties' expectations.

also questioned the continued viability of our decisions in *Vallera* and *Keene*; commentators have argued the need to reconsider those precedents.[20] We should not, therefore, reject the authority of *Cary* and *Atherley* without also examining the deficiencies in the former law which led to those decisions.

The principal reason why the pre-*Cary* decisions result in an unfair distribution of property inheres in the court's refusal to permit a nonmarital partner to assert rights based upon accepted principles of implied contract or equity. We have examined the reasons advanced to justify this denial of relief, and find that none have merit.

First, we note that the cases denying relief do not rest their refusal upon any theory of "punishing" a "guilty" partner. Indeed, to the extent that denial of relief "punishes" one partner, it necessarily rewards the other by permitting him to retain a disproportionate amount of the property. Concepts of "guilt" thus cannot justify an unequal division of property between two equally "guilty" persons.[21]

Other reasons advanced in the decisions fare no better. The principal argument seems to be that "[e]quitable considerations arising from the reasonable expectation of * * * benefits attending the status of marriage * * * are not present [in a nonmarital relationship]." (*Vallera v. Vallera, supra,* 21 Cal.2d at p. 685, 134 P.2d 761, 763.) But, although parties to a nonmarital relationship obviously cannot have based any expectations upon the belief that they were married, other expectations and equitable considerations remain. The parties may well expect that property will be divided in accord with the parties' own tacit understanding and that in the absence of such understanding the courts will fairly apportion property accumulated through mutual effort. We need not treat nonmarital partners as putatively married persons in order to apply principles of implied contract, or extend equitable remedies; we need to treat them only as we do any other unmarried persons.[22]

The remaining arguments advanced from time to time to deny remedies to the nonmarital partners are of less moment. There is no more reason to presume that services are contributed as a gift than to presume that funds are contributed as a gift; in any event the better approach is to presume, as Justice Peters suggested, "that the parties intend to deal fairly with each other." (*Keene v. Keene, supra,* 57 Cal.2d 657, 674, 21 Cal. Rptr. 593, 603, 371, P.2d 329, 339 (dissenting opn.); see Bruch, *op. cit., supra,* [10] FAMILY L.Q. [101].)

---

[20]See Bruch, *op. cit., supra,* [10] FAMILY L.Q. [101]; Article, *op. cit., supra,* 6 U.C. DAVIS L. REV. 354; Comment (1975) 6 GOLDEN GATE L. REV. 179, 197–201; Comment, *op. cit., supra,* 12 SAN DIEGO L. REV. 4356; Note, *op. cit., supra,* 25 HASTINGS L.J. 1226, 1246.

[21] Justice Finley of the Washington Supreme Court explains:

"Under such circumstances [the dissolution of a nonmarital relationship], this court and the courts of other jurisdictions have, in effect, sometimes said, 'We will wash our hands of such disputes. The parties should and must be left to their own devices, just where they find themselves.' To me, such pronouncements seem overly fastidious and a bit fatuous. They are unrealistic and, among other things, ignore the fact that an unannounced (but nevertheless effective and binding) rule of law is inherent in any such terminal statements by a court of law. The unannounced but inherent rule is simply that the party who has title, or in some instances who is in possession, will enjoy the rights of ownership of the property concerned. The rule often operates to the great advantage of the cunning and the shrewd, who wind up with possession of the property, or title to it in their names, at the end of a so-called meretricious relationship. So, although the courts proclaim that they will have nothing to do with such matters, the proclamation in itself establishes, as to the parties involved, an effective and binding rule of law which tends to operate purely by accident or perhaps by reason of the cunning, anticipatory designs of just one of the parties."

(*West v. Knowles* (1957) 50 Wash.2d 311, 311 P.2d 689, 692 (conc. opn.).)

[22] In some instances a confidential relationship may arise between nonmarital partners, and economic transactions between them should be governed by the principles applicable to such relationships.

The argument that granting remedies to the nonmarital partners would discourage marriage must fail; as *Cary* pointed out, "with equal or greater force the point might be made that the pre-1970 rule was calculated to cause the income producing partner to avoid marriage and thus retain the benefit of all of his or her accumulated earnings." (34 Cal. App.3d at p. 353, 109 Cal. Rptr. at p. 866.) Although we recognize the well-established public policy to foster and promote the institution of marriage [citation omitted], perpetuation of judicial rules which result in an inequitable distribution of property accumulated during a nonmarital relationship is neither a just nor an effective way of carrying out that policy.

In summary, we believe that the prevalence of nonmarital relationships in modern society and the social acceptance of them, marks this as a time when our courts should by no means apply the doctrine of the unlawfulness of the so-called meretricious relationship to the instant case. As we have explained, the nonenforceability of agreements expressly providing for meretricious conduct rested upon the fact that such conduct, as the word suggests, pertained to and encompassed prostitution. To equate the nonmarital relationship of today to such a subject matter is to do violence to an accepted and wholly different practice.

We are aware that many young couples live together without the solemnization of marriage, in order to make sure that they can successfully later undertake marriage. This trial period,[23] preliminary to marriage, serves as some assurance that the marriage will not subsequently end in dissolution to the harm of both parties. We are aware, as we have stated, of the pervasiveness of nonmarital relationships in other situations.

The mores of the society have indeed changed so radically in regard to cohabitation that we cannot impose a standard based on alleged moral considerations that have apparently been so widely abandoned by so many. Lest we be misunderstood, however, we take this occasion to point out that the structure of society itself largely depends upon the institution of marriage, and nothing we have said in this opinion should be taken to derogate from that institution. The joining of the man and woman in marriage is at once the most socially productive and individually fulfilling relationship that one can enjoy in the course of a lifetime.

We conclude that the judicial barriers that may stand in the way of a policy based upon the fulfillment of the reasonable expectations of the parties to a nonmarital relationship should be removed. As we have explained, the courts now hold that express agreements will be enforced unless they rest on an unlawful meretricious consideration. We add that in the absence of an express agreement, the courts may look to a variety of other remedies in order to protect the parties' lawful expectations.[24]

The courts may inquire into the conduct of the parties to determine whether that conduct demonstrates an implied contract or implied agreement of partnership or joint venture (see *Estate of Thornton* (1972) 81 Wash.2d 72, 499 P.2d 864), or some other tacit understanding between the parties. The courts may, when appropriate, employ principles of constructive trust (see *Omer v. Omer* (1974) 11 Wash. App. 386, 523 P.2d 957) or resulting trust (see *Hyman v. Hyman* (Tex. Civ. App. 1954) 275 S.W.2d 149). Finally, a nonmarital partner may recover in quantum meruit for the reasonable value of household services rendered less the reasonable value of support received

---

[23]Toffler, FUTURE SHOCK (Bantam Books, 1971) page 253.

[24]We do not seek to resurrect the doctrine of common law marriage, which was abolished in California by statute in 1895. (See *Norman v. Thomson* (1898) 121 Cal. 620, 628, 54 P. 143; *Estate of Abate* (1958) 166 Cal. App.2d 282, 292, 333 P.2d 200.) Thus we do not hold that plaintiff and defendant were "married," nor do we extend to plaintiff the rights which the Family Law Act grants valid or putative spouses; we hold only that she has the same rights to enforce contracts and to assert her equitable interest in property acquired through her effort as does any other unmarried person.

if he can show that he rendered services with the expectation of monetary reward. (See *Hill v. Estate of Westbrook, supra*, 39 Cal.2d 458, 462, 247 P.2d 19.)[25]

Since we have determined that plaintiff's complaint states a cause of action for breach of an express contract, and, as we have explained, can be amended to state a cause of action independent of allegations of express contract,[26] we must conclude that the trial court erred in granting defendant a judgment on the pleadings.

The judgment is reversed and the cause remanded for further proceedings consistent with the views expressed herein.

CLARK, Justice (concurring and dissenting).

The majority opinion properly permits recovery on the basis of either express or implied in fact agreement between the parties. These being the issues presented, their resolution requires reversal of the judgment. Here, the opinion should stop.

This court should not attempt to determine all anticipated rights, duties and remedies within every meretricious relationship—particularly in vague terms. Rather, these complex issues should be determined as each arises in a concrete case.

The majority broadly indicates that a party to a meretricious relationship may recover on the basis of equitable principles and *in quantum meruit*. However, the majority fails to advise us of the circumstances permitting recovery, limitations on recovery, or whether their numerous remedies are cumulative or exclusive. Conceivably, under the majority opinion a party may recover half of the property acquired during the relationship on the basis of general equitable principles, recover a bonus based on specific equitable considerations, and recover a second bonus *in quantum meruit*.

The general sweep of the majority opinion raises but fails to answer several questions. First, because the Legislature specifically excluded some parties to a meretricious relationship from the equal division rule of Civil Code section 4452, is this court now free to create an equal division rule? Second, upon termination of the relationship, is it equitable to impose the economic obligations of lawful spouses on meretricious parties when the latter may have rejected matrimony to avoid such obligations? Third, does not application of equitable principles—necessitating examination of the conduct of the parties—violate the spirit of the Family Law Act of 1969, designed to eliminate the bitterness and acrimony resulting from the former fault system in divorce? Fourth, will not application of equitable principles reimpose upon trial courts the unmanageable burden of arbitrating domestic disputes? Fifth, will not a *quantum meruit* system of compensation for services—discounted by benefits received—place meretricious spouses in a better position than lawful spouses? Sixth, if a *quantum meruit* system is to be allowed, does fairness not require inclusion of all services and all benefits regardless of how difficult the evaluation?

When the parties to a meretricious relationship show by express or implied in fact agreement they intend to create mutual obligations, the courts should enforce the agreement. However, in the absence of agreement, we should stop and consider the ramifications before creating economic obligations which may violate legislative intent, contravene the intention of the parties, and surely generate undue burdens on our trial courts.

---

[25] Our opinion does not preclude the evolution of additional equitable remedies to protect the expectations of the parties to a nonmarital relationship in cases in which existing remedies prove inadequate; the suitability of such remedies may be determined in later cases in light of the factual setting in which they arise.

[26] We do not pass upon the question whether, in the absence of an express or implied contractual obligation, a party to a nonmarital relationship is entitled to support payments from the other party after the relationship terminates.

By judicial overreach, the majority perform a *nunc pro tunc* marriage, dissolve it, and distribute its property on terms never contemplated by the parties, case law or the Legislature.

Marvin v. Marvin [II]

Superior Court of the State of California

5 FAM. L. REP. 3077 (1979)

MARSHALL, J.

April 18, 1979

The Supreme Court in *Marvin v. Marvin* (1976) 18 C.3d 660, 665, 134 Cal. Rptr. 815, 557 P.2d 106, decided that an unmarried person may recover from a person, with whom the former had lived, in accordance with any written contract between them unless the agreement "rest(s) on an unlawful meretricious consideration." (p. 684.) That court also determined that a nonmarital partner may recover if the conduct of the couple was such that a trial court could imply therefrom either "an implied contract, agreement of partnership or joint venture, or some other tacit understanding between the parties." (pp. 665, 682.) Lacking evidence which would support any such finding, "(T)he courts may also employ the doctrine of *quantum meruit*, or equitable remedies such as constructive or resulting trusts, when warranted by the facts of the case." (pp. 665, 677, 682, 684.)

Finally, the Supreme Court declared that a nonmarital partner may recover *in quantum meruit* for the reasonable value of household services less the reasonable value of support received. (p. 684.) The action was remanded to the Superior Court where evidence has been taken in implementation of the above described decision. The last mentioned remedy, *quantum meruit*, need not be considered here inasmuch as the plaintiff has dismissed her fourth and fifth causes of action based on such ground.

The first three causes of action, amended to reflect the remedies described by the Supreme Court, allege contractual, express and implied and equitable bases for judgment in favor of plaintiff.

In order to comply with the Supreme Court mandate, the trial court collected all available evidence which might bear on the relationship established after defendant allegedly promised plaintiff half of his property or which might serve as a basis for a tacit agreement or for equitable relief.

FACTS

In June, 1964, the parties met while they both were working on a picture called "Ship of Fools," he as a star and she as a stand-in. (She also was employed as a singer at the "Little Club" in Los Angeles.) A few days after their first meeting, they lunched together, then dined together. In a short time they saw each other on a daily basis after work. Sexual intimacy commenced about 2 weeks after their first date. During these early meetings, there was much conversation about their respective marital problems. The defendant said that, although he loved his wife and children, communication between him and his spouse had failed and he was unhappy. Plaintiff said that her marriage had been dissolved but her husband sought reconciliation.

Plaintiff testified that defendant told her that as soon as two people sign "a piece of paper," (meaning a marriage certificate) they waved that paper at each other whenever any problem arose instead of attempting to settle the problem. Defendant allegedly said that a license is a woman's insurance policy and he did not like that. Defendant further stated to plaintiff that when two people loved each other, there is no need for a license. Plaintiff declared that she told him that she did not necessarily agree with him.

Plaintiff testified that she hoped to secure a part in "Flower Drum Song" and was to journey to New York City for that purpose, but defendant did not want her to go as, he said, it was hard to conduct a romance at long distance. She did not go to New York. She rented an apartment for approximately one month. Defendant stayed with her from time to time.

In October, 1964, the plaintiff rented and moved into a house. The defendant moved in with her although he also maintained a room at a nearby hotel and occasionally stayed at the home where he lived with his wife and children. Plaintiff told defendant that they were not "living together." His response was, "What does it mean when your blouse and my suit come back (from) to the cleaners together?" He inquired, "Does it mean that I live here?" She testified that she replied, "Well, I guess it does."

Defendant allegedly repeated again and again, his opinion that a piece of paper, a marriage certificate, is not needed by people in love. Plaintiff testified that at first she thought he was crazy and asked him to explain. She did not think it would work without the "paper." Defendant responded that marriage was lacking in communication and that he was unhappy about it.

The defendant went to San Blas, Mexico in November or December of 1964 for sport fishing. He later invited plaintiff to join him, which she did. There, the defendant allegedly told her that he was unhappily married, that he might be terminating his marriage, and that he and plaintiff could be together. She testified that she doubted his words. He declared again that a woman does not need a piece of paper, a marriage certificate, for security. He repeated his belief that whenever there was a misunderstanding, each waved the paper at each other instead of working hard at clearing up the misunderstanding. He allegedly said that he would never marry again because he did not like that kind of arrangement. He declared that he was almost positive that his marriage was not going to mend and asked whether plaintiff and defendant could share their lives. She inquired as to his meaning. He replied that after the divorce he would be left with only "the shirt on his back (and alimony)" but would she like to live on the beach. She initially responded she was going to New York. Two days later she asked defendant if he really thought living together without marriage would work out. He said that it would and she agreed to live with him.

Then defendant allegedly uttered the words which plaintiff contends constitute a contractual offer. He said, "what I have is yours and what you have is mine." She then accepted the alleged offer but declared that she had her own career and she did not want to depend on anyone. Defendant said that he had no objection to her career, that they still could share and build their lives. She told him that she loved him, that she would care for him and their home, and that she would cook and be his companion. She offered to learn how to fish, a sport of which he was quite fond, although she got seasick. He said that she would get over her seasickness.

The defendant was intoxicated in San Blas a "few times" to the point of losing control. She said that in subsequent years, 1965 and 1966, he lost control whenever he drank. She testified that she asked him to stop drinking and that he did not do so.

Defendant vigorously denies telling plaintiff, "what I have is yours and what you have is mine"; he declared that he never said he would support her for life and that he never stated "I'll take care of you always." He further denies saying that a marriage license is a piece of paper which stood in the way of working out problems. He testified that he decided to get a divorce from his wife after he arrived at his beach house, many months after his return from San Blas. During the examination of defendant under Evidence Code, Section 776, counsel for plaintiff read from defendant's deposition wherein defendant declared that he wanted a relationship of no responsibility and that the plaintiff agreed thereto.

The defendant rented and later purchased a house on the Malibu beach. Plaintiff moved in, bringing a bed, stereo equipment and kitchen utensils. A refrigerator and washing machine were purchased. She bought food, cooked meals for defendant, cleaned house (after the first year, she had the periodic help of a cleaning woman). On occasion, the couple had visitors and they in turn went together to the homes of friends. In the circle of their friends and their acquaintances in the theatrical world, the plaintiff was reputed not to be defendant's wife.

In the six years of their relationship, they did considerable traveling, over 30 months away from the beach house, for the most part on various film locations. Plaintiff usually accompanied the defendant except for the seven months devoted to the filming of "Dirty Dozen" in England (she visited him for about a month) and an exploratory trip to Micronesia preliminary to filming "Hell in the Pacific."

Plaintiff testified that her acquaintance with the theatre began in 1957 as a dancer. She danced with several troupes. She states that she was a featured dancer in a group organized by Barry Ashton, who produced shows in Las Vegas. She further alleges that she was also a singer from about 1957 and appeared in nightclubs in several states and abroad. Her compensation was usually "scale," ranging from $285 to $400 a week. As to motion pictures, she served as a "stand-in" or in background groupings until her appearance in "Synanon" (shortly after working in "Ship of Fools" where she met defendant) in which she spoke some lines but was not a featured performer.

After the parties moved into the beach house, plaintiff continued to have singing engagements, encouraged by the defendant who would frequently attend, bringing friends and buying drinks for them to lengthen their stay and thereby increase plaintiff's audience.

A decorator was hired to work on the beach house and, after some structural changes, a substantial amount of furniture was purchased. Plaintiff worked with the decorator; both consulted defendant on occasion as to the purchases and alterations.

In 1966, defendant contacted a friend in Hawaii and secured a singing engagement for plaintiff. Before she left for Hawaii Santana Records, Inc., was organized by defendant and defendant paid for the recordation of four songs by plaintiff under the Santana label. With the assistance of her manager, Mimi Marleaux, plaintiff visited disc jockeys in Hawaii and promoted the record.

In that same year, 1966, defendant went to London to make a picture entitled, "Dirty Dozen." During his stay in England he wrote eight letters to plaintiff wherein he expressed affection for the plaintiff and looked forward to her coming to London. In one letter, Exhibit 13, he portrays an imaginary scene wherein he was "found guilty of robbing a 33-year-old cradle" and he answers the judge, "absolutely guilty, your honor. * * * Yes sir, I accept life with her, thank you your honor and the court. Will the jury please get out of that cradle!"

After the filming of "Dirty Dozen" and the parties' return to Malibu, Miss Marleaux allegedly was present in the Malibu house when defendant said, after plaintiff told Marleaux she was sorry she let her (Marleaux) down (by the slump in her career), "I don't know what you're worrying about. I'll always take care of you. * * *"

While in Hawaii, plaintiff alleges that there was a ninth letter wherein defendant demanded that she give up her career, cut short her promotion of her record in Hawaii and come to London and if she did not, the relationship would be ended. At one point in the suit, plaintiff declared that she could not locate the letter. She now contends that it was destroyed by defendant. Miss Marleaux recollects a telephone call by defendant to the same effect but defendant introduced bills which indicate he made no such call.

In March of 1967, defendant testified that he told plaintiff that she would have to prepare for separation and that she should learn a trade. The plaintiff responded that if he left her, she would reveal his fears, his worries to the public and his career would be destroyed. She also threatened suicide.

In 1967, the plaintiff accompanied defendant to Baker, Oregon, where the latter made a film called "Paint Your Wagon." The parties rented a house in Baker and established a joint bank account. Plaintiff signed most of the checks drawn on that account.

The plaintiff returned to Los Angeles while "Paint Your Wagon" was still being filmed in Oregon in order to confer with one of the defendant's attorneys, Louis L. Goldman. She asked him whether it would be any trouble to change her name to "Marvin" as their different names were embarrassing to her as well as defendant in a place like Baker. Goldman said if the change was approved by defendant, it was agreeable with him. She then requested him to arrange with defendant for the placement of some property or a lump sum in her name. She declared to him that she did not know whether the relationship would last forever, that she had talked to defendant about conveying the house to her but that he had absolutely said no. She requested Goldman to persuade defendant to do something for her. Goldman later telephoned plaintiff to inform her that defendant had refused to agree to any of her requests.

Goldman testified that plaintiff told him that neither she nor defendant wanted to get married, that each wanted to be free to come and go as they please and to terminate the relationship if they wished. The subject of defendant's frequent intoxication was discussed.

On cross-examination, plaintiff testified that they were "always very proud of the fact that nothing held us. We weren't—we weren't legally married." After the breakup she declared to an interviewer: "We used to laugh and feel a great warmth about the fact that either of us could walk out at anytime."

Following the completion of "Paint Your Wagon" (after additional work in Los Angeles), defendant made a picture entitled, "Hell in the Pacific" on the island of Palau in Micronesia. The parties again opened a joint account on location and drew funds therefrom for payment of food, clothing, etc. The plaintiff issued the greater number of checks.

She alleges that defendant introduced her as "Mrs. Marvin" although most of the American community on the island knew that they were not married, including the crew filming the picture and the cast. The defendant denies that he so introduced her.

The parties returned to Palau for a second sojourn. The parties enjoyed the fishing and the defendant supervised and assisted in the completion of a fishing boat which he hoped would vitalize the Palauan fishing industry. The parties talked to an architect about building a house, part of which they could occupy and part of which could be rented to visitors of Palau for the fishing.

Marriage was far from the thoughts of the parties. On the second visit to Palau plaintiff testified that defendant asked her to marry him but she thought he was joking and laughed. A few weeks later plaintiff allegedly asked defendant to marry her and *he* laughed.

On Palau, the parties met Richard Doughty, a member of the Peace Corps fishery department. Doughty testified that he had sexual relations with plaintiff approximately twenty times, on the island, and additional times later in Los Angeles and Tucson. Plaintiff vigorously denied this and claimed that Doughty was a homosexual, offering supporting witnesses.

This in turn was vigorously denied by Doughty who also offered witnesses who would rebut such a charge. Doughty's testimony was corroborated by Carol Clark who testified that plaintiff admitted to her that she (plaintiff) had "an affair" with him.

Doughty's testimony is weakened by his denial of such relationship when defendant's counsel, A. David Kagon, first questioned him prior to the trial. He explained that he decided to tell the truth at the trial because he did not wish defendant to be railroaded and because he now was more willing to accept responsibility after he had recovered from a serious illness.

LaVerna Hogan, wife of the production manager of "Hell in the Pacific," accompanied plaintiff on a trip from Palau to Hawaii. They stayed overnight in Guam where plaintiff told Mrs. Hogan that she was to meet two men in Hawaii. Mrs. Hogan asked plaintiff why she was going to meet them in view of her relationship with defendant and plaintiff responded,"We (plaintiff and defendant) have an understanding. He does his thing and I do mine." Plaintiff denies any such Hawaiian meeting.

In 1969, defendant filmed "Monte Walsh" on locations approximately two hours from Tucson. He rented a house in Tucson for the ten to twelve weeks of shooting. Doughty secured employment in "Monte Walsh" as a dialogue coach and lived with the parties. A joint bank account was again opened and funded by Edward Silver, defendant's business manager. Plaintiff signed most of the checks.

At the end of the shooting of the pictures, "Hell in the Pacific," "Paint Your Wagon" and "Monte Walsh," the Palau, Baker and Tucson Joint bank accounts were closed and the balances transferred to defendant's account.

Plaintiff had a separate account in Malibu in which defendant's business manager deposited $400 per month for her personal use.

The plaintiff testified that in May, 1970, defendant left the Malibu beach house upon her request. Later, she was told by defendant's agent, Mishkin, that defendant wished that they separate (Mishkin had referred to a "divorce" but testified that he was mistaken in his use of the term). The plaintiff later sought and found defendant in La Jolla. There he told her, plaintiff alleges, that he would not give up drinking, that it was part of his life and that his relationship with plaintiff was no longer enjoyable because of her frequent admonitions as to his drinking.

In May, 1970, plaintiff went to the office of defendant's attorney, Goldman. He informed her that defendant wanted her out of the house and out of his life and that defendant would pay her $833 per month (net after deduction of taxes from a gross of $1050) for five years. Plaintiff testified that she told Goldman she could not exist on such a stipend. Goldman responded that defendant could not afford to pay more because of the alimony which he paid to his former wife. Plaintiff testified that she replied that defendant had promised to take care of her for life. Goldman, however, testified that she had simply thanked him for the arrangement and said that $833 would be enough for her needs.

She returned to the beach house but finally departed after an emotional confrontation with defendant and his attorneys, Goldman and Kagon. Checks for $833 each began to arrive. According to defendant, the payments were made on condition that she removed herself from his life and not discuss with anyone anything she learned about defendant during their relationship. Defendant said that plaintiff thought this was fair. According to the plaintiff, the checks were stopped when defendant saw an item about him in one of the Hollywood columns. Defendant did send one more check but again stopped payment because, plaintiff declares, defendant was angered by her suit against Roberts. She told her attorney (then Howard L. Rosoff) to dismiss the action but, when no more checks came, she reversed her instructions. According to Goldman, plaintiff said she had nothing to do with the item in the column (re defendant's marriage to Pamela breaking up).

He testified that she also said that she would not do it again and to give her another chance. Goldman replied that defendant "was at the end of the road."

The plaintiff filed an application dated March 26, 1970 to change her name to Michelle Triola Marvin. The verified application declared that she had been known professionally as "Marvin" and that she used the name in her acting and singing career.

Plaintiff stated in her deposition that she never used the name "Marvin" professionally. She now declares that she meant (in her application) that she used "Marvin" *during* her career but only socially.

The plaintiff also declared in her deposition that she had asked for a written agreement as to property shortly after moving into the beach house. Defendant allegedly said an agreement was being prepared but they did not need any papers. The plaintiff said they did. Plaintiff said nothing further about the nonappearance of an agreement during 1968, 1969 and 1970.

The defendant stated in his deposition that he wanted a relationship of no responsibility and that the plaintiff agreed with him.

On trips out of town, plaintiff was introduced on occasion as Michelle Marvin to avoid embarrassment in hotels, but defendant contends he never introduced her as *Mrs.* Marvin. Bills were rarely addressed to Mrs. Lee Marvin, but rather to Michelle Marvin. In the Malibu community and the actor-producer circles in which they moved, the couple's relationship was known not to be that of husband and wife.

The plaintiff testified that she never told the defendant that she would hold herself out as his wife, that the parties never used the terms "husband and wife," those words were not in their vocabulary and that they never used the word "homemaker."

Defendant testified that in the winter of 1969 plaintiff wanted him to finance a European trip at $10,000–$15,000 per month as the price for separation. Later, she offered to "get out of your (his) life for $50,000" and he would never hear from her again. Still later, she requested $100,000. Plaintiff denies that she made any such offer.

Rather than review the great number of allegations by plaintiff as to defendant's drinking to excess, it is enough to observe that defendant admits that he was frequently intoxicated. It is a reasonable inference therefrom that in such condition he needed care and that plaintiff provided it.

TESTIMONIAL INCONSISTENCIES

The weight of the testimony of the plaintiff is lessened by several inconsistencies.

Plaintiff claims to have had considerable help from Gene Kelly in the procurement of employment in "Flower Drum Song" in New York City. He however, denied that he hired plaintiff. He further testified that he never talked to plaintiff about "Flower Drum Song" in 1963 or 1964 and that at that time the play was not being performed in New York City. In later testimony plaintiff altered her allegation of employment by Kelly to an offer of letters of introduction by him. She also modified her declaration that she was going to New York City to appear in "Flower Drum Song" to say that she did not know whether it was then being performed on Broadway.

Plaintiff's contention of many weeks of employment of Playboy clubs in Chicago, Phoenix, Miami, New York City, San Francisco and three other clubs and repeated in Chicago, Phoenix and San Francisco is countered by evidence from Playboy records of only one engagement, in Phoenix, and then for only two weeks. In fact, Noel Stein testified that the San Francisco club did not open until years after plaintiff's alleged engagement there. As for her allegation of employment by "Dino's Lodge" for 24 weeks in 1961 and 1962, its manager from 1958 on, Paul Wexler, declares that he recollects no employment of her by "Dino's Lodge" before 1965.

The testimony of plaintiff as to her right to compensation from Bobby Roberts, the producer of Monte Walsh, contains three variations as to the type of compensation sought. At first she was to receive a Rolls Royce, then a 10% finders fee and lastly 50% of the producer's fee in return for informing Roberts as to the availability of the Monte Walsh script. Also, she testified that she met Roberts and Landers in their offices on or about March 15, 1968 whereas she was in Palau from Christmas of 1967 to April or May of 1968.

According to the records of Sears Roebuck, an account had been opened in the name of Lee Marvin (Exhibit 117; the application was signed by Betty Marvin, defendant's former wife). Plaintiff testified, however, that an account was opened by her with defendant present in the name of "Mr. and Mrs. Marvin" or Lee Marvin. Sears records do not list her on any application nor as an authorized signator (Exhibit 119).

Plaintiff testified that she "never had an apartment while I was with Lee." However, Exhibit 151 dated May 1, 1965 and signed by plaintiff is a lease of an apartment at 8633 West Knoll Drive, West Hollywood. Plaintiff contends she signed the lease on behalf of her manager, Mimi Marleaux, and that she, the plaintiff, had no belongings there nor did she make any rent payments. Yet, testimony by Marleaux reveals that plaintiff did have some clothes in the apartment and that she, Marleaux, had only stayed a month or two in the apartment. On cross-examination, plaintiff admitted that she may have paid the rent and on direct rebuttal she testified that she did pay the rent two or three times. Exhibit 186 indicates that a Continental Bank signature card signed on December 28, 1965 bore the West Knoll address as plaintiff's residence. At a later time, that address was crossed off and that of the Malibu Beach house was inserted.

Plaintiff testified that she asked defendant for a written agreement to protect her rights. The defendant responded that it was not necessary and she believed him. In her deposition, however, she stated that she continued to request such agreement.

LAW

Is There An Express Contract?

An express contract must be founded on a promise directly or indirectly enforceable at law. (1 CORBIN ON CONTRACTS, §11.) Every contract requires, *inter alia* the mutual consent of the parties. (Civil Code §§1550, 1565.)

A review of the extensive testimony clearly leads this court to the conclusion that no express contract was negotiated between the parties. Neither party entertained any expectations that the property was to be divided between them.

Further, before mutual consent can exist, an intent to contract must be present. Also, the meaning of the agreement must be ascertainable and both parties must have the same understanding of its meaning. *Merrit & Co.* (1959) 176 C.A. 2d 719, 1 Cal. Rptr. 500. The basic statement on which plaintiff relies is the one which she says (and defendant denies) was made by defendant at San Blas—"What I have is yours and what you have is mine."

Considering the circumstances from which it allegedly sprung, the lack of intent to make a contract is immediately apparent. In 1964-1965 defendant was married; he had considerable unresolved financial problems; he had repeatedly informed plaintiff that he did not believe in marriage because of the property rights which a wife thereby acquires. Plaintiff could not have understood that phrase to accord the same rights to one who was *not* defendant's wife. If those words had been spoken, they were not spoken under circumstances in which either party would be entitled to believe that an offer of a contract was intended. (See *Fowler v. Security Pacific Bank* (1956) 146 C.A.2d 37, 47, 303 P.2d 565.)

In addition, the meaning of the phrase is difficult to ascertain. Does it mean a sharing of future as well as presently owned property? Does it mean a sharing of the *use* of property or is title to be extended to both parties? Does it mean that all property is shared even though the relationship may be terminated in a week or weekend? These are all unanswered questions. It is more reasonable to conclude that the declaration is simply hyperbole typical of persons who live and work in the entertainment field. It was defendant's way of expressing his affection for the plaintiff. As the defendant testified, in his business terms of affection are bandied about freely; one "loves" everyone and calls everybody "sweetheart."

Also, after hearing defendant's views on marriage and noting his antagonism against a person acquiring any rights by means of a certificate of marriage, it is not reasonable to believe that plaintiff understood that defendant intended to give her such rights even without a certificate. Without intent to contract and with no clearly ascertainable meaning of the contractual phrase, no express contract exists.

During a meeting with Marleaux in the fall of 1966 and in the presence of the defendant, the plaintiff told Marleaux that she (plaintiff) was sorry she had let Marleaux down by not pursuing her career. Defendant then allegedly stated, "I don't know what you're worrying about. I'll always take care of you."

Corbin has this to say about remarks of that sort: "The law does not attempt the realization of every expectation that has been induced by a promise; the expectation must be a reasonable one. Under no system of law that has ever existed are all promises enforceable. The expectation must be one that most people would have, and the promise must be one that most people would perform." (CORBIN ON CONTRACTS, p. 2 [West Pub. Co. 1852].) Surely plaintiff had no expectation that defendant would extend such care to her after separation, remembering defendant's antagonism to such automatic rights in a wife if the relationship failed (and to which she testified).

In addition, the phrase "I'll always take care of you" leaves many questions unanswered: Does defendant mean that plaintiff has the right to care even if separation is caused by plaintiff? What level of care? What if plaintiff marries, does the care continue? An offer as indefinite as this cannot be the basis of an enforceable contract (*Apablasa, supra* at 723).

Further, the alleged promise lacks mutuality; the plaintiff made no enforceable promise in response. Even if, *arguendo*, she had promised to forego her career, defendant could not have legally enforced such promise. (See *Mattei v. Hopper* (1959) 51 C.2d 119, 122, 330 P.2d 625.) Actually, plaintiff's career, never very brisk-paced, was sputtering and not because of any act of defendant; it came to an end unmourned and unattended by plaintiff who made no attempt to breathe life into it.

Doubt is cast upon the Marleaux testimony as to the alleged promise. The statement was allegedly made in the presence of Marleaux. The plaintiff testified that she remembers the event very clearly and that it was very important in her life. Yet in plaintiff's deposition of October, 1978, she was asked whether anyone other than the defendant was present and she responded, "I can't recall if anyone was present." (Deposition, p. 66, lines 19–23, read into the trial record at Vol. 30, p. 5490, lines 25–28, p. 5491, lines 1–3.)

The phrase, "Yes sir. I accept life with her, thank you. Your Honor, and the court" contained in Exhibit 13 (a letter written from London in 1966) adds no legal basis for a contract. It was a letter portraying an imaginary court scene from which one can infer the affection of defendant for plaintiff but from which one certainly cannot believe an offer of a contract was intended. (See *Fowler v. Security Pacific Bank, supra.*)

Is There an Implied Contract?

The conduct of the parties after the San Blas conversation certainly does not reveal any implementation of any contract nor does such conduct give rise to an implied contract. No joint bank accounts were established and no real property was placed in joint tenancy or tenancy in common. Plaintiff used a separate bank account for her allowance of $400 per month, her earnings from the Hawaii engagement and her settlement of the Roberts suit. When defendant bought real property, he placed it in his own name. Their tax returns were separate.

In plaintiff's letter to defendant dated November 2, 1971, (Ex. 67) she describes her activities after their separation, thanks defendant for his "financial help" (monthly payments for five years) and says nothing about any contract or agreement. In Ex. 155, a page from a book by plaintiff's counsel, he declares that plaintiff only asked him how to enforce defendant's promise to make payments pursuant to the five-year arrangement. Nothing was said then to counsel about any agreement to divide property. Plaintiff's attorney sent a letter to defendant's attorney, demanding recommencement of the payments for the five-year period. Plaintiff was quoted in an interview recorded in the Brenda Shaw article (Ex. 37) as follows: "We were always very proud of the fact that nothing really held us. We both agreed, and we were really pleased with the fact that you work harder at a relationship when you know that there is nothing really holding you." This evidence bars the finding of any contract.

The very fact that plaintiff pursued a claim for compensation from Roberts makes it plain that she expected no part of any earnings of defendant from the picture. Otherwise, why would she commence a lawsuit to recover a finder's fee or half of a producer's fee when she would have rights to half of the million dollars paid to defendant for the picture?[9]

The evidence does not support plaintiff's contention that she gave up her career in order to care for defendant and on his demand that she do so.

She claimed that defendant demanded that plaintiff give up her career and join him in London or else the relationship would end. Looking at the facts, she did go to London but remained only a few weeks. She declares that she returned because defendant was drinking heavily, and it was then too late to resume promotion of her record. Yet in her 1978 deposition she stated that she returned because her manager wanted her to come home to promote her record and in fact she did attempt to do so, but discovered that the radio stations were not interested. As for loss of momentum, in the promotion of her record by reason of her London trip, witnesses for defendant as well as one for plaintiff testified that no loss occurred. Contrary to any ultimatum, a witness for defendant declared that the latter expressed hope that she would have a successful career.

Plaintiff testified that the ultimatum was delivered to her by letter.[10]

However, her witness, Marleaux, declared that it came by way of telephone. One must doubt that the defendant issued an ultimatum (allegedly in the missing letter) demanding that plaintiff come to London when he writes

---

[9]After plaintiff and defendant separated, plaintiff testified she heard from Roberts many times. In her deposition (April 15, 1972, p. 44, lines 9–15) she said she never heard from Roberts after separation. Another inconsistency.

[10]The letter has been allegedly destroyed by defendant although at first the plaintiff declared that it was missing.

in Ex. 12, "only a month and a half to go, w(h)oopee," indicating that plans for her coming to London had already been made by the parties.

The plaintiff's testimony as to defendant's drinking habits would indicate that he was virtually awash with alcohol. Yet during this same period, defendant starred in several major films, all demanding of him physical stamina, a high degree of alertness and verbal as well as physical concentration. Her portrayal of large-scale and all pervasive inebriation raises doubt as to her accuracy of observation.

An implied as well as an express agreement must be founded upon mutual consent. Such consent may be inferred from the conduct of the parties. Proof of introductions of plaintiff as Mrs. Marvin, and the occasional registrations at hotels as Mrs. Marvin and evidence of a relationship wherein plaintiff furnishes companionship, cooking and home care do not establish that defendant agreed to give plaintiff half of his property. Those services may be rendered out of love or affection and are indeed so rendered in a myriad of relationships between man and woman which are not contractual in nature. They may be consideration for a contract to receive property but the other elements of such contract remain to be established. Discussion of an equitable basis for an award because of homemaking services is to be found in a later portion of his opinion.

The change of name to Marvin appears to have had one motivation to avoid embarrassment when traveling. It ended the awkwardness occurring when, for example, plaintiff's passport was examined in customs. Coming at a time so close to the date of separation and after some indication of difficulties between the parties, the change of name does raise a question whether plaintiff sought relief from embarrassment or whether she wished to acquire the right to use defendant's name after separation.

The evidence of a contract as to property may be imputed from a change in the manner of holding, such as joint tenancy bank accounts, but not such joint accounts as were set up on the various filming locations (Tucson, Baker, Palau). These accounts were transient, employed solely for the convenience of attending to current needs away from California. The disposition of funds remaining after the film was completed underlined the single purpose of the accounts: upon completion the funds were placed not in a joint account in Los Angeles but in defendant's separate account.

Plaintiff's use of charge accounts certainly does not establish that defendant by his alleged consent to such use intended that half of his property be given to plaintiff.

Registering at hotels as Mr. and Mrs. Marvin does not indicate that defendant intended to give plaintiff one-half of the property. Such evidence may assist in proving a relationship which on its surface resembles marriage in areas away from home, but relationships resembling marriage may exist without any property arrangements. Hence more must be proved by a preponderance of evidence, that is, that plaintiff used the charge accounts *because defendant had agreed to give her half of the property.*

Plaintiff proved that she acted as companion and homemaker, that she prepared a number of defendant's meals and that she cleaned house or supervised a cleaning woman. That she did so in consideration of a contract, express, implied, or tacit, with respect to disposing of property, remains unproven. The existence of such property agreement has not been established by the requisite preponderance of the evidence. The decision of *In re Marriage of Cary* (1973) 34 Cal. App. 3d 345, 109 Cal. Rptr. 862 and *Estate of Atherley* (1975) 44 Cal. App. 3d 758, 119 Cal. Rptr. 41 afford no comfort to the plaintiff as their facts distinguish them from the instant case. In *Cary*, the disputed property was placed in the joint names of both parties, joint income tax returns were filed, money was borrowed and business was conducted as husband and wife. In *Atherley*, both parties pooled earnings accumulated for 13 years and bought property as joint tenants. Both worked and contributed funds to the construction of improvements on land bought with such earnings. None of these facts were established in this case; there was no pooling of earnings, no property was purchased in joint names, and no joint income tax returns were executed. Joint accounts set up on filming locations were only used as convenient and transient methods of payment of bills with the balance returned to the separate account of the defendant when the film was completed.

As for pooling of earnings, the bulk of plaintiff's compensation for singing was used to pay her musician and arrangers. When she did achieve a net income in the Hawaiian engagement, she placed the money in her separate account. Defendant's income was deposited in his own bank account and used to buy property in his own name. This case therefore bears little resemblance either to *Cary* or *Atherley*.

Finding no contract, the testimony of Doughty is not evaluated as that relates to an alleged breach of contract.

It is clear that the parties came together because of mutual affection and not because of mutual consent to a contract. Nothing else, certainly no contract, kept them together and, when that affection diminished, they separated.

EQUITABLE REMEDIES

If no contract, express or implied, is to be found, the Supreme Court adjures the trial court to ascertain whether any equitable remedies are applicable. The high court suggests constructive and resulting trusts as well as *quantum meruit*. The court also declares: "Our opinion does not preclude the evolution of additional equitable remedies to protect the expectations of the parties to a nonmarital relationship in cases in which existing remedies prove inadequate; the suitability of such remedies may be determined in later cases in light of the factual setting in which they arise."[11]

The plaintiff has, by her dismissal of her fourth and fifth causes of action—both for *quantum meruit*—removed that remedy from the court's consideration.

If a resulting trust is to be established, it must be shown that property was intended by the parties to be held by one party in trust for the other and that consideration was provided by the one not holding title to purchase the property. As Witkin puts it, there must be "circumstances showing that the transferee (holder of title) was not intended to take the beneficial interest."[12]

No evidence has been adduced to show such consideration having been provided by the plaintiff to buy property.[13] It may be contended that as the defendant did not need to expend funds to secure homemaking services elsewhere, she thereby enhanced the financial base of the defendant and enabled him to increase his property purchases. (See Bruch, *supra*, p. 123.) Such alleged enhancement, however, would appear to be offset by the considerable flow of economic benefits in the other direction. Those benefits include payments for goods and services for plaintiff up to $72,900 for the period from 1967–1970 alone (Ex. 194). Exhibit 196 indicates that living expenses for the parties were $221,400 for the period from 1965 to 1970. Among such benefits were a Mercedes Benz automobile for plaintiff, fur coats, travel to London, Hawaii, Japan, Micronesia, and the pleasures of life

---

[11] *Marvin v. Marvin, supra*, p. 684, footnote 25.

[12] 7 Witkin, SUMMARY OF CALIF. LAW. §123, p. 5481.

[13] Such establishment must be by clear and convincing proof. (G. G. Bogert and G. T. Bogert, HANDBOOK OF THE LAW OF TRUSTS, §74 at p. 279 (5th edition 1973); *Moulton v. Moulton* (1920) 182 Cal. 185, 187 p. 421; Bruch, *Property Rights of De Facto Spouses*, 10 FAMILY LAW QUARTERLY, p. 101.)

on the California beach in frequent contact with many film and stage notables. Further, defendant made a substantial financial effort to launch plaintiff's career as a recording singer. No equitable basis for an expansion of the resulting trust theory is afforded in view of this evidence.

A constructive trust, pleaded in the second cause of action, is "equity's version of implied-in-law recovery" (see Bruch, *supra*, 125) based on unjust enrichment. This is a trust imposed to force restitution of something that in fairness and good conscience does not belong to its owner. (See Bruch, *supra*, p. 125). However, the defendant earned the money by means of his own effort, skill and reputation. The money was then invested in the properties now held by him. It cannot be said in good conscience that such properties do not belong to him.

As Witkin points out, such a trust is an equitable remedy imposed where a person obtains property by fraudulent misrepresentation or concealment or by some wrongful act.[14] No such wrongdoing can be elicited from the facts of this case.

Plaintiff contends that the Supreme Court by its opinion in *Marvin v. Marvin, supra*, requires that plaintiff receive a reasonable proportion of the property in defendant's name because of her performance of the homemaker-companion-cook and other wife-like functions even though no contract, express or implied, exists and even though no basis for a constructive or resulting trust can be found. To accede to such a contention would mean that the court would recognize each unmarried person living together to be automatically entitled by such living together, and performing spouse-like functions, to half of the property bought with the earnings of the other non-marital partner. This is tantamount to recognition of common law marriages in California. As they were abolished in 1895, the Supreme Court surely does not mean to resurrect them by its opinion in *Marvin v. Marvin*.[15] The trial court's understanding of *Marvin v. Marvin* is that if there is mutual consent or proof of the mutual intent of the parties, by reason of their conduct or because of surrounding circumstances, to share the property or if the plaintiff directly participated in the procurement of or the nurturing of investments, or if there has been mutual effort (which will be discussed later) the property should be divided. None of these conditions pertains here.

While the Supreme Court directs under certain circumstances a fair apportionment of property even though there is no express of implied contract, it has imposed a condition, that such property be "accumulated through mutual effort." (p. 682.) Plaintiff declares that her work as homemaker, cook and companion constituted "mutual effort."

The two cases cited as examples of mutual effort, *In re Marriage of Cary* (1973) 34 Cal. App. 3d 345, 109 Cal. Rptr. 862 and *Estate of Atherley* (1975) 44 Cal. App. 3d 758, 119 Cal. Rptr. 41, reveal considerably more involvement on the part of the woman in the accumulation of property. In the first place, Paul Cary and Janet Forbes (in *Cary, supra*) held themselves out to be husband and wife. That is not the case here. The reputation of the parties in the community in which they settled was not that they were a married couple. Not only did Cary and Forbes purchase a home, but they also borrowed money, obtained

---

[14]Civil Code, §§2223, 2224: 7 Witkin. Summary of Calif. Law, §§131, 132, pp. 5487, 5488.

[15]Footnote 24 of *Marvin v. Marvin, supra*, expressly denies any intent to revive the relationship:

"We do not seek to resurrect the doctrine of common law marriage, which was abolished in California by statute in 1885. (See *Norman v. Thomson* (1898) 121 Cal. 620, 628, [54 F. 143]; *Estate of Abate* (1958) 166 Cal. App. 2d 282, 292 [333 P.2d 200].) Thus we do not hold that plaintiff and defendant were 'married,' nor do we extend to plaintiff the rights which the Family Law Act grants valid or putative spouses; we hold only that she has the same rights to enforce contracts and to assert her equitable interest in property acquired *through her effort* as does any other unmarried person." (emphasis added)

credit, and filed joint income tax returns. Four children were born to the couple. The children's birth certificates and school registration recorded them as Paul and Janet Cary. None of these facts are present in the instant case.

In *Atherley,* the parties, Harold and Annette, lived together for 22 years; after 14 years Harold divorced a prior wife *ex parte* in Juarez, Mexico and then married Annette in Reno, Nevada. Both were employed and pooled their earnings in various bank accounts. They had been advised by a Los Angeles attorney that the Mexican divorce was valid. Both contributed services to the construction of improvements on land purchased by them. Funds used to purchase both land and materials can be traced to their accumulated earnings. Two bank accounts were established with funds accumulated by Harold and Annette. Upon the sale of an improved parcel, a promissory note representing part of the sales price was held in joint tenancy. None of these facts is present in the instant case.[16]

In this case we have all assets bought solely with the earnings of the defendant. The plaintiff had no net earnings except from the Hawaiian engagement and those funds went into her own account. Plaintiff secured $750 from the settlement of her suit against Roberts and those funds also did not go into defendant's account. There were, on the other hand, funds that were expended by defendant to further plaintiff's career. The defendant also persuaded a friend to employ plaintiff in Hawaii. He brought people to hear her sing and bought drinks to keep them in attendance. It was the plaintiff who stopped trying to sell her record and get singing engagements. The evidence does not establish that such cessation was caused by defendant.

It would be difficult to deem the singing career of plaintiff to be the "mutual effort" required by the Supreme Court. Certainly, where both wanted to be free to come and go without obligation, the basis of any division of property surely cannot be her "giving up" her career for him. It then can only be her work as cook, homemaker and companion that can be considered as plaintiff's contribution to the requisite "mutual effort." Yet, where $72,000 has been disbursed by defendant on behalf of plaintiff in less than six years, where she has enjoyed a fine home and travel throughout the world for about 30 months, where she acquired whatever clothes, furs and cars she wished and engaged in a social life amongst screen and stage luminaries, such services as she has rendered would appear to have been compensated. Surely one cannot glean from such services her participation in a "mutual effort" between the parties to earn funds to buy property as occurred in *Cary* and *Atherley, supra.*

The Supreme Court doubtless intended by the phrase "mutual effort" to mean the relationship of a man and woman who have joined together to make a home, who act together to earn and deposit such earnings in joint accounts, who pay taxes together, who make no effort to gain an advantage by reason of the association, (such as informing a producer of a script for a fee and taking defendant's name without his consent), who have children if possible and bring them up together. *Cary* and *Atherley* in fact demands more of the partners; they require participation in money-earning activities. Plaintiff's fundraising put money in her own account.

To construe "mutual effort" to mean services as homemaker, cook and companion and nothing else[17] would be tantamount to the grant of the benefits of the Family Law Act to the nonmarital partner as well as to the married person. This the Supreme Court has refused to do. Therefore, one must seek and find in each case those additional factors which indicate the expenditure

---

[16]Mere possession of property or the holding of title is not a determinant if standing alone. See *Marvin v. Marvin, supra,* footnote 21, p. 682.

[17]This is not to gainsay that an express or implied contract may be valid and enforceable where the consideration is ordinary homemaking services. (*Marvin v. Marvin, supra,* footnote 5, p. 670)

of "mutual effort," such as those present in *Cary* and *Atherley*. Such factors are not present in this case.

The court is aware that Footnote 25, *Marvin v. Marvin, supra,* p. 684, urges the trial court to employ whatever equitable remedy may be proper under the circumstances. The court is also aware of the recent resort of plaintiff to unemployment insurance benefits to support herself and of the fact that a return of plaintiff to a career as a singer is doubtful. Additionally, the court knows that the market value of defendant's property at time of separation exceeded $1,000,000.

In view of these circumstances, the court in equity awards plaintiff $104,000[18] for rehabilitation purposes so that she may have the economic means to re-educate herself and to learn new, employable skills or to refurbish those utilized, for example, during her most recent employment[19] and so that she may return from her status as companion of a motion picture star to a separate, independent but perhaps more prosaic existence.

---

[18] Plaintiff should be able to accomplish rehabilitation in less than two years. The sum awarded would be approximately equivalent to the highest scale that she ever earned as a singer, $1,000 per week, for two years.

[19] While part of the funds may be used for living expenses, the primary intent is that they be employed for retraining purposes.

Marvin v. Marvin [III]

California Court of Appeal, Second District

122 Cal. App.3d 871, 176 Cal. Rptr. 555 (1981)*

COBEY, Associate Justice.

Defendant, Lee Marvin, appeals from that portion of a judgment ordering him to pay to plaintiff, Michelle Marvin, the sum of $104,000, to be used by her primarily for her economic rehabilitation.

Defendant contends, among other things, that the challenged award is outside the issues of the case as framed by the pleadings of the parties (see Code Civ.Proc., §588) and furthermore lacks any basis in equity or in law.[1] We agree and will therefore modify the judgment by deleting therefrom the challenged award.

FACTS

This statement of facts is taken wholly from the findings of the trial court, which tried the case without a jury. The parties met in June 1964 and started living together occasionally in October of that year. They lived together almost continuously (except for business absences of his) from the spring of 1965 to May or June of 1970, when their cohabitation was ended at his insistence. This cohabitation was the result of an initial agreement between them to live together as unmarried persons so long as they both enjoyed their mutual companionship and affection.

---

*[Plaintiff's request for review denied by the Supreme Court of California without comment. See Los Angeles Times, Oct. 8, 1981, Part II, at 3, col. 6.]

[1] Defendant challenges the constitutionality of the award on various grounds, but we will not reach the issues there raised because it is unnecessary to do so. (See *People v. Green* (1980) 27 Cal.3d 1, 50, 164 Cal Rptr. 1, 609 P.2d 468; *People v. Kozden* (1974) 36 Cal. App.3d 918, 123, 111 Cal. Rptr. 826.)

More specifically, the parties to this lawsuit never agreed during their cohabitation that they would combine their efforts and earnings or would share equally in any property accumulated as a result of their efforts, whether individual or combined. They also never agreed during this period that plaintiff would relinquish her professional career as an entertainer and singer in order to devote her efforts full time to defendant as his companion and homemaker generally. Defendant did not agree during this period of cohabitation that he would provide all of plaintiff's financial needs and support for the rest of her life.

Furthermore, the trial court specifically found that: (1) defendant has never had any obligation to pay plaintiff a reasonable sum as and for her maintenance;[2] (2) plaintiff suffered no damage resulting from her relationship with defendant, including its termination and thus defendant did not become monetarily liable to plaintiff at all; (3) plaintiff actually benefited economically and socially from the cohabitation of the parties, including payment by defendant for goods and services for plaintiff's sole benefit in the approximate amount of $72,900.00, payment by defendant of the living expenses of the two of them of approximately $221,400.00, and other substantial specified gifts;[3] (4) a confidential and fiduciary relationship never existed between the parties with respect to property; (5) defendant was never unjustly enriched as a result of the relationship of the parties or of the services performed by plaintiff for him or for them; (6) defendant never acquired any property or money from plaintiff by any wrongful act.

The trial court specifically found in support of its challenged rehabilitation award that the market value of defendant's property at the time the parties separated exceeded $1 million, that plaintiff at the time of the trial of this case had been recently receiving unemployment insurance benefits, that it was doubtful that plaintiff could return to the career that she had enjoyed before the relationship of the parties commenced, namely, that of singer, that plaintiff was in need of rehabilitation—i.e., to learn new employable skills, that she should be able to accomplish such rehabilitation in two years and that the sum of $104,000 was not only necessary primarily for such rehabilitation, but also for her living expenses (including her debts) during this period of rehabilitation, and that defendant had the ability to pay this sum forthwith.

Moreover, the trial court concluded as a matter of law that inasmuch as defendant had terminated the relationship of the parties and plaintiff had no visible means of support, "in equity," she had a right to assistance by defendant until she could become self-supporting. The trial court explained that it fixed the award at the highest salary that the plaintiff had ever earned, namely, $1,000 a week for two years, although plaintiff's salary had been at that level for only two weeks and she ordinarily had earned less than one-half that amount weekly.

DISCUSSION

1. *The challenged rehabilitation award is not within the issues framed by the pleadings.*

This is a judgment roll appeal in the sense that we have no transcript of the evidence taken at the apparently lengthy trial below. The issues in a law-

---

[2]The judgment under appeal tracks this finding in the following language: "Defendant never had, and does not now have, the duty and obligation to pay to plaintiff a reasonable sum as and for her support and maintenance."

[3]The trial court also found that "Defendant made a substantial financial effort to launch Plaintiff's career as a recording singer and to continue her career as a nightclub singer."

suit are, aside from those added by a pretrial order, either those framed by the pleadings or as expanded at trial. (See 4 Witkin, CAL. PROCEDURE (2d ed. 1971) Trial, §336, p. 3138.) Here, however, since we do not have before us the evidence taken at trial and there was no pretrial order expanding the issues, we can look only to the pleadings to determine the issues between the parties.

Plaintiff's amended complaint, upon which this action went to trial, asks, with respect to the support of plaintiff by defendant, only that defendant be ordered to pay to plaintiff a reasonable sum per month as and for her support and maintenance. Plaintiff did not ask in this basic pleading for any limited rehabilitative support of the type the trial court apparently on its own initiative subsequently awarded her. Consequently, the special findings of fact and conclusions of law in support of this award must be disregarded as not being within the issues framed by the pleadings. (See *Crescent Lumber Co. v. Larson* (1913) 166 Cal. 168, 171, 135 P. 502; *Gardiana v. Small Claims Court* (1976) 59 Cal. App.3d 412, 421, 130 Cal. Rptr. 675.) When this is done, the challenged portion of the judgment becomes devoid of any support whatsoever and therefore must be deleted.

2. *In any event there is no equitable or legal basis for the challenged rehabilitative award.*

The trial court apparently based its rehabilitative award upon two footnotes in the opinion of our Supreme Court in this case. (*Marvin v. Marvin* (1976) 18 Cal.3d 660, 134 Cal. Rptr. 815, 557 P.2d 106.) These are footnotes 25 and 26, which respectively read as follows:

> "Our opinion does not preclude the evolution of additional equitable remedies to protect the expectations of the parties to a nonmarital relationship in cases in which existing remedies prove inadequate; the suitability of such remedies may be determined in later cases in light of the factual setting in which they arise." (*Id.* at p. 684, 134 Cal. Rptr. 815, 557 P.2d 106.)
>
> "We do not pass upon the question whether, in the absence of an express or implied contractual obligation, a party to a nonmarital relationship is entitled to support payments from the other party after the relationship terminates." (*Id.* at p. 685, 134 Cal. Rptr. 815, 557 P.2d 106.)

There is no doubt that footnote 26 opens the door to a support award in appropriate circumstances. Likewise, under footnote 25, equitable remedies should be devised "to protect the expectations of the parties to a nonmarital relationship." The difficulty in applying either of these footnotes in the manner in which the trial court has done in this case is that, as already pointed out, the challenged limited rehabilitative award of the trial court is not within the issues of the case as framed by the pleadings and there is nothing in the trial court's findings to suggest that such an award is warranted to protect the expectations of *both* parties.

Quite to the contrary, as already noted, the trial court expressly found that plaintiff benefited economically and socially from her relationship with defendant and suffered no damage therefrom, even with respect to its termination. Furthermore, the trial court also expressly found that defendant never had any obligation to pay plaintiff a reasonable sum as and for her maintenance and that defendant had not been unjustly enriched by reason of the relationship or its termination and that defendant had never acquired anything of value from plaintiff by any wrongful act.

Furthermore, the special findings in support of the challenged rehabilitative award merely established plaintiff's need therefor and defendant's ability to respond to that need. This is not enough. The award, being nonconsensual in nature, must be supported by some recognized underlying obligation in law or in equity. A court of equity admittedly has broad powers, but it may not create totally new substantive rights under the guise of doing equity. (See *Rosenberg v. Lawrence* (1938) 10 Cal.2d 590, 594–595, 75 P.2d 1082; *Lande v. Jurisich* (1943) 59 Cal. App.2d 613, 618, 139 P.2d 657.)

The trial court in its special conclusions of law addressed to this point attempted to state an underlying obligation by saying that plaintiff had a right to assistance from defendant until she became self-supporting. But this special conclusion obviously conflicts with the earlier, more general, finding of the court that defendant has never had and did not then have any obligation to provide plaintiff with a reasonable sum for her support and maintenance and, in view of the already-mentioned findings of no damage (but benefit instead), no unjust enrichment and no wrongful act on the part of defendant with respect to either the relationship or its termination, it is clear that no basis whatsoever, either in equity or in law, exists for the challenged rehabilitative award. It therefore must be deleted from the judgment.[4]

DISPOSITION

The judgment under appeal is modified by deleting therefrom the portion thereof under appeal, namely, the rehabilitative award of $104,000 to plaintiff, Michelle Marvin. As modified it is affirmed. Costs on appeal are awarded to defendant, Lee Marvin.

POTTER, J., concurs.

KLEIN, Presiding Justice, dissenting.

I dissent.

This case was tried by the court sitting without a jury over a three-month period, during which time presumably extensive evidence was taken. The trial court was able to evaluate the parties and witnesses as they appeared and gave testimony. However, since the record on this appeal consists only of the judgment roll rather than a reporter's transcript, we do not know the extent and nature of the evidence presented, or whether the issues as framed by the pleadings were expanded during the trial.

We do know that at the conclusion of the trial, the trial court awarded Michelle $104,000 pursuant to finding number 26 that: "Plaintiff is in need of funds to be used in the course of rehabilitation, so that she may re-educate herself and learn new employable skills . . .," and finding number 27 that: "The sum of $104,000.00 is necessary primarily for rehabilitation and also living expenses and debts to be paid during such rehabilitation."

In her first amended complaint, Michelle pled as follows:

"That in order that Plaintiff would be able to devote her full time to Defendant Marvin as a companion, homemaker, housekeeper and cook, it was further agreed that Plaintiff would give up her lucrative career as an entertainer/singer.

"That in return, Defendant Marvin would provide for all of Plaintiff's financial support and needs for the rest of her life."

Michelle prayed for "such other relief as this Court deems just and proper."

We are also made aware of the fact that Marvin was paying Michelle monies on a monthly basis after their separation pursuant to some kind of an "arrangement."

---

[4] We obviously disagree with our dissenting colleague regarding the clarity and consistency (with the judgment) of the trial court's special findings of fact and conclusions of law in support of the challenged rehabilitative award. There is no need to remand this case to the trial court for correction of these matters since the award itself is without support in either equity or law.

The trial court in its memorandum opinion recognizes that *Marvin v. Marvin* (1976) 18 Cal.3d 660, 134 Cal. Rptr. 815, 557 P.2d 106, "* * * urges the trial court to employ whatever equitable remedy may be proper under the circumstances."

Marvin v. Marvin, supra, at page 685, footnote 26, 134 Cal. Rptr. 815, 557 P.2d 106, specifically states: "We do not pass upon the question whether, in the absence of an express or implied contractual obligation, a party to a non-marital relationship is entitled to support payments from the other party after the relationship terminates."

In finding number 3, the trial court herein concludes: "The parties did not enter into any agreement to the following effect: That Plaintiff would give up any career which she might have had, whether as an entertainer/singer, or in any other calling, in order to enable Plaintiff to devote her full time to Defendant as a companion, homemaker, housekeeper and cook of Defendant," the contents of which finding was echoed in finding numbers 6 and 7. In finding number 18(c), the trial court found that the plaintiff did not in fact give up her career at the defendant's request in order to devote her full time and attention to defendant's personal needs.

In view of all the evidence that the trial court had before it, including the plaintiff's sex, age, earning ability and career status, the length of the relationship, and other circumstances of the factual setting, *Marvin v. Marvin, supra,* seems to say that the trial court was authorized by way of remedy to provide support payments from the other party after the relationship terminated, provided it also found some equitable right to such a remedy. Apparently, this is what the trial court herein attempted to do in granting a support-type award for rehabilitation for a two-year period, which seemed to reinstate to some extent the prior "arrangement" the parties had.

However, it is the trial court's responsibility to provide findings of fact and conclusions of law which are consistent with the judgment in order that we may conduct proper appellate review. (*Spaulding v. Cameron* (1952) 38 Cal.2d 265, 270, 239 P.2d 625; *Kaiser Foundation Hospitals v. Workers' Comp. Appeals Bd.* (Fuchs) (1979) 91 Cal. App.3d 501, 506, fn. 5, 154 Cal. Rptr. 765; *Machado v. Machado* (1914) 26 Cal. App. 16, 18, 145 P. 738.)

Indeed, " 'it is essential that [the trial court's findings of fact and conclusions of law] be sufficient in form and substance so that by reading them and referring to the record the parties can tell and this court can tell with reasonable certainty not only the theory upon which the [trial court] has arrived at its ultimate finding and conclusion but that the [trial court] has in truth found those facts which as a matter of law are essential to sustain its award.' (*Mercer-Fraser Co. v. Industrial Acc. Com.* [1953] 40 Cal.2d [102,] 124 [251 P.2d 955].'" (*Kaiser Foundation Hospitals v. Workers' Comp. Appeals Bd. (Fuchs),* supra, 91 Cal. App.3d at p. 506, fn. 5, 154 Cal. Rptr. 765.)

As "it is impossible to reconcile this judgment with the findings * * *, it is clearly the duty of this court to reverse this judgment and remand the case to the trial court for * * * correction * * * of the [inconsistencies] in its findings [and conclusions] or its judgment or both." (*Machado v. Machado, supra,* 26 Cal. App. at p. 18, 145 P. 738; 6 Witkin, CAL. PROCEDURE (2d ed. 1971) Appeal, §541, pp. 4482–4483.)

I would reverse the judgment and remand for further proceedings consistent with this dissent.

Comments

Peck, decided 84 years earlier than *Marvin* by the Supreme Judicial Court of Massachusetts, involved a clear case of contract cohabitation. The relationship was based on an express contract—witnessed and in writing—founded on love and terminable at the will of either party. The contract, styled as a partnership, provided for equal division of mutually acquired property and for mutual support obligations should there be children. In *Marvin,* on the other hand, the plaintiff alleged a mere oral contract which, ultimately, she could not prove. Her recovery, after the case was remanded to the trial court, was purely under the most general equitable considerations. (See p. 198.) Even this recovery was reversed on further appeal. (See pp. 198–202.)

There are procedural differences between *Peck* and *Marvin. Peck* involved a request for a divorce. It was dismissed because the pleadings, based on contract, did not conform to a theory of marriage. Whether any recovery would have been possible under contract was not in issue. In a sense, the woman had adhered to the contract by leaving after the union had become disagreeable to her. *Marvin,* on the other hand, was an action based on contract, not on marriage. Had the plaintiff requested a dissolution of marriage, it would also have been dismissed. It is unlikely that any form of recovery would have been possible in contract or equity under the facts recited in *Peck,* as the contract was probably against public policy in 1892. Yet, aside from its social-historical context, *Peck* is a much stronger case for contract cohabitation than *Marvin.*

Michelle Marvin was interested in economic benefits from the relationship. Why the male party in *Peck* filed a divorce action is less clear; perhaps it was brought to clarify status. Since a valid marriage is a prerequisite to a divorce action, a dismissal of the request for lack of marriage can have some of the legal effects of a declaration of non-marital status. Yet if the plaintiff in *Peck* was merely interested in testing the validity of a possible marriage, it is still left unclear why he appealed the dismissal. Perhaps he was concerned primarily about the status of property in the various jurisdictions in which he and his companion had lived. Many of them, including California, still recognized common law marriages in 1892. The plaintiff may also have been concerned about the full faith and credit effects of a judgment dismissing his complaint.

The significance of *Marvin* is somewhat affected by the way the case was continued after the Supreme Court of California had reversed and remanded it "for further proceedings consistent with the views expressed herein." Trial courts frequently attempt to minimize the impact of an appellate reversal, trying to reach a decision as close as possible to their original holdings without incurring the danger of a renewed appeal. After extensive findings of fact that cover more than half his opinion, the trial judge came to the conclusion that none of the suggested remedies was supported by the facts as found—no express contract, no implied contract, no unjust enrichment, no resulting or constructive trust. He then seized upon footnote 25 of the mandating opinion of the Supreme Court of California, which contemplates the possibility of additional equitable remedies as they "may be determined in later cases in light of the factual setting in which they arise."

In applying undefined equitable standards, the trial court awarded $104,000 to the plaintiff for rehabilitation purposes. Two short concluding paragraphs were felt to be sufficient for this result, although they contradict the earlier portions of the opinion that question the veracity of the plaintiff. In effect, Michelle Marvin was awarded rights comparable to rehabilitative alimony, although no marriage existed. Whatever one may think of the logic of the trial court, it may have been designed to prevent further appeals by permitting some recovery. Yet this hope proved to be unrealistic. (See pp. 198–202.)

Marvin emerges as an appellate opinion for the abstract proposition that cohabitation contracts are possible, although no such contract was found to exist in the specific case. To this the trial court added a remedy, erroneously as it seems, that has been called "palimony." Quite apart from the technical limits of *stare decisis,* three main consequences may acquire significance beyond California. First, parties may be induced to enter express cohabitation contracts to avoid the unlimited judicial discretion that could come into play if "additional equitable remedies" (footnote 25) were applicable. Second, in the absence of an express contract, the courts may imply one if they wish, since cohabitation always involves some consensus. A finding of an implied contract, based on facts relating to the conduct of the parties, would also be difficult to reverse on appeal. Obviously a great deal of discretion would be involved. Third, the portion of the appellate opinion that permitted "additional equitable remedies," as demonstrated by the trial court opinion, could invite a judge's discretionary application of power in cohabitation cases. The question to be answered is: what does the *Marvin* result mean in terms of legal theory and practice?

An express contract of cohabitation is not likely to raise serious problems; courts will be increasingly inclined to enforce well-drafted ones. Since one of the many functions of express contracts of cohabitation is to refute any presumption of marriage, as well as limit judicial discretion, express contract may become an alternative available to the literate American middle classes. That is, if they choose not to protect themselves by formal marriage, they will be able to protect themselves through written contractual stipulation.

On the other hand, implied contract, although viewed under contract theory as having the same conceptual basis as express contract, may break away from traditional theory and become a vehicle for subtly applying public policy through the legal fiction of an imposed consensual relationship. In other words, parties to cohabitation arrangements, based purely on ambiguous behavior and not on express agreement, may be treated by the courts as if they had entered a legal contract of cohabitation. Implied contract could thus become a tool for judicial intervention that allocates some of the social costs of a relationship to the appropriate party by way of contractual fiction. If this method appears too strained in an individual case, as in *Marvin,* the judge can still apply general equitable principles, although perhaps within limits, as indicated in the most recent appellate reversal.

One further aspect of *Marvin* requires discussion, namely, the revived importance of fault, a possibility foreseen by Mr. Justice Clark in his concurring and dissenting opinion. He pointed out that any resort to equity necessitates an examination of the conduct of parties, thus resurrecting the bitterness and acrimony of litigation that was common prior to the legislative adoption of no-fault divorce. The opinion of the trial court, following the mandate of the appellate court in *Marvin,* seemed to bear this out. The complete life patterns of the plaintiff and defendant were examined in detail, including alleged conduct of the plaintiff which, had there been a marriage, would have been adultery. Her defense was denial and an assertion that the alleged co-respondent was a homosexual. The trial court allowed the testimony under a theory that the sexual conduct of the plaintiff could amount to a breach of contract. While the court's finding was no contract, and it did not evaluate the testimony, it could nevertheless have been relevant under other headings, for instance, to prove that the plaintiff had not intended to be contractually bound and that she lacked clean hands for purposes of equitable remedies. It is possible therefore that evidence to demonstrate fault can be relevant in a breach of contract action based on nonmarital cohabitation, while the same evidence is excluded in California in a suit for no-fault divorce. Requiring a more stringent standard of conduct for cohabitation than for marriage lacks plausibility. We will see, however, that it is difficult to eradicate fault from human relations. There seems to be a strong emotional need to blame a party if a breakup occurs, regardless of whether there was or, as in *Marvin,* was not a marriage.

References

Population Div., Bureau of the Census, U.S. Dep't of Commerce, MARITAL STATUS AND LIVING ARRANGEMENTS: MARCH 1980 (Current Population Reports, Population Characteristics, Series P-20, No. 365, October 1981).

Putzel & Thurlow, *Marital and Cohabitation Contracts,* 6 FAM. L. REP. 4067 (1980).

Weitzman, L., THE MARRIAGE CONTRACT—SPOUSES, LOVERS, AND THE LAW (1981).

Hewitt v. Hewitt

Supreme Court of Illinois

77 Ill.2d 49, 394 N.E.2d 1204 (1979)

UNDERWOOD, Justice:

The issue in this case is whether plaintiff Victoria Hewitt, whose complaint alleges she lived with defendant Robert Hewitt from 1960 to 1975 in an unmarried, family-like relationship to which three children have been born, may recover from him "an equal share of the profits and properties accumulated by the parties" during that period.

Plaintiff initially filed a complaint for divorce, but at a hearing on defendant's motion to dismiss, admitted that no marriage ceremony had taken place and that the parties have never obtained a marriage license. In dismissing that complaint the trial court found that neither a ceremonial nor a common law marriage existed; that since defendant admitted the paternity of the minor children, plaintiff need not bring a separate action under the Paternity Act [citation omitted] to have the question of child support determined; and directed plaintiff to make her complaint more definite as to the nature of the property of which she was seeking division.

Plaintiff thereafter filed an amended complaint alleging the following bases for her claim: (1) that because defendant promised he would "share his life, his future, his earnings and his property" with her and all of defendant's property resulted from the parties' joint endeavors, plaintiff is entitled in equity to a one-half share; (2) that the conduct of the parties evinced an implied contract entitling plaintiff to one-half the property accumulated during their "family relationship"; (3) that because defendant fraudulently assured plaintiff she was his wife in order to secure her services, although he knew they were not legally married, defendant's property should be impressed with a trust for plaintiff's benefit; (4) that because plaintiff has relied to her detriment on defendant's promises and devoted her entire life to him, defendant has been unjustly enriched.

The factual background alleged or testified to is that in June 1960, when she and defendant were students at Grinnell College in Iowa, plaintiff became pregnant; that defendant thereafter told her that they were husband and wife and would live as such, no formal ceremony being necessary, and that he would "share his life, his future, his earnings and his property" with her; that the parties immediately announced to their respective parents that they were married and thereafter held themselves out as husband and wife; that in reliance on defendant's promises she devoted her efforts to his professional education and his establishment in the practice of pedodontia, obtaining financial assistance from her parents for this purpose; that she assisted defendant in his career with her own special skills and although she was given payroll checks for these services she placed them in a common fund; that defendant, who was without funds at the time of the marriage, as a result of her efforts now earns over $80,000 a year and has accumulated large amounts of property, owned either jointly with her or separately; that she has given him every assistance a wife and mother could give, including social activities designed to enhance his social and professional reputation.

The amended complaint was also dismissed, the trial court finding that Illinois law and public policy require such claims to be based on a valid marriage. The appellate court reversed, stating that because the parties had outwardly lived a conventional married life, plaintiff's conduct had not "so affronted public policy that she should be denied any and all relief" (62 Ill. App.3d 861, 869, 20 Ill. Dec. 476, 482, 380 N.E.2d 454, 460), and that plaintiff's complaint stated a cause of action on an express oral contract. We granted leave to appeal. Defendant apparently does not contest his obligation to support the children, and that question is not before us.

The appellate court, in reversing, gave considerable weight to the fact that the parties had held themselves out as husband and wife for over 15 years. The court noted that they lived "a most conventional, respectable and ordinary family life" (62 Ill. App.3d 861, 863, 20 Ill. Dec. 476, 478, 380 N.E.2d 454, 457) that did not openly flout accepted standards, the "single flaw" being the lack of a valid marriage. Indeed the appellate court went so far as to say that the parties had "lived within the legitimate boundaries of a marriage and family relationship of a most conventional sort" (62 Ill. App.3d 861, 864, 20 Ill. Dec. 476, 479, 380 N.E.2d 454, 457), an assertion which that court cannot have intended to be taken literally. Noting that the Illinois Marriage and Dissolution of Marriage Act (Ill. Rev. Stat. 1977, ch. 40, par. 101 *et seq.*)

does not prohibit nonmarital cohabitation and that the Criminal Code of 1961 (Ill. Rev. Stat. 1977, ch. 38, par. 11–8(a)) makes fornication an offense only if the behavior is open and notorious, the appellate court concluded that plaintiff should not be denied relief on public policy grounds.

In finding that plaintiff's complaint stated a cause of action on an express oral contract, the appellate court adopted the reasoning of the California Supreme Court in the widely publicized case of *Marvin v. Marvin* (1976), 18 Cal.3d 660, 134 Cal. Rptr. 815, 557 P.2d 106, quoting extensively therefrom. In *Marvin*, Michelle Triola and defendant Lee Marvin lived together for 7 years pursuant to an alleged oral agreement that while "the parties lived together they would combine their efforts and earnings and would share equally any and all property accumulated as a result of their efforts whether individual or combined." (18 Cal.3d 660, 666, 134 Cal. Rptr. 815, 819, 557 P.2d 106, 110.) In her complaint she alleged that, in reliance on this agreement, she gave up her career as a singer to devote herself full time to defendant as "companion, homemaker, housekeeper and cook." (18 Cal.3d 660, 666, 134 Cal. Rptr. 815, 819, 557 P.2d 106, 110.) In resolving her claim for one-half the property accumulated in defendant's name during that period the California court held that "The courts should enforce express contracts between nonmarital partners except to the extent that the contract is explicitly founded on the consideration of meretricious sexual services" and that "In the absence of an express contract, the courts should inquire into the conduct of the parties to determine whether that conduct demonstrates an implied contract, agreement of partnership or joint venture, or some other tacit understanding between the parties. The courts may also employ the doctrine of quantum meruit, or equitable remedies such as constructive or resulting trusts, when warranted by the facts of the case." (18 Cal.3d 660, 665, 134 Cal. Rptr. 815, 819, 557 P.2d 106, 110.) The court reached its conclusions because:

> "In summary, we believe that the prevalence of nonmarital relationships in modern society and the social acceptance of them, marks this as a time when our courts should by no means apply the doctrine of the unlawfulness of the so-called meretricious relationship to the instant case. * * *
>   * * *
> "The mores of the society have indeed changed so radically in regard to cohabitation that we cannot impose a standard based on alleged moral considerations that have apparently been so widely abandoned by so many."

18 Cal.3d 660, 683–84, 134 Cal. Rptr. 815, 831, 557 P.2d 106, 122.

It is apparent that the *Marvin* court adopted a pure contract theory, under which, if the intent of the parties and the terms of their agreement are proved, the pseudo-conventional family relationship which impressed the appellate court here is irrelevant; recovery may be had unless the implicit sexual relationship is made the explicit consideration for the agreement. In contrast, the appellate court here, as we understand its opinion, would apply contract principles only in a setting where the relationship of the parties outwardly resembled that of a traditional family. It seems apparent that the plaintiff in *Marvin* would not have been entitled to recover in our appellate court because of the absence of that outwardly appearing conventional family relationship.

The issue of whether property rights accrue to unmarried cohabitants can not, however, be regarded realistically as merely a problem in the law of express contracts. Plaintiff argues that because her action is founded on an express contract, her recovery would in no way imply that unmarried cohabitants acquire property rights merely by cohabitation and subsequent separation. However, the *Marvin* court expressly recognized and the appellate court here seems to agree that if common law principles of express contract govern express agreements between unmarried cohabitants, common law principles of implied contract, equitable relief and constructive trust must govern the parties' relations in the absence of such an agreement. (18 Cal.3d 660, 678, 134 Cal. Rptr. 815, 827, 557 P.2d 106, 118; 62 Ill. App.3d 861, 867–68, 20 Ill. Dec. 476, 380 N.E.2d 454.) In all probability the latter case will be much the more common, since it is unlikely that most couples who live together will enter into express agreements regulating their property rights. (Bruch, *Property Rights of De Facto Spouses, Including Thoughts on the Value of Homemakers' Services,* 10 FAM. L.Q. 101, 102 (1976).) The increasing incidence of nonmarital cohabitation referred to in *Marvin* and the variety of legal remedies therein sanctioned seem certain to result in substantial amounts of litigation, in which, whatever the allegations regarding an oral contract, the proof will necessarily involve details of the parties' living arrangements.

Apart, however, from the appellate court's reliance upon *Marvin* to reach what appears to us to be a significantly different result, we believe there is a more fundamental problem. We are aware, of course, of the increasing judicial attention given the individual claims of unmarried cohabitants to jointly accumulated property, and the fact that the majority of courts considering the question have recognized an equitable or contractual basis for implementing the reasonable expectations of the parties unless sexual services were the explicit consideration. (See cases collected in Annot., 31 A.L.R.2d 1255 (1953) and A.L.R.2d Later Case Service supplementing vols. 25 to 31.) The issue of unmarried cohabitants' mutual property rights, however, as we earlier noted, cannot appropriately be characterized solely in terms of contract law, nor is it limited to considerations of equity or fairness as between the parties to such relationships. There are major public policy questions involved in determining whether, under what circumstances, and to what extent it is desirable to accord some type of legal status to claims arising from such relationships. Of substantially greater importance than the rights of the immediate parties is the impact of such recognition upon our society and the institution of marriage. Will the fact that legal rights closely resembling those arising from conventional marriages can be acquired by those who deliberately choose to enter into what have heretofore been commonly referred to as "illicit" or "meretricious" relationships encourage formation of such relationships and weaken marriage as the foundation of our family-based society? In the event of death shall the survivor have the status of a surviving spouse for purposes of inheritance, wrongful death actions, workmen's compensation, etc.? And still more importantly: what of the children born of such relationships?

What are their support and inheritance rights and by what standards are custody questions resolved? What of the sociological and psychological effects upon them of that type of environment? Does not the recognition of legally enforceable property and custody rights emanating from nonmarital cohabitation in practical effect equate with the legalization of common law marriage—at least in the circumstances of this case? And, in summary, have the increasing numbers of unmarried cohabitants and changing mores of our society (Bruch, *Property Rights of De Facto Spouses Including Thoughts on the Value of Homemakers' Services,* 10 FAM. L.Q. 101, 102–03 (1976); Nielson, *In re Cary: A Judicial Recognition of Illicit Cohabitation,* 25 HASTINGS L.J. 1226 (1974)) reached the point at which the general welfare of the citizens of this State is best served by a return to something resembling the judicially created common law marriage our legislature outlawed in 1905?

Illinois' public policy regarding agreements such as the one alleged here was implemented long ago in *Wallace v. Rappleye* (1882), 103 Ill. 229, 249, where this court said: "An agreement in consideration of future illicit cohabitation between the plaintiffs is void." This is the traditional rule, in force until recent years in all jurisdictions. (See, *e.g., Gauthier v. Laing* (1950), 96 N.H. 80, 70 A.2d 207; *Grant v. Butt* (1941), 198 S.C. 298, 17 S.E.2d 689.) Section 589 of the Restatement of Contracts (1932) states, "A bargain in whole or in part for or in consideration of illicit sexual intercourse or of a promise thereof is illegal." See also 6A Corbin, CONTRACTS sec. 1476 (1962), and cases cited therein.

It is true, of course, that cohabitation by the parties may not prevent them from forming valid contracts about independent matters, for which it is said the sexual relations do not form part of the consideration. (RESTATEMENT OF CONTRACTS secs. 589, 597 (1932); 6A Corbin, CONTRACTS sec. 1476 (1962).) Those courts which allow recovery generally have relied on this principle to reduce the scope of the rule of illegality. Thus, California courts long prior to *Marvin* held that an express agreement to pool earnings is supported by independent consideration and is not invalidated by cohabitation of the parties, the agreements being regarded as simultaneous but separate. (See, *e.g.*, *Trutalli v. Meraviglia* (1932), 215 Cal. 698, 12 P.2d 430; see also Annot., 31 A.L.R.2d 1255 (1953), and cases cited therein.) More recently, several courts have reasoned that the rendition of housekeeping and homemaking services such as plaintiff alleges here could be regarded as the consideration for a separate contract between the parties, severable from the illegal contract founded on sexual relations. (*Kozlowski v. Kozlowski* (1979), 80 N.J. 378, 403 A.2d 902; *Marvin v. Marvin* (1976), 18 Cal.3d 660, 670 n.5, 134 Cal. Rptr. 815, 822 n.5, 557 P.2d 106, 113 n.5; *Tyranski v. Piggins* (1973), 44 Mich. App. 570, 205 N.W.2d 595, 597; *contra, Rehak v. Mathis* (1977), 239 Ga. 541, 238 S.E.2d 81.) In *Latham v. Latham* (1976), 274 Or. 421, 547 P.2d 144, and *Carlson v. Olson* (Minn. 1977), 256 N.W.2d 249, on allegations similar to those in this case, the Minnesota Supreme Court adopted *Marvin* and the Oregon court expressly held that agreements in consideration of cohabitation were not void, stating:

> "We are not validating an agreement in which the only or primary consideration is sexual intercourse. The agreement here contemplated all the burdens and amenities of married life."

274 Or. 421, 427, 547 P.2d 144, 147.

The real thrust of plaintiff's argument here is that we should abandon the rule of illegality because of certain changes in societal norms and attitudes. It is urged that social mores have changed radically in recent years, rendering this principle of law archaic. It is said that because there are so many unmarried cohabitants today the courts must confer a legal status on such relationships. This, of course, is the rationale underlying some of the decisions and commentaries. (See, *e.g.*, *Marvin v. Marvin* (1976), 18 Cal.3d 660, 683, 134 Cal. Rptr. 815, 831, 557 P.2d 106, 122; *Beal v. Beal* (1978), 282 Or. 115, 577 P.2d 507; Kay & Amyx, *Marvin v. Marvin: Preserving the Options*, 65 CAL. L. REV. 937 (1977).) If this is to be the result, however, it would seem more candid to acknowledge the return of varying forms of common law marriage than to continue displaying the naivete we believe involved in the assertion that there are involved in these relationships contracts separate and independent from the sexual activity, and the assumption that those contracts would have been entered into or would continue without that activity.

Even if we were to assume some modification of the rule of illegality is appropriate, we return to the fundamental question earlier alluded to: If resolution of this issue rests ultimately on grounds of public policy, by what body should that policy be determined? *Marvin*, viewing the issue as governed solely by contract law, found judicial policy-making appropriate. Its decision was facilitated by California precedent and that State's no-fault divorce law. In our view, however, the situation alleged here was not the kind of arm's length bargain envisioned by traditional contract principles, but an intimate arrangement of a fundamentally different kind. The issue, realistically, is whether it is appropriate for this court to grant a legal status to a private arrangement substituting for the institution of marriage sanctioned by the State. The question whether change is needed in the law governing the rights of parties in this delicate area of marriage-like relationships involves evaluations of sociological data and alternatives we believe best suited to the superior investigative and fact-finding facilities of the legislative branch in the exercise of its traditional authority to declare public policy in the domestic relations field. (*Strukoff v. Strukoff* (1979), 76 Ill.2d 53, 27 Ill. Dec. 762, 389 N.E.2d 1170; *Siegall v. Solomon* (1960), 19 Ill.2d 145, 166 N.E.2d 5.) That belief is reinforced by the fact that judicial recognition of mutual property rights between unmarried cohabitants would, in our opinion, clearly violate the policy of our recently enacted Illinois Marriage and Dissolution of Marriage Act. Although the Act does not specifically address the subject of nonmarital cohabitation, we think the legislative policy quite evident from the statutory scheme.

The Act provides:

"This Act shall be liberally construed and applied to promote its underlying purposes, which are to:

"(1) provide adequate procedures for the solemnization and registration of marriage;

"(2) strengthen and preserve the integrity of marriage and safeguard family relationships."

(Ill. Rev. Stat. 1977, ch. 40, par. 102.)
We cannot confidently say that judicial recognition of property rights between unmarried cohabitants will not make that alternative to marriage more attractive by allowing the parties to engage in such relationships with greater security. As one commentator has noted, it may make this alternative especially attractive to persons who seek a property arrangement that the law does not permit to marital partners. (Comment, 90 HARV. L. REV. 1708, 1713 (1977).) This court, for example, has held void agreements releasing husbands from their obligation to support their wives. (*Vock v. Vock* (1937), 365 Ill. 432, 6 N.E.2d 843; *VanKoten v. VanKoten* (1926), 323 Ill. 323, 154 N.E. 146; see also *Rhodes v. Rhodes* (1967), 82 Ill. App.2d 435, 225 N.E.2d 802, RESTATEMENT OF CONTRACTS sec. 587 (1932); Weitzman, *Legal Regulation of Marriage: Tradition and Change*, 62 CAL. L. REV. 1169, 1259–63 (1974).) In thus potentially enhancing the attractiveness of a private arrangement over marriage, we believe that the apellate court decision in this case contravenes the Act's policy of strengthening and preserving the integrity of marriage.

The Act also provides: "Common law marriages contracted in this State after June 30, 1905 are invalid." (Ill. Rev. Stat. 1977, ch. 40, par. 214.) The doctrine of common law marriage was a judicially sanctioned alternative to formal marriage designed to apply to cases like the one before us. In *Port v. Port* (1873), 70 Ill. 484, this court reasoned that because the statute governing marriage did not "prohibit or declare void a marriage not solemnized in accordance with its provisions, a marriage without observing the statutory regulations, if made according to the common law, will still be a valid marriage." (70 Ill. 484, 486.) This court held that if the parties declared their present intent to take each other as husband and wife and thereafter did so a valid common law marriage existed. (*Cartwright v. McGown* (1887), 121 Ill. 388, 398, 12 N.E. 737.) Such marriages were legislatively abolished in 1905, presumably because of the problems earlier noted, and the above-quoted language expressly reaffirms that policy.

While the appellate court denied that its decision here served to rehabilitate the doctrine of common law marriage, we are not persuaded. Plaintiff's allegations disclose a relationship that clearly would have constituted a valid common law marriage in this State prior to 1905. The parties expressly manifested their present intent to be husband and wife; immediately thereafter they assumed the marital status; and for many years they consistently held themselves out to their relatives and the public at large as husband and wife. Revealingly, the appellate court relied on the fact that the parties were, to the public, husband and wife in determining that the parties living arrangement did not flout Illinois public policy. It is of course true, as plaintiff argues, that unlike a common law spouse she would not have full marital rights in that she could not, for example, claim her statutory one-third share of defendant's property on his death. The distinction appears unimpressive, however, if she can claim one-half of his property on a theory of express or implied contract.

Further, in enacting the Illinois Marriage and Dissolution of Marriage Act, our legislature considered and rejected the "no-fault" divorce concept that has been adopted in many jurisdictions, including California. (See Uniform Marriage and Divorce Act secs. 302, 305.) Illinois appears to be one of three States retaining fault grounds for dissolution of marriage. (Ill. Rev. Stat. 1977, ch. 40, par. 401; Comment, *Hewitt v. Hewitt, Contract Cohabitation and Equitable Expectations Relief for Meretricious Spouses,* 12 J. MAR. J. PRAC. & PROC. 435, 452–53 (1979).) Certainly a significantly stronger pro-marriage policy is manifest in that action, which appears to us to reaffirm the traditional doctrine that marriage is a civil contract between three parties— the husband, the wife and the State. (*Johnson v. Johnson* (1942), 381 Ill. 362, 45 N.E.2d 625; *VanKoten v. VanKoten* (1926), 323 Ill. 323, 154 N.E. 146.) The policy of the Act gives the State a strong continuing interest in the institution of marriage and prevents the marriage relation from becoming in effect a private contract terminable at will. This seems to us another indication that public policy disfavors private contractual alternatives to marriage.

Lastly, in enacting the Illinois Marriage and Dissolution of Marriage Act, the legislature adopted for the first time the civil law concept of the putative spouse. The Act provides that an unmarried person may acquire the rights of a legal spouse only if he goes through a marriage ceremony and cohabits with another in the good-faith belief that he is validly married. When he learns that the marriage is not valid his status as a putative spouse terminates; common law marriages are expressly excluded. (Ill. Rev. Stat. 1977, ch. 40, par. 305.) The legislature thus extended legal recognition to a class of nonmarital relationships, but only to the extent of a party's good-faith belief in the existence of a valid marriage. Moreover, auring the legislature's deliberations on the Act *Marvin* was decided and received wide publicity. (See Note, 12 J. MAR. J. PRAC. & PROC. 435, 450 (1979).) These circumstances in our opinion constitute a recent and unmistakeable legislative judgment disfavoring the grant of mutual property rights to knowingly unmarried cohabitants. We have found no case in which recovery has been allowed in the face of a legislative declaration as recently and clearly enacted as ours. Even if we disagreed with the wisdom of that judgment, it is not for us to overturn or erode it. *Davis v. Commonwealth Edison Co.* (1975), 61 Ill.2d 494, 496–97, 336 N.E.2d 881.

Actually, however, the legislature judgment is in accord with the history of common law marriage in this country. "Despite its judicial acceptance in many states, the doctrine of common-law marriage is generally frowned on in this country, even in some of the states that have accepted it." (52 AM. JUR.2d 902 *Marriage* sec. 46 (1970).) Its origins, early history and problems are detailed in *In re Estate of Soeder* (1966), 7 Ohio App.2d 271, 220 N.E.2d 547, where that court noted that some 30 States did not authorize common law marriage. Judicial criticism has been widespread even in States recognizing the relationship. (See, *e.g., Baker v. Mitchell* (1941), 143 Pa. Super. 50, 54, 17 A.2d 738, 741, "a fruitful source of perjury and fraud * * *"; *Sorensen v. Sorensen* (1904), 68 Neb. 500, 100 N.W. 930.) "It tends to weaken the public estimate of the sanctity of the marriage relation. It puts in doubt the certainty of the rights of inheritance. It opens the door to false pretenses of marriage and the imposition on estates of suppositious heirs." 7 Ohio App.2d 271, 290, 220 N.E.2d 547, 561.

In our judgment the fault in the appellate court holding in this case is that its practical effect is the reinstatement of common law marriage, as we earlier indicated, for there is no doubt that the alleged facts would, if proved, establish such a marriage under our pre-1905 law. (*Cartwright v. McGown* (1887), 121 Ill. 388, 12 N.E. 737.) The concern of both the *Marvin* court and the appellate court on this score is manifest from the circumstance that both courts found it necessary to emphasize marital values ("the structure of society itself largely depends upon the institution of marriage" (*Marvin v. Marvin* (1976), 18 Cal.3d 660, 684, 134 Cal. Rptr. 815, 831, 557 P.2d 106, 122) and to deny any intent to "derogate from" (18 Cal.3d 660, 684, 134 Cal. Rptr. 815, 831, 557 P.2d 106, 122) or "denigrate" (*Hewitt v. Hewitt* (1978), 62 Ill. App.3d 861, 868, 20 Ill. Dec. 476, 380 N.E.2d 454) that institution. Commentators have expressed greater concern: "[T]he effect of these cases is to reinstitute common-law marriage in California after it has been abolished by the legislature." (Clark, *The New Marriage*, WILLAMETTE L.J. 441, 449 (1976).) "*[Hewitt]* is, if not a direct resurrection of common-law marriage contract principles, at least a large step in that direction." Reiland, *Hewitt v. Hewitt: Middle America, Marvin and Common-Law Marriage*, 60 CHI. B. REC. 84, 88–90 (1978).

We do not intend to suggest that plaintiff's claims are totally devoid of merit. Rather, we believe that our statement in *Mogged v. Mogged* (1973), 55 Ill.2d 221, 225, 302 N.E.2d 293, 295, made in deciding whether to abolish a judicially created defense to divorce, is appropriate here:

> "Whether or not the defense of recrimination should be abolished or modified in Illinois is a question involving complex public-policy considerations as to which compelling arguments may be made on both sides. For the reasons stated hereafter, we believe that these questions are appropriately within the province of the legislature, and that, if there is to be a change in the law of this State on this matter, it is for the legislature and not the courts to bring about that change."

We accordingly hold that plaintiff's claims are unenforceable for the reason that they contravene the public policy, implicit in the statutory scheme of the Illinois Marriage and Dissolution of Marriage Act, disfavoring the grant of mutually enforceable property rights to knowingly unmarried cohabitants. The judgment of the appellate court is reversed and the judgment of the circuit court of Champaign County is affirmed.

Appellate court reversed; circuit court affirmed.

Cohabitation Contract as Partnership, Joint Venture, or Joint Enterprise

Poole v. Schrichte

Supreme Court of Washington

39 Wash.2d 558, 236 P.2d 1044 (1951)

HILL, Justice.

The respondent, Irene M. Poole, and the appellant, Herbert A. Schrichte, lived together without the formality of a marriage ceremony, from 1935 to

1941 in Chicago and from 1941 to 1947 in Seattle. The present action is to determine their respective interests in a tavern and certain household furniture and personal property in Mr. Schrichte's possession.

In January, 1942, they combined their limited resources to acquire a beauty shop, which Mrs. Poole operated under the name of "Crosley Beauty Salon." (Their resources were then so limited that Mrs. Poole had to borrow fifty dollars to help pay the first month's rent.) During 1942, 1943 and part of 1944, Mr. Schrichte worked as a railroad switchman. In his spare time he constructed living quarters in back of the beauty shop, assisted Mrs. Poole in its business management, and did maintenance work in connection with its operation.

She opened a bank account, which will be referred to as the "Crosley account," and into it went the proceeds from the operation of the beauty shop and Mr. Schrichte's earnings, and the funds so deposited were used for their living expenses and for the operation of the shop. Mrs. Poole alone could write checks on this account.

In June, 1944, Mr. Schrichte sustained an injury that marked the termination of his employment with the railroad. In August of that year they made a three-thousand-dollar payment from the Crosley account on the purchase of a tavern, and borrowed ten thousand dollars to pay the balance of the purchase price. The loan was secured by two chattel mortgages, one on the fixtures and equipment in the beauty shop and one on the fixtures and equipment in the tavern. The bill of sale to the tavern, the lease, and the liquor licenses were in Mr. Schrichte's name, as was a bank account that was opened with six hundred dollars from the Crosley account and into which most of the tavern proceeds went. Checks signed "Herbert A. Schrichte, by Mrs. Herbert A. Schrichte" were honored on the tavern account.

For almost two years, until the beauty shop was sold in 1946, she ran the salon while he ran the saloon. Both before and after the sale of the beauty shop, because of Mr. Schrichte's frequent asthmatic seizures, which necessitated trips to Arizona, California, Canada and eastern Washington for relief, Mrs. Poole devoted considerable time to the tavern's operation and business management.

They purchased a house in January, 1946. The down payment and some of the monthly payments on the mortgage were made from the proceeds of the tavern. When the beauty shop was sold, some $1,534 from the proceeds of the sale was used to accelerate the payments on the house, and the remainder, like the proceeds from the operation of the shop, was used for living expenses. The Crosley account was closed in September, 1947, the balance in the account, $844, finding its way into the tavern account.

Differences arose between the parties and they separated October 9, 1947. He testified, "She left me"; her testimony was that he "threw me out bag and baggage.* * * He hit me until I couldn't walk, and I had to go to the hospital." A friend of hers testified that when Mrs. Poole left the hospital, "She was in bad condition. Her mouth was swollen and her face was in a bad mess."

Under those circumstances, the separation justifiably terminated any attempt by Mrs. Poole to participate in the operation of the tavern.

She instituted the present action to establish her interest in the tavern and in the household furniture and personal property which remained in Mr. Schrichte's possession. The trial court gave her a judgment for five thousand dollars against Mr. Schrichte in lieu of a half interest in the tavern and the profits thereof subsequent to her exclusion from any participation in its operation, and also gave her a half interest in the furniture and personal property. He has appealed.

The theory of both parties as to the proper disposition of this case stems from the fact of their cohabitation, concededly meretricious in its inception in Chicago in 1935, as Mrs. Poole had not at that time secured a final divorce from her second husband.

* * *

We have here a situation in which, if the parties to this action had not been living together, there would be no question but that Mrs. Poole had at least a one-half interest in the tavern. Her rights do not stem from cohabitation or the meretricious relationship, but from the fact that the proceeds from the beauty shop she operated clearly constituted a larger proportion of the Crosley account than did Mr. Schrichte's earnings as a railroad switchman. The undisputed testimony is that the money that went into the down payment on the tavern was at least half hers; that her credit was pledged to make its purchase possible, and that she assisted in its operation during Mr. Schrichte's frequent illnesses and absences from the city. The other payments on the purchase price came from the operation of the tavern. We know of no rule of law or equity that says that if she lived with Mr. Schrichte knowing that she was not married to him, she thereby forfeited her interest in the tavern because he had the foresight to see that the legal title thereto stood in his name.

The evidence establishes here a joint venture if not a partnership between the parties so far as their interests in the tavern are concerned. Their social relationships, legal or illegal, moral or immoral, are not material on this phase of the case. Mr. Schrichte chose to exclude Mrs. Poole from any voice in the operation of the tavern, and that she has made no contribution to its operation since October, 1947, is his fault, not hers. We would, therefore, not have allowed him the sum of $1,372 with which the trial court credited him for his services to the joint venture in the operation of the tavern.

Mr. Schrichte urges that the trial court having found that he was entitled to $39.80 a month for his services in the operation of the tavern and Mrs. Poole not having appealed from that finding, the law of the case is that he is entitled to compensation for his services to the joint venture; and that it is obvious that $39.80 a month is an arbitrary and not an adequate allowance, and, since he is entitled to compensation, the case should be remanded for the taking of evidence as to the value of his services. The argument is that we should not only perpetuate what we conceive to be error in allowing Mr. Schrichte any compensation for his services, but we should remand the case so that the error might be augmented.

In an equity case the trial is *de novo* in this court, and, although the trial court's findings are given great weight, we do, so far as necessary, make our own findings and draw our own conclusions, and certainly we are not bound to perpetuate error. [Citation omitted.]

We fail to see how the trial court could have found Mrs. Poole's interest in the business and her share of the proceeds to be less than five thousand dollars. She seemingly is satisfied with that amount, or at least does not cross-appeal from the judgment awarding it to her. That portion of the trial court's judgment will therefore be affirmed.

It could likewise be affirmed on the theory adopted by Mrs. Poole and the trial court, *i.e.*, that she had actually believed that there was a common-law marriage and that in such a situation, although she was mistaken, a court of equity will protect the rights of the innocent party in the property accumulated by the joint efforts of both. While some skeptics might be dubious as to the good faith of Mrs. Poole, since there is no common-law marriage in either Illinois or Washington, the experienced trial judge was convinced that she believed she was married, and he so found; and he, though doubtless gallant, is not entirely naive and unacquainted with the ways of the world. After an examination of the record, we are agreed that there is credible evidence to support that finding and to establish that Mrs. Poole is an innocent party within the rule and that under such circumstances a court of equity will protect the rights of an innocent party in the property accumulated by the joint efforts of both.

* * *

The judgment is affirmed in its entirety.

Cohabitation Contract as Express, Resulting, or Constructive Trust

Omer v. Omer

Court of Appeals of Washington

11 Wash. App. 386, 523 P.2d 957 (1974)

PEARSON, Chief Judge.

This is an action by plaintiff, Helen Omer, claiming an interest in several parcels of real property held in the name of defendant, Daniel Omer, her former husband. From a decree awarding plaintiff a one-half interest in each of the parcels as tenant in common, defendant appeals.

* * *

The relationship of plaintiff and defendant was stated by the trial court to be "technically" meretricious. The wisdom of this denomination is apparent from a consideration of the established facts.

The parties were married in Israel in 1949. During the course of their marriage, they had two children. In 1959, at the urging of Daniel Omer, at that time employed by the United States embassy in Israel, the parties were divorced. It was the stated opinion of the defendant that the divorce would facilitate the entry of the parties and their children into the United States. Subsequent to this divorce, the parties continued to live together as husband and wife in Israel.

In early 1963, the plaintiff came to New York. The defendant arrived in New York with the children the following year. The parties lived together in New York and operated together a luncheonette in that city. Both parties further entered into sham marriages to expedite their plans to obtain United States citizenship. (These marriages were terminated after the parties obtained citizenship.)

The defendant moved to Washington some time later. The record discloses that at his request, the plaintiff remained in New York with the children and regularly sent portions of her earnings to him in this state. He assured her that he was building a "paradise" for the family here, that she must continue to work and remit money to him, and in no event to disclose their relationship to third parties so as to impair naturalization prospects.

The trial court found that the plaintiff had difficulty with the English language, and that she was reliant upon the defendant for guidance and advice.

At various times while plaintiff remained in New York, the children came to Washington and resided with their father. Eventually, the plaintiff moved to Washington. The parties continued to live together here; Mrs. Omer continued to work and to turn paychecks over to the defendant.

Throughout this period, the defendant acquired the parcels of real estate which are the subject of this action. In 1969 the relationship between the parties deteriorated seriously; plaintiff was abused and rejected by the defendant, and she eventually brought this action, seeking a division of the real property.

The trial court found that from the time of the divorce until 1969, the intent of the parties was to further the interests of their family community. Telling in this connection was the testimony of the children that they were unaware until 1969 that their parents were, in fact, not married. In light of this intent, and the labors and contributions made by the plaintiff in furtherance of it, the trial court entered this finding of fact:

"That the property mentioned above was acquired through the joint efforts, by the plaintiff and by the defendant, in which they combined their earnings and accumulations of labor and their skills, and the funds contributed by the plaintiff were used by the defendant in the acquisition and the payment of the properties mentioned and were so intended to be used."

The settlement of property rights arising out of meretricious relationships has had a busy history in this state. It has generally involved two classes of cases: (1) those involving the claim of a meretricious "spouse" against the estate of the deceased partner to the relationship who held title to assets acquired during the relationship (*Creasman v. Boyle*, 31 Wash.2d 345, 196 P.2d 835 (1948)); and (2) those, like the one at bench, involving the claim by a meretricious spouse who has become estranged from the one who holds title to property acquired during the relationship. *West v. Knowles*, 50 Wash.2d 311, 311 P.2d 689 (1957). Aside from the obvious difficulty in proving the claim where one party is deceased, there appears little other reason to differentiate between the rules applicable to the two classes of cases. See *In re Estate of Thornton*, 81 Wash.2d 72, 499 P.2d 864 (1972).

Much of the history has recently been reviewed by the Supreme Court in *Humphries v. Riveland*, 67 Wash.2d 376, 407 P.2d 967 (1965) and *In re Estate of Thornton, supra*. We offer a brief summary of that history by first considering the rule enunciated in *Creasman v. Boyle, supra*, which poses a difficult hurdle to an equitable adjustment of the property rights of meretricious spouses. In *Creasman* the Supreme Court at 351 of 31 Wash.2d, at 838 of 196 P.2d established the following legal presumption:

> "[P]roperty acquired by a man and a woman not married to each other, but living together as husband and wife, is not community property, and, *in the absence of some trust relation*, belongs to the one in whose name the legal title to the property stands."

Because of the harshness of the announced rule, certain theories have been established as exceptions. In many instances these theories require fictional applications. Examples are (1) implied partnership or joint venture, *In re Estate of Thornton, supra;* (2) constructive trust, *Humphries v. Riveland, supra;* (3) resulting trust, *Walberg v. Mattson*, 38 Wash.2d 808, 232 P.2d 827 (1951); (4) express or implied contract (to make a will), *In re Estate of Thornton, supra;* and (5) community property interest arising out of a long-term stable meretricious relationship, *In re Estate of Thornton, supra*.

Without intending to unduly generalize, it appears from our review of the cases that if the joint efforts of the meretricious spouses relates to a business enterprise of some kind, an implied partnership affords the most viable theory of recovery. *Poole v. Schrichte*, 39 Wash.2d 558, 236 P.2d 1044 (1951); *In re Estate of Thornton, supra*. Otherwise, the party seeking to establish the claim usually must rely on either a constructive trust theory with its requirement of fraud, overreaching, or inequitable conduct, *Humphries v. Riveland, supra*, or a resulting trust theory with its requirement that the parties must have intended one party would hold the property in trust for the other who furnished the consideration for its purchase. See *Creasman v. Boyle, supra; Walberg v. Mattson, supra*. Proof of these theories must meet the clear, cogent, and convincing standard of proof, as an additional hurdle. *Manning v. Mount St. Michael's*, 78 Wash.2d 542, 477 P.2d 635 (1970); *Humphries v. Riveland, supra*.

A theory which would appear to involve the least fictional analysis has so far not been adopted in this state. That theory would recognize that certain meretricious relationships of long and durable standing may give rise to community property rights similar to those which prevail between married persons. See *In re Estate of Thornton, supra*, where the Supreme Court expresses some reluctance to continue resistance to this theory, but still declines to overrule or modify *Creasman v. Boyle, supra*.

The case at bench affords cogent reasons for supporting plaintiff's claim by analogy to the community property laws. Here the parties appear to have been divorced solely for the expediency of gaining entry to and citizenship in this country. In all other respects they lived together, raised a family and acquired property through joint efforts and money, as though they were in fact married.

If, in passing upon this type of case, the court is truly exercising its inherent power to do justice between the parties, and is not making its judgment on the basis that the relationship is illicit, as many of the cases suggest, it seems unwise that we should require proof of some fictional relationship by clear, cogent and convincing evidence in order to escape the consequences of a rigid legal presumption. This approach may deny, rather than achieve justice between the parties. See both dissents in *Humphries v. Riveland, supra;* see *In re Estate of Thornton, supra.*

It seems to us that a better approach would be to let proof of the relationship itself, its purpose, duration, stability, and so forth, determine the merits of the claim, and then, if warranted by the facts, hold that the community property laws should be applied by analogy to determine the rights of the parties.

If our trial courts were free of rigid doctrinal analysis, legal presumptions, high standards of proof and so forth, and could make determinations on the basis of the facts and equity of the particular case, it is our opinion that a just result could be achieved more often than it is presently.

Since *In re Estate of Thornton, supra* compels adherence to the traditional approach, we now reach the question of whether or not the facts as found by the trial court are sufficient to justify the conclusion it reached. In other words, do those findings support either a constructive trust or an implied partnership, to justify the division of property decreed?

Perhaps the simplest theory for affirming the judgment would be for us to hold that the finding quoted above relating to the joint efforts of the parties is sufficient to establish an implied partnership or joint venture and rely upon the statements pertaining to that theory as enunciated in *In re Estate of Thornton, supra.*

The difficulty we have with this simplistic approach is that the parties clearly did not either expressly or impliedly intend a business relationship. The clear thrust of the findings was that the non-marital status of the parties was conceived by defendant and carried out under his direction for the sole purpose of allowing his family the benefits of United States immigration and citizenship. But for that purpose, the parties would not have divorced in Israel nor entered into sham marriages in this country. The property was acquired by the joint efforts of the parties with that goal in mind and with the ultimate goal of remarriage when citizenship was achieved.

Without rejecting an implied partnership out of hand, other findings convince us to affirm the judgment on a theory of constructive trust. The real intention of the parties appears in finding of fact 8:

> "That while the property was taken in the name of the defendant it was the intent of the parties that the property would be shared both by the plaintiff and the defendant when they would once again be reunited as husband and wife in this country, as they had been in Israel once their citizenship was acquired."

Inasmuch as the trial court also found that defendant initiated and directed the changes in marital status, allegedly to further the goal of United States citizenship, and since plaintiff followed his advice and directions and contributed to the goals with labor and money, it would be grossly inequitable to deny her the relief sought.

It was stated by Justice Cardozo that "A constructive trust is the formula through which the conscience of equity finds expression." *Beatty v.*

Guggenheim Exploration Co., 225 N.Y. 380, 386, 122 N.E. 378, 380 (1919). A further amplification of the doctrine appears in *Proctor v. Forsythe,* 4 Wash. App. 238, 242, 480 P.2d 511, 514 (1971):

> "A constructive trust arises where a person holding title to property is subject to an equitable duty to convey it to another on the ground that he would be unjustly enriched if he were permitted to retain it. Restatement of Restitution §160 (1937). Our court has noted that constructive trusts are those which arise purely by construction of equity and are entirely independent of any actual or presumed intention of the parties and are often directly contrary to such intention. They are entirely in invitum and are forced upon the conscience of the trustee for the purpose of working out right and justice or frustrating fraud."

Carkonen v. Alberts, 196 Wash. 575, 83 P.2d 899, 135 A.L.R. 209 (1938). This description of the doctrine of constructive trusts describes rather well the circumstances of this case and we believe the findings of the trial court justify its application.

It is true, there is no specific finding of fraud or misrepresentation or overreaching. There is, however, a clear element of unconscionability inherent in the findings of the trial court which, in our view, justifies application of the doctrine of constructive trust.

Judgment affirmed.

Cohabitation Contract as Property Transaction, Specific Performance, and Suit to Quiet Title

Tyranski v. Piggins

Court of Appeals of Michigan

44 Mich. App. 570, 205 N.W.2d 595 (1973)

LEVIN, Presiding Judge.

The plaintiff, Mrs. Helen Tyranski, commenced this action in January, 1970, claiming that she was entitled to a house located on Blue Skies Avenue, Livonia, Michigan, which was held in the name of Alfred P. Lattavo. Mr. Lattavo had died in October, 1969.

At the conclusion of the trial, the judge, who sat without a jury, found that Mrs. Tyranski was entitled to the house and its furnishings. A judgment was entered for specific performance of an oral agreement the judge found Lattavo had made with Mrs. Tyranski to convey the house to her.

The defendant, the ancillary administrator of Lattavo's estate, does not, on appeal, dispute the claimed oral agreement. He contends that the judge should have refused to enforce the agreement because of the meretricious relationship of the parties. We affirm.

Lattavo, who traveled frequently in connection with his trucking business, met Mrs. Tyranski in 1963, while she was working as a cocktail waitress. They were attracted to one another and shortly thereafter began living together in Mrs. Tyranski's rented Detroit home, and later in an apartment. After they had been living together for nearly four years, Lattavo had the Blue Skies house built. There is evidence that tends to show that $10,000 of the required funds was contributed by Mrs. Tyranski. Mrs. Tyranski decorated the house and selected the furniture. They lived together in the Blue Skies home from 1967 until Lattavo's death.

Lattavo had married Rosella Lattavo in 1941. He made trips to their home in Canton throughout the period of his relationship with Mrs. Tyranski, though by 1967 he spent only a few days a month in Canton. The rest of the time he spent in Livonia.

Mrs. Tyranski is a married woman and the mother of two children. She has been separated from her husband for many years, but never secured a divorce. Lattavo acted as a father to her children, and gave away her daughter, Laura, in marriage. While Lattavo was in Michigan, he and Mrs. Tyranski lived together as man and wife, and at least one mutual friend testified that she knew Mrs. Tyranski as "Mrs. Lattavo."

Rosella Lattavo testified that she did not learn about Mrs. Tyranski or the Blue Skies house until she went to an attorney to file for a divorce and had her husband investigated in August, 1969.

The issue is whether Mrs. Tyranski's claim under the agreement is defeated by the meretricious relationship.

While the parties illicitly cohabited over a period of years, that does not render all agreements between them illegal. Professor Corbin and the drafters of the Restatement of Contracts both write that while bargains in whole or in part in consideration of an illicit relationship are unenforceable, agreements between parties to such a relationship with respect to money or property will be enforced if the agreement is independent of the illicit relationship.[1]

Neither these authorities nor the large body of case law in other jurisdictions—there is no Michigan authority dealing with this precise issue—articulate a guideline for determining when the consideration will be regarded as "independent," and when it is so coupled with the meretricious acts that the agreement will not be enforced. A pattern does, however, emerge upon reading the cases.

Neither party to a meretricious relationship acquires, by reason of cohabitation alone, rights in the property accumulations of the other during the period of the relationship. But where there is an express agreement to accumulate or transfer property following a relationship of some permanence and an additional consideration in the form of either money or of services, the courts tend to find an independent consideration.

Thus, a plaintiff who can show an actual contribution of money, pursuant to an agreement to pool assets and share accumulations, will usually prevail. Services, such as cooking meals, laundering clothes, "caring" for the decedent through sickness, have been found to be adequate and independent considerations in cases where there was an express agreement.

An express agreement to convey the Blue Skies house was established by testimony at the trial. There was also evidence that Mrs. Tyranski had "changed the tenor of her life" in performance of the agreement so as to make reasonable the inference that there was such an agreement. See *In re Cramer's Estate*, 296 Mich. 44, 49, 295 N.W. 553 (1941).

Mrs. Tyranski cleaned the house, did the marketing, cooked the food, did Mr. Lattavo's personal laundry, and acted as his hostess. She cared for him when he was sick, especially during the last year and a half of his life when his condition required greater attention and care. There was also the evidence of the $10,000 claimed to have been contributed by Mrs. Tyranski to Lattavo in April or May of 1967.

It has been said that "equity does not demand that its suitors shall have led blameless lives." *Loughran v. Loughran*, 292 U.S. 216, 229, 54 S.Ct. 684,

---

[1] 6A Corbin, CONTRACTS, §1476, p. 622; 2 RESTATEMENT CONTRACTS, §§589, 597, pp. 1098, 1108.

689, 78 L.Ed. 1219, 1227 (1934). The Michigan case law is in accord. In *Burns v. Stevens,* 236 Mich. 447, 452–453, 210 N.W. 483, 485 (1926), the plaintiff (the man) and the defendant (the woman) lived together for three years. They made a $1,000 down payment on a cottage. They signed a land contract "jointly." After the man tired of the woman, he brought suit claiming the cottage was his property and that her name was put on the contract to secure repayment to her of $400 she had advanced. He sought to have her interest in the contract declared to be a mortgage. In upholding the trial court's determination in his favor, the Michigan Supreme Court said:

> "[T]he rule that if the parties to a suit are *in pari delicto* a court of equity will leave them where they have placed themselves should not be here applied. * * * The question to be determined in this case * * * is whether the party acquired an interest in the property or a security for the money advanced. *The manner in which they were then living is immaterial to the issue* except in its bearing upon the weight to be given to their testimony. The doors of courts are not closed to people who lead immoral lives when contracts between them untainted with illegality or fraud are involved." (Emphasis supplied.)

* * *

Where a meretricious relationship has already been entered upon, to penalize one of the parties by striking down their otherwise lawful promises, will not undo the relationship, nor is it likely to discourage others from entering upon such relationships. It appears on examination of the cases that the courts have, on various theories, allotted to the woman a share of the property in cases thought to be meritorious. We are persuaded, as was the trial judge, that this is such a case.

Affirmed. * * *

Trutalli v. Meraviglia

Supreme Court of California

215 Cal. 698, 12 P.2d 430 (1932)

CURTIS, J.

This appeal is taken upon the judgment roll alone. The action was brought by plaintiff to quiet his title to certain real property situated in the city and county of San Francisco. The defendant answered, and, in addition to her answer, filed a cross-complaint in which she claimed to be the owner of an undivided one-half of said real property, and also the owner of an undivided one-half of another parcel of land situated in the county of Santa Clara. Each of said two parcels of real property stood upon the public records in the name of the plaintiff who claimed to be the sole owner of the same. The court made findings of fact upon which judgment was entered in favor of the defendant upon her cross-complaint. Two of these findings are as follows:

"II.

> "That in the year nineteen sixteen (1916) the plaintiff and defendant, without the performance of a marriage ceremony, agreed to become and live together and assume the marital relation between themselves and the world, as husband and wife; that thereupon said plaintiff and defendant did assume said marital relation openly, publicly and notoriously,

and were known to the public in general, and their friends in particular, as husband and wife, living and cohabiting together as such, and so continued until the latter part of the year nineteen twenty-seven (1927); that during said time there were born to plaintiff and defendant, as the issue of said cohabitation, two (2) children, to-wit: Alma, a girl, of the age of twelve (12) years, and Disma, a girl, of the age of eleven (11) years.

"III.

"That it was mutually agreed by and between the plaintiff and defendant herein, upon the making and entering into of said agreement set forth in paragraph one (1) herein, that the defendant would perform all the necessary household services, and that all monies derived by either, or both, of said parties would be paid to the plaintiff to be invested by him for the benefit of both parties from time to time; and that all property, real and personal, acquired by said plaintiff should be held by him for the joint benefit of the said parties, each having an undivided one-half (½) interest therein."

The court further found: "Finding V. That as a result of the joint efforts of plaintiff and defendant, under and by virtue of said agreement, and while they were living and cohabiting together as husband and wife, the plaintiff purchased, with funds accumulated through the joint efforts of plaintiff and defendant," the real property described in said cross-complaint.

Plaintiff now seeks to set aside this judgment in favor of the defendant on the ground that the agreement under which said parties acquired said real property was based upon an immoral consideration, and is therefore unenforceable against either party thereto. We do not so understand the findings. The agreement to live together as husband and wife without the formality of a marriage ceremony is set forth in finding II, quoted above. The agreement to invest their separate earnings for their joint benefit, and that all property so acquired should be owned by them jointly, is set forth in finding III. While the court found that the parties agreed "upon the making and entering into" the agreement of cohabitation that they would invest their earnings in property to be held jointly by them, it did not find that this latter agreement was a part of, or that it was in any manner connected with, their agreement to unlawfully cohabit together. The two agreements, although made at the same time, are separate and distinct contracts, and neither is made dependent upon the other. Therefore it cannot be said that the consideration of the latter agreement was the unlawful cohabitation assented to in the agreement set forth in finding II. It clearly appears from finding III that the consideration of plaintiff's agreement to hold all property for their joint benefit, which was acquired by their joint efforts, was the agreement on defendant's part that all moneys earned by her should be paid to plaintiff and invested by him in property of which each party was to be the owner of an undivided half.

* * *

The authorities cited by plaintiff and relied upon by him in support of his contention that the agreement upon which the defendant relies was based upon an immoral consideration are not applicable to the facts in the present action. They simply hold, as stated by the plaintiff in his brief, "that agreeing to live and cohabit together as man and wife, without the performance of a marriage ceremony constitutes an illegal and immoral consideration for the basis of a contract, and is, therefore, a void consideration." There is no question but that this statement of law is correct, but, as we have shown, the facts as found by the court in this action do not bring this case within the principles of law there enunciated.

* * *

The judgment is affirmed.

Comments

Poole, Omer, Tyranski, and *Trutalli* illustrate the infinite variety of fact and law attendant upon nonmarital cohabitation.

In *Poole,* parties of modest means joined their resources to acquire a beauty shop and a tavern. The business ventures may have facilitated the findings that there was "a joint venture if not a partnership" or a bona fide marital relationship. The alternative reasoning made it immaterial whether the parties actually believed themselves to be married. *Omer* and *Tyranski* involve meretricious relationships. *Omer* concerns cohabitation and pooling of resources between parties who had formerly been married in Israel, and who had obtained a divorce, thereafter entering sham marriages to facilitate immigration and naturalization in the United States. That this entails a conspiracy under federal law did not seem to disturb the state courts in Washington, which gave the former wife the full protection of equity. This decision was also cited in *Marvin.* Perhaps its most outstanding feature is that it gives a full enumeration of legal theories in support of claims based on cohabitation and, at the same time, recognizes the fictitious character of these remedies. Yet the court concluded by finding a constructive trust, perhaps the most fictitious alternative of all, especially since fraud was not alleged between the parties.

Tyranski, by comparison, was based on a common occurrence—a relationship between two parties already married to other persons. Since no divorces were argued, the cohabitation was found to be illegal under traditional views. Nevertheless the trial judge granted specific performance on an oral contract to convey title to land, thus benefiting a woman who knew that she was married to somebody else and that her deceased friend had also been married. Factors of social class were implied in the facts, the deceased apparently having been a teamster and the plaintiff a cocktail waitress. Since the two families of the deceased were in different locations, the facts are reminiscent of those in *Walker v. Matthews* (pp. 131–136), although the possibility of presumption of divorce was not in issue. Obviously, specific performance of the agreement underlying the cohabitation would not have been possible, but death changed the relationship to a purely proprietary one.

Property was also involved in *Trutalli,* a cohabitation of 11 years, short of marriage, resulting in two children. The mere assumption that a contract to live together may violate public policy does not necessarily invalidate a contract relating to property, although it may have been made simultaneously. The parallel contracts can be viewed as "separate and distinct," provided of course that the court considers them so. Apart from this the case relates to the fundamental problem of how such relationships should be terminated. The term "nonmarital cohabitation" seems to imply that mere factual termination is sufficient, but this is not necessarily true if issues of property are involved. Divorce or dissolution is not available because the parties are not legally married. The male party's suit to quiet title in *Trutalli* can be viewed as a functional equivalent to an action for annulment of marriage. The theory of the complaint is that there was no valid agreement to begin with, and that the unjustified claims of the woman clouded title in real property. The woman's cross-complaint, on the other hand, proceeded under a theory that some aspects of the relationship were valid and permitted splitting the mutually acquired assets. Seen in this light, the cross-complaint is similar to a request for divorce. The possibilities of legally adjudicated termination are infinite. If there is the possibility of a "marriage by presumption," for example, evidence can be introduced to rebut the presumption. The results of successful introduction of evidence may be comparable to those of divorce. The presence of children, as in *Trutalli*, is always a complicating factor. Obviously, a custody dispute, as well as requests for support, may ensue. Here, too, the functional differences between marriage and nonmarital cohabitation are fewer than may initially appear.

Bibliography

Bartke, *Marital Sharing—Why Not Do It by Contract?*, 67 Geo. L.J. 1131 (1979).

Blumberg, *Cohabitation Without Marriage: A Different Perspective*, 28 UCLA L. Rev. 1125 (1981).

Bruch, *Nonmarital Cohabitation in the Common Law Countries: A Study in Judicial-Legislative Interaction*, 29 Am. J. Comp. L. 217 (1981).

Eekelaar, J. & Katz, S., Marriage and Cohabitation in Contemporary Societies (1980).

Fineman, *Law and Changing Patterns of Behavior: Sanctions on Non-Marital Cohabitation*, 1981 Wis. L. Rev. 275.

Folberg & Buren, *Domestic Partnership: A Proposal for Dividing the Property of Unmarried Families*, 12 Willamette L.J. 453 (1976).

Hunter, *An Essay on Contract and Status: Race, Marriage and the Meretricious Spouse*, 64 Va. L. Rev. 1039 (1978).

Kay & Amyx, *Marvin v. Marvin: Preserving the Options*, 65 Calif. L. Rev. 937 (1977).

Levin & Spak, *Judicial Enforcement of Cohabitation Agreements: A Signal to Purge Marriage From the Statute of Frauds*, 12 Creighton L. Rev. 499 (1979).

Massey, C., & Warner, R., Sex, Living Together, and the Law—A Legal Guide for Unmarried Couples (and Groups) (1974).

Note, *Beyond Marvin: A Proposal for Quasi-Spousal Support*, 30 Stan. L. Rev. 359 (1978).

Note, *Marvin v. Marvin: The Scope of Equity With Respect to Non-Marital Relationships*, 5 Pepperdine L. Rev. 49 (1977).

Note, *Property Rights of a Same-Sex Couple: The Outlook After Marvin*, 12 Loy. L. Rev. 409 (1979).

Note, *Rehak v. Mathis*, 12 GA. L. REV. 361 (1978).

Putzel & Thurlow, *Marital and Cohabitation Contracts*, 6 FAM. L. REP. 4067 (1980).

Shultz, *Contractual Ordering of Marriage: A New Model for State Policy*, 70 CALIF. L. REV. 204 (1982).

Skolnick A., *The Social Contexts of Cohabitation*, 29 AM. J. COMP. L. 339 (1981).

VanDeusen, E., CONTRACT COHABITATION—AN ALTERNATIVE TO MARRIAGE (1974).

Weitzman, *Legal Regulation of Marriage: Tradition and Change—A Proposal for Individual Contracts and Contracts in Lieu of Marriage*, 62 CALIF. L. REV. 1169 (1974).

Weitzman, L., THE MARRIAGE CONTRACT—SPOUSES, LOVERS, AND THE LAW (1981).

Younger, *Marital Regimes: A Story of Compromise and Demoralization, Together With Criticism and Suggestions for Reform*, 67 CORNELL L. REV. 45 (1981).

3

Equality in Marriage

The incidents of marriage, whether formal or informal, are increasingly governed by concepts that support the equality of spouses. According to these concepts, the wife is not a subordinate in a master-servant relationship, but a person who enters a voluntary association that implies rights, duties, and contributions equal in value to those of the husband.

The Conceptual Sources of Equality. There are several conceptual sources of the new balance between husband and wife: freedom of contract, constitutional ideals of equality and civil rights, and respect for the privacy and autonomy of the individual. Although their legal consequences are often similar, these are not necessarily similar philosophies. The respective styles of legal reasoning associated with them—deriving from the law of contracts, from the Fourteenth Amendment's Equal Protection Clause, and from the constitutional right of privacy—occasionally may result in seemingly contradictory approaches, although again the legal outcome may not be affected. For example, the contractual style of reasoning relies on a theoretical assumption of equal bargaining power, regardless of whether it has in fact been achieved; while reasoning rooted in the constitutional demand for equality in marriage begins with an overt admission that the reality falls short of the ideal.

A host of new problems is opened up for discussion and decision. When men and women are treated alike to avoid sexual stereotyping, sometimes this may benefit men. Fathers may, at least in theory, be treated as equal to mothers of children in being awarded custody; men may receive alimony in case of need. Women, on the other hand, may be dealt with as members of a minority that has been discriminated against and is now entitled to a sort of "affirmative action" within the realm of marriage. Such affirmative action creates a greater potential for at least rehabilitative alimony and recognizes special equities for purposes of property division by courts in case of divorce. Thus it may resemble earlier judicial paternalism, under which women were seen

225

as the inherently weaker sex and permanently entitled to special judicial protection. But unlike paternalism, affirmative action is intended to be temporary and remedial to rectify past wrongs. In reality, however, paternalism and affirmative action are likely to coexist as long as women earn less than men, have fewer opportunities, and, as a consequence, expect preferential and compensatory treatment in marriage. As the earnings and opportunities of women approach those of men, the different shades of constitutional reasoning should give way to reasoning based on contract.

But mere equal treatment could simply result in a perpetuation of interdependencies in marriage. It might be argued, for example, that the disabilities of married women inherited from the common law apply equally to both spouses. Real equality, on the other hand, requires the autonomy of the spouses in making decisions. The most important instrument for achieving it may prove to be the right of privacy. The wife's autonomy in deciding about abortion, based on an argument of privacy, thus becomes an important judicial instrument for the protection of the female partner in marriage in her equal role. An expansion of the privacy argument to bring about equality between the sexes is likely to occur.

In its effects upon marriage, the ideal of privacy is somewhere between constitutional argument and contract theory. It pronounces the autonomy of the individual in the right to be left alone, and it may be inimical to traditional marriage. Illustrations are the freedom to prevent conception and to abort without consent of the husband and father, and homosexual marriage. On the other hand, the autonomy of spouses supports the contractual theory of marriage insofar as it assumes the mutual freedom of will essential both for entering any genuine agreement and also for terminating it.

Equality and Sharing. The ideal of equality of bargaining power merges inevitably into legal theories of marriage as contract and even as a copartnership for mutual benefit and profit. Although written articles of partnership, as in ordinary business partnership, are not essential, contractual regulation of certain aspects of marriage is judicially encouraged. The more literate members of the population thus have an advantage in this regard.

In this view of marriage, its mutual fiduciary aspects gain in legal recognition. Marriage as a community of purpose becomes, like partnership, a relation in which the parties are principals and agents of each other. The scope of a specific marriage, like the scope of a partnership, determines the extent of the shared authority. How many resources are to be surrendered to the common purpose, and are in fact pooled, can no longer be determined in the abstract but depends on individual circumstances as reflected in implicit understandings.

In aid of adjudication a new set of presumptions of equality is now emerging. For example, although in a marital partnership the contributions of the spouses and their share in partnership property may appear to be unequal, in absence of stipulation to the contrary equality may be presumed. More specifically, as the contributions of the homemaker and mother are increasingly recognized, they may be presumed to be equal in value to the contributions of the breadwinner. Furthermore, it may be presumed that husband and wife are to share in all tasks, including homemaking, child care, and earning. Straight refusal of any of these tasks may conceivably be viewed as a violation of the marital compact. There is less inclination than in the past to presume that spouses make gifts to each other, especially in regard to services. Instead the courts may impose a presumption of partnership and of equal sharing for mutual profit.

The presumed equality of spouses and even of participants in informal cohabitation facilitates decisions in cases in which bookkeeping on the respective contributions proves to be less than adequate. The marital property found upon dissolution is often presumed to have been acquired by joint effort. In effect this heralds the spread of conceptions of community property.

Antisocial Implications. The right of spouses to participate in the management of marriage and to share equally in decision making has consequences that may disrupt and eventually destroy a going concern. If marriage is considered a partnership of two, an impasse may result because a decision by majority is not possible. If the value conflict remains unsettled, it may cause the breakup of marriage. Thus equality in marriage increases the probability, statistically already a reality, that a marriage will come to dissolution and liquidation of the assets.

The unity of the family is also broken in other ways. Husbands and wives may not only contract with each other, they may also compete in the market for jobs. Because of job opportunities, they may live in different locations. They may have different names. In some jurisdictions even their children, upon birth, may be given separate and distinct last names. Much of the traditional symbolic content of marriage and the family is affected by these legal possibilities, even though the vast majority of the population continues to adhere to established practices.

Inevitably the laws of divorce and annulment are affected by equality in marriage. With voluntary termination of marriage relatively easy, annulment becomes an anachronism and divorce assumes the characteristics of a dissolution of partnership. Indeed, the preference for the term "dissolution of marriage," as well as the efforts to eliminate fault, are borrowed from the laws of business associations. Here too the consequences are not exclusively positive. The fault concept in divorce, in its functions and practical consequences, often protected the economic stake of women in marriage. The possibility of treating men punitively, to the point of sometimes assuming their fundamental wickedness, gave judges a legal tool for equalizing wealth upon divorce. In jurisdictions, like California, that have no-fault divorce and community property, the struggle may shift from who is at fault to what exactly is half of the marital assets. Other no-fault jurisdictions, like Florida, may face a transitional problem. Elimination of fault without guarantee of equal division of assets, at least at the present time, is likely to hurt women more often than men.

In other words, the legally assumed but in fact not yet achieved equality of women may, in the absence of corrective legal recognition of "fault" in men, lead to harsh results for women in case of family disruption. Whoever has title to marital property and is managing the assets—more often than not the husband—is likely to prevail. Some courts try to avoid these consequences and to reinject fault into no-fault divorce.

Transitional Solutions. Reestablishment of fault, as a concept deeply embedded in our culture, is relatively easy. The judge who is sympathetic to an aging wife may, for example, require an explanation for the marriage's "irretrievable breakdown." Once the precedent is set, attorneys may be inclined to negotiate divorce settlements at a price in order to avoid disclosure of fault in court. The "adjudication" of fault in no-fault jurisdictions may be transferred from the court to a lawyer's office. Furthermore, the contractual aspects of marriage invite argument essentially raising breach of contract, perhaps in the Holmesian sense that everyone has the right to breach a contract so long as he pays damages.

In other respects, too, efforts to eliminate fault do not necessarily result in elimination of controversy. As in partnership dissolution, the questions to be litigated or settled gravitate toward splitting the assets "down the middle." It can be difficult or impossible to determine what is exactly half if the property involved is not divisible or does not have a market value. If fault is resurrected for negotiation purposes in a lawyer's office, the old defenses to divorce, regardless of their express legislative abolition, may also lead a shadow existence. Fault may continue to determine the best interests of the children and the adjudication of their custody.

In general, children seem to be strangely untouched by any benefits that equality may provide to their parents. Privacy of women may exclude children from being born or even conceived. If they are born they appear as intruders, not being parties to the contract between their parents. As assets of the marriage they are, upon dissolution, subject to distribution upon principles that may continue to be concerned with the fault of their parents.

The various ingenious ways of resurrecting fault in family disputes indicate that, although the thrust of the argumentation is toward equality of the spouses, it has not yet been achieved. Faced with this reality, the legal system reacts with a compromise. It insists on the rhetoric of equality but at the same time demands the continued relevance of fault. Thus it can be maintained that the resurrection of fault as an equitable tool in marital disputes is a negative consequence of a not yet achieved equality between the "partners in marriage."

Privacy and Equality in Marriage

Freedom to Marry as a Fundamental Human Right

Loving v. Commonwealth of Virginia

United States Supreme Court

388 U.S. 1 (1967)

Mr. Chief Justice WARREN delivered the opinion of the Court.

This case presents a constitutional question never addressed by this Court: whether a statutory scheme adopted by the State of Virginia to prevent marriages between persons solely on the basis of racial classifications violates the Equal Protection and Due Process Clauses of the Fourteenth Amendment. * * *

In June 1958, two residents of Virginia, Mildred Jeter, a Negro woman, and Richard Loving, a white man, were married in the District of Columbia pursuant to its laws. Shortly after their marriage, the Lovings returned to Virginia and established their marital abode in Caroline County. At the October Term, 1958, of the Circuit Court of Caroline County, a grand jury issued an indictment charging the Lovings with violating Virginia's ban on interracial marriages. On January 6, 1959, the Lovings pleaded guilty to the charge and were sentenced to one year in jail; however, the trial judge suspended the sentence for a period of 25 years on the condition that the Lovings leave the State and not return to Virginia together for 25 years. He stated in an opinion that:

> "Almighty God created the races white, black, yellow, malay and red, and he placed them on separate continents. And but for the interference with his arrangement there would be no cause for such marriages. The fact that he separated the races shows that he did not intend for the races to mix."

After their convictions, the Lovings took up residence in the District of Columbia. On November 6, 1963, they filed a motion in the state trial court to vacate the judgment and set aside the sentence on the ground that the statutes which they had violated were repugnant to the Fourteenth Amendment. The motion not having been decided by October 28, 1964, the Lovings instituted a class action in the United States District Court for the Eastern District of Virginia requesting that a three-judge court be convened to declare the Virginia antimiscegenation statutes unconstitutional and to enjoin state officials from enforcing their convictions. On January 22, 1965, the state trial judge denied the motion to vacate the sentences, and the Lovings perfected an appeal to the Supreme Court of Appeals of Virginia. On February 11, 1965, the three-judge District Court continued the case to allow the Lovings to present their constitutional claims to the highest state court.

The Supreme Court of Appeals upheld the constitutionality of the antimiscegenation statutes and, after modifying the sentence, affirmed the convictions. The Lovings appealed this decision. * * *

The two statutes under which appellants were convicted and sentenced are part of a comprehensive statutory scheme aimed at prohibiting and punishing interracial marriages. The Lovings were convicted of violating §20–58 of the Virginia Code:

"*Leaving State to evade law.* If any white person and colored person shall go out of this State, for the purpose of being married, and with the intention of returning, and be married out of it, and afterwards return to and reside in it, cohabitating as man and wife, they shall be punished as provided in §20-59, and the marriage shall be governed by the same law as if it had been solemnized in this State. The fact of their cohabitation here as man and wife shall be evidence of their marriage."

Section 20-59, which defines the penalty for miscegenation, provides:

"*Punishment for marriage.* If any white person intermarry with a colored person, or any colored person intermarry with a white person, he shall be guilty of a felony and shall be punished by confinement in the penitentiary for not less than one nor more than five years."

Other central provisions in the Virginia statutory scheme are §20-57, which automatically voids all marriages between "a white person and a colored person" without any judicial proceeding, and §§20-54 and 1-14 which, respectively, define "white persons" and "colored persons and Indians" for purposes of the statutory prohibitions.[4] The Lovings have never disputed in the course of this litigation that Mrs. Loving is a "colored person" or that Mr. Loving is a "white person" within the meanings given those terms by the Virginia statutes.

Virginia is now one of 16 States which prohibit and punish marriages on the basis of racial classifications.[5] Penalties for miscegenation arose as an

---

[4] Section 20-54 of the Virginia Code provides:

"*Intermarriage prohibited; meaning of term 'white persons.'* It shall hereafter be unlawful for any white person in this State to marry any save a white person, or a person with no other admixture of blood than white and American Indian. For the purpose of this chapter, the term 'white person' shall apply only to such person as has no trace whatever of any blood other than Caucasian; but persons who have one-sixteenth or less of the blood of the American Indian and have no other non-Caucasic blood shall be deemed to be white persons. All laws heretofore passed and now in effect regarding the intermarriage of white and colored persons shall apply to marriages prohibited by this chapter."

Va. Code Ann. §20-54 (1960 Repl. Vol.).

The exception for persons with less than one-sixteenth "of the blood of the American Indian" is apparently accounted for, in the words of a tract issued by the Registrar of the State Bureau of Vital Statistics, by "the desire of all to recognize as an integral and honored part of the white race the descendants of John Rolfe and Pocahontas * * *." Plecker, *The New Family and Race Improvement*, 17 Va. Health Bull., Extra No. 12 at 25-26 (New Family Series No. 5, 1925), cited in Wadlington, *The Loving Case; Virginia's Anti-Miscegenation Statute in Historical Perspective*, 52 Va. L. Rev. 1189, 1202, n.93 (1966).

Section 1-14 of the Virginia Code provides:

"*Colored persons and Indians defined.* Every person in whom there is ascertainable any Negro blood shall be deemed and taken to be a colored person, and every person not a colored person having one fourth or more of American Indian blood shall be deemed an American Indian; except that members of Indian tribes existing in this Commonwealth having one fourth or more of Indian blood and less than one sixteenth of Negro blood shall be deemed tribal Indians."

Va. Code Ann. §1-14 (1960 Repl. Vol.).

[5] After the initiation of this litigation, Maryland repealed its prohibitions against interracial marriage, Md. Laws 1967, c. 6, leaving Virginia and 15 other States with statutes outlawing interracial marriage: Alabama, Ala. Const., Art. 4, §102, Ala. Code, Tit. 14, §360 (1958); Arkansas, Ark. Stat. Ann. §55-104 (1947); Delaware, Del. Code Ann., Tit. 13, §101 (1953); Florida, Fla. Const., Art. 16, §24, F.S.A., Fla. Stat. §741.11 (1965) F.S.A.; Georgia, Ga. Code Ann. §53-106 (1961); Kentucky, Ky. Rev. Stat. Ann. §402.020 (Supp. 1966); Louisiana, La. Rev. Stat. §14:79 (1950); Mississippi, Miss. Const., Art. 14, §263, Miss. Code Ann. §459 (1956); Missouri, Mo. Rev. Stat. §451.020 (Supp. 1966), V.A.M.S.; North Carolina, N.C. Const., Art. XIV, §8, N.C. Gen. Stat. §14-181 (1953); Oklahoma, Okla. Stat., Tit. 43, §12 (Supp. 1965); South Carolina, S.C. Const., Art. 3, §33, S.C. Code Ann. §20-7 (1962); Tennessee, Tenn. Const., Art. 11, §14, Tenn. Code Ann. §36-102 (1955); Vernon's Ann. Texas, Tex. Pen. Code, Art. 492 (1952); West Virginia, W.Va. Code Ann. §4697 (1961).

Over the past 15 years, 14 States have repealed laws outlawing interracial marriages: Arizona, California, Colorado, Idaho, Indiana, Maryland, Montana, Nebraska, Nevada, North Dakota, Oregon, South Dakota, Utah, and Wyoming.

The first state court to recognize that miscegenation statutes violate the Equal Protection Clause was the Supreme Court of California. *Perez v. Sharp*, 32 Cal.2d 711, 198 P.2d 17 (1948).

incident to slavery and have been common in Virginia since the colonial period.[6] The present statutory scheme dates from the adoption of the Racial Integrity Act of 1924, passed during the period of extreme nativism which followed the end of the First World War. The central features of this Act, and current Virginia law, are the absolute prohibition of a "white person" marrying other than another "white person," a prohibition against issuing marriage licenses until the issuing official is satisfied that the applicants' statements as to their race are correct, certificates of "racial composition" to be kept by both local and state registrars, and the carrying forward of earlier prohibitions against racial intermarriage.

I

In upholding the constitutionality of these provisions in the decision below, the Supreme Court of Appeals of Virginia referred to its 1955 decision in *Naim v. Naim,* 197 Va. 80, 87 S.E.2d 749, as stating the reasons supporting the validity of these laws. In *Naim,* the state court concluded that the State's legitimate purposes were "to preserve the racial integrity of its citizens," and to prevent "the corruption of blood," "a mongrel breed of citizens," and "the obliteration of racial pride," obviously an endorsement of the doctrine of White Supremacy. *Id.,* at 90, 87 S.E.2d, at 756. The court also reasoned that marriage has traditionally been subject to state regulation without federal intervention, and, consequently, the regulation of marriage should be left to exclusive state control by the Tenth Amendment.

While the state court is no doubt correct in asserting that marriage is a social relation subject to the State's police power, *Maynard v. Hill,* 125 U.S. 190, 8 S. Ct. 723, 31 L.Ed. 654 (1888), the State does not contend in its argument before this Court that its powers to regulate marriage are unlimited notwithstanding the commands of the Fourteenth Amendment. Nor could it do so in light of *Meyer v. State of Nebraska,* 262 U.S. 390, 43 S. Ct. 625, 67 L.Ed. 1042 (1923), and *Skinner v. State of Oklahoma,* 316 U.S. 535, 62 S. Ct. 1110, 86 L.Ed. 1655 (1942). Instead, the State argues that the meaning of the Equal Protection Clause, as illuminated by the statements of the Framers, is only that state penal laws containing an interracial element as part of the definition of the offense must apply equally to whites and Negroes in the sense that members of each race are punished to the same degree. Thus, the State contends that, because its miscegenation statutes punish equally both the white and the Negro participants in an interracial marriage, these statutes, despite their reliance on racial classifications do not constitute an invidious discrimination based upon race. The second argument advanced by the State assumes the validity of its equal application theory. The argument is that, if the Equal Protection Clause does not outlaw miscegenation statutes because of their reliance on racial classifications, the question of constitutionality would thus become whether there was any rational basis for a State to treat interracial marriages differently from other marriages. On this question, the State argues, the scientific evidence is substantially in doubt and, consequently, this Court should defer to the wisdom of the state legislature in adopting its policy of discouraging interracial marriages.

Because we reject the notion that the mere "equal application" of a statute containing racial classifications is enough to remove the classifications from the Fourteenth Amendment's proscription of all invidious racial discriminations, we do not accept the State's contention that these statutes should be upheld if there is any possible basis for concluding that they serve a rational purpose. * * *
       * * *

---

[6]For a historical discussion of Virginia's miscegenation statutes, see Wadlington, *supra,* n.4.

* * * We have rejected the proposition that the debates in the Thirty-ninth Congress or in the state legislatures which ratified the Fourteenth Amendment supported the theory advanced by the State, that the requirement of equal protection of the laws is satisfied by penal laws defining offenses based on racial classifications so long as white and Negro participants in the offense were similarly punished. *McLaughlin v. State of Florida,* 379 U.S. 184, 85 S. Ct. 283, 13 L.Ed.2d 222 (1964).

The State finds support for its "equal application" theory in the decision of the Court in *Pace v. State of Alabama,* 106 U.S. 583, 1 S. Ct. 637, 27 L.Ed. 207 (1883). In that case, the Court upheld a conviction under an Alabama statute forbidding adultery or fornication between a white person and a Negro which imposed a greater penalty than that of a statute proscribing similar conduct by members of the same race. The Court reasoned that the statute could not be said to discriminate against Negroes because the punishment for each participant in the offense was the same. However, as recently as the 1964 Term, in rejecting the reasoning of that case, we stated *"Pace* represents a limited view of the Equal Protection Clause which has not withstood analysis in the subsequent decisions of this Court." *McLaughlin v. Florida, supra,* 379 U.S. at 188, 85 S. Ct. at 286. As we there demonstrated, the Equal Protection Clause requires the consideration of whether the classifications drawn by any statute constitute an arbitrary and invidious discrimination. The clear and central purpose of the Fourteenth Amendment was to eliminate all official state sources of invidious racial discrimination in the States. [Citations omitted.]

There can be no question but that Virginia's miscegenation statutes rest solely upon distinctions drawn according to race. The statutes proscribe generally accepted conduct if engaged in by members of different races. Over the years, this Court has consistently repudiated "[d]istinctions between citizens solely because of their ancestry" as being "odious to a free people whose institutions are founded upon the doctrine of equality." *Hirabayashi v. United States,* 320 U.S. 81, 100, 63 S. Ct. 1375, 1385, 87 L.Ed. 1774 (1943). At the very least, the Equal Protection Clause demands that racial classifications, especially suspect in criminal statutes, be subjected to the "most rigid scrutiny," *Korematsu v. United States,* 323 U.S. 214, 216, 65 S. Ct. 193, 194, 89 L.Ed. 194 (1944), and, if they are ever to be upheld, they must be shown to be necessary to the accomplishment of some permissible state objective, independent of the racial discrimination which it was the object of the Fourteenth Amendment to eliminate. Indeed, two members of this Court have already stated that they "cannot conceive of a valid legislative purpose * * * which makes the color of a person's skin the test of whether his conduct is a criminal offense." *McLaughlin v. Florida, supra,* 379 U.S. at 198, 85 S. Ct. at 292, (Stewart, J., joined by Douglas, J., concurring).

There is patently no legitimate overriding purpose independent of invidious racial discrimination which justifies this classification. The fact that Virginia prohibits only interracial marriages involving white persons demonstrates that the racial classifications must stand on their own justification, as measures designed to maintain White Supremacy.[11] We have consistently denied the constitutionality of measures which restrict the rights of citizens

---

[11]Appellants point out that the State's concern in these statutes, as expressed in the words of the 1924 Act's title, "An Act to Preserve Racial Integrity," extends only to the integrity of the white race. While Virginia prohibits whites from marrying any nonwhite (subject to the exception for the descendants of Pocahontas), Negroes, Orientals, and any other racial class may intermarry without statutory interference. Appellants contend that this distinction renders Virginia's miscegenation statutes arbitrary and unreasonable even assuming the constitutional validity of an official purpose to preserve "racial integrity." We need not reach this contention because we find the racial classifications in these statutes repugnant to the Fourteenth Amendment, even assuming an even-handed state purpose to protect the "integrity" of all races.

on account of race. There can be no doubt that restricting the freedom to marry solely because of racial classifications violates the central meaning of the Equal Protection Clause.

II

These statutes also deprive the Lovings of liberty without due process of law in violation of the Due Process Clause of the Fourteenth Amendment. The freedom to marry has long been recognized as one of the vital personal rights essential to the orderly pursuit of happiness by free men.

Marriage is one of the "basic civil rights of man," fundamental to our very existence and survival. *Skinner v. State of Oklahoma*, 316 U.S. 535, 541, 62 S. Ct. 1110, 1113, 86 L.Ed. 1655 (1942). See also *Maynard v. Hill*, 125 U.S. 190, 8 S. Ct. 723, 31 L.Ed. 654 (1888). To deny this fundamental freedom on so unsupportable a basis as the racial classifications embodied in these statutes, classifications so directly subversive of the principle of equality at the heart of the Fourteenth Amendment, is surely to deprive all the State's citizens of liberty without due process of law. The Fourteenth Amendment requires that the freedom of choice to marry not be restricted by invidious racial discriminations. Under our Constitution, the freedom to marry or not marry, a person of another race resides with the individual and cannot be infringed by the State.

These convictions must be reversed. It is so ordered.

Reversed.

Comments

Loving and *Maynard v. Hill* (pp. 45–49) are interrelated. *Maynard* proclaims marriage as the most important relation in life, while *Loving* speaks of marriage as a basic civil right and a fundamental freedom. Consequently, *Loving* is more frequently invoked when freedom from restrictive legislation is claimed. *Maynard,* on the other hand, retains practical value for the support of such legislation. The very importance of marriage for society was viewed as making it subject to State regulation. Although this injects an element of contradiction between the two cases, they are frequently cited in the same breath. For example, whenever an attempt is made to broaden the concept of marriage to include categories earlier excluded, such as marriage between homosexuals or closely related persons, both cases tend to be cited. For the time being, however, the power of the State to regulate and prohibit is likely to prevail.

The importance of *Loving* should not, however, be seen in its ability to support a winning argument in court. In our view, its function is to signal potential changes in the law of marriage. These changes favor the increased autonomy of the parties and the decline of State involvement in marriage. There are other, more indirect, consequences of *Loving*: for instance, when the courts uphold contract cohabitation between parties who would be prohibited from marrying. In other words, the power of the State to regulate marriage, following

Maynard, is likely to be strictly construed and not necessarily extended to cover nonmarital cohabitation. If formal and informal marriage are viewed as being functionally related, the permissive message of *Loving* seems to prevail over restrictive State regulation insofar as informal marriage is concerned.

Compared to these fundamental questions, the problem of interracial marriage that gave rise to *Loving* appears to be of less significance. Since *Loving,* although the process took some time and sometimes new litigation, antimiscegenation statutes have been repealed or ruled unconstitutional in all states. The question of interracial marriage continues, however, to have social significance. Racial classifications are still emphasized. In some states information on race, ostensibly for identification, is requested for driver's licenses and applications for marriage licenses. Racial classifications continue to be legally relevant, if only for purposes of compensatory education and affirmative action. Nevertheless, the state statutes defining race referred to in *Loving* have all been repealed; and most racial classifications, for example, in the United States Census, appear to be based today on self-classification. To a large extent, individuals belong to the racial group they say they belong to.

Polls among college students have also demonstrated that both black and white students are expressing an increasing disinclination to enter interracial marriages. Moreover, race continues to be relevant in child custody matters and in placing children for adoption. Thus the impact of *Loving* on race relations so far is limited. As long as social pressures maintain the demographic patterns that obtained prior to *Loving,* it is possible for those patterns to form the bases of legal arguments. In light of the continued relevance of the racial issues in *Loving,* the decision of the California Supreme Court in *Perez v. Sharp** should be read together with *Loving.* It held the California antimiscegenation statute to be unconstitutional almost 20 years before the ruling of the United States Supreme Court and with reasoning that has not lost its poignancy.

References

Karst, *The Freedom of Intimate Association,* 89 YALE L.J. 624 (1980).
Wadlington, *The Loving Case: Virginia's Anti-Miscegenation Statute in Historical Perspective,* 52 VA. L. REV. 1189 (1966).

---

*32 Cal.2d 711, 198 P.2d 17 (1948).

Freedom to Prevent Conception

Griswold v. State of Connecticut

United States Supreme Court

381 U.S. 479 (1965)

Mr. Justice Douglas delivered the opinion of the Court.

Appellant Griswold is Executive Director of the Planned Parenthood League of Connecticut. Appellant Buxton is a licensed physician and a professor at the Yale Medical School who served as Medical Director for the League at its Center in New Haven—a center open and operating from November 1 to November 10, 1961, when appellants were arrested.

They gave information, instruction, and medical advice to *married persons* as to the means of preventing conception. They examined the wife and prescribed the best contraceptive device or material for her use. Fees were usually charged, although some couples were serviced free.

The statutes whose constitutionality is involved in this appeal are §§53-32 and 54-196 of the General Statutes of Connecticut (1958 rev.). The former provides:

"Any person who uses any drug, medicinal article or instrument for the purpose of preventing conception shall be fined not less than fifty dollars or imprisoned not less than sixty days nor more than one year or be both fined and imprisoned."

Section 54-196 provides:

"Any person who assists, abets, counsels, causes, hires or commands another to commit any offense may be prosecuted and punished as if he were the principal offender."

The appellants were found guilty as accessories and fined $100 each, against the claim that the accessory statute as so applied violated the Fourteenth Amendment. The Appellate Division of the Circuit Court affirmed. The Supreme Court of Errors affirmed that judgment. 151 Conn. 544, 200 A.2d 479. * * *

* * *

Coming to the merits, we are met with a wide range of questions that implicate the Due Process Clause of the Fourteenth Amendment. * * * We do not sit as a super-legislature to determine the wisdom, need, and propriety of laws that touch economic problems, business affairs, or social conditions. This law, however, operates directly on an intimate relation of husband and wife and their physician's role in one aspect of that relation.

The association of people is not mentioned in the Constitution nor in the Bill of Rights. The right to educate a child in a school of the parents' choice— whether public or private or parochial—is also not mentioned. Nor is the right to study any particular subject or any foreign language. Yet the First Amendment has been construed to include certain of those rights.

By *Pierce v. Society of Sisters, supra,* the right to educate one's children as one chooses is made applicable to the States by the force of the First and Fourteenth Amendments. By *Meyer v. State of Nebraska, supra,* the same dignity is given the right to study the German language in a private school. In other words, the State may not, consistently with the spirit of the First Amendment, contract the spectrum of available knowledge. * * *

In *NAACP v. State of Alabama*, 357 U.S. 449, 462, 78 S. Ct. 1163, 1172, we protected the "freedom to associate and privacy in one's associations," noting that freedom of association was a peripheral First Amendment right. Disclosure of membership lists of a constitutionally valid association, we held, was invalid "as entailing the likelihood of a substantial restraint upon the exercise by petitioner's members of their right to freedom of association."*Ibid.* In other words, the First Amendment has a penumbra where privacy is protected from governmental intrusion. In like context, we have protected forms of "association" that are not political in the customary sense but pertain to the social, legal, and economic benefit of the members. *NAACP v. Button*, 371 U.S. 415, 430–431, 83 S. Ct. 328, 336–337. * * *

Those cases involved more than the "right of assembly"—a right that extends to all irrespective of their race or idealogy. *De Jonge v. State of Oregon*, 299 U.S. 353, 57 S. Ct. 255, 81 L.Ed. 278. The right of "association," like the right of belief (*West Virginia State Board of Education v. Barnette*, 319 U.S. 624, 63 S. Ct. 1178), is more than the right to attend a meeting; it includes the right to express one's attitudes or philosophies by membership in a group or by affiliation with it or by other lawful means. Association in that context is a form of expression of opinion; and while it is not expressly included in the First Amendment its existence is necessary in making the express guarantees fully meaningful.

The foregoing cases suggest that specific guarantees in the Bill of Rights have penumbras, formed by emanations from those guarantees that help give them life and substance. See *Poe v. Ullman*, 367 U.S. 497, 516–522, 81 S. Ct. 1752, 6 L.Ed.2d 989 (dissenting opinion). Various guarantees create zones of privacy. The right of association contained in the penumbra of the First Amendment is one, as we have seen. The Third Amendment in its prohibition against the quartering of soldiers "in any house" in time of peace without the consent of the owner is another facet of that privacy. The Fourth Amendment explicitly affirms the "right of the people to be secure in their persons, houses, papers, and effects, against unreasonable searches and seizures." The Fifth Amendment in its Self-Incrimination Clause enables the citizen to create a zone of privacy which government may not force him to surrender to his detriment. The Ninth Amendment provides: "The enumeration in the Constitution, of certain rights, shall not be construed to deny or disparage others retained by the people."

The Fourth and Fifth Amendments were described in *Boyd v. United States*, 116 U.S. 616, 630, 6 S. Ct. 524, 532, 29 L.Ed. 746, as protection against all governmental invasions "of the sanctity of a man's home and the privacies of life." We recently referred in *Mapp v. Ohio*, 367 U.S. 643, 656, 81 S. Ct. 1684, 1692, 6 L.Ed.2d 1081, to the Fourth Amendment as creating a "right to privacy, no less important than any other right carefully and particularly reserved to the people." See Beaney, *The Constitutional Right to Privacy*, 1962 SUP. CT. REV. 212; Griswold, *The Right to be Let Alone*, 55 Nw. U.L. REV. 216 (1960).

* * *

The present case, then, concerns a relationship lying within the zone of privacy created by several fundamental constitutional guarantees. And it concerns a law which, in forbidding the *use* of contraceptives rather than regulating their manufacture or sale, seeks to achieve its goals by means having a maximum destructive impact upon that relationship. Such a law cannot stand in light of the familiar principle, so often applied by this Court, that a "governmental purpose to control or prevent activities constitutionally subject to state regulation may not be achieved by means which sweep unnecessarily broadly and thereby invade the area of protected freedoms." *NAACP v. Alabama*, 377 U.S. 288, 307, 84 S. Ct. 1302, 1314, 12 L.Ed.2d 325. Would we allow the police to search the sacred precincts of marital bedrooms for telltale signs of the use of contraceptives? The very idea is repulsive to the notions of privacy surrounding the marriage relationship.

We deal with a right of privacy older than the Bill of Rights—older than our political parties, older than our school system. Marriage is a coming together for better or for worse, hopefully enduring, and intimate to the degree of being sacred. It is an association that promotes a way of life, not causes; a harmony in living, not political faiths; a bilateral loyalty, not commercial or social projects. Yet it is an association for as noble a purpose as any involved in our prior decisions.

Reversed.

Mr. Justice GOLDBERG, whom THE CHIEF JUSTICE and Mr. Justice BRENNAN join, concurring.

* * *

My Brother STEWART, while characterizing the Connecticut birth control law as "an uncommonly silly law," *post*, at 1705, would nevertheless let it stand on the ground that it is not for the courts to " 'substitute their social and economic beliefs for the judgment of legislative bodies, who are elected to pass laws.' " *Post*, at 1705. * * *

The logic of the dissents would sanction federal or state legislation that seems to me even more plainly unconstitutional than the statute before us. Surely the Government, absent a showing of a compelling subordinating state interest, could not decree that all husbands and wives must be sterilized after two children have been born to them. Yet by their reasoning such an invasion of marital privacy would not be subject to constitutional challenge because, while it might be "silly," no provision of the Constitution specifically prevents the Government from curtailing the marital right to bear children and raise a family. While it may shock some of my Brethren that the Court today holds that the Constitution protects the right of marital privacy, in my view it is far more shocking to believe that the personal liberty guaranteed by the Constitution does not include protection against such totalitarian limitation of family size, which is at complete variance with our constitutional concepts. Yet, if upon a showing of a slender basis of rationality, a law outlawing voluntary birth control by married persons is valid, then, by the same reasoning, a law requiring compulsory birth control also would seem to be valid. In my view, however, both types of law would unjustifiably intrude upon rights of marital privacy which are constitutionally protected.

* * *

Although the Connecticut birth-control law obviously encroaches upon a fundamental personal liberty, the State does not show that the law serves any "subordinating [state] interest which is compelling" or that it is "necessary * * * to the accomplishment of a permissible state policy." The State, at most, argues that there is some rational relation between this statute and what is admittedly a legitimate subject of state concern—the discouraging of extra-marital relations. It says that preventing the use of birth-control devices by married persons helps prevent the indulgence by some in such extra-marital relations. The rationality of this justification is dubious, particularly in light of the admitted widespread availability to all persons in the State of Connecticut, unmarried as well as married, of birth-control devices for the prevention of disease, as distinguished from the prevention of conception, see *Tileston v. Ullman*, 129 Conn. 84, 26 A.2d 582. But, in any event, it is clear that the state interest in safeguarding marital fidelity can be served by a more discriminately tailored statute, which does not, like the present one, sweep unnecessarily broadly, reaching far beyond the evil sought to be dealt with and intruding upon the privacy of all married couples. * * *

Finally, it should be said of the Court's holding today that it in no way interferes with a State's proper regulation of sexual promiscuity or misconduct. As my Brother HARLAN so well stated in his dissenting opinion in *Poe v. Ullman, supra*, 367 U.S. at 553, 81 S. Ct. at 1782:

> "Adultery, homosexuality and the like are sexual intimacies which the State forbids * * * but the intimacy of husband and wife is necessarily an essential and accepted feature of the institution of marriage, an institution which the State not only must allow, but which always and in every age it has fostered and protected. It is one thing when the State exerts its power either to forbid extra-marital sexuality * * * or to say who may marry, but it is quite another when, having acknowledged a marriage and the intimacies inherent in it, it undertakes to regulate by means of the criminal law the details of that intimacy."

* * *

Freedom of Women to Decide on Termination of Pregnancy

Roe v. Wade

United States Supreme Court

410 U.S. 113 (1973)

Mr. Justice BLACKMUN delivered the opinion of the Court.

* * *

The Texas statutes that concern us here are Arts. 1191–1194 and 1196 of the State's Penal Code, Vernon's Ann. P.C. These make it a crime to "procure an abortion," as therein defined, or to attempt one, except with respect to "an abortion procured or attempted by medical advice for the purpose of saving the life of the mother." Similar statutes are in existence in a majority of the States.

* * *

The American law. In this country the law in effect in all but a few States until mid-19th century was the pre-existing English common law. Connecticut, the first State to enact abortion legislation, adopted in 1821 that part of Lord Ellenborough's Act that related to a woman "quick with child." The death penalty was not imposed. Abortion before quickening was made a crime in that State only in 1860. In 1828 New York enacted legislation that, in two respects, was to serve as a model for early anti-abortion statutes. First, while barring destruction of an unquickened fetus as well as a quick fetus, it made the former only a misdemeanor, but the latter second-degree manslaughter. Second, it incorporated a concept of therapeutic abortion by providing that an abortion was excused if it "shall have been necessary to preserve the life of such mother, or shall have been advised by two physicians to be necessary for such purpose." By 1840, when Texas had received the common law, only eight American States had statutes dealing with abortion. It was not until after the War Between the States that legislation began generally to replace the common law. Most of these initial statutes dealt severely with abortion after quickening but were lenient with it before quickening. Most punished attempts equally with completed abortions. While many statutes included the exception for an abortion thought by one or more physicians to be necessary to save the mother's life, that provision soon disappeared and the typical law required that the procedure actually be necessary for that purpose.

Gradually, in the middle and late 19th century the quickening distinction disappeared from the statutory law of most States and the degree of the offense and the penalties were increased. By the end of the 1950's a large majority of the States banned abortion, however and whenever performed, unless done to save or preserve the life of the mother. The exceptions, Alabama and the District of Columbia, permitted abortion to preserve the mother's health. Three other States permitted abortions that were not "unlawfully" performed or that were not "without lawful justification," leaving interpretation of those standards to the courts. In the past several years, however, a trend toward liberalization of abortion statutes has resulted in adoption, by about one-third of the States, of less stringent laws.

It is thus apparent that at common law, at the time of the adoption of our Constitution, and throughout the major portion of the 19th century, abortion was viewed with less disfavor than under most American statutes currently in effect. Phrasing it another way, a woman enjoyed a substantially broader right to terminate a pregnancy than she does in most States today. At least with respect to the early stage of pregnancy, and very possibly without such a limitation, the opportunity to make this choice was present in this country well into the 19th century. Even later, the law continued for some time to treat less punitively an abortion procured in early pregnancy.

The position of the American Medical Association. The anti-abortion mood prevalent in this country in the late 19th century was shared by the medical profession. Indeed, the attitude of the profession may have played a significant role in the enactment of stringent criminal abortion legislation during that period.

* * *

The position of the American Public Health Association. In October 1970, the Executive Board of the APHA adopted Standards for Abortion Services. These were five in number:

> "a. Rapid and simple abortion referral must be readily available through state and local public health departments, medical societies, or other non-profit organizations.

* * *

The position of the American Bar Association. At its meeting in February 1972 the ABA House of Delegates approved, with 17 opposing votes, the Uniform Abortion Act that had been drafted and approved the preceding August by the Conference of Commissioners on Uniform State Laws.

* * *

VIII

The Constitution does not explicitly mention any right of privacy. In a line of decisions, however, going back perhaps as far as *Union Pacific R. Co. v. Botsford,* 141 U.S. 250, 251, 11 S. Ct. 1000, 1001, 35 L.Ed. 734 (1891), the Court has recognized that a right of personal privacy, or a guarantee of certain areas or zones of privacy, does exist under the Constitution. In varying contexts, the Court or individual Justices have, indeed, found at least the roots of that right in the First Amendment, *Stanley v. Georgia,* 394 U.S. 557, 564, 89 S. Ct. 1243, 1247, 22 L.Ed.2d 542 (1969); in the Fourth and Fifth Amendments, *Terry v. Ohio,* 392 U.S. 1, 8-9, 88 S. Ct. 1868, 1872-1873, 20 L.Ed.2d 889 (1968); *Katz v. United States,* 389 U.S. 347, 350, 88 S. Ct. 507, 510, 19 L.Ed.2d 576 (1967); *Boyd v. United States,* 116 U.S. 616, 6 S. Ct. 524, 29 L.Ed. 746 (1886), see *Olmstead v. United States,* 277 U.S. 438, 478, 48 S. Ct. 564, 572, 72 L.Ed. 944 (1928) (BRANDEIS J., dissenting); in the penumbras of the Bill of Rights, *Griswold v. Connecticut,* [p. 250], in the Ninth Amendment, *id.,* (GOLDBERG, J., concurring); or in the concept of liberty guaranteed by the first section of the Fourteenth Amendment, see *Meyer v. Nebraska,* 262 U.S. 390, 399, 43 S. Ct. 625, 626, 67 L.Ed. 1042 (1923). These decisions make it clear that only personal rights that can be deemed "fundamental" or "implicit in the concept of ordered liberty," * * * are included in this guarantee of personal privacy. They also make it clear that the right has some extension to activities relating to marriage, *Loving v. Virginia,* [p. 10]; procreation, *Skinner v. Oklahoma,* [p. 328]; contraception, *Eisenstadt v. Baird,* [p. 257]; (WHITE, J., concurring in result); family relationships, *Prince v. Massachusetts,* 321 U.S. 158, 166, 64 S. Ct. 438, 442, 88 L.Ed. 645 (1944); and child rearing and education, *Pierce v. Society of Sisters,* 268 U.S. 510, 535, 45 S. Ct. 571, 573, 69 L.Ed. 1070 (1925); *Meyer v. Nebraska, supra.*

This right of privacy, whether it be founded in the Fourteenth Amendment's concept of personal liberty and restrictions upon state action, as we feel it is, or, as the District Court determined, in the Ninth Amendment's reservation of rights to the people, is broad enough to encompass a woman's decision whether or not to terminate her pregnancy. The detriment that the State would impose upon the pregnant woman by denying this choice altogether is apparent. Specific and direct harm medically diagnosable even in early pregnancy may be involved. Maternity, or additional offspring, may force upon the woman a distressful life and future. Psychological harm may be imminent. Mental and physical health may be taxed * * * by child care. There is also the distress, for all concerned, associated with the unwanted child, and there is the problem of bringing a child into a family already unable, psychologically and otherwise, to care for it. In other cases, as in this one, the additional difficulties and continuing stigma of unwed motherhood may be involved. All these are factors the woman and her responsible physician necessarily will consider in consultation.

On the basis of elements such as these, appellants and some *amici* argue that the woman's right is absolute and that she is entitled to terminate her pregnancy at whatever time, in whatever way, and for whatever reason she alone chooses. With this we do not agree. Appellant's arguments that Texas either has no valid interest at all in regulating the abortion decision, or no interest strong enough to support any limitation upon the woman's sole determination, is unpersuasive. The Court's decisions recognizing a right of privacy also acknowledge that some state regulation in areas protected by that right is appropriate. As noted above, a state may properly assert important interests in safeguarding health, in maintaining medical standards, and in protecting potential life. At some point in pregnancy, these respective interests become sufficiently compelling to sustain regulation of the factors that govern the abortion decision. The privacy right involved, therefore, cannot be said to be absolute. In fact, it is not clear to us that the claim asserted by some *amici* that one has an unlimited right to do with one's body as one pleases bears a close relationship to the right of privacy previously articulated in the Court's decisions. The Court has refused to recognize an unlimited right of this kind in the past.

We therefore conclude that the right of personal privacy includes the abortion decision, but that this right is not unqualified and must be considered against important state interests in regulation. * * *

Where certain "fundamental rights" are involved, the Court has held that regulation limiting these rights may be justified only by a "compelling state interest."
    * * *

IX

The District Court held that the appellee failed to meet his burden of demonstrating that the Texas statute's infringement upon Roe's rights was necessary to support a compelling state interest, and that, although the defendant presented "several compelling justifications for state presence in the area of abortions," the statutes outstripped these justifications and swept "far beyond any areas of compelling state interest." 314 F. Supp., at 1222-1223. Appellant and appellee both contest that holding. Appellant, as has been indicated, claims an absolute right that bars any state imposition of criminal penalties in the area. Appellee argues that the State's determination to recognize and protect prenatal life from and after conception constitutes a compelling state interest. As noted above, we do not agree fully with either formulation.

A. The appellee and certain *amici* argue that the fetus is a "person" within the language and meaning of the Fourteenth Amendment. In support of this they outline at length and in detail the well-known facts of fetal development. If this suggestion of personhood is established, the appellant's case, of course, collapses, for the fetus' right to life is then guaranteed specifically by the Amendment. The appellant conceded as much on reargument. On the other hand, the appellee conceded on reargument that no case could be cited that holds that a fetus is a person within the meaning of the Fourteenth Amendment.

The Constitution does not define "person" in so many words. Section 1 of the Fourteenth Amendment contains three references to "person." The first, in defining "citizens," speaks of "persons born or naturalized in the United States." The word also appears both in the Due Process Clause and in the Equal Protection Clause. "Person" is used in other places in the Constitution: in the listing of qualifications for representatives and senators, Art. I, §2, cl. 2, and §3, cl. 3; in the Apportionment Clause, Art. I, §2, cl. 3; in the Migration and Importation provision, Art. I, §9, cl. 1; in the Emolument Clause, Art. I, §9, cl 8; in the Electors provisions, Art. II, §1, cl. 2, and the superseded cl. 3; in the provision outlining qualifications for the office of President, Art. II, §1, cl. 5; in the Extradition provisions, Art. IV, §2, cl. 2, and the superseded Fugitive Slave cl. 3; and in the Fifth, Twelfth, and Twenty-second Amendments as well as in §§2 and 3 of the Fourteenth Amendment. But in nearly all these instances, the use of the word is such that it has application only post-natally. None indicates, with any assurance, that it has any possible pre-natal application.

All this, together with our observation, that throughout the major portion of the 19th century prevailing legal abortion practices were far freer than they are today, persuades us that the word "person," as used in the Fourteenth Amendment, does not include the unborn. This is in accord with the results reached in those few cases where the issue has been squarely presented.

* * *

This conclusion, however, does not of itself fully answer the contentions raised by Texas, and we pass on to other considerations.

B. The pregnant woman cannot be isolated in her privacy. She carries an embryo and, later, a fetus, if one accepts the medical definitions of the developing young in the human uterus. The situation therefore is inherently different from marital intimacy, or bedroom possession of obscene material, or marriage, or procreation, or education, with which *Eisenstadt, Griswold, Stanley, Loving, Skinner, Pierce,* and *Meyer* were respectively concerned. As we have intimated above, it is reasonable and appropriate for a State to decide that at some point in time another interest, that of health of the mother or that of potential human life, becomes significantly involved. The woman's privacy is no longer sole and any right of privacy she possesses must be measured accordingly.

Texas urges that, apart from the Fourteenth Amendment, life begins at conception and is present throughout pregnancy, and that, therefore, the State has a compelling interest in protecting that life from and after conception. We need not resolve the difficult question of when life begins. When those trained in the respective disciplines of medicine, philosophy, and theology are unable to arrive at any consensus, the judiciary, at this point in the development of man's knowledge, is not in a position to speculate as to the answer.

It should be sufficient to note briefly the wide divergence of thinking on this most sensitive and difficult question. There has always been strong support for the view that life does not begin until live birth. This was the belief of the Stoics. It appears to be the predominant, though not the unanimous, attitude of the Jewish faith. It may be taken to represent also the position of a large segment of the Protestant community, insofar as that can be ascertained; organized groups that have taken a formal position on the abortion issue have generally regarded abortion as a matter for the conscience of the individual and her family. As we have noted, the common law found greater significance in quickening. Physicians and their scientific colleagues have regarded that event with less interest and have tended to focus either upon conception or upon live birth or upon the interim point at which the fetus becomes "viable," that is, potentially able to live outside the mother's womb, albeit with artificial aid. Viability is usually placed at about seven months (28 weeks) but may occur earlier, even at 24 weeks. The Aristotelian theory of "mediate animation," that held sway throughout the Middle Ages and the Renaissance in Europe, continued to be official Roman Catholic dogma until the 19th century, despite opposition to this "ensoulment" theory from those in the Church who would recognize the existence of life from the moment of conception. The latter is now, of course, the official belief of the Catholic Church. As one of the briefs *amicus* discloses, this is a view strongly held by many non-Catholics as well, and by many physicians. Substantial problems for precise definition of this view are posed, however, by new embryological data that purport to indicate that conception is a "process" over time, rather than an event, and by new medical techniques such as menstrual extraction, the "morning-after" pill, implantation of embryos, artificial insemination, and even artificial wombs.

In areas other than criminal abortion the law has been reluctant to endorse any theory that life, as we recognize it, begins before live birth or to accord legal rights to the unborn except in narrowly defined situations and except when the rights are contingent upon live birth. For example, the traditional rule of tort law had denied recovery for prenatal injuries even though the child was born alive. That rule has been changed in almost every jurisdiction. In most States recovery is said to be permitted only if the fetus was viable, or at least quick, when the injuries were sustained, though few courts have squarely so held. In a recent development, generally opposed by the commentators, some States permit the parents of a stillborn child to maintain an action for wrongful death because of prenatal injuries. Such an action, however, would appear to be one to vindicate the parents' interest and is thus consistent with the view that the fetus, at most, represents only the potentiality of life. Similarly, unborn children have been recognized as acquiring rights or interests by way of inheritance or other devolution of property, and have been represented by guardians *ad litem*. Protection of the interests involved, again, has generally been contingent upon live birth. In short, the unborn have never been recognized in the law as persons in the whole sense.

X

In view of all this, we do not agree that, by adopting one theory of life, Texas may override the rights of the pregnant woman that are at stake. We repeat, however, that the State does have an important and legitimate interest in preserving and protecting the health of the pregnant woman, whether she be a resident of the State or a nonresident who seeks medical consultation and treatment there, and that it has still *another* important and legitimate interest in protecting the potentiality of human life. These interests are separate and distinct. Each grows in substantiality as the woman approaches term and, at a point during pregnancy, each becomes "compelling."

With respect to the State's important and legitimate interest in the health of the mother, the "compelling" point, in the light of present medical knowledge, is at approximately the end of the first trimester. This is so because of the now established medical fact * * * that until the end of the first trimester mortality in abortion is less than mortality in normal childbirth. It follows that, from and after this point, a State may regulate the abortion procedure to the extent that the regulation reasonably relates to the preservation and protection of maternal health. Examples of permissible state regulation in this area are requirements as to the qualifications of the person who is to perform the abortion; as to the licensure of that person; as to the facility in which the procedure is to be performed, that is, whether it must be a hospital or may be a clinic or some other place of less-than-hospital status; as to the licensing of the facility; and the like.

This means, on the other hand, that, for the period of pregnancy prior to this "compelling" point, the attending physician, in consultation with his patient, is free to determine, without regulation by the State, that in his medical judgment the patient's pregnancy should be terminated. If that decision is reached, the judgment may be effectuated by an abortion free of interference by the State.

With respect to the State's important and legitimate interest in potential life, the "compelling" point is at viability. This is so because the fetus then presumably has the capability of meaningful life outside the mother's womb. State regulation protective of fetal life after viability thus has both logical and biological justifications. If the State is interested in protecting fetal life after viability, it may go so far as to proscribe abortion during that period except when it is necessary to preserve the life or health of the mother.

Measured against these standards, Art. 1196 of the Texas Penal Code, in restricting legal abortions to those "procured or attempted by medical advice for the purpose of saving the life of the mother," sweeps too broadly. The statute makes no distinction between abortions performed early in pregnancy and those performed later, and its limits to a single reason, "saving" the mother's life, the legal justification for the procedure. The statute, therefore, cannot survive the constitutional attack made upon it here.

    * * *

XI

To summarize and to repeat:

1. A state criminal abortion statute of the current Texas type, that excepts from criminality only a *life saving* procedure on behalf of the mother, without regard to pregnancy stage and without recognition of the other interests involved, is violative of the Due Process Clause of the Fourteenth Amendment.

(a) For the stage prior to approximately the end of the first trimester, the abortion decision and its effectuation must be left to the medical judgment of the pregnant woman's attending physician.

(b) For the stage subsequent to approximately the end of the first trimester, the State, in promoting its interest in the health of the mother, may, if it chooses, regulate the abortion procedure in ways that are reasonably related to maternal health.

(c) For the stage subsequent to viability the State, in promoting its interest in the potentiality of human life, may, if it chooses, regulate, and even proscribe, abortion except where it is necessary, in appropriate medical judgment, for the preservation of the life or health of the mother.

* * *

It is so ordered.

Affirmed in part and reversed in part.

Mr. Justice STEWART, concurring.

* * *

Mr. Justice REHNQUIST, dissenting.

* * *

Privacy Rights of Women Versus State Intervention, Spousal, or Parental Consent

Planned Parenthood of Central Missouri v. Danforth

United States Supreme Court

428 U.S. 52 (1976)

Mr. Justice BLACKMUN delivered the opinion of the Court.

This case is a logical and anticipated corollary to *Roe v. Wade,* 410 U.S. 113, 93 S. Ct. 705, 35 L.Ed.2d 147 (1973), and *Doe v. Bolton,* 410 U.S. 179, 93 S. Ct. 739, 35 L.Ed.2d 201 (1973), for it raises issues secondary to those that were then before the Court. * * *

* * *

In June 1974, somewhat more than a year after *Roe* and *Doe* had been decided, Missouri's 77th General Assembly, in its Second Regular Session, enacted House Committee Substitute for House Bill No. 1211 (hereinafter Act). The legislation was approved by the Governor on June 14, 1974, and became effective immediately by reason of an emergency clause contained in §A of the statute.* * * It imposes a structure for the control and regulation of abortions in Missouri during all stages of pregnancy.

II

Three days after the Act became effective, the present litigation was instituted in the United States District Court for the Eastern District of Missouri. The plaintiffs are Planned Parenthood of Central Missouri, a not-for-profit Missouri corporation which maintains a facility in Columbia, Mo., for the performance of abortions; David Hall, M.D.; and Michael Freiman, M.D. Doctor Hall is a resident of Columbia, is licensed as a physician in Missouri, is chairman of the Department and Professor of Obstetrics and Gynecology at the University of Missouri Medical School at Columbia, and supervises abortions at the Planned Parenthood facility. * * *

The named defendants are the Attorney General of Missouri and the Circuit Attorney of the city of St. Louis "in his representative capacity" and "as the representative of the class of all similar Prosecuting Attorneys of the various counties of the State of Missouri." Complaint 10.

The plaintiffs brought the action on their own behalf and, purportedly, "on behalf of the entire class consisting of duly licensed physicians and surgeons presently performing or desiring to perform the termination of pregnancies and on behalf of the entire class consisting of their patients desiring the termination of pregnancy, all within the State of Missouri." *Id.*, at 9. Plaintiffs sought declaratory relief and also sought to enjoin enforcement of the Act on the ground, among others, that certain of its provisions deprived them and their patients of various constitutional rights: "the right to privacy in the physician-patient relationship"; the physicians' "right to practice medicine according to the highest standards of medical practice"; the female patients' right to determine whether to bear children; the patients' "right to life due to the inherent risk involved in childbirth" or in medical procedures alternative to abortion; the physicians' "right to give and plaintiffs' patients' right to receive safe and adequate medical advice and treatment, pertaining to the decision of whether to carry a given pregnancy to term and the method of termination"; the patients' right under the Eighth Amendment to be free from cruel and unusual punishment "by forcing and coercing them to bear each pregnancy they conceive"; and, by being placed "in the position of decision making beset with * * * inherent possibilities of bias and conflict of interest," the physician's right to due process of law guaranteed by the Fourteenth Amendment. *Id.*, at 10–11.

* * *

In No. 74–1151, the plaintiffs appeal from that part of the District Court's judgment upholding sections of the Act as constitutional and denying injunctive relief against their application and enforcement. In No. 74–1419, the defendant Attorney General cross-appeals from that part of the judgment holding §6(1) unconstitutional and enjoining enforcement thereof. * * *.

For convenience, we shall usually refer to the plaintiffs as "appellants" and to both named defendants as "appellees."

* * *

Our primary task, then, is to consider each of the challenged provisions of the new Missouri abortion statute in the particular light of the opinions and decisions in *Roe* and in *Doe*. To this we now turn, with the assistance of helpful briefs from both sides and from some of the *amici*.

A

The definition of viability. Section 2(2) of the Act defines "viability" as "that stage of fetal development when the life of the unborn child may be continued indefinitely outside the womb by natural or artificial life-supportive systems." Appellants claim that this definition violates and conflicts with the discussion of viability in our opinion in *Roe*. 410 U.S., at 160, 163, 93 S. Ct., at 730, 731. In particular, appellants object to the failure of the definition to contain any reference to a gestational time period, to its failure to incorporate and reflect the three stages of pregnancy, to the presence of the word "indefinitely," and to the extra burden of regulation imposed. It is suggested that the definition expands the Court's definition of viability, as expressed in *Roe*, and amounts to a legislative determination of what is properly a matter for medical judgment. It is said that the "mere possibility of momentary survival is not the medical standard of viability." Brief for Appellants 67.

In *Roe*, we used the term "viable," properly we thought, to signify the point at which the fetus is "potentially able to live outside the mother's womb, albeit with artificial aid," and presumably capable of "meaningful life outside the mother's womb," 410 U.S., at 160, 163, 93 S. Ct. at 730, 732. We noted that this point "is usually placed" at about seven months or 28 weeks, but may occur earlier. *Id.*, at 160, 93 S. Ct., at 730.

We agree with the District Court and conclude that the definition of viability in the Act does not conflict with what was said and held in *Roe*. In fact, we believe that §2(2), even when read in conjunction with §5 (proscribing an abortion "not necessary to preserve the life or health of the mother * * * unless the attending physician first certifies with reasonable medical certainty that the fetus is not viable"), the constitutionality of which is not explicitly challenged here, reflects an attempt on the part of the Missouri General Assembly to comply with our observations and discussion in *Roe* relating to viability. Appellant Hall, in his deposition, had no particular difficulty with the statutory definition. As noted above, we recognized in *Roe* that viability was a matter of medical judgment, skill, and technical ability, and we preserved the flexibility of the term. Section 2(2) does the same. Indeed, one might argue, as the appellees do, that the presence of the statute's words "continued indefinitely" favor, rather than disfavor, the appellants, for, arguably, the point when life can be "continued indefinitely outside the womb" may well occur later in pregnancy than the point where the fetus is "potentially able to live outside the mother's womb." *Roe v. Wade*, 410 U.S., at 160, 93 S. Ct., at 730.

In any event, we agree with the District Court that it is not the proper function of the legislature or the courts to place viability, which essentially is a medical concept, at a specific point in the gestation period. The time when viability is achieved may vary with each pregnancy, and the determination of whether a particular fetus is viable is, and must be, a matter for the judgment of the responsible attending physician. The definition of viability in §2(2) merely reflects this fact. * * *

* * *

We conclude that the definition in §2(2) of the Act does not circumvent the limitations on state regulation outlined in *Roe*. We therefore hold that the Act's definition of "viability" comports with *Roe* and withstands the constitutional attack made upon it in this litigation.

B

The woman's consent. Under §3(2) of the Act, a woman, prior to submitting to an abortion during the first 12 weeks of pregnancy, must certify in writing her consent to the procedure and "that her consent is informed and freely given and is not the result of coercion." Appellants argue that this requirement is violative of *Roe v. Wade*, 410 U.S., at 164–165, 93 S. Ct., at 732–733, by imposing an extra layer and burden of regulation on the abortion decision. See *Doe v. Bolton*, 410 U.S., at 195–200, 93 S. Ct., at 749–751. Appellants also claim that the provision is overbroad and vague.

The District Court's majority relied on the propositions that the decision to terminate a pregnancy, of course, "is often a stressful one," and that the consent requirement of §3(2) "insures that the pregnant woman retains control over the discretions of her consulting physician." 392 F. Supp., at 1368, 1369. The majority also felt that the consent requirement "does not single out the abortion procedure, but merely includes it within the category of medical operations for which consent is required." *Id.*, at 1369. The third judge joined the majority in upholding §3(2), but added that the written consent requirement was "not burdensome or chilling" and manifested "a legitimate interest of the state that this important decision has in fact been made by the person constitutionally empowered to do so." 392 F. Supp., at 1374. He went on to observe that the requirement "in no way interposes the state or third parties in the decision-making process." *Id.*, at 1375.

We do not disagree with the result reached by the District Court as to §3(2). It is true that *Doe* and *Roe* clearly establish the State may not restrict the decision of the patient and her physician regarding abortion during the first stage of pregnancy. Despite the fact that apparently no other Missouri statute, with the exceptions referred to in n.6, *supra*, requires a patient's prior written consent to a surgical procedure, the imposition by §3(2) of such a requirement for termination of pregnancy even during the first stage, in our view, is not in itself an unconstitutional requirement. The decision to abort, indeed, is an important, and often a stressful one, and it is desirable and imperative that it be made with full knowledge of its nature and consequences. The woman is the one primarily concerned, and her awareness of the decision and its significance may be assured, constitutionally, by the State to the extent of requiring her prior written consent.

We could not say that a requirement imposed by the State that a prior written consent for any surgery would be unconstitutional. As a consequence, we see no constitutional defect in requiring it only for some types of surgery as, for example, an intracardiac procedure, or where the surgical risk is elevated above a specified mortality level, or, for that matter, for abortions.

C

The spouse's consent. Section 3(3) requires the prior written consent of the spouse of the woman seeking an abortion during the first 12 weeks of pregnancy, unless "the abortion is certified by a licensed physician to be necessary in order to preserve the life of the mother."

* * *

In *Roe* and *Doe* we specifically reserved decision on the question whether a requirement for consent by the father of the fetus, by the spouse, or by the parents, or a parent, of an unmarried minor, may be constitutionally imposed. 410 U.S., at 165 n.67, 93 S. Ct., at 733. We now hold that the State may not constitutionally require the consent of the spouse, as is specified under §3(3) of the Missouri Act, as a condition for abortion during the first 12 weeks of pregnancy. We thus agree with the dissenting judge in the present case, and with the courts whose decisions are cited above, that the State cannot "delegate to a spouse a veto power which the state itself is absolutely and totally prohibited from exercising during the first trimester of pregnancy." 392 F. Supp., at 1375. Clearly, since the State cannot regulate or proscribe abortion during the first stage, when the physician and his patient make that decision, the State cannot delegate authority to any particular person, even the spouse, to prevent abortion during that same period.

We are not unaware of the deep and proper concern and interest that a devoted and protective husband has in his wife's pregnancy and in the growth and development of the fetus she is carrying. Neither has this Court failed to appreciate the importance of the marital relationship in our society. See, *e.g., Griswold v. Connecticut,* 381 U.S. 479, 486, 85 S. Ct. 1678, 1682, 14 L.Ed.2d 510 (1965); *Maynard v. Hill,* 125 U.S. 190, 211, 8 S. Ct. 723, 729, 31 L.Ed. 654 (1888). Moreover, we recognize that the decision whether to undergo or to forego an abortion may have profound effects on the future of any marriage, effects that are both physical and mental, and possibly deleterious. Notwithstanding these factors, we cannot hold that the State has the constitutional authority to give the spouse unilaterally the ability to prohibit the wife from terminating her pregnancy, when the State itself lacks that right. See *Eisenstadt v. Baird,* 405 U.S. 438, 453, 92 S. Ct. 1029, 1038, 31 L.Ed.2d 349 (1972).[11]

---

[11] As the Court recognized in *Eisenstadt v. Baird,*
> "the marital couple is not an independent entity with a mind and heart of its own, but an association of two individuals each with a separate intellectual and emotional makeup. If the right of privacy means anything, it is the right of the *individual,* married or single, to be free from unwarranted governmental intrusion into matters so fundamentally affecting a person as the decision whether to bear or beget a child."

405 U.S., at 453, 92 S. Ct., at 1038 (emphasis in original).

The dissenting opinion of our Brother WHITE appears to overlook the implications of this statement upon the issue whether §3(3) is constitutional. This section does much more than

It seems manifest that, ideally, the decision to terminate a pregnancy should be one concurred in by both the wife and her husband. No marriage may be viewed as harmonious or successful if the marriage partners are fundamentally divided on so important and vital an issue. But it is difficult to believe that the goal of fostering mutuality and trust in a marriage, and of strengthening the marital relationship and the marriage institution, will be achieved by giving the husband a veto power exercisable for any reason whatsoever or for no reason at all. Even if the State had the ability to delegate to the husband a power it itself could not exercise, it is not at all likely that such action would further, as the District Court majority phrased it, the "interest of the state in protecting the mutuality of decisions vital to the marriage relationship." 392 F. Supp., at 1370.

We recognize, of course, that when a woman, with the approval of her physician but without the approval of her husband, decides to terminate her pregnancy, it could be said that she is acting unilaterally. The obvious fact is that when the wife and the husband disagree on this decision, the view of only one of the two marriage partners can prevail. Inasmuch as it is the woman who physically bears the child and who is the more directly and immediately affected by the pregnancy, as between the two, the balance weighs in her favor. *Cf. Roe v. Wade,* 410 U.S., at 153, 93 S. Ct., at 726.

We conclude that §3(3) of the Missouri Act is inconsistent with the standards enunciated in *Roe v. Wade,* 410 U.S., at 164–165, 93 S. Ct., at 732–733, and is unconstitutional. * * *

D

Parental consent. Section 3(4) requires, with respect to the first 12 weeks of pregnancy, where the woman is unmarried and under the age of 18 years, the written consent of a parent or person *in loco parentis* unless, again, "the abortion is certified by a licensed physician as necessary in order to preserve the life of the mother." It is to be observed that only one parent need consent.
* * *
We agree with appellants * * * that the State may not impose a blanket provision, such as §3(4), requiring the consent of a parent or person *in loco parentis* as a condition for abortion of an unmarried minor during the first 12 weeks of her pregnancy. Just as with the requirement of consent from the spouse, so here, the State does not have the constitutional authority to give a third party an absolute, and possibly arbitrary, veto over the decision of the physician and his patient to terminate the patient's pregnancy, regardless of the reason for withholding the consent.

Constitutional rights do not mature and come into being magically only when one attains the state-defined age of majority. Minors, as well as adults, are protected by the Constitution and possess constitutional rights. [Citations omitted.] The Court indeed, however, long has recognized that the State has somewhat broader authority to regulate the activities of children than of adults. *Prince v. Massachusetts,* 321 U.S., at 170, 64 S. Ct., at 444; *Ginsberg v. New York,* 390 U.S. 629, 88 S. Ct. 1274, 20 L.Ed.2d 195 (1968). It remains, then, to examine whether there is any significant state interest in condition-

---

insure that the husband participate in the decision whether his wife should have an abortion. The State, instead, has determined that the husband's interest in continuing the pregnancy of his wife always outweighs any interest on her part in terminating it irrespective of the condition of their marriage. The State, accordingly, has granted him the right to prevent unilaterally, and for whatever reason, the effectuation of his wife's and her physician's decision to terminate her pregnancy. This state determination not only may discourage the consultation that might normally be expected to precede a major decision affecting the marital couple but also, and more importantly, the State has interposed an absolute obstacle to a woman's decision that *Roe* held to be constitutionally protected from such interference.

ing an abortion on the consent of a parent or person *in loco parentis* that is not present in the case of an adult.

One suggested interest is the safeguarding of the family unit and of parental authority. 392 F. Supp., at 1370. It is difficult, however, to conclude that providing a parent with absolute power to overrule a determination, made by the physician and his minor patient, to terminate the patient's pregnancy will serve to strengthen the family unit. Neither is it likely that such veto power will enhance parental authority or control where the minor and the nonconsenting parent are so fundamentally in conflict and the very existence of the pregnancy already has fractured the family structure. Any independent interest the parent may have in the termination of the minor daughter's pregnancy is no more weighty than the right of privacy of the competent minor mature enough to have become pregnant.

We emphasize that our holding that §3(4) is invalid does not suggest that every minor, regardless of age or maturity, may give effective consent for termination of her pregnancy. See *Bellotti v. Baird,* 428 U.S. 132, 96 S. Ct. 2857, 49 L.Ed.2d 844. The fault with §3(4) is that it imposes a special-consent provision, exercisable by a person other than the woman and her physician, as a prerequisite to a minor's termination of her pregnancy and does so without a sufficient justification for the restriction. It violates the strictures of *Roe* and *Doe.*

E

Saline amniocentesis. Section 9 of the statute prohibits the use of saline amniocentesis, as a method or technique of abortion, after the first 12 weeks of pregnancy. It describes the method as one whereby the amniotic fluid is withdrawn and "a saline or other fluid" is inserted into the amniotic sac. The statute imposes this proscription on the ground that the technique "is deleterious to maternal health," and places it in the form of a legislative finding. * * *

We held in *Roe* that after the first stage, "the State, in promoting its interest in the health of the mother, may, if it chooses, regulate the abortion procedure in ways that are reasonably related to maternal health." 410 U.S., at 164, 93 S. Ct., at 732. The question with respect to §9 therefore is whether the flat prohibition of saline amniocentesis is a restriction which "reasonably relates to the preservation and protection of maternal health." *Id.,* at 163, 93 S. Ct., at 732. The appellees urge that what the Missouri General Assembly has done here is consistent with that guideline and is buttressed by substantial supporting medical evidence in the record to which this Court should defer.

The District Court's majority determined, on the basis of the evidence before it, that the maternal mortality rate in childbirth does, indeed, exceed the mortality rate where saline amniocentesis is used. Therefore, the majority acknowledged, §9 could be upheld only if there were safe alternative methods of inducing abortion after the first 12 weeks. 392 F. Supp., at 1373. Referring to such methods as hysterotomy, hysterectomy, "mechanical means of inducing abortion," and prostaglandin injection, the majority said that at least the latter two techniques were safer than saline. Consequently, the majority concluded, the restriction in §9 could be upheld as reasonably related to maternal health.

We feel that the majority, in reaching its conclusion, failed to appreciate and to consider several significant facts. First, it did not recognize the prevalence, as the record conclusively demonstrates, of the use of saline amniocentesis as an accepted medical procedure in this country; the procedure, as noted above, is employed in a substantial majority (the testimony from both sides ranges from 68% to 80%) of all post-first-trimester abortions. Second, it failed to recognize that at the time of trial, there were severe limitations on the availability of the prostaglandin technique, which, although promising, was used only on an experimental basis until less than two years before. * * * Third, the statute's reference to the insertion of "a saline or other fluid" appears to include within its proscription the intra-amniotic injection of prostaglandin itself and other methods that may be developed in the future and that may prove highly effective and completely safe. Finally, the majority did not consider the anomaly inherent in §9 when it proscribes the use of saline but does not prohibit techniques that are many times more likely to result in maternal death. See 392 F. Supp., at 1378 n.8 (dissenting opinion).

These unappreciated or overlooked factors place the State's decision to bar use of the saline method in a completely different light. The State, through §9, would prohibit the use of a method which the record shows is the one most commonly used nationally by physicians after the first trimester and which is safer, with respect to maternal mortality, than even continuation of the pregnancy until normal childbirth. Moreover, as a practical matter, it forces a woman and her physician to terminate her pregnancy by methods more dangerous to her health than the method outlawed.

As so viewed, particularly in the light of the present unavailability—as demonstrated by the record—of the prostaglandin technique, the outright legislative proscription of saline fails as a reasonable regulation for the protection of maternal health. * * *

* * *

The judgment of the District Court is affirmed in part and reversed in part, and the case is remanded for further proceedings consistent with this opinion.

It is so ordered.

Comments

Griswold, Roe, and *Planned Parenthood* are frequently referred to as extending the constitutional right of privacy as emanating from the "penumbras" of the First, Third, Fourth, Fifth, and Ninth Amendments. The privacy rights of married persons to use contraceptives as proclaimed in *Griswold* were later extended to cover the rights of unmarried persons to receive contraceptive information.* This extension was not necessarily dictated by any inherent logic, since *Griswold* emphasized in its concluding paragraphs the fundamental nature of the marriage relationship and did not address itself to the rights of unmarried persons at all. Rather, the Court's opinions seemed to be based on value choices—quite independent of (and perhaps incidentally contrary to) more traditional views of marriage and procreation—that ultimately favor the equality of women in their relations to men. But we are less concerned here with the constitutional ramifications of these cases than with their inevitable impact on marriage and the family.

The tensions between the institution of marriage and the rights of individuals are accentuated by the later extension of privacy, supported by the Fourteenth Amendment's command that personal lib-

---

*Eisenstadt v. Baird, 405 U.S. 438 (1972).

erty not be denied without due process of law, to cover the various phases and aspects of abortion. Again we are dealing with implicit value choices that lie deeper than the text of the opinions in *Roe v. Wade* and *Doe v. Bolton.** In *The Brethren*, Woodward and Armstrong give an account of the tortuous ways in which the majority opinions in *Roe* and *Doe* were assigned to and drafted by Mr. Justice Blackmun. The original draft memorandum did not even contain a reference to a constitutional right of privacy. Later drafts incorporated suggestions from other Justices in an effort to accommodate them and gain their votes. Originally, only viability of the fetus was perceived by Mr. Justice Blackmun as a factor limiting abortion. Reference to trimesters of pregnancy was included at a later phase in an effort to gain the vote of Mr. Chief Justice Burger. The majority opinions were thus not the product of a cohesive intellectual effort, but had more the nature of a compromise. To some extent this is true of many opinions of collegial courts, but the patchwork is more obvious in these lengthy abortion decisions.

Because of their compromise language based on underlying but not fully articulated value preferences, it was probably inevitable that the abortion decisions spawned further controversy, especially over the question of whether public funds should be made available for abortions in case of poverty.† Opposition has been voiced by Catholics and Protestants and by scholars. Although statistics on abortions vary regionally and may not be fully reliable, it has been estimated by Wood and Durham that fetal deaths probably exceed the number of live births in the United States. Psychoanalyst Erik Erikson has deplored the repression of the urge to procreate which, like the earlier repression of sexuality, could lead to emotional harm on a large scale.

Yet the ongoing controversy over the abortion decisions—reflected in numerous often critical law review articles—seems largely confined to the realm of theory. In the world of legal practice, the reaction seems to have been relatively calm. The lower federal courts have followed the holding, sometimes perhaps indiscriminately, thus giving it greater weight. At the same time, the Court's controversial language seems to have faded in significance. Thus the trend has been toward striking simplicity, at least as compared to the reasoning in the original Blackmun opinions: a woman, regardless of age and whether married or not, may terminate her pregnancy within the first trimester; state regulation of abortion, reasonably related to the mother's health, may continue throughout the second trimester of pregnancy; interest in the potential human life of the fetus is to be given dominant consideration in the third trimester. Parental or spousal consent is not always required. Such simplicity is of course more imaginary than real, but it may provide the tool for a slow adjustment in the family relations of men and women.

---

*410 U.S. 179 (1973).
†See *Maher v. Roe*, 432 U.S. 464 (1977); *Harris v. McRae*, 448 U.S. 297 (1980).

More important, however, than the specific holdings in the contraception and abortion decisions are their indirect consequences for marriage and the family. The cases may have significance, at least for argumentative purposes, in areas that have nothing to do with abortion. The penumbra of privacy rights established by *Griswold* is a prime illustration. *Eisenstadt* held that married and unmarried persons cannot be treated differently in regard to contraceptive articles. The Supreme Court of New Jersey in *Application of Ellen Gaulkin* (see pp. 261–265) dealt with the question of whether the wife of a judge could be a candidate for public office. The court referred to the holding in *Eisenstadt* that even in marriage two individuals, each with a separate intellectual and emotional makeup, can be distinguished. Consequently, the court reasoned, the wife could have legitimate career goals apart from her husband. The holding in *Planned Parenthood* that married women may obtain abortions without spousal consent could be used to modify the laws of child support. An argument could be made by a husband that he is not required to support an unwanted child since he had no control over his wife. He might grant that he should pay the costs of an abortion, because he caused the pregnancy; but why should he pay for the costs of the child? At least he could argue that he should not be burdened with the support costs alone, as is still the case in many jurisdictions.

The constitutionality of statutes that irrebuttably presume the husband to be the father of a child could also be questioned because the privacy rights of married women weaken the control of husbands over procreation. Is it consistent to require spousal consent for artificial insemination, as is provided in many states, while spousal consent is irrelevant for abortion decisions?

These questions influence not only support obligations but also the nature of marriage and may even change the legal consequences of nonmarital relations. To the extent that fundamental questions relating to freedom from state intrusion are involved, it still has to be determined whether the autonomy of the marital institution or of the individuals who participate in it is concerned. The case law seems to be ambivalent when it speaks of privacy both of marriage and of the individual. Clearly, many important decisions within the sphere of intimate relations have been surrendered by the State. The inquiry into what is left for assertion of State power can thus be viewed as related to the expanding boundary of private autonomy.

References

Ely, *The Wages of Crying Wolf: A Comment on Roe v. Wade*, 82 YALE L.J. 920 (1973).

Erikson, E.H., Address, 31st Congress of the International Psycho-Analytical Association (Aug. 3, 1979), *quoted in* Adams, *Erikson Sees Psychological Danger in Trend of Having Fewer Children*, N.Y. Times, Aug. 4, 1979, at 17, col. 3.

Noonan, J., A PRIVATE CHOICE: ABORTION IN AMERICA IN THE SEVENTIES (1979).

Tribe, *The Supreme Court 1972 Term—Foreword: Toward a Model of Roles in the Due Process of Life and Law,* 87 Harv. L. Rev. 1 (1973).

Uddo, *A Wink From the Bench: The Federal Courts and Abortion,* 53 Tul. L. Rev. 398 (1979).

Wood & Durham, *Counseling, Consulting, and Consent: Abortion and the Doctor-Patient Relationship,* 1978 B.Y.U. L. Rev. 783.

Woodward, B., & Armstrong, S., The Brethren—Inside the Supreme Court 165–89, 229–40, 413–16 (1979).

Bibliography

Ely, *The Wages of Crying Wolf: A Comment on Roe v. Wade,* 82 Yale L.J. 920 (1973).

Foster, *Marriage: A "Basic Civil Right of Man,"* 37 Fordham L. Rev. 51 (1968).

Kurtz, *The State Equal Rights Amendments and Their Impact on Domestic Relations Law,* 11 Fam. L.Q. 101 (1977).

Noonan, J., A Private Choice: Abortion in America in the Seventies (1979).

Strickman, *Marriage, Divorce and the Constitution,* 22 B.C.L. Rev. 934 (1981), reprinted in 5 Fam. L.Q. 259 (1982).

Tribe, *The Supreme Court 1972 Term—Foreword: Toward a Model of Roles in the Due Process of Life and Law,* 87 Harv. L. Rev. 1 (1973).

Uddo, *A Wink From the Bench: The Federal Courts and Abortion,* 53 Tul. L. Rev. 398 (1979).

Wardle, L., The Abortion Privacy Doctrine: A Compendium and Critique of Federal Court Abortion Cases (1980).

Wood & Durham, *Counseling, Consulting, and Consent: Abortion and the Doctor-Patient Relationship,* 1978 B.Y.U. L. Rev. 783.

Incidents of Equality

Family Name

Stuart v. Board of Supervisors of Elections

Court of Appeals of Maryland

266 Md. 440, 295 A.2d 223 (1972)

Murphy, Chief Judge.

Mary Emily Stuart and Samuel H. Austell, Jr., were married in Virginia on November 13, 1971 and, shortly thereafter, took up residence in Columbia, Howard County, Maryland. In accordance with the couple's oral antenuptial agreement, Stuart continued, after the marriage, to use and be exclusively known by her birth given ("maiden") name and not by the legal surname of her husband.

On March 2, 1972, Stuart undertook to register to vote in Howard County in her birth given name. After disclosing to the registrar that she was married to Austell but had consistently and nonfraudulently used her maiden name, she was registered to vote in the name of Mary Emily Stuart.

On March 16, 1972 the Board of Supervisors of Elections for Howard County notified Stuart by letter that since under Maryland law "a woman's legal surname becomes that of her husband upon marriage," she was required by Maryland Code, Article 33, §3–18(c) to complete a "Request for Change of Name" form or her registration would be cancelled. Stuart did not complete the form and her registration was cancelled on April 4, 1972.

Stuart promptly challenged the Board's action by two petitions filed in the Circuit Court for Howard County, the first entitled "Petition to correct [the voter] registry," and the second "Petition to restore name to registry of voters in Howard County." In each petition Stuart maintained that she was properly registered to vote in her birth given name, that being her true and correct name; that under the English common law, in force in Maryland, a wife could assume the husband's name if she desired, or retain her own name, or be known by any other name she wished, so long as the name she used was not retained for a fraudulent purpose; and that since the only name she ever used was Mary Emily Stuart the Board had no right to cancel her voter registration listed in that name.

* * * Evidence was adduced showing that the oral antenuptial agreement between Stuart and Austell that she would retain her maiden name was a matter of great importance to both parties. Stuart testified that her marriage to Austell was "based on the idea that we're both equal individuals and our names symbolize that." There was evidence that prior to the marriage lawyers were consulted on the parties' behalf who indicated that Stuart had the right to retain her own name after the marriage. Stuart testified, and Austell corroborated her testimony, that she would not have gotten married "if * * * [the marriage] would have jeopardized my name." She testified that after the marriage she continued to use her own name on charge accounts, on her driver's license and Social Security registration and in "every legal document I've ever had." "Everybody" she said, "knows me by the name Mary Stuart."

There was evidence showing that the practice of the Board requiring a married woman to use the surname of her husband dated back to 1936; that the practice was a uniform one throughout the State and was adopted to provide some trail of identification to prevent voter fraud; that if a married woman could register under different names the identification trail would be lost; and that the only exception permitted to the requirement that married women register under their husbands' surnames was if the name was changed by court order.

By opinion filed May 10, 1972, Judge Mayfield concluded "that a person may adopt and use any name chosen in the absence of fraudulent intent or purpose"; that the use by Stuart of her maiden name was without fraudulent intent or purpose; that it is the law of Maryland that "the use by the wife of the husband's surname following marriage, while the same have been initially based upon custom and usage, is now based on the common law of England, which law has been duly adopted as the law of this State"; that under the provisions of the Code, Article 33, §3–18(a)(3) clerks of courts, as therein designated, are required to notify Boards of Supervisors of Elections of the "present names" of females over the age of eighteen years residing within the State "whose names have been changed by marriage"; that by subsection (c) of §3–18, the Boards, upon being advised of a "change of name by marriage," are required to give notification "that such * * * change of name by marriage * * * has been reported to the board, and shall require the voter to show cause within two weeks * * * why his registration should not be cancelled"; that §3-18 appeared "to be in conformity with the common law," as espoused in such cases as *People ex rel. Rago v. Lipsky,* 327 Ill. App. 63, 63 N.E.2d 642 (1945) and *Forbush v. Wallace,* 341 F. Supp. 217 (M.D. Ala. 1971), *aff'd per curiam,* 405 U.S. 970, 92 S. Ct. 1197, 31 L.Ed.2d 246 (1972); that the "statutory requirements [of §3-18] are in accordance with the law which says that upon marriage the wife takes the surname of her husband"; that the provisions of §3-18 do not deprive Stuart of her right to use her maiden name, nor of her right to vote, but require only that she "register to vote under her 'legal' name, * * * based upon the broad general principle of the necessity for proper record keeping and the proper and most expedient way of identifying the person who desires to vote."

From the court's order denying her petitions to correct the voter registry and to restore her name thereto, Stuart has appealed. She claims on appeal, as she did below, that a woman's surname upon marriage does not become that of her husband by operation of the common law in force in Maryland and that nothing in the provisions of §3-18(a)(3) and (c) mandates a contrary result.

What constitutes the correct legal name of a married woman under common law principles is a question which has occasioned a sharp split of authorities, crystallized in the conflicting cases of *State ex rel. Krupa v. Green,* 114 Ohio App. 497, 177 N.E.2d 616 (1961), relied upon by Stuart, and *People ex rel. Rago v. Lipsky, supra,* adopted by the lower court as its principal authority for denying the petitions. *Green* approved the voter registration of a married woman in her birth given name which she had openly, notoriously and exclusively used subsequent to her marriage, and held that she could use that name as a candidate for public office. The court held:

> "It is only *by custom,* in English speaking countries, that a woman, upon marriage, adopts the surname of her husband in place of the surname of her father."

Id. 177 N.E.2d at 619 (Emphasis in original.)

Lipsky refused to allow a married woman to remain registered to vote under her birth given name on the basis of

> "* * * the long-established custom, policy and rule of the common law among English-speaking peoples whereby a woman's name is changed by marriage and her husband's surname becomes *as a matter of law* her surname."

Id. 63 N.E.2d at 645 (Emphasis supplied.)
> * * *

We think the lower court was wrong in concluding that the principles enunciated in *Lipsky* represent the law of Maryland. We have heretofore unequivocally recognized the common law right of any person, absent a statute to the contrary, to "adopt any name by which he may become known, and by which he may transact business and execute contracts and sue or be sued." *Romans v. State,* 178 Md. 588, 597, 16 A.2d 642, 646. In the context of the name used in an automobile liability insurance contract, we approved the consistent nonfraudulent use by a married woman of a surname other than that of her lawful husband in *Erie Insurance Exchange v. Lane,* 246 Md. 55, 227 A.2d 231. Citing with approval *Everett v. Standard Acc. Ins. Co.,* 45 Cal. App. 332, 187 P. 996 (1919), we summarized its holding as follows:

> "The court * * * held that because the insured had been known as Everett for twenty-two years before the policy was issued, a representation that his name was Everett was not a misrepresentation, although his name before had been Cowie, since a man may lawfully change his name without resorting to legal proceedings and by general usage or habit acquire another."

Erie 246 Md. at 62–63, 227 A.2d at 236. If a married woman may lawfully adopt an assumed name (which, in *Erie,* was neither her birth given name nor the name of her lawful husband) without legal proceedings, then we think Maryland law manifestly permits a married woman to retain her birth given name by the same procedure of consistent, nonfraudulent use following her marriage. In so concluding, we note that there is no statutory requirement in the Code, in either Article 62 (Marriages) or Article 45 (Husband and Wife), that a married woman adopt her husband's surname.[3] Consistent with the common law principle referred to in the Maryland cases, we hold that a married woman's surname does not become that of her husband where, as here, she evidences a clear intent to consistently and nonfraudulently use her birth given name subsequent to her marriage. Thus, while under *Romans,* a married woman may choose to adopt the surname of her husband—this being the longstanding custom and tradition which has resulted in the vast majority of married women adopting their husbands' surnames as their own—the mere fact of the marriage does not, as a matter of law, operate to establish the custom and tradition of the majority as a rule of law binding upon all.

From a study of the English authorities cited to us by the parties and amici curiae, we believe the rule we enunciate today is founded upon the English common law incorporated into the laws of Maryland by Article 5 of the Maryland Declaration of Rights. The question of English common law was considered by the Ohio Court of Appeals in *State ex rel. Krupa v. Green, supra,* 177 N.E.2d at 619:

> "In England, from which came our customs with respect to names, a woman is permitted to retain her maiden surname upon marriage if she so desires.
>
> "M. Turner-Samuels, in his book on 'The Law of Married Women' at page 345, states:
>
>> " 'In England, custom has long since ordained that a married woman takes her husband's name. This practice is not invariable; not compellable by law. * * * A wife may continue to use her maiden, married, or any other name she wishes to be known by. * * *' "

* * * Other English text writers have expressed a similar view of English law:

> "In England (followed by the United States of America) practice has crept in, though apparently comparatively recently, for a woman upon marriage to merge her identity in that of her husband, and to substitute his name for her father's acquiring the new surname by repute."

C. Ewen, A History of British Isles 391 (London 1931).
To the same effect see 19 Halsbury's Laws of England 829 (3d 1957):

> "1350. Assumption by wife of husband's name. When a woman on her marriage assumes, as she usually does in England, the surname of her husband in substitution of her father's name, it may be said that she acquires a new name by repute. The change of name is in fact, rather than in law, a consequence of the marriage. * * * " (Footnotes omitted.)

Under the common law of Maryland, as derived from the common law of England, Mary Emily Stuart's surname thus has not been changed by operation of law to that of Austell solely by reason of her marriage to him. On the contrary, because of her exclusive, consistent, nonfraudulent use of her

---

[3] Compare Hawaii Rev. Stat., Title 31, §574–1 (1968): "Every married woman shall adopt her husband's name as a family name." Hawaii appears to be the only state with a statutory provision determinative of the issue.

maiden name, she is entitled to use the name Mary Emily Stuart unless there is a statute to the contrary. * * *

Nothing in the language of §3–18(a)(3) or (c) purports to compel *all* married women to register to vote in their husbands' surname. Since Mary Emily Stuart did not undergo a "change of name by marriage," this Section merely requires her to show cause to the Board that she consistently and nonfraudulently used her birth given name rather than her husband's surname following marriage. * * *

In light of our disposition of the common law issue, we find it unnecessary to reach the constitutional issues raised by the appeal.

Order dismissing petitions vacated; * * *

SMITH, Judge.

I would affirm.

I do not see a constitutional issue in this case other than that of judicial legislation.

* * *

It is interesting to note that in 1931 the Attorney General was asked to advise "as to the proper name to be used by a Catholic Sister or a Brother in a religious order when registering for voting purposes." In 16 Op. Atty. Gen. 144 (1931), he replied:

> "The law requires the giving of the correct legal name, and until a person's name has been changed in the manner provided by law, this name should be given when applying for registration purposes." *Id.* at 144.

2 Bishop, MARRIAGE, DIVORCE AND SEPARATION §1622 (1891), states:

> "The rule of law and custom is familiar, that marriage confers on the woman the husband's surname."

In re Kayaloff, 9 F. Supp. 176 (S.D.N.Y. 1934), is interesting in this regard. There a married woman was seeking naturalization. She was a musician "known professionally by her maiden name." She feared that she might possibly suffer financial loss if her naturalization certificate showed her surname to be that of her husband. She saw another problem in that a discrepancy would exist between her musical union card and her naturalization certificate. The court, after stating that "[t]he union card should conform to the naturalization certificate rather than that the latter should yield to the union card," said:

> "Under the law of New York, as pronounced in *Chapman v. Phoenix National Bank,* 85 N. Y. 437, a woman, at her marriage, takes the surname of her husband. 'That,' it was there said, 'becomes her legal name, and she ceases to be known by her maiden name. By that name she must sue and be sued, make and take grants and execute all legal documents. Her maiden surname is absolutely lost, and she ceases to be known thereby.'"

Id. 9 F. Supp. at 176.

The exact point here involved was before the court in *People ex rel. Rago v. Lipsky,* 327 Ill. App. 63, 63 N.E.2d 642 (1945). Antonia E. Rago, admitted to the bar of Illinois in 1938, married MacFarland in 1944. She was admitted to practice under the name of Rago in the federal courts in Chicago and before the Supreme Court of the United States, in addition to the Illinois courts. She practiced under the name of Rago. She claimed that her husband expressly approved of her plans to continue her practice of law and her other business affairs under the name of Rago. She sought to register under that name and challenged a provision of the Illinois law which provided that any registered voter who changed her name by marriage should "be required to register anew and authorize the cancellation of the previous registration." In holding that she was obliged to register under her married name, the court said:

> "Notwithstanding petitioner's contention to the contrary, it is well settled by common-law principles and immemorial custom that a woman upon marriage abandons her maiden name and takes the husband's surname, with which is used her own given name."

Id. 327 Ill. at 67, 63 N.E.2d at 644.

* * *

I am not impressed by the comment, citing *Romans v. State,* 178 Md. 588, 597, 16 A.2d 642 (1940), that a person has a common law right, absent a statute to the contrary, to "adopt any name by which he may become known, and by which he may transact business and execute contracts and sue or be sued." Rather, the question is, as I see it, what the General Assembly meant in the registration laws when "name" was mentioned.

It is conceded by all concerned that the uniform practice in Maryland has been for a married woman to register under the surname of her husband. This is in accordance with what I understand to be the authorities on the subject of name. It certainly is in accordance with custom. Therefore, I believe that to permit a married woman to register under a surname other than that of her husband she must either go through the process of having her name changed or the General Assembly must so provide. A holding to the contrary is in my humble opinion judicial legislation which is forbidden by the Maryland Declaration of Rights.

1976 Florida Attorney General Annual Report 462

December 21, 1976

BIRTH CERTIFICATES

BUREAU OF VITAL STATISTICS—NO POWER TO PROHIBIT ISSUANCE OF CERTIFICATES WITH HYPHENATED COMBINATION OF MOTHER'S MAIDEN NAME AND FATHER'S SURNAME

To: Lori Wilson, Senator, 16th District, Cocoa Beach

Prepared by: Sharyn L. Smith, Assistant Attorney General

QUESTION:

Is the Bureau of Vital Statistics empowered to require that birth certificates be issued only in the surname of the father as opposed to a hyphenated combination of the mother's maiden name and the father's surname?

SUMMARY:

Pending legislative or judicial clarification, the Bureau of Vital Statistics is not empowered to require that birth certificates be issued only in the surname of the father as opposed to a hyphenated combination of the mother's maiden name and the father's surname.

Section 382.18, F. S., provides as follows:

Certificate of birth to show given name of child.—

(1) When any certificate of birth of a living child is presented without the statement of the given name, then the local registrar shall make out and deliver to either parent of the child a special blank for supplemental report of the given name of the child which will be filled out as directed and returned to the local registrar as soon as the child shall have been named.

(2) The mother of a child born out of wedlock should enter on the birth certificate the surname by which she desires the child to be known. The registrar, upon presentation of proof that said child has acquired another name through usage, court order, or otherwise, shall correct the original birth certificate as hereinafter provided for to show the name by which said child is known.

Section 382.20, F. S., empowers the state registrar to make and enforce appropriate rules and regulations to carry out Ch. 382, F. S., and to prevent *fraud* and *deception* from being committed under the same.

An examination of Ch. 382, F. S., fails to disclose any statute that requires a registrar to issue a birth certificate in the surname of the father. Similarly, I have been unable to find any rule promulgated pursuant to s. 382.20 which administratively purports to impose such a requirement.

It is well settled than an administrative agency possesses only so much authority as is delegated to it by statute. Greenberg v. State Board of Dentistry, 297 So.2d 628 (1 D.C.A. Fla., 1974), *cert. dismissed* 300 So.2d 900 (Fla. 1974). If there is reasonable doubt as to the lawful existence of a particular power being exercised by an administrative agency, the further exercise of that power should be arrested. Edgerton v. Int'l Col., 89 So.2d 488 (Fla. 1956). *Also see* AGO 075-94.

While the Legislature has specifically addressed the issues of requiring the "given name" of all living children to be recorded and permitting the mother of a child born out of wedlock to select the name under which she desires the child to be known, it has not addressed the issue of whether to permit married parents to select the surname of their children. Significantly, however, the only specific administrative limitation which has been imposed by the Legislature has been to permit the state registrar to administer Ch. 382, F. S., to prevent fraud and deception.

A similar situation arose in Davis v. Roos, 326 So.2d 226 (1 D.C.A. Fla., 1976), in which the court held a woman by custom and usage generally adopts her husband's name upon marriage, but no Florida law compelled her to do so. The same appears to be true regarding registration of birth. While customarily a child assumes the surname of its father, there is no statute or existing rule which requires the same.

Accordingly, until legislatively or judicially clarified to the contrary, I do not believe that a registrar may require that parents use only the surname of the husband in registering the birth of their children.

Nothing herein should be construed to prohibit in an appropriate case the registrar from refusing to accept a particular name in order to permit fraud or deceit.

Comments

The changed position of women in marriage has found expression in extensive litigation relating to their right to retain their birth names. The result has been increased recognition of that right by federal authorities in the context of filing joint income tax returns or obtaining passports and by many state authorities in other contexts. On occasion, however, there are factual difficulties. For one thing, joint income tax returns under different last names may be returned by the computers for a closer check. Moreover, because every state has the power to develop its own notions of the local common law on marital names, there is the problem of 51 separate laws of marital names, with different lines of reasoning applied in individual cases. Thus, some states permit variations of the husband's and wife's names in hyphenated form, while other jurisdictions still adhere to the custom that the wife takes the husband's name upon marriage.

In a nation with a high degree of mobility, differences in the law of marital names pose problems. State authorities are often inclined, mainly with respect to voter registration and issuance of driver's licenses, to impose local law on women who have married elsewhere. A married woman could thus face the dilemma of the common law in a particular state being retroactively applied to her and to a marriage contracted in another jurisdiction at an earlier time. State administrative agencies, as well as the courts, are prone to overlook the questions of conflict of laws in this area. Attorneys representing married women in mandamus actions of this sort, perhaps in their zeal to get a ruling on local law, do not argue the conflict of laws question, namely, the right of women not to have different names imposed on them when they cross borders after marriage.

Stuart involved a marriage contracted in Virginia, after which the husband and wife moved to Maryland; yet the question of Virginia law on marital names was never examined. Similarly, in *Davis v. Roos,** the court did not even mention the marriage locale of the petitioning wife although the record disclosed that she was originally from Oklahoma and had, after her marriage, legally retained her birth name in Michigan, her state of domicile before moving to Florida. Neither the Florida Department of Highway Safety and Motor Vehicles nor the court checked whether the wife was entitled to retain her birth name under some out-of-state common law. The attorney for the petitioning wife reported that he had never thought of attempting to apply the laws of the state where the marriage took place, and that he had never seen this point argued in cases from other jurisdictions. Although this matter illustrates the unconscious preference for local rules, which counteracts the impact of conflict of laws in family law, it also demonstrates that conflicts are still perceived as being professorial law, at least in large segments of legal practice.

If a married woman may retain her birth name and perhaps even use a new form, such as a hyphenated combination of the husband's and the wife's last names, the question arises as to what names should be given to children. Those states where the question has been ad-

---

*326 So.2d 229 (1st D.C.A. Fla. 1976).

dressed have concluded that any name is permissible under common law, even an entirely new one, as long as its adoption does not result in fraud or deceit.* See, e.g., Op. Fla. Att'y Gen. (Dec. 21, 1976) (pp. 258–259).

The possibility that children may be given any surname of the parents' choice seems to have inflamed legislatures more than the right of women to retain their birth names after marriage. The Florida legislature reacted promptly to the opinion of the Attorney General of Florida of December 21, 1976, implying that any name is permissible as long as there is no intent to defraud. It passed a statute in 1977 that, in case of marriage, "the surname of the child shall be entered on the certificate as that of the husband."† The statute has been under constitutional attack for abridging due process and equal protection, as well as marital privacy.‡ Behind the constitutional argument are fundamental value choices relating to the nature of marriage that were also at stake in the abortion cases.

Reference

McDougall, *The Right of Women to Determine Their Own Names Irrespective of Marital Status*, 1 Fam. L. Rep. 4005 (1974).

Married Women and Work

Application of Ellen Gaulkin

Supreme Court of New Jersey

69 N.J. 185, 351 A.2d 740 (1976)

Hughes, C.J.

This application for the review and relaxation of an administrative policy enunciated by the Court is somewhat unusual in nature. It was initiated by a petition filed by one affected by the policy, Mrs. Ellen Gaulkin, wife of a Judge of the New Jersey Superior Court. In a most appropriate way she had sought the views of the Supreme Court as to the propriety of her intended candidacy for public office in view of her husband's judicial position. Upon the expression of our negative opinion, she acceded for the time, although disagreeing with it, and reserved the right to contest further. She is properly here now, as are the *amici* who have also briefed and argued the cause, which in itself is not adversarial in nature. *Cf. In re National Broadcasting Co.*, 64 N.J. 476, 317 A.2d 695 (1974). Through its chairman the Supreme Court's Advisory Committee on Professional Ethics joined in argument for explication of the reasons relevant to the origin and existence of the policy. There has been no adjudicatory hearing as such, nor indeed is such hearing necessary where the Court is exercising legislatively its constitutional power to formulate court rules and policy. *Cf. American Trial Lawyers Assoc. v. New Jersey Supreme Court*, 66 N.J. 258, 330 A.2d 350 (1974).

---

*See *Secretary of the Commonwealth v. City Clerk of Lowell*, 373 Mass. 178, 366 N.E.2d 717 (1977).

†See Fla. Stat. §382.16(5)(a) (1981).

‡See *Rice v. Department of Rehabilitative Serv.*, 386 So.2d 844 (1st D.C.A. Fla. 1980).

I

Since 1948, when the judicial system created by Article VI of the 1947 Constitution came into existence, judges and others officially associated with that court system have been wholly divorced from involvement in partisan or other political activity, as a necessary sacrifice for the sake of judicial integrity and the public appearance thereof. This separation is thought in this State (all judges in New Jersey are appointed) to be indispensable to public confidence in the courts and their probity, impartiality, disinterested objectivity and freedom from outside pressures in their dealing with causes coming before them. Such public confidence in judicial integrity is the foundation (along with Constitution and law) of our courts' power, influence and acceptance as necessary instruments in the effective administration of justice.

In recognition of that concept the people of New Jersey, in adopting our present Constitution, reposed in the New Jersey Supreme Court, a non-political entity, exclusive responsibility for the making of rules concerning practice and procedure in the courts thereby created, and for the admission and discipline of those admitted to the practice of the law. N.J. Const. (1947), Art. VI, §II, par. 3. * * *

It was to implement this mandate that our Court perceived the need for extension of the judge's disqualification from political involvement to include that of the spouse. (To avoid confusion, this opinion will refer to the wife or husband of a judge as the "non-judicial spouse.")

In reaffirming this policy the present Court, through a letter to Judge Gaulkin on December 31, 1973, opined that the candidacy for public office of his spouse represented "a form of political activity which would, unintentionally but seriously, affect public confidence in the judicial system." This was then our position despite an assurance that such candidacy would not involve the typical indicia of political campaigns, such as association with a slate, or acceptance of campaign financing, or solicitation of endorsements, and Mrs. Gaulkin's further belief that her tenure and its incidents would not be subversive of the policy of the Court.

* * *

II

It goes without saying that our system of government is predicated upon the premise that every citizen shall have the right to engage in political activity. It is a basic freedom enshrined in the First Amendment. * * * This important right (except of course for the private exercise of the voting franchise) is relinquished by our judges upon ascendancy to the bench. In this state, at least, it has been clearly established that courts do not belong in politics, that the independence of the judiciary depends upon that separation, and that political ties and debts and their accommodation would demean and degrade the courts and ultimately corrupt them. * * *

* * *

III

But the years which demonstrated the wisdom of this basic policy have also wrought other changes bearing upon the question now directly before us, namely, whether and to what extent the proscription of all political activity on the part of a judge should extend to the non-judicial spouse.

We focus first upon the trend of modern law which reflects society's realistic appreciation of the independence of both spouses in marriage and more specifically represents modern awareness and sensitivity to individual free-

doms, rights, responsibilities and development. A married woman in New
Jersey has the right to own property individually, N.J.S.A. 37:2-12; is liable
for debts contracted in her own name, N.J.S.A. 37:2-10; may enter into a
partnership with her husband, N.J.S.A. 37:2-16.1; may even enter into a
criminal conspiracy with him, *State v. Pittman,* 124 N.J. Super. 334, 338-40,
306 A.2d 500 (Law Div. 1973); may testify in court against her husband in
certain cases, *Evid. R.* 23(2); and is not compelled to assume her husband's
surname as her legal name, *In re Application of Lawrence,* 133 N.J. Super.
408, 412, 337 A.2d 49 (App. Div. 1975). The coexistence of separate and different interests in an ongoing marriage has also been recognized. In *Immer v.
Risko,* 56 N.J. 482, 267 A.2d 481 (1970), the Court limited the doctrine of
interspousal immunity in a woman's negligence action against a defendant
who became her husband. The Court rejected the assumption that interspousal tort actions would inevitably disrupt marital harmony. [*Id.* at 488-
490, 267 A.2d 481]. See also *Small v. Rockfeld,* 66 N.J. 231, 241, 330 A.2d
335 (1974). In *King v. Greene,* 30 N.J. 395, 412, 153 A.2d 49 (1959), the Court
held that a wife's interest in property held in a tenancy by the entirety could
be alienated. We notice too that the evolving recognition of individual
spousal interests has resulted in their being viewed as well from the perspective of the male and his role as husband and father. He too is being relieved of
the consequences of being fitted into a stereotypic mold. See, *e.g., Weinberger
v. Wiesenfeld,* 420 U.S. 636, 95 S. Ct. 1225, 43 L.Ed.2d 514 (1975); *Stanley v.
Illinois,* 405 U.S. 645, 92 S. Ct. 1208, 31 L.Ed.2d 551 (1972).

All of this bespeaks a realist appreciation of the marriage relationship
and the nature of the partnership it embodies:

> [T]he marital couple is not an independent entity with a mind and heart of
> its own, but an association of two individuals each with a separate intel-
> lectual and emotional makeup. [*Eisenstadt v. Baird,* 405 U.S. 438, 453, 92
> S. Ct. 1029, 1038, 31 L.Ed.2d 349, 362 (1972)].

And so it is with an appreciation of the emergence and the social and legal
recognition of spousal autonomy and retention of separate identities and interests, not withstanding the sympathetic relationship of an ongoing marriage, that we turn to the question of spousal political activity, as seen by
others in the judicial and professional world.

IV

The record before us indicates that no other American jurisdiction,
whether by a court having administrative responsibility for the conduct of
judges, a judicial ethics commission, or otherwise, has ever undertaken to
forbid or limit spousal public or political activity, with the exception of the
Association of the Bar of the City of New York, Committee on Professional
Ethics, whose Opinion No. 865, 20 *Record of N.Y.C.B.A.* 52 (1965), sought to
control political activity of a judge's spouse. It is pointed out to us that such
opinion has never been cited with approval in any opinion or other writing
since. On the contrary, in voluminous writings of recent years concerning
judicial ethics there does not seem to be the slightest suggestion that any
prohibition of a spouse's service in or candidacy for public office is either
necessary or appropriate.

* * *

Ours, then, has been a conspicuously minority position, designed however to meet a plain exigency, namely, the need to extricate our courts from
the sort of pre-1948 entanglements to which we have referred. It reflected as
well our determination, to which we still firmly adhere, not to move one inch
from the principle of total separation of the judiciary itself from involvement,
directly or indirectly, in political activities.

Upon the most careful reconsideration, however, we no longer see any confirmed justification for extending that prohibition to the non-judicial spouse. The reasoning supporting extension of the basic policy was based upon our perception that the spousal political activity would seem to embroil the judge in politics, because of an inevitable public belief that the publicly stated views of the political spouse would or must implicate the fundamental thinking of the judge and the court represented by that judge.

In light of the strong admonitions of Canon 7 adjuring the abstention by the judge from political activity and the Court's undoubted power and determination to enforce such a rule vigorously, we express doubt that spousal political activity per se would involve the judge in the political stream. Where a court is dealing with a First Amendment right (here the political involvement of the non-judicial spouse), fears that its exercise will have undesirable consequences cannot inhibit judicial vindication thereof. * * *

As to the community's perception of the spouse's exercise of that right, emerging concepts of spousal independence and autonomy in activities, development, interests, rights and responsibilities lead us to appraise our earlier assessment of probable public discernment and sophistication as no longer realistic. Furthermore, certain disqualification provisions under the Code provide an avenue for appropriate withdrawal of the judge from any matter which would or could embarrass the court, an implicit burden always resting on the judge to be vigilant in detecting possible impropriety or the likelihood of public appearance thereof. * * *

Additionally, our previous position now lacks a persuasive ring when we consider the impact on our judicial system of the publicly expressed views of the wife or husband of a judge as stated in the political forum, and those of a non-judicial spouse who is, let us say, an author, playwright, lecturer, newspaper editor or the like. The former would seem no more invidious than the latter. And one can hardly suppose that the latter, ordinarily, could come within the orbit of legitimate spousal control or judicial concern.

V

We think we have been explicit enough to indicate that while we now see the need and justice of withdrawing the Court's previous disapproval of spousal political involvement, which we do by this opinion, we are equally determined that every precaution shall be taken to assure that the judiciary itself shall continue its careful separation from direct or indirect involvement in politics. We consider that certain amenities of life, and perhaps even some legal rights, have to be sacrificed or curtailed for the larger purpose of avoiding the fact or appearance of participation by the judge in the political effort of a spouse. The administration of justice must be free of such appearance, as well as the fact. * * * Thus, for instance, despite the theory of *Painter v. Painter*, 65 N.J. 196, 320 A.2d 484 (1974), recognizing the contribution of both spouses to the marital assets, we would regard the use of any part thereof in the political forum as degrading to the court and plainly within the reach of the adjuration that the judge abstain from politics. Such assets normally are marked by a lack of an identifiable interest of either spouse, thus at least suggesting indirect involvement of the judge. The use of the marital home for a political or fundraising meeting or the making of political contributions from the common family funds would come within this objection. The ordinary courtesy of the judge in accompanying his or her spouse to a political gathering of any kind, or being seen as a political adviser, would have to be foregone. The making of political contributions to the campaign of a spouse of a judge by attorneys or litigants who are or may be involved in practice before that judge would be particularly offensive from an ethical standpoint. A myriad of other circumstances apt to involve the judge or give the public appearance of such political involvement may be imagined, but need not here be enumerated. Suffice it to say that notwithstanding the present relaxation of the policy with regard to the non-judicial spouse, the Court will be vigilant and will deal most strenuously with respect to any encroachment, actual or apparent, of politics upon the judiciary of New Jersey.

* * *

AMERICAN BAR ASSOCIATION
Committee on Ethics and Professional Responsibility
Formal Opinion 340*

September 23, 1975

Where both husband and wife are lawyers but they are not practicing in association with one another, they are not necessarily prohibited from representing different interests or from being associated with firms representing differing interests. Like all lawyers, they must obey all disciplinary rules; a particular situation may be inherently difficult because of the close relationship between husband and wife. In any situation where a client or potential client might question the loyalty of the lawyer representing him, the situation should be fully explained to the client and the question of acceptance or continuance of representation left to the client for decision.

Where both husband and wife are lawyers but they are not practicing in association with one another, may they or their firms represent differing interests?

This question, in varying forms, has been presented to this Committee with some frequency recently. Some firms apparently have been reluctant to employ one spouse-lawyer where that person's husband or wife is, or may soon be, practicing with another firm in the same city or area. On the other hand, some law schools have expressed disapproval of the practice by some firms in their hiring practices of attaching grave importance to the fact that the law student under consideration is married to a lawyer or a law student. Some law firms are concerned whether a law firm is disqualified, by reason of its employment of one spouse, to represent a client opposing an interest represented by another law firm that employs the husband or wife of the inquiring firm's associate. Some of the circumstances bearing on this question include whether the fee of either firm is contingent, whether the disputed matter is one of negotiation or litigation, and whether the married lawyer in question will or will not actually be working on the particular matter. Another variation of the problem is the situation in which a governmental agency, such as a district attorney or an attorney general, is the employer of either the husband or the wife, and the spouse is associated with a law firm in the same community.

The problem undoubtedly will arise with increasing frequency and in different settings, for it is a fact of modern society that women are entering the profession in increasing numbers and that increasing numbers of these women are married to lawyers. Clearly, today it is not uncommon for husband

---

*[Excerpted from Recent Ethics Opinions, September 23, 1975, copyright of 1975, American Bar Association, National Center for Professional Responsibility.]

and wife lawyers to be practicing in different offices in the same city, and the current enrollment of women in law schools indicates that women lawyers will constitute a greater percentage of the bar in the future than now.

It is not necessarily improper for husband-and-wife lawyers who are practicing in different offices or firms to represent differing interests. No disciplinary rule expressly requires a lawyer to decline employment if a husband, wife, son, daughter, brother, father, or other close relative represents the opposing party in negotiation or litigation. Likewise, it is not necessarily improper for a law firm having a married partner or associate to represent clients whose interests are opposed to those of other clients represented by another law firm with which the married lawyer's spouse is associated as a lawyer.

A lawyer whose husband or wife is also a lawyer must, like every other lawyer, obey all disciplinary rules, for the disciplinary rules apply to all lawyers without distinction as to marital status. We cannot assume that a lawyer who is married to another lawyer necessarily will violate any particular disciplinary rule, such as those that protect a client's confidences, that proscribe neglect of a client's interest, and that forbid representation of differing interests. Yet it also must be recognized that the relationship of husband and wife is so close that the possibility of an inadvertent breach of a confidence or the unavoidable receipt of information concerning the client by the spouse other than the one who represents the client (for example, information contained in a telephoned message left for the lawyer at home) is substantial. Because of the closeness of the husband-and-wife relationship, a lawyer who is married to a lawyer must be particularly careful to observe the suggestions and requirements of EC 4-1, EC 4-5, EC 5-1, EC 5-2, EC 5-3, EC 5-7, DR 4-101, and DR 5-101.

Even though the representation by husband and wife of opposing parties is not a violation of any disciplinary rule, the possibility of a violation of DR 5-101, in particular, is real and must be carefully considered in each instance. If the interest of one of the marriage partners as attorney for an opposing party creates a financial or personal interest that reasonably might affect the ability of a lawyer to represent fully his or her client with undivided loyalty and free exercise of professional judgment, the employment must be declined. We cannot assume, however, that certain facts, such as a fee being contingent or varying according to results obtained, necessarily will involve a violation of DR 5-101(A). In some instances the interest of one spouse in the other's income resulting from a particular fee may be such that professional judgment may be affected, while in other situations it may not be; the existence of such interest is a fact determination to be made in each individual case. Wherever one spouse is disqualified under DR 5-101(A), the entire firm is disqualified under DR 5-105(D).[1]

In any event, the advice contained in EC 5-3 and EC 5-16 is apropos; the lawyer should advise the client of all circumstances that might cause one to question the undivided loyalty of the law firm and let the client make the decision as to its employment. If the client prefers not to employ a law firm containing a lawyer whose spouse is associated with a firm representing an opposing party, that decision should be respected.

The views expressed in this opinion are consistent with the views expressed by other committees in regard to the close relationships of opposing lawyers. For example, it has been held that a father and son may represent opposite sides in litigation: See Opinion 19 (January 23, 1963), Professional Ethics Committee of the Kansas Bar Association; Opinion 48, Missouri Ad-

---

[1] As amended February, 1974, DR 5-105(D) provides: "If a lawyer is required to decline employment or to withdraw from employment under a Disciplinary Rule, no partner, or associate, or any other lawyer affiliated with him or his firm, may accept or continue such employment."

visory Opinions. In its Opinion No. 170 (1970), the New Jersey Advisory Committee on Professional Ethics held it is not improper for a lawyer to represent an indigent when the lawyer's brother is employed by the prosecutor's office.[2]

Accordingly, we conclude that a law firm employing a lawyer whose spouse is a lawyer associated with another local law firm need not fear consistent or mandatory disqualification when the two firms represent opposing interests; yet it is both proper and necessary for the firm always to be sensitive to both the possibility of disqualification and the wishes of its clients. Marriage partners who are lawyers must guard carefully at all times against inadvertent violations of their professional responsibilities arising by reason of the marital relationship.

---

[2]But *see* Opinion No. 288 (1974) of the New Jersey Advisory Committee on Professional Ethics which held that a "wife should not be permitted to practice criminal defense law in New Jersey while her husband is" a deputy attorney general assigned to the Appellate Section of the Division of Criminal Justice.

Comments

The *Application of Ellen Gaulkin* and the American Bar Association Committee on Ethics and Professional Responsibility Formal Opinion No. 340 present matters in a nonadversary context, and are seemingly narrow in scope. *Gaulkin* dealt with the issue of whether the wife of a New Jersey judge may run for public office, specifically, seek election to the Weehawken Board of Education. Opinion 340 was concerned with the question whether husband and wife, both lawyers but not associated with each other, may represent opposing interests. In addition to these issues, there are numerous other problems posed by dual career marriages. Husband and wife may find themselves professors on the same law faculty or they may be prevented from such employment by antinepotism policies. While protégé relationships do not result in automatic exclusion, marriage often does.

Even if there is no legal restriction against activities of husband and wife within the same professional and occupational context, it may still be customary to exclude one of the spouses—usually the wife—from employment. The implication is that marriage may result in an appearance of undue influence or at least the possibility of corruption. While this reasoning is contemporary, it results in disabilities similar to those incurred by married women under archaic beliefs that merged the wife's individuality into the husband's. Under somewhat less ancient conceptions, a wife was presumed not to have a mind of her own, but to be under coercion by her husband. None of this conforms to the realities of modern life, but the persistence of the effect illustrates a frequent occurrence in family law: that older policies, though they may take a different form, remain essentially unchanged or are modified only slowly.

Progress may also have negative implications. Referring to *Eisenstadt v. Baird, Gaulkin* stressed that marriage is not an independent entity but an association of two individuals "each with a separate intellectual and emotional makeup." Both in *Gaulkin* and in Opinion 340 marriage is referred to as partnership, following an aggregate, rather than an entity, theory of partnership. Inevitably, such emphasis on the individual in marriage may mean that husband and wife grow apart and that the centrifugal forces in modern marriage tend to result in dissolution, winding up of the marital business, and distribution of assets. A state can be reached in marriage in which legally the spouses are no longer identified by a common name or abode, do not want to have children, do not share common interests or property, and are not in any sense liable for each other. If all these factors coincide, we have a marriage in name only, yet as an institution it still is legally recognized, more so than cohabitation arrangements of sometimes considerable mutual involvement. This state of affairs could become an issue of significance to legislators and to judges in their lawmaking role. It could result in extreme reactions: a return to traditional conceptions of marriage with all its negative connotations; or the opposite, a weakening of traditional marriage, perhaps even a further encouragement of nonmarital cohabitation. More likely a compromise will become institutionalized. Examples for extreme positions in regard to marriage can be found in the laws of Illinois and California, while other states try to work out a compromise.

References

Bird, *Lawyer Couples*, CALIF. LAW., Sept. 1981, at 26.
Karst, *The Freedom of Intimate Association*, 89 YALE L.J. 624 (1980).
Kay, *Legal and Social Impediments to Dual Career Marriages*, 12 U.C.D. L. REV. 207 (1979).

Married Men and Children

State ex rel. Watts v. Watts

Family Court, City of New York, New York County

77 Misc.2d 178, 350 N.Y.S.2d 285 (1973)

SYBIL HART KOOPER, Judge.

The Family Court is now vested with original jurisdiction to determine custody of children (Chapter 535 of the Laws of 1972 amending section 651 of the Family Court Act). This is such an action between the mother and father of three infant children who are each suing for custody.

Although in theory, a father has an equal right with the mother to the custody of his children, in well over ninety percent of the cases adjudicated, the mother is awarded custody. (THE RIGHT OF CHILDREN IN MODERN AMERICAN FAMILY LAW, Drinan.)

Yet, sound application of the "best interests of the child" criteria requires that the court not place a greater burden on the father in proving suitability for custody than on the mother.

Application of a presumption favoring the mother violates the law of New York State. Both section 240 of the Domestic Relations Law, dealing with custody of children in matrimonial actions and section 70 of the Domestic Relations Law, dealing with habeas corpus for a child detained by a parent provides in relevant part:

> "In all cases there shall be no prima facie right to the custody of the child in either parent, but the court shall determine solely what is for the best interest of the child, and what will best promote its welfare and happiness. * * *"

* * *

Until recently, however, there has been a pattern of at least cursory invocation by the courts in New York and elsewhere, of the presumption that children of tender years, all other things being equal, should be given into the custody of their mother. In fact, this approach to deciding custody cases, since the Domestic Relations Law was amended to forbid such preference, constitutes judicial error—error, moreover, which does not promote the best interests of the children involved. As Foster and Freed, authors of the comprehensive treatise *Law and the Family*, New York, Vol. 2 (1967) stated:

> "The statutory mandate in practice is ignored and instead of equality as between the parents, the mother's claim to the child is paramount. In reality instead of "best interests of the child" serving as the test, the "unfitness" rule which was designed to serve in all custody contests between parents and non-parents is being applied * * *."

The "tender years presumption" is actually a blanket judicial finding of fact, a statement by a court that, until proven otherwise by the weight of substantial evidence, mothers are always better suited to care for young children than fathers. This flies in the face of the legislative finding of fact underlying the explicit command of section 240 and section 70 of the Domestic Relations Law, that the best interests of the child are served by the court's approaching the facts of the particular case before it without sex preconceptions of any kind.

However, the trend in legislation, legal commentary, and judicial decisions is away from the "tender years presumption."

Recent amendments of the Domestic Relations Law of several other states have codified as explicitly as New York the view that the child's best interest requires that neither parent have preference. In Florida, for example, the relevant provision, effective July 1, 1971, states:

> "The court shall award custody and visitation rights of minor children of the parties as a part of proceeding for dissolution of marriage in accordance with the best interests of the child. Upon considering all relevant factors, the father of the child shall be given the same consideration as the mother in determining custody."

Fla. Stat. 61.13(2), F.S.A. (1971).

Wisconsin's law also revised in 1971, provides in relevant part:

> "In determining the parent with whom a child shall remain, the court shall consider all facts in the best interest of the child and shall not prefer one parent over the other solely on the basis of the sex of the parent."

Wis. Stat. 247.24(3) (1971).

Colorado Rev. Stats. 46–1–5(7) provides:

> "No party shall be presumed to be able to serve the best interests of the child better than any other party because of sex."

Legal scholars advocate this evenhanded approach with near virtual una-
nimity. See *e.g.*, Podell, Peck and First, *Custody to Which Parent?* 56 MAR-
QUETTE UNIV. L. REV. Fall 1972; Foster and Freed, *Child Custody*, 39 N.Y.U.
L. REV. 422, 411, 1964; Polow, *Child Custody—The Law and Changing Social
Attitudes*; ABA Family Law Newsletter, November 1972. Evidence that the
courts are taking long strides toward abandoning the "tender years presumption" in favor of an unbiased consideration of the best interests of the children solely on the basis of the individual characteristics and relationships of
the parents and children involved is found in the large number of recent custody cases in which the parents were treated equally and the father prevailed.
(See the 48 cases collected in Footnote 23, Podell, Peck and First, *supra*.)

Apart from the question of legality, the "tender years presumption"
shoud be discarded because it is based on outdated social stereotypes rather
than on rational and up-to-date consideration of the welfare of the children
involved.

The simple fact of being a mother does not, by itself, indicate a capacity
or willingness to render a quality of care different from that which the father
can provide. The traditional and romantic view, at least since the turn of the
century, has been that nothing can be an adequate substitute for mother love.

> "For a boy of such tender years nothing can be an adequate substitute
> for mother love—for that constant ministration required during the per-
> iod of nurture [she] can give because * * * in her alone is service ex-
> pressed in terms of love. She alone has the patience and sympathy re-
> quired to mold and soothe the infant mind in its adjustment to its
> environment. The difference between fatherhood and motherhood in this
> respect is fundamental, and the law should recognize it unless offset by
> undesirable traits in the mother."

(*Jenkins v. Jenkins*, 173 Wis. 592, 181 N.W. 826, 827, 1921).

Later decisions have recognized that this view is inconsistent with informed application of the best interests of the child doctrine and out of touch
with contemporary thought about child development and male and female
stereotypes.

In *Garrett v. Garrett* (464 S.W.2d 740, 742, Mo. App., 1971), the court
stated:

> "The rule giving the mother preferential right to custody is considerably
> softened by the realization that 'all things never are exactly equal' and is
> predicated upon the acts of motherhood—not *the fact of motherhood*.
> Likewise, the rule will yield if the welfare of the children demands it,
> because this is not a presumption of law but a simple fact of life gleaned
> from human experience, and the courts are not timid in entrusting chil-
> dren into their father's care and custody when their best interests will be
> served thereby." (Citations omitted and emphasis added.)

Eminent psychologists and anthropologists, including Margaret Mead,
have also acknowledged and asserted that both female and male parents are
equally able to provide care and perform child-rearing functions.

> "At present, the specific biological situation of the continuing relationship
> of the child to the biological mother and its need for care by human beings
> are being hopelessly confused in the * * * insistence that the child and
> mother or mother surrogate must never be separated; that all separation
> even for a few days is ultimately damaging and that if long enough it does
> irreversible damage. This is a mere and subtle form of anti-feminism which
> men—under the guise of exalting the importance of maternity—are tying
> women more tightly to their children than has been thought necessary since
> the invention of bottle feeding and baby carriages."

Margaret Mead, *Some Theoretical Considerations of the Problems of Mother-Child Separation*, 24 AMER. JRL. OF ORTHOPSYCHIATRY 24 (1954).

Studies of maternal deprivation have shown that the essential experience for the child is that of mothering—the warmth, consistency and continuity of the relationship rather than the sex of the individual who is performing the mothering function. (See, *e.g.,* R.A. Spitz and Katherine Wolf, *Anaclitic Depression*, PSYCHOANALYTIC STUDY OF THE CHILD, 1946, pages 313–342; Leon J. Yarrow, *Maternal Deprivation: Toward an Empirical and Conceptual Reevaluation*, PSYCHOLOGICAL BULL., 58, 1961.)

Finally, application of the "tender years presumption" would deprive respondent of his right to equal protection of the law under the Fourteenth Amendment to the United States Constitution.

* * * Recent decisions of the Supreme Court of the United States make clear that differential treatment on the basis of sex of the kind created by the "tender years presumption" is "suspect" and therefore subject to the strictest judicial scrutiny. In *Frontiero v. Richardson* (411 U.S. 677, 93 S. Ct. 1764, 1770, 36 L.Ed.2d 583, 1973) the court made explicit the incurable flaw in rules of law which accord different treatment to men and women on the basis of rigid and outdated sexual stereotypes:

"Since sex, like race and national origin, is an immutable characteristic determined solely by the accident of birth, the imposition of special disabilities upon the members of a particular sex because of their sex would seem to violate 'the basic concept of our system that legal burdens should bear some relationship to individual responsibility (citation omitted) * * *.' And what differentiates sex from such nonsuspect statutes as intelligence or physical disability, and aligns it with the recognized suspect criteria, is that the sex characteristic frequently bears no relation to ability to perform or to contribute to society."

The message of *Frontiero* is clear: persons similarly situated, whether male or female, must be accorded evenhanded treatment by the law. Legislative classifications may legitimately take account of need or ability; they may not be premised on unalterable sex characteristics that bear no necessary relationship to the individual's need, ability or life situation. * * *

Classifications subject to "strict scrutiny" under the Fourteenth Amendment pass constitutional muster only if a "compelling state interest" requires their existence. (See *Frontiero v. Richardson*, 411 U.S. at 682, 93 S. Ct. at 1768, 36 L.Ed.2d at 589; *McLaughlin v. Florida*, 379 U.S. 184, 85 S. Ct. 283, 13 L.Ed.2d 222, 1964; *Loving v. Virginia*, 388 U.S. 1, 87 S. Ct. 1817, 18 L.Ed.2d 1010, 1967.) The "best interests" of the child might well qualify as such a compelling state interest if, in fact, it were served by the "tender years presumption." But since, as has been shown, the presumption does not in fact serve the child's interests, it does not constitute a compelling state interest justifying the different treatment of parents on the basis of sex. Thus the "tender years presumption" in addition to its other faults, works an unconstitutional discrimination against the respondent.

In this connection, even before *Frontiero*, the Federal District Court for the Southern District of New York indicated that governmental authorities could not, without violating the Fourteenth Amendment, make employee leaves for the purpose of caring for newborn infants available to mothers unless they also make them available to fathers. *(Danielson v. Board of Higher Education of the City of New York*, 358 F. Supp. 22, S.D.N.Y., 1972.) Ruling on a motion to dismiss, the court held that the Board of Higher Education of the City of New York's policy of granting such leaves only to mothers but not to fathers presented a colorable constitutional claim. The case was not pushed to a final decision because the board changed its policies to make such leave available for men.

Arbitrary assumptions about which spouse is better suited to care for young children are no more permissible in the case at bar than they are in the child care leave situation just described.

This court, in arriving at its decision, has applied one criteria only—the best interests of the children.

Having listened to all the testimony, having read all the medical reports and records and having observed the demeanor and responses of the parties on the witness stand, this court concludes that it is in the best interests of the children for them to be in their father's custody.

Danielson v. Board of Higher Education

United States District Court, Southern District, New York

358 F. Supp. 22 (S.D.N.Y. 1972)

MOTLEY, District Judge.

This is an action by Ross Danielson, a lecturer in sociology at City College, a branch of the City University of New York. Mr. Danielson's challenge is to the constitutionality of defendants' maternity leave provision on its face and as applied. The essence of Danielson's claim is that women faculty members are permitted to take a leave of absence in connection with pregnancy, up to three semesters, for the purpose, among others, of caring for a new born infant, without adversely affecting their tenure rights, but the same child care leave privilege is denied to men.

This action is also brought by Mr. Danielson's wife, Susan Danielson, who is a lecturer in English at Lehman College, another branch of the City University of New York. Her challenge is to the constitutionality of defendants' refusal to treat her 12-day leave, during which she gave birth to a child, as sick leave.

Defendants are the Board of Higher Education which governs the City University of New York, the chairman of that Board, the chancellor of the University, the president of City College, and the dean of faculties of Lehman College.

* * *

The action is presently before the court on the motion of plaintiffs for summary judgment in their favor and the motion of defendants to dismiss or, alternatively, for summary judgment in their favor. Defendants have moved to dismiss the complaint on two grounds: 1) the court lacks jurisdiction of the subject matter and, 2) the complaint fails to state a claim upon which relief may be granted. For the reasons set forth below, the motion to dismiss is denied. The motions for summary judgment are also denied on the ground that there are several disputed issues of fact.

Mr. Danielson commenced teaching in the City College in the fall semester of 1969. His wife, Susan Danielson, who was teaching at Lehman College at the same time became pregnant in the early spring of 1970. Upon discovering her pregnancy, Susan and her husband discussed the matter at great length. They weighed the options available to them with respect to the care of their child and the pursuit of their respective careers. They decided that Susan would continue her teaching duties throughout her pregnancy and after childbirth. Then, for at least the first six months after the child was born, Mr. Danielson would stay home and assume the primary responsibility for the care of their infant. Susan Danielson consulted her physician who assured her that such conduct on her part would in no way be injurious to her health.

Mr. Danielson then made every effort to obtain "parental leave of absence" from City College. He claims such "parental leave" is available for women faculty members pursuant to Article XIII, Section 13.4, of the By-Laws of the Board of Higher Education and should be equally available to men.

* * *

On or about December 21, 1970 Mr. Danielson learned that the president's Review Committee had rejected his application without stating any reason. Mr. Danielson appealed to the chancellor of the University and the chairman of the Board of Higher Education but received no reply to his letters.

Ross Danielson took a leave during the spring 1971 semester and alleges he assumed primary responsibility for the care of his child. His wife resumed her teaching duties. His application for maternity leave was treated as a resignation. Thus, although he was rehired for the fall 1971 term, the computation of his continuous service time has been affected.

Susan Danielson, who had a right to do so, did not request the maternity leave permitted under Section 13.4. The president's office, however, sent her a form for such leave on numerous occasions. Maternity leaves which are granted under Section 13.4 are leaves without pay. If Mrs. Danielson had chosen to take maternity leave as of September 1, 1970 and had requested the one year extension, she could have remained away from her post until February 1, 1972 without loss of accrued time towards tenure requirements. It appears that no doctor's certificate in support of her request for extension would have been required. However, there is no proof one way or the other on this question. During this time away from her position, Mrs. Danielson apparently would have been free to devote all her time to the care of her newborn infant or, it appears, she could also have worked on her Ph.D. But, again, there is no firm proof one way or the other on this crucial question.

Defendants say that "* * * Ross Danielson might have obtained a leave for special purposes under Section 13.6 if he so requested, for the purpose of taking care of his child." (Defendants' Brief, p. 18.) They also assert that "If any parent desires to take leave solely for childrearing purposes, they must proceed under By-Law §13.6, leave for special purposes." (*Id.* p. 24.)

Section 13.6b provides: "On the recommendation of the relevant departmental committee concerned with appointments, the relevant college committee and the president, the Board may grant to members of the instructional staff leaves of absence for special purposes such as study, writing, research, the carrying out of a creative project or a public service of reasonable duration. Such leaves shall be *without* pay." (Emphasis added.)

Mr. Danielson was not advised of this "administrative procedure * * * available to accommodate him" prior to suit (*Id.* pp. 18–19.) Such leave, of course, does affect the computation of the five years of continuous service required for tenure.

It should be noted also that defendants' statement, that *any* parent who desires leave "solely" for childrearing purposes may apply for same under Section 13.6, does not square with defendants' assertion on the same page of their brief (p. 24) which reads as follows: "Defendant's By-Law provides a mother with the option to recuperate from pregnancy. If she utilizes this leave period to also care for her child, this is her own determination." This latter statement is consistent with the former if the former refers to women who desire to take child-care leave unconnected with childbirth. Thus from reading defendants' brief, it is clear to this court that defendants have not made up their collective minds as to what their child-care leave policies really are in the face of this men's liberation request for equal treatment with women.

Consequently, summary judgment cannot be granted for either party. Not only is it unclear what defendants' policies really are, but the central fact is plainly in dispute, i.e., whether women faculty members are permitted leaves up to three semesters under Section 13.4 to care for their newborn children when there is no unusual medical disability resulting from the birth of the child and, during this period, may also do work toward a Ph.D. degree without loss of time served, as it relates to tenure.

Mrs. Danielson made arrangements with other teachers to cover her classes during her brief leave for the birth of her child. She was absent from work for 12 days, from December 8, 1970 to December 23, 1970. She requested that her absence be credited against her allotted sick leave with pay. Instead of treating her absence as sick leave, Lehman College recorded the leave as a "special leave without pay for emergency purposes (maternity)." The special leave section, Section 13.6a, provides for special leaves for personal emergencies of not more than 10 working days *with pay* at the discretion of the president. Despite the express terms of this provision, Mrs. Danielson was not paid.

Again it is clear defendants were confused about their own policy. Mrs. Danielson's claim that the leave which she took should be treated as any other illness is disputed by defendants on the ground that pregnancy is not an illness. With respect to Mrs. Danielson's claim we thus have another central disputed issue of fact, i.e., whether the period immediately following childbirth unattended by other complications is a medical disability or illness for which a woman is entitled to sick leave. Mrs. Danielson's claim for sick leave pay is a claim which has been previously recognized by a federal court, *Cohen v. Chesterfield County School Board*, 326 F. Supp. 1159 (E.D. Va. 1971), and has been bolstered by recently adopted Rules and Regulations of the Equal Employment Opportunity Commission. 37 FED. REG. 6837 (April 5, 1972).

On this motion to dismiss it is only necessary to determine whether Mr. and Mrs. Danielson's allegations raise "colorable" constitutional claims.
* * *

Mr. Danielson's primary claim is that his right to equal protection of the laws has been violated by defendants' refusal to extend to him the same child-care leave privilege which they extend to women solely because he is a man. He claims that by so discriminating against men who seek to fully participate in the care of their children, defendants are effectively denying men the right to play a full and equal role in their families. He then argues that the fact that child care has traditionally been considered women's work is no more an answer here than were the use of such sex stereotypes in an attempt to bar women from certain kinds of employment. * * * He also argues that he and other men are perfectly capable of caring for infant children and have a right to elect to do so without arbitrary interference with this choice by the state.

Very recently, the Supreme Court ruled that a state may not arbitrarily prefer men over women similarly situated in determining appointments to positions of administrator of decedent's estates. *Reed v. Reed*, 404 U.S. 71, 92 S. Ct. 251, 30 L.Ed.2d 225 (1971). There the Court ruled that where the state provides that different treatment be accorded to persons similarly situated, such a classification is subject to scrutiny under the equal protection clause. The Court held that a classification must be reasonable, not arbitrary, and must rest upon some ground of difference having a fair and substantial relation to the object of the legislation, so that all persons similarly circumstanced shall be treated alike. If upon a trial it is proved that the purpose of Section 13.4 leave is to give women an opportunity to care for infant children, and since it is not claimed that Mr. Danielson is incapable of such child care, then Mr. Danielson would have presented at least a "colorable" constitutional claim. Whether he will succeed with his claim is another matter not here decided.
* * *

For all of the foregoing reasons, the motions for summary judgment and to dismiss are denied.

Support and Alimony for Men

Pfohl v. Pfohl

District Court of Appeal of Florida

345 So.2d 371 (3d D.C.A. Fla. 1977)

HUBBART, Judge.

This is an action for dissolution of marriage in which the husband was awarded lump sum and rehabilitative alimony as well as attorneys' fees. The wife appeals and the husband cross appeals, raising questions which go to the propriety and sufficiency of such awards.

On May 28, 1966, the parties were married. At the time of the marriage, the wife owned a one third interest in a trucking company given to her by her father, which interest she sold in 1972 for seven million dollars. The husband had no assets going into the marriage except for a one half interest in one hundred shares of Sears Roebuck stock. He had been employed for four and one half years as a toy salesman for Strombecker Toy Co. earning a salary of approximately $9,000–$10,000 a year plus expenses and bonus. He resigned this job after one and a half years of marriage to satisfy the wife's wishes. She did not like his traveling which was necessary to pursue his line of work, and refused to move to New York with him to accept a promotion. Prior to the marriage, he had finished three years of college and received an honorable discharge from the marines. The couple had two sons, now ages 8 and 2.

The parties lived a life of extreme luxury and comfort during a marriage which lasted nine years prior to the parties' final separation. The wife supported the family at first through contributions from her father, and from 1972–75 from her own separate estate.

Both the husband and wife had an unlimited joint checking account. Both had access to the wife's extensive properties; a one hundred acre farm in Elgin, Illinois, purchased for $500,000; a five bedroom house in Chicago; and two homes in Bal Harbour, Florida, purchased for $140,000, and $60,000 respectively. Both had access to a six bedroom home and an eighty acre farm in Crystal Lake, Illinois, in which the wife gave the husband one half interest.

The husband had all the major credit cards with unlimited credit plus charge accounts at many luxury stores where he regularly shopped. He maintained extensive clothing in their Florida and Illinois homes. Several times each year he paid substantial entry fees so he could participate in celebrity golf tournaments such as the Bob Hope and Andy Williams Classics.

The parties were members of seven luxury country clubs in Chicago and Miami for which the wife paid substantial initial membership sums and all the subsequent dues and bills incurred. They traveled extensively throughout the country and the world, and because of the wife's substantial interest in race horses, routinely traveled to the Kentucky Derby and other races in New York, California and Illinois. They were attended by servants in their homes in Florida and Illinois. They entertained extensively at home and various clubs at which they were members. They had full access to the seventy-five foot family yacht on which they maintained a full crew, contributing $3,000 a month to the operation of the vessel. In addition, they had two late model Cadillacs, a Buick stationwagon and a speedboat.

The husband estimated that his living expenses during the marriage were over $5,000 a month. The wife estimated that the family's total monthly living expenses were approximately $15,000 including income taxes. The wife could not have provided the foregoing fantasy-land existence for the husband on anything less than enormous resources. At the time of the final hearing, she had a net worth of $4,250,000 including cash and marketable securities of $3,325,000 plus an annual net income of $200,000.

During the marriage the husband dabbled, but never seriously participated in various business ventures provided by his wife's family. He was a figurehead president of the Antioch Insurance Agency for four years. Following this venture, he was a treasurer and director in the Antioch Savings and Loan Association from which he was eventually removed for failure to attend meetings.

The parties ceased living together as husband and wife on May 6, 1975. At that time the wife forbade the husband to return to their home in Florida or to live in any other of her properties. She removed his clothes therefrom and the husband has remained unemployed living with friends at a drastically reduced living style ever since. He unsuccessfully sought employment on several occasions in Florida and Chicago. There is evidence that the husband presently suffers from a mental disorder requiring professional treatment, but that at 37 he is in excellent physical health.

At the time of the dissolution, the husband held the following assets, all provided to him by the wife during the marriage: an undivided one half interest in an eighty acre farm in Crystal Lake, Illinois, his interest valued at $160,000; a 1974 and 1975 Cadillac valued together at a total of $12,000; and a twenty-five foot power boat valued at $6,000. In addition, he leaves the marriage with his original one half interest in one hundred shares of Sears Roebuck stock valued at $6,000 and an 80 percent ownership interest in a Ft. Lauderdale lounge known as the "Filling Station." The husband owes the wife $60,000 for the purchase of this lounge which at the time of the final hearing was up for sale for $110,000. He, therefore, has approximately $200,000 in assets, almost all of which are non-liquid and non-income producing.

The wife filed a petition for dissolution of marriage seeking the dissolution of the marriage, custody of the parties' two minor children and an adjudication of her rights as to the $60,000 loan which she had made to the husband. The husband answered denying that the marriage was irretrievably broken as well as the allegations concerning the loan. He requested alimony, attorneys fees and suit monies. The wife replied denying the husband's need for alimony, suit monies, and attorneys fees, which reply was amended to assert adultery as a defense to his claim for alimony, suit monies and attorneys fees.

* * *

The major question presented for review is whether it is an abuse of discretion in a dissolution of marriage action for a trial court to award the husband $30,000 in lump sum alimony and $5,000 a month rehabilitative alimony for 18 months when: (1) the wife has a net worth of $4,250,000; (2) the parties shared an extremely high standard of living at first supported by the wife based on contributions to her from her father and thereafter based entirely on her own wealth during a nine year marriage; (3) the husband is 37 years old, unemployed with limited employment skills, in good physical, but impaired mental health, and in possession of approximately $200,000 assets most of which were received during the marriage from the wife.

Both parties contend that the trial judge abused his discretion. The wife argues that the husband is not entitled to any alimony; the husband argues that the amount of lump sum alimony is inadequate and that permanent, rather than rehabilitative alimony should have been awarded. We reject all these contentions and hold that the alimony awards herein were well within the discretion of the trial judge to make under the circumstances of this case.

Alimony has been traditionally considered an allowance which a husband is required to make in order to maintain his wife in the event of separation or divorce and is based on the common law obligation of a husband to support his wife. *Floyd v. Floyd*, 91 Fla. 910, 108 So. 896 (1926). In determining the amount of such alimony, the courts have established two criteria: (1) the husband's ability to pay, and (2) the needs of the wife, taking into consideration the standard of living shared by the parties to the marriage. *Sisson v. Sisson*, 336 So.2d 1129 (Fla. 1976); *Firestone v. Firestone*, 263 So.2d 223 (Fla. 1972); [citations omitted].

Quite properly, these are criteria of the broadest nature, not susceptible to a precise formula automatically translatable into dollars and cents. We are dealing with a tragically human problem which touches peoples' lives during a period of immense personal crisis. One cannot dispense substantial justice in such explosive cases as if the answer lies in a computer or a rigid rule book. Mathematical exactness is neither possible nor desirable. The trial court of necessity has a wide discretion to apply the established criteria in fashioning a fair and equitable alimony award in the infinite variety of cases which come before it. Absent a showing that the trial court exercised this discretion arbitrarily or unfairly, alimony awards made pursuant to such criteria must be sustained on appeal. [Citations omitted.]

The so-called "no fault" divorce law enacted by the Florida Legislature in 1971, represents a significant, but not totally radical departure from the historic conception of alimony. Section 61.08, Florida Statutes (1975) provides as follows:

> "(1) In a proceeding for dissolution of marriage, the court may grant alimony to either party, which alimony may be rehabilitative or permanent in nature. In any award of alimony, the court may order periodic payments or payments in lump sum or both. The court may consider the adultery of a spouse and the circumstances thereof in determining whether alimony shall be awarded to such spouse and the amount of alimony, if any, to be awarded to such spouse.
> "(2) In determining a proper award of alimony, the court may consider any factor necessary to do equity and justice between the parties."

Under this statute, it is provided for the first time that a wife may be required to support her husband through alimony payments. This is in keeping with a current social trend toward establishing a more equitable relationship between the sexes. The First District Court of Appeal pointed out in *Beard v. Beard*, 262 So.2d 269 (Fla. 1st DCA 1972):

> "In this era of women's liberation movements and enlightened thinking, we have almost universally come to appreciate the fallacy of treating the feminine members of our society on anything but a basis of complete equality with the opposite sex. Any contrary view would be completely anachronistic. In this day and time, women are well educated and trained in the arts, sciences, and professions as are their male counterparts. The law properly protects them in their right to independently acquire, encumber, accumulate, and alienate property at will. They now occupy a position of equal partners in the family relationship resulting from marriage, and more often than not contribute a full measure to the economic well-being of the family unit."

Id. at 271-72.

The First District Court of Appeal further elaborated on this theme in *Thigpen v. Thigpen*, 277 So.2d 583 (Fla. 4th DCA 1973) as follows:

> "The new concept of marriage relation implicit in the so-called 'no fault' divorce law enacted by the legislature in 1971 places both parties to the

> marriage on a basis of complete equality as partners sharing equal rights
> and obligations in the marriage relationship and sharing equal burdens
> in the event of dissolution."

Id. at 585.

Although this historic change in alimony law is far-reaching and we have
not yet chartered its full effects, we can at least begin by stating that a husband's entitlement to alimony must stand on the same criteria as that of a
wife. *Lefler v. Lefler,* 264 So.2d 112 (Fla. 4th DCA 1972). To be entitled to
alimony, the husband must show a financial ability by the wife to pay for such
an award coupled with a demonstrated need of the husband for support, taking into consideration the standard of living shared by the parties to the
marriage.

Although in most marriages, the husband remains the sole provider of
the family, with the wife making the home and raising the children, if any, an
increasing number of marriages do not fit this mold. In some marriages, both
parties work and jointly support the family, although the degree of support
by either party may vary. In others, the wife is the sole support of the family
unit with the husband fulfilling some non-economic role. It is in these non-
traditional type marriages where the question of alimony for the husband
may arise.

In the instant case, we are faced with such a non-traditional type of marriage. Although neither party did any serious work to financially support
the family unit, the wife, rather than the husband, was the sole provider in
this marriage. The husband resigned his employment at the request of the
wife to live a life of luxury with his wife and family. Such fabulous wealth on
the part of a woman who supports a marriage in which the husband is of modest means is not unknown in our society, but it certainly presents a case of
unusual dimensions which we think the trial judge handled most reasonably
upon the marriage's dissolution under the traditional criteria for awarding
alimony.

As to the first criterion for awarding alimony, it is undisputed that the
wife easily has the financial ability to pay for the alimony award in this case.
She has a financial worth in excess of $4,000,000 and regularly maintains a
checking account considerably greater than the total $120,000 alimony
award for the husband. The award is therefore immune from attack as being
beyond the financial means of the wife. See: *Sisson v. Sisson,* 336 So.2d 1129
(Fla. 1976).

As to the second criterion for awarding alimony, the lump sum and rehabilitative alimony awards herein were commensurate with the need of the
husband for temporary, although not permanent support, taking into consideration the standard of living shared by the parties to the marriage. The husband's limited employment opportunities, his impaired mental condition,
and the very high standard of living to which the wife accustomed the husband to live during the marriage, are all critical factors in sustaining the trial
court's exercise of discretion in fashioning the alimony award in this case.

The husband was a toy salesman for six years earning a modest salary
which job he gave up at the request of the wife to devote full time to his life
with the wife and family after a year and a half of marriage. Save for this
limited service mainly as a figurehead in the businesses of his wife's family,
he has been out of the employment market for the last seven and a half years
of the marriage. At the time of the final hearing, he was unemployed, living
with friends at a drastically reduced life style, having unsuccessfully attempted on a number of occasions to obtain employment, since the wife
barred him from the marital homes. This impairment in a spouse's otherwise
modest employment capacities caused in part by the supporting spouse's
insistence that such work be terminated in favor of the family is a significant
factor in sustaining an alimony award. *Brook v. Brook,* 289 So.2d 766 (Fla. 3d
DCA 1974).

Added to this, is the husband's impaired mental condition. According to the uncontradicted testimony of an industrial psychologist, Dr. Marquit, the husband is suffering from a mental disorder which will require at least a year of intensive psychotherapy at considerable expense. He further testified that at present the husband is ill-suited for the employment market. We are in no position to second guess the trial judge's acceptance of this testimony based on his personal evaluation of Dr. Marquit as well as that of the husband. Certainly it is not beyond the realm of reasonable inference for the trial judge to have concluded that the husband's nine years of leisure class idleness followed by an abrupt end to his male cinderella existence when the wife literally threw him out of her home, at least partially brought on his current mental problems for which some period of rehabilitation is necessary. Such mental impairment, although temporary rather than permanent in nature, is a significant factor in sustaining an alimony award. *Baker v. Baker*, 229 So.2d 276 (Fla. 3d DCA 1974).

The husband's financial needs must also be measured in part by taking into consideration the extremely high standard of living to which the wife accustomed the husband through nine years of marriage. [Citations omitted.] The wife accustomed the husband to a life style which costs over $5,000 a month to maintain during a marriage which can hardly be described as a "marry in June and sue the following September" situation. *Firestone v. Firestone, supra.* In view of this fact, we cannot say that the limited eighteen month rehabilitative alimony plus lump sum alimony fashioned by the trial judge herein was an abuse of discretion. It was reasonably commensurate with the parties' high life style without at the same time creating an unreasonable charge on the wife for the rest of her life.

The wife argues that she accustomed the husband to such a high life style based on money she received from her father. It is true that the wife supported the marriage at first through contributions from the wife's father, but from 1972–1975 she supported the family unit entirely from her own separate estate. In our judgment, it is irrelevant how the wife lawfully acquired the money on which she supported the husband and family. The fact is she supported the family unit, not the husband. And despite the wife's protests, a high standard of living remains a significant factor in setting an alimony award, which result is unchanged by the fact that the paying spouse acquired his or her wealth by gift or inheritance. See: *Firestone v. Firestone*, 263 So.2d 223 (Fla. 1972).

Rehabilitative alimony has been awarded to supplement means already available in an amount reasonably required during the post-marriage period to maintain a spouse until he or she in the exercise of reasonable efforts and endeavors is in a position of self support. *Cann v. Cann*, 334 So.2d 325 (Fla. 1st DCA 1976). It necessarily presupposes the potential for self support which is presently impaired. *Reback v. Reback*, 296 So.2d 541 (Fla. 3d DCA 1974). Lump sum alimony has been awarded as a payment of a definite sum or property in the nature of a final property settlement which serves a reasonable purpose such as rehabilitation or where the marriage's duration or the parties' financial position would make such an award advantageous to both parties. *Cann v. Cann*, 334 So.2d 325 (Fla. 1st DCA 1976); *Calligarich v. Calligarich*, 256 So.2d 60 (Fla. 4th DCA 1971). The alimony awards herein fit these traditional patterns and purposes for alimony.

The wife argues that the husband's $200,000 in assets acquired mainly by gift from the wife during the marriage, disqualifies the husband from receiving any alimony. We disagree. Although this is a significant factor in upholding the trial court's refusal to make the alimony permanent, we cannot say that this compels the result urged by the wife, particularly in view of the husband's demonstrated need for temporary, rehabilitative support. Except for the Sears stock, the husband's assets are non-income producing. And it has been held that a spouse is not required to deplete capital assets in order to maintain a prior standard of living. *Gordon v. Gordon*, 204 So.2d 734 (Fla. 3d

DCA 1967). Moreover, alimony awards have been upheld where the spouse seeking alimony possessed assets comparable to that of the husband in this case. *Harrison v. Harrison,* 314 So.2d 812 (Fla. 3d DCA 1975).

The wife throughout these proceedings has attacked the husband's life style as parasitic and has warned that he should not be able to parlay such an existence into a $120,000 alimony award. The same criticism could be made of a good many wives who upon dissolution of a tragically flawed marriage have received alimony awards. We pass no judgment on the morality or social value of the marriage herein. Many Americans might very well regard the conduct of either party to this marriage with some cynicism. The work ethic is, after all, deeply ingrained in our mores. But we must take the marriage as we find it without passing judgment on the life style of either party. In a free society, there is room enough for many kinds of marriages, including this one. If and when such a marriage dissolves, it must be accorded equal treatment according to the standards for determining alimony set for all marriage dissolutions.

Moreover, the limited nature of the alimony awards herein should allay any fears that it will encourage any type of parasitic conduct. The husband has hardly been given a meal ticket for life; he has been given a temporary and limited assist to rehabilitate himself to a position of eventual self-support based on a demonstrated need. In this, we can find no abuse of discretion.

Turning now to the husband's cross appeal, we are not persuaded that the husband's demonstrated needs are so great that the trial court abused its discretion in refusing to make the alimony award permanent rather than rehabilitative and in refusing to award a greater lump sum alimony. As the wife accurately points out, the husband is a relatively young, well-educated man of 37, has excellent physical health although temporarily impaired mental health, has $200,000 in assets of his own, has some employment skills if only limited ones, and lives alone without custody of the parties' two children. We can see no reason why he could not properly rehabilitate himself within eighteen months with the alimony awarded herein. See: *Cann v. Cann,* 334 So.2d 325 (Fla. 1st DCA 1976). In the event that substantial rehabilitation does not occur by the end of eighteen months despite the husband's reasonable and diligent efforts, the husband can petition the court for modification of the alimony award. Section 61.14 Florida Statutes (1975); *Lee v. Lee,* 309 So.2d 26 (Fla. 2d DCA 1975).

The second question presented for review is whether it is an abuse of discretion in a dissolution of marriage action for a trial judge a set a $30,000 attorneys fee to be paid by the wife for the husband's attorneys where: (1) the wife has a net worth of $4,250,000; (2) the husband has a net worth of $200,000; (3) the husband's attorneys secure lump sum and rehabilitative alimony for the husband worth $120,000; (4) the husband's attorneys are eminent counsel who spent one hundred working hours plus twenty more hours of associate and law clerk time preparing for a unique, but not protracted or unduly complex litigation; and (5) the expert testimony puts a reasonable attorneys fee at $30,000.

The wife contends that she should not be required to pay the fee and that in any event, the fee was excessive. We reject these contentions and hold that the award of attorneys fees was well within the discretion of the trial judge to set under the circumstances of this case.

Affirmed.

Comments

Watts, Danielson, and *Pfohl* all deal with the changed position of men in marriage and the family. The excessive rights of married men under common law were accompanied by excessive imposition of legal burdens. For example, since the husband acquired the property of his wife at marriage, it followed that he had an absolute duty to support her, as she had no property left to contribute to the costs of the marriage. Under these rules, formulated in England, it would have been considered illogical that a wife could ever be obligated to support her husband or herself. A case like *Pfohl* would have been a factual and legal impossibility. Absolute divorce was not available then, and even if there had been a divorce from bed and board, the husband, who retained control over the marital assets, would have been exclusively responsible for support. In reality the dichotomy between rights and duties of the husband proved to be artificial, because what appeared to be his rights were inseparable from the responsibilities flowing from his status within the family.

His position as the father of his children was governed by somewhat different perceptions. He was historically perceived to have all the rights and duties toward them, but nineteenth century English legislation established the rights of mothers to custody.* Thus, as far as children were concerned, the father lost many of his rights but ordinarily continued to be burdened with the duty to support his children as well as his wife.

In America, while women acquired more and more rights because their dependent position was increasingly understood to be socially undesirable, the duties of husbands and fathers remained relatively unchanged. Men were primarily responsible for the burdens of marriage while at the same time they lost much of their preferred status. In the public mind too, and in the minds of elected state court judges, men were still expected to live up to their responsibilities. Not inconsequentially, society was and still is inclined to grant them higher wages, with the implicit understanding that the bonus will be applied to the care of dependents. We thus face an irregular legal situation in which married men, having lost their absolute rights, are burdened with severe disabilities within the family. At the same time women continue to be subjected to discrimination in the labor market. The issue of women's liberation is complemented, as stated in *Danielson,* by an issue of men's liberation that is of equal weight but less visible.

The Equal Rights Amendment proposed in the 1970s provided that "Equality of Rights under the law shall not be denied or abridged by the United States or by any State on account of sex." Such a legal statement would provide a vehicle for removing the disabilities of both men and women. Some of the opposition against adoption of the ERA originated from the traditional feeling that men ought to be

---

*2 and 3 Vict., c. 54 in 1839 and 36 & 37 Vict., c. 12 in 1873.

made to live up to their responsibilities. However, it is an economic reality that they can do so more effectively if they retain their favored position for higher earnings and better career opportunities than those considered socially desirable for women. As job opportunities for women improve, however, the social climate will slowly change in favor of also giving men more equal rights. This will mean fewer burdens for men resulting from marriage and more rights for them in questions of child custody. Obviously this process, which is reflected in *Watts, Danielson,* and *Pfohl,* will cause substantial and prolonged strain because it runs counter to traditional roles of men and women and to traditional perspectives on marriage, the family, and social institutions. The hostile attitude of the defendant Board of Education in *Danielson* against the argument of the husband and father requesting "maternity leave" is symptomatic. It is not accidental that the opinion in *Watts* was written by a female judge. The strong language disfavoring the presumption benefiting the mother would not have been likely to emerge had the judge been a man; a male judge might have feared that his motives would be found suspect.

The language in *Watts* referring the the best interest of the child obscures more than it enlightens. It has strong emotional appeal, but in fact invites decisions according to prevailing social stereotypes of sex roles. This is a fact borne out by the situation in Florida. In spite of the statutory provision that the father shall be given the same consideration as the mother in determining custody, the trial courts, at least until July 1, 1982 when new legislation went into effect, have continued to grant custody to the mother in the overwhelming number of cases. The statutory invocation of "the best interest of the child," combined with the request that "all relevant factors" must be considered, effectively resulted in a continuation of the judicial preference for mothers.* The interpretation given by the New York court in *Watts* to this provision did not correspond to Florida practice. This is only one illustration of the inclination of the courts in common law jurisdictions to continue established judicial patterns regardless of legislative efforts to bring about change. Even *Pfohl,* granting substantial rehabilitative alimony to the husband, is in fact not as progressive a decision as it appears to be. Had the husband been a multimillionaire instead of the wife, with other facts reversed, namely, the wife being unemployable because of a mental disorder requiring professional treatment, there can be little doubt that the court would have granted her substantially higher alimony payments, perhaps of a permanent nature, than were granted in this case to the husband. In other words, although the trend is toward greater equality of the spouses, even the more advanced decisions often fall short of that goal.

---

*See Fla. Stat. §61.13(2)(b) (1981).

Orr v. Orr
United States Supreme Court
440 U.S. 268 (1979)

MR. JUSTICE BRENNAN delivered the opinion of the Court.

The question presented is the constitutionality of Alabama alimony statutes which provide that husbands, but not wives, may be required to pay alimony upon divorce.[1]

On February 26, 1974, a final decree of divorce was entered, dissolving the marriage of William and Lillian Orr. That decree directed appellant, Mr. Orr, to pay appellee, Mrs. Orr, $1,240 per month in alimony. On July 28, 1976, Mrs. Orr initiated a contempt proceeding in the Circuit Court of Lee County, Ala., alleging that Mr. Orr was in arrears in his alimony payments. On August 19, 1976, at the hearing on Mrs. Orr's petition, Mr. Orr submitted in his defense a motion requesting that Alabama's alimony statutes be declared unconstitutional because they authorize courts to place an obligation of alimony upon husbands but never upon wives. The Circuit Court denied Mr. Orr's motion and entered judgment against him for $5,524, covering back alimony and attorney fees. Relying solely upon his federal constitutional claim, Mr. Orr appealed the judgment. On March 16, 1977, the Court of Civil Appeals of Alabama sustained the constitutionality of the Alabama statutes, 351 So.2d 904 (1977). On May 24, the Supreme Court of Alabama granted Mr. Orr's petition for a writ of certiorari, but on November 10, without court opinion, quashed the writ as improvidently granted. 351 So.2d 906 (1977). We noted probable jurisdiction. 436 U.S. 924 (1978). We now hold the challenged Alabama statutes unconstitutional and reverse.

* * *

II

In authorizing the imposition of alimony obligations on husbands, but not on wives, the Alabama statutory scheme "provides that different treatment be accorded * * * on the basis of * * * sex; it thus establishes a classification subject to scrutiny under the Equal Protection Clause," *Reed v. Reed*, 404 U.S. 71, 75 (1971). The fact that the classification expressly discriminates against men rather than women does not protect it from scrutiny. *Craig v. Boren*, 429 U.S. 190 (1976). "To withstand scrutiny" under the equal protection clause, " 'classifications by gender must serve important governmental objectives and must be substantially related to achievement of those ob-

---

[1] The statutes, Ala. Code, Tit. 30, provide that:

"§30-2-51. If the wife has no separate estate or if it be insufficient for her maintenance, the judge, upon granting a divorce, at his discretion, may order to the wife an allowance out of the estate of the husband, taking into consideration the value thereof and the conditions of his family.

"§30-2-52. If the divorce is in favor of the wife for the misconduct of the husband, the judge trying the case shall have the right to make an allowance to the wife out of the husband's estate, or not make her an allowance as the circumstances of the case may justify, and if an allowance is made, it must be as liberal as the estate of the husband will permit, regard being had to the condition of his family and to all the circumstances of the case.

"§30-2-53. If the divorce is in favor of the husband for the misconduct of the wife and if the judge in his discretion deems the wife entitled to an allowance, the allowance must be regulated by the ability of the husband and the nature of the misconduct of the wife."

The Alabama Supreme Court has held that "there is no authority in this state for awarding alimony against the wife in favor of the husband. * * * The statutory scheme is to provide alimony only in favor of the wife." *Davis v. Davis*, 279 Ala. 643, 644, 189 So.2d 158, 160 (1966).

jectives.' " *Califano v. Webster*, 430 U.S. 313, 316-317 (1977). We shall, therefore, examine the three governmental objectives that might arguably be served by Alabama's statutory scheme.

Appellant views the Alabama alimony statutes as effectively announcing the State's preference for an allocation of family responsibilities under which the wife plays a dependent role, and as seeking for their objective the reinforcement of that model among the State's citizens. *Cf. Stern v. Stern,* 165 Conn. 190, 332 A.2d 78 (1973). We agree, as he urges, that prior cases settle that this purpose cannot sustain the statutes.[9] *Stanton v. Stanton,* 421 U.S. 7, 10 (1975), held that the "old notion" that "generally it is the man's primary responsibility to provide a home and its essentials," can no longer justify a statute that discriminates on the basis of gender. "No longer is the female destined solely for the home and the rearing of the family, and only the male for the marketplace and world of ideas," *id.,* at 14–15. See also *Craig v. Boren,* 429 U.S., at 198. If the statute is to survive constitutional attack, therefore, it must be validated on some other basis.

The opinion of the Alabama Court of Civil Appeals suggests other purposes that the statute may serve. Its opinion states that the Alabama statutes were "designed" for "the wife of a broken marriage who needs financial assistance," 351 So.2d, at 905. This may be read as asserting either of two legislative objectives. One is a legislative purpose to provide help for needy spouses, using sex as a proxy for need. The other is a goal of compensating women for past discrimination during marriage, which assertedly has left them unprepared to fend for themselves in the working world following divorce. We concede, of course, that assisting needy spouses is a legitimate and important governmental objective. We have also recognized "[r]eduction of the disparity in economic condition between men and women caused by the long history of discrimination against women * * * as * * * an important governmental objective," *Califano v. Webster,* 430 U.S., at 317. It only remains, therefore, to determine whether the classification at issue here is "substantially related to achievement of those objectives." *Ibid.*[10]

Ordinarily, we would begin the analysis of the "needy spouse" objective by considering whether sex is a sufficiently "accurate proxy," *Craig v. Boren,* 429 U.S., at 204, for dependency to establish that the gender classification rests " 'upon some ground of difference having a fair and substantial relation to the object of the legislation,' " *Reed v. Reed,* 404 U.S., at 76. Similarly, we would initially approach the "compensation" rationale by asking whether women had in fact been significantly discriminated against in the sphere to which the statute applied a sex-based classification, leaving the sexes "*not similarly situated with respect to opportunities*" in that sphere. *Schlesinger v. Ballard,* 419 U.S. 498, 508 (1975). Compare *Califano v. Webster,* 430 U.S.,

---

[9] Appellee attempts to buttress the importance of this objective by arguing that while "[t]he common law stripped the married woman of many of her rights and most of her property, * * * it attempted to partially compensate by giving her the assurance that she would be supported by her husband." Br. for Appellee 11–12. This argument, that the "support obligation was imposed by the common law to compensate the wife for the discrimination she suffered at the hands of the common law," *id.,* at 11, reveals its own weakness. At most it establishes that the alimony statutes were part and parcel of a larger statutory scheme which invidiously discriminated against women, removing them from the world of work and property and "compensating" them by making their designated place "secure." This would be reason to invalidate the entire discriminatory scheme—not a reason to uphold its separate invidious parts. But appellee's argument is even weaker when applied to the facts of this case, as Alabama has long ago removed, by statute, the elements of the common law appellee points to as justifying further discrimination. See Ala. Const., Art. 10, §209 (married women's property rights).

[10] Of course, if upon examination it becomes clear that there is no substantial relationship between the statutes and their purported objectives, this may well indicate that these objectives were not the statutes' goals in the first place. See Ely, *The Centrality and Limits of Motivation Analysis,* 15 SAN DIEGO L. REV. 1155 (1978).

at 318, and *Kahn v. Shevin*, 416 U.S. 351, 353 (1974), with *Weinberger v. Wiesenfeld*, 420 U.S. 636, 648 (1975).[11]

But in this case, even if sex were a reliable proxy for need, and even if the institution of marriage did discriminate against women, these factors still would "not adequately justify the salient features of" Alabama's statutory scheme, *Craig v. Boren*, 429 U.S., at 202. Under the statute, individualized hearings at which the parties' relative financial circumstances are considered *already* occur. See *Russell v. Russell*, 247, Ala. 284, 286, 24 So.2d 124, 126 (1945); *Ortman v. Ortman*, 203 Ala. 167, 82 So. 417 (1919). There is no reason, therefore, to use sex as a proxy for need. Needy males could be helped along with needy females with little if any additional burden on the State. In such circumstances, not even an administrative convenience rationale exists to justify operating by generalization or proxy.[12] Similarly, since individualized hearings can determine which women were in fact discriminated against vis à vis their husbands, as well as which family units defied the stereotype and left the husband dependent on the wife, Alabama's alleged compensatory purpose may be effectuated without placing burdens solely on husbands. Progress toward fulfilling such a purpose would not be hampered, and it would cost the State nothing more, if it were to treat men and women equally by making alimony burdens independent of sex. "Thus, the gender-based distinction is gratuitous; without it the statutory scheme would only provide benefits to those men who are in fact similarly situated to the women the statute aids," *Weinberger v. Wiesenfeld*, 420 U.S., at 653, and the effort to help those women would not in any way be compromised.

Moreover, use of a gender classification actually produces perverse results in this case. As compared to a gender-neutral law placing alimony obligations on the spouse able to pay, the present Alabama statutes give an advantage only to the financially secure wife whose husband is in need. Although such a wife might have to pay alimony under a gender-neutral statute, the present statutes exempt her from that obligation. Thus, "[t]he [wives] who benefit from the disparate treatment are those who were * * * nondependent on their husbands," *Califano v. Goldfarb*, 430 U.S. 199, 221 (1977) (STEVENS, J., concurring). They are precisely those who are not "needy spouses" and who are "least likely to have been victims of * * * discrimination," *ibid.*, by the institution of marriage. A gender-based classification which, as compared to a gender-neutral one, generates additional benefits only for those it has no reason to prefer cannot survive equal protection scrutiny.

Legislative classifications which distribute benefits and burdens on the basis of gender carry the inherent risk of reinforcing stereotypes about the "proper place" of women and their need for special protection. Cf. *United Jewish Organizations v. Carey*, 430 U.S. 144, 173–174 (1977) (concurring opinion). Thus, even statutes purportedly designed to compensate for and ameliorate the effects of past discrimination must be carefully tailored. Where, as here, the State's compensatory and ameliorative purposes are as

---

[11]We would also consider whether the purportedly compensatory "classifications in fact penalized women," and whether "the statutory structure and its legislative history revealed that the classification was not enacted as compensation for past discrimination." *Califano v. Webster*, 430 U.S. 313, 317 (1977).

[12]It might be argued that Alabama's rule at least relieves the State of the administrative burden of actions by husbands against their wives for alimony. However, when the wife is also seeking alimony, no savings will occur, as a hearing will be required in any event. But even when the wife is willing to forego alimony, it appears that under Alabama law savings will still not accrue, as Alabama courts review the financial circumstances of the parties to a divorce despite the parties' own views—even when settlement is reached. See *Russell v. Russell*, 247 Ala. 284, 24 So.2d 124, 126 (1946). Even were this not true, and some administrative time and effort were conserved, "[t]o give a mandatory preference to members of either sex * * * merely to accomplish the elimination of hearings on the merits, is to make the very kind of arbitrary legislative choice forbidden by the Equal Protection Clause," *Reed v. Reed*, 404, U.S. 71, 76 (1971).

well served by a gender-neutral classification as one that gender-classifies and therefore carries with it the baggage of sexual stereotypes, the State cannot be permitted to classify on the basis of sex. And this is doubly so where the choice made by the State appears to redound—if only indirectly— to the benefit to those without need for special solicitude.

III

Having found Alabama's alimony statutes unconstitutional, we reverse the judgment below and remand the cause for further proceedings not inconsistent with this opinion. That disposition, of course, leaves the state courts free to decide any questions of substantive state law not yet passed upon in this litigation. *Indiana ex rel. Anderson v. Brand*, 303 U.S., at 109; C. Wright, FEDERAL COURTS, at 544. See *South Dakota v. Opperman*, 428 U.S. 364, 396 (1976) (MARSHALL, J., dissenting); *United Air Lines, Inc. v. Mahin*, 410 U.S., at 632; *California v. Green*, 399 U.S. 149, 169–170 (1970); *Schuylkill Trust Co. v. Pennsylvania*, 302 U.S. 506, 512 (1938); *Georgia Ry. & Elec. Co. v. Decatur*, 297 U.S. 620, 623–624 (1936). Therefore, it is open to the Alabama courts on remand to consider whether Mr. Orr's stipulated agreement to pay alimony, or other grounds of gender-neutral state law, bind him to continue his alimony payments.

Reversed.

Interspousal Immunity

Klein v. Klein

Supreme Court of California

58 Cal.2d 692, 26 Cal. Rptr. 102, 376 P.2d 70 (1962)

PETERS, J.

This case involves the rule of interspousal immunity for personal torts. In this respect it is similar to *Self v. Self*, Cal. App., 20 Cal. Rptr. 781. The instant case, however, unlike the *Self* case, involves a negligent tort rather than an intentional one. We are of the opinion that insofar as interspousal liability for tort is concerned there is no logical or legal reason for drawing a distinction between the two, and that for that reason, the rule announced in *Self v. Self, supra*, is here controlling.

In the instant case, Thelma Klein filed her complaint against Joseph Klein on January 5, 1962. The complaint contains two causes of action. The first alleges that for some time prior to April 15, 1961, defendant owned and possessed a certain pleasure boat; that on April 15, 1961, plaintiff and defendant were married; that plaintiff has no right, title or interest in the pleasure boat; that on July 8, 1961, defendant invited plaintiff on the boat for a fishing trip; that after the trip was completed and the boat moored, plaintiff commenced to clean the exterior of the pleasure boat with the approval and consent of defendant; that defendant knew that the exterior deck of the boat was covered with a covering that when wet became so slippery and slick that it was difficult to maintain footing thereon; that in cleaning the pleasure boat it was necessary for plaintiff to use the exterior deck; that defendant knew that this was so; that prior to plaintiff walking on the exterior deck, defendant with full knowledge that plaintiff would have to use that deck, and contrary to his former practices and customs, did so negligently, carelessly and recklessly cause water to be placed on certain parts of the boat so that water ran down over the exterior deck so that it was not safe to walk on; that plaintiff while walking on the deck fell and broke her leg as a proximate result of the defendant's negligence.

The second cause of action is predicated upon the same facts as the first except that it is alleged that defendant, knowing plaintiff would walk upon the deck in question, failed to warn her of the slippery and unsafe condition of which he had knowledge.

The defendant demurred to this complaint on several grounds, among which was the alleged incapacity of the plaintiff to sue defendant because of the marital status of the parties. The demurrer was sustained without leave to amend on the ground that one spouse may not sue the other in California for a personal tort. Judgment was entered in favor of defendant and the plaintiff has appealed.

In *Self v. Self, supra,* Cal. App., 20 Cal. Rptr. 781, it was held that because the reasons for the rule of interspousal immunity for torts no longer exists, and because of certain legislative changes in recent years, that rule should be abandoned.

Respondent contends that even if the rule of *Peters v. Peters,* 156 Cal. 32, 103 P. 219, 23 L.R.A., N.S., 699, is to be abandoned as to intentional torts, it should be retained as to negligent torts. It is argued that to permit tort actions based on negligence to be maintained between spouses will cause the courts to be inundated with trifling suits, will tend to destroy conjugal harmony, and, because of the possibility of insurance, will encourage collusion, fraud and perjury. These arguments are not convincing. Similar arguments were advanced in the *Self* case as reasons for maintaining the old rule as to intentional torts and such arguments were there found not to be convincing. They are not any more convincing here. It is our opinion that the logical and legal reasons set forth in the *Self* case that cause us to abandon the old rule as to intentional torts apply with equal force to negligent torts.

* * *

The argument about inundating the courts with trifling suits is palpably unsound. We have not been informed that such result has followed in any of the 18 states that have repudiated the old rule. In response to this same argument, in *Spellens v. Spellens,* 49 Cal.2d 210, 317 P.2d 613, Justice Schauer, in his concurring and dissenting opinion, at page 241, at page 632 of 317 P.2d, stated: "The court should not decline to entertain a meritorious action against a spouse * * * because of the dubious apprehension that in some future case trifling domestic difficulties may become the subject of litigation." That is a sound argument.

The contention that there may be insurance involved, and that to permit such actions in such cases will encourage collusion, fraud and perjury, is also not convincing. Such arguments should be advanced to the Legislature, and not to the courts. Where such a danger is made clear to the Legislature it has not been slow to act.[1]

It is, of course, fundamental in the law of torts that any person proximately injured by the act of another, whether that act be willful or negligent, should, in the absence of statute or compelling reasons of public policy, be compensated. The possibility of fraud or perjury exists to some degree in all cases. But we do not deny a cause of action to a party because of such a danger. There is no contention that any collusion is involved in the present

---

[1] Thus the Legislature enacted the guest law, now section 17158, Vehicle Code, abolishing causes of action by guests in an automobile against the host for simple negligence, but retaining such an action based on the intoxication or willful misconduct of the host.

case. When, as and if that issue does arise in future cases the courts are equipped to meet it. As was said in *Emery v. Emery*, 45 Cal.2d 421, 289 P.2d 218, a case that held that an unemancipated minor could sue his minor brother or sister and parent for an intentional tort (pp. 431–432, 289 P.2d pp. 224–225):

> "Defendants' second argument, that tort actions between minor brothers and sisters will encourage fraud and collusion, is based on assumptions opposite from those on which their first argument is based. This argument assumes that the action is not in reality directed against the minor brother or sister of the plaintiff, but is in fact directed at his liability insurer. If this assumption is correct, maintenance of such a tort action would not disturb the family peace and harmony; on the contrary, the 'domestic harmony will not be disrupted so much by allowing the action as by denying it.' (PROSSER ON TORTS [2d ed.] 677.) Moreover, although defendants' statement that the existence of insurance, of which there is no evidence in the present case, 'gives no cause of action where one did not exist before' is correct, by the same token the mere possibility of fraud or collusion because of the possible existence of liability insurance does not warrant immunity from liability where it would otherwise exist. The interest of the child in freedom from personal injury caused by the tortious conduct of others is sufficient to outweigh any danger of fraud or collusion. As the Supreme Court of Washington said in reply to the same argument in a case involving an analogous situation [action by a child to recover for injuries caused by its parent's negligent operation of a truck for business purposes], 'The courts may and should take cognizance of fraud and collusion when found to exist in a particular case. However, the fact that there may be greater opportunity for fraud or collusion in one class of cases than another does not warrant courts of law in closing the door to all cases of that class. Courts must depend upon the efficacy of the judicial processes to ferret out the meritorious from the fraudulent in particular cases. *Rozell v. Rozell, supra* [281 N.Y. 106, 22 N.E.2d 254, 123 A.L.R. 1015]. If those processes prove inadequate, the problem becomes one for the Legislature. * * * Courts will not immunize tortfeasors from liability in a whole class of cases because of the possibility of fraud, but will depend upon the legislature to deal with the problem as a question of public policy.' *Borst v. Borst, supra*, 41 Wash.2d 642, 653–654, 251 P.2d 149, 155."

This is a complete answer to the contentions of respondent. It would be a sad commentary on the law if we were to admit that the judicial processes are so ineffective that we must deny relief to a person otherwise entitled simply because in some future case a litigant may be guilty of fraud or collusion. Once that concept were accepted, then all causes of action should be abolished. Our legal system is not that ineffectual.

It is true that in some respects the law has drawn a distinction between intentional and negligent torts. It has been held in California that a child may sue his parent for an intentional tort, contrary to the common law rule, but may not sue him for a negligent tort. (*Emery v. Emery, supra*, 45 Cal.2d 421, 289 P.2d 218 (a case involving an intentional tort); *Trudell v. Leatherby*, 212 Cal. 678, 300 P. 7 (a case denying to a minor any recovery against a defendant who was standing in the position of one *in loco parentis*); *Gillett v. Gillett*, 168 Cal. App.2d 102, 335 P.2d 736 (a case involving an intentional tort); *Perkins v. Robertson*, 140 Cal. App.2d 536, 295 P.2d 972 (a case involving both an intentional and negligent tort).)

But, because these cases have made a distinction between the two types of tort in the parent-child relationship, there is no logical basis for extending the distinction to the husband-wife relationship. As already pointed out, as to such relationship, the doctrines of identity of the persons, and of maintenance of the sanctity of the home, are no longer applicable. This being so, and there being no other argument to the contrary that is convincing, we are of the view that the rule of *Self v. Self, supra*, is here applicable.

Judgment reversed.

SCHAUER, J. (dissenting).

While I concur in the adoption of the rule of interspousal liability for intentional torts to the person announced in *Self v. Self*, Cal., 26 Cal. Rptr. 97, 376 P.2d 65, I believe it ill-advised for this court to undertake to extend that rule to interspousal liability for simple negligence. Inherent in every assertion of the latter liability are opportunities and incentives for—and hence probabilities of—collusion and fraud far more real than those involved in claims based on intentional torts. For this among other reasons, if the proposed extension is to become law it should be so declared by the Legislature after proper study of the problem and formulation of such specific rules as may be found necessary to protect all parties. [Citations omitted.]

* * *

Indeed, judicial interference in this sensitive area of substantive law may well have the opposite effect: e.g., within a few months after the Supreme Court of Illinois judicially abrogated in that state the common law rule of interspousal immunity in an action based on "wilful and wanton" conduct resulting in an automobile accident (*Brandt v. Keller* (1953) 413 Ill. 503, 109 N.E.2d 729) the Illinois Legislature reinstated the immunity rule as to all personal torts between spouses, enacting that "neither husband nor wife may sue the other for a tort to the person committed during coverture." (Ill. Rev. Stats. 1953, ch. 68, §1; see *Hindman v. Holmes* (1955, 4 Ill. App.2d 279) 124 N.E.2d 344, 345.) * * *

* * *

The distinction in this regard between intentional torts and negligent torts is a valid one, grounded on hard facts. Accident liability policies do not ordinarily insure against intentionally inflicted injuries, and hence the incentives for trumped up actions against insurers based on intentional tort are few or non-existent. But negligent injuries offer a fertile field for conjugal collusion and fraud. The wife—to take as example the suspiciously frequent case—is shaken up in an automobile accident caused by the husband's inattentive driving. Perhaps, on reflection, she discovers symptoms of a whiplash injury. An action for damages is brought nominally against the husband who, being insured, stands only to gain by losing and hence willingly plays the role of defendant. The resultant judgment for the "plaintiff" wife is collected from the "defendant" husband's insurer, and provides a tidy sum which both spouses may then enjoy as the fruits of conjugal cooperation. Or, conversely, the husband sues the wife for injuries allegedly caused when he slipped on a highly polished kitchen floor, tripped over the wife's mop, or suffered a similar household mishap. The variations on this theme are limited only by the ingenuity of the parties and the patience of the insurance company.

* * *

For the reasons stated I would affirm the judgment.

Comments

Klein represents the trend toward abolishing the vestiges of marital immunity by judicial decree. State legislatures are traditionally reluctant to change the law in this area, partly because of an effective insurance lobby; the common law disabilities of married women in

bringing actions for damages against their husbands have therefore
continued, except where the courts have intervened. Marital immunity illustrates the persistence of common law theories of marriage
which, although based on religious dogma and the economic needs of
feudal times, sometimes resurface in modern times, changed in appearance but with similar legal effects.

One of these ancient conceptions was the ideal of marital unity,
based on the legal fiction that husband and wife are one. This theory
rendered a lawsuit by the wife against the husband based on tort or
contract inconceivable; and in the earlier days of the law's evolution,
common law judges had no opportunity to think about the problem
resulting from this fact. Strictly speaking, neither issues of marital
immunity nor questions of policy were involved. The disability of the
wife resulted from the nature of marriage and from logic and reason as
they were then perceived.

The passage of married women's property acts brought about
new legal fictions, such as treating married women in regard to their
separate property as if they were unmarried. The first such statute,
passed in 1839 in Mississippi, applied only to white women, and was
probably meant to remove their disabilities in the exercise of ownership of slaves. Although the policies behind these statutes broadened
as they spread across the country, judges tended to interpret them
strictly because they viewed them as being in derogation of common
law. Thus tort actions by a wife against her husband were not covered
because they related not to property but to choses in action, while
marital immunity was invoked to prevent a wife from suing her husband, even though she could sue outsiders. When the concept of immunity lost its persuasive power, social policies such as the maintenance of marital peace or, as expressed in *Klein*, conjugal harmony
and the sanctity of the home rose to the fore and led to the same
results.

Closer examination of these social policies reveals that they
hardly convey a true picture. The lawyer for the defendant husband,
who raised these arguments by way of demurrer or motion to dismiss,
was in fact representing the interests of an insurance company that
would have to pay if the plaintiff wife were to prevail against her husband. Insurance contracts contained clauses that the insured had to
collaborate with the lawyer furnished by the company in case of a
claim. Although the interests of the husband and the insurance company would often appear to conflict, defense lawyers were permitted
to argue the virtues of marital peace for the ulterior purpose of avoiding liability on the insurance policy.

Compared to this legal situation, the latest arguments for preserving the disabilities of married women are bluntly to the point and
coincide with the views expressed in the dissenting opinion in *Klein*.
According to this view, lawsuits by wives against husbands encourage collusion, perjury, and fraud to the detriment of insurance companies. Of course, this issue is not likely to arise in the case of inten-

tional torts by a husband against his wife. Thus, this argument, like that of the insurance lawyer representing the husband in *Klein*, emphasizes the analytical distinction between intentional and negligent torts. There remains the power of insurance companies to exclude liability in case of injury to a spouse or other specified members of the family. Whether such clauses are valid depends on one's views on freedom of contract and contracts of adhesion.

The lesson to be learned is that legal concepts sometimes acquire a life of their own that enables them to persevere in spite of drastic changes in social conditions and underlying policies. Indeed, they sometimes appear to be independent even of the logic or rationality of any given period of time. Of course, the chain of events depicted here does not mean that older notions, such as unity of husband and wife, marital immunity, the maintenance of marital peace, and the prevention of fraud and collusion to the detriment of insurers, are necessarily ineffective. All of them are to some extent still viable and can be argued by lawyers in appropriate cases, depending on whom they are representing. The courts, especially on the trial level, may still give them some weight. Since the vast majority of all accident cases result in a negotiated settlement, all the theories on marital disabilities are also viable within the context of negotiations. In other words, in their pretrial negotiations lawyers are still likely to argue those legal theories that might persuade a conservative trial judge, even if those theories may not succeed in the relatively rare appeals in matters of this kind.

The picture that emerges is complex. That the law on the books differs from the law in action is no surprise. Less obvious is that the law in action has several levels. In *Klein*, for example, the trial court adhered to the notion that a spouse cannot sue the other for a personal tort. On the appellate level a more progressive court permitted such an action. Yet a lawyer would be ill-advised to overlook the attitudes of the lower courts. Even after *Klein*, in settlement negotiations defense lawyers are likely to argue the view of marriage espoused by the lower court and by the dissenting judge on appeal, while plaintiff lawyers can counter with reference to the Supreme Court of California.

References

Ashdown, *Intra-family, Pure Compensation, and the Family Exclusion Clause*, 60 Iowa L. Rev. 239 (1974).

Note, *Husband and Wife—Memorandum on the Mississippi Women's Law of 1839*, 42 Mich. L. Rev. 1110 (1944).

Note, *Litigation Between Husband and Wife*, 79 Harv. L. Rev. 1650 (1966).

Interference in Marriage

Gates v. Foley

Supreme Court of Florida

247 So.2d 40 (Fla. 1971)

ADKINS, J.

* * *

Plaintiff, Hilda I. Gates, sued the Defendant, alleging that the Defendant negligently operated his automobile causing a collision with an automobile operated by the husband of Plaintiff. It is further alleged that as a result of the accident Plaintiff's husband was rendered totally disabled and the Plaintiff claimed damages for "the loss of consortium and other services from her said husband."

In other words, a wife is suing for damages for loss of consortium as a result of injuries to her husband proximately caused by the negligence of the Defendant which rendered the husband totally disabled.

A motion to dismiss the complaint was granted on the ground that it failed to state a cause of action. Plaintiff appealed from the final judgment of dismissal. The District Court of Appeal affirmed the judgment.

At common law the wife could not maintain such an action. In 1950 the United States District Court of Appeal for the District of Columbia decided *Hitaffer v. Argonne Company*, 87 U.S. App. D.C. 57, 183 F.2d 811, 23 A.L.R.2d 1366, *cert. den.*, 340 U.S. 852, 71 S. Ct. 80, 95 L.Ed. 624, in which the Court updated the common law of the District of Columbia by acknowledging a cause of action in the wife for loss of consortium.

This court, in *Ripley v. Ewell*, 61 So.2d 420 (Fla. 1952), rejected the reasoning in the *Hitaffer* case and followed the common law doctrine.

* * *

Since *Hitaffer v. Argonne Company, supra*, a flood of authorities in other jurisdictions have overturned the common law rule and, on various grounds, allowed the wife to recover for loss of consortium.

Moreover, the overwhelming legal literature favors the position that the wife should have such a cause of action where the husband does.[2]

* * *

It should be specifically noted that the suit is for "loss of consortium" and not loss of support or earnings which the husband might recover in his own right. We are only concerned with loss of consortium, by which is meant, the companionship and fellowship of husband and wife and the right of each to the company, cooperation and aid of the other in every conjugal relation. Consortium means much more than mere sexual relation and consists, also, of that affection, solace, comfort, companionship, conjugal life, fellowship, soci-

[2] 1 Harper & James, TORTS, §8.9, p. 641–643 (1956); Prosser, TORTS 916–19 (3rd ed. 1964); Holbrook, *The Change in the Meaning of Consortium*, 22 MICH. L. REV. 1 (1923); Lippman, *The Breakdown of Consortium*, 30 COLUM. L. REV. 651, 664–68 (1930); Simone, *The Wife's Action for Loss of Consortium—Progress or No?*, 4 ST. LOUIS U.L.J. 424 (1957); Kinnird, *Right of Wife to Sue for Loss of Consortium Due to Negligent Injury to Her Husband*, 35 KY. L.J. 220, 223 (1946); Foster, *Relational Interests of the Family* , 1962, U. ILL. L.F. 403, 525–27 (1962); Note, *Judicial Treatment of Negligent Invasion of Consortium*, 61 COLUM. L. REV. 1341, 1352–57 (1961); Friedman, *Consortium as an "Interest" in the Law of Torts*, 32 CAN. B. REV. 1065 (1954); Brett, *Consortium and Servitium, A History and Some Proposals* (Pts. 1–3, 20 AUSTL. L.J. 321, 389, 428 (1955); 64 HARV. L. REV. 672 (1951); 39 CORNELL L.Q. 761 (1954); 39 MICH. L. REV. 820 (1941); 55 MICH. L. REV. 721 (1957); 1 U.C.L.A. L. REV. 223 (1954); 20 FORDHAM L. REV. 342 (1951); 41 GEO. L.J. 443 (1953); 86 A.L.R.2d 1184 (1980); 23 A.L.R.2d 1366 (1950).

ety and assistance so necessary to a successful marriage. *Lithgow v. Hamilton*, 69 So.2d 776 (Fla. 1954).

As discussed in *Ripley v. Ewell, supra*, Fla. Stat. §2.01, F.S.A., adopts the common law of England. The Court recognized the principle that if the inability of the wife to recover in a case of this kind is due to some reason of the common law which has disappeared, the rule denying her the right to maintain the action may have disappeared with it. This principle is a part of the common law which was adopted by the Florida Statute.

The law is not static. It must keep pace with changes in our society, for the doctrine of stare decisis is not an iron mold which can never be changed. Holmes, in his *The Common Law* (1881), p. 5, recognizes this in the following language:

> "The customs, beliefs, or needs of a primitive time establish a rule or a formula. In the course of centuries the customs, belief, or necessity disappear, but the rule remains. The reason which gave rise to the rule has been forgotten, and ingenious minds set themselves to inquire how it is to be accounted for. Some ground of policy is thought of, which seems to explain it and to reconcile it with the present state of things; and then the rule adapts itself to the new reasons which have been found for it, and centers on a new career. The old form receives a new content, and in time even the form modifies itself to fit the meaning which it has received."

It may be argued that any change in this rule should come from the Legislature. No recitation of authority is needed to indicate that this Court has not been backward in overturning unsound precedent in the area of tort law. Legislative action could, of course, be taken, but we abdicate our own function, in a field peculiarly nonstatutory, when we refuse to reconsider an old and unsatisfactory court-made rule.

* * *

The recent changes in the legal and societal status of women in our society forces us to recognize a change in the doctrine with which this opinion is concerned. The Florida Constitution (1968) contained the following significant clauses:

> "All natural persons are equal before the law." Article 1, Section 2.

> "No person shall be deprived of life, liberty or property without due process of law." Article 1, Section 9.

> "The courts shall be open to every person for redress of any injury and justice shall be administered without sale, denial or delay." Article 1, Section 21.

> "There shall be no distinction between married women and married men in the holding, control, disposition, or encumbering of their property, both real and personal." Article 10, Section 5.

Prior to the 1968 revision, the Florida Constitution always contained a provision that *all men* are equal before the law (Fla. Const., Declaration of Rights, §1 (1885)); and that every person could have a remedy for injury done *him* by due course of law (Fla. Const., Declaration of Rights, §4 (1885)).

The Florida Legislature has enacted the married woman's property act (Fla. Stat., Ch. 708, F.S.A.), and the United States Congress has passed the Civil Rights Act (U.S.C.A. Title 42, Ch. 21). Discrimination on the basis of sex has been proscribed by the United States Congress. U.S. Code Title 42, §2000c *et seq*.

So it is that the unity concept of marriage has in a large part given way to the partner concept whereby a married woman stands as an equal to her husband in the eyes of the law. By giving the wife a separate equal existence, the law created a new interest in the wife which should not be left unprotected by the courts. Medieval concepts which have no justification in our present society should be rejected. We therefore hold that deprivation to the wife of the husband's companionship, affection and sexual relation (or consortium, as above defined) constitutes a real injury to the marital relationship and one which should be compensable at law if due to the negligence of another.

A husband, of course, has a cause of action for loss of consortium of his wife when she suffers personal injury through the negligence of another, *Busby v. Winn & Lovett Miami, Inc.*, 80 So.2d 675 (Fla. 1955). No reasonable suggestion can be offered any longer to explain the disparity in the spouses' relative rights to secure damages for loss of consortium. No reasonable distinctions may be made between the wife's claim for negligent impairment of consortium and a similar claim by her husband. As consortium is defined above, the interests of the husband and wife are the same and it necessarily follows that negligent impairment of those interests by an outsider ought to have the same legal consequences.

* * *

The intangible segments of the elements comprising a cause of action for loss of consortium are equally precious to both husband and wife. The classification by sex formerly made by this Court discriminates unreasonably and arbitrarily against women and must be abolished. We recede from *Riley v. Ewell, supra.*

There are practical difficulties in allowing a consortium action, especially with respect to retrospective application. The problem has not troubled other courts seriously and may be easily resolved. Where there is a cause of action brought by the injured husband pending, the wife's consortium action, if not time barred, may be joined with her husband's claim, or, if separate suit has been filed, consolidated for the purpose of trial. The Defendant has the right to request joinder of the wife as a proper party to an action brought by her husband, if she has not filed suit in her own behalf. Where the husband's cause of action has been terminated by adverse judgment on the merits, this should bar the wife's cause of action for consortium.

The rule that we now recognize is that the wife of a husband injured as a proximate result of the negligence of another shall have a right of action against that same person for her loss of consortium. We further hold that her right of action is a derivative right and she may recover only if her husband has a cause of action against the same defendant. This means that the tortfeasor was negligent and the husband was free from contributory negligence.

In such actions by the wife, the trial court should carefully caution the jury that any loss to the wife of her husband's material support is fully compensated by any award to him for impairment of his lost earning and that the wife is entitled to recover only for loss of consortium as defined in this opinion.

The decision of the District Court of Appeal is quashed and the cause is remanded to that court with instructions to further remand same to the trial court for further proceedings not inconsistent with this opinion.

It is so ordered.

Comments

Gates deals with the question of whether a wife, too, is entitled to an action for loss of consortium based on an injury to her husband by a third person. At common law only the husband was permitted such recovery if his wife were injured. It is not clear whether the disability of the wife was procedural or substantive in nature. She could not have a cause of action in her own name. Perhaps her injury—loss of consortium of her husband—was not perceived to be distinguishable from the injury to the husband. Perhaps, since she had no rights for services and comfort against her husband, she could not claim loss of such rights against a third person who had injured her husband. The husband, of course, could always sue for his own damages as well as for damages to the extent that his wife was injured. In any event, there was concern at a later phase of the law's development that extension of recovery might result in double compensation.

A more realistic picture emerges if we look at the problems from the perspective of attorney strategies. The plaintiff's attorney has a natural interest in having as many causes of action against the wrongdoer as possible. Furthermore, if multiple counts are permissible, recovery is likely to be higher than for a single count. The defendant's attorney, on the other hand, is interested in keeping the causes of action and the counts at the lowest level possible. Thus, the question of whether the husband and wife can sue separately, each on multiple counts, is possibly related not so much to the nature of the marital relationship but to how much protection should be given to the outsider who causes an injury to either spouse. Under contemporary conditions these questions are related to policies sometimes referred to as socialization of risks. Should the parties to a marriage absorb at least part of the risk of injury, or should the risk be distributed, with the aid of insurance companies, to a large group of persons? Equality of spouses has little bearing on this fundamental problem. If equal treatment were the only issue, it would have been possible, for example, to abolish the cause of action for loss of consortium by both the husband and the wife. Yet by not pursuing this solution, an implicit choice was made by the legislature and the courts that preferred wide distribution of the risk of injury to letting the risk fall on the marital unit.

The question of what is to be contained in an action for loss of consortium and how to avoid double recovery of husband and wife is related to the basic problem of allocation of risks. Instead of viewing "consortium" purely as a single item of recovery, the inclination has been, even when the action could be brought only by the husband, to break consortium down into multiple components, each with a separate count of damages. Although sometimes reduced to loss of society, services, and sexual rights, other losses might be added, such as loss of love, companionship, affection, comfort, and solace. Each of these items may enlarge claims of both husband and wife. While the right for services is retained, perhaps in a form of legal fiction, other rights, such as those for sexual relations, may encourage dual recovery for both husband and wife.

Additional complications may arise because some claims can traditionally be raised only by the husband because of his duty to support the wife. Thus, if the wife has medical bills, it would be the duty of the husband to pay them, and he is entitled to demand compensation whether in fact he pays them or not. If the wife inadvertently claims damages that fall under the husband's duty to support, her claim could still be subject to a motion to dismiss. Many jurisdictions, including Florida in *Gates*, also view the cause of action as derivative. Contributory negligence of the husband in causing an accident would therefore negate the wife's recovery. Or, if today comparative negligence of the husband is at issue, it could affect the wife's recovery in the same degree.

An interesting aspect of *Gates* is its value as precedent. It is cited less for its holding than for its dictum. Once the right of married women to recover for loss of consortium is judicially recognized, the need to cite the opinion for this purpose will dissipate. The most durable part of the opinion, and the most frequently cited, is the paragraph proclaiming "that the unity concept of marriage has in large part given way to the partner concept whereby a married woman stands as an equal to her husband in the eyes of the law." *Gates* could, however, become a stepping-stone toward recognition of rights of children for loss of consortium if one or both parents were injured.

Fadgen v. Lenkner

Supreme Court of Pennsylvania

469 Pa. 272, 365 A.2d 147 (1976)

JONES, Chief Justice.

Appellee, James T. Fadgen, brought an action in trespass against appellant, George Lenkner, based upon the theory of criminal conversation. The complaint alleged that appellee and one Bonnie Hoch Fadgen were married in 1972 and that during the period of this marriage, the appellant, without the consent of appellee Fadgen, criminally conversed with Ms. Fadgen.

* * *

This Court last reviewed an action similar to the one presently at bar in 1959. In *Karchner v. Mumie*, 398 Pa. 13, 156 A.2d 537 (1959), the court upheld a jury verdict in favor of the plaintiff-wife based upon the tort of criminal conversation where appellant-defendant had sought reversal on the ground that that cause of action as developed at common law was only available to married men as against an erring spouse's paramour. The Court reasoned that the Married Women's Property Act of June 8, 1893, P.L. 344, *as amended* by the Act of May 17, 1945, P.L. 625, mandated the extension to married women of the right to bring such an action on their own behalf.

It is clear, however, that that first step directed towards fusing the ancient with the "modern" of 1959 was not sufficient revitalization such as to weather the rapid legal and societal changes witnessed over the past fifteen years. We might look back and well appreciate that, absent the benefit of attitudes reflected in the passage of the Equal Rights Amendment, the Court in 1959 nevertheless laudably rejected the fictitious notion that a wife, like a servant, was the personal property (chattel as it were) of the husband and that an action in criminal conversation was a right sacrosanct to none but the master. Still, the Court's extension to married women of the right to bring such a cause of action only delayed what today demands; that is, the total abolition of a pious yet unrighteous cause of action.

* * *

One of several civil actions directed at protecting against intentional interferences with the marital relationship,[4] criminal conversation comes closest in form to a strict liability tort. The cause of action is made out upon plaintiff's proof that while married to plaintiff, plaintiff's spouse and the defendant engaged in at least a single act of sexual intercourse without the consent of plaintiff. [Citations omitted.] There are but two possible complete defenses to the action: one, obviously, is an outright denial by the defendant of having had any such relation with plaintiff's spouse; the other occurs upon proof that the *plaintiff* consented to the adulterous relation. Prosser, LAW OF TORTS, §124, at p. 879 (Fourth Ed. 1971); [citations omitted].

It is no defense to the action, however, that the plaintiff's spouse consented nor in fact that the spouse was the aggressor or seducer. [Citations omitted.] As to the former, it was thought at common law that a wife was not competent to give her consent so as to defeat her husband's interest. *Tinker v. Colwell*, 193 U.S. 473, 483, 24 S. Ct. 505, 48 L.Ed. 754 (1903).[5]

As to the justification for eliminating the defense that the wife initiated and pursued the adulterous relationship, in addition to the belief at common law that she was incapable of prejudicing her husband's rights, the law burdensomely presuming the superiority of men over women chastised:

> "The man who breaks up the home of his neighbor by debauching his wife, rendering his children worse than motherless, is not excused because he is weak, and, being tempted by the woman, falls."

Seiber v. Pettit, 200 Pa. 58 at 67, 49 A.763 (1901).

> "* * * it is but the old cowardly excuse set up by the first man, 'The woman gave me of the tree, and I did eat.' It did not save from the penalty the first defendant, and cannot, under the law, save this one."

Id. at p. 69, 49 A. at 765. [Citations omitted.]
Moreover, a man could not plead ignorance of the marital status of the adulterer: "A man who has sexual relations with a woman, not his wife, assumes the risk that she is married. Even her misrepresentation that she is single affords the offender no defense to liability for criminal conversation. * * *" *Antonelli v. Xenakis, supra*, 363 Pa. at 378, 69 A.2d at 103.

We, of course, in no way condone sexual promiscuity and continue to hold the institution of marriage in the highest regard. However, the reasoning developed at common law behind stripping a defendant of all defenses to an action in criminal conversation, save the plaintiff's consent, no longer merits endorsement.

Damages alleged in an action for criminal conversation are compensatory, covering injury to the plaintiff's social position, disgrace in the community where he or she lives or was in business and dishonor to plaintiff and plaintiff's family. [Citations omitted.] "And, a single act of adultery is sufficient to entitle the husband of the woman to damages in an action against the adulterer for criminal conversation even though the husband sustains no further loss: *Antonelli v. Xenakis, supra*, 363 Pa. at 377, 69 A.2d 102; RESTATEMENT, TORTS, §683, Comment c; §685, Comment b." *DiSanti v. Cassidy, supra*, 63 Pa. D & C 2d at 9. Punitive damages have been held to be appropriate

---

[4] See Note, *The Case for Retention of Causes of Action for Intentional Interference with the Marital Relationship*, 48 NOTRE DAME LAW. 426, 427 (1972), wherein the author posits that statutory and judicial abolition of the tort actions known as "alienation of affections" and "enticement" is uncalled for and unfairly undermines the marriage institution. However, the author shows no like sympathy for criminal conversation. *Id.* at 433–34.

[5] Prosser, citing 8 Holdsworth, HISTORY OF ENGLISH LAW, 2d Edition 1937, 430, provides us with the following choice tidbit: "* * * it was considered that she was no more capable of giving a consent which would prejudice the husband's interests than was his horse." Prosser, *supra*, at 875.

as well. [Citations omitted.] Computations for the type of injury alleged here is always inexact and as Blackstone warned "usually very large and exemplary." This is so not only by virtue of the abstract nature of the injuries alleged but is further exacerbated by the emotion-laden nature of the proceedings. [Citations omitted.]

* * * Prosser succinctly summarizes:

"Those actions for interference with domestic relations which carry an accusation of sexual misbehavior—that is to say, criminal conversation, seduction, and to some extent alienation of affections—have been peculiarly susceptible to abuse. Together with the action for breach of promise to marry, it is notorious that they have afforded a fertile field for blackmail and extortion by means of manufactured suits in which the threat of publicity is used to force a settlement. There is good reason to believe that even genuine actions of this type are brought more frequently than not with purely mercenary or vindictive motives; that it is impossible to compensate for such damage with what has derisively been called 'heart-balm'; that people of any decent instincts do not bring an action which merely adds to the family disgrace; and that no preventive purpose is served, since such torts seldom are committed with deliberate plan."

Prosser, *supra*, at 887 and authorities cited therein.

We in no way intend to infer such motives on the part of the appellee in the instant case by pointing to the potential abuses to which this action is susceptible. However, we believe the cause of action itself is an anachronism and that in today's society it is unreasonable to impose upon a defendant such harsh results without affording any real opportunity to interject logically valid defenses on the merits such as the role of the plaintiff's spouse in the adulterous relationship or the quality of the plaintiff's marriage prior to the occurrence of the acts constituting the tort.

The total abolition of this cause of action is well within the bounds of our judicial powers. In fact, it is our duty to so act with regard to court-made rules where "reason and a right sense of justice recommend it." *Ayala v. Philadelphia Board of Public Education*, 453 Pa. 584, 600, 305 A.2d 877, 885 (1973); * * *

* * * As we said in *Flagiello v. Pennsylvania Hospital*, 417 Pa. 486, 208 A.2d 193 (1965), quoting Justice Cardozo:

" '[W]hen a rule, after it has been duly tested by experience, has been found to be inconsistent with the sense of justice or with the social welfare, there should be less hesitation in frank avowal and full abandonment. * * * There should be greater readiness to abandon an untenable position when the rule to be discarded may not reasonably be supposed to have determined the conduct of the litigants, and *particularly when in its origin it was the product of institutions or conditions which have gained a new significance or development with the progress of the years.*' " (Emphasis added).

Id. at 514, 208 A.2d at 207.

" 'Precedent speaks for the past; policy for the present and the future. The goal which we seek is a blend which takes into account in due proportion the wisdom of the past and the needs of the present.' "

Ayala v. Philadelphia Board of Public Education, supra, 453 Pa. at 603–04, 305 A.2d at 887.

The Order of the court below is vacated and the case remanded for the entry of judgment in favor of the appellant. The civil cause of action based upon the tort of criminal conversation is hereby abolished.

MANDERINO, J. (concurring).

I concur in the result reached by the majority opinion because I believe that result mandated by the decisions of the United States Supreme Court in

Roe v. Wade, 410 U.S. 113, 93 S. Ct. 705, 35 L.Ed.2d 147 (1973), in which the court held that the right of privacy was broad enough to preclude interference by the state in a woman's decision whether or not to terminate her pregnancy, and in *Cleveland Board of Education v. La Fleur*, 414 U.S. 632, 94 S. Ct. 791, 39 L.Ed.2d 52 (1974). In the latter case the court stated its recognition "* * * that freedom of personal choice in matters of marriage and family life is one of the liberties protected by the Due Process Clause of the Fourteenth Amendment." *Id.* at 639, 94 S. Ct. at 796, 39 L.Ed.2d at 60. If a married man or woman chooses to engage in sexual activity with one other than his or her spouse, I believe such a choice is protected by the right to privacy guaranteed by the Constitution and there is no "compelling state interest" involved which would justify the state's limiting the exercise of such rights. * * *

I also comment on the dissenting opinion of Mr. Justice Roberts. By "abolishing" the cause of action for criminal conversation, the majority at last recognizes that one's spouse no longer suffers a compensable injury when the other engages in sexual activity outside the marriage relationship. Such a recognition is long overdue. In fact, I believe that were we to apply Mr. Justice Roberts' three part inquiry the result would be the same: (1) society no longer has any interest in protecting one spouse against extramarital sexual activity by the other; (2) since there is no longer any interest to protect, there has been no invasion of such interest; and (3) no injury has resulted.

* * *

ROBERTS, J. (dissenting).

I dissent. The majority totally abolishes the cause of action for criminal conversation without any statutory or any other authority for doing so other than its own inclinations that the tort is an "anachronism." I cannot agree that the marital relationship—which has been protected in this Commonwealth for more than two centuries—is no longer deserving of the protection of our law.

* * *

The true inquiry here should be: (1) Is there an interest which society should protect? (2) Has there been an invasion of that interest which cannot be excused or justified? (3) Has the invasion produced an injury for which the law can provide a remedy?

The first inquiry has been answered in the affirmative for more than two hundred years. Whether the interest is no longer worthy of protection is a public policy decision only the Legislature should make. Since a legally protected interest exists and an invasion of that interest has been admitted in this case, the trial court should determine whether the invasion can be excused or justified. Likewise, the trial court should determine whether the injury sustained is one for which the court should provide a remedy.

The judgment on that issue of liability should be affirmed and the case remanded to the trial court for a determination of damages.

[Justice Pomeroy's dissenting opinion omitted.]

Comments

The common law action for criminal conversation has been legislatively abolished in a number of states, together with the causes of action for alienation of affection, seduction, and breach of contract to marry. In all instances the legislatures have acted out of concern that the danger of punitive and excessive jury verdicts might lead to extortion. The fact that the legislatures were predominantly male, as were the defendants in such actions, may have been of help. *Fadgen* follows this pattern of abolition; but this time we have a court abolishing a common law action in tort as no longer appropriate to contemporary conditions.

The Equal Protection Clause did not necessarily mandate this result. In fact, an earlier Pennsylvania Supreme Court case, *Karchner v. Mumie*, cited in *Fadgen*, in 1959 extended the cause of action that under common law was available only to men, and permitted married women to recover. Thus equal protection could mean extension to both spouses as well as abolition as to either. In *Fadgen*, however, the majority opinion seemed to recognize an inherent power of the courts to abolish such judge-made law, regardless of precedent, if it "is no longer in accord with modern realities."

The reasoning of Mr. Justice Manderino in his concurring opinion, referring to freedom of choice, privacy, and the liberties protected by the Due Process Clause of the Fourteenth Amendment, accords with contemporary legal theory. The reference to abortion appears to be particularly apt. Although *Fadgen* was argued before the decision of the U.S. Supreme Court was handed down in *Planned Parenthood of Central Missouri v. Danforth* (see pp. 244–250), the two cases appear to have been governed by the same reasoning: If a married woman can have an abortion without consent of the husband, perhaps her freedom of choice and individual privacy also cover choice of sexual partner. *Fadgen* did not actually make such drastic pronouncements; it merely abolished a common law cause of action against an outsider intervening in the marriage. Yet the concurring opinion, in response to the dissenting opinion of Mr. Justice Roberts, seems to say that the rights of privacy of married women (and consequently of married men) prevail over other considerations, and that, since society no longer has an interest in protecting a spouse against extramarital sexual activity by the other, one can no longer speak of any injury that has resulted. Obviously this view of marriage, although a consequence of the reasoning in the abortion decisions, has not yet been accepted by the general public.

A question not addressed in *Fadgen* is whether husband or wife may have remedies other than criminal prosecution and damages for criminal conversation. In light of *Bauman v. Bauman*,* it is unlikely that an injunction against the intervening outsider is possible. While in the past injunctive relief was denied on the ground that no property rights were involved and that conduct which merely injures a person's feelings cannot be restrained, *Fadgen* gave sufficient cues as to contemporary limitations on injunctive relief: the change of conditions in the relations of husband and wife, freedom of choice and rights of privacy of either spouse, and a declining social concern with intimate relations.

An interesting problem arises if husband and wife are viewed as partners in more than one sense—perhaps with respect to a jointly

*250 N.Y. 382, 165 N.E. 819 (1929).

owned and operated business. Interference by an outsider in a business relationship continues to be subject to a cause of action in tort for damages as well as injunctive relief. Traditional legal theory would probably justify this result by arguing that the marital and business interests can be treated separately. In reality, as we have seen in Chapter 2, it becomes increasingly difficult to make such a distinction. The same remedies that have declined within the realm of the family and marriage have survived in business as interference with contract, although both originate from the same historical source—the protection in Roman law of the pater familias from outside interference. It would be interesting to see whether the Supreme Court of Pennsylvania would adhere to the reasoning in *Fadgen* if an outsider were to interfere in a husband-and-wife-operated business by alienating one of the partners.

References

Karst, *The Freedom of Intimate Association*, 89 YALE L.J. 624 (1980).
Prosser. W., TORTS 929–931 (4th ed. 1971).

Bibliography

Clark, H., THE LAW OF DOMESTIC RELATIONS IN THE UNITED STATES chs. 6, 7, & 9 (1968).
Eekelaar, J., & Katz, S., FAMILY VIOLENCE (1978).
Gutman, *Loss of Consortium*, 43 ALB. L. REV. 1 (1978).
Karst, *The Freedom of Intimate Association*, 89 YALE L.J. 624 (1980).
Kay, *Legal and Social Impediments to Dual Career Marriages*, 12 U.C.D. L. REV. 207 (1979).
McCurdy, *Property Torts Between Spouses and Use During Marriage of the Matrimonial Home Owned by the Other*, 2 VILL. L. REV. 447 (1957).
Note, *Alienation of Affections: Flourishing Anachronism*, 13 WAKE FOREST L. REV. 585 (1977).
Note, *The Case for Retention of Causes of Action for Intentional Interference With the Marital Relationship*, 48 NOTRE DAME LAW. 426 (1972).
Note, *Loss of Consortium—Either Spouse Is Entitled to Recover*, 15 SANTA CLARA L. REV. 495 (1975).
Note, *Married Women and the Name Game*, 11 U. RICH. L. REV. 121 (1976).
Note, *The Tort of Criminal Conversation in Nebraska*, 58 NEB. L. REV. 595 (1979).
Note, *Women's Name Rights*, 59 MARQ. L. REV. 876 (1976).
Weitzman, L., THE MARRIAGE CONTRACT—SPOUSES, LOVERS, AND THE LAW (1981).

Divorce as Dissolution of Marital Partnership

"Pure" No-Fault Reasoning and Its Consequences for Distribution of Assets

*Manning v. Manning**

Supreme Court of Georgia

237 Ga. 746, 229 S.E.2d 611 (1976)

PER CURIAM.

This appeal by the wife is from a summary judgment entered in Bibb Superior Court which granted a divorce at the request of the husband on the ground that the marriage was irretrievably broken. The wife opposed the grant of the divorce. She denied the marriage was irretrievably broken and denied that there were no prospects for a reconciliation. The wife sought to have the trial court deny a divorce and also sought a jury trial on this issue. We affirm the grant of the divorce by the trial judge as we find this case is controlled by *Harwell v. Harwell*, 233 Ga. 89, 209 S.E.2d 625 (1974), and *McCoy v. McCoy*, 236 Ga. 633, 225 S.E.2d 682 (1976).

The husband filed an affidavit in support of the motion for summary judgment seeking a divorce. In it, the husband swore, in pertinent part, as follows: "The separation between us is complete and permanent. I am unwilling to live with the defendant [wife] at the present time. I am unwilling, and I refuse, to live with her at any time in the future. There is no possibility whatever of a reconciliation ever taking place between us. The marriage * * * is irretrievably broken."

This affidavit by the husband which was submitted to the trial judge brought the case squarely within the language of *McCoy* that, "Just as it takes two consenting parties to make a contract, it takes two consenting parties to make a reconciliation. Just as one party cannot make a contract, one party cannot make a marriage or a reconciliation thereof." We find no error, as there was no issue for a jury to decide on the question of the divorce.

Judgment affirmed.

ON MOTION FOR REHEARING

Appellant insists in a vigorous motion for rehearing that we have overlooked the provisions of Code Ann. §30–109, and *Williford v. Williford*, 230 Ga. 543, 198 S.E.2d 181 (1973) which, if applied, would require a different judgment in this case. In *Williford*, the husband sought a divorce on the grounds of desertion and cruel treatment by the wife. The wife did not ask for a divorce and sought to have a divorce denied to the husband because of his alleged adultery and cruel treatment.

The majority of this court is of the opinion that the Code section and decision noted above have no application in this no-fault divorce case. The rule urged by appellant and recognized by this court in fault ground divorce cases is that the court (or jury) is authorized to refuse a divorce to the party seeking the divorce when the evidence shows such party is guilty of adultery. Code Ann. §30–109 allows the opposite party to show "the conduct of

---

* [Overruled by *Dickson v. Dickson*, 238 Ga. 672, 235 S.E.2d 479 (1977).]

the party suing" for divorce and *Williford* holds that such evidence authorizes, but does not require, the court (or jury) to refuse a divorce in these circumstances.

These authorities have no application to no-fault divorce cases which this court has held involve only whether "either or both parties are unable or refuse to cohabit and there are no prospects for a reconciliation." *Harwell v. Harwell*, 233 Ga. 89, 91, 209 S.E.2d 625, 627 (1974). In summary, a majority of this court thinks that the traditional rules which have been applied in fault ground divorce cases should not be applied when the divorce is granted on the no-fault ground.

Motion for rehearing denied.

GUNTER, Justice. (concurring specially).

In this case the husband filed a complaint for divorce against his wife; he alleged that their marriage was irretrievably broken; the wife filed responsive pleadings in which she denied the irretrievable brokenness of the marriage; she further affirmatively alleged: "* * * contrary to the allegations of the plaintiff in the complaint, the marriage between the plaintiff and defendant is not irretrievably broken, and further that there are reasonable prospects for a reconciliation between the parties"; by counterclaim the wife sought temporary and permanent alimony for her separate support and maintenance irrespective of whether a divorce was granted; by counterclaim she also sought the vesting of fee simple title in her to the family residence and all furniture and furnishings situated therein; she alleged that she was entitled to be awarded temporary and permanent alimony for her support and maintenance because the parties were living separate and apart, and that the separation was caused by the misconduct of the husband in that he "wilfully and without just cause abandoned defendant against her wishes"; and she further alleged that her entitlement to temporary and permanent alimony was based on the fact that her husband "in the past wilfully and repeatedly inflicted and continues to inflict mental pain and anguish upon defendant such as reasonably justifies defendant's being apprehensive of danger to her life, limb and health."

The husband filed a motion for summary judgment on the sole issue of the irretrievable brokenness of the marriage; he filed a supporting affidavit set forth in part in the court's opinion; the wife filed an opposing affidavit in which she testified that "she personally knows that the marriage between herself and William S. Manning is not irretrievably broken inasmuch as a reconciliation may be possible between deponent and her said husband"; and she concluded her opposing affidavit by testifying that "she desires and is willing to reconcile and continue the marriage between the plaintiff and herself."

The husband contended that on the basis of the pleadings and affidavits he was entitled to a judgment in his favor as a matter of law on the issue of the irretrievable brokenness of the marriage. The wife contended that the issue of irretrievable brokenness was one of fact for determination by a jury, and that it could not be resolved on motion for summary judgment.

The trial judge granted the husband's motion for summary judgment on this sole issue, and he reserved for future determination the issues with respect to alimony and division of property. The wife has appealed, and her sole contention here is that the issue of irretrievable brokenness, a fact issue, was erroneously decided as a matter of law by the trial judge on a motion for summary judgment.

As I read the pleadings and affidavits in this case, there is no issue of fact as to the irretrievable brokenness of this marriage. In *Harwell v. Harwell*, 233 Ga. 89, 209 S.E.2d 625 (1974) this court said: "An 'irretrievably broken' marriage is one where either or both parties are unable or refuse to cohabit and there are no prospects for a reconciliation." P. 91, 209 S.E.2d p. 627.

In *McCoy v. McCoy*, 236 Ga. 633, 225 S.E.2d 682 (1976), this court said:

"In the case before us, we make explicit that which was implicit in *Harwell*, to wit: where one of the parties to a marriage refuses to cohabit with the other and testifies that the marriage is irretrievably broken, the fact that the other party maintains hope for a reconciliation will not support a finding under *Harwell* that there are 'prospects for a reconciliation.' Just as it takes two consenting parties to make a contract, it takes two consenting parties to make a reconciliation. Just as one party cannot make a contract, one party cannot make a marriage or a reconciliation thereof. If the General Assembly had intended that the thirteenth ground for divorce be consensual, it would have provided that 'The parties agree that the marriage is irretrievably broken.' "

P. 634, 225 S.E.2d p. 683.

Under the verified pleadings and the affidavits of record in this case by both parties, there are no real or practical prospects for a reconciliation. Stripped of all conclusions that project a mere glimmer of hope at reconciliation, this record eliminates any fact issue on the subject of irretrievable brokenness, and the trial judge correctly granted summary on this issue.

I therefore concur in the judgment of affirmance.

INGRAM, J. (concurring specially).

I concur in the judgment not because I think it is right but because it is based on case law decided by a majority of this court and I am bound by it. This court now holds that the mere assertion by one of the parties to a marriage that the marriage is irretrievably broken is sufficient not just to authorize, but to require the grant of a divorce.

Obviously, I think the court has gone too far in giving expression to this ground of divorce. Without repeating what I have said in previous dissents in these cases, I feel I must point out that the result in this case classically illustrates how generally beneficent legislation can be distorted beyond all reasonable intendment by judicial construction. Perhaps I am wrong, but I thought the primary purpose behind the addition of the no-fault ground for divorce was to cleanse our divorce law of the hypocrisy we previously indulged in the use of cruel treatment as a ground for divorce by parties who wanted a quiet, decent and friendly termination of their marriage without attacking one another in the process.

In other words, I see the use of the no-fault ground as a good and honest solution for ending a marriage where both parties agree it is finished, and in cases where one of the parties asserts the marriage is over and the other tacitly admits it by failing to contest it. What I find difficult to accept is this court's implicit holding that there can never be any serious judicial inquiry about prospects for reconciliation.[1]

To my mind, this encourages divorce and is inconsistent with the state's traditional, and I think wise, policy of encouraging efforts toward resolution of domestic disputes through reconciliation and continuation of the marriage, particularly where there are children.

I do not believe that anyone could reasonably foresee that the addition of the no fault ground for divorce by the legislature would lead this court to deny a party the opportunity to have this issue presented to a jury in a proper

---

[1] Intellectual candor compels me to note that the present decision by this court seems to fit an existing trend in divorce law. There is evidence of "the diminishing willingness of the state(s) to be involved in the matter of marriage termination" as a corollary to the states' "gradual divestment of its marriage regulation business." *Marriage and The State: The Withering Away of Marriage*, Professor Mary Ann Glendon, VIRGINIA LAW REVIEW, Vol. 62, May, 1976, No. 4, pp. 703–706. Even so, I maintain that this is such a fundamental issue of profound public importance that it should be decided in the General Assembly rather than in this court on a case by case basis.

case. But, it has happened in this case. In effect, this court holds here that where one party says there are no prospects for reconciliation and the other one says there are, the court has no alternative except to grant a divorce. This is too cold and hard for me to accept because the message it conveys is that our society has no interest in preserving marriages, but, on the contrary, encourages one of the parties to end it quickly and officially on the slightest caprice by merely asserting the marriage is irretrievably broken and without ever appearing in court to prove it. I see little difference between this and permitting one of the parties to write "Canceled" on the marriage license and mail it in to the judge of the probate court. If we have come to that, then I think the legislature ought to say so in plain and unmistakable language.

The judgment we have previously required trial judges to use in deciding these cases has been removed from them. I cannot agree this was intended merely by adding the no fault ground, but I concur in the judgment in this case as our decisions require it.

[Justice Hill's dissenting opinion omitted.]

Comments

Manning is included in this book although it was overruled by decision of the Supreme Court of Georgia in *Dickson v. Dickson.** It expresses most clearly a fundamental problem in no-fault divorce, present to various degrees in other jurisdictions: how to interpret a legislative clause that requires proof that a marriage is "irretrievably broken." The standard of interpretation could relate to external factors—determinable by the fact finder according to more or less objective criteria—or it could be purely subjective, that is, entirely dependent on the petitioner's state of mind. *Manning* took the extreme position that, in case of appropriate pleading supported by an affidavit of the petitioner, the court has no choice but to grant the dissolution. The opposing affidavit of the respondent wife, who believed in the possibility of reconciliation, could not shake the husband's express determination to end the marriage. Fault was to have no relevance whatsoever; and summary judgment on the pleadings, according to this view, had to be given to the petitioner regardless of whether or not he was to blame. The court apparently differentiated between facts and feelings, and found that the petitioner's subjective view of the state of his marriage entitled him to a judgment as a matter of law.

The opposite interpretation had been made three years earlier by the Supreme Court of Florida in *Ryan v. Ryan* (see pp. 53–59). The court posited that the judge should not act merely as a ministerial officer who accepts the magic words "irretrievably broken" from the petitioner, but that he should inquire objectively into what happened in the marriage. Inquiries into the causes of marital breakdown inevitably lead to resurrection of the fault concept, if only in an adumbrated form. This was demonstrated, again in Florida, in *McClelland*

---

*235 S.E.2d 479 (1977).

v. McClelland, where the court permitted the petitioner to plead adultery as the cause of an irretrievably broken marriage (see pp. 332–333).

Georgia itself retreated from its initial conception of "pure" no-fault, expressed in *Manning.* In *Dickson* the court held that a respondent can counter the pleadings of the petitioner by an affidavit that the marriage is not irretrievably broken—because the petitioner has shown prospects for reconciliation, for instance. The internal state of mind thus becomes a disputed issue to be resolved by the fact finder. In spite of the radical holding of *Manning,* Georgia has never entirely abandoned considerations of fault. It has retained the traditional divorce grounds based on fault in addition to the new ground of irretrievable breakdown of marriage. Since in mixed jurisdictions of this kind fault and no-fault can be linked together in the same proceedings by way of petition and counterclaim, it appears analytically to be difficult to eliminate fault altogether, especially in view of the consequences of dissolution, financial and otherwise.

But even in the aftermath of *Manning* overruled, it is still possible to differentiate between a few jurisdictions that adhere to a relatively pure concept of no-fault dissolution and those that have more or less openly reestablished considerations of fault. Mostly, rather than a dichotomy of fault and no-fault jurisdictions, we face various degrees of judicial adjustment to legislative demands. Perhaps one should then ask why it is so difficult to eradicate considerations of fault in the dissolution of marriage. On a superficial level it appears that judges have resented what they may view as legislative intrusion upon their prerogatives. Clearly judges do not want to be subservient to the demands of the petitioner but prefer to have a say in the matter that has been brought before them—or at least, in these cases, the power to inquire into the causes of irretrievable breakdown of marriage. However, the reasons for the continued emphasis on or need for moral blame in connection with divorce are deeper. In particular, considerations of fault and moral blame must have economic consequences in the vast majority of cases that are bargained over in lawyers' offices and then merely processed through the courts.

Complete eradication of fault interferes in this bargaining process and, is likely to lead to financial complications. The nature of these complications is hinted at in *Manning* in the concurring opinion of Mr. Justice Gunter. By way of counterclaim the respondent wife had asked for temporary and permanent alimony and for title in the family home and all furniture. It was not accidental that she raised misconduct of the husband petitioner in this context. Indeed in terms of social functions, fault may be related to considerations of a proprietary nature, as this book will demonstrate. In this connection, perhaps *Manning* had to be overruled because it did not consider adequately the proprietary consequences of granting a petitioner for dissolution of marriage a judgment on his pleadings alone. The misgivings about these pleadings are further accentuated if consideration is given to

their nature and to the problem of the exent to which obviously fictitious pleadings and affidavits should be taken at face value by the
courts. The language in the husband's sworn affidavit was clearly not
his, but that of the lawyer who, with distinct legal and financial consequences in mind, was speaking through the mouth of his client. The
language used is deliberately meant to foreclose any possibility of reconciliation, regardless of any argument the respondent wife might
make. If a lawyer is to prevail with this strategy, as he did in *Manning*,
it must affect not only the dissolution as such but, more importantly,
its proprietary consequences.

References

Comment, *The End of Innocence; Elimination of Fault in California Divorce
Law*, 17 UCLA L. REV. 1306 (1970).
Mnookin & Kornhauser, *Bargaining in the Shadow of the Law: The Case of
Divorce*, 88 YALE L.J. 950 (1979).

In re Marriage of Williams

Supreme Court of Iowa

199 N.W.2d 339 (Iowa 1972)

MASON, Judge.
Elmer Williams, respondent, appeals from decree entered in dissolution
of marriage proceedings brought under the provisions of what is now chapter
598, The Code, 1971.
    * * * The revised statute makes the breakdown of the marriage the sole
basis for termination of the marital relationship and eliminates the specific
categories of fault grounds enumerated in section 598.8, The Code, 1966, as a
standard for granting dissolution.
    * * *
    * * * [O]nly those propositions which deal with that portion of the de-
cree ordering alimony and support payments by respondent remain for consideration. These assignments are closely related. Perhaps it will tend to a
better understanding of the problem if respondent's fourth proposition is
considered first.
    * * * After entry of the decree of dissolution, defendant filed motion
asking the court to include in its findings a determination of whether petitioner had committed acts of adultery while married to respondent, had been
dating a named individual during this period and had written and received
letters from the person with whom she was inferentially accused of committing adultery. * * *
    The trial court denied the motion on the basis that if it were to comply
with the request, it would be necessary in fairness to the petitioner to also
enlarge the findings to detail misconduct on respondent's part and any testimony by respondent deemed by the court to be untrue. In its order the court
made this statement:

> "The court did determine that fault lay with both parties, although
> perhaps more heavily upon the petitioner than upon the respondent and

did accord fault some consideration in its determination of * * *, support and alimony, and property division."

In his second assignment respondent contends the property settlement and alimony and support payments are not equitable since the award does not take into account petitioner's fault for the marriage breakdown. In this connection respondent argues that although chapter 598, The Code, 1971, would seem, in effect, to remove the element of fault as a basis for dissolution of the marriage, nothing in the statute removes from the court's consideration the conduct of the spouses and particularly that of the guilty party as a criterion in determining the equitable disposition of property.

I. In support of his position respondent relies on *Schantz v. Schantz,* 163 N.W.2d 398, 405 (Iowa 1968), which was decided at a time divorces were based on the fault grounds enumerated in section 598.8, The Code, 1966. The opinion sets forth several factors as a suggested aid to trial courts in adjusting the rights and obligations of the parties upon judicial termination of the marriage relationship. *Loc. cit.* 163 N.W.2d at 405. Before listing the factors to be evaluated, the court gave this caveat:

> "This court has also repeatedly taken the position that in resolving the troublesome problem inherent in awarding alimony and effecting a distribution of property rights, *many factors* must be considered. See *Gerk v. Gerk,* Iowa, 158 N.W.2d 656, and citations.

> "Use of the following general formula may be helpful in arriving at an equitable determination of financial or property rights and obligations of the parties to a divorce action, though each element is not always present or important." (emphasis supplied)

The court then proceeds to set forth five premarital criteria and ten post-marital criteria which will not be repeated here.

Fault was never the sole criterion for an award or property settlement or an allowance of alimony or support under our previous statute. True, it did enter into the determination along with other factors.

The issue presented by this appeal is what, if any, consideration fault of the spouses is to be given in awarding property settlement, alimony or support payments under the revised statute.

This is a matter of first impression for this court. The courts of other jurisdictions which have adopted no-fault divorce statutes have not considered the precise problem so far as our research discloses.

Section 598.14, The Code, 1966, provided:

> "Alimony—custody of children—changes. When a divorce is decreed, the court may make such order in relation to the children, property, parties, and the maintenance of the parties as shall be *right.*

> "Subsequent changes may be made by it in these respects when circumstances render them expedient." (emphasis supplied)

The above section was repealed by chapter 1266 and section 598.21, The Code, 1971, was enacted in lieu thereof. It provides:

> "Alimony—custody of children—changes. When a dissolution of marriage is decreed, the court may make such order in relation to the children, property, parties, and the maintenance of the parties as shall be *justified.*

> "Subsequent changes may be made by the court in these respects when circumstances render them expedient." (emphasis supplied)

The only significant change made by the revision is substitution of the word "justified" for the word "right."

This language in section 598.17, The Code, 1971, is new:

"Dissolution of marriage—evidence. A decree dissolving the marriage may be entered when the court is satisfied from the evidence presented that there has been a breakdown of the marriage relationship to the extent that the legitimate objects of matrimony have been destroyed and there remains no reasonable likelihood that the marriage can be preserved.

"The court shall, based upon competent and relevant evidence, in such decree provide for the division of the assets of the parties and reasonable support or maintenance of any dependent children or either spouse.

"No marriage dissolution granted due to the mental illness of one of the spouses shall relieve the other spouse of any obligation imposed by law as a result of the marriage for the support of the mentally ill spouse, and the court may make an order for such support."

Originally, the Divorce Laws Study Committee of Iowa in its report said that all evidence should be permitted in determining marital breakdown. The committee specifically mentioned certain kinds of evidence which were to be included in the scope of review:

"1. Commission of adultery; 2. Willful desertion without reasonable cause for a period of two years; 3. Conviction of a felony after the marriage; 4. Chronic alcoholism; 5. Inhuman treatment affecting physical or mental wellbeing; 6. Incurable mental illness for a continuous period of three years immediately preceding the filing of the action, requiring confinement to an institution, home, or other facility and based upon the testimony of a qualified member of the medical profession that such spouse is incurably mentally ill; 7. Pregnancy of the wife at the time of the marriage, unknown by the husband, by a person other than the husband; 8. That the spouses have voluntarily lived entirely separate for three years next preceding the commencement of the action; and 9. The existence of an illegitimate child or children of one of the spouses, then living, which was unknown to the other spouse at the time of the marriage."

Peters, *Iowa Reform of Marriage Termination*, 20 Drake L. Rev. 211, 215–216. The legislature, however, declined to follow its recommendation, electing, instead, to eliminate fault grounds. One writer suggests this be interpreted as an attempt to truly effectuate the purpose of the modern approach to divorce. Note, *The No Fault Concept: Is This the Final Stage in the Evolution of Divorce?*, 47 Notre Dame Law. 959, 969 (1972).

The first paragraph of section 598.17 makes breakdown of the marriage relationship the sole basis for termination of the marriage. The decree neither favors a petitioner nor is against a respondent. It acts only upon the status of the parties with relation to one another and consists in the granting of a judgment of dissolution of the marriage.

The second paragraph of this section directs that the division of assets of the parties, support or maintenance of either spouse be "based on competent and relevant evidence." It does not specifically prohibit the use of fault evidence. This might logically be interpreted as leaving the court some flexibility in individual cases in arriving at a proper adjustment of the rights and obligations of the parties upon judicial termination of the marriage.

The contents of the petition for dissolution of marriage are specifically set out in subparagraph 7 of section 598.5, The Code, 1971, in this manner:

"7. Allege that there has been a breakdown of the marriage relationship to the extent that the legitimate objects of matrimony have been destroyed and there remains no reasonable likelihood that the marriage can be preserved."

The statute does not allow for the introduction of fault grounds in the petition.

Since the statute does not provide any specific guidelines, we turn to the efforts of legal writers in this field who have commented on similar no-fault dissolution statutes enacted in other jurisdictions as an aid in construing our statute. In addition to those already cited, we have examined: Clark, *Divorce Policy and Divorce Reform,* 42 COLO. L. REV. 403 (1971); Tenney, *Divorce Without Fault: The Next Step,* 46 NEB. L. REV. 24 (1967); Comment, 17 U.C.L.A. L. REV. 1306 (1969–1970); Hayes, *California Divorce Reform: Parting Is Sweeter Sorrow,* 56 A.B.A.J. 660; Walker, *Beyond Fault: An Examination of Patterns of Behavior in Response to Present Divorce Laws,* 10 J. FAM. L. 267 (1971). An article, "The New California Divorce Law," 1969, by Walter T. Winter is of interest.

In addition to Iowa, California (Calif. Civ. Code sections 4500–40); Florida (Florida Statutes, Title 6, chapter 61); Idaho (chapter 6, Title 32, Idaho Code); Michigan (Michigan Comp. Laws Ann. section 552.6 (Supp. 1971)); New Jersey (N.J. Rev. Stat. section 2A:34–2 (Supp. 1972)) and West Virginia (W.Va. Code chapter 48), are among the states that have taken steps to revise their state laws governing divorce.

California was the first to make the move in 1969 followed by Iowa and Michigan in 1970. The Florida statute became effective July 1, 1971; Idaho in February 1971 and New Jersey, September 1971. The West Virginia statute was partially rewritten by the 1969 legislature.

These statutes vary from state to state with Michigan's being the most similar to the Iowa statute upon which it based the format of its law for the new dissolution of marriage procedure. They each present problems of interpretation and administration.

In criticizing the various enactments, authors of the legal periodicals referred to, supra, agree the most significant aspect of the new law is the attempt to eliminate the notion of fault or marital guilt from marital dissolution proceedings, and to substitute the marital-breakdown approach as a standard for granting dissolution. Generally, they maintain the marital-breakdown approach does away "with the hypocrisy of the fault approach, and, more importantly, it can be used to limit the bitterness and emotional stress associated with the fault system." 47 NOTRE DAME LAW. at 970. The writer in another place in the cited note expresses the view that it was the hope of the legislatures this approach would eliminate the finger-pointing and thus reduce the bitterness and conflict.

These and other expressions found in the cited materials make it clear the overriding legislative purpose of the dissolution act is to remove fault-based standards for termination of marriages.

* * *

However, respondent's argument that the conduct of the spouses and particularly that of the guilty party has not been removed as a criterion in determining the equitable disposition of property remains. He directs attention to the fourth factor of the post-marital criteria, "conduct of the spouses and particularly that of the guilty party," as listed in the Schantz opinion. * * *

* * *

Unless the purpose of this enactment as determined from legislative history in the report of the Divorce Study Committee is to be defeated, the "guilty party" concept must be discarded as a factor for consideration in providing an award or an allowance of alimony or support money.

The author of the comment in 17 U.C.L.A. L. REV. at 1316–1317, expresses the belief, "Alimony, now called 'support,' will be determined by fairness rather than fault. Three factors must be taken into account: (a) the duration of the marriage, (b) the ability of the supported spouse to engage in gainful employment, and (c) the economic condition of the parties."

* * *

In order to carry out this obvious legislative intent and give effect to the object sought to be accomplished, we hold not only the "guilty party" concept must be eliminated but evidence of the conduct of the parties insofar as it tends to place fault for the marriage breakdown on either spouse must also be rejected as a factor in awarding property settlement or an allowance of alimony or support money. Usually both spouses contribute to a breakdown of the marital relations which makes necessary an adjustment of their rights and obligations. In other words, evidence bearing on the fourth factor listed in the Schantz decision of postmarital criteria is not admissible on this issue.

* * *

Nevertheless, as noted, the trial court in overruling respondent's motion to amend and enlarge the court's findings stated fault had been given some consideration in its determination of alimony and property division. It was error to do so.

II. Having arrived at the conclusion that fault is not a factor to be considered in awarding property settlement or an allowance of alimony under chapter 598, The Code, 1971, we proceed to consider respondent's other contention that the award was otherwise inequitable and unjust since it leaves him in an almost impossible financial position in view of his mortgage indebtedness.

In equity it is our duty in a *de novo* review to examine the whole record and adjudicate rights anew on those propositions properly presented, provided issue has been raised and error, if any, preserved in the course of trial proceedings. * * *

Petitioner and respondent were married February 25, 1950 and lived together as husband and wife until September 1970. Petitioner was 41 years of age at time of trial and respondent was 48 and a high school graduate. At the time of marriage the parties had few assets and only minor financial liabilities. During the course of the marriage virtually no contributions were received by them from outside sources. By virtue of hard work and conservative management of their finances, they had been able to accumulate a personal residence having a reasonable market value of $18,500 subject to a mortgage of $2659; an apartment house consisting of four two-bedroom first floor units having a reasonable market value of $33,500 subject to a mortgage of $24,017; a vacant lot valued at $1000; a Dodge automobile having a market value of $1875; a Chevrolet valued at $100; and 100 shares of National Mobile Home stock with a reasonable market value of $275. The parties had various other stocks totaling $1394, a bank account of $40 and respondent's carpenter tools and maintenance equipment valued at $750. Household goods and furnishings were valued at $1500. At time of trial they were indebted to a bank in the sum of $700.

* * *

Our examination of the record discloses that petitioner has had virtually no job training and at time of trial was employed part time as a nurses' aide at a rate of $1.65 per hour. She estimated her earnings at approximately $25 per week and the cost of a babysitter for their ten-year-old daughter at $10. Respondent, a skilled journeyman carpenter, is capable of earning in excess of $4.00 per hour. In 1969 he earned approximately $9000 as a carpenter and approximately $8500 in 1970.

The gross income from the apartment house building was $100 per month per rented unit and there had been no problem in keeping three units occupied. Respondent was living in the fourth unit. In addition to payment of taxes and insurance premiums, monthly payments of $221 on principal and interest were required by the mortgage on this property. The insurance premiums were $150 per year and the taxes were just a few dollars less than $800, including the curb and gutter tax. Tenants in the apartments are furnished some utilities which run approximately $87 per month.

Taxes on the personal residence where petitioner resides are $404 and insurance, $47.50. Monthly payments on this mortgage were $84.84.

Although the health of both parties seems to be affected by their marital difficulties, there appear no health or mental problems which will interfere with their employment once the marital difficulties have been resolved. All indications are that their earnings will increase in the future.

The custody of Tamela Sue Williams, born January 25, 1961, was awarded to petitioner. * * *

* * *

Respondent was ordered to pay as alimony and for the support of their minor daughter the sum of $200 per month commencing June 15, 1971. These payments were to cease when Tamela reached the age of 18 or sooner died, married or became self-supporting. However, termination of such payments was not to take place as long as Tamela was in full-time attendance at an accredited college, university or trade school, the period of such attendance not to exceed four years in any event and should be continuous following graduation from high school, vacation periods excepted.

Occupancy of the personal residence of the parties was awarded to petitioner with respondent being required to maintain the same, pay taxes, insurance premiums and principal and interest payments coming due on the mortgage on this residence.

Respondent was awarded the use and income from the apartment house building, being required to maintain the same, pay taxes, insurance premiums and mortgage payments.

Use of the properties by the parties was to terminate at the same time as payments of alimony and support money. Upon termination of the use and maintenance of the properties, the same were to be sold and after the payment of expenses, proceeds were to be divided 25 percent to petitioner and 75 percent to respondent.

Provision was made for the distribution of the net proceeds from the sale of these properties in the event either party should die prior to the termination date as fixed.

Petitioner was also awarded the vacant lot, Chevrolet automobile, household goods and furnishings and her personal belongings in the personal residence.

Respondent was awarded all other property including his tools and maintenance equipment. He was also required to pay the bank note, all expenses incurred by petitioner after September 1, 1971, remaining unpaid, costs of the action, $1000 toward the fee of petitioner's attorney and $100 as a fee for the attorney appointed to represent Tamela at the dissolution proceedings.

In summary, respondent is required under the terms of the court's decree to make the following annual payments on both pieces of real estate until the termination date fixed therein: taxes $1204, insurance $197.50, and mortgage loans $3670. In addition there is an estimated utility bill of $1044. Taxes and insurance premiums are, of course, approximate figures. Added to this amount are alimony and support money payments of $2400 per year. He is thus required to pay $8515.50. To do this he has his income of approximately $9000 as a carpenter and rent of $3600 from the three apartment units assuming they remain occupied. Subtracting the payments required of him from this $12,600, respondent is left with the sum of $4084.50.

Respondent was given stocks and bonds of approximately $1675 and was required to pay a bank note of $700, attorney fees and court costs.

We appreciate that this does not leave respondent with much money. On the other hand, petitioner is furnished a residence for herself and daughter with the taxes and insurance being paid by respondent. She has $200 per month to maintain herself and child in addition to such income as she is able to produce. We also realize that under the terms of the decree the respondent cannot use the real estate during the period payments are required in any financial transactions. This court has said many times under the old divorce statute that there is seldom enough money to support two families in these situations. It appears in this case the same is true.

In our *de novo* review of this record we have eliminated any consideration of the fault concept and reached our determination on the basis of the criteria otherwise suggested in *Schantz v. Schantz*, 163 N.W.2d at 405 and conclude that respondent's contention the decree was inequitable and unjust as it related to the division of property and alimony and support payments is without merit under the circumstances presented by this record.

Except for the monthly payments of alimony and support money the adjudication of the rights and obligations of the parties relating to the distribution of their property rights was just and fair.

As to those payments, we believe the decree should be modified by striking the provision requiring respondent to pay $200 per month as alimony and for the support of Tamela and that in lieu thereof the decree provide respondent make monthly payments of $100 as alimony with a further sum of $100 as support for Tamela. The decree insofar as it fixes the dates and conditions under which said payments are to continue shall remain unchanged.

* * *

Except as modified with respect to an allocation of a definite amount for alimony and support money and the additional allowances made herein, the decree is affirmed.

* * *

UHLENHOPP, Justice (dissenting from division I but concurring in result).

The question is whether the parties' *conduct* with respect to each other—not merely "fault" for the marital breakdown—may be considered as one factor on the issue of fair and equitable alimony. ("Alimony" is used here in the broad sense to include both property division and monetary payments.)

The question may be brought into focus by two rather extreme but not rare examples, in which all factors are equal except the parties' conduct. In one, the husband in frequent fits of rage visits violent physical abuse on his blameless wife and children, eventually driving them from the home by his cruelty. In the other, the wife carries on with a paramour, frequently spending nights and weekends with him to the knowledge of the blameless husband and children. Is the court to be allowed to know these facts along with the other equities in the case in deciding upon a fair adjustment of the parties' financial rights and obligations? Or is the court to function in a vacuum so far as the parties' conduct is concerned? Compare facts in *Caldwell v. Caldwell*, 5 Wis.2d 146, 92 N.W.2d 356, with *Manske v. Manske*, 6 Wis.2d 605, 95 N.W.2d 401.

* * *

Does the change in the basis for terminating marriage—from specified wrongs to irretrievable marital breakdown—constitute an enactment by implication that the parties' conduct shall no longer be considered on alimony?

Domestic relations cases ordinarily involve three main issues: dissolution of the marriage, child custody, and alimony. The legislature made a basic change in the law on the first issue, but it did not deal or purport to deal with the latter two.

The issue of custody is governed by what is in the best interest of the children. *Utter v. Utter*, 261 Iowa 683, 155 N.W.2d 419. The new act did not abolish that rule, nor did the act provide that the parties' conduct cannot be considered in determining the children's best interest.

Similarly, the issue of alimony is governed by what is just, fair, and equitable between the parties. The new act did not abolish that rule either, nor did it provide that the parties' conduct cannot be considered in determining what is a just, fair, and equitable adjustment of their financial affairs. The parties' conduct is just as relevant today as it was yesterday in resolving the custody and alimony issues. If evidence of that conduct also happens to disclose the cause of the marital breakdown, that is merely incidental.

Decreeing alimony is not as mechanical as fixing the award in other no-fault proceedings such as workmen's compensation, where the scale of payments is set by statute. In domestic relations cases, adjustment of the parties' financial rights and obligations is much more delicate and imprecise. The proceeding is in equity, and "the equities on both sides are to be considered. * * * A court of equity is a court of conscience; it seeks to do justice and equity between all parties; it seeks to strike a balance of convenience as between litigants; and *it looks at the whole situation.*" 30 C.J.S. *Equity* §89 at 976, 978–979. (Italics added.)

Under the new act, the chancellor is searching as he was before for a fair, just, and equitable determination of the parties' financial rights and duties. In that search he still needs to be placed in the position of the parties and to know what they know. To do equity, he still needs to be allowed to see the full picture.

Finally, a rule against considering the parties' conduct will not work in practice. Thus in a case involving a custody contest, a chancellor hearing evidence that the wife is living with another man will in fact be unable to blot that evidence from his mind when he comes to the alimony issue. The law in books and the law in action will not be the same. In the absence of direction by the legislature, courts of equity should continue to be permitted, in word as well as in fact, to consider the parties' conduct in decreeing alimony. They should continue to weigh all the equities.

Comments

In re Williams illustrates the strains that result from the introduction of no-fault divorce into jurisdictions, such as California and Iowa, that have traditionally been governed by conceptions of fault in marital breakdown. It becomes apparent that in practice, moral blame is related less to marital ethics than to issues of allocation of property. In this context the dominant position of the husband under common law should be recalled. As soon as absolute divorce through the courts was made available, it became necessary to create equitable means to provide for formerly married women. Since by virtue of marriage husbands owned or controlled most of the property, women, especially in long-term marriages, would have been left with little or nothing after divorce. Fault as a concept, even if it sometimes resulted in punitive awards, gave the chancellor the power to grant alimony and distribute property according to equitable standards.

Specifically, the concept of fault has been useful as an equitable tool for balancing the power of men in divorce proceedings by finding in favor of women. Other factors helped bring about this result. Statistically women were petitioners in divorce proceedings more often than men, although their husbands often instigated the filing of complaints. Also, cultural patterns, perhaps from the Puritan heritage, tended to fix the blame for marital breakdown on men.

Since pure no-fault divorce more often than not works to the disadvantage of women when accompanied by mere rehabilitative alimony or none at all and an unclear situation in regard to marital property, it will take considerable time and experimentation to bring about adjustments. The most obvious solution might be to give women a vested right in marital property, perhaps an equal share as now existing in community-property states, or as a possibility in equitable distribution jurisdictions. Experience in California indicates, however, that mandatory equal distribution of community property does not necessarily relieve the acrimony of marital disputes.* The emphasis shifts from blame to determining exactly what constitutes half of the assets. If equitable distribution governs, marital behavior becomes relevant, as pointed out in *Williams*, and considerations of fault are resurrected. Intricate problems of bookkeeping arise. Questions are raised about how assets should be evaluated and which assets to include. Divorce practice increasingly acquires aspects of business practice, and the emotional factors, at least outwardly, lose in significance. (See *In re Marriage of Mix*, pp. 100–105.)

Williams illustrates another problem of a pure no-fault approach in a noncommunity-property jurisdiction like Iowa. A strict elimination of any consideration of fault, especially if the marital assets are limited, may put the relatively blameless party in an untenable financial position. In *Williams*, it appears to have been the wife who benefited from no-fault. Testimony about her alleged adultery could not be considered at all, while her husband continued to be burdened with alimony and support obligations with hardly enough left for himself to live on. More usual is the reverse situation: A husband after a 20-year marriage with limited assets demands his freedom. In this context, substantial obligations he may face appear to be more palatable; at least they were brought about by his own actions. *Williams* illustrates this difficulty of disregarding behavior altogether, even good behavior. It leaves the impression of an inequitable and unfair result. Yet the invocation of equity seems to reestablish fault, at least in the phase when the consequences of dissolution are to be considered.

Many no-fault jurisdictions choose a compromise that permits consideration of some fault. Or they may recognize, as does Florida, so-called "special equities"; or they may consider, as does Massachusetts, "conduct of the parties" possibly leading to a reward for unusual efforts beyond the call of ordinary marital duties or to a penalty in cases in which the conduct of the spouse involved the wasting of assets (e. g., gambling) or physical absence from the home. To the extent that rights in marital property are "vested," they are not subject to the limitations that apply to alimony. Yet a pattern can be discerned. The inchoate rights resulting from marriage, like the possiblility of alimony, are declining in importance. Even lump-sum alimony, where permitted, increasingly acquires the characteristics of equitable property distribution. In the not-too-distant future, both husband and wife may, after divorce, be left with their capacity to work and a portion of whatever assets can be found. Whether this will lead to further adop-

*See Diamond, *No-Fault: New Emphasis in Divorce Cases*, L.A. Times, Feb. 14, 1977, §1 at 1, col. 1.

tion of community property or equitable distribution laws has not yet been determined. Whatever the outcome, courts appear to be decreasingly important. Even under fault regimes, the grounds for a divorce have been largely bargaining tools. Today the real decisions are likely to be made in lawyers' offices by way of complex property settlements or, at an earlier stage, by antenuptial agreements. That cohabitation short of marriage is not necessarily a safe alternative has already been discussed in connection with *Marvin v. Marvin* (see pp. 172–185).

The problem posed by *Williams* remains unresolved. What should be done if, after the "split," the marital assets are insufficient to support two new families? None of the traditional civil enforcement remedies are practical (e.g., voluntary wage assignments, mandatory wage withholding, liens, security or a bond to guarantee payment, setoff of tax refunds, registration of support orders in another state), and criminal prosecution under nonsupport laws is ineffective. Statistics indicate that males on the whole do not pay support or alimony. If they pay at all, they discontinue after a short period. Five years after divorce most males do not pay anything and enforcement is unrealistic in most cases. Consequently it is only natural that the financial position of males improves by divorce, because, regardless of what the courts say, they are effectively rid of obligations (publicized enforcement attempts in individual cases notwithstanding). The overwhelming burden of divorce continues to fall on women, especially if they have custody of minor children, as is usually the case. Thus *Williams* is an irregular case, and we do not know how Mr. Williams was in fact financially situated, apart from what the court said about his plight.

To the extent that members of the original family unit are in distress, with the government increasingly unwilling to assume the burden of such families, marriage can be a speculative investment that does not pay off. The same applies to a former spouse who, in addition to having to live on insufficient assets, does not have the capacity to work.

References

Chambers, D., MAKING FATHERS PAY—THE ENFORCEMENT OF CHILD SUPPORT 48 (1979).

Eekelaar, J., & Katz, S., MARRIAGE AND COHABITATION IN CONTEMPORARY SOCIETIES (1980).

Glendon, *Modern Marriage Law and Its Underlying Assumptions: The New Marriage and the New Property*, 13 FAM. L.Q. 441 (1980).

Glendon, M., STATE, LAW AND FAMILY: FAMILY LAW IN TRANSITION IN THE UNITED STATES AND WESTERN EUROPE (1977).

Glendon, M., THE NEW FAMILY AND THE NEW PROPERTY (1981).

Inker, Walsh, & Perocchi, *Alimony and Assignment of Property: The New Statutory Scheme in Massachusetts,* 10 SUFFOLK U.L. REV. 1 (1975) reprinted and updated in Katz, S. & Inker, M., FATHERS, HUSBANDS AND LOVERS 237–260 (1979).

Krause, *Child Support Enforcement: Legislative Tasks for the Early 1980s*, 15 FAM. L.Q. 349 (1982).

Weitzman, *The Economics of Divorce: Social and Economic Consequences of Property, Alimony and Child Support Awards*, 28 UCLA L. REV. 1181, 1211, 1249–56 (1981).

Weitzman & Dixon, *The Alimony Myth: Does No-Fault Divorce Make a Difference?*, 14 FAM. L.Q. 141, 172–79 (1980).

Rehabilitative Alimony

Dakin v. Dakin

Supreme Court of Washington

62 Wash.2d 687, 384 P.2d 639 (1963)

HUNTER, Judge.

Olcott W. Dakin, the husband (defendant), appeals from a decree awarding a divorce to Catherine M. Dakin, his wife (plaintiff), and dismissing his cross complaint for divorce with prejudice.

Olcott and Catherine Dakin were married at Watertown, New York, in 1936. They moved to Seattle where the defendant worked at various jobs until, in 1957, he purchased a small transfer and storage company. The plaintiff also obtained employment during this period in various positions within the general field of social work.

The defendant is presently the president and manager of three transfer businesses. He purchased Chesley Transfer Company, Inc., in 1957 and, shortly thereafter, organized Chesley Overseas, Inc. Later, he bought Yukon Transfer Company which, unlike the other two companies, is a sole proprietorship. These three businesses are one-man businesses which completely depend upon the defendant's attention.

In 1939, the plaintiff invited Karen Frolund, a co-worker at the Welfare Department, to be a guest at her home. After Karen married in 1941, the two families remained close friends and saw each other often. Sometime in 1948 (approximately), the defendant commenced seeing Karen privately despite the fact the plaintiff previously had remonstrated his excessive attentions to her. From 1949 on, the defendant and Karen secretly met at various locations in and around Seattle to prevent the plaintiff from discovering their relationship. Despite the couple's caution, the plaintiff suspected that her husband was meeting another woman and accused him of it. The defendant denied her accusations and, in rebuff, told her she was obsessed with jealousy.

In the fall of 1957, the defendant and Karen told the plaintiff that they had been in love with each other for nine years. They requested her to give the defendant a divorce, but she refused to do so. Despite her refusal, the defendant continued to live, off and on, with the plaintiff. Sometimes he abused her, both physically and mentally; other times he was very attentive and kind. During this period, however, the defendant kept up his relationship with Karen. This conduct left the plaintiff in a state of emotional turmoil.

Mr. and Mrs. Dakin separated permanently in 1959, in which year the defendant agreed to pay to the plaintiff $300 per month for temporary support money provided a divorce action was commenced prior to February 18, 1960.

* * *

The trial court found that the plaintiff should be granted a decree of divorce and that the defendant's cross complaint for divorce should be dismissed with prejudice; that the plaintiff should be given the family residence and vacant lot, together with certain household furnishings, an automobile, $7,500 in cash and alimony in the amount of $300 per month until she should remarry or die; that the defendant should be given the interests in the transfer businesses, his separate property, and the remaining community property; and that the defendant should be required to maintain the life insurance until the plaintiff should remarry or die, to pay certain debts, and to pay $1,000 as reasonable attorneys' fees as well as $400 for suit money previously allowed. A decree of divorce incorporating the above findings was entered from which the defendant appeals.

The defendant assigns error to the trial court's awarding of $300 per month as alimony for the plaintiff until she marries or dies.

The defendant contends the evidence does not support the trial court's finding that, during 1960, he earned $18,000 from his businesses and that the sum of $300 per month as alimony is reasonable. He contends the evidence shows that he made only $575 per month and that it is therefore inequitable to require him to pay alimony in the sum of $300 per month.

* * *

* * * He argues that, if justified at all, the plaintiff should be granted alimony of a temporary nature to be received during the period of her readjustment and rehabilitation and no longer.

The criterion adopted by this court for the allowance of alimony includes two factors: (1) the necessities of the wife, and (2) the financial ability of the husband.

The record shows that the plaintiff has no children to support or care for; that she was 53 years of age at the commencement of this action; that she was extremely nervous and upset at the time of the trial; but, otherwise, she is an able-bodied woman; that, because of her past condition, she has been unable to maintain steady employment; that she attended teacher's college for two years and taught school for four years thereafter; and that she has had considerable experience as a social worker, although no formal training.

It is the policy of this state to place a duty upon the wife to gain employment, if possible. In *Morgan v. Morgan, supra,* we said:

> "Alimony is not a matter of right. When the wife has the ability to earn a living, it is not the policy of the law of this state to give her a perpetual lien on her divorced husband's future income. *Warning v. Warning,* 40 Wash.2d 903, 247 P.2d 249 (1952); *Lockhart v. Lockhart,* 145 Wash. 210, 259 P. 385 (1927)."

We are of the opinion that the plaintiff in the instant case should not receive alimony until her remarriage or until her death. We think that she should be encouraged to rehabilitate herself and that, within a reasonable period, she may become self supporting. Although she may have been nervous and upset prior to her decree of divorce, there is no evidence which indicates this condition is of a permanent nature. Except for this condition, she appears to be an able-bodied woman capable of future employment. We conclude that alimony should be awarded which is adequate for the purpose of providing for her during her transitional period. We cannot say, under the state of this record, what this period should be. Therefore, the trial court should be in a position to modify or terminate the alimony upon competent proof of changed conditions, if any, that may be established at future modification hearings. The divorce decree is therefore modified by awarding the plaintiff alimony in the amount of $300 per month until further order of the court.

* * *

The judgment of the trial court is affirmed as modified by this opinion which provides that the alimony award shall be in the sum of $300 per month until further order of the court.

* * *

Comments

Alimony awards are essentially discretionary decisions. This realization has several consequences that are sometimes overlooked. Alimony controversies are won or lost on the trial court level. As in a case of a jury verdict, a judge's or chancellor's decision can be attacked only if it is clearly unreasonable, is unsupported by sufficient findings of fact, or involves an abuse of discretion. Appellate judges are prone to rule that since trial judges have observed the parties, heard their testimony, and studied their financial statements firsthand, their decisions should ordinarily be upheld. Knowing this, it is relatively easy for a trial judge to inject sufficient findings of fact into the trial record to support his decision and make it immune to appeal. On the other hand, it is exactly this discretionary power of the trial judge that encourages divorce settlements between the parties. By such settlement agreement, the parties avoid the risks of judicial discretion.

Trial judges themselves appear to be uneasy with an unfettered exercise of discretionary powers. They develop rules of thumb, sometimes even formulas, as to how they will ordinarily exercise their discretion. Important factors in their decisions are the husband's ability to pay and the wife's needs. Other factors have been added, such as conduct of the parties, duration of the marriage, standard of living during the marriage, age and health of the spouses, financial resources, needs for education or training, and contributions of each party to the marriage. Most important, fault of the parties continues to be significant, even if the courts no longer acknowledge it openly under conceptions of no-fault divorce. This does not mean that the courts will necessarily articulate that fault had any relevance; more likely they will not do so, because such articulation could encourage appeals.

Since the circumstances of a marriage are usually relevant for alimony claims, regardless of whether the divorce is based on the no-fault concept, good or bad conduct can be pleaded. Even if *Dakin* had been decided today, the plaintiff wife could have set forth her husband's conduct which resulted in her extreme nervousness and perhaps continued need for medical attention. On the other hand, her own "fault" may have a bearing too, even though it may not fit into traditional categories of improper conduct. For more than a decade she was "sleeping on her rights," apparently being unusually gullible, although her friend Karen carried on an affair with her husband. A judge may be influenced by such conduct under some theory that the

wife brought the marital problem upon herself, although he would be
unwise to express such an opinion because it could lead to an appeal
for an abuse of discretion.

To the extent that patterns of judicial discretion have become settled in a given jurisdiction—for example, in regard to need for alimony
and ability to pay it—exercise of discretion may be restricted by precedent. The legislature may also assert itself and restate major judicial
patterns as to alimony, perhaps following the catalogue contained in
§308 of the Uniform Marriage and Divorce Act. But it takes some
time for such legislation to become truly effective. Lower courts in
particular tend to follow traditional patterns of discretion. Even appellate courts are hesitant to surrender judicial prerogatives to the
legislature. The structuring of alimony requirements by new legislation is probably most effective in its impact on lawyers conducting
divorce negotiations. The new statutory requirements for alimony
furnish them a check list of factors to be considered in divorce
settlements.

The concept of "rehabilitative alimony" is part of the development described. It grew out of the exercise of judicial discretion. *Dakin* illustrates early judicial demands that women should participate
in their rehabilitation after divorce. No statute was needed for this
pronouncement. The wife's needs and the husband's limited financial
ability, in the court's view, made it desirable that she be self-supporting after a reasonable period. Once the concept of "rehabilitation" had
been judicially developed, it could be legislatively adopted. No-fault
divorce legislation provided an opportunity to make rehabilitative alimony the norm rather than the exception. Of course, this opened the
door to no alimony at all in the many cases in which judicial discretion
or the divorce settlement results in a decision that no rehabilitation is
needed.

The shift from permanent to rehabilitative alimony has, however,
a deeper meaning. It relates to the evolution of marriage toward a
contractual relationship. Permanent alimony was part of a husband's
obligation to support his wife, even after divorce. By requiring divorced women not to be idle but to become self-supporting, their status in marriage is altered. They lose some of the characteristics of
wives and acquire those of employees. Dissolution of marriage, on the
other hand, acquires characteristics of breach of contract. Since the
days of the Industrial Revolution employees have been under a duty
to mitigate damages, even if their dismissal were unjustified; in other
words, they had to seek other employment in an effort to keep the
damages low. In writing about contemporary affairs, Glendon has
noted that while it has become increasingly difficult to sever employment relationships, it has become increasingly easy to dissolve a marriage. Thus the concept of mitigation of damages, which seems archaic under modern conditions, has been revived in the context of
marriage and divorce as "rehabilitative alimony." Underlying this revival are economic conditions that affect the nature of marriage and

the status of women. However, if a married woman is more than a mere employee of sorts, namely, a person with an equal share in a marital partnership, the concept of "rehabilitative alimony" does not seem to fit. In this case, her status is more akin to that of an entrepreneur. If the marriage fails, the venture did not succeed. In that case there is no need to rehabilitate the wife because she carried her own risk. To carry the analogy further, she may not be granted severance pay unless it was bargained for prior to marriage in an antenuptial agreement. Division of property then becomes the only remaining issue.

References

Comment, *Alimony in Florida: No-Fault Stops at the Courthouse Door*, 28 U. FLA. L. REV. 521 (1976).

Glendon, M., STATE, LAW AND FAMILY: FAMILY LAW IN TRANSITION IN THE UNITED STATES AND WESTERN EUROPE (1977).

Glendon, M., THE NEW FAMILY AND THE NEW PROPERTY 1, 53 (1981).

Glendon & Lev, *Changes in the Bonding of the Employment Relationship: An Essay on the New Property*, 20 B.C.L. REV. 457 (1979).

Lepis v. Lepis

Supreme Court of New Jersey

83 N.J. 139, 416 A.2d 45 (1980)

PASHMAN, J.

Long after the bonds of matrimony are dissolved, courts of equity are frequently called upon to reassess the persisting obligations of financial support. This case presents for review the standards and procedures for modifying support and maintenance arrangements after a final judgment of divorce.

The parties were married in 1961 and had three children. After a period of marital discord, on January 8, 1974, the wife obtained from the Superior Court, Chancery Division, a judgment of divorce on grounds of desertion. The court incorporated as part of the judgment a detailed agreement governing property distribution, alimony, child custody and support.

Under the terms of the agreement, the wife retained all the household items and "any and all other tangible personal property" located at the marital home. She received title to the marital home and the husband's two-year old automobile. Upon entry of a final judgment of divorce and judicial ratification of the agreement, the husband would make a single payment of $22,000 "in settlement of the Wife's claim to her right for equitable distribution and any other support claims of the Wife now or at any time in the future except as provided herein."

The agreement permitted the wife to retain custody of the children and provided flexible visitation provisions. The husband agreed to pay $120 per week for alimony and $210 per week for child support—$70 per week for each unemancipated child. A child's attendance at college, business or trade school would not terminate support payments. The husband was obligated to maintain health insurance for the wife until her death or remarriage and for each child until emancipated. He was also responsible for all necessary medical, dental and prescription drug expenses of the children and for the wife's medical, dental and prescription drug expenses in excess of $50 per illness. The husband promised to pay all expenses for four years of college or professional education for each child. If a child lived away at school, child support would be reduced by some "appropriate" amount.

Looking to future uncertanties, the agreement sought to remove some of them from consideration if questions regarding modification arose. It specified that the presence or absence of separate earnings by the wife, or changes in the husband's income, would be irrelevant to a decision to alter or halt the husband's payments. The agreement also contained a provision governing modification by consent:

> "This Agreement shall not be varied, modified or annulled by the Husband or the Wife except by written instrument voluntarily executed and acknowledged by both."

On February 1, 1978, plaintiff moved to modify the support and alimony provisions of the agreement. She sought increased support for herself and the three children, a single, additional payment of $1,500 for household repairs and furniture, and counsel fees. Plaintiff also sought production of defendant's 1976 and 1977 income tax returns before a hearing on the modification motion. The trial court denied the motion without requiring defendant to disclose actual earnings. Plaintiff's request for counsel fees was also denied.

Plaintiff appealed from these rulings to the Appellate Division on April 19, 1978. On the following day she filed a notice of motion for rehearing of her motion for modification. Defendant responded by filing a notice of cross-motion for counsel fees and costs on the ground that plaintiff's motion for rehearing was frivolous. The trial court denied a rehearing, noting that by virtue of the pending appeal the court lacked jurisdiction to grant it. Because the application for a rehearing was clearly without merit, the court granted defendant's cross-motion for counsel fees. Plaintiff sought review in the Appellate Division of this second determination which was consolidated with her earlier appeal.

In an unreported opinion, the Appellate Division reversed the trial court's dispositions. The court held that "[o]nly after the discovery process is complete should the former wife's application for increased alimony and child support be determined." The Appellate Division concluded that refusing discovery of defendant's income despite plaintiff's showing of increased need "effectively denied her any opportunity to prove changed circumstances * * *" Since the court viewed plaintiff's application as requiring further examination, it held that the award of counsel fees was premature. It therefore vacated the trial court's orders and remanded the case with directions to order production of all tax returns of defendant since 1973.

This Court granted defendant's petition for certification. 81 N.J. 281 (1979). We now affirm. Before addressing whether the summary rejection of plaintiff's claims was proper, we first discuss the effect of a consensual agreement upon the court's power to modify obligations of support and maintenance. Secondly, we examine generally what constitutes "changed circumstances" so as to warrant a modification of those obligations. We then consider the procedures that a court should employ when passing upon a modification petition—particularly the allocation of the burdens of proof and the conditions for compelling production of tax returns. Finally, we apply the results of this analysis to the facts of the present case.

I.

Modification of Spousal Agreements

The equitable power of the courts to modify alimony and support orders at any time is specifically recognized by N.J.S.A. 2A:34-23:

> "Pending any matrimonial action brought in this State or elsewhere, or after judgment of divorce or maintenance, whether obtained in this State or elsewhere, the court may make such order as to the alimony or maintenance of the parties, and also as to the care, custody, education and maintenance of the children, or any of them, as the circumstances of the parties and the nature of the case shall render fit, reasonable and just, and require reasonable security for the due observance of such orders. * * * Orders so made may be revised and altered by the court from time to time as circumstances may require."

As a result of this judicial authority, alimony and support orders define only the present obligations of the former spouses. Those duties are always subject to review and modification on a showing of "changed circumstances." [Citations omitted.]

Divorcing spouses have often attempted to temper the flexibility of the court's power to modify with greater predictability by entering into separation agreements. In the past, such agreements have had significant and varying impact on the availability of post-judgment modification. Specific performance of spousal support agreements was once thought to be barred by the flexible approach to modification embodied in N.J.S.A. 2A:34-23. *Apfelbaum v. Apfelbaum*, 111 N.J. Eq. 529 (E & A 1932). Although not specifically enforceable, such agreements could be regarded by the court as relevant to the issue of support, and could be incorporated in a divorce decree. "The fact that [a] court took over the terms of the contract did not impair the power of the court to alter such provisions to accord with the equity of unfolding circumstance." *Corbin v. Mathews*, 129 N.J. Eq. 549, 554 (E & A 1941). The agreement was said to merge into the divorce decree, thereby losing its contractual nature. [Citations omitted.]

The rule against specific enforcement was later rejected by this Court in *Schlemm v. Schlemm*, 31 N.J. 557 (1960). That decision recognized that apart from its statutory authority, the Superior Court may exercise its "highly flexible" remedial powers to enforce the terms of interspousal support agreements "to the extent that they are just and equitable." *Id.* at 581-582. Later decisions continued to recognize the courts' power to modify such agreements "upon a showing of changed circumstances." *Berkowitz v. Berkowitz*, 55 N.J. 564, 569 (1970); see *Gulick v. Gulick*, 113 N.J. Super. 366, 370 (Ch. Div. 1971). The rule which developed, however, required that "[a] far greater showing of changed circumstances must be made before the court can modify a separation agreement than need be shown to warrant the court amending an order for alimony or support." *Schiff v. Schiff*, 116 N.J. Super. 546, 561 (App. Div. 1971), *certif. den.* 60 N.J. 139 (1972). Applying the "same standard that is applied by courts of equity to the specific enforcement of contracts in other fields [,]" the Appellate Division in *Schiff* held that modification of a spousal agreement required a showing of changed circumstances "such as to convince the court that to enforce the agreement would be *unconscionable*." 116 N.J. Super. at 561 (emphasis supplied). "Subsequent events which should have been in contemplation of the parties as possible contingencies when they entered into the contract [would] not excuse performance." *Id.*

Although this standard was never expressly adopted by the Supreme Court, it has been followed by lower courts.[1] [Citations omitted.]

In *Smith v. Smith*, 72 N.J. 350 (1977), this Court considered whether the *Schiff* standard applied when the trial court was effecting equitable distribution of marital property pursuant to N.J.S.A. 2A:34-23. Noting that "support payments are intimately related to equitable distribution" and that "trial judges should have the utmost leeway and flexibility in determining what is just and equitable in making allocations of marital assets," we disapproved of the *Schiff* rule:

> "Henceforth the extent of the change in circumstances, whether urged by plaintiff or defendant, shall be the same, regardless of whether the support payments being questioned were determined consensually or by judicial decree. In each case the court must determine what, in the light of all the facts presented to it, is equitable and fair, giving due weight to the strong public policy favoring stability of arrangements."

[72 N.J. at 360]

The rule announced in *Smith* is fully applicable when considering postjudgment modification. Consensual agreements and judicial decrees should be subject to the same standard of "changed circumstances." Initially it might appear that this rule would diminish the advantages of separation and property settlement agreements, since they would provide no greater certainty or stability than a judicial determination. However, granting a greater degree of permanence to negotiated agreements would tend to make them a riskier arrangement for spouses who are likely to be harmed by changed circumstances. Typically, they have been spouses who are economically dependent; they generally have been wives with custody of children. Often consensual agreements would not be in their best interests if only "unconscionable" circumstances would warrant modification.[2] As we recognized in rejecting *Schiff*, contract principles have little place in the law of domestic relations. See *Smith*, 72 N.J. at 360.

When we first upheld the specific enforceability of spousal agreements in *Schlemm*, we relied on the flexible power of equity to enforce such agreements only to the extent that they were fair and equitable. Similarly, the terms of such agreements should receive continued enforcement without modification only so long as they remain fair and equitable. The equitable authority of a court to modify support obligations in response to changed circumstances, regardless of their source, cannot be restricted. *Smith*, 72 N.J. at 360; *Berkowitz*, 55 N.J. at 569; *Schlemm*, 31 N.J. at 581; *Parmly*, 125 N.J. Eq. at 548. We therefore find no reason to distinguish between judicial decrees and consensual agreements when "changed circumstances" call for the modification of either.

II

Changed Circumstances

The parties here disagree over what constitutes "changed circumstances" sufficient to justify modification of alimony and child support.

---

[1] The *Schiff* rule, however, was not extended to modification of child support provisions. See *Clayton v. Muth*, 144 N.J. Super. 491 (Ch. Div. 1976).

[2] Commentators have addressed similar arguments to the *Schiff* rule of unconscionability. See Skoloff, *Schiff—Unconscionable Obstacle to Matrimonial Settlements*, 99 N.J.L.J. 553 (1976) ("The undue burden placed on counsel as well as the parties by this *Schiff* requirement is itself unconscionable. * * * The result: a decided chilling effect on the negotiation of such agreements * * *." *Id.* at 553–566); Meth, *Matrimonial Arbitration*, 99 N.J.L.J. 409 (1976) (noting that the impossibility of providing for every future contingency made "Schiff seem like a voice from a very ivory tower." *Id.*)

Plaintiff claims that her detailed demonstration of the increased needs resulting from maturation of the children and severe inflation justifies discovery of defendant's tax returns. Such increased needs and her husband's substantiated ability to pay would, according to plaintiff, constitute "changed circumstances" warranting upward modification of alimony and child support. Defendant responds that an increase in the cost of living and the "normal wear and tear" alleged here does not even entitle plaintiff to discovery of his present earnings. He argues that the increase in need alleged, even if coupled with proof of his increased ability to pay, would not constitute "changed circumstances."

According to defendant, plaintiff's position and the Appellate Division disposition are contrary to prior caselaw and will result in an avalanche of unwarranted petitions for modification.

The frequency with which courts are called upon to make or modify support awards needs no documentation. The lack of uniformity in their approaches and predictability in their decisions is similarly widely recognized. See generally Note, *Modification of Spousal Support: A Survey of a Confusing Area of the Law*, 17 J. FAM. LAW 711 (1979). In part, the inability to predict dispositions is responsible for the volume of modification motions. The solution to the problem of predictability would be a just accommodation of the power of the courts to adjust support obligations with the desirable features of stable arrangements and spousal cooperation. We conclude such an accommodation is possible through an approach linking the notion of "changed circumstances" to the initial support determination, be it judicial or consensual. This case presents an appropriate opportunity for us to clarify the proper set of coordinated standards.

A

The Elements of "Changed Circumstances"

The supporting spouse's obligation is mainly determined by the quality of economic life during the marriage, not bare survival. The needs of the dependent spouse and children "contemplate their continued maintenance at the standard of living they had become accustomed to prior to the separation." *Khalaf v. Khalaf*, 58 N.J. 63, 69 (1971); see *Bonanno v. Bonanno*, 4 N.J. 268, 274 (1950).[3]

> "The amount is not fixed *solely* with regard, on the one hand, to the actual needs of the wife, nor, on the other, to the husband's actual means. There should be taken into account the physical condition and social position of the parties, the husband's property and income (including what he could derive from personal attention to business), and also the separate property and income of the wife. Considering all these, and any other factors bearing upon the question, the sum is to be fixed at what the wife would have the right to expect as support, if living with her husband."

[*Bonanno*, 4 N.J. at 274 (quoting *Dietrick v. Dietrick*, 88 N.J. Eq. 560, 561–562 (E & A 1917)]

In accordance with this general principle, courts have recognized "changed circumstances" that warrant modification in a variety of settings. Some of them include

---

[3] These cases actually phrased this entitlement in terms of what a husband owes a wife. As we will discuss below, this is no longer a sound statement of contemporary domestic relations law. See *infra* at ___(slip op. at 21–22).

(1) an increase in the cost of living [citation omitted]
(2) increase or decrease in the supporting spouse's income [citations omitted]
(3) illness, disability or infirmity arising after the original judgment [citations omitted]
(4) the dependent spouse's loss of a house or apartment, *Jackson v. Jackson*, 140 N.J. Eq. 124 (E & A 1947); *McLeod v. McLeod*, 131 N.J. Eq. 44 (E & A 1942);
(5) the dependent spouse's cohabitation with another[4] [citations omitted]
(6) subsequent employment by the dependent spouse [citations omitted]
(7) changes in federal income tax law [citation omitted]

Courts have consistently rejected requests for modification based on circumstances which are only temporary or which are expected but have not yet occurred. [Citations omitted.]

When children are involved an increase in their needs—whether occasioned by maturation, the rising cost of living or more unusual events—has been held to justify an increase in support by a financially able parent. [Citations omitted.] Their emancipation and employment may warrant reduction in their support. [Citations omitted.]

This review of New Jersey decisions reveals the factors that a court of equity must assess when determining whether the former marital standard of living is being maintained. When support of an economically dependent spouse is at issue, the general considerations are the dependent spouse's needs, that spouse's ability to contribute to the fulfillment of those needs, and the supporting spouse's ability to maintain the dependent spouse at the former standard. The decision to modify child support requires a similar examination of the child's needs and the relative abilities of the spouses to supply them.

Our analysis makes clear that "changed circumstances" are not limited in scope to events that were unforeseeable at the time of divorce. This is particularly obvious in cases involving modification of child support orders, where maturation is cited as justifying an increase in support by a financially able parent. See, e.g., *Shaw v. Shaw, supra.* The supporting spouse has a continuing obligation to contribute to the maintenance of the dependent spouse at the standard of living formerly shared. So long as this duty continues, objective notions of foreseeability—what the parties or the court could or should have foreseen—are all but irrelevant. The proper criteria are whether the change in circumstance is continuing and whether the agreement or decree has made explicit provision for the change. An increase in support becomes necessary whenever changed circumstances substantially impair the dependent spouse's ability to maintain the standard of living reflected in the original decree or agreement. Conversely, a decrease is called for when circumstances render all or a portion of support received unnecessary for maintaining that standard. After finding that the dependent spouse cannot maintain the original standard of living, the court must consider the extent to which the supporting spouse's ability to pay permits modification.

If the existing support arrangement has in fact provided for the circumstances alleged as "changed," it would not ordinarily be "equitable and fair," *Smith*, 72 N.J. at 360, to grant modification. For example, although a spouse cannot maintain the marital standard of living on the support payments received, this would not ordinarily warrant modification if it were shown that a single large cash payment made at the time of divorce was included with the

---

[4] If the dependent spouse remarries, the court must modify any order or judgment to eliminate the alimony obligation on application by the supporting spouse, N.J.S.A. 2A:34–25; see *Sharpe v. Sharpe*, 109 N.J. Super. 410 (Ch. Div. 1970).

express intention of meeting the rising cost of living.[6] In other cases, the equitable distribution award—which we have recognized is intimately related to support, *Id.*—might have been devised to provide a hedge against inflation. The same might be true with respect to child support. A lump sum payment or a trust established for the benefit of the children could be shown to have been designed to cover the certain eventuality of increasing needs.

B

Judicial Provision for Changed Circumstances

As a practical matter, spousal agreements have great potential for ensuring the desired degree of stability in support arrangements. [Citations omitted.] Such agreements have traditionally been more comprehensive and particularized than court orders, and thus more carefully tailored to the peculiar circumstances of the parties' lives.[7] In view of the current economic conditions and the changing social structure of the family—particularly with regard to women's roles, *cf. Orr v. Orr*, 440 U.S. 268, 59 L.Ed.2d 306 (1979)—courts, too, should make greater efforts to provide in advance for change. This would enhance the stability of judicially fashioned arrangements and make unnecessary a return to court. The power to distribute property equitably should be exercised to relieve the strain of total reliance on support payments for financial security. See *Rothman v. Rothman*, 65 N.J. 219, 229 (1974); see also *Smith*, 72 N.J. at 360; *Painter v. Painter*, 65 N.J. 196, 218 (1974). Courts have refused to consider an alimony award in isolation; the earnings received from investments funded by an equitable distribution award have been considered when determining the adequacy of the dependent spouse's income. *Esposito v. Esposito*, 158 N.J. Super. 285, 300 (App. Div. 1978). "As a result of the equitable distribution plaintiff will have available a substantial capital fund to invest in order to produce additional income." *Lavene v. Lavene*, 162 N.J. Super. at 203.

A closer look should also be taken at the supported spouse's ability to contribute to his or her own maintenance, both at the time of the original judgment and on applications for modification.[8] The fact that our State's alimony and support statute is phrased without reference to gender, N.J.S.A. 2A:34-23, will accomplish little if judicial decision making continues to employ sexist stereotypes. The extent of actual economic dependency, not one's status as a wife, must determine the duration of support as well as its amount. [Citations omitted.][9]

---

[6] Of course under the standard for modification stated in *Smith*, should such a provision later prove inadequate, the court is free to require greater support if it is warranted in the light of prevailing circumstances. See 72 N.J. at 360.

[7] For examples of separation and property settlement agreements, see G. Skoloff, FAMILY LAW PRACTICE 330-349 (1976 ed.); 11 D. Herr, NEW JERSEY PRACTICE—MARRIAGE, DIVORCE AND SEPARATION §789 (3d ed. 1963) and §793.7 (Supp. 1978). See also *Berkowitz*, 55 N.J. at 569-570. In that case the parties provided that on the wife's remarriage the husband would convey his interest in the residence to the wife in return for cancellation of his obligations regarding it. They also made financial arrangements for the children's attendance at college away from home and a consequent reduction in child support. The court therefore denied the husband's motion for reduction of child support on grounds of the wife's remarriage: "[A]ll of the alleged 'changed circumstances' were envisioned by the parties and *dealt with* specifically in the Agreement." *Id.* at 570 (emphasis supplied).

[8] At times courts have found it necessary to assess the *supporting* spouse's ability to pay without regard to current earnings to determine fair and equitable support. See, *e.g.*, *Hess v. Hess*, 134 N.J. Eq. 360 (E & A 1944). The same should be done when the *supported* spouse's earning potential is an issue.

[9] In *Arnold v. Arnold*, 167 N.J. Super. 478 (App. Div. 1979), the Appellate Division concluded that in the absence of unusual facts, automatic cutoff dates for alimony should be

Not only the realities of the marketplace, but also the constitutional guarantee of "the equal protection of the laws," U.S. Const., Amend. XIV, compels this approach. It is no longer permissible to ground the law of domestic relations in the " 'old notio[n]' that 'generally it is the man's primary responsibility to provide a home and its essentials.' " *Orr v. Orr*, 440 U.S. at 279–280, 59 L.Ed.2d at 319 (quoting *Stanton v. Stanton*, 421 U.S. 7, 10, 43 L.Ed.2d 688, 692 (1975)). "No longer is the female destined solely for the home and the rearing of the family, and only the male for the marketplace and the world of ideas." *Orr*, 440 U.S. at 280, 59 L.Ed. at 319 (quoting *Stanton*, 421 U.S. at 14–15); see *Taylor v. Louisiana*, 419 U.S. 522, 535 n.17 91975); *Craig v. Boren*, 429 U.S. 190, 198 (1976). The law must be concerned with the economic realities of contemporary married life, not a model of domestic relations that provided women with security in exchange for economic dependence and discrimination. This does not mean that relative economic dependence—when proven—is irrelevant to the determination of support obligations. But a court of equity cannot rely on antiquated presumptions; gender is no longer a permissible proxy for economic need. See *Orr*, 440 U.S. at 281, 59 L.Ed.2d at 320. The need for support must be assessed with a view towards the earning capacity of the individual woman in the marketplace.

Careful consideration of all these factors at the time of divorce and at the time modification is sought will eventually reduce the necessity for otherwise well-founded postjudgment applications. It may also lessen the need for plenary hearings on modification motions. We are confident that any increased expenditure of judicial time necessitated by this expanded inquiry will be more than offset by savings from a reduced need for modification hearings.

III

Procedural Guidelines

The parties here disagree on the proper procedure for courts to follow on modification motions. In particular they dispute both the necessity and the elements of a *prima facie* showing of changed circumstances prior to discovery of the respondent's financial status. We therefore think it appropriate to explain procedures to be followed in the postjudgment setting.

The party seeking modification has the burden of showing such "changed circumstances" as would warrant relief from the support of maintenance provisions involved. *Martindell*, 21 N.J. at 353. A *prima facie* showing of changed circumstances must be made before a court will order discovery of an ex-spouse's financial status. When the movant is seeking modification of an alimony award, that party must demonstrate that changed circumstances have substantially impaired the ability to support himself or herself. This requires full disclosure of the dependent spouse's financial status, including tax returns. When the movant is seeking modification of child support, the guiding principle is the "best interests of the children." See *Hallberg v. Hallberg*, 113 N.J. Super. 205, 209 (App. Div. 1971); *Clayton v. Muth*, 144 N.J. Super. at 493. A *prima facie* showing would then require a demonstration that the child's

avoided. While we disapprove of the general approach in *Arnold*, the trial court in that case made no investigation of the nature of the wife's employment potential, and for this reason the 30-month limitation was justifiably seen as arbitrary. Careful and explicit factfinding on the earning ability of the dependent spouse is of paramount importance in such cases.

We do not share the view that only unusual cases will warrant the "rehabilitative alimony" approach. We note that other states permit such awards. See, *e.g.*, Fla. Stat. Ann. §61.08 (West Supp. 1979); Haw. Rev. Stat. Ann. §580–47 (Supp. 1979). See also Cal. Civ. Code §4806 (Supp. 1980) (court may withhold support allowance to a party who is "earning his or her own livelihood"); Ind. Code Ann. §31-1-11.5-9 (Burns 1979) (prohibiting maintenance of party unless he or she is physically or mentally incapable of supporting himself or herself).

needs have increased to an extent for which the original arrangement does not provide.

Only after the movant has made this *prima facie* showing should the respondent's ability to pay become a factor for the court to consider. Therefore, once a *prima facie* case is established, tax returns or other financial information should be ordered. We recognize that individuals have a legitimate interest in the confidentiality of their income tax returns. However, without access to such reliable indicia of the supporting spouse's financial ability, the movant may be unable to prove that modification is warranted. Similarly, without knowledge of the financial status of both parties, the court will be unable to make an informed determination as to "what, in light of all the circumstances is equitable and fair." *Smith*, 72 N.J. at 360. Courts have recognized that discovery and inspection of income tax returns should only be permitted for good cause. See *DeGraaff v. DeGraaff*, 163 N.J. Super. 578 (App. Div. 1978); see also *Ullmann v. Hartford Fire Ins. Co.*, 87 N.J. Super. 409 (App. Div. 1965); *Finnegan v. Coll*, 59 N.J. Super. 353 (Law Div. 1960). Because financial ability of the supporting spouse may be crucial to the proper disposition of a motion for modification, we conclude that a *prima facie* showing of changed circumstances meets this good cause standard. We also recognize, however, that the financial information of other individuals may be necessarily involved, as where the supporting spouse has remarried and filed joint returns with the new spouse. In such circumstances the court should follow the procedures outlined by the court in *DeGraaff*: the trial judge should examine the tax return *in camera* and excise irrelevant matters before giving the return to the plaintiff. 163 N.J. Super. at 583.

Once the above steps have been completed, the court must decide whether to hold a hearing. Although equity demands that spouse be afforded an opportunity to seek modification, the opportunity need not include a hearing when the material facts are not in genuine dispute. We therefore hold that a party must clearly demonstrate the existence of a genuine issue as to a material fact before a hearing is necessary. See *Shaw v. Shaw*, 138 N.J. Super. at 440; *Hallberg v. Hallberg*, 113 N.J. Super. at 208; *Tancredi v. Tancredi*, 101 N.J. Super. 259, 262 (App. Div. 1968). Without such a standard, courts would be obligated to hold hearings on every modification application. The application of the equitable principles we have outlined does not require elaborate procedures in every case. Courts should be free to exercise their discretion to prevent unnecessary duplication of proofs and arguments. The volume of post-judgment litigation provides additional, practical support for this approach.

In determining whether a material fact is in dispute, a court should rely on the supporting documents and affidavits of the parties. Conclusory allegations would, of course, be disregarded. Only statements to which a party could testify should be considered. Thus, if the sole dispute centered around the supporting spouse's earnings, the disclosure of income tax returns might render a hearing unnecessary.

IV

The Present Motion for Modification

Applying the foregoing standards and guidelines to the facts of this case, we conclude that the Appellate Division was correct in reversing the trial court's denial of plaintiff's motion and directing production of defendant's tax returns. Plaintiff has alleged with specificity the increases in her own and her children's needs caused by substantial inflation and the rising costs of supporting growing children. These changes in circumstances will apparently continue. They clearly warrant court inquiry into whether plaintiff's ability to maintain herself and her children has been substantially impaired.

By reason of plaintiff's *prima facie* showing, defendant should be required to disclose the requested evidence of his income, subject to the protections outlined above. See *supra* at ___(slip op. at 25). On remand, the trial court must then determine, among other things, whether the earlier agreement, as incorporated in the divorce judgment, provided for the present circumstances. Since the record clearly discloses genuine disputes as to material facts other than defendant's earnings, a hearing will be necessary.

As defendant points out, the agreement provided that the increased income of either spouse "shall not be a consideration to change or modify the support and maintenance payments for the Wife or the Wife and children." This might appear to be a valid accommodation of contingencies which otherwise would support modification based on "changed circumstances"—the wife's post-divorce employment or an increase in the husband's earnings. But as we have stated, the court is not bound by such provisions. It should scrutinize carefully the dependent spouse's ability to contribute to her own and her children's maintenance. The court must determine whether there has been substantial impairment of their ability to maintain the standard of living to which they are entitled.

Plaintiff, who was a teacher before her marriage, holds a Master's degree in Speech Communication and is continuing her education towards earning a Ph.D. She contends, however, that she has been unable to find substantial employment to bridge the gap between needs and expenses, and that employment in positions for which she is substantially overqualified would diminish her self image or esteem. Defendant asserts that plaintiff has unreasonably restricted her choice of employment fields. He points out that plaintiff's background and age and the children's maturity and attendance in school make her failure to find full-time employment while continuing her education unreasonable. These disputes must be addressed by the trial court on remand.

Defendant alleges that a $22,000 lump sum payment to plaintiff incorporated in their agreement should be recognized as the agreed means for covering the increased needs which plaintiff alleges—especially with respect to repairs to her present home. Whether this amount should be so considered is a question of fact for the court. While the supported spouse need not completely deplete savings to qualify for increased support, see *Capodanno v. Capodanno*, 58 N.J. 113, 118 (1971); *Khalaf*, 58 N.J. at 70; *Martindell*, 21 N.J. at 354, neither can that spouse be permitted unilaterally to designate her funds, as plaintiff attempts to do here, for the children's college education. This is so particularly in light of defendant's obligation under the agreement to pay for the expense of higher education. Any contention that the defendant will not perform this duty must be rejected as premature. When and if such college expenses arise and defendant fails to fulfill his obligation, a court is free to order defendant to make the required payments.[11]

* * *

[Discussion of child support and counsel fees has been omitted.]

For the foregoing reasons, the judgment of the Appellate Division is affirmed. The matter is remanded for further proceedings in accordance with this opinion.

---

[11] If circumstances have changed in such a way that requiring defendant to pay for college would no longer be equitable and fair, the court also remains free to alter the prior arrangement. See *Rufner v. Rufner*, 131 N.J. Eq. at 196; see also *Khalaf*, 58 N.J. at 71-72.

Comments

Lepis illustrates a conservative approach to the relation between divorce settlements and alimony decrees. According to this case, judicial discretion continues to prevail over the power of the parties to regulate their affairs by contract. In view of the fact that in any jurisdiction, regardless of its classification as conservative or liberal in divorce matters, the overwhelming majority of dissolutions are bargained for, the court's pronouncements in *Lepis* appear to be more ceremonial than real. On the other hand, court opinions still furnish the signposts for the bargaining that takes place between the parties or, more appropriately, between the lawyers representing them.

From this perspective it might be interesting to consider what effect an opinion like *Lepis* might have on the process of divorce bargaining in that jurisdiction. Obviously, a husband may be less inclined to make a large payment in settlement of his wife's future claims. Thus the result of *Lepis* does not necessarily favor the recipients of alimony and support, although the case seems to protect the rights of a divorced wife and of children. Yet leaving the matter entirely to the courts and to their relatively unpredictable discretion may not be in the best interest of either party. In the future, after a husband argues *Lepis* as a reason for not making a large payment "in settlement," the wife's lawyer may be willing to make concessions in order to avoid the negative consequences of *Lepis* for his client. Clearly, a married woman may prefer to receive a fixed sum of money or other property allocation at divorce rather than depend on judicial discretion in future requests for modification of alimony. The issue for the negotiations in lawyers' offices is, what concessions can still be validly made by a married woman in a post-*Lepis* situation?

Since the court in *Lepis* seems to foreclose any binding force of agreements provided they have merged into a divorce decree—at least to the extent that they appear to oust the court of jurisdiction or interfere with the power of the court to modify alimony and support obligations—lawyers for both husband and wife may be willing to try to prevent such merger, conceivably by not incorporating the divorce settlement in the decree. Of course, it could not then be enforced by contempt measures but only by ordinary contractual remedies. A further alternative is to avoid the language of alimony and support altogether in the settlement and refer only to mutual allocation of property rights. Since property rights "vest" upon execution of the settlement, it would be difficult for a court to modify what appears to be a certain and final situation proprietary in nature. Needless to say, the lawyer for the husband will attempt to use as much property language as possible, while the lawyer representing the wife will try to retain reference to "alimony and support." Sometimes this may bring about a compromise that deliberately confounds the language in the agreement, for instance, referring to "lump-sum property" or to real estate transfer as "alimony." In spite of the strong language in *Lepis*, it appears that the courts' power is limited.

Quite generally, the concept of alimony is waning and with it the protective discretionary powers of the courts. What we then have is a trend towards equitable distribution of proprietary rights leading to increased negotiations between lawyers. Since the development is in flux, it continues to be possible, for the time being, to argue *Lepis* considerations even in jurisdictions other than New Jersey—if not in court, then in negotiations with opposing counsel.

Reference

Clark, H., THE LAW OF DOMESTIC RELATIONS IN THE UNITED STATES 557–64 (1968).

Lingering Concepts of Fault

McClelland v. McClelland
District Court of Appeal of Florida
318 So.2d 160 (1st D.C.A. Fla. 1975)

SMITH, Judge.
Confronted with an unresolved conflict between decisions of two sister District Courts of Appeal,[1] we are asked to determine whether, in the consideration of a petition for dissolution of marriage and for alimony, child custody and child support, a trial court may hear evidence of allegedly persistent adultery by a respondent husband who seeks no alimony for himself and who does not deny that the marriage is irretrievably broken. Affirming the trial judge, we hold that the court may properly consider such evidence for the light it sheds on the condition of the marriage and on the equities of the necessary financial adjustment to be made between the parties.

The petition for dissolution filed by Ms. McClelland, appellee here, alleged:

> "7. Petitioner alleges that the Respondent has been involved in adulterous relationships for many years. The Petitioner has implored the Respondent to cease these activities, and even now he is engaged in an adulterous relationship. Although the Petitioner would gladly reconcile with the Respondent if he would cease his immoral behavior, he has indicated he does not intend to do so, and the Petitioner thus is reluctantly forced to conclude that the marriage is irretrievably broken."

Responding, appellant William J. McClelland admitted that the marriage is broken and moved to strike as irrelevant all of the quoted allegations except the last six words. The trial court denied that motion and the husband appealed from the interlocutory order. Appellant's answer seeks neither ali-

---

[1] *Pro v. Pro*, 300 So.2d 288 (Fla. App. 4th, 1974) and *Escobar v. Escobar*, 300 So.2d 702 (Fla. App. 3rd, 1974).

mony [as to which see §61.08(1), F.S. 1973] nor child custody and it does not dispute that the marriage is broken. Appellant therefore complains that a foray into the matter of his alleged adultery is not only irrelevant but also potentially destructive of the legislative goals to promote the amicable settlement of the marriage dispute and to minimize the hurt inflicted by the legal process itself. Secs. 61.001(2)(b), (c), F.S. 1973.

* * *

It is evident that the principal issue to be determined by the trial judge in this case, should he agree with the parties that the marriage is irretrievably broken, is the nature and the amount of alimony. Because in making these determinations the trial judge will be guided by evidence of the need of the demanding spouse for support and the ability of the other to respond [*Thigpen v. Thigpen*, 277 So.2d 583 (Fla. App. 1st, 1973)], the District Court of Appeal, Third District, held that a trial judge properly excluded evidence of a respondent husband's adultery when considering whether and in what amount the wife should receive alimony. "Here the wife hoped to obtain alimony," the Court observed, "by showing her husband's adultery." *Escobar v. Escobar*, 300 So.2d 702, 703 (Fla. App. 3rd, 1974). It may be that our Ms. McClelland is similarly motivated and that, while pleading that the marriage is broken for grave cause from which even now she seeks relief short of dissolution, her real intention is to be compensated and to punish her husband financially for his past offenses.

But we must give face value to appellee's declared reluctance to seek dissolution. Although husband and wife may agree in pleadings that the marriage is irretrievably broken, the statute does not require a circuit judge sitting with the historic discretion of a chancellor to find that to be a fact simply because the parties have said so. Secs. 61.011, 61.052(2)(a), F.S. 1973. Such a finding remains a judicial act; and it follows, even in the absence of a pleaded issue on the subject, that the court may consider at least some evidence of whether the marriage is irretrievably broken. The Court must therefore be permitted to learn from the parties the depth of the breach and, inevitably, its cause. [Citation omitted.]

While there is no contest in this case that Ms. McClelland shall have custody of the minor children, the award of custody is also a judicial act which is not woodenly to be performed as stipulated by the parents. For that act also discretion must be informed; and evidence of a parent's persistent adultery could be pertinent to the inquiry.

Finally, we agree with the District Court of Appeal, Fourth District, that evidence of adulterous activities may be pertinent to the question of alimony. *Pro v. Pro*, 300 So.2d 288 (Fla. App. 4th, 1974). The legislative mandate is that the court "consider any factor necessary to do equity and justice between the parties" in respect to alimony. Sec. 61.08(2), F.S. 1973.

We do not share appellant's apprehension that the trial court's decision will resurrect a system of divorce based on fault and, with it, all of the old agonies of accusation and recrimination. The trial judge in this case cautioned against "an unlimited foray into the details" of the alleged adultery and indicated a determination to restrict the inquiry "within reasonable bounds." It is unnecessary, undesirable and improper for the trial judge "to sit and hear every jit and jot of testimony offered by a party as to the other's misconduct" [*Oliver v. Oliver*, 285 So.2d 638, 641, (Fla. App. 4th, 1973)], and there are no circuit judges who, remembering such experiences, will now willingly relive them. "It is enough," the District Court, Fourth District, held in *Oliver* in connection with alimony questions, "that he simply get a broad picture and understanding of the relative equities and factors necessary to do justice."

The interlocutory appeal is dismissed.

McAllister v. McAllister

District Court of Appeal of Florida

345 So.2d 352 (4th D.C.A. Fla. 1977)

LETTS, Judge.

This appeal stems from a dissolution of marriage in which the wife of a successful doctor received a $500.00 per month award of permanent alimony.

This cause is reversed in part.

The McAllisters were married in 1951 while he was a medical student and she an employed pharmacist. The record reflects that the wife worked, to assist her husband finish school,[1] for over a year after the marriage, and almost immediately thereafter, bore the first of four children. Subsequently, until now, she pursued the outmoded profession of housewife and mother, only once working during a vacation period, in 24 years of marriage. Upon receiving his medical degree, the husband commenced to build a medical practice, equipping his office with the aid of a loan secured by the meager inherited stocks and bonds owned by the wife. His practice became successful and Doctor McAllister's 1973 corporate income tax return, for his single P.A., reflected a gross income of over $200,000. Moreover, his personal return for that same year, even after his accountants had done with their computations, reflected a payment to himself of a $75,000 salary. By contrast, the wife's income from dividends and interest totalled less than $2,200 in that same year.

The record reflects that Doctor McAllister is a good father, 49 years old and a man's man, who goes elk hunting in Wyoming, dove shooting in Mexico, fishing, belongs to the yacht club and enjoys many skiing excursions. Vacations have included several trips to the Bahamas, Canada and to Europe. He breeds horses, co-owns cattle, and he himself claims that his monthly personal living expenses add up to over $2,600. There can be no doubt that he enjoys a style of living and social prestige which, by the rest of society's standards, must be termed both generous and glamorous, and which can continue completely unaffected by the permanent alimony award in the court below. The wife, on the other hand, aged 48, although also able bodied and capable of employment, will, in terms of permanent alimony awarded, be receiving only $500.00 per month, plus her private income of $175.00, for a grand total, before taxes, of $675.00 per month, plus whatever she can earn. She claims her knowledge of pharmacology is so outdated that she cannot resume her former profession, but regardless of the truth of this, there is no suggestion that she cannot procure work. (Pharmacologists are paid $6.00 per hour, according to the record). The wife, apparently, has latterly continued her education, part-time, and now holds a degree in anthropology from Florida Atlantic University, but neither she, nor any of her graduate classmates, have been able to secure a job in this field.

The final judgment, insofar as alimony is concerned, awarded the wife $500.00 a month rehabilitative alimony for five years, and $500.00 a month permanent alimony, until his death or her remarriage. In addition, she was given possession of the house for five years (she was already the owner of record of an undivided one-half thereof and her assets were used to collateralize a second mortgage when it was purchased) and the husband required to pay the mortgage and taxes during that period, which he can deduct. At the end of the five years, the house is to be sold and the proceeds equally divided.

---

[1] It is not reflected in the record that he could not have finished his education but for her earnings.

The foregoing recitation of facts and circumstances in the case now before us, is laborious and detailed; however, we find it neither a waste of time nor paper, because we would hope by this opinion to help clarify the law regarding alimony where a breakup of a long term family marriage is involved, and we perceive a tendency by some trial courts, to undercompensate the wife. It would appear that, in some instances at the trial level, the result has very much hinged upon the luck of the draw depending upon which division in the courthouse gets the case; however, we see no such variation at the appellate level, where the recent case law on this kind of long term family marriage breakup has been reasonably uniform. * * *

The history of the change in alimony concept, up through the new dissolution of marriage law and beyond, is best set forth by Judge Rawls in the case of *Brown v. Brown*, 300 So.2d 719 (Fla. 1st DCA 1974), and we see no purpose to repeat it here. Suffice it to say that reasonable permanent alimony still lives, especially, in dissolutions involving the long time role of a mother and housewife.

Alimony is traditionally predicated on three criteria: (1) the ability of the husband to pay it, (2) the needs of the wife compared to reasonable expectations from her own income, and (3) the standard of living enjoyed by the wife during marriage. *Caracristi v. Caracristi*, 324 So.2d 634 (Fla. 2nd DCA 1976). In turn, these three criteria have, in developing case law, been supplemented by six more: (4) the length of the marriage; (5) the number of children. (Included in this category should be the extent to which the wife has been required to do the actual housework and perform the chore of raising the children, vis a vis the amount of outside domestic assistance paid for by the husband;) (6) the relative health and physical condition of both the wife and the husband, and (7) the extent of the contribution by the wife to her husband's successful career.

An eighth factor considered by the courts concerns the conduct, or misconduct, of the parties during the marriage. *Oliver v. Oliver*, 285 So.2d 638 (Fla. 4th DCA 1973). This particular category is cited with some reluctance, (although in the light of case law, it would be remiss to exclude it) for we recognize that, inevitably, a consideration of conduct involves a retrogression back to the fault concept and away from no fault; however, in *Oliver* the Court was careful to point out that the extent of such evidence should be limited, at the trial judge's discretion. Moreover, in *Oliver*, it would appear that the misconduct was gross, for the wife claiming alimony was all the time drunk, repeatedly threatened to kill her husband and made no effort whatever to keep house. The *Oliver* court permitted such testimony to be considered by the chancellor below on the basis of Florida Statute §61.08(2) (1975), which says:

"In determining a proper award of *alimony*, the court may consider *any factor necessary to do equity* and justice between the parties." (emphasis supplied).

By contrast, there is no suggestion in the record now before us of any misconduct by Dr. McAllister, but likewise, there is no indication that Mrs. McAllister was other than a good spouse. At all events, we would urge that evidence of misconduct be limited to gross situations such as existed in *Oliver*, with no mitigating circumstances, otherwise, as was conceded in that case, we will return to the very type of "* * * often sordid and provocative testimony of fault * * * that lead to the enactment of the so-called no-fault dissolution of marriage chapter." *Id.* at 640.

Finally, there is a ninth catchall consideration set forth in *Kennedy v. Kennedy*, 303 So.2d 629 (Fla. 1974), where the Supreme Court said that while alimony should not result in one spouse having to "* * * pass automatically from misfortune to prosperity, neither should a good [spouse] suffer a shocking change from prosperity to misfortune."

In the case now before us, we find all nine of these criteria present, in one form or another, although we quickly point out that the list is intended only as exemplary and neither exclusive nor demanding of the presence of all nine. Mrs. McAllister contributed to the early success of her healthy husband, who is well able to provide support, was married to him for 24 years, enjoyed a high standard of living and community prestige as his wife, will need financial help desperately at the end of five years, and bore her husband four children. By including the number of children as one of the nine significant factors, we do not mean to promote child bearing as an indirect form of future planning in order to insure alimony. After all, child support payments are more appropriate for that; however, it is axiomatic that a husband is a willing participant in the very existence of offspring, and their pre- and post-natal presence, in significant numbers, is a formidable obstacle to the mother pursuing a more financially rewarding career.

The award of permanent alimony in this case was $6,000 per year. The tax laws permit a deduction for that and the award will only actually cost Doctor McAllister half that sum, which in net effect, will hardly discomfit his life style by more than the sacrifice of one elk hunting trip to Wyoming a year. His wife, by contrast, will be devastated, and Mrs. McAllister, her children now adult, (the last is 18 this year), is left with little but her memories. Such is neither just, nor proper, nor is it the law of this State. Indeed, a ruling to the contrary would require society to re-classify the traditional all-American concept of Mom and apple pie and re-label it a most hazardous occupation that all young girls should be dissuaded from.

It is normally not our function to set the amount of the award, but in a case such as this, the trial court must allow a wife to continue with some semblance of her former standards while at the same time ensuring that the husband is not strapped so that his incentive to strive forward and his lust for life are seriously impaired. By so ruling, we do not intend to lend support to the thought that a middle aged healthy woman need not go out to work. In our society, today, women, more often than not, are required to work until retirement and there is no reason to excuse Mrs. McAllister from doing the same just because her former position allowed her to follow a more traditional role. On the other hand, it must be remembered that at her age and level of earning experience, Mrs. McAllister is unlikely to become a great financial success story, and in all probability she will not achieve other than a very modest income.

Accordingly, mere rehabilitative alimony is not enough; however, the award of reasonable permanent periodic alimony does not forever enslave the husband, because significantly changed circumstances, either his or hers, are well settled in the law as a basis for later modification thereof. As was said in *Wilson v. Wilson*, 279 So.2d 893 (Fla. 4th DCA 1973), "Nil prospects to the contrary notwithstanding, if she should somehow blossom into a financially productive member of society and other material changes occur, the husband can obtain a trial court review of the award."

We therefore reverse and direct an increase in the permanent periodic alimony from $500.00 to $1,000.00 per month during the first five years encompassed by the judge's final order. At the end of said period, after, and not before, the house has been sold and the husband no longer required to pay the mortgage payments and taxes on the house, the permanent periodic alimony shall be increased to $1,500.00 per month, until his death or her remarriage. The $500.00 per month rehabilitative alimony is hereby cancelled.

In so holding, we recognize that this decision does little more than repeat the same award as was made by the trial court, except that the total sum arrived at is permanent, rather than a combination of permanent and rehabilitative. Such a similar result is reached by us in deference to the trier of the fact who was out there on the firing line, which we were not; however we would comment that the award is low.

* * *
In all other respects, the final judgment is affirmed.

Comments

McClelland and *McAllister,* from the supposedly no-fault jurisdiction of Florida, illustrate the resurrection of fault by judicial interpretation of the dissolution statute. This development in Florida was initiated by a decision of the Florida State Supreme Court in *Ryan v. Ryan* (see pp. 53–59), which encouraged judicial inquiry into the causes of irretrievable breakdown of marriage. The cases also illustrate that the return to fault is dictated by economic considerations, namely, the amount of alimony to be awarded and the equitable distribution of property. Moral considerations appear to be secondary, although the preference of the judges for traditional values regarding marriage and the family is made quite clear, for example, in the ways husband and wife are described by the court in *McAllister.* This was a "good marriage," with the wife performing the traditional role of homemaker and mother; her conduct was considered laudable. The husband was not depicted as a bad person, although fault is hinted at and, under the facts as pointed out by the court, he appeared to be less than generous with his wife.

McClelland more directly permits the pleading of adultery in a no-fault jurisdiction for three reasons: (1) the chancellor should continue to have discretionary powers in establishing why a marriage is irretrievably broken; (2) adultery and other fault could be relevant in custody of children; (3) the legislature had empowered the courts to "consider any factor necessary to do equity and justice between the parties."

In spite of *McClelland* and *Ryan,* the position of lower courts in Florida is not uniform. Some judges continue to permit motions to strike pleadings based on fault concepts. *McClelland* mentions such a litigation, in which the trial judge properly excluded evidence of the husband's adultery because the pleadings introduced such facts solely for purposes of obtaining alimony. Although the court felt some discomfort about the wife's motivations in the instant case, it concluded that her pleadings had to be taken at face value. She had stated that she would gladly have reconciled if the respondent had ceased his immoral behavior, and that she brought this action reluctantly after the respondent had failed to do so. Reality, however, may be more complex than these pleadings indicate. As discussed in connection with *Manning v. Manning* (see pp. 302–305), pleadings often contain a fictitious element. Rather than giving the genuine reasons for a client's complaint, they reflect the language of the lawyer, who paraphrases legal requirements. The pleadings in *McClelland* could have been skillfully designed to inject adultery into the discussion and to preclude its being stricken as irrelevant under the no-fault statute. Certainly after *McClelland* attorneys would be aware that it is advisable to plead fault with an appearance of hesitation combined with fictitious offers of reconciliation. Judges, on the other hand, may listen to such pleadings if they feel like it. More often than not, they will be so inclined if the marriage in question is of some duration and if substantial economic factors are involved.

The most important effect of cases like *McClelland* and *McAllister* is that they shift proceedings even further from the courts and into lawyers' offices, where all the fault will be discussed in an effort to reach an agreement. Adultery is a good example. According to divorce statistics, it was rarely used by the courts in granting divorces except in New York, where until 1967 it was the sole ground for divorce. More often the threat to file a divorce action based on adultery was used for purposes of pressure in divorce negotiations or, as sometimes stated from a male perspective, for purposes of extortion. Even if the pleadings referred to adultery, they usually contained other divorce grounds, and the claim of adultery could still be withdrawn from consideration. The main effect of *McClelland* is to permit the continued use of adultery and other traditional divorce grounds as bargaining tools in a jurisdiction that seemingly adheres to an irretrievable breakdown standard. Only if the negotiations fail, in a small minority of cases, will it become necessary to plead adultery or other fault as alleged reasons for an irretrievably broken marriage. As in *McClelland*, such pleading is likely to be fictitious to the extent that it tries to avoid the consequences of pure no-fault in regard to alimony and property distribution.

McAllister, which is less visibly concerned with fault, exemplifies a different trend, in which the court can go into the elaborate marital history only because the petitioner has pleaded it. Because the "equities" continue to be relevant, they must be pleaded in great detail, often using the same style and reasoning that was customary before no-fault divorce. In effect this means that the content of the negotiations between the participating lawyers spills over into the pleadings because the negotiations outside of the court have not been successful. It would be a mistake to reproach lawyers for this state of affairs. They perform a valuable and necessary social function, and in continuing to apply conceptions of fault in their negotiations and pleadings, they act under the direction of cases like *McClelland* and *McAllister*. In the last analysis conceptions of moral blame still seem to be needed emotionally, although the underlying issues are more often than not economic.

References

Comment, *Alimony in Florida: No-Fault Stops at the Courthouse Door*, 28 U. Fla. L. Rev. 521 (1976).

Mnookin & Kornhauser, *Bargaining in the Shadow of the Law: The Case of Divorce*, 88 Yale L.J. 950 (1979).

Defenses Against Fault

Nardone v. Nardone

Superior Court of New Jersey

134 N.J. Super. 478, 341 A.2d 698 (1975)

McKENZIE, J.C.C.

The parties were married July 2, 1949. In June 1971 defendant wife advised plaintiff husband that she was involved in an adulterous relationship with the co-respondent. The relationship continued until June 1972, when plaintiff joined defendant in inviting the co-respondent to reside with them. The co-respondent and defendant occupied the master bedroom while plaintiff slept in another bedroom in the house. About January, 1974 plaintiff moved from the marital home to Pennsylvania after accepting employment in that state. At no time did plaintiff object to the relationship between defendant and the co-respondent, and in fact it is clear that he consented to it impliedly, if not expressly.

Is plaintiff entitled to a judgment for divorce on the grounds of adultery based on the above circumstances?

The 1971 revision of our Divorce Law was based primarily on the present-day concept that the viability of the marriage, rather than the assessment of fault, should be the principal factor to be considered in determining whether a marriage should be dissolved. [Citation omitted.] Accordingly, in addition to the introduction of the nonfault ground for divorce based on separation (N.J.S.A. 2A:34-2(d)), the Legislature abolished the defenses of condonation, recrimination and unclean hands in divorce cases. [Citation omitted.]

Previously, connivance in or consent to the adulterous conduct of the wife was a bar to the right of the husband to obtain a divorce on adultery grounds. This rule was grounded on the premise that it was the duty of a husband "to protect his wife's fair name, and to see that she was not improperly led into temptation." *Atha v. Atha,* 94 N.J. Eq. 692, 121 A.301 (Ch. 1923); *aff'd* 95 N.J. Eq. 275, 122 A. 926 (E. & A. 1923). A husband who failed to perform his duty to so protect his wife was held to have unclean hands, barring him from the relief to which he would otherwise be entitled.

In abolishing the unclean hands doctrine, the Legislature has adopted the view that to withhold relief in such circumstances is simply the infliction of punishment by the State. [Citation omitted.] Clearly the marriage is not "less dead" because the husband does not object to the wife's adultery. *Volenti non fit injuria* is now substantially inapplicable in the field of divorce law.

Plaintiff is granted a judgment for divorce.

Mogged v. Mogged

Supreme Court of Illinois

55 Ill.2d 221, 302 N.E.2d 293 (1973)

UNDERWOOD, Chief Justice:

The circuit court of Iroquois County entered a decree of divorce in favor of both parties on the grounds of mental cruelty.

* * *

In his complaint, plaintiff Roy Mogged alleged that his wife, defendant Wilma Mogged, was guilty of extreme and repeated mental cruelty. Defendant filed an answer denying the allegations of the complaint and counterclaimed for divorce from plaintiff alleging that plaintiff had been guilty of extreme and repeated mental cruelty toward her. After hearing a portion of the plaintiff's case, which included examination of the defendant as an adverse witness, the trial judge called a halt to the proceedings, over plaintiff's objection, and granted a decree of divorce to each party after stating that it was his opinion that both parties were at fault and that nothing would be accomplished by hearing further testimony.

On appeal by the plaintiff, the appellate court held that the evidence heard by the trial court was sufficient to establish extreme and repeated mental cruelty on the part of each party and stated that "the real question involved * * * is whether the doctrine of recrimination in Illinois * * * should be maintained inviolate, thus automatically precluding the divorce of parties who have been guilty of marital misconduct of equal stature toward the other, or whether that doctrine must be reexamined, and, in the light of present day reality, be rejected as unsound." (5 Ill. App.3d at 583, 284 N.E.2d at 664.) The court answered this question by concluding that the doctrine of recrimination should not be applied in those cases where, in the exercise of sound judicial discretion, it would be unwarranted. In affirming the trial court, the appellate court held further that the trial judge did not err in exercising his discretion in favor of the dual decree of divorce.

* * *

The doctrine of recrimination has been the subject of extensive analysis and commentary over the years with most writers recommending its modification or abolition. [Citations omitted.] Also, some courts have re-examined their States' respective divorce laws and have found them susceptible of an interpretation which modified and limited the previous application of the doctrine. Notable in this respect is the decision of the California Supreme Court in *DeBurgh v. DeBurgh* (1952), 39 Cal.2d 858, 250 P.2d 598, where that court analyzed in depth the origin and development of the doctrine as well as the public-policy considerations involved. The court concluded that the California statute which was then in existence did not require the automatic application of the doctrine of recrimination but instead left to the discretion and duty of the trial judge "to determine whether or not the fault of the plaintiff in a divorce action is to be regarded as 'in bar' of the plaintiff's cause of divorce based upon the fault of the defendant." (39 Cal.2d at 871, 250 P.2d at 605.) The court went on to state that dual divorces were permissible in appropriate circumstances. The Florida Supreme Court in *Stewart v. Stewart* (1946), 158 Fla. 326, 328, 29 So.2d 247, 249, has also held that "[t]he application of the doctrine of recrimination like the doctrine of clean hands is a matter of sound judicial discretion dependent upon public policy, public welfare and the exigencies of the case at bar." Other courts have reached similar conclusions. * * * We also note that in the Uniform Marriage and Divorce Act (1970), sec. 303(e), the National Conference of Commissioners on Uniform State Laws has recommended abolition of recrimination as a defense in divorce proceedings.

In Illinois, recrimination has long been recognized as a bar to divorce. (See *Davis v. Davis* (1857), 19 Ill. 333.) After adoption of the 1874 Divorce Act (Rev. Stat. 1874, ch. 40, par. 1 *et seq.*), which is the basis of our existing act, this court reaffirmed the doctrine. (*Bast v. Bast* (1876), 82 Ill. 584.) The subject was reviewed again in *Duberstein v. Duberstein* (1897), 171 Ill. 133, where the court defined the doctrine in the following terms:

" 'A party charged with cruelty may justify himself or herself by showing that the other party was equally to blame. * * * The law is for the relief of an oppressed party, and the courts will not interfere in quarrels where both parties commit reciprocal excesses and outrages.' * * * Divorce is a remedy provided for an innocent party; (5 AM. & ENG. ENCY. OF LAW, 825, note 6); so that, when each party has committed a cause for divorce, the causes being of the same statutory character, neither can complain of the other."

(171 Ill. at 144–145.) The court concluded that when parties are *in pari delicto* they must be left to themselves. * * *

Whether or not the defense of recrimination should be abolished or modified in Illinois is a question involving complex public-policy considerations as to which compelling arguments may be made on both sides. For the reasons stated hereafter, we believe that these questions are appropriately within the province of the legislature, and that, if there is to be a change in the law of this State on this matter, it is for the legislature and not the courts to bring about that change.

* * *

* * * What we stated in *Maki v. Frelk* (1968), 40 Ill.2d 193, 196–197, 239 N.E.2d 445, 447, is pertinent here: "Where it is clear that the court has made a mistake it will not decline to correct it, even though the rule may have been re-asserted and acquiesced in for long number of years. (*Neff v. George*, 364 Ill. 306, 4 N.E.2d 388.) No person has a vested right in any rule of law entitling him to insist that it shall remain unchanged for his benefit. (*Grasse v. Dealer's Transport Co.*, 412 Ill. 179, 190, 106 N.E.2d 124.) But when a rule of law has once been settled, contravening no statute or constitutional principle, such rule ought to be followed unless it can be shown that serious detriment is thereby likely to arise prejudicial to public interests. [Citations omitted.] The rule of *stare decisis* is founded upon sound principles in the administration of justice, and rules long recognized as the law should not be departed from merely because the court is of the opinion that it might decide otherwise were the question a new one. [Citation omitted.]"

Furthermore, we believe it is significant that over a period of almost one hundred years during which the doctrine of recrimination as enunciated in the *Duberstein* case has been established law of this State our legislature has in no manner acted to either abolish or modify the doctrine, although it has limited its application. This occurred most recently in 1967 when the legislature amended the Act by the addition of section 8a, which provides: "In every action for a divorce commenced on or after the effective date of this amendatory Act of 1967, the fault or conduct of the plaintiff, unless raised by the pleadings, is not a bar to the action nor a proper basis for the refusal of a decree of divorce." (Ill. Rev. Stat. 1971, ch. 40, par. 9a.) This provision, while limiting the application of the defense of recrimination, clearly recognizes its existence and contemplates its application in cases such as the one before us where recriminatory conduct on the part of the plaintiff is raised by the pleadings.

* * *

Accordingly, the judgments of the appellate court and the circuit court of Iroquois County are reversed. It seems appropriate, however, in view of the fact that the action of the trial court prevented the parties from completing the presentation of evidence, to afford an opportunity for the submission of such additional pleadings and evidence, if any, as the parties may desire and the trial court deems appropriate. We accordingly remand the cause to the circuit court of Iroquois County.

Reversed and remanded.

KLUCZYNSKI, Justice (dissenting):
I would affirm the judgment of the appellate court. It is my opinion that the trial court in its sound discretion should decide whether a recriminatory defense is permissible based solely upon the facts of each case. * * *

* * *

In a comment in the *Journal of Family Law,* the trend toward abolition or modification of the recrimination doctrine was examined. The author stated,

> "Whatever value may be gained in the application of the 'clean hands' doctrine in mutual fault divorces, it must be weighed against the ramifications of denial of relief. It must be remembered that if relief is denied, the state is in effect forcing two people to live together after they have decided that their continued relationship is no longer viable. It is very conceivable that this forced relationship could lead to increased hatred between parties, fostering of adulterous relationships, and destruction of home life to the detriment of the children."

Albers, *Judicial Discretion and the Doctrine of Recrimination* (1972), 11 J. FAM. L. 737, 739.

    * * *

The majority remands to afford the parties an opportunity to introduce any additional evidence despite their recognition that the findings that both parties committed wrongs of an equal stature is adequately established by the present record. It is unclear what the majority contemplates. Additional evidence of mental cruelty would be useless for it has been determined that if both parties are guilty of positive acts of the same statutory nature, recrimination must bar a divorce. (*Garrett v. Garrett,* 252 Ill. 318, 322, 96 N.E. 882) To say now that a divorce should be granted to the party who might ultimately be determined to have occasioned a lesser degree of mental cruelty would be to adopt the concept of comparative rectitude, which was designed to ameliorate the harsh injustice created by recrimination. [Citations omitted.] This doctrine has not previously been applied in Illinois.

Thus it would appear that in order to obtain a divorce in this jurisdiction one of the present parties must plead and prove a ground for divorce not subject to a recriminatory defense of mental cruelty or have the opposing party acquiesce in the divorce by voluntarily amending the pleadings to exclude the allegation of a recriminatory defense. The former seems unlikely at this juncture, the latter might be subject to criticism as a product of collusion.

    * * * The doctrine of recrimination is rooted in antiquity and has attained its initial status by judicial action. The present authorities are extremely critical of the harsh, unjust ramifications of this outmoded concept. Finally, our present Divorce Act does not preclude judicial modification or limitation of the doctrine, and the intent of recent legislative action can be reasonably interpreted as contrary to the strict application adopted by the majority.

This case is particularly appropriate to the comments of Justice Oliver Wendell Holmes. "It is revolting to have no better reason for a rule of law than that so it was laid down in the time of Henry IV. It is still more revolting if the grounds upon which it was laid down have vanished long since, and the rule simply persists from blind imitation of the past." *The Path of the Law,* 10 HARV. L. REV. 457, 469 (1897).

Simonson v. Simonson

Appellate Court of Illinois

128 Ill. App.2d 39, 262 N.E.2d 326 (1970)

STAMOS, Presiding Justice.

Defendant appeals from a decree that awarded plaintiff a divorce based upon mental cruelty, denied defendant a divorce based upon desertion and awarded custody of their six year old daughter to plaintiff. The decree also directed defendant to pay the sum of $40.00 per week to plaintiff for child support and provided that the court retain jurisdiction to hear evidence regarding alimony.

Defendant argues the following contentions:

(1) There is a total lack of evidence that defendant's conduct caused plaintiff's life or health to be endangered;
(2) Plaintiff condoned all of the acts complained of;
(3) Plaintiff's departure and her living separate and apart from defendant were unjustified and entitled defendant to a decree of divorce on the grounds of desertion;
(4) The court abused its discretion in awarding custody of their child to plaintiff; and
(5) Plaintiff failed to allege and prove lack of provocation.

Plaintiff's complaint alleged fifteen specific allegations of defendant's conduct toward plaintiff that allegedly caused her severe and extreme mental anguish. It was further alleged that as a result plaintiff suffered a severe breakdown that required her hospitalization and placed her in great fear for her mental and physical well being.

Defendant answered and denied each specific allegation of misconduct toward plaintiff; that if the allegations were true, they were all condoned by plaintiff and are of themselves glaring evidence of the emotional instability and mental incapacity of plaintiff and not sufficient to establish a cause of action for mental cruelty.

The allegations and proof of defendant's misconduct, with the exception of a few instances, related to a period of time of approximately a year before the parties separated. The parties were married on May 11, 1961, after a 4 month courtship and separated on August 30, 1967.

Plaintiff testified and also called upon next door neighbors, a family friend and two treating psychiatrists to testify in support of her allegations.

Defendant testified and denied each accusation of misconduct toward defendant and related general and specific instances of his devotion, affection and concern for plaintiff and his efforts to accommodate her personality. A salesman who frequented the parties' home and delicatessen testified that defendant always treated plaintiff with respect and decency and never cursed or abused her.

Plaintiff's evidence revealed that defendant criticized plaintiff in public and private regarding her housekeeping abilities, repeatedly boasted about his pre-marital relations, unfavorably compared plaintiff with these other women, struck her with a rolled up newspaper on the face and head causing her great pain and twisted her leg on another occasion causing her great pain and anguish. The evidence further revealed that defendant called her "nuts" threatening to send her to the "nut house," advised others that plaintiff was "nuts," constantly cursed and swore at plaintiff repeatedly telling her to return to Norway, constantly remained out late at night, possessed and publicly displayed pornograhic pictures and magazines in her presence, refused to introduce plaintiff as his wife and constantly caused her humiliation and embarrassment before their friends, relatives, customers and employees at defendant's delicatessen store.

Plaintiff testified that shortly after her marriage she realized her husband was a personality with three sides and that she had made a bad marriage, but endeavored to make it work although she was very unhappy because he mistreated her.

In 1964 plaintiff developed nervousness and on medical advice took tranquilizers and sleeping pills for a few days. She had no further difficulty until February, 1967, when plaintiff became very nervous and experienced vomiting spells and diarrhea. She lost her appetite, became nauseous, suffered from insomnia and began to lose weight. She prevailed upon her mother-in-law to drive her to the Edgewater Hospital, and testified that she did not have anyone else to assist her and could not rely upon defendant. After a two week period of hospitalization it was determined that plaintiff was in need of psychiatric care to prevent her "anxiety reactions" and was referred to the Northwestern University Clinic for examination and treatment. Plaintiff made some visits to the clinic during the summer of 1967 but felt she was not being helped. Plaintiff testified that during this period of her illness, she pleaded with defendant on her knees and implored him to at least treat her as his friend. She told defendant that she was desperate and needed his help, but defendant laughed and threatened her with incarceration in an institution for the mentally ill. Plaintiff testified that defendant's threat was the "biggest scare" in her life.

In September, 1967, plaintiff's condition had not improved and she prevailed upon her sister-in-law to drive her to Billings Hospital where plaintiff was hospitalized and treated in the psychiatric clinic for six weeks. Her symptoms were similar to those she exhibited in February, 1967, and her condition was diagnosed as "depressive reaction" for which she was afforded treatment. It was the opinion of the psychiatrists that her marital difficulties were a major contributor to the need for hospitalization. Two other emotional events in plaintiff's life they deemed significant were plaintiff's miscarriage in August, 1966, and the fact that her daughter in February, 1967, attained the same age that plaintiff had when plaintiff's first sibling was born. Plaintiff was discharged from the hospital on October 26, 1967.

After plaintiff's separation from defendant in August, 1967, and her subsequent hospital care, she was greatly improved and exhibited none of the symptoms for which she was given treatment. Her mood was considerably improved and the psychiatric impairment was minimal. Plaintiff was also examined on July 25, 1968, and no evidence of any psychiatric disorder was discovered.

During her hospitalization the psychiatrists discerned that plaintiff was a person who tended to keep resentment to herself, not being open and expressive about it, with a tendency to handle stressful relationships, inner distresses and nervousness by pleasantness and carefree amiability.

There is no dispute that plaintiff suffered a mental illness that required her hospitalization on more than one occasion. Plaintiff's condition was diagnosed as "depressive reaction." Defendant contends that there is a total lack of evidence that his conduct caused plaintiff's mental health to be endangered, but that plaintiff was a victim of her own frail personality and emotional instability. Defendant further contends that none of his conduct, that plaintiff complains about, if true, would be sufficient to meet the legal requirement for mental cruelty.

In *Hayes v. Hayes*, 117 Ill. App.2d 211 at page 215, 254 N.E.2d 288 at page 290 the court expressed the following language we find appropriate to the case at bar:

* * *

" 'Whether certain acts will constitute physical or mental cruelty still depends upon the total factual background surrounding the conduct under question. This includes the particular emotional and personal makeup of the parties and the varying circumstances under which any of the incidents occurred that may have given rise to the acts.' *Stanard v. Stanard*, 108 Ill. App.2d 240, 247 N.E.2d 438 (1969). In this case the emotional makeup of the plaintiff must be considered in determining the effect of the conduct of defendant in providing grounds for the mental cruelty allegation. Plaintiff's testimony, taken with the psychiatrist's reports, furnish an adequate basis for the court's findings."

We find that the evidence in the case at bar is sufficient to establish that defendant has been guilty of extreme and repeated mental cruelty. (Ill. Rev. Stat., ch. 40 §1 (1967)).

Defendant contends that the continued cohabitation and sexual relations of the parties constituted condonation of defendant's alleged misconduct. Condonation is a question of intent to be shown by words and deeds that reflect full, free and voluntary forgiveness and continued cohabitation will not necessarily amount to condonation. *Collinet v. Collinet,* 31 Ill. App.2d 72, 78, 175 N.E.2d 659. Plaintiff in the case at bar testified that she engaged in sexual relations, relied upon by defendant as condonation, against her wishes and that she was afraid of him.

In *Rasgaitis v. Rasgaitis,* 347 Ill. App. 477, at page 482, 107 N.E.2d 273, at page 275, the court said: "The law will not presume that a wronged wife condones the actions of her guilty husband simply because the difficulty of finding another place to live, the welfare of her child, and other factors beyond her control, force her to remain temporarily in the same house with him." Condonation is an affirmative defense which defendant pleaded but failed to prove by a preponderance of evidence.

In view of the foregoing, defendant's contention that plaintiff's departure and her living separate and apart were unjustified and entitled defendant to a decree of divorce on grounds of desertion, is of no merit.

The Chancellor elicited an opinion from one of plaintiff's psychiatrists that plaintiff was capable of caring for her minor child. The Chancellor also asked questions of the same witness which revealed that the witness was not surprised to learn that plaintiff filed a separate maintenance action while she was hospitalized. Defendant complains and contends that the answers were both bottomed on conversations the witness had with plaintiff and were hearsay and should not have been admitted into evidence. We find no error in the admission of an expression of the medical opinion and as to the other point, we observe that it was on defendant's own motion that voluminous medical records of both the Edgewater Hospital and the University of Chicago Hospitals and Clinics were received into evidence. These exhibits reflected countless recitations of conversations plaintiff had with the witness and other medical personnel regarding her illness, treatment, prognosis, symptoms and her marital disharmony and discontent. We also note that defendant's cross-examination prior to the Chancellor's questions delved into conversations this psychiatrist had with plaintiff regarding her marital difficulties.

There is no evidence in the record that would justify this court in finding that the Chancellor abused his discretion in awarding custody of the minor child to plaintiff. The psychiatric testimony established that plaintiff was not emotionally unstable but had in fact recovered from her illness and was clearly able to function and assume responsibility for the care of her minor child. The paramount consideration in determining custody is the welfare and best interest of the child. *Nye v. Nye,* 411 Ill. 408, 105 N.E.2d 300. We cannot set aside this award unless it was entered against the manifest weight of the evidence. * * *

Defendant contends that plaintiff's complaint lacks an essential element in failing to allege a lack of provocation and thus does not state a cause of action and that therefore, the complaint may be successfully attacked on appeal as not justifying the decree. *Stanard v. Stanard,* 108 Ill. App.2d 240, 247 N.E.2d 438.

* * *

In the case at bar plaintiff's evidence more than adequately depicted that defendant's misconduct was not caused or provoked by plaintiff and defendant averred and adduced evidence and conducted his cross-examination on the theory that the acts and misconduct of purported extreme and repeated mental cruelty charged by plaintiff never occurred—a theory which, by its nature, is inconsistent with a defense of provocation.

* * *
The judgment is affirmed.

Comments

The continued significance of fault and moral blame, even in many no-fault jurisdictions, raises the question of the extent to which these residual conceptions are related to the original, now seemingly abolished, divorce grounds (e.g., adultery, desertion, extreme cruelty). It also must be examined whether any of the traditional defenses has survived, and if so in what form. Obviously, as long as courts continue to discuss adultery, as in *McClelland* (see pp. 332–333), or talk about facts that may be the equivalent of mental cruelty, as in *McAllister* (see pp. 334–337), lawyers will have to be concerned with what now constitutes adultery or cruelty, even though they practice in a no-fault divorce jurisdiction. They also will have to be concerned with the kinds of defenses that are still available even though those defenses, such as condonation, collusion, connivance, recrimination, and unclean hands, may have been legislatively abolished.

Because of the difficulties involved in eliminating conceptions of fault altogether, it is submitted that an effective law practice in any jurisdiction must include a knowledge of the traditional divorce grounds and the defenses, regardless of what a given statute states. Even in apparently pure no-fault jurisdictions fault may resurface, for example, in custody proceedings involving children. And even in community-property jurisdictions such as California, which first legislated on no-fault divorce, a judge may be moved by the equities of a case in determining what is half of such property (see *In re Marriage of Mix*, pp. 100–105). In any event, the traditional definitions of fault grounds and defenses continue to be relevant for divorce negotiations. More important, failure to inform a client of the lingering relevance of adultery and other fault grounds may constitute malpractice. From that perspective the mechanical application of no-fault statutes in some law firms, in which paraprofessionals record the history of the marriage and fill in form pleadings in the interest of low-cost divorce and rapid turnover, is dangerous and may backfire, with suits eventually being brought against lawyers.

To the extent that a given jurisdiction has retained traditional divorce grounds in addition to a newly adopted no-fault statute, it is clear that preexisting case law on adultery, cruelty, and so on, as well as in regard to the defenses, continues to be applicable. Not quite so clear is what happens in such mixed jurisdictions if fault and no-fault grounds are linked together in the same proceedings by way of petition and counterclaim. Even though logic seems to dictate that no-fault prevail in such situations, it is more likely that fault will spill over into the whole proceeding with all the defenses then still available.

Even more complex is the situation if a no-fault divorce jurisdiction has legislatively abolished all defenses, but insists judicially that fault continues to be relevant (see *Ryan*, pp. 53–59, and *McClelland*, pp. 332–333). In *McClelland* it was made clear that courts should be interested only in the broad picture of why the marriage is irretrievably broken and refrain from going into details. Actual proof of sexual intercourse, as was necessary under the traditional divorce ground of adultery, or minute establishment of "reasonable apprehension of bodily harm," as under the divorce ground of cruelty, may no longer be required. Yet if moral blame has a bearing on the outcome, the traditional defenses must continue to be available in some form to the person who is accused of misconduct. *Ryan* makes it clear as to how this is to come about. Accordingly, not only is the chancellor permitted to continue to inquire into fault by asking why the marriage is irretrievably broken, but the respondent must have the right to demonstrate why it is not. The breakdown standard implicitly incorporates the possibility of fault and the traditional defenses against it. The legislative abolition of these defenses is, however, not entirely ineffective. What has been binding law has probably now become discretionary. The judge is not likely to refer expressly to condonation, collusion, connivance, recrimination, and unclean hands, because that might lead to a reversal on appeal. Instead he will state as a finding of fact that the marriage is or is not irretrievably broken.

If the husband was facilitating the adultery of his wife, a judge might at least theoretically continue to deny relief even in a no-fault jurisdiction. More likely, as in *Nardone*, a dissolution will be granted. If husband and wife engage consensually in "swinging," a judge, without reference to recrimination, may deny their request for dissolution because the marriage is not irretrievably broken. A more natural course of events would be for the judge to give a moral lecture to the parties and grant the request. In either case the fault of the parties and the nature of their defenses have a definite bearing on the remaining equities of the requests, particularly in regard to alimony, property distribution, and child custody.

It should be remembered that the opinion in *Mogged* originated in Illinois, a jurisdiction without no-fault divorce. The traditional defenses were still fully in force. Yet even with respect to recrimination, the approach of the Supreme Court of Illinois was not as orthodox as it appears. In its concluding paragraph the majority opinion remanded the case to the trial court to facilitate additional pleadings and evidence by the parties, which in effect amounted to an implicit invitation to the lawyers to engage in negotiations about the divorce grounds and defenses. The outcome of this litigation may thus be similar to that in a no-fault jurisdiction, although probably at a much higher cost. Yet it seems clear that the Supreme Court of Illinois perceived its primary function in this case to be one of maintaining principle.

Simonson injected the problem of insanity, which can come up in multiple fashions. In this instance it was used to demonstrate the extreme and repeated mental cruelty of the husband, which resulted in a "depressive reaction." It could also have been used as a defense by the wife that, because of her condition, she could not be cruel or commit desertion, nor could she commit any other act based on fault. She could also have used insanity as a reply to the husband's defense that she had "condoned," in other words, forgiven, his misconduct by continuing to live and have sexual relations with him. Condonation would also require legal capacity at the time in question. In addition, insanity could have an impact on alimony, equitable distribution of property, and child custody. Had this been a no-fault jurisdiction, the pleadings could have been quite similar in an effort to show irretrievable breakdown of marriage, although express reference to condonation might have been avoided. Continued sexual intercourse, if voluntary, could show that a marriage is salvageable. Hence lawyers in any jurisdiction should continue to include in their check lists inquiry about intercourse and when it last took place.

An additional problem with insanity may arise in some no-fault jurisdictions. California and Florida, for example, have two no-fault grounds, one based on ordinary breakdown of marriage, the other on insanity. The question of how the two grounds relate to each other could arise. For instance, if a husband were to bring a request for dissolution of marriage in Florida, based on the alleged mental incompetence of his wife, he would have to satisfy specific statutory requirements, for example, that the wife must have been adjudged incompetent for a preceding period of at least three years.* If such adjudication is missing or if it is less than three years in the past, could the husband base his request for dissolution on the first ground, namely, that his marriage is "irretrievably broken"? It can be argued that the wife, in such an instance, could defend herself by stating that an action must satisfy the requirements of the insanity ground. Assuming this defense prevails, the first ground should really read, "The marriage is irretrievably broken, unless the other party is mentally incompetent, in which case the petitioner must proceed under the requirements of that ground." Yet this interpretation injects a further element of residual fault into the statute: that the respondent in a no-fault action must be legally competent, that is, responsible for the breakdown of marriage. Whether actual litigation will often reach such a level of conceptual refinement is doubtful. Attorneys are likely to proceed under a simple theory of breakdown of marriage in cases of insanity. However, if a lawyer who represents an insane person does not raise the conceptual problems resulting from mental incompetence, he may become susceptible to substantial claims of malpractice.

Reference

Comment, *The End of Innocence: Elimination of Fault in California Divorce Law,* 17 UCLA L. Rev. 1306 (1970).

---

*Fla. Stat. §61.052(1)(b) (1981).

Bibliography

Atkin, *Survival of Fault in Contemporary Family Law in New Zealand*, 10 VICT. U. WELLINGTON L. REV. 93 (1979).

Clark, H., THE LAW OF DOMESTIC RELATIONS IN THE UNITED STATES chs. 12 & 13 (1968).

Comment, *The Development of Sharing Principles in Common Law Marital Property States*, 28 UCLA L. REV. 1269 (1981).

Comment, *The End of Innocence: Elimination of Fault in California Divorce Law*, 17 UCLA L. REV. 1306 (1970).

Diamond, *No-Fault: New Emphasis in Divorce Cases*, Los Angeles Times, Feb. 14, 1977, §1 at 1, col. 1.

Feldman, *A Statutory Proposal to Remove Divorce From the Courtroom*, 29 ME. L. REV. 25 (1977).

Frank, Berman, & Mazur-Hart, *No Fault Divorce and the Divorce Rate*, 58 NEB. L. REV. 1 (1979).

Freed & Foster, *Divorce in the Fifty States: An Overview as of 1978*, 13 FAM. L.Q. 105 (1979).

Freeman, *When Marriage Fails*, 31 CURRENT LEGAL PROB. 109 (1978).

Glendon, *Modern Marriage Law and Its Underlying Assumptions: The New Marriage and the New Property*, 13 FAM. L.Q. 441 (1980).

Glendon, M., THE NEW FAMILY AND THE NEW PROPERTY (1981).

Inker, Perocchi, & Maloney, *Alimony and Assignment of Property: The Massachusetts Experience*, 26 BOSTON B.J. March 1982, at 4.

Inker, Walsh, & Perocchi, *Alimony Orders Following Short-Term Marriages*, 12 FAM. L.Q. 91 (1978).

Mnookin & Kornhauser, *Bargaining in the Shadow of the Law: The Case of Divorce*, 88 YALE L.J. 950 (1979).

Note, *Are Fault Requirements in Divorce Actions Unconstitutional?* 16 J. FAM. L. 265 (1977).

A PRACTICAL GUIDE TO THE NEW YORK EQUITABLE DISTRIBUTION DIVORCE LAW (H. Foster ed.) (1980).

Project, *The Unauthorized Practice of Law and Pro Se Divorce: An Empirical Analysis*, 86 YALE L.J. 104 (1976).

Raphael, Frank, & Wilder, *Divorce in America: The Erosion of Fault*, 81 DICK. L. REV. 719 (1977).

Rheinstein, M., MARRIAGE STABILITY, DIVORCE AND THE LAW (1972).

Wadlington, *Divorce Without Fault Without Perjury*, 52 VA. L. REV. 32 (1966).

Wadlington, *Sexual Relations After Separation or Divorce*, 63 VA. L. REV. 249 (1977).

Weitzman, *The Economics of Divorce: Social and Economic Consequences of Property, Alimony and Child Support Awards*, 28 UCLA L. REV. 1181 (1981).

Weitzman & Dixon, *The Alimony Myth: Does No-Fault Divorce Make a Difference?*, 14 FAM. L.Q. 141 (1980).

4

State Involvement in Marriage

Whenever any form of state action has an impact on individual marriage, in any context whatsoever, one may speak of state involvement in marriage as an institution. State intervention, consequently, is diffuse and derives from multiple legislative, executive, and judicial sources. Perhaps in marriage more than anywhere else the express legal purposes of this state involvement are divergent from the actual social functions of regulation.

Underlying Conceptions of Property. Legal materials in treatises on the family and in casebooks that begin with courtship and engagement are usually arranged so that marriage is viewed mainly as a "live organism" or "going concern." This is probably misleading. True, the impact of legal regulation of marriage may be felt throughout life, but a closer look at litigated cases arising from law practice gives a different picture. Marriage becomes a matter of active legal concern chiefly when it is in trouble, breaking up, or terminated by death. Even then the primary interest appears to be to allocate and distribute property rights, and marriage itself is incidental to such disposition. Engagement is of no legal concern until it is broken. Formal requirements to obtain a marriage license and the capacity to marry are ordinarily of no serious legal import—except in an occasional mandamus action against a recalcitrant county judge—unless years have passed and an action for annulment of marriage is brought or the alleged invalidity of marriage is claimed to affect devolution of property upon death. The state is interested in and regulates these proprietary issues, and in doing so it regulates marriage.

To this practical concern, which views marriage as essentially a prelude to potential issues of property, a new concern has been added in the past decade. Marital property, not being present in substantial amounts in most cases, has become secondary to the expectation of private and public entitlements. The whole population, not just the poor, participates in this hope. Prime examples are social security benefits and other measures that secure minimum income and access to consumer goods and adequate housing. In this context, marriage or membership in a family or household again is a prelude to potential issues of property in the transformed appearance of entitlements.

This is not to say that property is the only societal concern in marriage, but merely that in law it seems to be a dominant issue. In medieval England, the laws of the family and of inheritance were closely allied with feudalism and land tenure. It may be felt that the persistent prevalence of property as an analytic principle for relationships based on love and affection is cynical. Yet the experience of actual law practice confirms that the law is not interested in happy marriages. It leaves them alone—in fact increasingly so under concepts of privacy.

Decline of a Dual System of Family Law. Since the Elizabethan poor laws, there has been justification for speaking of a dual system of family law: the courts and private law dealing with the rights of the reasonably affluent, on the one hand, and the legislative and executive branches of government concerned with the duties of the less fortunate, on the other. The nature of state involvement in these two spheres has been changing, and so has the corresponding involvement of lawyers. The wall separating the well-off from the poor is crumbling, and we may be standing at the threshold of what promises to be a uniform law of the family, governing all segments of the population equally.

As we have seen, privacy has influenced equality between spouses; this same privacy also has procedural aspects. No longer is it up to the courts to protect the privacy of middle-class families by low visibility of adjudication. There is now a strengthened right to privacy which deflects government intrusion into all families, no matter where positioned in the social structure.

The emphasis on personal rights and privacy has inevitable consequences. Relative freedom from investigation through various state branches means greater autonomy for all members of the family than in the past. The disbursing of public funds to both the poor and the more affluent is facilitated. Although hopefully in its aggregate effect this involves a redistribution of national wealth toward a more even spread, it has not seemed to result in a decline of private property. Rather one could say that the focus of proprietary concern is shifting to universal entitlements. In particular, the importance of property distribution upon death is being slowly replaced by a growing list of entitlements during life. The amalgamation of formal marriage and informal cohabitation can be seen from this new perspective, as well as an end to the legal relevance of illegitimacy of children. Since this process is not confined to any particular segment of the population, the modern middle-class family is acquiring some of the characteristics of welfare recipients; on the other hand, the legitimate expectations, aspirations, and rights of the lower classes are increasing.

Waning State Involvement in Formation and Termination of Marriage. The consequences of this evolution, which is by no means complete, are making themselves felt in decreased legislative and judicial regulation of marriage. The capacity to marry has been substantially broadened, even at the risk of greater expenditure of tax funds. Age requirements have been lowered. Mental competence to marry is assumed, not only in the young, but also in the mentally retarded, infirm, and senile. For some relationships and some purposes, incest taboos appear less serious than a generation ago because procreation is no longer always a primary concern of marriage. Past prohibitions against interracial marriage are so obsolete that some of the leading treatises hardly mention them. Requirements for marriage that appear on the books are held to be directory only, addressed to state authorities. Violations that would have voided marriages in the past are no longer seen as affecting the essence of the relationship. After the death of a party it no longer matters whether or not there was a marriage so long as there was a relationship worthy of legal recognition. Thus any past defects tend to be cured. Even marriages that are bigamous at their inception may be upheld for certain purposes, for instance, distribution of "marital" property.

Jurisdictional requirements for termination of marriage have also been affected. If the legal consequences of marriage and nonmarriage are assimilated to each other, it no longer makes as much sense as it once did to speak of a "marital *res*" and to determine where exactly a particular cohabitation is located, where the parties are domiciled, and where they reside. Nor is conflict of laws now a matter of paramount concern, except perhaps when it becomes important for the allocation of funds. On the whole, the decline of fault and of the use of moral yardsticks in the last 10 years has tended to neutralize the differences between state governments in their approach to marriage and divorce. In the foreseeable future no particular state law of dissolution of marriage may appear to be more "significant" than any other. If all governmental interests, at least among sister states, are essentially similar, it will no longer make sense for lawyers to speak of conflict of laws or for parties to go elsewhere for a divorce. As a result, American courts will increasingly apply their own jurisdictional and substantive laws of the family, and sister states will more or less automatically grant full faith and credit.

Continued Impact of Traditional Notions. Moral considerations, of course, continue to be prevalent in personal relations, but on a social and religious level rather than as a matter of governmental intervention. The same applies to marriage and sexual relations across barriers of race. While no longer subject to legislated prohibitions, however, such interracial relations may still be rare because of continuing, though slowly declining, social taboos.

Traditional legal practice may, for the present, continue relatively unaffected by the lessening of state involvement. For many lawyers marriage will remain what it always was, a matter that comes up incidentally in distribution and adjudication of rights to private property. On the other hand, specialized legal practice in social security, welfare rights, and consumer protection, particularly in legal clinics and legal aid offices, is now dealing with the new forms of entitlements. Thus conceptions of property, in various manifestations, serve as bridges between the past and today, between marriage and informal cohabitation, and between traditional law practice and social concerns.

Form Requirements

Mandamus

F.A. Marriage License
District Court of Pennsylvania
4 Pa. D. & C.2d 1 (1955)

KLEIN, P. J., and LEFEVER, J., May 19, 1955.
Application for a marriage license was filed by the applicants on April 30, 1955. It appears from the statements made by the female applicant (herein referred to as F.A.), that she was a mental patient in St. Mary's Hospital, Philadelphia, for a period of two months in 1951.

Mr. MacDonnell, assistant orphans' court clerk, pursuant to the provisions of section 9 of The Marriage Law of August 22, 1953, P.L. 1344, 48 PS §1, *et seq.*, refused to issue the license and certified the matter to this court for hearing.

This is the first time that this court has been asked to construe the provisions of the new marriage law, pertaining to the issuance of a marriage license to a person who has been afflicted with mental illness within a period of five years prior to the date of application for the license.

* * *

The legislature has thus placed a great social responsibility on the orphans' court. It is our duty to determine whether "it is for the best interest of such applicant and the general public to issue the license." Yet, the statute contains no criteria, standards or rules for determining this fact; and no definition of crucial terms used in the statute. This is perhaps necessary, for the broad discretion vested in the courts, will enable them, in true common-law tradition, to progress with the advances of science in this difficult and inexact field of law and medicine and decide each case on its own facts.

A vast, hazy shadowland exists between mental health and mental illness. The gradations of abnormalities are as varied and diffused as the merging colors of the rainbow. The most illustrious and respected psychiatrists often disagree radically in their opinions with respect to the sanity of an individual.

The following extract from the *Encyclopaedia Britannica*, vol. 12, p. 383 (14th ed.) points up the difficulty very sharply:

"INSANITY. This term ordinarily connotes more or less severe unsoundness of mind. Though its loose usage is almost synonymous with mental disease, scientifically the term should only be applied to the mental condition of an individual who, through socially inefficient conduct, has to be placed under supervision and control. The mind is the mechanism by means of which we adapt adequately to our environment and when, through its derangement, conduct is exhibited which the community looks upon as evidence of disease and as implying irresponsibility, the individual concerned is said to be insane and the law steps in to certify him as such. Strictly speaking, then, insanity is really a social and legal term and not medical. Mental illness is a broad concept which may include very efficient members of society. No satisfactory definition can therefore be arrived at, since it would be necessary to define what we mean by sanity, which would involve us in equal difficulties."

The phrase "an inmate of an institution for weakminded, insane, or persons of unsound mind" is, likewise, subject to interpretation. Institutions for the insane are no longer regarded merely as places in which persons of unsound mind are confined as custodial cases to rid the general public of their troublesome presence. Today, great progress is being made toward curing the mentally sick and the establishments in which they are housed are usually called "hospitals." In fact, many general hospitals have departments set aside for the care of the mentally sick. Furthermore, in present day usage the word "inmate" has been generally replaced by the more charitable word "patient." The language of the statute is general, but we believe that the legislature intended to include all cases in which the applicant has been hospitalized for treatment of some form of mental illness or deficiency in any mental institution, including a general hospital which conducts a department for the care of the mentally sick.

Basically, the problem which confronts us is one for the medical profession. A diagnosis by judicial decree should not be made except with the advice, and upon the recommendation of, trained psychiatrists.

The statute does not in so many words state that an applicant who has been in a mental institution must be cured permanently at the time the application is made. However, because the issuance of a license to a person who is weak-minded, insane or of unsound mind is absolutely prohibited by the statute, the legislature must have intended that a license is to be issued only to a person who has been completely cured of his mental illness or whose condition has so improved that he can be expected to lead a normal life and to take his place in society without serious risk to himself or to the community generally.

Leading members of the medical profession freely admit that the science of caring for the mentally ill is in its infancy. Much research and investigation has been undertaken recently which has resulted in tremendously enhancing the chances of curing or, at least, improving the condition of persons suffering from mental sickness.

It seems clear that under no circumstances should a marriage license be issued to persons having a mental deficiency of severe degree, *e.g.*, an idiot or imbecile. It is also apparent that persons suffering irremedial brain injury, or deteriorating organic brain syndromes which are of progressive or irreversible nature, *e.g.*, senile dementia, should not be permitted to marry.

On the other hand, many persons who are unable to cope with the intense pressures of the modern age, suffer what is commonly designated as "mental breakdowns" and are institutionalized. Most of these people respond favorably to therapy; many are completely cured. These obviously are the persons whom the legislature intended to benefit primarily and furnish no serious problem when they apply for marriage licenses.

The real difficulties arise with respect to persons who suffer moderate mental deficiency or who have been hospitalized because of the more serious mental illnesses, such as manic-depressive psychosis, schizophrenia (dementia praecox), post-partum psychosis, and involutional melancholia. Although many of these cases are completely hopeless, a great number show marked improvement under modern therapy, such as shock treatment, psychotherapy, and the use of newly discovered drugs. Some of these persons are able to leave the mental hospitals and, at least temporarily, take their places in society as useful citizens. Some apparently have complete remission from their malady. Whether they have recovered sufficiently to assume the responsibilities of marriage presents an extremely delicate question.

No general rule can be handed down. Each case is sui generis and must be decided upon its own facts. The discretion vested in the orphans' court must be carefully exercised in order to protect not only the applicants and their issue, but the general public as well.

Three preliminary requirements seem to be indicated in every case before a license should issue: (1) Full disclosure must be made to both applicants of all of the details of the case history of the applicant who has been mentally afflicted; (2) the court must be satisfied that such applicant has recovered sufficiently to adjust normally to the problems of everyday living, particularly those arising from the marriage relationship, and (3) the court must be reasonably assured that if children are born of the marriage, such children will be normal, healthy children, free from the taint of mental illness or deficiency.

With these principles in mind, let us examine the factual situation existing in the present case.

* * *

F.A. is 30 years of age. She was graduated from a Catholic parochial grade school and attended Little Flower High School for two years. She left school when she was about 17 years old and took a job in a hosiery mill, "sewing on piece-work." She continued in the hosiery industry until, apparently, the pressure of "piece-work" caused her to have a mental breakdown. She was hospitalized at St. Mary's Hospital in Philadelphia for a period of eight weeks with a diagnosis of dementia praecox. While in the hospital she received a full course of electric shock treatments, following which she received treatments as an out-patient until December 1953, when she was pronounced well. It appears, further, from the testimony that since her discharge from the hospital she has managed the household of her invalid sister satisfactorily and efficiently and has given no evidence of any recurrence of her malady.

* * *

After a careful study of the record in this case we make the following findings of fact:

1. That St. Mary's Hospital, Philadelphia, is an institution for persons who are insane or of unsound mind, within the purview of The Marriage Law of 1953;

2. That F.A. was an inmate of the mental department of that institution from April 16, 1951, to June 16, 1951;

3. That F.A. was an out-patient of the mental department of that institution from June 1951 until December 1953, when she was discharged as cured;

4. That F.A. is not at this time weak-minded, insane, or a person of unsound mind;

5. That the male applicant is fully aware of the entire history of F.A.'s mental illness, and

6. That there is no compelling evidence that children, if any, born of this marriage will be mentally deficient or predisposed to mental illness.

This is a borderline case and we confess that we are beset with doubts. However, life at its very best is uncertain. Probably in a strictly disciplined society persons of defective mentality would be deprived of the blessings of matrimony. This, however, is an imperfect world. It is difficult to foretell the unhappy consequences which might result from our refusing to issue a marriage license in this case in view of the fact that the marriage banns have been posted, and all of the arrangements for the marriage have been made. The applicants are obviously in love with each other. If they cannot be married in this State, they may be tempted to live together without the benefit of marriage, or to seek a marriage license in another State where the restrictions are less stringent. Under all of the existing circumstances, we are of the opinion that it is for the best interest of the applicants and the general public to issue the marriage license.

Comments

F.A. Marriage License is similar to a mandamus proceeding, although it is governed by local state statute and seems to have been initiated ex officio. Many states still require aggrieved parties who are refused a marriage license to file a formal action. There are other possibilities as well. Sometimes a lower-level judge, before refusing to issue a license, may request an opinion of the state attorney general on the legal issues involved. Indeed, much law on questions relating to marriage licenses is hidden away in poorly indexed opinions of state attorneys general. Such matters are perceived to be administrative tasks delegated in part to the courts rather than genuine judicial activities. These are artificial classifications, and many activities of state attorneys general are quasi-judicial. According to the Pennsylvania statute in question, the judicial nature of the proceedings is more openly recognized.

Substantively, *F.A. Marriage License* is a mixture of archaic and progressive notions. While ultimately directing the clerk of the court to issue a marriage license in spite of the medical history of the female applicant, it did so only after elaborate and strained reasoning, using dated classifications such as "mental breakdown" and "dementia praecox." The court also appears to have been concerned about the fact that the applicant received "a full course of electric shock treatments." The classifications of the statute itself in reference to the weak-minded, insane, or persons of unsound mind are behind the times. On the other hand, the court recognized that no strict demarcations exist between mental health and illness and that, in the last analysis, insanity is more a social and legal term than a medical term. However, following the general judicial inclination, this progressive reasoning is only a preface to the statement that each case is sui generis and must be decided on its own facts. In effect this means that judicial discretion, rather than the actual language of the legislature, governs the outcome. More likely than not, as in this case, the marriage license will be granted.

Nevertheless, the opinion is retrogressive in many respects. The factual account of the 17-year-old working girl who, while sewing on piecework in a hosiery mill, had a mental breakdown, sounds as if it had been written in the nineteenth century. The court maximized language that stigmatizes persons who have been hospitalized and received shock treatment in mental institutions. That such stigmatization is still alive was demonstrated, within a political context, in the McGovern-Eagleton presidential campaign in 1972. The requirements implicit in the findings of fact set forth by the court for issuance of a marriage license must also have a chilling effect on the parties and on future applicants. The female applicant was told that she was not "at this time" insane and that there was "no compelling evidence" that her children would be mentally deficient. The Court also established a requirement that the other applicant, here the male party, must be fully informed of all the details of the medical history. It is conceivable that in the process of such discovery parties will withdraw their request for a license or, in case of marriage, refrain from having children. Perhaps this was a calculated risk that the court was willing to take. Yet many states do not inquire into the mental conditions of the applicants at all, and severe character defects are usually not relevant to the capacity to marry.

Apart from the statutory requirements in Pennsylvania, the capacity to marry seems to imply a capacity to contract, at least in many jurisdictions. Yet even in this respect a minimum level of understanding, less than in ordinary contracts, appears to be considered sufficient. What is important, however, is the context in which this issue is likely to be raised. It would probably not be raised upon application for a marriage license, more likely if the issue is divorce or annulment of a marriage already entered. Except in a rare instance like *F.A. Marriage License*, a license is usually granted without delay. Questions are not likely to be asked or decided by minor court officials who accept and process applications. Even mental institutions are known to avoid potential complications by releasing patients who express an intention to marry. Much of the recommended procedure consists of treating patients as normally as possible and includes sex education and preparation for relationships that may result in marriage.

Thus inertia and design may lead to the common practical result that licenses to marry can be obtained without difficulty. As indicated above, the question of the capacity to marry is somewhat more likely to be raised successfully after the fact of marriage in the context of dissolution or annulment of marriage. The standards in such cases are not necessarily identical with those that apply, at least in theory, to the application for a marriage license. This is also the phase where attorneys are more likely to become active.

References

Hollingshead, A., & Redlich, F., SOCIAL CLASS AND MENTAL ILLNESS (1958).
Katz, J., Goldstein, J., & Dershowitz, A., PSYCHOANALYSIS, PSYCHIATRY AND LAW 676–679 (1967).
Note, *The Right of the Mentally Disabled to Marry: A Statutory Evaluation*, 15 J. FAM L. 463 (1976–1977).

Annulment

Wilkins v. Zelichowski

Supreme Court of New Jersey

26 N.J. 370, 140 A.2d 65 (1958)

J‌ACOBS, J.

* * *

The plaintiff and the defendant were domiciled in New Jersey as were their respective parents. They ran away from New Jersey to marry and they chose Indiana because they believed "it was the quickest place." The Indiana statutes provide that "females of the age of sixteen" are capable of marriage although they also provide that where the female is within the age of 18 the required marriage license shall not be issued without the consent of her parents. See Burns, Indiana Statutes Annotated, §§44–101, 44–202. After their marriage in Indiana on April 23, 1954 the plaintiff and defendant returned immediately to New Jersey where they set up their home. On February 22, 1955 the plaintiff bore the defendant's child. On April 22, 1955 the defendant, having been convicted on several independent charges of automobile theft, was sent to Bordentown Reformatory where he was still confined at the time of the hearing in the Chancery Division. On January 4, 1956 the plaintiff filed her annulment complaint under N.J.S. 2A:34–1(e), N.J.S.A., which provides that a judgment of nullity may be rendered on the wife's application upon a showing that she was under the age of 18 years at the time of her marriage and that the marriage has not been "confirmed by her after arriving at such age"; the statute also provides that where a child has been born there shall be no judgment of nullity unless the court is of the opinion that the judgment "will not be against the best interests of the child." Although the defendant was duly served he did not file any answer and he chose not to contest the plaintiff's proceeding.

The plaintiff's evidence adequately established that she was 16 years of age when she was married and that she did not confirm her marriage after she had reached 18 years of age and the Chancery Division expressly found that an annulment would be "for the best interests of the child"; nevertheless it declined to grant the relief sought by the plaintiff on the ground that the marriage was valid in Indiana and should therefore, under principles of the conflict of laws, not be nullified by a New Jersey court because of the plaintiff's non-age. In reaching the same result the Appellate Division recognized that the Chancery Division had ample power to nullify the Indiana marriage of the New Jersey domiciliaries [citations omitted], but expressed the view that comity dictated that it should not take such action unless there was an imperative New Jersey policy (which it did not find) against marriages of 16-year-old females. [Citations omitted.]

* * *

The vigor of New Jersey's policy against marriages by persons under the prescribed age is evidenced not only by the breadth of the statutory language but also by the judicial decisions. * * *

It is undisputed that if the marriage between the plaintiff and the defendant had taken place here, the public policy of New Jersey would be applicable and the plaintiff would be entitled to the annulment; and it seems clear to us that if New Jersey's public policy is to remain at all meaningful it must be considered equally applicable though their marriage took place in Indiana. While that State was interested in the formal ceremonial requirements of the marriage it had no interest whatever in that marital status of the parties. Indeed, New Jersey was the only State having any interest in that status, for both parties were domiciled in New Jersey before and after the marriage and their matrimonial domicile was established here. The purpose in having the ceremony take place in Indiana was to evade New Jersey's marriage policy and we see no just or compelling reason for permitting it to succeed. [Citations omitted.]

In the *Cunningham* case [206 N.Y. 341, 99 N.E. 848] the New York Court of Appeals annulled a marriage between New York residents who married outside the state to evade New York's age policy; the court expressed the view that the marriage was "repugnant to our public policy and legislation, and in view of the fact that the parties were, and ever since have been, residents of this state, our courts have the power to relieve the plaintiff by annulling the marriage." In the *Mitchell* case [63 Misc. 580, 117 N.Y.S. 676], the New York Supreme Court annulled a Canadian marriage of New York residents because the plaintiff was under the age of 18 at the time of her marriage; Justice Wheeler found that there was ample power in the New York court to annul the marriage though it was valid under Canadian law; in the course of his opinion he stressed that the New York Legislature had "seen fit in its wisdom to discourage marriages contracted by immature persons" and had provided for "the annulment of such marriages under certain circumstances and conditions," and he concluded that there would be neither reason nor justification for judicially permitting New York residents to evade the Legislature's age policy and defeat annulments contemplated by it.

* * *

* * * We are not here concerned with a collateral attack on an Indiana marriage or with a direct attack on an Indiana marriage between domiciliaries of Indiana or some state other than New Jersey. We are concerned only with a direct and timely proceeding, authorized by the New Jersey statute (N.J.S. 2A:34–1(e), N.J.S.A.), by an underage wife for annulment of an Indiana marriage between parties who have at all times been domiciled in New Jersey. We are satisfied that at least in this situation the strong public policy of New Jersey (see RESTATEMENT, CONFLICT OF LAWS §132(b), comment b) requires that the annulment be granted. The annulment will not render the plaintiff's child illegitimate (N.J.S. 2A:34–20, N.J.S.A.) and, as the Chancery Division found, it will be for his best interests. The annulment will also serve the plaintiff's best interests for it will tend to reduce the tragic consequences of her immature conduct and unfortunate marriage. The Legislature has clearly fixed the State's policy in her favor and has granted her the right to apply for a judgment nullifying her marriage; we know of no considerations of equity or justice or overriding principles of the law which would lead us to deprive her of the relief she seeks under the circumstances she presents. See Taintor, *supra*, 9 VAND. L. REV., at 624.

Reversed.

Comments

Wilkins has significance beyond the jurisdiction of New Jersey. It exemplifies a problem that may occur in various forms in any state, although often the problem does not pose itself as severely as it does in *Wilkins*. The issue is whether marriages contracted elsewhere to avoid local restrictions are to be recognized in the domiciliary state of the parties. Nevada, for example, is not only a state where people used to go for easy divorces, but also a jurisdiction attracting "migratory marriages." Some persons may find it objectionable to be married by a judge or a minister, or they may wish to avoid other burdensome restrictions such as waiting periods. A state's interest in having marriages of domiciliaries performed within its borders is substantially less than its interest in having a say in prospective divorces. Consequently, in many instances no question as to the validity of a marriage contracted out-of-state is likely to be raised.

Teenage runaway marriages in neighboring states pose special problems. In a typical situation the young parties leave their home state for a day or two and falsify their ages across the border. Whether the neighboring laws are more lenient than the laws regarding the capacity to marry at home then becomes irrelevant. The license-granting officials in border towns are often less than ardent about checking whether requirements under their own laws have been complied with. Of course, criminal prosecution of applicants who falsify their ages in order to avoid restrictions of parental consent is theoretically possible. Such prosecution, however, would have to take place where the crime has been committed, and parties to a runaway marriage ordinarily leave the neighboring jurisdiction soon thereafter. The home state cannot prosecute because the crime was not committed there.

The question of whether a crime was committed and, if so, whether it can realistically be prosecuted anywhere, has to be distinguished from the issue of whether a valid marriage has been contracted at the place where the license was obtained. In *Wilkins*, for example, even under Indiana law a falsification of age must have occurred to avoid consent of the parents, at least in regard to the young woman. If Indiana authorities had been concerned with the matter, they might have concluded that the statutory requirements are merely directory and thus do not affect the validity of the marriage. Thus the marriage of the parties may have been valid under Indiana law regardless of what position is taken by New Jersey thereafter. *Wilkins* does not address itself to this problem because it assumes that only New Jersey had an interest in this matter. Probably no further complication arose because of the nature of the parties. In fact, the husband's being in a reformatory for automobile theft may have facilitated granting the annulment. Had the parties been of different social status, the legal issue of whether the Indiana marriage was to be recognized in New Jersey, not to mention other jurisdictions, might not have been as clearly decided in favor of an annulment. That this was an executed transaction, namely a marriage that had taken place four years earlier in another state and had resulted in the birth of a child, could also be of significance.

Many states do not have legislation dealing with the possibility of annulment in case of underage marriages. On the other hand, many states do have statutes that provide for emancipation of minors upon marriage. Even a voidable marriage, since it is valid until voided, would have this effect. This could have a bearing on who has standing to sue for an annulment. It also could have a bearing on whether an annulment is possible at all. One could take the position that age requirements themselves, just as requirements for parental consent, are merely directory and that, in case of actual marriage, original common law should govern. That could mean that marriages are fully valid if the common law requirements of 12 years for the female party and 14 years for the male party are met. We do not take the position that these arguments would necessarily prevail in any given jurisdiction. It could speak, however, for obtaining judicial dissolutions in runaway marriages of this kind before any new marriage is entered. Such precautionary divorces have functions comparable to actions in real property law to remove a cloud and to clear title. In other words, it is important for lawyers to realize that cases of this nature can never be clear enough, for practical purposes, to disregard what has taken place in another jurisdiction simply because that jurisdiction supposedly had no interest in the matter.

In the light of these problems *Wilkins* can be viewed as an effort to clear the record. The state statute did authorize an annulment action. Yet, at least in some cases of this nature the alternative of a divorce action may be more appropriate. In this instance, it would have conflicted less with possible interests of the state of Indiana in the integrity of its public records. Although complications are not likely to arise in the present case, they may arise if the states involved are in closer proximity and if property is involved. Not infrequently the validity of an underage marriage and of subsequent proceedings to avoid its consequences comes up years later in an inheritance situation. It should also be remembered that in *Wilkins* the husband was apparently in no position to answer. The case was therefore not truly contested. A lawyer representing the plaintiff should also consider, in counseling a party whether to file for annulment or divorce, that the full faith and credit consequences of an annulment might not be as clear as those of a divorce.

As seen from these perspectives, *Wilkins* is less persuasive than its strong pronouncement of policy makes it appear. The case also loses significance because of a change in mores. The need for marriage, and consequently the need to run away to neighboring jurisdictions for purposes of getting married, has declined. Alternatives short of marriage are available, and if they result in legal complications they are of a different nature.

Reference

Baade, *Marriage and Divorce in American Conflicts Law: Governmental-Interests Analysis and the Restatement (Second)*, 72 Colum. L. Rev. 329 (1972).

Bilowit v. Dolitsky

Superior Court of New Jersey

124 N.J. Super. 101, 304 A.2d 774 (1973)

McKENZIE, J.C.C.

On the representation of defendant that he was a practicing Orthodox Jew, plaintiff married him on January 23, 1971. Thereafter plaintiff discovered that defendant did not in fact adhere to the tenets of Orthodox Judaism and had misrepresented his religious connections to plaintiff because he was in love with her, wished to marry her, and was aware that she would not marry him otherwise. The marriage was admittedly consummated. Plaintiff seeks an annulment, and her cause of action is not contested.

Our courts have long required a more substantial quantum of fraud to entitle a party to an annulment where the marriage has been consummated than where it has not. Any kind of fraud which would render a contract voidable may be the basis for the annulment of a marriage similarly infected. [Citations omitted.]

Where the marriage has been consummated, the fraud of defendant will entitle plaintiff to an annulment only when the fraud is of an extreme nature, going to one of the essentials of marriage. [Citations omitted.]

As to what constitutes the "essentials" of the marriage relation, it has been observed that the guidelines are vague and not fully delineated by our decisional law. [Citations omitted.] This is as it should be. What is essential to the relationship of the parties in one marriage may be of considerably less significance in another. For this reason a determination of whether a fraud goes to the essentials of the marriage must rest upon the facts in each case. [Citations omitted.]

Here plaintiff, corroborated by her rabbi, testified that she has been a deeply religious Orthodox Jew throughout her life. Her beliefs were made known to defendant and he, representing himself to be an Orthodox Jew, agreed to follow the requirements of that religion. As testified to by the rabbi, they are many and far-reaching, touching virtually all aspects of everyday life. Although for a few weeks following the marriage defendant adhered to them, it soon became apparent that he was not in fact an Orthodox Jew, and never sincerely intended to follow that religion. Plaintiff promptly separated from him.

The reported cases on this subject are meager. In both *Akrep v. Akrep*, 1 N.J. 268, 63 A.2d 253 (1949), and *Nocenti v. Ruberti*, 17 N.J. Misc. 21, 3 A.2d 128 (Ch. 1933), our courts granted annulments where the defendant misrepresented his intention to enter into a religious ceremony of marriage following the civil ceremony. However, in both cases the marriage was not consummated.

Numerous cases in New York indicate that annulments have been granted under circumstances similar to those in the instant case. [Citations omitted.] This court is aware, however, that these decisions were reported during the period preceding the reform of the New York divorce law, and this court is satisfied that under the circumstances they should not be given great weight here at this time. See Note, *Annulments for Fraud—New York's Answer to Reno?*, 48 COLUMBIA L. REV. 900 (1948).

* * *

* * * To plaintiff the religious beliefs and convictions of her husband were essential to her marriage. She could not have properly performed the duties of a wife and mother, following the rules and teachings of her faith, without the support of a husband holding the same beliefs. Defendant, having substantially and knowingly misrepresented the same to her, and plaintiff having relied thereon in entering into the marriage, this court holds the fraud to which plaintiff was subjected to be "gross and far-reaching," * * *. [Citations omitted.]

That a subjective test may render more difficult the fact-finding process of the court should not prevent a litigant from obtaining relief where justice dictates. Our requirement that the fraud alleged must be proved by clear and convincing evidence should be noted. [Citations omitted.]

A judgment for annulment of the marriage will be entered.

Comments

Bilowit illustrates some of the problems of actions for annulment of marriage as distinguished from divorce actions. The plaintiff wife proceeded under a theory that her marriage was void. The title of the case in the official reports reflects this theory. It is styled *"Anne Bilowit, falsely known as Ann Dolitsky v. Michael Dolitsky."* The findings of the court are largely based on her pleadings and testimony, corroborated by her rabbi, that she had always been a deeply religious Orthodox Jew, and that the defendant husband induced her to marry by the fraudulent representation that he also was an Orthodox Jew. The outcome of the case, the entering of a judgment for annulment, may have been influenced by the fact that the husband did not contest the suit. As a result several issues that could have been raised remained in the dark, and others were somewhat summarily disposed of by the court in favor of the plaintiff wife. Although the point was not argued, an inference from the case is that the husband was in fact Jewish but, after an unsuccessful attempt of a few weeks to follow the requirements of orthodoxy, discontinued his efforts. This factor, if the case had been contested, could have affected the outcome in a direction of not permitting an annulment, perhaps under a theory that the plaintiff had not satisfied her burden of proof that a misrepresentation had taken place prior to marriage.

A traditional difference between actions for annulment and for divorce is that the grounds for annulment must have occurred prior to the marriage, such as preexisting insanity or fraud, often combined with an allegation that as a result marital consent has been impaired. Divorce, on the other hand, conceptually requires grounds that have occurred after marriage. In *Bilowit* this distinction could mean viewing the unsuccessful attempt of the husband to conform to orthodox customs in two contradictory ways, either as an attempted cover-up of a preexisting fraud or as a good-faith attempt to live up to a marital promise that failed. Only in the former situation of an attempted cover-up could the annulment action succeed. Since wrongdoing cannot be presumed, any uncertainty of fact ordinarily would have to be interpreted in favor of the husband. However, in practice the chancellor in equity, having jurisdiction in annulment actions, can do as he pleases, for example, by taking the position that the evidence submitted by the plaintiff wife was sufficient to prove her allegations. There is yet an additional difficulty to overcome, mentioned by the court, namely, whether the fraud was of an extreme nature going to the essentials of marriage.

This language, sometimes referred to as the Massachusetts rule, originates from *Reynolds v. Reynolds*.* It took the position followed in many jurisdictions that no misrepresentation as to character, fortune, health, or temper would support a dissolution of the marriage, once it is executed. Rather, the misrepresentation must go to the essence of marriage, not to mere personal traits or attributes. A certain degree of misrepresentation, consequently, is considered excusable by *Reynolds*, and perhaps even permissible so that a person may be able, so to speak, to be rehabilitated from past weaknesses or misconduct through marriage. The startling aspect of this holding, which in *Reynolds* was meant to apply to sexual misconduct of women, is that it seems to establish at least an excuse to lie, provided that the misrepresentation does not go to the essence of marriage. The essence in turn was perceived mainly in terms of procreation. Although this holding has been criticized, it could be defended under traditional views of marriage. Basically it held that certain forms of misrepresentation are likely to occur in courtship when both parties are inclined to present themselves in the most favorable light. If any untruth in this context could lead to annulment actions at a later time, many marriages would be in jeopardy from the start. To translate this view into terms of contract law, it is like saying that materiality of the misrepresentation is missing.

Bilowit, while applying the test of essentiality of misrepresentation, extends it to cover matters of intense belief or feeling. Conceivably this could cover not only strongly felt religious beliefs but also personal predispositions of a less laudable nature. In this regard, courts are likely to reflect whatever might be considered in a given community as going to the essence of marriage. The more dubious aspects of such annulments are, however, somewhat mitigated by changed attitudes toward courtship. In fact this may mean that the rule as such—that the misrepresentation must go to the essentials of marriage—remains unchanged in form but is slowly given a different substantive content. The availability of no-fault divorce may also result in a change of approach and reasoning. A court in a situation comparable to *Bilowit* could, for example, take the position today that the allegations of the complaint merely state character flaws of the defendant husband, and the plaintiff consequently should be limited to claiming irretrievable breakdown of marriage. To avoid the need for filing new complaints, attorneys are inclined to combine requests for annulment with alternative requests for dissolution of marriage. As soon as a judge is faced with this alternative, it is likely that he will grant divorce rather than an annulment, simply because it appears to

---

*85 Mass. (3 Allen) 605 (1862).

be the more customary remedy. Requests for annulment alone are rare and often involve cases in which one party, because of strong feelings, is particularly aggrieved. Perhaps also annulments are brought so that an effort can be made to revive a pension or social security benefits from a preexisting marriage.

Other reasons may speak in favor of abolishing annulment actions altogether. It is impossible to void long-term contractual relations retroactively. Too many factors may have changed from the time when the contract was entered. Thus even in case of annulment or rescission, a de facto relationship remains which in one form or other must be legally recognized. Courts and the legislatures have, for instance, provided that children should not become illegitimate in case of annulment. Furthermore, most defects in the marriage contract are increasingly viewed as resulting not in void marriages, but in marriages valid until voided. Thus, the differences between annulment and divorce decrease to the point that it becomes arguable as a matter of policy that dissolution for irretrievable breakdown of marriage should be the only available remedy. In effect this means that policies on marriage, as perceived by the state, lose ground and that the fate of the marriage increasingly depends on the parties themselves.

Bibliography

Clark, H., The Law of Domestic Relations in the United States ch. 2 (1968).

Harding & Levy, *Marriage License Fees: Are They Constitutional?*, 17 J. Fam. L. 703 (1979).

Nagan, *Conflict of Laws: Group Discrimination and the Freedom to Marry—A Policy Science Prologue to Human Rights Decisions*, 21 How. L.J. 1 (1978).

Reese, *Marriage in American Conflict of Laws*, 26 Int'l & Comp. L.Q. 952 (1977).

Government Largess

Unemployment Compensation

Briggs v. Industrial Commission

Court of Appeals of Colorado

539 P.2d 1303 (Colo. App. 1975)

Smith, Judge.

Claimant, James M. Briggs, was employed by Hi Land Dairyman's Association in Durango from April of 1971 until his termination on September

13, 1973. Claimant had supplemented his income by working for one Ron Vesper, beginning in August 1973 and continuing after his termination from Hi Land until October 23, 1973. On this date claimant terminated his employment with Ron Vesper and left Durango to join his wife who had been promoted and transferred to Denver by her employer, Mountain Bell. Upon his arrival in Denver, claimant secured full-time employment which lasted until June 1974. Upon termination of this job, claimant sought unemployment compensation. Claimant was 55 years old at the time and had been married for 32 years.

The findings of the referee, subsequently affirmed by order of the Industrial Commission, determined (1) that because the employment with Ron Vesper did not last 90 days and consequently could not qualify as a better job as provided in §8–73–108(4)(f), C.R.S. 1973, claimant was disqualified from the receipt of benefits for 13 weeks because of his separation from Hi Land; and (2) that since claimant quit his employment with Vesper for personal reasons, he is disqualified from benefits for an additional period of 20 weeks because of that separation. See §8–73–108(6)(e), C.R.S. 1973.

* * *

First of all, we rule that one who becomes unemployed as the result of leaving employment in order to travel to another place to live with his or her spouse has not "voluntarily" left work. The pressure of family and marital responsibilities and claimant's capitulation to them transforms what is ostensibly voluntary unemployment into involuntary unemployment. *Bliley Electric Co. v. Unemployment Compensation Board of Review*, 158 Pa. Super. 548, 45 A.2d 898. Indeed, it would be repugnant to public policy, which encourages and promotes the family as a social unit in society, to require that a husband, in certain circumstances, be denied unemployment benefits merely because he chooses to live with his wife.

* * *

* * * The statute expressly provides for a special award where marital and familial responsibilities compel a worker to terminate employment. Living with one's spouse is one of the basic responsibilities in the marital relationship which compelled claimant to quit his job. Accordingly, claimant was entitled to a special award of unemployment benefits and the failure to make such an award was error.

Although claimant concedes that his termination from Hi Land is governed by the "better job" rule, he contends that it was error for the Commission to conclude that the Ron Vesper job was not a "better job" solely because he did not remain in that employment for more than 90 days. Thus, he argues that the penalty imposed for leaving the Hi Land job to work for Ron Vesper should be reversed. We agree.

Under §8–73–108(4)(f)(I), C.R.S. 1973, an exception exists to the statutory requirement that a job must last at least 90 days in order to constitute a "better" job where the job is terminated before the end of the 90-day period under conditions concerning which the worker had no knowledge or over which he had no control at the time he accepted the job. There is no dispute that claimant's employment with Ron Vesper did not last 90 days and that claimant left that job to join his wife in Denver. Thus, the issue is whether the promotion and transfer of claimant's wife and his decision to live with her in Denver, constitutes circumstances about which claimant had no knowledge, or over which he had no control.

At the time claimant began working for Vesper, his wife's transfer and promotion to Denver was only a possibility. Likewise, the promotion and transfer to Denver inured to the benefit of claimant's wife and the move to Denver was her decision, and thus we must assume, for purposes of the statute, was beyond the control of claimant.

To be sure, claimant could have remained in Durango and completed the 90 days and thus avoided the penalty of the "90 day" rule. However, as we have already stated, the compulsion to move was legitimate and consistent with public policy. Under these circumstances, to require him to remain long enough to comply with the technicality of the statute, in order to avoid the penalty, would be to put form before substance and would not accomplish the purpose intended to be furthered by the statute. Thus, the facts presented constitute a situation where the department and commission abused their discretion in not finding that the Ron Vesper job was a better job and in imposing a period of disqualification on claimant relative to that job.

The order of the Industrial Commission is therefore set aside and the cause is remanded for further proceedings not inconsistent herewith.

Food Stamps

United States Department of Agriculture v. Murry

United States Supreme Court

413 U.S. 508 (1973)

Mr. Justice DOUGLAS delivered the opinion of the Court.

Appellee Murry has two sons and ten grandchildren in her household. Her monthly income is $57.50, which comes from her ex-husband as support for her sons. Her expenses far exceed her monthly income. By payment, however, of $11 she received $128 in food stamps. But she has now been denied food stamps because her ex-husband (who has remarried) had claimed her two sons and one grandchild as tax dependents in his 1971 income tax return. That claim, plus the fact that her eldest son is 19 years old, disqualified her household for food stamps under §5(b) of the Act. Appellee Alderete is in comparable straits because her ex-husband claimed the five children, who live with their mother, as tax dependents, the oldest being 18 years old. Appellee Beavert's case is similar. Appellee Lee is the mother of five children, her entire income per month being $23 derived from public assistance. Her five children live with her. Her monthly bills are $249, of which $148 goes for food. Her husband is not a member of her household; he in fact deserted her and has supplied his family with no support. But he claimed the two oldest sons, ages 20 and 18, as tax dependents in his 1971 tax return, with the result that the wife's household was denied food stamps. Appellee Nevarez is in comparable straits.

Appellee Joe Valdez is 18 years old and married; and he and his wife have a child. He lives wholly on public assistance and applied for food stamps. His application was rejected because his father Ben claimed him as a tax dependent in his 1971 income tax return. Joe receives no support from Ben because Ben is in debt and unable to help support Joe.

Appellee Broderson is 18 and married to a 16-year-old wife and they have a small child. Their monthly income is $110 consisting of his wages at a service station. He cannot get food stamps because his father claimed him as a tax dependent. The father, however, gives him no support.

Appellee Schultz is 19 years old and she resides with a girl friend and the latter's two children. Appellee Schultz has no income of any kind but received food stamps for the household where she lived. Food stamps, however, were discontinued when her parents claimed her as a tax dependent but refused to give her any aid. She soon got married, but she and her husband were denied food stamps because her parents had claimed her for tax dependency.

These appellees brought a class action to enjoin the enforcement of the tax dependency provision of the Act; and, as noted, the three-judge court granted the relief.

Appellees are members of households that have been denied food stamp eligibility solely because the households contain persons 18 years or older who have been claimed as "dependents" for federal income tax purposes by taxpayers who are themselves ineligible for food stamp relief. Section 5(b) makes the entire household of which a "tax dependent" was a member ineligible for food stamps for two years: (1) during the tax year for which the dependency was claimed and (2) during the next 12 months. During these two periods of time §5(b) creates a conclusive presumption that the "tax dependent's" household is not needy and has access to nutritional adequacy.

The Acting Administrator of the Food and Nutrition Service of the Department of Agriculture admitted in this case that:

> "[I]n the case of households which have initially been determined to be ineligible for participation in the program on the basis of tax dependency, there are no factual issues to be presented or challenged by the household at such a hearing, other than the issue of whether or not a member of the household has been claimed as a dependent child by a taxpayer who is not a member of a household eligible for food assistance (a fact the household, in most cases, already will have disclosed in its application). If a household states that it has such a tax dependent member, the household is, in conformity with the Food Stamp Act, the program regulations, and the instructions of FNS governing the program administration by State agencies, determined to be ineligible."

App. 83.

Thus, in the administration of the Act, a hearing is denied, and is not available as the dissent implies. As stated by the District Court the Act creates "an irrebuttable presumption contrary to fact." 348 F. Supp., at 243. Moreover, an income tax return is filed, say in April 1973, for the year 1972. When the dependency deduction is filed, the year for which the dependency claim was made has already passed. Therefore the disqualification for food stamps cannot apply to 1972 but only to 1973.

The tax dependency provision was generated by congressional concern about nonneedy households participating in the food stamp program. The legislative history reflects a concern about abuses of the program by "college students, children of wealthy parents." But, as the District Court said, the Act goes far beyond that goal and its operation is inflexible. "Households containing no college student, that had established clear eligibility for Food Stamps and which still remain in dire need and otherwise eligible are now denied stamps if it appears that a household member 18 years or older is claimed by someone as a tax dependent." 348 F. Supp., at 243.

Tax dependency in a prior year seems to have no relation to the "need" of the dependent in the following year. It doubtless is much easier from the administrative point of view to have a simple tax "dependency" test that will automatically—without hearing, without witnesses, without findings of fact—terminate a household's claim for eligibility for food stamps. Yet, as we recently stated in *Stanley v. Illinois*, 405 U.S. 645, 656, 92 S. Ct. 1208, 1215, 31 L.Ed.2d 551:

> "[I]t may be argued that unmarried fathers are so seldom fit that Illinois need not undergo the administrative inconvenience of inquiry in any case, including Stanley's. The establishment of prompt efficacious procedures to achieve legitimate state ends is a proper state interest worthy of congnizance in constitutional adjudication. But the Constitution recog-

nizes higher values than speed and efficiency. Indeed, one might fairly say of the Bill of Rights in general, and the Due Process Clause in particular, that they were designed to protect the fragile values of a vulnerable citizenry from the overbearing concern for efficiency and efficacy that may characterize praiseworthy government officials no less, and perhaps more, than mediocre ones.''

We have difficulty in concluding that it is rational to assume that a child is not indigent this year because the parent declared the child as a dependent in his tax return for the prior year. But even on that assumption our problem is not at an end. Under the Act the issue is not the indigency of the child but the indigency of a different household with which the child happens to be living. Members of that different household are denied food stamps if one of its present members was used as a tax deduction in the past year by his parents even though the remaining members have no relation to the parent who used the tax deduction, even though they are completely destitute, and even though they are one, or 10 or 20 in number. We conclude that the deduction taken for the benefit of the parent in the prior year is not a rational measure of the need of a different household with which the child of the tax-deducting parent lives and rests on an irrebuttable presumption often contrary to fact. It therefore lacks critical ingredients of due process found wanting in *Vlandis v. Kline*, 412 U.S. 441, 452, 93 S. Ct. 2230, 37 L.Ed.2d 63; *Stanley v. Illinois, supra*; and *Bell v. Burson*, 402 U.S. 535, 91 S. Ct. 1586, 29 L.Ed.2d 90. Affirmed.

[Concurring and dissenting opinions omitted.]

Aid to Dependent Children

King v. Smith

United States Supreme Court

392 U.S. 309 (1968)

Mr. Chief Justice WARREN delivered the opinion of the Court.

Alabama, together with every other State, Puerto Rico, the Virgin Islands, the District of Columbia, and Guam, participates in the Federal Government's Aid to Families With Dependent Children (AFDC) program, which was established by the Social Security Act of 1935. 49 Stat. 620, as amended, 42 U.S.C. §§301–1394. This appeal presents the question whether a regulation of the Alabama Department of Pensions and Security, employed in that Department's administration of the State's federally funded AFDC program, is consistent with Subchapter IV of the Social Security Act, 42 U.S.C. §§601–609, and with the Equal Protection Clause of the Fourteenth Amendment. At issue is the validity of Alabama's so-called "substitute father" regulation which denies AFDC payments to the children of a mother who "cohabits" in or outside her home with any single or married able-bodied man. Appellees brought this class action against appellants, officers, and members of the Alabama Board of Pensions and Security, in the United States District Court for the Middle District of Alabama, under 42 U.S.C. §1983, seeking declaratory and injunctive relief. A properly convened three-judge District

Court correctly adjudicated the merits of the controversy without requiring appellees to exhaust state administrative remedies, and found the regulation to be inconsistent with the Social Security Act and the Equal Protection Clause. We noted probable jurisdiction, 390 U.S. 903, 88 S. Ct. 821, 19 L.Ed.2d 869 (1968), and, for reasons which will appear, we affirm without reaching the constitutional issue.

I

The AFDC program is one of three major categorical public assistance programs established by the Social Security Act of 1935. See U.S. Advisory Commission Report on Intergovernmental Relations, Statutory and Administrative Controls Associated with Federal Grants for Public Assistance 5–7 (1964) (hereafter cited as Advisory Commission Report). The category singled out for welfare assistance by AFDC is the "dependent child," who is defined in §406 of the Act, 49 Stat. 629, as amended, 42 U.S.C. §606(a) (1964 ed., Supp. II), as an age-qualified "needy child * * * who has been deprived of parental support or care by reason of the death, continued absence from the home or physical or mental incapacity of a parent, and who is living with" any one of several listed relatives. Under this provision, and, insofar as relevant here, aid can be granted only if "a parent" of the needy child is continually absent from the home. Alabama considers a man who qualifies as a "substitute father" under its regulation to be a nonabsent parent within the federal statute. The State therefore denies aid to an otherwise eligible needy child on the basis that his substitute parent is not absent from the home.

Under the Alabama regulation, an "able-bodied man, married or single, is considered a substitute father of *all the children of the applicant * * * mother*" in three different situations: (1) if "he lives in the home with the child's natural or adoptive mother for the purpose of cohabitation"; or (2) if "he visits [the home] frequently for the purpose of cohabiting with the child's natural or adoptive mother"; or (3) if "he does not frequent the home but cohabits with the child's natural or adoptive mother elsewhere." Whether the substitute father is actually the father of the children is irrelevant. It is also irrelevant whether he is legally obligated to support the children, and whether he does in fact contribute to their support. What is determinative is simply whether he "cohabits" with the mother.

The testimony below by officials responsible for the administration of Alabama's AFDC program establishes that "cohabitation," as used in the regulation, means essentially that the man and woman have "frequent" or "continuing" sexual relations. With regard to how frequent or continual these relations must be, the testimony is conflicting. One state official testified that the regulation applied only if the parties had sex at least once a week; another thought once every three months would suffice: and still another believed once every six months sufficient. The regulation itself provides that pregnancy or a baby under six months of age is prima facie evidence of a substitute father.

Between June 1964, when Alabama's substitute father regulation became effective, and January 1967, the total number of AFDC recipients in the State declined by about 20,000 persons, and the number of children recipients by about 16,000 or 22%. As applied in this case, the regulation has caused the termination of all AFDC payments to the appellees, Mrs. Sylvester Smith and her four minor children.

Mrs. Smith and her four children, ages 14, 12, 11, and 9, reside in Dallas County, Alabama. For several years prior to October 1, 1966, they had received aid under the AFDC program. By notice dated October 11, 1966, they were removed from the list of persons eligible to receive such aid. This action was taken by the Dallas County welfare authorities pursuant to the substitute father regulation, on the ground that a Mr. Williams came to her home on weekends and had sexual relations with her.

Three of Mrs. Smith's children have not received parental support or care from a father since their natural father's death in 1955. The fourth child's father left home in 1963, and the child has not received the support or care of his father since then. All the children live in the home of their mother, and except for the substitute father regulation are eligible for aid. The family is not receiving any other type of public assistance, and has been living, since the termination of AFDC payments, on Mrs. Smith's salary of between $16 and $20 per week which she earns working from 3:30 a.m. to 12 noon as a cook and waitress.

Mr. Williams, the alleged "substitute father" of Mrs. Smith's children, has nine children of his own and lives with his wife and family, all of whom are dependent upon him for support. Mr. Williams is not the father of any of Mrs. Smith's children. He is not legally obligated, under Alabama law, to support any of Mrs. Smith's children. Further, he is not willing or able to support the Smith children, and does not in fact support them. His wife is required to work to help support the Williams household.

II

The AFDC program is based on a scheme of cooperative federalism. See generally Advisory Commission Report, *supra*, at 1-59. It is financed largely by the Federal Government, on a matching fund basis, and is administered by the States. States are not required to participate in the program, but those which desire to take advantage of the substantial federal funds available for distribution to needy children are required to submit an AFDC plan for the approval of the Secretary of Health, Education, and Welfare (HEW). 49 Stat. 627 (1935) 42 U.S.C. §§601, 602, 603, and 604. See Advisory Commission Report, *supra*, at 21-23. The plan must conform with several requirements of the Social Security Act and with rules and regulations promulgated by HEW. 49 Stat. 627, as amended, 42 U.S.C. §602 (1964 ed., Supp. II). See also HEW, HANDBOOK OF PUBLIC ASSISTANCE ADMINISTRATION, pt. IV, §§2200, 2300 (hereafter cited as HANDBOOK).

One of the statutory requirements is that "aid to families with dependent children * * * shall be furnished with reasonable promptness to all eligible individuals * * *." 64 Stat. 550, as amended, 42 U.S.C. §602(a) (9) (1964 ed., Supp. II). As noted above, §406(a) of the Act defines a "dependent child" as one who has been deprived of "parental" support or care by reason of the death, continued absence, or incapacity of a "parent." 42 U.S.C. §606(a) (1964 ed., Supp. II). In combination, these two provisions of the Act clearly require participating States to furnish aid to families with children who have a parent absent from the home, if such families are in other respects eligible. See also HANDBOOK, pt. IV, §2200(b) (4).

The State argues that its substitute father regulation simply defines who is a nonabsent "parent" under §406(a) of the Social Security Act. 42 U.S.C. §606(a) (1964 ed., Supp. II). The State submits that the regulation is a legitimate way of allocating its limited resources available for AFDC assistance, in that it reduces the caseload of its social workers and provides increased benefits to those still eligible for assistance. Two state interests are asserted in support of the allocation of AFDC assistance achieved by the regulation: first, it discourages illicit sexual relationships and illegitimate births; second, it puts families in which there is an informal "marital" relationship on a par with those in which there is an ordinary marital relationship, because families of the latter sort are not eligible for AFDC assistance.

We think it well to note at the outset what is *not* involved in this case. There is no question that States have considerable latitude in allocating their

AFDC resources, since each State is free to set its own standard of need and to determine the level of benefits by the amount of funds it devotes to the program. See Advisory Commission Report, *supra*, at 30–59. Further, there is no question that regular and actual contributions to a needy child, including contributions from the kind of person Alabama calls a substitute father, can be taken into account in determining whether the child is needy. In other words, if by reason of such a man's contribution, the child is not in financial need, the child would be ineligible for AFDC assistance without regard to the substitute father rule. The appellees here, however, meet Alabama's need requirements; their alleged substitute father makes no contribution to their support; and they have been denied assistance solely on the basis of the substitute father regulation. Further, the regulation itself is unrelated to need, because the actual financial situation of the family is irrelevant in determining the existence of a substitute father.

Also not involved in this case is the question of Alabama's general power to deal with conduct it regards as immoral and with the problem of illegitimacy. This appeal raises only the question whether the State may deal with these problems in the manner that it has here—by flatly denying AFDC assistance to otherwise eligible dependent children.

Alabama's argument based on its interests in discouraging immorality and illegitimacy would have been quite relevant at one time in the history of the AFDC program. However, subsequent developments clearly establish that these state interests are not presently legitimate justifications for AFDC disqualification. Insofar as this or any similar regulation is based on the State's asserted interest in discouraging illicit sexual behavior and illegitimacy, it plainly conflicts with federal law and policy.

* * *

Congress has determined that immorality and illegitimacy should be dealt with through rehabilitative measures rather than measures that punish dependent children, and that protection of such children is the paramount goal of AFDC. In light of the Fleming Ruling and the 1961, 1962, and 1968 amendments to the Social Security Act, it is simply inconceivable, as HEW has recognized, that Alabama is free to discourage immorality and illegitimacy by the device of absolute disqualification of needy children. Alabama may deal with these problems by several different methods under the Social Security Act. But the method it has chosen plainly conflicts with the Act.

III

Alabama's second justification for its substitute father regulation is that "there is a public interest in a State not undertaking the payment of these funds to families who because of their living arrangements would be in the same situation as if the parents were married, except for the marriage." In other words, the State argues that since in Alabama the needy children of married couples are not eligible for AFDC aid so long as their father is in the home, it is only fair that children of a mother who cohabits with a man not her husband and not their father be treated similarly. The difficulty with this argument is that it fails to take account of the circumstance that children of fathers living in the home are in a very different position from children of mothers who cohabit with men not their fathers: the child's father has a legal duty to support him, while the unrelated substitute father, at least in Alabama, does not. We believe Congress intended the term "parent" in §406(a) of the Act, 42 U.S.C. §606(a), to include only those persons with a legal duty of support.

The Social Security Act of 1935 was part of a broad legislative program to counteract the depression. Congress was deeply concerned with the dire straits in which all needy children in the Nation then found themselves. In agreement with the President's Committee on Economic Security, the House Committee Report declared, "the core of any social plan must be the child." H.R. Rep. No. 615, 74th Cong., 1st Sess., 10 (1935). The AFDC program, however, was not designed to aid all needy children. The plight of most children was caused simply by the unemployment of their fathers. With respect to these children, Congress planned that "the work relief program and * * * the revival of private industry" would provide employment for their fathers. S. Rep. No. 628, 74th Cong., 1st Sess., 17 (1935). As the Senate Committee Report stated: "Many of the children included in relief families present no other problem than that of providing work for the breadwinner of the family." *Ibid.* Implicit in this statement is the assumption that children would in fact be supported by the family "breadwinner."

The AFDC program was designed to meet a need unmet by programs providing employment for breadwinners. It was designed to protect what the House Report characterized as "[o]ne clearly distinguishable group of children." H.R. Rep. No. 615, 74th Cong., 1st Sess., 10 (1935). This group was composed of children in families without a "breadwinner," "wage earner," or "father," as the repeated use of these terms throughout the Report of the President's Committee, Committee Hearings and Reports and the floor debates makes perfectly clear. To describe the sort of breadwinner that it had in mind, Congress employed the word "parent." 49 Stat. 629 as amended, 42 U.S.C. §606(a). A child would be eligible for assistance if his parent was deceased, incapacitated or continually absent.

The question for decision here is whether Congress could have intended that a man was to be regarded as a child's parent so as to deprive the child of AFDC eligibility despite the circumstances: (1) that the man did not in fact support the child; and (2) that he was not legally obligated to support the child. The State correctly observes that the fact that the man in question does not actually support the child cannot be determinative, because a natural father at home may fail actually to support his child but his presence will still render the child ineligible for assistance. On the question whether the man must be legally obligated to provide support before he can be regarded as the child's parent, the State has no such cogent answer. We think the answer is quite clear: Congress must have meant by the term "parent" an individual who owed to the child a state-imposed legal duty of support.

It is clear, as we have noted, that Congress expected "breadwinners" who secured employment would support their children. This congressional expectation is most reasonably explained on the basis that the kind of breadwinner Congress had in mind was one who was legally obligated to support his children. We think it beyond reason to believe that Congress would have considered that providing employment for the paramour of a deserted mother would benefit the mother's children whom he was not obligated to support.

By a parity of reasoning, we think that Congress must have intended that the children in such a situation remain eligible for AFDC assistance notwithstanding their mother's impropriety. AFDC was intended to provide economic security for children whom Congress could not reasonably expect would be provided for by simply securing employment for family breadwinners. We think it apparent that neither Congress nor any reasonable person would believe that providing employment for some man who is under no legal duty to support a child would in any way provide meaningful economic security for that child.

A contrary view would require us to assume that Congress, at the same time that it intended to provide programs for the economic security and protection of *all* children, also intended arbitrarily to leave one class of destitute children entirely without meaningful protection. Children who are told, as Alabama has told these appellees, to look for their food to a man who is not in the least obliged to support them are without meaningful protection. Such an interpretation of congressional intent would be most unreasonable, and we decline to adopt it.

Our interpretation of the term "parent" in §406(a) is strongly supported by the way the term is used in other sections of the Act. Section 402(a) (10) requires that, effective July 1, 1952, a state plan must:

"provide for prompt notice to appropriate law-enforcement officials of the furnishing of aid to families with dependent children in respect of a child who has been deserted or abandoned by a *parent.*" 64 Stat. 550, 42 U.S.C. §602(a) (10). (Emphasis added.)

The "parent" whom this provision requires to be reported to law enforcement officials is surely the same "parent" whose desertion makes a child eligible for AFDC assistance in the first place. And Congress obviously did not intend that a so-called "parent" who has no legal duties of support be referred to law enforcement officials (as Alabama's own welfare regulations recognize) for the very purpose of such referrals is to institute non-support proceedings. See HANDBOOK, pt. IV, §§8100–8149. Whatever doubt there might have been over this proposition has been completely dispelled by the 1968 amendments to the Social Security Act, which provide that the States must develop a program:

"(i) in the case of a child born out of wedlock who is receiving aid to families with dependent children, to establish the *paternity of such child and secure support for him,* and

"(ii) in the case of any child receiving such aid who has been deserted or abandoned *by his parent, to secure support for such child from such parent (or from any other person legally liable for such support)* * * *." §402(a), as amended by §201(a) (1) (C), 81 Stat. 878, 42 U.S.C. §602(a) (17) (1964 ed., Supp. III). (Emphasis added.)

* * * Consequently, if Alabama believes it necessary that it be able to disqualify a child on the basis of a man who is not under such a duty of support, its arguments should be addressed to Congress and not this Court.

IV

Alabama's substitute father regulation, as written and as applied in this case, requires the disqualification of otherwise eligible dependent children if their mother "cohabits" with a man who is not obligated by Alabama law to support the children. The regulation is therefore invalid because it defines "parent" in a manner that is inconsistent with §406(a) of the Social Security Act. 42 U.S.C. §606(a). In denying AFDC assistance to appellees on the basis of this invalid regulation, Alabama has breached its federally imposed obligation to furnish "aid to families with dependent children * * * with reasonable promptness to all eligible individuals * * *." 42 U.S.C. §602(a) (9) (1964 ed., Supp. II). Our conclusion makes unnecessary consideration of appellees' equal-protection claim, upon which we intimate no views.

We think it well, in concluding, to emphasize that no legitimate interest of the State of Alabama is defeated by the decision we announce today. The State's interest in discouraging illicit sexual behavior and illegitimacy may be protected by other means, subject to constitutional limitations, including state participation in AFDC rehabilitative programs. Its interest in economically allocating its limited AFDC resources may be protected by its undisputed power to set the level of benefits and the standard of need, and by its taking into account in determining whether a child is needy all actual and regular contributions to his support.

All responsible governmental agencies in the Nation today recognize the enormity and pervasiveness of social ills caused by poverty. The causes of

and cures for poverty are currently the subject of much debate. We hold today only that Congress has made at least this one determination: that destitute children who are legally fatherless cannot be flatly denied federally
funded assistance on the transparent fiction that they have a substitute
father.

Affirmed.

New Jersey Welfare Rights Organization v. Cahill

United States Supreme Court

411 U.S. 619 (1973)

Per Curiam.

This case presents the question of the constitutionality under the Equal
Protection Clause of the Fourteenth Amendment of the New Jersey "Assistance to Families of the Working Poor" program, N.J. Stat. Ann. §44:13-1 *et
seq.*, that allegedly discriminates against illegitimate children in the provision of financial assistance and other services. Specifically, appellants challenge that aspect of the program that limits benefits to only those otherwise
qualified families "which consist of a household composed of two adults of
the opposite sex ceremonially married to each other who have at least one
minor child * * * of both, the natural child of one and adopted by the other,
or a child adopted by both * * *." N.J. Stat. Ann. §44:13-3(a). Appellants
do not challenge the statute's "household" requirement. Rather, they argue
that although the challenged classification turns upon the marital status of
the parents as well as upon the parent-child relationship, in practical effect it
operates almost invariably to deny benefits to illegitimate children while
granting benefits to those children who are legitimate. Although apparently
conceding the correctness of this position, the United States District Court
for the District of New Jersey, sitting as a three-judge court, upheld the statutory scheme on the ground that it was designed "to preserve and strengthen
traditional family life." 349 F. Supp. 491, 496 (1972).

Confronted with similar arguments in the past, we have specifically declared that:

> "The status of illegitimacy has expressed through the ages society's con-
> demnation of irresponsible liaisons beyond the bonds of marriage. But
> visiting this condemnation on the head of an infant is illogical and unjust.
> Moreover, imposing disabilities on the illegitimate child is contrary to
> the basic concept of our system that legal burdens should bear some rela-
> tionship to individual responsibility or wrongdoing. Obviously, no child
> is responsible for his birth and penalizing the illegitimate child is an inef-
> fectual—as well as an unjust—way of deterring the parent."

Weber v. Aetna Casualty & Surety Co., 406 U.S. 164, 175, 92 S. Ct. 1400,
1406, 31 L.Ed.2d 768 (1972). Thus, in *Weber* we held that under the Equal
Protection Clause a State may not exclude illegitimate children from sharing
equally with other children in the recovery of workmen's compensation benefits for the death of their parent. Similarly, in *Levy v. Louisiana*, 391 U.S. 68,
88 S. Ct. 1509, 20 L.Ed.2d 436 (1968), we held that a State may not create a
right of action in favor of children for the wrongful death of a parent and
exclude illegitimate children from the benefit of such a right. And only this

Term, in *Gomez v. Perez*, 409 U.S. 535, 93 S. Ct. 872, 35 L.Ed.2d 56 (1973), we held that once a State posits a judicially enforceable right on behalf of children to needed support from their natural father, there is no constitutionally sufficient justification for denying such an essential right to illegitimate children. See also *Davis v. Richardson*, 342 F. Supp. 588 (D.C. Conn.), *aff'd*, 409 U.S 1069, 93 S. Ct. 678, 34 L.Ed.2d 659 (1972); *Griffin v. Richardson*, 346 F. Supp. 1226 (D.C. Md.), *aff'd*, 409 U.S. 1069, 93 S. Ct. 689, 34 L.Ed.2d 660 (1972).

Those decisions compel the conclusion that appellants' claim of the denial of equal protection must be sustained, for there can be no doubt that the benefits extended under the challenged program are as indispensable to the health and well-being of illegitimate children as to those who are legitimate. Accordingly, we grant the motion for leave to proceed *in forma pauperis*, reverse the judgment of the District Court, and remand for further proceedings consistent with this opinion.

Reversed and remanded.

[Dissenting opinion omitted.]

Social Security

Bryan v. Mathews

United States District Court, District of Columbia

427 F. Supp. 1263 (D.D.C. 1977)

MEMORANDUM

GASCH, District Judge.

* * *

Mr. Bryan filed his application for retirement benefits under section 202 of the Act, 42 U.S.C. §402, on April 5, 1971.[1] The Social Security Administration (hereinafter "Administration") began paying Mr. Bryan such benefits, including certain retroactive payments, in September of 1971.[2] Thereafter, the Administration discontinued payment of plaintiff's retirement benefits effective September 1973 because it had determined that he had been receiving wages in excess of the allowable monthly limit under section 203 of the Act, 42 U.S.C. §403, for the period in question. Section 203 provides for the

---

[1] Tr. 72–75. Mr. Bryan, who was born on April 6, 1906, attained the age of 65 on April 6, 1971. *Id.*

[2] In his initial application, Mr. Bryan reported that he would be earning wages in the first eight months of 1971 which would exceed the amount permitted by section 203 of the Act, 42 U.S.C. §403. Tr. 74. The Administration notified Mr. Bryan by letter dated May 19, 1971 that he was eligible to receive retirement benefits under the Act, but that no payments would be made because he had indicated in his application that his earnings did and would exceed the allowable maximum. Tr. 115. By letter dated July 6, 1971, Mr. Bryan notified the Administration that he had not received his salary for the months of February through June of 1971 due to adverse business conditions. Tr. 99–100. Thereafter, a series of letters passed between the Administration and plaintiff concerning a dispute as to the amount of Mr. Bryan's benefits.

deduction of certain wages earned by an individual from his retirement benefits under the Act. * * *
* * *
Mr. Bryan then requested a hearing which was held on May 7, 1975 before an Administrative Law Judge. The evidence before the Administrative Law Judge can be summarized as follows:

Mr. Bryan had been for many years the sole shareholder and president of a corporation which provided administrative and consulting services, primarily to medical societies. In 1970, the corporation suffered from business reverses, losing a portion of its clientele, and was obliged to separate its two executive employees.

In 1971, Mr. Bryan married his present wife, Helen Bryan. Prior to their marriage, Mrs. Bryan had been employed by the corporation on a part-time basis. In 1971, she became a full-time employee of the corporation assuming the duties of the departed executives, including bookkeeping, accounting, writing, and organizing duties. She was also made Vice President and Secretary of the corporation. During the period at issue, 1971 to 1973, Mrs. Bryan received an annual salary from the corporation ranging from about $20,000 to $24,000 per year, which apparently represented the entire net earnings of the corporation.

Subsequent to January 1971, and during the period in question, Mr. Bryan received no salary from the corporation. He admitted that during the period in question his duties did not materially change from those he had performed when he was receiving a salary and that he continued to perform substantial services for and was active in the corporation. Plaintiff also conceded that he controlled the corporation's salary arrangement and was responsible for the salary arrangement at issue.

Mr. Bryan and his wife maintained separate checking accounts. Mrs. Bryan's salary check was deposited into her account, and household expenses were also paid out of this account. Mrs. Bryan's salary was also used to make plaintiff's alimony payments to his former wife.

The Administrative Law Judge determined that the salary arrangement between plaintiff and his wife was only a pretext to enable plaintiff to receive retirement benefits and that at least 50 percent of the income[7] must be reallocated to the plaintiff. The Administrative Law Judge further determined that, as a result of this reallocation, Mr. Bryan had earned wages which required a 100 percent deduction of the retirement benefits paid to him and directed the plaintiff to repay the amount of the benefits previously paid to him. The Appeals Council affirmed the Administrative Law Judge's decision on January 10, 1976.

MERITS

The Secretary, of course, has the authority in determining eligibility for retirement benefits under the Act to pierce fictitious family salary arrangements and to reallocate income from one family member to another when the salary arrangement is not in accord with reality. [Citations omitted.]
* * * The principal questions presented here are whether the reasons relied upon by the Secretary in support of his determination that the salary arrangement was fictitious and that Mr. Bryan was indirectly receiving wages are valid and whether this decision was supported by substantial evidence.

---

[7]It is unclear from the Administrative Law Judge's opinion whether he was referring to the corporation's net income or Mrs. Bryan's income. See Tr. 24. However, there is no practical difference between these two incomes in the instant case since Mrs. Bryan's income represented the corporation's net income.

The Administrative Law Judge made no finding that Mrs. Bryan's salary was excessive or not earned by her, and the reasonableness of her salary was not a factor in his decision. * * *
He reasoned that:

> "The Administrative Law Judge must find that the claimant continued to be employed during all the period he was receiving benefits, and that he was not retired, and that the allocation of the income to his wife was fiction and a device to enable the claimant to draw benefits. It is clear from the evidence that he continued to be supported by the business and that his alimony payments were paid through the business income, as were all household expenses, and the fact that the income was paid through his wife, Helen Bryan, cannot be used as a pretext for obtaining retirement benefits. This is a wholly owned corporation, and the income thereof can be allocated as Mr. Bryan desires. Whatever the worth of Mrs. Bryan's services, for the purpose of this proceeding, there must be at least a 50 percent allocation of the income to Mr. Bryan, and it must be found that he was receiving each month an amount of money which required 100 percent deduction of the benefits paid to him."

Tr. 24. These reasons do not warrant the conclusion that the salary arrangement between Mr. and Mrs. Bryan was fictitious, or that Mr. Bryan was receiving wages for his services, and the reallocation of income in the instant case.

Where, as here, the Secretary seeks to attribute wages to an applicant for retirement benefits by reallocating income actually paid by the applicant's corporation to another person to the applicant, this salary arrangement must be a fictitious or unrealistic one. The fact that Mr. Bryan was performing substantial services for the corporation without remuneration, which services were worth at least as much as those performed by Mrs. Bryan, does not warrant a finding that the salary arrangement was fictitious or justify attributing a portion of the corporation's or Mrs. Bryan's income to him. Mr. Bryan was free to provide significant or substantial services to his corporation without jeopardizing his entitlement to retirement benefits, as long as he did not receive remuneration therefor, either directly or indirectly. [Citations omitted.]

The fact that Mrs. Bryan's salary was used to pay household expenses and satisfy Mr. Bryan's alimony obligation does not, without more, warrant a conclusion that Mr. Bryan was receiving wages indirectly through Mrs. Bryan's income or that the salary arrangement was fictitious. As long as Mrs. Bryan's salary was not unreasonable in light of the services performed by her, it was her salary. It cannot be said to be indirect wages for the plaintiff, and the salary arrangement cannot be said to be fictitious. [Citations omitted.] Mrs. Bryan is free to use the salary she earns as she sees fit, including contributing it to Mr. Bryan's support.

The final reason set forth by the Administrative Law Judge to justify his conclusion, that Mr. Bryan controlled the corporation, also does not warrant the reallocation of income. An applicant for retirement benefits may arrange his income for the avowed purpose of qualifying for such benefits. As long as no fraud is involved, there is nothing improper in such an arrangement and it does not warrant reallocation.

The Court is not intimating that the fact that Mr. Bryan was performing substantial services whose value exceeded his remuneration and that Mrs. Bryan's salary was used for his support are not important considerations. These are relevant considerations, but they do not alone warrant a determination that Mr. Bryan was indirectly receiving wages from the corporation and reallocating income to Mr. Bryan. There is a third consideration which was critical in the instant case and which the Administrative Law Judge did not take into consideration, the reasonableness of Mrs. Bryan's salary. As noted, if her salary was reasonable, the salary arrangement cannot be said to be unrealistic or fictitious and a portion of it, or of the corporation's net income, cannot be attributed or reallocated to plaintiff as wages received for his services. If her salary was unreasonable or excessive, then, in light of the fact that Mrs. Bryan's salary was used for plaintiff's support and that plaintiff's services were worth more than his wages, the salary arrangement could be said to be fictitious and Mr. Bryan could be found to be receiving wages indirectly through his wife's salary. However, the Administrative Law Judge failed to make any findings concerning the reasonableness of Mrs. Bryan's wages.

* * *

* * * Mrs. Bryan first came to work for the corporation on a part-time basis in 1968. In 1971, she began working for the corporation on a full-time basis and her salary increased to about $22,000 to $24,000 per year. This increase in her salary coincided with a marked increase in her duties. She assumed the duties of both the corporation's general assistant and bookkeeper and was Vice President and Secretary of the corporation. The corporation's previous general assistant had been paid $18,000 in 1968. She handled all of the corporation's accounts and bookkeeping, wrote minutes for some of the corporation's clients, did the work of an Executive Secretary for one of the corporation's clients, the American Academy for Cerebral Palsy, and performed some secretarial work, sometimes working 15 hours a day.

Neither party has requested this Court to remand this action to the agency for further consideration or for the taking of additional evidence. The Administration terminated plaintiff's retirement benefits because, although he was otherwise entitled to such benefits, he had been receiving wages in excess of the amount permitted by the Act. In light of the Court's determination that the Secretary employed an improper legal standard in reaching this conclusion and that had the proper standard been applied, there was not substantial evidence in the record to support a finding of indirect remuneration or that the salary arrangement was fictitious, no useful purpose would be served by remanding the case to the agency. The Court will, therefore, reverse the Secretary's decision and direct reinstatement of Mr. Bryan's retirement benefits.

Comments

Briggs, Murry, King, Cahill, and *Bryan* demonstrate the transformation from concern with marital property rights toward concern with entitlements. As Glendon has maintained, these new forms of property increasingly are taking the place of the traditional forms of wealth that were formerly the mainstay of the law of the family and of marriage (see References). These entitlements—though always subject to the winds of political and economic change—tend to originate from employment relationships or, in the case of indigency, from the relationship to government. *Briggs* deals with unemployment benefits, *Murry* with the right to obtain food stamps, *King* with aid to families with dependent children, *Cahill* with assistance to families of the working poor, and *Bryan* with social security payments. What all these cases have in common is that entitlements were extended judicially while the combined efforts of the legislature and the executive branch of government tried to apply restrictive standards in an effort to keep public expenditures low. It also appears that, in the relationship between federal and state authorities, and certainly within the judicial branch, the flow of entitlements tends to be expanded on the federal level.

The described strains can perhaps be explained by conflicts between the conceptions of "new property," namely, of entitlements, with policies of minimizing the spending and possible wasting of tax moneys. Since the Elizabethan poor laws, fiscal considerations have dominated public aid. The legislature combines with the police power of the government, as tenBroek demonstrated (see References), in an effort to secure the comfort and wealth of the affluent against those who are in need. This conflict, as daily political experience shows, is still unresolved and can be observed in the ambivalent reasoning of the courts. Yet *Briggs, Murry, King, Cahill,* and *Bryan* illustrate that the judicial trend tends, although less so in the lower courts, to favor rights to assistance over efforts to keep expenditures low.

Marriage and the family are intrinsically involved in the conflict of policies, although direct reference to these institutions is often avoided by legislatures. Marital obligations were involved in *Briggs*, the meaning of the word "household" in *Murry* and *Cahill*, and the meaning of "cohabitation" in *King*. *Bryan* concerned the relationship of the wife's earnings to her husband's claims for social security. In all these cases the underlying concepts of marriage and the family were, at least initially, interpreted so as to make it more difficult for claimants to obtain public assistance. That is, in the beginning the policy of saving tax moneys prevailed.

The legislative purposes, although they varied in the five cases, were often overinclusive, having purportedly a narrow goal but then depriving a large group of potential beneficiaries of their entitlements. For example, in the statutory scheme underlying *United States Department of Agriculture v. Moreno,** Congress made an effort in 1971 to exclude "hippies" and "hippie communes" from obtaining food stamps. Similarly, as indicated in *Murry*, an attempt was made to exclude campus activists—children of wealthy parents—from participation in the food-stamp program. *King* dealt with disguised racial discrimination against black recipients of welfare aid to families with dependent children. Beyond the constitutional concerns were broader and unarticulated issues of what kinds of living arrangements should be recognized for purposes of entitlements. *Briggs* and *Bryan* dealt with questions about the extent to which marital circumstances can be used to limit benefits. The cases discussed here, however, stand for a broad principle of universal validity: Whatever changes are observed in the family and in property, they do not apply across the board but are limited to specific purposes. While some of these purposes reflect progressive policies in varying degrees, others still adhere to more traditional views.

---

*413 U.S. 530 (1973).

References

Glendon, *Modern Marriage Law and Its Underlying Assumptions: The New Marriage and the New Property*, 13 FAM. L.Q. 441 (1980).

Glendon, M., THE NEW FAMILY AND THE NEW PROPERTY (1981).

Reich, *The New Property*, 73 YALE L.J. 733 (1964).

tenBroek, *California's Dual System of Family Law: Its Origin, Development, and Present Status* (pts. 1 & 2), 16 STAN. L. REV. 257, 900 (1964); (pt. 3), 17 STAN. L. REV. 614 (1965).

Weyrauch, *Dual Systems of Family Law: A Comment*, 54 CALIF. L. REV. 781 (1966).

Bibliography

Glendon, *Modern Marriage Law and Its Underlying Assumptions: The New Marriage and the New Property*, 13 FAM. L.Q. 441 (1980).

Glendon, M., THE NEW FAMILY AND THE NEW PROPERTY (1981).

Mess, *For Richer, for Poorer: Federal Taxation and Marriage*, 28 CATH. L. REV. 87 (1978).

Rombauer, *Marital Status and Eligibility for Federal Statutory Income Benefits*, 52 WASH. L. REV. 227 (1977).

Sackville, *Social Security and Family Law in Australia*, 27 INT'L & COMP. L.Q. 127 (1978).

tenBroek, *California's Dual System of Family Law: Its Origin, Development, and Present Status* (pts. 1 & 2), 16 STAN. L. REV. 257, 900 (1964); (pt. 3), 17 STAN. L. REV. 614 (1965).

Weyrauch, *Dual Systems of Family Law: A Comment*, 54 CALIF. L. REV. 781 (1966).

Waning State Involvement in Formation of Marriage

Lower Age Requirement

Short v. Hotaling

Supreme Court of New York

32 Misc.2d 933, 225 N.Y.S.2d 53 (1962)

BENJAMIN BRENNER, Justice.

The father and guardian *ad litem* of the infant wife seeks to annul her marriage, pursuant to section 7, subdivision 1 of the Domestic Relations Law. In the exercise of the discretion provided by that section, I believe that the dissolution here sought would not be in the public interest nor that of the married couple.

The facts as adduced upon the trial are as follows: In October of 1960, after dating one another for about a year, the girl, then 16, and the boy, then 19, eloped and married in the State of Virginia. On their return the following day, the parents of the boy accepted the situation, but not so the parents of the girl, who refused to allow them to stay in their home on the night of their return. After an unsuccessful attempt to separate them, the father suggested that the couple stay at a hotel, and on the following night both he and his wife brought them to another hotel to spend a second night together. Thereafter, the father finally prevailed upon his daughter to separate from her husband, to continue attendance at high school and remain at home. He unsuccessfully sought to prosecute the husband for abduction and, when, on a subsequent occasion, the couple contrived to be together at the home of the boy's parents, he again sought a solution through criminal action.

The couple cohabited at the time of their elopement as well as on the nights they stayed at the hotels. They probably also cohabited at the home of the husband's parents. Despite his disclaimer of knowledge, the further consummation of the marriage at the hotels should reasonably have been anticipated by the father. The husband is now of age and has taken part in the alteration of his parent's home to create a separate, if not a legally independent basement apartment, thus hopefully readying it for its prospective use by himself and his wife. He is capable of substantial earnings and, at the trial, appeared to me to be an upright, responsible individual who is most anxious to take on the burdens of married life and, when reunited, to adequately support his wife. So desirous is he of pleasing her and her parents that he has indicated a willingness to convert from Protestantism to Catholicism when so reunited. His love for her was freely professed in open court. The young lady, for her part, has made like professions of love for the husband. She appears to be quite dutiful, is now graduating high school and, except for the elopement and her understandable impatience, she has in large part exercised considerable restraint and complied with the wishes of her parents.

The marital status should be upheld, when the underaged persons involved show willingness and capacity for enduring marital life and for the building of a family unit (*Magee v. Nealon*, 108 Misc. 396, 177 N.Y.S. 517). This is the very discretion mandated by the section and repeatedly exercised in favor of validity when the circumstances so required (*Magee v. Nealon, supra; Allerton v. Allerton*, 104 Misc. 627, 172 N.Y.S. 152; *Marone v. Marone*, 105 Misc. 371, 174 N.Y.S. 151). It is also to be noted that while parental consent was here lacking, the consummation of the marital relationship was furthered by the father and mother of the wife when they suggested that the couple spend several nights together at hotels. This, it seems to me, constituted a measure of ratification of the matrimonial status (*Magee v. Nealon, supra*).

We know from our experience in the matrimonial courts that maturity of body alone is no sure foundation for a satisfactory marriage. What is needed is maturity of both body and mind, which quite often does occur in the case of a youthful couple while sometimes absent in people of age. Where it is present, as it is here, though it be a marriage without parental consent, the marriage deserves to be sustained.

Mindful as I am of all the reasons advanced by the father for the abrogation of the marriage, and giving due consideration to the duty of a parent to guide his child and to prevent her from an improvident marriage, I nevertheless find that the evidence presented by him upon trial offers little more than mere non-age and relentless opposition to the husband, which alone form no basis for the action. (*Todaro v. Todaro*, 120 Misc. 807, 200 N.Y.S. 567). This couple has now been forcefully parted for some fifteen months. Evidence usually needed to annul for non-age, similar to that which constitutes grounds for a decree of divorce or separation, does not exist. Nor do the circumstances warrant their continued enforced separation. They have already been sorely tried and they plainly deserve to put their marriage to the ultimate test of a single residence without parental interference, for which, in the light of their heartbreaking experience, they deserve the whole-hearted support of all involved.

The defendant is therefore entitled to a dismissal of the complaint. The motion for a counsel fee to him is denied.

* * *

Lovato v. Evans

District Court of Utah (3d District)

1 FAM. L. REP. 2848 (1975)

CROFT, J.

Plaintiff, 19 years old and not previously married, applied for a marriage license in the Salt Lake County Clerk's office which license was refused because plaintiff was a male under the age of 21 years and did not have the consent of his father, mother, or guardian to the marriage as required by Section 30-1-9 UCA as amended. Plaintiff asks the court to declare that section unconstitutional and to order defendants to issue a marriage license to plaintiff.

In 1975 the Legislature amended the statute on minority of children to read as follows: "The period of minority extends in males and females to the age of eighteen years, but all minors obtain their majority by marriage. It is further provided that courts in divorce actions may order support to age 21."

The legislature did not amend Section 30-1-9 which since statehood has fixed the age of applying for a marriage license without parental consent at 18 for females and 21 for males.

Prior to the 1975 amendment, Section 15-2-1 fixed the period of minority in males at 21 years and in females at 18. With respect to this statute the Supreme Court of the United States on April 15, 1975 ruled in *Stanton v. Stanton*, 43 L.Ed.2d 689, that in the context of child support the classification effectuated by Section 15-2-1 denied equal protection of the laws, as guaranteed by the Fourteenth Amendment. The *Stanton* case involved only the question of child support in divorce cases. The court said the test in *Stanton* was whether the difference in sex between children warranted the distinction in a father's obligation to support boys to 21 but girls only until 18 as drawn in Section 15-2-1 (before 1975 amendment). In reaching its conclusion that it did not, the court in *Stanton* said the section imposes "criteria wholly unrelated to the objective of that statute" for the need of support was equally great for girls as for boys.

In *Stanton* the court said it had held in *Reed v. Reed*, 404 U.S. 71.30 L.Ed.2d 225, that an Idaho statute (preference to males over females in probate matters) accorded different treatment on the basis of sex and that it "thus establishes a classification subject to scrutiny under the Equal Protection Clause." * * *

It thus appears that the test here, then, is whether the difference in sex between children warrants the distinction in the requirement of parental consent to a marriage of a male under 21 when it is required only for females under 18. In other words, is this classification "reasonable, not arbitrary" and does the classification "rest upon some ground of difference having a fair and substantial relation to the objection of the legislation?"

Undoubtedly, convincing arguments may be advanced on either side of the controversy. As one sits upon the bench of this court and witnesses the daily parade of divorce cases that are handled by the court, one longs for a means of making the stability of the home stronger and the marriage ties more lasting. But statistics in the past show that the divorce rate in Utah exceeds the national average and thus it does not appear that if the "object of the legislation" in Section 30-1-9 was to bring stability into marriage, it has achieved that goal. * * *

If Section 30-1-9 be held constitutional, this case would thus appear to put a premium upon falsifying one's age when the required written consent is not forthcoming, for he who lies about his age and gets a license, even though he may be guilty of perjury (Sec. 30-1-10), may thus enter into a valid marriage while he who truthfully admits to being "under age" cannot get a license without the written consent and thus cannot marry. This hardly smacks of "equal protection," or at least of the kind that ought to exist. * * *

As a judge I strongly oppose legislation by judicial fiat and I do not look lightly upon declaring existing statutes unconstitutional, particularly those of long standing. The Supreme Court of this state, or the United States or the legislature, should ultimately decide this question, but as a judge I cannot do other than declare the law as I believe it to be and to thus rule accordingly.

It is therefore my opinion that Section 30-1-9 denies equal protection of the law to males between the ages of 18 and 21 and is therefore unconstitutional and that the plaintiff is entitled to the relief prayed for in his complaint, subject, however, to a stay of one month from entry of judgment pending possible appeal by the defendants.

Comments

A number of questions relating to teenage marriages, especially in the area of conflict of laws, were dealt with in *Wilkins v. Zelichowski* (see pp. 358–359). Much in these cases depends on the wording used in an individual state statute establishing age limits for marriage. If such statutes use language to the effect that a state official or judge shall not issue a license unless certain requirements in regard to age and parental consent are met, it seems clear that no absolute bar to marriage is established. Such language appears to be directed toward the issuing officials who may be subject to state sanctions if they violate their obligations. To the extent that such statutes are silent, the traditional common law limits of 12 years of age for the female party to marriage and 14 for the male may still apply. Even parental consent may be viewed as being irrelevant to the validity of a marriage, although it may be relevant to the question of whether the issuing official has violated his obligations. Popular opinion treats the age requirements for marriage as more important than statutes and case law necessarily do.

The factual power of parents and the state to "terminate" an underage marriage by physical separation of the parties should be distinguished from the legal validity of the marriage. In *Short* the teenage bride's father succeeded in separating her from her husband, although there was an initial period of cohabitation in hotel rooms. The father attempted sanctions, but without success. Even so, the factual power of the police to break up marriages should not be underestimated. Realistically, much erroneous parental and official behavior may acquire all appearances of law because there is no effective power to challenge it. In *Short* an unusually persistent young couple combined their efforts with those of a benevolent court to overcome factual obstacles to the marriage.

In many jurisdictions a father's standing to sue for annulment in behalf of his daughter would be questionable, but New York has a statute that empowers him to bring such an action. The action failed not on procedural grounds, but because of the ways the facts were perceived by the court. The young woman's parents facilitated the consummation of marriage by permitting the couple to stay in a hotel together. Consummation, although the judge did not say it explicitly, involves sexual intercourse, which was presumed by the court in these circumstances. The courts have traditionally been inclined to give special weight to such consummation of marriage. Thus what may make the difference between a marriage subject to annulment and one that continues to be valid is the act of the parties that is presumed to have taken place in the privacy of the bedroom. Because of the continued legal significance of sexual intercourse in a marital context, attorneys should still inquire about this aspect in their interviews with clients. In *Short* the father's ratification was an additional concept in sustaining the marriage. Although the parties, at the time in question, did not have the power to ratify, the father himself ratified their conduct. Nevertheless it should not be overlooked that the court viewed the actions of the parties to the marriage in the most favorable light. Factors that could have spoken against them were neglected, for example, that in all probability the parties committed perjury in Virginia about their respective ages.

No perjury was committed in *Lovato*. The plaintiff, who had apparently remained in his home jurisdiction of Utah, had stated his proper age at all times. The objective of the suit was to declare that the different treatment of males and females in Utah in regard to parental consent is unconstitutional because it violates the Equal Protection Clause. In permitting the action, the Utah court set the stage for what might become a national trend, namely, making the requirements of age for marriage equal for males and females.

Yet again, both *Short* and *Lovato* appear somewhat dated in other respects. The behavior of the parties to the marriages no longer corresponds to contemporary mores. Young adults are more inclined to delay marriage regardless of the legal or constitutional situation. Consummation of marriage is also a dated concept because sexual intercourse short of marriage is frequent and, although "consummation" continues to be stressed by the courts, it increasingly acquires elements of a legal fiction that, as in *Short*, facilitates reaching an equitable result.

Reference

Clark, H., THE LAW OF DOMESTIC RELATIONS IN THE UNITED STATES 77–86 (1968).

Lower Mental Competence

Larson v. Larson

Appellate Court of Illinois

42 Ill. App.2d 467, 192 N.E.2d 594 (1963)

CROW, Presiding Justice.

This is an appeal by the plaintiff, Sidney F. Larson, from a decree dismissing a suit for want of equity on a complaint for annulment of a marriage between the plaintiff and the defendant, Myrtle Larson.

The pertinent evidence offered by the plaintiff disclosed that the plaintiff was 48 years of age and the defendant 39 years of age on March 21, 1950, the date of the marriage. The plaintiff had known the defendant for about two years, but had known her well for only about one month before the marriage. During that period he noticed nothing abnormal about her. He knew nothing of her having any mental disability, if she had any. A few months after the marriage the defendant once in a while thought police officers were watching her, although they were not. During the following months she thought the house was wired with electricity from which she was receiving electric shocks, but the house was not so wired. In the middle of the night sometimes she thought she heard people running around on the roof and around the house, but there were no people on the roof or around the house. In the nighttime on one occasion she ran to a neighbor's house where she was not known, and the police brought her home. The plaintiff thought it was a nervous condition. She ran away a second time. She was then committed to Elgin State Hospital for treatment on July 22, 1952, by the Winnebago County Court as a mentally ill person, incapable of managing and caring for her own estate. She was there about four months. Subsequently, on March 17, 1954, the County Court of Winnebago County, on the defendant's petition, found that she had recovered from her mental illness and was capable of caring for her own estate and restored her to all her civil rights. The plaintiff said she got along good for awhile. But, on November 9, 1956, she was again committed by the County Court of Winnebago County to the Elgin State Hospital, again as a mentally ill person. During the time between the first discharge and the second commitment, March 17, 1954 and November 9, 1956, she accused the plaintiff of having women around, when he did not, and sometimes said the police were watching her. Sometimes when the plaintiff came home from work she chased him with a broom. Once she locked him out of the house. The defendant had previously been married to another party and had been divorced by him on the ground of desertion in 1942. The plaintiff lived with the defendant as husband and wife until she was committed to the Hospital in 1952, and thereafter whenever she was at intervals permitted to come home on week-ends, and again after she was restored in 1954 and until the second commitment in 1956, and again thereafter when she was at times given conditional discharges on week-ends at home.

Dr. Curt Steffen, called as a witness on behalf of the plaintiff, testified that he was a physician and surgeon specializing in mental disorders. He had never personally examined or treated Mrs. Larson. She was diagnosed by some other doctor or doctors as a schizophrenic (apparently at the time of the 1952 or 1956 commitments), and, from an hypothetical question which took certain evidentiary facts into account alleged to have taken place before and after her marriage, he said all of her symptoms appeared to be schizophrenic symptoms, persecution ideas, delusions, and depressions. Such a psychosis usually starts earlier in life than 39 years of age he said. With this type of psychosis, he said, patients have so-called lucid intervals. Those intervals may last for months or even for years and then they go back into depression or insanity. Very few schizophrenics are cured, he said. They may be discharged from a hospital but after a time they have attacks again and have to be recommitted. He said he would assume she had been mentally sick for quite a while but she might not have had such outspoken symptoms that a layman would be able to recognize such as insanity. She might be all right for two years—a layman's cure. Outspoken symptoms usually come on very gradually. During the cross-examination, the doctor was asked:

"Q. Then is it your opinion, Doctor, that a schizophrenic can never be cured?
"A. I would say—I wouldn't say never, but I would say it is a rarity if they can ever cure a schizophrenic completely.
* * *
"Q. Then is it your opinion a schizophrenic is in the way of medically always insane?
"A. One doesn't have to be insane. There are a lot of symptoms between sanity and insanity, and you cannot just say sane and insane. It might be legally all right, but medically it is very difficult to say."

A brother of the defendant's first husband (from whom she was divorced in 1942, 8 years before the present marriage) said that while she was married to his brother she would about once a year just flare up, not talk to anyone, and run off and leave her family. He said she just didn't act normally. Once after she was married to the plaintiff Larson this witness said she came to the witness' home and accused his oldest son of improprieties towards her—that was in 1958. He said at one Christmas time she was good one day and not the next. He had no trouble with her.

It is this medical testimony and the other evidence referred to that the plaintiff insists is sufficient evidence of insanity of the defendant on March 21, 1950 to justify decreeing an annulment of the marriage.

When the celebration of a marriage is shown, the contract of marriage, the capacity of the parties, and, in fact, everything necessary to the validity of the marriage, in the absence of proof to the contrary, will be presumed; the burden of proof was upon the plaintiff to show the marriage was invalid; to enable a party legally to contract a marriage he or she must be capable of understanding the nature of the act: *Flynn et al. v. Troesch et al.* (1940) 373 Ill. 275, 26 N.E.2d 91. When a marriage is shown the law raises a strong presumption in favor of its validity, and the burden is upon the party objecting thereto to prove such facts and circumstances as necessarily establish its invalidity; there is no clear dividing line between competency and incompetency, and each case must be judged by its own peculiar facts; the parties must have sufficient mental capacity to enter into the status, but proof of lack of mental capacity must be clear and definite; if the party possesses sufficient mental capacity to understand the nature, effect, duties, and obligation of the marriage contract into which he or she is entering, the marriage contract is binding, as long as they are otherwise legally competent to enter into the relation: *Ertel v. Ertel* (1942) 313 Ill. App. 326, 40 N.E.2d 85. A marriage contract will be invalidated by the want of consent of capable persons; it requires the mutual consent of two persons of sound mind, and if at the time one is mentally incapable of giving an intelligent consent to what is done, with an understanding of the obligations assumed, the solemnization is a mere idle ceremony—they must be capable of entering understandingly into the relation: *Hagenson v. Hagenson et al.* (1913) 258 Ill. 197, 101 N.E. 606. It is impossible to prescribe a definite rule by which the mental condition as to sanity or insanity in regard to a marriage can in every case be tested; the question is not altogether of brain quantity or quality in the abstract, but whether the mind could and did act rationally regarding the precise thing in contemplation—marriage—and the particular marriage in dispute—not whether his or her conduct was wise, but whether it proceeded from a mind sane as respects the particular thing done: [citations omitted].

The decree here is not contrary to the manifest weight of the evidence or to the law. Prior to and at the time of the marriage the plaintiff noticed nothing abnormal about the defendant. There is no evidence that any of the unusual things she thought and did some months after the marriage had also occurred prior to and at the time of the marriage. Her first commitment to Elgin State Hospital was in 1952, more than two years after the marriage. In 1954 she was found to have recovered and was restored to all her civil rights. She got along good for awhile thereafter. Her second commitment was in 1956, more than four and one-half years after the marriage. The plaintiff continued to live regularly with the defendant as husband and wife except for such times as she was actually physically confined at the Hospital. The doctor who testified had never examined, or treated the defendant and his entire testimony is based, necessarily, on an hypothetical question. The ostensible diagnosis was evidently made by another or other doctors, who were not available or did not testify here. No doctor, nurse, or attendant at the Hospital who might have observed, examined, or treated her testified. In this doctor's opinion, even, a patient of that type may have lucid intervals for months or years—she may not have had any symptoms which a layman would recognize as insanity—she might be all right for years—and he would not say a patient of such type could never be cured. Even he said such a patient might be legally all right—not legally insane—though medically it may be very difficult to say. The other witness' testimony was either quite remote in point of time, or related to an incident eight years after the marriage, or had to do with matters having no great legal significance.

The plaintiff has not satisfied the burden of proving, clearly and definitely, that the defendant was an "insane person" at the particular time of this marriage, March 21, 1950—that she was at that time incapable of understanding the nature of the act, that she had insufficient mental capacity to enter into the status and understand the nature, effect, duties, and obligations of the marriage contract, that she was mentally incapable of giving an intelligent, understanding consent, or that her mind could not and did not act rationally regarding the precise thing in contemplation, marriage, and this particular marriage in dispute.

The decree is correct and it will be affirmed.

Comments

Theoretically, as the court states in *Larson*, marriage requires the mutual consent of two persons of sound mind; otherwise the solemnization of marriage "is a mere idle ceremony." Yet the capacity to contract is not necessarily identical with the capacity to marry; a more lenient standard may be applied to the latter. Futhermore, the substantive requirement of insanity of one of the spouses for purposes of an annulment action is not necessarily identical with the psychiatric conceptions of mental illness. Thus considerable diversification in analysis is possible. A person may be sane for purposes of entering a marriage, but not necessarily for entering a major contract of a commercial nature; and the medical characterization may vary for either legal classification. The legal conceptions of insanity are also, as are many legal terms, based on an implicit dichotomy of reasoning—that a person either is or is not sane for a particular purpose. As the expert stated in *Larson*, medical judgment is more tentative for a variety of reasons, one of which being that doctors are not concerned with solving specific issues. Further complications arise, as in *Larson*, from the psychiatric classification of schizophrenia, which includes a wide range of human behavior.

Although legal and medical classifications may vary in an individual case as well as in general, courts have developed procedural devices that facilitate an adjustment between differing professional judgments in law and medicine. In *Larson*, for example, the court concluded that the plaintiff had not satisfied the burden of proof that the defendant was "clearly and definitely" an insane person. A rule of evidence, rather than a substantive legal rule of insanity, permitted the court to reach a conclusion that can be compared in its tentative nature to the substantive medical diagnosis. While the evaluation of the psychiatric condition of the defendant wife remained inconclusive, for legal purposes a definite outcome of the litigation was still assured: the plaintiff lost. The lesson to be learned for legal analysis is that controversies have to be analyzed in their totality, including all aspects of substantive and procedural law. To the practicing lawyer this reflects the common experience that except for appellate strategy it does not matter whether a case is won or lost on procedural grounds or on substantive ones.

There is also an aspect of laches in *Larson*. More than 10 years had elapsed after the marriage. The defendant wife had been in and out of mental hospitals and, during this time, cohabitation between her and the plaintiff husband had taken place. Contrary to older views, even if one assumes that the wife was insane at the time of marriage, the marriage was considered to be merely voidable. This means in effect that the marriage was valid, and continued to be valid after the husband had lost his remedy of annulment by his conduct. The court did not stress this point, but it may have helped in coming to the conclusion that the complaint was to be dismissed. Here too there is a procedural side of a related nature. The plaintiff's lawyer had prepared the case poorly. He tried to prove his case by posing hypothetical questions to an expert who had never examined the defendant wife. Obviously better evidence was available but he neglected to pursue it. For example, he could have requested the doctors and nurses who had actually treated the wife to testify.

Today an additional aspect has to be considered: the impact of grounds for dissolution of marriage on annulment actions. Conceptually the two types of remedies have nothing to do with each other because dissolution arises from facts that occur after a marriage has been entered while annulment actions relate to facts prior to marriage. Nevertheless, courts can hardly overlook that even in no-fault jurisdictions a dissolution of marriage for insanity is regularly possible only if very specific and stringent statutory conditions have been met. If in comparison annulment were easily available without such conditions, plaintiffs could choose this avenue in an effort to avoid the pitfalls of dissolution. This does not mean of course that the same conditions have to be met in annulment actions that apply to divorce for insanity, but a court may again use stringent standards of proof as a means of reaching similar results.

References

Clark, H., THE LAW OF DOMESTIC RELATIONS IN THE UNITED STATES 95–99 (1968).

Katz, J., Goldstein, J., & Dershowitz, A., PSYCHOANALYSIS, PSYCHIATRY AND LAW 506–526 (1967).

Incestuous Marriage

Israel v. Allen

District Court of Colorado

3 FAM. L. REP. 2601 (1977)

The parties hereto agree to the fact that parties' plaintiffs are brother and sister only by adoption.

The plaintiffs applied to the Clerk and Recorder of Jefferson County for a marriage license and same was denied under the provisions of 14-2-110(1)(b), which states as follows:

> "Prohibited marriages: (1) The following marriages are prohibited:
> "(b) A marriage between an ancestor and a descendant or between a brother and a sister whether relationship is by the half or the whole blood or by adoption;"

The parties hereto agree that the portion of the statute pertaining to "relationship by half or whole blood" is constitutional in that there is a furtherance of a compelling state interest.

The question presented to the Court is whether or not that part of 14-2-110(1) (b), or "adoption;" is constitutional. * * *

The Court concludes that creation of a "marriage relationship" is a fundamental right in this jurisdiction. * * *

In concluding that marriage is a fundamental right the presumption of constitutionality is overcome and the test of a rational relationship to a legitimate state purpose is not applicable. Compelling the Court to strictly scrutinize that portion of the law and require the State to prove this provision is necessary to the furtherance of a compelling state interest. *Roe v. Wade*, 410 U.S. 113 (1973). *Shapiro v. Thomspon*, 394 U.S. 618 (1969). *Romero v. Schauer*, 386 F. Supp. 851.

The thrust of the argument for the State is that marriage of brothers and sisters by adoption are prohibited because of social interest in discouraging romantic attachments between such persons even if there is no genetic risk. 9 Uniform Laws Anno. 470 (1973).

This argument is devoid of any logic or showing of a compelling state interest. * * *

This Court concludes that there is no compelling state interest being served to warrant the denial of the parties' constitutional rights and liberties.

The Court concludes that portion of 14-2-110(1) (b) "or by adoption" denies the plaintiffs equal protection under the Constitution.—VOLLACK, J.

In re MEW and MLB

Pennsylvania Court of Common Pleas

3 FAM. L. REP. 2602 (1977)

The question to be determined on this record is whether two persons who are unrelated by blood but who become brother and sister by reason of an adoption of the male applicant by the natural mother of the female applicant may lawfully obtain a license to marry under the provisions of "The Marriage Law," Act of August 22, 1953, P.L. 1344, Sec. 5, 48 P.S. 1-5. * * *

In the light of the foregoing principles of law and there being no specific statutory prohibition of a marriage between two persons who are brother and sister by adoption, we come face to face with the proposition as to whether this relationship constitutes an impediment which bars the issuance of a marriage license in Pennsylvania.

The policy of the law of the Commonwealth is to impose upon adopted children all of the rights and duties of a natural child of an adoptive parent or parents. Correspondingly, an adopted child has imposed upon him or her all of the obligations and disabilities which accompany the relationship of parent and child. * * *

The hearing judge, in the case at bar, perceives the present application for a license to marry to be an entirely different problem than the one presented in *Enderle, supra*. Here the applicants are brother and sister by reason of the male applicant's adoption by the mother of the female applicant. While the applicants did not live and grow up together in the same household from early childhood, they have for at least part of their lives lived together as brother and sister in the family residence of their respective parents. An important consideration in this case is the integrity of the family which the law has a duty to protect. To authorize and encourage marriages of brothers and sisters by adoption would undermine the fabric of family life and would be the antithesis of the social aims and purposes which the adoption process is intended to serve.

The hearing judge holds that an adoption imposes on an adopted child a constructive relationship with the natural children of his adoptive parent equal to a relationship by consanguinity. In these circumstances the Court is obliged to sustain the action of the Clerk of the Orphan's Court Division, who has refused to issue a marriage license in this case.—BOYLE, J.

Concurrence: I agree with the result reached by Judge Boyle and join in his decree sustaining the refusal of the requested marriage license. Here, as in *Enderle*, 1 D&C 2nd 114, there appears at first blush no reason to prevent the marriage of the above applicants since their relationship arises from adoption and is not based on consanguinity. There are, however, other complex facets inherent in this matter, one of which concerned both Judge Boyle and Judge Klein, Judge Klein expressing his concern by stating that the sanctity of the home should be maintained and there should not be competition for sexual companionship between members of the same household or family, while Judge Boyle indicated that the duty of the law is to protect the integrity of the family with the law not encouraging marriages of brothers and sisters by adoption as this would undermine the family life and be antithesis of the adoption process purpose.

To this I would add my concern that if this license is granted, the marriage code will have preference over the adoption act. The adoption act makes the applicants brother and sister and since a man may not marry his sister, to hold that the marriage code means only a man and his sister by blood, would make the adoption process meaningless for the purposes of marriage. A person should not be able to consent to an adoption, receive the benefits of an adoption and then pretend that the adoption does not exist or does not affect the family relationship all for the purpose of obtaining a marriage license.—ZAVARELLA, J.

Dissent: The majority deny the parties the right to marry on the ground that the marriage "would undermine the fabric of family life and would be the antithesis of the social aim and purposes which the adoption process is intended to serve."

I do not believe that this would follow if a license were to be issued in the case at bar. Prior to the wedding above referred to, the parties were as strangers to each other. The fact that they lived in the same household for "a short period" in 1973 does not in my judgment make them "de facto" brother and sister. This is not a case where a male infant and a female infant were adopted and raised to maturity by the adopting parents in the same household. In a case of this nature the reasoning of the majority might be applicable.

The parties are not related by blood or affinity. Therefore, there is in law no obstacle to their marriage.

The purpose of the adoption law is to provide a secure home and loving parents to a child not wanted, or abandoned by his natural parents. I do not believe it should be construed in such a manner as to prevent a marriage between two persons, who, I believe, are legally entitled to marry. Therefore, I dissent.—MCKENNA, J.

Comments

Israel and *In re MEW* deal not with incest as traditionally understood, that is, as prohibitions against marriage in case of consanguinity or affinity, but with statutory prohibitions against marriage between adopted siblings. As in affinity, questions of genetics are not involved because adoption does not involve a blood relationship. *Israel* stressed the fundamental right to marry and permitted a marriage when the relationship of brother and sister resulted from adoption. *MEW* came to the opposite conclusion. There the court viewed the integrity of the family to be at stake. Inevitably this raises questions of conflict of laws since two different jurisdictions, Colorado and Pennsylvania, were involved. A question that may arise is, what effects should be given to a "migratory marriage"? For example, could the adoptive brother and sister in *MEW* go from Pennsylvania to Colorado to marry, and would their out-of-state marriage in the more liberal jurisdiction of Colorado be recognized if they were to return to Pennsylvania? A further question could arise if they were to leave Colorado for a third jurisdiction. Actually, these questions are simplistic and unanswerable unless further facts are given.

Most discussions of incest do not differentiate sufficiently between the numerous factual and legal variations that are possible. Obviously, legal characterizations of incest do not necessarily coincide with social understanding. The social understanding of incest is sometimes broader, sometimes narrower, than the legal prohibitions. Although society may disapprove of stepfather-stepdaughter relationships, some jurisdictions, such as Florida, may prohibit marriages only in case of consanguinity. On the other hand, society may be tolerant toward marriages between cousins, but statutes may prohibit them.

To the variables of legal policies and social understandings others should be added. The outcome of cases, regardless of statutory language, may depend on whether and to what degree consanguinity is involved or whether affinity is merely established by marriage. Whether the marriage establishing the relationship still exists or has been terminated by death or divorce may make a difference. Yet a close relationship, such as that between stepfather and stepdaughter, may be considered a continuing impediment, even if the mother has died. In adoption it may make a difference whether the issue involves a father and adoptive daughter, a brother and adoptive sister, or cousins who are merely related by adoption. Even more remote, and thus not necessarily effective in the courts, might be prohibitions of marriage if affinity established only by adoption is involved. Thus a marriage between a man and the widow of his deceased adoptive brother may technically be prohibited. Yet courts may be inclined to grant relief under reasoning similar to that in *Israel*.

The outcome of cases is further influenced by the purpose of the litigation. In applying the same statute, courts may be more stringent in permitting a marriage than in declaring it valid once it has been entered. It may be more difficult to enter an incestuous marriage than to stay in it. As in ordinary contract law, the level of execution can have a bearing on whether a marriage contract is upheld. It does make a difference when a marriage entered in violation of law has lasted for many years and has resulted in children and in the accumulation of property. Most jurisdictions will consider an uncle-niece marriage void for any purpose. Yet such a union may be upheld, as if it had been merely voidable, if the only issue is whether a past real estate transaction is valid after the death of both spouses. In this case cohabitation is no longer a problem, and courts may relax legislative prohibitions.* It is not likely that an incestuous marriage would have been permitted upon mandamus action. It also may have resulted in criminal prosecution during the life of the parties. Whether an incestuous marriage is absolutely void or merely voidable—in other words, valid until annulled—cannot be answered in the abstract.

Although everybody agrees that close blood relationships should be absolutely prohibited in marriage and sexual relations, the volume of civil litigation relating to incest is not concerned with these. Leaving criminal cases aside, the courts are involved in matters relating to adoption (as in *Israel* and *MEW*), to affinity relationships established by marriage, and to attempted marriages between cousins and, occasionally, between uncle and niece. It may become necessary for a lawyer then to delve into the underlying considerations of policy. Strong religious and social taboos are involved. Further considerations have been added, many of them relating to bygone times. It is no longer a matter of survival to establish a wide network of relationships through marriage outside the family or clan. Genetic considerations, for example, that incestuous marriages may result in defective offspring, have no bearing on relationships based on affinity and adoption. Even in the case of marriages between cousins, genetic theories are not conclusive. In the last analysis it is the taboo itself, whether or not it conforms to scientific knowledge, that provides the justification.

Nevertheless, any of the theories on incest is valid enough for a legal argument, especially in borderline cases. In other words, scientific evidence is good for argumentation, but the decision is likely to be made on another level. It is not the practicing lawyer's task to resolve deeply controversial matters beyond the resolution of a specific case at hand.

References

Goode, W., THE FAMILY 24 (1964).

Levi-Strauss, C., *The Family*, in MAN, CULTURE AND SOCIETY 261, 276–278 (Shapiro ed. 1956).

Mead, M., *Anomalies in American Post-Divorce Relationships*, in DIVORCE AND AFTER 97, 106–112 (1970).

Nagan, *Conflict of Laws and Proximate Relations: A Policy-Science Perspective*, 8 RUT.-CAM. L. REV. 416 (1977).

Packer, H., THE LIMITS OF THE CRIMINAL SANCTION 312–316 (1968).

Storke, *The Incestuous Marriage—Relic of the Past*, 36 U. COLO. L. REV. 473 (1964).

---

*See *Johnson v. Landefeld*, 138 Fla. 511, 189 So. 666 (1939).

Interracial Marriage

See *Loving v. Virginia*, Chapter 3, *supra* at p. 229.

Prisoner's Marriage

In re Carrafa

Court of Appeals of California

77 Cal. App.3d 788, 143 Cal. Rptr. 848 (1978)

REYNOSO, J.

Petitioner, Victor Carrafa, an inmate at Folsom State Prison, by his habeas corpus proceeding challenges the actions of the Department of Corrections (Department). The Department has prohibited, at least temporarily, his marriage with his fiancée, Joan Vibbard.

The right to marry is a statutorily recognized fundamental constitutional guarantee. The right was impermissibly infringed. Prison authorities erroneously ruled that denial of general visitation rights to the bride also justified the denial of the marriage request. We conclude that the Department must permit petitioner's marriage. Prison security may properly be considered by the Department in making arrangements for the ceremony.

Petitioner requested permission to marry his fiancée. The request, dated May 23, 1977, was to marry on June 29, the date already set for weddings. Permission was denied.

On June 4, 12 days after the request, a pistol and other contraband were found in prison. Petitioner was immediately placed in an isolated security unit. The next day he was informed in writing that he had been placed in the security unit pending the investigation. Prison authorities later advised petitioner that his "lock-up" was for his protection; they had received information that his murder was planned by other inmates. After 15 days, on June 20, petitioner was placed back in the general prison population.

Petitioner's fiancée's visitation rights were suspended apparently between June 20 and June 28. On the 28th she was advised in writing that the suspension was "due to information leading us to believe that you were involved [in] the smuggling of a firearm and narcotics" into prison. The suspension was also based on falsification of her residence address on the "visiting questionnaire."

Two further letters from prison authorities to petitioner's fiancée explained the suspension. During the investigation, according to a July 15 letter, "reliable information" revealed that she, Joan Vibbard, was involved in the introduction of large amounts of marijuana to the prison. Further, the method of introduction (hiding marijuana in prison service vehicle tire) was the same as that used to introduce the pistol. Secondly, the pistol found by prison authorities had been serviced prior to its introduction to prison. The repair "tag" listed Sharon Smith as the person who had the gun serviced. During that period the same address was used by Joan Vibbard. On July 25 yet another letter was sent. She was advised that she could not visit the prison until the investigation was complete. The letter explained that the investigation dealt with the "smuggling of a gun" and that she was "implicated" as being possibly involved.

In addition to the explanations contained in the letters, the record reveals that prison authorities had other information. They considered the inmate, whom they believed to be involved in the gun incident, petitioner's "associate." Further, no person by the name of Sharon Smith had been found who lived at the address listed on the "tag" at the time the pistol was serviced.

The petition to marry, as previously indicated, was denied. The letter sent Joan Vibbard dated July 25 also responded to her complaint that she was unable to marry petitioner. She was told that she could renew her application to marry when her visitation rights were restored. The date of the actual denial is July 29, 1977; petitioner's uncontradicted assertion is that he was not advised until August 19. The denial appears on the bottom of the internal memorandum recommending approval of the "marriage request"—the denial reads: "Denied. Bride not approved visitor."

Meanwhile, on July 27, petitioner filed a writ of habeas corpus before the Superior Court of Sacramento County. The writ was denied August 11, 1977. The petition for writ of habeas corpus before this court followed. As of December 15, the date of oral argument, permission to marry had apparently not been granted.

The right of prisoners to marry has been codified (Pen. Code, §§2600–2601.) Section 2601 declares: "Notwithstanding any other provision of law, each such person shall have the following civil rights: [* * *] (f) [t]o marry." Our Supreme Court has explained the historical setting of this statutory declaration: "We have, in this state, 'long since abandoned the medieval concept of strict "civil death" and have replaced it with statutory provisions seeking to insure that the civil rights of those convicted of crime be limited only in accordance with legitimate penal objectives.' [Citation omitted.] To that end, the Legislature, in 1968, amended the 'Civil Death' statute, section 2600, to provide that certain basic rights be retained by prisoners." (*In re Van Geldern* (1971) 5 Cal.3d 832, 836 [97 Cal. Rptr. 698, 489 P.2d 578].)

The right to marry is a fundamental constitutional right (*Perez v. Sharp* (1948) 32 Cal.2d 711, 714 [198 P.2d 17]; *Loving v. Virginia* (1967) 388 U.S. 1, 12 [18 L.Ed.2d 1010, 1018, 87 S. Ct. 1817].) The codification of that right emphasizes its fundamental nature. "The civil rights set forth in section 2600 are fundamental guarantees which may not arbitrarily be infringed." (*In re Van Geldern, supra*, 5 Cal.3d 832, 836.)

A prisoner may not be deprived of such a right except "as is necessary in order to provide for the reasonable security of the institution in which he is confined and for the reasonable protection of the public." (Pen. Code, §2600.) Such a limitation is not a " 'straightjacket limiting the ability of the prison authorities to deal with institutional realities.' " (*In re Van Geldern, supra*, at p. 837.) Rather "[v]alid and compelling institutional considerations may necessitate certain *limited inroads* upon the exercise of the prisoner's civil rights." (*Ibid.*; italics added.)

However, when state action infringes a fundamental right of the petitioner, the state action can be upheld only if necessary to effect an overriding governmental interest. The government must show that its interest cannot be satisfied by alternative methods less restrictive of the individual right abridged. Otherwise, the infringement must fail. (*Payne v. Superior Court* (1976) 17 Cal.3d 908, 914 [132 Cal. Rptr. 405, 553 P.2d 565].) As we explain below, the government has failed to meet that burden.

The Department argues that it is not depriving petitioner of the right to marry. Rather the marriage is delayed only until the conclusion of a pending investigation. The delay, the Department argues, is essential to prison security.

We disagree. We deal with the reality that delay prevents exercise of that right. (See *In re Harrell, supra*, 2 Cal.3d 675, 703.) Denial of petitioner's right to marry does not appear to be the only alternative available to the state in protecting its legitimate interest in prison security. First, his fiancée indicated her willingness to submit to a body search and noncontact visits if that would improve prison security. Thus, the possibility of smuggled contraband is virtually eliminated. Second, the mere fact of marriage does not preclude the Department from excluding the marriage partner if it believes that there is a legitimate security risk. (Cal. Admin. Code, tit. 15, §3176.) The Department has failed to demonstrate the unavailability of any reasonable alternative to protect prison security.

As indicated, a spouse may be excluded when appropriate. Thus, we draw a clear distinction, not recognized by the Department in this case, between the right to marry and the right of visitation. The right to marry may not be impinged or delayed unless security is endangered at the time and place of the marriage. Visitation rights are quite another matter.

A writ of habeas corpus will issue directing the Department of Corrections to permit petitioner's marriage under such circumstances as will respect prison security.

* * *

Comments

In re Carrafa deals with the power of prison authorities to prohibit prisoners from marrying. To be distinguished is the question of the extent to which existing marriages are affected by conviction or imprisonment. *In re Carrafa* represents the modern view, emphasizing the prisoner's civil rights including his fundamental right to marry. California is probably more progressive in these respects than other American jurisdictions, which uphold the right of prison authorities to refuse their consent to a prisoner's marriage. A state statute, changed in 1968, facilitated the liberal decision. The more restrictive traditional view, expressed with a certain grimness, can be found in *In re Goalen.** An extreme, unlitigated case occurred in Florida, where two death-row inmates, Jessie Tafero and Sonia Jacobs, requested permission to marry. The petitioners, who had lived together for about 10 years, desired to legitimatize their 21-month-old child. The petition was denied by the Department of Offender Rehabilitation because, it was said, the marriage would serve no useful purpose and would be an inappropriate expenditure of tax money.†

Somewhat related policy questions are involved in regard to the impact of conviction for crime on marriages. In many states conviction of a felony is a special divorce ground. *In re Carrafa* mentions the concept of "civil death," which, in a few jurisdictions, may apply to prisoners who have received a life term. Under this theory such prisoners not only are prohibited from marrying, but their existing marriages are perceived to be terminated.

---

*30 Utah 2d 27, 512 P.2d 1028 (1973), *cert. denied*, 414 U.S. 1148 (1974) (Stewart, Douglas, Brennan, JJ., dissenting).

†See Shields, *Prison Director Bans Death Row Wedding*, Gainesville Sun, Feb. 3, 1977, §D at 1, col. 3.

In spite of such sentencing practices—America's are among the harshest in the Western world—it is nevertheless likely that the California view, as expressed in *Carrafa*, will eventually prevail.

A lawyer has to be concerned not merely with the law in his jurisdiction but also with the legal myths, sometimes quite unsupported, that exist in the population. Perhaps as a result of theories of "civil death," many people believe that a felony conviction for a lengthy prison term frees the other party from marital obligations. The presumption of death after seven years' absence is also erroneously thought to be applicable in such cases if the conviction is for a term longer than seven years. Sometimes spouses remarry on the basis of a mistaken understanding of the law. Some authors have written in this context about "common law divorce," which is not actual law but a popular myth. This so-called "prison divorce" is only one illustration among many of how persons, because of their misinterpretation of law, feel free to remarry. It is the lawyer's obligation to be aware of the actual legal situation and at the same time of the ways in which it is reflected in the minds of clients who, in these kinds of cases, may well be from a lower-educated stratum of society.

References

Comment, *Civil Death—A New Look at an Ancient Doctrine*, 11 Wm. & Mary L. Rev. 988 (1970).

Foster, *Common Law Divorce*, 46 Minn. L. Rev. 43 (1961).

Jordan, *The Doctrine of Common Law Divorce*, 14 U. Fla. L. Rev. 264 (1961).

Special Project, *The Collateral Consequences of a Criminal Conviction*, 23 Vand. L. Rev. 929 (1970).

Bigamous Marriage

Davis v. Davis

Supreme Court of Texas

521 S.W.2d 603 (Tex. 1975)

Reavley, Justice.

Charles Davis was killed by shipwreck in the Sea of Java on December 24, 1970, at the age of 36 years. The Probate Court of Chambers County, where the administration of his estate is pending, is in possession of the small amount of his personal property, together with wages due from his employer, Reading & Bates Offshore Drilling Company, and the proceeds of a group accidental death insurance policy which was purchased by that employer and issued a few days prior to the death of Charles. The insurer has paid $51,031.38 into the registry of the Chambers County Court. This litigation will determine the heirship of Charles Davis and the manner of division of this property.

Charles married Mary Nell in Liberty County in 1966, and in 1967 he departed for Australia without her on an assignment with Reading & Bates.

After a year or so in Australia he was in Iran briefly, and then in August of 1968 he was assigned to Singapore. On October 2, 1968, a Buddhist wedding ceremony was performed to unite Charles and Nancy, and they lived together as man and wife in Singapore from that time until his death. Approximately one month after his death, both Mary Nell and Nancy gave birth to daughters.

This controversy ensues over the status and rights of Mary Nell and Nancy, and of the daughter of each. The County Probate Court held that Nancy was the lawful widow of Charles and that both of these daughters were entitled to inherit as children of Charles. The District Court, after an appeal and *de novo* trial without a jury, decided that Mary Nell was the widow, that Nancy was the putative wife, but that the daughter born to Mary Nell after the death of Charles was not his child and was not entitled to inherit any portion of his estate. The Court of Civil Appeals agreed that Mary Nell was the lawful widow and that her daughter was not the child of Charles, but it held that Nancy was not the putative wife at the time of the death of Charles. 507 S.W.2d 841. The only difference between the District Court and the Court of Civil Appeals in the division of the property was in the allotment to Nancy. What did not go to Nancy, under either judgment, went one-half to Mary Nell and the remaining one-half in equal parts to the children of Charles. The District Court awarded Nancy one-half of the wages due and the insurance proceeds; the Court of Civil Appeals judgment gave her nothing. Both Courts ruled that Mary Nell's daughter was not the child of Charles, and both ruled that Nancy's daughter inherited as a child of Charles. Even though the Court of Civil Appeals held that Nancy's putative status was terminated prior to the death of Charles, that holding would not prevent the daughter from being a legitimate child of their marriage. V.A.T.S. Probate Code, §42.

Nancy is here contending that she is the lawful widow or, at least, that she was the putative wife. Mary Nell's daughter contends that she is the legitimate child of Charles.

We hold, first, that Nancy was not the lawful widow of Charles. While it is initially presumed that Charles and Mary Nell were divorced prior to the wedding ceremony between Charles and Nancy (*Texas Employers' Insurance Ass'n v. Elder,* 155 Tex. 27, 282 S.W.2d 371, 1955; Vernon's Tex. Family Code Ann. §2.01, 1973), the evidence presented by Mary Nell was legally adequate to rebut that presumption. It is shown that the records in Chambers and Liberty Counties reflect no divorce between them, that the records of the State of Queensland, Australia, show no divorce during the period from September 1, 1967 to December 31, 1970, and that the records in Singapore show no divorce between them during that same period. It is not necessary in order to rebut the presumption that Mary Nell prove the nonexistence of divorce in every jurisdiction where proceedings could have been possible; it is only necessary to rule out those proceedings where Charles might reasonably have been expected to have pursued them. *Caruso v. Lucius,* 448 S.W.2d 711 (Tex. Civ. App. 1969, writ ref'd n.r.e.). The trial court was entitled to find that there had been no divorce between Charles and Mary Nell and that Mary Nell was therefore his lawful widow.

We next hold that Nancy was the putative wife of Charles. A written contract of marriage (the Chinese document and the English translation), signed by Charles and Nancy, together with her father and another witness, certifying the marriage as being solemnized on October 2, 1968, was placed in evidence. Nancy and two other witnesses testified to the full formality of the ceremony, which was held in the home of her parents with all of her family participating and with twenty persons in attendance. For more than two years thereafter, and until the date of his death, Charles and Nancy lived together as man and wife. Nancy testified that Charles told her of his previous marriage but also assured her that he was divorced and free to marry her. The evidence clearly warrants the finding that Nancy entered this relationship in good faith. The attorney for Mary Nell, however, having proved that official Singapore records show no registration of this marriage prior to the death of Charles, contends that the marriage was entirely void and of no legal effect under Singapore law. He placed in evidence photographic copies of a portion of the pages of what appears to be an official publication of the law of the Republic of Singapore. There was no pleading as to the law of Singapore, nor do these pages establish the total effect of that law as it pertains to Nancy and Charles. Even if there had been an adequate pleading and if we assume that these copies faithfully reflect some of the pages of an official publication, on this record the Texas courts cannot determine that the total law of Singapore would brand the relationship of Nancy and Charles as meretricious. See generally: Thomas, *Proof of Foreign Law in Texas*, 25 Sw. L.J. 554 (1971).

The Court of Civil Appeals has held that even though Nancy may have become the putative wife of Charles at the outset and continued in that relationship for two years thereafter, at a time prior to his death she was put on notice that he was not divorced from Mary Nell—whereupon her putative standing terminated. The evidence on this point turns on the following testimony by Nancy:

> "Q: Now, during—well—subsequent to April 2, 1968 and before December 23, 1970, you learned, did you not, that Mary Nell Davis was trying to get a divorce from Charles Davis?
> "A: I didn't learn nothing of that.
> "Q: Well, you remember you [sic] asking that question on your deposition?
> "A: You asking me whether I received—
> "Q: No ma'am, I didn't ask you if you received it. I asked you if you learned that Mary Nell Davis was trying to get a divorce from Charles?
> "A: I learned it.
> "Q: Yes.
> "A: I know it."

The interrogation on the occasion of Nancy's deposition, which was introduced at the trial by the lawyer for Nancy to show a waiver of the dead man's statute, does not throw much light on this matter except for her statements that she knew that Charles was asked to sign a paper which came in the mail at a time when she was pregnant with the child born after the death of Charles. This testimony does not establish conclusively her lack of good faith. In the first place, it is not clear when Nancy understood that Mary Nell was "trying to get a divorce." She appreciated the facts as of the time of the trial, but it is not clear that she did so prior to the death of Charles. And even if she knew that these were divorce papers, it does not necessarily follow that Nancy had any reason to believe that Charles had been dishonest with her and had not obtained a prior divorce from Mary Nell. Before we charge Nancy with bad faith or impose upon her a duty to investigate matters, we must take into account that she was in Singapore and not in Texas, that she knew nothing of Texas law, and that she was a 20 year old Chinese woman who had always lived in Singapore and was then expecting a child by a husband who had given her no reason to believe that he had another wife. The trial court was entitled to find in her favor; we hold that the record does not conclusively establish her lack of good faith.

As a putative wife Nancy is entitled to the same right in the property acquired during her marital relationship with Charles as if she were a lawful wife. [Citations omitted.] In her case it will be half of the wages owed by the employer at the date of his death as well as half of the proceeds from the insurance policy which was furnished by the employer as an incident of the employment.

This brings us to the question of the legitimacy of Mary Nell's daughter who was born a month after the death of Charles. We agree with the Court of Civil Appeals that impossibility of access between Charles and Mary Nell, during the time when this child might have been conceived, has not been proved unless we consider the testimony to that effect by Mary Nell herself. Whether her testimony may be considered depends on whether we apply the Rule of Lord Mansfield, so-called because it was Lord Mansfield in *Goodright v. Moss*, 98 Eng. Rep. 1257 who said in 1777 that husband and wife "shall not be permitted to say after marriage that they had no connection and therefore that the offspring is spurious." This rule has been applied to exclude testimony to facts that would bastardize one's own child as of the time of birth. *Esparza v. Esparza*, 382 S.W.2d 162 (Tex. Civ. App. 1964, no writ). It has even been used to exclude testimony on the ground that the effect would not be in accord with the innocence of married persons. [Citations omitted.]

* * *

Rules that exclude evidence bearing directly on the truth to be determined ought not to survive without very good cause. The testimony of a spouse on the matter of non-access by the other spouse is, subject to the usual tests of credibility, clearly the best evidence of that fact. The present case is one where all of the testimony establishes beyond any reasonable doubt that Mary Nell's daughter is not the child of Charles. Then why should the courts refuse to accept the truth? And is there not a valid objection to allowing the child of another father to inherit part of this estate? Some courts have said that the Rule is required for the protection of the child. This may or may not be its consequence. It may be harmful to the interest of the child. [Citations omitted.]

* * * The system and tradition that we call the "common law" is not a body of law which evolved within historic England or a bygone age to stand immutable ever afterward. It is the guide and governance of this Court today—in the absence of a mandate of the Constitution or statute. Learned Hand said that our common law is "a combination of custom and its successive adaptations. The judges receive it and profess to treat is as authoritative, while they gently mould it the better to fit changed ideas." THE SPIRIT OF LIBERTY p. 52 (1952). "This flexibility and capacity for growth and adaptation is the peculiar boast and excellence of the common law." *Hurtado v. California*, 110 U.S. 516, 530, 4 S. Ct. 111, 118, 28 L.Ed. 232 (1884). "[A]s life is always in flux, so the common law, which is merely life's explanation as the lawyer and the judge, law's spokemen, are always making it, must also be." Hutcheson, *The Common Law of the Constitution*, 15 TEX. L. REV. 317, 319 (1937).

* * *

It does not follow that this Court, or any court, is entitled to apply or not apply the rules of law according to preference in the individual case. Those who depend upon the law require continuity and predictability. If the administration of justice is to be effective in the trial courts, the rules must not be constantly shuffled. The appellate court must always start with the rule of precedent and either apply it faithfully or modify the rule if it is not consistent with the prevailing customs and precepts of the legal profession and of the community, giving particular attention to that portion of the community most concerned and affected by the rule.

If Lord Mansfield's Rule were one that had been counted upon in the planning of property rights, it should be left to the Legislature to change. That is no obstacle in this case. The Rule has never prevented proof of non-access of spouses for a determination of illegitimacy of a child born or conceived during wedlock. The exclusion has only applied to testimony by the spouses themselves. Proof of illegitimacy has been made more difficult, but there is no rule of law that prevents the fact from being shown if other evidence is available. Regarding blindfolds on triers of fact with disfavor, and finding no justification for perpetuating this decree by Lord Mansfield, we hold that testimony of non-access between man and woman is admissible from any witness knowledgeable of the fact.

The judgment of the Court of Civil Appeals is reversed; the judgment of the District Court is affirmed.

Comments

The substantive question of bigamy is often related to procedural questions, in particular in the application of presumptions. (Some aspects of this problem have been discussed earlier in the comments on *Campbell v. Christian, Thomson v. Thomson, Parkinson v. J. & S. Tool Company*, and *Walker v. Matthews*, pp. 119–136.) Rules relating to the putative wife, as well as the possibility of presumptions, were raised in connection with *Sousa v. Freitas* (pp. 150–153), *Sanguinetti v. Sanguinetti* (pp. 153–155), and *Lazzarevich v. Lazzarevich* (pp. 156–159). Whether bigamy was committed, with all the consequences of an illegal relationship, depends largely on questions of proof. In *Davis*, both the presumption of divorce and the conception of a putative wife are based on an underlying presumption of innocence. Whether this presumption, in its various manifestations, was overcome is left essentially to the discretion of the fact finder. Thus *Davis* refers repeatedly to the powers of the trial court, and mentions specifically that it "was entitled" to find in the second wife's favor. The Supreme Court of Texas was sympathetic to the 20-year-old second wife who had always lived in Singapore. It was less sympathetic to the first who, as the court was willing to accept, had conceived a child from another man.

It is customary to view substantive law and procedure separately. Analytically this is justified and necessary, yet in legal practice the questions of whether a given case contains the substantive elements of bigamy and whether bigamy can be proven are blurred. Failure on both levels results in a finding of no bigamy. As in *Davis*, courts indeed have a proclivity to resolve controversies on an evidentiary level. An argument of a lawyer that stresses the evidentiary aspects of the case—for example, the application of presumptions—has a good chance of persuading the court. In effect this means exactly what the Supreme Court of Texas is disclaiming in another context when discussing the Rule of Lord Mansfield (spouses "shall not be permitted to say after marriage that they had no connection and therefore that the offspring is spurious"), that is, that application of the rule of law depends on the court's preference in an individual case. Translating this premise and applying it to *Davis*, we see that the questions of whether the presumption of divorce is or is not applied, whether Nancy was a putative wife, and whether the child from the first marriage is presumed to be legitimate depend on what weight is given to the specific circumstances—in other words, on the preference of the court in this individual case.

Reference

Weyrauch, *Law as Mask—Legal Ritual and Relevance*, 66 CALIF. L. REV. 699 (1978).

Group Marriage

Village of Belle Terre v. Boraas
United States Supreme Court
416 U.S. 1 (1974)

Mr. Justice DOUGLAS delivered the opinion of the Court.

Belle Terre is a village on Long Island's north shore of about 220 homes inhabited by 700 people. Its total land area is less than one square mile. It has restricted land use to one-family dwellings excluding lodging houses, boarding houses, fraternity houses, or multiple-dwelling houses. The word "family" as used in the ordinance means, "[o]ne or more persons related by blood, adoption, or marriage, living and cooking together as a single housekeeping unit, exclusive of household servants. A number of persons but not exceeding two (2) living and cooking together as a single housekeeping unit though not related by blood, adoption, or marriage shall be deemed to constitute a family."

Appellees the Dickmans are owners of a house in the village and leased it in December 1971 for a term of 18 months to Michael Truman. Later Bruce Boraas became a colessee. Then Anne Parish moved into the house along with three others. These six are students at nearby State University at Stony Brook and none is related to the other by blood, adoption, or marriage. When the village served the Dickmans with an "Order to Remedy Violations" of the ordinance, the owners plus three tenants thereupon brought this action under 42 U. S. C. §1983 for an injunction and a judgment declaring the ordinance unconstitutional. * * *

* * *

The present ordinance is challenged on several gounds: that it interferes with a person's right to travel; that it interferes with the right to migrate to and settle within a State; that it bars people who are uncongenial to the present residents; that it expresses the social preferences of the residents for groups that will be congenial to them; that social homogeneity is not a legitimate interest of government; that the restriction of those whom the neighbors do not like trenches on the newcomers' rights of privacy; that it is of no rightful concern to villagers whether the residents are married or unmarried; that the ordinance is antithetical to the Nation's experience, ideology, and self-perception as an open, egalitarian, and integrated society.

We find none of these reasons in the record before us. It is not aimed at transients. Cf. *Shapiro v. Thompson,* 394 U.S. 618. It involves no procedural disparity inflicted on some but not on others such as was presented by *Griffin v. Illinois,* 351 U.S. 12. It involves no "fundamental" right guaranteed by the Constitution, such as voting, *Harper v. Virginia Board,* 383 U.S. 663; the right of association, *NAACP v. Alabama,* 357 U.S. 449; the right of access to the courts, *NAACP v. Button,* 371 U.S. 415; or any rights of privacy, *cf. Griswold v. Connecticut,* 381 U.S. 479; *Eisenstadt v. Baird,* 405 U.S. 438, 453–454. We deal with economic and social legislation where legislatures have historically drawn lines which we respect against the charge of violation of the Equal Protection Clause if the law be " 'reasonable, not arbitrary' " (quoting *Royster Guano Co. v. Virginia*, 253 U.S. 412, 415) and bears "a rational relationship to a [permissible] state objective." *Reed v. Reed*, 404 U.S. 71, 76.

It is said, however, that if two unmarried people can constitute a "family," there is no reason why three or four may not. But every line drawn by a legislature leaves some out that might well have been included. That exercise of discretion, however, is a legislative, not a judicial, function.

It is said that the Belle Terre ordinance reeks with an animosity to unmarried couples who live together. There is no evidence to support it; and the provision of the ordinance bringing within the definition of a "family" two unmarried people belies the charge.

The ordinance places no ban on other forms of association, for a "family" may, so far as the ordinance is concerned, entertain whomever it likes.

The regimes of boarding houses, fraternity houses, and the like present urban problems. More people occupy a given space; more cars rather continuously pass by; more cars are parked; noise travels with crowds.

A quiet place where yards are wide, people few, and motor vehicles restricted are legitimate guidelines in a land-use project addressed to family needs. This goal is a permissible one within * * *. The police power is not confined to elimination of filth, stench, and unhealthy places. It is ample to lay out zones where family values, youth values, and the blessings of quiet seclusion and clean air make the area a sanctuary for people.

Reversed.

* * *

MR. JUSTICE MARSHALL, dissenting.

This case draws into question the constitutionality of a zoning ordinance of the incorporated village of Belle Terre, New York, which prohibits groups of more than two unrelated persons, as distinguished from groups consisting of any number of persons related by blood, adoption, or marriage, from occupying a residence within the confines of the township. Lessor-appellees, the two owners of a Belle Terre residence, and three unrelated student tenants challenged the ordinance on the ground that it establishes a classification between households of related and unrelated individuals, which deprives them of equal protection of the laws. In my view, the disputed classification burdens the students' fundamental rights of association and privacy guaranteed by the First and Fourteenth Amendments. Because the application of strict equal protection scrutiny is therefore required, I am at odds with my Brethren's conclusion that the ordinance may be sustained on a showing that it bears a rational relationship to the accomplishment of legitimate governmental objectives.

* * *

* * * Zoning officials properly concern themselves with the uses of land—with, for example, the number and kind of dwellings to be constructed in a certain neighborhood or the number of persons who can reside in those dwellings. But zoning authorities cannot validly consider who those persons are, what they believe, or how they choose to live, whether they are Negro or white, Catholic or Jew, Republican or Democrat, married or unmarried.

My disagreement with the Court today is based upon my view that the ordinance in this case unnecessarily burdens appellees' First Amendment freedom of association and their constitutionally guaranteed right to privacy. * * *

* * * Constitutionally protected privacy is, in Mr. Justice Brandeis' words, "as against the Government, the right to be let alone * * * the right most valued by civilized man." *Olmstead v. United States*, 227 U.S. 438, 478 (1928) (dissenting opinion). The choice of household companions—of whether a person's "intellectual and emotional needs" are best met by living with

family, friends, professional associates, or others—involves deeply personal considerations as to the kind and quality of intimate relationships within the home. That decision surely falls within the ambit of the right to privacy protected by the Constitution. [Citations omitted.]

The instant ordinance discriminates on the basis of just such a personal lifestyle choice as to household companions. It permits any number of persons related by blood or marriage, be it two or twenty, to live in a single household, but it limits to two the number of unrelated persons bound by profession, love, friendship, religious or political affiliation, or mere economics who can occupy a single home. Belle Terre imposes upon those who deviate from the community norm in their choice of living companions significantly greater restrictions than are applied to residential groups who are related by blood or marriage, and compose the established order within the community. The village has, in effect, acted to fence out those individuals whose choice of lifestyle differs from that of its current residents.

* * *

A variety of justifications have been proffered in support of the village's ordinance. It is claimed that the ordinance controls population density, prevents noise, traffic and parking problems, and preserves the rent structure of the community and its attractiveness to families. As I noted earlier, these are all legitimate and substantial interests of government. But I think it clear that the means chosen to accomplish these purposes are both overinclusive and underinclusive, and that the asserted goals could be as effectively achieved by means of an ordinance that did not discriminate on the basis of constitutionally protected choices of lifestyle. The ordinance imposes no restriction whatsoever on the number of persons who may live in a house, as long as they are related by marital or sanguinary bonds—presumably no matter how distant their relationship. Nor does the ordinance restrict the number of income earners who may contribute to rent in such a household, or the number of automobiles that may be maintained by its occupants. In that sense the ordinance is underinclusive. On the other hand, the statute restricts the number of unrelated persons who may live in a home to no more than two. It would therefore prevent three unrelated people from occupying a dwelling even if among them they had but one income and no vehicles. While an extended family of a dozen or more might live in a small bungalow, three elderly and retired persons could not occupy the large manor house next door. Thus the statute is also grossly overinclusive to accomplish its intended purposes.

* * *

* * * I would find the challenged ordinance unconstitutional. But I would not ask the village to abandon its goal of providing quiet streets, little traffic, and a pleasant and reasonably priced environment in which families might raise their children. Rather, I would commend the village to continue to pursue those purposes but by means of more carefully drawn and evenhanded legislation.

I respectfully dissent.

Comments

The definition of the "family" is of legitimate concern to legislatures on all levels. It is an important tool in allocating government largess, although sometimes legislatures prefer the terms "household" or "cohabitation." (See the comments to *Briggs v. Industrial Commission, United States Department of Agriculture v. Murry,*

King v. Smith, New Jersey Welfare Rights Organization v. Cahill, and *Bryan v. Mathews,* pp. 365–379). The definition must depend on the purposes of the individual legislation—whether, for example, food stamps or zoning is involved. A further complication arises because more often than not the legislative history is not recorded and the purposes of the legislation are thus left to speculation. In the case of federal legislation we have clues; but in *Belle Terre* it is difficult if not impossible to ascertain what deliberations resulted in the specific wording of the ordinance of a small Long Island community of 700 people. Not unlikely, the ordinance was copied wholly or in part from some other ordinance, which in turn was copied from some preexisting form. Seemingly minor but nonetheless significant changes may have been made to adjust the form to local conditions, for instance, the proximity of a state university. The changes might have tried to cope with the influx of students and the fear that neighborhoods would deteriorate. Mr. Justice Douglas considered this fear legitimate.

Regardless of whether any forms were used, the defining of the "family" for zoning purposes, as for any other purpose, is a difficult task of drafting. Since, in the absence of a clear legislative history, any interpretation at a later stage must be left to the actual wording and speculation about the context, an ordinance of this nature is inevitably overinclusive or underinclusive, depending on the ways it is examined. To illustrate, the Belle Terre ordinance permits two unmarried people to constitute a family for zoning purposes. It is reasonably clear that unmarried cohabitation between a man and a woman are covered by the wording of the statute; but difference in sex does not seem to be required. The wording implies that the ordinance is directed against living arrangements of students and "hippie communes," but not against homosexual unions of two persons.

Constitutional adjudication necessarily proceeds from the wording of a statute or ordinance as a given fact. While this furnishes, as in *Belle Terre,* an important guideline to legal practice, it does not solve the problem of a lawyer who is requested to draft an ordinance of this kind. Only after it is clear what groups of persons are to be excluded and who is to be included in a definition of the family can the question be asked whether the wording is acceptable under constitutional standards. If the lawyer were to combine the two steps, he would be likely to neglect either the wishes of the community (assuming that they can be identified) or constitutional demands.

Returning to the speculative underlying purposes of the Belle Terre ordinance, like most zoning regulations it was probably concerned more with property values than with morality. In the vicinity of any university campus so-called "student ghettos" can be found. These ghettos have a tendency to spread. Their visual impact has some unique features, partly due to the transient nature of their occupants. The campus atmosphere tends to attract elements less desirable and stable than students. There is potential for drug dealing and rising crime rates. A further factor is the frequency of absentee landlords and therefore a lack of supervision of premises. Buildings deteriorate until they are finally condemned.

As pointed out by Mr. Justice Marshall, an ordinance can legitimately concern itself with these matters. To use a definition of the family within this context—that of regulating the external appearance of a neighborhood—may well be a subterfuge to reach a result that could be more appropriately reached by direct language. Yet the courts have permitted the use of definitions of the family for regulatory purposes that have little to do with the conception of the family as such.*

Future trends are perhaps indicated, especially in the light of rising costs for housing, in a recent decision of the Supreme Court of California, *City of Santa Barbara v. Adamson.*† In that case 12 unrelated persons were living in a large, 6,231 square foot house. They regarded themselves as a family. In its definition of the family for purposes of residential zoning, the city ordinance included only a group not to exceed five unrelated persons living together as a single housekeeping unit. By a narrow majority, the court held the ordinance invalid, as applied to the appellants, because it violated their broadly construed privacy rights, expressly protected in Article I of the California Constitution. *Belle Terre* does not preclude this holding because states may grant a higher degree of protection to their citizens than are constitutionally provided for on the federal level.

References

Comment, *All in the "Family": Legal Problems of Communes*, 7 HARV. C.R.-C.L. L. REV. 393 (1972).

Einbinder, *The Legal Family—A Definitional Analysis*, 13 J. FAM. L. 781 (1974).

Jensen, *From Belle Terre to East Cleveland: Zoning, the Family, and the Right of Privacy*, 13 FAM. L.Q. 1 (1979).

Kagy, *City of Santa Barbara v. Adamson: An Associational Right of Privacy and the End of Family Zones*, 69 CALIF. L. REV. 1052 (1981).

Karst, *The Freedom of Intimate Association*, 89 YALE L.J. 624 (1980).

Note, *Developments in the Law—The Constitution and the Family*, 93 HARV. L. REV. 1156 (1980).

Partridge, W., THE HIPPIE GHETTO—THE NATURAL HISTORY OF A SUBCULTURE (1973).

---

*See also *Palo Alto Tenants Union v. Morgan*, 321 F. Supp. 908 (N.D. Cal. 1970), *aff'd per curiam*, 487 F.2d 883 (9th Cir. 1973).

†27 Cal.3d 123, 610 P.2d 436, 164 Cal. Rptr. 539 (1980).

Remarriage

Zablocki v. Redhail

United States Supreme Court

434 U.S. 374 (1978)

Mr. Justice MARSHALL delivered the opinion of the Court.

At issue in this case is the constitutionality of a Wisconsin statute, Wis. Stat. §§245.10(1), (4), (5) (1973), which provides that members of a certain class of Wisconsin residents may not marry, within the State or elsewhere, without first obtaining a court order granting permission to marry. The class is defined by the statute to include any "Wisconsin resident having minor issue not in his custody and which he is under obligation to support by any court order or judgment." The statute specifies that court permission cannot be granted unless the marriage applicant submits proof of compliance with the support obligation and, in addition, demonstrates that the children covered by the support order "are not then and are not likely thereafter to become public charges." No marriage license may lawfully be issued in Wisconsin to a person covered by the statute, except upon court order; any marriage entered into without compliance with §245.10 is declared void; and persons acquiring marriage licenses in violation of the section are subject to criminal penalties.

After being denied a marriage license because of his failure to comply with §245.10, appellee brought this class action under 42 U.S.C. §1983, challenging the statute as violative of the Equal Protection and Due Process Clauses of the Fourteenth Amendment and seeking declaratory and injunctive relief. The United States District Court for the Eastern District of Wisconsin held the statute unconstitutional under the Equal Protection Clause and enjoined its enforcement. [Citations omitted.]

Appellee Redhail is a Wisconsin resident who, under the terms of §245.10, is unable to enter into a lawful marriage in Wisconsin or elsewhere so long as he maintains his Wisconsin residency. The facts, according to the stipulation filed by the parties in the District Court, are as follows. In January 1972, when appellee was a minor and a high school student, a paternity action was instituted against him in Milwaukee County Court, alleging that he was the father of a baby girl born out of wedlock on July 5, 1971. After he appeared and admitted that he was the child's father, the court entered an order on May 12, 1972, adjudging appellee the father and ordering him to pay $109 per month as support for the child until she reached 18 years of age. From May 1972 until August 1974, appellee was unemployed and indigent, and consequently was unable to make any support payments.

On September 27, 1974, appellee filed an application for a marriage license with appellant Zablocki, the County Clerk of Milwaukee County, and a few days later the application was denied on the sole ground that appellee had not obtained a court order granting him permission to marry, as required by §245.10. Although appellee did not petition a state court thereafter, it is stipulated that he would not have been able to satisfy either of the statutory prerequisites for an order granting permission to marry. First, he had not satisfied his support obligations to his illegitimate child, and as of December 1974 there was an arrearage in excess of $3,700. Second, the child had been a public charge since her birth, receiving benefits under the Aid to Families with Dependent Children program. It is stipulated that the child's benefit payments were such that she would have been a public charge even if appellee had been current in his support payments.

On December 24, 1974, appellee filed his complaint in the District Court, on behalf of himself and the class of all Wisconsin residents who had been refused a marriage license pursuant to §245.10(1) by one of the county clerks in Wisconsin. Zablocki was named as the defendant, individually and as representative of a class consisting of all county clerks in the State. The complaint alleged, among other things, that appellee and the woman he desired to marry were expecting a child in March 1975 and wished to be lawfully married before that time. The statute was attacked on the grounds that it deprived appellee, and the class he sought to represent of equal protection and due process rights secured by the First, Fifth, Ninth, and Fourteenth Amendments to the United States Constitution.

* * *

* * * Since our past decisions make clear that the right to marry is of fundamental importance, and since the classification at issue here significantly interferes with the exercise of that right, we believe that "critical examination" of the state interests advanced in support of the classification is required. [Citations omitted.]

The leading decision of this Court on the right to marry is *Loving v. Virginia*, 388 U.S. 1 (1967). In that case, an interracial couple who had been convicted of violating Virginia's miscegenation laws challenged the statutory scheme on both equal protection and due process grounds. The Court's opinion could have rested solely on the ground that the statutes discriminated on the basis of race in violation of the Equal Protection Clause. *Id.*, at 11–12. But the Court went on to hold that the laws arbitrarily deprived the couple of a fundamental liberty protected by the Due Process Clause, the freedom to marry. The Court's language on the latter point bears repeating:

> "The freedom to marry has long been recognized as one of the vital personal rights essential to the orderly pursuit of happiness by free men.
> "Marriage is one of the 'basic civil rights of man,' fundamental to our very existence and survival."

Id., at 12, quoting *Skinner v. Oklahoma ex rel. Williamson*, 316 U.S. 535, 541, (1942).

Although *Loving* arose in the context of racial discrimination, prior and subsequent decisions of this Court confirm that the right to marry is of fundamental importance for all individuals. Long ago, in *Maynard v. Hill*, 125 U.S. 190 (1888), the Court characterized marriage as "the most important relation in life," *id.*, at 205, and as "the foundation of the family and of society, without which there would be neither civilization nor progress," *id.*, at 211.

* * *

More recent decisions have established that the right to marry is part of the fundamental "right of privacy" implicit in the Fourteenth Amendment's Due Process Clause. In *Griswold v. Connecticut*, 381 U.S. 479 (1965), the Court observed:

> "We deal with a right of privacy older than the Bill of Rights—older than our political parties, older than our school system. Marriage is a coming together for better or for worse, hopefully enduring, and intimate to the degree of being sacred. It is an association that promotes a way of life, not causes; a harmony in living, not political faiths; a bilateral loyalty, not commercial or social projects. Yet it is an association for as noble a purpose as any involved in our prior decisions."

* * *

It is not surprising that the decision to marry has been placed on the same level of importance as decisions relating to procreation, childbirth, child rearing, and family relationships. As the facts of this case illustrate, it would make little sense to recognize a right of privacy with respect to other matters of family life and not with respect to the decision to enter the relationship that is the foundation of the family in our society. The woman whom appellee desired to marry had a fundamental right to seek an abortion of their expected child, see *Roe v. Wade*, or to bring the child into life to suffer the myriad social, if not economic, disabilities that the status of illegitimacy brings, see *Trimble v. Gordon*, 430 U.S. 762, 768–770, and n.13 (1977); *Weber v. Aetna Casualty & Surety Co.*, 406 U.S. 164, 175–176 (1972). Surely, a decision to marry and raise the child in a traditional family setting must receive equivalent protection. And, if appellee's right to procreate means anything at all, it must imply some right to enter the only relationship in which the State of Wisconsin allows sexual relations legally to take place.

By reaffirming the fundamental character of the right to marry, we do not mean to suggest that every state regulation which relates in any way to the incidents of or prerequisites for marriage must be subjected to rigorous scrutiny. To the contrary, reasonable regulations that do not significantly interfere with decisions to enter into the marital relationship may legitimately be imposed. See *Califano v. Jobst*, 434 U.S. 47, n.12, *infra*. The statutory classification at issue here, however, clearly does interfere directly and substantially with the right to marry.

Under the challenged statute, no Wisconsin resident in the affected class may marry in Wisconsin or elsewhere without a court order, and marriages contracted in violation of the statute are both void and punishable as criminal offenses. Some of those in the affected class, like appellee, will never be able to obtain the necessary court order, because they either lack the financial means to meet their support obligations or cannot prove that their children will not become public charges. These persons are absolutely prevented from getting married. Many others, able in theory to satisfy the statute's requirements, will be sufficiently burdened by having to do so that they will in effect be coerced into forgoing their right to marry. And even those who can be persuaded to meet the statute's requirements suffer a serious intrusion into their freedom of choice in an area in which we have held such freedom to be fundamental.[12]

When a statutory classification significantly interferes with the exercise of a fundamental right, it cannot be upheld unless it is supported by sufficiently important state interests and is closely tailored to effectuate only those interests. [Citations omitted.] Appellant asserts that two interests are served by the challenged statute: the permission-to-marry proceeding furnishes an opportunity to counsel the applicant as to the necessity of fulfilling his prior support obligations; and the welfare of the out-of-custody children is protected. We may accept for present purposes that these are legitimate and substantial interests, but, since the means selected by the State for achieving these interests unnecessarily impinge on the right to marry, the statute cannot be sustained.

There is evidence that the challenged statute, as originally introduced in the Wisconsin Legislature, was intended merely to establish a mechanism

---

[12] The directness and substantiality of the interference with the freedom to marry distinguish the instant case from *Califano v. Jobst*, 434 U.S. 47. In *Jobst*, we upheld sections of the Social Security Act providing, *inter alia*, for termination of a dependent child's benefits upon marriage to an individual not entitled to benefits under the Act. As the opinion for the Court expressly noted, the rule terminating benefits upon marriage was not "an attempt to interfere with the individual's freedom to make a decision as important as marriage." 434 U.S., at 54. The Social Security provisions placed no direct legal obstacle in the path of persons desiring to get married, and—notwithstanding our Brother REHNQUIST'S imaginative recasting of the case, see dissenting opinion, *post*, at 692—there was no evidence that the laws significantly discouraged, let alone made "practically impossible," any marriages. Indeed, the provisions had not deterred the individual who challenged the statute from getting married, even though he and his wife were both disabled. See *Califano v. Jobst*, 434 U.S., at 48. See also 434 U.S., at 57, n.17 (because of availability of other federal benefits, total payments to the Jobsts after marriage were only $20 per month less than they would have been had Mr. Jobst's child benefits not been terminated).

whereby persons with support obligations to children from prior marriages could be counseled before they entered into new marital relationships and incurred further support obligations. Court permission to marry was to be required, but apparently permission was automatically to be granted after counseling was completed. The statute actually enacted, however, does not expressly require or provide for any counseling whatsoever, nor for any automatic granting of permission to marry by the court, and thus it can hardly be justified as a means for ensuring counseling of the persons within its coverage. Even assuming that counseling does take place—a fact as to which there is no evidence in the record—this interest obviously cannot support the withholding of court permission to marry once counseling is completed.

With regard to safeguarding the welfare of the out-of-custody children, appellant's brief does not make clear the connection between the State's interest and the statute's requirements. At argument, appellant's counsel suggested that, since permission to marry cannot be granted unless the applicant shows that he has satisfied his court-determined support obligations to the prior children and that those children will not become public charges, the statute provides incentive for the applicant to make support payments to his children. Tr. of Oral Arg. 17–20. This "collection device" rationale cannot justify the statute's broad infringement on the right to marry.

First, with respect to individuals who are unable to meet the statutory requirements, the statute merely prevents the applicant from getting married, without delivering any money at all into the hands of the applicant's prior children. More importantly, regardless of the applicant's ability or willingness to meet the statutory requirements, the State already has numerous other means for exacting compliance with support obligations, means that are at least as effective as the instant statute's and yet do not impinge upon the right to marry. Under Wisconsin law, whether the children are from a prior marriage or were born out of wedlock, court-determined support obligations may be enforced directly via wage assignments, civil contempt proceedings, and criminal penalties. And, if the State believes that parents of children out of their custody should be responsible for ensuring that those children do not become public charges, this interest can be achieved by adjusting the criteria used for determining the amounts to be paid under their support orders.

There is also some suggestion that §245.10 protects the ability of marriage applicants to meet support obligations to prior children by preventing the applicants from incurring new support obligations. But the challenged provisions of §245.10 are grossly underinclusive with respect to this purpose, since they do not limit in any way new financial commitments by the applicant other than those arising out of the contemplated marriage. The statutory classification is substantially overinclusive as well: Given the possibility that the new spouse will actually better the applicant's financial situation, by contributing income from a job or otherwise, the statute in many cases may prevent affected individuals from improving their ability to satisfy their prior support obligations. And, although it is true that the applicant will incur support obligations to any children born during the contemplated marriage, preventing the marriage may only result in the children being born out of wedlock, as in fact occurred in appellee's case. Since the support obligation is the same whether the child is born in or out of wedlock, the net result of preventing the marriage is simply more illegitimate children.

The statutory classification created by §§245.10(1), (4), (5) thus cannot be justified by the interests advanced in support of it. The judgment of the District Court is, accordingly,

Affirmed.

[Mr. Chief Justice BURGER's concurring opinion omitted.]

* * *

Mr. Justice STEVENS, concurring in the judgment.

Because of the tension between some of the language in Mr. Justice MAR-SHALL's opinion for the Court and the Court's unanimous holding in *Califano v. Jobst*, 434 U.S. 47 (1977), a further exposition of the reasons why the Wisconsin statute offends the Equal Protection Clause of the Fourteenth Amendment is necessary.

When a State allocates benefits or burdens, it may have valid reasons for treating married and unmarried persons differently. Classification based on marital status has been an accepted characteristic of tax legislation, Selective Service rules, and Social Security regulations. As cases like *Jobst* demonstrate, such laws may "significantly interfere with decisions to enter into the marital relationship." *Ante*, at 681. That kind of interference, however, is not a sufficient reason for invalidating every law reflecting a legislative judgment that there are relevant differences between married persons as a class and unmarried persons as a class.[1]

A classification based on marital status is fundamentally different from a classification which determines who may lawfully enter into the marriage relationship. The individual's interest in making the marriage decision independently is sufficiently important to merit special constitutional protection. See *Whalen v. Roe*, 429 U.S. 589, 599–600. It is not, however, an interest which is constitutionally immune from evenhanded regulation. Thus, laws prohibiting marriage to a child, a close relative, or a person afflicted with venereal disease, are unchallenged even though they "interfere directly and substantially with the right to marry." *Ante*, at 681. This Wisconsin statute has a different character.

Under this statute, a person's economic status may determine his eligibility to enter into a lawful marriage. A noncustodial parent whose children are "public charges" may not marry even if he has met his court-ordered obligations. Thus, within the class of parents who have fulfilled their court-ordered obligations, the rich may marry and the poor may not. This type of statutory discrimination is, I believe, totally unprecedented, as well as inconsistent with our tradition of administering justice equally to the rich and to the poor.

The statute appears to reflect a legislative judgment that persons who have demonstrated an inability to support their offspring should not be permitted to marry and thereafter to bring additional children into the world. Even putting to one side the growing number of childless marriages and the burgeoning number of children born out of wedlock, that sort of reasoning cannot justify this deliberate discrimination against the poor.

The statute prevents impoverished parents from marrying even though their intended spouses are economically independent. Presumably, the Wisconsin Legislature assumed (a) that only fathers would be affected by the legislation, and (b) that they would never marry employed women. The first assumption ignores the fact that fathers are sometimes awarded custody, and the second ignores the composition of today's work force. To the extent that the statute denies a hard-pressed parent any opportunity to prove that an intended marriage will ease rather than aggravate his financial straits, it not only rests on unreliable premises, but also defeats its own objectives.

---

[1] In *Jobst*, we pointed out that "it was rational for Congress to assume that marital status is a relevant test of probable dependency * * *." We had explained:

"Both tradition and common experience support the conclusion that marriage is an event which normally marks an important change in economic status. Traditionally, the event not only creates a new family with attendant new responsibilities, but also modifies the pre-existing relationships between the bride and groom and their respective families. Frequently, of course, financial independence and marriage do not go hand in hand. Nevertheless, there can be no question about the validity of the assumption that a married person is less likely to be dependent on his parents for support than one who is unmarried."
At 53, 98 S. Ct., at 99.

These questionable assumptions also explain why this statutory blunderbuss is wide of the target in another respect. The prohibition on marriage applies to the noncustodial parent but allows the parent who has custody to marry without the State's leave. Yet the danger that new children will further strain an inadequate budget is equally great for custodial and non-custodial parents, unless one assumes (a) that only mothers will ever have custody and (b) that they will never marry unemployed men.

Characteristically, this law fails to regulate the marriages of those parents who are least likely to be able to afford another family, for it applies only to parents under a court order to support their children. Wis. Stat. §245.10(1) (1973). The very poorest parents are unlikely to be the objects of support orders. If the State meant to prevent the marriage of those who have demonstrated their inability to provide for children, it overlooked the most obvious targets of legislative concern.

In sum, the public-charge provision is either futile or perverse insofar as it applies to childless couples, couples who will have illegitimate children if they are forbidden to marry, couples whose economic status will be improved by marriage, and couples who are so poor that the marriage will have no impact on the welfare status of their children in any event. Even assuming that the right to marry may sometimes be denied on economic grounds, this clumsy and deliberate legislative discrimination between the rich and the poor is irrational in so many ways that it cannot withstand scrutiny under the Equal Protection Clause of the Fourteenth Amendment.

[Dissenting opinion of Mr. Justice REHNQUIST omitted.]

Comments

The statute involved in *Zablocki* had little chance of surviving constitutional attack. It was a clear illustration of what tenBroek called a dual system of family law: one law for the reasonably affluent and a separate law for the poor. (See References.) Even more significant than the outcome in this specific case, however, is the reasoning of the Court. It exemplifies the evolution of marriage toward recognition as a "fundamental right."

Maynard v. Hill (pp. 45–49), *Loving v. Virginia* (pp. 229–233), and *Griswold v. Connecticut* (pp. 235–238) are cited by the Court as way stations in this development. In their facts, these cases were quite unrelated. *Maynard* dealt with legislative divorce under frontier conditions, *Loving* with interracial marriage, and *Griswold* with the use of contraceptives in marriage. But they all stressed incidentally the importance of marriage as a social institution. It is perhaps not accidental that those portions of U.S. Supreme Court opinions that are traditionally classified as obiter dicta are often cited as significant statements in the evolution of law. They are the more speculative parts of the reasoning, not strictly essential to the exact point to be adjudicated, which tends to be narrow in scope and confined to one jurisdiction. Transcending, as they do, the case at hand, the speculative portions are just the ones likely to prove important in a wider context.

Related to the use of obiter dicta are the many hypotheticals employed by the Court. These hypotheticals go beyond the scope of the actual controversy and expand the factual basis of the decision. The hypotheticals are not necessarily phrased as such but appear in the opinion as a mere process of reasoning that tests the statute under attack. The Court asks, for example, to assume as a thinking construct that that the children to be supported were born of a prior marriage rather than out of wedlock. The Court also asks what would happen if the applicant for a marriage license were to take on new financial commitments other than those arising from the contemplated marriage. Suppose further, Mr. Justice Marshall hypothesizes in the majority opinion, that the new spouse will actually better the applicant's financial situation; would that not improve his ability to satisfy prior support obligations? Similar veiled hypotheticals are contained in the concurring opinions and the dissenting opinion of Mr. Justice Rehnquist.

On the one hand, the U.S. Supreme Court uses restraint in the exercise of its jurisdiction; on the other hand, once jurisdiction is taken, it broadens the scope of inquiry, also in regard to its factual basis, by the use of hypotheticals. While hypotheticals as analytical devices may well be introduced by the Court itself, they can also originate in the argument of counsel. They are thus an important tool of persuasion, especially in novel questions of law where precedent is scant or missing.

Zablocki, in conjunction with *Califano v. Jobst*,* may lead to a reexamination of restrictions on marriage. It would be wrong to assume, however, that recognition of marriage as a fundamental human right is firmly settled. *Zablocki* resulted in six separate opinions, each different in respect to the standard of review, ranging from "critical examination" in Mr. Justice Marshall's opinion to a test of minimal rationality in Mr. Justice Rehnquist's dissent. If the assumption is correct that state involvement in marriage is likely to decrease rather than increase, it is probable that critical examination of state regulations of marriage will prevail, as it did in the majority opinion of Mr. Justice Marshall, although this standard may still fall short of "strict scrutiny." The standards may also vary from case to case depending on what kind of regulation of marriage is involved. Even restrictions on marriage by persons of the same sex (see Comments, pp. 430–432) may be reexamined.

References

Foster, *Marriage: A "Basic Civil Right of Man,"* 37 Fordham L. Rev. 51 (1968–69).

---

*434 U.S. 47 (1977).

Karst, *The Freedom of Intimate Association*, 89 YALE L.J. 624 (1980).
Note, *Developments in the Law—The Constitution and the Family*, 93
   HARV L. REV. 1156 (1980).
Note, *Zablocki v. Redhail: Due Process or Equal Protection?*, 12 U.C.D.
   L. REV. 165 (1979).
tenBroek, *California's Dual System of Family Law: Its Origin, Develop-
   ment, and Present Status* (pts. 1 & 2), 16 STAN. L. REV. 257, 900 (1964);
   (pt. 3), 17 STAN. L. REV. 614 (1965).
Weyrauch, *Dual Systems of Family Law: A Comment*, 54 CALIF. L. REV.
   781 (1967).

Transsexual Marriage

M.T. v. J.T.

Superior Court of New Jersey

140 N.J. Super. 77, 355 A.2d 204 (1976)

HANDLER, J.A.D. This appeal presents the portentous problem of how to
tell the sex of a person for marital purposes. Involved is a post-operative
transsexual, born a male but now claiming to be a female.

The case started inauspiciously enough when plaintiff M.T. filed a simple
complaint in the Juvenile and Domestic Relations Court for support and
maintenance. The legal issue sharpened dramatically when defendant J.T.
interposed the defense that M.T. was a male and that their marriage was
void. Following a hearing the trial judge determined that plaintiff was a female and that defendant was her husband, and there being no fraud, ordered
defendant to pay plaintiff $50-a-week support. Notice of appeal was then filed
by defendant.

A careful recapitulation of the testimony is appropriate. M.T. testified
that she was born a male. While she knew that she had male sexual organs she
did not know whether she also had female organs. As a youngster she did not
participate in sports and at an early age became very interested in boys. At
the age of 14 she began dressing in a feminine manner and later began dating
men. She had no real adjustment to make because throughout her life she had
always felt that she was a female.

Plaintiff first met defendant in 1964 and told him about her feelings
about being a woman. Sometime after that she began to live with defendant.
In 1970 she started to go to Dr. Charles L. Ihlenfeld to discuss the possibility
of having an operation so that she could "be physically a woman." In 1971,
upon the doctor's advice, she went to a surgeon who agreed to operate. In
May of that year she underwent surgery for the removal of male sex organs
and construction of a vagina. Defendant paid for the operation. Plaintiff then
applied to the State of New York to have her birth certificate changed.

On August 11, 1972, over a year after the operation, plaintiff and defendant went through a ceremonial marriage in New York State and then moved
to Hackensack. They lived as husband and wife and had intercourse. Defendant supported plaintiff for over two years when, in October 1974, he left
their home. He has not supported plaintiff since.

Dr. Ihlenfeld, plaintiff's medical doctor with a specialty in gender identity, was accepted as an expert in the field of medicine and transsexualism. A
transsexual, in the opinion of this expert, was "a person who discovers some-

time, usually very early in life, that there is a great discrepancy between the physical genital anatomy and the person's sense of self-identity as a male or as a female. * * * [T]he transsexual is one who has a conflict between physical anatomy and psychological identity or psychological sex." Usually sexual anatomy was "normal" but for some reason transsexuals did not see themselves as members of the sex their anatomy seemed to indicate. According to Dr. Ihlenfeld, there are different theories to explain the origin of that conflict. There was, however, "very little disagreement" on the fact that gender identity generally is established "very, very firmly, almost immediately, by the age of 3 to 4 years." He defined gender identity as "a sense, a total sense of self as being masculine or female * * *"; it "pervades one's entire concept of one's place in life, of one's place in society and in point of fact the actual facts of the anatomy are really secondary * * *."

The doctor first saw and examined plaintiff in September 1970 and took a medical history from her. She told him that she had always felt like a woman and was living like a woman. She wanted sex reassignment surgery as well as treatments and hormones so that she could end the conflict she was feeling, "confronted with a male body," in order to live her life completely as the woman she thought herself to be. Dr. Ihlenfeld diagnosed her as a transsexual. He knew of no way to alter her sense of her own feminine gender identity in order to agree with her male body, and the only treatment available to her was to alter the body to conform with her sense of psyche gender identity. That regimen consisted of hormone treatment and sex reassignment surgery. Dr. Ihlenfeld recommended such an operation and treated plaintiff both before and after it.

The examination of plaintiff before the operation showed that she had a penis, scrotum and testicles. After the operation she did not have those organs but had a vagina and labia which were "adequate for sexual intercourse" and could function as any female vagina, that is, for "traditional penile/vaginal intercourse." The "artificial vagina" constructed by such surgery was a cavity, the walls of which are lined initially by the skin of the penis, often later taking on the characteristics of normal vaginal mucosa; the vagina, though at a somewhat different angle, was not really different from a natural vagina in size, capacity and "the feeling of the walls around it." Plaintiff had no uterus or cervix, but her vagina had a "good cosmetic appearance" and was "the same as a normal female vagina after a hysterectomy." Dr. Ihlenfeld had seen plaintiff since the operation and she never complained to him that she had difficulty having intercourse. So far as he knew, no one had tested plaintiff to find out what chromosomes she had. He knew that plaintiff had had silicone injections in her breasts; he had treated her continuously with female hormones to demasculinize her body and to feminize it at the same time. In the doctor's opinion plaintiff was a female; he no longer considered plaintiff to be a male since she could not function as a male sexually either for purposes of "recreation or procreation."

Plaintiff also produced Charles Annicello, a psychologist who worked at the gender identity clinic of The Johns Hopkins University Hospital. He was qualified as an expert in transsexualism. This witness demonstrated through slides the various methods by which scientists define whether a person is male or female. The witness said that transsexualism represented only one sexual variant although it was not known whether its cause was chromosomal, gonadal or hormonal. Annicello expressed the opinion that if a person had a female psychic gender and underwent a sex reassignment operation, that person would be considered female although no person is "absolutely" male or female.

Dr. Richard M. Samuels, a Ph.D. with a specialty in behavioral therapy and sexual dysfunctions, testified as an expert in psychology as it related to transsexualism. His definition of a transsexual was essentially the same as that given by the prior experts: "someone whose physical anatomy does not correspond to their [*sic*] sense of being, to their [*sic*] sense of gender." He also acknowledged that it was not known what caused that condition but he believed that it was probably a combination of neurological, chromosomal and environmental factors. Some psychological changes are noted following a sex reassignment operation. Thus, a transsexual was often depressed pre-operatively, but after the operation he or she lived a "fuller and richer life" and was better able to overcome obstacles in employment, housing, social security and welfare benefits; a sense of satisfaction and relief was felt since the body was now in line with the psyche. For Dr. Samuels the most important factor in determining whether a person should have a sex reassignment operation was how consistently the patient lived in the chosen gender role. A sex reassignment operation did not determine a person's gender. After a transsexual underwent a sex reassignment operation to remove male organs, Dr. Samuels would characterize that person as a female.

Defendant called as an expert witness Dr. T, a medical doctor who was defendant's adoptive father. Over plaintiffs objection he was allowed to testify as an expert. Dr. T classified sex at birth according to sexual anatomy. He described a female as "a person who has female organs in an anatomical sense, who has a vagina and a uterus and ovaries or at least has had them." The witness had heard all of the prior testimony and he said that in his opinion plaintiff was still a male because she did not have female organs. He did believe, however, that transsexuals existed and that they were people who had "the mental and emotional reactions of the opposite sex." On cross-examination Dr. T reiterated that it was the anatomy alone which determined the real sex of an individual and that gender in contrast to sex was not a significant factor. Although he was "very sympathetic to any male person" who had "the emotional and mental reactions of a female," since he knew that it was "very annoying," he still did not believe that that was determinative.

The trial judge made careful findings of fact on this evidential record. He accepted the testimony concerning M.T.'s personal and medical history as related by her and her doctor. He noted that defendant knew of her condition and cooperated in her sex reassignment surgery. The parties married in New York and subsequently consummated their marriage by engaging in sexual intercourse. The judge also found that defendant later deserted plaintiff and failed to support her.

Drawing from the opinions of the experts the judge defined a transsexual as "an individual anatomically of one sex who firmly believes he belongs to the other sex." He enumerated the seven factors considered generally relevant to the determination of sex. According to the judge, a preoperative transsexual would appropriately be classified according to his anatomical sex. After a successful sex reassignment operation, however, "psychological sex and anatomical sex become consistent as to outward appearances." The judge ruled that plaintiff was of the female psychic gender all her life and that her anatomical change through surgery required the conclusion that she was a female at the time of the marriage ceremony. He stated:

> "It is the opinion of the court that if the psychological choice of a person is medically sound, not a mere whim, and irreversible sex reassignment surgery has been performed, society has no right to prohibit the transsexual from leading a normal life. Are we to look upon this person as an exhibit in a circus side show? What harm has said person done to society? The entire area of transsexualism is repugnant to the nature of many persons within our society. However, this should not govern the legal acceptance of a fact. * * *"

Defendant's basic and continuing contention is that the marriage between him and plaintiff was a nullity because plaintiff was a male at the time of the ceremony. We disagree with this position and affirm the decision of the lower court.

We accept—and it is not disputed—as the fundamental premise in this case that a lawful marriage requires the performance of a ceremonial marriage of two persons of the opposite sex, a male and a female. Despite winds of change, this understanding of a valid marriage is almost universal. * * * [Citations omitted.]

There is not the slightest doubt that New Jersey follows the overwhelming authority.[1] * * *

The issue must then be confronted whether the marriage between a male and a postoperative transsexual, who has surgically changed her external sexual anatomy from male to female, is to be regarded as a lawful marriage between a man and a woman.

An English case, *Corbett v. Corbett*, 2 W.L.R. 1306, 2 All E.R. 33 (P. D. A. 1970) appears to be the only reported decision involving the validity of marriage of a true postoperative transsexual and a male person. The judge there held that the transsexual had failed to prove that she had changed her sex from male to female. The court subscribed to the opinion of the medical witnesses that "the biological sexual constitution of an individual is fixed at birth (at the latest), and cannot be changed, either by the natural development of organs of the opposite sex, or by medical or surgical means. The respondent's operation, therefore, cannot affect her true sex." 2 W.L.R. at 1323. It felt that three tests for sex should be used, the chromosomal, gonadal and genital, and when these were congruent sex for purposes of marriage should be determined accordingly. *Id.* at 1325. And, in view of the "essentially hetero-sexual character" of marriage, the test to determine sex must be biological, "for even the most extreme degree of transsexualism in a male or the most severe hormonal imbalance which could exist in a person with male chromosomes, male gonads, and male genitalia, cannot reproduce a person who is naturally capable of performing the essential role of a woman in marriage." *Id.* at 1324–1325. Based upon an assumed distinction between "sex" and "gender," the court held that "marriage is a relationship which depends on sex and not on gender." *Id.* at 1325. In addition, the judge was mindful that the marriage was unstable, brief and the sexual exchange between the parties—the husband was a transvestite—was ambivalent. He concluded on alternative grounds that the marriage had not been, and indeed could not be, consummated.

We cannot join the reasoning of the *Corbett* case. The evidence before this court teaches that there are several criteria or standards which may be relevant in determining the sex of an individual. It is true that the anatomical test, the genitalia of an individual, is unquestionably significant and probably in most instances indispensable. For example, sex classification of an individual at birth may as a practical matter rely upon this test. For other purposes, however, where sex differentiation is required or accepted, such as for public records, service in the branches of the armed forces, participation in certain regulated sports activities, eligibility for types of employment and the like, other tests in addition to genitalia may also be important. Comment, *Transsexualism, Sex Reassignment Surgery, and the Law*, 56 CORNELL L. REV. 963, 992–1002 (1971).

Against the backdrop of the evidence in the present record we must disagree with the conclusion reached in *Corbett* that for purposes of marriage

---

[1] No issue was raised below or on appeal as to the state law applicable to this case. Our courts would generally look to the law of the place of the marriage ceremony to determine its validity unless contrary to public policy. *Booker v. James Spence Iron Foundry*, 80 N. J. Super. 68, 77–78 (App. Div. 1963); *Winn v. Wiggins*, 47 N. J. Super. 215, 220 (App. Div. 1957). We have examined independently the statutory law of the State of New York (New York Domestic Relations Law, §§5 through 25) and are satisfied that by its literal terms the marriage in this case would not by statute be prohibited. The current decisional law of New York, discussed *infra*, is not dispositive of the legal issue as to whether this marriage would be void or voidable in that state. Hence, we are free to apply the law of the State of New Jersey.

sex is somehow irrevocably cast at the moment of birth, and that for adjudging the capacity to enter marriage, sex in its biological sense should be the
exclusive standard. On this score the case has not escaped critical review.
Comment, *supra*, 56 CORNELL L. REV. at 1003–1007; Note, *Transsexuals in
Limbo*, 31 MD. L. REV. 236, 244 (1971).

Our departure from the *Corbett* thesis is not a matter of semantics. It
stems from a fundamentally different understanding of what is meant by
"sex" for marital purposes. The English court apparently felt that sex and
gender were disparate phenomena. In a given case there may, of course, be
such a difference. A preoperative transsexual is an example of that kind of
disharmony, and most experts would be satisfied that the individual should
be classified according to biological criteria. The evidence and authority
which we have examined, however, show that a person's sex or sexuality
embraces an individual's gender, that is, one's self-image, the deep psychological or emotional sense of sexual identity and character. Indeed, it has
been observed that the "psychological sex of an individual," while not serv-
iceable for all purposes, is "practical, realistic and humane." Comment, *supra*, 56 CORNELL L. REV. at 969–970; *cf. In re Anonymous*, 57 Misc. 2d 813,
293 N.Y.S. 2d 834, 837 (Civ. Ct. 1968).

The English court believed, we feel incorrectly, that an anatomical
change of genitalia in the case of a transsexual cannot "affect her true sex."
Its conclusion was rooted in the premise that "true sex" was required to be
ascertained even for marital purposes by biological criteria. In the case of a
transsexual following surgery, however, according to the expert testimony
presented here, the dual tests of anatomy and gender are more significant. On
this evidential demonstration, therefore, we are impelled to the conclusion
that for marital purposes if the anatomical or genital features of a genuine
transsexual are made to conform to the person's gender, psyche or psychological sex, then identity by sex must be governed by the congruence of these
standards.

Implicit in the reasoning underpinning our determination is the tacit but
valid assumption of the lower court and the experts upon whom reliance was
placed that for purposes of marriage under the circumstances of this case, it
is the sexual capacity of the individual which must be scrutinized. Sexual
capacity or sexuality in this frame of reference requires the coalescence of
both the physical ability and the psychological and emotional orientation to
engage in sexual intercourse as either a male or a female.

Other decisions touching the marital status of a putative transsexual are
not especially helpful. *Anonymous v. Anonymous*, 67 Misc. 2d 982, 325
N.Y.S. 2d 499 (Sup. Ct. 1971), cited by defendant, held a marriage a nullity,
but there the two persons had never had sexual intercourse and had never
lived together. Although it was claimed that respondent was a transsexual
and had had an operation to remove his male organs after the marriage, there
was no medical evidence of this. In *B. v. B., supra*, a female transsexual had
had a hysterectomy and mastectomy but had not received any male organs
and was incapable of performing sexually as a male. He had then married a
normal female who later sued for an annulment on the ground that he had
defrauded her by not informing her of his transsexualism and of the operation. The judge there held that even if defendant were a male and trapped in
the body of a female, his attempted sex reassignment surgery had not successfully released him from that body.

Anonymous v. Weiner, 50 Misc. 2d 380, 270 N.Y.S. 2d 319 (Sup. Ct.
1966), sustained the refusal by the New York City Board of Health to amend
a sex designation on a birth certificate. The court acquiesced in the view of
the administrative agency that "male-to-female transsexuals are still chro-
mosomally males while ostensibly females" and that the desire of the transsexual for "concealment of a change of sex * * * is outweighed by the public
interest for protection against fraud." 270 N.Y.S. 2d at 322. To reiterate, the

chromosomal test of sex in this context is unhelpful. The potential for fraud, feared by the court, moreover, is effectively countered by the apt observation of the trial judge here: "The transsexual is not committing a fraud upon the public. In actuality she is doing her utmost to remove any false facade." Further, we note the *Weiner* case was sharply criticized *In re Anonymous, supra*, which ordered a change to a female name for a postoperative transsexual. The court concluded that the chromosomal test recommended by the New York Academy of Medicine and adopted by the court in *Weiner* was unrealistic and inhumane. It said:

> "It has been suggested that there is some middle ground between the sexes, a 'no-man's land' for those individuals who are neither truly 'male' nor truly 'female.' Yet the standard is much too fixed for such far-out theories. Rather the application of a simple formula could and should be the test of gender, and that formula is as follows: Where there is disharmony between the psychological sex and the anatomical sex, the social sex or gender of the individual will be determined by the anatomical sex. Where, however, with or without medical intervention, the psychological sex and the anatomical sex are harmonized, then the social sex or gender of the individual should be made to conform to the harmonized status of the individual and, if such conformity requires changes of a statistical nature, then such changes should be made. Of course, such changes should be made only in those cases where physiological orientation is complete. [293 N.Y.S. 2d at 837]"

* * *

In sum, it has been established that an individual suffering from the condition of transsexualism is one with a disparity between his or her genitalia or anatomical sex and his or her gender, that is, the individual's strong and consistent emotional and psychological sense of sexual being. A transsexual in a proper case can be treated medically by certain supportive measures and through surgery to remove and replace existing genitalia with sex organs which will coincide with the person's gender. If such sex reassignment surgery is successful and the postoperative transsexual is, by virtue of medical treatment, thereby possessed of the full capacity to function sexually as a male or female, as the case may be, we perceive no legal barrier, cognizable social taboo, or reason grounded in public policy to prevent that person's identification at least for purposes of marriage to the sex finally indicated.

In this case the transsexual's gender and genitalia are no longer discordant; they have been harmonized through medical treatment. Plaintiff has become physically and psychologically unified and fully capable of sexual activity consistent with her reconciled sexual attributes of gender and anatomy. Consequently, plaintiff should be considered a member of the female sex for marital purposes. It follows that such an individual would have the capacity to enter into a valid marriage relationship with a person of the opposite sex and did do so here. In so ruling we do no more than give legal effect to a *fait accompli*, based upon medical judgment and action which are irreversible. Such recognition will promote the individual's quest for inner peace and personal happiness, while in no way disserving any societal interest, principle of public order or precept of morality.

Accordingly, the court below correctly determined that plaintiff at the time of her marriage was a female and that defendant, a man, became her lawful husband, obligated to support her as his wife. The judgment of the court is therefore affirmed.

Homosexual Marriage

Jones v. Hallahan

Court of Appeals of Kentucky

501 S.W.2d 588 (Ky. 1973)

VANCE, Commissioner.

The appellants, each of whom is a female person, seek review of a judgment of the Jefferson Circuit Court which held that they were not entitled to have issued to them a license to marry each other.

Appellants contend that the failure of the clerk to issue the license deprived them of three basic constitutional rights, namely, the right to marry; the right of association; and the right to free exercise of religion. They also contend that the refusal subjects them to cruel and unusual punishment.

The sections of Kentucky statutes relating to marriage do not include a definition of that term. It must therefore be defined according to common usage.

Webster's New International Dictionary, Second Edition, defines marriage as follows:

"A state of being married, or being united to a person or persons of the opposite sex as husband or wife; also, the mutual relation of husband and wife; wedlock; abstractly, the institution whereby men and women are joined in a special kind of social and legal dependence, for the purpose of founding and maintaining a family."

The Century Dictionary and Encyclopedia defines marriage as:

"The legal union of a man with a woman for life; the state or condition of being married; the legal relation of spouses to each other; wedlock; the formal declaration or contract by which a man and a woman join in wedlock."

Black's Law Dictionary, Fourth Edition, defines marriage as:

"The civil status, condition or relation of one man and one woman united in law for life, for the discharge to each other and the community of the duties legally incumbent upon those whose association is founded on the distinction of sex."

Kentucky statutes do not specifically prohibit marriage between persons of the same sex nor do they authorize the issuance of a marriage license to such persons.

Marriage was a custom long before the state commenced to issue licenses for that purpose. For a time the records of marriage were kept by the church. Some states even now recognize a common-law marriage which has neither the benefit of license nor clergy. In all cases, however, marriage has always been considered as the union of a man and a woman and we have been presented with no authority to the contrary.

It appears to us that appellants are prevented from marrying, not by the statutes of Kentucky or the refusal of the County Court Clerk of Jefferson County to issue them a license, but rather by their own incapability of entering into a marriage as that term is defined.

A license to enter into a status or a relationship which the parties are incapable of achieving is a nullity. If the appellants had concealed from the clerk the fact that they were of the same sex and he had issued a license to them and a ceremony had been performed, the resulting relationship would not constitute a marriage.

This is a case of first impression in Kentucky. To our knowledge, only two other states have considered the question and both of them have reached the same result that we reach in this opinion. *Baker v. Nelson*, 291 Minn. 310, 191 N.W.2d 185 (1971), appeal dismissed for want of a substantial federal question, 409 U.S. 810, 93 S. Ct. 37, 34 L.Ed.2d 65; *Anonymous v. Anonymous*, 67 Misc.2d 982, 325 N.Y.S. 2d 499.

Baker v. Nelson considered many of the constitutional issues raised by the appellants here and decided them adversely to appellants. In our view, however, no constitutional issue is involved. We find no constitutional sanction or protection of the right of marriage between persons of the same sex.

The claim of religious freedom cannot be extended to make the professed doctrines superior to the law of the land and in effect to permit every citizen to become a law unto himself. *Reynolds v. United States*, 98 U.S. 145. We do not consider the refusal to issue the license a punishment.

In substance, the relationship proposed by the appellants does not authorize the issuance of a marriage license because what they propose is not a marriage.

The judgment is affirmed.

Singer v. Hara

Court of Appeals of Washington

11 Wash. App. 247, 522 P.2d 1187 (1974)

SWANSON, Chief Judge.

Appellants Singer and Barwick, both males, appeal from the trial court's order denying their motion to show cause by which they sought to compel King County Auditor Lloyd Hara to issue a marriage license to them. * * *

Appellants' argue three basic assignments of error, namely, (1) the trial court erred in concluding that the Washington marriage statutes, RCW 26.04.010 *et seq.*, prohibit same-sex marriages; (2) the trial court's order violates the Equal Rights Amendment (ERA) to the Washington State Constitution, Const. art. 31, §1; and (3) the trial court's order violates the eighth, ninth and fourteenth amendments to the United States Constitution.[1]

---

[1] Appellants also list as an "assignment of error" the assertion that the trial court's order "was based on the erroneous and fallacious conclusion that same-sex marriages are destructive to society." In support of this assertion, appellants devote nearly 40 pages of their brief to what they characterize as a discussion of "the concept of homosexuality and same-sex marriages through the eyes of other important disciplines—that of the sociologist, theologians, scientists, and doctors." Appellants state that "a basic understanding of homosexuals and society is a precondition to an enlightened discussion of the legal grounds raised * * *" Although we do not quarrel with that proposition, we deem it appropriate to observe that appellants' discussion in that regard does not present a legal argument, nor is there any evidence in the record to suggest that the trial court in fact based its order on the "erroneous and fallacious conclusion" to which appellants take exception. Therefore, while we recognize that appellants have presented a valuable context for the discussion of their legal points, we have endeavored to confine this opinion to discussion of the legal issues presented without attempting to present our views on matters of sociology, theology, science and medicine.

Directing our attention to appellants' first assignment of error, it is apparent from a plain reading of our marriage statutes that the legislature has not authorized same-sex marriages. Appellants argue that RCW 26.04.010 which authorizes marriages by "persons of the age of eighteen years, who are otherwise capable" includes no requirements that marriage partners be limited to one male and one female and that the phrase "who are otherwise capable" refers to the prohibitions of RCW 26.04.020–26.04.040 against certain marriages involving persons are habitual criminals, diseased, insane, etc., but there is no prohibition against same-sex marriages. Appellants argue that the legislature has not defined the competency of marriage but only the competency of individuals seeking to marry: inasmuch as the appellants are both legally "capable" of marriage, they argue state law permits them to marry each other. As the state points out, however, the statutory language of RCW 26.04.010 relied upon by the appellants merely reflects a 1970 amendment which substituted the word "persons" for the prior references to "males" "and females" to implement the legislature's elimination of differing age requirements for marriage by the respective sexes. Further, RCW 26.04.210, relating to the affidavits required for the issuance of a marriage license, makes reference to "the male" and "the female" which clearly dispels any suggestion that the legislature intended to authorize same-sex marriages. The trial court correctly concluded that the applicable marriage statutes do not permit same-sex marriage.

Appellants next argue that if, as we have held, our state marriage laws must be construed to prohibit same-sex marriages, such laws are unconstitutional when so applied. In this context, we consider appellants' second assignment of error which is directed to the proposition that the state prohibition of same-sex marriages violates the ERA which recently became part of our state constitution.[4] The question thus presented is a matter of first impression in this state and, to our knowledge, no court in the nation has ruled upon the legality of same-sex marriage in light of an equal rights amendment. The ERA provides, in relevant part:

> "Equality of rights and responsibility under the law shall not be denied or abridged on account of sex."

In seeking the protection of the ERA, appellants argue that the language of the amendment itself leaves no question of interpretation and that the essential thrust of the ERA is to make sex an impermissible legal classification. Therefore, they argue, to construe state law to permit a man to marry a woman but at the same time to deny him the right to marry another man is to construct an unconstitutional classification "on account of sex."[5] In response to appellants' contention, the state points out that all same-sex mar-

---

[4] HJR 61, commonly known as the "equal rights amendment," was approved by the voters November 7, 1972, and became effective December 7, 1972. Const. amend. 61, adding article 31. The language of the ERA is substantially similar to the federal ERA now before the states for ratification as the twenty-seventh amendment to the United States Constitution.

[5] Appellants also argue that prior to the November 7, 1972 election, the voters were advised that one effect of approval of the ERA (HJR 61) would be the legalization of same-sex marriages, but nevertheless voted in favor of the amendment. In this connection, appellants direct our attention to the following language in the "Statement against" HJR 61 contained in the 1972 Voters Pamphlet published by the Secretary of State:

"HJR 61 would establish rules in our society which were not intended and which the citizenry simply could not support. Examples are numerous:

* * *

"(3) Homosexual and lesbian marriage would be legalized, with further complication regarding adopting children into such a 'family.' People will live as they choose, but the beauty and sanctity of marriage must be preserved from such needless desecration; * * *"

We are not persuaded that voter approval of the ERA necessarily included an intention to permit same-sex marriages. On the contrary, the "Statement for" HJR 61 in the Voters Pamphlet indicated that the basic principle of the ERA

riages are deemed illegal by the state, and therefore argues that there is no violation of the ERA so long as marriage licenses are denied equally to both male and female pairs. In other words, the state suggests that appellants are not entitled to relief under the ERA because they have failed to make a showing that they are somehow being treated differently by the state than they would be if they were females. Appellants suggest, however, that the holdings in *Loving v. Virginia*, 388 U.S. 1, 9, 87 S. Ct. 1817, 18 L.Ed.2d 1010 (1967); *Perez v. Lippold*, 32 Cal.2d 711, 198 P.2d 17 (1948), and *J.S.K. Enterprises, Inc. v. City of Lacey*, 6 Wash. App. 43, 492 P.2d 600 (1971), are contrary to the position taken by the state. We disagree.

In *Loving*, the state of Virginia argued that its anti-miscegenation statutes did not violate constitutional prohibitions against racial classifications because the statutes affected both racial groups equally. The Supreme Court, noting that the fact of equal application does not immunize the statute from the very heavy burden of justification which the Fourteenth Amendment has traditionally required of state statutes drawn according to race, held that the Virginia laws were founded on an impermissible racial classification and therefore could not be used to deny interracial couples the "fundamental" right to marry. The California court made a similar ruling as to that state's anti-miscegenation law in *Perez*.

"is that both sexes be treated equally under the law. The States could not pass or enforce any law which places a legal obligation, or confers a special legal privilege on one sex but not the other."

Similarly, the Attorney General's explanation of the effect of HJR 61, also set forth in the Voters Pamphlet, focused on the idea that government "could not treat persons differently because they are of one sex or the other." In other words, as we discuss in the body of this opinion, to be entitled to relief under the ERA, appellants must make a showing that they are somehow being treated differently by the government than they would be if they were females.

Newspaper accounts published at the time of the November 7, 1972 election also tend to discount appellants' suggestion that the voters intended to approve same-sex marriage when they supported the ERA and make it apparent that proponents of the ERA were quick to point out their disagreement with opponents' speculation about the impact of the ERA and specifically with the "Statement against" in the Voters Pamphlet. Thus, for example, in an "Election Preview" supplement to the *Seattle Post-Intelligencer*, November 5, 1972, the following statement appears in an article describing HJR 61 at page 10:

"Opponents argue that passage [of HJR 61] would legalize homosexual marriage, deny preferential treatment to women in divorce settlements, make women eligible for Army combat duty, allow coed sports wrestling in schools, and eliminate preferential auto, health and life insurance rates for women.

"Proponents describe the foes' contentions as emotional, irresponsible fantasies, misleading, deceptive and incorrect. HJR 61 would have none of the affects [*sic*] listed above, they say."

Similarly, in the *Seattle Post-Intelligencer*, October 30, 1972, the following statement appears on page A-4:

"On home and social fronts, opponents [of HJR 61] fear the 'beauty and sanctity of marriage' would be destroyed. But proponents say the amendment will have no effect on private life, being concerned only with what happens under the law.

"They say the bill [HJR 61] would benefit both sexes and that it will have no effect on such things as homosexual marriage since laws against men or women marrying each other are not discriminating on the basis of sex."

A post-election survey of voter attitude toward HJR 61 reported in the *Seattle Times*, November 27, 1972, provides further evidence that public conception of HJR 61 involved its effect upon the rights of women in comparison with the rights of men and did not include any notion that HJR 61 would have an impact upon the interaction of members of the same sex. The following statement appears in the article at page A-20:

"Among those with negative attitudes toward HJR 61, men outnumbered women by almost 2 to 1.

"Among those with positive attitudes, there were five per cent more women than men.

"The idea of the 'woman as homemaker' was not a large factor among those who opposed the amendment. Most persons with negative attitudes said they took that view because they wanted to retain female legal advantages and expressed fear these would be abolished if the amendment became law.

"Most of those holding positive views toward sex equality and responsibility did so on economic grounds, feeling that equal pay should be given for equal work."

Although appellants suggest an analogy between the racial classification involved in *Loving* and *Perez* and the alleged sexual classification involved in the case at bar, we do not find such an analogy. The operative distinction lies in the relationship which is described by the term "marriage" itself, and that relationship is the legal union of one man and one woman. Washington statutes, specifically those relating to marriage (RCW 26.04) and marital (community) property (RCW 26.16), are clearly founded upon the presumption that marriage, as a legal relationship, may exist only between one man and one woman who are otherwise qualified to enter that relationship.[6] Similarly although it appears that the appellate courts of this state until now have not been required to define specifically what constitutes a marriage, it is apparent from a review of cases dealing with legal questions arising out of the marital relationship that the definition of marriage as the legal union of one man and one woman who are otherwise qualified to enter into the relationship not only is clearly implied from such cases, but also was deemed by the court in each case to be so obvious as not to require recitation. [Citations omitted.] Finally, the courts known by us to have considered the question have all concluded that same-sex relationships are outside of the proper definition of marriage. *Jones v. Hallahan*, 501 S.W.2d 588 (Ky. 1973); *Baker v. Nelson*, 291 Minn. 310, 191 N.W.2d 185 (1971); *Anonymous v. Anonymous*, 67 Misc.2d 982, 325 N.Y.S.2d 499 (1971). Appellants have cited no authority to the contrary.

Given the definition of marriage which we have enunciated, the distinction between the case presented by appellants and those presented in *Loving* and *Perez* is apparent. In *Loving* and *Perez*, the parties were barred from entering into the marriage relationship because of an impermissible racial classification. There is no analogous sexual classification involved in the instant case because appellants are not being denied entry into the marriage relationship because of their sex; rather, they are being denied entry into the marriage relationship because of the recognized definition of that relationship as one which may be entered into only by two persons who are members of the opposite sex.[8] As the court observed in *Jones v. Hallahan, supra*, 501 S.W.2d at 590: "In substance, the relationship proposed by the appellants does not authorize the issuance of a marriage license because what they propose is not a marriage." *Loving* and *Perez* are inapposite.

---

[6] In this regard, we are aided by the rule of statutory construction that words of a statute must be understood in their usual and ordinary sense in the absence of a statutory definition to the contrary. [Citations omitted.] We need not resort to the quotation of dictionary definitions to establish that "marriage" in the usual and ordinary sense refers to the legal union of one man and one woman.

[8] Appellants argue that *Loving* and *Perez* are analogous to the case at bar notwithstanding what might be the "definition" of marriage. They argue that at the time *Loving* and *Perez* were decided, marriage *by definition* barred interracial marriages and that the *Loving* and *Perez* courts changed that definition through their interpretation of the Fourteenth Amendment. Appellants suggest that the ERA operates in a manner analogous to the Fourteenth Amendment to require us to change the definition of marriage to include same-sex marriages. We disagree. The *Loving* and *Perez* courts did not change the basic definition of marriage as the legal union of one man and one woman; rather, they merely held that the race of the man or woman desiring to enter that relationship could not be considered by the state in granting a marriage license. In other words, contrary to appellants' contention, the Fourteenth Amendment did not require any change in the definition of marriage and, as we hold today, neither does the ERA.

To further illustrate our view, we suggest two examples of a situation which, contrary to the situation presented in the case at bar, would raise questions of possible sexual discrimination prohibited by the ERA. First, if the anti-miscegenation statutes involved in *Loving* and *Perez* had permitted white males to marry black females but prohibited white females from marrying black males, then it is arguable that the statutes would be invalid not only because of an impermissible racial classification under the Fourteenth Amendment but also because of an impermissible sexual classification under the ERA. Second, if the state legislature were to change the definition of marriage to include the legal union of members of the same sex but also provide that marriage licenses and the accompanying protections of the marriage laws could only be extended to male couples, then it is likely that the state marriage laws would be in conflict with the ERA for failure to provide equal benefits to female couples.

J.S.K. Enterprises, Inc. v. City of Lacey, supra, is also factually and legally dissimilar to the case at bar. In that case, this court held that a city ordinance which permitted massagists to administer massages only to customers of their own sex constituted discrimination on the basis of sex, prohibited by the equal protection clause of the fourteenth amendment to the United States Constitution, and also violated RCW 49.12.200, relating to the right of women to pursue any employment. We see no analogy between the right of women to administer massages to men and the question of whether the prohibition against same-sex marriages is unconstitutional. The right recognized in *J.S.K. Enterprises, Inc.* on the basis of principles applicable to employment discrimination has nothing to do with the question presented by appellants.

Appellants apparently argue, however, that notwithstanding the fact that the equal protection analysis applied in *Loving, Perez* and *J.S.K. Enterprises, Inc.* may render those cases distinguishable from the case at bar, the absolute language of the ERA requires the conclusion that the prohibition against same-sex marriages is unconstitutional. In this context, appellants suggest that definition of marriage, as the legal union of one man and one woman, in and of itself, when applied to appellants, constitutes a violation of the ERA. Therefore, appellants contend, persons of the same sex must be presumed to have the constitutional right to marry one another in the absence of a countervailing interest or clear exception to the ERA.

Appellants cite no case law in support of their position, but direct our attention to the analysis set forth in Note, *The Legality of Homosexual Marriage*, 82 YALE L.J. 573 (1973), and in Brown, Emerson, Falk & Freedman, *The Equal Rights Amendment: A Constitutional Basis for Equal Rights for Women*, 80 YALE L.J. 871 (1971). The latter article, however, is clearly written in the context of the impact of the ERA upon the rights of women and men as individuals and the authors make no suggestion that the ERA requires a change in the definition of marriage to include same-sex relationships. The authors suggest that the ERA prohibition of sex discrimination is "absolute," meaning that one person may not be favored over another where sex is the only distinguishing factor between the two. In that context, the authors state at 892:

> "From this analysis it follows that the constitutional mandate must be absolute. The issue under the Equal Rights Amendment cannot be different but equal, reasonable or unreasonable classification, suspect classification, fundamental interest, or the demands of administrative expediency. Equality of rights means that sex is not a factor. This at least is the premise of the Equal Rights Amendment."

The author of the note, *The Legality of Homosexual Marriage, supra*, applies the aforementioned analysis of the ERA in the totally different context of same-sex relationships and thus concludes that the ERA requires that such relationships be accommodated by state marriage laws. We are not persuaded by such reasoning. We do not believe that approval of the ERA by the people of this state reflects any intention upon their part to offer couples involved in same-sex relationships the protection of our marriage laws. A consideration of the basic purpose of the ERA makes it apparent why that amendment does not support appellants' claim of discrimination. The primary purpose of the ERA is to overcome discriminatory legal treatment as between men and women "on account of sex." The popular slogan, "Equal pay for equal work," particularly expresses the rejection of the notion that merely because a person is a woman, rather than a man, she is to be treated differently than a man with qualifications equal to her own.

Prior to adoption of the ERA, the proposition that women were to be accorded a position in the law inferior to that of men had a long history.[10] Thus, in that context, the purpose of the ERA is to provide the legal protection, as between men and women, that apparently is missing from the state and federal Bills of Rights, and it is in light of that purpose that the language of the ERA must be construed. To accept the appellants' contention that the ERA must be interpreted to prohibit statutes which refuse to permit same-sex marriages would be to subvert the purpose for which the ERA was enacted by expanding its scope beyond that which was undoubtedly intended by the majority of the citizens of this state who voted for the amendment.

We are of the opinion that a common-sense reading of the language of the ERA indicates that an individual is afforded no protection under the ERA unless he or she first demonstrates that a right or responsibility has been denied solely because of that individual's sex. Appellants are unable to make such a showing because the right or responsibility they seek does not exist. The ERA does not create any new rights or responsibilities, such as the conceivable right of persons of the same sex to marry one another; rather, it merely insures that existing rights and responsibilities, or such rights and responsibilities as may be created in the future, which previously might have been wholly or partially denied to one sex or to the other, will be equally available to members of either sex. The form of discrimination or difference in legal treatment which comes within the prohibition of the ERA necessarily is of an invidious character because it is discrimination based upon the fortuitous circumstance of one's membership in a particular sex per se. This is not to say, however, that the ERA prohibits all legal differentiations which might be made among males and females. A generally recognized "corollary" or exception to even an "absolute" interpretation of the ERA is the proposition that laws which differentiate between the sexes are permissible so long as they are based upon the unique physical characteristics of a particular sex, rather than upon a person's membership in a particular sex per se. See Brown, Emerson, Falk & Freedman, *The Equal Rights Amentment: A Constitutional Basis for Equal Rights for Women, supra* at 893–96.

In the instant case, it is apparent that the state's refusal to grant a license allowing the appellants to marry one another is not based upon appellants' status as males, but rather it is based upon the state's recognition that our society as a whole views marriage as the appropriate and desirable forum for procreation and the rearing of children. This is true even though married couples are not required to become parents and even though some couples are incapable of becoming parents and even though not all couples who produce children are married. These, however, are exceptional situations. The fact remains that marriage exists as a protected legal institution primarily because of societal values associated with the propagation of the human race. Further, it is apparent that no same-sex couple offers the possibility of the birth of children by their union. Thus the refusal of the state to authorize

---

[10] For example, Mr. Justice Bradley, in his concurring opinion upholding the refusal of a state court to license a woman to practice law in *Bradwell v. Illinois*, 83 U.S. (16 Wall.) 130, 21 L.Ed. 442 (1872), stated in part at 141:

"[T]he civil law, as well as nature herself, has always recognized a wide difference in the respective spheres and destinies of man and woman. Man is, or should be, woman's protector and defender. The natural and proper timidity and delicacy which belongs to the female sex evidently unfits it for many of the occupations of civil life. The constitution of the family organization, which is founded in the divine ordinance, as well as in the nature of things, indicates the domestic sphere as that which properly belongs to the domain and functions of womanhood. The harmony, not to say identity, of interests and views which belong, or should belong, to the family institution is repugnant to the idea of a woman adopting a distinct and independent career from that of her husband. * * *

"* * * The paramount destiny and mission of woman are to fulfil the noble and benign offices of wife and mother. This is the law of the Creator."

428   *American Family Law in Transition*

same-sex marriage results from such impossibilities of reproduction rather than from an invidious discrimination "on account of sex." Therefore, the definition of marriage as the legal union of one man and one woman is permissible as applied to appellants, notwithstanding the prohibition contained in the ERA, because it is founded upon the unique physical characteristics of the sexes and appellants are not being discriminated against because of their status as males per se. In short, we hold the ERA does not require the state to authorize same-sex marriage.

Appellants' final assignment of error is based primarily upon the proposition that the state's failure to grant them a marriage license violates the Equal Protection Clause of the Fourteenth Amendment to the United States Constitution.[11] The threshhold question presented involves the standard by which to measure appellants' constitutional argument. We have held that the effect of our state marriage statutes is to prohibit same-sex marriages, and as a general proposition such statutes must be presumed constitutional. See *Aetna Life Ins. Co. v. Washington Life & Disability Ins. Guar. Ass'n*, 83 Wash.2d 523, 520 P.2d 162 (1974). The operative effect of such a presumption is that the statutory classification in question—the exclusion of same-sex relationships from the definition of marriage—does not offend the Equal Protection Clause if it rests upon some reasonable basis. *Dandridge v. Williams*, 397 U.S. 471, 90 S. Ct. 1153, 25 L.Ed.2d 491 (1970); *Caughey v. Employment Sec. Dept.*, 81 Wash.2d 597, 503 P.2d 460 (1972).

Appellants contend, however, that a standard stricter than such a "reasonable basis" test must be applied to the operation of our state marriage laws. Appellants point out that a fundamental right—the right to marry—is at stake in the instant litigation, directing our attention to *Loving v. Virginia, supra*; *Skinner v. Oklahoma*, 316 U.S. 535, 62 S. Ct. 1110, 86 L.Ed. 1655 (1942), and *Meyer v. Nebraska*, 262 U.S. 390, 43 S. Ct. 625, 67 L.Ed. 1042 (1923). Moreover, appellants, reasoning primarily by analogy from *Loving* and related cases, argue that the statutory prohibition against same-sex marriages constitutes a classification based upon sex. Therefore, appellants urge that the applicable standard under the Equal Protection Clause requires that the classification be deemed "inherently suspect" and one which may not be sustained unless the state demonstrates that a "compelling state interest" so requires. See *Sail'er Inn, Inc. v. Kirby*, 5 Cal.3d 1, 95 Cal. Rptr. 329, 485 P.2d 529 (1971).

We do not take exception to the proposition that the Equal Protection Clause of the Fourteenth Amendment requires strict judicial scrutiny of legislative attempts at sexual discrimination. Our state Supreme Court has held that a legislative classification based upon sex is inherently suspect, *Hanson v. Hutt*, 83 Wash.2d 195, 517 P.2d 599 (1973), as has a plurality of the United States Supreme Court, *Frontiero v. Richardson*, 411 U.S. 677, 93 S. Ct. 1764, 36 L.Ed.2d 583 (1973). As we have already held in connection with our discussion of the ERA, however, appellants do not present a case of sexual discrimination. Appellants were not denied a marriage license because of their sex; rather, they were denied a marriage license because of the nature of marriage itself.

Appellants appear to recognize the distinction we make because they also argue that the definition of marriage as it is reflected in our marriage statutes constitutes an inherently suspect classification because it discrimi-

---

[11] Appellants also claim that their rights under the Eighth and Ninth Amendments, and under the Due Process Clause of the Fourteenth Amendment have been violated. In view of the conclusion we have reached with reference to appellants' claim under the Equal Protection Clause of the Fourteenth Amendment, we deem it unnecessary to discuss appellants' contentions with regard to the right to privacy under the Ninth Amendment and the right to due process under the Fourteenth Amendment. Further, we have determined that appellants' argument that denial of a marriage license to them constitutes cruel and unusual punishment prohibited by the Eighth Amendment is without merit.

nates against homosexuals as a group. In other words, appellants appear to present the alternative argument that although they are not being discriminated against because they are males, they are being discriminated against because they happen to be homosexual.

Although appellants present argument to the contrary,[12] we agree with the state's contention that to define marriage to exclude homosexual or any other same-sex relationships is not to create an inherently suspect legislative classification requiring strict judicial scrutiny to determine a compelling state interest. *Baker v. Nelson*, 291 Minn. 310, 191 N.W.2d 185 (1971); see *Jones v. Hallahan, supra; Anonymous v. Anonymous, supra;* see generally, Note, *The Legality of Homosexual Marriage, supra* at 574–83. The state contends that the exclusion of same-sex relationships from our marriage statutes may be upheld under the traditional "reasonable basis" or "rational relationship" test to which we have previously made reference. We agree.

There can be no doubt that there exists a rational basis for the state to limit the definition of marriage to exclude same-sex relationships. Although, as appellants contend, other cultures may have fostered differing definitions of marriage, marriage in this state, as elsewhere in the nation, has been deemed a private relationship of a man and a woman (husband and wife) which involves "interests of basic importance in our society." See *Boddie v. Connecticut*, 401 U.S. 371, 376, 91 S. Ct. 780, 785, 28 L.Ed.2d 113 (1971). Accordingly, subject to constitutional limitations, the state has exclusive dominion over the legal institution of marriage and the state alone has the "prerogative of creating and overseeing this important institution." *Coleman v. Coleman*, 32 Ohio St.2d 155, 160, 291 N.E.2d 530, 534 (1972). See also *O'Neil v. Dent*, 364 F. Supp. 565 (E.D.N.Y. 1973).

We do not seek to define in detail the "interests of basic importance" which are served by retaining the present definition of marriage as the legal union of one man and one woman. The societal values which are involved in this area must be left to the examination of the legislature. See *Moran v. School District #7*, 350 F. Supp. 1180 (D. Mont. 1972). For constitutional purposes, it is enough to recognize that marriage as now defined is deeply rooted in our society. Although, as appellants hasten to point out, married persons are not required to have children or even to engage in sexual relations, marriage is so clearly related to the public interest in affording a favorable environment for the growth of children that we are unable to say that there is not a rational basis upon which the state may limit the protection of its marriage laws to the legal union of one man and one woman. Under such circumstances, although the legislature may change the definition of marriage within constitutional limits, the constitution does not require the change sought by appellants. As the court observed in *Baker v. Nelson, supra*, 291 Minn. at 312, 313, 191 N.W.2d at 186:

> "The institution of marriage as a union of man and woman, uniquely involving the procreation and rearing of children within a family, is as old

---

[12] Appellants argue, in part, that homosexuals constitute a class having characteristics making any legislative classification applicable to them one having common denominators of suspectability. Thus, they argue homosexuals constitute "a politically voiceless and invisible minority," see *Hobson v. Hansen*, 269 F. Supp. 401, 508 (D.C. 1967); that being homosexual, generally speaking, is an immutable characteristic, see *Korematsu v. United States*, 323 U.S. 214, 65 S. Ct. 193, 89 L.Ed. 194 (1944); and that homosexuals are a group with a long history of discrimination subject to myths and stereotypes. See generally, Note, *The Legality of Homosexual Marriage, supra* at 575–78.

We are not unmindful of the fact that public attitude toward homosexuals is undergoing substantial, albeit gradual, change. See generally, Comment, *Homosexuality and the Law—A Right to be Different?* 38 ALBANY L. REV. 84 (1973). Notwithstanding these considerations, we express no opinion upon the desirability of revising our marriage laws to accommodate homosexuals and include same-sex relationships within the definition of marriage. That is a question for the people to answer through the legislative process. We merely hold such a legislative change is not constitutionally required.

as the book of Genesis. * * * This historic institution manifestly is more deeply founded than the asserted contemporary concept of marriage and societal interests for which petitioners contend. The due process clause of the Fourteenth Amendment is not a charter for restructuring it by judicial legislation.

　　* * *

　　"The equal protection clause of the Fourteenth Amendment, like the due process clause, is not offended by the state's classification of persons authorized to marry."

Thus, for the reasons stated in this opinion, we hold that the trial court correctly concluded that the state's denial of a marriage license to appellants is required by our state statutes and permitted by both the state and federal constitutions.

　　The judgment is affirmed.

Comments

　　The problems judges encounter in dealing with a theory of homosexual marriage are related to language. Note that *Jones v. Hallahan* relied primarily on *Webster's* and other dictionaries as authorities for its decision on what constitutes marriage. The justification for this procedure was seen in the need to determine "common usage." Since common usage appeared to exclude any definition of marriage other than one limited to heterosexuality, the court felt that no constitutional issue was involved. *Webster's*, however, is not necessarily concerned with the question whether a particular usage is constitutionally objectionable, or even discriminatory. A problem of linguistics becomes even more visible if one attempts to determine who is homosexual.

　　If there are conceptual difficulties with the terms "marriage" and "homosexual," there are of course greater difficulties with the combined term "homosexual marriage." Coming at the matter from a traditional direction, the tendency is strong, as illustrated by *Hallahan* and to a lesser degree also by *Singer*, to view such a combination as an absurdity. If the discussion were to stop at this point, the constitutional issue would indeed never be reached. Yet there have always been legal "homosexual marriages," if we agree to use this term for two persons of different sexes who are homosexually inclined and marry each other as a social accommodation. These unions may, of course, include affection and even procreation, and are not perceived as being homosexual. They seem to conform, at least outwardly, to the traditional heterosexual pattern. In fact, they include all the heterosexuality that the law asks for. Whether further pressure to conform is necessary or desirable is a matter to be examined, but it was not reached in *Hallahan* or *Singer*.

　　The transsexual marriage in *M.T. v. J.T.* was recognized because it did conform to a heterosexual pattern. An extraordinary procedure was necessary, however, to bring about full physical gender change, described in painful detail by the court. The male sexual organs were removed and an artificial vagina was surgically created. The trial judge found, as a matter of fact, that the plaintiff was a female. The appellate judge had no trouble consistently referring to the plaintiff as "she." Nevertheless it is possible that the case also had elements of estoppel. The defendant, after having paid for the operation prior to marriage, was in a bad position to raise the issue that the marriage was void. In other words, although the court did not use an estoppel rationale, it may have felt for this particular litigation that the defendant was precluded from raising the issue of homosexual marriage, and should support the plaintiff as if she were a woman and his wife. If the issue of homosexual marriage had been raised prior to marriage— perhaps in a mandamus action upon refusal of a clerk to grant a marriage license—it is probable that such refusal would have been upheld.

There is no certainty that other courts would treat a transsexual marriage as any different from an attempt to enter a homosexual union. For example, in the English case *Corbett v. Corbett,** a marriage was annulled because, in the opinion of the court, the participants in a transsexual union continued to be of the male sex. Indeed many courts, because of the ambiguity of the term "homosexual," may treat "transsexual" as a mere subspecies of homosexuality rather than recognizing legal effects of the operation. Courts have also been disinclined to recognize sex change operations of women.† Here too the conceptual problems related to language precede the legal characterizations. In *Corbett*, for instance, the court referred to the respondent by the male pronoun "he" up to the recital of the operation in the statement of facts, thereafter as "she." It recognized the operation as effective for linguistic purposes, but not for the legal purposes of marriage.

Since the courts seem to rely more on traditional community values on homosexuality than on an exhaustive exploration of the underlying issues in given cases, constitutional attacks on prohibitions of homosexual marriages are likely to continue. The imperfections of language provide a further stimulus for continued efforts at clarification. Further litigation relating to homosexual marriage is likely to rely on *Zablocki v. Redhail* (pp. 408–413), where Mr. Justice Marshall, in speaking for the majority, declared "that the decision to marry has been placed on the same level of importance as decisions relating to procreation, childbirth, child-rearing, and family relationships." Our legal system has shown an increasing inclination to embrace a larger and larger segment of human relationships, perhaps in an effort to "get them out of the closet" and to stabilize them. One of the questions to be asked is whether society is aided by laws that facilitate nonstable human associations. Another task is to ascertain the shifting community values in regard to marriage. It could be, for example, that marriage and nonmarriage are not the only alternatives. Contrac-

---

*[1970] 2 All E.R. 33, [1970] 2 W.L.R. 1306.
†See, *e.g., B. v. B.*, 355 N.Y.S.2d 712 (1974).

tual cohabitation may be an additional alternative that, short of actual marriage, could lend stability to the relationships of homosexual persons. It is conceivable that such contracts, express or implied, between persons of the same sex are more likely to be recognized, or at least to be recognized sooner, than homosexual marriage.

Adoption may be another alternative for legally recognizing a homosexual relationship. This is possible because in adult adoptions there is no test of best interests as found in child adoptions. So long as there is no obvious fraud (such as a lawyer attempting to be adopted by a wealthy octogenarian for purposes of inheritance) or a violation of a criminal statute (such as incest laws), a judge will ordinarily not inquire into matters other than whether the person being adopted is younger than the person adopting and whether the parties have technically complied with adoption laws.

References

Areen, J., CASES AND MATERIALS ON FAMILY LAW 25 (1978).

Dunlap, *The Constitutional Rights of Sexual Minorities: A Crisis of the Male/Female Dichotomy*, 30 HASTINGS L.J. 1131 (1979).

Karst, *The Freedom of Intimate Association*, 89 YALE L.J. 624 (1980).

Note, *Developments in the Law—the Constitution and the Family*, 93 HARV. L. REV. 1156 (1980).

Note, *Homosexuals' Right to Marry: A Constitutional Test and a Legislative Solution*, 128 U. PA. L. REV. 193 (1979).

Note, *The Law and Transsexualism: A Faltering Response to a Conceptual Dilemma*, 7 CONN. L. REV. 288 (1975).

Note, *The Legality of Homosexual Marriage*, 82 YALE L.J. 573 (1973).

Reese, *The Forgotten Sex: Lesbians, Liberation, and the Law*, 11 WILLAMETTE L.J. 354 (1975).

Rivera, *Our Straight-Laced Judges: The Legal Position of Homosexual Persons in the United States*, 30 HASTINGS L.J. 799 (1979).

Weitzman, *Legal Regulation of Marriage: Tradition and Change—A Proposal for Individual Contracts and Contracts in Lieu of Marriage*, 62 CALIF. L. REV. 1169 (1974).

Weitzman, L., THE MARRIAGE CONTRACT—SPOUSES, LOVERS, AND THE LAW 216–23, 316–19 (1981).

Bibliography

Brackel, S., & Rock, R., THE MENTALLY DISABLED AND THE LAW 240–43 (rev. ed. 1971).

Burgdorf & Burgdorf, *The Wicked Witch is Almost Dead: Buck v. Bell and the Sterilization of Handicapped Persons*, 50 TEMP. L.Q. 995 (1977).

Clark, H., THE LAW OF DOMESTIC RELATIONS IN THE UNITED STATES ch. 2 (1968).

Comment, *All in the "Family": Legal Problems of Communes*, 7 HARV. C.R.-C.L. L. REV. 393 (1972).

Comment, *Constitutional Aspects of the Homosexual's Right to a Marriage License*, 12 J. FAM. L. 607 (1973).

Comment, *Homosexuals' Right to Marry: A Constitutional Test and a Legislative Solution*, 128 U. PA. L. REV. 193 (1979).

Dunlap, *The Constitutional Rights of Sexual Minorities: A Crisis of the Male/Female Dichotomy*, 30 HASTINGS L.J. 1131 (1979).

Eekelaar, J., & Katz, S., MARRIAGE AND COHABITATION IN CONTEMPORARY SOCIETIES (1980).

Foster, *Common Law Divorce*, 46 MINN. L. REV. 43 (1961).

Jensen, *From Belle Terre to East Cleveland: Zoning, the Family, and the Right of Privacy*, 13 FAM. L.Q. 1 (1979).

Johns, *Right to Marry: Infringement by the Armed Forces*, 10 FAM. L.Q. 357 (1977).

Karst, *The Freedom of Intimate Association*, 89 YALE L.J. 624 (1980).

Knowles, *High Schools, Marriage and the Fourteenth Amendment*, 11 J. FAM. L. 711 (1972).

Knutson, D. (ed.), HOMOSEXUALITY AND THE LAW (1980).

Linn & Bowens, *Historical Fallacies Behind Legal Prohibitions Involving Mentally Retarded Persons*, 13 GONZ. L. REV. 624 (1978).

Nagan, *Conflict of Laws and Proximate Relations: A Policy-Science Perspective*, 8 RUT.-CAM. L.J. 416 (1977).

Note, *Adoptive Sibling Marriage in Colorado: Israel v. Allen*, 51 U. COLO. L. REV. 135 (1979).

Note, *Developments in the Law—The Constitution and the Family*, 93 HARV. L. REV. 1156 (1980).

Note, *The Legality of Homosexual Marriage*, 82 YALE L.J. 573 (1973).

Note, *The Right of the Mentally Disabled to Marry: A Statutory Evaluation*, 15 J. FAM. L. 463 (1976–77).

Note, *Standard of Review in Prisoner's Rights Litigation and the Constitutional Right to Marry*, 12 U.S.F.L. REV. 465 (1978).

Shaman, *Persons Who are Mentally Retarded: Their Right to Marry and Have Children*, 12 FAM. L.Q. 61 (1978).

Storke, *The Incestuous Marriage—Relic of the Past*, 36 U. COLO. L. REV. 473 (1964).

Strickman, *Marriage, Divorce and the Constitution*, 22 B.C.L. REV. 934 (1981), reprinted in 15 FAM. L.Q. 259 (1982).

Wald, *Basic Personal and Civil Rights*, in THE MENTALLY RETARDED CITIZEN AND THE LAW (M. Kindred ed. 1976).

Waning State Involvement in Termination of Marriage

Residency Requirements

Sosna v. Iowa

United States Supreme Court

419 U.S. 393 (1975)

Mr. Justice REHNQUIST delivered the opinion of the Court.

Appellant Carol Sosna married Michael Sosna on September 5, 1964, in Michigan. They lived together in New York between October 1967 and August 1971, after which date they separated but continued to live in New York. In August 1972, appellant moved to Iowa with her three children, and the following month she petitioned the District Court of Jackson County, Iowa, for a dissolution of her marriage. Michael Sosna, who had been personally served with notice of the action when he came to Iowa to visit his children, made a special appearance to contest the jurisdiction of the Iowa court. The Iowa court dismissed the petition for lack of jurisdiction, finding that Michael Sosna was not a resident of Iowa and appellant had not been a resident of the State of Iowa for one year preceding the filing of her petition. In so doing the Iowa court applied the provisions of Iowa Code §598.6 (1973) requiring that the petitioner in such an action be "for the last year a resident of the state."

* * *

The durational residency requirement under attack in this case is a part of Iowa's comprehensive statutory regulation of domestic relations, an area that has long been regarded as a virtually exclusive province of the States. Cases decided by this Court over a period of more than a century bear witness to this historical fact. In *Barber v. Barber*, 21 How. 582, 584, 16 L.Ed. 226 (1859), the Court said: "We disclaim altogether any jurisdiction in the courts of the United States upon the subject of divorce * * *." In *Pennoyer v. Neff*, 95 U.S. 714, 734–735, 24 L.Ed. 565 (1878), the Court said: "The State * * * has absolute right to prescribe the conditions upon which the marriage relation between its own citizens shall be created, and the causes for which it may be dissolved," and the same view was reaffirmed in *Simms v. Simms*, 175 U.S. 162, 167, 20 S. Ct. 58, 60, 44 L.Ed. 115 (1899).

The statutory scheme in Iowa, like those in other States, sets forth in considerable detail the grounds upon which a marriage may be dissolved and the circumstances in which a divorce may be obtained. Jurisdiction over a petition for dissolution is established by statute in "the county where either party resides," Iowa Code §598.2 (1973), and the Iowa courts have construed the term "resident" to have much the same meaning as is ordinarily associated with the concept of domicile. *Korsrud v. Korsrud*, 242 Iowa 178, 45 N.W.2d 848 (1951). Iowa has recently revised its divorce statutes, incorporating the no-fault concept, but it retained the one-year durational residency requirement.

The imposition of a durational residency requirement for divorce is scarcely unique to Iowa, since 48 States impose such a requirement as a condition for maintaining an action for divorce. As might be expected, the periods vary among the States and range from six weeks to two years. The one-year period selected by Iowa is the most common length of time prescribed.

Appellant contends that the Iowa requirement of one year's residence is unconstitutional for two separate reasons: *first*, because it establishes two classes of persons and discriminates against those who have recently exercised their right to travel to Iowa, thereby contravening the Court's holdings in *Shapiro v. Thompson*, 394 U.S. 618, 89 S. Ct. 1322, 22 L.Ed.2d 600 (1969); *Dunn v. Blumstein*, 405 U.S. 330, 92 S. Ct. 995, 31 L.Ed.2d 274 (1972); and *Memorial Hospital v. Maricopa County*, 415 U.S. 250, 94 S. Ct. 1076, 39 L.Ed.2d 306 (1974); and, *second*, because it denies a litigant the opportunity to make an individualized showing of bona fide residence and therefore denies such residents access to the only method of legally dissolving their marriage. [Citations omitted.]

State statutes imposing durational residency requirements were, of course, invalidated when imposed by States as a qualification for welfare payments, *Shapiro, supra*; for voting, *Dunn, supra*; and for medical care, *Maricopa County, supra*. But none of those cases intimated that the States might never impose durational residency requirements, and such a proposition was in fact expressly disclaimed.[19] What those cases had in common was that the durational residency requirements they struck down were justified on the basis of budgetary or recordkeeping considerations which were held insufficient to outweigh the constitutional claims of the individuals. But Iowa's divorce residency requirement is of a different stripe. Appellant was not irretrievably foreclosed from obtaining some part of what she sought, as was the case with the welfare recipients in *Shapiro*, the voters in *Dunn*, or the indigent patient in *Maricopa County*. She would eventually qualify for the same sort of adjudication which she demanded virtually upon her arrival in the State. Iowa's requirement delayed her access to the courts, but, by fulfilling it, she could ultimately have obtained the same opportunity for adjudication which she asserts ought to have been hers at an earlier point in time.

Iowa's residency requirement may reasonably be justified on grounds other than purely budgetary considerations or administrative convenience. *Cf. Kahn v. Shevin*, 416 U.S. 351, 94 S. Ct. 1734, 40 L.Ed.2d 189 (1974). A decree of divorce is not a matter in which the only interested parties are the State as a sort of "grantor," and a divorce petitioner such as appellant in the role of "grantee." Both spouses are obviously interested in the proceedings, since it will affect their marital status and very likely their property rights. Where a married couple has minor children, a decree of divorce would usually include provisions for their custody and support. With consequences of such moment riding on a divorce decree issued by its courts, Iowa may insist that one seeking to initiate such a proceeding have the modicum of attachment to the State required here.

Such a requirement additionally furthers the State's parallel interests both in avoiding officious intermeddling in matters in which another State has a paramount interest, and in minimizing the susceptibility of its own divorce decrees to collateral attack. A State such as Iowa may quite reasonably decide that it does not wish to become a divorce mill for unhappy spouses who have lived there as short a time as appellant had when she commenced her action in the state court after having long resided elsewhere. Until such time as Iowa is convinced that appellant intends to remain in the State, it lacks the "nexus between person and place of such permanence as to control the creation of legal relations and responsibilities of the utmost significance." *Williams v. North Carolina*, 325 U.S. 226, 229, 65 S. Ct. 1092, 1095, 89 L.Ed. 1577 (1945). Perhaps even more important, Iowa's interests extend beyond its borders and include the recognition of its divorce decrees by other States under the Full Faith and Credit Clause of the Constitution, Art. IV,

---

[19]*Shapiro*, 394 U.S. at 638 n.21, 89 S. Ct., at 1333; *Maricopa County*, 415 U.S., at 258–259, 94 S. Ct. at 1082–1083.

§1. For that purpose, this Court has often stated that "judicial power to grant a divorce—jurisdiction, strictly speaking—is founded on domicil." *Williams, supra; Andrews v. Andrews*, 188 U.S. 14, 23 S. Ct. 237, 47 L.Ed. 366 (1903); *Bell v. Bell*, 181 U.S. 175, 21 S. Ct. 551, 45 L.Ed. 804 (1901). Where a divorce decree is entered after a finding of domicile in *ex parte* proceedings,[20] this Court has held that the finding of domicile is not binding upon another State and may be disregarded in the face of "cogent evidence" to the contrary. *Williams, supra*, 325 U.S. at 236, 65 S. Ct. at 1098. For that reason, the State asked to enter such a decree is entitled to insist that the putative divorce petitioner satisfy something more than the bare minimum of constitutional requirements before a divorce may be granted. The State's decision to exact a one-year residency requirement as a matter of policy is therefore buttressed by a quite permissible inference that this requirement not only effectuates state substantive policy but likewise provides a greater safeguard against successful collateral attack than would a requirement of bona fide residence alone.[21] This is precisely the sort of determination that a State in the exercise of its domestic relations jurisdiction is entitled to make.

We therefore hold that the state interest in requiring that those who seek a divorce from its courts be genuinely attached to the State, as well as a desire to insulate divorce decrees from the likelihood of collateral attack, requires a different resolution of the constitutional issue presented than was the case in *Shapiro, supra, Dunn, supra*, and *Maricopa County, supra*.

Nor are we of the view that the failure to provide an individualized determination of residency violates the Due Process Clause of the Fourteenth Amendment. *Vlandis v. Kline*, 412 U.S. 441, 93 S. Ct. 2230, 37 L.Ed.2d 63 (1973), relied upon by appellant, held that Connecticut might not arbitrarily invoke a permanent and irrebuttable presumption of non-residence against students who sought to obtain in-state tuition rates when that presumption was not necessarily or universally true in fact. But in *Vlandis* the Court warned that its decision should not "be construed to deny a State the right to impose on a student, as one element in demonstrating bona fide residence, a reasonable durational residency requirement." *Id.*, at 452, 93 S. Ct. at 2236. See *Starns v. Malkerson*, 326 F. Supp. 234 (Minn. 1970), *aff'd*, 401 U.S. 985, 91 S. Ct. 1231, 28 L.Ed.2d 527 (1971). An individualized determination of

---

[20]When a divorce decree is not entered on the basis of *ex parte* proceedings, this Court held in *Sherrer v. Sherrer*, 334 U.S. 343, 351–352, 68 S. Ct. 1087, 1091, 92 L.Ed. 1429 (1948):

"[T]he requirements of full faith and credit bar a defendant from collaterally attacking a divorce decree on jurisdictional grounds in the courts of a sister State where there has been participation by the defendant in the divorce proceedings, where the defendant has been accorded full opportunity to contest the jurisdictional issues, and where the decree is not susceptible to such collateral attack in the courts of the State which rendered the decree."

Our Brother MARSHALL argues in dissent that the Iowa durational residency requirement "sweeps too broadly" since it is not limited to *ex parte* proceedings and could be narrowed by a waiver provision. *Post*, at 570. But Iowa's durational residency requirement cannot be tailored in this manner without disrupting settled principles of Iowa practice and pleading. Iowa's rules governing special appearances make it impossible for the state court to know, either at the time a petition for divorce is filed or when a motion to dismiss for want of jurisdiction is filed, whether or not a respondent will appear and participate in the divorce proceedings. Iowa Rules Civ. Proc. 66, 104. The fact that the state legislature might conceivably adopt a system of waivers and revise court rules governing special appearances does not make such detailed rewriting appropriate business for the federal judiciary.

[21]Since the majority of States require residence for at least a year, * * * it is reasonable to assume that Iowa's one-year "floor" makes its decrees less susceptible to successful collateral attack in other States. As the Court of Appeals for the Fifth Circuit observed in upholding a six-month durational residency requirement imposed by Florida, an objective test may impart to a State's divorce decrees "a verity that tends to safeguard them against the suspicious eyes of other states' prosecutorial authorities, the suspicions of private counsel in other states, and the post-decree dissatisfactions of parties to the divorce who wish a second bite. Such a reputation for validity of divorce decrees is not, then, merely cosmetic." *Makres v. Askew*, 500 F.2d 577, 579 (1974), *aff'g*, 359 F. Supp. 1225 (MD Fla. 1973).

physical presence plus the intent to remain, which appellant apparently seeks, would not entitle her to a divorce even if she could have made such a showing.[22] For Iowa requires not merely "domicile" in that sense, but residence in the State for a year in order for its courts to exercise their divorce jurisdiction.

In *Boddie v. Connecticut, supra*, this Court held that Connecticut might not deny access to divorce courts to those persons who could not afford to pay the required fee. Because of the exclusive role played by the State in the termination of marriages, it was held that indigents could not be denied an opportunity to be heard "absent a countervailing state interest overriding significance." 401 U.S., at 377, 91 S. Ct., at 785. But the gravamen of appellant Sosna's claim is not total deprivation, as in *Boddie*, but only delay. The operation of the filing fee in *Boddie* served to exclude forever a certain segment of the population from obtaining a divorce in the courts of Connecticut. No similar total deprivation is present in appellant's case, and the delay which attends the enforcement of the one-year durational residency requirement is, for the reasons previously stated, consistent with the provisions of the United States Constitution.

Affirmed.

* * *

Mr. Justice MARSHALL, with whom Mr. Justice BRENNAN joins, dissenting.

* * *

The Court omits altogether what should be the first inquiry: whether the right to obtain a divorce is of sufficient importance that its denial to recent immigrants constitutes a penalty on interstate travel. In my view, it clearly meets that standard. The previous decisions of this Court make it plain that the right of marital association is one of the most basic rights conferred on the individual by the State. The interests associated with marriage and divorce have repeatedly been accorded particular deference, and the right to marry has been termed "one of the vital personal rights essential to the orderly pursuit of happiness by free men." *Loving v. Virginia*, 388 U.S. 1, 12, 87 S. Ct. 1817, 1824, 18 L.Ed.2d 1010 (1967). In *Boddie v. Connecticut*, 401 U.S. 371, 91 S. Ct. 780, 28 L.Ed.2d 113 (1971), we recognized that the right to seek dissolution of the marital relationship was closely related to the right to marry, as both involve the voluntary adjustment of the same fundamental human relationship. *Id.*, at 383, 91 S. Ct. at 788. Without further laboring the point, I think it is clear beyond cavil that the right to seek dissolution of the marital relationship is of such fundamental importance that denial of this right to the class of recent interstate travelers penalizes interstate travel within the meaning of *Shapiro, Dunn*, and *Maricopa County*.

* * *

The Court proposes three defenses for the Iowa statute: first, the residency requirement merely delays receipt of the benefit in question—it does not deprive the applicant of the benefit altogether; second, since significant social consequences may follow from the conferral of a divorce, the State may legitimately regulate the divorce process; and third, the State has interests both in protecting itself from use as a "divorce mill" and in protecting its judgments from possible collateral attack in other States. In my view, the first two defenses provide no significant support for the statute in question here. Only the third has any real force.

---

[22] In addition to a showing of residence within the State for a year, Iowa Code §598.6 (1973) requires any petition for dissolution to state "that the maintenance of the residence has been in good faith and not for the purpose of obtaining a marriage dissolution only." In dismissing appellant's petition in state court, Judge Keck observed that appellant had failed to allege good-faith residence. (Jurisdictional Statement App.B. 2).

A

With the first justification, the Court seeks to distinguish the *Shapiro*, *Dunn*, and *Maricopa County* cases. Yet the distinction the Court draws seems to me specious. Iowa's residency requirement, the Court says, merely forestalls access to the courts; applicants seeking welfare payments, medical aid, and the right to vote, on the other hand, suffer unrecoverable losses throughout the waiting period. This analysis, however, ignores the severity of the deprivation suffered by the divorce petitioner who is forced to wait a year for relief. See *Stanley v. Illinois*, 405 U.S. 645, 647, 92 S. Ct. 1208, 1210, 31 L.Ed.2d 551 (1972). The injury accompanying that delay is not directly measurable in money terms like the loss of welfare benefits, but it cannot reasonably be argued that when the year has elapsed, the petitioner is made whole. The year's wait prevents remarriage and locks both partners into what may be an intolerable, destructive relationship. Even applying the Court's argument on its own terms, I fail to see how the *Maricopa County* case can be distinguished. A potential patient may well need treatment for a single ailment. Under Arizona statutes he would have had to wait a year before he could be treated. Yet the majority's analysis would suggest that Mr. Evaro's claim for nonemergency medical aid is not cognizable because he would "eventually qualify for the same sort of [service]," *ante*, at 561. The Court cannot mean that Mrs. Sosna has not suffered any injury by being foreclosed from seeking a divorce in Iowa for a year. It must instead mean that it does not regard that deprivation as being very severe.

B

I find the majority's second argument no more persuasive. The Court forgoes reliance on the usual justifications for durational residency requirements—budgetary considerations and administrative convenience, see *Shapiro*, 394 U.S., at 627–638, 89 S. Ct., at 1327–1333; *Maricopa County*, 415 U.S., at 262–269, 94 S. Ct., at 1084–1088. Indeed, it would be hard to make a persuasive argument that either of these interests is significantly implicated in this case. In their place, the majority invokes a more amorphous justification—the magnitude of the interest affected and resolved by a divorce proceeding. Certainly the stakes in a divorce are weighty both for the individuals directly involved in the adjudication and for others immediately affected by it. The critical importance of the divorce process, however, weakens the argument for a long residency requirement rather than strengthens it. The impact of the divorce decree only underscores the necessity that the State's regulation be evenhanded.[3]

It is not enough to recite the State's traditionally exclusive responsibility for regulating family law matters; some tangible interference with the State's regulatory scheme must be shown. Yet in this case, I fail to see how any legitimate objective of Iowa's divorce regulations would be frustrated by granting equal access to new state residents. To draw on an analogy, the States have great interest in the local voting process and wide latitude in regulating that process. Yet one regulation that the States may not impose is an unduly long residency requirement. *Dunn v. Blumstein*, 405 U.S. 330, 92 S. Ct. 995, 31 L.E.2d 274 (1972). To remark, as the Court does, that because of the consequences riding on a divorce decree "Iowa may insist that one seek-

---

[3]The majority identifies marital status, property rights, and custody and support arrangements as the important concerns commonly resolved by divorce proceedings. But by declining to exercise divorce jurisdiction over its new citizens, Iowa does not avoid affecting these weighty social concerns; instead, it freezes them in an unsatisfactory state that it would not require its long-time residents to endure.

ing to initiate such a proceeding have the modicum of attachment to the State required here" is not to make an argument, but merely to state the result.

C

The Court's third jurisdiction seems to me the only one that warrants close consideration. Iowa has a legitimate interest in protecting itself against invasion by those seeking quick divorces in a forum with relatively lax divorce laws, and it may have some interest in avoiding collateral attacks on its decree in other States. These interests, however, would adequately be protected by a simple requirement of domicile—physical presence plus intent to remain—which would remove the rigid one-year barrier while permitting the State to restrict the availability of its divorce process to citizens who are genuinely its own.

The majority notes that in *Williams v. North Carolina*, 325 U.S. 226, 65 S. Ct. 1092, 89 L.Ed. 1577 (1945), the Court held that for *ex parte* divorces one State's finding of domicile could, under limited circumstances, be challenged in the courts of another. From this, the majority concludes that since Iowa's findings of domicile might be subject to collateral attack elsewhere, it should be permitted to cushion its findings with a one-year residency requirement.

For several reasons, the year's waiting period seems to me neither necessary nor much of a cushion. First, the *Williams* opinion was not aimed at States seeking to avoid becoming divorce mills. Quite the opposite, it was rather plainly directed at States that had cultivated a "quickie divorce" reputation by playing fast and loose with findings of domicile. See *id.*, at 236–237, 65 S. Ct., at 1098–1099; *id.*, at 241, 65 S. Ct., at 1100 (Murphy, J., concurring). If Iowa wishes to avoid becoming a haven for divorce seekers, it is inconceivable that its good-faith determinations of domicile would not meet the rather lenient full faith and credit standards set out in *Williams*.

A second problem with the majority's argument on this score is that *Williams* applies only to *ex parte* divorces. This Court has held that if both spouses were before the divorcing court, a foreign State cannot recognize a collateral challenge that would not be permissible in the divorcing State. *Sherrer v. Sherrer*, 334 U.S. 343, 68 S. Ct. 1087, 92 L.Ed.2d 1429 (1948); *Coe v. Coe*, 334 U.S. 378, 68 S. Ct. 1094, 92 L.Ed. 1451 (1948); *Johnson v. Muelberger*, 340 U.S. 581, 71 S. Ct. 474, 95 L.Ed. 552 (1951); *Cook v. Cook*, 342 U.S. 126, 72 S. Ct. 157, 96 L.Ed. 146 (1951). Therefore, the Iowa statute sweeps too broadly even as a defense to possible collateral attacks, since it imposes a one-year requirement whenever the respondent does not reside in the State, regardless of whether the proceeding is *ex parte*.[7]

Third, even a one-year period does not provide complete protection against collateral attack. It merely makes it somewhat less likely that a second State will be able to find "cogent evidence" that Iowa's determination of domicile was incorrect. But if the Iowa court has erroneously determined the question of domicile, the year's residence will do nothing to preclude collateral attack under *Williams*.

Finally, in one sense the year's residency requirement may technically increase rather than reduce the exposure of Iowa's decrees to collateral attack. Iowa appears to be among the States that have interpreted their divorce residency requirements as being of jurisdictional import. Since a State's divorce decree is subject to collateral challenge in a foreign forum for any jurisdictional flaw that would void it in the State's own courts, *New York ex rel. Halvey v. Halvey*, 330 U.S. 610, 67 S. Ct. 903, 91 L.Ed. 1133 (1947), the residency requirement exposes Iowa divorce proceedings to attack both for

---

[7]This problem could be cured in large part if the State waived its year's residency requirement whenever the respondent agreed to consent to the court's jurisdiction.

failure to prove domicile and for failure to prove one year's residence. If nothing else, this casts doubt on the majority's speculation that Iowa's residency requirement may have been intended as a statutory shield for its divorce decrees. In sum, concerns about the need for a long residency requirement to defray collateral attacks on state judgments seem more fanciful than real. If, as the majority assumes, Iowa is interested in assuring itself that its divorce petitioners are legitimately Iowa citizens, requiring petitioners to provide convincing evidence of bona fide domicile should be more than adequate to the task.[9]

I conclude that the course Iowa has chosen in restricting access to its divorce courts unduly interferes with the right to "migrate, resettle, find a new job, and start a new life." *Shapiro v. Thompson*, 394 U.S., at 629, 89 S. Ct., at 1328 * * *.

---

[9]The majority argues that since most States require a year's residence for divorce, Iowa gains refuge from the risk of collateral attack in the understanding solicitude of States with similar laws. Of course, absent unusual circumstances, a judgment by this Court striking down the Iowa statute would similarly affect the other States with one- and two-year residency requirements. For the same reason, the risk of subjecting Iowa to an invasion of divorce seekers seems minimal. If long residency requirements are held unconstitutional, Iowa will not stand conspicuously alone without a residency requirement "defense." Moreover, its 90-day conciliation period, required of all divorce petitioners in the State, would still serve to discourage peripatetic divorce seekers who are looking for the quickest possible adjudication.

Leader v. Leader

Court of Appeals of Michigan

73 Mich. App. 276, 251 N.W.2d 288 (1977)

D.E. HOLBROOK, Presiding Judge.

Defendant appeals from an order of the trial court denying his motion to dismiss.

* * *

The only question we must decide is whether the trial court was correct in determining that plaintiff had met the jurisdictional prerequisite necessary to maintain her action for divorce. The controlling statute in pertinent part provides that: "A judgment of divorce shall not be granted * * * unless the complainant or defendant has resided in this state for 180 days immediately preceding the filing of the complaint." M.C.L.A. §552.9; M.S.A. §25.89. There is no disagreement as to any of the underlying facts herein. Plaintiff was physically outside the State of Michigan during most of the jurisdictional period.

Because of the unusual factual circumstances of this case, past precedent does not dictate a legal result. Plaintiff and defendant had lived in Michigan for a substantial period of time. They were married in Michigan in 1972. Defendant had three children by a prior marriage, and the parties had one child by this marriage. Plaintiff and defendant apparently had separated sometime prior to the instant action and filed for divorce in Michigan. However, a reconciliation was sought and the parties moved many of their belongings to Kentucky where defendant secured employment and the parties remained for a period of time.

Plaintiff left Michigan on or about October 1, 1975, and remained in Kentucky until January 21, 1976, with the exception of a two-day trip to Michigan. Plaintiff testified that she went to Kentucky with defendant specifically at his request in order to attempt a reconciliation, which she doubted would be successful. Plaintiff testified that she did not intend to stay in Kentucky, or anywhere else, with defendant if the reconciliation was unsuccessful. Plaintiff further testified that she intended to wait and see if the marriage could be saved before considering any place for residence. Plaintiff also testified that she only remained in Kentucky after the first two or three weeks because of a desire not to leave the children without a mother and because of threats which were later made to her by defendant. Finally, however, plaintiff did return to Michigan, her "home" state after almost a four-month absence. We must decide whether this absence is a jurisdictional defect which will defeat plaintiff's action for divorce.

An older Supreme Court case would appear to require reversal of the trial court. *Hoffman v. Hoffman*, 155 Mich. 328, 118 N.W. 990 (1909). In *Hoffman*, the plaintiff, a long-time resident of Michigan, married a resident of Chicago, Illinois. Apparently plaintiff and defendant both lived with their mothers, which came to be a source of trouble. There was a dispute as to where the parties would live. Finally plaintiff-wife went to Chicago where her husband lived and subsequently moved a good deal of her household furnishings there. Shortly thereafter she returned to Michigan, however, and instituted a divorce action. The Court found that she had not resided in Michigan for the requisite period of time. The following quotation is quite revealing:

"[T]here is nothing to indicate that, when she went to Chicago with the defendant, she had any other thought than to make her home with him, either at Chicago, where he then lived, or, if they should subsequently return to St. Joseph, at that place. She gave up her residence for that of the husband, and there is no room for saying that she continued her residence during this time at St. Joseph. A distinction is sought to be drawn between residence and domicile, complainant's counsel conceding that the rule is that the domicile of the husband is that of the wife, but, contending that, under the facts in this case, her residence continued to be in St. Joseph. We cannot assent to this view. Not only was her domicile in Chicago, but she undoubtedly intended to reside there, unless a certain contingency should happen, which did not occur."

Hoffman, supra, at 330, 118 N.W. at 990. This case, although factually similar, is necessarily distinguishable. As can be seen, Mrs. Hoffman at the time she left Michigan fully desired to live with her husband and make her home with him indefinitely and hopefully permanently. There was no indication of doubt or trouble at that time. In the instant case, plaintiff reluctantly went to Kentucky with the hope that the marital difficulties would be resolved and eventually a permanent, or at least indefinite, solution could be had. The establishment of a residence had not solidified and until such time as it did, her true residence according to her intent, remained in Michigan. We feel that the unusual facts surrounding this case require that it be distinguished from *Hoffman*. We do not rule that *Hoffman* is no longer the law, but obviously it must be considered in light of its facts and the characteristics of the time in which it was decided. Divorce rates, unfortunately, in our time have increased dramatically. Furthermore, even in a stable and healthy marriage, the residence and domicile of a wife are not necessarily the same as those of her husband. * * *

Residence in Michigan is defined as a place of abode accompanied with the intention to remain. *Hartzler v. Radeka*, 265 Mich. 451, 251 N.W. 554 (1933); *Reaume & Silloway, Inc. v. Tetzlaff*, 315 Mich. 95, 23 N.W.2d 219

(1946). Domicile and residence in Michigan are synonymous terms.[1] *Hartzler, supra,* and *Reaume & Silloway, supra.* Today in our mobile society physical presence for a longer period of time is no longer the key factor it once was.[2]

For many purposes, residence must be considered in light of a person's intent. *Grable v. City of Detroit*, 48 Mich. App. 368, 210 N.W.2d 379 (1973). Presence, abode, property ownership and other facts are often considered, yet intent is the key factor. This has been recognized in most jurisdictions and repeatedly cited. [Citations omitted.]][3]

The record amply supports plaintiff's claim that she did not abandon her Michigan residence and establish Kentucky as her place of residence. Plaintiff testified as follows:

"Q. *(by Mrs. Wright, plaintiff's attorney)* And would you tell the court how you happened to leave Michigan?

"A. On a reconciliation. We were going through a divorce proceeding, and we decided to try one more time, out of the state of Michigan. So we left and went to Kentucky because it was where Bob had always wanted to go, so I agreed Okay, fine.

"Q. Did you expect this reconciliation to work?

"A. No.

"Q. And how long after you got to Kentucky did you find that it was not working?

"A. I would say about two or three weeks, because there were things brought up that could not be forgotten about the past.

"Q. And why didn't you leave immediately?

"A. Well, as you know, there are four kids involved, and I couldn't just walk off on the kids and him."

Furthermore, plaintiff explained her reasons for not leaving Kentucky sooner than she did.

"Q. Did your husband ever beat you up?

"A. Yes.

---

[1] In 25 AM. JUR.2d, *Domicil*, §4, pp. 7–8, it was observed that:

"By comparison, domicil is said to be inclusive of residence, having a broader and more comprehensive meaning than residence. Residence, together with the requisite intent, is necessary to acquire domicil, but actual residence is not necessary to preserve a domicil after it is once acquired."

Recently, a Kentucky Court noted that while the term "residence" has a much narrower technical significance than the term "domicil", the two terms are almost universally used interchangeably. *St. John v. St. John*, 291 Ky. 363, 163 S.W.2d 820.

[2] The Minnesota Supreme Court recently noted:

"Domicile is the union of residence and intention, and residence without intention, or intention without residence, is of no avail. Mere change of residence, although continued for a long time, does not effect a change of domicile. 6A Dunnell, DIG. (3d ed.) §2816; *In re Estate of Smith*, 242 Minn. 85, 64 N.W.2d 129 (1954). Moreover, a domicile, once shown to exist, is presumed to continue until the contrary is shown. See, *Lusk v. Belote*, 22 Minn. 468 (1876)."

Davidner v. Davidner, 304 Minn. 491, ——, 232 N.W.2d 5, 7 (1975). This is particularly compelling because the Minnesota divorce statute contains a jurisdiction requirement which reads virtually the same as Michigan's, except that the period of time differs. 304 Minn. at ——, n.1, 232 N.W.2d at 6, n.1.

[3] The Iowa Supreme Court recently was faced with a problem concerning the change of domicile for divorce purposes and indicated:

"The change of a person's domicile is considered a serious matter. A domicile once acquired continues until a new one is perfected by the concurrence of three essential elements: (1) a definite abandonment of the former domicile; (2) actual removal to, and physical presence in the new domicile; (3) a bona fide intention to change and to remain in the new domicile permanently or indefinitely. * * *

"Domicile is largely a matter of intention, which must be freely and voluntarily exercised." (citations omitted)

Julson v. Julson, 255 Iowa 301, 122 N.W.2d 329, 331 (1963).

"Q. How many times?

"A. Once.

"Q. How badly did he beat you up?

"A. Well, it hurt. I tried to press charges, but I guess the police said it wasn't nothing too big.

"Q. Has he threatened to beat you up again?

"A. Oh, yes.

"Q. Did he threaten to beat you up in Kentucky?

"A. Yes, several times.

"Q. Did he threaten to bring suit against anyone here in Michigan?

"A. Yes.

"Q. Did he threaten to keep your baby from you?

"A. Yes.

"Q. And were you afraid that any or all of these things might happen?

"A. Yes.

"Q. Is that one of the reasons you didn't leave?

"A. Yes, it is.

"Q. Did you write your father you only wished you were brave enough to leave before you did?

"A. Yes, I did."

Plaintiff did not expect the reconciliation with her husband to be successful. Nevertheless, she made an effort. Almost immediately she discovered that the reconciliation would not work. Because of fear of harm to herself and fear of the loss of her child she was unable to return to Michigan. The trial court after a hearing on the matter made a proper finding. It is important to note that defendant did not testify at the hearing nor did he offer any other testimony which would contradict plaintiff's testimony. * * *

Affirmed.

Comments

In reconfirming the traditional position that jurisdiction in divorce proceedings is founded on domicile, *Sosna* mirrors a preference for social values that attach to persons who are settled firmly in one place. As noted in the dissenting opinion of Mr. Justices Marshall and Brennan, this value preference neglects the rights of recent immigrants and, implicitly, those aspects of American history that were based on large-scale migration of people. The views and interests of migratory persons tend to be underrepresented in the political process, especially on the state level where the policy considerations relating to jurisdiction in divorce matters are initiated. Yet lawyers are inevitably in contact with the flow of migration, regardless of stringent jurisdictional requirements of the courts. In fact, the more stringently the jurisdiction in divorce matters is perceived by local law, the more practicing lawyers will be concerned with finding solutions to the personal problems of their clients.

The group of persons neglected by the majority opinion in *Sosna* is large indeed. It includes all social strata of the population, from migrant workers and drifters to upper-class persons with multiple homes. The conception of domicile for jurisdictional purposes loses sight of persons in the military, in diplomacy, or in the employment of multinational corporations. As demonstrated by the facts of *Sosna* and *Leader*, it also neglects ordinary middle-class persons who get dislodged in the process of marital breakdown. *Sosna* takes the position that no denial of rights, but only a mere delay, is involved. Yet since the delay may involve a year or more of waiting out a statutory period of residence, lawyers will continue to try to find remedies for distraught clients who want to terminate their marriages and begin a new life in a new location.

The U.S. Supreme Court in *Sosna* falls short of establishing domicile as a due process requirement of jurisdiction in divorce matters. It merely holds that a state may reasonably be justified in requiring domicile and a one-year residence for those seeking a divorce. It also continues the theory that divorce actions are not transitory in nature but relate to a marital *res*. Yet in so holding the majority opinion fails to recognize fundamental changes in the law of marriage and divorce that have taken place. The jurisdictional requirement of domicile, enforced by statutory periods of residence, was meant to protect the interest of the state in marriage. Similarly the requirement that parties to a marriage may not agree to its dissolution, but must comply with statutory grounds, was meant to protect the state's interest. Yet with the adoption of no-fault divorce, much of the state's control over marriage was surrendered to the parties and their lawyers. Although lingering conceptions of fault and efforts of courts to reassert at least some of their powers show that this process of relinquishment is not yet complete, nonetheless it is evident that the state's interest in marriage and divorce is waning.

When it is no longer necessary to migrate to other jurisdictions to obtain divorces easily, the concern with domicile and residence periods for jurisdictional purposes loses much of its persuasive power. Iowa was one of the first jurisdictions adopting no-fault divorce and, at the time, may indeed have had an interest in retaining the one-year residence requirement for purposes of discouraging persons from elsewhere from seeking divorces in Iowa. With no-fault divorce available in most states, the reasons for stringent jurisdictional requirements have been weakened. This development illustrates the interdependence of procedure and substance, that is, the functional relation between jurisdictional requirements of domicile and substantive needs to establish fault.

A legal development in flux necessarily incorporates the old and the new conceptions. It provides strong stimuli to legal practice because the inherent strains must be resolved in individual cases as well as in the law. The lawyer who is in the middle of this evolution must know both where it came from and where it leads to. In other words, he must be equally versed in the traditional jurisdictional requirements and in the new conceptions that slowly take shape in a process of decisions. To the extent that jurisdiction and fault in divorce proceedings were meant to protect proprietary rights, lawyers have the choice of applying traditional reasoning or developing new alternatives, as the case may be.

References

Cromley, *Home Is Where I Hang My Divorce Decree: A Critical Appraisal of Sosna v. Iowa*, 12 CAL. W.L. REV. 452 (1976).
Garfield, *The Transitory Divorce Action: Jurisdiction in the No-Fault Era*, 58 TEX. L. REV. 501 (1980).
Stimson, *Jurisdiction in Divorce Cases: The Unsoundness of the Domiciliary Theory*, 42 A.B.A. J. 222 (1956).
Weintraub, *An Inquiry Into the Utility of "Domicile" as a Concept in Conflict Analysis*, 63 MICH. L. REV. 961 (1965).

Full Faith and Credit and Comity

Domestic Cases

Williams v. State of North Carolina [I]

United States Supreme Court

317 U.S. 287 (1942)

Mr. Justice DOUGLAS delivered the opinion of the Court.
Petitioners were tried and convicted of bigamous cohabitation under §4342 of the North Carolina Code, 1939, and each was sentenced for a term of years to a state prison. The judgment of conviction was affirmed by the Supreme Court of North Carolina. 220 N.C. 445, 17 S.E.2d 769. The case is here on certiorari. [Citations omitted.]
Petitioner Williams was married to Carrie Wyke in 1916 in North Carolina and lived with her there until May, 1940. Petitioner Hendrix was married to Thomas Hendrix in 1920 in North Carolina and lived with him there until May, 1940. At that time petitioners went to Las Vegas, Nevada and on June 26, 1940, each filed a divorce action in the Nevada court. The defendants in those divorce actions entered no appearance nor were they served with process in Nevada. In the case of defendant Thomas Hendrix service by publication was had by publication of the summons in a Las Vegas newspaper and by mailing a copy of the summons and complaint to his last post office address. In the case of defendant Carrie Williams a North Carolina sheriff delivered to her in North Carolina a copy of the summons and complaint. A decree of divorce was granted petitioner Williams by the Nevada court on August 26, 1940, on the grounds of extreme cruelty, the court finding that "the plaintiff has been and now is a bona fide and continuous resident of the County of Clark, State of Nevada, and had been such resident for more than six weeks immediately preceding the commencement of this action in the manner prescribed by law". The Nevada court granted petitioner Hendrix a divorce on October 4, 1940, on the grounds of wilful neglect and extreme cruelty and made the same finding as to this petitioner's bona fide residence in Nevada as it made in the case of Williams. Petitioners were married to each other in Nevada on October 4, 1940. Thereafter they re-

turned to North Carolina where they lived together until the indictment was returned. Petitioners pleaded not guilty and offered in evidence exemplified copies of the Nevada proceedings, contending that the divorce decrees and the Nevada marriage were valid in North Carolina as well as in Nevada. The State contended that since neither of the defendants in the Nevada actions was served in Nevada nor entered an appearance there, the Nevada decrees would not be recognized as valid in North Carolina. On this issue the court charged the jury in substance that a Nevada divorce decree based on substituted service where the defendant made no appearance would not be recognized in North Carolina under the rule of *Pridgen v. Pridgen*, 203 N.C. 533, 166 S.E. 591. The State further contended that petitioners went to Nevada not to establish a bona fide residence but solely for the purpose of taking advantage of the laws of that State to obtain a divorce through fraud upon that court. On that issue the court charged the jury that under the rule of *State v. Herron*, 175 N.C. 754, 94 S.E. 698, the defendants had the burden of satisfying the jury, but not beyond a reasonable doubt, of the bona fides of their residence in Nevada for the required time. Petitioners excepted to these charges. The Supreme Court of North Carolina in affirming the judgment held that North Carolina was not required to recognize the Nevada decrees under the full faith and credit clause of the Constitution (Art. IV, §1) by reason of *Haddock v. Haddock*, 201 U.S. 562, 26 S. Ct. 525, 50 L.Ed. 867, * * *.

* * * Accordingly, we cannot avoid meeting the *Haddock v. Haddock* issue in this case by saying that the petitioners acquired no bona fide domicil in Nevada. If the case had been tried and submitted on that issue only, we would have quite a different problem, * * *. We have no occasion to meet that issue now and we intimate no opinion on it. However it might be resolved in another proceeding, we cannot evade the constitutional issue in this case on the easy assumption that petitioners' domicil in Nevada was a sham and a fraud. Rather we must treat the present case for the purpose of the limited issue before us precisely the same as if petitioners had resided in Nevada for a term of years and had long ago acquired a permanent abode there. In other words, we would reach the question whether North Carolina could refuse to recognize the Nevada decrees because in its view and contrary to the findings of the Nevada court petitioners had no actual, bona fide domicil in Nevada, if and only if we concluded that *Haddock v. Haddock* was correctly decided. But we do not think it was.

The *Haddock* case involved a suit for separation and alimony brought in New York by the wife on personal service of the husband. The husband pleaded in defense a divorce decree obtained by him in Connecticut where he had established a separate domicil. This Court held that New York, the matrimonial domicil where the wife still resided, need not give full faith and credit to the Connecticut decree, since it was obtained by the husband who wrongfully left his wife in the matrimonial domicil, service on her having been obtained by publication and she not having entered an appearance in the action. But we do not agree with the theory of the *Haddock* case that, so far as the marital status of the parties is concerned, a decree of divorce granted under such circumstances by one state need not be given full faith and credit in another.

Article IV, §1 of the Constitution not only directs that "Full Faith and Credit shall be given in each State to the public Acts, Records, and Judicial Proceedings of every other State" but also provides that "Congress may by general Laws prescribe the Manner in which such Acts, Records and Proceedings shall be proved, and the Effect thereof." Congress has exercised that power. By the Act of May 26, 1790, c. 11, 28 U.S.C. §687, 28 U.S.C.A. §687, Congress has provided that judgments "shall have such faith and credit given to them in every court within the United States as they have by law or usage in the courts of the State from which they are taken." * * *

* * *
The historical view that a proceeding for a divorce was a proceeding *in rem* (2 Bishop, MARRIAGE & DIVORCE, 4th Ed., §164) was rejected by the *Haddock* case. We likewise agree that it does not aid in the solution of the problem presented by this case to label these proceedings as proceedings *in rem*. Such a suit, however, is not a mere in personam action. Domicil of the plaintiff, immaterial to jurisdiction in a personal action, is recognized in the *Haddock* case and elsewhere (Beale, CONFLICT OF LAWS, §110.1) as essential in order to give the court jurisdiction which will entitle the divorce decree to extraterritorial effect, at least when the defendant has neither been personally served nor entered an appearance. The findings made in the divorce decrees in the instant case must be treated on the issue before us as meeting those requirements. For it seems clear that the provision of the Nevada statute that a plaintiff in this type of case must "reside" in the State for the required period requires him to have a domicil as distinguished from a mere residence in the state. *Latterner v. Latterner*, 51 Nev. 285, 274 P. 194; *Lamb v. Lamb*, 57 Nev. 421, 65 P.2d 872. Hence the decrees in this case like other divorce decrees are more than in personam judgments. They involve the marital status of the parties. Domicil creates a relationship to the state which is adequate for numerous exercises of state power. [Citations omitted.] Each state as a sovereign has a rightful and legitimate concern in the marital status of persons domiciled within its borders. The marriage relation creates problems of large social importance. Protection of offspring, property interests, and the enforcement of marital responsibilities are but a few of commanding problems in the field of domestic relations with which the state must deal. Thus it is plain that each state by virtue of its command over its domiciliaries and its large interest in the institution of marriage can alter within its own borders the marriage status of the spouse domiciled there, even though the other spouse is absent. There is no constitutional barrier if the form and nature of the substituted service (see *Milliken v. Meyer, supra*, 311 U.S. at page 463, 61 S. Ct. at page 342, 85 L.Ed. 278, 132 A.L.R. 1357) meet the requirements of due process. [Citations omitted.]

Accordingly it was admitted in the *Haddock* case that the divorce decree though not recognized in New York was binding on both spouses in Connecticut where granted. * * * It therefore follows that, if the Nevada decrees are taken at their full face value (as they must be on the phase of the case with which we are presently concerned), they were wholly effective to change in that state the marital status of the petitioners and each of the other spouses by the North Carolina marriages. Apart from the requirements of procedural due process [citations omitted.] not challenged here by North Carolina, no reason based on the Federal Constitution has been advanced for the contrary conclusion. But the concession that the decrees were effective in Nevada makes more compelling the reasons for rejection of the theory and result of the *Haddock* case.

This Court stated in *Atherton v. Atherton, supra*, 181 U.S. at page 162, 21 S. Ct. at page 547, 45 L.Ed. 794, that "A husband without a wife, or a wife without a husband, is unknown to the law." But if one is lawfully divorced and remarried in Nevada and still married to the first spouse in North Carolina, an even more complicated and serious condition would be realized. We would then have what the Supreme Court of Illinois declared to be the "most perplexing and distressing complication in the domestic relations of many citizens in the different states." *Dunham v. Dunham*, 162 Ill. 589, 607, 44 N.E. 841, 847, 35 L.R.A. 70. Under the circumstances of this case, a man would have two wives, a wife two husbands. The reality of a sentence to prison proves that that is no mere play on words. Each would be a bigamist for living in one state with the only one with whom the other state would permit him lawfully to live. Children of the second marriage would be bastards in one state but legitimate in the other. And all that would flow from the legalistic notion that where one spouse is wrongfully deserted he retains power over the matrimonial domicil so that the domicil of the other spouse follows him wherever he may go, while if he is to blame, he retains no such power. But such considerations are inapposite. As stated by Mr. Justice Holmes in his dissent in the *Haddock* case, 201 U.S. at page 630, 26 S. Ct. at page 552, 50 L.Ed. 867, 5 Ann. Cas. 1, they constitute a "pure fiction, and fiction always is a poor ground for changing substantial rights." Furthermore, the fault or wrong of one spouse in leaving the other becomes under that view a jurisdictional fact on which this Court would ultimately have to pass. Whatever may be said as to the practical effect which such a rule would have in clouding divorce decrees, the question as to where the fault lies has no relevancy to the existence of state power in such circumstances. See Bingham, *In the Matter of Haddock v. Haddock*, 21 Corn. L.Q. 393, 426. The existence of the power of a state to alter the marital status of its domiciliaries, as distinguished from the wisdom of its exercise, is not dependent on the underlying causes of the domestic rift. As we have said, it is dependent on the relationship which domicil creates and the pervasive control which a state has over marriage and divorce within its own borders. *Atherton v. Atherton*, which preceded *Haddock v. Haddock*, and *Thompson v. Thompson*, 226 U.S. 551, 33 S. Ct. 129, 57 L.Ed. 347, which followed it, recognized that the power of the state of the matrimonial domicil to grant a divorce from the absent spouse did not depend on whether his departure from the state was or was not justified. As stated above, we see no reason, and none has here been advanced, for making the existence of state power depend on an inquiry as to where the fault in each domestic dispute lies. And it is difficult to pick out any such line of distinction in the generality of the words of the full faith and credit clause. Moreover, so far as state power is concerned no distinction between a matrimonial domicil and a domicil later acquired has been suggested or is apparent. See Mr. Justice Holmes dissenting, *Haddock v. Haddock, supra,* 201 U.S. at page 631, 26 S. Ct. at page 552, 50 L.Ed. 867, 5 Ann. Cas. 1; Goodrich, *Matrimonial Domicile,* 27 Yale L. Journ. 49. It is one thing to say as a matter of state law that jurisdiction to grant a divorce from an absent spouse should depend on whether by consent or by conduct the latter has subjected his interest in the marriage status to the law of the separate domicil acquired by the other spouse. Beale, Conflict of Laws, §113.11; Restatement, Conflict of Laws, §113. But where a state adopts, as it has the power to do, a less strict rule, it is quite another thing to say that its decrees affecting the marital status of its domiciliaries are not entitled to full faith and credit in sister states. Certainly if decrees of a state altering the marital status of its domiciliaries are not valid throughout the Union even though the requirements of procedural due process are wholly met, a rule would be fostered which could not help but bring "considerable disaster to innocent persons" and "bastardize children hitherto supposed to be the offspring of lawful marriage," (Mr. Justice Holmes dissenting in *Haddock v. Haddock, supra,* 201 U.S. at page 628, 26 S. Ct. at page 551, 50 L.Ed. 867, 5 Ann. Cas. 1), or else encourage collusive divorces. Beale, *Constitutional Protection of Decrees for Divorce,* 19 Harv. L. Rev. 586, 596. These intensely practical considerations emphasize for us the essential function of the full faith and credit clause in substituting a command for the former principles of comity [citations omitted] and in altering the "status of the several states as independent foreign sovereignties" by making them "integral parts of a single nation." *Milwaukee County v. M.E. White Co., supra,* 296 U.S. at page 277, 56 S. Ct. at page 234, 80 L.Ed. 220.

It is objected, however, that if such divorce decrees must be given full faith and credit, a substantial dilution of the sovereignty of other states will be effected. For it is pointed out that under such a rule one state's policy of strict control over the institution of marriage could be thwarted by the decree of a more lax state. But such an objection goes to the application of the full faith and credit clause to many situations. It is an objection in varying degrees of intensity to the enforcement of a judgment of a sister state based on a cause of action which could not be enforced in the state of the forum. Mississippi's policy against gambling transactions was overriden in *Fauntleroy v. Lum, supra,* when a Missouri judgment based on such a Mississippi contract was enforced by this Court. Such is part of the price of our federal system.

This Court, of course, is the final arbiter when the question is raised as to what is a permissible limitation on the full faith and credit clause. [Citations omitted.]

But the question for us is a limited one. In the first place, we repeat that in this case we must assume that petitioners had a bona fide domicil in Nevada, not that the Nevada domicil was a sham. We thus have no question on the present record whether a divorce decree granted by the courts of one state to a resident as distinguished from a domiciliary is entitled to full faith and credit in another state. Nor do we reach here the question as to the power of North Carolina to refuse full faith and credit to Nevada divorce decrees because, contrary to the findings of the Nevada court, North Carolina finds that no bona fide domicil was acquired in Nevada. In the second place, the question as to what is a permissible limitation on the full faith and credit clause does not involve a decision on our part as to which state policy on divorce is the more desirable one. It does not involve selection of a rule which will encourage on the one hand or discourage on the other the practice of divorce. That choice in the realm of morals and religion rests with the legislatures of the states. Our own views as to the marriage institution and the avenues of escape which some states have created are immaterial. It is a Constitution which we are expounding—a Constitution which in no small measure brings separate sovereign states into an integrated whole through the medium of the full faith and credit clause. Within the limits of her political power North Carolina may, of course, enforce her own policy regarding the marriage relation—an institution more basic in our civilization than any other. But society also has an interest in the avoidance of polygamous marriages [citations omitted] and in the protection of innocent offspring of marriages deemed legitimate in other jurisdictions. And other states have an equally legitimate concern in the status of persons domiciled there as respects the institution of marriage. So when a court of one state acting in accord with the requirements of procedural due process alters the marital status of one domiciled in that state by granting him a divorce from his absent spouse, we cannot say its decree should be excepted from the full faith and credit clause merely because its enforcement or recognition in another state would conflict with the policy of the latter. * * *

Haddock v. Haddock is overruled. The judgment is reversed and the cause is remanded to the Supreme Court of North Carolina for proceedings not inconsistent with this opinion.

* * *

Mr. Justice FRANKFURTER, concurring.

* * *

Article 91 of the British North America Act (1867) gives the Parliament of Canada exclusive legislative authority to deal with marriage and divorce. Similarly, Article 51 of the Australia Constitution Act (1900) empowers the Commonwealth Parliament to make laws with respect to marriage and divorce. The Constitution of the United States, however, reserves authority over marriage and divorce to each of the forty-eight states. That is our starting-point. In a country like ours where each state has the constitutional power to translate into law its own notions of policy concerning the family institution, and where citizens pass freely from one state to another, tangled marital situations, like the one immediately before us, inevitably arise. They arose before and after the decision in the *Haddock* case, 201 U.S. 562, 26 S. Ct. 525, 50 L.Ed. 867, 5 Ann. Cas. 1, and will, I daresay, continue to arise no matter what we do today. For these complications cannot be removed by any decisions this Court can make—neither the crudest nor the subtlest juggling of legal concepts could enable us to bring forth a uniform national law of marriage and divorce.

* * *

There is but one respect in which this Court can, within its traditional authority and professional competence, contribute uniformity to the law of marriage and divorce, and that is to enforce respect for the judgment of a state by its sister states when the judgment was rendered in accordance with settled procedural standards. As the Court's opinion shows, it is clearly settled that if a judgment is binding in the state where it was rendered, it is equally binding in every other state. * * *

The duty of a state to respect the judgments of a sister state arises only where such judgments meet the tests of justice and fair dealing that are embodied in the historic phrase, "due process of law." But in this case all talk about due process is beside the mark. If the actions of the Nevada court had been taken "without due process of law," the divorces which it purported to decree would have been without legal sanction in every state including Nevada. There would be no occasion to consider the applicability of the Full Faith and Credit Clause. It is precisely because the Nevada decrees do satisfy the requirements of the Due Process Clause and are binding in Nevada upon the absent spouses that we are called upon to decide whether these judgments, unassailable in the state which rendered them, are, despite the commands of the Full Faith and Credit Clause, null and void elsewhere.

* * *

For all but a very small fraction of the community the niceties of resolving such conflicts among the laws of the states are, in all likelihood, matters of complete indifference. Our occasional pronouncements upon the requirements of the Full Faith and Credit Clause doubtless have little effect upon divorces. Be this as it may, a court is likely to lose its way if it strays outside the modest bounds of its own special competence and turns the duty of adjudicating only the legal phases of a broad social problem into an opportunity for formulating judgments of social policy quite beyond its competence as well as its authority.

Mr. Justice MURPHY, dissenting.

I dissent because the Court today introduces an undesirable rigidity in the application of the Full Faith and Credit Clause to a problem which is of acute interest to all the states of the Union and on which they hold varying and sharply divergent views, the problem of how they shall treat the marriage relation.

* * *

In recognition of the paramount interest of the state of domicile over the marital status of its citizens, this Court has held that actual good faith domicile of at least one party is essential to confer authority and jurisdiction on the courts of a state to render a decree of divorce that will be entitled to extraterritorial effect under the Full Faith and Credit Clause [citations omitted], even though both parties personally appear [citations omitted]. When the doctrine of those cases is applied to the facts of this one, the question becomes a simple one: Did petitioners acquire a bona fide domicil in Nevada? I agree with my brother Jackson that the only proper answer on the record is, no. North Carolina is the state in which petitioners have their roots, the state to which they immediately returned after a brief absence just sufficient to achieve their purpose under Nevada's requirements. It follows that the Nevada decrees are entitled to no extraterritorial effect when challenged in another state. [Citations omitted.]

This is not to say that the Nevada decrees are without any legal effect in the State of Nevada. That question is not before us. It may be that for the purposes of that state the petitioners have been released from their marital vows, consistently with the procedural requirements of the Fourteenth Amendment, on the basis of compliance with its residential requirements and constructive service of process on the non-resident spouses. But conceding the validity in Nevada of its decrees dissolving the marriages, it does not mechanically follow that the Full Faith and Credit Clause compels North Carolina to accept them.

We have recognized an area of flexibility in the application of the Clause to preserve and protect state policies in matters of vital public concern.* * *

Prominent in the residuum of state power, as pointed out above, is the right of a state to deal with the marriage relations of its citizens and to pursue its chosen domestic policy of public morality in that connection. Both Nevada and North Carolina have rights in this regard which are entitled to recognition. The conflict between those rights here should not be resolved by extending into North Carolina the effects of Nevada's action through a perfunctory application of the literal language of the Full Faith and Credit Clause with the result that measures which North Carolina has adopted to safeguard the welfare of her citizens in this area of legitimate governmental concern are undermined. * * *

There is an element of tragic incongruity in the fact that an individual may be validly divorced in one state but not in another. But our dual system of government and the fact that we have no uniform laws on many subjects give rise to other incongruities as well—for example the common law took the logical position that an individual could have but one domicile at a time but this Court has nevertheless said that the Full Faith and Credit Clause does not prevent conflicting state decisions on the question of an individual's domicile. [Citations omitted.] In the absence of a uniform law on the subject of divorce this Court is not so limited in its application of the Full Faith and Credit Clause that it must force Nevada's policy upon North Carolina, any more than it must compel Nevada to accept North Carolina's requirements. The fair result is to leave each free to regulate within its own area the rights of its own citizens.

Mr. Justice JACKSON, dissenting.

I cannot join in exerting the judicial power of the Federal Government to compel the State of North Carolina to subordinate its own law to the Nevada divorce decrees. The Court's decision to do so reaches far beyond the immediate case. It subjects matrimonial laws of each state to important limitations and exceptions that it must recognize within its own borders and as to its own permanent population. It nullifies the power of each state to protect its own citizens against dissolution of their marriages by the courts of other states which have an easier system of divorce. It subjects every marriage to a new infirmity in that one dissatisfied spouse may choose a state of easy divorce, in which neither party has ever lived, and there commence proceedings without personal service of process. * * * To declare that a state is powerless to protect either its own policy or the family rights of its people against such consequences has serious constitutional implications. It is not an exaggeration to say that this decision repeals the divorce laws of all the states and substitutes the law of Nevada as to all marriages one of the parties to which can afford a short trip there. The significance of this decision is best appraised by orienting its facts with reference to the States involved, for the Court approves this concrete case as a pattern which anybody in any state may henceforth follow under the protection of the federal courts.

From the viewpoint of North Carolina, this is the situation: The Williamses, North Carolina people, were married in North Carolina, lived there twenty-five years, and have four children. The Hendrixes were also married in North Carolina and resided there some twenty years. In May of 1940, Mr.

Williams and Mrs. Hendrix left their homes and respective spouses, departed the state, but after an absence of a few weeks reappeared and set up housekeeping as husband and wife. North Carolina then had on its hands three marriages among four people in the form of two broken families, and one going concern. What problems were thereby created as to property or support and maintenance, we do not know. North Carolina, for good or ill, has a strict policy as to divorce. The situation is contrary to its laws, and it has attempted to vindicate its own law by convicting the parties of bigamy. * * * We turn to Nevada for that part of the episode.

Williams and Mrs. Hendrix appear in the State of Nevada on May 15, 1940. For barely six weeks they made their residences at the Alamo Auto Court on the Las Vegas—Los Angeles Road. On June 26, 1940, both filed bills of complaint for divorce through the same lawyer, and alleging almost identical grounds. No personal service was made on the home-staying spouse in either case; and service was had only by publication and substituted service. Both obtained divorce decrees. The Nevada policy of divorce is reflected in Mrs. Hendrix's case. Her grounds were "extreme mental cruelty." She sustained them by testifying that her husband was "moody"; did not talk or speak to her "often"; when she spoke to him he answered most of the time by a nod or shake of the head and "there was nothing cheerful about him at all." The latter of the two divorces was granted on October 4, 1940, and on that day in Nevada they had benefit of clergy and emerged as man and wife. Nevada having served its purpose in their affairs, they at once returned to North Carolina to live.

The question is whether this Court will now prohibit North Carolina from enforcing its own policy within that State against these North Carolinians on the ground that the law of Nevada under which they lived a few weeks is in some way projected into North Carolina to give them immunity.

* * *

The framers of the Constitution did not lay down rules to guide us in selecting which of two conflicting state judgments or public acts would receive federal aid in its extraterritorial enforcement. Nor was it necessary. There was, and is, an adequate body of law, if we do not reject it, by which to test jurisdiction or power to render the judgments in question so far as faith and credit by federal command is concerned. By the application of well established rules these judgments fail to merit enforcement for two reasons.

Lack of Due Process of Law

* * *

The opinion concedes that Nevada's judgment could not be forced upon North Carolina in absence of personal service if a divorce proceeding were an action in personam. In other words, settled family relationships may be destroyed by a procedure that we would not recognize if the suit were one to collect a grocery bill.

We have been told that this is because divorce is a proceeding *in rem*. The marriage relation is to be reified and treated as a *res*. Then it seems that this *res* follows a fugitive from matrimony into a state of easy divorce, although the other party to it remains at home where the *res* was contracted and where years of cohabitation would seem to give it local situs. Would it be less logical to hold that the continued presence of one party to a marriage gives North Carolina power to protect the *res*, the marriage relation, than to hold that the transitory presence of one gives Nevada power to destroy it? Counsel at the bar met this dilemma by suggesting that the *res* exists in duplicate—one for each party to the marriage. But this seems fatal to the decree, for if that is true the dissolution of the *res* in transit would hardly operate to dissolve the *res* that stayed in North Carolina. Of course this discussion is only to reveal the artificial and fictional character of the whole doctrine of a *res* as applied to a divorce action.

I doubt that it promotes clarity of thinking to deal with marriage in terms of a *res,* like a piece of land or a chattel. It might be more helpful to think of marriage as just marriage—a relationship out of which spring duties to both spouse and society and from which are derived rights,—such as the right to society and services and to conjugal love and affection—rights which generally prove to be either priceless or worthless, but which nonetheless the law sometimes attempts to evaluate in terms of money when one is deprived of them by the negligence or design or a third party.

It does not seem consistent with our legal system that one who has these continuing rights should be deprived of them without a hearing. Neither does it seem that he or she should be summoned by mail, publication, or otherwise to a remote jurisdiction chosen by the other party and there be obliged to submit marital rights to adjudication under a state policy at odds with that of the state under which the marriage was contracted and the matrimonial domicile was established.

Marriage is often dealt with as a contract. Of course a personal judgment could not be rendered against an absent party on a cause of action arising out of an ordinary commercial contract, without personal service of process. I see no reason why the marriage contract, if such it be considered, should be discriminated against, nor why a party to a marriage contract should be more vulnerable to a foreign judgment without process than a party to any other contract. I agree that the marriage contract is different, but I should think the difference would be in its favor.

* * *

* * * I cannot but think that in its pre-occupation with the full faith and credit clause the Court has slighted the due process clause.

Lack of Domicile

We should, I think, require that divorce judgments asking our enforcement under the full faith and credit clause, unlike judgments arising out of commercial transactions and the like, must also be supported by good-faith domicile of one of the parties within the judgment state. Such is certainly a reasonable requirement. A state can have no legitimate concern with the matrimonial status of two persons, neither of whom lives within its territory.

The Court would seem, indeed, to pay lip service to this principle. I understand the holding to be that it is domicile in Nevada that gave power to proceed without personal service of process. That being the course of reasoning, I do not see how we avoid the issue concerning the existence of the domicile which the facts on the face of this record put to us. Certainly we cannot, as the Court would, by-pass the matter by saying that "We must treat the present case for the purpose of the limited issue before us precisely the same as if petitioners had resided in Nevada for a term of years and had long ago acquired a permanent abode there." I think we should treat it as if they had done just what they have done.

The only suggestion of a domicile within Nevada was a stay of about six weeks at the Alamo Auto Court, an address hardly suggestive of permanence. Mrs. Hendrix testified in her case (the evidence in Williams' case is not before us) that her residence in Nevada was "indefinite permanent" in character. The Nevada court made no finding that the parties had a "domicile" there. It only found a residence—sometimes, but not necessarily, an equivalent. It is this Court that accepts these facts as enough to establish domicile.

While a state can no doubt set up its own standards of domicile as to its internal concerns, I do not think it can require us to accept and in the name of the Constitution impose them on other states. If Nevada may prescribe six weeks of indefinite permanent abode in a motor court as constituting domicile, she may as readily prescribe six days. Indeed, if the Court's opinion is carried to its logical conclusion, a state could grant a constructive domicile for divorce purposes upon the filing of some sort of declaration of intention. Then it would follow that we would be required to accept it as sufficient and to force all states to recognize mailorder divorces as well as tourist divorces. Indeed, the difference is in the bother and expense—not in the principle of the thing.

The concept of domicile as a controlling factor in choice of law to govern many relations of the individual was well known to the framers of the Constitution. It was hardly contemplated that a person should be subject at once to two conflicting state policies, such as those of Nevada and North Carolina. It was undoubtedly expected that the Court would in many cases of conflict use one's domicile as an appropriate guide in selecting the law to govern his controversies.

Domicile means a relationship between a person and a locality. It is the place, and the one place, where he has his roots and his real permanent home. The Fourteenth Amendment, in providing that one by residence in a state becomes a citizen thereof, probably used "residence" as synonymous with domicile. Thus domicile fixes the place where one belongs in our federal system. In some instances the existence of this relationship between the state and an individual may be a federal question, although this Court has been reluctant to accept that view.

If in testing this judgment to determine whether it qualifies for federal enforcement we should apply the doctrine of domicile to interpretation of the full faith and credit clause, Nevada would be held to a duty to respect the statutes of North Carolina and not to interfere with their application to those whose individual as well as matrimonial domicile is within that state unless and until that domicile has been terminated. And North Carolina would not be required to yield its policy as to persons resident there except upon a showing that Nevada had acquired a domiciliary right to redefine the matrimonial status.

* * *

In the application of the full faith and credit clause to the variety of circumstances that arise when families break up and separate domiciles are established there are, I grant, many areas of great difficulty. But I cannot believe that we are justified in making a demoralizing decision in order to avoid making difficult ones.

* * *

The Court advances two "intensely practical considerations" in support of its present decision. One is the "complicated and serious condition" if "one is lawfully divorced and remarried in Nevada and still married to the first spouse in North Carolina." This of course begs the question, for the divorces were completely ineffectual for any purpose relevant to this case. I agree that it is serious if a Nevada court without jurisdiction for divorce purports to say that the sojourn of two spouses gives four spouses rights to acquire four more, but I think it far more serious to force North Carolina to acquiesce in any such proposition. The other consideration advanced is that if the Court doesn't enforce divorces such as these it will, as it puts it, "bastardize" children of the divorcees. When thirty-seven years ago Mr. Justice Holmes perpetrated this quip, it had point, for the Court was then holding divorces invalid which many, due to the confused state of the law, had thought to be good. It is difficult to find that it has point now that the shoe is on the other foot. In any event I had supposed that our judicial responsibility is for the regularity of the law, not for the regularity of pedigrees.

Williams v. State of North Carolina [II]
United States Supreme Court
325 U.S. 226 (1945)

Mr. Justice FRANKFURTER delivered the opinion of the Court.

This case is here to review judgments of the Supreme Court of North Carolina, affirming convictions for bigamous cohabitation, assailed on the ground that full faith and credit, as required by the Constitution of the United States, was not accorded divorces decreed by one of the courts of Nevada. *Williams v. North Carolina,* 317 U.S. 287, 63 S. Ct. 207, 87 L.Ed. 279, 143 A.L.R. 1273, decided an earlier aspect of the controversy. It was there held that a divorce granted by Nevada, on a finding that one spouse was domiciled in Nevada, must be respected in North Carolina, where Nevada's finding of domicil was not questioned though the other spouse had neither appeared nor been served with process in Nevada and though recognition of such a divorce offended the policy of North Carolina. The record then before us did not present the question whether North Carolina had the power "to refuse full faith and credit to Nevada divorce decrees because, contrary to the findings of the Nevada court, North Carolina finds that no bona fide domicil was acquired in Nevada." *Williams v. North Carolina, supra,* 317 U.S. at page 302, 63 S. Ct. at page 215, 87 L.Ed. 279, 143 A.L.R. 1273. This is the precise issue which has emerged after retrial of the cause following our reversal. Its obvious importance brought the case here. [Citations omitted.]

* * *

* * * A judgment in one State is conclusive upon the merits in every other State, but only if the court of the first State had power to pass on the merits—had jurisdiction, that is, to render the judgment.

"It is too late now to deny the right collaterally to impeach a decree of divorce made in another state, by proof that the court had no jurisdiction, even when the record purports to show jurisdiction * * *." It was "too late" more than forty years ago. *German Savings & Loan Society v. Dormitzer,* 192 U.S. 125, 128, 24 S. Ct. 221, 222, 48 L.Ed. 373.

Under our system of law, judicial power to grant a divorce—jurisdiction, strictly speaking—is founded on domicil. [Citations omitted.] The framers of the Constitution were familiar with this jurisdictional prerequisite, and since 1789 neither this Court nor any other court in the English-speaking world has questioned it. Domicil implies a nexus between person and place of such permanence as to control the creation of legal relations and responsibilities of the utmost significance. The domicil of one spouse within a State gives power to that State, we have held, to dissolve a marriage wheresoever contracted. In view of *Williams v. North Carolina, supra,* the jurisdictional requirement of domicil is freed from confusing refinements about "matrimonial domicil," see *Davis v. Davis,* 305 U.S. 32, 41, 59 S. Ct. 3, 6, 83 L.Ed. 26, 118 A.L.R. 1518, and the like. Divorce, like marriage, is of concern not merely to the immediate parties. It affects personal rights of the deepest significance. It also touches basic interests of society. Since divorce, like marriage, creates a new status, every consideration of policy makes it desirable that the effect should be the same wherever the question arises.

It is one thing to reopen an issue that has been settled after appropriate opportunity to present their contentions has been afforded to all who had an interest in its adjudication. This applies also to jurisdictional questions. After a contest these cannot be relitigated as between the parties. [Citations omitted.] But those not parties to a litigation ought not to be foreclosed by the interested actions of others; especially not a State which is concerned with the vindication of its own social policy and has no means, certainly no effective means, to protect that interest against the selfish action of those outside its borders. The State of domiciliary origin should not be bound by an unfounded, even if not collusive, recital in the record of a court of another State. As to the truth or existence of a fact, like that of domicil, upon which depends the power to exert judicial authority, a State not a party to the exertion of such judicial authority in another State but seriously affected by it has a right, when asserting its own unquestioned authority, to ascertain the truth or existence of that crucial fact.

* * *

* * * In short, the decree of divorce is a conclusive adjudication of everything except the jurisdictional facts upon which it is founded, and domicil is a jurisdictional fact. To permit the necessary finding of domicil by one State to foreclose all States in the protection of their social institutions would be intolerable.

But to endow each State with controlling authority to nullify the power of a sister State to grant a divorce based upon a finding that one spouse had acquired a new domicil within the divorcing State would, in the proper functioning of our federal system, be equally indefensible. No State court can assume comprehensive attention to the various and potentially conflicting interests that several States may have in the institutional aspects of marriage. The necessary accommodation between the right of one State to safeguard its interest in the family relation of its own people and the power of another State to grant divorces can be left to neither State.

* * * The rights that belong to all the States and the obligations which membership in the Union imposes upon all, are made effective because this Court is open to consider claims, such as this case presents, that the courts of one State have not given the full faith and credit to the judgment of a sister State that is required by Art. IV, §1 of the Constitution.

* * *

What is immediately before us is the judgment of the Supreme Court of North Carolina. 224 N.C. 183, 29 S.E.2d 744. We have authority to upset it only if there is want of foundation for the conclusion that that Court reached. The conclusion it reached turns on its finding that the spouses who obtained the Nevada decrees were not domiciled there. The fact that the Nevada court found that they were domiciled there is entitled to respect, and more. The burden of undermining the verity which the Nevada decrees import rests heavily upon the assailant. But simply because the Nevada court found that it had power to award a divorce decree cannot, we have seen, foreclose reexamination by another State. Otherwise, as was pointed out long ago, a court's record would establish its power and the power would be proved by the record. Such circular reasoning would give one State a control over all the other States which the Full Faith and Credit Clause certainly did not confer. [Citations omitted.] If this Court finds that proper weight was accorded to the claims of power by the court of one State in rendering a judgment the validity of which is pleaded in defense in another State, that the burden of overcoming such respect by disproof of the substratum of fact—here domicil—on which such power alone can rest was properly charged against the party challenging the legitimacy of the judgment, that such issue of fact was left for fair determination by appropriate procedure, and that a finding adverse to the necessary foundation for any valid sister-State judgment was amply supported in evidence, we cannot upset the judgment before us. And we cannot do so even if we also found in the record of the court of original judgment warrant for its finding that it had jurisdiction. If it is a matter turning on local law, great deference is owed by the courts of one State to what a court of another State has done. [Citations omitted.] But when we are dealing as here with an historic notion common to all English-speaking courts, that of domicil, we should not find a want of deference to a sister State on the part of a court of another State which finds an absence of domicil where such a conclusion is warranted by the record.

When this case was first here, North Carolina did not challenge the finding of the Nevada court that petitioners had acquired domicils in Nevada. For her challenge of the Nevada decrees, North Carolina rested on *Haddock v. Haddock,* 201 U.S. 562, 26 S. Ct. 525, 50 L.Ed. 867, 5 Ann. Cas. 1. Upon retrial, however, the existence of domicil in Nevada became the decisive issue. The judgments of conviction now under review bring before us a record which may be fairly summarized by saying that the petitioners left North Carolina for the purpose of getting divorces from their respective spouses in Nevada and as soon as each had done so and married one another they left Nevada and returned to North Carolina to live there together as man and wife. Against the charge of bigamous cohabitation under §14-183 of the North Carolina General Statutes, petitioners stood on their Nevada divorces and offered exemplified copies of the Nevada proceedings. The trial judge charged that the State had the burden of proving beyond a reasonable doubt that (1) each petitioner was lawfully married to one person; (2) thereafter each petitioner contracted a second marriage with another person outside North Carolina; (3) the spouses of petitioners were living at the time of this second marriage; (4) petitioners cohabited with one another in North Carolina after the second marriage. The burden, it was charged, then devolved upon petitioners "to satisfy the trial jury, not beyond a reasonable doubt nor by the greater weight of the evidence, but simply to satisfy" the jury from all the evidence, that petitioners were domiciled in Nevada at the time they obtained their divorces. The court further charged that "the recitation" of bona fide domicil in the Nevada decree was "prima facie evidence" sufficient to warrant a finding of domicil in Nevada but not compelling "such an inference." If the jury found, as they were told, that petitioners had domicils in North Carolina and went to Nevada "simply and solely for the purpose of obtaining" divorces, intending to return to North Carolina on obtaining them, they never lost their North Carolina domicils nor acquired new domicils in Nevada. Domicil, the jury was instructed, was that place where a person "has voluntarily fixed his abode * * * not for a mere special or temporary purpose, but with a present intention of making it his home, either permanently or for an indefinite or unlimited length of time."

The scales of justice must not be unfairly weighted by a State when full faith and credit is claimed for a sister-State judgment. But North Carolina has not so dealt with the Nevada decrees. She has not raised unfair barriers to their recognition. North Carolina did not fail in appreciation or application of federal standards of full faith and credit. Appropriate weight was given to the finding of domicil in the Nevada decrees, and that finding was allowed to be overturned only by relevant standards of proof. There is nothing to suggest that the issue was not fairly submitted to the jury and that it was not fairly assessed on cogent evidence.

* * *

If a State cannot foreclose, on review here, all the other States by its finding that one spouse is domiciled within its bounds, persons may, no doubt, place themselves in situations that create unhappy consequences for them. This is merely one of those untoward results inevitable in a federal system in which regulation of domestic relations has been left with the States and not given to the national authority. But the occasional disregard by any one State of the reciprocal obligations of the forty-eight States to respect the constitutional power of each to deal with domestic relations of those domiciled within its borders is hardly an argument for allowing one State to deprive the other forty-seven States of their constitutional rights. Relevant statistics happily do not justify lurid forebodings that parents without number will disregard the fate of their offspring by being unmindful of the status of dignity to which they are entitled. But, in any event, to the extent that some one State may, for considerations of its own, improperly intrude into domestic relations subject to the authority of the other States, it suffices to suggest that any such indifference by a State to the bond of the Union should be discouraged not encouraged.

* * *

We conclude that North Carolina was not required to yield her State policy because a Nevada court found that petitioners were domiciled in Nevada when it granted them decrees of divorce. North Carolina was entitled to find, as she did, that they did not acquire domicils in Nevada and that the Nevada court was therefore without power to liberate the petitioners from amenability to the laws of North Carolina governing domestic relations. And, as was said in connection with another aspect of the Full Faith and Credit Clause, our conclusion "is not a matter to arouse the susceptibilities of the states, all of which are equally concerned in the question and equally on both sides." *Fauntleroy v. Lum*, 210 U.S. 230, 238, 28 S. Ct. 641, 643, 52 L.Ed. 1039.

* * *

Affirmed.

[Concurring opinion of Mr. Justice MURPHY omitted]

Mr. Justice RUTLEDGE, dissenting.

Once again the ghost of "unitary domicil" returns on its perpetual round, in the guise of "jurisdictional fact," to upset judgments, marriages, divorces, undermine the relations founded upon them, and make this Court the unwilling and uncertain arbiter between the concededly valid laws and decrees of sister states. From *Bell* and *Andrews* to *Davis* to *Haddock* to *Williams* and now back to *Haddock* and *Davis* through *Williams* again—is the maze the Court has travelled in a domiciliary wilderness, only to come out with no settled constitutional policy where one is needed most.

Nevada's judgment has not been voided. It could not be, if the same test applies to sustain it as upholds the North Carolina conviction.[2] It stands, with the marriages founded upon it, unimpeached. For all that has been determined or could be, unless another change is in the making, petitioners are lawful husband and wife in Nevada. *Williams v. North Carolina I*, 317 U.S. 287, 63 S. Ct. 207, 87 L.Ed. 279, 143 A.L.R. 1273; *Williams v. North Carolina II*, decided this day. They may be such everywhere outside North Carolina. Lawfully wedded also, in North Carolina, are the divorced spouse of one and his wife, taken for all we know in reliance upon the Nevada decree.[3] That is, unless another jury shall find they too are bigamists for their reliance. No such jury has been impanelled. But were one called, it could pronounce the Nevada decree valid upon the identical evidence from which the jury in this case drew the contrary conclusion. That jury or it and another, if petitioners had been tried separately, could have found one guilty, the other innocent, upon that evidence unvaried by a hair. And, by the Court's test, we could do nothing but sustain the contradictory findings in all these cases.

I do not believe the Constitution has thus confided to the caprice of juries the faith and credit due the laws and judgments of sister states. Nor has it

---

[2]Presumably it would be our function "to retry the facts" no more if the Nevada decree were immediately under challenge here than it is to do so when the North Carolina judgment is in issue. It would seem therefore that we owe the same deference to Nevada's finding of domicil as we do to North Carolina's. *Cf.* text at note 4 *et seq.*

[3]The record indicates that Mr. Hendrix "had brought no divorce proceeding against the feme defendant prior to the first trial of this cause, * * * but that he has since and remarried." Although the evidence shows institution of this proceeding, it does not show a decree was entered prior to his remarriage. Whether or not he actually relied upon the Nevada decree, thousands of spouses so divorced do so rely, thus founding new relations which are equally subject to invalidation by jury finding and are always beclouded by a judgment like that rendered in this case.

thus made that question a local matter for the states themselves to decide. Were all judgments given the same infirmity, the full faith and credit clause would be only a dead constitutional letter.

I agree it is not the Court's business to determine policies of divorce. But precisely its function is to lay the jurisdictional foundations upon which the states' determinations can be made effective, within and without their borders. For in the one case due process, in the other full faith and credit, commands of equal compulsion upon the estates and upon us, impose that duty.

I do not think we perform it, we rather abdicate, when we confide the ultimate decision to the states or to their juries. This we do when, for every case that matters, we make their judgment conclusive. It is so in effect when the crucial concept is as variable and amorphous as "domicil," is always a conclusion of "ultimate fact," and can be established only by proof from which, as experience shows, contradictory inferences may be made as strikes the local trier's fancy.* * *

* * *

Domicil, as a substantive concept, steadily reflects neither a policy of permanence nor one of transiency. It rather reflects both inconstantly. The very name gives forth the idea of home with all its ancient associations of permanence. But "home" in the modern world is often a trailer or a tourist camp. Automobiles, nation-wide business and multiple family dwelling units have deprived the institution, though not the idea, of its former general fixation to soil and locality. But, beyond this, "home" in the domiciliary sense can be changed in the twinkling of an eye, the time it takes a man to make up his mind to remain where he is when he is away from home. He need do no more than decide, by a flash of thought, to stay "either permanently or for an indefinite or unlimited length of time."[14] No other connection of permanence is required. All of his belongings, his business, his family, his established interests and intimate relations may remain where they have always been. Yet if he is but physically present elsewhere, without even bag or baggage, and undergoes the mental flash, in a moment he has created a new domicil though hardly a new home.

Domicil thus combines the essentially contradictory elements of permanence and instantaneous change. No legal conception, save possibly "jurisdiction," of which it is an elusive substratum, affords such possibilities for uncertain application. The only thing certain about it, beyond its uncertainty, is that one must travel to change his domicil. But he may travel without changing it, even remain for a lifetime in his new place of abode without doing so. Apart from the necessity for travel, hardly evidentiary of stabilized relationship in a transient age, the criterion comes down to a purely subjective mental state, related to remaining for a length of time never yet defined with clarity.

With the crux of power fixed in such a variable, small wonder that the states vacillate in applying it and this Court ceaselessly seeks without finding a solution for its quandary. But not all the vice lies in the substantive conception. Only lawyers know, unless now it is taxpayers and persons divorced, how rambling is the scope of facts from which proof is ever drawn to show and negate the ultimate conclusion of subjective "fact." They know, as do the courts and other tribunals which wrestle with the problem, how easily facts procreative of conflicting inferences may be marshalled and how conjectural is the outcome. There is no greater legal gamble. Rare is the situation, where much is at stake, in which conflicting circumstances cannot be shown and where accordingly conflicting ultimate inferences cannot be drawn.

* * *

---

[14]Citation of authority is hardly needed for reference to the difficulties courts have encountered in the effort to define this intent. "Animus manendi" is often a Latin refuge which succeeds only in evading not in resolving the question with which Job wrestled in his suffering.

With the subjective substratum removed, the largest source of variable and inconstant decision would disappear. This would be true, whether transiency guarded by due process or some more established but objectively determinable relation with the community were chosen for the standard to turn the existence of power. Either choice would be preferable to the variable which can give only inconstant and capricious effects, nullifying both policies.

If by one choice states of origin were forced to modify their local policies by giving effect to the different policies of other states when crystallized in valid judgments, that would be no more than the Constitution in terms purports to require. And it may be doubted their surrender would be much greater in practical effects than the present capricious and therefore deceptive system brings about. If by some more restrictive choice states now free to give essentially transient divorce were required to modify that policy for locally valid effects, within the limits of any objective standard that conceivably would be acceptable for constitutional purposes, the obligations they owe to the nation and to sister states would seem amply to justify that modest curtailment of their power. It is hard to see what legitimate substantial interest a state may have in providing divorces for persons only transiently there or for newcomers before they have created, by reasonable length of stay or other objective standards, more than fly-by-night connections.

I therefore dissent from the judgment which, in my opinion, has permitted North Carolina at her substantially unfettered will to deny all faith and credit to the Nevada decree, without in any way impeaching or attempting to impeach that judgment's constitutional validity. * * *

Mr. Justice BLACK, dissenting.

Anglo-American law has, until today, steadfastly maintained the principle that before an accused can be convicted of crime, he must be proven guilty beyond a reasonable doubt. These petitioners have been sentenced to prison because they were unable to prove their innocence to the satisfaction of the State of North Carolina. They have been convicted under a statute so uncertain in its application that not even the most learned member of the bar could have advised them in advance as to whether their conduct would violate the law. In reality the petitioners are being deprived of their freedom because the State of Nevada, through its legislature and courts, follows a liberal policy in granting divorces. They had Nevada divorce decrees which authorized them to remarry. Without charge or proof of fraud in obtaining these decrees, and without holding the decrees invalid under Nevada law, this Court affirms a conviction of petitioners, for living together as husband and wife. I cannot reconcile this with the Full Faith and Credit Clause and with congressional legislation passed pursuant to it.

It is my firm conviction that these convictions cannot be harmonized with vital constitutional safeguards designed to safeguard individual liberty and to unite all the states of this whole country into one nation. The fact that two people will be deprived of their constitutional rights impels me to protest as vigorously as I can against affirmance of these convictions. Even more, the Court's opinion today will cast a cloud over the lives of countless numbers of the multitude of divorced persons in the United States. * * *

* * *

The petitioners were married in Nevada. North Carolina has sentenced them to prison for living together as husband and wife in North Carolina. This Court today affirms those sentences without a determination that the Nevada marriage was invalid under that State's laws. This holding can be supported, if at all, only on one of two grounds: (1) North Carolina has extraterritorial power to regulate marriages within Nevada's territorial boundaries, or (2) North Carolina can punish people who live together in that state as husband and wife even though they have been validly married in Nevada. A holding based on either of these two grounds encroaches upon the general principle recognized by this Court that a marriage validly consummated under one state's laws is valid in every other state. If the Court is today abandoning that principle, it takes away from the states a large part of their hitherto plenary control over the institution of marriage. A further consequence is to subject people to criminal prosecutions for adultery and bigamy merely because they exercise their constitutional right to pass from a state in which they were validly married into another state which refuses to recognize their marriage. Such a consequence runs counter to the basic guarantees of our federal union. [Citations omitted.] It is true that persons validly married under the laws of one state have been convicted of crime for living together in other states. But those state convictions were not approved by this Court. And never before today has this Court decided a case upon the assumption that men and women validly married under the laws of one state could be sent to jail by another state for conduct which involved nothing more than living together as husband and wife.

The Court's opinion may have passed over the marriage question on the unspoken premise that the petitioners were without legal capacity to marry. If so, the primary question still would be whether that capacity, and other issues subsidiary to it, are to be determined under Nevada, North Carolina, or Federal law. Answers to these questions require a discussion of the divorce decrees awarded to the petitioners in a Nevada court prior to their marriage there.

When the Nevada decrees were granted, the petitioners' former spouses lived in North Carolina. When petitioners were tried and convicted, one of their former spouses was dead and the other had remarried. Under the legal doctrine prevailing in Nevada and in most of the states, these facts would make both the decrees immune from attack unless, perhaps, by persons other than the North Carolina spouses, whose property rights might be adversely affected by the decrees. So far as appears from the record no person's property rights were adversely affected by the dissolution decrees. None of the parties to the marriage, although formally notified of the Nevada divorce proceedings, made any protest before or after the decrees were rendered. The state did not sue here to protect any North Carolinian's property rights or to obtain support for the families which had been deserted. The result of all this is that the right of the state to attack the validity of these decrees in a criminal proceeding is today sustained, although the state's citizens, on whose behalf it purports to act, could not have done so at the time of the conviction in a civil proceeding. Furthermore, all of the parties to the first two marriages were apparently satisfied that their happiness did not lie in continued marital cohabitation. North Carolina claims no interest in abridging their individual freedom by forcing them to live together against their own desires. The state's interest at the time these petitioners were convicted thus comes down to its concern in preserving a bare marital status for a spouse who had already married again. If the state's interest before that time be considered, it was to preserve a bare marital status as to two persons who had sought a divorce and two others who had not objected to it. It is an extraordinary thing for a state to procure a retroactive invalidation of a divorce decree, and then punish one of its citizens for conduct authorized by that decree, when it had never been challenged by either of the people most immediately interested in it. I would not permit such an attenuated state interest to override the Full Faith and Credit Clause of the Constitution and an Act of Congress pursuant to it. Here again, North Carolina's right to attack this judgment, despite the Full Faith and Credit Clause and the Congressional enactment, is not based on Nevada law; nor could it be. For in Nevada, even the Attorney General could not have obtained a cancellation of the decree on the ground that it was rendered without jurisdiction. *State v. Moore*, 46 Nev. 65, 207 P.75, 22 A.L.R. 1101. This makes it clear beyond all doubt that North Carolina has not given these decrees the same effect that they would be given in the courts of Nevada.

* * *

This brings me to the Court's holding that Nevada decrees were "void." That conclusion rests on the premise that the Nevada court was without jurisdiction because the North Carolina Court found that the petitioners had no "domicile" in Nevada. The Nevada court had based its decree on a finding that "domicile" had been established by evidence before it. As I read that evidence, it would have been sufficient to support the findings, had the case been reviewed by us. Thus, this question of fact has now been adjudicated in two state courts with different results. It should be noted now that this Court very recently has said as to the Full Faith and Credit Clause and the 1790 Congressional enactment, that "From the beginning this Court has held that these provisions have made that which has been adjudicated in one state res judicata to the same extent in every other." *Magnolia Petroleum Co. v. Hunt, supra,* 320 U.S. at page 438, 64 S. Ct. at page 213, 88 L.Ed. 149, 150 A.L.R. 413. [10] That it was appropriate for the Nevada court to pass upon the question of domicile can hardly be doubted, since the concurring opinion in our first consideration of this case correctly said that the "Nevada decrees do satisfy the requirements of the Due Process Clause and are binding in Nevada upon the absent spouses * * *." 317 U.S. 287, 306, 63 S. Ct. 207, 217, 87 L.Ed. 279, 143 A.L.R. 1273. The Court today, however, seems to place its holding that the Nevada decrees are void on the basis that the Due Process Clause makes domicile an indispensable prerequisite to a state court's "jurisdiction" to grant divorce. It further holds that this newly created federal restriction of state courts projects fact issues which the state courts cannot finally determine for themselves. * * *

* * *

It is a drastic departure from former constitutional doctrine to hold that the Federal Constitution measures the power of state courts to pass upon petitions for divorce. The jurisdiction of state courts over persons and things within their boundaries has been uniformly acknowledged through the years, without regard to the length of their sojourn or their intention to remain. And that jurisdiction has not been thought to be limited by the Federal Constitution. Legislative dissolution of marriage was common in the colonies and the states up to the middle of the Nineteenth Century. A legislative dissolution of marriage, granted without notice or hearing of any kind, was sustained by this Court long after the Fourteenth Amendment was adopted. *Maynard v. Hill,* 125 U.S. 190, 8 S. Ct. 723, 31 L.Ed. 654; *cf. Pennoyer v. Neff,* 95 U.S. 714, 734, 735, 24 L.Ed. 565. The provision that made "due process of law" a prerequisite to deprivation of "life, liberty, or property" was not considered applicable to proceedings to sever the marital status. It was only when legislatures attempted to create or destroy financial obligations incident to marriage that courts began to conclude that their Acts encroached upon the

---

[10] The Nevada court had general jurisdiction to grant divorces, and the complaint was required to allege domicile along with the other requisite allegations. Domicile is as much an integral element in the litigation as the proof of cruelty or any of the other statutory grounds for divorce in Nevada. Labeling domicile as "jurisdictional" does not make it different from what it was before. Since the Nevada court had no power to render a divorce without proof of facts other than domicile, there is nothing to prevent this Court, under its expansive interpretation of the Due Process Clause, from labeling these other facts as "jurisdictional" and taking more state powers into the federal judicial orbit. Both these types of facts, however labeled, were part of the controversy which the Nevada legislature gave its courts power to resolve. The state could label them "jurisdictional" and having the exclusive power to grant divorces, could attach such consequences to them as it sees fit. But, while Congress might, under the Full Faith and Credit Clause, prescribe the "effect" in other states, of decrees based on the finding, I do not think the Federal courts can, by their mere label, attach jurisdictional consequences to the state's requirement of domicile. Hence, I think the quoted statement from the Magnolia Petroleum case should control this case.

right to a judicial trial in accordance with due process. The Court's holding now appears to overrule *Maynard v. Hill, sub silentio.* This perhaps is in keeping with the idea that the due process clause is a blank sheet of paper provided for courts to make changes in the Constitution and the Bill of Rights in accordance with their ideas of civilization's demands. I should leave the power over divorces in the states. And in the absence of further federal legislation under the Full Faith and Credit Clause, I should leave the effect of divorce decrees to be determined as Congress commanded—according to the laws and usages of the state where the decrees are entered.

Implicit in the majority of the opinions rendered by this and other courts, which, whether designedly or not, have set up obstacles to the procurement of divorces, is the assumption that divorces are an unmitigated evil, and that the law can and should force unwilling persons to live with each other. Others approach the problem as one which can best be met by moral, ethical and religious teachings. Which viewpoint is correct is not our concern. I am confident, however, that today's decision will no more aid in the solution of the problem than the Dred Scott decision aided in settling controversies over slavery. This decision, I think, takes the wrong road. Federal courts should have less, not more, to do with divorces. Only when one state refuses to give that faith and credit to a divorce decree which Congress and the Constitution command, should we enter this field.

Mr. Justice Douglas joins in this dissent.

Sherrer v. Sherrer

United States Supreme Court

334 U.S. 343 (1948)

Mr. Chief Justice Vinson delivered the opinion of the Court.

We granted certiorari in this case and in *Coe v. Coe*, 334 U.S. 378, 68 S. Ct. 1094, to consider the contention of petitioners that Massachusetts has failed to accord full faith and credit to decrees of divorce rendered by courts of sister States.

Petitioner Margaret E. Sherrer and the respondent, Edward C. Sherrer, were married in New Jersey in 1930, and from 1932 until April 3, 1944, lived together in Monterey, Massachusetts. Following a long period of marital discord, petitioner, accompanied by the two children of the marriage, left Massachusetts on the latter date, ostensibly for the purpose of spending a vacation in the State of Florida. Shortly after her arrival in Florida, however, petitioner informed her husband that she did not intend to return to him. Petitioner obtained housing accommodations in Florida, placed her older child in school, and secured employment for herself.

On July 6, 1944, a bill of complaint for divorce was filed at petitioner's direction in the Circuit Court of the Sixth Judicial Circuit of the State of Florida. The bill alleged extreme cruelty as grounds for divorce and also alleged that petitioner was a "bona fide resident of the State of Florida." The respondent received notice by mail of the pendency of the divorce proceedings. He retained Florida counsel who entered a general appearance and filed an answer denying the allegations of petitioner's complaint, including the allegation as to petitioner's Florida residence.

On November 14, 1944, hearings were held in the divorce proceedings. Respondent appeared personally to testify with respect to a stipulation entered into by the parties relating to the custody of the children. Throughout the entire proceedings respondent was represented by counsel. Petitioner introduced evidence to establish her Florida residence and testified generally to the allegations of her complaint. Counsel for respondent failed to crossexamine or to introduce evidence in rebuttal.

The Florida court on November 29, 1944, entered a decree of divorce after specifically finding "that petitioner is a bona fide resident of the State of Florida, and that this court has jurisdiction of the parties and the subject matter in said cause; * * *" Respondent failed to challenge the decree by appeal to the Florida Supreme Court.

On December 1, 1944, petitioner was married in Florida to one Henry A. Phelps, whom petitioner had known while both were residing in Massachusetts and who had come to Florida shortly after petitioner's arrival in that State. Phelps and petitioner lived together as husband and wife in Florida, where they were both employed, until February 5, 1945, when they returned to Massachusetts.

In June, 1945, respondent instituted an action in the Probate Court of Berkshire County, Massachusetts, which has given rise to the issues of this case. Respondent alleged that he is the lawful husband of petitioner, that the Florida decree of divorce is invalid, and that petitioner's subsequent marriage is void. Respondent prayed that he might be permitted to convey his real estate as if he were sole and that the court declare that he was living apart from his wife for justifiable cause. Petitioner joined issue on respondent's allegations.

In the proceedings which followed, petitioner gave testimony in defense of the validity of the Florida divorce decree. The Probate Court, however, resolved the issues of fact adversely to petitioner's contentions, found that she was never domiciled in Florida, and granted respondent the relief he had requested. The Supreme Judicial Court of Massachusetts affirmed the decree on the grounds that it was supported by the evidence and that the requirements of full faith and credit did not preclude the Massachusetts courts from reexamining the finding of domicile made by the Florida court.

At the outset, it should be observed that the proceedings in the Florida court prior to the entry of the decree of divorce were in no way inconsistent with the requirements of procedural due process. We do not understand respondent to urge the contrary. The respondent personally appeared in the Florida proceedings. Through his attorney he filed pleadings denying the substantial allegations of petitioner's complaint. It is not suggested that his rights to introduce evidence and otherwise to conduct his defense were in any degree impaired; nor is it suggested that there was not available to him the right to seek review of the decree by appeal to the Florida Supreme Court. It is clear that respondent was afforded his day in court with respect to every issue involved in the litigation, including the jurisdictional issue of petitioner's domicile. Under such circumstances, there is nothing in the concept of due process which demands that a defendant be afforded a second opportunity to litigate the existence of jurisdictional facts. [Citations omitted.]

It should also be observed that there has been no suggestion that under the law of Florida, the decree of divorce in question is in any respect invalid or could successfully be subjected to the type of attack permitted by the Massachusetts court. The implicit assumption underlying the position taken by respondent and the Massachusetts court is that this case involves a decree of divorce valid and final in the State which rendered it; and we so assume.

That the jurisdiction of the Florida court to enter a valid decree of divorce was dependent upon petitioner's domicile in that State is not disputed. This requirement was recognized by the Florida court which rendered the divorce decree, and the principle has been given frequent application in decisions of the State Supreme Court. But whether or not petitioner was domiciled in

Florida at the time the divorce was granted was a matter to be resolved by judicial determination. Here, unlike the situation presented in *Williams v. North Carolina*, 1945, 325 U.S. 226, 65 S. Ct. 1092, 89 L.Ed. 1577, 157 A.L.R. 1366, the finding of the requisite jurisdictional facts was made in proceedings in which the defendant appeared and participated. The question with which we are confronted, therefore, is whether such a finding made under the circumstances presented by this case may, consistent with the requirements of full faith and credit, be subjected to collateral attack in the courts of a sister State in a suit brought by the defendant in the original proceedings.

The question of what effect is to be given to an adjudication by a court that it possesses requisite jurisdiction in a case, where the judgment of that court is subsequently subjected to collateral attack on jurisdictional grounds, has been given frequent consideration by this Court over a period of many years. Insofar as cases originating in the federal courts are concerned, the rule has evolved that the doctrine of res judicata applies to adjudications relating either to jurisdiction of the person or of the subject matter where such adjudications have been made in proceedings in which those questions were in issue and in which the parties were given full opportunity to litigate. The reasons for this doctrine have frequently been stated. Thus in *Stoll v. Gottlieb*, 1938, 305 U.S. 165, 172, 59 S. Ct. 134, 138, it was said:

> "Courts to determine the rights of parties are an integral part of our system of government. It is just as important that there should be a place to end as that there should be a place to begin litigation. After a party has his day in court, with opportunity to present his evidence and his view of the law, a collateral attack upon the decision as to jurisdiction there rendered merely retries the issue previously determined. There is no reason to expect that the second decision will be more satisfactory than the first."

* * *

Applying these principles to this case, we hold that the Massachusetts courts erred in permitting the Florida divorce decree to be subjected to attack on the ground that petitioner was not domiciled in Florida at the time the decree was entered. Respondent participated in the Florida proceedings by entering a general appearance, filing pleadings placing in issue the very matters he sought subsequently to contest in the Massachusetts courts, personally appearing before the Florida court and giving testimony in the case, and by retaining attorneys who represented him throughout the entire proceedings. It has not been contended that respondent was given less than a full opportunity to contest the issue of petitioner's domicile or any other issue relevant to the litigation. There is nothing to indicate that the Florida court would not have evaluated fairly and in good faith all relevant evidence submitted to it. Respondent does not even contend that on the basis of the evidence introduced in the Florida proceedings, that court reached an erroneous result on the issue of petitioner's domicile. If respondent failed to take advantage of the opportunities afforded him, the responsibility is his own. We do not believe that the dereliction of a defendant under such circumstances should be permitted to provide a basis for subsequent attack in the courts of a sister State on a decree valid in the State in which it was rendered.

* * *

* * * We believe that in permitting an attack on the Florida divorce decree which again put in issue petitioner's Florida domicile and in refusing to recognize the validity of that decree, the Massachusetts courts have asserted a power which cannot be reconciled with the requirements of due faith and credit. We believe that assurances that such a power will be exercised sparingly and wisely render it no less repugnant to the constitutional commands.

It is one thing to recognize as permissible the judicial reexamination of findings of jurisdictional fact where such findings have been made by a court of a sister State which has entered a divorce decree in ex parte proceedings. It is quite another thing to hold that the vital rights and interests involved in divorce litigation may be held in suspense pending the scrutiny by courts of sister States of findings of jurisdictional fact made by a competent court in proceedings conducted in a manner consistent with the highest requirements of due process and in which the defendant has participated. We do not conceive it to be in accord with the purposes of the full faith and credit requirement to hold that a judgment rendered under the circumstances of this case may be required to run the gantlet of such collateral attack in the courts of sister States before its validity outside of the State which rendered it is established or rejected. That vital interests are involved in divorce litigation indicates to us that it is a matter of greater rather than lesser importance that there should be a place to end such litigation. And where a decree of divorce is rendered by a competent court under the circumstances of this case, the obligation of full faith and credit requires that such litigation should end in the courts of the State in which the judgment was rendered.

Reversed.

[Dissenting opinions by Mr. Justices FRANKFURTER and MURPHY omitted.]

Comments

Williams and *Sherrer* are still crucial for legal practice in spite of the availability of no-fault divorce in most jurisdictions. Although business in the so-called divorce-mill states has been drastically reduced by these legislative changes, marital breakdown is still often accompanied by change of abode by at least one of the spouses. Divorce is a traumatic experience for both parties to a marriage, and an adjustment to the new conditions appears to be facilitated by a change of environment. Numerous other factors induce people to move in case of marital breakdown, although easier divorce in another state may no longer be one of them. In other words, migratory divorce today is less institutionalized than it used to be under a fault regime, but it continues to be a matter of individual initiative. Furthermore, the legal situation under no-fault divorce is anything but uniform. Especially in regard to property division and alimony, considerable differences exist by way of judicial interpretation of statutes that outwardly may read quite similarly. As we have seen, fault conceptions persist in no-fault jurisdictions in various degrees.

The continued importance of *Williams* and *Sherrer* is perhaps felt most in a nonlitigative context. Past, present, and future conduct of clients is deeply influenced by their family relations, as well as their professional and business life. Proper legal advice in these matters necessitates knowledge of factors that may cause collateral attack on divorce decrees, even if such attack, under contemporary standards of no-fault, is less likely than in the past. The vitality of precedent, such as the *Williams* cases, may manifest itself on several levels. Even if a case, without being overruled, is no longer cited on the appellate level, it may continue to be effective for purposes of legal practice. In some respects—for example, in regard to the recognition of foreign divorce decrees—the significance of *Williams* and *Sherrer* has even increased, although the decisions were not originally meant to serve this purpose. In granting comity judges may be inclined to apply standards established in these cases. Any of the factors mentioned, whether they involve litigation, contemplated litigation, or mere conduct of clients, should still be incorporated into the intellectual check list of the practicing lawyer. To the extent that past migratory divorces have possibly affected the validity of marriages entered thereafter, the issues can be expected to be raised in years to come, if not in litigation then at least as a point of argument for purposes of reaching a favorable property settlement.

Although *Williams* and *Sherrer* are often cited as complementing each other, they arose in different factual contexts and involved different parties. *Williams* was a criminal prosecution for bigamy with the state of North Carolina as party; *Sherrer* was a civil litigation concerning not the marriage itself but rights of property. *Williams* was concerned with an ex parte divorce, while in *Sherrer* the defendant husband participated in the proceedings. In fact, the dichotomy between ex parte and bilateral divorces is false because there are multiple levels of participation. The facts in *Williams* make it clear that both Mrs. Williams and Mr. Hendrix had received notice of the Nevada proceedings. *Sherrer* involved a particularly high degree of participation. The respondent husband received notice by mail and retained Florida counsel, who entered an appearance denying the petitioner's domicile; in addition, the husband appeared personally and his counsel failed to cross-examine in regard to the petitioner's domicile and to introduce evidence in rebuttal; finally the husband failed to appeal the sentence. One could ask how many of these elements could be missing and the decision still have *res judicata* effects in regard to jurisdictional factors.

The concurring and dissenting opinions in *Williams I* and *II* and in *Sherrer* add further shades of reasoning. Mr. Justice Frankfurter, for example, concurred in the opinion of Mr. Justice Douglas in *Williams I*. Three years later in *Williams II*, Mr. Justice Frankfurter wrote for the majority with Mr. Justice Douglas dissenting. Again three years later, in *Sherrer*, Mr. Justice Douglas voted with the majority and Mr. Justice Frankfurter dissented. In this kind of situation it is impossible to ascertain whether the reasoning of the Court or of individual Justices is consistent. Rather than look for an elusive consistency, one should read the majority opinions in conjunction with the concurring and dissenting opinions for the extreme difficulties of the underlying problems. A few examples may demonstrate this complexity.

Mr. Justice Frankfurter stresses the point in his concurring opinion to *Williams I* that a divorce decree may satisfy the requirements under procedural due process in the state where it was rendered, in this instance Nevada, yet may be "null and void elsewhere" despite the commands of the Full Faith and Credit Clause. The reference to the decree being "null and void elsewhere," is probably misleading, because it is not within the jurisdiction of any decision maker to say that decrees from another sovereign are void. What is actually being referred to is the power to say that the foreign decree is not to be recognized. The nonspecific reference to "elsewhere" leaves open what states other than North Carolina might do in regard to the Nevada divorce decrees, not to mention foreign nations. According to Mr. Justice Frankfurter in writing for the majority in *Williams II*, any state may reexamine the jurisdictional fact of domicile in Nevada. The result could be that Mr. Williams is married to Mrs. Hendrix in some states and to Mrs. Williams in some others, depending on whether they follow the Nevada or the North Carolina holding. This compounds the problem of "a husband without a wife, or a wife without a husband," raised by Mr. Justice Douglas in *Williams I*. At least for purposes of bigamy, however, it is more likely that states other than North Carolina would recognize the Nevada divorces and choose not to prosecute, especially in light of the fact that North Carolina had at the time in question one of the most restrictive divorce laws in the United States.

Mr. Justice Rutledge and Mr. Justice Black in their dissenting opinions to *Williams II* shift the emphasis from the divorces to the valid marriage of Mr. Williams and Mrs. Hendrix in Nevada. They stress the conception that a marriage valid where entered is ordinarily to be recognized elsewhere. Both Justices stress also the underlying facts of the marriages involved. Mr. Hendrix, left behind in North Carolina, had meanwhile remarried. Mr. Justice Black reports in addition that the other spouse remaining in North Carolina, an obvious reference to Mrs. Williams, had died. In the light of this he questions the legitimate interest of the state in the prosecution. As a matter of principle, of course, the bigamy prosecution in North Carolina was not dependent on what happened to the deserted spouses. Nevertheless, the reality of the marriages seems to be out of line with the severity of the positions taken by the courts of North Carolina and by the Supreme Court of the United States in *Williams II*.

Perhaps some of the facts not mentioned in *Williams I* and *II* may throw light on the artificiality of the litigation. Not only had Mrs. Williams died, on June 24, 1943, but Mr. Hendrix had remarried after obtaining a divorce from his wife in North Carolina in May 1941 on the ground of adultery. Mr. Williams and Mrs. Hendrix did not return immediately after their marriage in Nevada to North Carolina, but were out of the state for the relatively respectable period of about six months. The ardor of the prosecution and the severity of the criminal sanctions applied by the North Carolina courts appears to have been prompted by some of the circumstances. Mr. Hendrix had been an employee in the store of Mr. Williams, located in Granite Falls, a rural town of little more than 2,000 inhabitants. After their return to North Carolina Mr. Williams and the former Mrs. Hendrix settled in the neighboring county in Pineola, a village of about 300 inhabitants. Since both families had been living in the area for many years, the local indignation appears to have been considerable. Unquestionably, the fact that state attorneys and judges hold elected offices must have had an impact on the prosecution and convictions. The sentences meted out were severe, not less than three nor more than 10 years at hard labor for Mr. Williams, and a corresponding sentence of not less than 3 years nor more than 5 years for Mrs. Hendrix. In the second trial the sentences were reduced to one to three years for Mr. Williams and 8 to 24 months for Mrs. Hendrix. After the fundamental power of North Carolina to reexamine the jurisdiction of the Nevada divorce courts was upheld in *Williams II*, much of the interest of North Carolina in punishing the offenders was gone. Before having served any part of their sentences and upon recommendation of the parole authorities, the parties remarried in North Carolina on August 18, 1945, and were thereafter paroled.

A further dimension is opened if the social class of the participants is considered. In all probability the Williams and Hendrix families belonged to the middle classes. After their return from Nevada to North Carolina, Mr. Williams and Mrs. Hendrix participated in church activities. Their ill-fated attempt to obtain divorces in Nevada was obviously dictated by a desire to conform at least to the appearances of law and respectability. Had they belonged to the lower classes, for example, as migrant workers, no legal issues would likely have arisen. Their intent to remain in North Carolina would have been in doubt. Family breakdown would have occurred without formal divorce or remarriage; in other words, the so-called poor men's divorce of factual desertion would have changed the relationship. Even if they had later returned to the same vicinity in North Carolina, the local community and officials would probably have reacted to their sexual mores with indifference. Had one of the participants been killed in an accident, the survivor might well have been presumed to have been validly married for purposes of legal recovery, if necessary by a presumption that somehow and somewhere legal divorces were obtained. The length of the North Carolina citizenship of Mr. Williams and Mrs. Hendrix worked against them. Had they been in the state for only a year, North Carolina would have been less interested in the prosecution. Even if they had conformed to a migrant pattern after leaving the state, for example, by driving around the country in a camper or mobile home, it would have been considerably more difficult for the state to prove bigamy. The presumption of divorce may have been more durable then than the Nevada divorces, known as a matter of record. As seen from this perspective, *Williams II* is perhaps directed toward a limited but important segment of the population, namely, middle-class persons who are likely to leave a clear documentary trail of their activities and travels. *Sherrer*, on the other hand, relieves some of the pressure in cases of participants to divorce proceedings who have established some measure of collaboration.

References

Baade, *Marriage and Divorce in American Conflicts Law: Governmental-Interests Analysis and the Restatement (Second)*, 72 COLUM. L. REV. 329 (1972).

Baer, *So Your Client Wants a Divorce! Williams v. North Carolina*, 24 N.C.L. REV. 1 (1945).

Clark, H., CASES AND PROBLEMS ON DOMESTIC RELATIONS 794–800 (3d ed. 1980).

Powell, *And Repent at Leisure: An Inquiry Into the Unhappy Lot of Those Whom Nevada Hath Joined Together and North Carolina Hath Put Asunder*, 58 HARV. L. REV. 930 (1945).

Rheinstein, M., MARRIAGE STABILITY, DIVORCE, AND THE LAW 63–81 (1972).

Rodgers & Rodgers, *The Disparity Between Due Process and Full Faith and Credit: The Problem of the Somewhere Wife*, 67 COLUM. L. REV. 1363 (1967).

Wheat v. Wheat

Supreme Court of Arkansas

229 Ark. 842, 318 S.W.2d 793 (1958)

GEORGE ROSE SMITH, Justice.

The only question here is the validity of Act 36 of 1957, which added the following provision to the statute governing the matter of residence in divorce cases: "The word 'residence' as used in Section 34–1208 is defined to mean actual presence and upon proof of such the party alleging and offering such proof shall be considered domiciled in the State and this is declared to be the legislative intent and public policy of the State of Arkansas." Ark. Stats. 1947, §34–1208.1. The effect of the 1957 statute is to substitute residence, in the sense of physical presence, for domicile as a jurisdictional requirement in divorce cases. The chancellor held the act unconstitutional and, finding that the plaintiff-appellant is not domiciled in Arkansas, dismissed his suit for divorce.

The parties were married in 1948 and were living in Maryland when they separated in 1952. The record does not show where the marriage ceremony was performed, but it was evidently in some state other than Arkansas. It is not contended that either of the parties had ever lived in Arkansas before the appellant came here in May of 1957. At that time he was transferred by his employer, a private corporation, to a station in Millington, Tennessee, which is some 20 miles northeast of West Memphis, Arkansas. Wheat rented an apartment in West Memphis and traveled back and forth each day to his work at Millington. After having thus resided in Arkansas for about three months Wheat filed this suit for a divorce, on the ground of three years separation. Mrs. Wheat, who is a resident of California, was served by warning order. She filed a cross-complaint asking for separate maintenance, but she denied the court's jurisdiction to grant a divorce. Although Wheat testified that he intends to make Arkansas his home, the weight of the evidence supports the chancellor's finding that Wheat has not established his domicile in this state. Hence the case turns upon the validity of Act 36, by which the jurisdictional requirement of domicile was abolished.

The legal history that lay behind Act 36 is well known. The Civil Code of 1869 required the plaintiff in a divorce case to prove residence in the state for one year next before the commencement of the action. C. & M. Dɪɢ. §3505. In 1931 the legislature amended the statute to require only that the plaintiff prove residence for three months next before the judgment and for two months next before the commencement of the action. Ark. Stats. §34–1208. In 1932 we held that the amended statute meant residence only, not domicile. *Squire v. Squire*, 186 Ark. 511, 54 S.W.2d 281. This interpretation was followed until 1947, when we overruled the Squire case and held that the statutory reference to residence meant domicile. *Cassen v. Cassen*, 211 Ark. 582, 201 S.W.2d 585, noted in 2 Aʀᴋ. L. Rᴇᴠ. 111. The *Cassen* case did not reach the constitutional question now presented, as the decision involved only an issue of statutory construction. It cannot be doubted that by Act 36 the legislature intended to restore the rule of the Squire case, for the emergency clause in the act refers specifically to that decision and to the *Cassen* case.

Although the wisdom of Act 36 is of no concern to the courts, since the law of divorce is purely statutory, *Squire v. Squire, supra, Young v. Young*, 207 Ark. 36, 178 S.W.2d 994, 152 A.L.R. 327, we may nevertheless observe that the act may well have been designed to prevent perjury. We know, of course, that the residential requirements for divorce vary greatly among the forty-nine states. In a decided majority of the states the plaintiff must have lived in the state for at least a year before filing suit. Louisiana and New York have no minimum period of residence, but their laws do not permit the courts to entertain cases where the state had no substantial connection with the marriage.

Arkansas is one of the five states in which the necessary period of residence is relatively short. In Idaho and Nevada the period is six weeks, in Wyoming sixty days, in Arkansas three months before judgment, and in Utah three months before the commencement of suit. At the time Act 36 was adopted all five of these states demanded proof of domicile as a condition to the granting of a divorce.

It is a matter of common knowledge that every year thousands of unhappily married persons, unable to obtain divorces at home, visit one or another of these five states in search of marital freedom. It is equally well known that the need for proof of domicile leads to perjury in a vast number of instances. The situation in Nevada, for example, has been described in these words:

> "It has been estimated that 8,616 divorces were granted in Nevada in 1942 and 11,399 in 1943, the great majority of which must have been obtained by non-residents who went to Nevada solely for divorce purposes, remaining there only the required six weeks. All the while they contemplated returning to their home states immediately after their divorces were secured, yet they all swore falsely that they intended to make Nevada their permanent home, having been warned by local counsel that, unless they did so, they would be out of court. On advice of counsel they also took steps which would be accepted by the Nevada courts as corroborating their sworn statement but were actually nothing more than sham and camouflage. Upon such evidence the courts find that they acquired a Nevada domicil."

Lorenzen, *Extraterritorial Divorce—Williams v. North Carolina II*, 54 Yᴀʟᴇ Lᴀᴡ Jᴏᴜʀɴᴀʟ 799, 801. We should be less than candid if we did not concede that similar instances of perjury have taken place in Arkansas. Act 36 goes far toward freeing litigants from the temptation to swear falsely on the issue of domicile.

To hold the act invalid we must be able to assert that it conflicts with some particular clause in the state or federal constitution. Only two clauses seem sufficiently pertinent to warrant discussion.

First is the full faith and credit clause of the federal constitution, art. 4, §1. This clause is now construed to mean that a divorce decree is not entitled to recognition in other states unless one of the parties was domiciled in the state where the decree was rendered, *Williams v. State of North Carolina*, 317 U.S. 287, 63 S. Ct. 207, 87 L.Ed. 279, 143 A.L.R. 1273, with an exception which precludes either party from attacking the decree if the question of domicile was actually put in issue. *Sherrer v. Sherrer*, 334 U.S. 343, 68 S. Ct. 1087, 92 L.Ed. 1429, 1 A.L.R.2d 1355.

The full faith and credit clause deals only with the extent to which the decree is entitled to recognition elsewhere. It does not purport to say that the decree is not valid in the state where rendered; still less does it intimate that the courts cannot be authorized to act at all in the absence of proof of domicile.

We do not question the desirability of having Arkansas divorce decrees receive recognition in other states. That wish was the basic reason for the *Cassen* decision. But it must be remembered that a decree is not entitled to respect elsewhere merely because the statute exacts a showing of domicile as a condition to the maintenance of the suit, and this is true even though the court makes a finding that domicile does exist. The decree is still not conclusive of the issue, which may be re-examined in other jurisdictions. *Williams v. State of North Carolina*, 325 U.S. 226, 65 S. Ct. 1092, 89 L.Ed. 1577. Although Nevada ostensibly requires proof of domicile, we have refused to recognize a Nevada decree when the court's finding of domicile was clearly unsupported. *Cooper v. Cooper*, 225 Ark. 626, 284 S.W.2d 617. With or without Act 36 the acceptance of any particular Arkansas decree by a court in another state will ultimately depend upon whether that court believes that an Arkansas domicile really existed. Even if the act deprives the decree of prima facie extraterritorial validity when the Arkansas court fails to make a finding of domicile, it was for the legislature to say whether this disadvantage is outweighed by the beneficial consequences of the statute.

The other constitutional provision to be considered is the due process clause, Amend. 14. On this point the arguments on each side are examined in detail in the majority and minority opinions in *Alton v. Alton*, 3 Cir., 207 F.2d 667, appeal dismissed as moot, 347 U.S. 610, 74 S. Ct. 736, 98 L.Ed. 987. See also *Granville-Smith v. Granville-Smith*, 349 U.S. 1, 75 S. Ct. 553, 99 L.Ed. 773. In the Alton case the Court of Appeals declared invalid a Virgin Islands statute which provided that six weeks residence should be prima facie evidence of domicile and, further, that if the defendant entered his appearance the court would have jurisdiction without reference to domicile. The facts were that Mrs. Alton brought suit for divorce after having resided in the Islands for the necessary six weeks. Her husband entered his appearance but made no defense. The trial court refused to grant a divorce without proof of domicile. The Court of Appeals, by a vote of four to three, sustained the trial court, holding that the statute denied due process of law.

We have studied the majority opinion in the *Alton* case with much care but do not find it convincing. The Fourteenth Amendment declares that no state shall deprive any person of life, liberty, or property without due process of law. The question at once arises: What person was denied due process in the *Alton* case? The majority's answer is hardly satisfying: "The question may well be asked as to what the lack of due process is. The defendant is not complaining. Nevertheless, if the jurisdiction for divorce continues to be based on domicile, as we think it does, we believe it to be lack of due process for one state to take to itself the readjustment of domestic relations between those domiciled elsewhere." [207 F.2d 677.] It will be seen that although Alton alone could have complained of a denial of due process and did not choose to do so, the court nevertheless found that his constitutional rights were somehow being violated.

In the case at bar Mrs. Wheat, unlike Alton, elects to contest the action for divorce and to attack the validity of Act 36. We may lay aside at the outset any question about procedural due process. It is not suggested that

Mrs. Wheat is being denied notice or an opportunity to be heard. To the contrary, she invokes the court's jurisdiction by her request for separate maintenance. We also assume that there is no doubt about the power of the Arkansas courts to determine Mrs. Wheat's marital rights in any Arkansas property her husband may own.

The difficult question is raised by the theory, which was the basis for the *Alton* decision, that the marriage relationship is a *res* that remains always at the parties' common domicile, or at their separate domiciles, and is therefore beyond the reach of courts in other jurisdictions. See REST., CONFLICT OF LAWS, §110; Leflar, ARKANSAS LAW OF CONFLICT OF LAWS, §133; and compare Corwin, *Out-Haddocking Haddock*, 93 PA. L. REV. 341. It will hardly do to sidestep this issue by merely observing that the marital status in the domiciliary jurisdiction will not be affected if our decree is not entitled to full faith and credit there.

With respect to the due process clause, as distinguished from the full faith and credit clause, we are not convinced that domicile must be the sole basis for the exercise of jurisdiction over the marriage relationship. As the court observed in *Wallace v. Wallace*, 63 N.M. 414, 320 P.2d 1020, 1022:

> "Where domicile is a statutory jurisdictional prerequisite it is quite correct to say that jurisdiction for divorce is founded on this concept. It is quite another matter to flatly declare that there may be no other relation between a state and an individual which will create a sufficient interest in the state under the due process clause to give it power to decree divorces. * * * Precedent is not lacking for the conclusion that divorce jurisdiction can be founded on circumstances other than domicile."

The court concluded that a soldier's residence in the state for a year, although insufficient to establish domicile, was a reasonable basis for the exercise of jurisdiction over the marital status.

The appellee relies strongly upon the decision in *Jennings v. Jennings*, 251 Ala. 73, 36 So.2d 236, 3 A.L.R.2d 662, where the court held invalid a statute permitting nonresident couples to confer jurisdiction by consent and thus obtain a divorce in Alabama with no residence there at all. We agree with that decision, for there was no reasonable basis for the exercise of jurisdiction over the marital status.

It has been pointed out repeatedly that the theory of basing divorce jurisdiction solely on domicile has led to conflicting decisions and to legal confusion ever since the theory was first formulated in connection with the full faith and credit clause. Domicile differs from residence only in the existence of a subjective intent to remain more or less permanently in the particular state. Whether that intent exists on the part of a person who comes to Arkansas can seldom be proved with any measure of certainty. Often it is only after the court has decided this perplexing question that the lack of intent becomes apparent, as when the successful plaintiff immediately leaves the state. Although the court reached its decision in the utmost good faith, the want of domicile becomes retroactively so demonstrable that the issue must be decided the other way when the decree is relied upon in another state.

By Act 36 the legislature has substituted the simple requirement of three months residence, which can be proved with certainty, for the nebulous concept of domicile, which usually cannot be proved. We concede that the period of residence might be shortened so unreasonably, as in the *Jennings* case, as to indicate that the state has no reasonable basis for exercising jurisdiction over the marriage. We are not convinced, however, that the act before us is open to that criticism. Under the holding in *Squire v. Squire, supra*, the rule of Act 36 actually prevailed in this state for fifteen years. Now that the legislature has unmistakably expressed its intention in the matter, we do not feel that the due process clause compels us to say that its action is arbitrary.

Reversed.

[Concurring and dissenting opinions omitted.]

Comments

Wheat exemplifies an alternative to the rigid conception of domicile for purposes of divorce jurisdiction. It also demonstrates that Mr. Justice Frankfurter's statement that no court in the English-speaking world has questioned the jurisdictional prerequisite of domicile cannot be maintained in its sweeping generality. According to the historical discussion in *Wheat*, Arkansas had a simple residence requirement at the time Mr. Justice Frankfurter made this assertion in *Williams v. North Carolina II* (pp. 455–463). The Arkansas legislature and the Supreme Court of Arkansas in *Wheat* confirmed that actual presence in the state is sufficient for domicile. Domicile for jurisdictional purposes is thereby openly reduced to a legal fiction; in other words, a party alleging and proving physical presence for the statutory period of time is deemed to be domiciled within Arkansas, although in fact this may not be the case. Nevada, by contrast, has retained the jurisdictional requirement of domicile, while the reality of migratory divorces might be similar there, at least in some of the cases, to the facts in *Wheat*.

The jurisdictional problem in *Wheat* is accentuated by further facts that appeared in the dissenting opinion, which quoted the trial court:

"* * * Mr. Wheat is a native of Oklahoma and was formerly a school teacher in that State. His mother still resides in Oklahoma. He has a married sister in Fort Smith, Arkansas.

"Mr. Wheat, now about 57 years old, is employed by North American Aviation Corporation, whose headquarters are in Columbus, Ohio. The company has places of business all over the nation, especially around U.S. Air Force bases, and in foreign countries. Mr. Wheat is subject to transfer to a new location on 24-hour notice.

"The present Mrs. Wheat is plaintiff's third wife. The first wife went by way of a divorce in the State of Illinois; and the second one by the same route in the State of California. Dates of these events are not in the record. Plaintiff married the present Mrs. Wheat in February, 1948, but the place is not revealed. It was not in Arkansas. The parties never lived in Arkansas during their married life. They separated around July or August, 1952, in Leonardtown, Maryland.

"Following this separation, Mr. Wheat was transferred from Maryland to Flordia, where he purchased a home and brought suit against the present Mrs. Wheat for divorce. Mrs. Wheat resisted the Florida suit and it was, on advice of Mr. Wheat's counsel, dismissed by Mr. Wheat. While living in Florida, Mr. Wheat wrote his wife and advised that he was finding happiness there and intended to make it his permanent home.

"After a little more than two years in Florida, Mr. Wheat was transferred to Columbus, Ohio, for two months and thence to California. Plaintiff volunteered the information that while in California he formed an intention to make that State his permanent home. Several months later he was transferred to Pennsylvania; and on May 1, 1957, his employer transferred Mr. Wheat to duty at the Naval Air Station, Millington, Tennessee (near Memphis).

"On the 3rd or 4th day of May, 1957, plaintiff rented a furnished apartment at a motel in West Memphis (Crittenden County), Arkansas, and has been using that as his home continuously since, to the extent that he sleeps there at night. He still (at the time of the depositions) has a Pennsylvania license plate on his automobile and operates under a California driver's license. He has not assessed his automobile or anything else for tax purposes in Arkansas. His official, and only, mail address is 'P.O. Box 7, Memphis, Tennessee.' He drives fifty miles daily to and from his work at Millington, Tennessee. He says he pays $110.00 a month rent for his furnished apartment; his landlady says he pays $80.00 a month. At least one or two other persons who came to Arkansas for a divorce have lived in the same motel but they do not still live there.

"Plaintiff makes no pretense that he intends to make Crittenden County his permanent home. Instead, he says, 'I intend to go to the Ozarks in Arkansas' and settle down to a little farming and fishing."

These facts, significantly not stated in this form in the majority opinion, demonstrate the trial judge's underlying hostility to the plaintiff's claim and his way of life. The selection of facts is meant to show that the plaintiff is an unstable person, of questionable veracity, and scheming to obtain a divorce. Even if plaintiff is telling the truth, the trial judge states derogatorily that he "makes no pretense that he intends to make Crittenden County his permanent home." Although there is no logical connection between the alleged characteristics of the plaintiff and the unconstitutionality of the Arkansas statute, the conclusion of the trial court appears to be foregone. The complaint was to be dismissed and, since this was the only way to reach this result, the Arkansas statute was held to be unconstitutional. Domicile was declared to be a jurisdictional requirement, albeit absent in this instance.

From a policy standpoint many factors, in addition to those stated in the majority opinion, speak for giving the plaintiff a forum for his request for divorce. Like military persons, with whom he is closely associated, he appears to be under a legal duty here, based on express contractual stipulation, not to have a domicile in any place. However, as an employee of a multinational enterprise—and there are thousands of them—he cannot claim the benefits of special jurisdictional statutes that have been enacted in many states for the military. A life subject to continued change, without this necessarily reflecting negatively on the plaintiff's character, is also likely to strain marriages. The plaintiff's earlier claims that he wanted to stay permanently in Florida or California may well have been true; his transfers were beyond his control. His declared intention to retire in Arkansas may have been equally true, because his sister was living in the state and he had been born in neighboring Oklahoma. To insist that he bring an action at his domicile of origin, Oklahoma, perhaps under a theory that he had not established any new domicile since he left, appears to be unreasonable because Mrs. Wheat had never had any relationship to that state, certainly no more than to Arkansas, and Mr. Wheat's may have been remote at this point.

On the other hand, it could be argued, in application of the traditional notions of fair play and substantial justice as pronounced in *International Shoe Co. v. Washington,** that the nonresident wife must have certain minimum contacts with the divorce forum; while here there were none whatsoever. Or perhaps divorce courts, especially if domicile is not an exclusive jurisdictional requirement, should, as a matter of policy, be more willing to apply *forum non conveniens* notions than they have been in the past. One dire prediction, by Mr. Chief Justice Harris in his concurring opinion to *Wheat,* that "any divorce granted under the provisions of this statute, in numerous of our sister states, will probably be worth only the paper it is written on," has not come true. Other states have recognized Arkansas divorces even though arguably their own domiciliaries were involved. For example see *Staples v. Staples,*† and *Reeves v. Reeves.*‡ *Reeves* involved a bilateral Arkansas divorce that could have been upheld under *Sherrer v. Sherrer,*** but *Staples* concerned recognition of an ex parte Arkansas divorce in Louisiana. However, in both instances the lower courts did not grant full faith and credit to the Arkansas divorces, further evidence that *Williams v. North Carolina II*†† continues to be important in legal practice.

Wheat prominently mentions as a policy sustaining the constitutional validity of the Arkansas statute that it is meant to prevent perjury. Yet whether perjury is actually committed in states like Nevada is at least subject to some question. Even the judges must be aware of the probable falsity of testimony that a petitioner intends to establish Nevada as a permanent home. What we may have is fictitious pleadings for purposes of obtaining jurisdiction. Such fictitious pleadings have a long history in English law. For example, the courts, in order to obtain jurisdiction, permitted pleas that the debtor was located in the county of Middlesex although in fact he was not. However, what may be a valid scholarly explanation may not necessarily be equally valid for legal practice. In some jurisdictions, such as Alabama, judges, acting within their inherent powers, have set aside divorces because an alleged fraud—false swearing to the jurisdictional facts—was perpetrated upon the court. In one instance, the judge acting ex officio vacated a divorce decree six years after the husband had remarried.‡‡

---

*326 U.S. 310, 316 (1945).
†232 So.2d 904 (Ct. App.2d Cir. La. 1970).
‡209 So.2d 554 (Ct. App.2d Cir. La. 1968).
**334 U.S. 343 (1948).
††325 U.S. 226 (1945).
‡‡See *Hartigan v. Hartigan,* 272 Ala. 67, 128 So.2d 725 (1961).

Such harsh decisions are to some extent beyond the control of the bar and also unrelated to the relative ease of grounds for divorce. They are the result of the political climate within a given state. Lower court judges are, as elected officials in most states, intensely dependent on local politics; they may be voted out of office following clean-up campaigns. The judge who sets aside a divorce judgment for an alleged fraud on the court may not be the same judge who rendered the decision years earlier. A lawyer would be ill-advised, even today, to make the fate of divorces and remarriage depend on such contingencies.

References

Furlong, *Dual Divorce Decrees and Conciliation in Contemporary Family Law*, 2 WILLAMETTE L.J. 134, 152–53 (1962) (account of the Nelson A. Rockefeller divorce at Reno, Nevada).

Garfield, *The Transitory Divorce Action: Jurisdiction in the No-Fault Era*, 58 TEX. L. REV. 501 (1980).

Note, *Migratory Divorce: The Alabama Experience*, 75 HARV. L. REV. 568 (1962).

Osgoode, *High Court Refuses to Stop Divorce Probe*, Montgomery Advertiser, Apr. 17, 1964, at 1, col. 5.

Estin v. Estin

United States Supreme Court

334 U.S. 541 (1948)

Mr. Justice DOUGLAS delivered the opinion of the Court.

This case, here on certiorari to the Court of Appeals of New York, presents an important question under the Full Faith and Credit Clause of the Constitution. Article IV, §1. It is whether a New York decree awarding respondent $180 per month for her maintenance and support in a separation proceeding survived a Nevada divorce decree which subsequently was granted petitioner.

The parties were married in 1937 and lived together in New York until 1942 when the husband left the wife. There was no issue of the marriage. In 1943 she brought an action against him for a separation. He entered a general appearance. The court, finding that he had abandoned her, granted her a decree of separation and awarded her $180 per month as permanent alimony. In January 1944 he went to Nevada where in 1945 he instituted an action for divorce. She was notified of the action by constructive service but entered no appearance in it. In May, 1945, the Nevada court, finding that petitioner had been a bona fide resident of Nevada since January 30, 1944, granted him an absolute divorce "on the ground of three years continual separation, without cohabitation." The Nevada decree made no provision for alimony, though the Nevada court had been advised of the New York decree.

Prior to that time petitioner had made payments of alimony under the New York decree. After entry of the Nevada decree he ceased paying. Thereupon respondent sued in New York for a supplementary judgment for the amount of the arrears. Petitioner appeared in the action and moved to eliminate the alimony provisions of the separation decree by reason of the Nevada decree. The Supreme Court denied the motion and granted respondent judgment for the arrears. Sup., 63 N.Y.S.2d 476. The judgment was affirmed by the Appellate Division, 271 App. Div. 829, 66 N.Y.S.2d 421, and then by the Court of Appeals. 296 N.Y. 308, 73 N.E.2d 113.

We held in *Williams v. North Carolina*, 317 U.S. 287, 143 A.L.R. 1273; 325 U.S. 226, 157 A.L.R. 1366, (1) that a divorce decree granted by a State to one of its domiciliaries is entitled to full faith and credit in a bigamy prosecution brought in another State, even though the other spouse was given notice of the divorce proceeding only through constructive service; and (2) that while the finding of domicile by the court that granted the decree is entitled to prima facie weight, it is not conclusive in a sister State but might be relitigated there. And see *Esenwein v. Pennsylvania*, 325 U.S. 279, 157 A.L.R. 1396. The latter course was followed in this case, as a consequence of which the Supreme Court of New York found, in accord with the Nevada court, that petitioner "is now and since January 1944, has been a bona fide resident of the State of Nevada." [63 N.Y.S.2d 482]

Petitioner's argument therefore is that the tail must go with the hide—that since by the Nevada decree, recognized in New York, he and respondent are no longer husband and wife, no legal incidence of the marriage remains. We are given a detailed analysis of New York law to show that the New York courts have no power either by statute or by common law to compel a man to support his ex-wife, that alimony is payable only so long as the relation of husband and wife exists, and that in New York, as in some other states, see *Esenwein v. Pennsylvania, supra*, 325 U.S. page 280, 157 A.L.R. 1396, a support order does not survive divorce.

The difficulty with that argument is that the highest court in New York has held in this case that a support order can survive divorce and that this one has survived petitioner's divorce. That conclusion is binding on us, except as it conflicts with the Full Faith and Credit Clause. It is not for us to say whether that ruling squares with what the New York courts said on earlier occasions. It is enough that New York today says that such is her policy. The only question for us is whether New York is powerless to make such a ruling in view of the Nevada decree.

We can put to one side the case where the wife was personally served or where she appears in the divorce proceedings. *Cf. Yarborough v. Yarborough*, 290 U.S. 202; *Davis v. Davis*, 305 U.S. 32, 118 A.L.R. 1518; *Sherrer v. Sherrer*, 334 U.S. 343; *Coe v. Coe*, 334 U.S. 378. The only service on her in this case was by publication and she made no appearance in the Nevada proceeding. The requirements of procedural due process were satisfied and the domicile of the husband in Nevada was foundation for a decree effecting a change in the marital capacity of both parties in all the other States of the Union, as well as in Nevada. *Williams v. North Carolina*, 317 U.S. 287, 143 A.L.R. 1273. But the fact that marital capacity was changed does not mean that every other legal incidence of the marriage was necessarily affected.

Although the point was not adjudicated in *Barber v. Barber*, 21 How. 582, 588, the Court in that case recognized that while a divorce decree obtained in Wisconsin by a husband from his absent wife might dissolve the vinculum of the marriage, it did not mean that he was freed from payment of alimony under an earlier separation decree granted by New York. An absolutist might quarrel with the result and demand a rule that once a divorce is granted, the whole of the marriage relation is dissolved, leaving no roots or tendrils of any kind. But there are few areas of the law in black and white. The greys are dominant and even among them the shades are innumerable. For the eternal problem of the law is one of making accommodations between conflicting interests. This is why most legal problems end as questions of degree. That is true of the present problem under the Full Faith and Credit Clause. The question involves important considerations both of law and of policy which it is essential to state.

The situations where a judgment of one State has been denied full faith and credit in another State, because its enforcement would contravene the latter's policy, have been few and far between. See *Williams v. North Carolina*, 317 U.S. 287, 294, 295, 143 A.L.R. 1273; *Magnolia Petroleum Co. v. Hunt*, 320 U.S. 430, 438, 439, 150 A.L.R. 413, and cases cited; *Sherrer v. Sherrer, supra*. The Full Faith and Credit Clause is not to be applied, accordion-like, to accommodate our personal predilections. It substituted a command for the earlier principles of comity and thus basically altered the status of the States as independent sovereigns. *Williams v. North Carolina*, 317 U.S. 287, 301, 302, 143 A.L.R. 1273; *Sherrer v. Sherrer, supra*. It ordered submission by one State even to hostile policies reflected in the judgment of another State, because the practical operation of the federal system, which the Constitution designed, demanded it. The fact that the requirements of full faith and credit, so far as judgments are concerned, are exacting, if not inexorable (*Sherrer v. Sherrer, supra*), does not mean, however, that the State of the domicile of one spouse may, through the use of constructive service, enter a decree that changes every legal incidence of the marriage relationship.

Marital status involves the regularity and integrity of the marriage relation. It affects the legitimacy of the offspring of marriage. It is the basis of criminal laws, as the bigamy prosecution in *Williams v. North Carolina* dramatically illustrates. The State has a considerable interest in preventing bigamous marriages and in protecting the offspring of marriages from being bastardized. The interest of the State extends to its domiciliaries. The State should have the power to guard its interest in them by changing or altering their marital status and by protecting them in that changed status throughout the farthest reaches of the nation. For a person domiciled in one State should not be allowed to suffer the penalties of bigamy for living outside the State with the only one which the State of his domicile recognizes as his lawful wife. And children born of the only marriage which is lawful in the State of his domicile should not carry the stigma of bastardy when they move elsewhere. These are matters of legitimate concern to the State of the domicile. They entitle the State of the domicile to bring in the absent spouse through constructive service. In no other way could the State of the domicile have and maintain effective control of the marital status of its domiciliaries.

Those are the considerations that have long permitted the State of the matrimonial domicile to change the marital status of the parties by an ex parte divorce proceeding, *Thompson v. Thompson*, 226 U.S. 551, considerations which in the *Williams* cases we thought were equally applicable to any State in which one spouse had established a bona fide domicile. See 317 U.S. pages 300–301, 143 A.L.R. 1273. But those considerations have little relevancy here. In this case New York evinced a concern with this broken marriage when both parties were domiciled in New York and before Nevada had any concern with it. New York was rightly concerned lest the abandoned spouse be left impoverished and perhaps become a public charge. The problem of her livelihood and support is plainly a matter in which her community had a legitimate interest. The New York court, having jurisdiction over both parties, undertook to protect her by granting her a judgment of permanent alimony. Nevada, however, apparently follows the rule that dissolution of the marriage puts an end to a support order. See *Herrick v. Herrick*, 55 Nev. 59, 68, 25 P.2d 378, 380. But the question is whether Nevada could under any circumstances adjudicate rights of respondent under the New York judgment when she was not personally served or did not appear in the proceeding.

Bassett v. Bassett, 9 Cir., 141 F.2d 954, held that Nevada could not. We agree with that view.

The New York judgment is a property interest of respondent, created by New York in a proceeding in which both parties were present. It imposed obligations on petitioner and granted rights to respondent. The property interest which it created was an intangible, jurisdiction over which cannot be exerted through control over a physical thing. Jurisdiction over an intangible can indeed only arise from control or power over the persons whose relationships are the source of the rights and obligations. Cf. *Curry v. McCanless*, 307 U.S. 357, 366, 123 A.L.R. 162.

Jurisdiction over a debtor is sufficient to give the State of his domicile some control over the debt which he owes. * * * But we are aware of no power which the State of domicile of the debtor has to determine the personal rights of the creditor in the intangible unless the creditor has been personally served or appears in the proceeding. The existence of any such power has been repeatedly denied. [Citations omitted.] We know of no source of power which would take the present case out of that category. The Nevada decree that is said to wipe out respondent's claim for alimony under the New York judgment is nothing less than an attempt by Nevada to restrain respondent from asserting her claim under that judgment. That is an attempt to exercise an in personam jurisdiction over a person not before the court. That may not be done. Since Nevada had no power to adjudicate respondent's rights in the New York judgment, New York need not give full faith and credit to that phase of Nevada's judgment. A judgment of a court having no jurisdiction to render it is not entitled to the full faith and credit which the Constitution and statute of the United States demand. *Hansberry v. Lee*, 311 U.S. 32, 40, 41, 132 A.L.R. 741; *Williams v. North Carolina*, 325 U.S. 226, 229, 157 A.L.R. 1366, and cases cited.

The result in this situation is to make the divorce divisible—to give effect to the Nevada decree insofar as it affects marital status and to make it ineffective on the issue of alimony. It accommodates the interests of both Nevada and New York in this broken marriage by restricting each State to the matters of her dominant concern.

Since Nevada had no jurisdiction to alter respondent's rights in the New York judgment, we do not reach the further question whether in any event that judgment would be entitled to full faith and credit in Nevada. [Citations omitted.] And it will be time enough to consider the effect of any discrimination shown to out-of-state ex parte divorces when a State makes that its policy.

Affirmed.

Mr. Justice FRANKFURTER, dissenting.

The Court's opinion appears to rest on three independent grounds:

(1) New York may, consistently with the Full Faith and Credit Clause, hold that a prior separate maintenance decree of one of its courts survives a decree of divorce within the scope of enforceability of the rule in *Williams v. North Carolina*, 317 U.S. 287, 143 A.L.R. 1273, whether such divorce is granted in New York or by a sister State;

(2) By virtue of its interest in preventing its citizens from becoming public charges, New York may constitutionally provide that a domestic separate maintenance decree survives a sister-State divorce decree which must be respected in New York under the rule in the first *Williams* case, *supra*;

(3) A separate maintenance decree creates an obligation which may not, consistently with due process, be extinguished by a court lacking personal jurisdiction of the obligee, though possessed of jurisdiction to terminate her marital status, and any judgment purporting to do so is not entitled to extra-State recognition.

To the first of these grounds I assent, and if such is the law of New York I agree that the decision of the New York Court of Appeals in this case must be upheld. It is for New York to decide whether its decrees for separate maintenance survive divorce or terminate with it, provided, of course, that its decision is not a mere attempt to defeat a federal right, given by the Full Faith and Credit Clause, under the guise of a determination of State law. Cf. *Davis v. Wechsler*, 263 U.S. 22, 24, 25.

The second ground presents difficulties. I cannot agree that New York's interest in its residents would justify New York in giving less effect to an enforceable Nevada divorce granted to one domiciled in Nevada, against a spouse not personally served, than it would give to a valid New York divorce similarly obtained. As to this, I agree with the views of by brother JACKSON. If, on the other hand, New York does not so discriminate against enforceable "ex parte" divorce decrees granted by a sister State, no problem under the Full Faith and Credit Clause arises.

Furthermore, if the respondent had obtained her separate maintenance decree in Pennsylvania—which treats such decrees as terminated by any valid divorce, see *Esenwein v. Commonwealth*, 325 U.S. 279, 157 A.L.R. 1396—and had subsequently moved to New York and there brought a suit based on the Pennsylvania decree, it is clear that New York's interest in preventing the respondent from becoming a public charge would not justify refusal to treat the separate maintenance decree as having been terminated. New York would be required to refer to the law of Pennsylvania to determine whether the maintenance decree of that Commonwealth had survived the Nevada divorce, and, finding that it had not, the New York courts could not enforce it.

My difficulty with the third ground of the Court's opinion is that Nevada did not purport, so far as the record discloses, to rule on the survival of the New York separate maintenance decree. Nevada merely established a change in status. It was for New York to determine the effect, with reference to its own law, of that change in status. If it was the law of New York that divorce put an end to its separate maintenance decree, the respondent's decree would have been terminated not by the Nevada divorce but by the consequences, under the New York law, of a change in status, even though brought about by Nevada. Similarly, Nevada could not adjudicate rights in New York realty, but, if New York law provided for dower, a Nevada divorce might or might not terminate a dower interest in New York realty depending on whether or not New York treated dower rights as extinguished by divorce.

If the Nevada decree, insofar as it affected the New York separate maintenance decree, were violative of due process, New York of course would not have to give effect to it. It could not do so even if it wished. If the Nevada decree involved a violation of due process there is an end of the matter and other complicated issues need not be considered! It would not matter whether New York had a special interest in preventing its residents from becoming public charges, or whether New York treated maintenance decrees as surviving a valid divorce.

Accordingly, the crucial issue, as I see it, is whether New York has held that *no* "ex parte" divorce decree could terminate a prior New York separate maintenance decree, or whether it has decided merely that no "ex parte" divorce decree of another State could. The opinion of the Court of Appeals leaves this crucial issue in doubt. The prior decisions of the New York courts do not dispel my doubts. Neither do the cases cited in the Court of Appeals' opinion, which, with the exception of *Wagster v. Wagster*, 193 Ark. 902, 103 S.W.2d 638, do not involve "ex parte" domestic divorces. New York may legitimately decline to allow any "ex parte" divorce to dissolve its prior separate maintenance decree, but it may not, consistently with *Williams v. North Carolina*, 317 U.S. 287, 143 A.L.R. 1273, discriminate against a Nevada decree granted to one there domiciled, and afford it less effect than it gives to a decree of its own with similar jurisdictional foundation. I cannot be sure which it has done.

I am reinforced in these views by Mr. Justice JACKSON's dissent. As a New York lawyer and the Justice assigned to the Second Circuit, he is presumably not without knowledge of New York law. The Court's opinion is written in a spirit of certitude that the New York law is contrary to that which Mr. Justice JACKSON assumes it to be. Thus, on the issue that I deem decisive of the question whether New York has given full faith and credit to the Nevada decree—namely, whether under New York's law divorce decrees based on publication terminate support—her law has thus far not spoken with ascertainable clarity. I would therefore remand the case to the New York Court of Appeals for clarification of its rationale. "* * * It is * * * important that ambiguous or obscure adjudications by state courts do not stand as barriers to a determination by this Court of the validity under the federal constitution of state action. Intelligent exercise of our appellate powers compels us to ask for the elimination of the obscurities and ambiguities from the opinions in such cases." *Minnesota v. National Tea Co.*, 309 U.S. 551, 557.

Mr. Justice JACKSON, dissenting.

If there is one thing that the people are entitled to expect from their lawmakers, it is rules of law that will enable individuals to tell whether they are married and, if so, to whom. Today many people who have simply lived in more than one state do not know, and the most learned lawyer cannot advise them with any confidence. The uncertainties that result are not merely technical, nor are they trivial; they affect fundamental rights and relations such as the lawfulness of their cohabitation, their children's legitimacy, their title to property, and even whether they are law-abiding persons or criminals. In a society as mobile and nomadic as ours, such uncertainties affect large numbers of people and create a social problem of some magnitude. It is therefore important that, whatever we do, we shall not add to the confusion. I think that this decision does just that.

These parties lived together in New York State during their entire married life. Courts of that State granted judgment of separation, with award of alimony to the wife, in October 1943. Three months later the husband journeyed to Nevada and in three more months began a divorce action. No process was served on the wife in Nevada; she was put on notice only by constructive service through publication in New York. Notified thus of what was going on, she was put to this choice: to go to Nevada and fight a battle, hopeless under Nevada laws, to keep her New York judgment, or to do nothing. She did nothing, and the Nevada court granted the husband a divorce without requiring payment of alimony.

Now the question is whether the New York judgment of separation or the Nevada judgment of divorce controls the present obligation to pay alimony. The New York judgment of separation is based on the premise that the parties remain husband and wife, though estranged, and hence the obligation of support, incident to marriage, continues. The Nevada decree is based on the contrary premise that the marriage no longer exists and so obligations dependent on it have ceased.

The Court reaches the Solomon-like conclusion that the Nevada decree is half good and half bad under the full faith and credit clause. It is good to free the husband from the marriage; it is not good to free him from its incidental obligations. Assuming the judgment to be one which the Constitution requires to be recognized at all, I do not see how we can square this decision with the command that it be given full faith and credit. For reasons which I stated in dissenting in *Williams v. North Carolina*, 317 U.S. 287, 143 A.L.R. 1273, I would not give standing under the clause to constructive service divorces obtained on short residence. But if we are to hold this divorce good, I do not see how it can be less good than a divorce would be if rendered by the courts of New York.

As I understand New York law, if, after a decree of separation and alimony, the husband had obtained a New York divorce against his wife, it would terminate her right to alimony. If the Nevada judgment is to have full faith and credit, I think it must have the same effect that a similar New York decree would have. I do not see how we can hold that it must be accepted for some purposes and not for others, that he is free of his former marriage but still may be jailed, as he may in New York, for not paying the maintenance of a woman whom the Court is compelled to consider as no longer his wife.

Comments

The question, already asked after *Williams v. North Carolina I* and *II*, whether no-fault legislation has affected the principles of migratory divorce pronounced by the U.S. Supreme Court arises again. In this instance "divisible divorce" is involved, that is, the theory that aspects of marriage related to status are to be treated differently from consequences of marriage considered to be proprietary in nature. The status aspects of divorce are supposed to be *in rem* or at least *quasi in rem*, while the proprietary matters are *in personam. Estin* characterizes support and alimony claims, if reduced to judgment, as proprietary in nature. Thus the claims of the out-of-state creditor, that is the wife, cannot be dismissed in an ex parte proceeding when the marital status is validly terminated. *Vanderbilt v. Vanderbilt** extends this holding, so far as New York law was concerned, to cover support claims not yet reduced to judgment. Conceivably the availability of no-fault divorce could have an impact. States might be more inclined to recognize the jurisdiction of a sister state in regard to adjudication of support and alimony claims. To the extent that the law of divorce becomes increasingly uniform, states may be less prone to take the extreme position of New York law expressed in *Estin* and *Vanderbilt*. At that time, much as Nevada was considered a divorce mill jurisdiction, New York could have been called a "support and alimony mill." In *Vanderbilt*, for example, the parties chose the jurisdictions likely to be favorable to their financial positions. After they separated in California, the husband moved to Nevada and the wife to New York. With considerable wealth at stake, they probably sought legal advice in contemplating their moves.

In spite of no-fault divorce forum shopping is still part of our reality. This does not necessarily mean that millions of dollars must be involved. Any accumulation of assets, including entitlements, may result in divorce planning by lawyers. A party may strengthen his or her bargaining position by being the first to file a divorce action in a jurisdiction more favorable in regard to alimony and property division than the jurisdiction of the opponent. The time of filing may be an important factor. If, for example, a spouse files in one state, that spouse may enjoin the other spouse from filing in another state, even if the second state has some interest in the marriage. The place of filing may be equally important because principles of "equitable distribution," even when adhered to by both jurisdictions, may be applied quite differently from state to state, regardless of uniform no-fault legislation.

Actually, divorce jurisdiction and the questions of choices involved may become additional bargaining tools in lawyers' offices, together with potential grounds that are more substantive in nature. Theoretically, of course, jurisdiction is not subject to negotiation in

---

*354 U.S. 449 (1957).

common law countries; but practically, it is within the power of clients to change residences and of lawyers, to some extent, to select and emphasize the facts that establish jurisdiction in one court rather than in another. Thus the whole jurisdictional problem inevitably becomes part of the bargaining process, especially in cases where reality is sufficiently ambiguous to permit multiple interpretations. What actually transpires before the trial courts may show nothing of these jurisdictional negotiations.

Perhaps one impact of no-fault divorce is that lawyers now resolve jurisdictional queries. Since they do not even reach the chancellor, much less the appellate courts, these issues have less visibility than at the time of *Estin* and *Vanderbilt*. But it would be a mistake to believe that problems have declined in importance simply because they have become less visible. A comparison of cases in this book shows the great divergence of jurisdictions in regard to consequences of no-fault divorce, for example, aspects of community property in California (see *In re Marriage of Mix*, pp. 100–105), pure no-fault in regard to proprietary consequences of divorce in Iowa (see *In re Marriage of Williams*, pp. 307–314), and the lingering concept of fault in Florida (see *McClelland v. McClelland*, pp. 332–333). Whether *Estin* and *Vanderbilt* continue to be important in these and other jurisdictions depends largely on how far a lawyer wishes to press his point in an appropriate case. Obviously, it still makes a difference, in terms of proprietary consequences of no-fault divorce, whether the action was filed in California, Iowa, Florida, or even in New York. In New York, much of the preexisting law of divorce consequences may still be effective, at least for purposes of argument, in spite of the availability of no-fault grounds.

The questions of continued interest can be summarized as follows: Is it realistic to differentiate between aspects of divorce that relate to status and those that relate to finances? If a divorce in one state is recognized in another for purposes of severing status, but disregarded in economical respects—an option that courts created to keep deserving wives from being cut off from support rights by a foreign divorce—what happens to the intervening equities of new spouses who may find that a prior marriage clouds their entitlements? What happens in jurisdictions other than the two competing states? That is, which position should they follow if a divorce is effective as to marital status, but not as to proprietary consequences of the dissolution of status? When, and in what jurisdictions, is support an incident of marriage and when is it a separate proprietary right? Which rights in marriage are "vested," and which are "inchoate"? The answers to these and other questions may continue to vary from jurisdiction to jurisdiction, and within each jurisdiction sometimes from case to case. Uniformity in answers, not yet achieved, is not necessarily desirable. Although it facilitates prediction and decisions, at the same time it damages the range of lawyers' arguments and limits the discretion of the courts.

References

Clark, H., THE LAW OF DOMESTIC RELATIONS IN THE UNITED STATES 314–319 (1968).

Ehrenzweig, A., A TREATISE ON THE CONFLICT OF LAWS 265–68 (1962).

Ritz, *Migratory Alimony: A Constitutional Dilemma in the Existence of In Personam Jurisdiction*, 29 FORDHAM L. REV. 83 (1960).

Foreign Cases

Hyde v. Hyde

Supreme Court of Tennessee

562 S.W.2d 194 (Tenn. 1978)

FONES, Justice.

Appellant, Divorce Referee of Shelby County, appeals from a declaratory judgment validating, "for reasons of equity and comity", a divorce awarded by a court in the Dominican Republic.

On November 21, 1974, Eleanor Lentz Hyde was awarded a decree of divorce by the Court of First Instance of the Judicial District of Santo Domingo, Dominican Republic. She appeared in person and was represented by an attorney. Joseph R. Hyde, III, was not personally present but was represented by his attorney in fact, by virtue of a power of attorney filed with the Court. These appearances fully satisfied the laws of the Dominican Republic with respect to jurisdiction of divorce actions. The divorce was granted on the ground of incompatibility of temperaments, making life together unbearable. Both parties to the marriage are residents of Memphis, and were residents of Memphis at the time of the divorce.

Joseph Hyde filed this suit in the Chancery Court of Shelby County on November 4, 1976, seeking a declaratory judgment that the Dominican Republic decree was valid, or in the alternative, seeking a divorce. He alleged that prior to October, 1974, the parties were preparing to file suit against each other in the courts of Shelby County, Tennessee, but they effected an agreement settling their property rights and providing for the support of their minor child; that they were then confronted by the prospect of an extensive delay before a divorce could be obtained due to the backlog of divorce cases in Shelby County. Being desirous of returning to the status of unmarried people, after an investigation, both parties submitted to the jurisdiction of the Dominican Republic court and obtained a no fault divorce, believed in good faith to be valid.

Eleanor Lentz Hyde answered, admitting those allegations and insisting that comity be granted the foreign decree, but in the alternative, also counterclaiming for divorce. Thus, in the Tennessee courts, both parties assert the validity of the foreign decree, neither raises any question as to the jurisdiction of the Dominican Republic court over the parties or the subject matter for the purpose of the 1974 proceeding, and they continue to assert that each is bound by the 1974 property settlement agreement. The Divorce Referee appeared in the action to contest the validity of the Dominican Republic decree. The Chancellor granted summary judgment for plaintiff in the declaratory judgment action, and the Divorce Referee perfected a direct appeal to this Court.

Because the decree for which recognition is sought is that of a foreign nation, the sole question here is whether Tennessee will grant comity to the divorce. We have not found any case in which Tennessee courts have considered the question of what effect should be given a judicial decree from a foreign nation, but the courts of this state have recognized the doctrine of comity in cases where the rights of parties under the laws of other states were at issue, and recognition was not obligatory under the Full Faith and Credit Clause. [Citations omitted.]

The rule of comity to be gleaned from these cases is that, where the law of another jurisdiction is applicable, Tennessee will enforce the substantive rights which litigants have under the laws of the other jurisdiction if such rights are not contrary to the policy of Tennessee. *Id.*

Resting as it does on the non-obligatory discretion of the forum, comity defies both precise definition and uniform rules of practice. The oft-cited case of *Hilton v. Guyot*, 159 U.S. 113, 16 S. Ct. 139, 40 L.Ed. 95 (1895), which contains a thorough examination of the basic principles of comity, defines it as follows:

> " 'Comity,' in the legal sense, is neither a matter of absolute obligation on the one hand, nor of mere courtesy and good will upon the other. But it is the recognition which one nation allows within its territory to the legislative, executive, or judicial acts of another nation, having due regard both to international duty and convenience, and to the rights of its own citizens, or of other persons who are under the protection of its laws.
>
> * * *
>
> "[S]peaking of the difficulty of applying the positive rules laid down by the Continental jurists, * * * [Mr. Justice Story] says that 'there is indeed great truth' in these remarks of Mr. Justice Porter, speaking for the supreme court of Louisiana: 'They have attempted to go too far, to define and fix that which cannot, in the nature of things, be defined and fixed. They seem to have forgotten that they wrote on a question which touched the comity of nations, and that that comity is, and ever must be, uncertain; that it must necessarily depend on a variety of circumstances which cannot be reduced to any certain rule; that no nation will suffer the laws of another to interfere with her own to the injury of her citizens' that whether they do or not must depend on the condition of the country in which the foreign law is sought to be enforced, the particular nature of her legislation, her policy, and the character of her institutions; that in the conflict of laws it must often be a matter of doubt which should prevail * * *.' " (citation omitted).

159 U.S. at 163–165, 16 S. Ct. at 143, 40 L.Ed. at 108–09.

Thus, comity is a discretionary doctrine and may be granted or withheld depending on the particular facts, laws and policies present in an individual case.

In this case, the public policy of this state as reflected by its grounds and jurisdictional requirements for divorce are the issues to be examined in determining the propriety of granting comity.

The majority of states do not grant comity to divorces rendered in foreign jurisdictions where neither spouse was actually domiciled, even where both parties voluntarily submitted to the jurisdiction of the rendering court. See Annotation, 13 A.L.R.3d 1419 (1967).

New York, on the other hand, recognizes foreign divorce decrees valid under the laws of the nation rendering them where the plaintiff spouse appeared personally and the defendant spouse voluntarily appeared through attorney, even though neither party was domiciled there in the Anglo-American legal sense, and the grounds on which the foreign divorce was granted were not recognized in New York. *Rosenstiel v. Rosenstiel*, 16 N.Y.2d 64, 262 N.Y.S.2d 86, 209 N.E.2d 709 (1965). Granting comity in the instant case will not require that we go as far from the majority rule as the New York courts have gone.

The public policy of a state is to be found in its constitution, its statutes, and the decisions of its courts. Primarily, it is for the legislature to determine the public policy of the state, and if there is a statute that addresses the subject in question, the policy reflected therein must prevail. [Citations omitted.]

The Tennessee legislature has authorized the granting of divorces on the ground of irreconcilable differences if the parties have, by written agreement, made provisions for the custody and maintenance of any children of the marriage and an equitable settlement of their property rights. Public Acts 1977, Chapter 107. The record in this case reflects compliance with these conditions and the incorporation of the settlement agreement of October 31, 1974, into the decree of divorce. Appellant suggests no distinction between the ground of irreconcilable differences and that of incompatibility of temperaments making life together unbearable, and in our opinion they are substantially equivalent. Thus, the grounds upon which the Dominican Republic decree was awarded cannot be said to be offensive to the public policy of Tennessee.

* * *

Appellant relies on the principle that a bona fide domicile in the divorce forum is essential to confer jurisdiction of the subject matter.

We note that, in the proper case, the domiciliary requirement may serve an important function; requiring domicile in the rendering jurisdiction as a prerequisite to granting comity may effectively prevent a jurisdiction with no legitimate interest in a particular controversy from fixing or altering legal relationships against the laws and policies of the jurisdiction which does have a legitimate interest in the parties, by virtue of their domiciliary status.

We would, of course, deny comity to a foreign nation decree if its lack of jurisdictional requirements equivalent to our own resulted in prejudice to any citizens of this State. It is clear that in this case the difference between Tennessee's jurisdictional requirements and those of the Dominican Republic have in no sense prejudiced the immediate parties. To the contrary, they contend that they have relied upon the validity of the Dominican Republic decree since its rendition more than three (3) years ago and will be prejudiced if we withhold comity.

Appellant contends that it is against public policy for the state as a third party to the marriage contract to "surrender its sovereignty" to a foreign nation whose laws evince no interest in maintaining the stability of marriage as an institution.

We recently had occasion to recognize and affirm that public policy. There is, however, another public policy consideration that is applicable in the aftermath of a hopelessly broken marriage, that was enunciated by this Court many years ago, a policy that also undergirds the legislative enactment allowing divorce on the ground of irreconcilable differences. In *Farrar v. Farrar*, 553 S.W.2d 741 (Tenn. 1977), Mr. Justice Henry, writing for the Court said:

> "We fully recognize that considerations of public policy demand that the institution of marriage be sheltered and safeguarded. But there is an obverse side to the coin of public policy and consideration must be given to the fact that society is illserved by a legally commanded continuance of a marriage which exists in name only. We quote from the opinion of the late Chief Justice Grafton Green, in *Lingner v. Lingner*, 165 Tenn. 525, 534, 56 S.W.2d 749, 752 (1933): As pointed out by another court, we must take into consideration 'the mischiefs arising from turning out into the world, in enforced celibacy, persons who are neither married nor unmarried.' (Citation omitted.) Society is not interested in perpetuating a status out of which no good can come and from which harm may result."

553 S.W.2d at 744, 745. * * *

* * *

Appellant argues that summary judgment was inappropriate in this case because appellees were not entitled to judgment "as a matter of law" as required by Rule 56.03, Tennessee Rules of Civil Procedure. This contention is without merit. Throughout the proceedings in the trial court and in this Court, there has been no hint that there was any issue as to any material fact. While Tennessee is not, as a matter of law, *required* to grant comity to any foreign decree, the decision to grant comity in a given situation is nevertheless purely a question of Tennessee law.

The judgment of the Chancery Court of Shelby County declaring the decree of the Court of First Instance, Santa Domingo, Dominican Republic, valid and enforceable is affirmed.

Yoder v. Yoder

Superior Court of Connecticut

31 Conn. Supp. 345, 330 A.2d 825 (1974)

SADEN, Judge.

This is an action instituted by the defendant's former wife individually and as parent and natural guardian of Martha Yoder, one of their minor children. In the interest of clarity, the parties will be referred to as "husband" and "wife."

In 1968 the couple obtained a Mexican divorce in which both parties appeared and fully participated. The validity of that divorce is not contested here. An agreement concerning the respective rights and duties regarding support and property was entered into shortly before the divorce and was made a part of the Mexican decree. That agreement provided in pertinent part that the husband would pay the medical expenses of his two minor children, Martha and Elizabeth, and educational expenses if they attend college. The wife alleges that Martha must attend a boarding school pursuant to doctor's orders. The expense of this school, she contends, is a medical one, properly payable by the husband, and not an educational one for which the husband would not be responsible.

In a motion dated October 26, 1972, the wife sought permission to amend her complaint by adding to the prayers for relief the following: " 'E.' That the decree of divorce entered by the Republic of Mexico be made a decree of this Court and enforced in the same manner as a final decree of this Court." The husband objected to this amendment on the ground, inter alia, that there was no authority for allowing such relief in our courts. The court nonetheless allowed the amendment. The husband now demurs to this prayer for relief, contending that, while our courts may recognize an alien decree, they cannot enforce it by making it a decree of the recognizing court. In order to make an alien decree a decree of this court, it is contended, there must be some statutory authority, which does not exist in Connecticut although it does in other states. See *Herczog v. Herczog*, 186 Cal. App.2d 318, 323, 9 Cal. Rptr. 5.

The question has never been squarely presented to our Supreme Court. This court is of the opinion that the reasoning in *Gagnon v. Gagnon*, 23 Conn. Sup. 368, 183 A.2d 858, is correct. Absent some statutory authorization, a decree of an out-of-state tribunal cannot be made that of a Connecticut court. Such a conclusion does not, however, bar the operation of the doctrine of comity.

Whether and to what extent American courts should recognize and enforce decrees of other nations has been a subject of voluminous concern to the commentators. See, *e.g.*, Yntema, *The Enforcement of Foreign Judgments in Anglo-American Law*, 33 MICH. L. REV. 1129; Peterson, *Foreign Country Judgments and the Second Restatement of Conflict of Laws*, 72 COLUM. L. REV. 220; Baade, *Marriage and Divorce in American Conflicts Law: Governmental-Interests Analysis and the Restatement (Second)*, 72 COLUM. L. REV. 329; von Mehren & Trautman, *Recognition of Foreign Adjudications: A Survey and a Suggested Approach*, 81 HARV. L. REV. 1601.

Over the years, the approach of the *Restatement (Second) of Conflict of Laws* appears to have prevailed. The *Restatement's* view is expressed in §§98 and 102. Section 98 provides: "A valid judgment rendered in a foreign nation after a fair trial in a contested proceeding will be recognized in the United States so far as the immediate parties and the underlying cause of action are concerned." Comment c to that section cites *Hilton v. Guyot*, 159 U.S. 113, 16 S. Ct. 139, 40 L.Ed. 95, from which comes the most often quoted list of requirements for "comity." The court said (p. 202, 16 S. Ct. p. 158) that

"where there has been opportunity for a full and fair trial abroad before a court of competent jurisdiction, conducting the trial upon regular proceedings, after due citation or voluntary appearance of the defendant, and under a system of jurisprudence likely to secure an impartial administration of justice between the citizens of its own country and those of other countries, and there is nothing to show either prejudice in the court or in the system of laws under which it was sitting, or fraud in procuring the judgment, or any other special reason why the comity of this nation should not allow it full effect, the merits of the case should not, in an action brought in this country upon the judgment, be tried afresh, as on a new trial or an appeal, upon the mere assertion of the party that the judgment was erroneous in law or in fact."

This rule is entirely sensible and has many policy considerations to recommend it. The commentators agree on several: (1) a desire to avoid the duplication of effort and consequent waste involved in reconsidering a matter which has been fully litigated; (2) a desire to protect the successful litigant from harassment or evasion by the other party; (3) a policy against making the availability of local enforcement the decisive element in the plaintiff's choice of forum; and (4) an interest in fostering stability and unity in an international society in which many aspects of life are multinational. See von Mehren & Trautman, *supra*, p. 1603-4.

As the decree rendered by the Republic of Mexico in the instant case appears to meet the requirements set down in *Hilton v. Guyot*, *supra*, it should be recognized in this state.

As to enforcement of that decree, §102, comment g, of the *Restatement (Second) of Conflict of Laws* says: "It can therefore be assumed that a decree rendered in a foreign nation which orders or enjoins the doing of an act will be enforced in this country provided that such enforcement is necessary to effectuate the decree and will not impose an undue burden upon the American court and provided further that in the view of the American court the decree is consistent with fundamental principles of justice and of good morals." In other words, an internationally foreign decree will be accorded treatment similar to a judgment of one of our sister states, unless it is found to be repugnant to some basic public property of the state.

No such repugnancy is found here. The divorce in the instant case was granted on grounds which, at the time of the rendition of the decree, would not have been considered proper under the Connecticut statute; that is, incompatibility of temperaments. Today, however, is the point in time from which we should evaluate the state's public policy regarding permissible grounds for divorce. Since the passage of Public Act 73-373, these grounds have included the irretrievable breakdown of the marriage. The grounds on which the Mexican divorce was granted do not differ so greatly from our current divorce law as to be considered repugnant.

There has been no claim made here that the Mexican court lacked jurisdiction to enter the decree. Some writers argue, however, that the state of the domicil of the parties has a paramount public interest in the status of the marriage and should refuse to recognize Mexican divorces or to enforce them since they are all too often procured on a divorce-mill basis. See Baade, *supra*. The court in *Rosenstiel v. Rosenstiel*, 16 N.Y.2d 64, 73, 262 N.Y.S.2d 86, 90, 209 N.E.2d 709, 712, remarked on that point: "The State or country of true domicile has the closest real public interest in a marriage but, where a New York spouse goes elsewhere to establish a synthetic domicile to meet technical acceptance of a matrimonial suit, our public interest is not affected differently by a formality of one day than by a formality of six weeks. Nevada gets no closer to the real public concern with the marriage than Chihuahua."

At present, of course, the Connecticut court's real concern is the best interests of the child. Apparently there is some medical problem, and the plaintiff mother seeks to have the court determine if the Mexican decree provides coverage for such treatment as the mother alleges is necessary, even though it involves special schooling not mentioned in the decree. This question, however, is beyond the scope of this memorandum.

In an analogous case, *Adamsen v. Adamsen*, 151 Conn. 172, 195 A.2d 418, custody of a child was awarded to the plaintiff as part of a Norwegian divorce decree. The defendant absconded from Norway to Connecticut with the child while an appeal was pending. The plaintiff, in a habeas corpus hearing, sought to have the Norwegian decree enforced here. The court said (p. 178, 195 A.2d p. 421):

> "The determination of the ultimate question as to the person in whom the custody should be reposed requires the court to exercise its discretion and to give paramount consideration to the welfare of the child. *Morrill v. Morrill*, * * * [83 Conn. 479] 489, 77 A. [1,] 4, 5; *Kelsey v. Green*, 69 Conn. 291, 301, 37 A.679 * * *. Where there is an outstanding foreign judgment determining custody, the effect to be accorded it as a matter of comity is the same whether it is the judgment of a foreign nation or of a sister state."

See *Litvaitis v. Litvaitis*, 162 Conn. 540, 545, 295 A.2d 519.

In *Adamsen v. Adamsen, supra*, 151 Conn. 180, 195 A.2d 418, the court makes it quite clear that while its ultimate conclusion coincided with that of the Norwegian court, the Connecticut hearing was an independent adjudication made after a full trial rather than a mere enforcement of the foreign judgment. In other words, had the Connecticut court seen fit to do so in the exercise of its discretion, it had the power and right to vary the custody provisions of the Norwegian decree.

Recognition of the Mexican decree in the instant case is a matter of comity among nations. This principle does not, however, require Connecticut to adopt an alien decree as its own, as the plaintiff requests in the relief challenged by demurrer. It is sufficient that Connecticut by virtue of the comity doctrine recognize the Mexican decree if it is not repugnant to the public policy of this state, and enforce it at law and in equity, including the remedy of contempt, if the circumstances warrant it. *German v. German*, 122 Conn. 155, 164, 188 A. 429.

The demurrer to the requested relief that the Mexican decree be made a decree of this court is sustained.

Comments

Hyde and *Yoder* involve the recognition of divorce decrees rendered by courts of foreign nations. In both instances, American domiciliaries had obtained bilateral divorces, with their respective spouses fully collaborating. The language in *Yoder* is somewhat myopic because the Supreme Court of Connecticut speaks of a divorce decree rendered by the Republic of Mexico, although in all probability a decree by the court in the Mexican state of Chihuahua was concerned. This oversight was harmless in *Yoder* because the Connecticut court recognized the foreign decree. However, failure to differentiate can sometimes facilitate nonrecognition. It would do so, for example, if the laws of divorce existing in Chihuahua until 1970 were given weight in determining whether divorces from other Mexican states or recent divorces from Chihuahua are to be recognized within the United States. As explained at the end of this Comment, an attitude of non-American courts similar to that of the Connecticut court here—speaking of "American" divorce decrees without differentiating between divorce jurisdictions of individual states—may sometimes lead to nonrecognition of "American" decrees abroad.

Until November 1970, the Mexican state of Chihuahua had a particularly liberal divorce law in two respects. It provided for a form of no-fault divorce on the ground of incompatibility of character, and for proving residence, and thereby jurisdiction, entry in the municipal register of the place of the divorce was sufficient. The courts of Ciudad Juárez, Chihuahua, across from El Paso, Texas, were most often invoked by New York residents at a time when divorce was difficult to obtain at home. After the divorce business declined in Chihuahua because of statutory change, it moved to Haiti and the Dominican Republic. This does not mean, however, that all migratory divorces in these countries originate from the United States. About half of them concern couples from Europe, Africa, and Latin America. *Hyde* illustrates why Americans may still prefer a Dominican or Haitian decree over a local divorce, especially if they are in full agreement on the divorce consequences. In this case a crowded docket would have imposed a waiting period on the parties. People from the world of entertainment appear also to prefer the remoteness of the forum from publicity.

Part of the problem of recognition of foreign divorce decrees is related to parochialism. It results from the isolation of many states from the rest of the world. As late as 1978 the Supreme Court of Tennessee found no single case from Tennessee dealing with the recognition of judicial decrees of any kind from foreign nations. The absence of binding legal authority favors an essentially discretionary judicial standard of comity among nations. Federal regulation—for example, akin to treaties recognizing foreign divorce judgments, which now exists in European countries—is unlikely because of local resentments against federal intrusion into matters traditionally perceived as belonging to the states. Thus the state courts will continue to deal with these matters haphazardly.

Although the full faith and credit clause does not apply to decrees from foreign nations, state courts apply standards of recognition developed among sister states. To the extent that this leads to reexamination of jurisdictional issues according to standards of domicile, regardless of whether the foreign country has a domicile requirement, it means the continued impact of *Williams v. North Carolina I* and *II* (see pp. 445–463) in an area for which it was not designed.

Sherrer v. Sherrer (see pp. 463–466) is of equal relevance because many foreign divorces are bilateral, as, for example, those in *Hyde* and *Yoder*. In fact, the laws of Haiti and the Dominican Republic appear to be designed to meet the requirements of *Sherrer*. If both parties to a foreign divorce have reached a settlement and are represented or appear in person, the danger of subsequent strife is minimized. Consequently, the majority of these foreign divorces, in the absence of controversy between the former spouses, are de facto effective although their legal validity may be subject to question. In *Hyde* the controversy was almost artificially created, against the wishes of the former spouses, by intervention of a Divorce Referee who appealed the recognizing lower court judgment in behalf of the interest of the State. Lack of controversy, however, does not alleviate the cloud on future marriages entered in reliance on foreign-country divorces. It appears also that at least some foreign divorces are fraudulent and ineffective under the laws of their origin, especially some divorces that continue to be issued to foreigners in a few Mexican states.

Hyde and *Yoder* refer to *Hilton v. Guyot** as the source for principles of comity in the recognition of foreign judgments. *Yoder*, in addition, quotes standards of fairness as enumerated in *Hilton* and supported by *Restatement (Second) of Conflict of Laws* §98. Yet *Hilton* involved a money judgment and was not meant to be binding on state courts, certainly not in regard to foreign divorce decrees. The references to *Hilton* and the *Restatement* are therefore probably intended only to articulate standards of discretion that the courts could have arrived at independently. Significantly, the requirement of reciprocity that was the basis of the decision in *Hilton*—that a foreign judgment is only to be recognized if the foreign country in question also recognizes American decrees—is omitted from the catalogue of factors needed for recognition. What seems to emerge is the absence of a national standard of binding force and at least the possibility of nonrecognition of the foreign divorce decree, although both *Hyde* and *Yoder*, with elaborate reasoning, came out in favor of recognition.

The question of recognition of the divorce decree by a foreign nation should be distinguished from the problem of whether a party can be estopped to attack collaterally the validity of a foreign divorce. Although such estoppel may lead to results comparable to recognition, it proceeds under a theory that, in spite of flaws in the local validity of the foreign decree, the party concerned is to be treated as if the

*159 U.S. 113 (1895).

decree were fully valid. If, for example, a voluntary party to a Haitian divorce, after remarriage, were to claim to his or her new spouse that the divorce, and therefore the remarriage, was invalid, he or she could be estopped by his prior conduct from raising this point. Even in a jurisdiction not recognizing the Haitian divorce, the subsequent remarriage could be treated by way of estoppel as if it were valid. Although this kind of case is conceptually different from actual recognition of the foreign divorce decree, its practical results are similar. The difference becomes apparent, however, if another party, for example, the bona fide new spouse, claims invalidity of the marriage. While genuine recognition affects all parties concerned, estoppel affects only the party whose present position is inconsistent with prior behavior.

Hyde and *Yoder* concerned American domiciliaries who obtained divorces in foreign countries, perhaps the most difficult situation for purposes of recognition. Other factual variations may prove to be less problematical: for example, American domiciliaries of foreign nationality who obtain a divorce in their country of origin; an American serviceman stationed abroad whose American domicile is difficult to ascertain and who obtains a divorce in the country where he is stationed; or two foreigners of the same nationality who have obtained divorces in their country of origin prior to coming to the United States. More complex situations may arise if foreigners of different nationality obtain a divorce in a third foreign country which may or may not be recognized in their countries of origin. Many of these questions are likely to arise in determining marital status for purposes of immigration.

One aspect of recognition of divorce decrees from foreign countries within the United States should not go unmentioned, namely, the reverse and indirect negative impact that these local American dispositions may have on recognition of American divorce decrees in foreign countries. If a foreign country is governed by conceptions of reciprocity, requiring proof that its own decrees will be recognized within the United States, severe complications may develop.

The workings of the American federal system are difficult to perceive for even sophisticated foreign lawyers and judges. *Williams v. North Carolina I* and *II* can be used to demonstrate in a foreign forum that no American divorce decree is immune from collateral attack, even if it originates within the United States. Since reciprocity does not exist between American states, the argument could go, how much less could it be expected in relation to foreign countries? The very concept of comity, which involves discretionary reexamination of the jurisdiction of foreign courts according to American notions and standards of fairness and American rather than foreign substantive law, seems to preclude, or at least impair, recognition of American judgments abroad. Much of the relevant American case law, including *Williams* and *Sherrer*, is partly responsible for bringing about this difficulty, albeit inadvertently. Most court opinions not involving foreign-country divorces use the term "foreign" only in relation to sister states, and might seem to the nonlegal reader to be speaking as if genuinely foreign countries do not exist. In fact, American courts tend to be more benevolent than they have given the appearance of being. The deplorable result is that foreign court decrees, including divorce judgments, are often more likely to be recognized within American states than our own judgments are likely to be recognized in foreign countries.

References

Baade, *Marriage and Divorce in American Conflicts Law: Governmental-Interests Analysis and the Restatement (Second)*, 72 COLUM. L. REV. 329 (1972).

Juenger, *Recognition of Foreign Divorces—British and American Perspectives*, 20 AM. J. COMP. L. 1 (1971).

Miller, *Mexican Divorces Revisited*, 84(4) CASE & COM. 43 (July-August 1979).

Note, *Caribbean Divorce for Americans: Useful Alternative or Obsolescent Institution?*, 10 CORNELL INT'L L.J. 116 (1976).

Note, *Foreign Nation Judgments: Recognition and Enforcement of Foreign Judgments in Florida and the Status of Florida Judgments Abroad*, 31 U. FLA. L. REV. 588 (1979).

Rheinstein, M., MARRIAGE STABILITY, DIVORCE, AND THE LAW 81–91 (1972).

Von Mehren & Trautman, *Recognition of Foreign Adjudications: A Survey and a Suggested Approach*, 81 HARV. L. REV. 1601 (1968).

Bibliography

Baade, *Marriage and Divorce in American Conflicts Law: Governmental-Interests Analysis and the Restatement (Second)*, 72 COLUM. L. REV. 329 (1972).

Clark, H., THE LAW OF DOMESTIC RELATIONS IN THE UNITED STATES chs. 11 & 13 (1968).

Cowley, *Home is Where I Hang My Divorce Decree: A Critical Appraisal of Sosna v. Iowa*, 12 CAL. W.L. REV. 452 (1976).

Garfield, *The Transitory Divorce Action: Jurisdiction in the No-Fault Era*, 58 TEX. L. REV. 501 (1980).

Juenger, *Recognition of Foreign Divorces—British and American Perspectives*, 20 AM. J. COMP. L. 1 (1971).

Lasok, D., *Reform of French Divorce Law*, 51 TUL. L. REV. 259 (1977).

Note, *Full Faith and Credit versus State Interest*, 55 TEX. L. REV. 127 (1976).

Note, *Marriage Dissolution Jurisdiction*, 52 WASH. L. REV. 369 (1977).

Note, *Migratory Divorce: The Alabama Experience*, 75 HARV. L. REV. 568 (1962).

Reese, *Marriage in American Conflict of Laws*, 26 INT'L & COMP. L.Q. 952 (1977).

Rheinstein, M., MARRIAGE STABILITY, DIVORCE, AND THE LAW (1972).

Von Mehren & Trautman, *Recognition of Foreign Adjudications: A Survey and a Suggested Approach*, 81 HARV. L. REV. 1601 (1968).

5

Children: In or Out of Privity

The legal position of children has been controversial through the ages and continues to be so today. Conflicting theories, each rooted in historical antecedents, seem to be reflected in the decisional law.

The Child as Chattel. Today's conceptions of child custody, as they in fact operate within the courts, cannot be understood without considering the historical importance of marriage for property and the rules governing succession upon death. Paternal power over children as the future heirs of property was essential to this system. Property itself was perceived in terms of relationships between persons. Yet, since they were subject to parental dominion, some of the persons—children—themselves acquired some of the characteristics of property, or chattels.

None of this would seem applicable to contemporary policies on child custody. But the traditional relations of land tenure are deeply embedded in common law; and American lawyers, especially within the jurisdiction of the state courts where custody battles are fought, are imbued with common law styles of reasoning borrowed from the law of property. Thus even the reformed law of custody, which urges that "the best interests of the child" should prevail over other considerations, is still argued not infrequently in the style of property adjudication.

The ancient paternal right to services of the child, compatible with feudal law, was likewise perceived as proprietary in nature. Children acquired characteristics of slaves who could be conveyed or of servants who could be exploited. In Massachusetts law during colonial times, the child could even be killed upon the father's request if the child disobeyed him. Slowly, and not before the nineteenth century, the wife and mother established competing rights in her children, which soon became superior to those of the husband and father, especially if the children were of "tender years." But even this shift took place in the style of a reallocation of property.

495

The presumption of the parent's fitness was, and still is, a rule of evidence in support of the custodial powers of the parent. Even the reasoning of contemporary psychoanalysts who have spoken on the question of what custodians are fit to have custody of a child is not entirely free of proprietary conceptions. While not using terms like "adverse possession," they argue that to disturb the emotional status quo, unless it is clearly required by circumstances of neglect, can only harm a child. According to this view, whoever has custody, no matter how obtained, is in a certain sense presumed to be fit, although there is an appearance of a shift of concern toward the child.

Custody therefore is still largely a matter of power, as in the past when it was founded on birth and blood ties. A custodian, even if his position is reached by questionable, perhaps even illegal means, enjoys quasi-parental rights of dominion over the child. The longer the custodian succeeds in maintaining possession of the child, regardless of bad faith, the more will contemporary law be inclined to leave the child for its own sake where it was found. While parental rights may have been weakened, the principle of "the best interests of the child" may inadvertently have brought about a result that sometimes resembles acquisition of title in real property by adverse possession. As in property adjudication, the disposition of custody is not supposed to have punitive elements.

The Child as Person. The 1960s, however, saw a shift in emphasis. Children were increasingly treated as persons rather than chattels. Their wishes became an important factor to be considered in child custody matters. Although they still were not recognized as parties in interest in divorce litigation, and were not entitled to representation, some measure of due process was accorded to them in juvenile proceedings. Their status, especially if they were older, was transformed. They were considered juveniles or adolescents earlier, and their status changed again to "young adults" when they reached 18. Children increasingly asserted themselves and challenged the authority of their parents and the State. They demonstrated in the streets and changed the course of national policies and elections.

The State, responded to these pressures, it appears, by lowering the age of majority. While this was part of the waning of parental rights, it can also be viewed in a different light. By treating children, almost overnight, as adults, parents acquired the legal power to "abandon" them at a time when they still needed guidance and support. The State too, while surrendering its power as *parens patriae*, gained the legal means to treat the former children as adults, fully responsible for their acts, and subject to severe discipline and punishment. The rebellious children were, so to speak, thrown to the wolves. They had gained constitutional protections as persons, but the emphasis was still, as in the past, on their responsibilities and subservient status.

The Child Not in Privity. Additional complicating factors in regard to children are introduced by the evolution of marriage toward partnership and contract. If marriage is viewed as contractual in nature, it is obvious that children do not participate in the agreement; they are born into it. Thus, at least under traditional views, they appear to be excluded as not being in privity of contract. On the other hand, the concept of privity has been slowly eroded in many areas of law, for example, in the protection of the consumer. Of course, the parallels between consumer protection and "best interests of the child" are hardly explicitly acknowledged by the courts. Yet if the courts increasingly treat marriage as a partnership—that is, as a co-ownership for profit between parties presumed to be equal who deal with each other at arm's length—then children acquire new and sometimes contradictory characteristics. They are "assets" of the marriage to be fought over in case of dissolution; they are also, in a sense, a "product" of marriage; and, if it comes to their protection as persons, they are "consumers" of marriage regardless of lack of privity of contract. Thus we witness conflicting trends in the law according to which children are increasingly recognized as persons, while at the same time they continue to be treated as if they were chattels.

The express or implied contractual aspects of cohabitation, whether the cohabitation is marital or not, and the view of marriage as a co-ownership for profit weaken the nature of marriage as traditionally perceived. The contemporary increase in illegitimate birth and in the neglect of children can be viewed this way. Large-scale state intervention becomes inevitable, leading to the creation of numerous foster parent-child relationships. Legal adoption is adjusting itself to this development, and now often results from a preexisting foster relationship. In such cases, of course, the adopted child is not newly born but older, and more likely, in the absence of rigid control by adoption authorities, to continue a relationship with his or her birth parents. Such adoption could be made "open," possibly with the opportunity for visitation rights with birth parents and even with all records open. In any event, as de facto relationships become assimilated with legal relationships—by a process discernible in the development of case law—illegitimacy of children becomes decreasingly significant as a concept and legal classification.

The Role of Legal Practice. As discussed at the onset hidden behind the benevolent principle of "the best interests of the child" is the maze of historical evolution including all its contradictory elements. It feeds into the ambivalent attitude of adults toward children. Faced with this situation contemporary courts may fall back on various historical policies or lines of reasoning. The facts of the individual case—whether a parent or an outsider, asserts rights, whether distribution of assets after dissolution of marriage or neglect is involved—may determine what particular historical style is activated for purposes of allocating power over the child.

It would be a mistake to view this complex situation pessimistically. At first blush it may seem appalling that notions of property and styles of reasoning continue to determine the fate of children. Yet it appears to have been impossible to dislodge the deep-rooted feelings that have held sway in this regard. Rather than experimenting with psychological and sociological approaches that ultimately lead to the same proprietary results, legal scholarship should reexamine the problem from the perspective of what practitioners have done in fact.

If proprietary conceptions of the parent-child relationship are here to stay, perhaps the extent to which they have valid functions should be considered more closely, for instance, from a procedural point of view in the adjudication of often untenable situations. Also, if proprietary styles of reasoning were openly acknowledged, the respects in which they fall short if children are involved could be judged more accurately. The assumed dehumanizing aspects of property could be more carefully scrutinized. For in fact, property law has always been concerned not with things but with relationships between people. It has also been viewed on occasion as an extension of one's personality, as are children, and as a means to extend life and control beyond one's death. The conceptual and rhetorical dichotomy between property and persons may therefore not be entirely realistic.

Obviously fundamental social changes in the structure of the family are taking place. The new theoretical structure is shaped by a myriad of decisions about children, with the legal practitioner in the forefront of a seemingly chaotic and ad hoc process that may nevertheless result in clarification.

Custodial Alternatives

Preference for the Mother

Dinkel v. Dinkel

Supreme Court of Florida

322 So.2d 22 (Fla. 1975)

ADKINS, Chief Justice.

Upon petition for certiorari to review the opinion of the District Court of Appeal, First District, at 305 So.2d 90 (1974), conflict appears with the myriad cases setting forth the rule that in the absence of a clear showing of abuse of discretion, the decision of the trial judge in a child custody case will not be reversed. *Grant v. Corbitt*, 95 So.2d (Fla. 1957); *Green v. Green*, 254 So.2d 860 (Fla. App. 1st, 1971); and *Harrison v. Harrison*, 165 So.2d 235 (Fla. App. 2nd 1966).

The only contested issue before the trial court in this proceeding for dissolution of marriage was the matter of custody of the parties' three-year-old child.

In any child custody proceeding, the welfare of the child is the prime consideration. *Green v. Green, supra.* Although a spouse has committed adultery, it may nonetheless be in the best interest of the child that custody be awarded to that spouse. *Anderson v. Anderson*, 205 So.2d 341 (Fla. App. 2nd, 1967). As stated in *McAnespie v. McAnespie*, 200 So.2d 606 (Fla. App. 2nd, 1957):

> "The fact that a mother is guilty of adultery does not necessarily disqualify her to have the custody of her children. Although she may have been a bad wife, she may be a good mother. *The moral unfitness of a mother must be such as has a direct bearing on the welfare of the child, if it is to deprive her of the custody of the child."* (Emphasis supplied) (p. 609)

The District Court of Appeal in the case *sub judice* recognized these rules. Although the District Court referred to the "moral unfitness" of the mother, there is nothing in the opinion which indicates that such "moral unfitness" had any "direct bearing on the welfare of the child." There is conflict and we have jurisdiction.

Petitioner admitted having sexual relations over a period of time with one man while she was married to respondent. During the time petitioner was having an affair with a co-teacher, respondent was overseas in military service. Although the sexual activity was carried on while the subject child was present in the two-bedroom mobile home, it was never performed in front of the child.

Although contradictory testimony was presented at the trial, the record contains competent substantial evidence to show that petitioner is an attentive, intelligent, loving and responsible parent whose adulterous activity did not adversely affect the child.

After holding two separate hearings and listening to twelve witnesses present over 230 pages of testimony, the trial judge entered a judgment awarding custody of the child to petitioner giving extensive visitation rights to respondent. In the final judgment, the trial judge found that although petitioner had committed adultery, it is in the best interest of the minor child that custody be awarded to petitioner.

The District Court reversed the award of custody of the minor child to petitioner and found that, because petitioner had committed adultery in the presence of her child, she was an unfit mother, and therefore not entitled to custody.

Adultery may or may not have a direct bearing on the welfare of a child of tender years. Engaging in sexual intercourse with someone other than one's spouse in the same household where the subject child is present does not necessarily affect the child's welfare. Whether the adultery has a direct bearing on the welfare of the child is a question for the trier of fact. Where the trier of fact determines that the spouse's adultery does not have any bearing on the welfare of the child, the act of adultery should not be taken into consideration in reaching the question of custody of the child.

Where the trier of fact reaches the conclusion that the adulterous conduct adversely affects the child, the scales are tipped against the award of custody to the adulterous spouse. Even if the trier of fact determines that the spouse's adultery has an adverse effect on the child, other factors, *i.e.*, cruelty, neglect, parental unfitness, exhibited by the other spouse, may be present to tip the scales back in favor of the award of custody to the adulterous spouse. In the latter event, it may be that the best interest of the child would be served by awarding custody to a third party.

While Fla. Stat. §61.13(2), F.S.A., provides for equal consideration of the spouses in the award of custody, it is still the law in this State that, other essential factors being equal, the mother of the infant of tender years should receive prime consideration for custody. *Anderson v. Anderson*, 309 So.2d 1 (Fla. 1975).

It is the function of the trial judge in a child custody proceeding to determine what is in the best interests of the child. An appellate court should not reverse the trial judge's findings absent a showing of abuse of discretion.

Green v. Green, supra; Harrison v. Harrison, supra. As stated in *Grant v. Corbitt, supra:*

> "[T]his court cannot, in any type of case, overturn the decision of a Chancellor made in the exercise of his judicial discretion in the absence of a clear showing of an abuse thereof; and, in a child custody case, the opportunity of the Chancellor to observe the demeanor and personalities of the parties and their witnesses and to feel forces, powers and influences that cannot be discerned by merely reading the record, assumes a new importance because of the many intangibles that must be evaluated in deciding the delicate question of child custody."

95 So.2d 25, p. 28.

Were this Court to sit as a trier of fact and hear all the evidence, we might have reached a conclusion different from that of the trial judge. However, neither this Court nor the district Court can substitute its judgment for that of the trier of fact, absent a finding of an abuse of discretion, which requires a lack of competent substantial evidence to sustain the findings of the trial judge.

In the case at bar, the trial judge heard extensive testimony and reached the conclusion that the child's welfare would be best served by awarding custody to the petitioner. Without even finding an abuse of discretion, the District Court substituted its opinion for that of the trial judge as to which parent would best satisfy the welfare of the child. Absent a showing of abuse of discretion, which was not shown before the District Court or this Court, the order of the trial judge was not reversible.

Accordingly, the decision *sub judice* is quashed and the cause is remanded to the District Court with instructions to reinstate that part of the order of the trial court awarding custody of the minor child to the petitioner.

It is so ordered.

Preference for the Father

Boroff v. Boroff

Supreme Court of Nebraska

197 Neb. 641, 250 N.W.2d 613 (1977)

BRODKEY, Justice.

This is an appeal from a District Court decree dissolving the marriage of the parties; granting custody of a daughter to the mother, and of a son to the father; and awarding alimony and child support to the wife. The husband has appealed, contesting the custody, alimony, and child support awards.

On November 18, 1975, Patricia Ann Boroff, the appellee herein, petitioned the District Court for Washington County to dissolve her marriage, alleging that the marriage was irretrievably broken. In her petition, she did not specifically request alimony, custody of her two children, child support, or a division of property, but prayed for other equitable relief. Respondent Eugene Allan Boroff, the appellant herein, answered the petition on November 19, 1975, admitting the allegations thereof, and prayed that the marriage be dissolved, that the custody of the children be awarded to him, and also for other equitable relief.

Hearing was had on February 12, 1976, at which time both parties and their children testified. Both parties acknowledged that their marriage was irretrievably broken, and that issue is not contested in this appeal. The Boroffs have two children, Vickie, a 12-year-old daughter who attends elementary school in Herman, Nebraska; and Robert, a 14-year-old son who attends Tekemah-Herman High School. The parties were married in 1961. Patricia is 36 years old, and Eugene is 34 years old.

Patricia is currently employed at a cafe in Herman, Nebraska, and earns $60 in net income each week. She works from 5:30 a.m. until 1p.m. 3 days a week, and from 5:30 a.m. until 2 p.m. 2 days a week. She has a high school education, and has previously worked for Western Electric, wiring PBX machines.

Patricia testified at trial that she was asking for custody of the children and an award of child support that would enable her to meet household expenses. She itemized monthly household expenses, totalling $511. Patricia stated that if she were to receive custody of the children, she was asking that she receive the parties' home as part of the property division. She acknowledged that she and her husband had agreed that the party who received custody of the children would remain in the home with the children until they were grown, and that the equity in the house would then be equally divided.

Patricia also asked that she receive a 1965 Buick automobile which the Boroffs owned, and that she receive necessary household furnishings. She stated that Eugene should receive the 1969 Chevrolet pickup they owned, and that he was entitled to the bonds that they jointly owned because he had paid for them. Patricia did not specifically request alimony either in her petition or at trial. In view of her prayer for equitable relief, this was not necessary. *Browers v. Browers*, 195 Neb. 743, 240 N.W.2d 585 (1976).

Finally, Patricia stated that Eugene had been a good father to the children, and that he was a fit person to have custody of the children. She did state, however, that she did not think that Eugene could do the wash, fix the children's meals, and keep the house clean; and she believed that she could provide a better home for the children than Eugene could provide.

Eugene stated that he is the postmaster at Herman, Nebraska, and that he earns $14,489 per year. With his deductions, he receives a monthly take-home pay of approximately $790. The house which the Boroffs own is worth approximately $12,000, and they owe a loan company $3,900.20 on the house, which is paid off at the rate of $61 per month, including real estate taxes and insurance.

Other assets of the Boroffs as testified to at the time of the divorce total $3,144.06. Eugene listed current debts such as oil bills, hospital bills, service station bills, mastercharge, etc., as being in the amount of approximately $600.

Eugene stated that he could do the household duties and take care of the children. He testified that the children got average grades in school, and that their grades had gone down due to domestic tensions over the divorce. Otherwise the children have no problems, and get along well in their community. Eugene agreed with Patricia that the person who is awarded custody of the children should be awarded the possession of the house until the children are grown, and that the equity in the house should then be divided equally between them.

The children testified outside the presence of each other and their parents. Robert stated that he wished to live with his father because his father could care for him better, and could understand his problems better. Robert had not discussed the matter of custody with his mother, but had talked with his father about who he wished to live with. Robert testified that he got along well with his sister, and wished to be together with her. Robert stated that he did not wish to live with his mother because "she goes places and leaves us at home sometimes." Robert stated that his mother had been doing this for 4 or 5 weeks, and that she would be away in the evening from 7 to 11. Robert is involved in scouting, and his father is scoutmaster.

Vickie also testified that she wished to live with her father, as she did not "like the friends my Mom hangs around with," and did not like her mother going to the bar. Vickie stated that her mother went to the bar on Wednesdays, when she went bowling. Vickie stated that she could talk to her father better than she could to her mother, and that she wanted to stay with her brother. Vickie had not talked with her mother about custody, but had talked with her father about it.

On redirect examination, Patricia stated that when she filed for divorce, she thought that the children should decide who they wanted to live with. She now thinks that the children would be better off with her, and particularly that Vickie needs a mother because she is entering her maturity. Patricia acknowledged that she bowls on Wednesday nights, and that she has a beer or two on such occasions. Ordinarily Patricia is home in the evenings with the children. Patricia admitted that Eugene had spent quite a bit of time with the children in recent years, and that he has been a good father.

In a decree dated February 12, 1976, the District Court dissolved the marriage, and made the following awards, which we summarize as follows:

(1) The parties shall receive the house and real estate as tenants in common, subject to the right of Patricia to live in the house rent free until Vickie becomes of legal age or fully self-supporting; Patricia shall pay the utilities and expenses of ordinary wear and tear on the house while she is in possession;

(2) Patricia shall receive the household goods subject to the indebtedness thereon, which she is to pay;

(3) Patricia is to receive the 1965 Buick;

(4) Patricia is to receive her checking account ($2.29), her credit union account ($24.39), and the savings account ($10.82);

(5) Eugene is to receive the pickup truck;

(6) Eugene is to receive his checking account ($203.86), his credit union account ($3.02), and the savings bonds ($380);

(7) Both parties are to equally pay the loan on the house (balance of $3,900.20) in $61 monthly installments;

(8) Eugene is to pay outstanding bills totalling approximately $600;

(9) Eugene is to pay Patricia alimony in the amount of $5,000 at the rate of $1,000 per year;

(10) Patricia shall have the custody of Vickie until she becomes of legal age, subject to reasonable visitation by Eugene;

(11) Patricia shall receive $300 child support per month until Vickie becomes of legal age or fully self-supporting;

(12) Eugene shall have custody of Robert until he becomes of legal age, subject to reasonable visitation by Patricia; and

(13) Eugene shall pay fees of $350 for Patricia's attorney and court costs of $26.

Eugene has appealed from the decree of the District Court, contending that the court erred: (1) In granting custody of Vickie to Patricia, thereby splitting the children contrary to their expressed wishes; (2) in awarding Patricia alimony when no alimony was asked for by Patricia and no evidence was adduced in support of an alimony award; (3) in awarding excessive alimony; (4) in awarding Patricia possession of the family dwelling; and (5) in awarding Patricia an excessive amount of child support.

The first issue to be addressed is whether the District Court erred in granting custody of Vickie to Patricia, thereby splitting the children contrary to their expressed wishes. Section 42-364, R.S. Supp., 1976, provides in part:

"(1) In determining with which of the parents the children, or any of them, shall remain, *the court shall consider the best interests of the children*, which shall include, but not be limited to:

"(a) The relationship of the children to each parent prior to the commencement of the action or any subsequent hearing;

"(b) The desires and wishes of the children if of an age of comprehension regardless of their chronological age, when such desires and wishes are based on sound reasoning; and

"(c) The general health, welfare, and social behavior of the children.

"(2) In determining with which of the parents the children, or any of them, shall remain, *the court shall not give preference to either parent based on the sex* of the parent and no presumption shall exist that either parent is more fit to have custody of the children than the other." (Emphasis supplied.)

The Nebraska cases are clear in holding that the mother and father have an equal and joint right to the custody of their children, and that custody shall be determined on the basis of the best interests of the child. *Young v. Young*, 195 Neb. 163, 237 N.W.2d 135 (1976).

In this case, both children expressed the wish to live with their father rather than their mother. The children were clearly of an age of comprehension, as required by section 42-364, R.S. Supp., 1976, and their wishes appear to have been based on sound reasoning. Both believed that social activities their mother engaged in were either improper or unnecessary. The wishes of the children, however, are not dispositive of the issue. " 'While the wishes of a child who has reached sufficient age, and has the ability to express an intelligent preference, are entitled to consideration, the wishes of the child are not controlling.' " *Miller v. Miller*, 196 Neb. 146, 241 N.W.2d 666 (1976). See, also, *Goodman v. Goodman*, 180 Neb. 83, 141 N.W.2d 445 (1966). Thus, although the wishes of the children in this case should have been considered by the trial court, they are not dispositive of what constitutes the best interests of the children.

In reference to the other factors listed in section 42-364(1), R.S. Supp., 1976, the evidence indicates that the relationship of the children to each parent prior to the commencement of the action was good, although the children expressed their disapproval of their mother's social activities. There was no evidence of any serious conflict between the children and either parent. Both children stated that they felt they could talk to their father more easily than they could talk to their mother. The general health, welfare, and social behavior of the children appeared to be normal, although the boy's grades at school were, at best, average.

In *Young v. Young, supra*, the court listed several other factors which are relevant in determining the best interests of a child: Moral fitness of each parent; the environment offered to the child by the parent; the emotional relationship of the children and each parent; the age, sex, and health of the child; the attitudes of each parent toward the child; each parent's capacity to furnish care to the child; and whether the child's social relationships would be disrupted by one parent having custody rather than the other parent. In this case, applying these factors does not result in a clear conclusion that one parent, rather than the other, should have custody of the children.

A final factor to consider is that the children will be split between the parents as the decree now stands. Although this court has acknowledged that it is sound public policy to keep children together when possible, considerations of public policy do not, in all cases, prevent the splitting of the custody of the children when a marriage is dissolved; rather, the ultimate standard is the best interests of the children. *Braeman v. Braeman*, 192 Neb. 510, 222 N.W.2d 811 (1974); *Humann v. Humann*, 180 Neb. 719, 144 N.W.2d 723 (1966).

The trial court, in splitting custody of the children, stated:

"I hate to do this, but I'm going to split these children. I think the boy has definitely indicated that he wanted to be with his father. He's over 14, I think, that his counsel's indication here about, thought he could pick his own guardian. * * * as far as the girl is concerned, I think it's paramount that she be with her mother until she gets through maturity. I have some personal experience with that. I've been guardian, but have had to exercise guardianship rights of both boys and girls and I think that that's very necessary that this girl get up to her maturity with the mother. They're both fit, and get up to age 16."

We call attention to section 42–364(2), R.S. Supp., 1976, which provides that "the court shall not give preference to either parent based on the sex of the parent and no presumption shall exist that either parent is more fit to have custody of the children than the other." The trial court gave no reason why the wishes of the children should be ignored, and why the custody of the children should be split, other than his belief that Vickie should be with her mother until she reached maturity. The trial court did not find that Vickie's wish to be with her father was not based on sound reasons, or that Vickie was not of an age of comprehension.

On balance, we believe that the court should have placed custody of both children in the father. If this were done, the wishes of the children would have been followed, the children would not have been split, and the father, who was admittedly a good father and fit parent, and who financially is probably in a better position to support the children, would have custody. This court clearly has the power to modify awards granting custody of children to a parent, as marriage dissolution actions are tried de novo by this court on appeal. *Schuller v. Schuller*, 191 Neb. 266, 214 N.W.2d 617 (1974). In this case the trial court's determination did not really turn on its accepting one version of the facts rather than another. The facts in this case are largely undisputed, and simply present a question of law as to who is entitled to custody of the children. In this case we conclude that Eugene should be given the custody of both children.

Since we determine that Eugene should be awarded the custody of Vickie, it is obvious that the award of child support to Patricia must be vacated; and pursuant to the agreement of the parties, Eugene should be awarded possession of the house until the children reach their majority. The parties clearly agreed that whoever received custody of the children should receive possession of the house until the children are of legal age or self-supporting, at which time the equity in the house would be divided equally between them. The question then arises as to whether the award of alimony should remain the same, and whether the household goods should be awarded to Eugene rather than to Patricia.

[Discussion of alimony omitted.]

* * *

In awarding custody of Vickie to Eugene, we also grant reasonable visitation rights to Patricia as to both the minor children. We do not modify the provisions of the divorce decree relative to payment of attorney's fees and costs, nor the provisions relative to division of property of the parties other than the house and household goods.

We affirm the decree of the District Court as modified above.

Affirmed as modified.

Comments

The vast majority of child custody matters are raised in the context of divorce. Those that do arise in the context of child neglect seemingly follow the same standards—that the welfare of the child is of prime consideration and that the best interests of the child should be the determinative factor. A closer look, however, shows that in actual practice, the two classes of child custody matters are treated quite differently. While child neglect cases are governed by state intervention under theories of *parens patriae* and are consequently of high visibility, the contrary is true in most dispositions of children after divorce.

Child custody cases in divorce are mostly handled by agreement between the parties, together with other stipulations relating to the division of marital property. Only a small number of cases are adjudicated by the courts; of these, an even smaller number are appealed—probably less than 1 percent of all custody matters. Since these appeals are taken against the dispositions of the trial judge, for reasons expressed in *Dinkel*, and have little chance of success unless it can be shown that the judge abused his discretion, the pressure on the parties and their lawyers to settle custody is increased. Their agreement shields them from the risks inherent in any exercise of judicial discretion.

Trial judges like to point out that since they are the ultimate decision makers, with the responsibility of looking out for a child's welfare, they are not bound by private agreements. They also reason that since a child is not a chattel, it cannot be bargained away for consideration. Yet these invocations are mostly ritualistic; the judge in fact incorporates the private agreement in his decree. The implication, at least outwardly, is that the parents' agreement coincides with the best interests of the child. Incorporation also establishes the power of the judge to modify the agreement later. The real effect, however, is that judges have surrendered much of their discretionary power to the parties, with the consequence that, within the domain of private divorce litigation, the autonomy of the family prevails over state intrusion. This procedure, which assures maximum privacy of the participants, essentially serves the needs of the middle classes; child neglect cases by their nature are more likely to involve the lower classes. This is not to say that divorce is confined to the middle classes or that child neglect occurs only in a lower-class environment. It merely reflects the reality in applying the best-interests standard.

While *Dinkel* illustrates a middle-class milieu with a schoolteacher mother, *Boroff* presents evidence of a class conflict. The mother's life style, working hours, and recreational preferences clashed with the more stable life of the postmaster husband and father. Not accidentally, the indiscretion of the mother in *Dinkel* received less weight than the irregularity of the mother in *Boroff*. The judge refrained from intervening in *Dinkel*, in spite of the adultery of the mother, while the judge in *Boroff* gave preference to the father. The two cases demonstrate that awareness of underlying issues of social class can substantially aid an attorney in preparing an argument and predicting outcomes in custody matters. Whether the custody of the children was given to the father or mother in *Boroff* was influenced by whether the parents were upwardly or downwardly mobile. That the children themselves preferred their father's middle-class environment to associating with a mother who worked odd hours in a cafe and in her free hours went bowling and drank beer could only help to tilt the decision in favor of the father. On the other hand, the fact that the child in *Dinkel* was only three years old had a bearing on favoring the mother. In fact, because the level of awareness of a child of such tender years is assumed to be low, the judge did not care to specify whether a boy or a girl was involved.

While it is easy to justify holdings of this kind in terms of the traditional best-interests standard, that standard is of little help in the preliminary phases of custody disputes when attorneys are making predictions, counseling their clients and negotiating with opponents. The difficulty of charting a course in these early stages is brought about by a standard which basically articulates the truism that the trial judge, in a controversy over child custody, will rule in favor of what he thinks is right.

In actuality, and perhaps especially under no-fault divorce, the best-interests standard is still concerned with the enforcement of social values, taking implicit punitive measures against one of the parents. It also relates to finances, for example, by covertly using the children to allocate wealth. *Boroff* illustrates the latter point. Custody of the children determined who got possession of the house and whether substantial payments were to be made to the mother. Financial considerations like those that surfaced in *Boroff* inevitably also affect the bargaining between the parties. Concern for children is often intertwined with these matters. In essence this means that children become both assets and liabilities of marriage and, upon divorce of the parents, a rearrangement must take place that often favors one party financially over the other.

While it is true that the best-interests standard is indeterminate and speculative, actual adjudication poses fewer problems than is commonly assumed. In fact, the standard is not applied to bring about a result, but merely serves as a convenient and useful justification for a decision reached on another level. Decision makers often feel uncomfortable with sweeping discretionary powers unless they have worked out more specific guidelines for exercising this seemingly unlimited discretion. To some extent these guidelines have found expression in legislative enactments in individual states and in the factor listings of §402 of the Uniform Marriage and Divorce Act.* Yet a statement that

---

*"Section 402. [Best Interest of Child.] The court shall determine custody in accordance with the best interest of the child. The court shall consider all relevant factors including:
    "(1) the wishes of the child's parent or parents as to his custody;
    "(2) the wishes of the child as to his custodian;

any other relevant factor may be considered is always included. In reality there is a substructure of guidelines—perhaps one could call them rules of thumb rather than rules of law—that are unlikely to be published cohesively, perhaps because once fully articulated they are inherently objectionable. Yet they can be extracted from an amorphous body of case law. Since they are not openly acknowledged in their totality as a cohesive body of regulations, they are relatively immune from efforts to change them. This explains why statutory pronouncements that no preference shall be given to either parent in custody disputes, as mentioned in *Dinkel* and *Boroff*, have had little practical effect in the majority of cases.

The following substructure of guidelines for continuing to exercise discretion, unless it is circumvented by settlement among the parties, can be discerned. The mother still has preference over the father in obtaining custody of children, regardless of their age and sex, particularly if the children are of tender years. The father's chances in a disputed case may not be much better than those of grandparents, unless he remarries. If he is not remarried he may sometimes get custody of a boy, especially a teenager, but only rarely of a girl, particularly one who is maturing. One unarticulated premise underlying this may be that because of the danger of sexual abuse, fathers cannot be fully trusted with girls unless a woman through remarriage resides in the house. A mother, on the other hand, may lose a custody battle over a teenage boy, perhaps because of the underlying fear that she will make a sissy of him. Socialization of children into their proper sexual roles is unquestionably an important factor. In *Boroff*, for instance, the fact—presumably introduced by the father's attorney—that the son was involved in scouting and that the father was a scoutmaster, probably weighed in his favor.

Blood relatives are preferred over outsiders. No splitting of custody should ordinarily take place, either in time or in space. Accordingly, in *Boroff*, the trial judge's ruling that the wife have custody of the daughter and the husband and father have custody of the son was not upheld. Shifting children back and forth between parents—for instance, six months with the mother and six months with the father—is also likely to be reversed. A mother's moral misconduct, such as indiscriminate promiscuity, is perceived to be serious, and may negate the preference that she normally has. An occasional indiscretion may be forgiven, especially if she maintains her decorum. Immorality of the mother tends to have greater weight when custody of a daughter is involved, especially if she is of an impressionable age, than if custody of a boy is concerned, perhaps because of the underlying notion that "boys will be boys." But a preference for maintaining an existing situ-

---

"(3) the interaction and interrelationship of the child with his parent or parents, his siblings, and any other person who may significantly affect the child's best interest;
"(4) the child's adjustment to his home, school, and community; and
"(5) the mental and physical health of all individuals involved.
"The court shall not consider conduct of a proposed custodian that does not affect his relationship to the child."

ation overrides any of these considerations. The child's status quo, even if it is less than ideal, is not disturbed unless child neglect becomes a factor. Thus a father who has taken care of a daughter for some time, for whatever reasons, is likely to retain custody of her.

A close examination of these guidelines or rules of thumb clarifies why they cannot be openly acknowledged. While they reflect arguable social values, in their totality they run counter to the demand for neutral adjudication. They violate admonitions against bias and stereotyping. But private and public acceptance of judicial decisions is facilitated because no single custody disposition is likely to offer more than a few of these justifications, which are introduced as part of the general and inconspicuous principle of best interests of the child. Indeed, the social usefulness of this principle is in its sweeping generality and positive stance. It invokes feelings that are universally shared; a palatable substitute is difficult to find. For example, no parent wants to be told that he or she was awarded custody because this was "the least detrimental alternative," although such a negatively phrased standard may make sense for analytical purposes. Consequently, decisions on the appellate level are more likely to refer to "the least detrimental alternative" standard than those in trial court custody proceedings. It would be hard to imagine a trial judge announcing from the bench to the litigants that one of them is "the least detrimental alternative" instead of enunciating the best interests of the child, which is more acceptable to parties and observers. Nor would it be wise to tell a father that he is denied custody of his teenage daughter because of some perceived potential for sexual abuse. Public sentiment, though tolerant of secret apprehensions, may find their overt application to an innocent father revolting and unfair.

The informal guidelines reflect widely shared popular feelings. Some of them are so firmly embedded in the public consciousness that no controversy about custody may arise in spite of a breakdown of marriage. That the mother continues to have preferential rights for the custody of children is probably responsible for the many tacit and express agreements to that effect that are entered into between parents. Fathers voluntarily submit to what they consider the inevitable. The evolving position of husband and wife in marriage and in postmarital adjustments may bring about changes, but no substantial statistical impact can as yet be discerned.

In the minority of cases in which custody is subject to dispute and adjudication, the guidelines must be balanced against one another. For example, in *Boroff* the preference for the mother had to be balanced against her conduct; the need to avoid contact between teenage daughters and fathers had to be balanced against the need to keep siblings together. One wonders, however, whether the decisive factor was the social class issue of preventing downward mobility of the children, which would have been likely had they been given to the mother. More simply stated, it was perceived to be in the best interests for both to stay with their father.

References

Clark, H., THE LAW OF DOMESTIC RELATIONS IN THE UNITED STATES 572–601 (1968).

Crouch, *An Essay on the Critical and Judicial Reception of Beyond the Best Interests of the Child*, 13 FAM. L.Q. 49 (1979).

Eekelaar, J., & Clive, E., CUSTODY AFTER DIVORCE (Oxford Centre for Socio-Legal Studies, Family Law Studies no. 1, 1977).

Goldstein, J., Freud, A., & Solnit, A., BEFORE THE BEST INTERESTS OF THE CHILD (1979).

Goldstein, J., Freud, A., & Solnit, A., BEYOND THE BEST INTERESTS OF THE CHILD (rev. ed. 1979).

Lowery, *Child Custody Decisions in Divorce Proceedings: A Survey of Judges*, 12 PROFESSIONAL PSYCHOLOGY 492 (August, 1981).

Mnookin, *Child Custody Adjudication: Judicial Functions in the Face of Indeterminacy*, 39 LAW & CONTEMP. PROBS. 226 (1975).

Weitzman & Dixon, *Child Custody Awards: Legal Standards and Empirical Patterns for Child Custody, Support and Visitation After Divorce*, 12 U.C.D. L. REV. 471 (1979).

Weyrauch, *Dual Systems of Family Law: A Comment*, 54 CALIF. L. REV. 781 (1967).

Equal Opportunity for Custody

People ex rel. Irby v. Dubois

Appellate Court of Illinois

41 Ill. App.3d 609, 354 N.E.2d 562 (1976)

DRUCKER, J.

Petitioner, appeals from a judgment denying her petition for a writ of habeas corpus and awarding custody of her twin daughters to respondent, the natural father.

The parties met in 1963 and respondent began residing with petitioner and her children soon thereafter. The parties never married. On July 21, 1973, petitioner gave birth to twin daughters. Respondent moved out of petitioner's home in March of 1974 and married Barbara Jean Dubois on April 11, 1974.

On April 14, 1974, respondent came to petitioner's apartment and, representing that he wanted to show the babies to friends, took the twins away. Although he stated that he would bring them home that evening, he never returned.

Petitioner, having failed to regain the children or contact respondent, filed a petition for habeas corpus on June 4, 1974. The trial court which initially heard the cause denied the petition and awarded temporary custody to respondent. That order was subsequently vacated and a new trial was granted. Prior to trial respondent filed a petition for adjudication of wardship in which he sought to have the children declared wards of the court and placed in his custody.

Since the facts adduced at trial were well stated in the trial court's memorandum opinion and are not now in dispute, we quote from it extensively:

"* * * The evidence reveals that both parents are fit to have custody, but that the natural father is married and can provide a more stable family life with more material advantages to the minor children than the mother can. However, the evidence also shows that the mother had physical custody of the children from birth until the time they were about nine months of age at which time the natural father obtained physical custody of the children by deceiving the mother. The children are now about twenty-one months of age.

"EDMUND DUBOIS is and for some time has been employed by Schenkers International Forwarders, Inc. as a driver-salesman. He testified that he is 53 and in good health. When he began living with petitioner in 1963 a divorce action was pending to dissolve his marriage of 14 years to one Gladys Branch Terrell. There were no children of that union. His present wife BARBARA DUBOIS appeared as a witness at the hearing and testified that she was educated in the Chicago Public Schools and received college training in several local schools including Moody Bible Institute. She further testified that she has been mothering the twins since they were nine months old; that she and DUBOIS want to keep them; and that she would give their care priority over her pastoral duties. DUBOIS, his wife and the twin girls live in a two apartment building at 834 East 88th Street in Chicago.

"Petitioner BARBARA IRBY lives in the Chicago Housing Authority Project at 220 East 63rd Street with four of her five children by her marriage to John H. Irby from whom she has been divorced since 1967. The ages of the four children range from 12 to 17. The fifth child, Belinda age 20, is married and out of the household. MRS. IRBY has not remarried. She is not employed. She receives public assistance. During the latter part of 1971 and the first six months of 1972 she was in a tuberculosis sanitarium. She testified that today the T.B. is inactive and her condition stable. She has no contact with the Sanitarium but goes to the Clinic at the Englewood Health Center every six months.

"This court ordered the probation department to make a social investigation that would include an assessment of the life patterns and the homes of the parties. Pursuant to this order an investigation was made by Probation Officer Birchette who testified at the hearing and submitted a written report which was received into evidence. The report states

'* * * that the best plan for the twins at this time would be to remain with their natural father who along with his wife and mother are providing adequate care and nurturing for the babies. However, it is felt that the mother should be granted visiting rights.'

"On the basis of all the facts and circumstances established by the evidence, this court finds that the interests of the twins would best be served by not disturbing the custody of the natural father. An order will issue denying the petition for Adjudication of Wardship, denying the petition for habeas corpus, fixing BARBARA IRBY's rights of visitation and assessing costs."

On appeal petitioner contends that (1) respondent's conduct in taking the children from her prejudicially altered her position before the trial court, (2) the judgment was against the manifest weight of the evidence and (3) the trial court improperly considered the probation officer's report which was not admitted into evidence.

Opinion

In *Vanderlaan v. Vanderlaan*, 9 Ill. App.3d 260, 292 N.E.2d 145, we held that the ruling by the Supreme Court of the United States in *Stanley v. Illinois*, 405 U.S. 645, indicates that in a custody proceeding a father is not barred from obtaining custody of his children born out of wedlock. Since our decision in that case, other jurisdictions have held similarly, considering the natural father of such children to have rights of custody as would a father of legitimate children upon a dissolution of a marriage. [Citations omitted.] This is in recognition of the principle that a determination concerning custody should be premised upon a consideration of what would be in the best interests of the children. As was stated in *E. v. T.*, 308 A.2d at 43, 44:

> "It is basic, however, that in all matters relating to the custody of minor children the paramount consideration of this and any other court is and should be the safety, happiness, physical, mental and moral welfare of the child. [Cites.] Each case must be decided on its own facts and circumstances, and neither parent has a superior right to custody."

We believe this to be the proper standard for determining who should be awarded custody, regardless of legitimacy.

In Illinois no presumption exists favoring custody in either parent. While giving custody to the mother may well be the usual result of a custody hearing, there is no rule requiring this finding. (*Anagnostopoulos v. Anagnostopoulos*, 22 Ill. App.3d 479, 317 N.E.2d 681.) In *Marcus v. Marcus*, 24 Ill. App.3d 401, 320 N.E.2d 581, 585, the court stated:

> "[I]t should be noted that there is today no inflexible rule which requires that custody of children, especially of tender age, be vested in the mother. Equality of the sexes has entered this field. The fact that a mother is fit is only one facet of the situation, and, standing by itself, it does not authorize a denial of custody to the father, when this appears necessary because of other considerations."

Although earlier cases did express a preference for the mother to be entrusted with the custody of children of tender years, (*Nye v. Nye*, 411 Ill. 408, 105 N.E.2d 300; *People ex rel. Bukovich v. Bukovich*, 39 Ill.2d 76, 233 N.E.2d 382) our 1970 Illinois constitution now provides that equal protection of the law shall not be denied or abridged because of sex. (Ill. Const. Art. 1, sec. 18, S.H.A.) As the trial court in the instant case properly concluded: "[N]o presumption of preference applies." The trial court arrived at its conclusion after a careful examination of this doctrine and its history:

> "The early Illinois case of *Wright v. Bennett*, 7 Ill. 587 (1845), in which the attorney for the defendant in error was a person named A. Lincoln, enunciated the common law rule that as between the mother and father of an illegitimate child the mother's right of custody is superior and the father's right secondary. A mother was assumed not to have outside employment. She was expected to be at home caring for the child. Further it was thought that if a young child could not have both maternal and paternal influences that it would benefit more from a mother's care. Today, women are often employed, and present day authorities assert that 'fathering' can be as essential as 'mothering' for both boys and girls.
> "Illinois courts have taken judicial notice of the recent emancipation of women socially and economically. * * * It is reasonable to expect that courts in awarding child custody will take judicial notice of the changing social and economic conditions of women. The factual basis, if there was one, for the so called 'tender years doctrine' is gone."

Petitioner initially contends that respondent's action in taking the children improperly altered the posture of the parties to her disadvantage. It is claimed that her burden of proof was increased from a mere showing of fitness to proving that she was more fit than respondent since the trial court erroneously applied a presumption favoring the custodial parent.
* * *

* * * The trial judge was aware of the existence of such a presumption but refused to apply it in favor of either party. It is true that once a right to custody has been *judicially* determined, the parent deprived of custody has a greater burden in subsequently proving that a change in custody is warranted. [Citations omitted.] However, in a proceeding to initially determine custody, no greater burden is placed on either parent. In the present case the trial court considered both parties to have equal standing to obtain custody.

Furthermore, although a suit involving custody presents an adversary proceeding between the parties, (*Henrikson v. Henrikson*, 26 Ill. App.3d 37, 324 N.E.2d 473) the State also has an interest in the outcome and the child is considered a ward of the court and is under its special protection. (*Gerst v. Gerst*, 349 Ill. App. 201, 110 N.E.2d 470; *Oakes v. Oakes*, 34 Ill. App.2d 387, 195 N.E.2d 840.) To the extent that there is a burden of proof in such matters, it is that each parent present the court with evidence that custody in that parent would be in the child's best interest. (*Anagnostopoulos; Henrikson.*) Therefore, although respondent's conduct necessitated that petitioner file an action, no greater amount of proof as to her fitness was required.

Petitioner next contends that the award of custody was against the manifest weight of the evidence. At the outset it should be noted that the determination of custody is within the discretion of the trial judge and will not be disturbed unless it appears that a manifest injustice has been done or that the trial court has abused its discretion. *Anagnostopoulos; Barbara v. Barbara*, 110 Ill. App.2d 189, 249 N.E.2d 269.

In the instant case the trial court's finding that it was in the best interests of the children that custody should be with the father was amply supported by the evidence. It was based upon more stable environment and family life which would be afforded the children were the father to be awarded custody. Stability of environment is an important factor to be considered in determining what is the best interests of the children. (*Holloway; Cave v. Cave*, 2 Ill. App.3d 782, 276 N.E.2d 793.) The court's conclusion was also premised upon the fact that respondent could provide more material advantages to the children, the health of the parents, and their past actions in affecting their fitness to have custody.

Although the trial court took cognizance of respondent's conduct in taking the children from petitioner, it was determined that such conduct should not preclude him from being awarded custody:

> "The fact that he obtained custody through deception, however unadmirable such conduct may have been, should not result in automatic award of custody to the mother. If such were to result the children become prizes to be awarded on the basis of parental misconduct not bearing any relevance to fitness. Parental misconduct, if any occurred, should be redressed in other ways and the court should focus only on which award of custody will best serve the interests of the children in this case."

Respondent's action was correctly viewed by the court as another factor to be considered in determining his fitness to have custody. What is of paramount importance is the welfare of the children, not punishment of the father. (*Fears v. Fears*, 5 Ill. App.3d 610, 283 N.E.2d 709.) The trial court's determination that respondent should have custody of the children, despite finding that petitioner was also fit to have custody, cannot be said to be against the manifest weight of the evidence.

Petitioner also contends that the trial court improperly considered the social investigator's report since it was not admitted into evidence.

The social investigator who prepared the report testified fully about its contents during petitioner's case in chief. An examination of the record reveals that the witness testified for 18 pages concerning matters contained in the report and the manner in which those facts were obtained. At one point her testimony concerning the recommendation that the children remain with respondent was virtually identical to that portion of the report quoted in the trial court's opinion:

> "THE WITNESS: * * * I did observe the DuBois home. I felt in terms of nurturing and mothering that his present wife was providing the children with love and attention."

We do not agree with petitioner's claim that it was reversible error for the trial court to consider the report. Petitioner has not indicated whether the witness' testimony failed to encompass any portions of the report, and in the absence of such a showing it must be assumed that the same or similar evidence was properly received during the social investigator's testimony. Therefore, prejudice to petitioner could not have resulted from a consideration of the report even if it were not formally admitted into evidence. [Citations omitted.]

The last issue to be decided is the contention that the trial court erred in considering the recommendation of the social investigator since her conclusion was based upon observations of the children solely in respondent's home thus depriving petitioner of the benefit of a fair comparison. The limitations which existed in the scope of the investigation were brought out and developed at trial during her testimony. Whatever weaknesses existed in this evidence affected the weight that it should be given. It was the function of the trial court, as the trier of fact, to weigh this evidence and determine its value. A court of review will not substitute its judgment for that of the trial court unless the ultimate decision was contrary to the manifest weight of the evidence. (*Anagnostopoulos*; *Hoffmann v. Hoffmann*, 40 Ill.2d 344, 239 N.E.2d 792.) Since we have held that the evidence amply supports the judgment, we must reject this claim.

The decree of the trial court awarding permanent custody of the children to respondent subject to specific visitation rights in petitioner was proper and therefore the judgment denying her application for a writ of habeas corpus is affirmed.

Affirmed.

Comments

Irby is noteworthy in several respects. It seems to establish equal opportunity for custody over twin daughters in the illegitimate father, and it proclaims that fault in achieving their physical custody should not preclude an award in his favor. Actually, the opinion is less progressive than it appears to be; it could have been reached and justified under the traditional guidelines that govern judicial discretion in custody matters. Numerous factors counteracted the usual preference for mothers in this instance. The father's chances were improved by his marriage to a woman with college training. Reference to religious factors, namely, the Moody Bible Institute and the unspecified pastoral duties of the stepmother, although seemingly submitted in a purely factual vein, was probably of at least some significance. The mother, on the other hand, was an unemployed welfare recipient living in public housing with four children from another relationship. Most important, she had tuberculosis, alleged but not proven to be inactive. Again, there were underlying considerations of social class. The father through marriage appeared to be leaning toward the middle classes, while the milieu and living conditions of the mother seemed to assure downward mobility for the children.

Had the father tried to obtain custody from the mother by legal means, he probably would have had a more difficult time. What really counted in his favor was the status quo he had created by his deception. The reference to the truism that children should not be "prizes to be awarded on the basis of parental misconduct" is not entirely persuasive. It is true that custody of children seems to be an issue removed from the question of damages for tort. To put the mother in the position she would have been in had the deception not been committed appears to be inappropriate. Yet leaving the children with the wrongdoing father, simply because the status quo is not to be disturbed, has elements of treating the children as chattels, as if there had been adverse possession. The courts do better to acknowledge this dilemma openly. The decisive factor is the traditional unarticulated guideline that the status quo in regard to children, even if less than ideal, is not to be altered unless the level of child neglect is reached, which clearly was not the case in *Irby*.

In view of these factors, the invocations of equal rights of fathers, even if they are illegitimate, appear to be ritualistic because the outcome was a foregone conclusion, in this instance favoring the father. In most cases, however, in spite of a supposedly equal position of the father, the outcome continues to be the opposite. The mother continues to win, even in jurisdictions, like Illinois, which have articulated the equal position of the father in custody disputes. The reasoning would go thus: upon consideration of all relevant factors, the best interests of the children still favor custody by the mother although—again ritualistically—the equal rights of the father are acknowledged as a matter of principle. It was the facts that dictated a different outcome in *Irby*.

The formal pronouncement of equal rights of fathers and mothers to custody is not entirely insignificant, however. It could be a bargaining tool of husbands and fathers for purposes of getting other, unrelated, advantages by way of settlement. It also encourages fathers to seek custody of children, even daughters, more actively than in the past. But the publicity connected with isolated cases is not yet reflected in a change of statistics in custody awards, which still favor mothers more than 90 percent of the time.

References

Note, *The Rights of Fathers of Non-Marital Children to Custody, Visitation, and to Consent to Adoption*, 12 U.C.D. L. REV. 523 (1979).

Pick, *Father Knows Best—When Parents Face Off in Court, the Odds Are Getting Better That Dad Will Keep the Kids*, STUDENT LAW., May 1978, at 38.

Equal Share in Custody: Joint Custody

Mayer v. Mayer

Superior Court of New Jersey

150 N.J. Super. 556, 376 A.2d 214 (1977)

DUFFY, J.S.C.

Plaintiff and defendant were married on January 13, 1962 and separated on December 1, 1973. Plaintiff wife filed her complaint for divorce on June 5, 1975, alleging a cause of action based on 18 months' separation. The parties were divorced by judgment of this court on November 23, 1976.

Two children were born of the marriage, Dana, 13 years of age, and William, 11. They are in the custody of plaintiff.

Defendant husband is now a practicing member of the Bar of this State, having successfully pursued various business ventures as a real estate broker and developer. At the present time he is attempting to develop several properties in the Livingston, New Jersey, area, and testified to possible ventures in Arizona and Pennsylvania.

Plaintiff has recently undergone an operation for cancer and is under continuing medical and psychiatric care. She is a licensed real estate saleswoman and is affiliated with a local agency, but she has not had a significant income from those efforts.

Trial of this matter consumed about three days. At the conclusion of oral testimony the court ordered counsel for the parties to submit summations as to law and fact covering equitable distribution, support and alimony, custody, counsel fees and costs. This opinion will dispose of those issues.

[The court here awarded plaintiff the marital residence and certain personal property by way of equitable distribution under N.J.S.A. 2A:34-23, applying the guidelines suggested in *Rothman v. Rothman*, 65 N.J. 219, 232, 320 A.2D 496 (1974), plaintiff to be solely responsible for the mortgage, taxes and upkeep of the home. The court also fixed the amounts of alimony and child support defendant is to pay plaintiff; he is to provide a policy insuring his life in an amount of at least $50,000, naming the children as irrevocable beneficiaries and to be maintained until the younger shall have become emancipated, as well as health and medical insurance for them, including major medical coverage, to be maintained until each is emancipated. In addition, he is to be responsible for any extraordinary medical expenses incurred by plaintiff for the treatment of her cancer.]

The issue of custody of the minor children of the marriage is seriously contested. During settlement negotiations held at a conference in chambers the court suggested that, in view of plaintiff's continuing health problems, an order of joint custody might be appropriate in this case.

Plaintiff, in her summation, requests that the court's order of joint custody, if entered, name one parent as the "primary custodian as a matter of law." Defendant "welcome[s] dual custody" in his summation.

Two questions are thus presented. Can this court order joint custody, that is, does the court have the authority to do so? If so, then in what fashion can an order of joint custody, if appropriate, best be implemented?

The question of joint custody has topical as well as legal significance, having been discussed recently in the *New York Times Sunday Magazine* (October 31, 1976) and being the subject of a pending suit naming the Chancery Division of Essex County as defendant. In addition, the concept of joint custody has never been fully explored in any reported decision of our courts.

The time is ripe for a full review of the legal and statutory bases for an award of custody, in general and joint custody, in particular.

The Superior Court of New Jersey has "original general jurisdiction throughout the State in all causes." N.J. Const. (1947), Art. VI, §III, par. 2. Further, the Legislature has vested in this court the authority to make such order, after judgment of divorce or maintenance, "as to the care, custody, education and maintenance of the children, or any of them, as the circumstances of the parties and the nature of the case shall render fit, reasonable and just * * *." N.J.S.A. 2A:34–23. Clearly, this legislative grant of authority would include the authority to order "joint," "divided" or "split" custody. Assuming, therefore, that the circumstances of the parties and the nature of the case render an award of joint custody, "fit, reasonable and just," there is no reason why such an order should not be entered.

New Jersey is in the majority of states which follow the traditional "best interests of the child" rule in custody determinations. The "best interests" doctrine was first announced by Judge (later Justice) Brewer in *Chapsky v. Wood*, 26 Kan. 650 (1881), in which the Kansas Supreme Court repudiated the rule which held that the rights of parents were primary over those of third parties to custody of their children. The doctrine gained popularity after the decision in *Finlay v. Finlay*, 240 N.Y. 429, 148 N.E. 624 (1925), in which the New York Court of Appeals held that the Chancellor acted as *parens patriae* to do what is best for the interests of the child.

The "best interests" standard is the one advocated by the Family Law Section of the American Bar Association in §402 of the Uniform Marriage and Divorce Act. That act has undergone a proposed revision, but §402 was left unmodified. See 7 FAM. L.Q. 135 (1973).

Other standards for placement of custody have been proposed, but they have not yet had as wide acceptance as the "best interests" test has had. Goldstein *et als.* propose the "least detrimental available alternative." Goldstein, Freud and Solnit, BEYOND THE BEST INTERESTS OF THE CHILD (1973). This choice would maximize,

> "* * * (i)n accord with the child's sense of time, the child's opportunity for being wanted and for maintaining on a continuous, unconditional, and permanent basis a relationship with at least one adult who is or will become the child's psychological parent." [at 99]

"Sense of time," "opportunity for being wanted" and "psychological parent" are terms of art coined by the authors.

Another approach is that of John Batt, who approaches child custody questions "from a psychologically oriented child development standpoint." Batt, *Child Custody Disputes: A Developmental-Psychological Approach to Proof and Decisionmaking*, 12 WILLAMETTE L.J. 491 (1976). He proposes that the court take into account five phases of development of the human child before making a custody placement. The phases generally follow the growth of the child from infancy to young adulthood.

The "best interests" standard was authoritatively announced in New Jersey in 1944 by the *Armour* decision and has since been followed by our courts. *Armour v. Armour*, 135 N.J. Eq. 47, 52, 37 A.2d 29 (E. & A. 1944). [Other citations omitted.] Other formulations of the "best interests" test require the court to consider the safety, happiness and physical, mental and moral welfare of the child. [Citations omitted.]

The court has broad discretion in dealing with the custody of a child, being always aware that the welfare and happiness (best interests) of the child is the controlling consideration. [Citation omitted.]

The court will consider the wishes of an infant child as to custody, if the child is of an age and capacity to form an intelligent preference as to custody.

[Citation omitted.] The preference of the young child has a place, although not a conclusive place, in determining custody. [Citations omitted.][2]

Commentators have suggested that a prerequisite to an award of custody should be the appointment of independent counsel for the child so as to safeguard his or her rights. Comment, *A Child's Right to Independent Counsel in Custody Proceedings: Providing Effective "Best Interest" Determination through the Use of a Legal Advocate*, 6 SETON HALL L. REV. 303 (1975); Inker and Peretta, *A Child's Right to Counsel in Custody Cases*, 5 FAM. L.Q. 108 (1971). While this court has assigned independent counsel for children in the past, such a procedure, which entails considerable expense, should be utilized only where the interests of the child are truly adverse to those of the parent(s). One example of such adverse interest would be the situation where neither parent is a fit custodian. That is not the case here.

To which parent, then, should custody be awarded? Our courts have long recognized that custody of a child of tender years ordinarily is awarded to the mother if she is a fit and proper person. *Esposito v. Esposito*, 41 N.J. 143, 145, 195 A.2d 295 (1963). The theory is that the mother will take better and more expert care of the small child than the father can. [Citations omitted.] These considerations must always be considered subordinate, however, to what is truly in the child's best interest. [Citations omitted.]

In the present case the question is not so much "to which parent should custody be awarded" as it is "should custody be awarded to both parents?" Nelson states that

> "Where both parents are suitable persons to have the custody of their children and are devoted to them, they should be given as nearly equal rights to the custody of the children as is practical and compatible with the convenience, education and welfare of the children, since it is against public policy to destroy or limit the relation of parent and child and the child is entitled to the love and training of both parents."

[2 Nelson, DIVORCE AND ANNULMENT (2 ed. 1961), §§15, 17, at 256–57]. N.J.S.A. 9:2-4 makes it clear that, with regard to an order or judgment of custody,

> "* * * the rights of both parents, in the absence of misconduct, shall be held to be equal, and they shall be equally charged with their care, nurture, education and welfare, and the happiness and welfare of the children shall determine the custody or possession."

This statutory grant of equal rights in both parents to custody effectively reversed the holding of the common law wherein the father had the preferred right to custody of his minor child, unless disqualified for same reason. [Citations omitted.]

Our case law is replete with decisions reaffirming the existence of equal rights to custody in both parents. [Citations omitted.] One of our later cases holds that the parental right to the care of his or her child is a fundamental right subject to constitutional protection. *In re J. S. & C.*, 129 N.J. Super. 486, 324 A.2d 90 (Ch. Div. 1974).

Notwithstanding the enlightened views of the Legislature and the courts of this State, no authoritative decision has ever been rendered by our courts on the subject of joint custody. It cannot be said, however, that joint ("dual," "alternating," "divided," "split") custody enjoys great popularity across the

---

[2] In the present case the court did not interview the infant children of the marriage. No evidence was adduced that either child preferred one parent over the other. The court is convinced that the parties have been careful to refrain from making the minds of the children their battleground. They have thus avoided creating the discord, mistrust and misery which forces a child to make a choice between his or her parents.

518 *American Family Law in Transition*

country. Decisions on joint custody in other jurisdictions demonstrate either a guarded acceptance or a clear dislike for the concept. See Annotation, 92 A.L.R.2d 691 (1963).

Courts approving joint custody generally agree that a child is entitled to the love, nurture, advice and training of both mother and father. The experience is said to give the child the experience of two separate homes. *Brock v. Brock*, 123 Wash. 450, 212 P. 550 (Sup. Ct. 1923); *Mullen v. Mullen*, 188 Va. 259, 49 S.E.2d 349 (Sup. Ct. App. 1948). Courts disapproving the concept point to the possibility of resentment against the parents who shuffle the child back and forth, *State ex rel. Larson v. Larson*, 190 Minn. 489, 252 N.W. 329 (Sup. Ct. 1934), the development of a sense of insecurity, *Heltsley v. Heltsley*, 242 S.W.2d 973 (Ky. Ct. App. 1951), and the destructive effect of instability in the human factors affecting a child's emotional life. *Kaehler v. Kaehler*, 219 Minn. 536, 18 N.W.2d 312 (Sup. Ct. 1945).

Two principles can be distilled from the reported cases. The first is that the primary consideration in an award of joint custody is the welfare and best interest of the child. *Bergerac v. Maloney*, 478 S.W.2d 111 (Tex. Civ. App. 1972); *Brocato v. Walker*, 220 So.2d 340 (Miss. Sup. Ct. 1969); *Davis v. Davis*, 354 S.W.2d 526 (Mo. App. 1962). The second principle is that decision must depend upon the facts of the particular case. [Citations omitted.]

Several factors are said to affect the decision to award joint custody. Among these are the wishes of the parents, as in *Ward v. Ward*, 88 Ariz. 130, 353 P.2d 895 (Sup. Ct. 1960), where the court stated that a sincere desire on the part of the parent to share his child's companionship should not be lightly dismissed. Another important factor is the age of the child, the general rule being that the courts should not divide the custody of a child of tender years. Even this rule is not absolute, as in *Lutker v. Lutker*, 230 S.W.2d 177 (Mo. App. 1950), where joint custody of a 2½-year-old was approved, largely because of the devotion of the parents to the child and the short distance between their respective homes.

The distance between the homes of the parents becomes an important factor if the distance is such as to prevent visitation by the noncustodial parent. In that case an award of joint custody may be appropriate. *Maxwell v. Maxwell*, 351 S.W.2d 192 (Ky. Ct. App. 1961).

Assuming that an order of joint custody is appropriate, most courts hold that a frequent shifting from home to home is unnecessarily harmful to the child and should not be permitted. Thus, in *Mason v. Mason*, 163 Wash. 539, 1 P.2d 885 (Sup. Ct. 1931), the court condemned an order of joint custody which gave custody of a two-year-old to the mother from noon on Sunday to noon on Thursday, and to the father from Thursday noon to Sunday noon. The Court said, "Thus the child becomes a perpetual traveler. This constant change in environment, discipline and control undoubtedly would prove to be harmful to the child." *Id.* at 886.

An award giving primary custody to one parent and giving the other parent custody on alternate weekends has been upheld. [Citations omitted.]

Courts sometimes disapprove custody arrangements which alternate custody between the parents for equal periods of time, especially where such shifts interfere with schooling. In *McLemore v. McLemore*, 346 S.W.2d 722, 92 A.L.R.2d 691 (Ky. Ct. App. 1961), an award of joint custody which shifted three young children every week was terminated because of the intolerable burden such frequent, though equal, shifts placed on the children. Periods of time of 6 months and 12 months have been approved for pre-school children.

The most widely accepted form of joint custody award is the one wherein one parent has custody during school months and the other custody during the summer. Annotation, 92 A.L.R.2d 691, §11(a), at 726 (1963). This form of award solves the problem of distance between the homes of the parents and generally avoids frequent shifts in custody. The attitude of courts granting this form of custody is well illustrated by *Fago v. Fago*, 250 S.W.2d 837 (Mo. App. 1952), where it was said:

> The pleasure and benefit of friendly association with both parents should be accorded to a child * * *. She needs to have the benefit of her father's guidance, love and affection as well as that of her mother and grandmother * * *. It will be a broadening and valuable experience for (the child) to spend a part of each summer in the State of New York with her father, leaving ten months of the year for the exertion on (the child) of the beneficent influence of mother, grandmother and aunt in her customary home surroundings in St. Louis. [at 842–43]

There is no doubt that the distance between the homes of the parents was an important factor in that case. [Citations omitted.]

In the present case, the minor children are 13 and 11 years of age and attend school in this State. Plaintiff has requested permission to move to Pittsburgh, Pennsylvania, to be near her parents. Under these circumstances, if plaintiff were given sole custody, visitation by defendant would be both difficult and expensive.

The children are not of such tender years that an award of joint custody would be detrimental to them. They are entitled to know, love and respect their father just as much as they know, love and respect their mother. No order of sole custody in the mother, even with unlimited visitation by the father, could possibly give these children the contact with their father that they need and have a right to. For that reason the court orders that the parties shall have joint custody of the children. Plaintiff will have physical custody from September to June, and defendant will have physical custody during July and August.

Plaintiff's request to move to Pittsburgh is granted. Defendant shall be permitted visitation one weekend a month in the Pittsburgh area during the school year. In addition, defendant shall have free access to the children via telephone at a reasonable hour and for reasonable lengths of time.

Defendant's visitation shall also include a four-day period of visitation during the Christmas and Easter vacations at either location. The parties are, of course, free to supplement this minimum visitation schedule as they may wish and are able to agree upon. Costs of transportation of the children between New Jersey and Pennsylvania will be borne equally by the parties.

[Discussion of counsel fees omitted.]

* * *

Comments

Mayer represents a modern trend that favors joint custody. The opinion is an excellent description of the historical evolution of, and the reasons for and against, joint awards. However, despite considerable intellectual thrust favoring this development, it has found more favor with state legislatures—27 by July, 1982—than with the practicing bar and the courts.*

Most of the custody matters successfully resolved in favor of joint custody are by way of settlement. In *Mayer* a continuing dispute

---

*See the alphabetical listing of state statutes in 8 FAM. L. REP. 2506, 2507 (1982).

between the parents was resolved by the court by an award of joint custody. Even this case contained some elements of settlement at the court's suggestion. The judge suggested in chambers that, in view of the mother's cancer and psychiatric problems, joint custody might be appropriate. The dispute then focused on the specifics of such an award. Some inherent weaknesses of the concept underlie these dynamics. The joint award in *Mayer* may have been a judicial compromise without which the mother might have lost custody altogether. Conceivably, it could also have been a device to give the father legal custody and supervisory functions, although the mother retained physical custody during the school year. Finally, joint custody could in general also be a device for the judge to avoid making a hard decision or sometimes an excuse for rendering no decision at all. As in *Mayer*, courts may choose this escape if their severe misgivings about the mother's suitability prevent application of the ordinary unarticulated guidelines favoring her sole custody. In other words, although joint custody clearly poses psychological advantages for the children, provided the parents are in a collaborative spirit, it also tends to sweep potential arguments under the rug and prevent their adjudication.

There are reasons that may speak against the concept of joint custody. Since the judicial guidelines or rules of thumb are relatively easy to apply, even in cases of severe controversy between the parties, it is not necessary, in the majority of cases, to avoid a clear decision in favor of one party or the other. Indeed, one of these guidelines disfavors any form of split custody. Underlying conceptions of a proprietary nature also disfavor joint custody awards. Although courts disclaim the influence of property notions when they state that the child is not a chattel, they are by a long historical development influenced by the styles of property adjudication. For example, following the imagery of property thinking, joint custody can be linked to a tenancy by the entireties that is transformed, upon divorce, to a tenancy in common, in this instance over children. Of course, this does not mean that courts and lawyers use property conceptions consciously, but awareness of this background helps in understanding their patterns of reasoning. Judges know that tenancy in common after divorce is only a way station to partition of property. Similarly, if marriage is perceived as partnership, dissolution of the partnership brings about an intermediary stage of liquidation when assets and liabilities are clarified, with the ultimate purpose of terminating the relationship for all intents and purposes. The ideal of joint custody of children after divorce, by comparison, appears to have a utopian quality. It pretends, for purposes of child custody, that the marriage continues. This unreality may be confusing to a child and indeed detrimental in that it prevents the child from confronting the divorce and its effect on the once intact family unit. Further complications arise when the child's parents remarry and form new relationships. In some cases, especially when remarriages do not occur, joint custody may be psychologically sound for the children. But, what may be psychologically desirable for children should not be confused with what in fact takes place in child custody proceedings and what actually happens thereafter.

Mayer enumerates some of the factors that favor joint custody. Most important is the willingness and capacity of the parents to collaborate willingly as they would, for example, in a divorce settlement. To impose joint custody in a strongly disputed case, as in *Mayer*, may invite future factual and legal complications. Another factor implicit in *Mayer* is the parents' relatively high socioeconomic status and high educational levels. Education in particular could possibly be linked to levels of tolerance toward nonconformity. The same capacity for tolerance could also affect the workings of joint custody. Age of the children and the logistics of geography may have a bearing too, affecting the children's schooling and the length of time they live in the physical custody of either parent. A crucial factor is the nature of the specific joint custody. Numerous distinct types of arrangements may be involved concerning either physical custody, as in *Mayer*, or aspects of shared decision making by the parents. The latter, though not foreclosed, was not emphasized in *Mayer* but is at the heart of new legislation.* Any of these elements of joint custody requires a degree of sophistication of parties and judges that cannot necessarily be expected. To the extent that joint custody is perceived as a trend of the future, expectations for its workability may be somewhat too high.

References

Bodenheimer, *The International Kidnapping of Children: The United States Approach*, 11 Fam. L.Q. 83, 84 n.5 (1977).
Bratt, *Joint Custody*, 67 Ky. L.J. 271 (1978–1979).
Folberg & Graham, *Joint Custody of Children Following Divorce*, 12 U.C.D. L. Rev. 523 (1979).
Holly, *Joint Custody: The New Haven Plan*, Ms. Magazine, Sept. 1976, at 70.
Kubie, *Provisions for the Care of Children of Divorced Parents: A New Legal Instrument*, 73 Yale L.J. 1197 (1964).
Levy & Chambers, *The Folly of Joint Custody*, Fam. Advoc., Spring, 1981, at 6.
Miller, *Joint Custody*, 13 Fam. L.Q. 345 (1979).
Roman & Haddad, *The Case for Joint Custody*, Psychology Today, Sept. 1978, at 102.

Bibliography

Bratt, *Joint Custody*, 67 Ky. L.J. 271 (1978–79).
Burt, *Developing Constitutional Rights Of, In, and For Children*, 39 Law & Contemp. Probs. 119 (1975).

*See, e.g., Cal. Civ. Code §4600.5, eff. Jan. 1, 1980; Fla. Stat. §61.13(2)(b) (1982), eff. July 1, 1982.

Clark, H., THE LAW OF DOMESTIC RELATIONS IN THE UNITED STATES ch. 17 (1968).

Crouch, *An Essay on the Critical and Judicial Reception of Beyond the Best Interests of the Child*, 13 FAM. L.Q. 49 (1979).

Folberg & Graham, *Joint Custody of Children Following Divorce*, 12 U.C.D. L. REV. 522 (1979).

Foster & Freed, *Life With Father: 1978*, 11 FAM. L.Q. 321 (1978).

Foster, H., A "BILL OF RIGHTS" FOR CHILDREN (1974).

Goldstein, J., Freud, A., & Solnit, A., BEFORE THE BEST INTERESTS OF THE CHILD (1979).

Goldstein, J., Freud, A., & Solnit, A., BEYOND THE BEST INTERESTS OF THE CHILD (rev. ed. 1979).

Katz, S. (ed.), 1 THE YOUNGEST MINORITY: LAWYERS IN DEFENSE OF CHILDREN (1974).

Katz, S. (ed.), 2 THE YOUNGEST MINORITY: LAWYERS IN DEFENSE OF CHILDREN (1977).

Katz, S., & Inker, M. (eds.), FATHERS, HUSBANDS AND LOVERS (1979).

Miller, *Joint Custody*, 13 FAM. L.Q. 345 (1979).

Mnookin, *Child Custody Adjudication: Judicial Functions in the Face of Indeterminacy*, 39 LAW & CONTEMP. PROBS. 226 (1975).

Note, *Developments in the Law—The Constitution and the Family*, 93 HARV. L. REV. 1156 (1980).

Orthner, *Evidence of Single-Father Competence in Childrearing*, 13 FAM. L.Q. 27 (1979).

Factors Influencing Custody Decisions

Psychological Attachment and the Uniqueness of the Individual Case

Seymour v. Seymour

Supreme Court of Connecticut

180 Conn. 705 (1980)

PETERS, J.

This is an appeal from a judgment awarding the custody of a minor child to her mother. The plaintiff, Dennis Seymour, brought an action against the defendant, Margaret Seymour, seeking dissolution of their marriage and custody of their minor child. The defendant's cross complaint did not contest that the marriage had irretrievably broken down, but sought an order that custody be awarded to the defendant as well as an order for ancillary financial relief. No appeal has been taken from the trial court's judgment insofar as it dissolved the parties' marriage and divided their joint assets. The parties continue to be at issue about the custody of their child, which the trial court, *Berdon, J.*, awarded to the defendant mother.

The trial court's extensive finding, corrected as appropriate,[1] establishes the following facts: The plaintiff (hereinafter the father) and the defendant (hereinafter the mother) were married in 1972. Their only child was born on February 4, 1975. The child's first year was a difficult one for her and therefore for her parents. She suffered from colic and from a hip problem that required the wearing of an orthopedic brace. As a result, the child cried often and slept irregularly. During this first year, the mother had primary responsibility for the care of the child, in part because she was nursing her and in part because the father, with a full time job outside of the home, was reluctant to assist in her care. Except for the assistance of friends, there was little outside help for the mother at this time. Within a year of the child's birth, the parents had separated.

The parties' living arrangements, and their arrangements for the care of their child, took various forms from the time of separation in January, 1976, to the time of trial, which began in July, 1977. In 1976, the mother and the child first lived in a variety of marginally adequate temporary quarters. In an effort to find more suitable quarters and to make more permanent plans, the mother, in May of that year, found a baby-sitter for the child during weekdays and asked the father to care for her at night. The father remained in sole custody of the child until some time in June, when the mother resumed personal responsibility for the care of the child for part of each week. The father's custody continued to include leaving the child on weekdays with the baby-sitter the mother had located. The mother's custody did not require the use of baby-sitters, since the mother was able to schedule her part-time work for the time when the child was with her father. Although both parents tried, in good faith, to make a success of joint custody, both had become persuaded, by the time of trial, that joint custody was not feasible.

Although all aspects of the issue of custody of the minor child, then two and one-half years old, were thoroughly and extensively contested at trial by all of the interested parties, there was widespread agreement on two crucial matters. Witness after witness testified that both the mother and the father were suitable and nurturing parents, that each loved the child, and that the child had significant psychological ties to each of them. The witnesses were equally in agreement that the two parents exhibited marked and irreconcilable differences in their personalities, in their life-styles, and in their child care practices. The father was characterized as orderly, well organized, responsible and inflexible, while the mother was described as energetic, impulsive, immature and open. These disparities in the parents' personal orientations led to opposing viewpoints with respect to the child's diet, health care and daily living arrangements, and hence to the breakdown of joint custody of the child.

To assist the court in its Solomonic responsibility to make a choice between the child's suitable but irreconcilable parents, the court appointed Attorney Peter A. Kelly as counsel for the minor child and conducted extensive hearings for seven trial days. The court received testimony not only from the parents and their friends but also from a number of professional experts. The court heard from Kay Shafer, a psychiatric social worker who had counseled extensively with the parents before and after the marital breakdown; she recommended that custody be awarded to the father. The court asked for a report from a family relations officer, Allen Rubin, who, after a custody investigation, also recommended that custody be awarded to the father. The court received reports, finally, from two psychiatrists. Earl S. Patterson, M.D., concluded from his psychiatric examination of the parents that psychiatrically it made no difference which parent was awarded custody. Kyle D.

---

[1] The appellant's effort to add fifty-two proposed draft findings, many of which are merely duplicative of findings actually made, is, as we have noted in the past, a singularly unhelpful approach to appellate review. See *Fucci v. Fucci*, 179 Conn. 174, 177, 425 A.2d 592 (1979).

Pruett, M.D., finding that the child's primary psychological attachment was to her mother, recommended that custody be awarded to the mother.

The court concluded, in accordance with the criteria of General Statutes §46b-56 (b),[2] that custody should be awarded to the mother because such an award would be in the best interests of the minor child. The appellants cannot and do not challenge the overall propriety of this standard, which this court has on innumerable occasions repeatedly affirmed. *Friedman v. Friedman*, 180 Conn. 132, 135–36, 429 A.2d 823 (1980); *Trunik v. Trunik*, 179 Conn. 287, 426 A.2d 274 (1979); *Joy v. Joy*, 178 Conn. 254, 257, 423 A.2d 895 (1979); *Stewart v. Stewart*, 177 Conn. 401, 408, 418 A.2d 62 (1979); *Spicer v. Spicer*, 173 Conn. 161, 162, 377 A.2d 259 (1977); *Simons v. Simons*, 172 Conn. 341, 347, 374 A.2d 1040 (1977). "It is settled that the determination of the custody of a minor child rests largely in the discretion of the trial court, and its decision cannot be overriden unless it abused its discretion." *Simons v. Simons, supra*, 348.

The appellants mount a twofold attack on the trial court's determination to award custody to the mother. First, the appellants argue that the custody statute's failure to provide guidelines for the exercise of the trial court's discretion makes the statute unconstitutionally vague. Second, the appellants contend that the trial court abused its discretion in relying too heavily on psychiatric testimony about the child's primary psychological parent. We find neither argument persuasive.

This is not the first occasion upon which this court has been asked to interpolate objective guidelines into the open-ended fact-oriented statutes which govern family disputes. In *Joy v. Joy*, 178 Conn. 254, 255, 423 A.2d 895 (1979), we declined to impose guidelines to constrain a trial court's inquiry into the irretrievable breakdown of a marriage. In *Posada v. Posada*, 179 Conn. 568, 573, 427 A.2d 406 (1980), and *Fucci v. Fucci*, 179 Conn. 174, 179–80, 425 A.2d 592 (1979), we refused to require specific findings concerning each of the factors that a trial court must consider in making financial statements persuant to General Statutes §§46b-81 (assignment of property) and 46b-82 (alimony). We continue to adhere to the view that the legislature was acting wisely in leaving the delicate and difficult process of fact-finding in family matters to flexible, individualized adjudication of the particular facts of each case without the constraint of objective guidelines. See Mnookin, *Child-Custody Adjudication: Judicial Functions in the Face of Indeterminacy*, 39 LAW & CONTEMP. PROBS. 226, 249–68 (Summer, 1975); Foster & Freed, *Child Custody*, 39 NYU L. REV. 423, 441 (1964). Certainly, a statute that vests discretion in the trial court to determine the best interests of a child in awarding custody is no more unconstitutional than is a statute that allows dissolution of a marriage without fault upon a factual finding that a marriage has irretrievably broken down. See *Joy v. Joy, supra*, 255, and cases there cited.

The contention that the trial court abused its discretion is based upon the appellants' allegation that insufficient weight was given to evidence concerning the parenting ability of the father and of the mother, and excessive weight was given to identification of the child's primary psychological parent. This claim is difficult to sustain in light of the trial court's express statement that it had taken into account the parents' past behavior as it related to their parenting ability and to their consistency in parenting and life style, insofar

---

[2] Section 46b-56 provides, in relevant part:

"SUPERIOR COURT ORDERS RE CUSTODY AND CARE OF MINOR CHILDREN IN ACTIONS FOR DISSOLUTION OF MARRIAGE, LEGAL SEPARATION AND ANNULMENT.* * * (b) In making or modifying any order with respect to custody or visitation, the court shall be guided by the best interests of the child, giving consideration to the wishes of the child if he is of sufficient age and capable of forming an intelligent preference, provided in making the initial order the court may take into consideration the causes for dissolution of the marriage or legal separation."

as these factors might affect the child's growth, development and well-being. It is true that the court assigned special significance to four additional factors: the emotional ties of the child to each parent; the emotional ties of each parent to the child; the time each parent would be able to devote to the child on a day-to-day basis; and the flexibility of each parent to best serve the psychological development and growth of the child. Even these factors, however, go beyond the single-minded attention to primary attachment to a psychological parent of which the appellants are critical.

The role that psychological evaluations play in the determination of the best interests of the child is not susceptible to generalization by appellate courts. It is significant that Goldstein, Freud & Solnit characterize as the "least detrimental available alternative" their suggestion that child placement should maintain "on a continuous, unconditional, and permanent basis a relationship with at least one adult who is or will become the child's psychological parent." Goldstein, Freud & Solnit, BEYOND THE BEST INTERESTS OF THE CHILD, p. 99 (1979). Such a characterization serves to emphasize that the concept of the psychological parent is not a fixed star by which custody decisions can invariably be guided. The notion of a person being or becoming a psychological parent properly emphasizes that nature and nurture both play a role in a child's psychological well-being. Nothing in BEYOND THE BEST INTERESTS OF THE CHILD is inconsistent with a child's having two psychological parents, as would normally be the case in an intact family. Furthermore, professionals in the field of child development remind us that a child may become deeply attached to a parent who is seriously inadequate, disturbed or abusive, so that "in some cases it is a disadvantage for the child to be in the care of the psychological parent." Leonard & Provence, *The Development of Parent-Child Relationships and the Psychological Parent*, 53 CONN. B.J. 320, 327 (1979). While psychological parenting is thus one indicator of the best interests of a child, a court has an independent responsibility to assure itself of the suitability of the parent to whom the child is primarily attached. *Cf. In re Juvenile Appeal (Anonymous)*, 177 Conn. 648, 667–68, 420 A.2d 875 (1979). On this record, the trial court exercised that responsibility.

The appellants challenge not only the concept of the psychological parent but also the methodology of the psychiatrist who presented the concept to the court. The weight to be given to psychological testimony by professionals in mental health is, in matters of custody, as it is elsewhere, a question for the trier of fact. It should be noted, however, that expert opinion must be evaluated in light of the expert's opportunity to come to a reasoned conclusion. *Duley v. Plourde*, 170 Conn. 482, 487, 365 A.2d 1148 (1976); *Stephanofsky v. Hill*, 136 Conn. 379, 384, 71 A.2d 560 (1950); see Tait and LaPlante, HANDBOOK OF CONNECTICUT EVIDENCE §7.16 (b) (1976). As this case illustrates, long-range forecasts about future child development are sometimes based upon relatively few and brief interviews and tests conducted under circumstances of stress.[3] It is not clear to what extent the analytic insights derived from long and intensive psychotherapy can readily be translated into an evaluative setting that is governed by a radically different time frame. None of these infirmities in the psychological testimony is, however, sufficient, singly or jointly, to have required exclusion of Pruett's testimony.

In the circumstances of the case before it, the trial court was certainly not unjustified in concluding that it was relevant to inquire as it did into the psychological relationship between the child and her parents. Once it is definitively established, as it was here, that each parent is loving, caring and otherwise entirely suitable, the court perforce must look to other factors to come to

---

[3] Pruett saw the child with her father on two occasions, and with her mother once. Each interview lasted between forty-five and fifty minutes. Pruett never saw the child in the company of both of her parents. Pruett supervised the administration of a development assessment for the child alone, which involved both interviews and observations of undisclosed length.

a decision about custody. The court was not in error in basing its award of custody to the mother on her strong and healthy relationship to her daughter, her willingness and ability to devote time to her daughter, and her willingness to facilitate visitation by the father.

There is no error.

In this opinion the other judges concurred.

Kinship and the Preference of the Child

McKay v. Mitzel

Supreme Court of North Dakota

137 N.W.2d 792 (N.D. 1965)

STRUTZ, J.

Petitioner brings habeas corpus proceedings to determine the custody of three minor children. The parents were divorced in 1955, and custody of the children was awarded to the mother by the decree. The petitioner is the natural father, who was remarried, in 1957, to a woman who had two children by a former marriage. Two other children have been born as the issue of this second marriage.

The natural mother, who also remarried following the divorce, died in 1963, and this proceeding was brought by the father to secure the custody of the three children by his first marriage.

The respondents in this proceeding are the parents of the mother, and the grandparents of the children involved. The children, two girls and a boy, presently are living with the respondents in Linton and are attending the public schools in that city. The petitioner, with his present family, is residing in the State of Colorado where he is employed by a construction firm. They reside in a trailer home, but the petitioner advised the trial court that, if he were awarded the custody of these three children, he would rent an apartment or a house. The record discloses that the petitioners's salary is adequate to care for these children in addition to his other obligations.

The record further discloses that the petitioner suffered an injury in connection with his employment which made it necessary for him to seek reductions in the amounts which he was required to pay for the support of these children, under the divorce decree. Such payments first were reduced to ninety dollars a month and thereafter to seventy-five dollars a month. It further appears that the children lived with the respondents during the period following the divorce of their parents and until their mother's remarriage, a period of approximately two years, and that, since their mother's remarriage, they have spent much time with the respondents.

At the time of the trial, the court, in the presence of counsel for both the petitioner and the respondents, talked to the children in chambers. At that time, the girls were fifteen and fourteen and the boy was approximately ten and one-half years of age. All of the children expressed a desire to remain with the respondents.

The trial court found that both the petitioner and the respondents were fit and proper persons to have the custody of such minor children. In its decision, the court pointed out that the petitioner's wife is a comparative stranger to the three children involved in this proceeding. The court noted that petitioner's wife has four children of her own and that, although she testified that her relations with the three children involved in this proceeding were excellent on those occasions when they visited their father and that she would try to treat them the same as if they were her own, she could not be expected to give them the same love and consideration that she would give to her own offspring.

Findings of fact and conclusions of law were made in favor of the respondents, and the petition for writ of habeas corpus was denied. The petitioner has appealed from the order denying his petition and has demanded a trial de novo of all the issues before this court.

It is the contention of the petitioner that, as the natural father of the children involved in this proceeding, he is entitled to their custody. Sec. 14-09-04, N.D.C.C. He points out that this court has held that, where the mother is dead, the father is entitled to the custody of the children. *Raymond v. Geving*, 74 N.D. 142, 20 N.W.2d 335.

This court has also held that, upon the death of the parent to whom custody of a child was awarded in a divorce proceeding, the surviving parent may be given custody in a habeas corpus proceeding upon a showing that such parent is a proper person. *Garrett v. Burbage*, 55 N.D. 926, 215 N.W. 479.

Our statute provides that, of two persons equally entitled to custody, preference is to be given to a parent. Sec. 30-10-07(1), N.D.C.C.

While a parent's right to the custody of a child is preferred by this section, in awarding custody the court will be guided by Section 30-10-06, North Dakota Century Code. This section provides that, in awarding custody of a minor, the court is to be guided by certain considerations:

"1. By what appears to be for the best interests of the child in respect to its temporal and its mental and moral welfare, and if the child is of sufficient age to form an intelligent preference, the court or judge may consider that preference in determining the question; * * *."

Thus the statutory right of the parent to primary consideration in the matter of custody is subject to a determination of what is best for the child, such best interests of the child being paramount. *Nelson v. Ecklund*, 68 N.D. 724, 283 N.W. 273. Consequently, where the mother is dead, the father has the right to custody superior to that of anyone else, unless the best interests of the child require that he be deprived of such custody. Thus, before the natural right of a parent to custody of a minor child may be set aside, it must appear that the best interests of the child require such action.

In the matter before us, the trial court found both the natural father, as the petitioner, and the maternal grandparents, as the respondents, fit to have custody of these children. If this were the only matter before the court, the father clearly would be entitled to the writ prayed for. But, in awarding custody, the court must weigh all of the conflicting rules and presumptions, together with all of the circumstances of the particular case. And, as has been pointed out, the controlling consideration of the court in determining custody should be the welfare and best interests of the children. Within the limits imposed by our statute, the trial court is vested with a large discretion in determining what is in the child's best interests and to whom custody should be awarded. The court, having had all of the parties before it, in this case determined that the best interests of the children required that the custody be awarded to the respondents. We cannot say that, in so finding, the court abused its discretion.

We would point to a further consideration which lends support to the court's decision in this matter. At the time of the trial, the two daughters whose custody was involved in this proceeding were fifteen and fourteen years of age, while the son was ten years and five months old. The court, in chambers, in the presence of counsel for both sides, asked these children what their wishes were in the matter of custody, and they stated that they preferred to remain with the respondents. In determining an award of custody, the court may consider the wishes of the children where such children have reached the age of discretion, although such preference is not controlling on the court. Since the children were fifteen, fourteen, and ten years of age, they were not too young to exercise some judgment in respect to their custody. This is especially true of the two older children, and we believe the court was right in determining that the best interests of the children required that they remain together. The desires of the children relative to custody were entitled to consideration. It was for the trial court, in the exercise of its discretion, to appraise the intelligence of the children and to decide what weight, if any, should be given to their wishes in determining the question of custody.

The welfare and best interests of the children, the fitness of the parties, and the right of custody of the parties were all before the trial court. The findings and conclusions of the court are well supported by the evidence, and we agree with these findings.

The order appealed from is affirmed.

Morality and Alternative Life Styles

Jarrett v. Jarrett

Supreme Court of Illinois

78 Ill.2d 337, 400 N.E.2d 421 (1979)

UNDERWOOD, Justice:

On December 6, 1976, Jacqueline Jarrett received a divorce from Walter Jarrett in the circuit court of Cook County on grounds of extreme and repeated mental cruelty. The divorce decree, by agreement, also awarded Jacqueline custody of the three Jarrett children subject to the father's right of visitation at reasonable times. Seven months later, alleging changed conditions, Walter petitioned the circuit court to modify the divorce decree and award him custody of the children. The circuit court granted his petition subject to the mother's right of visitation at reasonable times, but a majority of the appellate court reversed (64 Ill. App.3d 932, 21 Ill. Dec. 718, 382 N.E.2d 12), and we granted leave to appeal.

During their marriage, Walter and Jacqueline had three daughters, who, at the time of the divorce, were 12, 10 and 7 years old. In addition to custody of the children, the divorce decree also awarded Jacqueline the use of the family home, and child support; Walter received visitation rights at all reasonable times and usually had the children from Saturday evening to Sunday evening. In April 1977, five months after the divorce, Jacqueline informed Walter that she planned to have her boyfriend, Wayne Hammon, move into the family home with her. Walter protested, but Hammon moved in on May 1, 1977. Jacqueline and Hammon thereafter cohabited in the Jarrett home but did not marry.

The children, who were not "overly enthused" when they first learned that Hammon would move into the family home with them, asked Jacqueline if she intended to marry Hammon, but Jacqueline responded that she did not know. At the modification hearing Jacqueline testified that she did not want to remarry because it was too soon after her divorce; because she did not believe that a marriage license makes a relationship; and because the divorce decree required her to sell the family home within six months after remarriage. She did not want to sell the house because the children did not want to move and she could not afford to do so. Jacqueline explained to the children that some people thought it was wrong for an unmarried man and woman to live together but she thought that what mattered was that they loved each other. Jacqueline testified that she told some neighbors that Hammon would move in with her but that she had not received any adverse comments. Jacqueline further testified that the children seemed to develop an affectionate relationship with Hammon, who played with them, helped them with their homework, and verbally disciplined them. Both Jacqueline and Hammon testified at the hearing that they did not at that time have any plans to marry. In oral argument before this court Jacqueline's counsel conceded that she and Hammon were still living together unmarried.

Walter Jarrett testified that he thought Jacqueline's living arrangements created a moral environment which was not a proper one in which to raise three young girls. He also testified that the children were always clean, healthy, well dressed and well nourished when he picked them up, and that when he talked with his oldest daughter, Kathleen, she did not object to Jacqueline's living arrangement.

The circuit court found that it was "necessary for the moral and spiritual well-being and development" of the children that Walter receive custody. In reversing, the appellate court reasoned that the record did not reveal any negative effects on the children caused by Jacqueline's cohabitation with Hammon, and that the circuit court had not found Jacqueline unfit. It declined to consider potential future harmful effects of the cohabitation on the children. 64 Ill. App.3d 932, 937, 21 Ill. Dec. 718, 382 N.E.2d 12.

Both parties to this litigation have relied on sections 602 and 610 of the new Illinois Marriage and Dissolution of Marriage Act (Ill. Rev. Stat. 1977, ch. 40, pars. 602, 610), which provide:

"Sec. 602. Best interest of child.

"(a) The court shall determine custody in accordance with the best interest of the child. The court shall consider all relevant factors including:

"(1) the wishes of the child's parent or parents as to his custody;

"(2) the wishes of the child as to his custodian;

"(3) the interaction and interrelationship of the child with his parent or parents, his siblings and any other person who may significantly affect the child's best interest;

"(4) the child's adjustment to his home, school and community; and

"(5) the mental and physical health of all individuals involved.

"(b) The court shall not consider conduct of a present or proposed custodian that does not affect his relationship to the child."

"Sec. 610. Modification.

"(a) No motion to modify a custody judgment may be made earlier than 2 years after its date, unless the court permits it to be made on the basis of affidavits that there is reason to believe the child's present environment may endanger seriously his physical, mental, moral or emotional health.

"(b) The court shall not modify a prior custody judgment unless it finds, upon the basis of facts that have arisen since the prior judgment or that were unknown to the court at the time of entry of the prior judgment, that a change has occurred in the circumstances of the child or his custodian and that the modification is necessary to serve the best interest of the child. In applying these standards the court shall retain the custodian appointed pursuant to the prior judgment unless:

> * * *
> "(3) the child's present environment endangers seriously his physical, mental, moral or emotional health and the harm likely to be caused by a change of environment is outweighed by its advantages to him.
> "(c) * * *"

We note initially, however, that this appeal from the custody modification order was taken on August 11, 1977, two months before the effective date of the new act, and that the new act expressly provides that prior law shall govern such an appeal (Ill. Rev. Stat. 1977, ch. 40, par. 801(d)). While the sections of the new act governing modification of custody orders require explicit findings (see *In re Custody of Harne* (1979), 77 Ill.2d 414, 33 Ill. Dec. 110, 396 N.E.2d 499), we believe those sections in substance modify the prior decisional law, and that our decision in this appeal is not affected by the applicability or nonapplicability of the new act.

The standards applicable to petitions for modification of custody appearing in section 610(b) are substantially those to which Illinois courts have long adhered. In *Nye v. Nye* (1952), 411 Ill. 408, 416, 105 N.E.2d 300, 304, this court said that a divorce decree "is *res judicata* as to the facts which existed at the time it was entered" and that "[n]ew conditions must have arisen to warrant the court changing its prior custody determination." Moreover, the guiding principle in custody adjudications is the best interests of the child (411 Ill. 408, 415, 105 N.E.2d 300) and the change in conditions must adversely affect the best interests of the child (411 Ill. 408, 416, 105 N.E.2d 300). The prior statute also directed the attention of the court to the interests of the child in custody adjudication (sections 13 and 18 of the Divorce Act (Ill. Rev. Stat. 1975, ch. 40, pars. 14, 19), repealed by the Illinois Marriage and Dissolution of Marriage Act (Ill. Rev. Stat. 1977, ch. 40, pars. 101 to 802)). Although prior Illinois decisions did not explicitly articulate the new act's command that no change be made in custody unless the harm inherent in any change in custody is outweighed by the advantages to the child of the new environment, they did recognize that continuity in the child's environment is in itself important. (*Bergan v. Bergan* (1976), 42 Ill. App.3d 740, 743, 1 Ill. Dec. 485, 356 N.E.2d 673; *Holloway v. Holloway* (1973), 10 Ill. App.3d 662, 665, 294 N.E.2d 759; *Collings v. Collings* (1970), 120 Ill. App.2d 125, 128, 256 N.E.2d 108; *Jenkins v. Jenkins* (1967), 81 Ill. App.2d 67, 72, 74, 225 N.E.2d 698; *Leary v. Leary* (1965), 61 Ill. App.2d 152, 155, 209 N.E.2d 663.) Finally, the commands of sections 602 and 610 of the new act to consider only whether the child's environment endangers his physical, mental, moral and emotional health (Ill. Rev. Stat. 1977, ch. 40, par. 610) and to disregard any conduct of the custodian that does not affect his relationship with the child (Ill. Rev. Stat. 1977, ch. 40, par. 602) reemphasize the principle stated in *Nye v. Nye* (1952), 411 Ill. 408, 105 N.E.2d 300, that the focus of custody determinations must be the welfare of the child.

The chief issue in this case is whether a change of custody predicated upon the open and continuing cohabitation of the custodial parent with a member of the opposite sex is contrary to the manifest weight of the evidence in the absence of any tangible evidence of contemporaneous adverse effect upon the minor children. Considering the principles previously enunciated, and the statutory provisions, and prior decisions of the courts of this State, we conclude that under the facts in this case the trial court properly transferred custody of the Jarrett children from Jacqueline to Walter Jarrett.

The relevant standards of conduct are expressed in the statutes of this State: Section 11-8 of the Criminal Code of 1961 (Ill. Rev. Stat. 1977, ch. 38, par. 11-8) provides that "[a]ny person who cohabits or has sexual intercourse with another not his spouse commits fornication if the behavior is open and notorious." In *Hewitt v. Hewitt* (1979), 77 Ill.2d 49, 61-62, 31 Ill. Dec. 827,

394 N.E.2d 1204, we emphasized the refusal of the General Assembly in enacting the new Illinois Marriage and Dissolution of Marriage Act (Ill. Rev. Stat. 1977, ch. 40, par. 101 *et seq.*) to sanction any nonmarital relationships and its declaration of the purpose to "strengthen and preserve the integrity of marriage and safeguard family relationships" (Ill. Rev. Stat. 1977, ch. 40, par. 102(2)).

Jacqueline argues, however, that her conduct does not affront public morality because such conduct is now widely accepted, and cites 1978 Census Bureau statistics that show 1.1 million households composed of an unmarried man and woman, close to a quarter of which also include at least one child. This is essentially the same argument we rejected last term in *Hewitt v. Hewitt* (1979), 77 Ill.2d 49, 31 Ill. Dec. 827, 394 N.E.2d 1204, and it is equally unpersuasive here. The number of people living in such households forms only a small percentage of the adult population, but more to the point, the statutory interpretation urged upon us by Jacqueline simply nullifies the fornication statute. The logical conclusion of her argument is that the statutory prohibitions are void as to those who believe the proscribed acts are not immoral, or, for one reason or another, need not be heeded. So stated, of course, the argument defeats itself. The rules which our society enacts for the governance of its members are not limited to those who agree with those rules—they are equally binding on the dissenters. The fornication statute and the Illinois Marriage and Dissolution of Marriage Act evidence the relevant moral standards of this State, as declared by our legislature. The open and notorious limitation on the former's prohibitions reflects both a disinclination to criminalize purely private relationships and a recognition that open fornication represents a graver threat to public morality than private violations. Conduct of that nature, when it is open, not only violates the statutorily expressed moral standards of the State, but also encourages others to violate those standards, and debases public morality. While we agree that the statute does not penalize conduct which is essentially private and discreet (*People v. Cessna* (1976), 42 Ill. App.3d 746, 749, 1 Ill. Dec. 433, 356 N.E.2d 621), Jacqueline's conduct has been neither, for she has discussed this relationship and her rationalization of it with at least her children, her former husband and her neighbors. It is, in our judgment, clear that her conduct offends prevailing public policy. *Lyman v. People* (1902), 198 Ill. 544, 549–50, 64 N.E. 974; *Searls v. People* (1852), 13 Ill. 597, 598; *People v. Potter* (1943), 319 Ill. App. 409, 410–11, 416, 49 N.E.2d 307.

Jacqueline's disregard for existing standards of conduct instructs her children, by example, that they, too, may ignore them (see *Stark v. Stark* (1973), 13 Ill. App.3d 35, 299 N.E.2d 605; *Brown v. Brown* (1977), 218 Va. 196, 237 S.E.2d 89), and could well encourage the children to engage in similar activity in the future. That factor, of course, supports the trial court's conclusion that their daily presence in that environment was injurious to the moral well-being and development of the children.

It is true that, as Jacqueline argues, the courts have not denied custody to every parent who has violated the community's moral standards, nor do we now intimate a different rule. Rather than mechanically denying custody in every such instance, the courts of this State appraise the moral example currently provided and the example which may be expected by the parent in the future. We held in *Nye v. Nye* (1952), 411 Ill. 408, 415, 105 N.E.2d 300, that past moral indiscretions of a parent are not sufficient grounds for denying custody if the parent's present conduct establishes the improbability of such lapses in the future. This rule focuses the trial court's attention on the moral values which the parent is actually demonstrating to the children.

Since the decision in *Nye*, the appellate courts of this State have repeatedly emphasized this principle, particularly when the children were unaware of their parent's moral indiscretion. (*Hendrickson v. Hendrickson* (1977), 49 Ill. App.3d 160, 7 Ill. Dec. 405, 364 N.E.2d 566; *Strand v. Strand* (1976), 41 Ill.

App.3d 651, 355 N.E.2d 47; *Christensen v. Christensen* (1975), 31 Ill. App.3d 1041, 335 N.E.2d 581; *Huey v. Huey* (1975), 25 Ill. App.3d 20, 322 N.E.2d 560; *Mulvihill v. Mulvihill* (1974), 20 Ill. App.3d 440, 314 N.E.2d 342; *Hahn v. Hahn* (1966), 69 Ill. App.2d 302, 216 N.E.2d 229; *Leary v. Leary* (1965), 61 Ill. App.2d 152, 209 N.E.2d 663; *Jayroe v. Jayroe* (1965), 58 Ill. App.2d 79, 206 N.E.2d 266; *Arden v. Arden* (1960), 25 Ill. App.2d 181, 166 N.E.2d 111; *Wolfrum v. Wolfrum* (1955), 5 Ill. App.2d 471, 126 N.E.2d 34.) At the time of this hearing, however, and even when this case was argued orally to this court, Jacqueline continued to cohabit with Wayne Hammon and had done nothing to indicate that this relationship would not continue in the future. Thus the moral values which Jacqueline currently represents to her children, and those which she may be expected to portray to them in the future, contravene statutorily declared standards of conduct and endanger the children's moral development.

Jacqueline argues, however, that three recent cases—*Burris v. Burris* (1979), 70 Ill. App.3d 503, 26 Ill. Dec. 810, 388 N.E.2d 811; *In re Marriage of Farris* (1979), 69 Ill. App.3d 1042, 26 Ill. Dec. 608, 388 N.E.2d 232, and *Rippon v. Rippon* (1978), 64 Ill. App.3d 465, 21 Ill. Dec. 135, 381 N.E.2d 70—indicate that the moral indiscretion of a parent is not sufficient ground for denial of custody. In *Rippon* the mother who had committed the indiscretion planned to marry her paramour and there was no indication of future misconduct. *Rippon* therefore falls within the rule set out in *Nye*. Both *Farris* and *Burris* were rendered after, and relied upon, the appellate decisions in this case (64 Ill. App.3d 932, 21 Ill. Dec. 718, 382 N.E.2d 12) and in *Hewitt v. Hewitt* (1978), 62 Ill. App.3d 861, 20 Ill. Dec. 476, 380 N.E.2d 454, both of which we have now reversed.

Jacqueline also argues, and the appellate court agreed (64 Ill. App.3d 932, 937, 21 Ill. Dec. 718, 382 N.E.2d 12), that the trial court's decision to grant custody of the children to Walter Jarrett was an improper assertion by the trial judge of his own personal moral beliefs. She further argues that the assertion of moral values in this case, as in *Hewitt v. Hewitt* (1979), 77 Ill.2d 49, 31 Ill. Dec. 827, 394 N.E.2d 1204, is a task more appropriately carried out by the legislature. As pointed out earlier, however, it is the legislature which has established the standards she has chosen to ignore, and the action of the trial court merely implemented principles which have long been followed in this State.

The mother argues, too, that section 610 of the Illinois Marriage and Dissolution of Marriage Act (Ill. Rev. Stat. 1977, ch. 40, par. 610) requires the trial court to refrain from modifying a prior custody decree unless it finds that the children have suffered actual tangible harm. The statute, however, directs the trial court to determine whether "the child's present environment *endangers* seriously his physical, mental, moral or emotional health." (Emphasis added.) (Ill. Rev. Stat. 1977, ch. 40, par. 610(b)(3).) In some cases, particularly those involving physical harm, it may be appropriate for the trial court to determine whether the child is endangered by considering evidence of actual harm. In cases such as this one, however, such a narrow interpretation of the statute would defeat its purpose. At the time of the hearing the three Jarrett children, who were then 12, 10 and 7 years old, were obviously incapable of emulating their mother's moral indiscretions. To wait until later years to determine whether Jacqueline had inculcated her moral values in the children would be to await a demonstration that the very harm which the statute seeks to avoid had occurred. Measures to safeguard the moral well-being of children, whose lives have already been disrupted by the divorce of their parents, cannot have been intended to be delayed until there are tangible manifestations of damage to their character.

While our comments have focused upon the moral hazards, we are not convinced that open cohabitation does not also affect the mental and emotional health of the children. Jacqueline's testimony at the hearing indicated that when her children originally learned that Wayne Hammon would move in with them, they initially expected that she would marry him. It is difficult to predict what psychological effects or problems may later develop from their efforts to overcome the disparity between their concepts of propriety and their mother's conduct. (*Gehn v. Gehn* (1977), 51 Ill. App.3d 946, 949, 10 Ill. Dec. 120, 367 N.E.2d 508.) Nor will their attempts to adjust to this new environment occur in a vacuum. Jacqueline's domestic arrangements are known to her neighbors and their children; testimony at the hearing indicated that Wayne Hammon played with the Jarrett children and their friends at the Jarrett home and also engaged in other activities with them. If the Jarrett children remained in that situation, they might well be compelled to try to explain Hammon's presence to their friends and, perhaps, to endure their taunts and jibes. In a case such as this the trial judge must also weigh these imponderables, and he is not limited to examining the children for current physical manifestations of emotional or mental difficulties.

Finally, we do not believe that the United States Supreme Court's opinion in *Stanley v. Illinois* (1972), 405 U.S. 645, 92 S. Ct. 1208, 31 L.Ed.2d 551, requires a different result. In *Stanley* the Supreme Court found that Illinois statutes created a presumption that an unwed father is unfit to exercise custody over his children. The court held that depriving an unwed father of his illegitimate children without a prior hearing to determine his actual rather than presumptive unfitness, when the State accords that protection to other parents, deprives him of equal protection of the law.

The case before us is fundamentally different. The trial court did not presume that Jacqueline was not an adequate parent, as the juvenile court in effect did in *Stanley*. Rather the trial court recognized that the affection and care of a parent do not alone assure the welfare of the child if other conduct of the parent threatens the child's moral development. Since the evidence indicated that Jacqueline had not terminated the troublesome relationship and would probably continue it in the future, the trial court transferred custody to Walter Jarrett, an equally caring and affectionate parent whose conduct did not contravene the standards established by the General Assembly and earlier judicial decisions. Its action in doing so was not contrary to the manifest weight of the evidence.

Accordingly, we reverse the judgment of the appellate court and affirm the judgment of the circuit court of Cook County.

Appellate court reversed; circuit court affirmed.

GOLDENHERSH, Chief Justice, with whom THOMAS J. MORAN, Justice, joins, dissenting:

The majority states, "The chief issue in this case is whether a change of custody predicated upon the open and continuing cohabitation of the custodial parent with a member of the opposite sex is contrary to the manifest weight of the evidence in the absence of any tangible evidence of contemporaneous adverse effect upon the minor children." (78 Ill.2d at 345,——Ill. Dec. at——, 400 N.E.2d at 423.) An examination of the opinion fails to reveal any other issue, and the effect of the decision is that the plaintiff's cohabitation with Hammon *per se* was sufficient grounds for changing the custody order previously entered. This record shows clearly that the children were healthy, well adjusted, and well cared for, and it should be noted that both the circuit and appellate courts made no finding that plaintiff was an unfit mother. The majority, too, makes no such finding and based its decision on a nebulous concept of injury to the children's "moral well-being and development." (78 Ill.2d at 347,——Ill. Dec. at——, 400 N.E.2d at 424.) I question that any competent sociologist would attribute the increase of "live in" unmarried couples to parental example.

The fragility of its conclusion concerning "prevailing public policy" is demonstrated by the majority's reliance on cases decided by this court in 1852 (*Searls v. People*, 13 Ill. 597) and 1902 (*Lyman v. People*, 198 Ill. 544, 64 N.E. 974), and an appellate court decision (*People v. Potter* (1943), 319 Ill. App. 409, 49 N.E.2d 307) which, rather than "prevailing public policy," more clearly indicates the prejudice extant in that period against interracial sexual relations.

As the appellate court pointed out, the courts should not impose the personal preferences and standards of the judiciary in the decision of this case. Courts are uniquely equipped to decide legal issues and are well advised to leave to the theologians the question of the morality of the living arrangement into which the plaintiff had entered.

As a legal matter, simply stated, the majority has held that on the basis of her presumptive guilt of fornication, a Class B misdemeanor, plaintiff, although not declared to be an unfit mother, has forfeited the right to have the custody of her children. This finding flies in the face of the established rule that, in order to modify or amend an award of custody, the evidence must show that the parent to whom custody of the children was originally awarded is unfit to retain custody, or that a change of conditions makes a change of custody in their best interests. This record fails to show either. Mr. Justice Moran and I dissent and would affirm the decision of the appellate court.

MORAN, Justice, with whom GOLDENHERSH, Chief Justice, joins, dissenting:

I join in the dissent of the chief justice, but also dissent separately. My primary disagreement with the majority lies with its countenancing a change of custody based solely on a *conclusive presumption* that harm to the Jarrett children stemmed from Jacqueline's living arrangements. The majority purports to follow the Illinois Marriage and Dissolution of Marriage Act. Yet, under that act, only on the basis of fact can there be a finding that a change in circumstances has occurred and that modification of the prior custody judgment is necessary to serve the best interest of the children. (Ill. Rev. Stat. 1977, ch. 40, par. 610(b).) The court is not to consider conduct of a custodian if that conduct does not affect his relationship to the child. (Ill. Rev. Stat. 1977, ch. 40, par. 602(b).) In this case, not one scintilla of actual or statistical evidence of harm or danger to the children has been presented. To the contrary, all of the evidence of record, as related by the majority, indicates that under Jacqueline's custodianship the children's welfare and needs were met. Also, the trial court expressly declined to find Jacqueline unfit. Nevertheless, the majority's finding of a violation of the seldom-enforced fornification statute effectively foreclosed any further consideration of the custody issue. Instead of focusing solely on the best interest of the children—the "guiding star" (*Nye v. Nye* (1952), 411 Ill. 408, 415, 105 N.E.2d 300)—the majority has utilized child custody as a vehicle to punish Jacqueline for her "misconduct." Such selective enforcement of a statute is inappropriate and, especially in the child-custody context, unfortunate.

The majority decision also is at odds with the principle of *Stanley v. Illinois* (1972), 405 U.S. 645, 92 S. Ct. 1208, 31 L.Ed.2d 551. The constitutional infirmity of the statutory presumption in *Stanley* casts doubt on the validity of the judicially created conclusive presumption in this case. After *Stanley*, an unwed father may not be deprived of his illegitimate children without a prior hearing to determine his actual fitness. Similarly, Jacqueline should not be deprived of the children in the absence of evidence that a change is necessary to serve the best interest of the children. A hearing at which custody is determined on the basis of the conclusive presumption sanctioned by the majority amounts to no hearing at all.

Comments

Seymour, McKay, and *Jarrett* present cumulative evidence of the persistent effect of traditional internal guidelines or rules of thumb concerning the exercise of discretion in custody awards (see Comments, pp. 505–508, to *Dinkel v. Dinkel* and *Boroff v. Boroff*). In spite of the appearance of sophistication and progressive language, the outcome in these cases was fairly predictable under traditional standards. This is particularly noticeable in *Seymour,* where the Supreme Court of Connecticut used a panoply of modern vocabulary, such as "nurturing parents," "psychological parents," and "parenting ability," to reach its decision to uphold the custody award favoring the mother. One wonders whether all this judicial reasoning was necessary to arrive at the quite possibly foregone conclusion. The elaborate procedure may in fact have been inspired by another purpose, namely, assuring the parties that they have had a fair hearing and that due process prevailed. Yet the hearing was largely ritualistic, with its show of seemingly plausible and progressive steps, such as the appointment of counsel for the minor child and seven trial days of extensive hearings with expert opinions by a psychiatric social worker, family relations officer, and two psychiatrists. Of these experts two favored the father, one the mother, and one felt it made no difference which parent was awarded custody. The trial court, predictably, favored the expert statement preferring the mother and, equally predictably, was upheld on appeal.

In searching for the reasons for the extensive procedure in *Seymour* and the need for progressive language, one has to remember the nature of the internal guidelines. Not only are they based in part on archaic conceptions that reflect strongly held social value preferences, but they are also often in the unconsciousness of the judge and the lawyers who, more likely than not, would deny their influence. In *Seymour* the court also faced, as it often does in initial joint custody awards, parents who were high on the socioeconomic scale. Probably none of the reasoning, nor the battery of expert statements, would have applied to parents from a lower stratum of society. Consequently, the arguments of the lawyers in the case, as well as the opinion of the appellate court, stayed on the same elevated plane. Mere rubber-stamp reasoning that the chancellor was closer to the facts and that his disposition was not to be disturbed would have been unacceptable to these parties and might have led eventually to further complications. One may note in passing that the guideline fundamentally favoring the mother was not all that was involved in *Seymour.* Although in the initial phases of the opinion the sex of the child was unspecified, the last paragraph finally disclosed it by repeated reference to the relationship between a mother and her daughter. Thus the opinion also follows the ancient canon that a father, in a disputed case, has little chance of obtaining custody of girls. Compared with the power of these predispositions, the layer of modern reasoning is inevitably mere surface.

McKay also upheld the trial judge, in this instance favoring custody of the maternal grandparents over that of the father. This case involved some balancing of competing guidelines, yet the outcome here was also fairly predictable. The grandparents had cared for the children, two teenage daughters and one younger boy, prior to their mother's death. Thus the fundamental rule could be applied that, in case of doubt, the status quo in regard to children should not be disturbed. Another factor was only hinted at by the court, namely, that the father was a construction worker living in a trailer. Furthermore, the petitioning father had four children living with him: two from his present marriage and two from an earlier marriage of his present wife. Awarding him custody of the three children from his former marriage would have created a household with seven children. Why then, the court seems to have felt, should the status quo be disturbed, bringing about crowded conditions and uncertain new adjustments? Yet even in this case progressive reasoning was invoked, giving weight to the stated preference of the children. It is of course conceivable that in time what is now a mere makeweight argument will gain in significance.

That the court in *Jarrett* followed traditional guidelines is not surprising considering that it involved Illinois, a jurisdiction noted for its conservatism in family law matters. The Supreme Court of Illinois deliberately referred to its own earlier decision, *Hewitt v. Hewitt* (see pp. 205–212), by which it rejected mere cohabitation as a basis for legal claims. The language of the court, referring to "paramours" and "indiscretions," is significant for discerning the social values preferred by the majority opinion. The behavior of the mother, who did not maintain decorum and who proselytized her beliefs in relations based on nonmarital love to her neighbors and her three daughters, was clearly no help to her. The court applied the guideline that moral misconduct by the mother, referred to as fornication, may negate the preference for custody she may otherwise have, especially if daughters of impressionable age are involved. It is implicit in the decision that the judicial censure of the mother, who chose to live with her "boyfriend," not only cost her the custody of the three daughters, but also had financial consequences—loss of support money and, more important, loss of the house. Thoughts of loss of social status and downward mobility may also have been involved. None of this reasoning, of course, is part of the appellate process. However, the tone of the opinion in *Jarrett* makes it apparent that the court approved of the punitive consequences of what it considered to be immoral behavior.

References

Note, *Lawyering for the Child: Principles of Representation in Custody and Visitation Disputes Arising from Divorce,* 87 YALE L.J. 1126 (1978).
Weyrauch, *Law as Mask—Legal Ritual and Relevance,* 66 CALIF. L. REV. 699 (1978).

Respect for Another State's Decree

Palm v. Superior Court
Court of Appeal, Fourth District
97 Cal. App.3d 456, 158 Cal. Rptr. 786 (1979)

COLOGNE, Associate Justice.

Petitioner Franklin P. Palm seeks a writ of "prohibition/mandate" to compel the Superior Court of San Diego County to vacate its order and stay further proceedings in exercise of jurisdiction in a disputed child custody matter instituted by Rebecca Palm Moody in her complaint to establish a North Dakota divorce decree. That 1974 decree gave Rebecca custody of the parties' minor son who was then a year and a half old. Franklin seeks to stay these proceedings during the pendency of hearings concerned with the son's custody currently being conducted in the North Dakota courts. Franklin contends California's Uniform Child Custody Jurisdiction Act (Act) which North Dakota also adopted[1] requires the superior court to decline jurisdiction over the minor child and instead to abide by North Dakota's determination of the son's custodial fate.

Franklin married Rebecca in 1968. The parties separated in August 1974 and Rebecca moved to San Diego. When Franklin took the child back to North Dakota, she returned to North Dakota to regain custody. Franklin obtained a judgment of divorce on December 16, 1974, in the District Court of Cass County, Fargo, North Dakota. At that time, the North Dakota court awarded custody of their son to Rebecca with the right of reasonable visitation given to Franklin. In March 1976, Rebecca began living with a man named Ross Moody. On December 31, 1976, by stipulation, the parties agreed Franklin could have custody of the son for six months, after which time the custody would go to Rebecca with Franklin to have the right of reasonable visitation, eight consecutive weeks of visitation in the summer plus alternating Christmas and Easter holidays. Franklin took the boy for the agreed six months and immediately afterward kept the boy for the additional eight weeks to which he was entitled. On July 14, 1977, Franklin filed a petition in the District Court seeking an order to show cause why he should not have the son's custody. The matter was heard on August 19, both parties appearing in court personally and through counsel. On September 27, the court made an order amending the judgment to award Rebecca custody provided if she "resumes cohabitation with one Ross Moody, custody of the minor child * * * shall be changed" to Franklin.

Rebecca then took the son with her and the two lived in California where he began school. At this same time, she resumed cohabitation with Moody though at the time he was still married to another. On October 11, 1977, she "married" him and sent a certified copy of the marriage certificate to the court "in order to satisfy the order of the North Dakota Court." She admitted later this was tantamount to "fraud and deceit on the North Dakota court" because Moody was not yet free to marry. Since that time, however, Moody did obtain a divorce from his wife, the "marriage" to Rebecca was annulled and he legally married her.

---

[1] All references to sections of the Act are in the California Civil Code unless otherwise designated. The Act may be found in section 5150 *et seq.* The language of the Act adopted by California and North Dakota (NDCC 14–14–01 to 14–14–26) is not significantly different as it relates to the issues raised in this case.

In April 1978, Rebecca brought an action in California to establish the foreign judgment and to modify visitation. The superior court refused to exercise jurisdiction over the matter and dismissed the complaint with prejudice.

In June 1978, Franklin took the son back to North Dakota for his eight-week visitation period.

On August 14, before the end of that period, Franklin obtained an order to show cause from the North Dakota court for the purpose of securing full custody of the child. He obtained temporary custody and a temporary restraining order was issued to prohibit interference with his custody.

On August 18, Rebecca filed a second complaint against Franklin in San Diego seeking to establish the California court's jurisdiction over the issue of child custody, visitation and child support. On September 18, the court below determined California did have jurisdiction, California was the domiciliary of the child, it is the most convenient state to try the matter of custody, Rebecca has legal custody under the most recent North Dakota decree, the pending change of custody proceedings in North Dakota are not in substantial conformity with the Uniform Child Custody Jurisdiction Act, and the previous action of the California court dismissing Rebecca's action is not res judicata. It ordered Franklin to dismiss his North Dakota change of custody action, to refile it here and to transfer custody of the child to Rebecca to whom it advanced temporary custody pending a hearing on change of custody.

We are advised in November 1978, the son was picked up at school in North Dakota by his maternal grandmother and taken to California where he now resides with them at a place not revealed to Franklin and contrary to the California court order, he has not been allowed visitation privileges. Franklin characterizes this as an "abduction," Rebecca says the son "voluntarily left school." We take judicial notice of the fact North Dakota now has completed hearings on this matter. On May 8, 1979, that court granted full custody to Franklin subject to a right of visitation by Rebecca under Franklin's supervision. The court later adjudicated Rebecca in contempt for failure to appear with the child, punishment to be meted out when she appears before the North Dakota court.

The situation we review is a classic example of the interstate conflict which the Act was intended to obviate. [2] Although both California and North Dakota have adopted the Act, we are faced here with courts in absolute conflict, California exercising jurisdiction and awarding the child to the mother,

---

[2]Section 5150 of the Act reads as follows:

"(1) The general purposes of this title are to:

"(a) Avoid jurisdiction competition and conflict with courts of other states in matters of child custody which have in the past resulted in the shifting of children from state to state with harmful effects on their well-being.

"(b) Promote cooperation with the courts of other states to the end that a custody decree is rendered in that state which can best decide the case in the interest of the child.

"(c) Assure that litigation concerning the custody of a child take place ordinarily in the state with which the child and his family have the closest connection and where significant evidence concerning his care, protection, training, and personal relationships is most readily available, and that courts of this state decline the exercise of jurisdiction when the child and his family have a closer connection with another state.

"(d) Discourage continuing controversies over child custody in the interest of greater stability of home environment and of secure family relationships for the child.

"(e) Deter abductions and other unilateral removals of children undertaken to obtain custody awards.

"(f) Avoid relitigation of custody decisions of other states in this state insofar as feasible.

"(g) Facilitate the enforcement of custody decrees of other states.

"(h) Promote and expand the exchange of information and other forms of mutual assistance between the courts of this state and those of other states concerned with the same child.

"(i) To make uniform the law of those states which enact it.

"(2) This title shall be construed to promote the general purposes stated in this section."

a resident of this state, and North Dakota exercising jurisdiction and awarding the child to the father, a resident of that state. The jurisdictional facts are not in dispute and if the work of the Commission on Uniform State Laws and the respective state Legislatures is to have any relevance, this jurisdictional dispute should be resolved.

A state acquires jurisdiction under the provisions of section 5152. This reads in pertinent part as follows:

> "(1) A court of this state which is competent to decide child custody matters has jurisdiction to make a child custody determination by initial or modification decree if the conditions as set forth in any of the following paragraphs are met: "(a) This state (i) is the home state of the child at the time of commencement of the proceeding, or (ii) had been the child's home state within six months before commencement of the proceeding and the child is absent from this state because of his removal or retention by a person claiming his custody or for other reasons, and a parent or person acting as parent continues to live in this state.
> "(b) It is in the best interest of the child that a court of this state assume jurisdiction because (i) the child and his parents, or the child, and at least one contestant, have a significant connection with the state, and (ii) there is available in this state substantial evidence concerning the child's present or future care, protection, training, and personal relationships."
>
> * * *

"Home state" is defined in section 5151 as "the state in which the child immediately preceding the time involved lived with * * * a parent * * * for at least six consecutive months * * *. Periods of temporary absence of any of the named persons are considered as part of the six-month or other period."

Under the facts of this case, the child was clearly within the jurisdiction of the California courts under the provisions of section 5152, subdivision (1)(a), since he was with his mother in California continuously from August 1977 to June 1978, with the exception of the visit with his father at Christmas. This period, immediately before the commencement of these proceedings, qualifies California as the child's "home state."[3] A California court has the right to determine its jurisdiction (*Abelleira v. District Court of Appeal*, 17 Cal.2d 280, 302, 109 P.2d 942), and the superior court properly did so here.

Under the Act's provisions paralleling section 5152, subdivision (1)(b), North Dakota might well have determined it too has jurisdiction over the custody of the child. The courts of North Dakota could and properly did find it was in the best interests of the child[4] to assume jurisdiction because the child and the father had a significant connection with that state and the requirement of available evidence concerning the child is met. The evidence supporting such a finding may be seen from the fact the father is a resident of that state, maintains his home and business as a dry wall contractor in Fargo; the parties last lived together as man and wife there and obtained their divorce there giving that court jurisdiction to award custody in the first instance, their reputation and relationships are well established in that community; and the child lived there for ten of the last 22 months and even attended school there at least until his removal by the grandparents. During that period, the child obviously made contacts with neighbors, friends and others who could testify as to his behavior and adjustment. There is available in

---

[3]The court found the child was "domiciled" in California, a fact not necessary to finding jurisdiction (see Commissioner's Notes to §3 of the Uniform Act (our §5152); *A Legislative Remedy for Children Caught in the Conflict of Laws*, 22 VANDERBILT L. REVIEW 1207, 1224–1226).

[4]Jurisdiction exists only if it is in the *child's* best interest, not merely the interest or convenience of the contending parties (see Commissioner's Notes to §3 of the Uniform Child Custody Jurisdiction Act).

North Dakota substantial evidence concerning the child's present or future care, protection, housing and personal relationships.

Additionally, it should be noted the court in North Dakota which granted the dissolution has continuing jurisdiction over custody matters. This is the state of the law for California courts as well (Civ. Code, §4600;[5] *Clark v. Superior Court*, 73 Cal. App.3d 298, 304, 140 Cal. Rptr. 709; NDCC 14-05-22; *Moran v. Moran*, 200 N.W.2d 263 (N.D. 1972)).

Faced with a similar factual situation, though one not involving competing exercise of jurisdiction, the Court of Appeal in *Smith v. Superior Court*, 68 Cal. App.3d 457, 137 Cal. Rptr. 348, held California had jurisdiction of the custody question on the basis of the Act which controls over the more general continuing jurisdiction provision of Code of Civil Procedure section 410.50, subdivision (b).[6] In that case, the parties obtained a judgment in California dissolving their marriage. The mother received custody. She remarried and eventually moved to Oregon with the child. They lived there approximately five years, then entered a stipulation concerning custody and visitation, including a visit during Easter 1976. The judgment was modified according to the stipulation. The mother, on the child's strenuous resistance, and on the advice of a psychologist in Oregon, refused to send the child to California for the Easter visitation. The father sought an order of contempt against the mother in California. The trial court determined it had jurisdiction to modify the judgment and to hold the mother in contempt; it was affirmed on appeal.

In *Smith*, the reviewing court conceded Oregon was the "home state" of the child under the provisions of section 5152, subdivision (1)(a). The court concluded, however, under section 5152, subdivision (1)(b), the child had equal or stronger ties to California and "there is available in this state substantial evidence concerning the child's present or future care, protection, training, and personal relationships" in spite of the fact he had been absent for five years. The court relied on the language of the statute, the Code Commissioner's Notes and the facts, as earlier stated, among which were the facts the child's grandparents lived in San Francisco and his relatives there had a good relationship with him. It noted there is additional significance in the fact the parties themselves had submitted the issue of the child's custody and visitation rights to the California court and, while that does not confer jurisdiction, an inference may be reasonably drawn the parties themselves considered the ties to California are stronger. (*Smith v. Superior Court, supra,* 68 Cal. App.3d 457, 464-465, fn. 3, 137 Cal. Rptr. 348.)

By analogy it may be said, just as in *Smith* where California assumed jurisdiction though it was not the "home state" of the child, North Dakota also has the right to assume jurisdiction. North Dakota's jurisdiction in the case before us rests on the same basis as did California's jurisdiction in *Smith.*

It is apparent under the Act both California, as the home state, and North Dakota have jurisdiction over the custody of this child. The question remaining is which state should exercise it.

The Act authorizes a court to relinquish jurisdiction or to stay proceedings in favor of the proceedings in the court of a sister state if it finds it is an inconvenient forum[7] or if there is misconduct.[8] Our courts have on occa-

---

[5]Section 4600 provides in part, "In any proceeding where there is at issue the custody of a minor child, the court may, during the pendency of the proceeding or *at any time thereafter*, make such order for the custody * * *."
(Italics added.)

[6]Code of Civil Procedure section 410.50, subdivision (b), provides: "Jurisdiction of the court over the parties and the subject matter of an action continues throughout subsequent proceedings in the action."

[7]Section 5156 reads as follows:

"(1) A court which has jurisdiction under this title to make an initial or modification decree may decline to exercise its jurisdiction any time before making a decree if it finds that

sion held it an abuse of discretion not to stay proceedings where the other court is clearly the most convenient forum with access to relevant evidence (*Schlumpf v. Superior Court,* 79 Cal. App.3d 892, 145 Cal. Rptr. 190; *Clark v. Superior Court, supra,* 73 Cal. App.3d 298, 140 Cal. Rptr. 709). Nothing in the Act, however, gives a court the authority to determine it has a superior right to proceed where another court is also asserting jurisdiction. On the contrary, the Act provides a means to resolve the issue in an orderly manner without letting a state make factual rulings binding on another. Section 5155 reads as follows:

"(1) *A court of this state shall not exercise its jurisdiction under this title if at the time of filing the petition a proceeding concerning the custody of the child was pending in a court of another state exercising jurisdiction substantially in conformity with this title,* unless the proceeding is stayed by the court of the other state because this state is a more appropriate forum or for other reasons.

"(2) Before hearing the petition in a custody proceeding the court shall examine the pleadings and other information supplied by the parties under 5159 and shall consult the child custody registry established under 5165 concerning the pendency of proceedings with respect to the child in other states. If the court has reason to believe that proceedings may be

---

it is an inconvenient forum to make a custody determination under the circumstances of the case and that a court of another state is a more appropriate forum.

"(2) A finding of inconvenient forum may be made upon the court's own motion or upon motion of a party or a guardian ad litem or other representative of the child.

"(3) In determining if it is an inconvenient forum, the court shall consider if it is in the interest of the child that another state assume jurisdiction. For this purpose it may take into account the following factors, among others:

"(a) If another state is or recently was the child's home state.

"(b) If another state has a closer connection with the child and his family or with the child and one or more of the contestants.

"(c) If substantial evidence concerning the child's present or future care, protection, training, and personal relationships is more readily available in another state.

"(d) If the parties have agreed on another forum which is no less appropriate.

"(e) If the exercise of jurisdiction by a court of this state would contravene any of the purposes stated in Section 5150.

"(4) Before determining whether to decline or retain jurisdiction the court may communicate with a court of another state and exchange information pertinent to the assumption of jurisdiction by either court with a view to assuring that jurisdiction will be exercised by the more appropriate court and that a forum will be available to the parties.

"(5) If the court finds that it is an inconvenient forum and that a court of another state is a more appropriate forum, it may dismiss the proceedings, or it may stay the proceedings upon condition that a custody proceeding be promptly commenced in another named state or upon any other conditions which may be just and proper, including the condition that a moving party stipulate his consent and submission to the jurisdiction of the other forum.

"(6) The court may decline to exercise its jurisdiction under this title if a custody determination is incidental to an action for divorce or another proceeding while retaining jurisdiction over the divorce or other proceeding.

"(7) If it appears to the court that it is clearly an inappropriate forum it may require the party who commenced the proceedings to pay, in addition to the costs of the proceedings in this state, necessary travel and other expenses, including attorney's fees, incurred by other parties or their witnesses. Payment is to be made to the clerk of the court for remittance to the proper party.

"(8) Upon dismissal or stay of proceedings under this section the court shall inform the court found to be the more appropriate forum of this fact, or if the court which would have jurisdiction in the other state is not certainly known, shall transmit the information to the court administrator or other appropriate official for forwarding to the appropriate court.

"(9) Any communication received from another state informing the state of a finding of inconvenient forum because a court of this state is the more appropriate forum shall be filed in the custody registry of the appropriate court. Upon assuming jurisdiction the court of this state shall inform the original court of this fact."

The authority given is strictly to relinquish or stay when there is a finding it is an inconvenient forum. Subdivision (4) gives authority to communicate with the court of a sister state hopefully to reconcile any differences.

[8]Section 5157 deals generally with the clean hands doctrine which is not in issue in this case.

pending in another state it shall direct an inquiry to the state court administrator or other appropriate official of the other state.

"(3) If the court is informed during the course of the proceeding that a proceeding concerning the custody of the child was pending in another state before the court assumed jurisdiction it shall stay the proceeding and communicate with the court in which the other proceeding is pending to the end that the issue may be litigated in the more appropriate forum and that information be exchanged in accordance with Sections 5168 through 5171. If a court of this state has made a custody decree before being informed of a pending proceeding in a court of another state it shall immediately inform that court of the fact. If the court is informed that a proceeding was commenced in another state after it assumed jurisdiction it shall likewise inform the other court to the end that the issues may be litigated in the more appropriate forum." (Italics added.)

The Act was thus designed to solve this very problem of conflicting jurisdictions. The state which enjoys priority of time in initiating the proceedings will proceed if the dispute is not resolved by agreement or consent of the other court.[9]

Moreover, where a custody decree has been made, section 5163, subdivision (1), becomes relevant. That provision reads:

"(1) If a court of another state has made a custody decree, a court of this state shall not modify that decree unless (a) it appears to the court of this state that the court which rendered the decree does not now have jurisdiction under jurisdictional prerequisites substantially in accordance with this title or has declined to assume jurisdiction to modify the decree and (b) the court of this state has jurisdiction."

Professor Bodenheimer, the reporter for the committee which prepared the Uniform Law, interprets the effects of section 5163 (§14 of the Act) as follows:

"A typical example is the case of the couple who are divorced in state A, their matrimonial home state, and whose children are awarded to the wife, subject to visitation rights of the husband. Wife and children move to state B, with or without permission of the court to remove the children. State A has continuing jurisdiction and the courts in state B may not hear the wife's petition to make her the sole custodian, eliminate visitation rights, or make any other modification of the decree, even though state B has in the meantime become the 'home state' under section 3 [Civ. Code, §5151(5)]. The jurisdiction of state A continues and is exclusive as long as the husband lives in state A unless he loses contact

---

[9]The Code Commissioner's Notes to section 5155 (§6 of the Act) read in part:
"Because of the havoc wreaked by simultaneous and competitive jurisdiction * * * this section seeks to avoid jurisdictional conflict with all feasible means, including novel methods. Courts are expected to take an active part under this section in seeking out information about custody proceedings concerning the same child pending in other states. In a proper case jurisdiction is yielded to the other state either under this section or under section 7 [§5156]. Both sections must be read together.
"When the courts of more than one state have jurisdiction under sections 3 [§5152] or 14 [§5163], priority in time determines which court will proceed with the action, but the application of the inconvenient forum principle of section 7 [§5156] may result in the handling of the case by the other court.
"While jurisdiction need not be yielded under subsection (a) if the other court would not have jurisdiction under the criteria of this Act, the policy against simultaneous custody proceedings is so strong that it might in a particular situation be appropriate to leave the case to the other court even under such circumstances.
* * *
"Once a custody decree has been rendered in one state, jurisdiction is determined by sections 8 [§5157] and 14 [5163]."

with the children, for example, by not using his visitation privileges for three years."

(Bodenheimer, *Uniform Child Custody Jurisdiction Act* (1969) 22 VAND. L. REV. 1207, 1237; see similar examples in Commissioner's Notes to §3, Uniform Child Custody Jurisdiction Act.)

Substitute North Dakota for "A" and California for "B" and you have the present fact situation. All petitions for modification are to be addressed to the state which rendered the original decree if that state has jurisdiction under the standards of the Act (*In re Marriage of Schwander*, 79 Cal. App.3d 1013, 1019, 145 Cal. Rptr. 325).

We can understand the trial judge's concern over California not being able to determine custody of its own residents and the possibility of multiple proceedings in the action. This very concern states have for their residents or for those merely within their borders has caused the interstate conflicts and thus prompted the Legislature to adopt the Act.

The Act permits the state which first obtained jurisdiction to exercise it. It does not shock the conscience that California must bow to North Dakota and yet appear to have greater access to the facts.[10] The North Dakota court may have abused its discretion in not permitting California to exercise jurisdiction. "[T]here is no reason why [the] courts of one state should not be able to 'assume with confidence that the courts of the other jurisdiction will act with wisdom and sincerity in all matters pertaining to the welfare of this child.' [Citations.]" (*Ferreira v. Ferreira*, 9 Cal.3d 824, 841, fn. 21, 109 Cal. Rptr. 80, 91, fn. 21, 512 P.2d 304, 315, fn. 21; see also *In re Marriage of Steiner*, 89 Cal. App.3d 363, 372–373, 152 Cal. Rptr. 612.) In this connection, the statements of the referee related to the trial judge here do not necessarily establish the fact the North Dakota court will not exercise its jurisdiction substantially in conformity with this Act.

If California is the more appropriate forum for the custody decision because of the location of witnesses, etc., North Dakota should stay its proceedings and allow California to proceed (§5156). If the North Dakota trial court makes the wrong decision on whether to stay its proceedings, the appellate court of North Dakota should rectify the mistake. This is not the California trial or reviewing court function. The purpose of section 5156 is to provide the court with a tool to allow another court to go forward, not to create a confrontation or deny another court the authority to proceed. Were the roles of North Dakota and California reversed on these facts, we would expect the courts of North Dakota would require the proceedings in that state to be stayed (see *Bosse v. Superior Court*, 89 Cal. App.3d 440, 443–445, 152 Cal. Rptr. 665; *In re Marriage of Kern*, 87 Cal. App.3d 402, 150 Cal. Rptr. 860).

The only exception noted in the Act for a state exercising jurisdiction contrary to this provision giving priority to the time the proceeding is initiated is where the child is abandoned or endangered (§5152, subd. (1)(c)) or where *no* forum has jurisdiction under the provisions. Neither of these conditions exists (§5152, subd. (1)(d)). While full faith and credit has never been given to foreign custody decrees by California courts (see 53 HARVARD L. REV. 1024, 1029), foreign decrees must be given "due consideration" on the grounds of comity (*Sampsell v. Superior Court*, 32 Cal.2d 763, 780, 197 P.2d 739). The Act makes a comprehensive attempt to accommodate all these state interests (see the Uniform Child Custody Jurisdiction Act, 62 CAL. L. REV. 365). It should be adhered to by our courts.

We hold under the facts of this case the California court was required to stay its proceedings under Civil Code section 5155, subdivision (1), because a custody proceeding was already pending in North Dakota and the relief

---

[10]Section 5156, subdivision (7), allows necessary travel expenses and costs of the parties and their witnesses in the more convenient forum.

sought amounted to a modification of the North Dakota decree when that state still had jurisdiction and had assumed it (§5163, subd. (1)(a)). North Dakota has continuing jurisdiction under the Act and the right to exercise it. There is nothing in the record to show North Dakota was not acting substantially in conformity with this Act.

Let a writ of prohibition issue directing the respondent San Diego County Superior Court to stay all proceedings in case number 421423 until such time as it may resume such custody proceedings in accordance with Civil Code section 5155 and the other sections of the Uniform Child Custody Jurisdiction Act and to vacate all orders made in connection with such proceedings.

[Dissenting opinion omitted.]

Murphy v. Murphy

Supreme Judicial Court of Massachusetts

404 N.E.2d 69 (1980)

LIACOS, Justice.

Kevin L. Murphy (husband) appeals from a judgment of the Probate Court for Barnstable County granting custody of their minor child to Florence E. Murphy (wife). The husband argues that the Probate Court lacked jurisdiction because of an Arizona order pendente lite granting temporary custody of the child to him. We transferred the appeal here from the Appeals Court on our own motion.

We summarize the facts and the proceedings below. The parties were married in Barnstable, Massachusetts, in July, 1975. A child was born to the marriage in December, 1975, in Falmouth, Massachusetts. In February, 1976, the husband left Massachusetts to begin his tour of duty with the United States Air Force. His wife and child joined him in Texas in April of that year. Subsequently, in July, 1976, the husband was assigned to a military base in Tucson, Arizona, and his family joined him there. The parties purchased a house in Arizona where they lived together until their separation in April, 1978. On April 20, 1978, the husband filed a petition in the Arizona Superior Court (Pima County), seeking dissolution of the marriage, custody of the child, and division of the property and debts of the marriage. The wife retained counsel and filed a response seeking, inter alia, a dissolution of the marriage, custody of the child, support for herself and the child, division of the marital estate and the right to resume use of her maiden name. A hearing was held on June 22, 1978, before a Commissioner of the Arizona Superior Court where both parties were represented by counsel, gave testimony and presented evidence. On July 5, 1978, the Superior Court Commissioner entered an order pendente lite granting temporary custody of the child to the husband and prohibiting the wife from removing the child from Pima County without prior notice to the husband.

Two days later, without prior notice, the wife returned with the child to live at her parents' home in Massachusetts. On July 31, 1978, she filed a petition for separate support in the Barnstable Probate Court, together with a motion for temporary custody of the child. The husband's counsel filed on the same day a special appearance solely for the purpose of contesting jurisdiction. The motion for temporary custody was allowed on July 31, 1978, pending a hearing on the merits of the petition for separate support. After a hearing on August 10, in which the husband's attorney appeared, contested jurisdiction and "stood mute" as to the cross-examination of the plaintiff's two witnesses (herself and her sister), a temporary order awarding custody of the child to the plaintiff was entered. On September 26, 1978, judgment was entered for the wife, granting her custody of the child. The judgment granted the husband the right to see the child at the home of the wife, in the presence of the wife and two other witnesses, but contained no provision as to support of the wife or the child.

The husband claims error and argues that since both parties appeared in the Arizona court, admitted domicile in Arizona, and contested the issue of divorce, custody and support in an adversarial proceeding, the Arizona court had jurisdiction to determine the custody of the minor child. The husband further contends that the child was removed from Arizona contrary to the order of the Arizona court, that there was no change in circumstances warranting a reversal of that court's order by the Probate Court, and that the Massachusetts court was required to give full faith and credit to the order of the Arizona court under article IV, §1, of the Constitution of the United States. The wife argues that the Barnstable Probate Court had jurisdiction to entertain her petition for separate support, under G.L. c. 209, §32, where the plaintiff is domiciled in Massachusetts and both mother and child are residents of and physically present in the Commonwealth. She asserts that the orders and judgment of the Barnstable Probate Court were a proper exercise of its power to act in the best interests of the child. No argument is made by the wife that there had been a change of circumstance from the time of the entry of the Arizona order to the time of the filing of the petition for support and custody in the Barnstable Probate Court.

We first consider the question whether the Probate Court had jurisdiction to enter the custody judgment pursuant to G.L. c. 209, §32.[1] This court has held that under G.L. c. 209, §32, the Probate Court has jurisdiction over child custody matters, on substituted service, if either party is domiciled within the Commonwealth.[2] *Wiley v. Wiley*, 328 Mass. 348, 349, 103 N.E.2d 699 (1952). In *Wiley, supra* at 351, 103 N.E.2d 699, we held that reacquisition of a Massachusetts domicile was achieved where the wife returned here with the intention of remaining indefinitely. The record in the case at bar indicates that both parties were born in Massachusetts and resided in Massachusetts until their marriage, that the child of the marriage was born here, that defendant enlisted for military service from this State, that both parties have parents residing in this State, that both parties maintain a driver's license and

---

[1] General Laws c. 209, §32, as amended by St. 1977, c. 984, §1, provides in pertinent part: "If a spouse fails, without justifiable cause, to provide suitable support of the other spouse, or deserts the other spouse, or if a married person has justifiable cause for living apart from his spouse, whether or not the married person is actually living apart, the probate court may, upon the complaint of the married person, * * * prohibit the spouse from imposing any restraint upon the personal liberty of the married person during such time as the court by its order may direct or until further order of the court thereon. Upon the complaint of any such party or guardian of a minor child made in accordance with the Massachusetts Rules of Civil Procedure the court may make further orders relative to the support of the married person and the care, custody and maintenance of minor children, may determine with which of the parents the children or any of them shall remain and may, from time to time, upon similar complaint revise and alter such judgment or make a new order of judgment as the circumstances of the parents or the benefit of the children may require."

[2] *Green v. Green*, 351 Mass. 466, 221 N.E.2d 857 (1966), refers to another basis of jurisdiction in a proceeding under G.L. c. 209, §32, *i.e.*, personal jurisdiction over the parties. In both cases, the absent spouse had been served "in hand" in Massachusetts. We note that, despite the "special appearance" filed by the husband's attorney on July 31, 1978, to contest jurisdiction, the husband voluntarily accepted service of the petition in Arizona before a notary public on August 24, 1978 (prior to the entry of judgment). The parties do not argue the question whether such acceptance of service was sufficient to give the Probate Court jurisdiction, and we need not reach the question, since we hold jurisdiction to have been properly established on either the basis of domicile or presence of the child, or both.

motor vehicle registration in Massachusetts, and that the parties filed a joint income tax return in Massachusetts for the years 1976–1977 (even though located in Arizona). The record also indicates that the wife alleges that she returned to her parents' home in Massachusetts with an intent to reacquire a Massachusetts domicile. We note that the Murphy child is physically present in the Commonwealth and that the Probate judge took jurisdiction on this basis, although such presence is not necessarily required in order to meet the jurisdictional requirements of G.L. c. 209, §32. *Green v. Green*, 351 Mass. 466, 221 N.E.2d 857 (1966), cited in *Doe v. Roe*, —— Mass. ——, ——, 387 N.E.2d 143 (1979). We, therefore, conclude that the jurisdictional requirements of G.L. c. 209, §32, were met. See also G.L. c. 209, §37; *Schmidt v. Schmidt*, 280 Mass. 216, 182 N.E. 374 (1932).

The critical question, however, is whether the court should have exercised jurisdiction in this case. The exercise of jurisdiction is in no sense mandatory. As this court has stated,

> "surely we should not insist on exercising such jurisdiction whenever permissible as a matter of due process of law. Rather we should deal with the question as a prudential one which invites careful examination of the relation of the lawsuit to the Commonwealth, including such issues as access to evidence and convenience of management or administration; and it should count against assuming jurisdiction that there is another State better situated to deal with the matter. * * * Actually the whole trend of the law is, or ought to be, to pay less attention to formal jurisdictional tests and more to functional or pragmatic considerations about the comparative advantages of one forum over another."

Doe v. Roe, —— Mass. ——, ——, ——, 387 N.E.2d 143, 145 (1979). This discretionary approach to jurisdiction in child custody cases is in accord with the Uniform Child Custody Jurisdiction Act (1968), 9 Uniform Laws Annot. §§3, 7 (1973) (recodified in 1979 edition), not adopted in Massachusetts, but cited with approval in *Doe, supra at* —— n. 3, 387 N.E.2d 143.

We now apply the considerations enumerated above to the circumstances in the case at bar to determine whether the Probate Court judge's exercise of jurisdiction was proper. The full faith and credit clause of the United States Constitution, Art. IV, §1, does not require, as the husband argues, that Massachusetts give full faith and credit to the Arizona order for the reason that the Arizona order pendente lite is not a final judgment.[4] See *New York ex rel. Halvey v. Halvey*, 330 U.S. 610, 67 S. Ct. 903, 91 L.Ed. 1133 (1947); *Heard v. Heard*, 323 Mass. 357, 82 N.E.2d 219 (1948). However, the fact that the Arizona temporary order was incidental to an Arizona proceeding which was still in progress at the time the Massachusetts Probate Court entered its order is significant. See Uniform Child Custody Jurisdiction Act (1968), 9 Uniform Laws Annot. §6 (1979). Where a court of another State has validly assumed jurisdiction over a particular child custody matter, Massachusetts courts should seriously consider the propriety of entertaining a simultaneous custody proceeding in this State. See *Aufiero v. Aufiero*, 332 Mass. 149, 153, 123 N.E.2d 709 (1955); Uniform Child Custody Jurisdiction Act, *supra*, Commissioner's Note to §6. The wife, having submitted herself to the jurisdiction of the Arizona court, should not be allowed to seek relief in

---

[4]Arizona Rev. Stat. §25–315 (Supp. 1979) provides in pertinent part:
"In all actions for the dissolution of marriage or for legal separation, the clerk of court shall pursuant to order of the superior court issue a preliminary injunction * * *. A temporary order or preliminary injunction: 1. Does not prejudice the rights of the parties or any child which are to be adjudicated at the subsequent hearings in the proceeding. 2. May be revoked or modified before final decree on a showing by affidavit of the facts necessary to revocation or modification of a final decree under §25–327 and as provided in rule 65 of the Rules of Civil Procedure. 3. Terminates when the final decree is entered or when the petition for dissolution or legal separation is dismissed."

Massachusetts simply because she is dissatisfied with the preliminary determination of the Arizona court. She must base her request on the welfare of the child, focusing on such issues as the relative significance of the parties' jurisdictional contacts and the relative accessibility of evidence in the two States. See *Doe v. Roe, supra; Green v. Green, supra.*

The Arizona court clearly had jurisdiction over the child custody determination. Uniform Child Custody Jurisdiction Act, Ariz. Rev. Stat. §8–403 (Supp. 1979). The parents and the child were all physically present. The husband and wife bought a house and lived together in Arizona with their child from July, 1976, to April, 1978. During the Arizona proceeding, both parties alleged that they were Arizona domiciliaries. The Arizona temporary order was entered after a full day's hearing. A total of eight witnesses testified, four on behalf of the wife and four on behalf of the husband. The wife left Arizona with the child, in violation of the temporary order, only two days after entry of the order. She instituted proceedings in Massachusetts less than four weeks after her arrival here, while the proceeding in Arizona was still pending. The husband did not submit himself generally to the jurisdiction of the Massachusetts Probate Court.[5] The entire Probate Court hearing in Massachusetts consisted of arguments of counsel and testimony of the wife and her sister. No material change in circumstances was alleged other than the move from Arizona to Massachusetts. In light of the very brief lapse of time between the entry of the Arizona temporary order and the Massachusetts proceeding, it would be most unusual for a material change in circumstances to have occurred.

We conclude that maintenance of simultaneous custody proceedings in Arizona and Massachusetts cannot be justified factually on the basis of the parties' more significant contacts here[6] or better access to relevant evidence here. The record reveals circumstances to the contrary. Moreover, the wife has sought access to the courts of this State with "unclean hands." Her removal of the child from Arizona to Massachusetts was in flagrant defiance of the Arizona temporary order.[7] Such custodial interference is a crime in Arizona. Ariz. Rev. Stat. §13–1302 (1978).

This court has in the past developed rules aimed at discouraging "the despicable practice of child snatching." *Conley v. Conley*, 324 Mass. 530, 534, 87 N.E.2d 153 (1949). For example, a parent has no power to change the domicile of a child while both are subject to a valid decree awarding custody to the other parent. *Id.* Also a parent is not entitled as of right to press an appeal from a custody decree favorable to the other parent after removing the child from the jurisdiction in violation of that decree. *Henderson v. Henderson*, 329 Mass. 257, 107 N.E.2d 773 (1952). Cf. *Ellis v. Doherty*, 334 Mass. 466, 467, 136 N.E.2d 203 (1956). We believe that a parent's misconduct should likewise be considered in determining whether simultaneous custody proceedings are appropriate. See *Leathers v. Leathers*, 162 Cal. App.2d 768, 775, 328 P.2d 853 (1958); Ehrenzweig, *Interstate Recognition of Custody Decrees*, 51 MICH. L. REV. 345 (1953); Uniform Child Custody Jurisdiction Act (1968); 9 Uniform Laws Annot. §8 (1979). While such misconduct is a relevant consideration, it is not necessarily controlling. *Aufiero, supra.* See *Hersey v. Hersey*, 271

---

[5]But see footnote 2, *supra.*

[6]The wife urges this court to consider the parties' filing of Massachusetts Tax Returns in 1976 and 1977 and their maintenance of Massachusetts drivers licenses and motor vehicle registration as significant contacts to Massachusetts. We have considered these incidents of Massachusetts residence, and note the husband's enlistment in the Armed Services as a justification for them. See Soldiers' and Sailors' Civil Relief Act, 50 U.S.C. App. 501 *et seq.* (1976).

[7]The order states in pertinent part, "the Respondent is enjoined from leaving Pima County with the minor child, and should she desire to leave Pima County with the child, she is to notify the Petitioner/husband not less than forty-eight (48) hours in advance. * * * " The record reflects no such 48-hour advance notice, and, in any case, it is clear that the decree did not authorize the wife's permanent removal of the child to Massachusetts.

Mass. 545, 171 N.E. 815 (1930); *Gil v. Servizio*, —— Mass. ——,[d] 375 N.E.2d
716 (1978). As we indicated in *Aufiero*, the child "was not chargeable with the
misconduct of her mother in failing to return her * * * and ought not to be
compelled to suffer for it. Her welfare is the paramount consideration."
Aufiero, supra, 332 Mass. at 153, 123 N.E.2d at 712. The misconduct of the
parent may, nevertheless, adversely affect the welfare of the child. Captures
and possible recaptures of a child can be "harmful to the child and [can cause]
emotional and physical reactions in the child commensurate with these distresses." *Vilakezi v. Maxie,* 371 Mass. 406, 408, 357 N.E.2d 763, 764 (1976).

The parties have significant contacts to Arizona, and the Arizona proceeding appears thorough and complete. The wife alleged no material change
in circumstances since the time of that proceeding other than her illegal removal of the child.[8] The Probate Court judge's decision to allow a simultaneous custody proceeding in Massachusetts in the circumstances was an abuse
of discretion and cannot stand. The judgment of the Probate Court was entered on September 26, 1978. In light of the considerable passage of time
since the entry of that order, we think it appropriate to remand the case to the
Probate Court for a new hearing. The judge should consider, in addition to the
views expressed herein, any material change in circumstances since the entry
of the September 26, 1978, judgment.[9]

So ordered.

---

[d]Mass. Adv. Sh. (1978) 1222.

[8]The party seeking modification of a foreign custody decree is required to show a material
change in circumstances. *Buchanan v. Buchanan,* 353 Mass. 351, 231 N.E.2d 570 (1967). See also
G.L. c. 209, §§32, 37. This principle has particular relevance where the foreign decree is *pendente
lite,* in light of the policy against entertaining a custody proceeding in Massachusetts at the
same time a similar proceeding is pending in a competent court of a sister State.

[9]During oral argument the parties informed this court that a final Arizona decree of divorce
had been entered awarding custody of the child to the husband. This final decree was purportedly entered subsequent to the Massachusetts Probate Court proceeding. We note the absence
of the divorce decree in the record.

The wife's complaint under G.L. c. 209, §32, is no longer appropriate if the final Arizona
decree included dissolution of the marriage. It is a prerequisite under G.L. c. 209, §32, that the
parties be married. *Welker v. Welker,* 325 Mass. 738, 743, 92 N.E.2d 373 (1950). The wife may
consider whether she would be required to seek relief pursuant to G.L. c. 208, §29.

Comments

Both *Palm* and *Murphy* are governed by principles of the Uniform
Child Custody Jurisdiction Act (UCCJA), although Massachusetts,
as of late 1982, was one of the few states that had not adopted it
through legislation. The purpose of the Act is to prevent "child
snatching," which is likely to occur when multiple competing jurisdictions are involved. Whether the Act is as effective as it was meant to
be is subject to conjecture. Its language continues to invite judicial
discretion, as, for example, when it refers repeatedly to the "best interests of the child," to "significant connection" as a jurisdictional
alternative, or to the existence of an "emergency." The power to stay
proceedings because the court finds itself to be an "inconvenient forum" is essentially discretionary, as are the findings that the petitioner has engaged in "reprehensible conduct." In the latter instance,
the court may decline to exercise jurisdiction "if this is just and proper

under the circumstances." Any of these provisions can be used to foster parochial interests, especially in the lower courts. In fact, both *Palm* and *Murphy* illustrate the parochial bent of the lower courts, which later had to be corrected on the appellate level. The conflict between Florida and Georgia courts is an important illustration. Both lower state courts disregarded mandatory provisions of the UCCJA, and the Supreme Court of Georgia, after criticism, upheld a local decision favoring local interests.*

Nevertheless, it would be erroneous to assume that the Act is ineffective. Part of its effectiveness lies in the fact that people believe in it. Courts are more likely now than earlier to honor out-of-state custody decrees, even in jurisdictions like Florida and New York, which were traditionally disinclined to do so. The parties concerned may be more willing than in the past to follow legal procedures, although it is impossible to verify this fact statistically. If child snatching occurs, parties may go underground rather than to court to try to obtain a new decision in their favor. This, in a backhanded way, also attests to the Act's effectiveness, because parties may increasingly weigh the burdens of deviant behavior; and this, in the long run, is likely to lower its incidence. However, it is not so much the wording of the Act that achieves these positive results, but the mystique that surrounds its almost universal adoption, a situation that may require further explanation.

One of the characteristics of the best-interests standard in regard to custody decisions is its strong emotional appeal. It seems to disregard legal technicalities and to focus instead on what people feel to be of the essence—the good of the young. The use of procedural technicalities, if children are involved, is especially frowned on by lawyers and laymen alike. An inevitable side effect of this attitude is the possibility of multiple jurisdictions for controversies relating to children. Every court in the nation could potentially assume the power to relitigate custody disputes as though no decision had been rendered in another state. Any effort to claim *res judicata* or full faith and credit, according to this attitude, should be met with judicial disdain because it asserts the powers of a foreign sovereign over a child. The child, the reasoning would go, should not be treated as a chattel or custody as a chose in action. The whole concept of *res judicata*, following this extreme view, would be contrary to the best interests of the child because it would erect a procedural hurdle preventing reexamination of the ever-changing merits of the case. Any contact with the child, no matter how fleeting, would suffice to allow a court to take a second or third look at a disputed question of custody. Accordingly, the best-interests standard in its pure form can be viewed not merely as an invocation of unfettered judicial discretion but also, in a jurisprudential sense, as a demand for absolute justice by perpetual reexami-

---

Webb v. Webb, 245 Ga. 650, 266 S.E.2d 463 (1980), *cert. dismissed*, 451 U.S. 493 (1981).

nation that in no other area of law has met with such widespread approval.

However, the search for absolute justice, regardless of procedures and technical rules, must ultimately lead to lawlessness, especially by parties who take the law into their own hands. As exemplified by the facts of both *Palm* and *Murphy*, this may take the form of snatching the child and trying for justice in another jurisdiction or, more frequently, not returning the child after an authorized visit. Sooner or later such actions must lead the judiciary to realize that using the best-interests standard without qualification is not really in the children's best interests, and that the law, even in this area, is largely concerned with rendering peace even at the cost of occasional injustice. In the authors' view, the UCCJA is trying to achieve this result without openly acknowledging it. The reasons for this roundabout procedure are essentially political. It is impossible to tamper with the best-interests standard by direct legislation. The UCCJA therefore seemingly confirms the standard but tries to limit an excessive application of it that would be harmful to children's long-range interests in interstate cases.

Since jurisdictional competition is at the source of the problem of child snatching, a technique must be developed to minimize its effects. The Act tries to accomplish this result by differentiating between having jurisdiction on the one hand and exercising it on the other. In other words, a court, in a custody dispute, should engage in a two-pronged examination: first, determining whether it has jurisdiction, and second, if it finds it has, deciding whether to exercise it. Both *Palm* and *Murphy* illustrate that an erroneous exercise of jurisdiction may lead to appellate intervention under a theory that, although there is in fact jurisdiction, any exercise of it in the circumstances was an abuse of discretion. In effect this means that jurisdiction, which traditionally has been perceived as the unqualified power to hear and to decide a case, has been limited. It also means that in actual application the court that first becomes active in a custody dispute will prevail with greater frequency than in the past. Custody decisions will have *res judicata* effects, regardless of whether the parties concerned feel that justice has been done, and they will enjoy some measure of full faith and credit. The decisions will no longer be perceived as being *in personam* in precisely the way *May v. Anderson** saw them, but will be considered entitled to full faith and credit if the due process requirements of reasonable notice and opportunity to be heard are met.

The Federal Parental Kidnapping Prevention Act of 1980 is an attempt by Congress, reportedly of limited success so far, to intercede in local jurisdictional conflicts. The Act, in following UCCJA guidelines, calls for the granting of full faith and credit to foreign custody decrees that have respected due process requirements. In addition, the Federal Parent Locator Service can be used to locate a parent or

---

*345 U.S. 528 (1953).

other person who has violated a lawful custody order. The final provision of the Act applies the federal felony statute to parental kidnappings, thus drawing the resources of the FBI and the United States Attorney General into the conflict.

References

Bodenheimer, *The International Kidnapping of Children: The United States Approach*, 11 FAM. L.Q. 83 (1977).

Bodenheimer, *Progress Under the Uniform Child Custody Jurisdiction Act and Remaining Problems: Punitive Decrees, Joint Custody, and Excessive Modification*, 65 CALIF. L. REV. 978 (1977).

Bodenheimer & Neeley-Kvarme, *Jurisdiction Over Child Custody and Adoption After Shaffer and Kulko*, 12 U.C.D. L. REV. 229 (1979).

Crouch, R., INTERSTATE CUSTODY LITIGATION: A GUIDE TO USE AND COURT INTERPRETATION OF THE UNIFORM CHILD CUSTODY JURISDICTION ACT (1981).

Foster & Freed, *Child Snatching and Custodial Fights: The Case for the Uniform Child Custody Jurisdiction Act*, 28 HASTINGS L. REV. 1011 (1977).

Frumkes & Elser, *The Uniform Child Custody Jurisdiction Act—The Florida Experience*, 53 FLA. B.J. 684 (1979).

Katz, S., CHILD SNATCHING—THE LEGAL RESPONSE TO THE ABDUCTION OF CHILDREN (1981).

New Action Likely on Child-Snatching Law, 39 CONG. Q. WEEKLY REP. 2240 (Nov. 14, 1981).

Note, *Developments in the Law—The Constitution and the Family*, 93 HARV. L. REV. 1156, 1242–48 (1980).

Ratner, *Procedural Due Process and Jurisdiction to Adjudicate: (a) Effective Litigation Values vs. the Territorial Imperative; (b) The Uniform Child Custody Jurisdiction Act*, 75 NW. U.L. REV. 363 (1980).

Sampson, *What's Wrong With the UCCJA? Punitive Decrees and Hometown Decisions Are Making a Mockery of This Uniform Act*, FAM. ADVOC., Spring, 1981, at 28.

Minimum Jurisdiction for Custody and Support

*Kulko v. Superior Court of California
in and for the City and County of San Francisco*

(Horn, Real Party in Interest)

United States Supreme Court

436 U.S. 84 (1978)

Mr. Justice MARSHALL delivered the opinion of the Court.

The issue before us is whether, in this action for child support, the California state courts may exercise *in personam* jurisdiction over a nonresident, nondomiciliary parent of minor children domiciled within the State. For reasons set forth below, we hold that the exercise of such jurisdiction would violate the Due Process Clause of the Fourteenth Amendment.

I

Appellant Ezra Kulko married appellee Sharon Kulko Horn in 1959, during appellant's three-day stopover in California en route from a military base in Texas to a tour of duty in Korea. At the time of this marriage, both parties were domiciled in and residents of New York State. Immediately following the marriage, Sharon Kulko returned to New York, as did appellant after his tour of duty. Their first child, Darwin, was born to the Kulkos in New York in 1961, and a year later their second child, Ilsa, was born, also in New York. The Kulkos and their two children resided together as a family in New York City continuously until March 1972, when the Kulkos separated.

Following the separation, Sharon Kulko moved to San Francisco, Cal. A written separation agreement was drawn up in New York; in September 1972, Sharon Kulko flew to New York City in order to sign this agreement. The agreement provided, *inter alia*, that the children would remain with their father during the school year but would spend their Christmas, Easter, and summer vacations with their mother. While Sharon Kulko waived any claim for her own support or maintenance, Ezra Kulko agreed to pay his wife $3,000 per year in child support for the periods when the children were in her care, custody, and control. Immediately after execution of the separation agreement, Sharon Kulko flew to Haiti and procured a divorce there;[1] the divorce decree incorporated the terms of the agreement. She then returned to California, where she remarried and took the name Horn.

The children resided with appellant during the school year and with their mother on vacations, as provided by the separation agreement, until December 1973. At this time, just before Ilsa was to leave New York to spend Christmas vacation with her mother, she told her father that she wanted to remain in California after her vacation. Appellant bought his daughter a one-way plane ticket, and Ilsa left, taking her clothing with her. Ilsa then commenced living in California with her mother during the school year and spending vacations with her father. In January 1976, appellant's other child, Darwin, called his mother from New York and advised her that he wanted to live with her in California. Unbeknownst to appellant, appellee Horn sent a plane ticket to her son, which he used to fly to California where he took up residence with his mother and sister.

Less than one month after Darwin's arrival in California, appellee Horn commenced this action against appellant in the California Superior Court. She sought to establish the Haitian divorce decree as a California judgment; to modify the judgment so as to award her full custody of the children; and to increase appellant's child-support obligations.[2] Appellant appeared specially and moved to quash service of the summons on the ground that he was not a resident of California and lacked sufficient "minimum contacts" with the State under *International Shoe Co. v. Washington*, 326 U.S. 310, 316, 66 S. Ct. 154, 158, 90 L.Ed. 95 (1945), to warrant the State's assertion of personal jurisdiction over him.

---

[1]While the Jurisdictional Statement, at 5, asserts that "the parties" flew to Haiti, appellant's affidavit submitted in the Superior Court stated that Sharon Kulko flew to Haiti with a power of attorney signed by appellant. App. 28. The Haitian decree states that Sharon Kulko appeared "in person" and that appellant filed a "Power of Attorney and submission to jurisdiction," *Id.*, at 14.

[2]Appellee Horn's complaint also sought an order restraining appellant from removing his children from the State. The trial court immediately granted appellee temporary custody of the children and restrained both her and appellant from removing the children from the State of California. See 19 Cal.3d 514, 520, 138 Cal. Rptr. 586, 588, 564 P.2d 353, 355 (1977). The record does not reflect whether appellant is still enjoined from removing his children from the State.

The trial court summarily denied the motion to quash, and appellant sought review in the California Court of Appeal by petition for a writ of mandate. Appellant did not contest the court's jurisdiction for purposes of the custody determination, but, with respect to the claim for increased support, he renewed his argument that the California courts lacked personal jurisdiction over him. The appellate court affirmed the denial of appellant's motion to quash, reasoning that, by consenting to his children's living in California, appellant had "caused an effect in th[e] state" warranting the exercise of jurisdiction over him. 133 Cal. Rptr. 627, 628 (1976).

The California Supreme Court granted appellant's petition for review, and in a 4-2 decision sustained the rulings of the lower state courts. 19 Cal.3d 514, 138 Cal. Rptr. 586, 564 P.2d 353 (1977). * * *

* * *

* * * We have concluded that jurisdiction by appeal does not lie, but, treating the papers as a petition for a writ of certiorari, we hereby grant the petition and reverse the judgment below.

II

The Due Process Clause of the Fourteenth Amendment operates as a limitation on the jurisdiction of state courts to enter judgments affecting rights or interests of nonresident defendants. See *Shaffer v. Heitner*, 433 U.S. 186, 198-200, 97 S. Ct. 2569, 2577, 53 L.Ed.2d 683 (1977). It has long been the rule that a valid judgment imposing a personal obligation or duty in favor of the plaintiff may be entered only by a court having jurisdiction over the person of the defendant. *Pennoyer v. Neff*, 95 U.S. 714, 732-733, 24 L.Ed. 565, 572 (1878); *International Shoe Co. v. Washington*, 326 U.S., at 316, 66 S. Ct., at 158. The existence of personal jurisdiction, in turn, depends upon the presence of reasonable notice to the defendant that an action has been brought. *Mullane v. Central Hanover Trust Co.*, 339 U.S. 306, 313-314, 70 S. Ct. 652, 656-657, 94 L.Ed. 865 (1950), and a sufficient connection between the defendant and the forum State to make it fair to require defense of the action in the forum. *Milliken v. Meyer*, 311 U.S. 457, 463-464, 61 S. Ct. 339, 342-343, 85 L.Ed. 278 (1940). In this case, appellant does not dispute the adequacy of the notice that he received, but contends that his connection with the State of California is too attenuated, under the standards implicit in the Due Process Clause of the Constitution, to justify imposing upon him the burden and inconvenience of defense in California.

The parties are in agreement that the constitutional standard for determining whether the State may enter a binding judgment against appellant here is that set forth in this Court's opinion in *International Shoe Co. v. Washington, supra:* that a defendant "have certain minimum contacts with [the forum State] such that the maintenance of the suit does not offend 'traditional notions of fair play and substantial justice.' " 326 U.S., at 316, 66 S. Ct., at 158, quoting *Milliken v. Meyer, supra*, 311 U.S., at 463, 61 S. Ct., at 342. While the interests of the forum State and of the plaintiff in proceeding with the cause in the plaintiff's forum of choice are, of course, to be considered, see *McGee v. International Life Insurance Co.*, 355 U.S. 220, 223, 78 S. Ct. 199, 201, 2 L.Ed.2d 223 (1957), an essential criterion in all cases is whether the "quality and nature" of the defendant's activity is such that it is "reasonable" and "fair" to require him to conduct his defense in that State. *International Shoe Co. v. Washington, supra*, 326 U.S., at 316-317, 319, 66 S. Ct., at 158, 159. Accord, *Shaffer v. Heitner, supra*, 433 U.S., at 207-212, 97 S. Ct., at 2581-2584; *Perkins v. Benguet Mining Co.*, 342 U.S. 437, 445, 72 S. Ct. 413, 418, 96 L.Ed. 485 (1952).

Like any standard that requires a determination of "reasonableness," the "minimum contacts" test of *International Shoe* is not susceptible of mechanical application; rather, the facts of each case must be weighed to determine whether the requisite "affiliating circumstances" are present. *Hanson v. Denckla*, 357 U.S. 235, 246, 78 S. Ct. 1228, 1235, 2 L.Ed.2d 1283 (1958). We recognize that this determination is one in which few answers will be written "in black and white. The greys are dominant and even among them the shades are innumerable." *Estin v. Estin*, 334 U.S. 541, 545, 68 S. Ct. 1213, 1216, 92 L.Ed. 1561 (1948). But we believe that the California Supreme Court's application of the minimum-contacts test in this case represents an unwarranted extension of *International Shoe* and would, if sustained, sanction a result that is neither fair, just, nor reasonable.

A

In reaching its result, the California Supreme Court did not rely on appellant's glancing presence in the State some 13 years before the events that led to this controversy, nor could it have. Appellant has been in California on only two occasions, once in 1959 for a three-day military stopover on his way to Korea, see *supra*, at 1694, and again in 1960 for a 24-hour stopover on his return from Korean service. To hold such temporary visits to a State a basis for the assertion of *in personam* jurisdiction over unrelated actions arising in the future would make a mockery of the limitations on state jurisdiction imposed by the Fourteenth Amendment. Nor did the California court rely on the fact that appellant was actually married in California on one of his two brief visits. We agree that where two New York domiciliaries, for reasons of convenience, marry in the State of California and thereafter spend their entire married life in New York, the fact of their California marriage by itself cannot support a California court's exercise of jurisdiction over a spouse who remains a New York resident in an action relating to child support.

Finally, in holding that personal jurisdiction existed, the court below carefully disclaimed reliance on the fact that appellant had agreed at the time of separation to allow his children to live with their mother three months a year and that he had sent them to California each year pursuant to this agreement. As was noted below, 19 Cal.3d, at 523–524, 138 Cal. Rptr., at 590, 564 P.2d, at 357, to find personal jurisdiction in a State on this basis, merely because the mother was residing there, would discourage parents from entering into reasonable visitation agreements. Moreover, it could arbitrarily subject one parent to suit in any State of the Union where the other parent chose to spend time while having custody of their offspring pursuant to a separation agreement.[6] As we have emphasized:

> "The unilateral activity of those who claim some relationship with a nonresident defendant cannot satisfy the requirement of contact with the forum State. * * * [I]t is essential in each case that there be some act by which the defendant purposefully avails [him]self of the privilege of conducting activities within the forum State * * *."

Hanson v. Denckla, supra, 357 U.S., at 253, 78 S. Ct., at 1240.

The "purposeful act" that the California Supreme Court believed did warrant the exercise of personal jurisdiction over appellant in California was his "actively and fully consent[ing] to Ilsa living in California for the school year * * * and * * * sen[ding] her to California for that purpose." 19 Cal.3d, at 524, 138 Cal. Rptr., at 591, 564 P.2d, at 358. We cannot accept the proposi-

---

[6]Although the separation agreement stated that appellee Horn resided in California and provided that child-support payments would be mailed to her California address, it also specifically contemplated that appellee might move to a different State. The agreement directed appellant to mail the support payments to appellee's San Francisco address or "any other address which the Wife may designate from time to time in writing." App. 10.

tion that appellant's acquiescence in Ilsa's desire to live with her mother conferred jurisdiction over appellant in the California courts in this action. A father who agrees, in the interests of family harmony and his children's preferences, to allow them to spend more time in California than was required under a separation agreement can hardly be said to have "purposefully availed himself" of the "benefits and protections" of California's laws. See *Shaffer v. Heitner*, 433 U.S., at 216, 97 S. Ct., at 2586.[7]

Nor can we agree with the assertion of the court below that the exercise of *in personam* jurisdiction here was warranted by the financial benefit appellant derived from his daughter's presence in California for nine months of the year. 19 Cal.3d at 524–525, 138 Cal. Rptr., at 590–591, 564 P.2d, at 358. This argument rests on the premise that, while appellant's liability for support payments remained unchanged, his yearly expenses for supporting the child in New York decreased. But this circumstance, even if true, does not support California's assertion of jurisdiction here. Any diminution in appellant's household costs resulted, not from the child's presence in California, but rather from her absence from appellant's home. Moreover, an action by appellee Horn to increase support payments could now be brought, and could have been brought when Ilsa first moved to California, in the State of New York;[8] a New York court would clearly have personal jurisdiction over appellant and, if a judgment were entered by a New York court increasing appellant's child-support obligations, it could properly be enforced against him in both New York and California.[9] Any ultimate financial advantage to appellant thus results not from the child's presence in California, but from appellee's failure earlier to seek an increase in payments under the separation agreement.[10] The argument below to the contrary, in our view, confuses the question of appellant's liability with that of the proper forum in which to determine that liability.

B

In light of our conclusion that appellant did not purposefully derive benefit from any activities relating to the State of California, it is apparent that the California Supreme Court's reliance on appellant's having caused an "effect" in California was misplaced. See *supra*, at 1695. This "effects" test is derived from the American Law Institute's *Restatement (Second) of Conflict of Laws* §37 (1971), which provides:

"A state has power to exercise judicial jurisdiction over an individual who causes effects in the state by an act done elsewhere with respect to

---

[7]The court below stated that the presence in California of appellant's daughter gave appellant the benefit of California's "police and fire protection, its school system, its hospital services, its recreational facilities, its libraries and museums * * *." 19 Cal.3d, at 522, 138 Cal. Rptr., at 589, 564 P.2d at 356. But, in the circumstances presented here, these services provided by the State were essentially benefits to the child, not the father, and in any event were not benefits that appellant purposefully sought for himself.

[8]Under the separation agreement, appellant is bound to "indemnify and hold [his] Wife harmless from any and all attorney fees, costs and expenses which she may incur by reason of the default of [appellant] in the performance of any of the obligations required to be performed by him pursuant to the terms and conditions of this agreement." App. 11. To the extent that appellee Horn seeks arrearages, * * * her litigation expenses, presumably including any additional cost incurred by her as a result of having to prosecute the action in New York, would thus be borne by appellant.

[9]A final judgment entered by a New York court having jurisdiction over the defendant's person and over the subject matter of the lawsuit would be entitled to full faith and credit in any State. See *New York ex rel. Halvey v. Halvey*, 330 U.S. 610, 614, 67 S. Ct. 903, 905, 91 L.Ed. 1133 (1947). See also *Sosna v. Iowa*, 419 U.S. 393, 407, 95 S. Ct. 553, 561, 42 L.Ed.2d 532 (1975).

[10]It may well be that, as a matter of state law, appellee Horn could still obtain through New York proceedings additional payments from appellant for Ilsa's support from January 1974, when a *de facto* modification of the custody provisions of the separation agreement took place, until the present. See H. Clark, DOMESTIC RELATIONS §15.2, p. 500 (1968); *cf. In re Santa Clara County v. Hughes*, 43 Misc.2d 559, 251 N.Y.S.2d 579 (1964).

any cause of action arising from these effects unless the nature of the effects and of the individual's relationship to the state make the exercise of such jurisdiction unreasonable."[11]

While this provision is not binding on this Court, it does not in any event support the decision below. As is apparent from the examples accompanying §37 in the *Restatement*, this section was intended to reach wrongful activity outside of the State causing injury within the State, see, *e.g.*, Comment a, p. 157 (shooting bullet from one State into another), or commercial activitiy affecting state residents, *ibid*. Even in such situations, moreover, the Restatement recognizes that there might be circumstances that would render "unreasonable" the assertion of jurisdiction over the nonresident defendant.

The circumstances in this case clearly render "unreasonable" California's assertion of personal jurisdiction. There is no claim that appellant has visited physical injury on either property or persons within the State of California. Cf. *Hess v. Pawloski*, 274 U.S. 352, 47 S. Ct. 632, 71 L.Ed. 1091 (1927). The cause of action herein asserted arises, not from the defendant's commercial transactions in interstate commerce, but rather from his personal, domestic relations. It thus cannot be said that appellant has sought a commercial benefit from solicitation of business from a resident of California that could reasonably render him liable to suit in state court; appellant's activities cannot fairly be analogized to an insurer's sending an insurance contract and premium notices into the State to an insured resident of the State. Cf. *McGee v. International Life Insurance Co.*, 355 U.S. 220, 78 S. Ct. 199, 2 L.Ed.2d 223 (1957). Furthermore, the controversy between the parties arises from a separation that occurred in the State of New York; appellee Horn seeks modification of a contract that was negotiated in New York and that she flew to New York to sign. As in *Hanson v. Denckla*, 357 U.S., at 252, 78 S. Ct., at 1239, the instant action involves an agreement that was entered into with virtually no connection with the forum State. See also n.6, *supra*.

Finally, basic considerations of fairness point decisively in favor of appellant's State of domicile as the proper forum for adjudication of this case, whatever the merits of appellee's underlying claim. It is appellant who has remained in the State of the marital domicile, whereas it is appellee who has moved across the continent. Cf. *May v. Anderson*, 345 U.S. 528, 534–535, n.8, 73 S. Ct. 840, 843–844, 97 L.Ed. 1221 (1953). Appellant has at all times resided in New York State, and, until the separation and appellee's move to California, his entire family resided there as well. As noted above, appellant did no more than acquiesce in the stated preference of one of his children to live with her mother in California. This single act is surely not one that a reasonable parent would expect to result in the substantial financial burden and personal strain of litigating a child-support suit in a forum 3,000 miles away, and we therefore see no basis on which it can be said that appellant could reasonably have anticipated being "haled before a [California] court," *Shaffer v. Heitner*, 433 U.S., at 216, 97 S. Ct., at 2586.[12] To make jurisdiction in a case such as this turn on whether appellant bought his daughter her ticket or instead unsuccessfully sought to prevent her departure would impose an unreasonable burden on family relations, and one wholly unjustified by the "quality and nature" of appellant's activities on or relating to the State of California. *International Shoe Co. v. Washington*, 326 U.S., at 319, 66 S. Ct., at 159.

---

[11]Section 37 of the *Restatement* has effectively been incorporated into California law. See Judicial Council Comment (9) to Cal. Civ. Proc. Code Ann. §410.10 (West 1973).

[12]See also *Developments in the Law—State-Court Jurisdiction*, 73 HARV. L. REV. 909, 911 (1960).

III

In seeking to justify the burden that would be imposed on appellant were the exercise of *in personam* jurisdiction in California sustained, appellee argues that California has substantial interests in protecting the welfare of its minor residents and in promoting to the fullest extent possible a healthy and supportive family environment in which the children of the State are to be raised. These interests are unquestionably important. But while the presence of the children and one parent in California arguably might favor application of California law in a lawsuit in New York, the fact that California may be the " 'center of gravity' " for choice-of-law purposes does not mean that California has personal jurisdiction over the defendant. *Hanson v. Denckla, supra,* 357 U.S., at 254, 78 S. Ct., at 1240. And California has not attempted to assert any particularized interest in trying such cases in its courts by, *e.g.,* enacting a special jurisdictional statute. *Cf. McGee v. International Life Ins. Co., supra,* 355 U.S., at 221, 224, 78 S. Ct., at 200–201.

California's legitimate interest in ensuring the support of children resident in California without unduly disrupting the children's lives, moreover, is already being served by the State's participation in the Revised Uniform Reciprocal Enforcement of Support Act of 1968. This statute provides a mechanism for communication between court systems in different States, in order to facilitate the procurement and enforcement of child-support decrees where the dependent children reside in a State that cannot obtain personal jurisdiction over the defendant. California's version of the Act essentially permits a California resident claiming support from a nonresident to file a petition in California and have its merits adjudicated in the State of the alleged obligor's residence, without either party's having to leave his or her own State. Cal. Civ. Proc. Code Ann. §1650 *et. seq.* (West 1972 and Supp. 1978).[13] New York State is a signatory to a similar Act.[14] Thus, not only may

---

[13] In addition to California, 24 other States are signatories to this Act. 9 U.L.A. 473 (Supp. 1978). Under the Act, an "obligee" may file a petition in a court of his or her State (the "initiating court") to obtain support. 9 U.L.A. §§11, 14 (1973). If the court "finds that the [petition] sets forth facts from which it may be determined that the obligor owes a duty of support and that a court of the responding state may obtain jurisdiction of the obligor or his property," it may send a copy of the petition to the "responding state." §14. This has the effect of requesting the responding State "to obtain jurisdiction over the obligor." §18(b). If jurisdiction is obtained then a hearing is set in a court in the responding State at which the obligor may, if he chooses, contest the claim. The claim may be litigated in that court, with deposition testimony submitted through the initiating court by the initiating spouse or other party. §20. If the responding state court finds that the obligor owes a duty of support pursuant to the laws of the State where he or she was present during the time when support was sought, §7, judgment for the petitioner is entered. §24. If the money is collected from the spouse in the responding State, it is then sent to the court in the initiating State for distribution to the initiating party. §28.

[14] While not a signatory to the Uniform Reciprocal Enforcement of Support Act of 1968, New York is a party to the Uniform Reciprocal Enforcement of Support Act of 1950, as amended. N.Y. Dom. Rel. Law §30 *et seq.* (McKinney 1077) (Uniform Support of Dependents Law). By 1957 this Act, or its substantial equivalent, had been enacted in all States, organized Territorites, and the District of Columbia. 9 U.L.A. 885 (1973). The "two-state" procedure in the 1950 Act for obtaining and enforcing support obligations owed by a spouse in one State to a spouse in another is similar to that provided in the 1968 Act. See n.13, *supra.* See generally Note, 48 CORNELL L.Q. 541 (1963).

In *Landes v. Landes,* 1 N.Y.2d 358, 153 N.Y.S.2d 14, 135 N.E.2d 562, appeal dismissed, 352 U.S. 948, 77 S. Ct. 325, 1 L.Ed.2d 241 (1956), the court upheld a support decree entered against a divorced husband living in New York, on a petition filed by his former wife in California pursuant to the Uniform Act. No prior support agreement or decree existed between the parties; the California spouse sought support from the New York husband for the couple's minor child, who was residing with her mother in California. The New York Court of Appeals concluded that the procedures followed—filing of a petition in California, followed by its certification to New York's Family Court, the obtaining of jurisdiction over the husband, a hearing in New York on the merits of the petition, and entry of an award—were proper under the laws of both States and were constitutional. The constitutionality of these procedures has also been upheld in other

plaintiff-appellee here vindicate her claimed right to additional child support from her former husband in a New York court, see *supra*, at 1698–1699, but also the Uniform Acts will facilitate both her prosecution of a claim for additional support and collection of any support payments found to be owed by appellant.[15]

It cannot be disputed that California has substantial interests in protecting resident children and in facilitating child-support actions on behalf of those children. But these interests simply do not make California a "fair forum," *Shaffer v. Heitner, supra*, 433 U.S., at 215, 97 S. Ct., at 2586, in which to require appellant, who derives no personal or commercial benefit from his child's presence in California and who lacks any other relevant contact with the State, either to defend a child-support suit or to suffer liability by default.

IV

We therefore believe that the state courts in the instant case failed to heed our admonition that "the flexible standard of *International Shoe*" does not "heral[d] the eventual demise of all restrictions on the personal jurisdiction of state courts." *Hanson v. Denckla*, 357 U.S., at 251, 78 S. Ct., at 1238. In *McGee v. International Life Ins. Co.*, we commented on the extension of *in personam* jurisdiction under evolving standards of due process, explaining that this trend was in large part "attributable to the * * * increasing nationalization of commerce * * * [accompanied by] modern transportation and communication [that] have made it much less burdensome for a party sued to defend himself in a State where he engages in economic activity." 355 U.S., at 222–223, 78 S. Ct., at 201. But the mere act of sending a child to California to live with her mother is not a commercial act and connotes no intent to obtain or expectancy of receiving a corresponding benefit in the State that would make fair the assertion of that State's judicial jurisdiction.

Accordingly, we conclude that the appellant's motion to quash service, on the ground of lack of personal jurisdiction, was erroneously denied by the California courts. The judgment of the California Supreme Court is, therefore,

Reversed.

Mr. Justice BRENNAN, with whom Mr. Justice WHITE and Mr. Justice POWELL join, dissenting.

The Court properly treats this case as presenting a single narrow question. That question is whether the California Supreme Court correctly "weighed" "the facts," *ante*, at 1697, of this particular case in applying the settled "constitutional standard," *ibid.*, that before state courts may exercise *in personam* jurisdiction over a nonresident, nondomiciliary parent of minor children domiciled in the State, it must appear that the nonresident has "certain minimum contacts [with the forum State] such that the maintenance of the suit does not offend 'traditional notions of fair play and substantial justice.'" *International Shoe Co. v. Washington*, 326 U.S. 310, 316, 66 S. Ct. 154, 158, 90 L.Ed. 95 (1945). The Court recognizes that "this determination is one in which few answers will be written 'in black and white,'" *ante*, at 1697. I cannot say that the Court's determination against state-court *in personam* jurisdiction is implausible, but, though the issue is close, my indepen-

jurisdictions. See, *e.g.*, *Watson v. Dreadin*, 309 A.2d 493 (D.C. App. 1973), *cert. denied*, 415 U.S. 959, 94 S. Ct. 1488, 39 L.Ed.2d 574 (1974); *State ex rel. Terry v. Terry*, 80 N.M. 185, 453 P.2d 206 (1969); *Harmon v. Harmon*, 184 Cal. App.2d 245, 7 Cal. Rptr. 279 (1960), appeal dismissed and cert. denied, 366 U.S. 270, 81 S. Ct. 1100, 6 L.Ed.2d 382 (1961).
[15]Thus, it cannot here be concluded, as it was in *McGee v. International Life Insurance Co.*, 355 U.S. 220, 223–224, 78 S. Ct. 199, 201, 2 L.Ed.2d 223 (1957), with respect to actions on insurance contracts, that resident plaintiffs would be at a "severe disadvantage" if *in personam* jurisdiction over out-of-state defendants were sometimes unavailable.

dent weighing of the facts leads me to conclude, in agreement with the analysis and determination of the California Supreme Court, that appellant's connection with the State of California was not too attenuated, under the standards of reasonableness and fairness implicit in the Due Process Clause, to require him to conduct his defense in the California courts. I therefore dissent.

Comments

Following the language in *Shaffer v. Heitner*, the legal literature has perceived *Kulko* to be related to the "standards set forth in *International Shoe* and its progeny."* Indeed, the defendant invoked, successfully before the U.S. Supreme Court, that he lacked sufficient minimum contacts with the State of California and that the proceedings against him before the California courts did not comply with "traditional notions of fair play and substantial justice," as demanded by *International Shoe Co. v. Washington.*† In spite of the historical discussion in Mr. Justice Marshall's opinion in *Kulko*, going back more than 100 years to *Pennoyer v. Neff,*‡ it is probable that factors other than those discussed by the Court had an impact on the outcome, in particular the conduct of the plaintiff wife who throughout the controversy seemed to have aggressively pursued her self-interest. The statement of facts at the onset of the majority opinion in *Kulko* is symptomatic.

Mr. Justice Marshall set forth in minute detail the tragic events that brought about the gradual disintegration of the Kulko family. In each instance, Sharon Kulko was described, sometimes by implication, as having been the moving force. She moved away to San Francisco, California, while still married, leaving her husband behind in New York with the children. She came back to New York merely to sign the separation agreement thereby surrendering the custody of the children to her husband. Immediately thereafter she flew to Haiti to secure a divorce in person while (as indicated in footnote 1) the husband stayed behind in New York, and he merely filed a power of attorney which she had taken along for this purpose. Apparently without delay she returned to California, "where she remarried and took the name Horn." Having settled her own situation by remarrying, she then induced the children, first the daughter Ilsa, then the boy Darwin, to leave their father and join her and the stepfather in San Francisco. The contrary separation agreement seemed to have been a way station to facilitate the Haitian divorce and remarriage. Less than a month after she had spirited away the son from New York, she brought proceedings in California demanding *inter alia* a change in

---

*433 U.S. 186, 212 (1977).
†326 U.S. 310, 316 (1945) (quoting *Milliken v. Meyer*, 311 U.S. 457, 463 (1940)).
‡95 U.S. 714 (1877).

custody and an increase in support. The California trial court immediately granted her temporary custody and (as indicated in the here deleted footnote 5) increased substantially the defendant's support obligation.

As a matter of legal theory, the detailed factual account in *Kulko* can be justified, at least in part, as laying a foundation for jurisdictional conclusions, based on the requirement of "reasonableness" in *Shaffer* and *International Shoe*. More clearly, however, especially when the tone of the account is considered, it spells out fault. It is inferred that this woman had deserted her husband and temporarily abandoned her children in the interest of a new relationship and remarriage. The defendant, on the other hand, is depicted, again supposedly for jurisdictional purposes, as having remained passive and as having merely acquiesced in the progressively perplexing situation he found himself in. His motives are described as laudable, having in mind family harmony and the welfare of the children.

This particular discussion is geared by the Court to the additional jurisdictional requirement established in *Hanson v. Denckla** that the defendant must have *purposefully* availed himself of some benefits or privileges within the forum state, in this instance, California. Yet this jurisdictional factor imparts a subjective element, in this case the defendant's freedom from fault by staying passive in the interests of peace and for the good of the children. The plaintiff's conduct, by comparison, seems to be designed to maximize her strategic position with the aid of the California courts and to offend, in the language of *Shaffer* and *International Shoe*, "traditional notions of fair play and substantial justice." This concept too imparts possible consideration of fault or the freedom from it, especially within the realm of jurisdiction of state courts in family disputes.

One aspect of *Kulko* seems to be that it resurrects, albeit inadvertently, *Haddock v. Haddock*,[†] which was expressly overruled with detailed reasons in *Williams v. North Carolina I* (see pp. 445–454). A criticized aspect of *Haddock* was that it combined jurisdictional considerations with questions of who was at fault—in other words, the actual merits of the case. As Mr. Justice Douglas expressed in writing for the majority in *Williams I*, "the fault or wrong of one spouse in leaving the other becomes under that view a jurisdictional fact on which this Court would ultimately have to pass. Whatever may be said as to the practical effect which such would have in clouding divorce decrees, the question as to where the fault lies has no relevancy to the existence of state power in such circumstances." While the logic of this reasoning seems to be unassailable, its application poses practical problems, as *Kulko* demonstrates. The jurisdictional standards of *Shaffer* and *International Shoe* which may be relatively free of hidden substantive elements in financial or commercial transactions

---

*357 U.S. 235, 253 (1958).
[†]201 U.S. 562 (1906).

seem to invite substantive considerations of fault within the whole area of family law, regardless of whether an attempt is made to apply them to status questions, such as divorce and custody, or whether as in *Kulko* a mere monetary award is in issue.

In spite of legislative efforts to eliminate fault, family law continues to be permeated with submerged, essentially emotional, needs to apply moral standards of fault. As *Kulko* illustrates, even an elevated judicial forum, such as the U.S. Supreme Court, may follow this pattern. Independently, the conceptual distinction between procedure and substance has caused problems in other areas of law. Actually, both types of rules are equally concerned with the exercise of power. Practicing lawyers realize that it is sound strategy to support a seemingly purely technical jurisdictional argument with substantive reasons relating to the merits of the case. A judge may rule that these matters are irrelevant for the determination of the jurisdictional issues, yet he may nevertheless be swayed by broad considerations of fairness, as he understands them. Frequently substantive dispositions are made under color of procedure, and jurisdictional dispositions are particularly amenable to this, sometimes unconscious, judicial strategy.

The outcome of *Kulko* is an illustration for such a hidden substantive disposition of the case. That the California courts served the cause of the plaintiff is obvious. She obtained custody and a substantial increase in support, essentially all that she had asked for. Whether the New York courts would have been equally supportive of her claims is doubtful, the Uniform Reciprocal Enforcement of Support Act notwithstanding. The attorneys representing the parties were obviously aware of the respective merits and disadvantages of litigating the issues in California or in New York. By deciding the jurisdictional issue in favor of the defendant, the U.S. Supreme Court affected the merits of the case sufficiently to make it feasible for the plaintiff to settle the case for less than she could have obtained through the jurisdiction of the California courts. The reason why the fault aspect of *Kulko* and its relation to *Haddock* have not been sufficiently discussed in the literature lies in two factors—insufficient close analysis of the facts and concentration on the conceptual reasons given by the Court. Had Mr. Justice Marshall's factual account been matched with the legal conclusion, it would have become apparent that more was involved in the outcome favoring the defendant than jurisdictional considerations.

The mere fact that the legal analysis of *Kulko* has tended to be incomplete does not permit the conclusion, however, that the jurisdictional reasoning in the opinion can be disregarded. It encourages the reevaluation of the jurisdictional issues in status litigation from the perspective of due process as expressed in *Shaffer*. Technically, only child support was in issue before the U.S. Supreme Court in *Kulko*. But the litigation, as initiated by the plaintiff, had also included a request for change in custody. Although the appeal did not challenge the custody disposition, matters relating to custody continued to be significant for the adjudication of support. The Court did not limit itself in its reasoning to support, but implied a universally applicable theory of jurisdiction that required a nexus between the defendant and the forum state that is not too attenuated.

Bodenheimer has maintained that footnote 30 in *Shaffer* exempted status adjudications from the minimum contacts rule. Yet *Shaffer* involved a derivative shareholder's suit in a commercial context, and family or status was not in issue and not argued before the Court. Moreover, the passing reference to status in a footnote was not clear as an exemption. It was expressed in the form of a double negative: "We do not suggest that jurisdictional doctrines other than those discussed in text, such as the particularized rules governing adjudications of status, are inconsistent with the standard of fairness."* This is substantially less than a positive suggestion that jurisdictional doctrines, such as the rules governing adjudications of status, are consistent with the standard of fairness. In other words, jurisdiction in status litigation, for example, relating to divorce or custody, may or may not comport with the standards of fairness and reasonableness as demanded by due process. Or, to use the language of Mr. Justice Marshall in *Kulko*, "the facts of each case must be weighed to determine whether the requisite 'affiliating circumstances' are present."

Past case law in regard to status adjudication in family law, traditionally perceived as being in the nature of *in rem*, would have to be reexamined in the light of *Shaffer* and *Kulko* under the test of minimum contacts. For example, the jurisdictional requirement of domicile as developed in *Williams I* for ex parte divorces might continue to survive constitutional attack, perhaps even the three-month "actual presence" in Arkansas before judgment as the jurisdictional basis for divorce in *Wheat v. Wheat* (pp. 470–474). Yet a technical domicile might be an unreasonable basis for jurisdiction. Had the peripatetic Mr. Wheat, for instance, instead of pursuing his request for divorce in Arkansas, the state of his actual presence, filed for divorce in Oklahoma, the state of his original and probably continuing domicile, a sufficient jurisdictional nexus might have been missing. He did not reside within Oklahoma for years and Mrs. Wheat probably had no connection with that state whatsoever.

In regard to custody adjudications, the jurisdictional theories as expressed in *May v. Anderson*,† upon reexamination, may have to be modified. In that case a custody award by a Wisconsin divorce court, favoring the father, had been given full faith and credit in Ohio where the mother and children were living. In reversing the Ohio courts, the U.S. Supreme Court by a plurality of the Justices maintained that Wisconsin courts could not cut off the custody rights of a nonresident mother without *in personam* jurisdiction. The opinion could run counter to the suggestion in *Shaffer*, not contradicted in *Kulko*, that

---

*433 U.S. 186, 208 n. 30 (1977).
†345 U.S. 528 (1953).

at least some particularized rules governing status adjudications may not be inconsistent with the standard of fairness propagated by the minimum contacts test of jurisdiction. Custody adjudications, in which the status of children is determined, could be a prime illustration. A requirement of *in personam* jurisdiction over the parent could be an intolerable burden, especially in neglect and adoption cases.

References

Bodenheimer & Neeley-Kvarme, *Jurisdiction Over Child Custody and Adoption After Shaffer and Kulko*, 12 U.C.D. L. REV. 229 (1979).

Cardozo, *The Reach of the Legislature and the Grasp of Jurisdiction*, 43 CORNELL L.Q. 210 (1957).

Currie, *The Growth of the Long Arm: Eight Years of Extended Jurisdiction in Illinois*, 1963 U. ILL. L.F. 533.

Garfield, *The Transitory Divorce Action: Jurisdiction in the No-Fault Era*, 58 TEX. L. REV. 501 (1980).

Hazard, *May v. Anderson: Preamble to Family Law Chaos*, 45 VA. L. REV. 378 (1959).

Nagan, W., Jurisdiction: Domestic Relations in the Wake of Kulko and Shaffer (July 1982) (unpublished manuscript).

Note, *Developments in the Law—The Constitution and the Family*, 93 HARV. L. REV. 1156, 1242–1248 (1980).

Note, *The Long-Arm Reach of the Courts Under the Effect Test After Kulko v. Superior Court*, 65 VA. L. REV. 175 (1979).

Riesenfeld, *Shaffer v. Heitner: Holding, Implications, Forebodings*, 30 HASTINGS L.J. 1183 (1979).

Vernon, *State-Court Jurisdiction: A Preliminary Inquiry Into the Impact of Shaffer v. Heitner*, 63 IOWA L. REV. 997 (1978).

Woods, *Pennoyer's Demise: Personal Jurisdiction After Shaffer and Kulko and a Modest Prediction Regarding World-Wide Volkswagen Corp. v. Woodson*, 20 ARIZ. L. REV. 861, 890–898 (1978) (fairness factors).

Bibliography

Batt, *Child Custody Disputes: A Developmental-Psychological Approach to Proof and Decisionmaking*, 12 WILLAMETTE L.J. 491 (1976).

Bodenheimer, *The International Kidnapping of Children: The United States Approach*, 11 FAM. L.Q. 83 (1977).

Bodenheimer, *Interstate Custody: Initial Jurisdiction and Continuing Jurisdiction Under the UCCJA*, 14 FAM. L.Q. 203 (1981).

Bodenheimer, *Progress Under the Uniform Child Custody Jurisdiction Act and Remaining Problems: Punitive Decrees, Joint Custody, and Excessive Modification*, 65 CALIF. L. REV. 978 (1977).

Bodenheimer & Neeley-Kvarme, *Jurisdiction Over Child Custody and Adoption After Shaffer and Kulko*, U.C.D. L. REV. 229 (1979).

Coombs, *Interstate Child Custody: Jurisdiction, Recognition, and Enforcement*, 66 MINN. L. REV. 711 (1982).

Crouch, R., Interstate Custody Litigation: A Guide to Use and Court Interpretation of the Uniform Child Custody Jurisdiction Act (1981).

Foster & Freed, *Child Custody*, 39 N.Y.U. L. Rev. 423 (1964).

Foster & Freed, *Child Snatching and Custodial Flights: The Case for the Uniform Child Custody Jurisdiction Act*, 28 Hastings L.J. 1011 (1977).

Foster & Freed, *Grandparent Visitation: Vagaries and Vicissitudes*, 23 St. Louis U.L.J. 643 (1979).

Gault, *Statutory Grandchild Visitation*, 5 St. Mary's L.J. 474 (1973).

Hazard, *May v. Anderson: Preamble to Family Law Chaos*, 45 Va. L. Rev. 378 (1959).

Hoff, P., Schulman, J., & Volenik, A., Interstate Child Custody Disputes and Parental Kidnapping: Policy, Practice and Law (National Center on Women and Family Law, Inc., National Center for Youth Law, Legal Services Corporation, and American Bar Association, 1982).

Katz, S., Child Snatching—The Legal Response to the Abduction of Children (1981).

Mnookin, *Child-Custody Adjudication: Judicial Functions in the Face of Indeterminacy*, 39 Law & Contemp. Probs. 226 (1975).

Note, *Developments in the Law—The Constitution and the Family*, 93 Harv. L. Rev. 1156 (1980).

Note, *The Long-Arm Reach of the Courts Under the Effect Test After Kulko v. Superior Court*, 65 Va. L. Rev. 175 (1979).

Note, *Statutory Visitation of Grandparents: One Step Closer to the Best Interest of the Child*, 26 Cath. U.L. Rev. 387 (1977).

Weitzman & Dixon, *Child Custody Awards: Legal Standards and Empirical Patterns for Child Custody Support and Visitation After Divorce*, 12 U.C.D. L. Rev. 473 (1979).

Woods, *Pennoyer's Demise: Personal Jurisdiction After Shaffer and Kulko and a Modest Prediction Regarding World-Wide Volkswagen Corp. v. Woodson*, 20 Ariz. L. Rev. 861 (1978).

Zaharoff, *Access to Children: Towards a Model Statute for Third Parties*, 15 Fam. L.Q. 165 (1981).

Children as Persons

Freedom from Parental Support

White v. White

District Court of Appeal of Florida

296 So.2d 619 (1st D.C.A. Fla. 1974)

Boyer, Judge.

We are called upon to review an order of the trial court requiring a father to pay to the mother of a "child" over 18 years of age support for that "child." Dates are important. On April 28, 1969 a final judgment of divorce was entered in a proceeding in which the appellant here was plaintiff and the appellee defendant. The final judgment awarded to the defendant mother custody of the party's son, then 15 years of age. The final judgment was unusual in that although it required the payment of child support in a specified sum there was no provision for termination upon attaining age 18, age 21, upon becoming *sua juris*, self-supporting or otherwise. On January 5, 1970 an order was entered modifying the final judgment by reducing "child support" payments to $100 per month, which order provided that such payments should continue "until further order of the court." On August 31, 1971 another order modifying the final judgment was entered by which plaintiff father was required to pay to the defendant mother the sum of $115 "as and for support of the minor child of the parties." That order is silent as to any termination date and contains no provision that the payment shall continue "until further order of the court" as was provided in the previous order. On July 1, 1973 Chapter 73-21, removing the disability of non-age to persons 18 years of age became effective. That statute provides as follows:

"Section 1. Subsection (14) of section 1.01, Florida Statutes, is created to read:

"1.01 Definitions.—In construing these statutes and each and every word, phrase or part hereof, where the context will permit:
"(14) The word 'minor' includes any person who has not attained the age of 18 years.

"Section 2. The disability of nonage is hereby removed for all persons in this state who are 18 years of age or older and they shall enjoy and suffer the rights, privileges *and obligations* of all persons 21 years of age or older except as otherwise excluded by the Constitution of the State of Florida immediately preceding the effective date of this act. Provided, however, this act shall not prohibit any court of competent jurisdiction from requiring support for a *dependent* person beyond the age of 18 years; and provided further that any crippled child as defined in chapter 391, Florida Statutes, shall receive benefits under the provisions of said chapter until age 21, the provisions of this act to the contrary notwithstanding.

"Section 3. This act shall operate prospectively and not retrospectively and *shall not affect the rights and obligations existing prior to the effective date of this act.*

"Section 4. Any law inconsistent herewith is hereby repealed to the extent of such inconsistency. In editing the manuscript for the next revision of the Florida Statutes, the statutory revision and indexing service is hereby directed to conform existing statutes to the provisions of this act.

"Section 5. In the event that any provision or application of this act is held to be invalid, it is the legislative intent that the other provisions and applications hereof shall not be thereby affected.

"Section 6. This act shall take effect July 1, 1973.

"Approved by the Governor May 9, 1973." (Emphasis added)

The son of the parties became 18 years of age on February 6, 1972.

Following the effective date of the above mentioned statute plaintiff-father discontinued making payments, on advice of counsel, on the assumption that the "child" was then legally an adult and that therefore "child support payments" were not required. The defendant-mother procured the issuance of a rule to show cause and on October 5, 1973 the trial judge found the plaintiff to be in arrears in the total amount of $460 through the payment due August 2, 1973 and allowed 15 days for payment thereof. He further ordered the plaintiff to pay an attorney's fee of $50 for the defendant's attorney incident to the bringing of the rule to show cause.

Via some vehicle not quite clear in the record, a further hearing was held on October 7, 1973 at which hearing the evidence revealed that the son of the parties was a sophomore attending Florida Junior College; that he lived with his mother and stepfather who provided him with the necessities of life; that he had theretofore worked but had been injured on the job resulting in payment of $72 bi-weekly as workmen's compensation; that he had no permanent disability and since his injury had worked for a construction company as a laborer earning $3.80 per hour which job he had voluntarily quit to become a student. The son testified that he was enrolled taking prelaw courses with the anticipation of ultimately attending law school. The plaintiff did not contend that he was financially unable to make the payments but stated that he hadn't been "treated like a father" and essentially had lost control of his son.

On October 23, 1973 the trial judge entered an order finding that since the son was attending junior college and was not employed he was entitled to the support of $115 per month from plaintiff-father and further stating that the son "in the court's opinion, is entitled to a college education at the expense of his parents."

This appeal followed.

The Supreme Court of Florida, in *Perla v. Perla*, Sup. Ct. Fla. 1952, 58 So.2d 689, had occasion to consider a court's order wherein the father of a 33 year old mentally retarded child was sought to be required in a divorce proceeding to pay support to the mother of the child. The court there stated:

> "Generally, the obligation of a parent to support a child ceases when the child reaches majority, but an exception arises when the child is, from physical or mental deficiencies, unable to support himself. The overwhelming weight of authority supports the view, however, that a divorce suit is not the proper proceeding where the responsibility may be fixed and the burden imposed. *Borchert v. Borchert*, 185 Md. 586, 45 A.2d 463, 162 A.L.R. 1078.
>
> "An action for divorce is statutory, and we can find nothing in our laws * * * warranting an order requiring a father to pay to his erstwhile wife money for the support of an adult child, even though the child is mentally and physically afflicted. The mother should not, in a divorce proceeding, be made a medium through which payments coerced from the father would reach an adult child.
>
>   * * *
>
> "We do not hold that for all time the father, in the transaction with the mother, managed to shrug off any responsibility for supporting the child, but only that now, and by a decree in this suit, the court should not require him to compensate the mother for what the care and custody may be costing her." (at page 690, of 58 So.2d)

Again, in *Zalka v. Zalka*, Sup. Ct. Fla. 1958, 100 So.2d 157, that court, citing *Perla v. Perla, supra*, restated the proposition that a mother's right to receive support money "would automatically terminate upon the son's attaining his majority.'

This Court, in *Fincham v. Levin*, Fla. App. (1st) 1963, 155 So.2d 883, held that a divorced father may be required to contribute to the support of his unmarried adult daughter who was congenatively mentally and physically unable to care for and support herself, saying however:

> "* * * He [appellant] cites the annotation in 1 A.L.R.2d at page 914 in support of the proposition that the common law went no further than to impose on parents the duty of supporting their minor children, and that as a general rule there is no obligation on the part of a parent to support an adult child. *This is unquestionably the rule with respect to able-bodied children.* * * *" (at page 884) (Emphasis added)

In *Carmody v. Carmody*, Fla. App. (1st) 1970, 230 So.2d 40, this Court held that "by operation of law" a son 20 years of age whose disabilities of non-age had been removed, a sophomore in college with approximately $3,000 in savings was "not entitled to parental support as a matter of law."

In a *per curiam* opinion this Court, in *Register v. Register*, Fla. App. (1st) 1970, 230 So.2d 684, said:

> "It is discretionary with the trial court as to whether any allowance should be made to defray college expense, with many factors entering into the question, one being whether the child is college material or not. These factors as well as others will continue to exist *until a dependent child reaches his or her majority* and must be determined by the court periodically when and if the needs arise and shall be dependent also upon the father's financial ability to supply such needs." (at page 684) (Emphasis added)

In *Bosem v. Bosem*, Fla. App. (3d) 1972, 269 So.2d 758 the court, in considering an "open ended" support order, said:

> "* * * Of course, the provisions must be limited to the period of time before the children become twenty-one years old. * * *" (at page 763)

In *Field v. Field*, Fla. App. (2d) 1974, 291 So.2d 654, opinion filed March 22, 1974, our sister court of the Second District held that the trial court erred in modifying a final judgment by changing the termination date of child support payments from age 21, as provided in the final judgment of divorce, to age 18, saying:

> "* * * This modification, apparently made by the trial court sua sponte, is a misinterpretation of the applicable law. Chapter 73–21, Laws of Florida, provides that the change in the minimum age of majority is to operate prospectively and not retrospectively and is not to affect pre-existing rights. The change in the instant case is not justified by the record and must be reversed."

As noted, the final judgment in the Field case specifically provided that the child support payments continue until the child reached age 21. The final judgment in the case sub judice did not so provide.

In *Finn v. Finn*, Fla. App. (3d) 1974, 294 So.2d 57, opinion filed April 2, 1974, the Third District Court of Appeal had occasion to consider the exact point here involved under identical circumstances, except that it appears from a reading of that case that the initial final judgment provided for support payments until the children became 21 years of age. That court affirmed an order of the trial judge denying the father's post-judgment motion to terminate child support payments when the children attained 18 years of age and required such payments to continue until they attained age 21. The court there stated:

> "First, Section 2, Ch. 73–21, Fla. Stat. authorizes a court to provide dependent persons beyond the age of 18 with support and, second, Section 3 clearly indicates that the statute was not to have an impact on obligations existing prior to the effective date of the act. Prior to July 1, 1973, the appellant was obligated to support the children of the marriage until they reached the age of 21 years. Under the provisions of the act, these obligations were not to be disturbed."

It was stipulated in the Finn case that the subject children were neither physically nor mentally disabled. They were both over 18 years of age and were attending college. It would appear therefore that the court there considered the word "dependent" as used in Section 2 of Chapter 73–21, Laws of 1973, to mean without independent means of support as distinguished from physical or mental disability. We do not think that such was the legislative intent. The same sentence, which constituted the proviso in said Section 2, provides for court ordered support "for a dependent *person* beyond the age of 18 years" and for benefits under Chapter 391, Florida Statutes, for "any crippled child." It appears to us therefore that by use of the term "dependent person" the legislature intended a person over 18 years of age unable by reason of physical or mental incompetency or inability to be independent.

The court, in the Finn case, recited that Section 3 indicates that the statute was not to have an impact on obligations existing prior to its effective date and that prior to said date the father of said children was obligated to support said children until they attained age 21. However, *in the case* sub judice, *there was no such obligation.* As stated in the first paragraph of this opinion the original final judgment was silent as to the period for which the support payments were to continue. The first order of modification provided that said payments should continue "until further order of the court." The subsequent order of modification was, like the final judgment, silent as to any termination date. Accordingly, we find that Section 3 of Chapter 73-21, Laws of Florida 1973 has no application under the facts of the case *sub judice* inasmuch as there were no "rights and obligations existing prior to the effective date" of the Act.

As stated elsewhere in this opinion the trial judge's order giving rise to this appeal found that since the son was attending college and not employed he was entitled to support from his father, and further "in the court's opinion, is entitled to a college education at the expense of his parents." It is certainly desirable and laudable for parents to encourage their offspring to get a college education *if* he or she is college material. However, there are many parents who enjoy complete domestic tranquility but who do not, either from personal choice or inability or otherwise, give their children a college education. The fact that domestic whirlwinds cause a severance of the marriage does not enhance the rights of the children nor alter the obligations of the parents. Certainly if the parents were still married and enjoying domestic harmony a suit would not lie by the child or either parent to require parental support for a college education. Neither may such be accomplished in a dissolution of marriage forum.

When the legislature, in its infinite wisdom, emancipated 18 year old children, it specifically provided that they enjoy and *"suffer"* the rights, privileges *"and obligations"* of persons 21 years of age and older. We find nothing in the act which appears to us to have been intended to afford 18 year old adults any bonus rights or privileges not enjoyed by persons over 21 years of age.

In the case *sub judice* the harassed father testified that his son had ceased to treat him like a father and that he had essentially lost control of his son. The tightening of parental purse strings is often a very effective cure for such a disease. If the son deserves his father's financial help we would encourage and urge the father, appellant here, to respond. However, inasmuch as the 18 year old adult in the case *sub judice* is mentally and physically able and has demonstrated his ability to be gainfully employed, and since there was no requirement of support to age 21 nor requirement of support during the attaining of a college education in the orders of the Circuit Court which preceded the effective date of Chapter 73-21, F.S., we do not construe the law as empowering us, or the trial judge, to require the appellant so to do.

The appellee's motion for attorneys' fees incident to this appeal is denied. Reversed.

McCORD, Judge (dissenting).

We have before us an order of the trial judge entered after hearing on a rule to show cause why appellant should not be held in contempt for failure to pay support payments for his son as previously ordered by the court. The only basis appellant gave for abruptly discontinuing payments was that his son had reached the age of 18 years and under Chapter 73-21, Laws of Florida, he was no longer a minor. The previous support order directed that appellant pay $115 per month support and did not state a termination date. At the time of that order, a child did not reach his majority under the law until age 21.

Sections 2 and 3 of said Chapter 73-21 provide as follows:

"Section 2. The disability of nonage is hereby removed for all persons in this state who are 18 years of age or older and they shall enjoy and suffer the rights, privileges and obligations of all persons 21 years of age or older except as otherwise excluded by the Constitution of the State of Florida immediately preceding the effective date of this act. Provided, however, this act shall not prohibit any court of competent jurisdiction from requiring support for a dependent person beyond the age of 18 years; and provided further that any crippled child as defined in chapter 391, Florida Statutes, shall receive benefits under the provisions of said chapter until age 21, the provisions of this act to the contrary notwithstanding.

"Section 3. This act shall operate prospectively and not retrospectively and shall not affect the rights and obligations existing prior to the effective date of this act."

It is my view that since the operation of the new statute is prospective rather than retroactive, and under the previous order at the time it was entered the father was obligated to make support payments until his son reached age 21, and since the new statute further authorizes the court to require support for a dependent person beyond the age of 18 years, the statute did not nullify the court's previous support order upon the son reaching age 18. If appellant desired at that time to have the support modified or terminated on the ground that the former minor was self-supporting, he should have filed a petition seeking such relief. Upon the filing of such petition, it then would become the duty of the trial judge under the evidence presented at a hearing thereon to determine the question of dependency in the exercise of his sound discretion considering the circumstances of the parents and the needs of their offspring. The question of whether or not the offspring is satisfactorily pursuing an education to become better equipped for life and the reasonableness of such pursuit would be relevant to the question of his dependency. The legislature in the above quotation from Section 2 of the statute used the words "dependent person." It did not limit dependent persons to disabled persons or to disabled dependent persons, although it could have done so if it had intended such limited interpretation. It is my view that the legislature did not intend an abrupt and radical change in the law of support previously existing prior to the effective date of the new act.

In the absence of a petition for termination of support and a final order by the court approving same, appellant had no authority to terminate the support payments previously ordered. I would affirm.

Freedom to Make Their Own Decisions

Bellotti v. Baird

United States Supreme Court

443 U.S. 622 (1979)

Mr. Justice POWELL announced the judgment of the Court and delivered an opinion in which THE CHIEF JUSTICE, Mr. Justice STEWART, and Mr. Justice REHNQUIST, joined.

These appeals present a challenge to the constitutionality of a state statute regulating the access of minors to abortions. They require us to continue the inquiry we began in *Planned Parenthood v. Danforth*, 428 U.S. 52 (1976), and *Bellotti v. Baird*, 428 U.S. 132 (1976).

On August 2, 1974, the legislature of the Commonwealth of Massachusetts passed, over the Governor's veto, an act pertaining to abortions performed within the State. 1974 Mass. Acts, ch. 706. According to its title, the statute was intended to regulate abortions "within present constitutional limits." Shortly before the act was to go into effect, the class action from which these appeals arise was commenced in the District Court[1] to enjoin, as unconstitutional, the provision of the act now codified as Mass. Gen. Laws Ann., ch. 112, §12S (West).

Section 12S provides in part:

> "If the mother is less than eighteen years of age and has not married, the consent of both the mother and her parents [to an abortion to be performed on the mother] is required. If one or both of the mother's parents refuse such consent, consent may be obtained by order of a judge of the superior court for good cause shown, after such hearing as he deems necessary. Such a hearing will not require the appointment of a guardian for the mother. If one of the parents has died or has deserted his or her family, consent by the remaining parent is sufficient. If both parents have died or have deserted their family, consent of the mother's guardian or other person having duties similar to a guardian, or any person who had assumed the care and custody of the mother is sufficient. The commissioner of public health shall prescribe a written form for such consent. Such form shall be signed by the proper person or persons and given to the physician performing the abortion who shall maintain it in his permanent files."

* * *[3]

A child, merely on account of his minority, is not beyond the protection of the Constitution. As the Court said in *In re Gault*, 387 U.S. 1 (1967), "whatever may be their precise impact, neither the Fourteenth Amendment nor the Bill of Rights is for adults alone."[12] This observation, of course, is but the

---

[1]The court promptly issued a restraining order which remained in effect until its decision on the merits. Subsequent stays of enforcement were issued during the complex course of this litigation, with the result that Mass. Gen. Laws Ann., ch. 112, §12S (West), never has been enforced by Massachusetts.

[3]The proceedings before the court and the substance of its opinion are described in detail in *Bellotti v. Baird*, 428 U.S. 132, 136–143 (1976).

[12]Similarly, the Court said in *Planned Parenthood of Central Missouri v. Danforth*, 428 U.S. 52, 74 (1976):

beginning of the analysis. The Court long has recognized that the status of minors under the law is unique in many respects. As Mr. Justice Frankfurter aptly put it. "[c]hildren have a very special place in life which law should reflect. Legal theories and their phrasing in other cases readily lead to fallacious reasoning if uncritically transferred to determination of a State's duty towards children." *May v. Anderson*, 345 U.S. 528, 536 (1953) (concurring opinion). The unique role in our society of the family, the institution by which "we inculcate and pass down many of our most cherished values, moral and cultural," *Moore v. City of East Cleveland*, 431 U.S. 494, 503–504 (1977) (plurality opinion), requires that constitutional principles be applied with sensitivity and flexibility to the special needs of parents and children. We have recognized three reasons justifying the conclusion that the constitutional rights of children cannot be equated with those of adults: the peculiar vulnerability of children; their inability to make critical decisions in an informed, mature manner; and the importance of the parental role in child-rearing.

The Court's concern for the vulnerability of children is demonstrated in its decisions dealing with minors' claims to constitutional protection against deprivations of liberty or property interests by the State. With respect to many of these claims, we have concluded that the child's right is virtually coextensive with that of an adult. For example, the Court has held that the Fourteenth Amendment's guarantee against the deprivation of liberty without due process of law is applicable to children in juvenile delinquency proceedings. *In re Gault*, 387 U.S. 1 (1967). In particular, minors involved in such proceedings are entitled to adequate notice, the assistance of counsel, and the opportunity to confront their accusers. They can be found guilty only upon proof beyond a reasonable doubt, and they may assert the privilege against compulsory self-incrimination. [Citations omitted.]

These rulings have not been made on the uncritical assumption that the constitutional rights of children are indistinguishable from those of adults. Indeed, our acceptance of juvenile courts distinct from the adult criminal justice system assumes that juvenile offenders constitutionally may be treated differently from adults. In order to preserve this separate avenue for dealing with minors, the Court has said that hearings in juvenile delinquency cases need not necessarily "conform with all the requirements of a criminal trial or even of the usual administrative hearing." *In re Gault, supra*, 387 U.S., at 30, quoting *Kent v. United States*, 383 U.S. 541, 562 (1966). Thus, juveniles are not constitutionally entitled to trial by jury in delinquency adjudications. *McKeiver v. Pennsylvania*, 403 U.S. 528 (1978). Viewed together, our cases show that although children generally are protected by the same constitutional guarantees against governmental deprivations as are adults, the State is entitled to adjust its legal system to account for children's vulnerability and their needs for "concern, * * * sympathy, and * * * paternal attention." *Id.*, at 550 (plurality opinion).

Second, the Court has held that the States validly may limit the freedom of children to choose for themselves in the making of important, affirmative choices with potentially serious consequences. These rulings have been grounded in the recognition that, during the formative years of childhood and adolescence, minors often lack the experience, perspective, and judgment to recognize and avoid choices that could be detrimental to them.[13]

* * *

"Constitutional rights do not mature and come into being magically only when one attains the state-defined age of majority. Minors, as well as adults, are protected by the Constitution and possess constitutional rights."

[13]As Mr. Justice STEWART wrote of the exercise by minors of the First Amendment rights that "secur[e] * * * the liberty of each man to decide for himself what he will read and to what he will listen," *Ginsberg v. New York*, 390 U.S. 629, 649 (1968) (STEWART, J., concurring in the result):

Third, the guiding role of parents in the upbringing of their children justifies limitations on the freedoms of minors. The State commonly protects its youth from adverse governmental action and from their own immaturity by requiring parental consent to or involvement in important decisions by minors. But an additional and more important justification for state deference to parental control over children is that "[t]he child is not the mere creature of the state; those who nurture him and direct his destiny have the right, coupled with the high duty, to recognize and prepare him for additional obligations." *Pierce v. Society of Sisters*, 268 U.S. 510, 535 (1925). "The duty to prepare the child for 'additional obligations' * * * must be read to include the inculcation of moral standards, religious beliefs, and elements of good citizenship." *Wisconsin v. Yoder*, 406 U.S. 205, 233 (1972). This affirmative process of teaching, guiding, and inspiring by precept and example is essential to the growth of young people into mature, socially responsible citizens.

We have believed in this country that this process, in large part, is beyond the competence of impersonal political institutions. Indeed, affirmative sponsorship of particular ethical, religious, or political beliefs is something we expect the State *not* to attempt in a society constitutionally committed to the ideal of individual liberty and freedom of choice. Thus, "[i]t is cardinal with us that the custody, care and nurture of the child reside first in the parents, whose primary function and freedom include *preparation for obligations the state can neither supply nor hinder.*" *Prince v. Massachusetts, supra*, 321 U.S., at 166 (emphasis added).

Unquestionably, there are many competing theories about the most effective way for parents to fulfill their central role in assisting their children on the way to responsible adulthood. While we do not pretend any special wisdom on this subject, we cannot ignore that central to many of these theories, and deeply rooted in our nation's history and tradition, is the belief that the parental role implies a substantial measure of authority over one's children. Indeed, "constitutional interpretation has consistently recognized that the parents' claim to authority in their own household to direct the rearing of their children is basic in the structure of our society." *Ginsberg v. New York, supra*, 390 U.S., at 639.

Properly understood, then, the tradition of parental authority is not inconsistent with our tradition of individual liberty; rather, the former is one of the basic presuppositions of the latter. Legal restrictions on minors, especially those supportive of the parental role, may be important to the child's chances for the full growth and maturity that make eventual participation in a free society meaningful and rewarding. Under the Constitution, the State can "properly conclude that parents and others, teachers for example, who have [the] primary responsibility for children's well-being are entitled to the support of laws designed to aid discharge of that responsibility." *Ginsberg v. New York, supra*, at 639.

With these principles in mind, we consider the specific constitutional questions presented by these appeals. In §12S Massachusetts has attempted to reconcile the constitutional right of a woman, in consultation with her physician, to choose to terminate her pregnancy as established by *Roe v. Wade*, 410 U.S. 113 (1973) and *Doe v. Bolton*, 410 U.S. 179 (1973), with the special interest of the State in encouraging an unmarried pregnant minor to seek the advice of her parents in making the important decision whether or

---

"[A]t least in some precisely delineated areas, a child—like someone in a captive audience—is not possessed of that full capacity for individual choice which is the presupposition of First Amendment guarantees. It is only upon such a premise, I should suppose, that a State may deprive children of other rights—the right to marry, for example, or the right to vote—deprivations that would be constitutionally intolerable for adults."
Id., at 649–650 (footnotes omitted).

not to bear a child. As noted above, §12S was before us in *Bellotti I*, 428 U.S. 132 (1976), where we remanded the case for interpretation of its provisions by the Supreme Judicial Court of Massachusetts. We previously had held in *Planned Parenthood v. Danforth*, 428 U.S. 52 (1976), that a State could not lawfully authorize an absolute parental veto over the decision of a minor to terminate her pregnancy. *Id.*, at 74. In *Bellotti, supra*, we recognized that §12S could be read as "fundamentally different from a statute that creates a 'parental veto,' "*id.*, at 145, thus "avoid[ing] or substantially modify[ing] the federal constitutional challenge to the statute." *Id.*, at 148. The question before us—in light of what we have said in the prior cases—is whether §12S, as authoritatively interpreted by the Supreme Judicial Court, provides for parental notice and consent in a manner that does not unduly burden the right to seek an abortion. See *id.*, at 147.

Appellees and intervenors contend that even as interpreted by the Supreme Judicial Court of Massachusetts §12S does unduly burden this right. They suggest, for example, that the mere requirement of parental notice constitutes such a burden. As stated * * * above, however, parental notice and consent are qualifications that typically may be imposed by the State on a minor's right to make important decisions. As immature minors often lack the ability to make fully informed choices that take account of both immediate and long-range consequences, a State reasonably may determine that parental consultation often is desirable and in the best interest of the minor.[19] It may further determine, as a general proposition, that such consultation is particularly desirable with respect to the abortion decision—one that for some people raises profound moral and religious concerns.[20] As Mr. Justice STEWART wrote in concurrence in *Planned Parenthood v. Danforth*, 428 U.S., at 91:

"There can be little doubt that the State furthers a constitutionally permissible end by encouraging an unmarried pregnant minor to seek the help and advice of her parents in making the very important decision whether or not to bear a child. That is a grave decision, and a girl of tender years, under emotional stress, may be ill-equipped to make it without mature advice and emotional support. It seems unlikely that she will obtain counsel and support from the attending physician at an abortion clinic, where abortions for pregnant minors frequently take place." (Footnote omitted.)[21]

---

[19]In *Planned Parenthood v. Danforth*, 428 U.S., at 75, "[W]e emphasize[d] that our holding [did] not suggest that every minor, regardless of age or maturity, may give effective consent for termination of her pregnancy."

[20]The expert testimony at the hearings in the District Court uniformly was to the effect that parental involvement in a minor's abortion decision, if compassionate and supportive, was highly desirable. The findings of the court reflect this consensus. See *Baird I*, 393 F. Supp., at 853.

[21]Mr. Justice STEWART's concurring opinion in *Danforth* underscored the need for parental involvement in minors' abortion decisions by describing the procedures followed at the clinic operated by the Parents Aid Society and Dr. Gerald Zupnick:

"The counseling * * * occurs entirely on the day the abortion is to be performed * * *. It lasts for two hours and takes place in groups that include both minors and adults who are strangers to one another * * *. The physician takes no part in this counseling process * * *. Counseling is typically limited to a description of abortion procedures, possible complications, and birth control techniques * * *.

"The abortion itself takes five to seven minutes * * *. The physician has no prior contact with the minor, and on the days that abortions are being performed at the [clinic], the physician, * * * may be performing abortions on many other adults and minors * * *. On busy days patients are scheduled in separate groups, consisting usually of five patients * * *. After the abortion [the physician] spends a brief period with the minor and others in the group in the recovery room * * *." 428 U.S., at 91–92, n.2, quoting Brief for Appellants in *Bellotti I, supra*.
* * *

But we are concerned here with a constitutional right to seek an abortion. The abortion decision differs in important ways from other decisions that may be made during minority. The need to preserve the constitutional right and the unique nature of the abortion decision, especially when made by a minor, require a State to act with particular sensitivity when it legislates to foster parental involvement in this matter.

A

The pregnant minor's options are much different from those facing a minor in other situations, such as deciding whether to marry. A minor not permitted to marry before the age of majority is required simply to postpone her decision. She and her intended spouse may preserve the opportunity for later marriage should they continue to desire it. A pregnant adolescent, however, cannot preserve for long the possibility of aborting, which effectively expires in a matter of weeks from the onset of pregnancy.

Moreover, the potentially severe detriment facing a pregnant woman, see *Roe v. Wade*, 410 U.S., at 153, is not mitigated by her minority. Indeed, considering her probable education, employment skills, financial resources, and emotional maturity, unwanted motherhood may be exceptionally burdensome for a minor. In addition, the fact of having a child brings with it adult legal responsibility, for parenthood, like attainment of the age of majority, is one of the traditional criteria for the termination of the legal disabilities of minority. In sum, there are few situations in which denying a minor the right to make an important decision will have consequences so grave and indelible.

Yet, an abortion may not be the best choice for the minor. The circumstances in which this issue arises will vary widely. In a given case, alternatives to abortion, such as marriage to the father of the child, arranging for its adoption, or assuming the responsibilities of motherhood with the assured support of family, may be feasible and relevant to the minor's best interests. Nonetheless, the abortion decision is one that simply cannot be postponed, or it will be made by default with far-reaching consequences.

For these reasons, as we held in *Planned Parenthood v. Danforth, supra*, 428 U.S., at 74, "the State may not impose a blanket provision * * * requiring the consent of a parent or person *in loco parentis* as a condition for abortion of an unmarried minor during the first 12 weeks of her pregnancy." Although, as stated in Part II, *supra*, such deference to parents may be permissible with respect to other choices facing a minor, the unique nature and consequences of the abortion decision make it inappropriate "to give a third party an absolute, and possibly arbitrary, veto over the decision of the physician and his patient to terminate the patient's pregnancy, regardless of the reason for withholding consent." *Ibid*. We therefore conclude that if the State decides to require a pregnant minor to obtain one or both parents' consent to an abortion, it also must provide an alternative procedure[22] whereby authorization for the abortion can be obtained.

A pregnant minor is entitled in such a proceeding to show either: (1) that she is mature enough and well enough informed to make her abortion decision, in consultation with her physician, independently of her parents' wishes;[23] or (2) that even if she is not able to make this decision independently, the desired abortion would be in her best interests. The proceeding in

---

[22]As §12S provides for involvement of the state superior court in minors' abortion decisions, we discuss the alternative procedure described in the text in terms of judicial proceedings. We do not suggest, however, that a State choosing to require parental consent could not delegate the alternative procedure to a juvenile court or an administrative agency or officer. Indeed, much can be said for employing procedures and a forum less formal than those associated with a court of general jurisdiction.

[23]The nature of both the State's interest in fostering parental authority and the problem of determining "maturity" makes clear why the State generally may resort to objective, though

which this showing is made must assure that a resolution of the issue, and any appeals that may follow, will be completed with anonymity and sufficient expedition to provide an effective opportunity for an abortion to be obtained. In sum, the procedure must ensure that the provision requiring parental consent does not in fact amount to the "absolute, and possibly arbitrary, veto" that was found impermissible in *Danforth. Ibid.*

It is against these requirements that §12S must be tested. We observe initially that as authoritatively construed by the highest court of the State, the statute satisfies some of the concerns that require special treatment of a minor's abortion decision. It provides that if parental consent is refused, authorization may be "obtained by order of a judge of the superior court for good cause shown, after such hearing as he deems necessary." A superior court judge presiding over a §12S proceeding "must disregard all parental objections, and other considerations, which are not based exclusively on what would serve the minor's best interests."[24] *Attorney General* 371 Mass., at——, 360 N.E.2d, at 293. The Supreme Judicial Court also stated that "[p]rompt resolution of a [§12S] proceedings may be expected. * * * The proceeding need not be brought in the minor's name and steps may be taken, by impoundment or otherwise, to preserve confidentiality as to the minor and her parents. * * * [W]e believe that an early hearing and decision on appeal from a judgment of a Superior Court judge may also be achieved." *Id.,* at——, 360 N.E.2d, at 298. The court added that if these expectations were not met, either the Superior Court, in the exercise of its rulemaking power, or the Supreme Judicial Court would be willing to eliminate any undue burdens by rule or order. *Ibid.*

Despite these safeguards, which avoid much of what was objectionable in the statute successfully challenged in *Danforth* §12S falls short of constitutional standards in certain respects. We now consider these.

Among the questions certified to the Supreme Judicial Court was whether §12S permits any minors—mature or immature—to obtain judicial consent to an abortion without any parental consultation whatsoever. See n.9, *supra.* The state court answered that, in general, they may not. "[T]he consent required by [§12S must] be obtained for every nonemergency abortion where the mother is less than eighteen years of age and unmarried." *Attorney General, supra,* at ——, 360 N.E.2d, at 294. The text of §12S itself states an exception to this rule, making consent unnecessary from any parent who has "died or has deserted his or her family."[26] The Supreme Judicial

---

inevitably arbitrary, criteria such as age limits, marital status, or membership in the armed forces for lifting some or all of the legal disabilities of minority. Not only is it difficult to define, let alone determine, maturity, but the fact that a minor may be very much an adult in some respects does not mean that his need and opportunity for growth under parental guidance and discipline have ended. As discussed in the text, however, the peculiar nature of the abortion decision requires the opportunity for case-by-case evaluations of the maturity of pregnant minors.

[24] The Supreme Judicial Court held that §12S imposed this standard on the Superior Court in large part because it construed the statute as containing the same restriction on parents. * * * The court concluded that the judge should not be entitled "to exercise his authority on a standard broader than that to which a parent must adhere." *Attorney General, supra,* at ——, 360 N.E.2d, at 293.

Intervenors argue that, assuming state-supported parental involvement in the minor's abortion decision is permissible, the State may not endorse the withholding of parental consent for any reason not believed to be in the minor's best interests. They agree with the District Court that, even though §12S was construed by the highest state court to impose this restriction, the statute is flawed because the restriction is not apparent on its face. Intervenors thus concur in the District Court's assumption that the statute will encourage parents to withhold consent for impermissible reasons. See *Baird III,* 450 F. Supp., at 1004–1005, *Baird II,* 428 F. Supp., at 855–856.

* * *

[26] The statute also provides that "[i]f both parents have died or have deserted their family, consent of the mother's guardian or other person having duties similar to a guardian, or any person who has assumed the care and custody of mother is sufficient."

Court construed the statute as containing an additional exception: Consent need not be obtained "where no parent (or statutory substitute) is available." *Ibid.* The court also ruled that an available parent must be given notice of any judicial proceedings brought by a minor to obtain consent for an abortion.[27] *Id.,* at——, 360 N.E.2d, at 297.

We think that, construed in this manner, §12S would impose an undue burden upon the exercise by minors of the right to seek abortion. As the District Court recognized, "there are parents who would obstruct, and perhaps altogether prevent, the minor's right to go to court." *Baird III, supra,* at 1001. There is no reason to believe that this would be so in the majority of cases where consent is withheld. But many parents hold strong views on the subject of abortion, and young pregnant minors, especially those living at home, are particularly vulnerable to their parents' efforts to obstruct both an abortion and their access to court. It would be unrealistic, therefore, to assume that the mere existence of a legal right to seek relief in superior court provides an effective avenue of relief for some of those who need it the most.

We conclude, therefore, that under state regulation such as that undertaken by Massachusetts, every minor must have the opportunity—if she so desires—to go directly to a court without first consulting or notifying her parents. If she satisfies the court that she is mature and well-informed enough to make intelligently the abortion decision on her own, the court must authorize her to act without parental consultation or consent. If she fails to satisfy the court that she is competent to make this decision independently, she must be permitted to show that an abortion nevertheless would be in her best interest. If the court is persuaded that it is, the court must authorize the abortion. If, however, the court is not persuaded by the minor that she is mature or that the abortion would be in her best interest, it may decline to sanction the operation.

There is, however, an important state interest in encouraging a family rather than a judicial resolution of a minor's abortion decision. Also, as we have observed above, parents naturally take an interest in the welfare of their children—an interest that is particularly strong where a normal family relationship exists and where the child is living with one or both parents. These factors properly may be taken into account by a court called upon to determine whether an abortion in fact is in a minor's best interests. If, all things considered, the court determines that an abortion is in the minor's best interests, she is entitled to court authorization without any parental involvement. On the other hand, the court may deny the abortion request of an immature minor in the absence of parental consultation if it concludes that her best interests would be served thereby, or the court may in such a case defer deci-

---

[27] This reading of the statute requires parental consultation and consent more strictly than appellants themselves previously believed was necessary. In their first argument before this Court, and again before the Supreme Judicial Court, appellants argued that §12S was not intended to abrogate Massachusetts' common-law "mature minor" rule as it applies to abortions. See 428 U.S., at 144. They also suggested that, under some circumstances, §12S might permit even immature minors to obtain judicial approval for an abortion without any parental consultation. See 428 U.S., at 145; *Attorney General, supra,* 371 Mass., at——, 360 N.E.2d, at 294. The Supreme Judicial Court sketched the outlines of the mature minor rule that would apply in the absence of §12S: "The mature minor rule calls for an analysis of the nature of the operation, its likely benefit, and the capacity of the particular minor to understand fully what the medical procedure involves. * * * Judicial intervention is not required. If judicial approval is obtained, however, the doctor is protected from a subsequent claim that the circumstances did not warrant his reliance on the mature minor rule, and, of course, the minor patient is afforded advance protection against a misapplication of the rule." *Attorney General, supra,* at——, 360 N.E.2d, at 295. "We conclude that, apart from statutory limitations which are constitutional, where the best interests of a minor will be served by not notifying his or her parents of intended medical treatment and where the minor is capable of giving informed consent to that treatment, the mature minor rule applies in this Commonwealth." *Id.,* at——, 360 N.E.2d, at 296. The Supreme Judicial Court held that the common-law mature minor rule was inapplicable to abortions because it had been legislatively superseded by §12S.

sion until there is parental consultation in which the court may participate. But this is the full extent to which parental involvement may be required.[28] For the reasons stated above, the constitutional right to seek an abortion may not be unduly burdened by state-imposed conditions upon initial access to court.

Section 12S requires that both parents consent to a minor's abortion. The District Court found it to be "custom" to perform other medical and surgical procedures on minors with the consent of only one parent, and it concluded that "nothing about abortions * * * requires the minor's interest to be treated differently." *Baird I, supra*, at 852. See *Baird III, supra*, at 1004 n.9.

We are not persuaded that, as a general rule, the requirement of obtaining both parents' consent unconstitutionally burdens a minor's right to seek an abortion. The abortion decision has implications far broader than those associated with most other kinds of medical treatment. At least when the parents are together and the pregnant minor is living at home, both the father and mother have an interest—one normally supportive—in helping to determine the course that is in the best interest of a daughter. Consent and involvement by parents in important decisions by minors long have been recognized as protective of their immaturity. In the case of the abortion decision, for reasons we have stated, the focus of the parents' inquiry should be the best interests of their daughter. As every pregnant minor is entitled in the first instance to go directly to the court for a judicial determination without prior parental notice, consultation or consent, the general rule with respect to parental consent does not unduly burden the constitutional right. Moreover, where the pregnant minor goes to her parents and consent is denied, she still must have recourse to a prompt judicial determination of her maturity or best interests.[29]

Another of the questions certified by the District Court to the Supreme Judicial Court was the following: "If the superior court finds that the minor is capable [of making], and has, in fact, made and adhered to, an informed and reasonable decision to have an abortion, may the court refuse its consent on a finding that a parent's, or its own, contrary decision is a better one?" *Attorney General, supra*, 371 Mass., at——,360 N.E.2d, at 293 n.5. To this the state court answered:

> "[W]e do not view the judge's role as limited to a determination that the minor is capable of making, and has made, an informed and reasonable decision to have an abortion. Certainly the judge must make a determination of those circumstances, but, if the statutory role of the judge to determine the best interests of the minor is to be carried out, he must make a finding on the basis of all relevant views presented to him. We suspect that the judge will give great weight to the minor's determination, if informed and reasonable, but in circumstances where he determines that the best interests of the minor will not be served by an abortion, the judge's determination should prevail, assuming that his conclusion is supported by the evidence and adequate findings of fact."

Id., at——, 360 N.E.2d, at 293.

The Supreme Judicial Court's statement reflects the general rule that a State may require a minor to wait until the age of majority before being permitted to exercise legal rights independently. See n.23, *supra.* But we are concerned here with the exercise of a constitutional right of unique character. As stated above, if the minor satisfies a court that she has attained sufficient

---

[28] Of course, if the minor consults with her parents voluntarily and they withhold consent, she is free to seek judicial authorization for the abortion immediately.

[29] There will be cases where the pregnant minor has received approval of the abortion decision by one parent. In that event, the parent can support the daughter's request for a prompt judicial determination, and the parent's support should be given great, if not dispositive, weight.

maturity to make a fully informed decision, she then is entitled to make her abortion decision independently. We therefore agree with the District Court that §12S cannot constitutionally permit judicial disregard of the abortion decision of a minor who has been determined to be mature and fully competent to assess the implications of the choice she has made.

Although it satisfies constitutional standards in large part, §12S falls short of them in two respects: First, it permits judicial authorization for an abortion to be withheld from a minor who is found by the superior court to be mature and fully competent to make this decision independently. Second, it requires parental consultation or notification in every instance, without affording the pregnant minor an opportunity to receive an independent judicial determination that she is mature enough to consent or that an abortion would be in her best interests.[31] Accordingly, we affirm the judgment of the District Court insofar as it invalidates this statute and enjoins its enforcement.

Affirmed.

[Concurring opinion of Mr. Justice REHNQUIST and dissenting opinion of Mr. Justice STEVENS are omitted.]

---

[31] Section 12S evidently applies to all nonemergency abortions performed on minors, without regard to the period in pregnancy during which the procedure occurs. As the court below recognized, most abortions are performed during the early stages of pregnancy, before the end of the first trimester. See *Baird III, supra*, at 1001; see *Baird I, supra*, at 853. This coincides approximately with the previability period during which a pregnant woman's right to decide, in consultation with her physician, to have an abortion is most immune to state intervention. See *Roe v. Wade*, 410 U.S. 113, 164–165 (1973).

The propriety of parental involvement in a minor's abortion decision does not diminish as the pregnancy progresses and legitimate concerns for the pregnant minor's health increase. Furthermore, the opportunity for direct access to court which we have described is adequate to safeguard throughout pregnancy the constitutionally protected interests of a minor in the abortion decision. Thus, although a significant number of abortions within the scope of §12S might be performed during the later stages of pregnancy, we do not believe a different analysis of the statute is required for them.

Phelps v. Bing

Supreme Court of Illinois

58 Ill.2d 32, 316 N.E.2d 775 (1974)

UNDERWOOD, Chief Justice:

The plaintiffs, Larry Phelps, age 20, and Nikki Rexroad, age 19, sought a marriage license in Champaign County where both were residents. The defendant, Champaign County Clerk Dennis Bing, refused to issue the license because Phelps was not 21 years old and had no parent or legal guardian to give consent as required by the provisions of sections 3 and 6 of the Marriage Act (Ill. Rev. Stat. 1973, ch. 89, pars. 3, 6). Plaintiffs then filed a petition for a writ of *mandamus* alleging that section 3(b) of the Marriage Act is unconstitutional in that it discriminates in age requirements between males and females, and asking that the defendant clerk be ordered to issue a marriage license to the parties.

The trial court found that section 6 of the Marriage Act violated section 18 of article I of the Constitution of 1970, S.H.A., and was therefore invalid. While defendant objected that *mandamus* was not the proper remedy, the writ was awarded directing the county clerk to issue a marriage license.
* * *

The case comes to us on direct appeal pursuant to Rule 302, Ill. Rev. Stat. 1973, ch. 110A, §302. 50 Ill.2d R. 302.

Section 3 of the Marriage Act provides in pertinent part:

"The following persons may contract and be joined in marriage:
"(a) Male persons of 21 or more years and female persons of 18 or more years; or
"(b) Male persons of 18 or more years and female persons of 16 or more years. However, the parent or guardian of such person must appear before the county clerk in the county where either such minor person resides, or before the county clerk to whom application for a license under Section 6 is made, and make affidavit that he or she is the parent or guardian of such minor and give consent to the marriage. * * *"

Section 3.1 provides:

"Male persons of 16 or more years and female persons of 15 or more years may contract and be joined in marriage provided such persons first present to the county clerk who is requested to issue to them a marriage license, a certified copy of a court order which has been obtained pursuant to Section 3.2 of this Act. No county clerk shall issue a marriage license under this Section unless such order has been so obtained as provided in Section 3.2."

Section 6 provides:

"If the male is over the age of 18 years and under the age of 21 years, or the female is over the age of 16 years and under the age of 18 years, no license may be issued by the County Clerk, unless the consent in writing of the parents of the person under age, or one of such parents, or of his or her guardian, is presented to him, duly verified by such parents, or parent, or guardian, and such consent must be filed by the Clerk, and he must state such facts in the license."

The effect of this statutory scheme is that while a male must be 21 to obtain a license to marry without parental consent, 18 to marry with consent, and 16 to marry by court order, a female may obtain a license at 18 without parental consent, at 16 with consent, and at 15 by court order.

Section 18 of the Bill of Rights of the Constitution of 1970 (Ill. Const. (1970), art. I, sec. 18) provides:

"The equal protection of the laws shall not be denied or abridged on account of sex by the State or its units of local government and school districts."

In *People v. Ellis* (1974), 57 Ill.2d 127, 132, 133, 311 N.E.2d 98, 101, we found this section "was intended to supplement and expand the guaranties of the equal protection provision of the [Federal] Bill of Rights" and that any classification based on sex is a "suspect classification" which must withstand "strict judicial scrutiny" in order to be upheld. The age classifications found in sections 3, 3.1, and 6 of the Marriage Act are obviously based on sex.

It is not argued that there exists, and we do not find, any compelling State interest which justifies treating males and females of the same age differently for the purpose of determining their rights to a marriage license. Accordingly we hold the higher age limitations for males in sections 3, 3.1, and 6 are invalid and that the lesser age limits therein shall apply to both males and females.

Defendant urges that the relief granted was improper because *mandamus* may be used only to compel an official to act when it is his duty to do so, and in this case the county clerk had no duty to act since the statutory law forbade him to do so. We see no merit in this contention since *mandamus* has often been deemed to be an appropriate means "for the simultaneous determination of issues of statutory constitutionality and the enforcement of rights initially determined to exist in the proceeding awarding the writ." *People ex rel. Scott v. Kerner* (1965), 32 Ill.2d 539, 545, 208 N.E.2d 561, 565, and cases cited therein.

Accordingly, the judgment of the circuit court of Champaign County is affirmed.

Judgment affirmed.

Comments

Considerable ambivalence toward children prevails in contemporary law. Even though they are viewed as "our most valued possession," children are also a continued source of frustration. In the past decades they have persistently challenged the values held by adults, for example, in sexual and political matters. Treating them as persons can become a vehicle of control by parents and the State in trying to curb the subversive powers of youths. By being made responsible as adults, youths are deprived of the opportunity to engage in forays into adult territory with the option of retreating afterward into the sanctuary of childhood if an attack from established forces makes this feasible. *White* is an illustration of the ways the law has coped with this problem. By lowering the age of majority to 18 it gave parents the power to tighten the purse strings. It left to their discretion whether, and in what form, to furnish support to their offspring after they had been legally declared adults. The court made its position clear by identifying with the "harassed father" who "had essentially lost control of his son," and was now being asked to pay for a college education at a time when campuses had become sources of major political unrest.

The court in *White* also emphasized that young adults were meant to enjoy and *suffer* the rights, privileges, and *obligations* that apply to every citizen. It is the grimness of the court's language that conveys a message of potential cruelty to persons who are admittedly not yet fully mature and who continue to need moral and financial assistance. In a positive vein, children are at the same time emancipated to the advanced position of young adults. Many young persons, of course, still get financial support and voluntary contributions from their parents to further their education. More often, however, young adults struggle for themselves and may look to their peers for moral and financial support. For instance, young men may receive support from young women with whom they cohabit or whom they marry while attending college. In these instances, legal problems continue to exist in transmuted form, for example, in the question of the extent to which such women, on termination of the relationship, are entitled to some form of compensation for their contributions to another's education while often having to defer their own (see *Colvert v. Colvert* and *Morgan v. Morgan*, pp. 82–88). If marriage becomes a means of educational advancement of young men, financial support may sometimes devolve from young wives to their parents, who may feel inclined to invest in the future of a promising son-in-law. Leaving young adults to fend for themselves may therefore sometimes bring about results that legislatures and the judiciary did not foresee when they lowered the age of majority during the 1960s and early 1970s.

The legal situation is different if teenage pregnancy rather than education is involved. Parents are less inclined to let a pregnant child fend for herself. They may wish to intervene in the abortion decision by imposing their will. As *Bellotti* stressed, the courts are concerned with a matter that involves the exercise of constitutional rights of a unique character. The pregnant child is to be protected from the emotionalism of parents who may hold strong views on pregnancy or abortion. In addition, parents' judgment may be impaired because they face potential financial liabilities, such as medical expenses during pregnancy and additional support obligations after birth. If the child is mature enough to make the decision on abortion, then she should prevail, according to *Bellotti*, over any interest the parents may have; if not, the courts have to determine the pregnant child's best interests.

It is not clear whether *Bellotti* is based on an implicit bias favoring abortion in a situation in which the child-mother desires an abortion against the wishes of her parents or whether it emphasizes the privacy rights of a child comparable to those of adult pregnant women. A majority of pregnant teenagers, contrary to the underlying facts in *Bellotti*, prefer to keep their children against the wishes of parents who would prefer them to have abortions. Perhaps because of the language of the Massachusetts statute concerned with abortion, the Court did not address itself to such a reverse situation, that is, a 15-year-old girl who wished to have a child against the desires of her parents, who would have preferred she have an abortion. Maturity of the mother or, in its absence, her best interests, could govern here too. But how is a case to be resolved, if an immature mother wishes to have a child against her best interests, as determined by the court? In this hypothetical not covered in *Bellotti*, the choice may be between a compulsory abortion and the privacy rights of the mother. Perhaps the issue will rarely pose itself that clearly because courts may prefer to avoid abortion in such instances. It would be difficult to enforce an abortion against an unwilling mother, and the medical profession might be reluctant to collaborate. These complexities may affect the substantive considerations.

If the right to marry is involved, as in *Phelps*, courts may be inclined to lower age requirements to a common level for males and females. Since marriage in most states also means legal emancipation, this may in effect lower the age of majority too. This view, coming from Illinois—probably the most conservative jurisdiction in family law matters in the United States at this time—seems to correspond to the Florida position expressed in *White*. In other words, young men and women must enjoy and *suffer* the rights, privileges, and *obliga-*

tions of marriage equally, without regard to legislative attempts to differentiate on marital age.

References

Mnookin, R., CHILD, FAMILY AND STATE—PROBLEMS AND MATERIALS ON CHILDREN AND THE LAW 153-155 (1978) (Questions: Privacy Rights of Minors).

Note, *Developments in the Law—The Constitution and the Family*, 93 HARV. L. REV. 1156, 1372-1383 (1980).

Wald, *Children's Rights: A Framework for Analysis*, 12 U.C.D. L. REV. 255 (1979).

Bibliography

Brockelbank, W., INTERSTATE ENFORCEMENT OF FAMILY SUPPORT: THE RUN-AWAY PAPPY ACT (2d ed., F. Infausto ed. 1971).

Cady, *Emancipation of Minors,* 12 CONN. L. REV. 62 (1979).

Cassetty, J., CHILD SUPPORT AND PUBLIC POLICY: SECURING SUPPORT FROM ABSENT FATHERS (1978).

Chambers, D., MAKING FATHERS PAY—THE ENFORCEMENT OF CHILD SUPPORT (1979).

Katz, Schroeder, & Sidman, *Emancipating Our Children—Coming of Legal Age in America,* 3 FAM. L.Q. 211 (1969).

Krause, H., CHILD SUPPORT IN AMERICA (1981).

Marks, *Detours on the Road to Maturity: A View of the Legal Conception of Growing Up and Letting Go,* 39 LAW & CONTEMP. PROBS. 78 (1975).

Note, *The Emancipation of Minors Act: A California Solution for the Mature Minor,* 12 U.C.D. L. REV. 283 (1979).

Increased Rights for Children Born Outside of Marriage

Trimble v. Gordon

United States Supreme Court

430 U.S. 762 (1977)

Mr. Justice POWELL delivered the opinion of the Court.

At issue in this case is the constitutionality of §12 of the Illinois Probate Act[1] which allows illegitimate children to inherit by intestate succession only

---

[1] Ill. Rev. Stat. c. 3, §12 (1973). Effective January 1, 1976, §12 and the rest of the Probate Act of which it was a part were repealed and replaced by the Probate Act of 1975, Public Act 79-328. Section 12 has been replaced by Ill. Rev. Stat. c. 3, §2-2 (1976). Although §2-2 of the Probate Act of 1975 differs in some respects from the old §12, that part of §12 that is at issue here was recodified without material change in §2-2. As the opinions below and the briefs refer to the disputed statutory provision as §12, we will continue to refer to it that way.

from their mothers. Under Illinois law, legitimate children are allowed to inherit by intestate succession from both their mothers and their fathers.[2]

I

Appellant Deta Mona Trimble is the illegitimate daughter of appellant Jessie Trimble[3] and Sherman Gordon. Trimble and Gordon lived in Chicago with Deta Mona from 1970 until Gordon died in 1974, the victim of a homicide. On January 2, 1973, the Circuit Court of Cook County, Ill., had entered a paternity order finding Gordon to be the father of Deta Mona and ordering him to pay $15 per week for her support.[4] Gordon thereafter supported Deta Mona in accordance with the paternity order and openly acknowledged her as his child. He died intestate at the age of 28, leaving an estate consisting only of a 1974 Plymouth automobile worth approximately $2,500.

Shortly after Gordon's death, Trimble, as the mother and next friend of Deta Mona, filed a petition for letters of administration, determination of heirship, and declaratory relief in the Probate Division of the Circuit Court of Cook County, Ill. That court entered an order determining heirship, identifying as the only heirs of Gordon his father, Joseph Gordon, his mother, Ethel King, and his brother, two sisters, and a half brother.[5] * * *

The Circuit Court excluded Deta Mona on the authority of the negative implications of §12 of the Illinois Probate Act, which provides in relevant part:

"An illegitimate child is heir of his mother and of any maternal ancestor, and of any person from whom his mother might have inherited, if living; and the lawful issue of an illegitimate person shall represent such person and take, by descent, any estate which the parent would have taken, if living. A child who was illegitimate whose parents intermarry and who is acknowledged by the father as the father's child is legitimate."[6]

If Deta Mona had been a legitimate child, she would have inherited her father's entire estate under Illinois law.[7] In rejecting Deta Mona's claim of heirship, the court sustained the constitutionality of §12.

* * * [T]he Illinois Supreme Court entered an order allowing direct appeal * * * bypassing the Illinois Appellate Court. Appellants were granted leave to file an *amicus* brief in two pending consolidated appeals which presented similar challenges to the constitutionality of §12. On June 2, 1975, the Illinois Supreme Court handed down its opinion in *In re Estate of Karas*, * * *.

We noted probable jurisdiction to consider the arguments that §12 violates the Equal Protection Clause of the Fourteenth Amendment by invidiously discriminating on the basis of illegitimacy and sex.[10] 424 U.S. 964 (1976). We now reverse. As we conclude that the statutory discrimination against illegitimate children is unconstitutional, we do not reach the sex discrimination argument.

---

[2] Ill. Rev. Stat. c. 3, §2-1(b) (1976).

[3] There is some dispute over the status of Jessie Trimble in this litigation. It has been argued that she is in the case only as the next friend of her daughter. As the question is relevant only to the claim of sex discrimination against the mothers of illegitimate children, an issue we do not reach, we need not resolve the dispute.

[4] App. 8.

[5] *Id.*, at 14.

[6] See n.1, *supra.*

[7] See n.2, *supra.*

[10] Not presented here is the appellants' contention below that §12 discriminates on the basis of race because of its alleged disproportionate impact on Negroes.

In *Karas*, the Illinois Supreme Court rejected the equal protection challenge to the discrimination against illegitimate children on the explicit authority of *Labine v. Vincent*, 401 U.S. 532 (1971). The court found that §12 is supported by the state interests in encouraging family relationships and in establishing an accurate and efficient method of disposing of property at death. The court also found the Illinois law unobjectionable because no "insurmountable barrier" prevented illegitimate children from sharing in the estates of their fathers. By leaving a will, Sherman Gordon could have assured Deta Mona a share of his estate.

Appellees endorse the reasoning of the Illinois Supreme Court and suggest additional justifications for the statute. In weighing the constitutional sufficiency of these justifications, we are guided by our previous decisions involving equal protection challenges to laws discriminating on the basis of illegitimacy.[11] "[T]his Court requires, at a minimum, that a statutory classification bear some rational relationship to a legitimate state purpose." *Weber v. Aetna Casualty & Surety Co.*, 406 U.S. 164, 172 (1972). In this context, the standard just stated is a minimum; the Court sometimes requires more. "Though the latitude given state economic and social regulation is necessarily broad, when state statutory classifications approach sensitive and fundamental personal rights, this Court exercises a stricter scrutiny * * *." *Ibid.*

Appellants urge us to hold that classifications based on illegitimacy are "suspect," so that any justifications must survive "strict scrutiny." We considered and rejected a similar argument last Term in *Mathews v. Lucas*, 427 U.S. 495 (1976). As we recognized in *Lucas*, illegitimacy is analogous in many respects to the personal characteristics that have been held to be suspect when used as the basis of statutory differentiations. *Id.*, at 505. We nevertheless concluded that the analogy was not sufficient to require "our most exacting scrutiny." *Id.*, at 506. Despite the conclusion that classifications based on illegitimacy fall in a "realm of less than strictest scrutiny," *Lucas* also establishes that the scrutiny "is not a toothless one," *id.*, at 510, a proposition clearly demonstrated by our previous decisions in this area.[12]

The Illinois Supreme Court prefaced its discussion of the state interests served by §12 with a general discussion of the purpose of the statute. Quoting from its earlier opinions, the court concluded that the statute was enacted to ameliorate the harsh common-law rule under which an illegitimate child was *filius nullius* and incapable of inheriting from anyone. 61 Ill.2d, at 44–45, 329 N.E.2d, at 236–237. Although §12 did not bring illegitimate children into parity with legitimate children, it did improve their position, thus partially achieving the asserted objective. The sufficiency of the justifications ad-

---

[11] This case represents the 12th time since 1968 that we have considered the constitutionality of alleged discrimination on the basis of illegitimacy. The previous decisions are as follows: *Mathews v. Lucas*, 427 U.S. 495 (1976); *Beaty v. Weinberger*, 478 F.2d 300 (CA5 1973), summarily aff'd, 418 U.S. 901 (1974); *Jimenez v. Weinberger*, 417 U.S. 628 (1974); *New Jersey Welfare Rights Organization v. Cahill*, 411 U.S. 619 (1973); *Griffin v. Richardson*, 346 F. Supp. 1226 (Md.), summarily aff'd, 409 U.S. 1069 (1972); *Davis v. Richardson*, 342 F. Supp. 588 (Conn.), summarily aff'd, 409 U.S. 1069 (1972); *Gomez v. Perez*, 409 U.S. 535 (1973); *Weber v. Aetna Casualty & Surety Co.*, 406 U.S. 164 (1972); *Labine v. Vincent*, 401 U.S. 532 (1971); *Glona v. American Guarantee & Liability Ins. Co.*, 391 U.S. 73 (1968); *Levy v. Louisiana*, 391 U.S. 68 (1968).

[12] See cases cited n.11, *supra*. *Labine v. Vincent, supra*, is difficult to place in the pattern of this Court's equal protection decisions, and subsequent cases have limited its force as a precedent. In *Weber v. Aetna Casualty & Surety Co., supra*, we found in *Labine* a recognition that judicial deference is appropriate when the challenged statute involves the "substantial state interest in providing for 'the stability of * * * land titles and in the prompt and definitive determination of the valid ownership of property left by decedents' * * *." 406 U.S., at 170, quoting *Labine v. Vincent*, 229 So.2d 449, 452 (La. App. 1969). We reaffirm that view, but there is a point beyond which such deference cannot justify discrimination. Although the proposition is self-evident, *Reed v. Reed*, 404 U.S. 71 (1971), demonstrates that state statutes involving the disposition of property at death are not immunized from equal protection scrutiny. See also *Eskra v. Morton*, 524 F.2d 9, 13 (CA7 1975) (Stevens, J.). The more specific analysis of *Labine* is discussed throughout the remainder of this opinion.

vanced for the remaining discrimination against illegitimate children must be considered in light of this motivating purpose.

The Illinois Supreme Court relied in part on the State's purported interest in "the promotion of [legitimate] family relationships." 61 Ill.2d, at 48, 329 N.E.2d, at 238. Although the court noted that this justification had been accepted in *Labine*, the opinion contains only the most perfunctory analysis. This inattention may not have been an oversight, for §12 bears only the most attenuated relationship to the asserted goal.[13]

In a case like this, the Equal Protection Clause requires more than the mere incantation of a proper state purpose. No one disputes the appropriateness of Illinois' concern with the family unit, perhaps the most fundamental social institution of our society. The flaw in the analysis lies elsewhere. As we said in *Lucas*, the constitutionality of this law "depends upon the character of the discrimination and its relation to legitimate legislative aims." 427 U.S., at 504. The court below did not address the relation between §12 and the promotion of legitimate family relationships, thus leaving the constitutional analysis incomplete. The same observation can be made about this Court's decision in *Labine*, but that case does not stand alone. In subsequent decisions, we have expressly considered and rejected the argument that a State may attempt to influence the actions of men and women by imposing sanctions on the children born of their illegitimate relationships.

In *Weber* we examined a Louisiana workmen's compensation law which discriminated against one class of illegitimate children. Without questioning Louisiana's interest in protecting legitimate family relationships, we rejected the argument that "persons will shun illicit relations because the offspring may not one day reap the benefits of workmen's compensation." 406 U.S., at 173. Although *Weber* distinguished *Labine* on other grounds, the reasons for rejecting this justification are equally applicable here:

> "The status of illegitimacy has expressed through the ages society's condemnation of irresponsible liaisons beyond the bonds of marriage. But visiting this condemnation on the head of an infant is illogical and unjust. Moreover, imposing disabilities on the illegitimate child is contrary to the basic concept of our system that legal burdens should bear some relationship to individual responsibility or wrongdoing. Obviously, no child is responsible for his birth and penalizing the illegitimate child is an ineffectual—as well as an unjust—way of deterring the parent."

406 U.S., at 175 (footnote omitted).
The parents have the ability to conform their conduct to societal norms, but their illegitimate children can affect neither their parents' conduct nor their own status.

The Illinois Supreme Court relied on *Labine* for another and more substantial justification: the State's interest in "establish[ing] a method of property disposition." 61 Ill.2d, at 48, 329 N.E.2d, at 238. Here the court's analysis is more complete. Focusing specifically on the difficulty of proving paternity and the related danger of spurious claims, the court concluded that this interest explained and justified the asymmetrical statutory discrimina-

---

[13] This purpose is not apparent from the statute. Penalizing children as a means of influencing their parents seems inconsistent with the desire of the Illinois Legislature to make the intestate succession law more just to illegitimate children. Moreover, the difference in the rights of illegitimate children in the estates of their mothers and their fathers appears to be unrelated to the purpose of promoting family relationships. In this respect the Louisiana laws at issue in *Labine* were quite different. Those laws differentiated on the basis of the character of the child's illegitimacy. "Bastard children" were given no inheritance rights. "Natural children," who could be and were acknowledged under state law, were given limited inheritance rights, but still less than those of legitimate children. 401 U.S., at 537, and n.13. The Louisiana categories are consistent with a theory of social opprobrium regarding the parents' relationships and with a measured, if misguided, attempt to deter illegitimate relationships.

tion against the illegitimate children of intestate men. The more favorable treatment of illegitimate children claiming from their mothers' estates was justified because "proof of a lineal relationship is more readily ascertainable when dealing with maternal ancestors." *Id.*, at 52, 329 N.E.2d, at 240. Alluding to the possibilities of abuse, the court rejected a case-by-case approach to claims based on alleged paternity. *Id.*, at 52–53, 329 N.E.2d, at 240–241.

The more serious problems of proving paternity might justify a more demanding standard for illegitimate children claiming under their fathers' estates than that required either for illegitimate children claiming under their mothers' estates or for legitimate children generally. We think, however, that the Illinois Supreme Court gave inadequate consideration to the relation between §12 and the State's proper objective of assuring accuracy and efficiency in the disposition of property at death. The court failed to consider the possibility of a middle ground between the extremes of complete exclusion and case-by-case determination of paternity. For at least some significant categories of illegitimate children of intestate men, inheritance rights can be recognized without jeopardizing the orderly settlement of estates or the dependability of titles to property passing under intestacy laws. Because it excludes those categories of illegitimate children unnecessarily, §12 is constitutionally flawed.

The orderly disposition of property at death requires an appropriate legal framework, the structuring of which is a matter particularly within the competence of the individual States. In exercising this responsibility, a State necessarily must enact laws governing both the procedure and substance of intestate succession. Absent infringement of a constitutional right, the federal courts have no role here, and, even when constitutional violations are alleged, those courts should accord substantial deference to a State's statutory scheme of inheritance.

The judicial task here is the difficult one of vindicating constitutional rights without interfering unduly with the State's primary responsibility in this area. Our previous decisions demonstrate a sensitivity to "the lurking problems with respect to proof of paternity," *Gomez v. Perez*, 409 U.S. 535, 538 (1973), and the need for the States to draw "arbitrary lines * * * to facilitate potentially difficult problems of proof," *Weber*, 406 U.S., at 174. "Those problems are not to be lightly brushed aside, but neither can they be made into an impenetrable barrier that works to shield otherwise invidious discrimination." *Gomez, supra*, at 538. Our decision last Term in *Mathews v. Lucas, supra*, provides especially helpful guidance.

In *Lucas* we sustained provisions of the Social Security Act governing the eligibility for surviving children's insurance benefits. One of the statutory conditions of eligibility was dependency on the deceased wage earner. 427 U.S., at 498 and n.1. Although the Act presumed dependency for a number of categories of children, including some categories of illegitimate children, it required that the remaining illegitimate children prove actual dependency. The Court upheld the statutory classifications, finding them "reasonably related to the likelihood of dependency at death." *Id.*, at 509. Central to this decision was the finding that the "statute does not broadly discriminate between legitimates and illegitimates without more, but is carefully tuned to alternative considerations." *Id.*, at 513.

Although the present case arises in a context different from that in *Lucas*, the question whether the statute "is carefully tuned to alternative considerations" is equally applicable here. We conclude that §12 does not meet this standard. Difficulties of proving paternity in some situations do not justify the total statutory disinheritance of illegitimate children whose fathers die intestate. The facts of this case graphically illustrate the constitutional defect of §12. Sherman Gordon was found to be the father of Deta Mona in a state-court paternity action prior to his death. On the strength of that finding, he was ordered to contribute to the support of his child. That adjudication should be equally sufficient to establish Deta Mona's right to claim a child's share of Gordon's estate, for the State's interest in the accurate and efficient disposition of property at death would not be compromised in any way by allowing her claim in these circumstances.[14] The reach of the statute extends well beyond the asserted purposes. See *Jimenez v. Weinberger*, 417 U.S. 628, 637 (1974).

The Illinois Supreme Court also noted that the decedents whose estates were involved in the consolidated appeals could have left substantial parts of their estates to their illegitimate children by writing a will. The court cited *Labine* as authority for the proposition that such a possibility is constitutionally significant. 61 Ill.2d, at 52, 329 N.E.2d, at 240. The penultimate paragraph of the opinion in *Labine* distinguishes that case from *Levy v. Louisiana*, 391 U.S. 68 (1968),[15] because no insurmountable barrier prevented the illegitimate child from sharing in her father's estate. "There is not the slightest suggestion in this case that Louisiana has barred this illegitimate from inheriting from her father." 401 U.S., at 539. The Court then listed three different steps that would have resulted in some recovery by Labine's illegitimate daughter. Labine could have left a will; he could have legitimated the daughter by marrying her mother; and he could have given the daughter the status of a legitimate child by stating in his acknowledgment of paternity his desire to legitimate her. *Ibid.* In *Weber* our distinction of *Labine* was based in part on the fact that no such alternatives existed, as state law prevented the acknowledgment of the children involved. 406 U.S., at 170–171.

Despite its appearance in two of our opinions, the focus on the presence or absence of an insurmountable barrier is somewhat of an analytical anomaly. Here, as in *Labine*, the question is the constitutionality of a state intestate succession law that treats illegitimate children differently from legitimate children. Traditional equal protection analysis asks whether this statutory differentiation on the basis of illegitimacy is justified by the promotion of recognized state objectives. If the law cannot be sustained on this analysis, it is not clear how it can be saved by the absence of an insurmountable barrier to inheritance under other and hypothetical circumstances.

By focusing on the steps that an intestate might have taken to assure some inheritance for his illegitimate children, the analysis loses sight of the essential question: the constitutionality of discrimination against illegitimates in a state intestate succession law. If the decedent had written a will devising property to his illegitimate child, the case no longer would involve intestate succession law at all. Similarly, if the decedent had legitimated the child by marrying the child's mother or by complying with the requirements of some other method of legitimation, the case no longer would involve discrimination against illegitimates. Hard questions cannot be avoided by a hypothetical reshuffling of the facts. If Sherman Gordon had devised his estate to Deta Mona this case would not be here. Similarly, in *Reed v. Reed*, 404 U.S. 71 (1971), if the decedent had left a will naming an executor, the problem of the statutory preference for male administrators of estates of intestates would not have been presented. The opinion in *Reed* gives no indication that this available alternative had any constitutional significance. We think it has none in this case.

---

[14] Evidence of paternity may take a variety of forms, some creating more significant problems of inaccuracy and inefficiency than others. The States, of course, are free to recognize these differences in fashioning their requirements of proof. Our holding today goes only to those forms of proof which do not compromise the States' interests. This clearly would be the case, for example, where there is a prior adjudication or formal acknowledgment of paternity. Thus, we would have a different case if the state statute were carefully tailored to eliminate imprecise and unduly burdensome methods of establishing paternity.

[15] In *Levy* the Court struck down a Louisiana wrongful-death statute that gave legitimate, but not illegitimate, children a cause of action for the wrongful death of their parents.

Finally, appellees urge us to affirm the decision below on the theory that the Illinois Probate Act, including §12, mirrors the presumed intentions of the citizens of the State regarding the disposition of their property at death. Individualizing this theory, appellees argue that we must assume that Sherman Gordon knew the disposition of his estate under the Illinois Probate Act and that his failure to make a will shows his approval of that disposition. We need not resolve the question whether presumed intent alone can ever justify discrimination against illegitimates,[16] for we do not think that §12 was enacted for this purpose. The theory of presumed intent is not relied upon in the careful opinion of the Illinois Supreme Court examining both the history and the text of §12. This omission is not without significance, as one would expect a state supreme court to identify the state interests served by a statute of its state legislature. Our own examination of §12 convinces us that the statutory provisions at issue were shaped by forces other than the desire of the legislature to mirror the intentions of the citizens of the State with respect to their illegitimate children.

To the extent that other policies are not considered more important, legislators enacting state intestate succession laws probably are influenced by the desire to reflect the natural affinities of decedents in the allocation of estates among the categories of heirs. See *Mathews v. Lucas*, 427 U.S., at 514–515. A pattern of distribution favoring brothers and sisters over cousins is, for example, best explained on this basis. The difference in §12 between the rights of illegitimate children in the estates of their fathers and mothers, however, is more convincingly explained by the other factors mentioned by the court below. Accepting in this respect the views of the Illinois Supreme Court, we find in §12 a primary purpose to provide a system of intestate succession more just to illegitimate children than the prior law, a purpose tempered by a secondary interest in protecting against spurious claims of paternity. In the absence of a more convincing demonstration, we will not hypothesize an additional state purpose that has been ignored by the Illinois Supreme Court.

IV

For the reasons stated above, we conclude that §12 of the Illinois Probate Act[17] cannot be squared with the command of the Equal Protection Clause of

---

[16] Appellees characterize the Illinois intestate succession law as a "statutory will." Because intent is a central ingredient in the disposition of property by will, the theory that intestate succession laws are "statutory wills" based on the "presumed intent" of the citizens of the State may have some superficial appeal. The theory proceeds from the initial premise that an individual could, if he wished, disinherit his illegitimate children in his will. Because the statute merely reflects the intent of those citizens who failed to make a will, discrimination against illegitimate children in intestate succession laws is said to be equally permissible. The term "statutory will," however, cannot blind us to the fact that intestate succession laws are acts of States, not of individuals. Under the Fourteenth Amendment this is a fundamental difference.

Even if one assumed that a majority of the citizens of the State preferred to discriminate against their illegitimate children, the sentiment hardly would be unanimous. With respect to any individual, the argument of knowledge and approval of the state law is sheer fiction. The issue therefore becomes where the burden of inertia in writing a will is to fall. At least when the disadvantaged group has been a frequent target of discrimination, as illegitimates have, we doubt that a State constitutionally may place the burden on that group by invoking the theory of "presumed intent." See *Eskra v. Morton*, 524 F.2d, at 12–14 (Stevens, J.).

[17] The Illinois statute can be distinguished in several respects from the Louisiana statute in *Labine*. The discrimination in *Labine* took a different form, suggesting different legislative objectives. See, *e.g.*, n.13, *supra*. In its impact on the illegitimate children excluded from their parents' estates, the statute was significantly different. Under Louisiana law, all illegitimate children, "natural" and "bastard," were entitled to support from the estate of the deceased parent. 401 U.S., at 534, n.2. Despite these differences, it is apparent that we have examined the Illinois statute more critically than the Court examined the Louisiana statute in *Labine*. To the extent that our analysis in this case differs from that in *Labine* the more recent analysis controls.

the Fourteenth Amendment. Accordingly, we reverse the judgment of the Illinois Supreme Court and remand the case for further proceedings not inconsistent with this opinion.

So ordered.

THE CHIEF JUSTICE, Mr. Justice STEWART, Mr. Justice BLACKMUN, and Mr. Justice REHNQUIST dissent. Like the Supreme Court of Illinois, they find this case constitutionally indistinguishable from *Labine v. Vincent,* 401 U.S. 532 (1971). They would, therefore, affirm the judgment.

[Separate dissenting opinion by Mr. Justice REHNQUIST omitted.]

Lalli v. Lalli

United States Supreme Court

439 U.S. 259 (1978)

Mr. Justice POWELL announced the judgment of the Court in an opinion, in which THE CHIEF JUSTICE and Mr. Justice STEWART join.

This case presents a challenge to the constitutionality of §4-1.2 of New York's Estates, Powers, and Trusts Law,[1] which requires illegitimate children who would inherit from their fathers by intestate succession to provide a particular form of proof of paternity. Legitimate children are not subject to the same requirement.

Appellant Robert Lalli claims to be the illegitimate son of Mario Lalli who died intestate on January 7, 1973, in the State of New York. Appellant's mother, who died in 1968, never was married to Mario. After Mario's widow, Rosamond Lalli, was appointed administratrix of her husband's estate, appellant petitioned the Surrogate's Court for Westchester County for a compulsory accounting, claiming that he and his sister Maureen Lalli were entitled to inherit from Mario as his children. Rosamond Lalli opposed the petition. She argued that even if Robert and Maureen were Mario's children, they were not lawful distributees of the state because they had failed to comply with §4-1.2,[2] which provides in part:

---

[1] 1965 N.Y. Laws, ch. 958, §1. The statute was initially codified as N.Y. Decedent Est. Law §83-a. In 1968 it was recodified without material change as N.Y. Est., Powers and Trusts Law §4-1.2. 1966 N.Y. Laws, ch. 952. Further nonsubstantive amendments were made the next year. 1967 N.Y. Laws, ch. 686, §§28, 29.

[2] Section 4-1.2 in its entirety provides:

"(a) For the purposes of this article:

"(1) An illegitimate child is the legitimate child of his mother so that he and his issue inherit from his mother and from his maternal kindred.

"(2) An illegitimate child is the legitimate child of his father so that he and his issue inherit from his father if a court of competent jurisdiction has, during the lifetime of the father, made an order of filiation declaring paternity in a proceeding instituted during the pregnancy of the mother or within two years from the birth of the child.

"(3) The existence of an agreement obligating the father to support the illegitimate child does not qualify such child or his issue to inherit from the father in the absence of an order of filiation made as prescribed by subparagraph (2).

"(4) A motion for relief from an order of filiation may be made only by the father, and such motion must be made within one year from the entry of such order.

"(b) If an illegitimate child dies, his surviving spouse, issue, mother, maternal kindred and father inherit and are entitled to letters of administration as if the decedent were legitimate, provided that the father may inherit or obtain such letters only if an order of filiation has been made in accordance with the provisions of subparagraph (2)."

"An illegitimate child is the legitimate child of his father so that he and his issue inherit from his father if a court of competent jurisdiction has, during the lifetime of the father, made an order of filiation declaring paternity in a proceeding instituted during the pregnancy of the mother or within two years from the birth of the child."

Appellant conceded that he had not obtained an order of filiation during his putative father's lifetime. He contended, however, that §4-1.2, by imposing this requirement, discriminated against him on the basis of his illegitimate birth in violation of the Equal Protection Clause of the Fourteenth Amendment.[3] Appellant tendered certain evidence of his relationship with Mario Lalli, including a notarized document in which Lalli, in consenting to appellant's marriage, referred to him as "my son," and several affidavits by persons who stated that Lalli had acknowledged openly and often that Robert and Maureen were his children.

The Surrogate's Court noted that §4-1.2 had previously, and unsuccessfully, been attacked under the Equal Protection Clause. After reviewing recent decisions of this Court concerning discrimination against illegitimate children, particularly *Labine v. Vincent,* 401 U.S. 532 (1971), and three New York decisions affirming the constitutionality of the statute, *In re Belton,* 70 Misc.2d 814, 335 N.Y.S.2d 177 (Sur. Ct. 1972); *In re Hendrix,* 68 Misc.2d 439, 444, 326 N.Y.S.2d 646, 652 (Sur. Ct. 1971); *In re Crawford,* 64 Misc.2d 758, 762–763, 315 N.Y.S.2d 890, 895 (Sur. Ct. 1970), the court ruled that appellant was properly excluded as a distributee of Lalli's estate and therefore lacked status to petition for a compulsory accounting.

On direct appeal the New York Court of Appeals affirmed. *In re Lalli,* 38 N.Y.2d 77, 378 N.Y.S.2d 351, 340 N.E.2d 721 (1975). It understood *Labine* to require the State to show no more than that "there is a rational basis for the means chosen by the Legislature for the accomplishment of a permissible State objective." *In re Lalli, supra,* 38, N.Y.2d, at 81, 378 N.Y.S.2d, at 354, 340 N.E.2d, at 723. After discussing the problems of proof peculiar to establishing paternity, as opposed to maternity, the court concluded that the State was constitutionally entitled to require a judicial decree during the father's lifetime as the exclusive form of proof of paternity.

Appellant appealed the Court of Appeals' decision to this Court. While that case was pending here, we decided *Trimble v. Gordon,* 430 U.S. 762 (1977). Because the issues in these two cases were similar in some respects, we vacated and remanded to permit further consideration in light of *Trimble. Lalli v. Lalli,* 431 U.S. 911 (1977).

On remand,[4] the New York Court of Appeals, with one judge dissenting, adhered to its former disposition. *In re Lalli,* 43 N.Y.2d 65, 400 N.Y.S.2d 761, 371 N.E.2d 481 (1977). It acknowledged that *Trimble* contemplated a standard of judicial review demanding more than "a mere finding of some remote rational relationship between the statute and a legitimate State purpose," *id.,* at 67, 400 N.Y.S.2d at 762, 371 N.E.2d, at 482, though less than strictest scrutiny. Finding §4-1.2 to be "significantly and determinatively different" from the statute overturned in *Trimble,* the court ruled that the New York law was sufficiently related to the State's interest in "the orderly settlement of estates and the dependability of titles to property passing under intestacy

---

[3] Appellant also claimed that §4-1.2 was invalid under N.Y. Const., Art 1, §11. The New York Court of Appeals did not rule on this issue, nor do we. We also do not consider whether §4-1.2 unconstitutionally discriminates on the basis of sex or whether the administratrix of Mario's estate is required to account for her alleged failure to bring a wrongful death action on behalf of appellant. The latter question was not considered by the Court of Appeals, and the former was raised for the first time by a brief *amicus curiae* in this Court.

[4] On remand from this Court, the New York Attorney General was permitted to intervene as a defendant-appellee. He has filed a brief on the merits and argued the case in this Court. Appellee Rosamond Lalli did not present oral argument and has not filed a brief on the merits.

laws," *id.,* at 67, 69–70, 400 N.Y.S.2d at 763–764, 371 N.E.2d, at 482, 483, quoting *Trimble, supra,* 430 U.S. at 771, to meet the requirements of equal protection.

Appellant again sought review here, and we noted probable jurisdiction. *Lalli v. Lalli,* 435 U.S. 921 (1978). We now affirm.

We begin our analysis with *Trimble.* At issue in that case was the constitutionality of an Illinois statute providing that a child born out of wedlock could inherit from his intestate father only if the father had "acknowledged" the child and the child had been legitimated by the intermarriage of the parents. The appellant in *Trimble* was a child born out of wedlock whose father had neither acknowledged her nor married her mother. He had, however, been found to be her father in a judicial decree ordering him to contribute to her support. When the father died intestate, the child was excluded as a distributee because the statutory requirements for inheritance had not been met.

We concluded that the Illinois statute discriminated against illegitimate children in a manner prohibited by the Equal Protection Clause. Although, as decided in *Mathews v. Lucas,* 427 U.S. 495, 506 (1976), and reaffirmed in *Trimble, supra,* 430 U.S. at 767, classifications based on illegitimacy are not subject to "strict scrutiny," they nevertheless are invalid under the Fourteenth Amendment if they are not substantially related to permissible state interests. Upon examination, we found that the Illinois law failed that test.

Two state interests were proposed which the statute was said to foster: the encouragement of legitimate family relationships and the maintenance of an accurate and efficient method of disposing of an intestate decedent's property. Granting that the State was appropriately concerned with the integrity of the family unit, we viewed the statute as bearing "only the most attenuated relationship to the asserted goal." *Trimble, supra* at 768. We again rejected the argument that "persons will shun illicit relationships because the offspring may not one day reap the benefits" that would accrue to them were they legitimate. *Weber v. Aetna Casualty & Surety Co.,* 406 U.S. 164, 173 (1972). The statute therefore was not defensible as an incentive to enter legitimate family relationships.

Illinois' interest in safeguarding the orderly disposition of property at death was more relevant to the statutory classification. We recognized that devising "an appropriate legal framework" in the futherance of that interest "is a matter particularly within the competence of the individual States." *Trimble, supra,* 430 U.S. at 771. An important aspect of that framework is a response to the often difficult problem of proving the paternity of illegitimate children and the related danger of spurious claims against intestate estates. See *infra,* at 526. These difficulties, we said, "might justify a more demanding standard for illegitimate children claiming under their fathers' estates than that required either for illegitimate children claiming under their mothers' estates or for legitimate children generally." *Id.,* at 770.

The Illinois statute, however, was constitutionally flawed because, by insisting upon not only an acknowledgment by the father, but also the marriage of the parents, it excluded "at least some significant categories of illegitimate children of intestate men [whose] inheritance rights can be recognized without jeopardizing the orderly settlement of estates or the dependability of titles to property passing under intestacy laws." *Id.,* at 771. We concluded that the Equal Protection Clause required that a statute placing exceptional burdens on illegitimate children in the furtherance of proper State objectives must be more "carefully tuned to alternative considerations," *id.,* at 772, quoting *Mathews v. Lucas, supra,* 427 U.S. at 513, than was true of the broad disqualification in the Illinois law.

The New York statute, enacted in 1965, was intended to soften the rigors of previous law which permitted illegitimate children to inherit only from their mothers. See *infra,* at 527. By lifting the absolute bar to paternal inheritance, §4-1.2 tended to achieve its desired effect. As in *Trimble,* however, the question before us is whether the remaining statutory obstacles to inheritance by illegitimate children can be squared with the Equal Protection Clause.

At the outset we observe that §4-1.2 is different in important respects from the statutory provision overturned in *Trimble.* The Illinois statute required, in addition to the father's acknowledgment of paternity, the legitimation of the child through the intermarriage of the parents as an absolute precondition to inheritance. This combination of requirements eliminated "the possibility of a middle ground between the extremes of complete exclusion and case-by-case determination of paternity." *Trimble, supra,* 430 U.S. at 770–771. As illustrated by the facts in *Trimble,* even a judicial declaration of paternity was insufficient to permit inheritance.

Under §4-1.2, by contrast, the marital status of the parents is irrelevant. The single requirement at issue here is an evidentiary one—that the paternity of the father be declared in a judicial proceeding sometime before his death.[5] The child need not have been legitimated in order to inherit from his father. Had the appellant in *Trimble* been governed by §4-1.2, she would have been a distributee of her father's estate. See *In re Lalli,* 43 N.Y.2d at 68 n.2, 400 N.Y.S.2d at 762 n.2, 371 N.E.2d, at 482 n.2.

A related difference between the two provisions pertains to the state interests said to be served by them. The Illinois law was defended, in part, as a means of encouraging legitimate family relationships. No such justification has been offered in support of §4-1.2. The Court of Appeals disclaimed that the purpose of the statute, "even in small part, was to discourage illegitimacy, to mold human conduct or to set societal norms." *In re Lalli, supra,* 43 N.Y.2d, at 70, 400 N.Y.S.2d, at 764, 371 N.E.2d, at 483. The absence in §4-1.2 of any requirement that the parents intermarry or otherwise legitimate a child born out of wedlock and our review of the legislative history of the statute, *infra,* at 527, confirm this view.

Our inquiry, therefore, is focused narrowly. We are asked to decide whether the discrete procedural demands that §4-1.2 places on illegitimate children bear an evident and substantial relation to the particular state interests this statute is designed to serve.

The primary state goal underlying the challenged aspects of §4-1.2 is to provide for the just and orderly disposition of property at death.[6] We long have recognized that this is an area with which the States have an interest of considerable magnitude. *Trimble, supra,* 430 U.S. at 771; *Weber v. Aetna Casualty & Surety Co., supra,* 406 U.S. at 170; *Labine v. Vincent,* 401 U.S., at 538 (1971); see also *Lyeth v. Hoey,* 305 U.S. 188, 193 (1938); *Mager v. Grima,* 8 How. 490, 493, 12 L.Ed. 1168 (1850).

---

[5] Section 4-1.2 requires not only that the order of filiation be made during the lifetime of the father, but that the proceeding in which it is sought have been commenced "during the pregnancy of the mother or within two years from the birth of the child." The New York Court of Appeals declined to rule on the constitutionality of the two-year limitation in both of its opinions in this case because appellant concededly had never commenced a paternity proceeding at all. Thus, if the rule that paternity be judicially declared during his father's lifetime were upheld, appellant would lose for failure to comply with that requirement alone. If, on the other hand, appellant prevailed in his argument that his inheritance could not be conditioned on the existence of an order of filiation, the two-year limitation would become irrelevant, since the paternity proceeding itself would be unnecessary. See *In re Lalli,* 43 N.Y.2d 65, 68 n.1, 400 N.Y.S.2d 761, 762, n.1, 371 N.E.2d 481, 482 n.1 (1977); *In re Lalli,* 38 N.Y.2d 77, 80, 378 N.Y.S.2d 351, 353, 340 N.E.2d 721, 723 (1975). As the New York Court of Appeals has not passed upon the constitutionality of the two-year limitation, that question is not before us. Our decision today therefore sustains §4-1.2 under the Equal Protection Clause only with respect to its requirement that a judicial order of filiation be issued during the lifetime of the father of an illegitimate child.

[6] The presence in this case of the State's interest in the orderly disposition of a decedent's property at death distinguishes it from others in which that justification for an illegitimacy-based classification was absent. *E.g., Jimenez v. Weinberger,* 417 U.S. 628 (1974); *Gomez v. Perez,* 409 U.S. 535 (1973); *Weber v. Aetna Casualty & Surety Co.,* 406 U.S. 164, 170 (1972); *Levy v. Louisiana,* 391 U.S. 68 (1968).

This interest is directly implicated in paternal inheritance by illegitimate children because of the peculiar problems of proof that are involved. Establishing maternity is seldom difficult. As one New York Surrogate's Court has observed, "the birth of the child is a recorded or registered event usually taking place in the presence of others. In most cases the child remains with the mother and for a time is necessarily reared by her. That the child is the child of a particular woman is rarely difficult to prove." *In re Ortiz*, 60 Misc.2d 756, 761, 303 N.Y.S.2d 806, 812 (Sur. Ct. 1969). Proof of paternity, by contrast, frequently is difficult when the father is not part of a formal family unit. "The putative father often goes his way unconscious of the birth of a child. Even if conscious, he is very often totally unconcerned because of the absence of any ties to the mother. Indeed the mother may not know *who* is responsible for her pregnancy." *Ibid.* (emphasis in original); accord, *In re Flemm*, 85 Misc.2d 855, 861, 381 N.Y.S.2d 573, 576–577 (Sur. Ct. 1975); *In re Hendrix*, 68 Misc.2d, at 443, 326 N.Y.S.2d, at 650; cf. *Trimble, supra*, 430 U.S., at 770, 772.

Thus, a number of problems arise that counsel against treating illegitimate children identically to all other heirs of an intestate father. These were the subject of a comprehensive study by the Temporary State Commission on the Modernization, Revision and Simplification of the Law of Estates. This group, known as the Bennett Commission,[7] consisted of individuals experienced in the practical problems of estate administration. *In re Flemm, supra*, 85 Misc.2d, at 858, 381 N.Y.S.2d, at 575. The Commission issued its report and recommendations to the Legislature in 1965. See Fourth Report of the Temporary State Commission on the Modernization, Revision and Simplification of the Law of Estates, Legis. Doc. 1965, No. 19 (hereinafter Commission Report). The statute now codified as §4-1.2 was included.

Although the overarching purpose of the proposed statute was "to alleviate the plight of the illegitimate child," Commission Report 37, the Bennett Commission considered it necessary to impose the strictures of §4-1.2 in order to mitigate serious difficulties in the administration of the estates of both testate and intestate decedents. The Commission's perception of some of these difficulties was described by Surrogate Sobel, a member of "the busiest [surrogate's] court in the State measured by the number of intestate estates which traffic daily through this court," *In re Flemm, supra*, at 857, 381 N.Y.S.2d, at 574 (Sobel, S.), and a participant in some of the Commission's deliberations:

> "An illegitimate, if made an unconditional distributee in intestacy, must be served with process in the estate of his parent or if he is a distributee in the estate of the kindred of a parent. * * * And, in probating the will of his parent (though not named a beneficiary) or in probating the will of any person who makes a class disposition to 'issue' of such parent, the illegitimate must be served with process. * * * How does one cite and serve an illegitimate of whose existence neither family nor personal representative may be aware? And of greatest concern, how achieve finality of decree in *any* estate when there always exists the possibility however remote of a secret illegitimate lurking in the buried past of a parent or an ancestor of a class of beneficiaries? Finality in decree is essential in the Surrogate's Courts since title to real property passes under such decree. Our procedural statutes and the Due Process Clause mandate notice and opportunity to be heard to all necessary parties. Given the right to intestate succession, *all* illegitimates must be served with process. This would

---

[7] The Bennett Commission was created by the New York Legislature in 1961. It was instructed to recommend needed changes in certain areas of state law, including that pertaining to "the descent and distribution of property and the practice and procedure relating thereto." 1961 N.Y. Laws, ch. 731, §1.

be no real problem with respect to those few estates where there are 'known' illegitimates. But it presents an almost insuperable burden as regards 'unknown' illegitimates. The point made in the [Bennett] commission discussions was that instead of affecting only a few estates, procedural problems would be created for many—some members suggested a majority—of estates."

Id., at 859, 381 N.Y.S.2d, at 575–576; *cf. In re Leventritt,* 92 Misc.2d 598, 601–602, 400 N.Y.S. 298, 300–301 (Sur. Ct. 1977).

Even where an individual claiming to be the illegitimate child of a deceased man makes himself known, the difficulties facing an estate are likely to persist. Because of the particular problems of proof, spurious claims may be difficult to expose. The Bennett Commission therefore sought to protect "innocent adults and those rightfully interested in their estates from fraudulent claims of heirship and harassing litigation instituted by those seeking to establish themselves as illegitimate heirs." Commission Report 265.

As the State's interests are substantial, we now consider the means adopted by New York to further these interests. In order to avoid the problems described above, the Commission recommended a requirement designed to ensure the accurate resolution of claims of paternity and to minimize the potential for disruption of estate administration. Accuracy is enhanced by placing paternity disputes in a judicial forum during the lifetime of the father. As the New York Court of Appeals observed in its first opinion in this case, the "availability [of the putative father] should be a substantial factor contributing to the reliability of the fact-finding process." *In re Lalli,* 38 N.Y.2d, at 82, 378 N.Y.S.2d, at 355, 340 N.E.2d, at 724. In addition, requiring that the order be issued during the father's lifetime permits a man to defend his reputation against "unjust accusations in paternity claims," which was a secondary purpose of §4-1.2. Commission Report 266.

The administration of an estate will be facilitated, and the possibility of delay and uncertainty minimized, where the entitlement of an illegitimate child to notice and participation is a matter of judicial record before the administration commences. Fraudulent assertions of paternity will be much less likely to succeed, or even to arise, where the proof is put before a court of law at a time when the putative father is available to respond, rather than first brought to light when the distribution of the assets of an estate is in the offing.[8]

Appellant contends that §4-1.2, like the statute at issue in *Trimble,* excludes "significant categories of illegitimate children" who could be allowed to inherit "without jeopardizing the orderly settlement" of their intestate fathers' estates. *Trimble, supra,* 430 U.S. at 771. He urges that those in his position—"known" illegitimate children who, despite the absence of an order of filiation obtained during their fathers' lifetimes, can present convincing proof of paternity—cannot rationally be denied inheritance as they pose none of the risks §4-1.2 was intended to minimize.[9]

---

[8] In affirming the judgment below, we do not, of course, restrict a State's freedom to require proof of paternity by means other than a judicial decree. Thus a State may prescribe any *formal* method of proof, whether it be similar to that provided by §4-1.2 or some other regularized procedure that would assure the authenticity of the acknowledgment. As we noted in *Trimble,* 430 U.S., at 772 n.14, such a procedure would be sufficient to satisfy the State's interests. See also n.11, *infra.*

[9] Appellant claims that in addition to discriminating between illegitimate and legitimate children, §4-1.2, in conjunction with N.Y. Dom. Rel. Law §24 (McKinney 1977), impermissibly discriminates between classes of illegitimate children. Section 24 provides that a child conceived out of wedlock is nevertheless legitimate if, before or after his birth, his parents marry, even if the marriage is void, illegal or judicially annulled. Appellant argues that by classifying as "legiti-

We do not question that there will be some illegitimate children who would be able to establish their relationship to their deceased fathers without serious disruption of the administration of estates and that, as applied to such individuals, §4-1.2 appears to operate unfairly. But few statutory classifications are entirely free from the criticism that they sometimes produce inequitable results. Our inquiry under the Equal Protection Clause does not focus on the abstract "fairness" of a state law, but on whether the statute's relation to the state interests it is intended to promote is so tenuous that it lacks the rationality contemplated by the Fourteenth Amendment.

The Illinois statute in *Trimble* was constitutionally unacceptable because it effected a total statutory disinheritance of children born out of wedlock who were not legitimated by the subsequent marriage of their parents. The reach of the statute was far in excess of its justifiable purposes. Section 4-1.2 does not share this defect. Inheritance is barred only where there has been a failure to secure evidence of paternity during the father's lifetime in the manner prescribed by the State. This is not a requirement that inevitably disqualifies an unnecessarily large number of children born out of wedlock.

The New York courts have interpreted §4-1.2 liberally and in such a way as to enhance its utility to both father and child without sacrificing its strength as a procedural prophylactic. For example, a father of illegitimate children who is willing to acknowledge paternity can waive his defenses in a paternity proceeding, *e.g., In re Thomas,* 87 Misc.2d 1033, 387 N.Y.S.2d 216 (Sur. Ct. 1976), or even institute such a proceeding himself.[10] N.Y. Jud.; Fam. Ct. Act. §522 (McKinney Supp. 1977); *In re Flemm,* 85 Misc.2d, at 863, 381 N.Y.S.2d, at 578. In addition, the courts have excused "technical" failures by illegitimate children to comply with the statute in order to prevent unnecessary injustice. *E.g., In re Niles,* 53 A.D.2d 983, 385 N.Y.S.2d 876 (1976), *appeal den.,* 40 N.Y.2d 809, 392 N.Y.S.2d 1027, 360 N.E.2d 1109 (1977) (filiation order may be signed *nunc pro tunc* to relate back to period prior to father's death when court's factual finding of paternity had been made); *In re Kennedy,* 89 Misc.2d 551, 554, 392 N.Y.S.2d 365, 367 (Sur. Ct. 1977) (judicial support order treated as "tantamount to an order of filiation," even though paternity was not specifically declared therein).

As the history of §4-1.2 clearly illustrates, the New York Legislature desired to "grant to illegitimates *in so far as practicable* rights of inheritance on a par with those enjoyed by legitimate children," Commission Report 265 (emphasis added), while protecting the important state interests we have described. Section 4-1.2 represents a carefully considered legislative judgment as to how this balance best could be achieved.

Even if, as Mr. Justice BRENNAN believes, §4-1.2 could have been written somewhat more equitably, it is not the function of a court "to hypothesize independently on the desirability or feasibility of any possible alternative[s]" to the statutory scheme formulated by New York. *Mathews v. Lucas,* 427 U.S., at 515. "These matters of practical judgment and empirical calculation are for [the State]. * * * In the end, the precise accuracy of [the State's] calculations is not a matter of specialized judicial competence; and we have no

---

mate" children born out of wedlock whose parents later marry, New York has, with respect to these children, substituted marriage for §4-1.2's requirement of proof of paternity. Thus, these "illegitimate" children escape the rigors of the rule unlike their unfortunate counterparts whose parents never marry.

Under §24, one claiming to be the legitimate child of a deceased man would have to prove not only his paternity but also his maternity and the fact of the marriage of his parents. These additional evidentiary requirements make it reasonable to accept less exacting proof of paternity and to treat such children as legitimate for inheritance purposes.

[10] In addition to making intestate succession possible, of course, a father is always free to provide for his illegitimate child by will. See *In re Flemm,* 85 Misc.2d 855, 864, 381 N.Y.S.2d 573, 579 (Sur. Ct. 1975).

basis to question their detail beyond the evident consistency and substantiality." *Id.,* at 515–516.[11]

We conclude that the requirement imposed by §4-1.2 on illegitimate children who would inherit from their fathers is substantially related to the important state interests the statute is intended to promote. We therefore find no violation of the Equal Protection Clause.

The judgment of the New York Court of Appeals is
Affirmed.

For the reasons stated in his dissent in *Trimble v. Gordon,* 430 U.S. 762, 777 (1977), Mr. Justice REHNQUIST concurs in the judgment of affirmance.

Mr. Justice STEWART, concurring.

It seems to me that Mr. Justice POWELL'S opinion convincingly demonstrates the significant differences between the New York law at issue here and the Illinois law at issue in *Trimble v. Gordon,* 430 U.S. 762. Therefore, I cannot agree with the view expressed in the concurring opinion that *Trimble v. Gordon* is now "a derelict," or with the implication that in deciding the two cases the way it has this Court has failed to give authoritative guidance to the courts and legislatures of the several States.

Mr. Justice BLACKMUN, concurring in the judgment.

I agree with the result the Court has reached and concur in its judgment. I also agree with much that has been said in the plurality opinion. My point of departure, of course, is at the plurality's valiant struggle to distinguish, rather than overrule, *Trimble v. Gordon,* 430 U.S. 762 (1977), decided just last Term, and involving a small probate estate (an automobile worth approximately $2,500) and a sad and appealing fact situation. Four Members of the Court, like the Supreme Court of Illinois, found the case "constitutionally

---

[11] The dissent of Mr. Justice BRENNAN would reduce the opinion in *Trimble v. Gordon,* 430 U.S. 762 (1977), to a simplistic holding that the Constitution *requires* a State, in a case of this kind, to recognize as sufficient any "formal acknowledgment of paternity." This reading of *Trimble* is based on a single phrase lifted from a footnote. *Id.,* at 772 n.14. It ignores both the broad rationale of the Court's opinion and the context in which the note and the phrase relied upon appear. The principle that the footnote elaborates is that the States are free to recognize the problems arising from different forms of proof and to select those forms "carefully tailored to eliminate imprecise and unduly burdensome methods of establishing paternity." *Ibid.* The New York Legislature, with the benefit of the Bennett Commission's study, exercised this judgment when it considered and rejected the possibility of accepting evidence of paternity less formal than a judicial order. Fourth Report of the Temporary State Commission on the Modernization, Revision and Simplification of the Law of Estates, Legis. Doc. 1965, No. 19, at 266–267.

The "formal acknowledgment" contemplated by *Trimble* is such as would minimize post-death litigation, *i.e.,* a regularly prescribed, legally recognized method of acknowledging paternity. See n.8, *supra.* It is thus plain that footnote 14 in *Trimble* does not sustain the dissenting opinion. Indeed, the document relied upon by the dissent is not an acknowledgment of paternity at all. It is a simple "Certificate of Consent" that apparently was required at the time by New York for the marriage of a minor. It consists of one sentence:

"This is to certify that I, who have hereto subscribed my name, do hereby consent that Robert Lalli who is my son and who is under the age of 21 years, shall be united in marriage to Janice Bivens by a minister of the gospel or other person authorized by law to solemnize marriages." App. A-16.

Mario Lalli's signature to this document was acknowledged by a notary public, but the certificate contains no oath or affirmation as to the truth of its contents. The notary did no more than confirm the identity of Lalli. Because the certificate was executed for the purpose of giving consent to marry, not of proving biological paternity, the meaning of the words "my son" is ambiguous. One can readily imagine that had Robert Lalli's half-brother, who was not Mario's son but who took the surname Lalli and lived as a member of his household, sought permission to marry, Mario might also have referred to him as "my son" on a consent certificate.

The important state interests of safeguarding the accurate and orderly disposition of property at death, emphasized in *Trimble* and reiterated in our opinion today, could be frustrated easily if there were a constitutional rule that any notarized but unsworn statement identifying an individual as a "child" must be accepted as adequate proof of paternity regardless of the context in which the statement was made.

2

indistinguishable from *Labine v. Vincent,* 401 U.S. 532 (1971)," and were in dissent. 430 U.S., at 776, 777.

It seems to me that the Court today gratifyingly reverts to the principles set forth in *Labine v. Vincent.* What Mr. Justice Black said for the Court in *Labine* applies with equal force to the present case and, as four of us thought, to the Illinois situation with which *Trimble* was concerned.

I would overrule *Trimble,* but the Court refrains from doing so on the theory that the result in *Trimble* is justified because of the peculiarities of the Illinois Probate Act there under consideration. This, of course, is an explanation, but, for me, it is an unconvincing one. I therefore must regard *Trimble* as a derelict, explainable only because of the overtones of its appealing facts and offering little precedent for constitutional analysis of State intestate succession law. If *Trimble* is not a derelict, the corresponding statutes of other States will be of questionable validity until this Court passes them, one by one, as being on the *Trimble* side of the line, or the *Vincent-Lalli* side.

Mr. Justice BRENNAN, with whom Mr. Justice WHITE, Mr. Justice MARSHALL, and Mr. Justice STEVENS join, dissenting.

Trimble v. Gordon, 430 U.S. 762 (1977), declares that the state interest in the accurate and efficient determination of paternity can be adequately served by requiring the illegitimate child to offer into evidence a "formal acknowledgment of paternity." *Id.,* at 772 n.14. The New York statute is inconsistent with this command. Under the New York scheme, an illegitimate child may inherit intestate only if there has been a judicial finding of paternity during the lifetime of the father.

The present case illustrates the injustice of the departure from *Trimble* worked by today's decision sustaining the New York rule. All interested parties concede that Robert Lalli is the son of Mario Lalli. Mario Lalli supported Robert during his son's youth. Mario Lalli formally acknowledged Robert Lalli as his son. See *Matter of Lalli,* 38 N.Y.2d 77, 79, 378 N.Y.S.2d 351, 352, 340 N.E.2d 721, 722 (1975). Yet, for want of a judicial order of filiation entered during Mario's lifetime, Robert Lalli is denied his intestate share of his father's estate.

There is no reason to suppose that the injustice of the present case is aberrant. Indeed it is difficult to imagine an instance in which an illegitimate child acknowledged and voluntarily supported by his father, would ever inherit intestate under the New York scheme. Social welfare agencies, busy as they are with errant fathers, are unlikely to bring paternity proceedings against fathers who support their children. Similarly, children who are acknowledged and supported by their father are unlikely to bring paternity proceedings against him. First, they are unlikely to see the need for such adversary proceedings. Second, even if aware of the ruling requiring judicial filiation orders, they are likely to fear provoking disharmony by suing their father. For the same reasons, mothers of such illegitimates are unlikely to bring proceedings against the father. Finally, fathers who do not even bother to make out wills (and thus die intestate) are unlikely to take the time to bring formal filiation proceedings. Thus, as a practical matter, by requiring judicial filiation orders entered during the lifetime of the father, the New York statute makes it virtually impossible for acknowledged and freely supported illegitimate children to inherit intestate.

Two interests are said to justify this discrimination against illegitimates. First, it is argued, reliance upon mere formal public acknowledgements of paternity would open the door to fraudulent claims of paternity. I cannot accept this argument. I adhere to the view that when "a father has formally acknowledged his child * * * there is no possible difficulty of proof, and no opportunity for fraud or error. This purported interest [in avoiding fraud] * * * can offer no justification for distinguishing between a formally acknowledged illegitimate child and a legitimate one." *Labine v. Vincent,* U.S. 532, 552 (1971) (BRENNAN, J., dissenting).

But even if my confidence in the accuracy of formal public acknowledgments of paternity were unfounded, New York has available less drastic means of screening out fraudulent claims of paternity. In addition to requiring formal acknowledgments of paternity, New York might require illegitimates to prove paternity by an elevated standard of proof, *e.g.,* clear and convincing evidence, or even beyond a reasonable doubt. Certainly here, where there is no factual dispute as to the relationship between Robert and Mario Lalli, there is no justification for denying Robert Lalli his intestate share.

Second, it is argued, the New York statute protects estates from belated claims by unknown illegitimates. I find this justification even more tenuous than the first. Publication notice and a short limitations period in which claims against the estate could be filed could serve the asserted state interest as well, if not better, than the present scheme. In any event, the fear that unknown illegitimates might assert belated claims hardly justifies cutting off the rights of known illegitimates such as Robert Lalli. I am still of the view that the state interest in the speedy and efficient determination of paternity "is completely served by public acknowledgment of parentage and simply does not apply to the case of acknowledged illegitimate children." *Labine v. Vincent,* 401 U.S. 532, 558 n.30 (1971) (BRENNAN, J., dissenting).

I see no reason to retreat from our decision in *Trimble v. Gordon.* The New York statute on review here, like the Illinois statute in *Trimble,* excludes "forms of proof which do not compromise the State['s] interests." *Trimble v. Gordon,* 430 U.S. 762, 772 n.14. The statute thus discriminates against illegitimates through means not substantially related to the legitimate interests that the statute purports to promote. I would invalidate the statute.

Comments

After the decision in *Trimble* it appeared that little, if anything, was left of the law of illegitimacy. *Lalli,* however, indicates that serious questions of evidence concerning the parentage of an illegitimate child remain unresolved. The U.S. Supreme Court, by upholding the requirement of a judicial order of filiation during the father's lifetime, has permitted an impossible burden of proof. As Mr. Justice Brennan noted in his dissenting opinion in *Lalli,* it is unlikely that, in the case of an illegitimate child who is acknowledged and supported by his or her father, anybody would institute paternity proceedings. Consequently, under the New York scheme, such a child would be unable to inherit.

The shifting alliances in *Trimble* and *Lalli* reflect the underlying clash in values. Mr. Justice Powell delivered the opinion of the Court in both cases, but all other Justices changed positions. Mr. Justice Brennan, Mr. Justice White, Mr. Justice Marshall, and Mr. Justice Stevens voted with the majority in *Trimble,* but dissented in *Lalli.* Conversely, Mr. Chief Justice Burger, Mr. Justice Stewart, Mr. Justice Blackmun, and Mr. Justice Rehnquist dissented in *Trimble,* but were with the majority in *Lalli.* Perhaps this moved Mr. Justice Blackmun to take the position that *Trimble*, although it was not overruled, should be regarded "as a derelict." Yet the only prediction possible at this stage is that the Court will continue to vacillate in regard to illegitimate children.

The inconsistency of *Trimble* and *Lalli* in the Court's approach to illegitimacy exemplifies a decade of inconsistent Supreme Court decisions in the area of family law. While it is true that the laws of different states were at issue, as pointed out by Mr. Justice Stewart in his concurring opinion to *Lalli*, this in itself does not fully explain the differences in outcomes. The initial cases suggested that illegitimate children would be protected. In *Levy v. Louisiana*,* the Court reversed a district court's dismissal of a wrongful death action brought on behalf of five illegitimate children for the death of their mother on the grounds that illegitimacy had no relation to the cause of action. Conversely, in a companion case, *Glona v. American Guarantee & Liability Insurance Co.*,† the Court held that the mother of an illegitimate son must be permitted to sue for his wrongful death.

The Court then retreated in *Labine v. Vincent*,‡ which involved the constitutionality of a statute that barred intestate succession by an illegitimate child. In upholding the statute, the Court distinguished *Levy* and *Glona* as instances in which a state had created an "insurmountable barrier" to the illegitimate child, whereas in *Labine* the child would have been able to inherit if her father had executed a will, married her mother, or stated his desire to legitimize her in his acknowledgment of paternity. Mr. Justice Brennan, in dissenting with Mr. Justice Douglas, Mr. Justice White, and Mr. Justice Marshall, focused on the injustice of punishing illegitimate children for the "misdeeds of their parents." He and the dissenters rejected the rationale that punishing the child would encourage parents to marry and proposed that such an objective would be better achieved by focusing directly on the parents instead.

The pendulum then swung back to favor illegitimates. In *Weber v. Aetna Casualty & Surety Co.*,** a case involving a workmen's compensation statute that barred benefits to unacknowledged illegitimate children, the Court likened workmen's compensation benefits to wrongful death actions and held that there was no reasonable relation between the statute and the classification. Then, in *Gomez v. Perez*†† the Court struck down a Texas statute that obliged a father to support a legitimate, but not an illegitimate, child. In *New Jersey Welfare Rights Organization v. Cahill*,‡‡ the Court invalidated a New Jersey law for "Assistance to the Working Poor" that denied benefits to families composed of two adults who had not been ceremonially married.

---

* 391 U.S. 68 (1968).
† 391 U.S. 73 (1968).
‡ 401 U.S. 532 (1971).
** 406 U.S. 164 (1972).
†† 409 U.S. 535 (1973).
‡‡ 411 U.S. 619 (1973).

The trend of increased protection of an illegitimate child's right to government benefits was halted in *Mathews v. Lucas.** That case involved the constitutionality of provisions of the Social Security Act that conditioned an illegitimate child's rights to insurance benefits upon a showing that the deceased wage earner was either living with or contributing support to the claimants at the time of death. The Court rejected the appellee's claim that it was an unconstitutional violation of the Due Process Clause to make such a required showing for illegitimate children but not for legitimate ones. The Court held that illegitimacy was not a "suspect classification" and that it would therefore not use the "strict scrutiny" test. The Court found that the statutory presumption of dependency of legitimate children was valid and therefore upheld the statute. However, unlike *Labine* and *Lalli*, which operate to preclude any benefits, *Mathews* focused only on the evidentiary issue; that is, a child must prove more than a mere biological tie to receive benefits.

Mathews was followed by *Trimble*, which seems to have marked the crest of protection for the illegitimate. The Court, on the same day it decided *Trimble*, also decided *Fiallo v. Bell,*† in which it upheld a section of the Immigration and Nationality Act that discriminates against illegitimate children seeking to enter the country with their fathers. However, *Fiallo* actually accentuates the enormity of the change through *Trimble*. It is generally known that the area of immigration and naturalization law is a vestige of otherwise defunct archaic notions. Prejudices, and to some extent racism, are still permissible. That seems to be the main area, apart from social feelings, where illegitimacy of birth is still significant. Although there are occasional cases in which illegitimacy as a legal characterization has continued relevance,‡ the weight of the cases indicates that little is left of the substantive law of illegitimacy, especially if the child is acknowledged by the father. Further, state legislatures are beginning to eradicate the distinction between legitimate and illegitimate births by declaring all children legitimate.

The decline of illegitimacy as a legal factor has major consequences for marriage as a whole. The reason for legal marriage—namely, avoiding illegitimacy of children—is gone if support enforcement is ensured and the children are entitled to inherit anyway. A continuing benefit of marriage is that it raises a *presumption* of legitimacy, which also results in a presumption of inheritance rights; the illegitimate child continues to have the burden of proving that a person of means is actually the biological father. Marriage has thus been reduced from a sacrament to what might be called a mere evidentiary (procedural) convenience. Moreover, if *Marvin v. Marvin* (see pp. 172–185) becomes the national pattern, together with *Trimble*, a

---

*427 U.S. 495 (1976).
†430 U.S. 787 (1977).
‡See, e.g., *Labine v. Vincent* and more recently *Parham v. Hughes*, 441 U.S. 347 (1979).

woman may indeed be better off if she does not marry. She gets many rights anyway, and still has other options in case a better prospect comes along.

From the child's perspective, the contemporary decline of illegitimacy as a legal and social stigma makes marriage "for the children's sake" equally irrelevant. The child's rights to property and government benefits are no longer in jeopardy, providing there is proof of paternity. Even though *Stanley v. Illinois* (see pp. 602–609) gives the child a right to an undisturbed relationship with his or her father, if the father wants it, this evidentiary proviso is still important. Krause maintains that true equality of the illegitimate with the legitimate child would require the recognition of the child's procedural right to ascertain paternity (see References).

Perhaps it is appropriate to conclude this comment with a reexamination of the shifting legislative and judicial attitudes toward illegitimacy. What appear to be vacillating attitudes, as in *Trimble* and *Lalli*, may in part be dictated by a changeover from substantive to procedural considerations of an evidentiary nature. As long as illegitimate children were excluded from inheritance rights and governmental benefits, the question of who is actually illegitimate did not pose itself with the same urgency as it does today. As soon as the rights of illegitimate children were recognized, the question of evidence as to who is the illegitimate child of whom became inescapable. This emphasis on questions of evidence was also manifested in *Fiallo*, in which the Court was concerned with "the serious problems of proof that usually lurk in paternity determinations." The apprehensions in *Fiallo* about the vagaries of proof of paternity in foreign countries for immigration purposes are equally applicable locally. They may result in standardized requirements for benefits to illegitimate children by way of state legislation. While the need for such legislation is defensible, it may indirectly resurrect substantive disqualification of illegitimate children who cannot meet the new legislative standards.

Another aspect of this dilemma is that eventually various types of illegitimacies may emerge. A higher degree of protection may be given to illegitimate children who originate from durable relationships based on nonmarital cohabitation akin to marriage. These children will find it easier to establish their biological origin than those born from fleeting and casual sexual contacts. Since much contemporary state legislation on standardized requirements for inheritance rights and government benefits does not differentiate sufficiently between illegitimacy resulting from durable or casual relationships, continued constitutional attack in the courts is likely. In the judicial process, by which the more irrational legislative distinctions are eliminated, the more durable sexual unions, regardless of whether their basis is marital or nonmarital cohabitation, will become assimilated to each other in their legal consequences. Only illegitimate children resulting from casual sexual relations will continue to bear the brunt of the burden of proof to establish their rights.

References

Clark, *Constitutional Protection of the Illegitimate Child?*, 12 U.C.D. L. REV. 383 (1979).
Krause, H., FAMILY LAW 435 (1967).
Krause, H., ILLEGITIMACY: LAW AND SOCIAL POLICY (1971).
Note, *Illegitimacy and Equal Protection*, 49 N.Y.U. L. REV. 479 (1974).

Stanley v. Illinois

United States Supreme Court

405 U.S. 645 (1972)

Mr. Justice WHITE delivered the opinion of the Court.

Joan Stanley lived with Peter Stanley intermittently for 18 years, during which time they had three children.[1] When Joan Stanley died, Peter Stanley lost not only her but also his children. Under Illinois law, the children of unwed fathers become wards of the State upon the death of the mother. Accordingly, upon Joan Stanley's death, in a dependency proceeding instituted by the State of Illinois, Stanley's children[2] were declared wards of the State and placed with court-appointed guardians. Stanley appealed, claiming that he had never been shown to be an unfit parent and that since married fathers and unwed mothers could not be deprived of their children without such a showing, he had been deprived of the equal protection of the laws guaranteed him by the Fourteenth Amendment. The Illinois Supreme Court accepted the fact that Stanley's own unfitness had not been established but rejected the equal protection claim, holding that Stanley could properly be separated from his children upon proof of the single fact that he and the dead mother had not been married. Stanley's actual fitness as a father was irrelevant. *In re Stanley*, 45 Ill.2d 132, 256 N.E.2d 814 (1970).

Stanley presses his equal protection claim here. The State continues to respond that unwed fathers are presumed unfit to raise their children and that it is unnecessary to hold individualized hearings to determine whether particular fathers are in fact unfit parents before they are separated from their children. We granted certiorari, 400 U.S. 1020 (1971), to determine whether this method of procedure by presumption could be allowed to stand in light of the fact that Illinois allows married fathers—whether divorced, widowed, or separated—and mothers—even if unwed—the benefit of the presumption that they are fit to raise their children.

At the outset we reject any suggestion that we need not consider the propriety of the dependency proceeding that separated the Stanleys because Stanley might be able to regain custody of his children as a guardian or through adoption proceedings. The suggestion is that if Stanley has been treated differently from other parents, the difference is immaterial and not legally cognizable for the purposes of the Fourteenth Amendment. This Court has not, however, embraced the general proposition that a wrong may be done if it can be undone. *Cf. Sniadach v. Family Finance Corp. of Bay View*, 395 U.S. 337 (1969). Surely, in the case before us, if there is delay between the doing and the undoing petitioner suffers from the deprivation of his children, and the children suffer from uncertainty and dislocation.

---

[1] Uncontradicted testimony of Peter Stanley, App. 22.
[2] Only two children are involved in this litigation.

It is clear, moreover, that Stanley does not have the means at hand promptly to erase the adverse consequences of the proceeding in the course of which his children were declared wards of the State. It is first urged that Stanley could act to adopt his children. But under Illinois law, Stanley is treated not as a parent but as a stranger to his children, and the dependency proceeding has gone forward on the presumption that he is unfit to exercise parental rights. Insofar as we are informed, Illinois law affords him no priority in adoption proceedings. It would be his burden to establish not only that he would be a suitable parent but also that he would be the most suitable of all who might want custody of the children. Neither can we ignore that in the proceedings from which this action developed, the "probation officer," see App. 17, the assistant state's attorney, see *id.*, at 29–30, and the judge charged with the case, see *id.*, at 16–18, 23, made it apparent that Stanley, unmarried and impecunious as he is, could not now expect to profit from adoption proceedings.[3] The Illinois Supreme Court apparently recognized some or all of these considerations, because it did not suggest that Stanley's case was undercut by his failure to petition for adoption.

Before us, the State focuses on Stanley's failure to petition for "custody and control"—the second route by which, it is urged, he might regain authority for his children. Passing the obvious issue whether it would be futile or burdensome for an unmarried father—without funds and already once presumed unfit—to petition for custody, this suggestion overlooks the fact that legal custody is not parenthood or adoption. A person appointed guardian in an action for custody and control is subject to removal at any time without such cause as must be shown in a neglect proceeding against a parent. Ill. Rev. Stat., c. 37, §705–8. He may not take the children out of the jurisdiction without the court's approval. He may be required to report to the court as to his disposition of the children's affairs. Ill. Rev. Stat., c. 37, §705–8. Obviously then, even if Stanley were a mere step away from "custody and control," to give an unwed father only "custody and control" would still be to leave him seriously prejudiced by reason of his status.

We must therefore examine the question that Illinois would have us avoid: Is a presumption that distinguishes and burdens all unwed fathers constitutionally repugnant? We conclude that, as a matter of due process of law, Stanley was entitled to a hearing on his fitness as a parent before his children were taken from him and that, by denying him a hearing and extending it to all other parents whose custody of their children is challenged, the State denied Stanley the equal protection of the laws guaranteed by the Fourteenth Amendment.

Illinois has two principal methods of removing nondelinquent children from the homes of their parents. In a dependency proceeding it may demonstrate that the children are wards of the State because they have no surviving parent or guardian. Ill. Rev. Stat., c. 37, §§702–1, 702–5. In a neglect proceeding it may show that children should be wards of the State because the present parent(s) or guardian does not provide suitable care. Ill. Rev. Stat., c. 37, §§702–1, 702–4.

The State's right—indeed, duty—to protect minor children through a judicial determination of their interests in a neglect proceeding is not challenged here. Rather, we are faced with a dependency statute that empowers state officials to circumvent neglect proceedings on the theory that an unwed father is not a "parent" whose existing relationship with his children must be

---

[3] The Illinois Supreme Court's opinion is not at all contrary to this conclusion. That court said: "[T]he trial court's comments clearly indicate the court's willingness to consider *a future* request by the father for *custody and guardianship.*" 45 Ill.2d 132, 135, 256 N.E.2d 814, 816. (Italics added.) See also the comment of Stanley's counsel on oral argument: "If Peter Stanley could have adopted his children, we would not be here today." Tr. of Oral Arg. 7.

considered.[4] "Parents," says the State, "means the father and mother of a legitimate child, or the survivor of them, or the natural mother of an illegitimate child, and includes any adoptive parent," Ill. Rev. Stat., c. 37, §701-14, but the term does not include unwed fathers.

Under Illinois law, therefore, while the children of all parents can be taken from them in neglect proceedings, that is only after notice, hearing, and proof of such unfitness as a parent as amounts to neglect, an unwed father is uniquely subject to the more simplistic dependency proceeding. By use of this proceeding, the State, on showing that the father was not married to the mother, need not prove unfitness in fact, because it is presumed at law. Thus, the unwed father's claim of parental qualification is avoided as "irrelevant."

In considering this procedure under the Due Process Clause, we recognize, as we have in other cases, that due process of law does not require a hearing "in every conceivable case of government impairment of private interest." *Cafeteria and Restaurant Workers Union etc. v. McElroy*, 367 U.S. 886, 894 (1961). That case explained that "[t]he very nature of due process negates any concept of inflexible procedures universally applicable to every imaginable situation" and firmly established that "what procedures due process may require under any given set of circumstances must begin with a determination of the precise nature of the government function involved as well as of the private interest that has been affected by governmental action." *Id.*, at 895; *Goldberg v. Kelly*, 397 U.S. 254, 263 (1970).

The private interest here, that of a man in the children he has sired and raised, undeniably warrants deference and, absent a powerful countervailing interest, protection. It is plain that the interest of a parent in the companionship, care, custody, and management of his or her children "come[s] to this Court with a momentum for respect lacking when appeal is made to liberties which derive merely from shifting economic arrangements." *Kovacs v. Cooper*, 336 U.S. 77, 95 (1949) (Frankfurter, J. concurring).

The Court has frequently emphasized the importance of the family. The rights to conceive and to raise one's children have been deemed "essential," *Meyer v. Nebraska*, 262 U.S. 390, 399 (1923), "basic civil rights of man," *Skinner v. Oklahoma*, 316 U.S. 535, 541 (1942), and "[r]ights far more precious * * * than property rights," *May v. Anderson*, 345 U.S. 528, 533 (1953). "It is cardinal with us that the custody, care and nurture of the child reside first in the parents, whose primary function and freedom include preparation for obligations the state can neither supply nor hinder." *Prince v. Massachusetts*, 321 U.S. 158, 166 (1944). The integrity of the family unit has found protection in the Due Process Clause of the Fourteenth Amendment, *Meyer v. Nebraska, supra*, 262 U.S. at 399, the Equal Protection Clause of the Fourteenth Amendment, *Skinner v. Oklahoma, supra*, 316 U.S., at 541, and the Ninth Amendment, *Griswold v. Connecticut*, 381 U.S. 479, 496 (1965) (Goldberg, J., concurring).

Nor has the law refused to recognize those family relationships unlegitimized by a marriage ceremony. The Court has declared unconstitutional a state statute denying natural, but illegitimate, children a wrongful-death action for the death of their mother, emphasizing that such children cannot be denied the right of other children because familial bonds in such cases were often as warm, enduring, and important as those arising within a more formally organized family unit. *Levy v. Louisiana*, 391 U.S. 68, 71-72 (1968).

* * *

    * * *

---

[4]Even while refusing to label him a "legal parent," the State does not deny that Stanley has a special interest in the outcome of these proceedings. It is undisputed that he is the father of these children, that he lived with the two children whose custody is challenged all their lives, and that he has supported them.

For its part, the State has made its interest quite plain: Illinois has declared that the aim of the Juvenile Court Act is to protect "the moral, emotional, mental, and physical welfare of the minor and the best interests of the community" and to "strengthen the minor's family ties whenever possible, removing him from the custody of his parents only when his welfare or safety or the protection of the public cannot be adequately safeguarded without removal * * *" Ill. Rev. Stat., c. 37, §701-2. These are legitimate interests, well within the power of the State to implement. We do not question the assertion that neglectful parents may be separated from their children.

But we are here not asked to evaluate the legitimacy of the state ends, rather, to determine whether the means used to achieve these ends are constitutionally defensible. What is the state interest in separating children from fathers without a hearing designed to determine whether the father is unfit in a particular disputed case? We observe that the State registers no gain towards its declared goals when it separates children from the custody of fit parents. Indeed, if Stanley is a fit father, the State spites its own articulated goals when it needlessly separates him from his family.

In *Bell v. Burson*, 402 U.S. 535 (1971), we found a scheme repugnant to the Due Process Clause because it deprived a driver of his license without reference to the very factor (there fault in driving, here fitness as a parent) that the State itself deemed fundamental to its statutory scheme. Illinois would avoid the self-contradiction that rendered the Georgia license suspension system invalid by arguing that Stanley and all other unmarried fathers can reasonably be presumed to be unqualified to raise their children.[5]

It may be, as the State insists, that most unmarried fathers are unsuitable and neglectful parents.[6] It may also be that Stanley is such a parent and that his children should be placed in other hands. But all unmarried fathers are not in this category; some are wholly suited to have custody of their chil-

---

[5] Illinois says in its brief, at 21-23,
  "[T]he only relevant consideration in determining the propriety of governmental intervention in the raising of children is whether the best interests of the child are served by such intervention.
  "In effect, Illinois has imposed a statutory presumption that the best interests of a particular group of children necessitates some governmental supervision in certain clearly defined situations. The group of children who are illegitimate are distinguishable from legitimate children not so much by their status at birth as by the factual differences in their upbringing. While a legitimate child usually is raised by both parents with the attendant familial relationships and a firm concept of home and identity, the illegitimate child normally knows only one parent—the mother. * * *
  "* * * The petitioner has premised his argument upon particular factual circumstances—a lengthy relationship with the mother * * * a familial relationship with the two children, and a general assumption that this relationship approximates that in which the natural parents are married to each other.
  "* * * Even if this characterization were accurate (the record is insufficient to support it) it would not affect the validity of the statutory definition of parent. * * * The petitioner does not deny that the children are illegitimate. The record reflects their natural mother's death. Given these two factors, grounds exist for the State's intervention to ensure adequate care and protection for these children. This is true whether or not this particular petitioner assimilates all or none of the normal characteristics common to the classification of fathers who are not married to the mothers of their children."
See also Illinois' Brief 23 ("The comparison of married and putative fathers involves exclusively factual differences. The most significant of these are the presence or absence of the father from the home on a day-to-day basis and the responsibility imposed upon the relationship"), *id.*, at 24 (to the same effect), *id.*, at 31 (quoted below in n.6), *id.*, at 24-26 (physiological and other studies are cited in support of the proposition that men are not naturally inclined to childrearing), and Tr. of Oral Arg. 31 ("We submit that both based on history or [*sic*] culture the very real differences * * * between the married father and the unmarried father, in terms of their interests in children and their legal responsibility for their children, that the statute here fulfills the compelling governmental objective of protecting children * * *").
  [6] The State speaks of "the general disinterest of putative fathers in their illegitimate children" (Brief 8) and opines that "[i]n most instances the natural father is a stranger to his children." Brief 31.

dren.[7] This much the State readily concedes, and nothing in this record indicates that Stanley is or has been a neglectful father who has not cared for his children. Given the opportunity to make his case, Stanley may have been seen to be deserving of custody of his offspring. Had this been so, the State's statutory policy would have been furthered by leaving custody in him.

* * *

* * * [I]t may be argued that unmarried fathers are so seldom fit that Illinois need not undergo the administrative inconvenience of inquiry in any case, including Stanley's. The establishment of prompt efficacious procedures to achieve legitimate state ends is a proper state interest worthy of cognizance in constitutional adjudication. But the Constitution recognizes higher values than speed and efficiency. Indeed, one might fairly say of the Bill of Rights in general, and the Due Process Clause in particular, that they were designed to protect the fragile values of a vulnerable citizenry from the overbearing concern for efficiency and efficacy that may characterize praiseworthy government officials no less, and perhaps more, than mediocre ones.

Procedure by presumption is always cheaper and easier than individualized determination. But when, as here, the procedure forecloses the determinative issues of competence and care, when it explicitly disdains present realities in deference to past formalities, it needlessly risks running roughshod over the important interests of both parent and child. It therefore cannot stand.[9]

Bell v. Burson held that the State could not, while purporting to be concerned with fault in suspending a driver's license, deprive a citizen of his license without a hearing that would assess fault. Absent fault, the State's declared interest was so attenuated that administrative convenience was insufficient to excuse a hearing where evidence of fault could be considered. That drivers involved in accidents, as a statistical matter, might be very likely to have been wholly or partially at fault did not foreclose hearing and proof in specific cases before licenses were suspended.

We think the Due Process Clause mandates a similar result here. The State's interest in caring for Stanley's children is *de minimis* if Stanley is shown to be a fit father. It insists on presuming rather than proving Stanley's unfitness solely because it is more convenient to presume than to prove. Un-

---

[7] See *In re T.*, 8 Mich. App. 122, 154 N.W.2d 27 (1967). There a panel of the Michigan Court of Appeals in unanimously affirming a circuit court's determination that the father of an illegitimate son was best suited to raise the boy, said:

"The appellants' presentation in this case proceeds on the assumption that placing Mark for adoption is inherently preferable to rearing by his father, that uprooting him from the family which he knew from birth until he was a year and a half old, secretly institutionalizing him and later transferring him to strangers is so incontroveritbly better that no court has the power even to consider the matter. Hardly anyone would even suggest such a proposition if we were talking about a child born in wedlock.

"We are not aware of any sociological data justifying the assumption that an illegitimate child reared by his natural father is less likely to receive a proper upbringing than one reared by his natural father who was at one time married to his mother, or that the stigma of illegitimacy is so pervasive it requires adoption by strangers and permanent termination of a subsisting relationship with the child's father."

Id., at 146, 154 N.W.2d, at 39.

[9] We note in passing that the incremental cost of offering unwed fathers an opportunity for individualized hearings on fitness appears to be minimal. If unwed fathers, in the main, do not care about the disposition of their children, they will not appear to demand hearings. If they do care, under the scheme here held invalid, Illinois would admittedly at some later time have to afford them a properly focused hearing in a custody or adoption proceeding.

Extending opportunity for hearing to unwed fathers who desire and claim competence to care for their children creates no constitutional or procedural obstacle to foreclosing those unwed fathers who are not so inclined. The Illinois law governing procedure in juvenile cases, Ill. Rev. Stat., c. 37, §704-1 *et seq.*, provides for personal service, notice by certified mail, or for notice by publication when personal or certified mail service cannot be had or when notice is directed to unknown respondents under the style of "All whom it may Concern." Unwed fathers who do not promptly respond cannot complain if their children are declared wards of the State. Those who do respond retain the burden of proving their fatherhood.

der the Due Process Clause that advantage is insufficient to justify refusing a father a hearing when the issue at stake is the dismemberment of his family.

The State of Illinois assumes custody of the children of married parents, divorced parents, and unmarried mothers only after a hearing and proof of neglect. The children of unmarried fathers, however, are declared dependent children without a hearing on parental fitness and without proof of neglect. Stanley's claim in the state courts and here is that failure to afford him a hearing on his parental qualifications while extending it to other parents denied him equal protection of the laws. We have concluded that all Illinois parents are constitutionally entitled to a hearing on their fitness before their children are removed from their custody. It follows that denying such a hearing to Stanley and those like him while granting it to other Illinois parents is inescapably contrary to the Equal Protection Clause.

The judgment of the Supreme Court of Illinois is reversed and the case is remanded to that court for proceedings not inconsistent with this opinion. It is so ordered.

Reversed and remanded.

Mr. Justice POWELL and Mr. Justice REHNQUIST took no part in the consideration or decision of this case.

Mr. Justice DOUGLAS joins in Parts I and II of this opinion.

Mr. Chief Justice BURGER, with whom Mr. Justice BLACKMUN concurs, dissenting.

The only constitutional issue raised and decided in the courts of Illinois in this case was whether the Illinois statute that omits unwed fathers from the definition of "parents" violates the Equal Protection Clause. We granted certiorari to consider whether the Illinois Supreme Court properly resolved that equal protection issue when it unanimously upheld the statute against petitioner Stanley's attack.

No due process issue was raised in the state courts; and no due process issue was decided by any state court.

In the case now before us, it simply does not suffice to say, as the Court in a footnote does say, that "we dispose of the case on the constitutional premise raised below, reaching the result by a method of analysis readily available to the state court." *Ante*, at 1216 n.10. The Court's method of analysis seems to ignore the strictures of Justices Douglas and White, but the analysis is clear: the Court holds *sua sponte* that the Due Process Clause requires that Stanley, the unwed biological father, be accorded a hearing as to his fitness as a parent before his children are declared wards of the state court; the Court then reasons that since Illinois recognizes such rights to due process in married fathers, it is required by the Equal Protection Clause to give such protection to unmarried fathers. This "method of analysis" is, of course, no more or less than the use of the Equal Protection Clause as a shorthand condensation of the entire Constitution: a State may not deny *any* constitutional right to some of its citizens without violating the Equal Protection Clause through its failure to deny such rights to *all* of its citizens. The limits on this Court's jurisdiction are not properly expandable by the use of such semantic devices as that.

* * *

All of those persons in Illinois who may have followed the progress of this case will, I expect, experience no little surprise at the Court's opinion handed down today. Stanley will undoubtedly be surprised to find that he has prevailed on an issue never advanced by him. * * *

In regard to the only issue that I consider properly before the Court, I agree with the State's argument that the Equal Protection Clause is not violated when Illinois gives full recognition only to those father-child relationships that arise in the context of family units bound together by legal obligations arising from marriage or from adoption proceedings. Quite apart from the religious or quasi-religious connotations that marriage has—and has historically enjoyed—for a large proportion of this Nation's citizens, it is in law an essentially contractual relationship, the parties to which have legally enforceable rights and duties, with respect both to each other and to any children born to them. Stanley and the mother of these children never entered such a relationship. The record is silent as to whether they ever privately exchanged such promises as would have bound them in marriage under the common law. See *Cartwright v. McGown*, 121 Ill. 388, 398, 12 N.E. 737, 739 (1887). In any event, Illinois has not recognized common-law marriages since 1905. Ill. Rev. Stat., c. 89, §4. Stanley did not seek the burdens when he could have freely assumed them.

Where there is a valid contract of marriage, the law of Illinois presumes that the husband is the father of any child born to the wife during the marriage; as the father, he has legally enforceable rights and duties with respect to that child. When a child is born to an unmarried woman, Illinois recognizes the readily identifiable mother, but makes no presumption as to the identity of the biological father. It does, however, provide two ways, one voluntary and one involuntary, in which that father may be identified. First, he may marry the mother and acknowledge the child as his own; this is the legal effect of legitimating the child and gaining for the father full recognition as a parent. Ill. Rev. Stat., c. 3, §12, subd. 8. Second, a man may be found to be the biological father of the child pursuant to a paternity suit initiated by the mother; in this case, the child remains illegitimate, but the adjudicated father is made liable for the support of the child until the latter attains age 18 or is legally adopted by another. Ill. Rev. Stat., c. 106¾, §52.

Stanley argued before the Supreme Court of Illinois that the definition of "parents," set out in Ill. Rev. Stat., c. 37, §701-14, as including "the father and mother of a legitimate child, or the survivor of them, or the natural mother of an illegitimate child, [or] * * * any adoptive parent,"[3] violates the Equal Protection Clause in that it treats unwed mothers and unwed fathers differently. Stanley then enlarged upon his equal protection argument when he brought the case here; he argued before this Court that Illinois is not permitted by the Equal Protection Clause to distinguish between unwed fathers and any of the other biological parents included in the statutory definition of legal "parents."

The Illinois Supreme Court correctly held that the State may constitutionally distinguish between unwed fathers and unwed mothers. Here, Illinois' different treatment of the two is part of that State's statutory scheme for protecting the welfare of illegitimate children. In almost all cases, the unwed mother is readily identifiable, generally from hospital records, and alternatively by physicians or others attending the child's birth. Unwed fathers, as a class, are not traditionally quite so easy to identify and locate. Many of them either deny all responsibility or exhibit no interest in the child or its welfare; and, of course, many unwed fathers are simply not aware of their parenthood.

Furthermore, I believe that a State is fully justified in concluding, on the basis of common human experience, that the biological role of the mother in

---

[3] The Court seems at times to ignore this statutory definition of "parents," even though it is precisely that definition itself whose constitutionality has been brought into issue by Stanley. In preparation for finding a purported similarity between this case and *Bell v. Burson*, 402 U.S. 535 (1971), the Court quotes the legislatively declared aims of the Juvenile Court Act to "strengthen the minor's family ties whenever possible, removing him from the custody of his *parents* only when his welfare or safety or the protection of the public cannot be adequately safeguarded without removal." (Emphasis added.) The Court then goes on to find a "self-contradiction" between that stated aim and the Act's nonrecognition of unwed fathers. *Ante*, at 1213. There is, of course, no such contradiction. The word "parent" in the statement of legislative purpose obviously has the meaning given to it by the definitional provision of the Act.

carrying and nursing an infant creates stronger bonds between her and the child than the bonds resulting from the male's often casual encounter. This view is reinforced by the observable fact that most unwed mothers exhibit a concern for their offspring either permanently or at least until they are safely placed for adoption, while unwed fathers rarely burden either the mother or the child with their attentions or loyalties. Centuries of human experience buttress this view of the realities of human conditions and suggest that unwed mothers of illegitimate children are generally more dependable protectors of their children than are unwed fathers. While these, like most generalizations, are not without exceptions, they nevertheless provide a sufficient basis to sustain a statutory classification whose objective is not to penalize unwed parents but to further the welfare of illegitimate children in fulfillment of the State's obligations as *parens patriae*.[4]

Stanley depicts himself as a somewhat unusual unwed father, namely, as one who has always acknowledged and never doubted his fatherhood of these children. He alleges that he loved, cared for, and supported these children from the time of their birth until the death of their mother. He contends that he consequently must be treated the same as a married father of legitimate children. Even assuming the truth of Stanley's allegations, I am unable to construe the Equal Protection Clause as requiring Illinois to tailor its statutory definition of "parents" so meticulously as to include such unusual unwed fathers, while at the same time excluding those unwed, and generally unidentified, biological fathers who in no way share Stanley's professed desires.

Indeed, the nature of Stanley's own desires is less than absolutely clear from the record in this case. Shortly after the death of the mother, Stanley turned these two children over to the care of a Mr. and Mrs. Ness; he took no action to gain recognition of himself as a father, through adoption, or as a legal custodian, through a guardianship proceeding. Eventually it came to the attention of the state that there was no living adult who had any legally enforceable obligation for the care and support of the children; it was only then that the dependency proceeding here under review took place and that Stanley made himself known to the juvenile court in connection with these two children.[5] Even then, however, Stanley did not ask to be charged with the legal responsibility for the children. He asked only that such legal responsibility be given to no one else. He seemed, in particular, to be concerned with the loss of the welfare payments he would suffer as a result of the designation of others as guardians of the children.

Not only, then, do I see no ground for holding that Illinois' statutory definition of "parents" on its face violates the Equal Protection Clause; I see no ground for holding that any constitutional right of Stanley has been denied in the application of that statutory definition in the case at bar.

* * *

---

[4] When the marriage between the parents of a legitimate child is dissolved by divorce or separation, the State, of course, normally awards custody of the child to one parent or the other. This is considered necessary for the child's welfare, since the parents are no longer legally bound together. The unmarried parents of an illegitimate child are likewise not legally bound together. Thus, even if Illinois did recognize the parenthood of both the mother and father of an illegitimate child, it would for consistency with its practice in divorce proceedings, be called upon to award custody to one or the other of them, at least once it had by some means ascertained the identity of the father.

[5] As the majority notes, *ante*, at 1210, Joan Stanley gave birth to three children during the 18 years Peter Stanley was living "intermittently" with her. At oral argument, we were told by Stanley's counsel that the oldest of these three children had previously been declared a ward of the court pursuant to a neglect proceeding that was "proven against" Stanley at a time, apparently, when the juvenile court officials were under the erroneous impression that Peter and Joan Stanley had been married. Tr. of Oral Arg. 19.

Quilloin v. Walcott

United States Supreme Court

434 U.S. 246 (1978)

Mr. Justice MARSHALL delivered the opinion of the Court.

The issue in this case is the constitutionality of Georgia's adoption laws as applied to deny an unwed father authority to prevent adoption of his illegitimate child. The child was born in December 1964 and has been in the custody and control of his mother, appellee Ardell Williams Walcott, for his entire life. The mother and the child's natural father, appellant Leon Webster Quilloin, never married each other or established a home together, and in September 1967 the mother married appellee Randall Walcott.[1] In March 1976, she consented to adoption of the child by her husband, who immediately filed a petition for adoption. Appellant attempted to block the adoption and to secure visitation rights, but he did not seek custody or object to the child's continuing to live with appellees. Although appellant was not found to be an unfit parent, the adoption was granted over his objection.

In *Stanley v. Illinois*, 405 U.S. 645 (1972), this Court held that the State of Illinois was barred, as a matter of both due process and equal protection, from taking custody of the children of an unwed father, absent a hearing and a particularized finding that the father was an unfit parent. The Court concluded, on the one hand, that a father's interest in the "companionship, care, custody, and management" of his children is "cognizable and substantial," *id.*, at 651–652, and, on the other hand, that the State's interest in caring for the children is "*de minimis*" if the father is in fact a fit parent, *id.*, at 657–658. *Stanley* left unresolved the degree of protection a State must afford to the rights of an unwed father in a situation, such as that presented here, in which the countervailing interests are more substantial.

Generally speaking, under Georgia law a child born in wedlock cannot be adopted without the consent of each living parent who has not voluntarily surrendered rights in the child or been adjudicated an unfair parent.[2] Even where the child's parents are divorced or separated at the time of the adoption proceedings, either parent may veto the adoption. In contrast, only the consent of the mother is required for adoption of an illegitimate child. Ga. Code §74–403(3) (1975).[3] To acquire the same veto authority possessed by other parents, the father of a child born out of wedlock must legitimate his offspring, either by marrying the mother and acknowledging the child as his own, §74–101, or by obtaining a court order declaring the child legitimate and

---

[1] The child lived with his maternal grandmother for the intitial period of the marriage, but moved in with appellees in 1969 and lived with them thereafter.

[2] See Ga. Code §§74–403(1), (2) (1975). Section 74–403(1) sets forth the general rule that "no adoption shall be permitted except with the written consent of the living parents of a child." Section 74–403(2) provides that consent is not required from a parent who (1) has surrendered rights in the child to a child-placing agency or to the adoption court; (2) is found by the adoption court to have abandoned the child, or to have willfully failed for a year or longer to comply with a court-imposed support order with respect to the child; (3) has had his or her parental rights terminated by court order, see Ga. Code §24A–3201; (4) is insane or otherwise incapacitated from giving consent; or (5) cannot be found after a diligent search has been made.

[3] Section 74–403(3), which operates as an exception to the rule stated in §74–403(1), see n.2, *supra*, provides:

"Illegitimate children—If the child be illegitimate, the consent of the mother alone shall suffice. Such consent, however, shall not be required if the mother has surrendered all of her rights to said child to a licensed child-placing agency, or to the State Department of Family and Children Services."

Sections of Ga. Code (1975) will hereinafter be referred to merely by their numbers.

capable of inheriting from the father, §74-103.[4] But unless and until the child is legitimated, the mother is the only recognized parent and is given exclusive authority to exercise all parental prerogatives, §74-203,[5] including the power to veto adoption of the child.

Appellant did not petition for legitimation of his child at any time during the 11 years between the child's birth and the filing of Randall Walcott's adoption petition.[6] However, in response to Walcott's petition, appellant filed an application for a writ of habeas corpus seeking visitation rights, a petition for legitimation, and an objection to the adoption.[7] Shortly thereafter, appellant amended his pleadings by adding the claim that §§74-203 and 74-403(3) were unconstitutional as applied to his case, insofar as they denied him the rights granted to married parents, and presumed unwed fathers to be unfit as a matter of law.

The petitions for adoption, legitimation and writ of habeas corpus were consolidated for trial in the Superior Court of Fulton County, Ga. The court expressly stated that these matters were being tried on the basis of a consolidated record to allow "the biological father * * * a right to be heard with respect to any issue or other thing upon which he desire[s] to be heard, including his fitness as a parent * * *."[8] After receiving extensive testimony from the parties and other witnesses, the trial court found that, although the child had never been abandoned or deprived, appellant had provided support only on an irregular basis.[9] Moreover, while the child previously had visited with appellant on "many occasions," and had been given toys and gifts by appellant "from time to time," the mother had recently concluded that these con-

---

[4] Section 74-103 provides in full:
"A father of an illegitimate child may render the same legitimate by petitioning the superior court of the county of his residence, setting forth the name, age, and sex of such child, and also the name of the mother; and if he desires the name changed, stating the new name, and praying the legitimation of such child. Of this application the mother, if alive, shall have notice. Upon such application, presented and filed, the court may pass an order declaring said child to be legitimate, and capable of inheriting from the father in the same manner as if born in lawful wedlock, and the name by which he or she shall be known."

[5] Section 74-203 states:
"The mother of an illegitimate child shall be entitled to the possession of the child, unless the father shall legitimate him as before provided. Being the only recognized parent, she may exercise all the paternal power."
In its opinion in this case, the Georgia Supreme Court indicated that the word "paternal" in the second sentence of this provision is the result of a misprint, and was instead intended to read "parental." See 238 Ga. 230, 231, 232 S.E.2d 246, 247 (1977).

[6] It does appear that appellant consented to entry of his name on the child's birth certificate. See §88-1709(d)(2). The adoption petition gave the name of the child as "Darrell Webster Quilloin," and appellant alleges in his brief that the child has always been known by that name, see Brief for Appellant 11.

[7] Appellant had been notified by the State's Department of Human Resources that an adoption petition had been filed.

[8] *In re: Application of Randall Walcott for Adoption of Child*, Adoption Case No. 8466 (Ga. Super. Ct., July 12, 1976), App. 70.
Sections 74-103, 74-203, and 74-403(3) are silent as to the appropriate procedure in the event that a petition for legitimation is filed after an adoption proceeding has already been initiated. Prior to this Court's decision in *Stanley v. Illinois*, 405 U.S. 645 (1972), and without consideration of potential constitutional problems, the Georgia Supreme Court had concluded that an unwed father could not petition for legitimation after the mother had consented to an adoption. *Smith v. Smith*, 224 Ga. 442, 445-446, 162 S.E.2d 379, 383-384 (1968). But *cf. Clark v. Buttry*, 226 Ga. 687, 177 S.E.2d 89 (1970), *aff'g*, 121 Ga. App. 492, 174 S.E.2d 356. However, the Georgia Supreme Court had not had occasion to reconsider this conclusion in light of *Stanley*, and, in the face of appellant's constitutional challenge to §§74-203, 74-403(3), the trial court evidently concluded that concurrent consideration of the legitimation and adoption petitions was consistent with the statutory provisions. See also Tr. of Hearing before Superior Court, App., 34, 51; n.12, *infra*.

[9] Under §74-202, appellant had a duty to support his child, but for reasons not appearing in the record the mother never brought an action to enforce this duty. Since no court ever ordered appellant to support his child, denial of veto authority over the adoption could not have been justified on the ground of willful failure to comply with a support order. See n.2, *supra*.

tacts were having a disruptive effect on the child and on appellees' entire family.[10] The child himself expressed a desire to be adopted by Randall Walcott and to take on Walcott's name,[11] and the court found Walcott to be a fit and proper person to adopt the child.

On the basis of these findings, as well as findings relating to appellees' marriage and the mother's custody of the child for all of the child's life, the trial court determined that the proposed adoption was in the "best interests of [the] child." The court concluded, further, that granting either the legitimation or the visitation rights requested by appellant would not be in the "best interests of the child," and that both should consequently be denied. The court then applied §§74-203 and 74-403(3) to the situation at hand, and, since appellant had failed to obtain a court order granting legitimation, he was found to lack standing to object to the adoption. Ruling that appellant's constitutional claims were without merit, the court granted the adoption petition and denied the legitimation and visitation petitions.

Appellant took an appeal to the Supreme Court of Georgia, claiming that §§74-203 and 74-403(3), as applied by the trial court to his case, violated the Equal Protection and Due Process Clauses of the Fourteenth Amendment. In particular, appellant contended that he was entitled to the same power to veto an adoption as is provided under Georgia law to married or divorced parents and to unwed mothers, and, since the trial court did not make a finding of abandonment or other unfitness on the part of appellant, see n.2, *supra*, the adoption of his child should not have been allowed.

Over a dissent which urged that §74-403(3) was invalid under Stanley v. Illinois, the Georgia Supreme Court affirmed the decision of the trial court. 238 Ga. 230, 232 S.E.2d 246 (1977).[12] The majority relied generally on the strong state policy of rearing children in a family setting, a policy which in the court's view might be thwarted if unwed fathers were required to consent to adoptions. The court also emphasized the special force of this policy under the facts of this case, pointing out that the adoption was sought by the child's stepfather, who was part of the family unit in which the child was in fact living, and that the child's natural father had not taken steps to support or legitimate the child over a period of more than 11 years. The court noted in addition that, unlike the father in *Stanley*, appellant had never been a *de facto* member of the child's family unit.

Appellant brought this appeal pursuant to 28 U.S.C. §1257(2), continuing to challenge the constitutionality of §§74-203 and 74-403(3) as applied to his case, and claiming that he was entitled as a matter of due process and equal protection to an absolute veto over adoption of his child, absent a finding of his unfitness as a parent. In contrast to appellant's somewhat broader statement of the issue in the Georgia Supreme Court, on this appeal he focused his equal protection claim solely on the disparate statutory treatment of his

---

[10] In addition to Darrell, appellees' family included a son born several years after appellees were married. The mother testified that Darrell's visits with appellant were having unhealthy effects on both children.

[11] The child also expressed a desire to continue to visit with appellant on occasion after the adoption. The child's desire to be adopted, however, could not be given effect under Georgia law without divesting appellant of any parental rights he might otherwise have or acquire, including visitation rights. See §74-414.

[12] The Supreme Court addressed itself only to the constitutionality of the statutes as applied by the trial court and thus, at least for purposes of this case, accepted the trial court's construction of §§74-203 and 74-403(3), as allowing concurrent consideration of the adoption and legitimation petitions. See n.8, *supra*.

Subsequent to the Supreme Court's decision in this case, the Georgia Legislature enacted a comprehensive revision of the State's adoption laws, which became effective January 1, 1978. 1977 Ga. Laws 201. The new law expressly gives an unwed father the right to petition for legitimation subsequent to the filing of an adoption petition concerning his child. See Ga. Code §74-406 (1977 Supp.). The revision also leaves intact §§74-103 and 74-203, and carries forward the substance of §74-403(3), and thus appellant would not have received any greater protection under the new law than he was actually afforded by the trial court.

case and that of a married father.[13] We noted probable jurisdiction, 431 U.S. 937 (1977), and we now affirm.

At the outset, we observe that appellant does not challenge the sufficiency of the notice he received with respect to the adoption proceeding, see n.7, *supra*, nor can he claim that he was deprived of a right to a hearing on his individualized interests in his child, prior to entry of the order of adoption. Although the trial court's ultimate conclusion was that appellant lacked standing to object to the adoption, this conclusion was reached only after appellant had been afforded a full hearing on his legitimation petition, at which he was given the opportunity to offer evidence on any matter he thought relevant, including his fitness as a parent. Had the trial court granted legitimation, appellant would have acquired the veto authority he is now seeking.

The fact that appellant was provided with a hearing on his legitimation petition is not, however, a complete answer to his attack on the constitutionality of §§74-203 and 74-403(3). The trial court denied appellant's petition, and thereby precluded him from gaining veto authority, on the ground that legitimation was not in the "best interests of the child"; appellant contends that he was entitled to recognition and preservation of his parental rights absent a showing of his "unfitness." Thus, the underlying issue is whether, in the circumstances of this case and in light of the authority granted by Georgia law to married fathers, appellant's interests were adequately protected by a "best interests of the child" standard. We examine this issue first under the Due Process Clause and then under the Equal Protection Clause.

Appellees suggest that due process was not violated, regardless of the standard applied by the trial court, since any constitutionally protected interest appellant might have had was lost by his failure to petition for legitimation during the 11 years prior to filing of Randall Walcott's adoption petition. We would hesitate to rest decision on this ground, in light of the evidence in the record that appellant was not aware of the legitimation procedure until after the adoption petition was filed.[14] But in any event we need not go that far, since under the circumstances of this case appellant's substantive rights were not violated by application of a "best interests of the child" standard.

We have recognized on numerous occasions that the relationship between parent and child is constitutionally protected. See, *e.g.*, *Wisconsin v. Yoder*, 406 U.S. 205, 231-233 (1972); *Stanley v. Illinois, supra; Meyer v. Nebraska*, 262 U.S. 390, 399-401 (1923). "It is cardinal with us that the custody, care and nurture of the child reside first in the parents, whose primary function and freedom include preparation for obligations the state can neither supply nor hinder." *Prince v. Massachusetts*, 321 U.S. 158, 166 (1944). And it is now firmly established that "freedom of personal choice in matters of * * * family life is one of the liberties protected by the Due Process Clause of the Fourteenth Amendment." *Cleveland Board of Education v. LaFleur*, 414 U.S. 632, 639-640 (1974).

We have little doubt that the Due Process Clause would be offended "[i]f a State were to attempt to force the breakup of a natural family, over the objections of the parents and their children, without some showing of unfitness and for the sole reason that to do so was thought to be in the children's

---

[13] In the last paragraph of his brief, appellant raises the claim that the statutes make gender-based distinctions that violate the Equal Protection Clause. Since this claim was not presented in appellant's jurisdictional statement, we do not consider it. This Court's Rule 15(1)(c); see, *e.g.*, *Phillips Chem. Co. v. Dumas School Dist.*, 361 U.S. 376, 386, and n.12 (1960).

[14] At the hearing in the trial court, the following colloquy took place between appellees' counsel and appellant:

"Q. Had you made any effort prior to this time [prior to the instant proceedings], during the eleven years of Darrell's life to legitimate him?

"A. * * * I didn't know that was process even you went through [*sic*]." App. 58.

best interest." *Smith v. Organization of Foster Families*, 431 U.S. 816, 862–863 (1977) (Stewart, J., concurring in judgment). But this is not a case in which the unwed father at any time had, or sought, actual or legal custody of his child. Nor is this a case in which the proposed adoption would place the child with a new set of parents with whom the child had never before lived. Rather, the result of the adoption in this case is to give full recognition to a family unit already in existence, a result desired by all concerned, except appellant. Whatever might be required in other situations, we cannot say that the State was required in this situation to find anything more than that the adoption, and denial of legitimation, were in the "best interests of the child."

Appellant contends that even if he is not entitled to prevail as a matter of due process, principles of equal protection require that his authority to veto an adoption be measured by the same standard that would have been applied to a married father. In particular, appellant asserts that his interests are indistinguishable from those of a married father who is separated or divorced from the mother and is no longer living with his child, and therefore the State acted impermissibly in treating his case differently. We think appellant's interests are readily distinguishable from those of a separated or divorced father, and accordingly believe that the State could permissibly give appellant less veto authority than it provides to a married father.

Although appellant was subject, for the years prior to these proceedings, to essentially the same child-support obligation as a married father would have had, compare §74–202 with §74–105 and §30–301, he has never exercised actual or legal custody over his child, and thus has never shouldered any significant responsibility with respect to the daily supervision, education, protection, or care of the child. Appellant does not complain of his exemption from these responsibilities and, indeed, he does not even now seek custody of his child. In contrast, legal custody of children is, of course, a central aspect of the marital relationship, and even a father whose marriage has broken apart will have borne full responsibility for the rearing of his children during the period of the marriage. Under any standard of review, the State was not foreclosed from recognizing this difference in the extent of commitment to the welfare of the child.

For these reasons, we conclude that §§74–203 and 74–403(3), as applied in this case, did not deprive appellant of his asserted rights under the Due Process and Equal Protection Clauses. The judgment of the Supreme Court of Georgia is accordingly,

Affirmed.

Comments

The legal position of illegitimate children in regard to their rights is closely mirrored in the rights of the unwed father. To the extent that the courts are vacillating in their decision on inheritance rights and government benefits to the illegitimate, a similar vacillation can be observed with the rights of illegitimate fathers in their children. *Stanley* is an illustration of the pendulum swinging toward recognition of the unwed father's rights, while *Quilloin* seems to retract. Again it is possible to explain the difference in terms of facts and variations in state statutes. Yet there is an underlying legislative and judicial unease with questions of evidence. When illegitimate fathers did not have any rights whatsoever in their offspring, the question of their legal position, depending on the nature and quality of their relationship, was inevitably irrelevant. Since *Stanley* recognized the rights of some illegitimate fathers in their children, the question of which fathers, upon what evidence, deserve protection and which fathers do not has had to be approached and answered from case to case. This situation is further complicated because not only are economic rights involved, as in *Trimble v. Gordon* and *Lalli v. Lalli* (pp. 582 and 589), but also highly personal rights, this time of unwed fathers, such as the right to be notified and heard in adoption proceedings, visitation rights, and rights for custody.

Although there was some lingering doubt in *Stanley* about the quality of the relationship between the father and his children, the majority appears to have been willing to treat them as belonging to one family. Whether this ongoing family was based on ceremonial marriage, as required by Illinois law, then became irrelevant. This element was absent in *Quilloin*, in which the illegitimate father never had, or actually sought, custody of his child. His claimed rights were indeed in conflict with an existing family unit to which the child belonged, one based on the marriage of the child's mother to a third person. From another perspective we can view these court decisions as being concerned not merely with ongoing families but also with preservation of the status quo in regard to children, unless strong factors speak against it. To recognize the rights of illegitimate fathers indiscriminately, especially if the relationship is based on casual sexual relations, could lead to many situations felt to be undesirable, for example, harassment of the mother and prospective adoptive parents or the possibility of extortion by persons whose claim to paternity is subject to doubt.

On the other hand, if the positions of the illegitimate mother and father are comparable—for example, because they have cohabited and mutually contributed to the support and comfort of the child or children—then perhaps they should be treated alike and for legal purposes as if they had been married. In such situations, the position of the unwed father indeed becomes comparable to that of a divorced parent. If the development in the law continues to take this direction, as it seems to be doing, the stigma on casual sexual encounters remains, and the consequences for children of cohabitation arrangements and marriage become indistinguishable. *Stanley* illustrates this trend, resulting in some side effects that the court may not have contemplated. Illinois is a jurisdiction with strong legislative and judicial policies against common law marriage and cohabitation contracts. (See *Hewitt v. Hewitt*, pp. 205–212.) The due process and equal protection requirements in *Stanley* brought about one of the effects of common law marriage in a jurisdiction that does not permit it. That is, the court, in considering custody of the children, treated the relationship as though it were a marriage. As in marriage, the father's unfitness would have to be proved by the state.

The position taken in *Quilloin* poses problems too. Even though the illegitimate father had never sought custody of the child or had him timely legitimated, he nevertheless had visited him frequently and appears to have had a warm relationship with him. The adoption proceedings may have been prompted by the mother's ulterior motives, for example, avoiding personal contact with the natural father by cutting off his visitation rights. Although continuation of the unwed father's rights appears to have been considered by the Court as merely the less desirable alternative, the negative disposition can also be understood on the basis of the unfounded assumption that illegitimate fathers are irresponsible. *Quilloin* can be interpreted as encouraging parents to resolve their custody disputes by resorting to adoption as a strategy. Yet if unwed fathers were allowed to block adoption proceedings, it would have a chilling effect on all potential adoptions of illegitimate children. Few mothers of illegitimate children and prospective adoptive parents would risk proceedings that could be impeded or set aside if the rights of all unwed fathers were recognized without limitations. On another level of abstraction, it may be recalled that the "best interests of the child" standard, so much at the heart of the reasoning in *Quilloin*, though certainly qualified there, still contains aspects of treatment of the child as a chattel. To recognize fully the rights of unwed fathers in their offspring, by discouraging adoption, would have an effect similar to a restraint on alienation in the law of property.

Adoption agencies, like welfare agencies in general, are not necessarily concerned with the best interests of the child alone, but, as the opinion in *Stanley* noted, are also motivated by a desire for efficiency. This attitude "may characterize praiseworthy government officials no less, and perhaps more, than mediocre ones." If faced with resistance, they simply because of human nature may turn petty and vengeful. *Stanley* illustrates this problem too. The State of Illinois was engaged in a running battle with Peter Stanley over a prolonged period of time. Its welfare representatives had the power to shape the facts in a light unfavorable to the unwed father. Prior to the present litigation a neglect proceeding had been instituted for one of the children, apparently under the erroneous assumption that the parents had been married. The death of the mother, together with an irrebuttable presumption of unfitness of the father, seems to have furnished the State a new avenue of attack. After the unwed father prevailed in the U.S. Supreme Court, the State did not wait long before instituting new child neglect proceedings. Having lost this case again, the unwed father appealed. Only at this stage was the State willing to give in, returning the children and having the charges dismissed. There is even some indication that part of the aggravation was caused not so much by Peter Stanley and the conditions within his de facto family, but by the zealous representation of his rights by a Legal Service Office representing indigents. Lawyers who deal with welfare agencies know that, because some social workers may be used to considerable power in exercising their discretion, they are to be approached with caution. To the extent that new types of persons have been recruited into welfare agencies within the last decade, some of these problems may have been alleviated. Furthermore, the family situation that gave rise to *Stanley* was probably less than ideal.

The interdependence of the rights of illegitimate fathers and adoption is illustrated by footnote 9 in *Stanley*. Although this case involved possible child neglect and the fitness of an unwed father, the note sets forth the criteria of notice that, at low cost, could be used in various contexts—for example, adoption—to notify such fathers of pending proceedings. This passing suggestion by the Court was sufficiently effective to influence adoption proceedings throughout the nation. The underlying thought was that if the illegitimate father were not given any notice, adoption proceedings might prove to be defective. Yet the note was not addressed to problems involved in locating fathers whose whereabouts may be unknown and some of whom may not know about the child. There is, for example, the question of how much effort should be expended to locate fathers, and how much time should be set aside for such purpose at the cost of delaying adoption. Neither does the note answer what "a properly focused hearing," after notice, would entail; whether consent of the natural father to adoptions is necessary; and so on. We can, however, infer from the impact of this seemingly casual footnote that any suggestion relating to, or any regulation of, illegitimacy tends to have consequences in other areas of law, adoption being only one of them.

Ultimately, cases like *Stanley* and *Quilloin* affect the nature of marriage and of the family. One may perceive these problems as being definitional and implying value choices; or as evidentiary and relating to the question of who is a father; or perhaps even as quasi-proprietary in nature, relating to the seemingly technical issues of how much effort a natural father must invest to be given rights and at what point his rights "vest."

References

Areen, J., CASES AND MATERIALS ON FAMILY LAW 155 (1978) (Letter dated Mar. 23, 1976 from Patrick T. Murphy, attorney for Peter Stanley).

Barron, *Notice to the Unwed Father and Termination of Parental Rights: Implementing Stanley v. Illinois*, 9 FAM. L.Q. 527 (1975), *reprinted in* 2 THE YOUNGEST MINORITY 22 (S. Katz ed. 1977).

Howe, *Development of a Model Act to Free Children for Permanent Placement: A Case Study in Law and Social Planning*, 13, FAM. L.Q. 257, 301, 337–338 (1979).

Katz, *Freeing Children for Permanent Placement Through a Model Act*, 12 FAM. L.Q. 203, 231–235 (1978).

Katz, S., WHEN PARENTS FAIL (1971).

Note, *The Rights of Fathers of Non-Marital Children to Custody, Visitation, and to Consent to Adoption*, 12 U.C.D. L. REV. 412 (1979).

Note, *The Strange Boundaries of Stanley: Providing Notice of Adoption to the Unknown Putative Father*, 59 VA. L. REV. 517 (1973).

Schafrick, *The Emerging Constitutional Protection of the Putative Father's Parental Rights*, 7 FAM. L.Q. 75 (1973).

Wadlington, W. & Paulsen, M., CASES AND OTHER MATERIALS ON DOMESTIC RELATIONS 731, 1055–58 (3d ed. 1978) (impact of footnote 9 of *Stanley* on adoption).

Bibliography

Eekelaar, J. & Katz, S., MARRIAGE AND COHABITATION IN CONTEMPORARY SOCIETIES (1980).

Katz, S. & Inker, M., FATHERS, HUSBANDS AND LOVERS (1979).

Krause, H., ILLEGITIMACY—LAW AND SOCIAL POLICY (1971).

Stenger, *The Supreme Court and Illegitimacy: 1968-1977*, 11 FAM. L.Q. 365 (1978).

Table of Cases*

---

*Cases presented in text are printed in italics.

Index

623